Reading Feminist Theory
From Modernity to Postmodernity

Susan Archer Mann
University of New Orleans

Ashly Suzanne Patterson
Southeastern Louisiana University

New York   Oxford
OXFORD UNIVERSITY PRESS

Oxford University Press is a department of the University of Oxford.
It furthers the University's objective of excellence in research,
scholarship, and education by publishing worldwide.

Oxford   New York
Auckland   Cape Town   Dar es Salaam   Hong Kong   Karachi
Kuala Lumpur   Madrid   Melbourne   Mexico City   Nairobi
New Delhi   Shanghai   Taipei   Toronto

With offices in
Argentina   Austria   Brazil   Chile   Czech Republic   France   Greece
Guatemala   Hungary   Italy   Japan   Poland   Portugal   Singapore
South Korea   Switzerland   Thailand   Turkey   Ukraine   Vietnam

For titles covered by Section 112 of the US Higher Education
Opportunity Act, please visit www.oup.com/us/he for the
latest information about pricing and alternate formats.

Published by Oxford University Press
198 Madison Avenue, New York, New York 10016
http://www.oup.com

Oxford is a registered trademark of Oxford University Press

Library of Congress Cataloging-in-Publication Data
Reading feminist theory : from modernity to postmodernity / [edited by]
Susan Archer Mann, University of New Orleans, Ashly Suzanne Patterson,
Southeastern Louisiana University.
     pages cm
   Includes bibliographical references.
   ISBN 978-0-19-936498-5
  1. Feminist theory--History. 2. Feminism--History. I. Mann, Susan Archer.
II. Patterson, Ashly Suzanne.
   HQ1190.R433 2016
   305.4209--dc23
                                                                    2014043659

Dedicated with deepest love to our children,
Susan's son, Joshua Mann Sartisky
and
Ashly's daughter, Skylar Isabelle Rains

Contents

CHAPTER 3 — Radical Feminisms

We also thank the following reviewers commissioned by Oxford University Press:

Emma G. Bailey, Western New Mexico University
Bernadette Barton, Morehead State University
Garlena A. Bauer, Otterbein University
Eileen Boris, University of California, Santa Barbara
Colleen Coughlin, Davenport University
Deirdre M. Condit, Virginia Commonwealth University
Sara L. Crawley, University of South Florida
Karina Eileraas, University of Southern California
Abby Ferber, University of Colorado
Hawley Fogg-Davis, Temple University
Cecilia Herles, University of Georgia
Marie Laberge, University of Delaware
Kelly Pemberton, George Washington University
Cheryl L. Radeloff, Minnesota State University, Mankato

Acknowledgments

It is a privilege to have spent my adult life doing work that I love. It also is a privilege to have had the emotional, material, and intellectual support of so many dear friends, family members, and colleagues. I am not very well as I write this, so I will be brief. But you who are dear to me know who you are and how important our relationships have been over the years. I have wonderful memories of the childhood that shaped my life thanks to my family and best childhood friends, Ginny Brassel, Ellen Hoberman, Colleen Webster, Sally Livingston, and Cam Jackson. As an adult, I am most grateful to the women (past and present) involved in the University of New Orleans (UNO) Women's and Gender Studies Program and to my close colleagues in sociology during my sojourns in New Orleans, Toronto, and Washington, D.C. (especially Max) who supported my intellectual and political work for so many decades. Particular thanks to my women's writing group—D'Lane Compton, Rachel Luft, Renia Ehrenfeucht, Ana Croegaert, and Elizabeth Steeby—for their gentle support. I also thank the UNO Office of Research for a Creative Endeavor Award to work on this anthology. My graduate assistant, Heather Horton, deserves special thanks for scanning so many of the readings found in this anthology. Much gratitude also goes to my coauthor, Ashly Patterson, for hanging in there with her ceaseless enthusiasm, humor, and good heart through this rather arduous and, at times, frustrating process. To the crew at Oxford University Press—especially Katy Albis, Cari Heicklen, and Sherith Pankratz—please accept my appreciation for your hard work and sound advice. Heartfelt thanks go to Bunk, Shari, Michael, and Michelle Mann who took good care of my dear mother while I lived and worked thousands of miles away. My mother, Hannah Grashl Mann, passed away this fall, but her love and good mothering live on in her children, grandchildren and great-grandchildren. Finally, my innermost thanks go to Michael D. Grimes and Joshua Mann Sartisky, whose love kept the home-fires burning during the trials and tribulations of my many years of writing. I know I shall rest peacefully for raising a son of whom I am so deeply proud, for having the love of close friends and family, and for making even a small contribution to the women's movement and its long, proud struggle for bread and roses.

Susan Archer Mann, October 2014

Many people have aided and supported me during this work's production. First and foremost, I thank my teacher, mentor, collaborator, and friend, Susan Mann. Early on you saw a spark in me that I had yet to recognize and you nurtured that flickering flame with your years of experience, knowledge, and wisdom until it became a roaring fire. I thank you for your patience and for reeling me back to home plate every time I began to slide out-of-bounds. There are simply no words to truly articulate my gratitude in being asked to be part of the creation of this work. Thank you to our editors at Oxford University Press, Sherith Pankratz, Cari Heicklen, and Katy Albis, for your painstaking hard work and perseverance in obtaining permissions as well as your eagle-eye attention to detail. You, together, have been the backbone to this immense project.

I am also thankful for my many professors whose guidance and knowledgeable expertise transformed me along the way: Rachel Luft, Vern Baxter, D'Lane Compton, and Nicole Farris. I credit each of you with ripping off my many blindfolds, thereby forcing me to come to terms with and confront my world of privileged solipsism in its many forms. To my colleagues, Kenneth Bolton, Rebecca Hensley, and Marc Settembrino, your support and encouragement over this past year has kept me going in more ways than you will probably ever realize.

To my mother, Dianna Giardelli Pappas, you are my rock, my constant. You have loved me and believed in me in times when I could not do those things myself. Thank you for never turning away from me and for always allowing me to draw from your well of energy, strength, and wisdom even when my need depleted your own reserves. I am grateful beyond words. To my daughter, Skylar Rains, we have grown alongside one another during this process. Your teenage wisdom, wit, smarts, and fierce independence have been refreshing gifts as your level of patience, love, and understanding of my nontraditional ways are incommunicable. I stand in awe of you, every day. To my sister, Katie Landry, you have often surprised me with your love and kindness. Thank you for all your "good luck" phone calls and cards over the years. They have kept me going when I thought I had nothing left to give.

To my step-father, William Pappas, thank you for your silent support, love, and overwhelming generosity and care over the years. You are a man of few words, but when you speak I know that there is a lesson to be learned and it is in my best interest to stop running my mouth and listen. To my step-father, Steve Landry (Pappa), thank you for leading by example in teaching me early on the values of hard work, even though it took me years to appreciate the lessons. Being witness to your current fight inspires me to strive and *overcome* to *become* all that you ever dreamed for me. Thank you both for always loving me and believing in me.

Last, very special thanks to all of the contributors to this anthology. Your works have inspired, captivated, enraged, soothed, and challenged me to reach deep within as well as out to transform me into the woman I am becoming. It is through the literature contained in this text that I came to feminism in its vast and myriad forms. To these brilliant, eloquent minds, both past and present, I am forever indebted.

Ashly Suzanne Patterson, October 2014

Introduction

Toward a history of the vanishing present . . .

—Gayatri Chakravorty Spivak, 1999

Constructing feminist theory is a social practice and a form of labor. Just as textile workers weave yarn and thread to create fabrics, feminist theorists weave concepts and ideas to better understand the gendered fabric of social life. Although all knowledge is socially constructed, doing feminist theory is a *critical* social practice directed toward better understanding and improving the position of women in diverse social locations.

Like any social theory anthology, the readings in this text ask big questions: "What is going on just now? What is happening to us? What is this world, this period, this precise moment in which we are living?" (Foucault quoted in Best and Kellner, 2001: 5). To answer these questions, readers are provided with a diverse array of readings that attempt to understand and to analyze the social world and how it came to be. Because this is a *feminist* theory anthology, attention centers on what these various social transformations mean for gender relations and for women of different classes, races, sexualities, and global locations. These different social locations present a multiplicity of lenses for viewing the world and each theorist provides insights into her or his own "vanishing present" that helps us to better understand our own (Spivak, [1999] 2006).[1]

USING THIS TEXT TO NAVIGATE FEMINIST THOUGHT

This interdisciplinary text interweaves classical and contemporary writings from the social sciences and the humanities to represent feminist thought from the late eighteenth century to the present. Although the focus is on U.S. feminist thought, feminist writings from abroad that have substantially impacted U.S. feminism are included. Having studied and taught feminist theory either individually or collectively for decades, we are well aware of the trepidation with which many students approach theory as an intimidating subject and/or as an unnecessarily abstract, abstruse, and irrelevant one. Consequently, we have organized this text in a number of specific ways to make feminist thought more accessible to readers and to help them understand its value.

The first level of organization highlights the major feminist political perspectives that have characterized U.S. feminist thought. The importance of organizing the text in terms of political perspectives lies in the fact that *feminism is not simply a body of thought; it is a politics directed toward social change.* Here readers can see the political differences between various feminist perspectives and their strategies for social change. It will readily become apparent that feminism is not a monolithic theory; that all feminists do not think alike; and that, like all other time-honored modes of thinking, feminist thought has a past, as well as a present and a future (Tong, 1998: 1).

The second level of organization is historical in that the anthology covers feminist thought from the late eighteenth century to the present. The advantages of this historical approach are that readers can see how theories are constructed over time and how they often develop in response to concrete historical conditions, as well as to other perspectives and the debates they engender. Most importantly, it illuminates how theories are not "free floating ideas" (Morton, 2003: x) but are grounded in social, economic, and political conditions that influence their form and content.

Many histories of U.S. feminism employ a linear "wave approach." There are debates over the actual timing of different waves, but there is general consensus that the **first wave** designates the surge of women's rights activism beginning in the 1830s and culminating around the campaign for women's suffrage that ended or at least went into abeyance in 1920 with the passage of the Nineteenth Amendment to the U.S. Constitution (Taylor, 1989). The **second wave** denotes the resurgence of women's organizing in the 1960s that suffered major setbacks with the defeat of the Equal Rights Amendment (ERA) in 1982. The **third wave** refers to the resurgence of feminist activism in the 1990s by younger feminists who came of adult age after the second wave (Siegel, 1997). Although women's rights advocates of the first wave rarely used the term "feminist" (Cott, 1987: 13–14), we will take the liberty of using this term throughout the text.

At times, we will refer to these different waves. However, we chose not to foreground this oceanography of feminism for a number of reasons. First, wave approaches too often ignore feminist writings and activism before and between the different waves. Second, such approaches generally draw attention to the common themes that unify each wave and focus on the largest and most hegemonic feminist organizations. By doing so, they obscure the diversity of competing feminisms *within* each wave, as well as the contributions of more politically radical feminists and of women activists and theorists marginalized within each wave. Third, history itself does not develop in a cumulative, progressive, or linear fashion. Consequently, feminist writings are included that suggest alternative ways of viewing history where the uneven and contingent nature of societal development and the development of social thought are revealed. Fourth, "waves of feminism" are not synonymous with the history of feminism. Rather, just as ocean waves crest and subside, waves of feminism simply refer to those historical eras when the U.S. women's movement sufficiently crested to have an *activist mass-base.* Consequently, this anthology includes feminist writings prior to, during these crests, and in the periods of subsidence between the various waves.

The third level of organization focuses on theory applications or how feminist theorists have addressed specific topics over historical time. This is done in two different ways. First, rather than having a separate chapter on ecofeminism, ecofeminist writings are threaded throughout the text to show how different feminist political perspectives address the links between the domination of women and the domination of nature. Although the term ecofeminism was not coined until 1974, this text demonstrates how environmental concerns were addressed by diverse feminisms throughout the history of the U.S. women's movement.

Second, we focus on how feminists from the first through the third waves addressed the topics of colonialism, imperialism, and globalization. The choice of these topics and the space devoted to them reflect the importance of using a global perspective. Globalization is ubiquitous today. As the world economic system becomes increasingly integrated, the privileges and oppressions of women in the United States are tied increasingly to the privileges and oppressions of women across the globe; thus, it becomes ever more important to recognize the links between the global and the local.

UNIQUE FEATURES OF THIS ANTHOLOGY

A central tenet of this text is that the quest for social justice is the *raison d'etre* of feminist theory; thus, understanding the political implications of different feminist perspectives is imperative. Because the *emphasis is on the political*, this text differs from other feminist anthologies that simply list readings chronologically or by topic. We fear that when feminist writings are simply listed, it is more difficult for readers to distinguish between their underlying political assumptions and their strategies and goals for social change. In contrast, this text *highlights the relationship between feminist theory and political practice* so that these important distinctions do not remain obscured.

Second, particular *attention is paid to the multiplicity and diversity of feminist voices, visions and vantage points by race, class, gender, sexuality, and global location.* Whereas many other feminist anthologies focus on these important differences between women, this text links these diverse social locations to political concerns. We take as a central tenet that the particular problems people face in their everyday lives often reflect their different standpoints or social locations. Given the historical nature of this text, how these problems and political concerns change over time also become more visible.

Third, this anthology *calls for a broader description of the activity that customarily qualifies as theoretical—pointing to multiple sites of theory production both inside and outside of the academy.* Not only does it celebrate the value of socially lived knowledge or the knowledge garnered from everyday life, but also it celebrates forms of theorizing that are different from the Western form of abstract logic (Collins, 1990; King, 1990). *Along with more conventional forms of theorizing, this anthology includes personal narratives, poems, short stories, zines, lyrics from music, and even a cartoon.* By defending multiple sites of theorizing, we recognize that "doing theory" is an activity that extends well beyond the classroom, the seminar paper, or the academic journal and that alternative forms of theorizing also represent a "distillation of experience" that can serve as emancipatory projects for women (Lorde, 1984: 38).

Fourth, for readers interested in a deeper understanding of feminist theory, there is a *sister textbook* that provides a more detailed analysis of the writings in this anthology, as well as a more thorough grounding of these ideas in their historical context. *Reading Feminist Theory: From Modernity to Postmodernity* was actually designed to accompany its sister text *Doing Feminist Theory: From Modernity to Postmodernity* (2012) and Oxford University Press offers a discount for purchasing these two books together.

Fifth, to enhance the learning experience, there is an *online website that provides bibliographical information on the authors of the readings in this anthology*. Here readers can learn more about the lives and works of these feminist authors, as well as their various activities and accomplishments. The website link is http://www.oup.com/us/mann.

A sixth unique feature of this text is that it is organized so that readers can more clearly see *paradigm shifts in feminist thought*. A **paradigm shift** is a fundamental change in the theoretical assumptions underlying an entire school of thought or worldview. We argue that such a shift in feminist thought took place between the 1970s and the 1990s in U.S. feminism, when modern feminist thought was challenged by feminist perspectives that had taken the postmodern turn. By comparing and contrasting these two modes of social thought, readers will see how their distinctly different views on social life, social thought, and political practice hold the key to some of the major conflicts and debates within feminism today.

Seventh, this text *devotes three entire chapters and more than thirty readings to the topics of colonialism, imperialism, and globalization*. Here readers will learn how feminists from the first through the third waves addressed these issues and how feminist thought on these topics changed over time. Because the area we now call the United States has been both a colony and a colonizer, readers will better understand how this volatile history has affected women of different races, classes, sexualities, and nations.

Finally, *many of the chapters include readings that illustrate feminist critiques of other feminist theoretical perspectives*. For example, the reading by Uma Narayan in Chapter 1 shows how a non-Western, postcolonial theorist responds to various Western approaches to feminist epistemology. In Chapter 3, a reading by Suzanna Danuta Walters demonstrates how a radical feminist critiques queer theory. This *enables readers to see not only the strengths of various perspectives, but also their weaknesses*. Overall, the goal is to help readers develop the critical, analytical skills necessary to understand and to analyze new social conditions as they unfold. Such skills assist us in questioning conventional wisdoms about innumerable features of social life that we often take for granted. Using these skills results in a deeper understanding of what we already know, as well as new ideas and imperatives for social change.

NOTE

1. *Toward a History of the Vanishing Present* is the subtitle of Gayatri Chakravorty Spivak's *Critique of Postcolonial Reason* ([1999] 2006).

Reading Feminist Theory

CHAPTER 1

Doing Feminist Theory

> Making theory is the challenge before us. For in its production lies the hope of
> our liberation, in its production lies the possibility of naming our pain—of
> making our hurt go away.
>
> —bell hooks, 1994

INTRODUCTION

The earliest use of the term "feminist" in the United States is attributed to a 1906
article about Madeleine Pelletier—a socialist who used "militant" suffrage tactics
learned in France (Cott, 1987: 14–15). Prior to that, U.S. feminists referred to
themselves as "suffragists" or used the awkward term "women's righters." Nineteenth-
and early-twentieth-century women's rights activists also referred to their political
concerns as the "Woman Question," intentionally using the singular "woman" to
denote the unity women shared in their political cause and social movement (Cott,
1987: 3). After 1910, the term feminist became more frequently used in the United
States. Today "feminism" not only is used in academic and political discourses, but
also is part of everyday discourse. Whether used as a negative label to dismiss this
"ism" or as a positive label to empower women, feminism is often portrayed as a
single entity. In contrast, this text highlights the *multiplicity of feminist perspectives*
that exist today and that have existed in the past.

Precisely because there are many and diverse feminisms, the term feminism
defies any simple explanation. Indeed, it is common for contemporary feminist
texts to evade or elide the question of what feminism means—a situation that can
be frustrating for students. It is important to realize that the authors of these texts
may be intentionally avoiding the dangers of speaking for other feminists who have
different and equally viable definitions of feminism. Thus, rather than a weakness,
this evasion can reflect one of the feminist movement's strengths—namely a commitment to openness and inclusiveness. As an alternative, feminist texts often provide a list of definitions that have been used by a variety of feminists. Following

this well-traversed path, Reading 1 from Cheris Kramarae and Paula Treichler's *A Feminist Dictionary* (1985) illustrates how the terms woman, feminist, and feminism have been defined by feminists in different historical eras and representing diverse political perspectives.

HOW FEMINISTS DO THEORY AND FOR WHOM?

A key issue in debates over how we do feminist theory and for whom it is done is the *accessibility of feminist theory*. If feminist theory is a tool for social and political change, should it be accessible and understandable to the average person? Some of the most influential feminist theoretical perspectives today, such as feminist postmodernism, poststructuralism, and postcolonial theory, use extremely difficult scholarly language. Among their ranks are feminists who challenge the notion that theory should be written in a style accessible to all. For example, postcolonial theorist Gayatri Spivak argues that simple language is easily misconstrued and/or interpreted differently by different people and can mask real social and political inequalities in the contemporary world (Spivak quoted in Morton, 2003: 6). On the opposite end of the continuum are feminists who argue that we should abandon theory altogether—that theories themselves are simply powerful, elitist discourses that end up empowering some people and silencing others (Grimshaw, 1993). The difficult, abstruse language of academic theory especially has been criticized for failing to meet the needs of women "outside the ivied gates" (Wolf, [1993] 1994: 125) and for draining ideas of their relevance to real-world politics and action.

Reading 2 from "Theory as Liberatory Practice" by intersectionality theorist bell hooks [Gloria Jean Watkins][1] addresses this debate. Hooks takes a middle ground between those who engage in anti-intellectual theory bashing and those who treat theory as something that only elites can produce or understand. On the one hand, hooks argues that theory should be accessible to more than a small cadre of intellectuals and she criticizes theorists who use difficult language that leave readers "stumbling bleary-eyed" and "feeling humiliated" (1994: 65). On the other, she criticizes those who "trash" theory for promoting a "false dichotomy between theory and political practice" (1994: 65). She knows that theories entail important ideas that can serve a healing, liberatory function. Her conclusion implores feminists to call attention to the importance of theory because "in its production lies the possibility of naming our pain—of making our hurt go away" (hooks, 1994: 75).

FEMINIST EPISTEMOLOGIES

The term **epistemology** refers to the study of who can be a knowledge producer and how knowledge is produced. Because there is not one, but many feminisms, the writings presented in this text do not always agree on epistemological positioning. Major analysts of feminist epistemologies have divided feminist thought into three major camps—feminist empiricism, feminist standpoint epistemology, and feminist postmodern epistemology (Hesse-Biber et al., 2004; Harding, 2004; Hekman, 2004). Reading 3 from Sandra Harding's "The Woman Question in Science to the Science Question in Feminism" (1986) is one of the more influential works that highlighted this trio of epistemological stances underlying feminist thought.

FEMINIST EMPIRICISM

For feminist empiricists, theories are privileged when they are based on rational means for their construction, such as logic and/or empirical science. By privileged, we mean that they are given more status and credibility than other forms of knowledge such as intuition or common sense. By rational, we mean that they adhere to certain formal rules of procedure such as those that undergird the scientific method. For example, when one refers to **empirical** data, this means that evidence must be capable of being observed through one's senses (sight, sound, smell, and touch). Such rules are exclusive in that they exclude certain phenomena, such as the supernatural, that lie outside of the domain of scientific theories or methodological practices.

For feminist empiricists, logic and empirical evidence provide the bases for determining the greater "truth" or "falsity" of different knowledge claims and/or the success or failure of certain political policies or practices. Logic and science also are used to document existing inequalities between men and women and to empirically challenge claims that women are less capable than men. Here, scientific facts are viewed as subversive because they can undermine patriarchal assumptions about women. For feminist empiricists, theory and empirical evidence are powerful tools for understanding social reality, for guiding political practice, and for empowering women.

An example of an empiricist approach is provided in Reading 4 from Charlotte Bunch's "Not by Degrees: Feminist Theory and Education" ([1979] 1987). Bunch highlights how "theory is not just a body of facts or a set of personal options"; rather, "it involves explanations and hypotheses that are based on available knowledge and experience" ([1979] 1987: 12). Bunch sees emancipatory possibilities in developing a comprehensive feminist theory buttressed by logic and scientific evidence. For her, the main task of feminist theory is to develop a framework that can accurately describe the social realities of women's existence and subordination, provide a deep explanation of the origins of those realities, offer an alternative vision of how the social world could be better for women, and guide political strategies for ending or at least reducing women's subordination (Jaggar and Rothenberg, 1984: xvi).

Bunch's approach differs from positivist empiricism[2] in that she does not view herself as a neutral, objective, detached researcher. She explicitly recognizes that feminist research has political implications given its goal of improving the position of women. However, the other features of her article follow the logic of the empiricist camp.

STANDPOINT EPISTEMOLOGIES

Standpoint theorists highlight the differential privilege given to certain groups in knowledge production. For Sandra Harding, the starting point of standpoint theory is the recognition that in societies stratified by race, class, gender, and sexuality, socially marginalized people have been excluded from knowledge production because they are viewed as biologically or intellectually inferior (Harding, 1991: 140). The knowledge claims of these subordinate groups are often referred to as **subjugated knowledges** because they have been silenced, ignored, or deemed less credible. Standpoint epistemologies call for the retrieval of these subjugated knowledges as part of their demand for **polyvocality**, or the inclusion of many and diverse voices.

A powerful example of a standpoint approach can be found in Reading 5 from Maria Lugones and Elizabeth Spelman's "Have We Got a Theory for You!" ([1983] 2005). By interweaving Spanish and English, as well as counterposing different standpoints, both the form and the content of their article reveal their critical points. The Hispana voice argues,

> But you theorize about women and we are women, so you understand yourselves to be theorizing about us, and we understand you to be theorizing about us. Yet none of the feminist theories developed so far seems to me to help Hispanas in the articulation of our experience. We have a sense that in using them we are distorting our experiences. (Lugones and Spelman, [1983] 2005: 20)

Lugones and Spelman highlight how, by speaking for other women without understanding their lives and experiences, many feminist theorists from privileged social locations ended up using an imperial "we." This imperial, feminist we colonizes the visions and voices of women in less privileged social locations. A **colonialist stance** is discussed in more depth in Chapter 10. Suffice it to say here that it refers to representations that employ a type of "missionary framework" where women from subordinate social locations are viewed as victims who are unable to represent themselves and must be rescued and represented by more privileged others (Narayan, 1997: 48–49).

Some standpoint theorists argue that the knowledges of subjugated peoples entail the most critical insights, as we shall see in Chapters 4 and 5. Although not all standpoint theorists agree with **privileging the knowledge of the oppressed,** they all share the modernist view that feminists must judge between competing knowledge claims for theory to guide political practice. Science is one means for making judgments about the validity of knowledge claims, but it is not the only means. For standpoint theorists, alternative ways of knowing are also given credence, such as **socially lived knowledge** or the "wisdom" garnered from everyday life experiences (Collins, 1990). Thus science is not dismissed, but it is decentered. Standpoint epistemologies bridge modern and postmodern thought given their notion of multiple vantage points on reality. Yet, they maintain a foothold in modernism by not treating all knowledge claims as equally valid.

Today, most feminists recognize that there is no generic woman—every woman has specific class, race, sexuality, and global locations; hence, gender is always inflected by race, class, sexuality, and global location. Armed with this new understanding of gender, political concerns have moved away from considering women in general toward exploring the specificities of gender relations and the ways in which gender is necessarily shaped in conjunction with other systems of domination (Jaggar and Rothenberg, 1993: xvi). Feminist scholarship also has turned away from the foundational issues discussed by Charlotte Bunch, such as her call for understanding the origins of women's oppression to develop a universal, comprehensive theory of women's oppression. Instead, preference is given to **historical specificity**, meaning the analysis of a specific time and place.

Sandra Harding provides additional contrasts between standpoint epistemologies and positivist empiricist approaches. Unlike positivists who view scientific knowledge as value free or objective, standpoint theorists view all knowledge as socially situated and influenced by the knower's social location. No one—including scientists—can "erase the fingerprints" (Harding, 1993: 57) that underlie this production process. Harding uses the term **God trick** to refer to positivists' claims that scientists can view the world in a detached or impartial manner. In contrast, standpoint theorists advocate **reflexivity** where researchers acknowledge their roles in constructing knowledge, as well as how their own social locations may influence their studies and, conversely, how their studies may also affect their own views as knowledge producers as well as the views of other people.

POSTMODERN EPISTEMOLOGIES

Postmodern epistemologies agree with many of the features of standpoint approaches. They too use a social constructionist approach that highlights the relationship between knowledge and power. They accept the view that knowledges are socially situated and partial and they acknowledge that there are multiple vantage points on social reality. They also value polyvocality and call for the resuscitation of subjugated knowledges as a critical act. One of the major ways they differ is that postmodern epistemologies embrace **judgmental relativism**—meaning that no one vantage point or knowledge claim can be judged as more valid than any other.

This relativism is rooted in their rejection of the modernist assumption that reality has an inherent order or structure discernible through scientific inquiry. Rather, reality is open to a multitude of possible interpretations that are manifest in different vantage points and discourses of varying degrees of power and privilege. There is no way to adjudicate between them. Science and history—the evidentiary bases of modern thought—are all just narratives, just stories that silence some and give voice to others. There is no single truth, but many different truths situated in different discourses, some of which are more dominant than others. There is no uniquely privileged social standpoint from which a final, authoritative feminist theory can be constructed.

Reading 6 from Jane Flax's article "The End of Innocence" (1992) uses a postmodern lens to highlight some of the issues at stake in these epistemological debates. For example, Flax accuses modernists of having a naive or "innocent" faith in the Enlightenment ideas of a universal scientific method and a singular notion of truth—an innocence ended by the postmodern turn in social thought. For Flax, the belief that there is some sort of truth that can tell us how to act in the world in ways that are good for all people is a "dream" (446). This dream cannot be realized because "there is no stable, unchanging, and unitary Real against which our thoughts can be tested" (453). Truth claims are "undecidable" (452) outside of or between different discourses. In her view, a "dangerous consequence" (459) of modernist notions of universal truth, justice, and knowledge is that they release us from taking full responsibility for our actions. Modernists "remain children" waiting for these "higher authorities" (459) to save us from the consequences of our acts. Feminists must grow up; face the "end of innocence" and "resist the delusory and dangerous hope of redemption by science and logic" (460).

For these reasons, postmodernists are skeptical that science and rationality necessarily lead to social progress. They point to how these so-called rational means have ushered in some of the worst nightmares of the twentieth century, such as the ability to destroy our planet through environmental or nuclear disasters. Flax concludes, "At its best, postmodernism invites us to engage in a continual process of disillusionment with the grandiose fantasies that have brought us to the brink of annihilation" (1992: 460).

A POSTCOLONIAL RESPONSE TO WESTERN FEMINIST EPISTEMOLOGICAL DEBATES

Reading 7 from "The Project of Feminist Epistemology: Perspectives from a Non-western Feminist" ([1989] 2013) is by postcolonial theorist Uma Narayan. She begins by discussing the various assumptions and goals of feminist epistemologies and how they have fostered the efforts of oppressed groups to "reclaim for themselves the value of their own experience" (Narayan, [1989] 2013: 371). Although she lauds many of their achievements, she also examines the dangers of using these epistemologies in a "noncontextual" and "nonpragmatic" way (371). In particular, Narayan explores what these feminist epistemological stances might mean in non-Western contexts and for non-Western feminists. She has serious reservations about criticizing positivist empiricism as Western feminist standpoint and postmodern epistemologies do, particularly in societies where religion and traditional values prevail over secular and scientific thought. She fears that such attacks on empirical science might result in the further entrenchment of traditional values that may prove more oppressive to women. She also fears that feminist epistemologies that highlight the value of women's standpoint could be misconstrued and used to vindicate traditional beliefs that assign women to unequal roles in society.

Narayan also explores the "dark side of double vision" ([1989] 2013: 376), meaning the dangers of privileging the knowledge of oppressed groups, whether these groups are women, the poor, or racial minorities. She points to the costs of oppression that can render subjects devoid of the skills necessary to function as independent entities in a given culture or society. She warns feminists not to idealize or romanticize oppression in ways that "blind us to its real material and psychic deprivations" (378).

CONCLUSION

Overall the readings in this first chapter underscore the multiplicity and diversity of feminist perspectives and the debates between feminists in regard to theory construction, epistemology, and the accessibility of theory. Most of all, these readings should make readers ever mindful of the power dynamics involved in knowledge production and the integral relationship between knowledge and power.

NOTES

1. bell hooks is the pen name of Gloria Jean Watkins. She prefers that this pen name be typed in lowercase to highlight the content of her writings rather than herself as author.
2. Positivists believe that there is a single unitary scientific method that can be used to study the natural and the social sciences. They also believe in objectivity or that scientists can be detached, value-free observers.

"WOMAN," "FEMINISTS," AND "FEMINISM"

ON "WOMAN"

Is a "slave who has chains to break." (Margaret Fuller, 1843)

Is "in her sufferings bound hand and foot, unprotected by the law or public sentiment, dumb alike in Church, State, and at the domestic hearth." (Susan B. Anthony, 1852)

Regarded by men "as a breeding-machine and the necessary adjunct to a frying-pan." (Cicely Hamilton, 1909)

Is economically invisible. "To the androcentric mind she does not exist—women are females, and that's all." (Charlotte Perkins Gilman, 1911)

"A woman, unless she submits, is neither a mule
nor a queen
though like a mule she may suffer and like a queen
pace the floor." (Alice Walker, 1975)

Has been "obsolete since the beginning of the Glorious Age. Considered by many companion lovers as the most infamous designation. This word once applied to being fallen in an absolute state of servitude. Its meaning was, 'one who belongs to another.'" (Monique Wittig and Sande Zeig, 1976)

"Jill-of-all-trades
Lover, mother, housewife, friend, breadwinner
Heart and spade
A woman is a ritual
A house that must accommodate
A house that must endure
Generation after generation . . . " (Genny Lim, 1981)

"From father's house to husband's house to a grave that still might not be her own, a woman acquiesces to male authority in order to gain some protection from male violence. She conforms, in order to be as safe as she can be." (Andrea Dworkin, 1983: 14)

"What is a woman you ask. . . . Una mujer? . . . Are you like me, are you proud, brown, bilingual, confused and anxious? . . . The voices of our culture—our mothers and grandmothers—filter through the cracks of our personal feminism. . . . Independence. We want to be our mothers . . . crochet like our grandmothers—abuelita—and write reports and analytical studies." (Gladys Benavides Corbit, 1984)

ON "FEMINISM" AND "FEMINISTS"

Has as its goal to give every woman "the opportunity of becoming the best that her natural faculties make her capable of." (Millicent Garrett Fawcett, 1878)

"I myself have never been able to find out precisely what feminism is: I only know that people call me a feminist whenever I express sentiments that differentiate me from a doormat. . . ." (Rebecca West, 1913)

"Mother, what is a Feminist?"
  "A Feminist, my daughter, Is any woman now who
  cares To think about her own affairs
  As men don't think she oughter."
  (Alice Duer Miller, 1915)

"Begins but cannot end with the discovery by an individual of her self-consciousness as a woman. It is not, finally, even the recognition of her reasons for anger, or

Reprinted from *A Feminist Dictionary* edited by Paula Treichler and Cheris Kramarae. London: Pandora, 1985. pp. 158–161 and 492–494. Reprinted by permission of Cheris Kramarae.

the decision to change her life, to go back to school, to leave a marriage. . . . Feminism means finally that we renounce our obedience to the fathers and recognize that the world they have described is not the whole world. . . . Feminism implies that we recognize fully the inadequacy for us, the distortion, of male-created ideologies, and that we proceed to think, and act, out of that recognition." (Adrienne Rich, 1976)

A person who knows that we hold up half the sky and who is going to make everyone else notice it. (Dawn Russell, 1979: 75)

"Feminism is the political theory and practice to free all women: women of color, working-class women, poor women, physically challenged women, lesbians, old women, as well as white economically privileged heterosexual women. Anything less than this is not feminism, but merely female self-aggrandizement." (Barbara Smith, 1979)

"Is a commitment to eradicating the ideology of domination that permeates Western culture on various levels—sex, race, and class, to name a few—and a commitment to reorganizing U.S. society, so that the self-development of people can take precedence over imperialism, economic expansion, and material desires." (bell hooks, 1981)

"Is an entire worldview or *gestalt,* not just a laundry list of 'women's issues.' Feminist theory provides a basis for understanding every area of our lives, and a feminist perspective can affect the world politically, culturally, economically, and spiritually." (Charlotte Bunch, 1983)

"A set of beliefs and theoretical constructions about the nature of women's oppression and the part that this oppression plays within social reality more generally." (Liz Stanley and Sue Wise, 1983)

"Well, I'm convinced that many frustrated and crabby women are merely feminists in restraints." (Diane E. Germain, 1983)

(1985)

---

2 • *bell hooks*

"THEORY AS LIBERATORY PRACTICE"

I came to theory because I was hurting—the pain within me was so intense that I could not go on living. I came to theory desperate, wanting to comprehend— to grasp what was happening around and within me. Most importantly, I wanted to make the hurt go away. I saw in theory then a location for healing.

I came to theory young, when I was still a child. In *The Significance of Theory* Terry Eagleton says:

> Children make the best theorists, since they have not yet been educated into accepting our routine social practices as "natural," and so insist on posing to those practices the most embarrassingly general and fundamental questions,

regarding them with a wondering estrangement which we adults have long forgotten. Since they do not yet grasp our social practices as inevitable, they do not see why we might not do things differently.

Whenever I tried in childhood to compel folks around me to do things differently, to look at the world differently, using theory as intervention, as a way to challenge the status quo, I was punished. I remember trying to explain at a very young age to Mama why I thought it was highly inappropriate for Daddy, this man who hardly spoke to me, to have the right to discipline me, to punish me physically with

---

whippings. Her response was to suggest I was losing my mind and in need of more frequent punishment.

Imagine if you will this young black couple struggling first and foremost to realize the patriarchal norm (that is of the woman staying home, taking care of the household and children while the man worked) even though such an arrangement meant that economically, they would always be living with less. Try to imagine what it must have been like for them, each of them working hard all day, struggling to maintain a family of seven children, then having to cope with one bright-eyed child relentlessly questioning, daring to challenge male authority, rebelling against the very patriarchal norm they were trying so hard to institutionalize.

. . . How I envied Dorothy her journey in *The Wizard of Oz*, that she could travel to her worst fears and nightmares only to find at the end that "there is no place like home." Living in childhood without a sense of home, I found a place of sanctuary in "theorizing," in making sense out of what was happening. I found a place where I could imagine possible futures, a place where life could be lived differently. This "lived" experience of critical thinking, of reflection and analysis, because a place where I worked at explaining the hurt and making it go away. Fundamentally, I learned from this experience that theory could be a healing place.

Psychoanalyst Alice Miller lets you know in her introduction to the book *Prisoners of Childhood* that it was her own personal struggle to recover from the wounds of childhood that led her to rethink and theorize anew prevailing social and critical thought about the meaning of childhood pain, of child abuse. In her adult life, through her practice, she experienced theory as a healing place. Significantly, she had to imagine herself in the space of childhood, to look again from that perspective, to remember "crucial information, answers to questions which had gone unanswered throughout [her] study of philosophy and psychoanalysis." When our lived experience of theorizing is fundamentally linked to processes of self-recovery, of collective liberation, no gap exists between theory and practice. Indeed, what such experience makes more evident is the bond between the two—that ultimately reciprocal process wherein one enables the other.

Theory is not inherently healing, liberatory, or revolutionary. It fulfills this function only when we ask that it do so and direct our theorizing towards this end. When I was a child, I certainly did not describe the

processes of thought and critique I engaged in as "theorizing." Yet, as I suggested in *Feminist Theory: From Margin to Center*, the possession of a term does not bring a process or practice into being; concurrently one may practice theorizing without ever knowing/possessing the term, just as we can live and act in feminist resistance without ever using the word "feminism."

. . . Critical reflection on contemporary production of feminist theory makes it apparent that the shift from early conceptualizations of feminist theory (which insisted that it was most vital when it encouraged and enabled feminist practice) begins to occur or at least becomes most obvious with the segregation and institutionalization of the feminist theorizing process in the academy, with the privileging of written feminist thought/theory over oral narratives. Concurrently, the efforts of black women and women of color to challenge and deconstruct the category "woman"—the insistence on recognition that gender is not the sole factor determining constructions of femaleness—was a critical intervention, one which led to a profound revolution in feminist thought and truly interrogated and disrupted the hegemonic feminist theory produced primarily by academic women, most of whom were white.

In the wake of this disruption, the assault on white supremacy made manifest in alliances between white women academics and white male peers seems to have been formed and nurtured around common efforts to formulate and impose standards of critical evaluation that would be used to define what is theoretical and what is not. These standards often led to appropriation and/or devaluation of work that did not "fit," that was suddenly deemed not theoretical—or not theoretical enough. In some circles, there seems to be a direct connection between white feminist scholars turning towards critical work and theory by white men, and the turning away of white feminist scholars from fully respecting and valuing the critical insights and theoretical offerings of black women or women of color.

Work by women of color and marginalized groups of white women (for example, lesbians, sex radicals), especially if written in a manner that renders it accessible to a broad reading public, is often de-legitimized in academic settings, even if that work enables and promotes feminist practice. Though such work is often appropriated by the very individuals setting restrictive critical standards, it is this work that they most often claim is not really theory. Clearly, one of the uses these individuals make of theory is instrumental. They use it to set up unnecessary and competing hierarchies of thought which reinscribe the politics of domination by designating work as either inferior, superior, or more or less worthy of attention. King emphasizes that "theory finds different uses in different locations." It is evident that one of the many uses of theory in academic locations is in the production of an intellectual class hierarchy where the only work deemed truly theoretical is work that is highly abstract, jargonistic, difficult to read, and containing obscure references. In Childers and hooks's "A Conversation about Race and Class" (also in *Conflicts in Feminism*) literary critic Mary Childers declares that it is highly ironic that "a certain kind of theoretical performance which only a small cadre of people can possibly understand" has come to be seen as representative of any production of critical thought that will be given recognition within many academic circles as "theory." It is especially ironic when this is the case with feminist theory. And, it is easy to imagine different locations, spaces outside academic exchange, where such theory would not only be seen as useless, but as politically nonprogressive, a kind of narcissistic, self-indulgent practice that most seeks to create a gap between theory and practice so as to perpetuate class elitism. There are so many settings in this country where the written word has only slight visual meaning, where individuals who cannot read or write can find no use for a published theory however lucid or opaque. Hence, any theory that cannot be shared in everyday conversation cannot be used to educate the public.

Imagine what a change has come about within feminist movements when students, most of whom are female, come to Women's Studies classes and read what they are told is feminist theory only to feel that what they are reading has no meaning, cannot be understood, or when understood in no way connects to "lived" realities beyond the classroom. As feminist activists we might ask ourselves, of what use is feminist theory that assaults the fragile psyches of women struggling to throw off patriarchy's oppressive yoke? We might ask ourselves, of what use is feminist theory that literally beats them down, leaves them stumbling bleary-eyed from classroom settings feeling humiliated, feeling as though they could easily be standing in a living room or bedroom somewhere naked with someone who has seduced them or is going to, who also subjects them to a process of interaction that humiliates, that strips them

of their sense of value? Clearly, a feminist theory that can do this may function to legitimize Women's Studies and feminist scholarship in the eyes of the ruling patriarchy, but it undermines and subverts feminist movements. Perhaps it is the existence of this most highly visible feminist theory that compels us to talk about the gap between theory and practice. For it is indeed the purpose of such theory to divide, separate, exclude, keep at a distance. And because this theory continues to be used to silence, censor, and devalue various feminist theoretical voices, we cannot simply ignore it. Yet, despite its uses as an instrument of domination, it may also contain important ideas, thoughts, visions, that could, if used differently, serve a healing, liberatory function. However, we cannot ignore the dangers it poses to feminist struggle which must be rooted in a theory that informs, shapes, and makes feminist practice possible.

Within feminist circles, many women have responded to hegemonic feminist theory that does not speak clearly to us by trashing theory, and, as a consequence, further promoting the false dichotomy between theory and practice. Hence, they collude with those whom they would oppose. By internalizing the false assumption that theory is not a social practice, they promote the formation within feminist circles of a potentially oppressive hierarchy where all concrete action is viewed as more important than any theory written or spoken. Recently, I went to a gathering of predominantly black women where we discussed whether or not black male leaders, such as Martin Luther King and Malcolm X, should be subjected to feminist critiques that pose hard questions about their stance on gender issues. The entire discussion was less than two hours. As it drew to a close, a black woman who had been particularly silent, said that she was not interested in all this theory and rhetoric, all this talk, that she was more interested in action, in doing something, that she was just "tired" of all the talk.

This woman's response disturbed me: it is a familiar reaction. Perhaps in her daily life she inhabits a world different from mine. In the world I live in daily, there are few occasions when black women or women-of-color thinkers come together to debate rigorously issues of race, gender, class, and sexuality. Therefore, I did not know where she was coming from when she suggested that the discussion we were having was common, so common as to be something we could dispense with or do without. I felt that we were engaged in a process of critical dialogue and theorizing that has long been taboo. Hence, from my perspective we were charting new journeys, claiming for ourselves as black women an intellectual terrain where we could begin the collective construction of feminist theory.

In many black settings, I have witnessed the dismissal of intellectuals, the putting down of theory, and remained silent. I have come to see that silence is an act of complicity, one that helps perpetuate the idea that we can engage in revolutionary black liberation and feminist struggle without theory. Like many insurgent black intellectuals, whose intellectual work and teaching is often done in predominantly white settings, I am often so pleased to be engaged with a collective group of black folks that I do not want to make waves, or make myself an outsider by disagreeing with the group. In such settings, when the work of intellectuals is devalued, I have in the past rarely contested prevailing assumptions, or have spoken affirmatively or ecstatically about intellectual process. I was afraid that if I took a stance that insisted on the importance of intellectual work, particularly theorizing, or if I just simply stated that I thought it was important to read widely, I would risk being seen as uppity, or as lording it over. I have often remained silent.

These risks to one's sense of self now seem trite when considered in relation to the crises we are facing as African Americans, to our desperate need to rekindle and sustain the flame of black liberation struggle. At the gathering I mentioned, I dared to speak, saying in response to the suggestion that we were just wasting our time talking, that I saw our words as an action, that our collective struggle to discuss issues of gender and blackness without censorship was subversive practice. Many of the issues that we continue to confront as black people—low self-esteem, intensified nihilism and despair, repressed rage and violence that destroys our physical and psychological well-being—cannot be addressed by survival strategies that have worked in the past. I insisted that we needed new theories rooted in an attempt to understand both the nature of our contemporary predicament and the means by which we might collectively engage in resistance that would transform our current reality. I was, however, not as rigorous and relentless as I would have been in a different setting in my efforts to emphasize the importance of intellectual work, the production of theory as a social practice that can be liberatory. Though not afraid to

speak, I did not want to be seen as the one who "spoiled" the good time, the collective sense of sweet solidarity in blackness. This fear reminded me of what it was like more than ten years ago to be in feminist settings, posing questions about theory and practice, particularly about issues of race and racism that were seen as potentially disruptive of sisterhood and solidarity.

It seemed ironic that at a gathering called to honor Martin Luther King, Jr., who had often dared to speak and act in resistance to the status quo, black women were still negating our right to engage in oppositional political dialogue and debate, especially since this is not a common occurrence in black communities. Why did the black women there feel the need to police one another, to deny one another a space within blackness where we could talk theory without being self-conscious? Why, when we could celebrate together the power of a black male critical thinker who dared to stand apart, was there this eagerness to repress any viewpoint that would suggest we might collectively learn from the ideas and visions of insurgent black female intellectuals/theorists, who by the nature of the work they do are necessarily breaking with the stereotype that would have us believe the "real" black woman is always the one who speaks from the gut, who righteously praises the concrete over the abstract, the material over the theoretical?

Again and again, black women find our efforts to speak, to break silence and engage in radical progressive political debates, opposed. There is a link between the silencing we experience, the censoring, the anti-intellectualism in predominantly black settings that are supposedly supportive (like all-black woman space), and that silencing that takes place in institutions wherein black women and women of color are told that we cannot be fully heard or listened to because our work is not theoretical enough. In "Travelling Theory: Cultural Politics of Race and Representation," cultural critic Kobena Mercer reminds us that blackness is complex and multifaceted and that black people can be interpolated into reactionary and antidemocratic politics. Just as some elite academics who construct theories of "blackness" in ways that make it a critical terrain which only the chosen few can enter—using theoretical work on race to assert their authority over black experience, denying democratic access to the process of theory making—threaten collective black liberation struggle, so do those among us who react to this by promoting anti-intellectualism by declaring all theory as worthless. By reinforcing the idea that there is a split between theory and practice or by creating such a split, both groups deny the power of liberatory education for critical consciousness, thereby perpetuating conditions that reinforce our collective exploitation and repression. . . .

. . . Within revolutionary feminist movements, within revolutionary black liberation struggles, we must continually claim theory as necessary practice within a holistic framework of liberatory activism. We must do more than call attention to ways theory is misused. We must do more than critique the conservative and at times reactionary uses some academic women make of feminist theory. We must actively work to call attention to the importance of creating a theory that can advance renewed feminist movements, particularly highlighting that theory which seeks to further feminist opposition to sexism, and sexist oppression. Doing this, we necessarily celebrate and value theory that can be and is shared in oral as well as written narrative.

Reflecting on my own work in feminist theory, I find writing—theoretical talk—to be most meaningful when it invites readers to engage in critical reflection and to engage in the practice of feminism. To me, this theory emerges from the concrete, from my efforts to make sense of everyday life experiences, from my efforts to intervene critically in my life and the lives of others. This to me is what makes feminist transformation possible. Personal testimony, personal experience, is such fertile ground for the production of liberatory feminist theory because it usually forms the base of our theory making. While we work to resolve those issues that are most pressing in daily life (our need for literacy, an end to violence against women and children, women's health and reproductive rights, and sexual freedom, to name a few), we engage in a critical process of theorizing that enables and empowers. I continue to be amazed that there is so much feminist writing produced and yet so little feminist theory that strives to speak to women, men and children about ways we might transform our lives via a conversion to feminist practice. Where can we find a body of feminist theory that is directed toward helping individuals integrate feminist thinking and practice into daily life? What feminist theory, for example, is directed toward assisting women who live in sexist households in their efforts to bring about feminist change?

We know that many individuals in the United States have used feminist thinking to educate themselves in ways that allow them to transform their lives. I am often critical of a life-style-based feminism, because I fear that any feminist transformational process that seeks to change society is easily co-opted if it is not rooted in a political commitment to mass-based feminist movement. Within white supremacist capitalist patriarchy, we have already witnessed the commodification of feminist thinking (just as we experience the commodification of blackness) in ways that make it seem as though one can partake of the "good" that these movements produce without any commitment to transformative politics and practice. In this capitalist culture, feminism and feminist theory are fast becoming a commodity that only the privileged can afford. This process of commodification is disrupted and subverted when as feminist activists we affirm our commitment to a politicized revolutionary feminist movement that has as its central agenda the transformation of society. From such a starting point, we automatically think of creating theory that speaks to the widest audience of people. I have written elsewhere, and shared in numerous public talks and conversations, that my decisions about writing style, about not using conventional academic formats, are political decisions motivated by the desire to be inclusive, to reach as many readers as possible in as many different locations. This decision has had consequences both positive and negative. Students at various academic institutions often complain that they cannot include my work on required reading lists for degree-oriented qualifying exams because their professors do not see it as scholarly enough. Any of us who create feminist theory and feminist writing in academic settings in which we are continually evaluated know that work deemed "not scholarly" or "not theoretical" can result in one not receiving deserved recognition and reward.

Now, in my life these negative responses seem insignificant when compared to the overwhelmingly positive responses to my work both in and outside the academy. Recently, I have received a spate of letters from incarcerated black men who read my work and wanted to share that they are working to unlearn sexism. In one letter, the writer affectionately boasted that he has made my name a "household word around that prison." These men talk about solitary critical reflection, about using this feminist work to understand the implications of patriarchy as a force shaping their identities, their ideas of manhood. After receiving a powerful critical response by one of these black men to my book *Yearning: Race, Gender and Cultural Politics*, I closed my eyes and visualized that work being read, studied, talked about in prison settings. Since the location that has most spoken back to me critically about the study of my work is usually an academic one, I share this with you not to brag or be immodest, but to testify, to let you know from firsthand experience that all our feminist theory directed at transforming consciousness, that truly wants to speak with diverse audiences, does work: this is not a naive fantasy.

In more recent talks, I have spoken about how "blessed" I feel to have my work affirmed in this way, to be among those feminist theorists creating work that acts as a catalyst for social change across false boundaries. There were many times early on when my work was subjected to forms of dismissal and devaluation that created within me a profound despair. I think such despair has been felt by every black woman or woman-of-color thinker/theorist whose work is oppositional and moves against the grain. Certainly Michele Wallace has written poignantly in her introduction to the re-issue of *Black Macho and the Myth of the Superwoman* that she was devastated and for a time silenced by the negative critical responses to her early work.

I am grateful that I can stand here and testify that if we hold fast to our beliefs that feminist thinking must be shared with everyone, whether through talking or writing, and create theory with this agenda in mind we can advance feminist movement that folks will long—yes, yearn—to be a part of. I share feminist thinking and practice wherever I am. When asked to talk in university settings, I search out other settings or respond to those who search me out so that I can give the riches of feminist thinking to anyone. Sometimes settings emerge spontaneously. At a black-owned restaurant in the South, for instance, I sat for hours with a diverse group of black women and men from various class backgrounds discussing issues of race, gender and class. Some of us were college-educated, others were not. We had a heated discussion of abortion, discussing whether black women should have the right to choose. Several of the Afrocentric black men present were arguing that the male should have as much choice as the female. One of the feminist black women present, a director of a health clinic for women,

spoke eloquently and convincingly about a woman's right to choose.

During this heated discussion one of the black women present who had been silent for a long time, who hesitated before she entered the conversation because she was unsure about whether or not she could convey the complexity of her thought in black vernacular speech (in such a way that we, the listeners, would hear and understand and not make fun of her words), came to voice. As I was leaving, this sister came up to me and grasped both my hands tightly, firmly, and thanked me for the discussion. She prefaced her words of gratitude by sharing that the conversation had not only enabled her to give voice to feelings and ideas she had always "kept" to herself, but that by saying it she had created a space for her and her partner to change thought and action. She stated this to me directly, intently, as we stood facing one another, holding my hands and saying again and again, "there's been so much hurt in me." She gave thanks that our meeting, our theorizing of race, gender, and sexuality that afternoon had eased her pain, testifying that she could feel the hurt going away, that she could feel a healing taking place within. Holding my hands, standing body to body, eye to eye, she allowed me to share empathically the warmth of that healing. She wanted me to bear witness, to hear again both the naming of her pain and the power that emerged when she felt the hurt go away. . . .

. . . It is not easy to name our pain, to theorize from that location.

I am grateful to the many women and men who dare to create theory from the location of pain and struggle, who courageously expose wounds to give us their experience to teach and guide, as a means to chart new theoretical journeys. Their work is liberatory. It not only enables us to remember and recover ourselves, it charges and challenges us to renew our commitment to an active, inclusive feminist struggle. We have still to collectively make feminist revolution. I am grateful that we are collectively searching as feminist thinkers/theorists for ways to make this movement happen. Our search leads us back to where it all began, to that moment when an individual woman or child, who may have thought she was all alone, began a feminist uprising, began to name her practice, indeed began to formulate theory from lived experience. Let us imagine that this woman or child was suffering the pain of sexism and sexist oppression, that she wanted to make the hurt go away. I am grateful that I can be a witness, testifying that we can create a feminist theory, a feminist practice, a revolutionary feminist movement that can speak directly to the pain that is within folks, and offer them healing words, healing strategies, healing theory. There is no one among us who has not felt the pain of sexism and sexist oppression, the anguish that male domination can create in daily life, the profound and unrelenting misery and sorrow.

Mari Matsuda has told us that "we are fed a lie that there is no pain in war," and that patriarchy makes this pain possible. Catharine MacKinnon reminds us that "we know things with our lives and we live that knowledge, beyond what any theory has yet theorized." Making this theory is the challenge before us. For in its production lies the hope of our liberation, in its production lies the possibility of naming all our pain—of making all our hurt go away. If we create feminist theory, feminist movements that address this pain, we will have no difficulty building a mass-based feminist resistance struggle. There will be no gap between feminist theory and feminist practice.

(1994)

---

3 • *Sandra Harding*

"THE WOMAN QUESTION IN SCIENCE TO THE SCIENCE QUESTION IN FEMINISM"

Feminist scholars have studied women, men, and social relations between the genders within, across, and insistently against the conceptual frameworks of the disciplines. In each area we have come to understand that what we took to be humanly inclusive problematics, concepts, theories, objective methodologies, and transcendental truths are in fact far less than that. Instead, these products of thought bear the mark of their collective and individual creators, and the creators in turn have been distinctively marked as to gender, class, race, and culture.[1] We can now discern the effects of these cultural markings in the discrepancies between the methods of knowing and the interpretations of the world provided by the creators of modern Western culture and those characteristic of the rest of us. Western culture's favored beliefs mirror in sometimes clear and sometimes distorting ways not the world as it is or as we might want it to be, but the social projects of their historically identifiable creators.

The natural sciences are a comparatively recent subject of feminist scrutiny. The critiques excite immense anticipation—or fear—yet they remain far more fragmented and less clearly conceptualized than feminist analyses in other disciplines.

The anticipation and fear are based in the recognition that we are a scientific culture, that scientific rationality has permeated not only the modes of thinking and acting of our public institutions but even the ways we think about the most intimate details of our private lives. Widely read manuals and magazine articles on child rearing and sexual relations gain their authority and popularity by appealing to science. And during the last century, the social use of science has shifted: formerly an occasional assistant, it has become the

---

direct generator of economic, political, and social accumulation and control. Now we can see that the hope to "dominate nature" for the betterment of the species has become the effort to gain unequal access to nature's resources for purposes of social domination. No longer is the scientist—if he ever was—an eccentric and socially marginal genius spending private funds and often private time on whatever purely intellectual pursuits happen to interest him. Only very rarely does his research have no foreseeable social uses. Instead, he (or, more recently, she) is part of a vast work force, is trained from elementary school on to enter academic, industrial, and governmental laboratories where 99+ percent of the research is expected to be immediately applicable to social projects. If these vast industrialized empires, devoted—whether intentionally or not—to material accumulation and social control, cannot be shown to serve the best interests of social progress by appeal to objective, dispassionate, impartial, rational knowledge-seeking, then in our culture they cannot be legitimated at all. Neither God nor tradition is privileged with the same credibility as scientific rationality in modern cultures. . . .

FIVE RESEARCH PROGRAMS

To draw attention to the lack of a developed feminist theory for the critique of the natural sciences is not to overlook the contributions these young but flourishing lines of inquiry have made. In a very short period of time, we have derived a far clearer picture of the extent to which science, too, is gendered. Now we can begin to understand the economic, political, and psychological mechanisms that keep science sexist and that must be eliminated if the nature, uses, and valuations of knowledge-seeking are to become humanly inclusive ones. Each of these lines of inquiry raises intriguing political and conceptual issues, not only for the practices of science and the ways these practices are legitimated but also for each other. Details of these research programs are discussed in following chapters; I emphasize here the problems they raise primarily to indicate the undertheorization of the whole field.

First of all, equity studies have documented the massive historical resistance to women's getting the education, credentials, and jobs available to similarly talented men;[2] they have also identified the psychological and social mechanisms through which discrimination

is informally maintained even when the formal barriers have been eliminated. Motivation studies have shown why boys and men more often want to excel at science, engineering, and math than do girls and women.[3] But should women want to become "just like men" in science, as many of these studies assume? That is, should feminism set such a low goal as mere equality with men? And to which men in science should women want to be equal—to underpaid and exploited lab technicians as well as Nobel Prize winners? Moreover, should women want to contribute to scientific projects that have sexist, racist, and classist problematics and outcomes? Should they want to be military researchers? Furthermore, what has been the effect of women's naiveté about the depth and extent of masculine resistance—that is, would women have struggled to enter science if they had understood how little equity would be produced by eliminating the formal barriers against women's participation?[4] Finally, does the increased presence of women in science have any effect at all on the nature of scientific problematics and outcomes?

Second, studies of the uses and abuses of biology, the social sciences, and their technologies have revealed the ways science is used in the service of sexist, racist, homophobic, and classist social projects. Oppressive reproductive policies; white men's management of all women's domestic labor; the stigmatization of, discrimination against, and medical "cure" of homosexuals; gender discrimination in workplaces—all these have been justified on the basis of sexist research and maintained through technologies, developed out of this research, that move control of women's lives from women to men of the dominant group.[5] Despite the importance of these studies, critics of the sexist uses of science often make two problematic assumptions: that there is a value-free, pure scientific research which can be distinguished from the social uses of science; and that there are proper uses of science with which we can contrast its improper uses. Can we really make these distinctions? Is it possible to isolate a value-neutral core from the uses of science and its technologies? And what distinguishes improper from proper uses? Furthermore, each misuse and abuse has been racist and classist as well as oppressive to women. This becomes clear when we note that there are different reproductive policies, forms of domestic labor, and forms of workplace discrimination mandated for women of different classes and races even within U.S. culture at any single moment in history. (Think, for instance, of the current attempt to restrict the availability of abortion and contraceptive information for some social groups at the same time that sterilization is forced on others. Think of the resuscitation of scientifically supported sentimental images of motherhood and nuclear forms of family life for some at the same time that social supports for mothers and nonnuclear families are systematically withdrawn for others.) Must not feminism take on as a central project of its own the struggle to eliminate class society and racism, homophobia and imperialism, in order to eliminate the sexist uses of science?

Third, in the critiques of biology and the social sciences, two kinds of challenges have been raised not just to the actual but to the possible existence of any pure science at all.[6] The selection and definition of problematics—deciding what phenomena in the world need explanation, and defining what is problematic about them—have clearly been skewed toward men's perception of what they find puzzling. Surely it is "bad science" to assume that men's problems are everyone's problems, thereby leaving unexplained many things that women find problematic, and to assume that men's explanations of what they find problematic are undistorted by their gender needs and desires. But is this merely—or, perhaps, even—an example of bad science? Will not the selection and definition of problems always bear the social fingerprints of the dominant groups in a culture? With these questions we glimpse the fundamental value-ladenness of knowledge-seeking and thus the impossibility of distinguishing between bad science and science-as-usual. Furthermore, the design and interpretation of research again and again has proceeded in masculine-biased ways. But if problems are necessarily value-laden, if theories are constructed to explain problems, if methodologies are always theory-laden, and if observations are methodology-laden, can there be value-neutral design and interpretation of research? This line of reasoning leads us to ask whether it is possible that some kinds of value-laden research are nevertheless maximally objective. For example, are overtly anti-sexist research designs inherently more objective than overtly sexist or, more important, "sex-blind" (i.e., gender-blind) ones? And are antisexist inquiries that are also self-consciously antiracist more objective than those that

are not? There are precedents in the history of science for preferring the distinction between objectivity-increasing and objectivity-decreasing social values to the distinction between value-free and value-laden research. A different problem is raised by asking what implications these criticisms of biology and social science have for areas such as physics and chemistry, where the subject matter purportedly is physical nature rather than social beings ("purportedly" because, as we shall see, we must be skeptical about being able to make any clear distinctions between the physical and the nonphysical). What implications could these findings and this kind of reasoning about objectivity have for our understanding of the scientific world view more generally?

Fourth, the related techniques of literary criticism, historical interpretation, and psychoanalysis have been used to "read science as a text" in order to reveal the social meanings—the hidden symbolic and structural agendas—of purportedly value-neutral claims and practices.[7] In textual criticism, metaphors of gender politics in the writings of the fathers of modern science, as well as in the claims made by the defenders of the scientific world view today, are no longer read as individual idiosyncrasies or as irrelevant to the meanings science has for its enthusiasts. Furthermore, the concern to define and maintain a series of rigid dichotomies in science and epistemology no longer appears to be a reflection of the progressive character of scientific inquiry; rather, it is inextricably connected with specifically masculine—and perhaps uniquely Western and bourgeois—needs and desires. Objectivity vs. subjectivity, the scientist as knowing subject vs. the objects of his inquiry, reason vs. the emotions, mind vs. body—in each case the former has been associated with masculinity and the latter with femininity. In each case it has been claimed that human progress requires the former to achieve domination of the latter.[8]

Valuable as these textual criticisms have been, they raise many questions. What relevance do the writings of the fathers of modern science have to contemporary scientific practice? What theory would justify regarding these metaphors as fundamental components of scientific explanations? How can metaphors of gender politics continue to shape the cognitive form and content of scientific theories and practices even when they are no longer overtly expressed? And can we imagine what a scientific mode of knowledge-seeking would look like that was not concerned to distinguish between objectivity and subjectivity, reason and the emotions?

Fifth, a series of epistemological inquiries has laid the basis for an alternative understanding of how beliefs are grounded in social experiences, and of what kind of experience should ground the beliefs we honor as knowledge.[9] These feminist epistemologies imply a relation between knowing and being, between epistemology and metaphysics, that is an alternative to the dominant epistemologies developed to justify science's modes of knowledge-seeking and ways of being in the world. It is the conflicts between these epistemologies that generate the major themes of this study.

A GUIDE TO FEMINIST EPISTEMOLOGIES

The epistemological problem for feminism is to explain an apparently paradoxical situation. Feminism is a political movement for social change. But many claims, clearly motivated by feminist concerns, made by researchers and theorists in the social sciences, in biology, and in the social studies of the natural sciences appear more plausible—more likely to be confirmed by evidence—than the beliefs they would replace. How can such politicized research be increasing the objectivity of inquiry? On what grounds should these feminist claims be justified?

We can usefully divide the main feminist responses to this apparent paradox into two relatively well-developed solutions and one agenda for a solution. I will refer to these three responses as *feminist empiricism,* the *feminist standpoint,* and *feminist postmodernism.*

Feminist empiricism argues that sexism and androcentrism are social biases correctable by stricter adherence to the existing methodological norms of scientific inquiry. Movements for social liberation "make it possible for people to see the world in an enlarged perspective because they remove the covers and blinders that obscure knowledge and observation."[10] The women's movement produces not only the opportunity for such an enlarged perspective but more women scientists, and they are more likely than men to notice androcentric bias.

This solution to the epistemological paradox is appealing for a number of reasons, not the least because it appears to leave unchallenged the existing methodological norms of science. It is easier to gain acceptance

of feminist claims through this kind of argument, for it identifies only bad science as the problem, not science-as-usual.

Its considerable strategic advantage, however, often leads its defenders to overlook the fact that the feminist empiricist solution in fact deeply subverts empiricism. The social identity of the inquirer is supposed to be irrelevant to the "goodness" of the results of research. Scientific method is supposed to be capable of eliminating any biases due to the fact that individual researchers are white or black, Chinese or French, men or women. But feminist empiricism argues that women (or feminists, whether men or women) *as a group* are more likely to produce unbiased and objective results than are men (or nonfeminists) as a group.

Moreover, though empiricism holds that scientific method is sufficient to account for historical increases in the objectivity of the picture of the world that science presents, one can argue that history shows otherwise. It is movements for social liberation that have most increased the objectivity of science, not the norms of science as they have in fact been practiced, or as philosophers have rationally reconstructed them. Think, for instance, of the effects of the bourgeois revolution of the fifteenth to seventeenth centuries, which produced modern science itself; or of the effects of the proletarian revolution of the nineteenth and early twentieth centuries. Think of the effects on scientific objectivity of the twentieth-century deconstruction of colonialism.

We shall also see that a key origin of androcentric bias can be found in the selection of problems for inquiry, and in the definition of what is problematic about these phenomena. But empiricism insists that its methodological norms are meant to apply only to the "context of justification"—to the testing of hypotheses and interpretation of evidence—not to the "context of discovery" where problems are identified and defined. Thus a powerful source of social bias appears completely to escape the control of science's methodological norms. Finally, it appears that following the norms of inquiry is exactly what often results in androcentric results.

Thus, feminist attempts to reform what is perceived as bad science bring to our attention deep logical incoherences and what, paradoxically, we can call empirical inadequacies in empiricist epistemologies.

The feminist standpoint originates in Hegel's thinking about the relationship between the master and the slave and in the elaboration of this analysis in the writings of Marx, Engels, and the Hungarian Marxist theorist G. Lukacs. Briefly, this proposal argues that men's dominating position in social life results in partial and perverse understandings, whereas women's subjugated position provides the possibility of more complete and less perverse understandings. Feminism and the women's movement provide the theory and motivation for inquiry and political struggle that can transform the perspective of women into a "standpoint"—a morally and scientifically preferable grounding for our interpretations and explanations of nature and social life. The feminist critiques of social and natural science, whether expressed by women or by men, are grounded in the universal features of women's experience as understood from the perspective of feminism.[11]

While this attempted solution to the epistemological paradox avoids the problems that beset feminist empiricism, it generates its own tensions. First of all, those wedded to empiricism will be loath to commit themselves to the belief that the social identity of the observer can be an important variable in the potential objectivity of research results. Strategically, this is a less convincing explanation for the greater adequacy of feminist claims for all but the already convinced; it is particularly unlikely to appear plausible to natural scientists or natural science enthusiasts.

Considered on its own terms, the feminist standpoint response raises two further questions. Can there be *a* feminist standpoint if women's (or feminists') social experience is divided by class, race, and culture? Must there be Black and white, working-class and professional-class, American and Nigerian feminist standpoints? This kind of consideration leads to the postmodernist skepticism: "Perhaps 'reality' can have 'a' structure only from the falsely universalizing perspective of the master. That is, only to the extent that one person or group can dominate the whole, can 'reality' appear to be governed by one set of rules or be constituted by one privileged set of social relations."[12] Is the feminist standpoint project still too firmly grounded in the historically disastrous alliance between knowledge and power characteristic of the modern epoch? Is it too firmly rooted in a problematic politics of essentialized identities?

Before turning briefly to the feminist postmodernism from which this last criticism emerges, we should

note that both of the preceding epistemological approaches appear to assert that objectivity never has been and could not be increased by value-neutrality. Instead, it is commitments to antiauthoritarian, antielitist, participatory, and emancipatory values and projects that increase the objectivity of science. Furthermore, the reader will need to avoid the temptation to leap to relativist understandings of feminist claims. In the first place, feminist inquirers are never saying that sexist and antisexist claims are equally plausible—that it is equally plausible to regard women's situation as primarily biological *and* as primarily social, or to regard "the human" both as identical *and* nonidentical with "the masculine." The *evidence* for feminist vs. nonfeminist claims may be inconclusive in some cases, and many feminist claims that today appear evidentially secure will no doubt be abandoned as additional evidence is gathered and better hypotheses and concepts are constructed. Indeed, there should be no doubt that these normal conditions of research hold for many feminist claims. But agnosticism and recognition of the hypothetical character of all scientific claims are quite different epistemological stances from relativism. Moreover, whether or not feminists take a relativist stance, it is hard to imagine a coherent defense of cognitive relativism when one thinks of the conflicting claims.

Feminist postmodernism challenges the assumptions upon which feminist empiricism and the feminist standpoint are based, although strains of postmodernist skepticism appear in the thought of these theorists, too. Along with such mainstream thinkers as Nietzsche, Derrida, Foucault, Lacan, Rorty, Cavell, Feyerabend, Gadamer, Wittgenstein, and Unger, and such intellectual movements as semiotics, deconstruction, psychoanalysis, structuralism, archeology/genealogy, and nihilism, feminists "share a profound skepticism regarding universal (or universalizing) claims about the existence, nature and powers of reason, progress, science, language and the 'subject/self.' "[13]

This approach requires embracing as a fruitful grounding for inquiry the fractured identities modern life creates: black-feminist, socialist-feminist, women-of-color, and so on. It requires seeking a solidarity in our oppositions to the dangerous fiction of the naturalized, essentialized, uniquely "human" (read "manly") and to the distortion and exploitation perpetrated on behalf of this fiction. It may require rejecting fantasized returns to the primal wholeness of infancy, preclass societies, or pregender "unitary" consciousnesses of the species—all of which have motivated standpoint epistemologies. From this perspective, feminist claims are more plausible and less distorting only insofar as they are grounded in a solidarity between these modern fractured identities and between the politics they create.

Feminist postmodernism creates its own tensions. In what ways does it, like the empiricist and standpoint epistemologies, reveal incoherences in its parental mainstream discourse? Can we afford to give up the necessity of trying to provide "one, true, feminist story of reality" in the face of the deep alliances between science and sexist, racist, classist, and imperialist social projects?

Clearly, there are contradictory tendencies among the feminist epistemological discourses, and each has its own set of problems. The contradictions and problems do not originate in the feminist discourses, however, but reflect the disarray in mainstream epistemologies and philosophies of science since the mid-1960s. They also reflect shifting configurations of gender, race, and class—both the analytic categories and the lived realities. New social groups—such as feminists who are seeking to bridge a gap between their own social experience and the available theoretical frameworks—are more likely to hone in on "subjugated knowledge" about the world than are groups whose experience more comfortably fits familiar conceptual schemes. Most likely, the feminist entrance into these disputes should be seen as making significant contributions to clarifying the nature and implications of paradoxical tendencies in contemporary intellectual and social life.

The feminist criticisms of science have produced an array of conceptual questions that threaten both our cultural identity as a democratic and socially progressive society and our core personal identities as gender-distinct individuals. I do not mean to overwhelm these illuminating lines of inquiry with criticisms so early in my study—to suggest that they are not really feminist or that they have not advanced our understanding. On the contrary, each has greatly enhanced our ability to grasp the extent of androcentrism in science. Collectively, they have made it possible for us to formulate new questions about science.

It is a virtue of these critiques that they quickly bring to our attention the socially damaging incoherences in all the nonfeminist discourses. Considered in the sequence described in this chapter, they move us from the Woman Question in science to the more radical Science Question in feminism. Where the first three kinds of criticism primarily ask how women can be more equitably treated within and by science, the last two ask how a science apparently so deeply involved in distinctively masculine projects can possibly be used for emancipatory ends. Where the Woman Question critiques still conceptualize the scientific enterprise we have as redeemable, as reformable, the Science Question critiques appear skeptical that we can locate anything morally and politically worth redeeming or reforming in the scientific world view, its underlying epistemology, or the practices these legitimate.

(1986)

NOTES

1. I make a sharp distinction between "sex" and "gender" (even though this is a dichotomy I shall later problematize); thus I refer to "gender roles" rather than "sex roles," etc., retaining only a few terms such as "sexism," where the substitution seems more distracting than useful. Otherwise (except in direct quotations), I use "sex" only when it is, indeed, biology that is at issue. There are two reasons for this policy. First, in spite of feminist insistence for decades, perhaps centuries, that women's and men's "natures" and activities are primarily shaped by social relations, not by immutable biological determinants, many people still do not grasp this point or are unwilling to commit themselves to its full implications (the current fascination with sociobiology is just one evidence of this problem). Second, the very thought of sex exerts its own fatal attraction for many otherwise well-intentioned people: such phrases as "sexual politics," "the battle between the sexes," and "male chauvinism" make the continuation of gender hostilities sound far more exciting than feminism should desire.
2. See, e.g., Rossiter (1982b); Walsh (1977).
3. See Aldrich (1978).
4. Rossiter (1982b) makes this point.
5. See Tobach and Rosoff (1978; 1979; 1981; 1984); Brighton Women and Science Group (1980); Ehrenreich and English (1979); Rothschild (1983); Zimmerman (1983); Arditti, Duelli-Klein, and Minden (1984).
6. The literature here is immense. For examples of these criticisms, see Longino and Doell (1983); Hubbard, Henifin, and Fried (1982); Gross and Averill (1983); Tobach and Rosoff (1978; 1979; 1981; 1984); Millman and Kanter (1975); Andersen (1983); Westkott (1979).

7. Good examples are Keller (1984); Merchant (1980); Griffin (1978); Flax (1983); Jordanova (1980); Bloch and Bloch (1980); Harding (1980).

8. The key "object-relations" theorists among these textual critics are Dinnerstein (1976); Chodorow (1978); Flax (1983). See also Balbus (1982).

9. See Flax (1983); Rose (1983); Hartsock (1983); Smith (1974; 1977; 1979; 1981); Harding (1983); Fee (1981). Haraway (1985) proposes a somewhat different epistemology for feminism.

10. Millman and Kanter (1975, vii).

11. Flax (1983), Rose (1983), Hartsock (1983), and Smith (1974; 1977; 1979; 1981) all develop this standpoint approach.

12. Flax (1986, 17). Strains of postmodernism appear in all of the standpoint thinking. Of this group, Flax has most overtly articulated also the postmodernist epistemological issues.

13. Flax (1986, 3). This is Flax's list of the mainstream postmodernist thinkers and movements. See Haraway (1985), Marks and de Courtivron (1980), and *Signs* (1981) for discussion of the feminist postmodernist issues.

REFERENCES

Aldrich, Michele L. 1978. "Women in Science." *Signs: Journal of Women in Culture and Society* 4 (no. 1).

Andersen, Margaret. 1983. *Thinking about Women.* New York: Macmillan.

Arditti, Rita, Renate Duelli Klein, and Shelly Minden, eds. 1984. *Test-Tube Women: What Future for Motherhood?* Boston: Pandora Press.

Balbus, Isaac. 1982. *Marxism and Domination.* Princeton, N.J.: Princeton University Press.

Bloch, Maurice, and Jean Bloch. 1980. "Women and the Dialectics of Nature in Eighteenth Century French Thought." In *Nature, Culture and Gender*, ed. C. MacCormack and M. Strathern. Cambridge: Cambridge University Press.

Boch, Gisela. 1983. "Racism and Sexism in Nazi Germany: Motherhood, Compulsory Sterilization, and the State." *Signs: Journal of Women in Culture and Society* 8 (no. 3).

Brighton Women and Science Group. 1980. *Alice through the Microscope.* London: Virago Press.

Caulfield, Mina Davis. 1974. "Imperialism, the Family, and Cultures of Resistance," *Socialist Revolution* 4 (no. 2).

Chodorow, Nancy. 1978. *The Reproduction of Mothering.* Berkeley: University of California Press.

Davis, Angela. 1971. "The Black Woman's Role in the Community of Slaves." *Black Scholar* 2.

Dinnerstein, Dorothy. 1976. *The Mermaid and the Minotaur: Sexual Arrangements and Human Malaise.* New York: Harper & Row.

Ehrenreich, Barbara, and Deirdre English. 1979. *For Her Own Good: 150 Years of Experts' Advice to Women.* New York: Doubleday.

Fee, Elizabeth. 1981. "Women's Nature and Scientific Objectivity." In *Woman's Nature: Rationalizations of Inequality*, eds. M. Lowe and R. Hubbard. New York: Pergamon Press. Originally appeared as "Is Feminism a Threat to Scientific Objectivity?" in *International Journal of Women's Studies* 4 (no. 4).

Flax, Jane. 1983. "Political Philosophy and the Patriarchal Unconscious: A Psychoanalytic Perspective on Epistemology and Metaphysics." In *Discovering Reality: Feminist Perspectives on Epistemology, Metaphysics, Methodology and Philosophy of Science*, eds. S. Harding and M. Hintikka. Dordrecht: Reidel.

Flax, Jane. 1986. "Gender as a Social Problem: In and For Feminist Theory." *American Studies/Amerika Studien*, Journal of the German Association for American Studies.

Griffin, Susan. 1978. *Woman and Nature: The Roaring inside Her.* New York: Harper & Row.

Gross, Michael, and Mary Beth Averill. 1983. "Evolution and Patriarchal Myths of Scarcity and Competition." In *Discovering Reality: Feminist Perspectives on Epistemology, Metaphysics, Methodology and Philosophy of Science*, eds. S. Harding and M. Hintikka. Dordrecht: Reidel.

Haraway, Donna. 1985. "A Manifesto for Cyborgs: Science, Technology, and Socialist Feminism in the 1980's." *Socialist Review* 80.

Harding, Sandra. 1980. "The Norms of Social Inquiry and Masculine Experience." In *PSA 1980*, vol. 2, ed. P. D. Asquith and R. N. Giere. East Lansing, Mich.: Philosophy of Science Association.

Harding, Sandra. 1983. "Why Has the Sex–Gender System Become Visible Only Now?" In *Discovering Reality: Feminist Perspectives on Epistemology, Metaphysics, Methodology and Philosophy of Science*, eds. S. Harding and M. Hintikka. Dordrecht: Reidel.

Hartsock, Nancy. 1983. "The Feminist Standpoint: Developing the Ground for a Specifically Feminist Historical Materialism." In *Discovering Reality: Feminist Perspectives on Epistemology, Metaphysics, Methodology and Philosophy of Science*, eds. S. Harding and M. Hintikka. Dordrecht: Reidel.

Hubbard, Ruth, M.S. Henifin, and Barbara Fried, eds. 1982. *Biological Woman: The Convenient Myth.* Cambridge, Mass.: Schenkman. Earlier version published 1979 under the title *Women Look at Biology Looking at Women.*

Jordanova, L. J. 1980. "Natural Facts: A Historical Perspective on Science and Sexuality." In *Nature, Culture and Gender*, eds. C. MacCormack and M. Strathern. New York: Cambridge University Press.

Keller, Evelyn Fox. 1984. *Reflections on Gender and Science.* New Haven, Conn.: Yale University Press.

Longino, Helen, and Ruth Doell, 1983. "Body, Bias, and Be-havior: A Comparative Analysis of Reasoning in Two Areas of Biological Science." *Signs: Journal of Women in Culture and Society* 9 (no. 2).

McIntosh, Peggy. 1983. "Interactive Phases of Curricular Revision: A Feminist Perspective." Working paper no. 124. Wellesley, Mass.: Wellesley College Center for Research on Women.

Marks, Elaine, and Isabelle de Courtivron, eds. 1980. *New French Feminisms.* Amherst: University of Massachusetts Press.

Merchant, Carolyn. 1980: *The Death of Nature: Women, Ecology and the Scientific Revolution.* New York: Harper & Row.

Millman, Marcia, and Rosabeth Moss Kanter, eds. 1975. *Another Voice: Feminist Perspectives on Social Life and Social Science.* New York: Anchor Books.

Rose, Hilary, and Steven Rose, eds. 1976. *Ideology of/in the Natural Sciences.* Cambridge, Mass.: Schenkman.

Rossiter, Margaret. 1982a. "Fair Enough?" *Isis* 72.

Rossiter, Margaret. 1982b. *Women Scientists in America: Struggles and Strategies to 1940.* Baltimore, Md.: Johns Hopkins University Press.

Rothschild, Joan. 1983. *Machina ex Dea: Feminist Perspectives on Technology.* New York: Pergamon Press.

Signs: Journal of Women in Culture and Society. 1981. Special issue on French feminism, 7 (no. 1).

Smith, Dorothy. 1974. "Women's Perspective as a Radical Critique of Sociology." *Sociological Inquiry* 44.

Smith, Dorothy. 1977. "Some Implications of a Sociology for Women." In *Woman in a Man-Made World: A Socioeconomic Handbook,* eds. N. Glazer and H. Waehrer. Chicago: Rand McNally.

Smith, Dorothy. 1979. "A Sociology for Women." In *The Prism of Sex: Essays in the Sociology of Knowledge,* eds. J. Sherman and E. T. Beck. Madison: University of Wisconsin Press.

Smith, Dorothy. 1981. "The Experienced World as Problematic: A Feminist Method." Sorokin Lecture no. 12 Saskatoon: University of Saskatchewan.

Tobach, Ethel, and Betty Rosoff, eds. 1978, 1979, 1981, 1984. *Genes and Gender,* vols. 1–4. New York: Gordian Press.

Westkott, Marcia. 1979. "Feminist Criticism of the Social Sciences." *Harvard Educational Review* 49.

Zimmerman, Jan, ed. 1983. *The Technological Woman: Interfacing with Tomorrow.* New York: Praeger.

4 • *Charlotte Bunch*

NOT BY DEGREES: FEMINIST THEORY AND EDUCATION

. . .

THE FUNCTIONS OF FEMINIST THEORY

Theory enables us to see immediate needs in terms of long-range goals and an overall perspective on the world.* It thus gives us a framework for evaluating various strategies in both the long and the short run, and for seeing the types of changes that they are likely to produce. Theory is not just a body of facts or a set of personal opinions. It involves explanations and hypotheses that are based on available knowledge and experience. It is also dependent on conjecture and insight about how to interpret those facts and experiences and their significance.

---

*There are many approaches to theory, and those interested in exploring more about how theory is constructed should look at the literature of political philosophy. Another model for feminist theory similar to the one that I discuss in this paper was developed by Judy Smith of the Women's Resource Center, in Missoula, Montana.

No theory is totally "objective," since it reflects the interests, values, and assumptions of those who created it. Feminist theory relies on the underlying assumption that it will aid the liberation of women. Feminist theory, therefore, is not an unengaged study of women. It is an effort to bring insights from the movement and from various female experiences together with research and data-gathering to produce new approaches to understanding and ending female oppression.

While feminist theory begins with the immediate need to end women's oppression, it is also a way of viewing the world. Feminism is an entire world view or *gestalt*, not just a list of "women's issues." Feminist theory provides a basis for understanding every area of our lives, and a feminist perspective can affect the world politically, culturally, economically, and spiritually. The initial tenets of feminism have already been established—the idea that power is based on gender differences and that men's illegitimate power over women taints all aspects of society, for instance. But now we face the arduous task of systematically working through these ideas, fleshing them out and discovering new ones. . . .

A MODEL FOR THEORY

Theory doesn't necessarily progress in a linear fashion, but examining its components is useful in understanding existing political theory as well as in developing new insights. In the model I have developed, I divide theory into four interrelated parts: description, analysis, vision, and strategy.

1. Description: *Describing what exists* may sound simple, but the choices that we make about interpreting and naming reality provide the basis for the rest of our theory. Changing people's perceptions of the world through new descriptions of reality is usually a prerequisite for altering that reality. For example, fifteen years ago, few people would say that women in the United States were oppressed. Today, the oppression of women is acknowledged by a large number of people, primarily because of feminist work which described that oppression in a number of ways. This work has involved consciousness-raising, as well as gathering and interpreting facts about women in order to substantiate our assertions.

Description is necessary for all theory; unfortunately for feminism, much of our work has not yet gone beyond this point.

2. Analysis: *Analyzing why that reality exists* involves determining its origins and the reasons for its perpetuation. This is perhaps the most complex task of theory and is often seen as its entire function. In seeking to understand the sources of women's oppression and why it is perpetuated, we have to examine biology, economics, psychology, sexuality, and so on. We must also look at what groups and institutions benefit from oppression, and why they will, therefore, strive to maintain it. Analyzing why women are oppressed involves such things as sorting out how the forms of oppression change over time while the basic fact of oppression remains, or probing how the forms of oppression vary in different cultures while there are cross-cultural similarities.

Analysis of why something happens sometimes gets short-circuited by the temptation to ascribe everything to one single factor, such as capitalism or motherhood. In developing an analysis, I find that it is useful to focus initially on a phenomenon in a limited context and consider a wide range of factors that may affect it. Then, as that context is understood, the analysis can be expanded. Above all, we need not feel that we must answer the "why" of everything all at once with a single explanation.

3. Vision: *Determining what should exist* requires establishing principles (or values) and setting goals. In taking action to bring about change, we operate consciously or unconsciously out of certain assumptions about what is right or what we value (principles), and out of our sense of what society ought to be (goals). This aspect of theory involves making a conscious choice about those principles in order to make our visions and goals concrete. We must look at our basic assumptions about such things as "human nature" and how it can be changed, about the relationships of individuals to groups, about whether men and women are essentially different, for example. We may choose not to address some of these issues yet, but since every action carries implicit assumptions; we must be conscious of them so that we do not operate out of old theoretical frameworks by default. The clearer we are about our principles—for example, whether we think that women should gain as much power as possible in

every area, or believe, instead, that power itself should be eliminated—the more easily we can set our long-term goals. Immediate goals can then be based on an assessment of what can be accomplished that may be short of our long-term vision, but moves toward, not away, from it. Visions, principles, and goals will change with experience, but the more explicit we make them, the more our actions can be directed toward creating the society we want, as well as reacting to what we don't like.

4. Strategy: *Hypothesizing how to change what is to what should be* moves directly into questions of changing reality. Some people see strategy not as part of theory, but rather as a planning process based on theory. But I include strategy here in its broadest sense—the overall approach one takes to how to accomplish one's goals. The descriptive and analytic process of theory help develop a more systematic understanding of the way things work, but they usually do not make obvious what one should do. Developing a strategy requires that

we draw out the consequences of our theory and suggest general directions for change.

Like the other aspects of theory, this involves a combination of information-gathering and creative speculation. It entails making judgments about what will lead to change—judgments that are based both on description and analysis of reality, and on visions, principles, and goals. Developing a strategy also involves examining various tools for change—legislative, military, spiritual—and determining which are most effective in what situations. There are many questions to consider, such as what sectors of society can best be mobilized to carry out which types of action. In working out which strategies will be most effective, the interaction between developing theory and actively experimenting with it becomes most clear. For in all aspects of theory development, theory and activism continually inform and alter each other. . . .

(1979)

5 • *Maria C. Lugones and Elizabeth V. Spelman*

"HAVE WE GOT A THEORY FOR YOU! FEMINIST THEORY, CULTURAL IMPERIALISM AND THE DEMAND FOR 'THE WOMAN'S VOICE'"

PROLOGUE

(*In a Hispana voice*) A veces quisiera mezclar en una voz el sonido canyengue, tristón y urbano del porteñismo que llevo adentro con la cadencia apacible, serrana y llena de corage de la hispana nuevo mejicana. Contrastar y unir

    el piolin y la cuerda
    el traé y el pepéname
    el camion y la troca
    la lluvia y el llanto

Pero este querer se me va cuando veo que he confundido la solidaridad con la falta de diferencia. La solidaridad requiere el reconocer, comprender, respetar y amar lo que nos lleva a llorar en distintas cadencias. El imperialismo cultural desea lo contrario, por eso necesitamos muchas voces. Porque una sola voz nos mata a las dos.

No quiero hablar por ti sino contigo. Pero si no aprendo tus modos y tu los mios la conversación es sólo aparente. Y la apariencia se levanta como una barrera sin sentido entre las dos. Sin sentido y sin sentimiento.

Reprinted from *Women's Studies International Forum*, 6:6, 573–581, 1983. Used by permission of Elsevier.

Por eso no me debes dejar que te dicte tu ser y no me dictes el mio. Porque entonces ya no dialogamos. El diálogo entre nosotras requiere dos voces y no una.

Tal vez un día jugaremos juntas y nos hablaremos no en una lengua universal sino que vos me hablarás mi voz y yo la tuya.

PREFACE

This paper is the result of our dialogue, of our thinking together about differences among women and how these differences are silenced. (Think, for example, of all the silences there are connected with the fact that this paper is in English—for that is a borrowed tongue for one of us.) In the process of our talking and writing together, we saw that the differences between us did not permit our speaking in one voice. For example, when we agreed we expressed the thought differently; there were some things that both of us thought were true but could not express as true of each of us; sometimes we could not say "we"; and sometimes one of us could not express the thought in the first person singular, and to express it in the third person would be to present an outsider's and not an insider's perspective. Thus the use of two voices is central both to the process of constructing this paper and to the substance of it. We are both the authors of this paper and not just sections of it but we write together without presupposing unity of expression or of experience. So when we speak in unison it means just that—there are two voices and not just one.

INTRODUCTION

(*In the voice of a white/Anglo woman who has been teaching and writing about feminist theory*) Feminism is, among other things, a response to the fact that women either have been left out of or included in demeaning and disfiguring ways in what has been an almost exclusively male account of the world. And so while part of what feminists want and demand for women is the right to move and to act in accordance with our own wills and not against them, another part is the desire and insistence that we give our *own* accounts of these movements and actions. For it matters to us what is said about us, who says it, and to whom it is said: having the opportunity to talk about one's life, to give an account of it, to interpret it, is integral to leading that life rather than being led through it; hence our

distrust of the male monopoly over accounts of women's lives. To put the same point slightly differently, part of human life, human living, is talking about it, and we can be sure that being silenced in one's own account of one's life is a kind of amputation that signals oppression. Another reason for not divorcing life from the telling of it or talking about it is that as humans our experiences are deeply influenced by what is said about them, by ourselves or powerful (as opposed to significant) others. Indeed, the phenomenon of internalized oppression is only possible because this is so: one experiences her life in terms of the impoverished and degrading concepts others have found it convenient to use to describe her. We can't separate lives from the accounts given of them; the articulation of our experience is part of our experience.

Sometimes feminists have made even stronger claims about the importance of speaking about our own lives and the destructiveness of others presuming to speak about us or for us. First of all, the claim has been made that on the whole men's accounts of women's lives have been at best false, a function of ignorance, and at worst malicious lies, a function of a knowledgeable desire to exploit and oppress. Since it matters to us that falsehood and lies not be told about us, we demand, of those who have been responsible for those falsehoods and lies, or those who continue to transmit them, not just that we speak but that they learn to be able to hear us. It has also been claimed that talking about one's life, telling one's story, in the company of those doing the same (as in consciousness-raising sessions), is constitutive of feminist method.[1]

And so the demand that the woman's voice be heard and attended to has been made for a variety of reasons: not just so as to greatly increase the chances that true accounts of women's lives will be given, but also because the articulation of experience (in myriad ways) is among the hallmarks of a self-determining individual or community. There are not just epistemological but moral and political reasons for demanding that the woman's voice be heard, after centuries of androcentric din.

But what more exactly is the feminist demand that the woman's voice be heard? There are several crucial notes to make about it. First of all, the demand grows out of a complaint, and in order to understand the scope and focus of the demand we have to look at the scope and focus of the complaint. The complaint does not specify *which* women have been silenced, and in one way this is appropriate to the conditions it is a complaint about; virtually no women have had a voice, whatever their race, class, ethnicity, religion, sexual alliance, whatever place and period in history they lived. And if it is as women that women have been silenced, then of course the demand must be that women as women have a voice. But in another way the complaint is very misleading, insofar as it suggests that it is women as women who have been silenced, and that whether a woman is rich or poor, Black, brown or white, etc., is irrelevant to what it means for her to be a woman. For the demand thus simply made ignores at least two related points: (1) it is only possible for a woman who does not feel highly vulnerable with respect to other parts of her identity, e.g., race, class, ethnicity, religion, sexual alliance, etc., to conceive of her voice simply or essentially as a "woman's voice"; (2) just because not all women are equally vulnerable with respect to race, class, etc., some women's voices are more likely to be heard than others by those who have heretofore been giving—or silencing—the accounts of women's lives. For all these reasons, the women's voices most likely to come forth and the women's voices most likely to be heard are, in the United States anyway, those of white, middle-class, heterosexual Christian (or anyway not self-identified non-Christian) women. Indeed, many Hispanas, Black women, Jewish women—to name a few groups—have felt it an invitation to silence rather than speech to be requested—if they are requested at all—to speak about being "women" (with the plain wrapper—as if there were one) in distinction from speaking about being Hispana, Black, Jewish, working-class, etc., women.

The demand that the "woman's voice" be heard, and the search for the "woman's voice" as central to feminist methodology, reflects nascent feminist theory. It reflects nascent empirical theory insofar as it presupposes that the silencing of women is systematic, shows up in regular, patterned ways, and that there are discoverable causes of this widespread observable phenomenon; the demand reflects nascent political theory insofar as it presupposes that the silencing of women reveals a systematic pattern of power and authority; and it reflects nascent moral theory insofar as it presupposes that the silencing is unjust and that there are particular ways of remedying this injustice. Indeed, whatever else we know feminism to include—e.g., concrete direct political action—theorizing is integral to it: theories about the nature of oppression, the causes of it, the relation of the oppression of women to other forms of oppression. And certainly the concept of the woman's voice is itself a theoretical concept, in the sense that it presupposes a theory according to which our identities as human beings are actually compound identities, a kind of fusion or confusion of our otherwise separate identities as women or men, as Black or brown or white, etc. That is no less a theoretical stance than Plato's division of the person into soul and body or Aristotle's parceling of the soul into various functions.

The demand that the "woman's voice" be heard also invites some further directions in the exploration of women's lives and discourages or excludes others. For reasons mentioned above, systematic, sustained reflection on being a woman—the kind of contemplation that "doing theory" requires—is most likely to be done by women who vis-à-vis other women enjoy a certain amount of political, social and economic privilege because of their skin color, class membership, ethnic identity. There is a relationship between the content of our contemplation and the fact that we have the time to engage in it at some length—otherwise we shall have to say that it is a mere accident of history that white middle-class women in the United States have in the main developed "feminist theory" (as opposed to "Black feminist theory," "Chicana feminist theory," etc.) and that so much of the theory has failed to be relevant to the lives of women who are not white or middle class. Feminist theory—of all kinds—is to be based on, or anyway touch base with, the variety of real-life stories women provide about themselves. But in fact, because, among other things, of the structural political and social and economic inequalities among women, the tail has been wagging the dog: feminist theory has not for the most part arisen out of a medley of women's voices; instead, the theory has arisen out of the voices, the experiences, of a fairly small handful of women, and if other women's voices do not sing in harmony with the theory, they aren't counted as women's voices—rather, they are the voices of the woman as Hispana, Black, Jew, etc. There is another sense in which the tail is wagging the dog, too: it is presumed to be the case that those who do the theory know more about those who are theorized than vice versa; hence it ought to be the case that if it is white/Anglo women who write for and about all other women, the white/Anglo women must know more about all other women than other women know about them. But in fact just in order to survive, brown and Black women have to know a lot more about white/Anglo women—not through the sustained contemplation theory requires, but through the sharp observation stark exigency demands.

(*In an Hispana voice*) I think it necessary to explain why in so many cases when women of color appear in front of white/Anglo women to talk about feminism and women of color, we mainly raise a complaint: the complaint of exclusion, of silencing, of being included in a universe we have not chosen. We usually raise the complaint with a certain amount of disguised or un-disguised anger. I can only attempt to explain this phenomenon from a Hispanic viewpoint and a fairly narrow one at that: the viewpoint of an Argentinian woman who has lived in the U.S. for 16 years, who has attempted to come to terms with the devaluation of things Hispanic and Hispanic people in "America" and who is most familiar with Hispano life in the South-west of the U.S. I am quite unfamiliar with daily Hispano life in the urban centers, though not with some of the themes and some of the salient experiences of urban Hispano life.

When I say "we,"[2] I am referring to Hispanas. I am accustomed to use the "we" in this way. I am also pained by the tenuousness of this "we" given that I am not a native of the United States. Through the years I have come to be recognized and I have come to recognize myself more and more firmly as part of this "we." I also have a profound yearning for this firmness since I am a displaced person and I am conscious of not being of and I am unwilling to make myself of—even if this were possible—the white/Anglo community.

When I say "you" I mean not the non-Hispanic but the white/Anglo women that I address. "We" and "you" do not capture my relation to other non-white women. The complexity of that relation is not addressed here, but it is vivid to me as I write down my thoughts on the subject at hand.

I see two related reasons for our complaint-full discourse with white/Anglo women. Both of these reasons plague our world, they contaminate it through and through. It takes some hardening of oneself, some self-acceptance of our own anger to face them, for to face them is to decide that maybe we can change our situation in self-constructive ways and we know fully well that the possibilities are minimal. We know that we cannot rest from facing these reasons, that the tenderness

towards others in us undermines our possibilities, that we have to fight our own niceness because it clouds our minds and hearts. Yet we know that a thoroughgoing hardening would dehumanize us. So, we have to walk through our days in a peculiarly fragile psychic state, one that we have to struggle to maintain, one that we do not often succeed in maintaining.

We and you do not talk the same language. When we talk to you we use your language: the language of your experience and of your theories. We try to use it to communicate our world of experience. But since your language and your theories are inadequate in expressing our experiences, we only succeed in communicating our experience of exclusion. We cannot talk to you in our language because you do not understand it. So the brute facts that we understand your language and that the place where most theorizing about women is taking place is your place both combine to require that we either use your language and distort our experience not just in the speaking about it, but in the living of it, or that we remain silent. Complaining about exclusion is a way of remaining silent.

You are ill at ease in our world. You are ill at ease in our world in a very different way than we are ill at ease in yours. You are not of our world and again, you are not of our world in a very different way than we are not of yours. In the intimacy of a personal relationship we appear to you many times to be wholly there, to have broken through or to have dissipated the barriers that separate us because you are Anglo and we are raza. When we let go of the psychic state that I referred to above in the direction of sympathy, we appear to ourselves equally whole in your presence but our intimacy is thoroughly incomplete. When we are in your world many times you remake us in your own image, although sometimes you clearly and explicitly acknowledge that we are not wholly there in our being with you. When we are in your world we ourselves feel the discomfort of having our own being Hispanas disfigured or not understood. And yet, we have had to be in your world and learn its ways. We have to participate in it, make a living in it, live in it, be mistreated in it, be ignored in it, and, rarely, be appreciated in it. In learning to do these things or in learning to suffer them or in learning to enjoy what is to be enjoyed or in learning to understand your conception of us, we have had to learn your culture and thus your language and self-conceptions. But there is nothing that necessitates that you understand our world: understand, that is, not as an observer understands things, but as a participant, as someone who has a stake in them understands them. So your being ill at ease in our world lacks the features of our being ill at ease in yours precisely because you can leave and you can always tell yourselves that you will be soon out of there and because the wholeness of your selves is never touched by us, we have no tendency to remake you in our image.

But you theorize about women and we are women, so you understand yourselves to be theorizing about us, and we understand you to be theorizing about us. Yet none of the feminist theories developed so far seems to me to help Hispanas in the articulation of our experience. We have a sense that in using them we are distorting our experiences. Most Hispanas cannot even understand the language used in these theories—and only in some cases the reason is that the Hispana cannot understand English. We do not recognize ourselves in these theories. They create in us a schizophrenic split between our concern for ourselves as women and ourselves as Hispanas, one that we do not feel otherwise. Thus they seem to us to force us to assimilate to some version of Anglo culture, however revised that version may be. They seem to ask that we leave our communities or that we become alienated so completely in them that we feel hollow. When we see that you feel alienated in your own communities, this confuses us because we think that maybe every feminist has to suffer this alienation. But we see that recognition of your alienation leads many of you to be empowered into the remaking of your culture, while we are paralyzed into a state of displacement with no place to go.

So I think that we need to think carefully about the relation between the articulation of our own experience, the interpretation of our own experience, and theory making by us and other non-Hispanic women about themselves and other "women."

The only motive that makes sense to me for your joining us in this investigation is the motive of friendship, out of friendship. A non-imperialist feminism requires that you make a real space for our articulating, interpreting, theorizing and reflecting about the connections among them—a real space must be a noncoerced space—and/or that you follow us into our world out of friendship. I see the "out of friendship" as the only sensical motivation for this following because the task at hand for you is one of extraordinary difficulty.

It requires that you be willing to devote a great part of your life to it and that you be willing to suffer alienation and self-disruption. Self-interest has been proposed as a possible motive for entering this task. But self-interest does not seem to me to be a realistic motive, since whatever the benefits you may accrue from such a journey, they cannot be concrete enough for you at this time and they may not be worth your while. I do not think that you have any obligation to understand us. You do have an obligation to abandon your imperialism, your universal claims, your reduction of us to your selves, simply because they seriously harm us.

I think that the fact that we are so ill at ease with your theorizing in the ways indicated above does indicate that there is something wrong with these theories. But what is it that is wrong? Is it simply that the theories are flawed if meant to be universal but accurate so long as they are confined to your particular group(s)? Is it that the theories are not really flawed but need to be translated? Can they be translated? Is it something about the process of theorizing that is flawed? How do the two reasons for our complaint-full discourse affect the validity of your theories? Where do *we* begin? To what extent are our experience and its articulation affected by our being a colonized people, and thus by your culture, theories, and conceptions? Should we theorize in community and thus as part of community life and outside the academy and other intellectual circles? What is the point of making theory? Is theory making a good thing for us to do at this time? When are we making theory and when are we just articulating and/or interpreting our experiences?

SOME QUESTIONABLE ASSUMPTIONS ABOUT FEMINIST THEORIZING

(*Unproblematically in Vicky's and Maria's voice*) Feminist theories aren't just about what happens to the female population in any given society or across all societies; they are about the meaning of those experiences in the lives of women. They are about beings who give their own accounts of what is happening to them or of what they are doing, who have culturally constructed ways of reflecting on their lives. But how can the theorizer get at the meaning of those experiences? What should the relation be between a woman's own account of her experiences and the theorizer's account of it? . . .

Our suggestion in this paper, and at this time it is no more than a suggestion, is that only when genuine and reciprocal dialogue takes place between "outsiders" and "insiders" can we trust the outsider's account. At first sight it may appear that the insider/outsider distinction disappears in the dialogue, but it is important to notice that all that happens is that we are now both outsider and insider with respect to each other. The dialogue puts us both in position to give a better account of each other's and our own experience. Here we should again note that white/Anglo women are much less prepared for this dialogue with women of color than women of color are for dialogue with them in that women of color have had to learn white/Anglo ways, self-conceptions, and conceptions of them.

But both the possibility and the desirability of this dialogue are very much in question. We need to think about the possible motivations for engaging in this dialogue, whether doing theory jointly would be a good thing, in what ways and for whom, and whether doing theory is in itself a good thing at this time for women of color or white/Anglo women. In motivating the last question let us remember the hierarchical distinctions between theorizers and those theorized about and between theorizers and doers. These distinctions are endorsed by the same views and institutions which endorse and support hierarchical distinctions between men/women, master race/inferior race, intellectuals/manual workers. Of what use is the activity of theorizing to those of us who are women of color engaged day in and day out in the task of empowering women and men of color face to face with them? Should we be articulating and interpreting their experience for them with the aid of theories? Whose theories?

WAYS OF TALKING OR BEING TALKED ABOUT THAT ARE HELPFUL, ILLUMINATING, EMPOWERING, RESPECTFUL

(*Unproblematically in Maria's and Vicky's voice*) Feminists have been quite diligent about pointing out ways in which empirical, philosophical, and moral theories have been androcentric. They have thought it crucial to ask, with respect to such theories: who makes them? for whom do they make them? about what or whom are the theories? why? how are theories tested? what are the criteria for such tests and where did the criteria come

from? Without posing such questions and trying to answer them, we'd never have been able to begin to mount evidence for our claims that particular theories are androcentric, sexist, biased, paternalistic, etc. Certain philosophers have become fond of—indeed, have made their careers on—pointing out that characterizing a statement as true or false is only one of many ways possible of characterizing it; it might also be, oh, rude, funny, disarming, etc.; it may be intended to soothe or to hurt; or it may have the effect, intended or not, of soothing or hurting. Similarly, theories appear to be the kinds of things that are true or false; but they also are the kinds of things that can be, e.g., useless, arrogant, disrespectful, ignorant, ethnocentric, imperialistic. The immediate point is that feminist theory is no less immune to such characterizations than, say, Plato's political theory, or Freud's theory of female psychosexual development. Of course this is not to say that if feminist theory manages to be respectful or helpful it will follow that it must be true. But if, say, an empirical theory is purported to be about "women" and in fact is only about certain women, it is certainly false, probably ethnocentric, and of dubious usefulness except to those whose position in the world it strengthens (and theories, as we know, don't have to be true in order to be used to strengthen people's positions in the world).

Many reasons can be and have been given for the production of accounts of people's lives that plainly have nothing to do with illuminating those lives for the benefit of those living them. It is likely that both the method of investigation and the content of many accounts would be different if illuminating the lives of the people the accounts are about were the aim of the studies. Though we cannot say ahead of time how feminist theory making would be different if all (or many more) of those people it is meant to be about were more intimately part of the theory-making process, we do suggest some specific ways being talked about can be helpful:

1. The theory or account can be helpful if it enables one to see how parts of one's life fit together, for example, to see connections among parts of one's life one hasn't seen before. No account can do this if it doesn't get the parts right to begin with, and this cannot happen if the concepts used to described a life are utterly foreign.

2. A useful theory will help one locate oneself concretely in the world, rather than add to the mystification of the world and one's location in it. New concepts

may be of significance here, but they will not be useful if there is no way they can be translated into already existing concepts. Suppose a theory locates you in the home, because you are a woman, but you know full well that is not where you spend most of your time? Or suppose you can't locate yourself easily in any particular class as defined by some version of Marxist theory?

3. A theory or account not only ought to accurately locate one in the world but also enable one to think about the extent to which one is responsible or not for being in that location. Otherwise, for those whose location is as oppressed peoples, it usually occurs that the oppressed have no way to see themselves as in any way self-determining, as having any sense of being worthwhile or having grounds for pride, and paradoxically at the same time feeling at fault for the position they are in. A useful theory will help people work out just what is and is not due to themselves and their own activities as opposed to those who have power over them.

It may seem odd to make these criteria of a useful theory, if the usefulness is not to be at odds with the issue of the truth of the theory; for the focus on feeling worthwhile or having pride seems to rule out the possibility that the truth might just be that such-and-such a group of people has been under the control of others for centuries and that the only explanation of that is that they are worthless and weak people, and will never be able to change that. Feminist theorizing seems implicitly if not explicitly committed to the moral view that women *are* worthwhile beings, and the metaphysical theory that we are beings capable of bringing about a change in our situations. Does this mean feminist theory is "biased"? Not any more than any other theory, e.g., psychoanalytic theory. What is odd here is not the feminist presupposition that women are worthwhile but rather that feminist theory (and other theory) often has the effect of empowering one group and demoralizing another.

Aspects of feminist theory are as unabashedly value-laden as other political and moral theories. It is not just an examination of women's positions, for it includes, indeed begins with, moral and political judgments about the injustice (or, where relevant, justice) of them. This means that there are implicit or explicit judgments also about what kinds of changes constitute a better or worse situation for women.

4. In this connection a theory that is useful will provide criteria for change and make suggestions for

modes of resistance that don't merely reflect the situation and values of the theorizer. A theory that is respectful of those about whom it is a theory will not assume that changes that are perceived as making life better for some women are changes that will make, and will be perceived as making, life better for other women. This is *not* to say that if some women do not find a situation oppressive, other women ought never to suggest to the contrary that there might be very good reasons to think that the situation nevertheless *is* oppressive. But it is to say that, e.g., the prescription that life for women will be better when we're in the workforce rather than at home, when we are completely free of religious beliefs with patriarchal origins, when we live in complete separation from men, etc., are seen as slaps in the face to women whose life would be better if they could spend more time at home, whose identity is inseparable from their religious beliefs and cultural practices (which is not to say those beliefs and practices are to remain completely uncriticized and unchanged), who have ties to men—whether erotic or not—such that to have them severed in the name of some vision of what is "better" is, at that time and for those women, absurd. Our visions of what is better are always informed by our perception of what is bad about our present situation. Surely we've learned enough from the history of clumsy missionaries, and the white suffragists of the 19th century (who couldn't imagine why Black women "couldn't see" how crucial getting the vote for "women" was) to know that we can clobber people to destruction with our visions, our versions, of what is better. *But:* this does not mean women are not to offer supportive and tentative criticism of one another. But there is a very important difference between (a) developing ideas together, in a "pre-theoretical" stage, engaged as equals in joint enquiry, and (b) one group developing, on the basis of their own experience, a set of criteria for good change for women— and then reluctantly making revisions in the criteria at the insistence of women to whom such criteria seem ethnocentric and arrogant. The deck is stacked when one group takes it upon itself to develop the theory and then have others criticize it. Categories are quick to congeal, and the experiences of women whose lives do not fit the categories will appear as anomalous when in fact the theory should have grown out of them as much as others from the beginning. This, of course, is why any organization or conference having to do with "women"—with no qualification—that seriously does not want to be "solipsistic" will from the beginning be multicultural or state the appropriate qualifications. How we think and what we think about does depend in large part on who is there—not to mention who is expected or encouraged to speak. (Recall the boys in the *Symposium* sending the flute girls out.) Conversations and criticism take place in particular circumstances. Turf matters. So does the fact of who if anyone already has set up the terms of the conversations.

5. Theory cannot be useful to anyone interested in resistance and change unless there is reason to believe that knowing what a theory means and believing it to be true have some connection to resistance and change. As we make theory and offer it up to others, what do we assume is the connection between theory and consciousness? Do we expect others to read theory, understand it, believe it, and have their consciousnesses and lives thereby transformed? If we really want theory to make a difference to people's lives, how ought we to present it? Do we think people come to consciousness by reading? only by reading? Speaking to people through theory (orally or in writing) is a *very* specific context-dependent activity. That is, theory makers and their methods and concepts constitute a community of people and of shared meanings. Their language can be just as opaque and foreign to those not in the community as a foreign tongue or dialect.[3] Why do we engage in *this* activity and what effect do we think it ought to have? As Helen Longino has asked: "Is 'doing theory' just a bonding ritual for academic or educationally privileged feminist women?" Again, whom does our theory making serve?

SOME SUGGESTIONS ABOUT HOW TO DO THEORY THAT IS NOT IMPERALISTIC, ETHNOCENTRIC, DISRESPECTFUL

(*Problematically in the voice of a woman of color*) What are the things we need to know about others, and about ourselves, in order to speak intelligently, intelligibly, sensitively, and helpfully about their lives? We can show respect, or lack of it, in writing theoretically about others no less than in talking directly with them. This is not to say that here we have a well-worked-out concept of respect, but only to suggest that together all

of us consider what it would mean to theorize in a respectful way. . . .

. . . If white/Anglo women and women of color are to do theory jointly, in helpful, respectful, illuminating and empowering ways, the task ahead of white/Anglo women, because of this asymmetry, is a very hard task. The task is a very complex one. In part, to make an analogy, the task can be compared to learning a text without the aid of teachers. We all know the lack of contact felt when we want to discuss a particular issue that requires knowledge of a text with someone who does not know the text at all. Or the discomfort and impatience that arise in us when we are discussing an issue that presupposes a text and someone walks into the conversation who does not know the text. That person is either left out or will impose herself on us and either try to engage in the discussion or try to change the subject. Women of color are put in these situations by white/Anglo women and men constantly. Now imagine yourself simply left out but wanting to do theory with us. The first thing to recognize and accept is that you disturb our own dialogues by putting yourself in the left-out position and not leaving us in some meaningful sense to ourselves.

You must also recognize and accept that you must learn the text. But the text is an extraordinarily complex one: viz., our many different cultures. You are asking us to make ourselves more vulnerable to you than we already are before we have any reason to trust that you will not take advantage of this vulnerability. So you need to learn to become unintrusive, unimportant, patient to the point of tears, while at the same time open to learning any possible lessons. You will also have to come to terms with the sense of alienation, of not belonging, of having your world thoroughly disrupted, having it criticized and scrutinized from the point of view of those who have been harmed by it, having important concepts central to it dismissed, being viewed with mistrust, being seen as of no consequence except as an object of mistrust.

Why would any white/Anglo woman engage in this task? Out of self-interest? What in engaging in this task would be, not just in her interest, but perceived as such by her before the task is completed or well under way? Why should we want you to come into our world out of self-interest? Two points need to be made here. The task as described could be entered into with the intention of finding out as much as possible about us so as to better dominate us. The person engaged in this task would act as a spy. The motivation is not unfamiliar to us. We have heard it said that now that Third World countries are more powerful as a bloc, westerners need to learn more about them, that it is in their self-interest to do so. Obviously there is no reason why people of color should welcome white/Anglo women into their world for the carrying out of this intention. It is also obvious that white/Anglo feminists should not engage in this task under this description since the task under this description would not lead to joint theorizing of the desired sort: respectful, illuminating, helpful, and empowering. It would be helpful and empowering only in a one-sided way.

Self-interest is also mentioned as a possible motive in another way. White/Anglo women sometimes say that the task of understanding women of color would entail self-growth or self-expansion. If the task is conceived as described here, then one should doubt that growth or expansion will be the result. The severe self-disruption that the task entails should place a doubt in anyone who takes the task seriously about her possibilities of coming out of the task whole, with a self that is not as fragile as the selves of those who have been the victims of racism. But also, why should women of color embrace white/Anglo women's self-betterment without reciprocity? At this time women of color cannot afford this generous affirmation of white/Anglo women.

Another possible motive for engaging in this task is the motive of duty, "out of obligation," because white/Anglos have done people of color wrong. Here again two considerations: coming into Hispano, Black, Native American worlds out of obligation puts white/Anglos in a morally self-righteous position that is inappropriate. You are active, we are passive. We become the vehicles of your own redemption. Secondly, we couldn't want you to come into our worlds "out of obligation." That is like wanting someone to make love to you out of obligation. So, whether or not you have an obligation to do this (and we would deny that you do), or whether this task could even be done out of obligation, this is an inappropriate motive.

Out of obligation you should stay out of our way, respect us and our distance, and forgo the use of whatever power you have over us—for example, the power to use your language in our meetings, the power to overwhelm us with your education, the power to intrude in our communities in order to research us and to record the

supposed dying of our cultures, the power to engrain in us a sense that we are members of dying cultures and are doomed to assimilate, the power to keep us in a defensive posture with respect to our own cultures.

So the motive of friendship remains as both the only appropriate and understandable motive for white/Anglo feminists engaging in the task as described above. If you enter the task out of friendship with us, then you will be moved to attain the appropriate reciprocity of care for your and our well-being as whole beings, you will have a stake in us and in our world, you will be moved to satisfy the need for reciprocity of understanding that will enable you to follow us in our experiences as we are able to follow you in yours.

We are not suggesting that if the learning of the text is to be done out of friendship, you must enter into a friendship with a whole community and for the purpose of making theory. In order to understand what it is that we are suggesting, it is important to remember that during the description of her experience of exclusion, the Hispana voice said that Hispanas experience the intimacy of friendship with white/Anglo women friends as thoroughly incomplete. It is not until this fact is acknowledged by our white/Anglo women friends and felt as a profound lack in our experience of each other that white/Anglo women can begin to see us. Seeing us in our communities will make clear and concrete to you how incomplete we really are in our relationships with you. It is this beginning that forms the proper background for the yearning to understand the text of our cultures that can lead to joint theory making.

Thus, the suggestion made here is that if white/Anglo women are to understand our voices, they must understand our communities and us in them. Again, this is not to suggest that you set out to make friends with our communities, though you may become friends with some of the members, nor is it to suggest that you should try to befriend us for the purpose of making theory with us. The latter would be a perversion of friendship. Rather, from within friendship you may be moved by friendship to undergo the very difficult task of understanding the text of our cultures by understanding our lives in our communities. This learning calls for circumspection, for questioning of yourselves and your roles in your own culture. It necessitates a striving to understand while in the comfortable position of not having an official calling card (as "scientific" observers of our communities have); it demands recognition that you do not have the authority of knowledge; it requires coming to the task without ready-made theories to frame our lives. This learning is then extremely hard because it requires openness (including openness to severe criticism of the white/Anglo world), sensitivity, concentration, self-questioning, circumspection. It should be clear that it does not consist in a passive immersion in our cultures, but in a striving to understand what it is that our voices are saying. Only then can we engage in a mutual dialogue that does not reduce each one of us to an instance of the abstraction called "woman."

(1983)

NOTES

1. For a recent example, see MacKinnon, Catharine, 1982. Feminism, Marxism, Method and the State: An Agenda for Theory. *Signs* 7 (3): 515–544.

2. I must note that when I think this "we," I think it in Spanish—and in Spanish this "we" is gendered, "nosotras." I also use "nosotros" lovingly and with ease and in it I include all members of "La raza cosmica" (Spanish-speaking people of the Americas, la gente de colores: people of many colors). In the U.S., I use "we" contextually with varying degrees of discomfort: "we" in the house, "we" in the department, "we" in the classroom, "we" in the meeting. The discomfort springs from the sense of community in the "we" and the varying degrees of lack of community in the context in which the "we" is used.

3. See Bernstein, Basil. 1972. Social Class, Language, and Socialization. In Giglioli, Piet Paolo, ed., *Language and Social Context,* pp. 157–178. Penguin, Harmondsworth, Middlesex. Bernstein would probably, and we think wrongly, insist that theoretical terms and statements have meanings *not* "tied to a local relationship and to a local social structure," unlike the vocabulary of, e.g., working-class children.

---

6 • *Jane Flax*

"THE END OF INNOCENCE"

. . . Despite postmodernist challenges and their own deconstructions of the gender-based relations of power that generate the content and legitimacy of many forms of knowledge, many feminist theorists sustain the Enlightenment hope that it is possible to obtain "better" knowledge and epistemologies. By better, they mean (at minimum) knowledge and epistemologies less contaminated by false beliefs and dominating relations of power. They believe feminist theories are progressive; that is, they are freer from these effects than previous thinking and therefore represent a higher and more adequate stage of knowledge. Many feminists also continue to argue for the necessary relationships between better knowledge and better practices.[1] Without the secure ability to make truth

claims, the feminist project of ending gender-based domination is doomed.[2]

One of the most persuasive advocates of such positions, Sandra Harding, argues that epistemologies are partially justificatory schemes. Like moral codes, they challenge the idea of "might makes right" in the domain of knowledge claims. Access to such schemes is especially necessary when unequal power relations exist. It is in the interest of the weak to contest on the ground of truth rather than with force. Feminists also need some defense against and alternatives to traditional discourses about women and about means of obtaining truth, since both of these may be gender biased. We also need decision procedures articulable to other feminists to guide choices in theory, research, and

---

Reprinted from *Feminists Theorize the Political*, eds. Judith Butler and Joan Wallach Scott, 445–463. New York: Routledge, 1992. Used by permission of Jane Flax. Notes have been renumbered.

politics. When traditional grounds for knowledge claims are not adequate we need to justify our claims to ourselves and to others. This theory should be accountable to many different women. Difference should be taken into account, both as cultural variation and as domination. We also need decision procedures to guide practice; knowledge can be a resource to help organize strategies against domination. Ultimately Harding seems to think, as do Nancy Hartsock and others, that the success of the feminist projects of creating effective analyses of gender and of ending gender-based domination depends on our ability to make truth claims about the "objective" status or our knowledge and our rights.

I believe these arguments are profoundly mistaken and, to the extent to which they are (unconsciously) intended to maintain the innocence of feminist theories and politics, dangerous. Operating within the Enlightenment metanarrative, these feminist theorists confuse two different claims—that certain kinds of knowledge are generated by gender-based power relations and that correcting for these biases will necessarily produce "better," knowledge that will be purely emancipatory (that is, not generated by and generative of its own relations of noninnocent power). They are not content with constructing discourses which privilege some of those who have previously lacked power (at the necessary expense of others) but wish to claim discovery of ways to increase the general sum of human emancipation. These theorists assume that domination and emancipation are a binary pair and that to displace one necessarily creates new space for the other. They conceive disruption of the given as entailing an obligation to create something new. The legitimacy or justification of disruption depends in part on the nature of what is offered in place of the old. They fear what will emerge in disrupted spaces if they are not in feminist control. In order for the new to be secure and effective, it must be located and grounded within a new epistemological scheme. Like other Enlightenment thinkers, they believe innocent, clean knowledge is available somewhere for our discovery and use. Although the discovery of new knowledge may be dependent upon disruptions of previously existing power relations, the effects of its social origins are somehow transformed by epistemological means. Epistemology also gives a force to new knowledge (independent of politics) that it would otherwise lack.

These claims reflect the difficulties of abandoning the Enlightenment metanarrative that cannot, despite its promises, deliver us from domination or enable us to construct or exercise knowledge innocently. Harding and others assume (rather than demonstrate) that there are necessary connections between truth, knowledge, emancipation, and justice and that truth and force or domination are necessarily antinomies.

On the contrary, I believe we need to rethink all these concepts, let them float freely, and explore their differences. All epistemological talk is not useless or meaningless, but a radical shift of terrain is necessary. I would like to move the terms of the discussion away from the relations between knowledge and truth to those between knowledge, desire, fantasy, and power of various kinds. Epistemology should be reconceived as genealogy and the study of the social and unconscious relations of the production of knowledge. Philosophers would abandon wishes to adjudicate truth claims and instead would engage in linguistic, historical, political, and psychological inquiries into forms of knowledge construction and conflict within particular discursive formations. Such inquiries would include investigations into the philosopher's own desire and place within particular social locations and discourses. We can also analyze what has occurred within different discursive practices and articulate why one set of practices appears to be preferable for certain pragmatic purposes.

RESPONSIBILITY WITHOUT GROUNDS

A belief in the connections between truth and knowledge at this point in Western history seems far more likely to encourage a dangerously blind innocence rather than to prepare the ways for freedom or justice. We should take responsibility for our desire in such cases: what we really want is power in the world, not an innocent truth. The idea that truth is on one's side is a recurrent element in justificatory schemes for the actions of terrorists, fundamentalists, and producers of dangerous technologies. Part of the purpose of claiming truth seems to be to compel agreement with our claim (if it is true, then you as a "rational person" must agree with me and change your beliefs and behavior accordingly). We are often seeking a change in behavior or a win for our side. If so, there may be more effective ways to attain agreement or produce change than to argue about truth. Political action and change require and call upon many human capacities including empathy, anger, and disgust. There is no evidence that appeals to reason, knowledge or truth are uniquely effective or ought to occupy privileged positions in strategies for change. Nor do epistemologies necessarily reassure people that taking risks is worthwhile or convince them that political claims are justified. It is simply not necessarily the case (especially in politics) that appeals to truth move people to action, much less to justice.

Thus Harding confuses the need for justification with the need for power. Arguments can lack force (in the political sense) no matter how well they may be grounded in some epistemological scheme. Furthermore, arguments about knowledge are motivated in part by a wish to maintain an innocence and an innocent form of hope that are actually quite dangerous. Just because false knowledge can be utilized to justify or support domination, it does not follow that true knowledge will diminish it or that the possessor of "less false" knowledge will be free from complicity in the domination of others.

A concern for epistemology can mask the desire to claim a position of innocence in which one person's clarity does not rest on the exclusion of an other's experience. It can also be motivated by an illusory wish to discover a set of neutral rules which guarantee that adherence to them will not result in the distortion or erasure of someone's "truth." Speaking in knowledge's voice or on its behalf, we can avoid taking responsibility for locating our contingent selves as the producers of knowledge and truth claims. Talk of adjudication and justification assumes that neutrality, or at least consensus, is possible. But this in turn presupposes there are no irresolvable differences, that harmony and unity are desirable, and that effective knowledge and political action must rest on a secure, nonconflictual common ground. Consensus is privileged over conflict, rule following over anarchy.

Some negative consequences of these beliefs can be seen in contemporary feminist theory. As some feminists have argued recently, an intensified concern about epistemological issues emerged at the same time as women of color began to critique the writings of white feminists. The unity of categories such as "woman" or "gender" was found to depend upon the exclusion of many of the experiences of women of color (as well as women outside the overdeveloped world, poor women and lesbians).[3] As much if not more than postmodernism, the writings of women of color have compelled white feminists to confront problems of difference and the relations of domination that are the conditions of possibility for the coherence of our own theorizing and category formation. But our guilt and anxieties about racism (and our anger at the "others" for disturbing the initial pleasure and comfort of "sisterhood") also partially account for the discomfort and difficulties we white women have in rethinking differences and the nature of our own theorizing and statuses. Since the projects of postmodernism and women of color overlap here, I wonder whether there is a racial subtext at work that requires more attention. Since directly attacking women of color or voicing our resentment of them (in public) would be politically unthinkable, is it easier and more acceptable for white women to express our discomfort with difference discourses and the politics of knowledge claims by categorically rejecting postmodernism and branding it politically incorrect? Such constituting acts of exclusion or repression can only become evident when the power relations which enable the construction of knowledge claims are explicitly addressed.[4]

Establishing or adjudicating truth claims will not help us achieve a central feminist objective: to destroy all gender-based relations of domination. Claims about domination are claims about *injustice* and cannot be given extra force or justification by reference to Truth. Claims about injustice belong on the terrain of politics and in the realm of persuasive speech, action, and (sometimes) violence. As Machiavelli argues, politics requires a morality and knowledge appropriate to its unique domain. Claims about injustice can operate independently of "truth," or indeed any corresponding counterclaim about a transcendental good or (substantive) justice.[5]

Once we begin to make claims about gender injustice, we have irrevocably entered the realm of politics. We need to learn ways of making claims about and acting upon injustice without transcendental guarantees or illusions of innocence. One of the dangerous consequences of transcendental notions of justice or knowledge is that they release us as discrete persons from full responsibility for our acts. We remain children, waiting, if our own powers fail, for the higher authorities to save us from the consequences of our actions.

Such wishes depend on and express our complicity with what Nietzsche calls the "longest lie," the belief that "outside the haphazard and perilous experiments we perform there lies something (God, Science, Knowledge, Rationality, or Truth) which will, if only we perform the correct rituals, step in to save us."⁶

To take responsibility is to firmly situate ourselves within contingent and imperfect contexts, to acknowledge differential privileges of race, gender, geographic location, and sexual identities, and to resist the delusory and dangerous recurrent hope of redemption to a world not of our own making. We need to learn to make claims on our own and others' behalf and to listen to those which differ from ours, knowing that ultimately there is nothing that justifies them beyond each person's own desire and need and the discursive practices in which these are developed, embedded, and legitimated. Each person's well-being is ultimately dependent on the development of discursive communities which foster (among other attributes) an appreciation of and desire for difference, empathy, even indifference in the others. Lacking such feelings, as the Jews in Germany or people of color in the United States (among many others) have discovered, all the laws and culture civilization can offer will not save us. It is far from clear what contributions knowledge or truth can make to the development of such feelings and communities.

At its best, postmodernism invites us to engage in a continual process of dis-illusionment with the grandiose fantasies that have brought us to the brink of annihilation. For this is part of what is missing from Christa Wolf's equation: in different situations, people in the West are on both sides, the few and the many, and it is extremely difficult for us to accept and live such unstable and painful ambivalence. But these junctures are exactly where responsibility beyond innocence looms as a promise and a frightening necessity.

(1992)

NOTES

1. Such arguments have been made by Sandra Harding, "Feminism, Science, and the Anti-Enlightenment Critiques," and Christine Di Stefano, "Dilemmas of Difference: Feminism, Modernity, and Postmodernism," both in Linda J. Nicholson, ed., *Feminism/Postmodernism*; and by Mary E. Hawkesworth, "Knowers, Knowing, Known: Feminist Theory and the Claims of Truth," in *Feminist*

Theory in Practice and Process, edited by Micheline R. Malson, Jean F. O'Barr, Sarah Westphall-Wihl, Mary Wyer (Chicago: University of Chicago Press, 1989).

2. For strong statements of this position, see Nancy Hartsock, "Foucault on Power: A Theory for Women?," in Linda J. Nicholson, ed., *Feminism/Postmodernism*; and Mary E. Hawkesworth, "Knowers, Knowing, Known." Much of the feminist debate on postmodernism turns on a political question: whether the legitimacy and efficacy of feminist practices and claims require an epistemological justification/grounding. On this debate see Nancy Fraser and Linda J. Nicholson, "Social Criticism without Philosophy: An Encounter between Feminism and Postmodernism," and Seyla Benhabib, "Epistemologies of Postmodernism: A Rejoinder to Jean-François Lyotard," both in Linda J. Nicholson, *Feminism/Postmodernism*; Linda Alcoff, "Cultural Feminism versus Post-Structuralism: The Identity Crisis in Feminist Theory," in Micheline R. Malson, *et al.*, *Feminist Theory*; the essays in *Feminist Studies*, 14, 1 (Spring 1988); Donna Haraway, "Situated Knowledges: The Science Question in Feminism and the Privilege of Partial Perspective," *Feminist Studies*, 14, 3 (Fall 1988), pp. 575–99; Nancy Fraser, *Unruly Practices*; and Kathy E. Ferguson, "Interpretation and Genealogy in Feminism," *Signs*, 16, 2 (Winter 1991), pp. 322–39.

3. Barbara Christian, "The Race for Theory," *Feminist Studies,* 14, 1 (Summer 1988), pp. 67–79; Audre Lorde, *Sister Outsider* (Trumansburg, N.Y.: Crossing Press, 1984); Deborah K. King, "Multiple Jeopardy, Multiple Consciousness: The Context for a Black Feminist Ideology," in Micheline R. Malson *et al.*, *Feminist Theory*; Elizabeth V. Spelman, *Inessential Woman: Problems of Exclusion in Feminist Thought* (Boston: Beacon, 1988); Biddy Martin and Chandra Talpade Mohanty, "Feminist Politics: What's Home Got to Do With It?," in *Feminist Studies/Critical Studies*, edited by Teresa de Lauretis (Bloomington: Indiana University Press, 1986); and Bernice Johnson Reagon, "Coalition Politics: Turning the Century," in *Home Girls: A Black Feminist Anthology*, edited by Barbara Smith (New York: Kitchen Table: Women of Color Press, 1983).

4. As I argue in *Thinking Fragments* (Berkeley: University of California Press, 1990), postmodernism is not above criticism or without flaws. I would not claim that anxieties about race and other differences are the only source of its rejection. I am trying to make sense of part of the emotional vehemence with which some feminists reject these writings, sometimes with only minimal knowledge of them. The intensity of the emotional response is puzzling, especially among people who generally respond to ideas in a much more complex and

nuanced manner. On postmodernism, race, and gender see bell hooks, *Yearning* (Boston: South End Press, 1990).

5. See Stuart Hampshire, *Innocence and Experience*; Agnes Heller and Ferenc Feher, *The Postmodernism Political Condition* (New York: Columbia University Press, 1989); and Judith N. Shklar, "Injustice, Injury and Inequality:

An Introduction," in *Justice and Equality in the Here and Now*, edited by Frank S. Lucash (Ithaca: Cornell University Press, 1986).

6. Richard Rorty, "Method, Social Science, and Social Hope," in *Consequences of Pragmatism*, p. 208.

7 • *Uma Narayan*

"THE PROJECT OF FEMINIST EPISTEMOLOGY: PERSPECTIVES FROM A NONWESTERN FEMINIST"

A fundamental thesis of feminist epistemology is that our location in the world as women makes it possible for us to perceive and understand different aspects of both the world and human activities in ways that challenge the male bias of existing perspectives. Feminist epistemology is a particular manifestation of the general insight that the nature of women's experiences as individuals and as social beings, our contributions to work, culture, knowledge, and our history and political interests have been systematically ignored or misrepresented by mainstream discourses in different areas.

Women have been often excluded from prestigious areas of human activity (for example, politics or science) and this has often made these activities seem clearly "male." In areas where women were not excluded (for example, subsistence work), their contribution has been misrepresented as secondary and inferior to that of men. Feminist epistemology sees mainstream theories about various human enterprises, including mainstream theories about human knowledge, as one-dimensional and deeply flawed because of the exclusion and misrepresentation of women's contributions.

Feminist epistemology suggests that integrating women's contribution into the domain of science and knowledge will not constitute a mere adding of details; it will not merely widen the canvas but result in a shift of perspective enabling us to see a very different picture. The inclusion of women's perspective will not merely amount to women participating in greater numbers in the existing practice of science and knowledge, but it will change the very nature of these activities and their self-understanding.

It would be misleading to suggest that feminist epistemology is a homogenous and cohesive enterprise. Its practitioners differ both philosophically and politically in a number of significant ways (Harding 1986). But an important theme on its agenda has been to undermine the abstract, rationalistic, and universal image of the scientific enterprise by using several different strategies. It has studied, for instance, how contingent historical factors have colored both scientific theories and practices and provided the (often sexist) metaphors in which scientists have conceptualized their activity (Bordo 1986; Keller 1985; Harding and O'Barr 1987). It has tried to reintegrate values and emotions into our account of our cognitive activities, arguing for both the inevitability of their presence and the importance of the contributions they are capable of

Reprinted from *Gender/Body/Knowledge*, eds. A. M. Jaggar and S. R. Bordo, 256–269. New Brunswick: Rutgers University Press, 1989. Used by permission of Rutgers University Press.

making to our knowledge (Gilligan 1982; Jaggar [1989] and Tronto [1989]). It has also attacked various sets of dualisms characteristic of western philosophical thinking—reason versus emotion, culture versus nature, universal versus particular—in which the first of each set is identified with science, rationality, and the masculine and the second is relegated to the non-scientific, the nonrational, and the feminine (Harding and Hintikka 1983; Lloyd 1984; Wilshire [1989]).

At the most general level, feminist epistemology resembles the efforts of many oppressed groups to reclaim for themselves the value of their own experience. The writing of novels that focused on working-class life in England or the lives of black people in the United States shares a motivation similar to that of feminist epistemology—to depict an experience different from the norm and to assert the value of this difference.

In a similar manner, feminist epistemology also resembles attempts by third-world writers and historians to document the wealth and complexity of local economic and social structures that existed prior to colonialism. These attempts are useful for their ability to restore to colonized peoples a sense of the richness of their own history and culture. These projects also mitigate the tendency of intellectuals in former colonies who are westernized through their education to think that anything western is necessarily better and more "progressive." In some cases, such studies help to preserve the knowledge of many local arts, crafts, lore, and techniques that were part of the former way of life before they are lost not only to practice but even to memory.

These enterprises are analogous to feminist epistemology's project of restoring to women a sense of the richness of their history, to mitigate our tendency to see the stereotypically "masculine" as better or more progressive, and to preserve for posterity the contents of "feminine" areas of knowledge and expertise—medical lore, knowledge associated with the practices of childbirth and child rearing, traditionally feminine crafts, and so on. Feminist epistemology, like these other enterprises, must attempt to balance the assertion of the value of a different culture or experience against the dangers of romanticizing it to the extent that the limitations and oppressions it confers on its subjects are ignored.

My essay will attempt to examine some dangers of approaching feminist theorizing and epistemological values in a noncontextual and nonpragmatic way, which could convert important feminist insights and theses into feminist epistemological dogmas. I will use my perspective as a nonwestern, Indian feminist to examine critically the predominantly Anglo-American project of feminist epistemology and to reflect on what such a project might signify for women in nonwestern cultures in general and for nonwestern feminists in particular. I will suggest that different cultural contexts and political agendas may cast a very different light on both the "idols" and the "enemies" of knowledge as they have characteristically been typed in western feminist epistemology.

In keeping with my respect for contexts, I would like to stress that I do not see nonwestern feminists as a homogenous group and that none of the concerns I express as a nonwestern feminist may be pertinent to or shared by all nonwestern feminists, although I do think they will make sense to many. . . .

NONWESTERN FEMINIST POLITICS AND FEMINIST EPISTEMOLOGY

Some themes of feminist epistemology may be problematic for nonwestern feminists in ways that they are not problematic for western feminists. Feminism has a much narrower base in most nonwestern countries. It is primarily of significance to some urban, educated, middle-class, and hence relatively westernized women, like myself. Although feminist groups in these countries do try to extend the scope of feminist concerns to other groups (for example, by fighting for childcare, women's health issues, and equal wages issues through trade union structures), some major preoccupations of western feminism—its critique of marriage, the family, compulsory heterosexuality—presently engage the attention of mainly small groups of middle-class feminists.

These feminists must think and function within the context of a powerful tradition that, although it systematically oppresses women, also contains within itself a discourse that confers a high value on women's place in the general scheme of things. Not only are the roles of wife and mother highly praised, but women also are seen as the cornerstones of the spiritual well-being of their husbands and children, admired for their supposedly higher moral, religious, and spiritual qualities, and so on. In cultures that have a pervasive religious component, like the Hindu culture with which I am familiar, everything seems assigned a place and value as long as it keeps to its place. Confronted with a powerful traditional discourse that values woman's place as long as she keeps to the place prescribed, it may be politically counterproductive for nonwestern feminists to echo uncritically the themes of western feminist epistemology that seek to restore the value, cognitive and otherwise, of "women's experience."

The danger is that, even if the nonwestern feminist talks about the value of women's experience in terms totally different from those of the traditional discourse, the difference is likely to be drowned out by the louder and more powerful voice of the traditional discourse, which will then claim that "what those feminists say" vindicates its view that the roles and experiences it assigns to women have value and that women should stick to those roles. . . .

THE NONPRIMACY OF POSITIVISM AS A PROBLEMATIC PERSPECTIVE

As a nonwestern feminist, I also have some reservations about the way in which feminist epistemology seems to have picked positivism as its main target of attack. The choice of positivism as the main target is reasonable because it has been a dominant and influential western position and it most clearly embodies some flaws that feminist epistemology seeks to remedy.

But this focus on positivism should not blind us to the facts that it is not our only enemy and that nonpositivist frameworks are not, by virtue of that bare qualification, any more worthy of our tolerance. Most traditional frameworks that nonwestern feminists regard as oppressive to women are not positivist, and it would be wrong to see feminist epistemology's critique of positivism given the same political importance for nonwestern feminists that it has for western feminists. Traditions like my own, where the influence of religion is pervasive, are suffused through and through with values. We must fight not frameworks that assert the separation of fact and value but frameworks that are pervaded by values to which we, as feminists, find ourselves opposed. Positivism in epistemology flourished at the same time as liberalism in western political theory. Positivism's view of values as individual and subjective related to liberalism's political emphasis on individual rights that were supposed to protect an individual's freedom to live according to the values she espoused.

Nonwestern feminists may find themselves in a curious bind when confronting the interrelations between positivism and political liberalism. As colonized people, we are well aware of the facts that many political concepts of liberalism are both suspicious and confused and that the practice of liberalism in the colonies was marked by brutalities unaccounted for by its theory. However, as feminists, we often find some of its concepts, such as individual rights, very useful in our attempts to fight problems rooted in our traditional cultures.

Nonwestern feminists will no doubt be sensitive to the fact that positivism is not our only enemy. Western feminists too must learn not to uncritically claim any nonpositivist framework as an ally; despite commonalities, there are apt to be many differences. A temperate look at positions we espouse as allies is necessary since "the enemy of my enemy is my friend" is a principle likely to be as misleading in epistemology as it is in the domain of Realpolitik. . . .

THE DARK SIDE OF "DOUBLE VISION"

I think that one of the most interesting insights of feminist epistemology is the view that oppressed groups, whether women, the poor, or racial minorities, may derive an "epistemic advantage" from having knowledge of the practices of both their own contexts and those of their oppressors. The practices of the dominant groups (for instance, men) govern a society; the dominated group (for instance, women) must acquire some fluency with these practices in order to survive in that society.

There is no similar pressure on members of the dominant group to acquire knowledge of the practices of the dominated groups. For instance, colonized people had to learn the language and culture of their colonizers. The colonizers seldom found it necessary to have more than a sketchy acquaintance with the language and culture of the "natives." Thus, the oppressed are seen as having an "epistemic advantage" because they can operate with two sets of practices and in two different contexts. This advantage is thought to lead to critical insights because each framework provides a critical perspective on the other.

I would like to balance this account with a few comments about the "dark side," the disadvantages, of being able to or of having to inhabit two mutually incompatible frameworks that provide differing perspectives on social reality. I suspect that nonwestern feminists, given the often complex and troublesome interrelationships between the contexts they must inhabit, are less likely to express unqualified enthusiasm about the benefits of straddling a multiplicity of contexts. Mere access to two different and incompatible contexts is not a guarantee that a critical stance on the part of an individual will result. There are many ways in which she may deal with the situation.

First, the person may be tempted to dichotomize her life and reserve the framework of a different context for each part. The middle class of nonwestern countries supplies numerous examples of people who are very westernized in public life but who return to a very traditional lifestyle in the realm of the family. Women may choose to live their public lives in a "male" mode, displaying characteristics of aggressiveness, competition, and so on, while continuing to play dependent and compliant roles in their private lives. The pressures of jumping between two different lifestyles may be mitigated by justifications of how each pattern of behavior is appropriate to its particular context and of how it enables them to "get the best of both worlds."

Second, the individual may try to reject the practices of her own context and try to be as much as possible like members of the dominant group. Westernized intellectuals in the nonwestern world often may almost lose knowledge of their own cultures and practices and be ashamed of the little that they do still know. Women may try both to acquire stereotypically male characteristics, like aggressiveness, and to expunge stereotypically female characteristics, like emotionality. Or the individual could try to reject entirely the framework of the dominant group and assert the virtues of her own despite the risks of being marginalized from the power structures of the society; consider, for example, women who seek a certain sort of security in traditionally defined roles.

The choice to inhabit two contexts critically is an alternative to these choices and, I would argue, a more useful one. But the presence of alternative contexts does not by itself guarantee that one of the other choices will not be made. Moreover, the decision to inhabit two contexts critically, although it may lead to an "epistemic advantage," is likely to exact a certain price. It may lead to a sense of totally lacking roots or any space where one is at home in a relaxed manner.

This sense of alienation may be minimized if the critical straddling of two contexts is part of an ongoing critical politics, due to the support of others and a deeper understanding of what is going on. When it is not so rooted, it may generate ambivalence, uncertainty, despair, and even madness, rather than more positive critical emotions and attitudes. However such a person determines her locus, there may be a sense of being an outsider in both contexts and a sense of clumsiness or lack of fluency in both sets of practices. Consider this simple linguistic example: most people who learn two different languages that are associated with two very different cultures seldom acquire both with equal fluency; they may find themselves devoid of vocabulary in one language for certain contexts of life or be unable to match real objects with terms they have acquired in their vocabulary. For instance, people from my sort of background would know words in Indian languages for some spices, fruits, and vegetables that they do not know in English. Similarly, they might be unable to discuss "technical" subjects like economics or biology in their own languages because they learned about these subjects and acquired their technical vocabularies only in English.

The relation between the two contexts the individual inhabits may not be simple or straightforward. The individual subject is seldom in a position to carry out a perfect "dialectical synthesis" that preserves all the advantages of both contexts and transcends all their problems. There may be a number of different "syntheses," each of which avoids a different subset of the problems and preserves a different subset of the benefits.

No solution may be perfect or even palatable to the agent confronted with a choice. For example, some Indian feminists may find some western modes of dress (say trousers) either more comfortable or more their "style" than some local modes of dress. However, they may find that wearing the local mode of dress is less socially troublesome, alienates them less from more traditional people they want to work with, and so on. Either choice is bound to leave them partly frustrated in their desires.

Feminist theory must be temperate in the use it makes of this doctrine of "double vision"—the claim that oppressed groups have an epistemic advantage and access to greater critical conceptual space. Certain types and contexts of oppression certainly may bear out the truth of this claim. Others certainly do not seem to do so; and even if they do provide space for critical insights, they may also rule out the possibility of actions subversive of the oppressive state of affairs.

Certain kinds of oppressive contexts, such as the contexts in which women of my grandmother's background lived, rendered their subjects entirely devoid of skills required to function as independent entities in the culture. Girls were married off barely past puberty, trained for nothing beyond household tasks and the rearing of children, and passed from economic dependency on their fathers to economic dependency on their husbands to economic dependency on their sons in old age. Their criticisms of their lot were articulated, if at all, in terms that precluded a desire for any radical change. They saw themselves sometimes as personally unfortunate, but they did not locate the causes of their misery in larger social arrangements.

I conclude by stressing that the important insight incorporated in the doctrine of "double vision" should not be reified into a metaphysics that serves as a substitute for concrete social analysis. Furthermore, the alternative to "buying" into an oppressive social system need not be a celebration of exclusion and the mechanisms of marginalization. The thesis that oppression may bestow an epistemic advantage should not tempt us in the direction of idealizing or romanticizing oppression and blind us to its real material and psychic deprivations. . . .

(1989)

SECTION ONE

Modern Feminist Thought

CHAPTER 2

Liberal Feminisms

The true republic—men, their rights and nothing more; women, their rights and nothing less.

—Susan B. Anthony, 1868

INTRODUCTION

The most popular and hegemonic feminist perspective in the United States from the American Revolution to the present era has been liberal feminism. During the first wave, the liberal **National American Woman Suffrage Association (NAWSA)** was the largest women's rights organization in the United States. From the second wave to the present day, the liberal **National Organization for Women (NOW)** has been the largest feminist organization in the United States. Today NOW boasts more than 500,000 contributing members and more than 500 local and campus affiliates across the country.[1]

This chapter focuses on the contributions of liberal feminisms to the U.S. women's movement. In the eighteenth century, liberal ideas were revolutionary. They sparked the overthrow of absolute monarchy in France and the demise of Britain's colonial rule of the American colonies. However, once democratic republics were established, liberal feminists embraced a **reform-oriented politics** *that advocated working within the system through legitimate electoral, legislative, and judicial processes.* They did not argue that women's emancipation required qualitative changes in the economic or political system. They neither called for the demise of capitalism nor challenged the basic assumptions of a democratic republic so long as women enjoyed the same rights as men. Consequently, for most of American history they favored reform over revolution.

THE "WOMAN QUESTION" AND ENLIGHTENMENT THOUGHT

Liberal feminism has its deepest theoretical roots in Enlightenment thought—a body of thought that shook the foundations of social life in Europe and the American colonies in the eighteenth century. The term "Enlightenment" comes from the idea that this new social thought could lift the world from an age of darkness and ignorance into a world of science and rational thought (Zeitlin, 1981). These then-radical ideas provided the ideology and slogans for major eighteenth-century revolutions—namely the French Revolution and the American Revolution. For example, the American Declaration of Independence, as well as the U.S. Constitution and Bill of Rights, exemplify the Enlightenment idea of a "social contract" theory of the state. That is, to form governments, citizens should have a written contract that specifies the rights and responsibilities of both the government and its citizens, as does the U.S. Constitution. Citizens could not be governed without their consent and could even overthrow their government if it abrogated its responsibilities or citizens' rights. Enlightenment thinkers also maintained that citizens had "natural and inalienable rights" such as freedom of speech and freedom of assembly.

Yet, in regard to the "woman question," many Enlightenment thinkers held far less progressive views than their critical ideas would suggest (Knott and Taylor, 2005; O'Brien, 2009). This is evident in the correspondence between Abigail Adams and her husband John on the eve of the American Revolution found in Reading 8. Abigail asks her husband to "remember the ladies" when he is composing the Declaration of Independence. John replies that he "cannot but laugh" at Abigail's "extraordinary" and "saucy" request (John Adams quoted in Butterfield et al., 1975: 375). His views on voting rights were typical of Enlightenment thinkers and reveal how issues of gender, class, and race were imbricated in their refusal to grant women the vote. John Adams, like many other male Enlightenment thinkers, viewed property ownership as a qualification for voting. For him, people without property are "too dependent upon other men to have a will of their own" (375). Thus, although Enlightenment thought was radical for its era, many people were excluded from the rights it so proudly proclaimed.

THE RISE OF THE U.S. WOMEN'S MOVEMENT IN EARLY MODERNITY

The inability of married women to own property and to control their own income or wealth was rooted in the **doctrine of coverture** that governed marriage laws across most of the country.[2] This doctrine held that, once a man and woman were married, they were one in front of the law. This "one" was the man, who controlled the property and income of the household and legally had the right to chastise or punish his wife and children. Reading 16, "The Story of an Hour" written by Kate Chopin ([1894] 1975), depicts the constraints of the doctrine of coverture and the freedom the wife in this short story felt when she thought her husband had died in a train crash. The startling twist at the end is a signature of many of Chopin's short stories.

The temperance movement of the late nineteenth century was a direct response to the gender inequalities protected by the doctrine of coverture. Not only was alcohol abuse a serious issue associated with domestic violence, but also wives feared their husbands would drink up their households' wages. However, it was the abolitionist movement that was the major trigger for the rise of the nineteenth-century U.S. women's movement. In Reading 10, *Letters on the Equality of the Sexes and the Condition of Women* (1837), the renowned feminist and abolitionist Sarah

Grimké interweaves her feminist critique of the "miserably deficient" lives of free women in terms of their ability to gain intellect with powerful descriptions of the tyranny and sexual violence suffered by slave women ([1837] 1974: 311 and 315). Grimké asks: "Can any American woman look at these scenes of shocking licentiousness and cruelty, and fold her hands in apathy, and say, 'I have nothing to do with slavery'? *She cannot and be guiltless*" (315, her emphasis).

Within the abolitionist movement, women learned important political and organizing skills. However, they also learned that they could not function as equals alongside their male abolitionist counterparts. Not only were women barred from membership in some abolitionist organizations, but also they had to battle simply to speak in public. A major theme used by some white, liberal feminists to advance their feminist demands was to highlight the *similarities* between their own lack of freedom and that of slaves. This is exemplified in Reading 15, "Speech after Arrest for Illegal Voting" (1872), Susan B. Anthony's statement at a trial after she and fifteen other women were arrested for trying to vote in a presidential election. Here Anthony discusses how neither free women nor slaves could own their own property, control their own incomes, keep their own names, or have custody of their children (Anthony ([1872] 1992). As discussed in Chapter 5, many African American women did not appreciate such comparisons—given the stark differences in the lives of slaves and those of white, middle-class suffragists.

THE SENECA FALLS DECLARATION OF SENTIMENTS

The first women's rights convention in U.S. history was held at Seneca Falls, New York, in 1848 and their demands were stated in the famous "Declaration of Sentiments" found in Reading 11. This document, drafted by Elizabeth Cady Stanton, was modeled on the Declaration of Independence to highlight the contradictions between the rights espoused there and women's exclusion from these rights. The "Declaration of Sentiments" enumerated more than a dozen ways that men established "tyranny" over women, such as "depriving her of her inalienable right to elective franchise"; "taking from her all right to property, even to the wages she earns"; and "making her, if married, in the eye of the law, civilly dead" (Stanton, [1848] 2005: 72). They also strove for guardianship of their children because men received custody in the rare cases of divorce in this era.

These demands were made in opposition to the prevailing discourse of that era—often referred to as the "**cult of domesticity**" or the "**cult of true womanhood**"—which romanticized women's roles as housewives, homemakers, and mothers (Welter, 1973). This discourse was buttressed by the "**doctrine of separate spheres**," which deemed the private realm of the household the women's sphere and the public realm outside of the home the men's sphere (Lerner, 1979). The extent to which women's lives conformed to this ideal, of course, varied according to their social locations given that slave women, as well as most poor and working-class women, had to work outside of their homes. Although the cult of domesticity was designed to distinguish class-privileged "ladies" from other women, it nonetheless restricted the lives of middle-class women (Lerner, 1979: 190–192).

LIBERAL FEMINISTS ON LOVE, MARRIAGE, AND SEX IN EARLY MODERNITY[3]

Because England was the birthplace of the industrial revolution and entered the modern world before its former colony, which became the United States, some of the earliest writings by liberal feminists were penned by British feminists. Reading 9 is from the Introduction to Mary Wollstonecraft's *A Vindication of the Rights of Woman* ([1792] 1975). Wollstonecraft argued that women gained only superficial status by asserting themselves as the natural possessors of beauty, innocence, and delicacy. She emphasized the need for cultural, educational, and economic reforms that would allow women to cultivate their skills and assigned great significance to rationality and self-actualization. In these ways, Wollstonecraft offered a prescient feminist critique of the social construction of gender in her era.

Writing a half century later, British authors Harriet Taylor Mill and John Stuart Mill echoed these liberal ideas and highlighted how existing marriage laws often chained women to violent and oppressive relationships. Reading 12 is from Harriet Taylor Mill's "Enfranchisement of Women" ([1851] 1970), whereas Reading 13 is from John Stuart Mill's *The Subjection of Women* ([1869] 1972).[4] Both of these authors wrote extensively about the importance of reforming marriage, divorce, and child custody laws and the Enlightenment ideas of reason and self-determination are threaded throughout their works. Because many of these advocates of **sexual reformism** presented sexual violence as a symptom of the larger problem of unequal gender relations, they laid a crucial foundation for later feminist analyses of domestic violence and sexual assault.

Most women's rights activists of this era provided little insight into women's positive experiences of sexuality. Only a few made the then-radical claim that women should be able to experience sexual pleasure outside of marriage. At this time, **"free love"** or **"sex love"** referred to the right to have sex *with someone you loved* whether inside or outside of marriage. It did not refer to indiscriminate or casual sexual relations. The high priestess of free love among U.S. liberal feminists of this era was Victoria Claflin Woodhull.[5] For Woodhull, sex based upon mutual love and desire that provided reciprocal benefit was simply not possible within the institution of legal marriage at that time given that marriage was an economic necessity for most women. For this reason, Woodhull viewed marriage as no different from prostitution. In Reading 14, "And the Truth Shall Make You Free" (1871), Woodhull defends her position on free love and the influence of Enlightenment thought is evident when she writes: "I have an inalienable, constitutional, and natural right to love whom I may, to love as long or as short a period as I can" (Woodhull [1871] 2010: 51).

FIRST-WAVE ENVIRONMENTAL ACTIVISM[6]

Compared to moderate liberal feminists who worked mainly with people of their own social classes, many of the middle-class, left-liberal suffragists who engaged in environmental activism in this era worked in settlement houses or mutual aid societies and/or initiated various experiments in collective forms of living, as well as communal kitchens and child care (Hayden, 1982). Because the settlement houses and mutual aid societies were located in neighborhoods of poor and working-class people, these social reformers came face-to-face with the dire effects of poverty and squalor. The most famous settlement house, Hull House in Chicago founded by Jane Addams, provided poor and working-class families with health care, child care, and adult education and championed the rights of working-class people to unionize.

The Hull House women were heavily involved in addressing environmental issues. They worked under the banner of **municipal housekeeping** to highlight how these issues directly affected the safety of their homes and families. Thousands of women mobilized to address the environmental problems created by modernization and industrialization, such as air and water pollution, sanitation issues, safe food, and occupational safety. Reading 18 provides a brief excerpt from Jane Addams's writings on municipal housekeeping ([1907] 1973). Addams points not only to how women have traditionally dealt with the issues of health and sanitation, but also that they should have the right to vote on these issues that so severely affected their homes and communities.

Often overlooked in existing ecofeminist literature is how African American suffragists contributed significantly to the municipal housekeeping movement, usually through the black women's clubs and/or by establishing mutual aid societies.[7] Overall, the black women's club movement had more serious problems to deal with than did their white counterparts. Not only were health conditions perilous in the black shantytowns and ghettoes of apartheid America, but also issues like child care were far more compelling for the vast majority of black women (Olivia Davidson quoted in Giddings, 1984: 100).

Indeed, these women dealt with social problems that spanned the life cycle from day nurseries to old-age homes. Their activities helped compensate for poorly funded black schools, hospitals, and clinics (Shaw: 1995). One of the more remarkable institutions created during this era was the Atlanta Neighborhood Union—the black women's organization most similar to Hull House during this era (Lerner, 1979: 88–90). Organized in 1908 under the leadership of Lugenia Hope, it established a nursery, a kindergarten, and a medical center to treat tuberculosis and other filth diseases (Giddings, 1984: 136). Fannie Barrier Williams captures well the differences between the white and the black women's clubs when she writes: "The club movement among colored women reaches into the sub-social conditions of the entire race . . . Among white women the club is the forward movement of the already uplifted" (quoted in Giddings, 1984: 98).

WINNING SUFFRAGE

In 1890 the two major U.S. suffrage organizations merged to form the NAWSA and this organization focused its energies on winning the vote (Hole and Levine, 1979). A cartoon depicting this merger titled "American Suffragettes" (1896) can be found in Reading 17. The term "suffragettes" was originally a term used to diminish the activities of these women. Some British suffragists, and a few American ones, reclaimed the term to distinguish their more militant activism from the more staid constitutionalists who sought political equality through legislative means and lobbying. Most American suffragists, however, continued to use the term suffragist, choosing not to reclaim the earlier derogatory term.[8]

Regardless of whether the term was used, in the early twentieth century a new generation of more militant liberal suffragists came of age. Under the leadership of

Alice Paul, these suffragists formed the **Woman's Party.** They worked exclusively for a federal Woman Suffrage Amendment using a wider array of tactics than the NAWSA—tactics that Paul had learned from her contact with militant British suffragists. The Woman's Party organized parades and demonstrations. They picketed the White House and even engaged in hunger strikes. All of these activities were considered militant at this time and on several occasions these women were arrested and jailed.

The various forms of liberal activism undertaken to attain the vote were impressive and incredibly time-consuming. Seventy years had passed between the Seneca Falls Convention and the victory of women's suffrage with the passage of the Nineteenth Amendment in 1920. Carrie Chapman Catt, a former president of NAWSA, estimated that it took:

> 56 campaigns of referenda to male voters; 480 campaigns to get Legislatures to submit suffrage amendments to votes; 44 campaigns to get State constitutional conventions to write woman suffrage into state constitutions; 277 campaigns to get State party conventions to include woman suffrage planks; 30 campaigns to get presidential party conventions to adopt woman suffrage planks in party platforms, and 29 campaigns with 19 successive Congresses. (Catt quoted in Hole and Levine, 1979: 554)

After the passage of the Nineteenth Amendment, Alice Paul called for a new campaign to pass an Equal Rights Amendment (ERA) to the Constitution. This amendment simply stated that *equality of rights under the law shall not be denied or abridged by the United States or by any State on account of sex.*[9] Yet, by 1920 so much energy had been expended in achieving the vote that the woman's movement virtually collapsed with exhaustion (Hole and Levine, 1979). It would take more than four decades before a second wave of mass activism by U.S. feminists crested in the 1960s.

ADVANCES AND SETBACKS BETWEEN THE WAVES

Despite the decline of mass-based activism after the passage of the Nineteenth Amendment, U.S. women made some important strides in the period between 1920 and 1930. In particular, significant advances were made in educational attainment. A staggering 40 percent of the students who received college degrees in 1930 were women, a percentage twice as high as in 1900. Traditional areas of women's work—such as nursing and teaching—explain much of the increase in women's professional roles between the waves. In terms of advanced degrees, the fields of psychology and anthropology were most welcoming to women (Cott, 1987).

Among U.S. feminist academics, anthropologist Margaret Mead's writings gained the most widespread public and professional attention between the waves because of her focus on sexual practices and gender roles. Her reports of healthy and permissive attitudes toward sex in *Coming of Age in Samoa* (1928) earned Mead a reputation as a champion of liberal sexual practices. Reading 21 is from her book *Sex and Temperament in Three Primitive Societies* ([1935] 1963), where Mead highlights how gender is socially constructed based on her ethnographic studies of how gender roles vary in different cultures.

Another important influence on feminist thought between the waves was the work of British novelist and essayist Virginia Woolf. In Reading 19 from *A Room of One's Own* (1929) Woolf introduces **"Shakespeare's sister"**—a "poet who never wrote a word" and who "was buried at the cross-roads" without fame or fortune precisely because women of that era were precluded from opportunities for education and writing (2008: 148). But Woolf argues that Shakespeare's sister still "lives in you and me" (ibid) and here begins her clarion call for women to take up the pen, to make their voices heard, and to write their way into history. In Reading 20 from this same book and titled "A Room of One's Own," Woolf ponders why mothers have no wealth to leave to their daughters and discusses how women's relegation to child rearing and work in the home poses serious obstacles to producing both income and literature. She concludes that 500 pounds (economic independence) and a room of our own (a place free from the interruptions and demands of everyday life) are prerequisites for women's writing.

LIBERAL FEMINISMS IN LATE MODERNITY

World War II not only lifted the U.S. economy from the depths of the Great Depression, but also jettisoned vast numbers of women into the wartime economy and into occupations traditionally held by men. Yet when soldiers returned home, married and/or pregnant women often were forced to leave their jobs in favor of men by both private and public hiring policies (Cott, 1987: 225). This postwar era also witnessed a revival of the cult of domesticity that would become the target of many feminist writings during the second wave of the U.S. women's movement.

Indeed, the book often cited as triggering the second wave—Betty Friedan's *The Feminine Mystique* (1963)—directly addressed the cult of domesticity. Friedan's focus was on white, middle-class women who had achieved what was considered at that time the "American Dream" for women—being housewives and stay-at-home moms with breadwinner husbands, homes of their own, and sufficient disposable income to live comfortably. As Reading 22 from this book illustrates, Friedan documented how many housewives were experiencing deep and persistent depression. Because both these women and the doctors who examined them had a difficult time articulating the source of their depression, Friedan called this phenomenon **"the problem that has no name"** and rooted it in the lack of fulfillment associated with being housewives and mothers (Friedan [1963] 1997: 15). Later feminist authors would criticize Friedan for ignoring race and class differences between women, for not addressing whether it "was more fulfilling to be a maid, a babysitter, a factory worker, a clerk, or a prostitute, than to be a leisure class housewife" (hooks, 1984: 1–2). Nevertheless, Friedan's analysis spoke to the concerns of many women of that era—given how post–World War II prosperity had provided the high male wages that enabled the number of stay-at-home moms in the United States to reach one of its highest peaks.

Friedan ([1963] 1997) also contrasted how "a century earlier women had fought for higher education" (16), whereas in the 1950s they went to college "to get a husband." She lamented how young women were taught to pity "unfeminine" women who wanted to be poets, physicians, or presidents (ibid). In postwar America, "truly feminine" women did not want careers, higher education, political rights, or the opportunities that the first wave struggled to achieve (ibid). Friedan called this notion of femininity that crippled women's aspirations, reducing them to the size of a casserole dish, the **feminine mystique** (Friedan, [1963] 1997, 18). She blamed it on a systemic, gendered worldview that formed the normative core of U.S. society and called for women to strive for equality in the world outside the home.

In 1966, along with other women who shared these views, Friedan founded NOW and its first "Statement of Purpose" can be found in Reading 23. Other major liberal feminist organizations that fought for equal rights during this era were the League of Women Voters, Women's Equity Action League, and the organization of Federally Employed Women. A major liberal organization that focuses on constitutional rights—the American Civil Liberties Union—often provided feminists with legal services and waged their legal battles in the courts. The American Civil Liberties Union assisted in one of the second wave's major victories—the 1973 Supreme Court's Roe v. Wade decision that established a constitutional right to privacy, a woman's right to control her body, and the legalization of abortion.

LIBERAL PSYCHOANALYTIC FEMINISMS

Reading 24 is an excerpt from one of the most influential second-wave, liberal feminist psychoanalytic works—Carol Gilligan's *In a Different Voice: Psychological Theory and Women's Development* (1982). Gilligan critiqued earlier, male-authored psychoanalytic theories of moral development for being gender blind and for excluding women from their studies. Her research revealed that when girls made moral decisions, they were more concerned with relationships between people than were boys. She concluded that girls are oriented toward an "ethic of care," whereas boys are oriented toward an "ethic of justice." An **ethic of care** emphasizes interconnectedness and emerges to a greater degree in girls because of their early connection in identity formation with their mothers. An **ethic of justice** emerges from masculine identity formation that requires separation and individuation from the mother. Gilligan argued that this separation heightens boys' awareness of the differences in power relations between children and adults and creates a more intense concern with formal rules of justice. In contrast, girls' continued attachment to their mothers fosters an understanding of morality viewed within a web of social relations.

Whereas most liberal feminisms of the second wave highlighted the similarities between men and women, Gilligan's work focused on their differences. However, according to Gilligan's theory, these differences are socially constructed and her politics follow the liberal path of emphasizing the importance of male involvement in child care and gender equality in early childhood socialization.

CONCLUSION

A major contribution of liberal feminists was to make "gender" a core concept in feminist analysis. By highlighting the distinction between biological sex and socially learned gender, they focused on how gender roles could be socially transformed through conscious social and political action to foster a more egalitarian society. Indeed, the large, liberal feminist political organizations were central to changing federal and state laws that discriminated against women and for getting women elected to political offices.

Liberal feminists also were at the forefront of the long and difficult battle to pass the ERA, and the defeat of the ERA in 1982 was a crushing blow to the second wave. Yet by the late 1970s the political climate had drastically changed. The conservative Moral Majority's "family values" campaigns captured the national limelight and Republicans began to enjoy a sweep of electoral victories. These right-wing conservative successes were in large part the result of how Ronald Reagan's 1980 presidential campaign and the **STOP-ERA** movement[10] had united evangelical Christians and secular conservatives. Although the 1980s proved a bleak decade for feminist political agendas, it was a prolific era for feminist theories, as we shall see in later chapters of this anthology.

NOTES

1. See http://www.now.org (retrieved February 13, 2014).
2. A similar law called the Head and Master Law prevailed in Louisiana because Napoleonic law, rather than English common law, was the basis of this state's legislation.
3. Parts of this section are drawn from Jane Ward and Susan Mann (2012a).
4. The conventional view is that John and Harriet coauthored "Early Essays on Marriage and Divorce," Harriet wrote "Enfranchisement of Women," and John wrote *The Subjection of Women*. However, John claimed that everything he wrote after 1840 comprised "joint productions" based on ideas shared by both of them, thus giving Harriet credit for coauthoring *The Subjection of Women* (Rossi, 1970: 39). For an interesting discussion of the debates over the authorship of these writings see Rossi (1970).
5. Given her radical lifestyle views, it may appear odd to place Woodhull in the liberal feminist camp. However, she was not a political revolutionary like her socialist and anarchist peers who were advocates of free love (see Chapter 4). Woodhull made a fortune as the first woman to own an investment firm and was a free-market enthusiast. She also embraced political reform within the system and was the first woman nominated to run for president of the United States in 1872, although her name did not appear on the ballot (Goldsmith, 1988).
6. Parts of this section on first-wave women's environmental activism first appeared in S. A. Mann, "Pioneers of Ecofeminism & Environmental Justice," *Feminist Formations*, 2011. The author thanks Johns Hopkins University Press for permission to print them.
7. Even environmental historians most sensitive to issues of race, class, and gender often fail to include the black women's clubs in their discussions of environmental activism in the nineteenth and early twentieth centuries (Mann, 2011).
8. See http://coolbeanscool.blogspot.com/2003/09/suffragists-vs-suffragettes.html for this debate over the terms "suffragettes" versus "suffragists."
9. See http://www.equalrightsamendment.org/ (retrieved October 23, 2014).
10. In this antifeminist acronym, STOP stood for Stop Taking Our Privileges (meaning the privileges of being a stay-at-home mom), whereas ERA referred to the Extra Responsibilities Amendment (the extra responsibilities women would shoulder if they had to work inside and outside of the home) (Marshall [1989] 1995).

SELECTED LETTERS FROM THE ADAMS FAMILY CORRESPONDENCE

The following excerpts are from correspondences between Abigail and John Adams written on the eve of the American Revolution.

From Abigail Adams to John Adams, March 31, 1776:

I long to hear that you have declared an Independency—and by the way In the new Code of Laws which I suppose it will be necessary for you to make I desire you would Remember the Ladies and be more generous and favourable to them than your ancestors, Do not put such unlimited power into the hands of the Husbands. Remember all Men would be tyrants if they could. If perticullar care and attention Is not paid to the Laidies we are determined to foment a Rebellon, and will not hold ourselves bound by any Laws in which we have no voice, or Representation.

From John Adams to Abigail Adams, April 14, 1776:

As to your extraordinary Code of Laws, I cannot but laugh. We have been told that our Struggle has loosened the bands of Government every where. That Children and Apprentices were disobedient—that schools and Colledges were grown turbulent—that Indians slighted their Guardians and Negroes grew Insolent to their Masters. But your Letter was the first Intimation that another Tribe more numerous and powerfull than all the rest were grown discontented.— This is rather too coarse a Compliment but you are so saucy, I won't blot It out.

Depend upon it, We know better than to repeal our Masculine systems. Altho they are In full Force, you know they are little more than Theory. . . . We are the subjects. We have only the Name of Masters, and rather than give up this, which would compleatly subject us to the Despotism of the Peticoat, I hope General Washington, and all our brave Heroes would fight.

(1776)

Reprinted from *The Feminist Papers: From Adams to de Beauvoir*, ed. Alice S. Rossi, 10–11. New York: Bantam, 1974. Both letters reproduced as in the original.

9 • *Mary Wollstonecraft*

INTRODUCTION TO *A VINDICATION OF THE RIGHTS OF WOMAN*

After considering the historic page, and viewing the living world with anxious solicitude, the most melancholy emotions of sorrowful indignation have depressed my spirits, and I have sighed when obliged to confess that either Nature has made a great difference between man and man, or that the civilization which has hitherto taken place in the world has been very partial. I have turned over various books written on the subject of education, and patiently observed the conduct of parents and the management of schools; but what has been the result?—a profound conviction that the neglected education of my fellow-creatures is the grand source of the misery I deplore, and that women, in particular, are rendered weak and wretched by a variety of concurring causes, originating from one hasty conclusion. The conduct and manners of women, in fact, evidently prove that their minds are not in a healthy state; for, like the flowers which are planted in too rich a soil, strength and usefulness are sacrificed to beauty; and the flaunting leaves, after having pleased a fastidious eye, fade, disregarded on the stalk, long before the season when they ought to have arrived at maturity. One cause of this barren blooming I attribute to a false system of education, gathered from the books written on this subject by men who, considering females rather as women than human creatures, have been more anxious to make them alluring mistresses than affectionate wives and rational mothers; and the understanding of the sex has been so bubbled by this specious homage, that the civilized women of the present century, with a few exceptions, are only anxious to inspire love, when they ought to cherish a nobler ambition, and by their abilities and virtues exact respect.

In a treatise, therefore, on female rights and manners, the works which have been particularly written for their improvement must not be overlooked, especially when it is asserted, in direct terms, that the minds of women are enfeebled by false refinement; that the books of instruction, written by men of genius, have had the same tendency as more frivolous productions; and that, in the true style of Mahometanism,[1] they are treated as a kind of subordinate beings, and not as a part of the human species, when improvable reason is allowed to be the dignified distinction which raises men above the brute creation, and puts a natural sceptre in a feeble hand.

Yet, because I am a woman, I would not lead my readers to suppose that I mean violently to agitate the contested question respecting the quality or inferiority of the sex; but as the subject lies in my way, and I cannot pass it over without subjecting the main tendency of my reasoning to misconstruction, I shall stop a moment to deliver, in a few words, my opinion. In the government of the physical world it is observable that the female in point of strength is, in general, inferior to the male. This is the law of Nature; and it does not appear to be suspended or abrogated in favour of woman. A degree of physical superiority cannot, therefore, be denied, and it is a

Reprinted from *A Vindication of the Rights of Woman*, Boston: Peter Ides, 1792.

noble prerogative! But not content with this natural pre-eminence, men endeavour to sink us still lower, merely to render us alluring objects for a moment; and women, intoxicated by the adoration which men, under the influence of their senses, pay them, do not seek to obtain a durable interest in their hearts, or to become the friends of the fellow-creatures who find amusement in their society.

I am aware of an obvious inference. From every quarter have I heard exclamations against masculine women, but where are they to be found? If by this appellation men mean to inveigh against their ardour in hunting, shooting, and gaming, I shall most cordially join in the cry; but if it be against the imitation of manly virtues, or, more properly speaking, the attainment of those talents and virtues, the exercise of which ennobles the human character, and which raises females in the scale of animal being, when they are comprehensively termed mankind, all those who view them with a philosophic eye must, I should think, wish with me, that they may every day grow more and more masculine.

This discussion naturally divides the subject. I shall first consider women in the grand light of human creatures, who, in common with men, are placed on this earth to unfold their faculties; and afterwards I shall more particularly point out their peculiar designation.

I wish also to steer clear of an error which many respectable writers have fallen into; for the instruction which has hitherto been addressed to women, has rather been applicable to *ladies*, if the little indirect advice that is scattered through "Sandford and Merton"[2] be excepted; but, addressing my sex in a firmer tone, I pay particular attention to those in the middle class, because they appear to be in the most natural state. Perhaps the seeds of false refinement, immorality, and vanity, have ever been shed by the great. Weak, artificial beings, raised above the common wants and affections of their race, in a premature unnatural manner, undermine the very foundation of virtue, and spread corruption through the whole mass of society! As a class of mankind they have the strongest claim to pity; the education of the rich tends to render them vain and helpless, and the unfolding mind is not strengthened by the practice of those duties which dignify the human character. They

only live to amuse themselves, and by the same law which in Nature invariably produces certain effects, they soon only afford barren amusement.

But as I purpose taking a separate view of the different ranks of society, and of the moral character of women in each, this hint is for the present sufficient; and I have only alluded to the subject because it appears to me to be the very essence of an introduction to give a cursory account of the contents of the work it introduces.

My own sex, I hope, will excuse me, if I treat them like rational creatures, instead of flattering their *fascinating* graces, and viewing them as if they were in a state of perpetual childhood, unable to stand alone. I earnestly wish to point out in what true dignity and human happiness consists. I wish to persuade women to endeavour to acquire strength, both of mind and body, and to convince them that the soft phrases, susceptibility of heart, delicacy of sentiment, and refinement of taste, are almost synonymous with epithets of weakness, and that those beings who are only the objects of pity, and that kind of love which has been termed its sister, will soon become objects of contempt.

Dismissing, then, those pretty feminine phrases, which the men condescendingly use to soften our slavish dependence, and despising that weak elegancy of mind, exquisite sensibility, and sweet docility of manners, supposed to be the sexual characteristics of the weaker vessel. I wish to show that elegance is inferior to virtue, that the first object of laudable ambition is to obtain a character as a human being, regardless of the distinction of sex, and that secondary views should be brought to this simple touchstone.

This is a rough sketch of my plan; and should I express my conviction with the energetic emotions that I feel whenever I think of the subject, the dictates of experience and reflection will be felt by some of my readers. Animated by this important object, I shall disdain to cull my phrases or polish my style. I aim at being useful, and sincerity will render me unaffected; for wishing rather to persuade by the force of my arguments than dazzle by the elegance of my language, I shall not waste my time in rounding periods, or in fabricating the turgid bombast of artificial feelings, which, coming from the head, never reach the heart. I shall be employed about things, not words! and, anxious to render my sex more respectable members of society, I shall try to avoid that flowery diction which has slided from essays into novels, and from novels into familiar letters and conversations.

These pretty superlatives, dropping glibly from the tongue, vitiate the taste, and create a kind of sickly delicacy that turns away from simple unadorned truth; and a deluge of false sentiments and overstretched feelings, stifling the natural emotions of the heart, render the domestic pleasures insipid, that ought to sweeten the exercise of those severe duties, which educate a rational and immortal being for a nobler field of action.

The education of women has of late been more attended to than formerly; yet they are still reckoned a frivolous sex, and ridiculed or pitied by the writers who endeavour by satire or instruction to improve them. It is acknowledged that they spend many of the first years of their lives in acquiring a smattering of accomplishments; meanwhile strength of body and mind are sacrificed to libertine notions of beauty, to the desire of establishing themselves—the only way women can rise in the world—by marriage. And this desire making mere animals of them, when they marry they act as such children may be expected to act—they dress, they paint, and nickname God's creatures. Surely these weak beings are only fit for a seraglio! Can they be expected to govern a family with judgement, or take care of the poor babes whom they bring into the world?

If, then, it can be fairly deduced from the present conduct of the sex, from the prevalent fondness for pleasure which takes place of ambition and those nobler passions that open and enlarge the soul, that the instruction which women have hitherto received has only tended, with the constitution of civil society, to render them insignificant objects of desire—mere propagators of fools!—if it can be proved that in aiming to accomplish them, without cultivating their understandings, they are taken out of their sphere of duties, and made ridiculous and useless when the short-lived bloom of beauty is over,* I presume that *rational* men will excuse

me for endeavouring to persuade them to become more masculine and respectable.

Indeed the word masculine is only a bugbear; there is little reason to fear that women will acquire too much courage or fortitude, for their apparent inferiority with respect to bodily strength must render them in some degree dependent on men in the various relations of life; but why should it be increased by prejudices that give a sex to virtue, and confound simple truths with sensual reveries?

Women are, in fact, so much degraded by mistaken notions of female excellence, that I do not mean to add a paradox when I assert that this artificial weakness produces a propensity to tyrannize, and gives birth to cunning, the natural opponent of strength, which leads them to play off those contemptible infantine airs that undermine esteem even whilst they excite desire. Let men become more chaste and modest, and if women do not grow wiser in the same ratio it will be clear that they have weaker understandings. It seems scarcely necessary to say that I now speak of the sex in general. Many individuals have more sense than their male relatives; and, as nothing preponderates where there is a constant struggle for an equilibrium without it has naturally more gravity, some women govern their husbands without degrading themselves, because intellect will always govern.

(1792)

NOTES

1. *The true style of Mahometanism.* A common eighteenth-century misconception of Muslim doctrine that women have neither souls nor access to the afterlife.
2. *"Sandford and Merton."* Authored by Thomas Day (1748–1789), *The History of Sandford and Merton* was a popular and influential children's book series that provided children with lessons about morality and virtue.

---

*A lively writer (I cannot recollect his name) asks what business women turned of forty have to do in the world?

FROM *LETTERS ON THE EQUALITY OF THE SEXES AND THE CONDITION OF WOMEN*

LETTER VIII

Brookline, 1837

. . . I shall now proceed to make a few remarks on the condition of women in my own country.

During the early part of my life, my lot was cast among the butterflies of the *fashionable* world; and of this class of women, I am constrained to say, both from experience and observation, that their education is miserably deficient; that they are taught to regard marriage as the one thing needful, the only avenue to distinction; hence to attract the notice and win the attention of men, by their external charms, is the chief business of fashionable girls. They seldom think that men will be allured by intellectual acquirements, because they find, that where any mental superiority exists, a woman is generally shunned and regarded as stepping out of her "appropriate sphere," which, in their view, is to dress, to dance, to set out to the best possible advantage her person, to read the novels which inundate the press, and which do more to destroy her character as a rational creature, than any thing else. Fashionable women regard themselves, and are regarded by men, as pretty toys or as mere instruments of pleasure; and the vacuity of mind, the heartlessness, the frivolity which is the necessary result of this false and debasing estimate of women, can only be fully understood by those who have mingled in the folly and wickedness of fashionable life. . . .

There is another and much more numerous class in this country, who are withdrawn by education or circumstances from the circle of fashionable amusements, but who are brought up with the dangerous and absurd idea, that *marriage* is a kind of preferment; and that to be able to keep their husband's house, and render his situation comfortable, is the end of her being. Much that she does and says and thinks is done in reference to this situation; and to be married is too often held up to the view of girls as the sine qua non of human happiness and human existence. For this purpose more than for any other, I verily believe the majority of girls are trained. This is demonstrated by the imperfect education which is bestowed upon them, and the little pains taken to cultivate their minds, after they leave school, by the little time allowed them for reading, and by the idea being constantly inculcated, that although all household concerns should be attended to with scrupulous punctuality at particular seasons, the improvement of their intellectual capacities is only a secondary consideration, and may serve as an occupation to fill up the odds and ends of time. In most families, it is considered a matter of far more consequence to call a girl off from making a pie, or a pudding, than to interrupt her whilst engaged in her studies. This mode of training necessarily exalts, in their view, the animal above the intellectual and spiritual nature, and teaches women to regard themselves as a kind of machinery, necessary to keep the domestic engine in order, but of little value as the *intelligent* companions of men.

Reprinted from *The Feminist Papers: From Adams to de Beauvoir*, ed. Alice S. Rossi, 311–316. New York: Bantam, 1974. Reproduced as in the original.

Let no one think, from these remarks, that I regard a knowledge of housewifery as beneath the acquisition of women. Far from it: I believe that a complete knowledge of household affairs is an indispensable requisite in a woman's education,—that by the mistress of a family, whether married or single, doing her duty thoroughly and *understandingly*, the happiness of the family is increased to an incalculable degree, as well as a vast amount of time and money saved. All I complain of is, that our education consists so almost exclusively in culinary and other manual operations. I do long to see the time, when it will no longer be necessary for women to expend so many precious hours in furnishing "a well spread table," but that their husbands will forego some of their accustomed indulgences in this way, and encourage their wives to devote some portion of their time to mental cultivation, even at the expense of having to dine sometimes on baked potatoes, or bread and butter. . . .

The influence of women over the minds and character of *children* of both sexes, is allowed to be far greater than that of men. This being the case by the very ordering of nature, women should be prepared by education for the performance of their sacred duties as mothers and as sisters. . . .

There is another way in which the general opinion, that women are inferior to men, is manifested, that bears with tremendous effect on the laboring class, and indeed on almost all who are obliged to earn a subsistence, whether it be by mental or physical exertion—I allude to the disproportionate value set on the time and labor of men and of women. A man who is engaged in teaching, can always, I believe, command a higher price for tuition than a woman—even when he teaches the same branches, and is not in any respect superior to the woman. This I know is the case in boarding and other schools with which I have been acquainted, and it is so in every occupation in which the sexes engage indiscriminately. As for example, in tailoring, a man has twice, or three times as much for making a waistcoat or pantaloons as a woman, although the work done by each may be equally good. In those employments which are peculiar to women, their time is estimated at only half the value of that of men. A woman who goes out to wash, works as hard in proportion as a

wood sawyer, or a coal heaver, but she is not generally able to make more than half as much by a day's work. The low remuneration which women receive for their work, has claimed the attention of a few philanthropists, and I hope it will continue to do so until some remedy is applied for this enormous evil. . . . There is yet another and more disastrous consequence arising from this unscriptural notion—women being educated, from earliest childhood, to regard themselves as inferior creatures, have not that self-respect which conscious equality would engender, and hence when their virtue is assailed, they yield to temptation with facility, under the idea that it rather exalts than debases them, to be connected with a superior being.

There is another class of women in this country, to whom I cannot refer, without feelings of the deepest shame and sorrow. I allude to our female slaves. Our southern cities are whelmed beneath a tide of pollution; the virtue of female slaves is wholly at the mercy of irresponsible tyrants, and women are bought and sold in our slave markets, to gratify the brutal lust of those who bear the name of Christians. In our slave States, if amid all her degradation and ignorance, a woman desires to preserve her virtue unsullied, she is either bribed or whipped into compliance, or if she dares resist her seducer, her life by the laws of some of the slave States may be, and has actually been sacrificed to the fury of disappointed passion. Where such laws do not exist, the power which is necessarily vested in the master over his property, leaves the defenceless slave entirely at his mercy, and the sufferings of some females on this account, both physical and mental, are intense. Mr. Gholson, in the House of Delegates of Virginia, in 1832, said, "He really had been under the impression that he owned his slaves. He had lately purchased four women and ten children, in whom he thought he had obtained a great bargain; for he supposed they were his own property, *as were his brood mares.*" But even if any laws existed in the United States, as in Athens formerly, for the protection of female slaves, they would be null and void, because the evidence of a colored person is not admitted against a white, in any of our Courts of Justice in the slave States. "In Athens, if a female slave had cause to complain of any want of respect to the laws of modesty, she could seek the protection of the temple, and demand a change of owners; and such appeals were never discountenanced, or neglected by the magistrate." In Christian America, the slave has no refuge from unbridled cruelty and lust.

S. A. Forrall, speaking of the state of morals at the South, says, "Negresses when young and likely, are often employed by the planter, or his friends, to administer to their sensual desires. This frequently is a matter of speculation, for if the offspring, a mulatto, be a handsome female, 800 or 1000 dollars may be obtained for her in the New Orleans market. It is an occurrence of no uncommon nature to see a Christian father sell his own daughter and the brother his own sister." . . . I will add but one more from the numerous testimonies respecting the degradation of female slaves, and the licentiousness of the South. It is from the Circular of the Kentucky Union, for the moral and religious improvement of the colored race. "To the female character among our black population, we cannot allude but with feelings of the bitterest shame. A similar condition of moral pollution and utter disregard of a pure and virtuous reputation, is to be found *only without the pale of Christendom.* That such a state of society should exist in a Christian nation, claiming to be the most enlightened upon earth, without calling forth any *particular attention* to its existence, though ever before our eyes and *in our* families, is a moral phenomenon at once unaccountable and disgraceful." Nor does the colored woman suffer alone: the moral purity of the white woman is deeply contaminated. In the daily habit of seeing the virtue of her enslaved sister sacrificed without hesitancy or remorse, she looks upon the crimes of seduction and illicit intercourse without horror, and although not personally involved in the guilt, she loses that value for innocence in her own, as well as the other sex, which is one of the strongest safeguards to virtue. She lives in habitual intercourse with men, whom she knows to be polluted by licentiousness, and often is she compelled to witness in her own domestic circle, those disgusting and heart-sickening jealousies and strifes which disgraced and distracted the family of Abraham. In addition to all this, the female slaves suffer every species of degradation and cruelty, which the most wanton barbarity can inflict; they are indecently divested of their clothing, sometimes tied up and severely whipped, sometimes prostrated on the earth, while their naked bodies are torn by the scorpion lash.

> "The whip on woman's shrinking flesh!
> Our soil yet reddening with the stains
> Caught from her scourging warm and fresh."

Can any American woman look at these scenes of shocking licentiousness and cruelty, and fold her hands in apathy, and say, "I have nothing to do with slavery"? *She cannot and be guiltless.*

I cannot close this letter, without saying a few words on the benefits to be derived by men, as well as women, from the opinions I advocate relative to the equality of the sexes. Many women are now supported, in idleness and extravagance, by the industry of their husbands, fathers, or brothers, who are compelled to toil out their existence, at the counting house, or in the printing office, or some other laborious occupation, while the wife and daughters and sisters take no part in the support of the family, and appear to think that their sole business is to spend the hard bought earnings of their male friends. I deeply regret such a state of things, because I believe that if women felt their responsibility, for the support of themselves, or their families it would add strength and dignity to their characters, and teach them more true sympathy for their husbands, than is now generally manifested,—a sympathy which would be exhibited by actions as well as words. Our brethren may reject my doctrine, because it runs counter to common opinions, and because it wounds their pride; but I believe they would be "partakers of the benefit" resulting from the Equality of the Sexes, and would find that woman, as their equal, was unspeakably more valuable than woman as their inferior, both as a moral and an intellectual being.

Thine in the bonds of womanhood,

Sarah M. Grimké

(1838)

11 • *Elizabeth Cady Stanton*

"DECLARATION OF SENTIMENTS"

When, in the course of human events, it becomes necessary for one portion of the family of man to assume among the people of the earth a position different from that which they have hitherto occupied, but one to which the laws of nature and of nature's God entitle them, a decent respect to the opinions of mankind requires that they should declare the causes that impel them to such a course.

We hold these truths to be self-evident: that all men and women are created equal; that they are endowed by their Creator with certain inalienable rights; that among these are life, liberty, and the pursuit of happiness; that to secure these rights governments are instituted, deriving their just powers from the consent of the governed. Whenever any form of government becomes destructive of these ends, it is the right of those who suffer from it to refuse allegiance to it, and to insist upon the institution of a new government, laying its foundation on such principles, and organizing its powers in such form, as to them shall seem most likely to effect their safety and happiness. Prudence, indeed, will dictate that governments long established should not be changed for light and transient causes; and accordingly all experience hath shown that mankind are more disposed to suffer, while evils are sufferable, than to right themselves by abolishing the forms to which they were accustomed. But when a long train of abuses and usurpations, pursuing invariably the same object evinces a design to reduce them under absolute despotism, it is their duty to throw off such government, and to provide new guards for their future security. Such has been the patient sufferance of the women under this government, and such is now the necessity which constrains them to demand the equal station to which they are entitled.

The history of mankind is a history of repeated injuries and usurpations on the part of man toward woman, having in direct object the establishment of an absolute tyranny over her. To prove this, let facts be submitted to a candid world.

He has never permitted her to exercise her inalienable right to the elective franchise.

He has compelled her to submit to laws, in the formation of which she had no voice.

He has withheld from her rights which are given to the most ignorant and degraded men—both natives and foreigners.

Having deprived her of this first right of a citizen, the elective franchise, thereby leaving her without representation in the halls of legislation, he has oppressed her on all sides.

He has made her, if married, in the eye of the law, civilly dead.

He has taken from her all right in property, even to the wages she earns.

He has made her, morally, an irresponsible being, as she can commit many crimes with impunity, provided they be done in the presence of her husband. In the covenant of marriage, she is compelled to promise obedience to her husband, he becoming, to all intents and purposes, her master—the law giving him power to deprive her of her liberty, and to administer chastisement.

He has so framed the laws of divorce, as to what shall be the proper causes, and in case of separation, to whom the guardianship of the children shall be given, as to be wholly regardless of the happiness of women—the law, in all cases, going upon a false supposition of the supremacy of man, and giving all power into his hands.

After depriving her of all rights as a married woman, if single and the owner of property, he has taxed her to support a government which recognizes her only when her property can be made profitable to it.

Reprinted from *The History of Women's Suffrage*, eds. Stanton, Anthony, Gage. Rochester, NY, 1881.

He has monopolized nearly all the profitable employments, and from those she is permitted to follow, she receives but a scanty remuneration. He closes against her all the avenues to wealth and distinction which he considers most honorable to himself. As a teacher of theology, medicine, or law, she is not known.

He has denied her the facilities for obtaining a thorough education, all colleges being closed against her.

He allows her in Church, as well as State, but a subordinate position, claiming Apostolic authority for her exclusion from the ministry, and, with some exceptions, from any public participation in the affairs of the Church.

He has created a false public sentiment by giving to the world a different code of morals for men and women, by which moral delinquencies which exclude women from society are not only tolerated, but deemed of little account in man.

He has usurped the prerogative of Jehovah himself, claiming it as his right to assign for her a sphere of action, when that belongs to her conscience and to her God.

He has endeavored, in every way that he could, to destroy her confidence in her own powers, to lessen her self-respect, and to make her willing to lead a dependent and abject life.

Now, in view of this entire disfranchisement of one-half the people of this country, their social and religious degradation—in view of the unjust laws above mentioned, and because women do feel themselves aggrieved, oppressed, and fraudulently deprived of their most sacred rights, we insist that they have immediate admission to all the rights and privileges which belong to them as citizens of the United States.

In entering upon the great work before us, we anticipate no small amount of misconception, misrepresentation, and ridicule; but we shall use every instrumentality within our power to affect our object. We shall employ agents, circulate tracts, petition the State and National legislatures, and endeavor to enlist the pulpit and the press in our behalf. We hope this Convention will be followed by a series of Conventions embracing every part of the country.

* * *

Whereas, the great precept of nature is conceded to be, that "man shall pursue his own true and substantial happiness." Blackstone in his Commentaries

remarks, that this law of Nature being coeval with mankind, and dictated by God himself, is of course superior in obligation to any other. It is binding over all the globe, in all countries and at all times; no human laws are of any validity if contrary to this, and such of them as are valid, derive all their force, and all their validity, and all their authority, mediately and immediately, from this original; therefore,

Resolved, That such laws as conflict, in any way, with the true and substantial happiness of woman, are contrary to the great precept of nature and of no validity, for this is "superior in obligation to any other."

Resolved, That all laws which prevent woman from occupying such a station in society as her conscience shall dictate, or which place her in a position inferior to that of man, are contrary to the great precept of nature, and therefore of no force or authority.

Resolved, That woman is man's equal—was intended to be so by the Creator, and the highest good of the race demands that she should be recognized as such.

Resolved, That the women of this country ought to be enlightened in regard to the laws under which they live, that they may no longer publish their degradation by declaring themselves satisfied with their present position, nor their ignorance, by asserting that they have all the rights they want.

Resolved, That inasmuch as man, while claiming for himself intellectual superiority, does accord to woman moral superiority, it is pre-eminently his duty to encourage her to speak and teach, as she has an opportunity, in all religious assemblies.

Resolved, That the same amount of virtue, delicacy, and refinement of behavior that is required of woman in the social state, should also be required of man, and the same transgressions should be visited with equal severity on both man and woman.

Resolved, That the objection of indelicacy and impropriety, which is so often brought against woman when she addresses a public audience, comes with a very ill-grace from those who encourage, by their attendance, her appearance on the stage, in the concert, or in feats of the circus.

Resolved, That woman has too long rested satisfied in the circumscribed limits which corrupt customs and a perverted application of the Scriptures have marked out for her, and that it is time she should move in the enlarged sphere which her great Creator has assigned her.

Resolved, That it is the duty of the women of this country to secure to themselves their sacred right to the elective franchise.

Resolved, That the equality of human rights results necessarily from the fact of the identity of the race in capabilities and responsibilities.

Resolved, therefore, That, being invested by the Creator with the same capabilities, and the same consciousness of responsibility for their exercise, it is demonstrably the right and duty of woman, equally with man, to promote every righteous cause by every righteous means; and especially in regard to the great subjects of morals and religion, it is self-evidently her right to participate with her brother in teaching them, both in private and in public, by writing and by speaking, by any instrumentalities proper to be used, and in any assemblies proper to be held; and this being a self-evident truth growing out of the divinely implanted principles of human nature, any custom or authority adverse to it, whether modern or wearing the hoary sanction of antiquity, is to be regarded as a self-evident falsehood, and at war with mankind.

* * *

Resolved, That the speedy success of our cause depends upon the zealous and untiring efforts of both men and women, for the overthrow of the monopoly of the pulpit, and for the securing to woman an equal participation with men in the various trades, professions, and commerce.

* * *

(1848)

12 • *Harriet Taylor Mill*

"ENFRANCHISEMENT OF WOMEN"

Most of our readers will probably learn from these pages for the first time, that there has arisen in the United States, and in the most civilized and enlightened portion of them, an organized agitation on a new question—new, not to thinkers, nor to any one by whom the principles of free and popular government are felt as well as acknowledged, but new, and even unheard-of, as a subject for public meetings and practical political action. This question is, the enfranchisement of women; their admission, in law and in fact, to equality in all rights, political, civil, and social, with the male citizens of the community.

It will add to the surprise with which many will receive this intelligence, that the agitation which has commenced is not a pleading by male writers and orators for women, those who are professedly to be benefited remaining either indifferent or ostensibly hostile. It is a political movement, practical in its objects, carried on in a form which denotes an intention to persevere. And it is a movement not merely *for* women, but *by* them. Its first public manifestation appears to have been a Convention of Women, held in the State of Ohio, in the spring of 1850. Of this meeting we have seen no report. On the 23rd and 24th of October last, a succession of public meetings was held at Worcester in Massachusetts under the name of a "Women's Rights Convention," of which the president was a woman,[1] and nearly all the chief speakers women; numerously reinforced, however, by men, among whom were some of the most distinguished leaders in the kindred cause of negro emancipation. A general and four special committees were nominated, for the

Published in the *Westminster Review* (July, 1851). Notes have been renumbered.

purpose of carrying on the undertaking until the next annual meeting.

According to the report in the *New York Tribune,* above a thousand persons were present throughout, and "if a larger place could have been had, many thousands more would have attended." The place was described as "crowded from the beginning with attentive and interested listeners."[2] In regard to the quality of the speaking, the proceedings bear an advantageous comparison with those of any popular movement with which we are acquainted, either in this country or in America. Very rarely in the oratory of public meetings is the part of the verbiage and declamation so small, that of calm good sense and reason so considerable. The result of the Convention was in every respect encouraging to those by whom it was summoned: and it is probably destined to inaugurate one of the most important of the movements towards political and social reform, which are the best characteristics of the present age. . . .

Not only to the democracy of America, the claim of women to civil and political equality makes an irresistible appeal, but also to those Radicals and Chartists[3] in the British islands, and democrats on the continent, who claim what is called universal suffrage as an inherent right, unjustly and oppressively withheld from them. For with what truth or rationality could the suffrage be termed universal, while half the human species remained excluded from it? To declare that a voice in the government is the right of all, and demand it only for a part—the part, namely, to which the claimant himself belongs—is to renounce even the appearance of principle. The Chartist who denies the suffrage to women, is a Chartist only because he is not a lord: he is one of those levellers who would level only down to themselves.

Even those who do not look upon a voice in the government as a matter of personal right, nor profess principles which require that it should be extended of all, have usually traditional maxims of political justice with which it is impossible to reconcile the exclusion of all women from the common rights of citizenship. It is an axiom of English freedom that taxation and representation should be co-extensive. Even under the laws which give the wife's property to the husband, there are many unmarried women who pay taxes. It is one of the fundamental doctrines of the British Constitution, that all persons should be tried by their peers: yet women, whenever tried, are by male judges and a male jury. To foreigners the law accords the privilege of claiming that half the jury should be composed of themselves; not so to women. Apart from maxims of detail, which represent local and national rather than universal ideas; it is an acknowledged dictate of justice to make no degrading distinctions without necessity. In all things the presumption ought to be on the side of equality. A reason must be given why anything should be permitted to one person and interdicted to another. But when that which is interdicted includes nearly everything which those to whom it is permitted most prize, and to be deprived of which they feel to be most insulting; when not only political liberty but personal freedom of action is the prerogative of a caste; when even in the exercise of industry, almost all employments which task the higher faculties in an important field, which lead to distinction, riches, or even pecuniary independence, are fenced round as the exclusive domain of the predominant section, scarcely any doors being left open to the dependent class, except such as all who can enter elsewhere disdainfully pass by; the miserable expediencies which are advanced as excuses for so grossly partial a dispensation, would not be sufficient, even if they were real, to render it other than a flagrant injustice. While, far from being expedient, we are firmly convinced that the division of mankind into two castes, one born to rule over the other, is in this case, as in all cases, an unqualified mischief; a source of perversion and demoralization, both to the favoured class and to those at whose expense they are favoured; producing none of the good which it is the custom to ascribe to it, and forming a bar, almost insuperable while it lasts, to any really vital improvement, either in the character or in the social condition of the human race. . . .

When a prejudice, which has any hold on the feelings, finds itself reduced to the unpleasant necessity of assigning reasons, it thinks it had done enough when it has re-asserted the very point in dispute, in phrases which appeal to the pre-existing feeling. Thus, many persons think they have sufficiently justified the restrictions on women's field of action, when they have said that the pursuits from which women are excluded are *unfeminine,* and that the *proper sphere* of women is not politics or publicity, but private and domestic life.

We deny the right of any portion of the species to decide for another portion, or any individual for another individual, what is and what is not their "proper sphere." The proper sphere for all human beings is the largest and highest which they are able to attain to. What this is, cannot be ascertained, without complete liberty of choice. The speakers at the Convention in America have therefore done wisely and right, in refusing to entertain the question of the peculiar aptitudes either of women or of men, or the limits within this or that occupation may be supposed to be more adapted to the one or to the other. They justly maintain, that these questions can only be more adapted to the one or the other. They justly maintain, that these questions can only be satisfactorily answered by perfect freedom. Let every occupation be open to all, without favour or discouragement to any, and employments will fall into the hands of those men or women who are found by experience to be most capable of worthily exercising them. There need be no fear that women will take out of the hands of men any occupation which men perform better than they. Each individual will prove his or her capacities, in the only way in which capacities can be proved—by trial; and the world will have the benefit of the best faculties of all its inhabitants. But to interfere beforehand by an arbitrary limit, and declare that whatever be the genius, talent, energy, or force of mind of an individual of a certain sex or class, those faculties shall not be exerted, or shall be exerted only in some few of the many modes in which others are permitted to use theirs, is not only an injustice to the individual, and a detriment to society, which loses what it can ill spare, but is also the most effectual mode of providing that, in the sex or class so fettered, the qualities which are not permitted to be exercised shall not exist. . . .

But, in truth, none of these arguments and considerations touch the foundations of the subject. The real question is, whether it is right and expedient that one-half of the human race should pass through life in a state of forced subordination to the other half. If the best state of human society is that of being divided into two parts, one consisting of persons with a will and a substantive existence, the other of humble companions to these persons, attached, each of them to one, for the purpose of bringing up *his* children, and making *his* home pleasant to him; if this is the place assigned to women, it is but kindness to educate them for this; to make them believe that the greatest good fortune which can befal them, is to be chosen by some man for this purpose; and that every other career which the world deems happy or honourable, is closed to them by the law, not social institutions, but of nature and destiny.

When, however, we ask why the existence of one-half the species should be merely ancillary to that of the other—why each woman should be a mere appendage to a man, allowed to have no interest of her own, that there may be nothing to compete in her mind with his interests and his pleasure; the only reason which can be given is, that men like it. It is agreeable to them that men should live for their own sake, women for the sake of men: and the qualities and conduct in subjects which are agreeable to rulers, they succeed for a long time in making the subjects themselves consider as their appropriate virtues. Helvetius[4] has met with much obloquy for asserting, that persons usually mean by virtues the qualities which are useful or convenient to themselves. How truly this is said of mankind in general, and how wonderfully the ideas of virtue set afloat by the powerful, are caught and imbibed by those under the dominion, is exemplified by the manner in which the world were once persuaded that the supreme virtue of subjects was loyalty to kings, and are still persuaded that the paramount virtue of womanhood is loyalty to men. Under a nominal recognition of a moral code common to both, in practice self-will and self-assertion form the type of what are designated as manly virtues, while abnegation of self, patience, resignation, and submission to power, unless when resistance is commanded by other interests than their own, have been stamped by general consent as pre-eminently the duties and graces required of women. The meaning being merely, that power makes itself the centre of moral obligation, and that a man likes to have his own will, but does not like that his domestic companion should have a will different from his. . .

(1851)

NOTES

1. Paulina Kellogg Wright Davis (1813–76).
2. Jacob Gilbert Forman, *New York Daily Tribune,* 26 October 1850.
3. Chartism was a working-class movement for parliamentary reform, including suffrage. The movement began in the 1830s.
4. Claude Adrien Helvetius. *De L'esprit* (Paris: 1758). 53–55. (Cited in Robson, *Sexual Equality,* 192).

13 • *John Stuart Mill*

FROM *THE SUBJECTION OF WOMEN*

The object of this Essay is to explain as clearly as I am able, the grounds of an opinion which I have held from the very earliest period when I had formed any opinions at all on social or political matters, and which, instead of being weakened or modified, has been constantly growing stronger by the progress of reflection and the experience of life: That the principle which regulates the existing social relations between the two sexes—the legal subordination of one sex to the other—is wrong in itself, and now one of the chief hindrances to human improvement; and that it ought to be replaced by a principle of perfect equality, admitting no power or privilege on the one side, not disability on the other.

* * *

. . . Whatever gratification of pride there is in the possession of power, and whatever personal interest in its exercise, is in this case not confined to a limited class, but common to the whole male sex. Instead of being, to most of its supporters, a thing desirable chiefly in the abstract, or, like the political ends usually contended for by factions, of little private importance to any but the leaders; it comes home to the person and hearth of every male head of a family, and of every one who looks forward to being so. The clodhopper exercises, or is to exercise, his share of the power equally with the highest nobleman. And the case is that in which the desire of power is the strongest: for every one who desires power, desires it most over those who are nearest to him, with whom his life is passed, with whom he has most concerns in common, and in whom any independence of his authority is oftenest likely to interfere with his individual preferences. If, in the other cases specified, power manifestly grounded only on force, and having so much less to support them, are so slowly and with so much difficulty got rid of, much more must it be so with this, even if it rests on no better foundation than those. We must consider, too, that the possessors of the power have facilities in this case, greater than in any other, to prevent any uprising against it. Every one of the subjects lives under the very eye, and almost, it may be said, in the hands, of one of the masters—in closer intimacy with him than with any of her fellow-subjects; with no means of combining against him, no power of even locally overmastering him, and, on the other hand, with the strongest motives for seeking his favour and avoiding to give him offence. In struggles for political emancipation, everybody knows how often its champions are bought off by bribes, or daunted by terrors. In the case of women, each individual of the subject-class is in a chronic state of bribery and intimidation combined. In setting up the standard of resistance, a large number of the leaders, and still more of the followers, must make an almost complete sacrifice of the pleasures or the alleviations of their own individual lot. If ever any system of privilege and enforced subjection had its yoke tightly riveted on the necks of those who are kept down by it, this has. . . .

. . . But, it will be said, the rule of men over women differs from all these others in not being a rule of force: it is accepted voluntarily; women make no complaint, and are consenting parties to it. In the first place, a great number of women do not accept it. Ever since there have been women able to make their sentiments known by their writings (the only mode of publicity which society permits to them), an increasing number of them have recorded protests against their present social condition: and recently many thousands of them, headed by the most eminent women known

Reprinted from John Stuart Mill, *The Subjection of Women*, in Alice S. Rossi, ed., *Essays on Sex Equality.* Chicago, University of Chicago Press, 1972. Pp. 125–242.

to the public, have petitioned Parliament for their admission to the Parliamentary Suffrage. The claim of women to be educated as solidly, and in the same branches of knowledge, as men, is urged with growing intensity, and with a great prospect of success; while the demand for their admission into professions and occupations hitherto closed against them, becomes every year more urgent. Though there are not in this country, as there are in the United States, periodical Conventions and an organized party to agitate for the Rights of Women, there is a numerous and active Society organized and managed by women, for the more limited object of obtaining the political franchise. Nor is it only in our own country and in America that women are beginning to protest, more or less collectively, against the disabilities under which they labour. France, and Italy, and Switzerland, and Russia now afford examples of the same thing. How many more women there are who silently cherish similar aspirations, no one can possibly know; but there are abundant tokens how many *would* cherish them, were they not so strenuously taught to repress them as contrary to the proprieties of their sex. It must be remembered, also, that no enslaved class ever asked for complete liberty at once. . . .

. . . All causes, social and natural, combine to make it unlikely that women should be collectively rebellious to the power of men. They are so far in a position different from all other subject classes, that their masters require something more from them than actual service. Men do not want solely the obedience of women, they want their sentiments. All men, except the most brutish, desire to have, in the woman most nearly connected with them, not a forced slave but a willing one, not a slave merely, but a favourite. They have therefore put everything in practice to enslave their minds. The masters of all other slaves rely, for maintaining obedience, on fear; either fear of themselves, or religious fears. The masters of women wanted more than simple obedience, and they turned the whole force of education to effect their purpose. All women are brought up from the very earliest years in the belief that their ideal of character is the very opposite to that of men; not self-will, and government by self-control, but submission, and yielding to the control of others. All the moralities tell them that it is the duty of women, and all the current sentimentalities that it is their nature, to live for others; to make

complete abnegation of themselves, and to have no life but in their affections. And by their affections are meant the only ones they are allowed to have—those to the men with whom they are connected, or to the children who constitute an additional and indefeasible tie between them and a man. When we put together three things—first, the natural attraction between opposite sexes; secondly, the wife's entire dependence on the husband, every privilege or pleasure she has being either his gift, or depending entirely on his will; and lastly, that the principal object of human pursuit, consideration, and all objects of social ambition, can in general be sought or obtained by her only through him, it would be a miracle if the object of being attractive to men had not become the polar star of feminine education and formation of character. And, this great means of influence over the minds of women having been acquired, an instinct of selfishness made men avail themselves of it to the utmost as a means of holding women in subjection, by representing to them meekness, submissiveness, and resignation of all individual will into the hands of a man, as an essential part of sexual attractiveness. Can it be doubted that any of the other yokes which mankind have succeeded in breaking, would have subsisted till now if the same means had existed, and had been as sedulously used, to bow down their minds to it? . . .

The preceding considerations are amply sufficient to show that custom, however universal it may be, affords, in this case no presumption, and ought not to create any prejudice, in favour of the arrangements which place women in social and political subjection to men. But I may go farther, and maintain that the course of history, and the tendencies of progressive human society, afford not only no presumption in favour of this system of inequality of rights, but a strong one against it; and that, so far as the whole course of human improvement up to this time, the whole stream of modern tendencies, warrants any inference on the subject, it is, that this relic of the past is discordant with the future, and must necessarily disappear.

. . . The moral regeneration of mankind will only really commence, when the most fundamental of the social relations is placed under the rule of equal justice, and when human beings learn to cultivate their strongest sympathy with an equal in rights and in cultivation.

Thus far, the benefits which it has appeared that the world would gain by ceasing to make sex a disqualification for privileges and a badge of subjection, are social rather than individual; consisting in an increase of the general fund of thinking and acting power, and an improvement in the general conditions of the association of men with women. But it would be a grievous understatement of the case to omit the most direct benefit of all, the unspeakable gain in private happiness to the liberated half of the species; the difference to them between a life of subjection to the will of others, and a life of rational freedom. After the primary necessities of food and raiment, freedom is the first and strongest want of human nature. . . .

(1870)

14 • *Victoria Woodhull*

"AND THE TRUTH SHALL MAKE YOU FREE"
A Speech on the Principles of Social Freedom

It can now be asked: What is the legitimate sequence of Social Freedom? To which I unhesitatingly reply: Free Love, or freedom of the affections. "And are you a Free Lover?" is the almost incredulous query.

I repeat a frequent reply: "I am; and I can honestly, in the fulness of my soul, raise my voice to my Maker, and thank Him that *I am*, and that I have had the strength and the devotion to truth to stand before this traducing and vilifying community in a manner representative of that which shall come with healing on its wings for the bruised hearts and crushed affections of humanity."

And to those who denounce me for this I reply: "Yes, I am a Free Lover. I have an *inalienable, constitutional,* and *natural* right to love whom I may, to love as *long* or as *short* a period as I can; to *change* that love *every day* if I please, and with *that* right neither *you* nor any *law* you can frame have *any* right to interfere. And I have the *further* right to demand a free and unrestricted exercise of that right, and it is *your duty* not only to *accord* it, but as a community, to see that I am protected in it. I trust that I am fully understood, for I mean *just* that, and nothing less!

To speak thus plainly and pointedly is a *duty I owe* to myself. The press have stigmatized me to the world as an advocate, theoretically and practically, of the doctrine of Free Love, upon which they have placed their stamp of moral deformity; the vulgar and inconsequent definition which they hold makes the theory an abomination. And though this conclusion is a no more legitimate and reasonable one than that would be which should call the Golden Rule a general license to all sorts of debauch, since Free Love bears the *same* relations to the moral deformities of which it stands accused as does the Golden Rule to the Law of the Despot, yet it obtains among many intelligent people. But they claim, in the language of one of these exponents, that "Words belong to the people; they are the common property of the mob. Now the common use, among the mob, of the term Free Love, is a synonym for promiscuity." Against this absurd proposition I oppose the assertion that words *do not* belong to the

Reprinted from *Selected Writings of Victoria Woodhull: Suffrage, Free Love, and Eugenics* by Victoria C. Woodhull, ed. Cari M. Carpenter. Lincoln: University of Nebraska Press, 2010. Notes have been deleted.

mob, but to that which they represent. Words are the exponents and interpretations of ideas. If I use a word which exactly interprets and represents what I would be understood to mean, shall I go to the *mob* and *ask* of *them* what interpretation *they* choose to place upon it? If lexicographers, when they prepare their dictionaries, were to go to the mob for the rendition of words, what kind of language would we have? . . .

The good women of one of the interior cities of New York some two years since organized a movement to put down prostitution. They were, by stratagem, to find out who visited houses of prostitution, and then were to ostracise them. They pushed the matter until they found their own husbands, brothers, and sons involved, and then suddenly desisted, and nothing has since been heard of the eradication of prostitution in that city. If the same experiment were to be tried in New York, the result would be the same. The supporters of prostitution would be found to be those whom women cannot ostracise. The same disability excuses the presence of women in the very home, and I need not tell you that Mormonism is practised in *other* places beside Utah. But what is the logic of these things? Why, simply this: A woman, be she wife or mistress, who consorts with a man who consorts with *other* women, is equally, with *them and him*, morally responsible, since the receiver is held to be as culpable as the thief.

The false and hollow relations of the sexes are thus resolved into the mere question of the *dependence* of women upon men for support, and women, whether married or single, are supported *by* men because they *are* women and their opposites in sex. I can see no moral difference between a woman who marries and lives with a man because he can provide for her wants, and the woman who is *not* married, but who is provided for at the same price. There is a *legal* difference, to be sure, upon one side of which is set the seal of respectability, but there is no virtue in law. In the *fact* of law, however, is the evidence of the lack of virtue, since if the law be *required* to enforce virtue, its real presence is wanting; and women need to comprehend this truth.

The sexual relation must be rescued from this *insidious* form of slavery. Women must rise from their position as *ministers* to the passions of men to be their equals. Their entire system of education must be changed. They must be trained to be *like* men, permanent and independent individualities, and not their mere appendages or adjuncts, with them forming but

one member of society. They must be the companions of men from *choice, never* from necessity. . . .

Oh! my brothers and sisters, let me entreat you to have more faith in the self-regulating efficacy of freedom. Do you not see how beautifully it works among us in other respects? In America everybody is free to worship God according to the dictates of his own conscience, or even not to worship anything, notwithstanding you or I may think that very wicked or wrong. The respect for freedom we make paramount over our individual opinions, and the result is peace and harmony, when the people of other countries are still throttling and destroying each other to enforce their individual opinions on others. Free Love is only the appreciation of this beautiful principle of freedom. One step further I entreat you to trust it still, and though you may see a thousand dangers, I see peace and happiness and steady improvement as the result.

To more specifically define Free Love I would say that I prefer to use the word *love* with *lust* as its antithesis, *love* representing the spiritual and *lust* the animal; the perfect and harmonious interrelations of the two being the perfected human. . . .

I know full well how strong is the appeal that can be made in behalf of marriage, an appeal based on the sanctions of usage and inherited respect, and on the sanctions of religion reinforced by the sanctions of law. I know how much can be said, and how forcibly it can be said, on the ground that women, and especially that the children born of the union of the sexes, must be protected and must, therefore, have the solemn contract of the husband and father to that effect. I know how long and how powerfully the ideality and sentiment of mankind have clustered, as it were in a halo, around this time-honoured institution of marriage. And yet I solemnly believe that *all that* belongs to a dispensation of force and contract, and of a low and unworthy sense of mutual ownership, which is passing, and which is destined rapidly to pass, completely away; not to leave us without love, nor without the happiness and beauty of the most tender relation of human souls; nor without security for woman, and ample protection for children; but to lift us to a higher level in the enjoyment of every blessing. I believe in *love with liberty*; in *protection without slavery*; in *the care and culture of offspring by new and better methods, and without the tragedy of self-immolation on the part of parents.* I believe in the family, *spiritually constituted*, expanded, amplified, and scientifically and artistically organized, as a unitary home. I believe in the most wonderful transformation of human society as about to come, as even now at the very door, through general progress, science and the influential intervention of the spirit world. I believe in more than all that the millennium has ever signified to the most religious mind; and I believe that in order to prepare minds to contemplate and desire and enact the new and better life, it is necessary that the old and still prevalent superstitious veneration for the legal marriage tie be relaxed and weakened; not to pander to immorality, but as introductory to a nobler manhood and a more glorified womanhood; as, indeed, the veritable gateway to a paradise regained. . . .

Thus have I explained to you what Social Freedom or, as some choose to denominate it, Free Love, is, and what its advocates demand. Society says, to grant it is

to precipitate itself into anarchy. I oppose to this arbitrary assumption the logic of general freedom, and aver that order and harmony will be secured where anarchy now reigns. The order of nature will soon determine whether society is or I am right. Let that be as it may, I repeat: "The love that I cannot command is not mine; let me not disturb myself about it, nor attempt to filch it from its rightful owner. A heart that I supposed mine has drifted and gone. Shall I go in pursuit? Shall I forcibly capture the truant and transfix it with the barb of my selfish affection, and pin it to the wall of my chamber? Rather let me leave my doors and windows open, intent only on living so nobly that the best cannot fail to be drawn to me by an irresistible attraction."

(1871)

15 • *Susan B. Anthony*

SPEECH AFTER ARREST FOR ILLEGAL VOTING

Friends and Fellow-Citizens:—I stand before you under indictment for the alleged crime of having voted at the last presidential election, without having a lawful right to vote. It shall be my work this evening to prove to you that in thus doing, I not only committed no crime, but instead simply exercised my citizen's right, guaranteed to me and all United States citizens by the National Constitution beyond the power of any State to deny.

Our democratic-republican government is based on the idea of the natural right of every individual member thereof to a voice and a vote in making and executing the laws. We assert the province of government to be to secure the people in the enjoyment of their

inalienable rights. We throw to the winds the old dogma that government can give rights. No one denies that before governments were organized each individual possessed the right to protect his own life, liberty and property. When 100 to 1,000,000 people enter into a free government, they do not barter away their natural rights; they simply pledge themselves to protect each other in the enjoyment of them through prescribed judicial and legislative tribunals. They agree to abandon the methods of brute force in the adjustment of their differences and adopt those of civilization. . . . The Declaration of Independence, the United States Constitution, the constitutions of the several States and the organic laws of the Territories, all alike propose to

Reprinted from *The Life and Work of Susan B. Anthony* by Ida Husted Harper. Indianapolis: The Bowen–Merrill Company, 1898.

protect the people in the exercise of their God-given rights. Not one of them pretends to bestow rights.

> All men are created equal, and endowed by their Creator with certain inalienable rights. Among these are life, liberty and the pursuit of happiness. To secure these, governments are instituted among men, deriving their just powers from the consent of the governed.

Here is no shadow of government authority over rights, or exclusion of any class from their full and equal enjoyment. Here is pronounced the right of all men, and "consequently," as the Quaker preacher said, "of all women," to a voice in the government. And here, in this first paragraph of the Declaration, is the assertion of the natural right of all to the ballot; for how can "the consent of the governed" be given, if the right to vote be denied? . . . The women, dissatisfied as they are with this form of government, that enforces taxation without representation—that compels them to obey laws to which they never have given their consent—that imprisons and hangs them without a trial by a jury of their peers—that robs them, in marriage, of the custody of their own persons, wages and children—are this half of the people who are left wholly at the mercy of the other half, in direct violation of the spirit and letter of the declarations of the framers of this government, every one of which was based on the immutable principle of equal rights to all. By these declarations, kings, popes, priests, aristocrats, all were alike dethroned and placed on a common level, politically, with the lowliest born subject or serf. By them, too, men, as such, were deprived of their divine right to rule and placed on a political level with women. By the practice of these declarations all class and caste distinctions would be abolished, and slave, serf, plebeian, wife, woman, all alike rise from their subject position to the broader platform of equality.

The preamble of the Federal Constitution says:

> We, the people of the United States, in order to form a more perfect union, establish justice, insure domestic tranquillity, provide for the common defence, promote the general welfare and secure the blessings of liberty to ourselves and our posterity, do ordain and establish this Constitution for the United States of America.

It was we, the people, not we, the white male citizens, nor we, the male citizens; but we, the whole people, who formed this Union. We formed it not to give the blessings of liberty but to secure them; not to

the half of ourselves and the half of our posterity, but to the whole people—women as well as men. It is downright mockery to talk to women of their enjoyment of the blessings of liberty while they are denied the only means of securing them provided by this democratic-republican government—the ballot . . .

If, however, you will insist that the Fifteenth Amendment's emphatic interdiction against robbing United States citizens of their suffrage "on account of race, color or previous condition of servitude," is a recognition of the right of either the United States or any State to deprive them of the ballot for any or all other reasons, I will prove to you that the class of citizens for whom I now plead are, by all the principles of our government and many of the laws of the States, included under the term "previous conditions of servitude."

Consider first married women and their legal status. What is servitude? "The condition of a slave." What is a slave? "A person who is robbed of the proceeds of his labor; a person who is subject to the will of another." By the laws of Georgia, South Carolina and all the States of the South, the negro had no right to the custody and control of his person. He belonged to his master. If he were disobedient, the master had the right to use correction. If the negro did not like the correction and ran away, the master had the right to use coercion to bring him back. By the laws of almost every State in this Union today, North as well as South, the married woman has no right to the custody and control of her person. The wife belongs to the husband; and if she refuse obedience he may use moderate correction, and if she do not like his moderate correction and leave his "bed and board," the husband may use moderate coercion to bring her back. The little word "moderate," you see, is the saving clause for the wife, and would doubtless be overstepped should her offended husband administer his correction with the "cat-o'-nine-tails," or accomplish his coercion with blood-hounds.

Again the slave had no right to the earnings of his hands, they belonged to his master; no right to the custody of his children, they belonged to his master; no right to sue or be sued, or to testify in the courts. If he committed a crime, it was the master who must sue or be sued. In many of the States there has been special legislation, giving married women the right to property inherited or received by bequest, or earned by the pursuit of any avocation outside the home; also giving them the right to sue and be sued in matters pertaining to such separate property; but not a single State of this Union has ever secured the wife in the enjoyment of her right to equal ownership of the joint earnings of the marriage copartnership. And since, in the nature of things, the vast majority of married women never earn a dollar by work outside their families, or inherit a dollar from their fathers, it follows that from the day of their marriage to the day of the death of their husbands not one of them ever has a dollar, except it shall please her husband to let her have it. . . .

A good farmer's wife in Illinois, who had all the rights she wanted, had made for herself a full set of false teeth. The dentist pronounced them an admirable fit, and the wife declared it gave her fits to wear them. The dentist sued the husband for his bill; his counsel brought the wife as witness; the judge ruled her off the stand, saying, "A married woman can not be a witness in matters of joint interest between herself and her husband." Think of it, ye good wives, the false teeth in your mouths are a joint interest with your husbands, about which you are legally incompetent to speak! If a married woman is injured by accident, in nearly all of the States it is her husband who must sue, and it is to him that the damages will be awarded. . . . Isn't such a position humiliating enough

to be called "servitude?" That husband sued and obtained damages for the loss of the services of his wife, precisely as he would have done had it been his ox, cow or horse; and exactly as the master, under the old regime, would have recovered for the services of his slave.

I submit the question, if the deprivation by law of the ownership of one's own person, wages, property, children, the denial of the right as an individual to sue and be sued and testify in the courts, is not a condition of servitude most bitter and absolute, even though under the sacred name of marriage? . . . The facts also prove that, by all the great fundamental principles of our free government, not only married women but the entire womanhood of the nation are in a "condition of servitude" as surely as were our Revolutionary fathers when they rebelled against King George. Women are taxed without representation, governed without their consent, tried, convicted and punished without a jury of their peers. Is all this tyranny any less humiliating and degrading to women under our democratic-republican government today than it was to men under their aristocratic, monarchial government one hundred years ago? . . .

(1872)

"THE STORY OF AN HOUR"

Knowing that Mrs. Mallard was afflicted with a heart trouble, great care was taken to break to her as gently as possible the news of her husband's death.

It was her sister Josephine who told her, in broken sentences, veiled hints that revealed in half concealing. Her husband's friend Richards was there, too, near her. It was he who had been in the newspaper office when intelligence of the railroad disaster was received, with Brently Mallard's name leading the list of "killed." He

had only taken the time to assure himself of its truth by a second telegram, and had hastened to forestall any less careful, less tender friend in bearing the sad message.

She did not hear the story as many women have heard the same, with a paralyzed inability to accept its significance. She wept at once, with sudden, wild abandonment, in her sister's arms. When the storm of grief had spent itself she went away to her room alone. She would have no one follow her.

"The Story of an Hour" was first published in *Vogue* on December 6, 1894, under the title "The Dream of an Hour." It was reprinted in *St. Louis Life* on January 5, 1895.

There stood, facing the open window, a comfortable, roomy armchair. Into this she sank, pressed down by a physical exhaustion that haunted her body and seemed to reach into her soul.

She could see in the open square before her house the tops of trees that were all aquiver with the new spring life. The delicious breath of rain was in the air. In the street below a peddler was crying his wares. The notes of a distant song which some one was singing reached her faintly, and countless sparrows were twittering in the eaves.

There were patches of blue sky showing here and there through the clouds that had met and piled above the other in the west facing her window.

She sat with her head thrown back upon the cushion of the chair quite motionless, except when a sob came up into her throat and shook her, as a child who has cried itself to sleep continues to sob in its dreams.

She was young, with a fair, calm face, whose lines bespoke repression and even a certain strength. But now there was a dull stare in her eyes, whose gaze was fixed away off yonder on one of those patches of blue sky. It was not a glance of reflection, but rather indicated a suspension of intelligent thought.

There was something coming to her and she was waiting for it, fearfully. What was it? She did not know; it was too subtle and elusive to name. But she felt it, creeping out of the sky, reaching toward her through the sounds, the scents, the color that filled the air.

Now her bosom rose and fell tumultuously. She was beginning to recognize this thing that was approaching to possess her, and she was striving to beat it back with her will—as powerless as her two white slender hands would have been.

When she abandoned herself a little whispered word escaped her slightly parted lips. She said it over and over under her breath: "Free, free, free!" The vacant stare and the look of terror that had followed it went from her eyes. They stayed keen and bright. Her pulses beat fast, and the coursing blood warmed and relaxed every inch of her body.

She did not stop to ask if it were not a monstrous joy that held her. A clear and exalted perception enabled her to dismiss the suggestion as trivial.

She knew that she would weep again when she saw the kind, tender hands folded in death; the face that had never looked save with love upon her, fixed and gray and dead. But she saw beyond that bitter moment a long procession of years to come that would belong to her absolutely. And she opened and spread her arms out to them in welcome.

There would be no one to live for during those coming years; she would live for herself. There would be no powerful will bending her in that blind persistence with which men and women believe they have a right to impose a private will upon a fellow-creature. A kind intention or a cruel intention made the act seem no less a crime as she looked upon it in that brief moment of illumination.

And yet she had loved him—sometimes. Often she had not. What did it matter! What could love, the unsolved mystery, count for in face of this possession of self-assertion which she suddenly recognized as the strongest impulse of her being!

"Free! Body and soul free!" she kept whispering.

Josephine was kneeling before the closed door with her lips to the keyhole, imploring for admission. "Louise, open the door! I beg; open the door—you will make yourself ill. What are you doing, Louise? For heaven's sake open the door."

"Go away. I am not making myself ill." No; she was drinking in a very elixir of life through that open window.

Her fancy was running riot along those days ahead of her. Spring days, and summer days, and all sorts of days that would be her own. She breathed a quick prayer that life might be long. It was only yesterday she had thought with a shudder that life might be long.

She arose at length and opened the door to her sister's importunities. There was a feverish triumph in her eyes, and she carried herself unwittingly like a goddess of Victory. She clasped her sister's waist, and together they descended the stairs. Richards stood waiting for them at the bottom.

Some one was opening the front door with a latchkey. It was Brently Mallard who entered, a little travel-stained, composedly carrying his grip-sack and umbrella. He had been far from the scene of the accident, and did not even know there had been one. He stood amazed at Josephine's piercing cry; at Richards' quick motion to screen him from the view of his wife.

But Richards was too late.

When the doctors came they said she had died of heart disease—of joy that kills.

(1894)

17 •

"AMERICAN SUFFRAGETTES"

American suffragettes Elizabeth Cady Stanton (1815–1902) and Susan Brownell Anthony (1820–1906) at the 28th Annual Convention of the National American Woman Suffrage Association.

(1896)

18 • *Jane Addams*

"ON MUNICIPAL HOUSEKEEPING"

... It has been well said that the modern city is a stronghold of industrialism, quite as the feudal city was a stronghold of militarism, but the modern city fears no enemies, and rivals from without and its problems of government are solely internal. Affairs for the most part are going badly in these great new centres in which the quickly congregated population has not yet learned to arrange its affairs satisfactorily. Insanitary housing, poisonous sewage, contaminated water, infant mortality, the spread of contagion, adulterated food, impure milk, smoke-laden air, ill-ventilated factories, dangerous occupations, juvenile crime, unwholesome crowding, prostitution, and drunkenness are the enemies which the modern city must face and overcome would it survive. Logically, its electorate should be made up of those who can bear a valiant part in this arduous contest, of those who in the past have at least attempted to care for children, to clean houses, to prepare foods, to isolate the family from moral dangers, of those who have traditionally taken care of that side of life which, as soon as the population is congested, inevitably becomes the subject of municipal consideration and control.

To test the elector's fitness to deal with this situation by his ability to bear arms, is absurd. A city is in many respects a great business corporation, but in other respects it is enlarged housekeeping. If American cities have failed in the first, partly because office holders have carried with them the predatory instinct learned in competitive business, and cannot help "working a good thing" when they have an opportunity, may we not say that city housekeeping has failed partly because women, the traditional housekeepers, have not been consulted as to its multiform activities? The men of the city have been carelessly indifferent to much of this civic housekeeping, as they have always been indifferent to the details of the household. They have totally disregarded a candidate's capacity to keep the streets clean, preferring to consider him in relation to the national tariff or to the necessity for increasing the national navy, in a pure spirit of reversion to the traditional type of government which had to do only with enemies and outsiders.

It is difficult to see what military prowess has to do with the multiform duties, which, in a modern city, include the care of parks and libraries, superintendence of markets, sewers, and bridges, the inspection of provisions and boilers, and the proper disposal of garbage. Military prowess has nothing to do with the building department which the city maintains to see to it that the basements be dry, that the bedrooms be large enough to afford the required cubic feet of air, that the plumbing be sanitary, that the gas-pipes do not leak, that the tenement-house court be large enough to afford light and ventilation, and that the stairways be fireproof. The ability to carry arms has nothing to do with the health department maintained by the city, which provides that children be vaccinated, that contagious diseases be isolated and placarded, that the spread of tuberculosis be curbed, and that the water be free from typhoid infection. Certainly the military conception of society is remote from the functions of the school boards, whose concern it is that children be educated, that they be supplied with kindergartens and be given a decent place in which to play. The very multifariousness and complexity of a city government

Reprinted from *Newer Ideals of Peace* by Jane Addams. Chatauqua, New York: The Chatauqua Press, 1907.

demands the help of minds accustomed to detail and variety of work, to a sense of obligation for the health and welfare of young children, and to a responsibility for the cleanliness and comfort of others.

Because all these things have traditionally been in the hands of women, if they take no part in them now, they are not only missing the education which the natural participation in civic life would bring to them, but they are losing what they have always had. From the beginning of tribal life women have been held responsible for the health of the community, a function which is now represented by the health department; from the days of the cave dwellers, so far as the home was clean and wholesome, it was due to their efforts, which are now represented by the bureau of tenement-house inspection; from the period of the primitive village, the only public sweeping performed was what they undertook in their own dooryards, that which is now represented by the bureau of street cleaning. Most of the departments in a modern city can be traced to woman's traditional activity, but in spite of this, so soon as these old affairs were turned over to the care of the city, they slipped from woman's hands, apparently because they then became matters for collective action and implied the use of the franchise. Because the franchise had in the first instance been given to the man who could fight, because in the beginning he alone could vote who could carry a weapon, the franchise was considered an improper thing for a woman to possess.

Is it quite public spirited for women to say, "We will take care of these affairs so long as they stay in our own houses, but if they go outside and concern so many people that they cannot be carried on without the mechanism of the vote, we will drop them. It is true that these activities which women have always had, are not at present being carried on very well by the men in most of the great American cities, but because we do not consider it 'ladylike' to vote shall we ignore their failure"?

Because women consider the government men's affair and something which concerns itself with elections and alarms, they have become so confused in regard to their traditional business in life, the rearing of children, that they hear with complacency a statement made by Nestor of sanitary reformers, that one-half of the tiny lives which make up the city's death rate each year might be saved by a more thorough application of sanitary science. Because it implies the use of the suffrage, they do not consider it women's business to save these lives. Are we going to lose ourselves in the old circle of convention and add to that sum of wrong-doing which is continually committed in the world because we do not look at things as they really are? Old-fashioned ways which no longer apply to changed conditions are a snare in which the feet of women have always become readily entangled. . . .

Why is it that women do not vote upon the matters which concern them so intimately? Why do they not follow these vital affairs and feel responsible for their proper administration, even though they have become municipalized? What would the result have been could women have regarded the suffrage, not as a right or a privilege, but as a mere piece of governmental machinery without, which they could not perform their traditional functions under the changed conditions of city life? Could we view the whole situation as a matter of obligation and of normal development, it would be much simplified. We are at the beginning of a prolonged effort to incorporate a progressive developing life founded upon a response to the needs of all the people, into the requisite legal enactments and civic institutions. To be in any measure successful, this effort will require all the intelligent powers of observation, all the sympathy, all the common sense which may be gained from the whole adult population.

(1907)

19 • *Virginia Woolf*

"SHAKESPEARE'S SISTER"

. . . But what I find deplorable, I continued, looking about the bookshelves again, is that nothing is known about women before the eighteenth century. I have no model in my mind to turn about this way and that. Here am I asking why women did not write poetry in the Elizabethan age, and I am not sure how they were educated; whether they were taught to write; whether they had sitting-rooms to themselves; how many women had children before they were twenty-one; what, in short, they did from eight in the morning till eight at night. They had no money evidently; according to Professor Trevelyan they were married whether they liked it or not before they were out of the nursery, at fifteen or sixteen very likely. It would have been extremely odd, even upon this showing, had one of them suddenly written the plays of Shakespeare, I concluded, and I thought of that old gentleman, who is dead now, but was a bishop, I think, who declared that it was impossible for any woman, past, present, or to come, to have the genius of Shakespeare. He wrote to the papers about it. He also told a lady who applied to him for information that cats do not as a matter of fact go to heaven, though they have, he added, souls of a sort. How much thinking those old gentlemen used to save one! How the borders of ignorance shrank back at their approach! Cats do not go to heaven. Women cannot write the plays of Shakespeare.

Be that as it may, I could not help thinking, as I looked at the works of Shakespeare on the shelf, that the bishop was right at least in this; it would have been impossible, completely and entirely, for any woman to have written the plays of Shakespeare in the age of Shakespeare. Let me imagine, since facts are so hard to come by, what would have happened had Shakespeare had a wonderfully gifted sister, called Judith, let us say. Shakespeare himself went, very probably,—his mother was an heiress—to the grammar school, where he may have learnt Latin—Ovid, Virgil and Horace—and the elements of grammar and logic. He was, it is well known, a wild boy who poached rabbits, perhaps shot a deer, and had, rather sooner than he should have done, to marry a woman in the neighbourhood, who bore him a child rather quicker than was right. That escapade sent him to seek his fortune in London. He had, it seemed, a taste for the theatre; he began by holding horses at the stage door. Very soon he got work in the theatre, became a successful actor, and lived at the hub of the universe, meeting everybody, knowing everybody, practising his art on the boards, exercising his wits in the streets, and even getting access to the palace of the queen. Meanwhile his extraordinarily gifted sister, let us suppose, remained at home. She was as adventurous, as imaginative, as agog to see the world as he was. But she was not sent to school. She had no chance of learning grammar and logic, let alone of reading Horace and Virgil. She picked up a book now and then, one of her brother's perhaps, and read a few pages. But then her parents came in and told her to mend the stockings or mind the stew and not moon about with books and papers. They would have spoken sharply but kindly, for they were substantial people who knew the conditions of life for a woman and loved their daughter—indeed, more likely than not she was the apple of her father's eye. Perhaps she scribbled some pages up in an apple loft on the sly, but was careful to hide them or set fire to them. Soon, however, before she was out of her teens, she was to be betrothed to the son of a neighbouring wool-stapler. She cried out that marriage was hateful to her, and for that she was severely beaten by her father. Then he ceased to scold her. He begged her instead not to hurt him, not to shame him in this matter of her marriage. He would give her a chain of beads or a fine petticoat, he said; and there were tears in his eyes. How could she disobey him? How could she break his heart? The force of her own gift alone drove her to it. She made up a small parcel of her belongings, let herself down by a rope one summer's night and took the road to London. She was not seventeen. The birds that sang in the hedge were not more musical than she was. She had the quickest fancy, a gift like her brother's, for the tune of words. Like him, she had a taste for the theatre. She stood at the stage door; she wanted to act, she said. Men laughed in her face. The manager—a fat, loose-lipped man—guffawed. He bellowed something about poodles dancing and women acting—no woman, he said, could possibly be an actress. He hinted—you can imagine what. She could get no training in her craft. Could she even seek her dinner in a tavern or roam the streets at midnight? Yet her genius was for fiction and lusted to feed abundantly upon the lives of men and women and the study of their ways. At last—for she was very young, oddly like Shakespeare the poet in her face, with the same grey eyes and rounded brows—at last Nick Greene the actor–manager took pity on her; she found herself with child by that gentleman and so—who shall measure the heat and violence of the poet's heart when caught and tangled in a woman's body?—killed herself one winter's night and lies buried at some cross-roads where the omnibuses now stop outside the Elephant and Castle. . . .

This may be true or it may be false—who can say?—but what is true in it, so it seemed to me, re-viewing the story of Shakespeare's sister as I had made it, is that any woman born with a great gift in the sixteenth century would certainly have gone crazed, shot herself, or ended her days in some lonely cottage outside the village, half witch, half wizard, feared and mocked at. For it needs little skill in psychology to be sure that a highly gifted girl who had tried to use her gift for poetry would have been so thwarted and hin-dered by other people, so tortured and pulled asunder by her own contrary instincts, that she must have lost her health and sanity to a certainty. . . .

. . . I told you in the course of this paper that Shakespeare had a sister; but do not look for her in Sir Sidney Lee's life of the poet. She died young—alas, she never wrote a word. She lies buried where the omnibuses now stop, opposite the Elephant and Castle. Now my belief is that this poet who never wrote a word and was buried at the cross-roads still lives. She lives in you and in me, and in many other women who are not here tonight, for they are washing up the dishes and putting the children to bed. But she lives; for great poets do not die; they are continuing pres-ences; they need only the opportunity to walk among us in the flesh. This opportunity, as I think, it is now coming within your power to give her. For my belief is that if we live another century or so—I am talking of the common life which is the real life and not of the little separate lives which we live as individuals—and have five hundred a year each of us and rooms of our own; if we have the habit of freedom and the courage to write exactly what we think; if we escape a little from the common sitting-room and see human beings not always in their relation to each other but in rela-tion to reality; and the sky, too, and the trees or what-ever it may be in themselves; if we look past Milton's bogey, for no human being should shut out the view; if we face the fact, for it is a fact, that there is no arm to cling to, but that we go alone and that our relation is to the world of reality and not only to the world of men and women, then the opportunity will come and the dead poet who was Shakespeare's sister will put on the body which she has so often laid down. Drawing her life from the lives of the unknown who were her forerunners, as her brother did before her, she will be born. As for her coming without that preparation, with-out that effort on our part, without that determination that when she is born again she shall find it possible to live and write her poetry, that we cannot expect, for that would be impossible. But I maintain that she would come if we worked for her, and that so to work, even in poverty and obscurity, is worth while.

(1929)

20 • *Virginia Woolf*

"A ROOM OF ONE'S OWN"[1]

But, you may say, we asked you to speak about women and fiction—what has that got to do with a room of one's own? I will try to explain. When you asked me to speak about women and fiction I sat down on the banks of a river and began to wonder what the words meant. They might mean simply a few remarks about Fanny Burney; a few more about Jane Austen; a tribute to the Brontës and a sketch of Haworth Parsonage under snow; some witticisms if possible about Miss Mitford; a respectful allusion to George Eliot; a reference to Mrs Gaskell and one would have done. But at second sight the words seemed not so simple. The title women and fiction might mean, and you may have meant it to mean, women and what they are like, or it might mean women and the fiction that they write; or it might mean women and the fiction that is written about them; or it might mean that somehow all three are inextricably mixed together and you want me to consider them in that light. But when I began to consider the subject in this last way, which seemed the most interesting, I soon saw that it had one fatal drawback. I should never be able to come to a conclusion. I should never be able to fulfil what is, I understand, the first duty of a lecturer—to hand you after an hour's discourse a nugget of pure truth to wrap up between the pages of your notebooks and keep on the mantelpiece for ever. All I could do was to offer you an opinion upon one minor point—a woman must have money and a room of her own if she is to write fiction;

and that, as you will see, leaves the great problem of the true nature of woman and the true nature of fiction unsolved. I have shirked the duty of coming to a conclusion upon these two questions—women and fiction remain, so far as I am concerned, unsolved problems. But in order to make some amends I am going to do what I can to show you how I arrived at this opinion about the room and the money. I am going to develop in your presence as fully and freely as I can the train of thought which led me to think this. Perhaps if I lay bare the ideas, the prejudices, that lie behind this statement you will find that they have some bearing upon women and some upon fiction. . . .

. . . What had our mothers been doing then that they had no wealth to leave us? Powdering their noses? Looking in at shop windows? Flaunting in the sun at Monte Carlo? There were some photographs on the mantelpiece. Mary's mother—if that was her picture—may have been a wastrel in her spare time (she had thirteen children by a minister of the church), but if so her gay and dissipated life had left too few traces of its pleasures on her face. She was a homely body; an old lady in a plaid shawl which was fastened by a large cameo; and she sat in a basket-chair, encouraging a spaniel to look at the camera, with the amused, yet strained expression of one who is sure that the dog will move directly the bulb is pressed. Now if she had gone into business; had become a manufacturer of artificial silk or a magnate on the Stock Exchange; if she had left two or three hundred thousand pounds to Fernham, we could have been sitting at our ease tonight and the subject of our talk might have been archaeology, botany, anthropology, physics, the nature of the atom, mathematics, astronomy, relativity, geography.

---

[1]This essay is based upon two papers read to the Arts Society at Newnham and the Odtaa at Girton in October 1928. The papers were too long to be read in full, and have since been altered and expanded.

If only Mrs Seton and her mother and her mother before her had learnt the great art of making money and had left their money, like their fathers and their grandfathers before them, to found fellowships and lectureships and prizes and scholarships appropriated to the use of their own sex, we might have dined very tolerably up here alone off a bird and a bottle of wine; we might have looked forward without undue confidence to a pleasant and honourable lifetime spent in the shelter of one of the liberally endowed professions. We might have been exploring or writing; mooning about the venerable places of the earth; sitting contemplative on the steps of the Parthenon, or going at ten to an office and coming home comfortably at half-past four to write a little poetry. Only, if Mrs Seton and her like had gone into business at the age of fifteen, there would have been—that was the snag in the argument—no Mary. What, I asked, did Mary think of that? There between the curtains was the October night, calm and lovely, with a star or two caught in the yellowing trees. Was she ready to resign her share of it and her memories (for they had been a happy family, though a large one) of games and quarrels up in Scotland, which she is never tired of praising for the fineness of its air and the quality of its cakes, in order that Fernham might have been endowed with fifty thousand pounds or so by a stroke of the pen? For, to endow a college would necessitate the suppression of families altogether. Making a fortune and bearing thirteen children—no human being could stand it. Consider the facts, we said. First there are nine months before the baby is born. Then the baby is born. Then there are three or four months spent in feeding the baby. After the baby is fed there are certainly five years spent in playing with the baby. You cannot, it seems, let children run about the streets. People who have seen them running wild in Russia say that the sight is not a pleasant one. People say, too, that human nature takes its shape in the years between one and five. If Mrs Seton, I said, had been making money, what sort of memories would you have had of games and quarrels? What would you have known of Scotland, and its fine air and cakes and all the rest of it? But it is useless to ask these questions, because you would never have come into existence at all. Moreover, it is equally useless to ask what might have happened if Mrs Seton and her mother and her mother before her had amassed great wealth and laid it under the foundations of college and library, because, in the first place, to earn money was impossible for them, and in the second, had it been possible, the law denied them the right to possess what money they earned. It is only for the last forty-eight years that Mrs Seton has had a penny of her own. For all the centuries before that it would have been her husband's property—a thought which, perhaps, may have had its share in keeping Mrs Seton and her mothers off the Stock Exchange. Every penny I earn, they may have said, will be taken from me and disposed of according to my husband's wisdom—perhaps to found a scholarship or to endow a fellowship in Balliol or Kings, so that to earn money, even if I could earn money, is not a matter that interests me very greatly. I had better leave it to my husband. . . .

So I went back to my inn, and as I walked through the dark streets I pondered this and that, as one does at the end of the day's work. I pondered why it was that Mrs Seton had no money to leave us; and what effect poverty has on the mind; and what effect wealth has on the mind. . . .

(1929)

21 • *Margaret Mead*

"SEX AND TEMPERAMENT"

. . . We know that human cultures do not all fall into one side or the other of a single scale and that it is possible for one society to ignore completely an issue which two other societies have solved in contrasting ways. Because a people honour the old may mean that they hold children in slight esteem, but a people may also, like the Ba Thonga of South Africa, honour neither old people nor children; or, like the Plains Indians, dignify the little child and the grandfather; or, again, like the Manus and parts of modern America, regard children as the most important group in society. In expecting simple reversals—that if an aspect of social life is not specifically sacred, it must be specifically secular; that if men are strong, women must be weak—we ignore the fact that cultures exercise far greater license than this in selecting the possible aspects of human life which they will minimize, overemphasize, or ignore. And while every culture has in some way institutionalized the roles of men and women, it has not necessarily been in terms of contrast between the prescribed personalities of the two sexes, nor in terms of dominance or submission. With the paucity of material for elaboration, no culture has failed to seize upon the conspicuous facts of age and sex in some way, whether it be the convention of one Philippine tribe that no man can keep a secret, the Manus assumption that only men enjoy playing with babies, the Toda prescription of almost all domestic work as too sacred for women, or the Arapesh insistence that women's heads are stronger than men's. In the division of labour, in dress, in manners, in social and religious functioning—sometimes in only a few of these respects, sometimes in all—men and women are socially differentiated, and each sex, as a sex, forced to conform to the role assigned to it. In some societies, these socially defined roles are mainly expressed in dress or occupation, with no insistence upon innate temperamental differences. Women wear long hair and men wear short hair, or men wear curls and women shave their heads; women wear skirts and men wear trousers, or women wear trousers, and men wear skirts. Women weave and men do not, or men weave and women do not. Such simple tie-ups as these between dress and occupation and sex are easily taught to every child and make no assumptions to which a given child cannot easily conform.

It is otherwise in societies that sharply differentiate the behaviour of men and of women in terms which assume a genuine difference in temperament. Among the Dakota Indians of the Plains, the importance of an ability to stand any degree of danger or hardship was frantically insisted upon as a masculine characteristic. From the time that a boy was five or six, all the conscious educational effort of the household was bent towards shaping him into an indubitable male. Every tear, every timidity, every clinging to a protective hand or desire to continue to play with younger children or with girls, was obsessively interpreted as proof that he was not going to develop into a real man. . .

The knowledge that the personalities of the two sexes are socially produced is congenial to every programme that looks forward towards a planned order of society. It is a two-edged sword that can be used to hew a more flexible, more varied society than the human race has ever built, or merely to cut a narrow path down which one sex or both sexes will be forced to march, regimented, looking neither to the right nor to the left. . . .

There are at least three courses open to a society that has realized the extent to which male and female personality are socially produced. Two of these courses have been tried before, over and over again, at different

Pp. 143–7 from *Sex and Temperament in Three Primitive Societies* by Margaret Mead. Copyright © 1935, 1950, 1963 by Margaret Mead. Reprinted by permission of HarperCollins Publishers.

times in the long, irregular, repetitious history of the race. The first is to standardize the personality of men and women as clearly contrasting, complementary, and antithetical, and to make every institution in the society congruent with this standardization. If the society declared that women's sole function was motherhood and the teaching and care of young children, it could so arrange matters that every woman who was not physiologically debarred should become a mother and be supported in the exercise of this function. It could abolish the discrepancy between the doctrine that women's place is the home and the number of homes that were offered to them. It could abolish the discrepancy between training women for marriage and then forcing them to become the spinster supports of their parents.

Such a system would be wasteful of the gifts of many women who could exercise other functions far better than their ability to bear children in an already overpopulated world. It would be wasteful of the gifts of many men who could exercise their special personality gifts far better in the home than in the marketplace. It would be wasteful, but it would be clear. It could attempt to guarantee to each individual the role for which society insisted upon training him or her, and such a system would penalize only those individuals who, in spite of all the training, did not display the approved personalities. There are millions of persons who would gladly return to such a standardized method of treating the relationship between the sexes, and we must bear in mind the possibility that the greater opportunities open in the twentieth century to women may be quite withdrawn, and that we may return to a strict regimentation of women.

The waste, if this occurs, will be not only of many women, but also of as many men, because regimentation of one sex carries with it, to a greater or less degree, the regimentation of the other also. Every parental behest that defines a way of sitting, a response to a rebuke or a threat, a game, or an attempt to draw or sing or dance or paint, as feminine, is moulding the personality of each little girl's brother as well as moulding the personality of the sister. There can be no society which insists that women follow one special personality-pattern, defined as feminine, which does not do violence also to the individuality of many men.

Alternatively, society can take the course that has become especially associated with the plans of most

radical groups: admit that men and women are capable of being moulded to a single pattern as easily as to a diverse one, and cease to make any distinction in the approved personality of both sexes. Girls can be trained exactly as boys are trained; taught the same code, the same forms of expression, the same occupations. This course might seem to be the logic which follows from the conviction that the potentialities which different societies label as either masculine or feminine are really potentialities of some members of each sex, and not sex-linked at all. If this is accepted, is it not reasonable to abandon the kind of artificial standardizations of sex-differences that have been so long characteristic of European society, and admit that they are social fictions for which we have no longer any use? In the world today, contraceptives make it possible for women not to bear children against their will. The most conspicuous actual difference between the sexes, the difference in strength, is progressively less significant. Just as the difference in height between males is no longer a realistic issue, now that lawsuits have been substituted for hand-to-hand encounters, so the difference in strength between men and women is no longer worth elaboration in cultural institutions.

* * *

To break down one line of division, that between the sexes, and substitute another, that between classes, is no real advance. It merely shifts the irrelevancy to a different point. And meanwhile, individuals born in the upper classes are shaped inexorably to one type of personality, to an arrogance that is again uncongenial to at least some of them, while the arrogant among the poor fret and fume beneath their training for submissiveness. At one end of the scale is the mild, unaggressive young son of wealthy parents who is forced to lead, at the other the aggressive, enterprising child of the slums who is condemned to a place in the ranks. If our aim is greater expression for each individual temperament, rather than any partisan interest in one sex or its fate, we must see these historical developments which have aided in freeing some women as nevertheless a kind of development that also involved major social losses.

The second way in which categories of sex-differences have become less rigid is through a recognition of genuine individual gifts as they occurred in either sex. Here a real distinction has been substituted for an artificial one, and the gains are tremendous for society and for the individual. Where writing is accepted as a profession that may be pursued by either sex with perfect suitability, individuals who have the ability to write need not be debarred from it by their sex, nor need they, if they do write, doubt their essential masculinity or femininity. An occupation that has no basis in sex-determined gifts can now recruit its ranks from twice as many potential artists. And it is here that we can find a ground-plan for building a society that would substitute real differences for arbitrary ones. We must recognize that beneath the superficial classifications of sex and race the same potentialities exist, recurring generation after generation, only to perish because society has no place for them. Just as society now permits the practice of an art to members of either sex, so it might also permit the development of many contrasting temperamental gifts in each sex. It might abandon its various attempts to make boys fight and to make girls remain passive, or to make all children fight, and instead shape our educational institutions to develop to the full the boy who shows a capacity for maternal behaviour, the girl who shows an opposite capacity that is stimulated by fighting against obstacles. No skill, no special aptitude, no vividness of imagination or precision of thinking would go unrecognized because the child who possessed it was of one sex rather than the other. No child would be relentlessly shaped to one pattern of behaviour, but instead there should be many patterns, in a world that had learned to allow to each individual the pattern which was most congenial to his gifts.

Such a civilization would not sacrifice the gains of thousands of years during which society has built up standards of diversity. The social gains would be conserved, and each child would be encouraged on the basis of his actual temperament. Where we now have patterns of behaviour for women and patterns of behaviour for men, we would then have patterns of behaviour that expressed the interests of individuals with many kinds of endowment. There would be ethical codes and social symbolisms, an art and a way of life, congenial to each endowment.

Historically our own culture has relied for the creation of rich and contrasting values upon many artificial distinctions, the most striking of which is sex. It will not be by the mere abolition of these distinctions that society will develop patterns in which individual gifts are given place instead of being forced into an ill-fitting mould. If we are to achieve a richer culture, rich in contrasting values, we must recognize the whole gamut of human potentialities, and so weave a less arbitrary social fabric, one in which each diverse human gift will find a fitting place.

(1935)

"THE PROBLEM THAT HAS NO NAME"

The problem lay buried, unspoken, for many years in the minds of American women. It was a strange stirring, a sense of dissatisfaction, a yearning that women suffered in the middle of the twentieth century in the United States. Each suburban wife struggled with it alone.

As she made the beds, shopped for groceries, matched slipcover material, ate peanut butter sandwiches with her children, chauffeured Cub Scouts and Brownies, lay beside her husband at night—she was afraid to ask even of herself the silent question—"Is this all?"

For over fifteen years there was no word of this yearning in the millions of words written about women, for women, in all the columns, books and articles by experts telling women their role was to seek fulfillment as wives and mothers. Over and over women heard in voices of tradition and of Freudian sophistication that they could desire no greater destiny than to glory in their own femininity. Experts told them how to catch a man and keep him, how to breastfeed children and handle their toilet training, how to cope with sibling rivalry and adolescent rebellion; how to buy a dishwasher, bake bread, cook gourmet snails, and build a swimming pool with their own hands; how to dress, look, and act more feminine and make marriage more exciting; how to keep their husbands from dying young and their sons from growing into delinquents. They were taught to pity the neurotic, unfeminine, unhappy women who wanted to be poets or physicists or presidents. They learned that truly feminine women do not want careers, higher education, political rights—the independence and the opportunities that the old-fashioned feminists fought for. Some women, in their forties and fifties, still remembered painfully giving up those dreams, but most of the younger women no longer even thought about them. A thousand expert voices applauded their femininity, their adjustment, their new maturity. All they had to do was devote their lives from earliest girlhood to finding a husband and bearing children.

By the end of the nineteen-fifties, the average marriage age of women in America dropped to 20, and was still dropping, into the teens. Fourteen million girls were engaged by 17. The proportion of women attending college in comparison with men dropped from 47 percent in 1920 to 35 per cent in 1958. A century earlier, women had fought for higher education; now girls went to college to get a husband. By the mid-fifties, 60 per cent dropped out of college to marry, or because they were afraid too much education would be a marriage bar. Colleges built dormitories for "married students," but the students were almost always the husbands. A new degree instituted for the wives— "Ph.T." (Putting Husband Through).

Then American girls began getting married in high school. And the women's magazines, deploring the unhappy statistics about these young marriages, urged that courses on marriage, and marriage counselors, be installed in the high schools. Girls started going steady at twelve and thirteen, in junior high. Manufacturers

put out brassieres with false bosoms of foam rubber for little girls of ten. And an advertisement for a child's dress, sizes 3–6x, in the *New York Times* in the fall of 1960, said: "She Too Can Join the Man-Trap Set."

By the end of the fifties, the United States birthrate was overtaking India's. The birth-control movement, renamed Planned Parenthood, was asked to find a method whereby women who had been advised that a third or fourth baby would be born dead or defective might have it anyhow. Statisticians were especially astounded at the fantastic increase in the number of babies among college women. Where once they had two children, now they had four, five, six. Women who had once wanted careers were now making careers out of having babies. So rejoiced *Life* magazine in a 1956 paean to the movement of American women back to the home.

In a New York hospital, a woman had a nervous breakdown when she found she could not breastfeed her baby. In other hospitals, women dying of cancer refused a drug which research had proved might save their lives: its side effects were said to be unfeminine. "If I have only one life, let me live it as a blonde," a larger-than-life-sized picture of a pretty, vacuous woman proclaimed from newspaper, magazine, and drugstore ads. And across America, three out of every ten women dyed their hair blonde. They ate a chalk called Metrecal, instead of food, to shrink to the size of the thin young models. Department-store buyers reported that American women, since 1939, had become three and four sizes smaller. "Women are out to fit the clothes, instead of vice-versa," one buyer said.

Interior decorators were designing kitchens with mosaic murals and original paintings, for kitchens were once again the center of women's lives. Home sewing became a million-dollar industry. Many women no longer left their homes, except to shop, chauffeur their children, or attend a social engagement with their husbands. Girls were growing up in America without ever having jobs outside the home. In the late fifties, a sociological phenomenon was suddenly remarked: a third of American women now worked, but most were no longer young and very few were pursuing careers. They were married women who held part-time jobs, selling or secretarial, to put their husbands through school, their sons through college, or to help pay the mortgage. Or they were widows supporting families. Fewer and fewer women were entering professional work. The shortages in the nursing, social work, and teaching professions caused crises in almost every American city. Concerned over the Soviet Union's lead in the space race, scientists noted that America's greatest source of unused brain-power was women. But girls would not study physics: it was "unfeminine." A girl refused a science fellowship at Johns Hopkins to take a job in a real-estate office. All she wanted, she said, was what every other American girl wanted—to get married, have four children and live in a nice house in a nice suburb.

The suburban housewife—she was the dream image of the young American women and the envy, it was said, of women all over the world. The American housewife—freed by science and labor-saving appliances from the drudgery, the dangers of childbirth and the illnesses of her grandmother. She was healthy, beautiful, educated, concerned only about her husband, her children, her home. She had found true feminine fulfillment. As a housewife and mother, she was respected as a full and equal partner to man in his world. She was free to choose automobiles, clothes, appliances, supermarkets; she had everything that women ever dreamed of.

In the fifteen years after World War II, this mystique of feminine fulfillment became the cherished and self-perpetuating core of contemporary American culture. Millions of women lived their lives in the image of those pretty pictures of the American suburban housewife, kissing their husbands goodbye in front of the picture window, depositing their station-wagonsful of children at school, and smiling as they ran the new electric waxer over the spotless kitchen floor. They baked their own bread, sewed their own and their children's clothes, kept their new washing machines and dryers running all day. They changed the sheets on the beds twice a week instead of once, took the rug-hooking class in adult education, and pitied their poor frustrated mothers, who had dreamed of having a career. Their only dream was to be perfect wives and mothers; their highest ambition to have five children and a beautiful house, their only fight to get and keep their husbands. They had no thought for the unfeminine problems of the world outside the home; they wanted the men to make the major decisions. They gloried in their role as women, and wrote proudly on the census blank: "Occupation: housewife."

For over fifteen years, the words written for women, and the words women used when they talked to each other, while their husbands sat on the other side of the room and talked shop or politics or septic tanks, were about problems with their children, or how to keep their husbands happy, or improve their children's school, or cook chicken or make slipcovers. Nobody argued whether women were inferior or superior to men; they were simply different. Words like "emancipation" and "career" sounded strange and embarrassing; no one had used them for years. When a Frenchwoman named Simone de Beauvoir wrote a book called *The Second Sex,* an American critic commented that she obviously "didn't know what life was all about," and besides, she was talking about French women. The "woman problem" in America no longer existed.

If a woman had a problem in the 1950's and 1960's, she knew that something must be wrong with her marriage, or with herself. Other women were satisfied with their lives, she thought. What kind of a woman was she if she did not feel this mysterious fulfillment waxing the kitchen floor? She was so ashamed to admit her dissatisfaction that she never knew how many other women shared it. If she tried to tell her husband, he didn't understand what she was talking about. She did not really understand it herself. For over fifteen years women in America found it harder to talk about this problem than about sex. Even the psychoanalysts had no name for it. When a woman went to a psychiatrist for help, as many women did, she would say, "I'm so ashamed," or "I must be hopelessly neurotic." "I don't know what's wrong with women today," a suburban psychiatrist said uneasily. "I only know something is wrong because most of my patients happen to be women. And their problem isn't sexual." Most women with this problem did not go to see a psychoanalyst, however. "There's nothing wrong really," they kept telling themselves. "There isn't any problem." . . .

If I am right, the problem that has no name stirring in the minds of so many American women today is not a matter of loss of femininity or too much education, or the demands of domesticity. It is far more important than anyone recognizes. It is the key to these other new and old problems which have been torturing women and their husbands and children, and puzzling their doctors and educators for years. It may well be the key to our future as a nation and a culture. We can no longer ignore that voice within women that says: "I want something more than my husband and my children and my home."

(1963)

"1966 STATEMENT OF PURPOSE"

We, men and women who hereby constitute ourselves as the National Organization for Women, believe that the time has come for a new movement toward true equality for all women in America, and toward a fully equal partnership of the sexes, as part of the world-wide revolution of human rights now taking place within and beyond our national borders.

The purpose of NOW is to take action to bring women into full participation in the mainstream of American society now, exercising all the privileges and responsibilities thereof in truly equal partnership with men.

We believe the time has come to move beyond the abstract argument, discussion and symposia over the status and special nature of women which has raged in America in recent years; the time has come to confront, with concrete action, the conditions that now prevent women from enjoying the equality of opportunity and freedom of choice which is their right, as individual Americans, and as human beings.

NOW is dedicated to the proposition that women, first and foremost, are human beings, who, like all other people in our society, must have the chance to develop their fullest human potential. We believe that women can achieve such equality only by accepting to the full the challenges and responsibilities they share with all other people in our society, as part of the decision-making mainstream of American political, economic and social life.

We organize to initiate or support action, nationally, or in any part of this nation, by individuals or organizations, to break through the silken curtain of prejudice and discrimination against women in government, industry, the professions, the churches, the political parties, the judiciary, the labor unions, in education, science, medicine, law, religion and every other field of importance in American society.

Enormous changes taking place in our society make it both possible and urgently necessary to advance the unfinished revolution of women toward true equality, now. With a life span lengthened to nearly 75 years it is no longer either necessary or possible for women to devote the greater part of their lives to child-rearing; yet childbearing and rearing which continues to be a most important part of most women's lives—still is used to justify barring women from equal professional and economic participation and advance.

Today's technology has reduced most of the productive chores which women once performed in the home and in mass-production industries based upon routine unskilled labor. This same technology has virtually eliminated the quality of muscular strength as a criterion for filling most jobs, while intensifying American industry's need for creative intelligence. In view of this new industrial revolution created by automation in the mid-twentieth century, women can and must participate in old and new fields of society in full equality—or become permanent outsiders.

Despite all the talk about the status of American women in recent years, the actual position of women in the United States has declined, and is declining, to an alarming degree throughout the 1950's and 60's. Although 46.4% of all American women between the ages of 18 and 65 now work outside the home, the overwhelming majority—75%—are in routine clerical, sales, or factory jobs, or they are household workers, cleaning women, hospital attendants. About two-thirds of Negro women workers are in the lowest paid service occupations. Working women are becoming increasingly—not less—concentrated on the bottom of the job ladder. As a consequence full-time women workers today earn on the average only 60% of what men earn, and that wage gap has been increasing over the past twenty-five years

National Organization for Women Statement of Purpose (1966), reprinted with permission. This is a historical document and may not reflect the current language or priorities of the organization.

in every major industry group. In 1964, of all women with a yearly income, 89% earned under $5,000 a year; half of all full-time year round women workers earned less than $3,690; only 1.4% of full-time year round women workers had an annual income of $10,000 or more.

Further, with higher education increasingly essential in today's society, too few women are entering and finishing college or going on to graduate or professional school. Today, women earn only one in three of the B.A.'s and M.A.'s granted, and one in ten of the Ph.D.'s.

In all the professions considered of importance to society, and in the executive ranks of industry and government, women are losing ground. Where they are present it is only a token handful. Women comprise less than 1% of federal judges; less than 4% of all lawyers; 7% of doctors. Yet women represent 51% of the U.S. population. And, increasingly, men are replacing women in the top positions in secondary and elementary schools, in social work, and in libraries—once thought to be women's fields.

Official pronouncements of the advance in the status of women hide not only the reality of this dangerous decline, but the fact that nothing is being done to stop it. The excellent reports of the President's Commission on the Status of Women and of the State Commissions have not been fully implemented. Such Commissions have power only to advise. They have no power to enforce their recommendation; nor have they the freedom to organize American women and men to press for action on them. The reports of these commissions have, however, created a basis upon which it is now possible to build. Discrimination in employment on the basis of sex is now prohibited by federal law, in Title VII of the Civil Rights Act of 1964. But although nearly one-third of the cases brought before the Equal Employment Opportunity Commission during the first year dealt with sex discrimination and the proportion is increasing dramatically, the Commission has not made clear its intention to enforce the law with the same seriousness on behalf of women as of other victims of discrimination. Many of these cases were Negro women, who are the victims of double discrimination of race and sex. Until now, too few women's organizations and official spokesmen have been willing to speak out against these dangers facing women. Too many women have been restrained by the fear of being called "feminist." There is no civil rights movement to speak for women, as there has been for Negroes and other victims

of discrimination. The National Organization for Women must therefore begin to speak.

WE BELIEVE that the power of American law, and the protection guaranteed by the U.S. Constitution to the civil rights of all individuals, must be effectively applied and enforced to isolate and remove patterns of sex discrimination, to ensure equality of opportunity in employment and education, and equality of civil and political rights and responsibilities on behalf of women, as well as for Negroes and other deprived groups.

We realize that women's problems are linked to many broader questions of social justice; their solution will require concerted action by many groups. Therefore, convinced that human rights for all are indivisible, we expect to give active support to the common cause of equal rights for all those who suffer discrimination and deprivation, and we call upon other organizations committed to such goals to support our efforts toward equality for women.

WE DO NOT ACCEPT the token appointment of a few women to high-level positions in government and industry as a substitute for serious continuing effort to recruit and advance women according to their individual abilities. To this end, we urge American government and industry to mobilize the same resources of ingenuity and command with which they have solved problems of far greater difficulty than those now impeding the progress of women.

WE BELIEVE that this nation has a capacity at least as great as other nations, to innovate new social institutions which will enable women to enjoy the true equality of opportunity and responsibility in society, without conflict with their responsibilities as mothers and homemakers. In such innovations, America does not lead the Western world, but lags by decades behind many European countries. We do not accept the traditional assumption that a woman has to choose between marriage and motherhood, on the one hand, and serious participation in industry or the professions on the other. We question the present expectation that all normal women will retire from job or profession for 10 or 15 years, to devote their full time to raising children, only to reenter the job market at a relatively minor level. This, in itself, is a deterrent to the aspirations of women, to their acceptance into management or professional training courses, and to the very possibility of equality of opportunity or real choice, for all but a few women. Above all, we reject the assumption that these problems are the unique responsibility of each individual woman, rather than a basic social dilemma which society must solve. True equality of opportunity and freedom of choice for women requires such practical, and possible innovations as a nationwide network of child-care centers, which will make it unnecessary for women to retire completely from society until their children are grown, and national programs to provide retraining for women who have chosen to care for their children full-time.

WE BELIEVE that it is as essential for every girl to be educated to her full potential of human ability as it is for every boy—with the knowledge that such education is the key to effective participation in today's economy and that, for a girl as for a boy, education can only be serious where there is expectation that it will be used in society. We believe that American educators are capable of devising means of imparting such expectations to girl students. Moreover, we consider the decline in the proportion of women receiving higher and professional education to be evidence of discrimination. This discrimination may take the form of quotas against the admission of women to colleges, and professional schools; lack of encouragement by parents, counselors and educators; denial of loans or fellowships; or the traditional or arbitrary procedures in graduate and professional training geared in terms of men, which inadvertently discriminate against women. We believe that the same serious attention must be given to high school dropouts who are girls as to boys.

WE REJECT the current assumptions that a man must carry the sole burden of supporting himself, his wife, and family, and that a woman is automatically entitled to lifelong support by a man upon her marriage, or that marriage, home and family are primarily woman's world and responsibility—hers, to dominate—his to support. We believe that a true partnership between the sexes demands a different concept of marriage, an equitable sharing of the responsibilities of home and children and of the economic burdens of their support. We believe that proper recognition should be given to the economic and social value of homemaking and child-care. To these ends, we will seek to open a reexamination of laws and mores governing marriage and divorce, for we believe that the current state of "half-equity" between the sexes discriminates against both men and women, and is the cause of much unnecessary hostility between the sexes.

WE BELIEVE that women must now exercise their political rights and responsibilities as American citizens. They must refuse to be segregated on the basis of sex into separate-and-not-equal ladies' auxiliaries in the political parties, and they must demand representation according to their numbers in the regularly constituted party committees—at local, state, and national levels—and in the informal power structure, participating fully in the selection of candidates and political decision-making, and running for office themselves.

IN THE INTERESTS OF THE HUMAN DIGNITY OF WOMEN, we will protest, and endeavor to change, the false image of women now prevalent in the mass media, and in the texts, ceremonies, laws, and practices of our major social institutions. Such images perpetuate contempt for women by society and by women for themselves. We are similarly opposed to all policies and practices—in church, state, college, factory, or office—which, in the guise of protectiveness, not only deny opportunities but also foster in women self-denigration, dependence, and evasion of responsibility, undermine their confidence in their own abilities and foster contempt for women.

NOW WILL HOLD ITSELF INDEPENDENT OF ANY POLITICAL PARTY in order to mobilize the political power of all women and men intent on our goals. We will strive to ensure that no party, candidate, president, senator, governor, congressman, or any public official who betrays or ignores the principle of full equality between the sexes is elected or appointed to office. If it is necessary to mobilize the votes of men and women who believe in our cause, in order to win for women the final right to be fully free and equal human beings, we so commit ourselves.

WE BELIEVE THAT women will do most to create a new image of women by acting now, and by speaking out in behalf of their own equality, freedom, and human dignity—not in pleas for special privilege, nor in enmity toward men, who are also victims of the current, half-equality between the sexes—but in an active, self-respecting partnership with men. By so doing, women will develop confidence in their own ability to determine actively, in partnership with men, the conditions of their life, their choices, their future and their society.

This Statement of Purpose was written by Betty Friedan, author of *The Feminine Mystique*.

(1966)

FROM *IN A DIFFERENT VOICE*

Among the most pressing items on the agenda for research on adult development is the need to delineate *in women's own terms* the experience of their adult life. My own work in that direction indicates that the inclusion of women's experience brings to developmental understanding a new perspective on relationships that changes the basic constructs of interpretation. The concept of identity expands to include the experience of interconnection. The moral domain is similarly enlarged by the inclusion of responsibility and care in relationships. And the underlying epistemology correspondingly shifts from the Greek ideal of knowledge as a correspondence between mind and form to the Biblical conception of knowing as a process of human relationship.

Given the evidence of different perspectives in the representation of adulthood by women and men, there is a need for research that elucidates the effects of these differences in marriage, family, and work relationships. My research suggests that men and women may speak different languages that they assume are the same, using similar words to encode disparate experiences of self and social relationships. Because these languages share an overlapping moral vocabulary, they contain a propensity for systematic mistranslation, creating misunderstandings which impede communication and limit the potential for cooperation and care in relationships. At the same time, however, these languages articulate with one another in critical ways. Just as the language of responsibilities provides a weblike imagery of relationships to replace a hierarchical ordering that dissolves with the coming of equality, so the language of rights underlines the importance of including in the network of care not only the other but also the self.

As we have listened for centuries to the voices of men and the theories of development that their experience informs, so we have come more recently to notice not only the silence of women but the difficulty in hearing what they say when they speak. Yet in the different voice of women lies the truth of an ethic of care, the tie between relationship and responsibility, and the origins of aggression in the failure of connection. The failure to see the different reality of women's lives and to hear the differences in their voices stems in part from the assumption that there is a single mode of social experience and interpretation. By positing instead two different modes, we arrive at a more complex rendition of human experience which sees the truth of separation and attachment in the lives of women and men and recognizes how these truths are carried by different modes of language and thought.

To understand how the tension between responsibilities and rights sustains the dialectic of human development is to see the integrity of two disparate modes of experience that are in the end connected. While an ethic of justice proceeds from the premise of equality—that everyone should be treated the same—an ethic of care rests on the premise of nonviolence—that no one should be hurt. In the representation of maturity, both perspectives converge in the realization that just as inequality adversely affects both parties in an unequal relationship, so too violence is destructive for everyone involved. This dialogue between fairness and care not only provides a better understanding of relations between the sexes but also gives rise to a more comprehensive portrayal of adult work and family relationships.

As Freud and Piaget call our attention to the differences in children's feelings and thought, enabling us to respond to children with greater care and respect, so a recognition of the differences in women's experience and understanding expands our vision of maturity and points to the contextual nature of developmental truths. Through this expansion in perspective, we can begin to envision how a marriage between adult development as it is currently portrayed and women's development as it begins to be seen could lead to a changed understanding of human development and a more generative view of human life.

(1982)

CHAPTER 3

Radical Feminisms

> Sexism is the foundation on which all tyranny is built. Every social form of hierarchy and abuse is modeled on male-over-female domination.
>
> —Andrea Dworkin, 1976

INTRODUCTION

Of all the feminist perspectives that arose during the second wave of the U.S. women's movement, radical feminism was the most woman-centered approach. It also made the greatest strides in bridging the personal and the political. Radical feminists were foremost among second-wave feminists for emphasizing how women's emancipation required that women understand, protect, and control their own bodies. They also addressed various oppressions that previously had been relegated to the private realm of interpersonal life, such as rape, domestic violence, and sexual harassment. Whether highlighting the dangers or the pleasures associated with sexual practices, radical feminists exposed and analyzed issues that had been closeted or hidden in the household.

The term "**the personal is political**," first coined in 1969 by radical feminist Carol Hanisch, became a mantra of the second wave. On the one hand, it highlighted how many gender-related "personal" problems, such as domestic violence, should not be addressed individually, but rather collectively as problems rooted in social and political institutions. On the other hand, it enjoined feminists to live their politics in their everyday lives—to practice what they preached. Together these two dimensions of "the personal is political" formed a powerful duo. They linked the macro- and micro-levels of society, as well as social structure and human agency. Most importantly, they called for a feminism that transformed both the individual and society.

THE DIALECTIC OF SEX

One of the most influential statements of radical feminism was Shulamith Firestone's *Dialectic of Sex* (1970). Excerpts from its concluding chapter can be found in Reading 28 titled "Revolutionary Demands." Firestone viewed women's oppression as the earliest and most fundamental form of oppression that provides the model for all later forms of oppression, such as those based on class, race, or sexual orientation. Unlike most other feminist frameworks that root women's oppression in sociohistorical conditions, Firestone roots women's oppression in biology, arguing that through most of human history women had been at the mercy of "menstruation, menopause, and 'female ills,' constant painful childbirth, wetnursing and care of infants all of which made them dependent on males for survival" (Firestone, [1970] 2003: 9). In her view, the sexual division of labor was simply a reflection of these biological differences.

If the root of women's oppression is biological, this leaves little room for social change. For Firestone, the ultimate liberation of women would have to wait until new reproductive technologies could enable ex-utero reproduction whereby "genital differences between human beings would no longer matter culturally" (Firestone, [1970] 2003: 11). Then heterosexual intercourse would no longer be so important for procreation and people could experience many and diverse erotic experiences, which she referred to as "pansexuality" (ibid). Unlike Friedan, Firestone considers any image of "drafting women into a male world rather than the elimination of the sex class distinction altogether" as part of the "1984 nightmare" (188).[1] She does not want a society in which "women have become like men, crippled in the identical ways" (189). Rather, she calls for androgyny.

Firestone had been a key activist in founding the group Radical Women in New York. Their protest against the Miss America Pageant in 1968 was the first feminist demonstration of the second wave to receive front-page coverage in the national press (Deckard, [1979] 1983: 329). At this protest a sheep was crowned Miss America and a "Freedom Trash Can" was provided for women to throw away "women's garbage" such as "bras, girdles, curlers, false eyelashes and wigs" (329). Most likely this event contributed to the legendary labeling of second-wave feminists as "bra burners" (although the actual burning of bras was never documented). The tone and political stance of radical feminists in these early years is captured well in Reading 26, "The BITCH Manifesto" (1969), written by Joreen [Jo Freeman].

LESBIANISM, FEMINIST SEPARATISM, AND THE WOMAN-IDENTIFIED WOMAN

Radical feminists were key voices in the U.S. women's movement that drew attention to lesbian issues. Reading 25 provides excerpts from one of the earliest coming-out stories, "Miss Furr and Miss Skeene" (1922), by Gertrude Stein. Sometimes referred to as a prose poem, Stein plays with noun/adjective ambiguity and repetition to capture the coming together of two women who later part. One of the most famous early lesbian novels was written a few years later—Radclyffe Hall's *The Well of Loneliness* (1928). Although the main character's attitude toward her sexuality is anguished, Hall presents lesbianism as natural and makes a plea for greater tolerance.

However, it was not until the second wave of U.S. feminism that we began to see major radical feminist statements on the relationship between lesbianism and feminism. For example, in Reading 30 from "Lesbians in Revolt," Charlotte Bunch discusses the **woman-identified woman** who "commits herself to other women for political emotional, physical, and economic support" ([1972] 1987: 162). She contrasts the "woman-identified woman" with women who give their primary commitments to men. In her view, "giving support and love to men over women perpetuates the system that oppresses her" (Bunch, [1972] 1987: 162). Bunch argues that heterosexuality separates women from each other, forces women to compete for men, and encourages them to define themselves through men ([1972] 1987: 164). She also points to how heterosexual women gain privileges as compensation for their loss of freedom, such as being honored as mothers, socially accepted as wives, or lovers, and receiving some economic security (Bunch, [1972] 1987: 165). These privileges give heterosexual women a political stake in maintaining the status quo that may lead them to "betray their sisters, especially lesbian sisters who do not receive those benefits" (Bunch, [1972] 1987: 166). Thus, "woman-identified lesbianism is more than a sexual preference; *it is a political choice*" (Bunch, [1972] 1987: 162, our emphasis). Bunch and other radical feminists who shared her views called for **feminist separatism**, meaning women's conscious and willful separation from various forms of patriarchal control, including living separately from men in women-identified and women-controlled communities.

Similar views can be found in Reading 29, "The Woman-Identified Woman" (1970) by the Radicalesbians. This group grew out of the Lavender Menace protest in New York—a protest against the invisibility of lesbians in the women's movement that especially focused its attacks on NOW's refusal to address lesbian issues. The term "**lavender menace**" referred to Betty Friedan's remark that lesbianism was a "lavender herring" for the women's movement that would distract attention from more serious and more widely shared women's issues (Deckard, [1979] 1983: 340–342). It was not until radical feminists, such as the Radicalesbians, staged a number of protests at national women's conferences that NOW finally agreed to address lesbian issues in 1971 (ibid).

Nevertheless, the heated debates over the relationship between lesbianism and feminism continued to simmer. On one side, distrust of feminism among lesbians was high because NOW—the largest feminist organization in the United States—initially eschewed lesbian issues. On the other side, many heterosexual women were threatened by radical feminists' claim that only heterosexual women who cut their ties with male privilege could be trusted. These polarized positions created one of the most serious splits in the U.S. second wave—the lesbian-versus-straight split.

MENDING THE LESBIAN/STRAIGHT SPLIT IN THE SECOND WAVE

Perhaps the most successful radical feminist to mend the lesbian/straight split within the second wave was Adrienne Rich, who also was renowned for her poetry and prose. Reading 35 provides excerpts from her widely read "Compulsory Heterosexuality and Lesbian Existence" (1980), where Rich tries to unify heterosexual and lesbian women. Her notion of women-identified women entailed a wide spectrum of female-to-female relationships. Although she refers to this as a "**lesbian continuum**," her women-to-women relationships ranged from sexual intimacy with women to mother–daughter relations, sister-to-sister relations, and best friend relations (Rich, [1980] 1994: 51). Thus it included relationships that all women have had or could have with other women.

Although a lesbian herself, Rich argued that *gender is more important than sexual orientation* and urged lesbians to politically ally with heterosexual feminists rather than with gay males. She highlighted the privileges enjoyed by both straight and gay males—such as their higher incomes and earning power. She pointed to "qualitative differences in female and male sexual relationships," citing how males engage in more "anonymous sex," whereas females are more relationship oriented (Rich, [1980] 1994: 53). She criticized gay males for a number of practices such as pedophilia and sadomasochism, as well as "the pronounced ageism in male homosexual standards of sexual attractiveness" (ibid). For Rich, being lesbian is a "profoundly *female* experience" (ibid, her emphasis); to "equate lesbian existence with male homosexuality because each is stigmatized" (Rich, [1980] 1994: 52) erases female reality. Indeed, she argues that "the term *gay* may serve the purpose of blurring the very outlines we need to discern, which are of crucial value for feminism and for the freedom of women as a group" (Rich, [1980] 1994: 53). Many of Rich's views here would be heavily criticized in the 1990s by feminist queer theorists (see Chapter 6). However, in the early 1980s they soothed some of the tensions within the U.S. second wave.

Rich's approach to radical feminism is also distinctly different from that of Firestone. Rather than biological determinism driving her writings, Rich takes a *social constructionist approach to gender and sexuality.* For Rich, heterosexuality is not a natural emotional and sensual inclination, but rather it is "forcibly and subliminally imposed on women" ([1980] 1994: 57). **Compulsory heterosexuality** refers to how heterosexuality has been created and rigidly enforced by various institutional, ideological, and normative means to achieve women's subservience through emotional and erotic loyalty to men. Rich points to how historically many women have resisted heterosexuality at great costs, such as imprisonment, physical torture, psychosurgery, social ostracism, and poverty (ibid). She asks, if heterosexuality is so natural, why do societies need such violent strictures to enforce it?

In *Of Woman Born: Motherhood as Experience and Institution* ([1976] 1977), Rich takes a different approach to childbirth and mothering than Firestone. Rich highlights the trials and tribulations, as well as the sheer joy, entailed in biological gestation, childbirth, nursing, and nurturing children. This warm, emotional, and socially lived approach to motherhood contrasts sharply with Firestone's rather cold, analytical, and impersonal call for women to free themselves from the chains of biological reproduction—a freedom not likely to be relished by many women, including feminists. Rich also distinguishes between motherhood as experience or the "potential relationship" of any women to her powers of reproduction and to her children and motherhood as a "patriarchal institution," which aims at ensuring that this potential remains under male control ([1976] 1977: xv). Rich makes clear that she is critiquing patriarchal institutions and is not calling for an end to women's role in reproduction ([1976] 1977: xvi).

In contrast, earlier radical feminists directed their attacks against men, rather than against patriarchal institutions. The 1969 "Redstockings Manifesto" in Reading 27 takes this latter position. **Redstockings** was a short-lived radical feminist organization that reclaimed the pejorative label "bluestockings" used for educated women in the nineteenth century with the color red to signify their radical politics. Members of this group viewed all men as benefiting from women's oppression and all men as oppressors. They explicitly state that shifting the burden of responsibility from men to institutions is an evasion that excuses men for their oppressive actions. It is men who need to change.

The presence of such distinctly different positions *within* the radical feminist camp is also visible in another battle that split the second wave, the so-called "sex wars."

THE "SEX WARS"

The term "sex wars" has been used to describe heated debates that took place *within* the second wave of U.S. feminism from the late 1970s through the mid-1980s. These debates focused on the implications of various sexual practices for women's liberation. Feminists argued over pornography, sex work, censorship, sadomasochism, and other erotic practices in terms of what constituted nonpatriarchal forms of sex or whether there should even be such a notion (Henry, 2004: 89). The "pro-sex" side of this debate rejected any form of censorship or restrictions on sexual practices in the interests of more openness and freedom. In contrast, their opponents—often referred to as "victim feminists" today—highlighted the violence and danger associated with certain sexual practices and had definite opinions about what constituted patriarchal and nonpatriarchal forms of sex. Although feminists from a wide array of feminist perspectives participated in these debates, the focus below is on the diverse voices of radical feminists. Not only were their voices among the most vocal on *both* sides of this debate, but also radical feminism became fractured from *within* during these internecine battles.

SEX AS A REALM OF PLEASURE

We already have seen above how Firestone took a pro-sex approach in her call for freedom of sexual expression and her vision of pansexuality as integral to women's liberation. Another key voice in the pro-sex chorus was Gayle Rubin, who argued that ending sexual repression was central to ending women's oppression. In her widely read article "Thinking Sex: Notes for a Radical Theory of the Politics of Sexuality" (1984), Rubin attacks all ideologies of sexual repression—whether they come from the left, the right, or from feminists themselves. After studying the hierarchies of sexual values in religious, medical, psychiatric, and popular discourses on sexuality, she argues that there appears to "be a need to draw and maintain an imaginary line between good and bad sex"—a line that stands between "sexual order and chaos" (Rubin, 1984: 282).

Rubin stood steadfast against any ideologies that attempted to describe sex in terms "of sin, disease, neurosis, pathology, decadence, pollution, or the decline and fall of empires" (1984: 278). Convinced that sexual repression was one of the most irrational ways for civilizations to control human behavior, she views sexual permissiveness as in the best interests of all people. In Reading 37 from "Thinking Sex" Rubin discusses how misguided it is for feminists to dictate which types of sex are patriarchal or liberatory. For her, sexual repression is repression regardless of who makes the rules. Her views here have much in common with later queer theory.

SEX AS A REALM OF DANGER

The second-wave radical feminists who delineated certain sexual practices as violent and/or patriarchal were motivated by their desire to end unequal power relations and violence against women. They were not victim feminists in the sense of presenting women as passive or weak victims in the face of sexual violence, as some contemporary feminists have claimed.[2] On the contrary, they named certain sexual practices as violent and patriarchal to illuminate injustices so that women would refuse to be victims. What divided the second wave and caused deep splits within radical feminism were two major issues: (1) whether feminists should legislate that certain sexual practices constituted patriarchal and/or violent forms; and (2) whether feminists should censor violent and degrading images or just concern themselves with violent acts and behaviors.

In the 1980s, the most vocal feminists on the topic of pornography were Andrea Dworkin and Catharine MacKinnon. These radical feminists placed pornography "at the center of a cycle of abuse" and viewed it as a "core constitutive practice" (Dworkin and MacKinnon, 1988: 47) that helped to institutionalize and legitimize gender inequality by creating a social climate in which sexual assault and abuse were tolerated. They argued that pornography was not merely a fantasy, a simulation, or an idea. Rather, it was a concrete discriminatory social practice that institutionalizes the inferiority and subordination of one group to another and they demanded laws to deal with this discrimination (Berger et al., 1991: 37). Reading 38 is an excerpt from "Model Antipornography Civil Rights Ordinance" ([1988] 2013) coauthored by Dworkin and MacKinnon. Although often misinterpreted as advocating censorship of pornography, this ordinance simply allowed civil suits for discrimination to be filed by those who could prove harm through pornography.

Indeed, the responses to pornography were many and varied. One of the bolder responses was by Robin Morgan and her famous statement, "Pornography is the theory, and rape the practice" ([1977] 1992: 88), can be found in Reading 31. Some antipornography feminists, such as Gloria Steinem, the founder of *Ms. Magazine*, made distinctions between "erotica" as images of mutually pleasurable sexual expression between equal and consenting subjects and "pornography" as objectifying women and portraying sex as violent, degrading, or dehumanizing (Steinem, 1980). To provide readers with an example of erotica, Reading 34 "Mandra, II" is a short story from *Little Birds: Erotica* ([1979] 1995) by Anaïs Nin, who has been hailed as one of the finest writers of female erotica in the twentieth century. In turn, to counter the stereotype of radical feminists as austere women who lack humor and police political correctness, we included Gloria Steinem's "If Men Could Menstruate" ([1983] 1995) in Reading 36.

CULTURAL AND SPIRITUAL ECOFEMINISMS

The major ecofeminist perspectives with roots in radical feminism are cultural ecofeminism and spiritual ecofeminism. Both of these forms of ecofeminism are essentialist in that they view women as closer to the natural world than men because of their embodiment as women and potential mothers. Rather than denigrate this relationship between women and nature as patriarchal cultures historically have done, they celebrate it as a source of female power.

Cultural and spiritual ecofeminists focus heavily on symbolic and cultural connections between women and nature. They portray women as oriented toward nurturing and caring and, thereby, as providing a more symbiotic relationship between humans and nature. In contrast, men are portrayed as more rationally oriented and more prone to uncritically use science and technology to dominate women and nature. Whereas patriarchal cultures historically have used the binary polarizations, such as men/women, mind/body, rational/irrational, and culture/nature to argue for the subordination of women, cultural and spiritual ecofeminists invert these dualisms and herald women's traits as sources of their empowerment and ecological sensitivity. Such dualistic thought in cultural ecofeminism is exemplified in Reading 32, "Use," from Susan Griffin's *Woman and Nature: The Roaring inside Her* (1978). Through the use of powerful metaphorical images, Griffin describes man's conquest of women and nature and demonstrates how language and culture buttress patriarchal oppression.

In contrast to the negative, critical approach used by Griffin to expose how patriarchal culture exploits women and the environment, the spiritual ecofeminists employ a positive, functional approach to women and nature. They call for retrieving ancient rituals centered on natural cycles that they link to women's reproductive cycles. Especially popular are rituals from premodern cultures that were matrilineal or that worshipped female deities. Native American traditions have inspired many spiritual ecofeminists, as have Celtic and ancient Greek cultures. Reading 33 from Carol Christ's "Why Women Need the Goddess" (1978) illustrates this perspective.

A RADICAL FEMINIST RESPONSE
TO QUEER THEORY

Given how radical feminism was one of the major second-wave feminist perspectives to draw attention to lesbian issues, it is important to understand how this perspective differs from later queer theory, which arose in the 1990s. In Reading 39, "From Here to Queer: Postmodernism and the Lesbian Menace" ([1996] 2013), Suzanna Walters points out major differences between a radical feminist approach to lesbian theory and politics and the basic assumptions of queer theory. Whereas Walters praises some advances made by queer theorists, overall she views queer theory and politics as well intentioned, but "misguided" and "theoretically suspect" (Walters, [1996] 2013: 554). Not only does she think queer theorists paint an "unfair picture of feminism as rigid, homophobic and sexless" (558), but also she argues that queer theory erases lesbian specificity and the enormous difference that gender makes in people's lives. Thus, it "evacuates the importance of feminism" (558). Walters laments the way that the images/signifiers of gender transcendence are "suspiciously male"—such as the notion of "going fag" or emulating gay male sexual practices proclaimed as empowering by many contemporary queer women (560).[3] She also grieves the way today's sexual "bad girls" rebel as much against their feminist predecessors as against male power (561). She even asks whether their "vision of a genderless nonnormativity is a worthwhile goal" (560).

Walters further argues that deconstructing and destabilizing gender by making its social construction apparent is not the same as overthrowing its power (Walters [1996] 2013: 569). For her, the gender performance motif embraced by queer theorists is vacuous unless it is systematically connected with an understanding of complex sociopolitical realities. Performance tropes alone are ultimately ahistorical, "depoliticized academic exercises" (564). She decries the "relentless narcissism and individualism" of queer theory narratives as an "obsessive focus on self" (564–565), where rather than the personal becoming political, the political becomes personal.

Finally, because queer theorists position themselves on the margins as permanent critics of normativity, Walters fears these theorists "romanticize the margins" (564), ignoring their actual psychic and material costs.

CONCLUSION

This chapter includes writings by a diverse array of radical feminists who often held conflicting positions on a number of issues. Indeed, the common ground shared by radical feminists is a fairly narrow isthmus. Many share the view that women's oppression is the earliest and most fundamental form of oppression that serves as a model for all other forms of oppression. Many also share an essentialist approach to gender that highlights core traits that all women share. This approach has been heavily criticized by other feminists for ignoring differences between women by race, class, and global location (Lorde, 1984; Mohanty, 1984).

Yet their positive contributions were many. Their voices were central in drawing U.S. feminists' attention to compulsory heterosexuality, as well as to how the personal is political. They exposed how oppressions previously treated as personal problems such as rape, incest, domestic violence, and sexual harassment were political issues that should be dealt with collectively. They also empowered women by celebrating women's bodies and culture, as well as women's relationships with other women. Even their essentialist slogans such as "sisterhood is powerful" and "sisterhood is global" did much to build community and collectivity among women of the U.S. second wave.

NOTES

1. Firestone is referring here to the totalitarian, repressive, and bleak social world portrayed in George Orwell's dystopian novel *1984* (Firestone, [1970] 2003: 238).
2. See Wolf ([1993] 1994); Roiphe (1993); and Denfeld (1995).
3. For more on these issues of younger queer women "going fag" and rebelling against their lesbian feminist predecessors see Henry (2004: 115–131).

FROM "MISS FURR AND MISS SKEENE"

Helen Furr had quite a pleasant home. Mrs. Furr was quite a pleasant woman. Mr. Furr was quite a pleasant man. Helen Furr had quite a pleasant voice a voice quite worth cultivating. She did not mind working. She worked to cultivate her voice. She did not find it gay living in the same place where she had always been living. She went to a place where some were cultivating something, voices and other things needing cultivating. She met Georgine Skeene there who was cultivating her voice which some thought was quite a pleasant one. Helen Furr and Georgine Skeene lived together then. Georgine Skeene liked travelling. Helen Furr did not care about travelling, she liked to stay in one place and be gay there. They were together then and travelled to another place and stayed there and were gay there.

They stayed there and were gay there, not very gay there, just gay there. They were both gay there, they were regularly working there both of them cultivating their voices there, they were both gay there. Georgine Skeene was gay there and she was regular, regular in being gay, regular in not being gay, regular in being a gay one who was one not being gay longer than was needed to be one being quite a gay one. They were both gay then there and both working there then.

They were in a way both gay there where there were many cultivating something. They were both regular in being gay there. Helen Furr was gay there, she was gayer and gayer there and really she was just gay there, she was gayer and gayer there, that is to say she found ways of being gay there that she was using in being gay there. She was gay there, not gayer and gayer, just gay there, that is to say she was not gayer by using the things she found there that were gay things, she was gay there, always she was gay there.

They were quite regularly gay there, Helen Furr and Georgine Skeene, they were regularly gay there where they were gay. They were very regularly gay.

To be regularly gay was to do every day the gay thing that they did every day. To be regularly gay was to end every day at the same time after they had been regularly gay. They were regularly gay. They were gay every day. They ended every day in the same way, at the same time, and they had been every day regularly gay . . .

(1922)

Reprinted from *Geography and Plays* by Gertrude Stein. Boston: The Four Seas Company, 1922.

26 • *Joreen (Jo Freeman)*

FROM "THE BITCH MANIFESTO"

Written in the fall of 1968, this paper was first published in *Notes from the Second Year* ed. by Shulamith Firestone and Anne Koedt, 1970. It was later reprinted as a pamphlet by KNOW, Inc., and reprinted in several books.

> ". . . man is defined as a human being and woman is defined as a female. Whenever she tries to behave as a human being she is accused of trying to emulate the male . . ."
>
> —Simone de Beauvoir

BITCH is an organization which does not yet exist. The name is not an acronym. It stands for exactly what it sounds like.

BITCH is composed of Bitches. There are many definitions of a bitch. The most complimentary definition is a female dog. Those definitions of bitches who are also homo-sapiens are rarely as objective. They vary from person to person and depend strongly on how much of a bitch the definer considers herself. However, everyone agrees that a bitch is always a female, dog, or otherwise.

It is also generally agreed that a Bitch is aggressive and therefore unfeminine (ahem). She may be sexy, in which case she becomes a Bitch Goddess, a special case which will not concern us here. But she is never a "true woman." . . .

A true Bitch is self-determined, but the term "bitch" is usually applied with less discrimination. It is a popular derogation to put down uppity women that was created by man and adopted by women. . . .

BITCH does not use this word in the negative sense. A woman should be proud to declare she is a Bitch, because Bitch is Beautiful. It should be an act of affirmation by self and not negation by others. . . .

The most prominent characteristic of all Bitches is that they rudely violate conceptions of proper sex role behavior. They violate them in different ways, but they all violate them. Their attitudes towards themselves and other people, their goal orientations, their personal style, their appearance and way of handling their bodies, all jar people and make them feel uneasy. Sometimes it's conscious and sometimes it's not, but people generally feel uncomfortable around Bitches. They consider them aberrations. They find their style disturbing. So they create a dumping ground for all who they deplore as bitchy and call them frustrated women. Frustrated they may be, but the cause is social not sexual.

What is disturbing about a Bitch is that she is androgynous. She incorporates within herself qualities traditionally defined as "masculine" as well as "feminine." A Bitch is blunt, direct, arrogant, at times egoistic. She has no liking for the indirect, subtle, mysterious ways of the "eternal feminine." She disdains the vicarious life deemed natural to women because she wants to live a life of her own.

Our society has defined humanity as male, and female as something other than male. In this way, females could be human only by living vicariously thru a male. To be able to live, a woman has to agree to serve, honor, and obey a man and what she gets in exchange is at best a shadow life. Bitches refuse to serve, honor or obey anyone. They demand to be fully functioning human beings, not just shadows. They want to be both female and human. This makes them social contradictions. The mere existence of Bitches negates the idea that a woman's reality must come thru her relationship to a man and defies the belief that women are perpetual children who must always be under the guidance of another.

Therefore, if taken seriously, a Bitch is a threat to the social structures which enslave women and the social values which justify keeping them in their place. She is living testimony that woman's oppression does not have to be, and as such raises doubts about the validity of the whole social system. Because she is a threat she is not taken seriously. Instead, she is dismissed as a deviant. Men create a special category for her in which she is accounted at least partially human, but not really a woman. To the extent to which they relate to her as a human being, they refuse to relate to her as a sexual being. Women are even more threatened because they cannot forget she is a woman. They are afraid they will identify with her too closely. She has a freedom and an independence which they envy and challenges them to forsake the security of their chains. Neither men nor women can face the reality of a Bitch because to do so would force them to face the corrupt reality of themselves. She is dangerous. So they dismiss her as a freak.

This is the root of her own oppression as a woman. Bitches are not only oppressed as women, they are oppressed for not being like women. Because she has insisted on being human before being feminine, on being true to herself before kowtowing to social pressures, a Bitch grows up an outsider . . .

Bitches are good examples of how women can be strong enough to survive even the rigid, punitive socialization of our society. As young girls it never quite penetrated their consciousness that women were supposed to be inferior to men in any but the mother/helpmate role. They asserted themselves as children and never really internalized the slave style of wheedling and cajolery which is called feminine. Some Bitches were oblivious to the usual social pressures and some stubbornly resisted them. Some developed a superficial feminine style and some remained tomboys long past the time when such behavior is tolerated. All Bitches refused, in mind and spirit, to conform to the idea that there were limits on what they could be and do. They placed no bounds on their aspirations or their conduct.

For this resistance they were roundly condemned. They were put down, snubbed, sneered at, talked about, laughed at and ostracized. Our society made women into slaves and then condemned them for acting like slaves. It was all done very subtly. Few people were so direct as to say that they did not like Bitches because they did not play the sex role game.

In fact, few were sure why they did not like Bitches. They did not realize that their violation of the reality structure endangered the structure. Somehow, from early childhood on, some girls didn't fit in and were good objects to make fun of. But few people consciously recognized the root of their dislike. The issue was never confronted. If it was talked about at all, it was done with snide remarks behind the young girl's back. Bitches were made to feel that there was something wrong with them; something personally wrong.

Teenage girls are particularly vicious in the scapegoat game. This is the time of life when women are told they must compete the hardest for the spoils (i.e., men) which society allows. They must assert their femininity or see it denied. They are very unsure of themselves and adopt the rigidity that goes with uncertainty. They are hard on their competitors and even harder on those who decline to compete. Those of their peers who do not share their concerns and practice the arts of charming men are excluded from most social groupings. If she didn't know it before, a Bitch learns during these years that she is different.

As she gets older she learns more about why she is different. As Bitches begin to take jobs, or participate in organizations, they are rarely content to sit quietly and do what they are told. A Bitch has a mind of her own and wants to use it. She wants to rise high, be creative, assume responsibility. She knows she is capable and wants to use her capabilities. This is not pleasing to the men she works for, which is not her primary goal.

When she meets the hard brick wall of sex prejudice she is not compliant. She will knock herself out batting her head against the wall because she will not accept her defined role as an auxiliary. Occasionally she crashes her way thru. Or she uses her ingenuity to find a loophole, or creates one. Or she is ten times better than anyone else competing with her. She also accepts less than her due. Like other women her ambitions have often been dulled for she has not totally escaped the badge of inferiority placed upon the "weaker sex" . . . Because she has been put down most of her life, both for being a woman and for not being a true woman, a Bitch will not always recognize that what she has achieved is not attainable by the typical woman . . .

As adults, Bitches may have learned the feminine role, at least the outward style but they are rarely comfortable in it. This is particularly true of those women who are physical Bitches. They want to free their bodies as well as their minds and deplore the effort they must waste confining their physical motions or dressing the role in order not to turn people off. Too, because they violate sex role expectations physically, they are not as free to violate them psychologically or intellectually. A few deviations from the norm can be tolerated but too many are too threatening. It's bad enough not to think like a woman, sound like a woman or do the kinds of things women are supposed to do. To also not look like a woman, move like a woman or act like a woman is to go way beyond the pale. Ours is a rigid society with narrow limits placed on the extent of human diversity. . . .

Bitches were the first women to go to college, the first to break thru the Invisible Bar of the professions, the first social revolutionaries, the first labor leaders, the first to organize other women. Because they were not passive beings and acted on their resentment at being kept down, they dared to do what other women would not. They took the flak and the shit that society dishes out to those who would change it and opened up portions of the world to women that they would otherwise not have known. They have lived on the fringes. And alone or with the support of their sisters they have changed the world we live in.

By definition Bitches are marginal beings in this society. They have no proper place and wouldn't stay in it if they did. They are women but not true women. They are human but they are not male. . . . They may play the feminine game at times, but they know it is a game they are playing. Their major psychological oppression is not a belief that they are inferior but a belief that they are not. Thus, all their

lives they have been told they were freaks. More polite terms were used of course, but the message got thru. Like most women they were taught to hate themselves as well as all women. In different ways and for different reasons perhaps, but the effect was similar. Internalization of a derogatory self-concept always results in a good deal of bitterness and resentment. This anger is usually either turned in on the self—making one an unpleasant person or on other women—reinforcing the social cliches about them. Only with political consciousness is it directed at the source—the social system.

The bulk of this Manifesto has been about Bitches. The remainder will be about BITCH. The organization does not yet exist and perhaps it never can. Bitches are so damned independent and they have learned so well not to trust other women that it will be difficult for them to learn to even trust each other. This is what BITCH must teach them to do. Bitches have to learn to accept themselves as Bitches and to give their sisters the support they need to be creative Bitches. Bitches must learn to be proud of their strength and proud of themselves. They must move away from the isolation which has been their protection and help their younger sisters avoid its perils. They must recognize that women are often less tolerant of other women than are men because they have been taught to view all women as their enemies. And Bitches must form together in a movement to deal with their problems in a political manner. They must organize for their own liberation as all women must organize for theirs. We must be strong, we must be militant, we must be dangerous. We must realize that Bitch is Beautiful and that we have nothing to lose. Nothing whatsoever.

This manifesto was written and revised with the help of several of my sisters, to whom it is dedicated.

(1969)

"REDSTOCKINGS MANIFESTO"

Redstockings, also known as Redstockings of the Women's Liberation Movement, is a radical feminist group that was founded in January 1969. The name is a left-wing play on "Blue Stockings," a pejorative term for intelligent women, combined with "red," for its association with the revolutionary left.

I After centuries of individual and preliminary political struggle, women are uniting to achieve their final liberation from male supremacy. [Redstockings is dedicated to building this unity and winning our freedom.]

II Women are an oppressed class. Our oppression is total, affecting every facet of our lives. We are exploited as sex objects, breeders, domestic servants, and cheap labor. We are considered inferior beings, whose only purpose is to enhance men's lives.] Our humanity is denied. Our prescribed behavior is enforced by the threat of physical violence.

Because we have lived so intimately with our oppressors, in isolation from each other, we have been kept from seeing our personal suffering as a political condition. This creates the illusion that a woman's relationship with her man is a matter of interplay between two unique personalities, and can be worked out individually. In reality, every such relationship is a *class* relationship, and the conflicts between individual men and women are *political* conflicts that can only be solved collectively.

III We identify the agents of our oppression as men. [Male supremacy is the oldest, most basic form of domination.] All other forms of exploitation and oppression (racism, capitalism, imperialism, etc.) are extensions of male supremacy: [men dominate women, a few men dominate the rest.] All power structures throughout history have been male-dominated and male-oriented. Men have controlled all political, economic and cultural institutions and backed up this control with physical force. They have used their power to keep women in an inferior position. *All men* receive economic, sexual, and psychological benefits from male supremacy. *All men* have oppressed women.

IV Attempts have been made to shift the burden of responsibility from men to institutions or to women themselves. We condemn these arguments as evasions. Institutions alone do not oppress; they are merely tools of the oppressor. [To blame Institutions implies that men and women are equally victimized,] obscures the fact that men benefit from the subordination of women, and gives men the excuse that they are forced to be oppressors. On the contrary, any man is free to renounce his superior position, provided that he is willing to be treated like a woman by other men.

We also reject the idea that women consent to or are to blame for their own oppression. Women's submission is not the result of brain-washing, stupidity or mental illness but of continual, daily pressure from men. We do not need to change ourselves, but to change men.

The most slanderous evasion of all is that women can oppress men. The basis for this illusion is the isolation of individual relationships from their political context and the tendency of men to see any legitimate challenge to their privileges as persecution.

The Redstockings Manifesto was issued in New York City on July 7, 1969. It first appeared as a mimeographed flyer, designed for distribution at women's liberation events. Further information about the Manifesto and other materials from the 1960's rebirth years of feminism is available from the Redstockings Women's Liberation Archives for Action at **www.redstockings.org** or PO Box 744 Stuyvesant Station, New York, NY 10009.

V We regard our personal experience, and our feelings about that experience, as the basis for an analysis of our common situation. We cannot rely on existing ideologies as they are all products of male supremacist culture. We question every generalization and accept none that are not confirmed by our experience.

[Our chief task at present is to develop female class consciousness through sharing experience and publicly exposing the sexist foundation of all our institutions.] Consciousness-raising is not "therapy," which implies the existence of individual solutions and falsely assumes that the male–female relationship is purely personal, but the only method by which we can ensure that our program for liberation is based on the concrete realities of our lives.

The first requirement for raising class consciousness is honesty, in private and in public, with ourselves and other women.

VI We identify with all women. We define our best interest as that of the poorest, most brutally exploited woman.

We repudiate all economic, racial, educational or status privileges that divide us from other women. We are determined to recognize and eliminate any prejudices we may hold against other women.

We are committed to achieving internal democracy. We will do whatever is necessary to ensure that every woman in our movement has an equal chance to participate, assume responsibility, and develop her political potential.

VII We call on all our sisters to unite with us in struggle.

We call on all men to give up their male privilege and support women's liberation in the interest of our humanity and their own.

In fighting for our liberation we will always take the side of women against their oppressors. We will not ask what is "revolutionary" or "reformist," only what is good for women.

The time for individual skirmishes has passed. This time we are going all the way.

(July 7, 1969, New York City)

28 • *Shulamith Firestone*

"REVOLUTIONARY DEMANDS"

Women, biologically distinguished from men, are culturally distinguished from "human." Nature produced the fundamental inequality—half the human race must bear and rear the children of all of them—which was later consolidated, institutionalized, in the interests of men. Reproduction of the species cost women dearly, not only emotionally, psychologically, culturally but even in strictly material (physical) terms: before recent methods of contraception, continuous childbirth led to constant "female trouble," early ageing, and death. Women were the slave class that maintained the species in order to free the other half for the business of the world—admittedly often its drudge aspects, but certainly all its creative aspects as well.

This natural division of labour was continued only at great cultural sacrifice: men and women developed only half of themselves. The division of the psyche into male and female to better reinforce the reproductive division was tragic: the hypertrophy in men of rationalism, aggressive drive, the atrophy of their emotional sensitivity, was a physical (war) as well as a cultural disaster. The emotionalism and passivity of women increased their suffering (we cannot speak of them in a symmetrical way, since they were victimized as a class by the division). Sexually men and women were channelled into a highly ordered—time, place, procedure, even dialogue—heterosexuality restricted to the genitals, rather than diffused over the entire physical being.

I submit, then, that the first demand for any alternative system must be:

1. *The freeing of women from the tyranny of reproduction by every means possible, and the diffusion of the child-rearing role to the society as a whole, men as well as women.*

There are many degrees of this. Already we have a (hard-won) acceptance of "family planning," if not contraception for its own sake. Proposals are imminent for day-care centres, perhaps even twenty-four-hour childcare centres staffed by men as well as women. But this, in my opinion, is timid if not entirely worthless as a transition. We're talking about *radical* change. And though indeed it cannot come all at once, radical goals must be kept in sight at all times. Day-care centres buy women off. They ease the immediate pressure without asking why that pressure is on *women.*

At the other extreme there are the more distant solutions based on the potentials of modern embryology, that is, artificial reproduction, possibilities still so frightening that they are seldom discussed seriously. We have seen that the fear is to some extent justified: in the hands of our current society and under the direction of current scientists (few of whom are female or even feminist), any attempted use of technology to "free" anybody is suspect. But we are speculating about post-revolutionary systems, and for the purposes of our discussion we shall assume flexibility and good intentions in those working out the change.

To free women thus from their biology would be to threaten the *social* unit that is organized around biological reproduction and the subjection of women to their biological destiny, the family. Our second demand also will come as a basic contradiction to the family, this time the family as an *economic* unit.

2. *The political autonomy, based on economic independence, of both women and children.*

To achieve this goal would require revolutionary changes in our social and economic structure. That is why we must talk about, in addition to radically new forms of breeding, a cybernetic communism. For without advanced technology, even eliminating capitalism,

we could withstand only a marginal integration of women into the labour force. Margaret Benston has pointed out the importance of distinguishing between the industrial economy based on commodity production, and the pre-industrial economy of the family, production for immediate use: because the work of women is not part of the modern economy, its function as the very basis of that economy is easily overlooked. Talk of drafting women *en masse* into the superstructure economy thus fails to deal with the tremendous amount of labour of the more traditional kind that—prior to full cybernation—still must be done. Who will do it?

Even paying the masses of women for doing this labour, could we swing it—multiply the 99.6 woman-hours per week (conservatively estimated by the Chase Manhattan Bank) by even a minimum hourly wage, times half the (previously slave) population, and you are calculating the overthrow of capitalism—would constitute only a reform in revolutionary feminist terms, for it does not begin to challenge the root division of labour and thus could never eradicate its disastrous psycho-cultural consequences.

As for the independence of children, that is really a pipe dream, realized as yet nowhere in the world. For, in the case of children, too, we are talking about more than a fair integration into the labour force; we are talking about the obsolescence of the labour force itself through cybernation, the radical restructuring of the economy to make "work," i.e., compulsory labour, particularly alienated "wage" labour, no longer necessary.

We have now attacked the family on a double front, challenging that around which it is organized: reproduction of the species by females and its outgrowth, the dependence of women and children. To eliminate these would be enough to destroy the family, which breeds the psychology of power. However, we will break it down still further.

3. *The complete integration of women and children into society.*

All institutions that segregate the sexes, or bar children from adult society, must be destroyed. (Down with school!)

And if male/female–adult/child cultural distinctions are destroyed, we will no longer need the sexual repression that maintains these unequal classes, uncovering for the first time natural sexual freedom. Thus we arrive at:

4. *The sexual freedom of all women and children.* Now they can do whatever they wish to do sexually. There

will no longer be any reason *not* to. Past reasons: full sexuality threatened the continuous reproduction necessary for human survival, and thus, through religion and other cultural institutions, sexuality had to be restricted to reproductive purposes, all non-reproductive sex pleasure considered deviation or worse: the sexual freedom of women would call into question the fatherhood of the child, thus threatening patrimony; child sexuality had to be repressed by means of the incest taboo because it was a threat to the precarious internal balance of the family. These sexual repressions increased proportionately to the degree of cultural exaggeration of the biological family.

But in our new society, humanity could finally revert to its natural polymorphous sexuality—all forms of sexuality would be allowed and indulged. The fully sexuate mind, realized in the past in only a few individuals (survivors), would become universal. Artificial cultural achievement would no longer be the only avenue to sexuate self-realization: one could now realize oneself fully, simply in the process of being and acting.

THREE FAILED EXPERIMENTS

These structural imperatives must form the basis of any more specific radical feminist programme. But our revolutionary demands are likely to meet anything from mild balking ("utopian . . . unrealistic . . . far-fetched . . . too far in the future . . . impossible . . . so, the system stinks, but you haven't got anything better . . .") to hysteria ("inhuman . . . unnatural . . . sick . . . perverted . . . communistic . . . 1984 . . . what? creative motherhood destroyed for babies in glass tubes, monsters made by scientists?, etc."). But we have seen that such defensive reactions on the contrary may signify how close we are hitting: revolutionary feminism is the only radical programme that immediately cracks through to the emotional strata underlying "serious" politics, thus reintegrating the personal with the public, the subjective with the objective, the emotional with the rational—the female principle with the male. . . .

(1970)

29 • *Radicalesbians*

"THE WOMAN IDENTIFIED WOMAN"

Our awareness is due to all women who have struggled and learned in consciousness raising groups, but particularly to gay women whose path has delineated and focused the women's movement on the nature and underlying causes of our oppression.

What is a lesbian? A lesbian is the rage of all women condensed to the point of explosion. She is the woman who, often beginning at an extremely early age, acts in accordance with her inner compulsion to be a more complete and freer human being than her society—perhaps then, but certainly later—cares to allow her. These needs and actions, over a period of years, bring

her into painful conflict with people, situations, the accepted ways of thinking, feeling and behaving, until she is in a state of continual war with everything around her, and usually with her self. She may not be fully conscious of the political implications of what for her began as personal necessity, but on some level she has not been able to accept the limitations and oppression laid on her by the most basic role of her society—the female role. The turmoil she experiences tends to induce guilt proportional to the degree to which she feels she is not meeting social expectations, and/or eventually drives her to question and analyze what the rest of her society more or less accepts. She is forced to

Published by KNOW, Inc., 1970.

evolve her own life pattern, often living much of her life alone, learning usually much earlier than her "straight" (heterosexual) sisters about the essential aloneness of life (which the myth of marriage obscures) and about the reality of illusions. To the extent that she cannot expel the heavy socialization that goes with being female, she can never truly find peace with herself. For she is caught somewhere between accepting society's view of her—in which case she cannot accept herself—and coming to understand what this sexist society has done to her and why it is functional and necessary for it to do so. Those of us who work that through find ourselves on the other side of a tortuous journey through a night that may have been decades long. The perspective gained from that journey, the liberation of self, the inner peace, the real love of self and of all women, is something to be shared with all women—because we are all women.

It should first be understood that lesbianism, like male homosexuality, is a category of behavior possible only in a sexist society characterized by rigid sex roles and dominated by male supremacy. Those sex roles dehumanize women by defining us as a supportive/serving caste *in relation to* the master caste of men, and emotionally cripple men by demanding that they be alienated from their own bodies and emotions in order to perform their economic/political/military functions effectively. Homosexuality is a by-product of a particular way of setting up roles (or approved patterns of behavior) on the basis of sex as such it is an inauthentic (not consonant with "reality") category. In a society in which men do not oppress women, and sexual expression is allowed to follow feelings, the categories of homosexuality and heterosexuality would disappear.

But lesbianism is also different from male homosexuality, and serves a different function in the society. "Dyke" is a different kind of put-down from "faggot," although both imply you are not playing your socially assigned sex role . . . are not therefore a "real woman" or a "real man." The grudging admiration felt for the tomboy, and the queasiness felt around a sissy boy point to the same thing: the contempt in which women—or those who play a female role—are held. And the investment in keeping women in that contemptuous role is very great. Lesbian is the word, the label, the condition that holds women in line. When a woman hears this word tossed her way, she knows she is stepping out of line. She knows that she has crossed the terrible

boundary of her sex role. She recoils, she protests, she reshapes her actions to gain approval. Lesbian is a label invented by the Man to throw at any woman who dares to be his equal, who dares to challenge his prerogatives (including that of all women as part of the exchange medium among men), who dares to assert the primacy of her own needs. To have the label applied to people active in women's liberation is just the most recent instance of a long history; older women will recall that not so long ago, any woman who was successful, independent, not orienting her whole life about a man, would hear this word. For in this sexist society, for a woman to be independent means she *can't be* a woman—she must be a dyke. That in itself should tell us where women are at. It says as clearly as can be said: women and person are contradictory terms. For a lesbian is not considered a "real woman." And yet, in popular thinking, there is really only one essential difference between a lesbian and other women: that of sexual orientation—which is to say, when you strip off all the packaging, you must finally realize that the essence of being a "woman" is to get fucked by men.

"Lesbian" is one of the sexual categories by which men have divided up humanity. While all women are dehumanized as sex objects, as the objects of men they are given certain compensations: identification with his power, his ego, his status, his protection (from other males), feeling like a "real woman," finding social acceptance by adhering to her role, etc. Should a woman confront herself by confronting another woman, there are fewer rationalizations, fewer buffers by which to avoid the stark horror of her dehumanized condition. Herein we find the overriding fear of many women toward being used as a sexual object by a woman, which not only will bring her no male-connected compensations, but also will reveal the void which is woman's real situation. This dehumanization is expressed when a straight woman learns that a sister is a lesbian; she begins to relate to her lesbian sister as her potential sex object, laying a surrogate male role on the lesbian. This reveals her heterosexual conditioning to make herself into an object when sex is potentially involved in a relationship, and it denies the lesbian her full humanity. For women, especially those in the movement, to perceive their lesbian sisters through this male grid of role definitions is to accept this male cultural conditioning and to oppress their sisters much as they themselves have been oppressed by men. Are we going to continue the male classification system of defining all females in sexual relation to some other category of people? Affixing the label lesbian not only to a woman who aspires to be a person, but also to any situation of real love, real solidarity, real primacy among women, is a primary form of divisiveness among women: it is the condition which keeps women within the confines of the feminine role, and it is the debunking/scare term that keeps women from forming any primary attachments, groups, or associations among ourselves.

Women in the movement have in most cases gone to great lengths to avoid discussion and confrontation with the issue of lesbianism. It puts people up-tight. They are hostile, evasive, or try to incorporate it into some "broader issue." They would rather not talk about it. If they have to, they try to dismiss it as a "lavender herring." But it is no side issue. It is absolutely essential to the success and fulfillment of the women's liberation movement that this issue be dealt with. As long as the label "dyke" can be used to frighten a woman into a less militant stand, keep her separate from her sisters, keep her from giving primacy to anything other than men and family—then to that extent she is controlled by the male culture. Until women see in each other the possibility of a primal commitment which includes sexual love, they will be denying themselves the love and value they readily accord to men, thus affirming their second class status. As long as male acceptability is primary—both to individual women and to the movement as a whole—the term lesbian will be used effectively against women. Insofar as women want only more privileges within the system, they do not want to antagonize male power. They instead seek acceptability for women's liberation, and the most crucial aspect of the acceptability is to deny lesbianism—i.e., to deny any fundamental challenge to the basis of the female. It should also be said that some younger, more radical women have honestly begun to discuss lesbianism, but so far it has been primarily as a sexual "alternative" to men. This, however, is still giving primacy to men, both because the idea of relating more completely to women occurs as a negative reaction to men, and because the lesbian relationship is being characterized simply by sex, which is divisive and sexist. On one level, which is both personal and political, women may withdraw emotional and sexual energies from men, and work out various alternatives for those energies in their own lives. On a different political/psychological level, it must be understood that

what is crucial is that women begin disengaging from male-defined response patterns. In the privacy of our own psyches, we must cut those cords to the core. For irrespective of where our love and sexual energies flow, if we are male-identified in our heads, we cannot realize our autonomy as human beings.

But why is it that women have related to and through men? By virtue of having been brought up in a male society, we have internalized the male culture's definition of ourselves. That definition consigns us to sexual and family functions, and excludes us from defining and shaping the terms of our lives. In exchange for our psychic servicing and for performing society's non-profitmaking functions, the man confers on us just one thing: the slave status which makes us legitimate in the eyes of the society in which we live. This is called "femininity" or "being a real woman" in our cultural lingo. We are authentic, legitimate, real to the extent that we are the property of some man whose name we bear. To be a woman who belongs to no man is to be invisible, pathetic, inauthentic, unreal. He confirms his image of us—of what we have to be in order to be acceptable by him—but not our real selves; he confirms our womanhood—as he defines it, in relation to him—but cannot confirm our personhood, our own selves as absolutes. As long as we are dependent on the male culture for this definition, for this approval, we cannot be free.

The consequence of internalizing this role is an enormous reservoir of self-hate. This is not to say the self-hate is recognized or accepted as such; indeed most women would deny it. It may be experienced as discomfort with her role, as feeling empty, as numbness, as restlessness, as a paralyzing anxiety at the center. Alternatively, it may be expressed in shrill defensiveness of the glory and destiny of her role. But it does exist, often beneath the edge of her consciousness, poisoning her existence, keeping her alienated from herself, her own needs, and rendering her a stranger to other women. They try to escape by identifying with the oppressor, living through him, gaining status and identity from his ego, his power, his accomplishments. And by not identifying with other "empty vessels" like themselves. Women resist relating on all levels to other women who will reflect their own oppression, their own secondary status, their own self-hate. For to confront another woman is finally to confront oneself—the self we have gone to such lengths to avoid. And in the mirror we know we cannot really respect and love that which we have been made to be.

As the source of self-hate and the lack of real self are rooted in our male-given identity, we must create a new sense of self. As long as we cling to the idea of "being a woman," we will sense some conflict with that incipient self, that sense of I, that sense of a whole person. It is very difficult to realize and accept that being "feminine" and being a whole person are irreconcilable. Only women can give to each other a new sense of self. That identity we have to develop with reference to ourselves, and not in relation to men. This consciousness is the revolutionary force from which all else will follow, for ours is an organic revolution. For this we must be available and supportive to one another, give our commitment and our love, give the emotional support necessary to sustain this movement. Our energies must flow toward our sisters, not backward toward our oppressors. As long as woman's liberation tries to free women without facing the basic heterosexual structure that binds us in one-to-one relationship with our oppressors, tremendous energies will continue to flow into trying to straighten up each particular relationship with a man, into finding how to get better sex, how to turn his head around—into trying to make the "new man" out of him, in the delusion that this will allow us to be the "new woman." This obviously splits our energies and commitments, leaving us unable to be committed to the construction of the new patterns which will liberate us.

It is the primacy of women relating to women, of women creating a new consciousness of and with each other, which is at the heart of women's liberation, and the basis for the cultural revolution. Together we must find, reinforce, and validate our authentic selves. As we do this, we confirm in each other that struggling, incipient sense of pride and strength, the divisive barriers begin to melt, we feel this growing solidarity with our sisters. We see ourselves as prime, find our centers inside of ourselves. We find receding the sense of alienation, of being cut off, of being behind a locked window, of being unable to get out what we know is inside. We feel a realness, feel at last we are coinciding with ourselves. With that real self, with that consciousness, we begin a revolution to end the imposition of all coercive identifications, and to achieve maximum autonomy in human expression.

(1970)

---

30 • *Charlotte Bunch*

"LESBIANS IN REVOLT"*

The development of lesbian-feminist politics as the basis for the liberation of women is our top priority; this article outlines our present ideas. In our society, which defines all people and institutions for the benefit of the rich, white male, the lesbian is in revolt. In revolt because she defines herself in terms of women and rejects the male definitions of how she should feel, act, look, and live. To be a lesbian is to love oneself, woman, in a culture that denegrates and despises women. The lesbian rejects male sexual/political domination; she defies his world, his social organization, his ideology, and his definition of her as inferior. Lesbianism puts women first while the society declares the male supreme. Lesbianism threatens male supremacy at its core. When politically conscious and organized, it is central to destroying our sexist, racist, capitalist, imperialist system.

---

*"Lesbians in Revolt" first appeared in *The Furies,* vol. 1, no. 1 (January 1972).

LESBIANISM IS A POLITICAL CHOICE

Male society defines lesbianism as a sexual act, which reflects men's limited view of women: they think of us only in terms of sex. They also say lesbians are not real women, so a real woman is one who gets fucked by men. We say that a lesbian is a woman whose sense of self and energies, including sexual energies, center around women—she is woman-identified. The woman-identified-woman commits herself to other women for political, emotional, physical, and economic support. Women are important to her. She is important to herself. Our society demands that commitment from women be reserved for men.

The lesbian, woman-identified-woman, commits herself to women not only as an alternative to oppressive male/female relationships but primarily because she *loves* women. Whether consciously or not, by her actions, the lesbian has recognized that giving support and love to men over women perpetuates the system that oppresses her. If women do not make a commitment to each other, which includes sexual love, we deny ourselves the love and value traditionally given to men. We accept our second-class status. When women do give primary energies to other women, then it is possible to concentrate fully on building a movement for our liberation.

Woman-identified lesbianism is, then, more than a sexual preference; it is a political choice. It is political because relationships between men and women are essentially political: they involve power and dominance. Since the lesbian actively rejects that relationship and chooses women, she defies the established political system.

LESBIANISM, BY ITSELF, IS NOT ENOUGH

Of course, not all lesbians are consciously woman-identified, nor are all committed to finding common solutions to the oppression they suffer as women and lesbians. Being a lesbian is part of challenging male supremacy, but not the end. For the lesbian or heterosexual woman, there is no individual solution to oppression.

The lesbian may think that she is free since she escapes the personal oppression of the individual male/female relationship. But to the society she is still a woman, or worse, a visible lesbian. On the street, at the job, in the schools, she is treated as an inferior and is at the mercy of men's power and whims. (I've never

heard of a rapist who stopped because his victim was a lesbian.) This society hates women who love women, and so, the lesbian, who escapes male dominance in her private home, receives it doubly at the hands of male society; she is harassed, outcast, and shuttled to the bottom. Lesbians must become feminists and fight against woman oppression, just as feminists must become lesbians if they hope to end male supremacy.

U.S. society encourages individual solutions, apolitical attitudes, and reformism to keep us from political revolt and out of power. Men who rule, and male leftists who seek to rule, try to depoliticize sex and the relations between men and women in order to prevent us from acting to end our oppression and challenging their power. As the question of homosexuality has become public, reformists define it as a private question of whom you sleep with in order to sidetrack our understanding of the politics of sex. For the lesbian-feminist, it is not private; it is a political matter of oppression, domination, and power. Reformists offer solutions that make no basic changes in the system that oppresses us, solutions that keep power in the hands of the oppressor. The only way oppressed people end their oppression is by seizing power: people whose rule depends on the subordination of others do not voluntarily stop oppressing others. Our subordination is the basis of male power.

SEXISM IS THE ROOT OF ALL OPPRESSION

The first division of labor, in prehistory, was based on sex: men hunted, women built the villages, took care of children, and farmed. Women collectively controlled the land, language, culture, and the communities. Men were able to conquer women with the weapons that they developed for hunting when it became clear that women were leading a more stable, peaceful, and desirable existence. We do not know exactly how this conquest took place, but it is clear that the original imperialism was male over female: the male claiming the female body and her service as his territory (or property).

Having secured the domination of women, men continued this pattern of suppressing people, now on the basis of tribe, race, and class. Although there have been numerous battles over class, race, and nation during the past three thousand years, none has brought the liberation of women. While these other forms of oppression must be ended, there is no reason to believe that our liberation will come with the smashing of capitalism, racism, or imperialism today. Women will be free only when we concentrate on fighting male supremacy.

Our war against male supremacy does, however, involve attacking the latter-day dominations based on class, race, and nation. As lesbians who are outcasts from every group, it would be suicidal to perpetuate these man-made divisions among ourselves. We have no heterosexual privileges, and when we publicly assert our Lesbianism, those of us who had them lose many of our class and race privileges. Most of our privileges as women are granted to us by our relationships to men (fathers, husbands, boyfriends) whom we now reject. This does not mean that there is no racism or class chauvinism within us, but we must destroy these divisive remnants of privileged behavior among ourselves as the first step toward their destruction in the society. Race, class, and national oppressions come from men, serve ruling-class white male interests, and have no place in a woman-identified revolution.

LESBIANISM IS THE BASIC THREAT TO MALE SUPREMACY

Lesbianism is a threat to the ideological, political, personal, and economic basis of male supremacy. The lesbian threatens the ideology of male supremacy by destroying the lie about female inferiority, weakness, passivity, and by denying women's "innate" need for men. Lesbians literally do not need men, even for procreation.

The lesbian's independence and refusal to support one man undermines the personal power that men exercise over women. Our rejection of heterosexual sex challenges male domination in its most individual and common form. We offer all women something better than submission to personal oppression. We offer the beginning of the end of collective and individual male supremacy. Since men of all races and classes depend on female support and submission for practical tasks and feeling superior, our refusal to submit will force some to examine their sexist behavior, to break down their own destructive privileges over other humans, and to fight against those privileges in other men. They will have to build new selves that do not depend on oppressing women and learn to live in social structures that do not give them power over anyone.

Heterosexuality separates women from each other; it makes women define themselves through men; it

forces women to compete against each other for men and the privilege that comes through men and their social standing. Heterosexual society offers women a few privileges as compensation if they give up their freedom: for example, mothers are "honored," wives or lovers are socially accepted and given some economic and emotional security, a woman gets physical protection on the street when she stays with her man, etc. The privileges give heterosexual women a personal and political stake in maintaining the status quo.

The lesbian receives none of these heterosexual privileges or compensations since she does not accept the male demands on her. She has little vested interest in maintaining the present political system since all of its institutions—church, state, media, health, schools—work to keep her down. If she understands her oppression, she has nothing to gain by supporting white rich male America and much to gain from fighting to change it. She is less prone to accept reformist solutions to women's oppression.

Economics is a crucial part of woman oppression, but our analysis of the relationship between capitalism and sexism is not complete. We know that Marxist economic theory does not sufficiently consider the role of women or lesbians, and we are presently working on this area.

However, as a beginning, some of the ways that lesbians threaten the economic system are clear: in this country, women work for men in order to survive, on the job and in the home. The lesbian rejects this division of labor at its roots; she refuses to be a man's property, to submit to the unpaid labor system of housework and child care. She rejects the nuclear family as the basic unit of production and consumption in capitalist society.

The lesbian is also a threat on the job because she is not the passive/part-time woman worker that capitalism counts on to do boring work and be part of a surplus labor pool. Her identity and economic support do not come through men, so her job is crucial and she cares about job conditions, wages, promotion, and status. Capitalism cannot absorb large numbers of women demanding stable employment, decent salaries, and refusing to accept their traditional job exploitation. We do not understand yet the total effect that this increased job dissatisfaction will have. It is, however, clear that as women become more intent upon taking control of their lives, they will seek more control over their jobs, thus increasing the strains on capitalism and enhancing the power of women to change the economic system.

LESBIANS MUST FORM OUR OWN MOVEMENT TO FIGHT MALE SUPREMACY

Feminist-lesbianism, as the most basic threat to male supremacy, picks up part of the women's liberation analysis of sexism and gives it force and direction. Women's liberation lacks direction now because it has failed to understand the importance of heterosexuality in maintaining male supremacy, and because it has failed to face class and race as real differences in women's behavior and political needs. As long as straight women see lesbianism as a bedroom issue, they hold back the development of politics and strategies that would put an end to male supremacy and they give men an excuse for not dealing with their sexism.

Being a lesbian means ending identification with, allegiance to, dependence on, and support of heterosexuality. It means ending your personal stake in the male world so that you join women, individually and collectively, in the struggle to end your oppression. Lesbianism is the key to liberation and only women who cut their ties to male privilege can be trusted to remain serious in the struggle against male dominance. Those who remain tied to men, individually or in political theory, cannot always put women first. It is not that heterosexual women are evil or do not care about women. It is because the very essence,

definition, and nature of heterosexuality is men first. Every woman has experienced that desolation when her sister puts her man first in the final crunch: heterosexuality demands that she do so. As long as women still benefit from heterosexuality, receive its privileges and security, they will at some point have to betray their sisters, especially lesbian sisters who do not receive those benefits.

Women in women's liberation have understood the importance of having meetings and other events for women only. It has been clear that dealing with men divides us and saps our energies, and that it is not the job of the oppressed to explain our oppression to the oppressor. Women also have seen that collectively, men will not deal with their sexism until they are forced to do so. Yet, many of these same women continue to have primary relationships with men individually and do not understand why lesbians find this oppressive. Lesbians cannot grow politically or personally in a situation which denies the basis of our politics: that lesbianism is political, that heterosexuality is crucial to maintaining male supremacy.

Lesbians must form our own political movement in order to grow. Changes that will have more than token effects on our lives will be led by woman-identified lesbians who understand the nature of our oppression and are therefore in a position to end it.

(1972)

---

31 • *Robin Morgan*

"THEORY AND PRACTICE: PORNOGRAPHY AND RAPE"

. . . Knowing our place is the message of rape—as it was for blacks the message of lynchings. Neither is an act of spontaneity or sexuality—they are both acts of political terrorism, designed consciously *and* unconsciously to keep an entire people in its place by continual reminders. For the attitudes of racism and sexism are twined

together in the knot of rape in such a way as to constitute *the* symbolic expression of the worst in our culture.*

---

*Susan Brownmiller has since demonstrated this point in depth, with courage and clarity, in her book *Against Our Will: Men, Women and Rape* (Simon & Schuster, New York, 1975).

Reprinted by permission of the author from her collection of essays, *The Word of a Woman: Feminist Dispatches* (2nd edition), W. W. Norton, 1992; Copyright 1977 by Robin Morgan.

These "reminders" are perpetrated on victims selected sometimes at random, sometimes with particular reason. So we have the senseless rape murders of children and of seventy-year-old women—whom no one can salaciously claim were enticing the rapist—and we also have the deliberate "lesson-rapes" that feminist students have been prey to on their campuses for the past four years—acts based on the theory that all these frustrated feminists need is a good rape to show 'em the light.

Thus, the woman is rarely unknown to her attacker, nor need the rapist be a stranger to his victim—although goddess help her deal with the more-than-usual scorn of the police if she reports rape by a former jealous boyfriend, or an ex-husband, or her faculty advisor or boss or psychiatrist. Many policemen already delight in asking the victim such sadistic and illegal questions as, "Did you enjoy it?" Consequently, any admission on her part, whether elicited or volunteered, that the rapist was actually an acquaintance seems to invite open season on *her* morals.

But radical feminists see the issue of rape as even more pervasive than these examples. For instance, I would define rape not only as the violation taking place in the dark alley or after breaking into and entering a woman's home. I claim that rape exists any time sexual intercourse occurs when it has not been initiated by the woman out of her own genuine affection and desire. This last qualifier is important because we are familiar with the cigarette commercial of the "Liberated Woman," she who is the nonexistent product of the so-called sexual revolution: a Madison Avenue–spawned male fantasy of what the liberated woman should be—a glamorous lady slavering with lust for his paunchy body. We also know that many women, in responding to this new pressure to be "liberated initiators," have done so *not* out of their own desire but for the same old reasons—fear of losing the guy, fear of being a prude, fear of hurting his fragile feelings, *fear.* So it is vital to emphasize that when we say she must be the initiator (in tone if not in actuality) we mean because *she* wants to be. Anything short of that is, in a radical feminist definition, rape. Because *the pressure is there*, and it need not be a knife blade against the throat; it's in his body language, his threat of sulking, his clenched or trembling hands, his self-deprecating humor or angry put-down or silent self-pity at being rejected. How many millions of times have women had sex "willingly" with men they didn't

want to have sex with? Even men they loved? How many times have women wished just to sleep instead or read or watch "The Late Show"? It must be clear that, under this definition, most of the decently married bedrooms across America are settings for nightly rape.

This normal, corn-fed kind of rape is less shocking if it can be realized and admitted that the act of rape is merely the expression of the standard, "healthy" even encouraged male fantasy in patriarchal culture—that of aggressive sex. And the articulation of that fantasy into a billion-dollar industry is pornography.

Civil libertarians recoil from linking the issues of rape and pornography, dredging out their yellowing statistics from the Scandinavian countries which appear to show that acts of rape decline where pornography is more easily procured. This actually ought to prove the connection. I am not suggesting that censorship should rule the day here—I abhor censorship in any form (although there was a time when I felt it was a justifiable means to an end—which is always the devil's argument behind thought control, isn't it?). I'm aware, too, that a phallocentric culture is more likely to begin its censorship purges with books on pelvic self-examination for women, or books containing lyrical paeans to lesbianism than with *See Him Tear and Kill Her* or similar Spillane-esque titles. Nor do I place much trust in a male-run judiciary, and I am less than reassured by the character of those who would pretend to judge what is fit for the public to read or view. On the contrary, I feel that censorship often boils down to some male judges sitting up on their benches, getting to read a lot of dirty books with one hand. This hardly appears to me to be the solution. Some feminists have suggested that a Cabinet-level woman in charge of Women's Affairs (in itself a controversial idea) might take pornography regulation into her portfolio. Others hark back to the idea of community control. Both approaches give me unease, the first because of the unlikeliness that a Cabinet-level woman appointee these days would have genuine feminist consciousness, or, if she did, have the power and autonomy from the administration to act upon it; the second because communities can be as ignorant and totalitarian in censorship as individual tyrants. A lot of education would have to precede community-controlled regulation to win that proposal my paranoid support. Certainly this is one problem to which simple solutions are just nonexistent, rhetoric to the contrary.

But women seem to be moving on the issue with a different strategy, one that circumvents censorship and instead is aimed at hurting the purveyors themselves, at making the business less lucrative by making the clients less comfortable. In one Southern town, women planned their action with considerable wit; they took up positions on their local porn strip and politely photographed each man as he entered or left the bookstores and movie houses. They used a very obvious camera—the large, newspaper-photographer type—sometimes chasing the man for a block as he fled in chagrin. One group of women who used this tactic deliberately worked with cameras that had no film—scaring and embarrassing the men was their aim. Another group, however, did use film and developed the shots. They then made up Wanted Posters of the men, which they plastered all over town—to the acute humiliation of the porn-purchasers, some of whom turned out to be influential and upstanding citizens of the community. In Seattle women's anti-pornography squads have stink-bombed smut bookstores—and the local papers were filled with approving letters to the editors. In New York three porn movie houses have been fire-bombed.

The massive porn industry grinds on, of course. In a replay of the liberated-woman shill, we are now being sold so-called female-oriented pornography, as if our sexuality were as imitative of patriarchal man's as *Playgirl* is of *Playboy*. It must be frustrating to the pushers of such tacky trash to realize that for most women *Wuthering Heights* is still a *real* turn-on, or that there are quite a few of us who remained loyal to Ashley Wilkes (especially as portrayed by Leslie Howard) and never were fooled by that gross Rhett Butler. Yet pornography today is becoming chic—serious movie houses, which usually run art films, are now cashing in on so-called art-porn. The Mick Jagger/sadism fad, the popularity of transvestite entertainers, and the resurgence of "Camp" all seem to me part of an unmistakable backlash against what feminists have been demanding. It is no coincidence that FBI statistics indicate the incidence of rape *increased 93 percent* in the 1960's. When people refuse to stay in their place, the message must be repeated in a louder tone . . .

. . . So we can admit that pornography is sexist propaganda, no more and no less. [There is no comparison here with genuine erotic art—such as *The Tale of Genji* by Lady Shikibu Murasaki (c. 978–1031 A.D.), the great Japanese novelist of the Heian period.]

Pornography is the theory, and rape the practice. And what a practice. The violation of an individual woman is *the* metaphor for man's forcing himself on whole nations (rape as the crux of war), on nonhuman creatures (rape as the lust behind hunting and related carnage), and on the planet itself (reflected even in our language—carving up "virgin territory," with strip-mining often referred to as a "rape of the land"). Elaine Morgan, in her book *The Descent of Woman* (New York: Stein & Day, 1972), posits that rape was the initial crime, not murder, as the Bible would have it. She builds an interesting scientific argument for her theory. In *The Mothers* (1927; New York: Grosset & Dunlap Universal Library edition, 1963), Robert Briffault puts forward much the same hypothesis for an evolutionary "fall" from the comparable grace of the animal realm; his evidence is anthropological and mythohistoric. In more than one book, Claude Lévi-Strauss has pursued his complex theory of how men use women as the verbs by which they communicate with one another (they themselves are the nouns, of course), rape being the means for communicating defeat to the men of a conquered tribe, so overpowered that they cannot even defend "their" woman from the victors. That theory, too, seems relevant here. The woman may serve as a vehicle for the rapist expressing his rage against a world which gives him pain—because he is poor, or oppressed, or mad, or simply human. Then what of *her*? We have waded in the swamp of compassion for him long enough. It is past time we stopped him.

The conflict is escalating now because we won't cast our glances down any more to avoid seeing the degrading signs and marquees. We won't shuffle past the vulgarity of the sidewalk verbal hassler, who is not harmless but who is broadcasting the rapist's theory and who is backed up by *the threat of the capacity to carry out the practice* itself. We will no longer be guilty about being victims of ghastly violations on our spirits and bodies merely because we are female. Whatever their age and origin, the propaganda and act which transform that most intimate, vulnerable, and tender of physical exchanges into one of conquest and humiliation is surely the worse example patriarchy has to offer women of the way it truly regards us.

(1977)

32 • *Susan Griffin*

"USE"

On the arable land the cultivators will be increasingly mechanized, the management and operation of the machines being the responsibility of one group of workers. Field sizes will have been reshaped and enlarged to make cultivation easier. . . . Weeds will be almost entirely controlled by means of herbicides. . . . Crop varieties bred to meet the needs of mechanized fanning. . . . The crops will be protected against pests and diseases, from seed time to harvest, by insecticides and fungicides.

—Sir William Slater, "Farming as a Science-Based
Industry," *The World in 1984*, vol. 1 (1964)

The very use man makes of woman destroys her most pernicious power: weighed down by maternities, she loses her erotic attraction.

—Simone de Beauvoir, *The Second Sex*

Putting virgin soil under cultivation initiates a breakdown of what may be called the "body" of the soil.

—William A. Albrecht, "Physical, Chemical, Biological Changes
in Soil Community," *Man's Role in Changing the Face of the Earth*

He breaks the wilderness. He clears the land of trees, brush, weed. The land is brought under his control; he has turned waste into a garden. Into her soil he places his plow. He labors. He plants. He sows. By the sweat of his brow, he makes her yield. She opens her broad lap to him. She smiles on him. She prepares him a feast. She gives up her treasures to him. She makes him grow rich. She yields. She conceives. Her lap is fertile. Out of her dark interior, life arises. What she does to his seed is a mystery to him. He counts her yielding as a miracle. He sees her workings as effortless. Whatever she brings forth he calls his own. He has made her conceive. His land is a mother. She smiles on the joys of her children. She feeds him generously. Again and again, in his hunger, he returns to her. Again and again she gives to him. She is his mother. Her powers are a mystery to him. Silently she works miracles for him. Yet, just as silently, she withholds from him. Without reason, she refuses to yield.

She is fickle. She dries up. She is bitter. She scorns him. He is determined he will master her. He will make her produce at will. He will devise ways to plant what he wants in her, to make her yield more to him.

He deciphers the secrets of the soil. (He knows why she brings forth.) He recites the story of the carbon cycle. (He masters the properties of chlorophyll.) He recites the story of the nitrogen cycle. (He brings nitrogen out of the air.) He determines the composition of the soil. (Over and over he can plant the same plot of land with the same crop.) He says that the soil is a lifeless place of storage, he says that the soil is what is tilled by farmers. He says that the land need no longer lie fallow. That what went on in her quietude is no longer a secret, that the ways of the land can be managed. That the farmer can ask whatever he wishes of the land. (He replaces the fungi, bacteria, earthworms, insects, decay.) He names all that is necessary, nitrogen, phosphorus, potassium, and these he says he can make. He increases the weight of kernels of barley with potash; he makes a more mealy potato with nitrate of potash, he makes the color of cabbage bright green with nitrate, he makes onions which live longer with phosphates, he makes the cauliflower head early by withholding nitrogen. His powers continue to grow.

Phosphoric acid, nitrogen fertilizers, ammonium sulfate, white phosphate, potash, iron sulfate, nitrate of soda, superphosphate, calcium cynanamide, calcium oxide, calcium magnesium, zinc sulfate, phenobarbital, amphetamine, magnesium, estrogen, copper sulfate, meprobamate, thalidomide, benzethonium chloride, Valium, hexachlorophene, diethylstilbestrol.

What device she can use to continue she does. She says that the pain is unbearable. *Give me something*, she says. What he gives her she takes into herself without asking why. She says now that the edges of what she sees are blurred. The edges of what she sees, and what she wants, and what she is saying, are blurred. *Give me something*, she says. What he gives her she takes without asking. She says that the first pain is gone, or that she cannot remember it, or that she cannot remember why this began, or what she was like before, or if she will

survive without what he gives her to take, but that she does not know, or cannot remember, why she continues.

He says she cannot continue without him. He says she must have what he gives her. He says also that he protects her from predators. That he gives her dichlorodiphenyltrichloroethane, dihedron, chlorinated naphthalenes, chlordan, parathion, Malathion, selenium, pentachlorophenol, arsenic, sodium arsenite, amitrole. That he has rid her of pests, he says.

And he has devised ways to separate himself from her. He sends machines to do his labor. His working has become as effortless as hers. He accomplishes days of labor with a small motion of his hand. His efforts are more astonishing than hers. No longer praying, no longer imploring, he pronounces words from a distance and his orders are carried out. Even with his back turned to her she yields to him. And in his mind, he imagines that he can conceive without her. In his mind he develops the means to supplant her miracles with his own. In his mind, he no longer relies on her. What he possesses, he says, is his to use and to abandon.

(1978)

---

33 • *Carol P. Christ*

"WHY WOMEN NEED THE GODDESS: PHENOMENOLOGICAL, PSYCHOLOGICAL, AND POLITICAL REFLECTIONS"

. . . The sources for the symbol of the Goddess in contemporary spirituality are traditions of Goddess worship and modern women's experience. The ancient Mediterranean, pre-Christian European, native American, Mesoamerican, Hindu, African, and other traditions are rich sources for Goddess symbolism. But these traditions are filtered through modern women's experiences. Traditions of Goddesses, subordination to Gods, for example, are ignored. Ancient traditions are tapped selectively and eclecticly, but they are not considered

Excerpts from the keynote address at the University of California at Santa Cruz Extension conference "The Great Goddess Re-Emerging," Spring, 1978. The essay appeared in a slightly different form in *Heresies*, Spring, 1978. Reprinted by permission of Carol P. Christ. Notes have been renumbered.

authoritative for modern consciousness. The Goddess symbol has emerged spontaneously in the dreams, fantasies, and thoughts of many women around the country in the past several years. Kirsten Grimstad and Susan Rennie reported that they were surprised to discover widespread interest in spirituality, including the Goddess, among feminists around the country in the summer of 1974.[1] *WomanSpirit* magazine, which published its first issue in 1974 and has contributors from across the United States, has expressed the grass roots nature of the women's spirituality movement. In 1976, a journal, *Lady Unique,* devoted to the Goddess emerged. In 1975, the first women's spirituality conference was held in Boston and attended by 1,800 women. In 1978, a University of Santa Cruz course on the Goddess drew over 500 people. Sources for this essay are these manifestations of the Goddess in modern women's experiences as reported in *WomanSpirit, Lady Unique,* and elsewhere, and as expressed in conversations I have had with women who have been thinking about the Goddess and women's spirituality.

The simplest and most basic meaning of the symbol of Goddess is the acknowledgement of the legitimacy of female power as a beneficent and independent power. A woman who echoes Ntosake Shange's dramatic statement, "I found God in myself and I loved her fiercely," is saying "Female power is strong and creative." She is saying that the divine principle, the saving and sustaining power, is in herself, that she will no longer look to men or male figures as saviors. The strength and independence of female power can be intuited by contemplating ancient and modern images of the Goddess. This meaning of the symbol of Goddess is simple and obvious, and yet it is difficult for many to comprehend. It stands in sharp contrast to the paradigms of female dependence on males that have been predominant in Western religion and culture. . . .

. . . A second important implication of the Goddess symbol for women is the affirmation of the female body and the life cycle expressed in it. Because of women's unique position as menstruants, birthgivers, and those who have traditionally cared for the young and the dying, women's connection to the body, nature, and this world has been obvious. Women were denigrated because they seemed more carnal, fleshy, and earthy than the culture-creating males.[2] The misogynist anti*body* tradition in Western thought is symbolized in the myth of Eve who is traditionally viewed

as a sexual temptress, the epitome of women's carnal nature. This tradition reaches its nadir in the *Malleus Maleficarum* (*The Hammer of Evil-Doing Women*), which states, "All witchcraft stems from carnal lust, which in women is insatiable."[3] The Virgin Mary, the positive female image in Christianity does not contradict Christian denigration of the female body and its powers. The Virgin Mary is revered because she, in her perpetual virginity, transcends the carnal sexuality attributed to most women.

The denigration of the female body is expressed in cultural and religious taboos surrounding menstruation, childbirth, and menopause in women. While menstruation taboos may have originated in a perception of the awesome powers of the female body,[4] they degenerated into a simple perception that there is something "wrong" with female bodily functions. Menstruating women were forbidden to enter the sanctuary in ancient Hebrew and premodern Christian communities. Although only Orthodox Jews still enforce religious taboos against menstruant women, few women in our culture grow up affirming their menstruation as a connection to sacred power. Most women learn that menstruation is a curse and grow up believing that the bloody facts of menstruation are best hidden away. Feminists challenge this attitude to the female body. Judy Chicago's art piece "Menstruation Bathroom" broke these menstrual taboos. In a sterile white bathroom, she exhibited boxes of Tampax and Kotex on an open shelf, and the wastepaper basket was overflowing with bloody tampons and sanitary napkins.[5] Many women who viewed the piece felt relieved to have their "dirty secret" out in the open. . . .

. . . A third important implication of the Goddess symbol for women is the positive valuation of will in a Goddess-centered ritual, especially in Goddess-centered ritual magic and spellcasting in womanspirit and feminist witchcraft circles. The basic notion behind ritual magic and spellcasting is energy as power. Here the Goddess is a center or focus of power and energy; she is the personification of the energy that flows between beings in the natural and human worlds. In Goddess circles, energy is raised by chanting or dancing. According to Starhawk, "Witches conceive of psychic energy as having form and substance that can be perceived and directed by those with a trained awareness. The power generated within the circle is built into a cone form, and at its peak is released—to the Goddess, to reenergize the members of the coven, or to do a specific work such as healing."[6] In ritual magic, the energy raised is directed by willpower. Women who celebrate in Goddess circles believe they can achieve their wills in the world.

The emphasis on the will is important for women, because women traditionally have been taught to devalue their wills, to believe that they cannot achieve their will through their own power, and even to suspect that the assertion of will is evil. Faith Wildung's poem "Waiting," from which I will quote only a short segment, sums up women's sense that their lives are defined not by their own will, but by waiting for others to take the initiative.

Waiting for my breasts to develop
Waiting to wear a bra
Waiting to menstruate

. . .

Waiting for life to begin. Waiting—
Waiting to be somebody

. . .

Waiting to get married
Waiting for my wedding day
Waiting for my wedding night

. . .

Waiting for the end of the day
Waiting for sleep. Waiting . . .[7]

. . . The fourth and final aspect of Goddess symbolism that I will discuss here is the significance of the Goddess for a revaluation of woman's bonds and heritage. As Virginia Woolf has said, "Chloe liked Olivia," a statement about a woman's relation to another woman, is a sentence that rarely occurs in fiction. Men have written the stories, and they have written about women almost exclusively in their relations to men.[8] The celebrations of women's bonds to each other, as

mothers and daughters, as colleagues and coworkers, as sisters, friends, and lovers, is beginning to occur in the new literature and culture created by women in the women's movement. . . .

. . . The symbol of Goddess has much to offer women who are struggling to be rid of the "powerful, pervasive, and long-lasting moods and motivations" of devaluation of female power, denigration of the female body, distrust of female will, and denial of the women's bonds and heritage that have been engendered by patriarchal religion. As women struggle to create a new culture in which women's power, bodies, will, and bonds are celebrated, it seems natural that the Goddess would reemerge as symbol of the newfound beauty, strength, and power of women.

(1978)

NOTES

1. See Susan Rennie and Kirsten Grimstad, "Spiritual Exploration Cross-Country," *Quest* I, no. 4 (1975): 49–51; and *WomanSpirit* magazine.
2. This theory of the origins of the Western dualism is stated by Rosemary Ruether in *New Woman: New Earth* (New York: Seabury Press, 1975), and elsewhere.
3. Heinrich Kramer and Jacob Sprenger (New York: Dover, 1971), p. 47.
4. See Rita M. Gross, "Menstruation and Childbirth as Ritual and Religious Experience in the Religion of the Australian Aborigines," in *The Journal of the American Academy of Religion*, 1977, 45 (4), Supplement 1147–1181.
5. *Through the Flower* (New York: Doubleday & Company, 1975), plate 4, pp. 106–107.
6. Starhawk, "Witchcraft and Women's Culture" in this volume.
7. In Judy Chicago, pp. 213–217.
8. *A Room of One's Own* (New York: Harcourt Brace Jovanovich, 1928), p. 86.

"MANDRA, II"

I am invited one night to the apartment of a young society couple, the H's. It is like being on a boat because it is near the East River and the barges pass while we talk, the river is alive. Miriam is a delight to look at, a Brunhilde, full-breasted, with sparkling hair, a voice that lures you to her. Her husband, Paul, is small and of the race of the imps, not a man but a faun—a lyrical animal, quick and humorous. He thinks I am beautiful. He treats me like an objet d'art. The black butler opens the door. Paul exclaims over me, my Goyaesque hood, the red flower in my hair, and hurries me into the salon to display me. Miriam is sitting cross-legged on a purple satin divan. She is a natural beauty, whereas I, an artificial one, need a setting and warmth to bloom successfully.

Their apartment is full of furnishings I find individually ugly—silver candelabra, tables with nooks for trailing flowers, enormous mulberry satin poufs, rococo objects, things full of chic, collected with snobbish playfulness, as if to say "We can make fun of everything created by fashion, we are above it all."

Everything is touched with aristocratic impudence, through which I can sense the H's fabulous life in Rome, Florence; Miriam's frequent appearances in *Vogue* wearing Chanel dresses; the pompousness of their families; their efforts to be elegantly bohemian; and their obsession with the word that is the key to society—everything must be "amusing."

Miriam calls me into her bedroom to show me a new bathing suit she has bought in Paris. For this, she undresses herself completely, and then takes the long piece of material and begins rolling it around herself like the primitive draping of the Balinese.

Her beauty goes to my head. She undrapes herself, walks naked around the room, and then says, "I wish

I looked like you. You are so exquisite and dainty. I am so big."

"But that's just why I like you, Miriam."

"Oh, your perfume, Mandra."

She pushes her face into my shoulder under my hair and smells my skin.

I place my hand on her shoulder.

"You're the most beautiful woman I've ever seen, Miriam."

Paul is calling out to us, "When are you going to finish talking about clothes in there? I'm bored!"

Miriam replies, "We're coming." And she dresses quickly in slacks. When she comes out Paul says, "And now you're dressed to stay at home, and I want to take you to hear the String Man. He sings the most marvelous songs about a string and finally hangs himself on it."

Miriam says, "Oh, all right. I'll get dressed." And she goes into the bathroom.

I stay behind with Paul, but soon Miriam calls me. "Mandra, come in here and talk to me."

I think, by this time she will be half-dressed, but no, she is standing naked in the bathroom, powdering and fixing her face.

She is as opulent as a burlesque queen. As she stands on her toes to lean towards the mirror and paint her eyelashes more carefully, I am again affected by her body. I come up behind her and watch her.

I feel a little timid. She isn't as inviting as Mary. She is, in fact, sexless, like the women at the beach or at the Turkish bath, who think nothing of their nakedness. I try a light kiss on her shoulder. She smiles at me and says, "I wish Paul were not so irritable. I would have liked to try the bathing suit on you. I would love to see you wearing it." She returns my kiss, on the mouth, taking care not to disturb her lipstick outline. I do not know what to do next. I want to take hold of her. I stay near her.

Then Paul comes into the bathroom without knocking and says, "Miriam, how can you walk around like this? You mustn't mind, Mandra. It is a habit with her. She is possessed with the need to go around without clothes. Get dressed, Miriam."

Miriam goes into her room and slips on a dress, with nothing underneath, then a fox cape, and says, "I'm ready."

In the car she places her hand over mine. Then she draws my hand under the fur, into a pocket of the dress, and I find myself touching her sex. We drive on in the dark.

Miriam says she wants to drive through the park first. She wants air. Paul wants to go directly to the nightclub, but he gives in and we drive through the park, I with my hand on Miriam's sex, fondling it and feeling my own excitement gaining so that I can hardly talk.

Miriam talks, wittily, continuously. I think to myself, "You won't be able to go on talking in a little while." But she does, all the time that I am caressing her in the dark, beneath the satin and the fur. I can feel her moving upwards to my touch, opening her legs a little so I can fit my entire hand between her legs. Then she grows tense under my fingers, stretching herself, and I know she is taking her pleasure. It is contagious. I feel my own orgasm without even being touched.

I am so wet that I am afraid it will show through my dress. And it must show through Miriam's dress, too. We both keep our coats on as we go into the nightclub.

Miriam's eyes are brilliant, deep. Paul leaves us for a while and we go into the ladies' room. This time Miriam kisses my mouth fully, boldly. We arrange ourselves and return to the table.

(1979)

35 • Adrienne Rich

"COMPULSORY HETEROSEXUALITY AND LESBIAN EXISTENCE"

Biologically men have only one innate orientation—a sexual one that draws them to women,—while women have two innate orientations, sexual toward men and reproductive toward their young.[1]

. . . I was a woman terribly vulnerable, critical, using femaleness as a sort of standard or yardstick to measure and discard men. Yes—something like that. I was an Anna who invited defeat from men without ever being conscious of it. (But I am conscious of it. And being conscious of it means I shall leave it all behind me and become—but what?) I was stuck fast in an emotion common to women of our time, that can turn them bitter, or Lesbian, or solitary. Yes, that Anna during that time was . . .[2]

The bias of compulsory heterosexuality, through which lesbian experience is perceived on a scale ranging from deviant to abhorrent, or simply rendered invisible, could be illustrated from many other texts than the two just preceding. The assumption made by Rossi, that women are "innately sexually oriented" toward men, or by Lessing, that the lesbian choice is simply an acting-out of bitterness toward men, are by no means theirs alone; they are widely current in literature and in the social sciences.

I am concerned here with two other matters as well: first, how and why women's choice of women as passionate comrades, life partners, co-workers, lovers, tribe, has

Excerpts from "Compulsory Heterosexuality and Lesbian Existence," from BLOOD, BREAD, AND POETRY: Selected Prose 1979–1985 by Adrienne Rich, 1994. Used by permission of W. W. Norton & Company, Inc. Notes have been renumbered.

been crushed, invalidated, forced into hiding and disguise; and second, the virtual or total neglect of lesbian existence in a wide range of writings, including feminist scholarship. Obviously there is a connection here. I believe that much feminist theory and criticism is stranded on this shoal.

My organizing impulse is the belief that it is not enough for feminist thought that specifically lesbian texts exist. Any theory or cultural/political creation that treats lesbian existence as a marginal or less "natural" phenomenon, as mere "sexual preference," or as the mirror image of either heterosexual or male homosexual relations, is profoundly weakened thereby, whatever its other contributions. Feminist theory can no longer afford merely to voice a toleration of "lesbianism" as an "alternative life-style," or make token allusion to lesbians. A feminist critique of compulsory heterosexual orientation for women is long overdue. In this exploratory paper, I shall try to show why. . . .

II

. . . The assumption that "most women are innately heterosexual" stands as a theoretical and political stumbling block for many women. It remains a tenable assumption, partly because lesbian existence has been written out of history or catalogued under disease; partly because it has been treated as exceptional rather than intrinsic; partly because to acknowledge that for women heterosexuality may not be a "preference" at all but something that has had to be imposed, managed, organized, propagandized, and maintained by force, is an immense step to take if you consider yourself freely and "innately" heterosexual. Yet the failure to examine heterosexuality as an institution is like failing to admit that the economic system called capitalism or the caste system of racism is maintained by a variety of forces, including both physical violence and false consciousness. To take the step of questioning heterosexuality as a "preference" or "choice" for women—and to do the intellectual and emotional work that follows—will call for a special quality of courage in heterosexually identified feminists but I think the rewards will be great: a freeing-up of thinking, the exploring of new paths, the shattering of another great silence, new clarity in personal relationships.

III

I have chosen to use the terms *lesbian existence* and *lesbian continuum* because the word *lesbianism* has a clinical and limiting ring. *Lesbian existence* suggests both the fact of the historical presence of lesbians and our continuing creation of the meaning of that existence. I mean the term *lesbian continuum* to include a range—through each woman's life and throughout history—of woman-identified experience; not simply the fact that a woman has had or consciously desired genital sexual experience with another woman. If we expand it to embrace many more forms of primary intensity between and among women, including the sharing of a rich inner life, the bonding against male tyranny, the giving and receiving of practical and political support; if we can also hear in it such associations as *marriage resistance* and the "haggard" behavior identified by Mary Daly (obsolete meanings: "intractable," "willful," "wanton," and "unchaste" . . . "a woman reluctant to yield to wooing")[3]—we begin to grasp breadths of female history and psychology which have lain out of reach as a consequence of limited, mostly clinical, definitions of "lesbianism."

Lesbian existence comprises both the breaking of a taboo and the rejection of a compulsory way of life. It is also a direct or indirect attack on male right of access to women. But it is more than these, although we may first begin to perceive it as a farm of nay-saying to patriarchy, an act of resistance. It has of course included role playing, self-hatred, breakdown, alcoholism, suicide, and intrawoman violence; we romanticize at our peril what it means to love and act against the grain, and under heavy penalties; and lesbian existence has been lived (unlike, say, Jewish or Catholic existence) without access to any knowledge of a tradition, a continuity, a social underpinning. The destruction of records and memorabilia and letters documenting the realities of lesbian existence must be taken very seriously as a means of keeping heterosexuality compulsory for women, since what has been kept from our knowledge is joy, sensuality, courage, and community, as well as guilt, self-betrayal, and pain.[4]

Lesbians have historically been deprived of a political existence through "inclusion" as female versions of male homosexuality. To equate lesbian existence with male homosexuality because each is stigmatized is to deny and erase female reality once again. To separate those women stigmatized as "homosexual" or "gay" from the complex continuum of female resistance to enslavement, and attach them to a male pattern, is to falsify our history. Part of the history of lesbian existence is, obviously, to be found where lesbians, lacking a coherent female community, have shared a kind of social life and common cause with homosexual men. But this has to be seen against the differences: women's lack of economic and cultural privilege relative to men; qualitative differences in female and male relationships, for example, the prevalence of anonymous sex and the justification of pederasty among male homosexuals, the pronounced ageism in male homosexual standards of sexual attractiveness, etc. In defining and describing lesbian existence I would hope to move toward a dissociation of lesbian from male homosexual values and allegiances. I perceive the lesbian experience as being, like motherhood, a profoundly *female* experience, with particular oppressions, meanings, and potentialities we can not comprehend as long as we simply bracket it with other sexually stigmatized existences. Just as the term "parenting" serves to conceal the particular and significant reality of being a parent who is actually a mother, the term "gay" serves the purpose of blurring the very outlines we need to discern, which are of crucial value for feminism and for the freedom of women as a group.

As the term "lesbian" has been held to limiting, clinical associations in its patriarchal definition, female friendship and comradeship have been set apart from the erotic, thus limiting the erotic itself. But as we deepen and broaden the range of what we define as lesbian existence, as we delineate a lesbian continuum, we begin to discover the erotic in female terms: as that which is unconfined to any single part of the body or solely to the body itself, as an energy not only diffuse but, as Audre Lorde has described it, omnipresent in "the sharing of joy, whether physical, emotional, psychic," and in the sharing of work; as the empowering joy which "makes us less willing to accept powerlessness, or those other supplied states of being which are not native to me, such as resignation, despair, self-effacement, depression, self-denial."[5] In another context, writing of women and work, I quoted the autobiographical passage in which the poet H.D. described how her friend Bryher supported her in persisting with the visionary experience which was to shape her mature work:

. . . I knew that this experience, this writing-on-the-wall before me, could not be shared with anyone except the girl who stood so bravely there beside me. This girl had said without hesitation, "Go on." It was she really who had the detachment and integrity of the Pythoness of Delphi. But it was I, battered and dissociated . . . who was seeing the pictures, and who was reading the writing or granted the inner vision. Or perhaps, in some sense, we were "seeing" it together, for without her, admittedly, I could not have gone on. . . .[6]

If we consider the possibility that all women—from the infant suckling her mother's breast, to the grown woman experiencing orgasmic sensations while suckling her own child, perhaps recalling her mother's milk-smell in her own; to two women, like Virginia Woolf's Chloe and Olivia, who share a laboratory;[7] to the woman dying at ninety, touched and handled by women—exist on a lesbian continuum, we can see ourselves as moving in and out of this continuum, whether we identify ourselves as lesbian or not. It allows us to connect aspects of woman-identification as diverse as the impudent, intimate girl-friendships of eight- or nine-year olds and the banding together of those women of the twelfth and fifteenth centuries known as Beguines who "shared houses, rented to one another, bequeathed houses to their room-mates . . . in cheap subdivided houses in the artisans' area of town," who "practiced Christian virtue on their own, dressing and living simply and not associating with men," who earned their livings as spinners, bakers, nurses, or ran schools for young girls, and who managed—until the Church forced them to disperse—to live independent both of marriage and of conventual restrictions.[8] It allows us to connect these women with the more celebrated "Lesbians" of the women's school around Sappho of the seventh century B.C.; with the secret sororities and economic networks reported among African women; and with the Chinese marriage resistance sisterhoods—communities of women who refused marriage, or who if married often refused to consummate their marriages and soon left their husbands—the only women in China who were not footbound and who, Agnes Smedley tells us, welcomed the births of daughters and organized successful women's strikes in the silk mills.[9] It allows us to connect and compare disparate individual instances of marriage resistance: for example, the type of autonomy claimed by Emily Dickinson, a nineteenth-century white woman genius, with the strategies available to Zora Neale Hurston, a twentieth-century black woman genius. Dickinson never married, had tenuous intellectual friendships with men, lived self-convented in her genteel father's house, and wrote a lifetime of passionate letters to her sister-in-law Sue Gilbert and a smaller group of such letters to her friend Kate Scott Anthon. Hurston married twice but soon left each husband, scrambled her way from Florida to Harlem to Columbia University to Haiti and finally back to Florida, moved in and out of white patronage and poverty, professional success, and failure; her survival relationships were all with women, beginning with her mother. Both of these women in their vastly different circumstances were marriage resisters, committed to their own work and selfhood, and were later characterized as "apolitical." Both were drawn to men of intellectual quality; for both of them women provided the on-going fascination and sustenance of life.

If we think of heterosexuality as the "natural" emotional and sensual inclination for women, lives such as these are seen as deviant, as pathological, or as emotionally and sensually deprived. Or, in more recent and permissive jargon, they are banalized as "life-styles." And the work of such women—whether merely the daily work of individual or collective survival and resistance, or the work of the writer, the activist, the reformer, the anthropologist, or the artist—the work of self-creation—is undervalued, or seen as the bitter fruit of "penis envy," or the sublimation of repressed eroticism, or the meaningless rant of a "manhater." But when we turn the lens of vision and consider the degree to which, and the methods whereby, heterosexual "preference" has actually been imposed on women, not only can we understand differently the meaning of individual lives and work, but we can begin to recognize a central fact of women's history: that women have always resisted male tyranny. A feminism of action, often, though not always, without a theory, has constantly reemerged in every culture and in every period. We can then begin to study women's struggle against powerlessness, women's radical rebellion, not just in male-defined "concrete revolutionary situations"[10] but in all the situations male ideologies have not perceived as revolutionary; for example, the refusal of some women to produce children, aided at great risk by other women; the refusal to produce a higher standard of living and leisure for men (Leghorn and

Parker show how both are part of women's unacknowledged, unpaid, and ununionized economic contribution); that female antiphallic sexuality which, as Andrea Dworkin notes, has been "legendary," which, defined as "frigidity" and "puritanism," has actually been a form of subversion of male power—"an ineffectual rebellion, but . . . rebellion nonetheless."[11] We can no longer have patience with Dinnerstein's view that women have simply collaborated with men in the "sexual arrangements" of history; we begin to observe behavior, both in history and in individual biography, that has hitherto been invisible or misnamed; behavior which often constitutes, given the limits of the counterforce exerted in a given time and place, radical rebellion. And we can connect these rebellions and the necessity for them with the physical passion of woman for woman which is central to lesbian existence: the erotic sensuality which has been, precisely, the most violently erased fact of female experience.

Heterosexuality has been both forcibly and subliminally imposed on women, yet everywhere women have resisted it, often at the cost of physical torture, imprisonment, psychosurgery, social ostracism, and extreme poverty. "Compulsory heterosexuality" was named as one of the "crimes against women" by the Brussels Tribunal on Crimes against Women in 1976. Two pieces of testimony, from women from two very different cultures, suggest the degree to which persecution of lesbians is a global practice here and now. A report from Norway relates:

> A lesbian in Oslo was in a heterosexual marriage that didn't work, so she started taking tranquillizers and ended up at the health sanatorium for treatment and rehabilitation. . . . The moment she said in family group therapy that she believed she was a lesbian, the doctor told her she was not. He knew from "looking into her eyes," he said. She had the eyes of a woman who wanted sexual intercourse with her husband. So she was subjected to so-called "couch therapy." She was put into a comfortably heated room, naked, on a bed, and for an hour her husband was to . . . try to excite her sexually. . . . The idea was that the touching was always to end with sexual intercourse. She felt stronger and stronger aversion. She threw up and sometimes ran out of the room to avoid this "treatment." The more strongly she asserted that she was a lesbian, the more violent the forced heterosexual intercourse became. This

treatment went on for about six months. She escaped from the hospital, but she was brought back. Again she escaped. She has not been there since. In the end she realized that she had been subjected to forcible rape for six months.

(This, surely, is an example of female sexual slavery according to Barry's definition.) And from Mozambique:

> I am condemned to a life of exile because I will not deny that I am a lesbian, that my primary commitments are, and will always be to other women. In the new Mozambique, lesbianism is considered a left-over from colonialism and decadent Western civilization. Lesbians are sent to rehabilitation camps to learn through self-criticism the correct line about themselves. . . . If I am forced to denounce my own love for women, if I therefore denounce myself, I could go back to Mozambique and join forces in the exciting and hard struggles of rebuilding a nation, including the struggle for the emancipation of Mozambiquan women. As it is, I either risk the rehabilitation camps, or remain in exile. . . .[12]

IV

Woman-identification is a source of energy, a potential springhead of female power, violently curtailed and wasted under the institution of heterosexuality. The denial of reality and visibility to women's passion for women, women's choice of women as allies, life companions, and community; the forcing of such relationships into dissimulation and their disintegration under intense pressure have meant an incalculable loss to the power of all women *to change the social relations of the sexes, to liberate ourselves and each other.* The lie of compulsory female heterosexuality today afflicts not just feminist scholarship, but every profession, every reference work, every curriculum, every organizing attempt, every relationship or conversation over which it hovers. It creates, specifically, a profound falseness, hypocrisy, and hysteria in the heterosexual dialogue, for every heterosexual relationship is lived in the queasy strobelight of that lie. However we chose to identify ourselves, however we find ourselves labeled, it flickers across and distorts our lives.[13]

The lie keeps numberless women psychologically trapped, trying to fit mind, spirit, and sexuality into a prescribed script because they cannot look beyond the parameters of the acceptable. It pulls on the energy of such women even as it drains the energy of "closeted" lesbians—the energy exhausted in the double-life.

The lesbian trapped in the "closet," the woman imprisoned in prescriptive ideas of the "normal," share the pain of blocked options, broken connections, lost access to self-definition freely and powerfully assumed.

The lie is many-layered. In Western tradition, one layer—the romantic—asserts that women are inevitably, even if rashly and tragically, drawn to men; that even when that attraction is suicidal (e.g., *Tristan und Isolde*, Kate Chopin's *The Awakening*) it is still an organic imperative. In the tradition of the social sciences it asserts that primary love between the sexes is "normal," that women *need* men as social and economic protectors, for adult sexuality, and for psychological completion; that the heterosexually constituted family is the basic social unit; that women who do not attach their primary intensity to men must be, in functional terms, condemned to an even more devastating outsiderhood than their outsiderhood as women. Small wonder that lesbians are reported to be a more hidden population than male homosexuals. The black lesbian/feminist critic, Lorraine Bethel, writing on Zora Neale Hurston, remarks that for a black woman—already twice an outsider—to choose to assume still another "hated identity" is problematic indeed. Yet the lesbian continuum has been a lifeline for black women both in Africa and the United States.

> Black women have a long tradition of bonding together . . . in a Black/women's community that has been a source of vital survival information, psychic and emotional support for us. We have a distinct Black woman-identified folk culture based on our experiences as Black women in this society; symbols, language and modes of expression that are specific to the realities of our lives. . . . Because Black women were rarely among those Blacks and females who gained access to literary and other acknowledged forms of artistic expression, this Black female bonding and Black woman-identification has often been hidden and unrecorded except in the individual lives of Black women through our own memories of our particular Black female tradition.[14]

Another layer of the lie is the frequently encountered implication that women turn to women out of hatred for men. Profound skepticism, caution, and righteous paranoia about men may indeed be part of any healthy woman's response to the woman-hatred embedded in male-dominated culture, to the forms assumed by "normal" male sexuality, and to *the failure even of "sensitive" or "political" men to perceive or find these troubling.*

Yet woman-hatred is so embedded in culture, so "normal" does it seem, so profoundly is it neglected as a social phenomenon, that many women, even feminists and lesbians, fail to identify it until it takes, in their own lives, some permanently unmistakable and shattering form. Lesbian existence is also represented as mere refuge from male abuses, rather than as an electric and empowering charge between women. I find it interesting that one of the most frequently quoted literary passages on lesbian relationship is that in which Colette's Renée, in *The Vagabond*, describes "the melancholy and touching image of two weak creatures who have perhaps found shelter in each other's arms, there to sleep and weep, safe from man who is often cruel, and there to taste *better than any pleasure, the bitter happiness of feeling themselves akin, frail and forgotten* [emphasis added]."[15] Colette is often considered a lesbian writer; her popular reputation has, I think, much to do with the fact that she writes about lesbian existence as if for a male audience; her earliest "lesbian" novels, the Claudine series, were written under compulsion for her husband and published under both their names. At all events, except for her writings on her mother, Colette is a far less reliable source on lesbian existence than, I would think, Charlotte Brontë, who understood that while women may, indeed must, be one another's allies, mentors, and comforters in the female struggle for survival, there is quite extraneous delight in each other's company and attraction to each others' minds and character, which proceeds from a recognition of each others' strengths.

By the same token, we can say that there is a *nascent* feminist political content in the act of choosing a woman lover or life partner in the face of institutionalized heterosexuality.[16] But for lesbian existence to realize this political content in an ultimately liberating form, the erotic choice must deepen and expand into conscious woman-identification—into lesbian/feminism.

The work that lies ahead, of unearthing and describing what I call here "lesbian existence" is potentially liberating for all women. It is work that must assuredly move beyond the limits of white and middle-class Western women's studies to examine women's lives, work, and groupings within every racial, ethnic, and political structure. There are differences, moreover, between "lesbian existence" and the "lesbian continuum"—differences we can discern even in the movement of our own lives. The lesbian continuum, I suggest, needs delineation in light of the "double-life" of women, not only women self-described as heterosexual but also of self-described lesbians.

We need a far more exhaustive account of the forms the double-life has assumed. Historians need to ask at every point how heterosexuality as institution has been organized and maintained through the female wage scale, the enforcement of middle-class women's "leisure," the glamorization of so-called sexual liberation, the withholding of education from women, the imagery of "high art" and popular culture, the mystification of the "personal" sphere, and much else. We need an economics which comprehends the institution of heterosexuality, with its doubled workload for women and its sexual divisions of labor, as the most idealized of economic relations.

The question inevitably will arise; Are we then to condemn all heterosexual relationships, including those which are least oppressive? I believe this question, though often heartfelt, is the wrong question here. We have been stalled in a maze of false dichotomies which prevents our apprehending the institution as a whole: "good" versus "bad" marriages; "marriage for love" versus arranged marriage; "liberated" sex versus prostitution; heterosexual intercourse versus rape; Liebeschmerz versus humiliation and dependency. Within the institution exist, of course, qualitative differences of experience; but the absence of choice remains the great unacknowledged reality, and in the absence of choice, women will remain dependent upon the chance or luck of particular relationships and will have no collective power to determine the meaning and place of sexuality in their lives. As we address the institution itself, moreover, we begin to perceive a history of female resistance which has never fully understood itself because it has been so fragmented, miscalled, erased. It will require a courageous grasp of the politics and economics, as well as the cultural propaganda, of heterosexuality to carry us beyond individual cases or diversified group situations into the complex kind of overview needed to undo the power men everywhere wield over women, power which has become a model for every other form of exploitation and illegitimate control.

(1980)

NOTES

1. Alice Rossi, "Children and Work in the Lives of Women" (paper delivered at the University of Arizona, Tucson, February 1976).
2. Doris Lessing, *The Golden Notebook* (New York: Bantam Books [1962] 1977), p. 480.
3. Daly. *Gyn/Ecology*, p. 15.

4. "In a hostile world in which women are not supposed to survive except in relation with and in service to men, entire communities of women were simply erased. History tends to bury what it seeks to reject" (Blanche W. Cook," " 'Women Alone Stir My Imagination': Lesbianism and the Cultural Tradition." *Signs: Journal of Women in Culture and Society* 4, no. 4 [Summer 1979]: 719–20). The Lesbian Herstory Archives in New York City is one attempt to preserve contemporary documents on lesbian existence—a project of enormous value and meaning, still pitted against the continuing censorship and obliteration of relationships, networks, communities, in other archives and elsewhere in the culture.

5. Audre Lorde, *Uses of the Erotic: The Erotic as Power*, Out & Out Books Pamphlet no. 3 (New York: Out & Out Books [476 2d Street, Brooklyn, New York 11215], 1979).

6. Adrienne Rich, "Conditions for Work: The Common World of Women," in *On Lies, Secrets and Silence* (p. 209); H. D., *Tribute to Freud* (Oxford: Carcanet Press, 1971), pp. 50–54.

7. Woolf, *A Room of One's Own*, p. 126.

8. Gracia Clark, "The Beguines: A Mediaeval Women's Community," *Quest: A Feminist Quarterly* 1, no. 4 (1975): 73–80.

9. See Denise Paulmé, ed., *Women of Tropical Africa* (Berkeley: University of California Press, 1963), pp. 7, 266–67. Some of these sororities are described as "a kind of defensive syndicate against the male element"—their aims being "to offer concerted resistance to an oppressive patriarchate," "independence in relation to one's husband and with regard to motherhood, mutual aid, satisfaction of personal revenge." See also Audre Lorde, "Scratching the Surface: Some Notes on Barriers to Women and Loving," *Block Scholar* 9, no. 7 (1978): 31–35; Marjorie Topley, "Marriage Resistance in Rural Kwangtung." in *Women in Chinese Society*, ed. M. Wolf and R. Witke (Stanford, Calif.: Stanford University Press, 1978), pp. 67–89; Agnes Smedley, *Portraits of Chinese Women in Revolution*, ed. J. MacKinnon and S. MacKinnon (Old Westbury, N.Y.: Feminist Press, 1976), pp. 103–10.

10. See Rosalind Petchesky, "Dissolving the Hyphen: A Report on Marxist-Feminist Groups 1–5," In *Capitalist Patriarchy and the Case for Socialist Feminism*, ed. Zillah Eisenstein (New York: Monthly Review Press, 1979), p. 387.

11. Andrea Dworkin, *Chains of Iron, Chains of Grief* (Garden City, N.Y.: Doubleday & Co., in press).

12. Russell and van de Ven, pp. 42–43, 56–57.

13. See Russell and van de Ven, p. 40: ". . . few heterosexual women realize their lack of free choice about their sexuality, and few realize how and why compulsory heterosexuality is also a crime against them."

14. Lorraine Bethel. "This Infinity of Conscious Pain" (see unnumbered n. above).

15. Dinnerstein, the most recent writer to quote this passage, adds ominously: "But what has to be added to her account is that these 'women enlaced' are sheltering each other not just from what men want to do to them, but also from what they want to do to each other" (Dinnerstein, p. 103). The fact is, however, that woman-to-woman violence is a minute grain in the universe of male-against-female violence perpetrated and rationalized in every social institution.

16. Conversation with Blanche W. Cook, New York City, March 1979.

36 • *Gloria Steinem*

"IF MEN COULD MENSTRUATE"

Living in India made me understand that a white minority of the world has spent centuries conning us into thinking a white skin makes people superior, even though the only thing it really does is make them more subject to ultraviolet rays and wrinkles.

Reading Freud made me just as skeptical about penis envy. The power of giving birth makes "womb envy" more logical, and an organ as external and unprotected as the penis makes men very vulnerable indeed.

But listening recently to a woman describe the unexpected arrival of her menstrual period (a red stain had spread on her dress as she argued heatedly on the public stage) still made me cringe with embarrassment.

That is, until she explained that, when finally informed in whispers of the obvious event, she had said to the all-male audience, "and you should be *proud* to have a menstruating woman on your stage. It's probably the first real thing that's happened to this group in years!"

Laughter. Relief. She had turned a negative into a positive. Somehow her story merged with India and Freud to make me finally understand the power of positive thinking. Whatever a "superior" group has will be used to justify its superiority, and whatever an "inferior" group has will be used to justify its plight. Black men were given poorly paid jobs because they were said to be "stronger" than white men, while all women were relegated to poorly paid jobs because they were said to be "weaker." As the little boy said when asked if he wanted to be a lawyer like his mother. "Oh no, that's women's work." Logic has nothing to do with oppression.

So what would happen if suddenly, magically, men could menstruate and women could not?

Clearly, menstruation would become an enviable, boast-worthy, masculine event:

Men would brag about how long and how much.

Young boys would talk about it as the envied beginning of manhood. Gifts, religious ceremonies, family dinners, and stag parties would mark the day.

To prevent monthly work loss among the powerful, Congress would fund a National Institute of Dysmenorrhea. Doctors would research little about heart attacks, from which men were hormonally protected, but everything about cramps.

Sanitary supplies would be federally funded and free. Of course, some men would still pay for the prestige of such commercial brands as Paul Newman Tampons, Muhammad Ali's Rope-a-Dope Pads, John Wayne Maxi Pads, and Joe Namath Jock Shields— "For Those Light Bachelor Days."

Statistical surveys would show that men did better in sports and won more Olympic medals during their periods.

Generals, right-wing politicians, and religious fundamentalists would cite menstruation ("*men*-struation") as proof that only men could serve God and country in combat ("You have to give blood to take blood"), occupy high political office ("Can women be properly fierce without a monthly cycle governed by the planet Mars?"), be priests, ministers, God Himself ("He gave this blood for our sins"), or rabbis ("Without a monthly purge of impurities, women are unclean").

Male liberals or radicals, however, would insist that women are equal, just different; and that any woman could join their ranks if only she were willing to recognize the primacy of menstrual rights ("Everything else is a single issue") or self-inflict a major wound every month ("You *must* give blood for the revolution").

Street guys would invent slang ("He's a three-pad man") and "give fives" on the corner with some exchange like, "Man, you lookin' *good!*"

"Yeah, man, I'm on the rag!"

TV shows would treat the subject openly. (*Happy Days:* Richie and Potsie try to convince Fonzie that he is still "The Fonz," though he has missed two periods in a row. *Hill Street Blues:* The whole precinct hits the same cycle.)

So would newspapers. (SUMMER SHARK SCARE THREATENS MENSTRUATING MEN, JUDGE CITES MONTHLIES IN PARDONING RAPIST.) And so would movies. (Newman and Redford in *Blood Brothers!*)

Men would convince women that sex was *more* pleasurable at "that time of the month." Lesbians would be said to fear blood and therefore life itself, though all they needed was a good menstruating man.

Medical schools would limit women's entry ("they might faint at the sight of blood").

Of course, intellectuals would offer the most moral and logical arguments. Without that biological gift for measuring the cycles of the moon and planets, how could a woman master any discipline that demanded a sense of time, space, mathematics—or the ability to measure anything at all? In philosophy and religion, how could women compensate for being disconnected from the rhythm of the universe? Or for their lack of symbolic death and resurrection every month?

Menopause would be celebrated as a positive event, the symbol that men had accumulated enough years of cyclical wisdom to need no more.

Liberal males in every field would try to be kind. The fact that "these people" have no gift for measuring life, the liberals would explain, should be punishment enough.

And how would women be trained to react? One can imagine right-wing women agreeing to all these arguments with a staunch and smiling masochism. ("The ERA would force housewives to wound themselves every month": Phyllis Schlafly. "Your husband's blood is as sacred as that of Jesus—and so sexy, too!": Marabel Morgan.)

Reformers and Queen Bees would adjust their lives to the cycles of the men around them. Feminists would explain endlessly that men, too, needed to be liberated from the false idea of Martian aggressiveness, just as women needed to escape the bonds of "menses-envy." Radical feminists would add that the oppression of the nonmenstrual was the pattern for all other oppressions. ("Vampires were our first freedom fighters!") Cultural feminists would exalt a female bloodless imagery in art and literature. Socialist feminists would insist that, once capitalism and imperialism were overthrown, women would menstruate, too. ("If women aren't yet menstruating in Russia," they would explain, "it's only because true socialism can't exist within capitalist encirclement.")

In short, we would discover, as we should already guess, that logic is in the eye of the logician. (For instance, here's an idea for theorists and logicians: If women are supposed to be less rational and more emotional at the beginning of our menstrual cycle when the female hormone is at its lowest level, then why isn't it logical to say that, in those few days, women behave the most like the way men behave all month long? I leave further improvisations up to you.)

The truth is that, if men could menstruate, the power justifications would go on and on.

If we let them.

(1983)

---

37 • *Gayle Rubin*

"THINKING SEX: NOTES FOR A RADICAL THEORY OF THE POLITICS OF SEXUALITY"

I THE SEX WARS

Asked his advice, Dr. J. Guerin affirmed that, after all other treatments had failed, he had succeeded in curing young girls affected by the vice of onanism by burning the clitoris with a hot iron. . . . I apply the hot point three times to each of the large labia and another on the clitoris. . . . After the first operation, from forty to fifty times a day, the number of voluptuous spasms was reduced to three or four. . . . We believe, then, that in cases similar to those submitted to your consideration, one should not hesitate to resort to the hot iron, and at an early hour, in order to combat clitoral and vaginal onanism in little girls.

Demetrius Zambaco[1]

The time has come to think about sex. To some, sexuality may seem to be an unimportant topic, a frivolous diversion from the more critical problems of poverty, war, disease, racism, famine, or nuclear annihilation. But it is precisely at times such as these, when we live with the possibility of unthinkable destruction, that people are likely to become dangerously crazy about sexuality. Contemporary conflicts over sexual values and erotic conduct have much in common with the religious disputes of earlier centuries. They acquire immense symbolic weight. Disputes over sexual behavior often become the vehicles for displacing social anxieties, and discharging their attendant emotional intensity. Consequently, sexuality should be treated with special respect in times of great social stress.

The realm of sexuality also has its own internal politics, inequities, and modes of oppression. As with other aspects of human behavior, the concrete institutional forms of sexuality at any given time and place are products of human activity. They are imbued with conflicts of interest and political maneuvering, both deliberate and incidental. In that sense, sex is always political. But there are also historical periods in which sexuality is more sharply contested and more overtly politicized. In such periods, the domain of erotic life is, in effect, renegotiated. . . .

VI THE LIMITS OF FEMINISM

We know that in an overwhelmingly large number of cases, sex crime is associated with pornography. We know that sex criminals read it, are clearly influenced by it. I believe that, if we can eliminate the distribution of such items among impressionable children, we shall greatly reduce our frightening sex-crime rate.

J. Edgar Hoover[2]

In the absence of a more articulated radical theory of sex, most progressives have turned to feminism for guidance. But the relationship between feminism and sex is complex. Because sexuality is a nexus of the relationships between genders, much of the oppression of women is borne by, mediated through, and constituted within, sexuality. Feminism has always been vitally interested in sex. But there have been two strains of feminist thought on the subject. One tendency has criticized the restrictions on women's sexual behavior and denounced the high costs imposed on women for being sexually active. This tradition of feminist sexual thought has called for a sexual liberation that would work for women as well as for men. The second tendency has considered sexual liberalization to be inherently a mere extension of male privilege. This tradition resonates with conservative, anti-sexual discourse. With the advent of the anti-pornography movement, it achieved temporary hegemony over feminist analysis.

The anti-pornography movement and its texts have been the most extensive expression of this discourse.[3] In addition, proponents of this viewpoint have condemned virtually every variant of sexual expression as anti-feminist. Within this framework, monogamous lesbianism that occurs within long-term, intimate relationships and which does not involve playing with polarized roles, has replaced married, procreative heterosexuality at the top of the value hierarchy. Heterosexuality has been demoted to somewhere in the middle. Apart from this change, everything else looks more or less familiar. The lower depths are occupied by the usual groups and behaviors: prostitution, transsexuality, sadomasochism, and cross-generational activities.[4] Most gay male conduct, all casual sex, promiscuity, and lesbian behavior that does involve roles or kink or non-monogamy are also censured.[5] Even sexual fantasy during masturbation is denounced as a phallocentric holdover.[6]

This discourse on sexuality is less a sexology than a demonology. It presents most sexual behavior in the worst possible light. Its descriptions of erotic conduct always use the worst available example as if it were representative. It presents the most disgusting pornography, the most exploited forms of prostitution, and the least palatable or most shocking manifestations of sexual variation. This rhetorical tactic consistently misrepresents human sexuality in all its forms. The picture of human sexuality that emerges from this literature is unremittingly ugly.

In addition, this anti-porn rhetoric is a massive exercise in scapegoating. It criticizes non-routine acts of love rather than routine acts of oppression, exploitation, or violence. This demon sexology directs legitimate anger at women's lack of personal safety against innocent individuals, practices, and communities. Anti-porn propaganda often implies that sexism originates within the commercial sex industry and subsequently infects the rest of society. This is sociologically nonsensical. The sex industry is hardly a feminist utopia. It reflects the sexism that exists in the society as a whole. We need to analyze and oppose the manifestations of gender inequality specific to the sex industry. But this is not the same as attempting to wipe out commercial sex.

Similarly, erotic minorities such as sadomasochists and transsexuals are as likely to exhibit sexist attitudes or behavior as any other politically random social grouping. But to claim that they are inherently anti-feminist is sheer fantasy. A good deal of current feminist literature attributes the oppression of women to graphic representations of sex, prostitution, sex education, sadomasochism, male homosexuality, and transsexualism. Whatever happened to the family, religion, education, child-rearing practices, the media, the state, psychiatry, job discrimination, and unequal pay?

Finally, this so-called feminist discourse recreates a very conservative sexual morality. For over a century, battles have been waged over just how much shame, distress, and punishment should be incurred by sexual activity. The conservative tradition has promoted opposition to pornography, prostitution, homosexuality, all erotic variation, sex education, sex research, abortion, and contraception. The opposing, pro-sex tradition has included individuals like Havelock Ellis, Magnus Hirshfeld, Alfred Kinsey, and Victoria Woodhull, as well as the sex education movement, organizations of militant prostitutes and homosexuals, the reproductive rights movement, and organizations such as the Sexual Reform League of the 1960s. This motley collection of sex reformers, sex educators, and sexual militants has mixed records on both sexual and feminist issues. But surely they are closer to the spirit of modern feminism than are moral crusaders, the social purity movement, and anti-vice organizations. Nevertheless, the current feminist sexual demonology generally elevates the anti-vice crusaders to positions of ancestral honor, while condemning the more liberatory tradition as anti-feminist. In an essay that exemplifies some of these trends, Sheila Jeffreys blames Havelock Ellis, Edward Carpenter, Alexandra Kollantai, "believers in the joy of sex of every possible political persuasion," and the 1929 congress of the World League for Sex Reform for making "a great contribution to the defeat of militant feminism."[7]

The anti-pornography movement and its avatars have claimed to speak for all feminism. Fortunately, they do not. Sexual liberation has been and continues to be a feminist goal. The women's movement may have produced some of the most retrogressive sexual thinking this side of the Vatican. But it has also produced an exciting, innovative, and articulate defense of sexual pleasure and erotic justice. This "pro-sex" feminism has been spearheaded by lesbians whose sexuality does not conform to movement standards of purity (primarily lesbian sadomasochists and butch/femme dykes), by unapologetic heterosexuals, and by women who adhere to classic radical feminism rather than to the revisionist celebrations of femininity which have become so common.[8] Although the anti-porn forces have attempted to weed anyone who disagrees with them out of the movement, the fact remains that feminist thought about sex is profoundly polarized.[9]

Whenever there is polarization, there is an unhappy tendency to think the truth lies somewhere in between. Ellen Willis has commented sarcastically that "the feminist bias is that women are equal to men and the male chauvinist bias is that women are inferior. The unbiased view is that the truth lies somewhere in between."[10] The most recent development in the feminist sex wars is the emergence of a "middle" that seeks to evade the dangers of anti-porn fascism, on the one hand, and a supposed "anything goes" libertarianism, on the other.[11] Although it is hard to criticize a position that is not yet fully formed, I want to draw attention to some incipient problems.

The emergent middle is based on a false characterization of the poles of the debate, construing both sides as equally extremist. According to B. Ruby Rich, "the desire for a language of sexuality has led feminists into locations (pornography, sadomasochism) too narrow or overdetermined for a fruitful discussion. Debate has collapsed into a rumble."[12] True, the fights between Women Against Pornography (WAP) and lesbian sadomasochists have resembled gang warfare. But the responsibility for this lies primarily with the anti-porn movement, and its refusal to engage in principled discussion. S/M lesbians have been forced into a struggle to maintain their membership in the movement, and to defend themselves against slander. No major spokeswoman for lesbian S/M has argued for any kind of S/M supremacy, or advocated that everyone should be a sadomasochist. In addition to self-defense, S/M lesbians have called for appreciation for erotic diversity and more open discussion of sexuality.[13] Trying to find a middle course between WAP and Samois is a bit like saying that the truth about homosexuality lies somewhere between the positions of the Moral Majority and those of the gay movement.

In political life, it is all too easy to marginalize radicals, and to attempt to buy acceptance for a moderate position by portraying others as extremists. Liberals have done this for years to communists. Sexual radicals have opened up the sex debates. It is shameful to deny their contribution, misrepresent their positions, and further their stigmatization.

In contrast to cultural feminists, who simply want to purge sexual dissidents, the sexual moderates are willing to defend the rights of erotic non-conformists to political participation. Yet this defense of political rights is linked to an implicit system of ideological condescension. The argument has two major parts. The first is an accusation that sexual dissidents have not paid close enough attention to the meaning, sources, or historical construction of their sexuality. This emphasis on meaning appears to function in much the same way that the question of etiology has functioned in discussions of homosexuality. That is, homosexuality, sadomasochism, prostitution, or boy-love are taken to be mysterious and problematic in some way that more respectable sexualities are not. The search for a cause is a search for something that could change so that these "problematic" eroticisms would simply not occur. Sexual militants have replied to such exercises that although the question of etiology or cause is of intellectual interest, it is not high on the political agenda and that, moreover, the privileging of such questions is itself a regressive political choice.

The second part of the "moderate" position focuses on questions of consent. Sexual radicals of all varieties have demanded the legal and social legitimation of consenting sexual behavior. Feminists have criticized them for ostensibly finessing questions about "the limits of consent" and "structural constraints" on consent.[14] Although there are deep problems with the political discourse of consent, and although there are certainly structural constraints on sexual choice, this criticism has been consistently misapplied in the sex debates. It does not take into account the very specific semantic content that consent has in sex law and sex practice.

As I mentioned earlier, a great deal of sex law does not distinguish between consensual and coercive behavior. Only rape law contains such a distinction. Rape law is based on the assumption, correct in my view, that heterosexual activity may be freely chosen or forcibly coerced. One has the legal right to engage in heterosexual behavior as long as it does not fall under the purview of other statutes and as long as it is agreeable to both parties.

This is not the case for most other sexual acts. Sodomy laws, as I mentioned above, are based on the assumption that the forbidden acts are an "abominable and detestable crime against nature." Criminality is intrinsic to the acts themselves, no matter what the desires of the participants. "Unlike rape, sodomy or an unnatural or perverted sexual act may be committed between two persons both of whom consent, and, regardless of which is the aggressor, both may be prosecuted."[15] Before the consenting adults statute was

passed in California in 1976, lesbian lovers could have been prosecuted for committing oral copulation. If both participants were capable of consent, both were equally guilty.[16]

Adult incest statutes operate in a similar fashion. Contrary to popular mythology, the incest statutes have little to do with protecting children from rape by close relatives. The incest statutes themselves prohibit marriage or sexual intercourse between adults who are closely related. Prosecutions are rare, but two were reported recently. In 1979, a 19-year-old Marine met his 42-year-old mother, from whom he had been separated at birth. The two fell in love and got married. They were charged and found guilty of incest, which under Virginia law carries a maximum ten-year sentence. During their trial, the Marine testified, "I love her very much. I feel that two people who love each other should be able to live together."[17] In another case, a brother and sister who had been raised separately met and decided to get married. They were arrested and pleaded guilty to felony incest in return for probation. A condition of probation was that they not live together as husband and wife. Had they not accepted, they would have faced twenty years in prison.[18]

In a famous S/M case, a man was convicted of aggravated assault for a whipping administered in an S/M scene. There was no complaining victim. The session had been filmed and he was prosecuted on the basis of the film. The man appealed his conviction by arguing that he had been involved in a consensual sexual encounter and had assaulted no one. In rejecting his appeal, the court ruled that one may not consent to an assault or battery "except in a situation involving ordinary physical contact or blows incident to sports such as football, boxing, or wrestling."[19] The court went on to note that the "consent of a person without legal capacity to give consent, such as a child or insane person, is ineffective," and that "It is a matter of common knowledge that a normal person in full possession of his mental faculties does not freely consent to the use, upon himself, of force likely to produce great bodily injury."[20] Therefore, anyone who would consent to a whipping would be presumed *non compos mentis* and legally incapable of consenting. S/M sex generally involves a much lower level of force than the average football game, and results in far fewer injuries than most sports. But the court ruled that football players are sane, whereas masochists are not.

Sodomy laws, adult incest laws, and legal interpretations such as the one above clearly interfere with consensual behavior and impose criminal penalties on it. Within the law, consent is a privilege enjoyed only by those who engage in the highest-status sexual behavior. Those who enjoy low-status sexual behavior do not have the legal right to engage in it. In addition, economic sanctions, family pressures, erotic stigma, social discrimination, negative ideology, and the paucity of information about erotic behavior, all serve to make it difficult for people to make unconventional sexual choices. There certainly are structural constraints that impede free sexual choice, but they hardly operate to coerce anyone into being a pervert. On the contrary, they operate to coerce everyone toward normality.

The "brainwash theory" explains erotic diversity by assuming that some sexual acts are so disgusting that no one would willingly perform them. Therefore, the reasoning goes, anyone who does so must have been forced or fooled. Even constructivist sexual theory has been pressed into the service of explaining away why otherwise rational individuals might engage in variant sexual behavior. Another position that is not yet fully formed uses the ideas of Foucault and Weeks to imply that the "perversions" are an especially unsavory or problematic aspect of the construction of modern sexuality.[21] This is yet another version of the notion that sexual dissidents are victims of the subtle machinations of the social system. Weeks and Foucault would not accept such an interpretation, since they consider all sexuality to be constructed, the conventional no less than the deviant.

Psychology is the last resort of those who refuse to acknowledge that sexual dissidents are as conscious and free as any other group of sexual actors. If deviants are not responding to the manipulations of the social system, then perhaps the source of their incomprehensible choices can be found in a bad childhood, unsuccessful socialization, or inadequate identity formation. In her essay on erotic domination, Jessica Benjamin draws upon psychoanalysis and philosophy to explain why what she calls sadomasochism "is alienated, distorted, unsatisfactory, numb, purposeless, and an attempt to "relieve an original effort at differentiation that failed."[22] This essay substitutes a psychophilosophical inferiority for the more usual means of devaluing dissident eroticism. One reviewer has already construed Benjamin's argument as showing that

sadomasochism is merely an "obsessive replay of the infant power struggle."[23]

The position which defends the political rights of perverts but which seeks to understand their "alienated" sexuality is certainly preferable to the WAP-style bloodbaths. But for the most part, the sexual moderates have not confronted their discomfort with erotic choices that differ from their own. Erotic chauvinism cannot be redeemed by tarting it up in Marxist drag, sophisticated constructivist theory, or retro-psychobabble.

Whichever feminist position on sexuality—right, left, or center—eventually attains dominance, the existence of such a rich discussion is evidence that the feminist movement will always be a source of interesting thought about sex. Nevertheless, I want to challenge the assumption that feminism is or should be the privileged site of a theory of sexuality. Feminism is the theory of gender oppression. To automatically assume that this makes it the theory of sexual oppression is to fail to distinguish between gender, on the one hand, and erotic desire, on the other.

In the English language, the word "sex" has two very different meanings. It means gender and gender identity, as in "the female sex" or "the male sex." But sex also refers to sexual activity, lust, intercourse, and arousal, as in "to have sex." This semantic merging reflects a cultural assumption that sexuality is reducible to sexual intercourse and that it is a function of the relations between women and men. The cultural fusion of gender with sexuality has given rise to the idea that a theory of sexuality may be derived directly out of a theory of gender.

In an earlier essay, "The Traffic in Women," I used the concept of a sex/gender system, defined as a "set of arrangements by which a society transforms biological sexuality into products of human activity."[24] I went on to argue that "Sex as we know it—gender identity, sexual desire and fantasy, concepts of childhood—is itself a social product."[25] In that essay, I did not distinguish between lust and gender, treating both as modalities of the same underlying social process.

"The Traffic in Women" was inspired by the literature on kin-based systems of social organization. It appeared to me at the time that gender and desire were systemically intertwined in such social formations. This may or may not be an accurate assessment of the relationship between sex and gender in tribal organizations. But it is surely not an adequate formulation for sexuality in Western industrial societies. As Foucault has pointed out, a system of sexuality has emerged out of earlier kinship forms and has acquired significant autonomy.

Particularly from the eighteenth century onward, Western societies created and deployed a new apparatus which was superimposed on the previous one, and which, without completely supplanting the latter, helped to reduce its importance. I am speaking of the deployment of sexuality. . . . For the first [kinship], what is pertinent is the link between partners and definite statutes; the second [sexuality] is concerned with the sensations of the body, the quality of pleasures, and the nature of impressions.[26]

The development of this sexual system has taken place in the context of gender relations. Part of the modern ideology of sex is that lust is the province of men, purity that of women. Women have been to some extent excluded from the modern sexual system. It is no accident that pornography and the perversions have been considered part of the male domain. In the sex industry, women have been excluded from most production and consumption, and allowed to participate primarily as workers. In order to participate in the "perversions," women have had to overcome serious limitations on their social mobility, their economic resources, and their sexual freedoms. Gender affects the operation of the sexual system, and the sexual system has had gender-specific manifestations. But although sex and gender are related, they are not the same thing, and they form the basis of two distinct arenas of social practice.

In contrast to my perspective in "The Traffic in Women," I am now arguing that it is essential to separate gender and sexuality analytically to more accurately reflect their separate social existence. This goes against the grain of much contemporary feminist thought, which treats sexuality as a derivation of gender. For instance, lesbian feminist ideology has mostly analyzed the oppression of lesbians in terms of the oppression of women. However, lesbians are also oppressed as queers and perverts, by the operation of sexual, not gender, stratification. Although it pains many lesbians to think about it, the fact is that lesbians have shared many of the sociological features and suffered from many of the same social penalties as have gay men, sadomasochists, transvestites, and prostitutes.

Catherine MacKinnon has made the most explicit theoretical attempt to subsume sexuality under feminist thought. According to MacKinnon, "Sexuality is to feminism what work is to marxism . . . the molding, direction, and expression of sexuality organizes society into two sexes, women and men."[27] This analytic strategy in turn rests on a decision to "use sex and gender relatively interchangeably."[28] It is this definitional fusion that I want to challenge.

There is an instructive analogy in the history of the differentiation of contemporary feminist thought from Marxism. Marxism is probably the most supple and powerful conceptual system extant for analyzing social inequality. But attempts to make Marxism the sole explanatory system for all social inequalities have been dismal exercises. Marxism is most successful in the areas of social life for which it was originally developed— class relations under capitalism.

In the early days of the contemporary women's movement, a theoretical conflict took place over the applicability of Marxism to gender stratification. Since Marxist theory is relatively powerful, it does in fact detect important and interesting aspects of gender oppression. It works best for those issues of gender most closely related to issues of class and the organization of labor. The issues more specific to the social structure of gender were not amenable to Marxist analysis.

The relationship between feminism and a radical theory of sexual oppression is similar. Feminist conceptual tools were developed to detect and analyze gender-based hierarchies. To the extent that these overlap with erotic stratifications, feminist theory has some explanatory power. But as issues become less those of gender and more those of sexuality, feminist analysis becomes irrelevant and often misleading. Feminist thought simply lacks angles of vision which can encompass the social organization of sexuality. The criteria of relevance in feminist thought do not allow it to see or assess critical power relations in the area of sexuality.

In the long run, feminism's critique of gender hierarchy must be incorporated into a radical theory of sex, and the critique of sexual oppression should enrich feminism. But an autonomous theory and politics specific to sexuality must be developed.

It is a mistake to substitute feminism for Marxism as the last word in social theory. Feminism is no more capable than Marxism of being the ultimate and complete account of all social inequality. Nor is feminism the residual theory which can take care of everything to which Marx did not attend. These critical tools were fashioned to handle very specific areas of social activity. Other areas of social life, their forms of power, and their characteristic modes of oppression, need their own conceptual implements. In this essay, I have argued for theoretical as well as sexual pluralism.

VII CONCLUSION

. . . these pleasures which we lightly call physical . . .

Colette[29]

Like gender, sexuality is political. It is organized into systems of power, which reward and encourage some individuals and activities, while punishing and suppressing others. Like the capitalist organization of labor and its distribution of rewards and powers, the modern sexual system has been the object of political struggle since it emerged and as it has evolved. But if the disputes between labor and capital are mystified, sexual conflicts are completely camouflaged.

The legislative restructuring that took place at the end of the nineteenth century and in the early decades of the twentieth was a refracted response to the emergence of the modern erotic system. During that period, new erotic communities formed. It became possible to be a male homosexual or a lesbian in a way it had not been previously. Mass-produced erotica became available, and the possibilities for sexual commerce expanded. The first homosexual rights organizations were formed, and the first analyses of sexual oppression were articulated.[30]

The repression of the 1950s was in part a backlash to the expansion of sexual communities and possibilities which took place during World War II.[31] During the 1950s, gay rights organizations were established, the Kinsey reports were published, and lesbian literature flourished. The 1950s were a formative as well as a repressive era.

The current right-wing sexual counter-offensive is in part a reaction to the sexual liberalization of the 1960s and early 1970s. Moreover, it has brought about a unified and self-conscious coalition of sexual radicals. In one sense, what is now occurring is the emergence of a new sexual movement, aware of new issues and seeking a new theoretical basis. The sex wars out on the streets have been partly responsible for provoking a new intellectual focus on sexuality. The sexual system is shifting once again, and we are seeing many symptoms of its change.

In Western culture, sex is taken all too seriously. A person is not considered immoral, is not sent to prison, and is not expelled from her or his family, for enjoying spicy cuisine. But an individual may go through all this and more for enjoying shoe leather. Ultimately, of what possible social significance is it if a person likes to masturbate over a shoe? It may even be non-consensual, but since we do not ask permission of our shoes to wear them, it hardly seems necessary to obtain dispensation to come on them.

If sex is taken too seriously, sexual persecution is not taken seriously enough. There is systematic mistreatment of individuals and communities on the basis of erotic taste or behavior. There are serious penalties for belonging to the various sexual occupational castes. The sexuality of the young is denied, adult sexuality is often treated like a variety of nuclear waste, and the graphic representation of sex takes place in a mire of legal and social circumlocution. Specific populations bear the brunt of the current system of erotic power, but their persecution upholds a system that affects everyone.

The 1980s have already been a time of great sexual suffering. They have also been a time of ferment and new possibility. It is up to all of us to try to prevent more barbarism and to encourage erotic creativity. Those who consider themselves progressive need to examine their preconceptions, update their sexual educations, and acquaint themselves with the existence and operation of sexual hierarchy. It is time to recognize the political dimensions of erotic life.

A NOTE ON DEFINITIONS

Throughout this essay, I use terms such as homosexual, sex worker, and pervert. I use "homosexual" to refer to both women and men. If I want to be more specific, I use terms such as "lesbian" or "gay male." "Sex worker" is intended to be more inclusive than "prostitute," in order to encompass the many jobs of the sex industry. Sex worker includes erotic dancers, strippers, porn models, nude women who will talk to a customer via telephone hook-up and can be seen but not touched, phone partners, and the various other employees of sex businesses such as receptionists, janitors, and barkers. Obviously, it also includes prostitutes, hustlers, and "male models." I use the term "pervert" as a shorthand for all the stigmatized sexual orientations. It used to cover male and female homosexuality as well but as these become less disreputable, the term has increasingly referred to the other "deviations." Terms such as "pervert" and "deviant" have, in general use, a connotation of disapproval, disgust, and dislike. I am using these terms in a denotative fashion, and do not intend them to convey any disapproval on my part.

(1984)

NOTES

1. Demetrius Zambaco, "Onanism and Nervous Disorders in Two Little Girls," in François Peraldi (ed.), *Polysexuality, Semiotext(e)*, vol. IV, no. 1, 1981, pp. 31, 36.

2. Cited in H. Montgomery Hyde, *A History of Pornography*, New York. Dell, 1965, p. 31.

3. See for example Laura Lederer (ed.), *Take Back the Night*, New York, William Morrow, 1980; Andrea Dworkin, *Pornography*, New York, Perigee, 1981. The *Newspage* of San Francisco's Women Against Violence in Pornography and Media and the *Newsreport* of New York Women Against Pornography are excellent sources.

4. Kathleen Barry, *Female Sexual Slavery*, Englewood Cliffs, New Jersey, Prentice-Hall, 1979; Janice Raymond, *The Transsexual Empire*, Boston, Beacon, 1979; Kathleen Barry, "Sadomasochism: The New Backlash to Feminism," *Trivia*, no. 1, fall 1982; Robin Ruth Linden, Darlene R. Pagano, Diana E. H. Russell, and Susan Leigh Starr (eds), *Against Sadomasochism*, East Palo Alto, CA, Frog in the Well, 1982; and Florence Rush, *The Best Kept Secret*, New York, McGraw–Hill, 1980.

5. Sally Gearhart. "An Open Letter to the Voters in District 5 and San Francisco's Gay Community," 1979; Adrienne Rich, *On Lies, Secrets, and Silence*, New York, W. W. Norton, 1979, p. 225. ("On the other hand, there is homosexual patriarchal culture, a culture created by homosexual men, reflecting such male stereotypes as dominance and submission as modes of relationship, and the separation of sex from emotional involvement—a culture tainted by profound hatred for women. The male 'gay' culture has offered lesbians the imitation role-stereotypes of 'butch' and 'femme,' 'active' and 'passive,' cruising, sado-masochism, and the violent, self-destructive world of 'gay' bars."); Judith Pasternak, "The Strangest Bedfellows: Lesbian Feminism and the Sexual Revolution," *WomanNews*, October 1983; Adrienne Rich, "Compulsory Heterosexuality and Lesbian Existence," in Ann Snitow, Christine Stansell, and Sharon Thompson (eds). *Powers of Desire: The Politics of Sexuality*, New York, Monthly Review Press, 1983.

6. Julia Penlope, op. cit.

7. Sheila Jeffreys, "The Spinster and Her Enemies: Sexuality and the Last Wave of Feminism," *Scarlet Woman*, no. 13, part 2, July 1981, p. 26; a further elaboration of this tendency can be found in Judith Pasternak, op. cit.

8. Pat Califia, "Feminism vs. Sex: A New Conservative Wave," *Advocate*, February 21, 1980; Pat Califia, "Among Us, Against Us—The New Puritans," *Advocate*, April 17, 1980; Califia, "The Great Kiddy Porn Scare of '77 and Its Aftermath," op. cit.; Califia, "A Thorny Issue Splits a Movement," op. cit.; Pat Califia, *Sapphistry*, Tallahassee, Florida, Naiad, 1980; Pat Califia, "What Is Gay Liberation," *Advocate*, June 25, 1981; Pat Califia, "Feminism and Sadomasochism," *Co-Evolution Quarterly*, no. 33, spring 1981; Pat Califia, "Response to Dorchen Leidholdt," *New Women's Times*, October 1982; Pat Califia, "Public Sex," *Advocate*, September 30, 1982; Pat Califia, "Doing It Together: Gay Men, Lesbians, and Sex," *Advocate*, July 7, 1983; Pat Califia, "Gender-Bending," *Advocate*, September 15, 1983; Pat Califia, "The Sex Industry," *Advocate*, October 13, 1983; Deirdre English, Amber Hollibaugh, and Gayle Rubin, "Talking Sex," *Socialist Review*, July–August 1981; "Sex Issue," *Heresies*, no. 12, 1981; Amber Hollibaugh, "The Erotophobic Voice of Women: Building a Movement for the Nineteenth Century," *New York Native*, September 26–October 9, 1983; Maxine Holz, "Porn: Turn On or Put Down, Some Thoughts on Sexuality," *Processed World*, no. 7, spring 1983; Barbara O'Dair, "Sex, Love, and Desire: Feminists Struggle Over the Portrayal of Sex," *Alternative Media*, spring 1983; Lisa Orlando, "Bad Girls and 'Good' Politics," *Village Voice*, Literary Supplement, December 1982; Joanna Russ, "Being Against Pornography," *Thirteenth Moon*, vol. VI, nos 1 and 2, 1982; Samois, *What Color Is Your Handkerchief*, Berkeley, Samois, 1979; Samois, *Coming to Power*, Boston, Alyson, 1982; Deborah Sundahl, "Stripping For a Living," *Advocate*, October 13, 1983; Nancy Wechsler. "Interview with Pat Califia and Gayle Rubin," part I, *Gay Community News*, Book Review, July 18, 1981, and part II, *Gay Community News*, August 15, 1981; Ellen Willis, *Beginning to See the Light*, New York, Knopf, 1981; for an excellent overview of the history of the ideological shifts in feminism which have affected the sex debates, see Alice Echols, "Cultural Feminism: Feminist Capitalism and the Anti-Pornography Movement," *Social Text*, no. 7, spring and summer 1983.

9. Lisa Orlando, "Lust at Last! Spandex Invades the Academy," *Gay Community News*, May 15, 1982; Ellen Willis. "Who Is a Feminist? An Open Letter to Robin Morgan," *Village Voice*, Literary Supplement, December 1982.

10. Ellen Willis, *Beginning to See the Light*, op. cit., p. 146. I am indebted to Jeanne Bergman for calling my attention to this quote.

11. See, for example, Jessica Benjamin, "Master and Slave: The Fantasy of Erotic Domination," in Snitow et al.,

op. cit., p. 297; and B. Ruby Rich, review of *Powers of Desire. In These Times*, November 16–22, 1983.

12. B. Ruby Rich, op. cit., p. 76.

13. Samois, *What Color Is Your Handkerchief*, op. cit.; Samois, *Coming To Power*, op. cit.; Pat Califia, "Feminism and Sadomasochism," op. cit.; Pat Califia, *Sapphistry*, op. cit.

14. Lisa Orlando, "Power Plays: Coming To Terms With Lesbian S/M," *Village Voice*, July 26, 1983; Elizabeth Wilson, *"The Context of 'Between Pleasure and Danger': The Barnard Conference on Sexuality," Feminist Review*, no. 13, spring 1983, especially pp. 35–41.

15. *Taylor v. State*, 214 Md. 156, 165, 133 A. 2d 414, 418. This quote is from a dissenting opinion, but it is a statement of prevailing law.

16. Bessera, Jewel, Matthew, and Gatov, op. cit., pp. 163–5. See note 55 above.

17. "Marine and Mom Guilty of Incest," *San Francisco Chronicle*, November 16, 1979, p. 16.

18. Norton, op. cit., p. 18.

19. *People v. Samuels*, 250 Cal. App. 2d 501, 513, 58 Cal. Rptr. 439, 447 (1967).

20. *People v. Samuels*, 250 Cal. App. 2d. at 513–514, 58 Cal. Rptr. at 447.

21. Mariana Valverde, "Feminism Meets Fist-Fucking: Getting Lost in Lesbian S & M," *Body Politic*, February 1980; Wilson, op. cit., p. 38.

22. Benjamin, op. cit. p. 292, but see also pp. 286, 291–7.

23. Barbara Ehrenreich, "What Is This Thing Called Sex," *Nation*, September 24, 1983, p. 247.

24. Gayle Rubin, "The Traffic in Women," in Rayna R. Reiter (ed.), *Toward an Anthropology of Women*, New York, Monthly Review Press, 1975, p. 159.

25. Rubin, "The Traffic in Women," op. cit., p. 166.

26. Foucault, op. cit., p. 106.

27. Catherine MacKinnon, "Feminism, Marxism, Method and the State: An Agenda for Theory," *Signs*, vol. 7, no. 3, spring 1982, pp. 515–16.

28. Catherine MacKinnon, "Feminism, Marxism, Method, and the State: Toward Feminist Jurisprudence," *Signs*, vol. 8, no. 4, summer 1983, p. 635.

29. Colette. *The Ripening Seed*, translated and cited in Hannah Alderfer, Beth Jaker, and Marybeth Nelson, *Diary of a Conference on Sexuality*, New York, Faculty Press, 1982, p. 72.

30. John Lauritsen and David Thorstad, *The Early Homosexual Rights Movement in Germany*, New York, Times Change Press, 1974.

31. D'Emilio, *Sexual Politics, Sexual Communitie*s, op. cit.; Bérubé, "Behind the Spectre of San Francisco," op. cit.; Bérubé, "Marching to a Different Drummer," op. cit.

38 • *Andrea Dworkin and Catharine MacKinnon*

"MODEL ANTIPORNOGRAPHY CIVIL RIGHTS ORDINANCE"

SECTION 1. STATEMENT OF POLICY

1. Pornography is a practice of sex discrimination. It exists in [place], threatening the health, safety, peace, welfare, and equality of citizens in our community. Existing laws are inadequate to solve these problems in [place].

2. Pornography is a systematic practice of exploitation and subordination based on sex that differentially harms and disadvantages women. The harm of pornography includes dehumanization, psychic assault, sexual exploitation, forced sex, forced prostitution, physical injury, and social and sexual terrorism and inferiority presented as entertainment. The bigotry and

contempt pornography promotes, with the acts of aggression it fosters, diminish opportunities for equality of rights in employment, education, property, public accommodations, and public services; create public and private harassment, persecution, and denigration; promote injury and degradation such as rape, battery, sexual abuse of children, and prostitution, and inhibit just enforcement of laws against these acts; expose individuals who appear in pornography against their will to contempt, ridicule, hatred, humiliation, and embarrassment and target such women in particular for abuse and physical aggression; demean the reputations and diminish the occupational opportunities of individuals and groups on the basis of sex; contribute significantly to restricting women in particular from full exercise of citizenship and participation in the life of the community; lower the human dignity, worth, and civil status of women and damage mutual respect between the sexes; and undermine women's equal exercise of rights to speech and action guaranteed to all citizens under the [Constitutions] and [laws] of [place].

SECTION 2. DEFINITIONS

1. "Pornography" means the graphic sexually explicit subordination of women through pictures and/or words that also includes one or more of the following:

a. women are presented dehumanized as sexual objects, things or commodities; or

b. women are presented as sexual objects who enjoy humiliation or pain; or

c. women are presented as sexual objects experiencing sexual pleasure in rape, incest, or other sexual assault; or

d. women are presented as sexual objects tied up or cut up or mutilated or bruised or physically hurt; or

e. women are presented in postures or positions of sexual submission, servility, or display; or

f. women's body parts—including but not limited to vaginas, breasts, or buttocks—are exhibited such that women are reduced to those parts; or

g. women are presented being penetrated by objects or animals; or

h. women are presented in scenarios of degradation, humiliation, injury, torture, shown as filthy or inferior, bleeding, bruised or hurt in a context that makes these conditions sexual.

2. The use of men, children, or transsexuals in the place of women in (a) of this definition is also pornography for purposes of this law.

* * *

SECTION 3. CAUSES OF ACTION

1. Coercion into pornography. It is sex discrimination to coerce, intimidate, or fraudulently induce . . . any person into performing for pornography, which injury may date from any appearance or sale of any product(s) of such performance(s). . . .

2. Forcing pornography on a person. It is sex discrimination to force pornography on a person in any place of employment, education, home or any public place. Complaints may be brought only against the perpetrator of the force and/or the entity or institution responsible for the force.

3. Assault or physical attack due to pornography. It is sex discrimination to assault, physically attack, or injure any person in a way that is directly caused by specific pornography. . . .

4. Defamation through pornography. It is sex discrimination to defame any person through the unauthorized use in pornography of their proper name, image, and/or recognizable personal likeness. . . .

5. Trafficking in pornography. It is sex discrimination to produce, sell, exhibit, or distribute pornography, including through private clubs. . . . (b) Isolated passages or isolated parts shall not be the sole basis for complaints under this section. (c) Any woman may bring a complaint hereunder as a woman acting against the subordination of women. Any man, child, or transsexual who alleges injury by pornography in the way women are injured by it may also complain.

* * *

SECTION 5. ENFORCEMENT

1. Civil Action. Any person who has a cause of action under this law may complain directly to a court of competent jurisdiction for relief.

* * *

(1988)

"FROM HERE TO QUEER: RADICAL FEMINISM, POSTMODERNISM, AND THE LESBIAN MENACE (OR, WHY CAN'T A WOMAN BE MORE LIKE A FAG?)"

. . . I want to examine the relationship between new queer developments and feminism and feminist theory, with a specific focus on the displacements of radical and lesbian feminism by a queer theory that often posits itself as the antidote to a "retrograde" feminist theorizing. Let me begin by laying my cards on the table: I am wary of this phenomenon.[1] These new developments are not wholly propitious for the (shared, I hope) goals of ending homophobia, confronting compulsory heterosexuality, liberating sexuality. Nevertheless (and I would hope this goes without saying, but I will say it anyway), this critique should be taken as an immanent one, from someone who lives within the gay and lesbian movement and who believes the new queer politics and theory to be largely well intentioned, however misguided and theoretically suspect.[2]

While my criticisms stand, I am also aware of the real strengths and possibilities embodied in the new queer designations. The full exploration of sexual desire in all its complexity is of course an important move, particularly as a neglected aspect of progressive discourse. And the queer challenge to the notion of sexual identity as monolithic, obvious, and dichotomous is a healthy corrective to our vexing inability to see beyond the limitations of the homo/hetero opposition. In addition, the openness of the term *queer* seems to many to provide the possibility of theorizing "beyond the hyphen," beyond the additive models (race, class, gender, sexual orientation = oppressed identity) that have so often seemed to set up new hierarchies or retreated instead into an empty recitation of "difference." Indeed, race critiques have consistently insisted on challenging binary models of identity in the development of concepts of positionality and intersectionality. Queer discourse is clearly not "the enemy,"[3] but neither is it unambiguously the new hope for a theory and/or politics to lead us into the next century. . . .

THE CASE OF THE DISAPPEARING LESBIAN (OR, WHERE THE BOYS ARE)

My main critique of the new popularity of "queer" (theory and, less so, politics) is that it often (and once again) erases lesbian specificity and the enormous difference that gender makes, evacuates the importance of feminism, and rewrites the history of lesbian feminism and feminism generally. Now this is not to say that strongly identified lesbians have not embraced queer theory and politics, or that those who do so are somehow acting in bad faith or are "antifeminist." Indeed, what makes queer theory so exciting in part is the way in which so many different kinds of theorists have been attracted to its promise. Many lesbians

From *Signs: Journal of Women in Culture and Society* 21.4 (Summer 1996): 830–869. Copyright © 1996 by the University of Chicago Press. Reprinted with permission. Notes have been renumbered.

(including myself) have been attracted to queer theory out of frustration with a feminism that, they believe, either subsumes lesbianism under the generic category woman or poses gender as the transcendent category of difference, thus making cross-gender gay alliances problematic. To a certain extent, I, too, share this excitement and embrace the queer move that can complicate an often too-easy feminist take on sexual identity that links lesbianism (in the worst-case scenario) to an almost primordial and timeless mother-bond or a hazy woman-identification. At the same time, however, I fear that many lesbians' engagement with queer theory is informed itself by a rudimentary and circumscribed (revisionist) history of feminism and gender-based theory that paints an unfair picture of feminism as rigid, homophobic, and sexless. . . .

The story, alluded to above, goes something like this: once upon a time there was this group of really boring ugly women who never had sex, walked a lot in the woods, read bad poetry about goddesses, wore flannel shirts, and hated men (even their gay brothers). They called themselves lesbians. Then, thankfully, along came these guys named Foucault, Derrida, and Lacan dressed in girls' clothes riding some very large white horses. They told these silly women that they were politically correct, rigid, frigid, sex-hating prudes who just did not GET IT—it was all a game anyway, all about words and images, all about mimicry and imitation, all a cacophony of signs leading back to nowhere. To have a politics around gender was silly, they were told, because gender was just a performance anyway, a costume one put on and, in drag performance, wore backward. And everyone knew boys were better at dress up.

So, queerness is theorized as somehow beyond gender, a vision of a sort of transcendent polymorphous perversity deconstructing as it slips from one desiring/desired object to the other. But this forgets the very real and felt experience of gender that women, particularly, live with quite explicitly. Indeed, one could argue that this is really the dividing line around different notions of queer; to what extent do theorists argue *queer* as a term beyond (or through) gender? "Where de Lauretis retains the categories 'gay' and 'lesbian' and some notion of gender division as parts of her discussion of what 'queerness' is (or might be), Judith Butler and Sue-Ellen Case have argued that queerness is something that is ultimately beyond gender—it is an

attitude, a way of responding, that begins in a place not concerned with, or limited by, notions of a binary opposition of male and female or the homo versus hetero paradigm usually articulated as an extension of this gender binarism" (Doty 1993, xv). But, again, this seems to assume that feminists (or gays and lesbians) have somehow created these binarisms.

Unlike the terms *gay* and *lesbian*, *queer* is not gender specific, and this of course has been one of its selling points, as it purports to speak to the diversity of the gay and lesbian community and to dethrone gender as the significant marker of sexual identity and sexual expression. . . .

. . . But in a culture in which male is the default gender, in which *homosexual* (a term that also does not specify gender) is all too often imaged as male, and *gay* as both, to see queer as somehow gender *neutral* is ludicrous and willfully naive. Feminism has taught us that the idea of gender neutrality is not only fictitious but a move of gender domination. I applaud queer theory's expansion of the concept of difference but am concerned that, too often, gender is not *complicated* but merely ignored, dismissed, or "transcended." In contradistinction, I would argue that the critique of gender theory from the perspective of women of color has done precisely what the queer critique of gender is only partially and incompletely able to do. In other words, gender in black feminist writing is not "transcended" or somehow deemed an "enemy" concept. Rather, the concept of gender—and feminist theory more generally—is complicated, expanded, deepened both to challenge its "privileged" status and to render it susceptible to theories of intersectionality and multiplicity. The queer critique of the feminist mantra of the separation of sex and gender (sex being the biological "raw material" and gender the socially constructed edifice that creates masculinity and femininity) is helpful in complicating what has become a somewhat rote recitation of social constructionist argument, an argument that too often leaves the body and its various constructions unexamined. But in the light of recently resurgent theories of biological determinism, . . . the insistence on a righteous social constructionism (women are made, not born; we are not simply an expression of our biological makeup, etc.) might be important strategically and politically. Too often in these queer challenges to this dichotomy, sex becomes the grand force of excess that can offer more possibilities for liberatory culture, and gender the constraint on that which would (naturally?) flow freely and polymorphously if left to its own devices. Biddy Martin has made the argument that, for Sedgwick and others, race and gender often assume a fixity, a stability, a ground, whereas sexuality (typically thematized as male) becomes the "means of crossing" and the figure of mobility. In the process of making the female body the "drag" on the (male) play of sexuality, "the female body appears to become its own trap, and the operations of misogyny disappear from view" (Martin 1994, 104, 109–10).

But it is also not clear to me that this vision of a genderless nonnormativity is a worthwhile goal. Is a degendered idea of sexual identity/sexual desire what we strive for? Is this just a postmodern version of a liberal pluralist "if it feels good, do it" ethos? Also, the images/signifiers for this transcendence (of gender) are suspiciously male (why can't a woman be more like a fag?). If the phallus has been replaced by the dildo as the prime signifier of sexual transgression, of queerness, how far have we really come, so to speak?

Queer discourse sets up a universal (male) subject, or at least a universal gay male subject, as its implicit referent. (It is interesting to note in this regard that the 1993 summer special "Queer Issue" of the *Village Voice* was called "Faith Hope & Sodomy.") We cannot deny the centrality of gay maleness to this reconstruction of queer as radical practice. For example, Sue-Ellen Case discusses her engagement with the word *queer* by saying that "I became queer through my readerly identification with a male homosexual author" (1991, 1). . . .

Although lesbians are occasionally mentioned (usually when speaking of S/M), gay men most assuredly have become the model for lesbian radical sex (e.g., the celebration of pornography, the "reappropriation" of the phallus in the fascination with the dildo, the "daddy" fantasies, and reverence for public sex of Pat Califia, etc.).[4] This has entailed a denigration of lesbian attempts to rethink sexuality within a feminist framework. Granted (and we do not need to go through this one more time), lesbian sexuality has suffered from both a discursive neglect and an idealization on the part of lesbians themselves. The image of hand-holding, eye-gazing, woodsy eroticism, however, is not wholly the creation of lesbians but part of the devaluation and stereotyping of all women's sexuality by male-dominant culture. Even in that haven of supposedly uptight, separatist nonsex

(Northampton, Massachusetts, in the late 1970s and early 1980s), I seem to remember we were all doing the nasty fairly well, and, for all the talk of the "lesbian sex police," no girl ever banged down my door and stymied my sexual expression. The straight gaybashers, however, did. We should never forget this difference as we glibly use words like *police*.

. . . Do we really want to relinquish a critique of male identification? After all, the feminist insight that a central impediment to women's liberation (yes, liberation) is an identification with and dependence on males and male approval, desire, status, and so on is so obvious as to be banal. Charges of male identification may have been spuriously made at times, but the *analysis* of male identification is central and important.

The construction of an old, bad, exclusive, policing lesbian feminism is necessary for the "bad girl" (dildo in tow) to emerge as the knight in leather armor, ready to make the world safe for sexual democracy . . .

Even further, not only are those repressed and repressive lesbians responsible for putting a major damper on our nascent sexuality, but feminism itself is responsible for that horror of all horrors: THE BINARY. Bensinger indicts "the binaries generated within feminist movement: feminism/patriarchy, inside/outside, and porn/erotica" (1992, 88). Certain strands of feminism might indeed have perpetuated some of these oppositions (and is feminism *not* opposed to patriarchy?), but, alas, they long predate second-wave feminism. Seventies feminism here becomes the ogre that haunts queer kids of today. "By the seventies feminism had sanitized lesbianism. Lesbophobia forced lesbians to cling to feminism in an attempt to retain respectability. However, in the eighties, discussions of sadomasochism permanently altered the relationship of many lesbians to feminism" (Morgan 1993, 39). I would have hoped most politically astute lesbians (and gay men, for that matter) were/are feminists; this should be a theory we embrace (not "cling to") and, of course, transform and challenge in that embrace.

Many queer activists and theorists seem to believe the media fiction that feminism is either (*a*) dead because we lost or (*b*) dead because we won: "1988. So feminism is dead, or it has changed, or it is still meaningful to some of us but its political currency in the world is weak, its radical heart excised, its plodding middle-class moderation now an acceptable way of life. Feminism has been absorbed by the same generation that so proudly claims to reject it, and instead of women's liberation I hear, 'Long live the Queer nation!'" (Maggenti 1993, 250). As Whisman notes, "Today's 'bad girls' rebel as much against their feminist predecessors as against male power" (1993, 48). In her review of the *differences* issue on queer theory, Hennessy challenges those writers who set up feminism as the enemy, "substitut[ing] feminism (the Symbolic Mother) for patriarchy as the most notable oppressive force that lesbian sexual politics and eroticism must contend with. For feminists this should seem a very disturbing perspective shift, especially when feminism, among young people in particular, is more than ever a bad word" (1993, 969) . . .

I CROSS-DRESS, THEREFORE I AM

I worry about the centrality of drag and camp to queer signification.[5] . . . From "Chicks with Dicks" to Ru Paul to butch/femme bravado, crossing has become the metaphor of choice and the privileged sign of the new queer sensibility. As much as lesbians may now be "playing" with these signifiers (and given the reality that there are women who cross-dress, etc.), these are, after all, historically primarily male activities, particularly in the mode of public performance. In addition, "playing gender" for male drag queens or cross-dressers cannot, in a world marked by the power of gender within patriarchy, be the same for women. As much as we might intellectually want to talk about a more fluid and shifting continuum of both gender and sexual desire (and the separation of the two) we cannot afford to slip into a theory of gender as simply play and performance, a theory that, albeit attired in postmodern garb, appears too much like the old "sex roles" framework or even an Erving Goffman-type "presentation of self" paradigm. . . .

The concept of "performance" has dominated recent feminist theory as well as gay/lesbian/queer theory. Butler is obviously key here, as her work has come to signify a radical move in both theoretical arenas, and the notions of gender play and performance that she elaborates have found themselves the starting points for any number of new works in feminist theory and queer theory. I want to be careful not to simplify her complex and compelling contributions to these discussions. I think she is much more careful about theorizing "performance" than many others who have constructed a less nuanced analysis. Indeed, in *Bodies That Matter*, Butler sets out to clarify what she sees as a misconstrual of her stance on performativity, particularly when it comes to the question of drag. Just as she is explicit that the performance of gender is never a simple voluntary act (like choosing the clothes one puts on in the morning) and is always already constituted by the rules and histories of gender, she reiterates that ambiguity of drag, arguing carefully that "drag is not unproblematically subversive . . . [and] there is no guarantee that exposing the naturalized status of heterosexuality will lead to its subversion" (1993a, 231). Yet, provisos (as in "performance is never simply voluntaristic action") do little when the performances remain removed from a social and cultural context that either enables or disenables their radical enactment.

Clearly, cross-dressing, passing, and assorted tropes of postmodern delight are sexier, more fun, more inventive than previous discourses of identity and politics. Indeed, I think the performance motif the perfect trope for our funky times, producing a sense of enticing activity amid the depressing ruins of late capitalism. . . . [Y]et this hand can, and has, been overplayed. In particular, this trope becomes vacuous when it is decontextualized, bandied about as the new hope for a confused world. Theories of gender as play and performance need to be intimately and systematically connected with the *power* of gender (really, the power of *male* power) to constrain, control, violate, and configure. Too often, mere lip service is given to the specific historical, social, and political configurations that make certain conditions possible and others constrained. . . . Without substantive engagement with complex sociopolitical realities, those performance tropes appear as entertaining but ultimately depoliticized academic exercises.

There is great insight and merit in understanding gender and sexual identity as processes, acquisitions, enactments, creations, processes (and Butler is right to credit Simone de Beauvoir with this profound insight), and Butler and others have done us a great service in elaborating the dissimulating possibilities of simulation. But this insight gets lost if it is not theorized with a deep understanding of the limitations and constraints within which we "perform" gender. And without some elaborated social and cultural context, this theory of performance is deeply ahistorical and, therefore, ironically (because postmodernism fashions itself as particularism par excellence) universalistic, avoiding a discussion of the contexts (race, class, ethnicity, etc.) that make particular "performances" more or less likely to be possible in the first place. It is not enough to assert that all performance of gender takes place within complex and specific regimes of power and domination; those regimes must be explicitly part of the analytic structure of the performance trope, rather than asides to be tossed around and then ignored.[6]

I worry, too, about the romanticization of the margins and of the outlaw that this emphasis on "gender bending" often accompanies. Rearranging the signs of gender too often becomes a substitute for challenging gender inequity. Wearing a dildo will not stop me from being raped as a woman or being harassed as a lesbian. And while donning the accoutrements of masculinity might make me feel more powerful, it will not, short of "passing," keep me out of the ghettos of female employment. This deconstruction of signs—this exploration of the fictitious and constructed nature of gender encoding and gender itself—must be a part of any radical gay politics, but if it *becomes* radical gay politics, we are in trouble. . . . So, I have a concern here about queer political activism (and theory) degenerating into a self-styled rebel stance. . . .

Reading these tales of modern queer life reveals the obsessive focus on the self, the relentless narcissism and individualism of narratives of queer theory: "I pack a dildo, therefore I am." It is sort of like, let us make a theory from our own sexual practices (e.g., "I'm a cross-dressing femme who likes to use a dildo while watching gay male porn videos with my fuck buddy who sometimes likes to do it with gay men. Hmm, what kind of a theory can I make from that?"). But, in my reading, the notion of the "personal is political" did not mean let us construct a theory from individual personal experiences. Rather, there was some notion of collective experience, shared experience. . . .

Now, I would be the last to decry experience, to want to rope it off, out of the reach of theory. Indeed, one of the strongest and most lasting aspects of feminist theorizing has been an adamant refusal to isolate personal narratives out of the reach of theory making. But I fear that much of this work is taking "the personal is political" in an unintended direction: my life, my personal story is theory: I am the world. In addition, I think these are personal stories *designed* to be outrageous, to articulate the author as inheritor of the mantle of Sadean dissidence. . . .

. . . Again, personal transgression or predilection has metamorphosed into political and theoretical action. Sexual hobbies do not a theory make.

FROM QUEER TO WHERE? MURMURS OF DISSENT

. . . The "answer," such as it is, is surely not to dismiss queer theory altogether, as I think I have made clear throughout the course of this article. But the part of "queer" that hinges on a separation from feminism (both theory and politics) seems to me misguided at best. A more profitable direction might be the constant and creative renegotiation of the relationship between feminism and queer theory and politics, with the "goal" not being a severance but rather more meaningful and substantive ties. . . . I think it needs reiterating that there can be no radical theory and surely no radical politics without feminism, however much that feminism might be rendered plural and reconfigured. This is nowhere more true than in recent right-wing rhetoric regarding "the family" and the scary discourse of family values. Here, a nuanced and subtle understanding of the ways in which both patriarchy and heterosexism construct the discourse and produce the politics would be fruitful. For example, in analyzing the attacks on lesbian and gay parents . . ., we might develop frameworks of knowledge that explicitly address the mutual "concatenation" of both gender discourses and sexuality discourses. . . . A feminist queer theory might focus more on the material realities of lives lived under patriarchal, capitalist, racist regimes, not as background or aside, but as the very stuff of a political and politicized analysis. . . .

Destabilizing gender (or rendering its artifice apparent) is not the same as overthrowing it; indeed, in a culture in which drag queens can become the hottest fashion, commodification of resistance is an omnipresent threat. Moreover, a queer theory that posits

feminism (or lesbian theory) as the transcended enemy
is a queer that will really be a drag.

(1996)

NOTES

1. Let me note here, too, that I am most assuredly not alone
   in my critique of "queer." Indeed, feminists have already
   initiated a substantial body of work that takes issue with
   the construction of "queer theory" as the "replacement" for
   feminist and lesbian and gay studies. Often, but not
   always, these critiques of "queer" dovetail with critiques of
   postmodernism, as will be brought out in the course of this
   article. See particularly Modleski 1991; and Bordo 1990.
   Biddy Martin's work (1993, 1994) has been particularly
   helpful. Wilson's 1992 critique of bisexuality and de
   Lauretis's 1991 thoughtful introduction to the *differences* issue
   on queer theory have also added to the growing discourse.
2. I should note here that queer theory and queer politics are
   not, of course, identical. . . . Nevertheless, the two are, as
   are most theories and practices, intimately connected,
   albeit often in an implicit manner. . . . While I do
   not mean to conflate the two, I *am* interested in
   discussing the connections between them and the
   implications for a radical politics given these newer
   developments. . . .
3. Indeed, one of my chief concerns here is the danger of
   "queer" being used to construct an enemy of feminism.
4. See particularly Creet 1991; Reich 1992; Hall 1993; and
   Roy 1993.
5. I will forgo here any substantive discussion of the long
   and complicated history of drag and camp (themselves
   not synonymous, of course) within the lesbian and gay
   movement. . . .
6. Again, I would note here that Butler's most recent
   work seems to address, rather successfully, many of
   my concerns. Nevertheless, I still am concerned that
   much of the discussion around drag, performance,
   crossing, etc., remains deeply decontextualized or
   that the context seems to be solely a textual and
   representational one.

CHAPTER 4

Marxist, Socialist, and Anarchist Feminisms

If voting changed anything, they'd make it illegal.

—Emma Goldman, 1912

INTRODUCTION

This chapter examines how the Old and New Left have influenced U.S. feminist thought. Marxism and anarchism were the major **Old Left** theoretical perspectives that impacted U.S. feminism in the nineteenth and early twentieth centuries. Marxism highlighted social class—specifically the battle between the **proletariat** (wage laborers) and the **bourgeoisie** (the capitalist business owners who hired wage labor)—as the primary axis of oppression in modern societies and championed the industrial working class as their major agent of revolutionary social change. Whereas anarchists sought to rid the world of all forms of domination, they too focused primarily on class conflict and the struggles between labor and capital in the nineteenth and early twentieth centuries. The **New Left** refers to the new social movements of late modernity such as the civil rights movement, the women's movement, the gay and lesbian rights movement, and the anti-Vietnam war movement. Along with a focus on social class, the New Left addressed the conflicts and cleavages generated by inequalities of race, gender, sexuality, and global location that tore at the fabric of American society in that era.

Although the distinction between Marxist feminism and socialist feminism did not become part of the feminist lexicon until the second wave, there were some precursors to socialist feminism in the first wave as we shall see below. We also will explore how anarchist theory injected a radical thrust into the women's movement that was distinct from Marxism. The term anarchism derives from the word "anarchos," meaning "without rulers" and, unlike Marxists, anarchists reject all forms of hierarchy and government (including socialist governments). Anarchists advocate spontaneous, militant, direct-action politics and are less willing than Marxists and socialists to engage in reformist measures on their path to revolution. Yet, despite their differences, Marxist, socialist, and anarchist feminists *all share a heavy focus on class and gender.*

THE ORIGINS OF WOMEN'S OPPRESSION

It was rare for male theorists to address women's oppression in the nineteenth and early twentieth centuries. Aside from John Stuart Mill, who was discussed in Chapter 2, the other male theorists who made the most significant contributions during this era were Marxists.[1] One of the most influential works was Friedrich Engels's *The Origin of the Family, Private Property, and the State* ([1884] 1972).[2] As shown in Reading 41, Engels locates the roots of women's oppression not in biology, but rather in sociohistorical developments. He argues that the earliest human societies—hunting-and-gathering societies—did not have developed systems of stratification based on class or gender. Rather, they were organized in matrilineal clans where both men and women had significant roles in providing economic subsistence. Because hunting and gathering is risky and vulnerable to the vagaries of nature, it entailed more sharing or mutual aid than did later modes of production. His analysis was based on existing anthropological data, such as Henry Louis Morgan's research on Native American tribes. As discussed in Chapter 8, Morgan's work was familiar to some U.S. suffragists who also were interested in the greater gender equality found in these tribes (Landsman, 1992).

According to Engels, gender oppression arose alongside class oppression in ancient agricultural societies based on private property in land and slaves, as well as their state systems that enforced property rights and patriarchal dominion. To reproduce class systems over generational time, private property had to be passed down to one's children. This required the establishment of patriarchal institutions to control women's sexuality, such as restricting women in propertied classes to the household and laws that punished women but not men for adultery. Thus, **patriarchy**—meaning institutionalized male dominion over women and children and women's relegation to the home—originally arose to protect property rights and class privilege. In this way, Engels tied the rise of women's oppression to the rise of class oppression. The Marxist path to women's emancipation required the abolition of private property through a socialist revolution and the overthrow of patriarchal domination in the family and in state laws.

WOMEN'S WORK IN THE HOME

Charlotte Perkins Gilman's *Women and Economics* (1898) provided the most substantial feminist analysis of housework and child care written in the nineteenth century. Gilman was inspired by utopian and Fabian socialism, which embraced cooperative and collective forms of social life, but rejected revolutionary approaches to social change. However, they shared with Marxism the view that labor is fundamental to the existential well-being of human beings. Like Marx, Gilman assigns much weight to human labor in giving meaning to human life. The relation between gender and the economy or what she calls the "sexuo-economic relation" provides the conceptual framework for *Women and Economics* ([1898] 1966) and selections from this work can be found in Reading 43.

Gilman primarily rooted women's oppression in their relegation to housework and child care. Many of her writings call for more collective ways of providing child care, food, and cleaning services to enable women to realize themselves in other forms of labor.[3] Reading 42 provides excerpts from her most widely read work—"The Yellow Wallpaper" ([1892] 1995). This feminist novella highlights the depression that some women experience when they are relegated to the home and are allowed few outlets to realize themselves—a phenomenon Betty Friedan, a half century later, would call **the problem that has no name**" (Friedan, [1963] 1997).

The major character in "The Yellow Wallpaper" is an upper-class woman whose efforts to write are obstructed by her husband (a doctor) and by the medical establishment of her era. This novella critiques not only the paucity of options open for women's work, but also medical practices of late nineteenth century where doctors prescribed a "rest cure" for women with nervous disorders or "hysteria" (a word derived from the Latin for womb). Under this rest cure (which Gilman had experienced) women were forbidden from doing any labor, a cure that Gilman thought only made women's depression worse. In "The Yellow Wallpaper", the wife is relegated not only to the home, but also to a former nursery with barred windows that symbolizes how the husband treated his wife like a child. The wallpaper in the nursery has intricate designs that appear to the wife as a maze that imprisons women's desire for freedom. Thus the wallpaper becomes a metaphor for the way the home and decorative femininity stifle women's creativity and self-actualization.

CLASS DIFFERENCES IN WOMEN'S LIVES AND WORK

Reading 40 is a poem titled "The New Colossus" written by socialist Emma Lazarus in 1883.[4] It is one of the most famous poems in American history because its stanzas "Give me your tired, your poor and your huddled masses . . ." are enshrined on the Statue of Liberty. Inspired by the utopian socialism of William Morris, as well as the writings of Henry George, Lazarus embraced the importance of labor for self-realization and creativity and lamented the stark class inequalities she witnessed. Her contributions to helping working-class immigrants and combatting anti-Semitism were recognized in 1944 when the Emma Lazarus Division of the Jewish People's Fraternal Order of the International Workers Order (IWO) was founded.[5]

Many first-wave Marxist, socialist, and anarchist feminists were labor organizers whose writings focused attention on the plight of working-class and poor women. Reading 44, "Girl Slaves of the Milwaukee Breweries" ([1910] 1990), is by Mother (Mary) Jones, who was a founder of the anarchist Industrial Workers of the World and a community activist who fought to end child labor. Reading 48, "Working Woman and Mother" ([1914] 2005), was written by Alexandra Kollontai, a Marxist feminist who was a key figure in the Russian revolution and the establishment of the first socialist country in the world—the Union of Soviet Socialist Republics (U.S.S.R). Although both of their works are more descriptive than theoretical, they poignantly highlight significant class differences that existed between women in the early twentieth century. These feminist labor organizers called for various policies designed to assist working-class women such as protective labor legislation for pregnant women, maternity insurance, and state-subsidized child care.

The distinction between Marxist feminism and socialist feminism was not introduced until the second wave. However, Crystal Eastman's writings closely mirror what would later be called a socialist feminist perspective. Eastman was a labor lawyer, socialist, suffragist, and one of four authors of the Equal Rights

Amendment when it was first introduced in the 1920s. She also was the author of New York's first workman's (sic) compensation law in 1907, which became a model for other state laws across the United States. In Reading 49 from *On Women and Revolution* ([1919] 1978), Eastman argues that a socialist revolution would not be sufficient to end women's oppression. She challenges Marxist feminists' prioritization of class oppression over gender oppression. Like later socialist feminists, Eastman demands that *equal* consideration be given to gender and class.

Some of the most famous icons of the U.S. women's movement are based on the struggles of working-class women during the first wave. **International Women's Day**, which falls annually on March 8, was established in 1910 to commemorate major strikes by women workers. It was proposed by the German socialist feminist Clara Zetkin, who was well known in Europe for championing women's rights. "**Bread and Roses**," first published as a poem by James Oppenheim (1911), later became an anthem for working women's rights. It is often associated with a strike of women textile workers in Lawrence, Massachusetts, in 1912 called the "Bread and Roses Strike." The first stanzas of this famous anthem can be found in Reading 46.

LOVE, MARRIAGE, AND SEXUAL PRACTICES IN EARLY MODERNITY

Marxist, socialist, and anarchist feminists called for "**free love**" or "**sex love**," which, in that era, meant that people had the right to have sex with and marry people they loved. They also argued that, because women had few opportunities for economic independence, they were forced to marry for financial security. It is for this reason that some of these left-wing feminists likened conventional marriage to a form of prostitution.

Reading 45 from Emma Goldman's "The Traffic in Women" from *Anarchism and Other Essays* ([1910] 1917), is one of the most famous first-wave writings to make this point. Moreover, Goldman leveled a scathing critique against existing prostitution laws in that era. She discussed how poor and working-class women were often the victims of these laws, whereas wealthy men who paid for sex received no penalty. She also chastised the wives of these wealthy men for holding prostitutes in disdain and for lauding their falsely assumed greater virtue. By rooting prostitution in poverty and/or lack of employment options for women, Goldman linked gender oppression to class oppression.

Marxist, socialist, and anarchist feminists were among the first U.S. feminists to demand women's rights to birth control and abortion. Most liberal feminists of this era only supported **voluntary motherhood**—or the right to abstain from sex with their husbands. The most prominent birth control advocate of that era— Margaret Sanger—was a socialist feminist who worked as a nurse with poor and working-class women. As Reading 50, "My Fight for Birth Control" ([1920] 1974), reveals, Sanger saw firsthand how maternal deaths from childbirth, as well as uncontrolled fertility, seriously impacted the lives of these women and their families. At this time, it was illegal even for married couples to use birth control except in emergencies. Because birth control information was viewed as pornography, it was illegal to distribute it. Nevertheless, Sanger published the *Woman Rebel*, a magazine that provided birth control information, and was arrested for opening a birth control clinic that gave poor and working-class women medical check-ups and birth control pamphlets. Many years later, Sanger founded the organization that would eventually become known as Planned Parenthood.

PRECURSORS TO ECOFEMINISM
IN EARLY MODERNITY[6]

Because many Marxist, socialist, and anarchist feminists were directly involved in labor organizing, they were among some of the earliest activists to focus attention on hazards in the workplace (Mann, 2011). By the late nineteenth century, the United States had one of the highest industrial accidents rates in the world. One of the most serious industrial accidents involving women was the 1911 Triangle Factory fire, which killed 146 women garment workers. Reading 47, "We Have Found You Wanting" ([1911] 1962), is a speech by feminist labor organizer Rose Schneiderman, who spoke at the memorial for these women. Schneiderman helped to organize the International Ladies Garment Workers Union and led its 1913 strike.

As noted in Chapter 2, environmental issues in the nineteenth and early twentieth centuries were diverse; they included air and water pollution, garbage and sanitation issues, safe food, and industrial health and safety. Although these problems affected the entire population, they most seriously affected poor and working-class people who lived near industrial factories and/or in overcrowded, urban areas (Merchant, 2007: 120). Because the municipal housekeeping activities of Marxist and socialist feminists focused on the concerns of working-class and poor people, they were referred to derogatorily as "sewer socialists" and became victims of red-baiting during the Red Scare of 1919–1920.

The Red Scare is the name given to the increased police surveillance and arrests of left-wing radicals—especially labor organizers—in 1919 and 1920. Like the McCarthy era after World War II, the Red Scare had a crippling effect on the American Left. For example, Crystal Eastman and Emma Goldman came under surveillance from the newly formed Federal Bureau of Investigation. Eastman's radical journal *The Liberator* was banned and she was blacklisted. Goldman was arrested and deported to the Soviet Union with more than 200 other foreign-born radicals in 1919.

MARXIST, SOCIALIST, AND ANARCHIST
FEMINISMS BETWEEN THE WAVES

From the 1930s through the 1950s, Marxist, socialist, and anarchist feminists turned their attention to the immense problems bequeathed by the Great Depression, the rise of fascism, and World War II. After the war, these radicals had to contend with the Cold War and McCarthyism:

> The radicalism of the 1930s concentrated on unemployment and, in the late 1930s, on the threat of fascism to the practical exclusion of all other issues. The postwar 1946–1960 period was a time of U.S. economic expansion and world dominance, of the cold war and super-patriotism ensured by the witch-hunting of McCarthyism. All radical and liberal groups suffered repression; and possible women's liberation causes . . . were smothered with the rest. (Deckard: [1979] 1983: 316)

One of the most influential feminist works written between the waves was Simone de Beauvoir's *The Second Sex*, first published in French in 1949 and in English in 1952. Here de Beauvoir develops her socialist existential feminism. One of her most famous quotes (1949/2011: 283), "One is not born, but rather becomes, a woman," states not only that gender is socially constructed, but also how woman is defined and differentiated with reference to man and not he with reference to her; she is the incidental, the inessential as opposed to the essential. For de Beauvoir, *otherness* is a fundamental category of human thought that affects all subordinate groups (6).

A basic assumption of existentialism is that humans are defined by what they do and by how they act. Reality and existence are expressed by action and engagement. For de Beauvoir, the gendered world of the home cripples women's ability to act on and to engage in the world. Reading 52 from *The Second Sex* ([1949] 2011) illustrates the existential repercussions of the cyclical, repetitive, and invisible nature of housework. De Beauvoir's prose captures not only the rhythms of this work, but also the frustrations and monotony experienced by housewives in their day-to-day lives. A striking feature of de Beauvoir's work is how she articulates the embodied, situated nature of human consciousness "whereby experience and perception are never wholly detachable from the flesh and blood in which human agency is embroiled, nor indeed from the material contexts in which they occur" (Cavallaro, 2003: 15).

Novels, short stories, and poems written by feminists of this era also captured the existential dimensions of women's work. Tillie Olsen's portrayals of working-class women's lives and labor in her short stories were favorites among feminists of the second wave. A member of the Communist Party, Olsen was arrested many times for her labor organizing. Reading 51, "I Want You Women up North to Know" ([1934] 1990), illustrates how her work explored not only the "fraying seams of blue collar life," but also the silencing of those on the margins. Indeed, Olsen played an important role in highlighting the *politics of voice* (Holley, 2007).

WOMEN'S WORK IN LATE MODERNITY

Marxist and socialist feminists' major contributions were their analyses of women's work inside and outside of the home. In late modernity, they provided detailed historical data on gendered inequalities in the workplace and developed the theoretical underpinnings for feminist issues such as **equal pay, comparable worth,** and **sex-segregated occupations.**[7] Because they viewed women's labor *within* the home as a major obstacle to their emancipation, they also devoted much attention to analyzing women's work that was "hidden in the household" (Fox, 1980). During the 1970s, the debates that ensued over how to analyze women's work in the home came to be known as the "domestic labor debates" and drew contributors from many different countries.[8]

Margaret Benston's "The Political Economy of Women's Liberation" (1969) found in Reading 53 exemplifies a classic second-wave Marxist feminist approach. According to Benston, because women have been historically relegated to primary responsibility for housework and child care, women and men have a different relationship to the means of production. This difference centers around the distinction Marx made between production for use and production for exchange. Work outside of the home is **production for exchange** because this labor produces commodities and garners direct income in the form of wages. By contrast, housework and child care (when not done by paid servants) are forms of **production for use**—labor directed toward immediate use rather than sale. Benston sees this distinction as the structural basis for women's inequality in modern societies because production for use is unpaid labor and provides no basis for women's economic independence. Even for women employed outside of the home, having major responsibility for housework and child care inhibits, interrupts, and reduces the attention and time they can give to their jobs, thus placing them on an unequal playing field relative to men in terms of earning power.

Benston contrasts work inside and outside of the home. For example, in factories, workers work together in a highly specialized division of labor. By contrast, housewives labor in relative isolation, which makes them more difficult to politically organize. In nonspecialized domestic labor a woman is expected to be a Jill of all trades—cook, cleaner, nurse, and nanny—but a recognized expert at none. In turn, because there are no set hours, woman qua housewife is expected to be on call at any hour, day or night, for sick family members or hungry infants. What distinguishes Benston's piece as a Marxist feminist analysis is the way she describes *unpaid domestic labor as primarily serving the capitalist class*. Rather than highlighting how it serves all men, she emphasizes how it serves the capitalist class in a number of ways, such as providing a reserve labor force that could be called on in times of labor shortages or wars and keeping wages low because housework and child care are unpaid labor.

Socialist feminist Heidi Hartmann criticizes this type of Marxist feminist analysis in her article, "The Unhappy Marriage of Marxism and Feminism: Towards a More Progressive Union" (1979). Reading 55, from this work, shows how Hartmann uses the notion of the doctrine of coverture to argue that wedding Marxist theory and feminist theory together ends up in an "unhappy marriage" (1979: 1), where Marxism ends up dominating feminism. Like Eastman before her, Hartmann argues that capitalists are not the only beneficiaries of women's relegation to domestic labor; rather, *all* men are beneficiaries—including working-class men. For Marxists to ignore these gender realities is to be gender blind.

Hartmann's theory of "**capitalist-patriarchy**" gives gender and class *equal* importance (1979: 30). It requires that two spheres of social life be examined: the sphere of production (the basis of capitalist domination) and the sphere of the reproduction (the basis of patriarchal domination). Hartmann's term the **social reproduction of labor power** has two dimensions. First, it refers to the day-to-day labor involved in housework or child care that enables people to replenish their labor power or their ability to work each day. Second, it refers to the intergenerational reproduction of labor power through childbirth and childrearing, which provides society with new members. Every society requires these dimensions of social life to function adequately. Although Marx had examined the sphere of production at great length, socialist feminists demanded that both spheres be examined to reveal the integral relationship between capitalism and patriarchy.

FEMINIST EXISTENTIAL PHENOMENOLOGY

Coupling insights from Simone de Beauvoir's existentialism with Maurice Merleau-Ponty's phenomenological approach, political philosopher Iris Marion Young centered her work on how human consciousness was situated in the lived body. Reading 56 is from her famous piece "Throwing like a Girl: A Phenomenology of Feminine Body Comportment, Motility, and Spaciality" (1980). Echoing de

Beauvoir, Young discusses how the constraints of gender and femininity define woman as "Other" and constrain the subjectivity, autonomy, and creativity that are definitive of being human beings. Young focuses on how women's actual bodily movements exhibit tensions between being an active, creative subject and a mere object to others (2005: 29).

Young uses the description of "throwing like a girl" as just one example of physical activities that reflect the constraints of feminine bodily comportment. She argues that feminine bodily movements, unlike those of males, often do not engage the entire body in directed motion. Women lack trust in their bodies and often approach tasks with "timidity, immobility, and uncertainty" (Young, 2005: 40). Women also restrict their use of space; they wait and react rather than going forth to act (2005: 39–41). Young makes clear that these modalities of feminine bodily comportment are socially constructed and "have their source in the particular situation of women as conditioned by their sexist oppression in contemporary society" (2005: 42). For her, the root of this problem "lies in the fact that woman lives her body as *object* as well as subject" (2005: 44, her emphasis). She describes how this objectification is manifest in women's fear of bodily invasion such as rape and in the "threat of being seen" (2005: 44–45) given the heavy role played by beauty and appearance in women's lives. As a result, "Women in sexist society are physically handicapped" (2005: 42).

PSYCHOANALYTIC APPROACHES OF THE FEMINIST NEW LEFT

Although a number of Marxist and socialist feminists in late modernity wed the works of Marx and Freud, among the most influential feminist psychoanalytic approaches was Nancy Chodorow's *The Reproduction of Mothering: Psychoanalysis and the Sociology of Gender* (1978). Excerpts from her book can be found in Reading 54. Chodorow's theory builds upon Melanie Klein's neo-Freudian, object relations theory where deep-seated, gendered psychosocial orientations are created in the process of an infant or child's separation from their primary object of affection—the mother. She links these psychosocial orientations to sex role theory and to capitalism by arguing that **instrumental roles** provide the basis for capitalist production, whereas **expressive roles** provide the basis for the social reproduction of labor power.

Chodorow argues that it is women who primarily rear children and who provide them with "affective bonds and a diffuse, multifaceted, ongoing personal relationship" that helps them form their "core gender identity" and "sense of self" ([1978] 1999: 3). Although all infants and toddlers must separate from their primary caregivers to begin the process of becoming separate selves, girls and boys experience this separation differently. Because boys have to separate from their mothers to take on adult male gender roles, they break the ties between affect (emotion) and sex role learning. This break enables them to be independent social actors who engage in the impersonal, instrumental, or task-oriented social action required by capitalist production. In contrast, because girls enact adult female gender roles, the tie between affect and role learning is maintained. Women see themselves primarily in relation to others, and their social actions are more personal, expressive, or people oriented than those of men. Using this analysis, Chodorow links sex role socialization to the requirements of the capitalist system.

SOCIALIST FEMINIST STANDPOINT THEORIES

The intellectual roots of feminist standpoint epistemologies are often traced to G. W. F. Hegel's master/slave dialectic and his reflections on how the vantage point of the slave informed this relationship of servitude. Marxist theorists used these insights to discuss the standpoint of the working class. It was only a short leap in logic for feminists to apply these insights to women. Reading 58 is from Dorothy Smith's *The Everyday World as Problematic: A Feminist Sociology* (1987). A unique feature of Smith's work is how she interweaves Marxism, feminism, and ethnomethodology. Smith emphasizes how beginning research from the standpoint and practices of everyday life marks a departure from the procedures of more conventional social science, or what she refers to as "objectified forms of knowledge" (Mann and Kelley, 1997). She highlights how the knowledge people have by virtue of their concrete, everyday experiences is for the most part "tacit knowledge"—a knowing of what we do, how we go about things, and what we get done, such as where to go shopping, how to catch a bus, how to wash dishes, or how to sweep floors (D. E. Smith, 2004: 265–266). She argues that such knowledge is rarely discursively appropriated because it is seen as uninteresting, unimportant, or routine.

Smith analytically distinguishes between the "extralocal" world and the world of "everyday/everynight life" (D. E. Smith, 1990: 18). The latter is subordinate, suppressed, and ignored although it is the social grounding—the taken-for-granted social context—for its superior. If we start from women's everyday lives, we see how they are assigned the work of caring for the bodies of men, children, and the elderly, as well as their own bodies. They also are assigned responsibility for the local places—namely the home—where these activities take place. Not only does women's everyday work free men from these tasks, but also the more successful women are at this concrete work, the more invisible it becomes to men as distinctively social labor (D. E. Smith, 1990: 19). Conventional forms of knowledge produced by men fail to understand both women's standpoint and the world of everyday life. Smith refers to her work as **institutional ethnography** because it examines how the scenes of everyday life are knitted into broader forms of social organization—moving from everyday practices in households, to those in local neighborhoods and schools, to those in larger bureaucracies and the state (D. E. Smith, 2005; Grahame, 1998).

Because standpoint and postmodern epistemologies are often confused, a common thread running through socialist feminist standpoint approaches is their critique of the **judgmental relativism** in postmodern epistemology. In "Telling the Truth after Postmodernism" (1996) and "High Noon in Textland" (1993), Dorothy Smith mocks the political impotency of postmodern relativism. She argues that, if knowledge is to have an impact on politics, there must exist the practical possibility that one account can invalidate another. In Reading 59, "Foucault on Power: A Theory for Women?" ([1990] 1993), Nancy Hartsock points to the political impotency of poststructuralism when she distinguishes between socialist feminist standpoint theory and Foucault's approach to power. She views the postmodern turn in social thought as a "dangerous approach" for any marginalized group to adopt (546). In particular, she criticizes Foucault's poststructuralist approach for focusing only on resistance to power, rather than a transformation of existing power relations. Hartsock discusses how a "theory of power for women" (553) (or for other marginalized groups) should lead to a call for social transformation, as well as a vision of the means necessary for altering existing power relations.

MARXIST, SOCIALIST, AND ANARCHIST ECOFEMINISMS

Marxist and socialist ecofeminists see environmental problems as rooted in a specific mode of production—capitalism. They view capitalism's insatiable drive for private profits as the major source of environmental degradation. This does not mean that there were no preindustrial forms of environmental despoliation. However, these premodern environmental problems pale beside the massive destruction of the environment that has occurred over the past few centuries since the birth of industrial capitalism.

In contrast, anarchist-ecofeminists view socialist societies as just as guilty of environmental degradation as capitalist ones—pointing to ecological disasters such as the nuclear fallout at Chernobyl. They typically support small, decentralized, democratic social organizations centered on local and community politics and consider large, centralized, bureaucratic forms antithetical to their goals. Slogans, such as "small is beautiful" or "simple living," resonate strongly with them (Merchant, 1995).

Marxist and socialist ecofeminists counter this anarchist preference for the small and local by arguing that the vast majority of economic, social, and ecological problems cannot be adequately addressed at the local level. They point to pollution of all kinds that spills over local, regional, and national boundaries and argue that problems like acid rain, ozone depletion, nuclear disasters, and global warming are simply beyond the scope of small-scale, local solutions (O'Connor, 1997; Merchant, 1999).

The first ecofeminist course in the United States was taught by Ynestra King at the Center for Social Ecology founded by the anarchist theorist Murray Bookchin. Rather than engaging in what she views as internecine debates between ecofeminists, King's approach is more inclusive. In Reading 57, "Feminism and the Revolt of Nature" (1981), King calls for ecofeminists to garner insights from socialist ecofeminists' materialist approach, as well as from radical ecofeminists' cultural and spiritual approaches. She argues that, although women are as rational as men, as socialist feminists claim, they should not lose sight of their emotional sides highlighted by cultural feminists. She calls for a merger of these two perspectives: "To fulfill its liberatory potential, ecofeminism needs to pose a rational reenchantment that brings together spiritual and material, being and knowing. This is the promise of ecological feminism" (King quoted in Merchant, 1999: 202).

In contrast to King's call for a harmonious merger of spiritual and materialist ecofeminisms, socialist feminist Donna Haraway launches a scathing critique of spiritual ecofeminists' mythology. Reading 60, titled "The Cyborg Manifesto and Fractured Identities," is from her book *Simians, Cyborgs, and Women: The Reinvention of Nature* (1991).[9] Haraway calls for an updated socialist feminism that can analyze the shift from modern, industrial societies to the new postindustrial, information-based societies wrought by the new digital technologies. Her term "cyborg" refers to a mythic creature that is part human/part machine. The cyborg serves as a metaphor for technocratic approaches that falsely assume that science can fix all environmental problems. Haraway counterposes this technocratic approach to spiritual ecofeminists' vision of women saving the planet through embracing goddess worship and rejecting science, technology, and industry. Haraway views both paths as dangerous for women and the environment. However, if forced to choose, she finds the irrational, antiscience, spiritual ecofeminist path more reactionary and ineffective politically.

CONCLUSION

This chapter has presented a vast array of feminist writings that bear the imprint of the Old Left theories of Marxism and anarchism. Readers can see how the conceptual tools provided by both the Old and the New Left have been valuable for understanding women's oppression—its historical origins as well as the various ways women's labor is exploited in modern societies by capitalism and patriarchy. In addition, the Old and New Left fostered new directions in feminist thought that ranged from developing standpoint approaches to novel ways of looking at the relationship between women and nature.

NOTES

1. Other famous late nineteenth- and early-twentieth-century feminist works by male Marxists include August Bebel's *Women under Socialism* (1904);[1] V. I. Lenin's writings collected in *The Emancipation of Women: From the Writings of V. I. Lenin* ([1934] 1995); and Leon Trotsky's works, which can be found in *Women and the Family* (1973).
2. Engels' work is based on Marx's *Ethnological Notebooks* ([1882] 1986). The importance of these writings is discussed in Jacqueline Solway's *The Politics of Egalitarianism: Theory and Practice* (2006).
3. Charlotte Gilman discusses these transformations of home in *Concerning Children* (1900), *The Home* (1903), *Human Work* (1904), and her utopian novel *Herland* (1915).
4. A special thanks to John Dixon for introducing me to Emma Lazarus's work and activism.
5. When the IWO was deemed a subversive institution during the McCarthy era, it reorganized as the independent Emma Lazarus Federation of Jewish Women's Clubs. See http://jwa.org/encyclopedia/article/emma-lazarus-federation-of-jewish-womens-clubs (retrieved October 28, 2014).
6. Parts of this section were first published in "Pioneers of Ecofeminism & Environmental Justice," *Feminist Formations*, 2011, 23 (2). The author thanks Johns Hopkins University Press for permission to print them.
7. Excellent summaries of their research on women's work can be found in Natalie Sokoloff's *Between Money and Love: The Dialectic of Women's Home and Market Work* (1980); Paula England's *Comparable Worth: Theories and Evidence* (1992), and Alice Kemp's *Women's Work: Devalued and Degraded* (1993).
8. From the United States, see Lise Vogel ([1973] 1983, 1981), Zillah Eisenstein (1979), and Heidi Hartmann (1979). From abroad, see Mariarosa Dalla Costa and Selma James from Italy (1975); Sheila Rowbotham (1975, 1978), Ann Oakley (1974a, 1974b), and Michele Barrett (1980) from Great Britain; and Margaret Benston (1969), Wally Seccombe (1973), and Bonnie Fox (1980) from Canada.
9. This piece is also based on Haraway's earlier article, "A Manifesto for Cyborgs: Science, Technology and Socialist Feminism in the 1980s" (1985).

40 • *Emma Lazarus*

"THE NEW COLOSSUS"

Not like the brazen giant of Greek fame
With conquering limbs astride from land to land;
Here at our sea-washed, sunset gates shall stand
A mighty woman with a torch, whose flame
Is the imprisoned lightning, and her name
Mother of Exiles. From her beacon-hand
Glows world-wide welcome; her mild eyes command
The air-bridged harbor that twin cities frame,

"Keep, ancient lands, your storied pomp!" cries she
With silent lips. "Give me your tired, your poor,
Your huddled masses yearning to breathe free,
The wretched refuse of your teeming shore,
Send these, the homeless, tempest-tossed to me,
I lift my lamp beside the golden door!"

(1883)

Emma Lazarus, New York City, 1883. This poem is mounted on the Statue of Liberty monument in New York City.

41 • *Friedrich Engels*

FROM *THE ORIGIN OF THE FAMILY, PRIVATE PROPERTY, AND THE STATE*

. . . According to the materialistic conception, the determining factor in history is, in the final instance, the production and reproduction of immediate life. This, again, is of a twofold character: on the one side, the production of the means of existence, of food, clothing and shelter and the tools necessary for that production; on the other side, the production of human beings themselves, the propagation of the species. The social organization under which the people of a particular historical epoch and a particular country live is determined by both kinds of production: by the stage of development of labor on the one hand and of the family on the other. The lower the development of labor and the more limited the amount of its products, and consequently, the more limited also the wealth of the society, the more the social order is found to be dominated by kinship groups. However, within this structure of society based on kinship groups the productivity of labor increasingly develops, and with it private property and exchange, differences of wealth, the possibility of utilizing the labor power of others, and hence the basis of class antagonisms: new social elements, which in the course of generations strive to adapt the old social order to the new conditions, until at last their incompatibility brings about a complete upheaval. In the collision of the newly developed social

Reprinted by permission from Friedrich Engels, *The Origin of the Family, Private Property, and the State.*
International Publishers Company, Inc., New York, 1972.

classes, the old society founded on kinship groups is broken up. In its place appears a new society, with its control centered in the state, the subordinate units of which are no longer kinship associations, but local associations; a society in which the system of the family is completely dominated by the system of property, and in which there now freely develop those class antagonisms and class struggles that have hitherto formed the content of all *written* history. . . .

. . . One of the most absurd notions taken over from 18th century enlightenment is that in the beginning of society woman was the slave of man. Among all savages and all barbarians of the lower and middle stages, and to a certain extent of the upper stage also, the position of women is not only free, but honorable. . . .

. . . Among peoples where the women have to work far harder than we think suitable, there is often much more real respect for women than among our Europeans. The lady of civilization, surrounded by false homage and estranged from all real work, has an infinitely lower social position than the hard-working woman of barbarism, who was regarded among her people as a real lady (lady, *frowa*, *Frau*—mistress) and who was also a lady in character. . . .

The first beginnings of the pairing family appear on the dividing line between savagery and barbarism; they are generally to be found already at the upper stage of savagery, but occasionally not until the lower stage of barbarism. . . .

Unless new, *social* forces came into play, there was no reason why a new form of family should arise from the single pair. But these new forces did come into play . . .

Here the domestication of animals and the breeding of herds had developed a hitherto unsuspected source of wealth and created entirely new social relations. Up to the lower stage of barbarism, permanent wealth had consisted almost solely of house, clothing, crude ornaments and the tools for obtaining and preparing food—boat, weapons, and domestic utensils of the simplest kind. Food had to be won afresh day by day. Now, with their herds of horses, camels, asses, cattle, sheep, goats, and pigs, the advancing pastoral peoples—the Semites on the Euphrates and the Tigris, and the Aryans in the Indian country of the Five Streams (Punjab), in the Ganges region, and in the steppes then much more abundantly watered by the Oxus and the Jaxartes—had acquired property which only needed supervision and the rudest care to

reproduce itself in steadily increasing quantities and to supply the most abundant food in the form of milk and meat. All former means of procuring food now receded into the background; hunting, formerly a necessity, now became a luxury . . .

For now slavery had also been invented. To the barbarian of the lower stage, a slave was valueless. Hence the treatment of defected enemies by the American Indians was quite different from that at a higher stage. The men were killed or adopted as brothers into the tribe of the victors; the women were taken as wives or otherwise adopted with their surviving children. At this stage human labor power still does not produce any considerable surplus over and above its maintenance costs. That was no longer the case after the introduction of cattle breeding, metalworking, weaving, and lastly, agriculture. Just as the wives whom it had formerly been so easy to obtain had now acquired an exchange value and were bought, so also with labor power, particularly since the herds had definitely become family possessions. The family did not multiply so rapidly as the cattle. More people were needed to look after them; for this purpose use could be made of the enemies captured in war, who could also be bred just as easily as the cattle themselves.

Once it had passed into the private possession of families and there rapidly begun to augment, this wealth dealt a severe blow to the society founded on pairing marriage and the matriarchal gens. Pairing marriage had brought a new element into the family. By the side of the natural mother of the child it placed its natural and attested father with a better warrant of paternity, probably, than that of many a "father" today. According to the division of labor within the family at that time, it was the man's part to obtain food and the instruments of labor necessary for the purpose. He therefore also owned the instruments of labor, and in the event of husband and wife separating, he took them with him, just as she retained her household goods. Therefore, according to the social custom of the time, the man was also the owner of the new source of subsistence, the cattle, and later of the new instruments of labor, the slaves. But according to the custom of the same society, his children could not inherit from him. For as regards inheritance, the position was as follows:

At first, according to mother right—so long, therefore, as descent was reckoned only in the female line—and according to the original custom of inheritance within the gens, the gentile relatives inherited from a deceased fellow member of their gens. His property had to remain within the gens. His effects being insignificant, they probably always passed in practice to his nearest gentile relations—that is, to his blood relations on the mother's side. The children of the dead man, however, did not belong to his gens, but to that of their mother; it was from her that they inherited, at first conjointly with her other blood-relations, later perhaps with rights of priority; they could not inherit from their father because they did not belong to his gens within which his property had to remain. When the owner of the herds died, therefore, his herds would go first to his brothers and sisters and to his sister's children, or to the issue of his mother's sisters. But his own children were disinherited.

Thus on the one hand, in proportion as wealth increased it made the man's position in the family more important than the woman's, and on the other hand created an impulse to exploit this strengthened position in order to overthrow, in favor of his children, the traditional order of inheritance. This, however, was impossible so long as descent was reckoned according to mother right. Mother right, therefore, had to be overthrown, and overthrown it was. This was by no means so difficult as it looks to us today. For this revolution—one of the most decisive ever experienced by humanity—could take place without disturbing a single one of the living members of a gens. All could remain as they were. A simple decree sufficed that in the future the offspring of the male members should remain within the gens, but that of the female should be excluded by being transferred to the gens of their father. The reckoning of descent in the female line and the matriarchal law of inheritance were thereby overthrown, and the male line of descent and the paternal law of inheritance were substituted for them. As to how and when this revolution took place among civilized peoples, we have no knowledge. It falls entirely within prehistoric times. But that it *did* take place is more than sufficiently proved by the abundant traces of mother right which have been collected. . . .

The overthrow of mother right was the *world historical defeat of the female sex.* The man took command in the home also; the woman was degraded and reduced to servitude; she became the slave of his lust and a mere instrument for the production of children. This degraded position of the woman, especially conspicuous among the Greeks of the heroic and still more of the classical age, has gradually been palliated and

glossed over, and sometimes clothed in a milder form; in no sense has it been abolished.

The establishment of the exclusive supremacy of the man shows its effects first in the patriarchal family, which now emerges as an intermediate form. Its essential characteristic is not polygyny, of which more later, but "the organization of a number of persons, bond and free, into a family under paternal power for the purpose of holding lands and for the care of flocks and herds. . . . (In the Semitic form) the chiefs, at least, lived in polygamy. . . . Those held to servitude and those employed as servants lived in the marriage relation" [Morgan, 1963: 474].

Its essential features are the incorporation of unfree persons and paternal power; hence the perfect type of this form of family is the Roman. The original meaning of the word "family" (*familia*) is not that compound of sentimentality and domestic strife which forms the ideal of the present-day philistine; among the Romans it did not at first even refer to the married pair and their children but only to the slaves. *Famulus* means domestic slave, and *familia* is the total number of slaves belonging to one man. As late as the time of Gaius, the *familia, id est patrimonium* (family, that is, the patrimony, the inheritance) was bequeathed by will. The term was invented by the Romans to denote a new social organism whose head ruled over wife and children and a number of slaves, and was invested under Roman paternal power with rights of life and death over them all.

> This term, therefore, is no older than the ironclad family system of the Latin tribes, which came in after field agriculture and after legalized servitude, as well as after the separation of the Greeks and Latins [Morgan, 1963: 478].

Marx adds:

> The modern family contains in germ not only slavery (*servitus*) but also serfdom, since from the beginning it is related to agricultural services. It contains *in miniature* all the contradictions which later extend throughout society and its state.

Such a form of family shows the transition of the pairing family to monogamy. In order to make certain of the wife's fidelity and therefore of the paternity of the children, she is delivered over unconditionally into the power of the husband; if he kills her, he is only exercising his rights. . . .

Thus when monogamous marriage first makes its appearance in history, it is not as the reconciliation of man and woman, still less as the highest form of such a reconciliation. Quite the contrary monogamous marriage comes on the scene as the subjugation of the one sex by the other; it announces a struggle between the sexes unknown throughout the whole previous prehistoric period. In an old unpublished manuscript written by Marx and myself in 1846, I find the words: "The first division of labor is that between man and woman for the propagation of children." And today I can add: The first class opposition that appears in history coincides with the development of the antagonism between man and woman in monogamous marriage, and the first class oppression coincides with that of the female sex by the male. Monogamous marriage was a great historical step forward; nevertheless, together with slavery and private wealth, it opens the period that has lasted until today in which every step forward is also relatively a step backward, in which prosperity and development for some is won through the misery and frustration of others. It is the cellular form of civilized society in which the nature of the oppositions and contradictions fully active in that society can be already studied. . . .

(1884)

42 • *Charlotte Perkins Gilman*

FROM "THE YELLOW WALLPAPER"

It is very seldom that mere ordinary people like John and myself secure ancestral halls for the summer.

A colonial mansion, a hereditary estate, I would say a haunted house, and reach the height of romantic felicity—but that would be asking too much of fate!

Still I will proudly declare that there is something queer about it.

Else, why should it be let so cheaply? And why have stood so long untenanted?

John laughs at me, of course, but one expects that in marriage.

John is practical in the extreme. He has no patience with faith, an intense horror of superstition, and he scoffs openly at any talk of things not to be felt and seen and put down in figures.

John is a physician, and *perhaps*—(I would not say it to a living soul, of course, but this is dead paper and a great relief to my mind—) *perhaps* that is one reason I do not get well faster.

You see he does not believe I am sick!

And what can one do?

If a physician of high standing, and one's own husband, assures friends and relatives that there is really nothing the matter with one but temporary nervous depression—a slight hysterical tendency[1]—what is one to do?

My brother is also a physician, and also of high standing, and he says the same thing.

So I take phosphates or phosphites—whichever it is, and tonics, and journeys, and air, and exercise, and am absolutely forbidden to "work" until I am well again.

Personally, I disagree with their ideas.

Personally, I believe that congenial work, with excitement and change, would do me good.

But what is one to do?

I did write for a while in spite of them; but it *does* exhaust me a good deal—having to be so sly about it, or else meet with heavy opposition.

Reprinted from *The Oxford Book of Women's Writing in the United States*, eds. Linda Wagner-Martin and Cathy N. Davidson. New York: Oxford University Press, 1995. pp. 41–43, 52.

I sometimes fancy that in my condition if I had less opposition and more society and stimulus—but John says the very worst thing I can do is to think about my condition, and I confess it always makes me feel bad.

So I will let it alone and talk about the house.

The most beautiful place! It is quite alone, standing well back from the road, quite three miles from the village. It makes me think of English places that you read about, for there are hedges and walls and gates that lock, and lots of separate little houses for the gardeners and people.

There is a *delicious* garden! I never saw such a garden—large and shady, full of box-bordered paths, and lined with long grape-covered arbors with seats under them.

There were greenhouses, too, but they are all broken now.

There was some legal trouble, I believe, something about the heirs and coheirs; anyhow, the place has been empty for years.

That spoils my ghostliness, I am afraid, but I don't care—there is something strange about the house—I can feel it.

I even said so to John one moonlight evening, but he said what I felt was a *draught*, and shut the window.

I get unreasonably angry with John sometimes. I'm sure I never used to be so sensitive. I think it is due to this nervous condition.

But John says if I feel so, I shall neglect proper self-control; so I take pains to control myself—before him, at least, and that makes me very tired.

I don't like our room a bit. I wanted one downstairs that opened on the piazza and had roses all over the window, and such pretty old-fashioned chintz hangings! but John would not hear of it.

He said there was only one window and not room for two beds, and no near room for him if he took another.

He is very careful and loving, and hardly lets me stir without special direction.

I have a schedule prescription for each hour in the day, he takes all care from me, and so I feel basely ungrateful not to value it more.

He said we came here solely on my account, that I was to have perfect rest and all the air I could get. "Your exercise depends on your strength, my dear," said he, "and your food somewhat on your appetite; but air you can absorb all the time." So we took the nursery at the top of the house.

It is a big, airy room, the whole floor nearly, with windows that look all ways, and air and sunshine galore. It was nursery first and then playroom and gymnasium, I should judge; for the windows are barred for little children, and there are rings and things in the walls.

The paint and paper look as if a boys' school had used it. It is stripped off—the paper—in great patches all around the head of my bed, about as far as I can reach, and in a great place on the other side of the room low down. I never saw a worse paper in my life.

One of those sprawling flamboyant patterns committing every artistic sin.

It is dull enough to confuse the eye in following, pronounced enough to constantly irritate and provoke study, and when you follow the lame uncertain curves for a little distance they suddenly commit suicide—plunge off at outrageous angles, destroy themselves in unheard of contradictions.

The color is repellant, almost revolting; a smouldering unclean yellow, strangely faded by the slow-turning sunlight.

It is a dull yet lurid orange in some places, a sickly sulphur tint in others.

No wonder the children hated it! I should hate it myself if I had to live in this room long.

There comes John, and I must put this away,—he hates to have me write a word.

* * *

(weeks later . . .)

I really have discovered something at last.

Through watching so much at night, when it changes so, I have finally found out.

The front pattern *does* move—and no wonder! The woman behind shakes it!

Sometimes I think there are a great many women behind, and sometimes only one, and she crawls around fast, and her crawling shakes it all over.

Then in the very bright spots she keeps still, and in the very shady spots she just takes hold of the bars and shakes them hard.

And she is all the time trying to climb through. But nobody could climb through that pattern—it strangles so; I think that is why it has so many heads.

They get through, and then the pattern strangles them off and turns them upside down, and makes their eyes white!

If those heads were covered or taken off it would not be half so bad.

I think that woman gets out in the daytime!

And I'll tell you why—privately—I've seen her!

I can see her out of every one of my windows!

It is the same woman, I know, for she is always creeping, and most women do not creep by daylight.

I see her in that long shaded lane, creeping up and down. I see her in those dark grape arbors, creeping all around the garden.

I see her on that long road under the trees, creeping along, and when a carriage comes she hides under the blackberry vines.

I don't blame her a bit. It must be very humiliating to be caught creeping by daylight!

I always lock the door when I creep by daylight. I can't do it at night, for I know John would suspect something at once.

And John is so queer now, that I don't want to irritate him. I wish he would take another room! Besides,

I don't want anybody to get that woman out at night but myself.

I often wonder if I could see her out of all the windows at once.

But, turn as fast as I can, I can only see out of one at one time.

And though I always see her, she *may* be able to creep faster than I can turn!

I have watched her sometimes away off in the open country, creeping as fast as a cloud shadow in a high wind.

If only that top pattern could be gotten off from the under one! I mean to try it, little by little.

(1892)

NOTE

1. Many women's ailments were diagnosed as coming from the womb (*hyster*). This ineffectual diagnosis often led to mistreatment.

---

43 • *Charlotte Perkins Gilman*

FROM *WOMEN AND ECONOMICS*

A Study of the Economic Relation between Men and Women as a Factor in Social Evolution

Economic independence for women necessarily involves a change in the home and family relation. But, if that change is for the advantage of individual and race, we need not fear it. It does not involve a change in the marriage relation except in withdrawing the element of economic dependence, nor in the relation of mother to child save to improve it. But it does involve the exercise of human faculty in women, in social service and exchange rather than in domestic service solely. This will of course require the introduction of some other form of living than that which now obtains. It will render impossible the present method of feeding the world by means of millions of private servants, and bringing up children by the same hand. . . .

If there should be built and opened in any of our large cities to-day a commodious and well-served apartment house for professional women with families, it would be filled at once. The apartments would be without kitchens; but there would be a kitchen belonging to the house from which meals could be served to the families in their rooms or in a common

Reprinted from *The Feminist Papers: From Adams to de Beauvoir*, ed. Alice S. Rossi, 591–593, 596–598. New York: Bantam, 1974. Reproduced as in the original.

dining-room, as preferred. It would be a home where the cleaning was done by efficient workers, not hired separately by the families, but engaged by the manager of the establishment; and a roof-garden, day nursery, and kindergarten, under well-trained professional nurses and teachers, would insure proper care of the children. The demand for such provision is increasing daily, and must soon be met, not by a boarding-house or a lodging-house, a hotel, a restaurant, or any makeshift patching together of these; but by a permanent provision for the needs of women and children, of family privacy with collective advantage. This must be offered on a business basis to prove a substantial business success; and it will so prove, for it is a growing social need. . . .

In suburban homes this purpose could be accomplished much better by a grouping of adjacent houses, each distinct and having its own yard, but all kitchenless, and connected by covered ways with the eating-house. No detailed prophecy can be made of the precise forms which would ultimately prove most useful and pleasant; but the growing social need is for the specializing of the industries practised in the home and for the proper mechanical provision for them. . . .

Meals could of course be served in the house as long as desired; but, when people become accustomed to pure, clean homes, where no steaming industry is carried on, they will gradually prefer to go to their food instead of having it brought to them. It is a perfectly natural process, and a healthful one, to go to one's food. And, after all, the changes between living in one room, and so having the cooking most absolutely convenient; going as far as the limits of a large house permit, to one's own dining-room; and going a little further to a dining-room not in one's own house, but near by,—these differ but in degree. Families could go to eat together, just as they can go to bathe together or to listen to music together; but, if it fell out that different individuals presumed to develop an appetite at different hours, they could meet it without interfering with other people's comfort or sacrificing their own. Any housewife knows the difficulty of always getting a family together at meals. Why try? Then arises sentiment, and asserts that family affection, family unity, the very existence of the family, depend on their being together at meals. A family

unity which is only bound together with a table-cloth is of questionable value. . . .

It is not the home as a place of family life and love that injures the child, but as the centre of a tangled heap of industries, low in their ungraded condition, and lower still because they are wholly personal. Work the object of which is merely to serve one's self is the lowest. Work the object of which is merely to serve one's family is the next lowest. Work the object of which is to serve more and more people, in widening range . . . is social service in the fullest sense, and the highest form of service that we can reach. . . .

We suffer also, our lives long, from an intense self-consciousness, from a sensitiveness beyond all need; we demand measureless personal attention and devotion, because we have been born and reared in a very hot-bed of these qualities. A baby who spent certain hours of every day among other babies, being cared for because he was a baby, and not because he was "my baby," would grow to have a very different opinion of himself from that which is forced upon each new soul that comes among us by the ceaseless adoration of his own immediate family. What he needs to learn at once and for all, to learn softly and easily, but inexorably, is that he is one of many. We all dimly recognize this in our praise of large families, and in our saying that "an only child is apt to be selfish." So is an only family. The earlier and more easily a child can learn that human life means many people, and their behavior to one another, the happier and stronger and more useful his life will be.

This could be taught him with no difficulty whatever, under certain conditions, just as he is taught his present sensitiveness and egotism by the present conditions. It is not only temperature and diet and rest and exercise which affect the baby. "He does love to be noticed," we say. "He is never so happy as when he has a dozen worshippers around him." But what is the young soul learning all the while? What does he gather, as he sees and hears and slowly absorbs impressions? With the inflexible inferences of a clear, young brain, unsupplied with any counter-evidence until later in life, he learns that women are meant to wait on people, to get dinner, and sweep and pick up things; that men are made to bring home things, and are to be begged of according to circumstances; that babies are the object of concentrated admiration; that their hair, hands, feet, are specially attractive; that they are the heated focus of attention, to be passed from hand to hand, swung and danced and amused most violently, and also be laid aside and have nothing done to them, with no regard to their preference in either case. . . .

. . . [W]hile we flatter ourselves that things remain the same, they are changing under our very eyes from year to year, from day to day. Education, hiding itself behind a wall of books, but consisting more and more fully in the grouping of children and in the training of faculties never mentioned in the curriculum,— education, which is our human motherhood, has crept nearer and nearer to its true place, its best work,—the care and training of the little child. Some women there are, and some men, whose highest service to humanity is the care of children. Such should not concentrate their powers upon their own children alone,— a most questionable advantage,—but should be so placed that their talent and skill, their knowledge and experience, would benefit the largest number of children. . . .

As we now arrange life, our children must take their chances while babies, and live or die, improve or deteriorate, according to the mother to whom they chance to be born. An inefficient mother does not prevent a child from having a good college education; but the education of babyhood, the most important of all, is wholly in her hands. It is futile to say that mothers should be taught how to fulfil their duties. You cannot teach every mother to be a good school educator or a good college educator. Why should you expect every mother to be a good nursery educator? . . .

The growth and change in home and family life goes steadily on under and over and through our prejudices and convictions; and the education of the child has changed and become a social function, while we still imagine the mother to be doing it all. . . .

We think no harm of motherhood because our darlings go out each day to spend long hours in school. The mother is not held neglectful, nor the child bereft. It is not called a "separation of mother and child." There would be no further harm or risk or loss in a babyhood passed among such changed surroundings and skilled service as should meet its needs more perfectly than it is possible for the mother to meet them alone at home.

Better surroundings and care for babies, better education, do not mean, as some mothers may imagine, that the tiny monthling is to be taught to read, or even that it is to be exposed to cabalistical arrangements of color and form and sound which shall mysteriously force the young intelligence to flower. It would mean, mainly, a far quieter and more peaceful life than is possible for the heavily loved and violently cared for baby in the busy household; and the impressions which it did meet would be planned and maintained with an intelligent appreciation of its mental powers. The mother would not be excluded, but supplemented, as she is now, by the teacher and the school. . . .

. . . The mother as a social servant instead of a home servant will not lack in true mother duty. She will love her child as well, perhaps better, when she is not in hourly contact with it, when she goes from its life to her own life, and back from her own life to its life, with ever new delight and power. She can keep the deep, thrilling joy of motherhood far fresher in her heart, far more vivid and open in voice and eyes and tender hands, when the hours of individual work give her mind another channel for her own part of the day. From her work, loved and honored though it is, she will return to the home life, the child life, with an eager, ceaseless pleasure, cleansed of all the fret and fraction and weariness that so mar it now.

(1898)

44 • *Mother (Mary) Jones*

"GIRL SLAVES OF THE MILWAUKEE BREWERIES"

It is the same old story, as pitiful as old, as true as pitiful.

When the whistle blows in the morning it calls the girl slaves of the bottle-washing department of the breweries to don their wet shoes and rags and hustle to the bastile to serve out their sentences. It is indeed true, they are *sentenced* to hard, brutal labor—labor that gives no cheer, brings no recompense. Condemned for life, to slave daily in the washroom in wet shoes and wet clothes, surrounded with foul-mouthed, brutal foremen, whose orders and language would not look well in print and would surely shock over-sensitive ears or delicate nerves! And their crime? Involuntary poverty. It is hereditary. They are no more to blame for it than is a horse for having the glanders. It is the accident of birth. This accident that throws them into the surging, seething mass known as the working class is what forces them out of the cradle into servitude, to be willing(?) slaves of the mill, factory, department store, hell, or bottling shop in Milwaukee's colossal breweries; to create wealth for the brewery barons, that they may own palaces, theaters, automobiles, blooded stock, farms, banks, and Heaven knows what all, while the poor girls slave on all day in the vile smell of sour beer, lifting cases of empty and full bottles weighing from 100 to 150 pounds, in their wet shoes and rags, for God knows they cannot buy clothes on the miserable pittance doled out to them by their soulless master class. The conscienceless rich see no reason why the slave should not be content on the crust of bread for its share of all the wealth created. That these slaves of the dampness should contract rheumatism is a foregone conclusion. Rheumatism is one of the chronic ailments, and is closely followed by consumption. Consumption is well known to be only a disease of poverty. The Milwaukee lawmakers, of course, enacted an antispit ordinance to protect the public health, and the brewers contributed to the Red Cross Society to make war on the shadow of tuberculosis, and all the while the big capitalists are setting out incubators to hatch out germs enough among the poor workers to destroy the nation. Should one of these poor girl slaves spit on the sidewalk, it would cost her more than she can make in two weeks' work. Such is the *fine* system of the present-day affairs. The foreman even regulates the time that they may stay in the toilet room, and in the event of overstaying it gives the foreman an opportunity he seems to be looking for to indulge in indecent and foul language. Should the patient slave forget herself and take offense, it will cost her the job in that prison. And after all, bad as it is, it is all that she knows how to do. To deprive her of the job means less crusts and worse rags in "the land of the free and the home of the brave." Many of the girls have no home nor parents and are forced to feed and clothe and shelter themselves, and all this on an average of $3.00 per week. Ye Gods! What a horrible nightmare! What hope is there for decency when unscrupulous wealth may exploit its producers so shamelessly?

No matter how cold, how stormy, how inclement the weather, many of these poor girl slaves must walk from their shacks to their work, for their miserable stipend precludes any possibility of squeezing a street car ride out of it. And to this is due our much-vaunted greatness. Is this civilization? If so, what, please, is barbarism?

As an illustration of what these poor girls must submit to, one about to become a mother told me with tears in her eyes that every other day a depraved specimen of mankind took delight in measuring her girth

First published in *United Mine Workers Journal*. 1910 Apr 7; 20(47): 2.

and passing such comments as befits such humorous(?) occasion.

While the wage paid is 75 to 85 cents a day, the poor slaves are not permitted to work more than three or four days a week, and the continual threat of idle days makes the slave much more tractable and submissive than would otherwise obtain. Often when their day's work is done they are put to washing off the tables and lunch room floors and the other odd jobs, for which there is not even the suggestion of compensation. Of course, abuse always follows power, and nowhere is it more in evidence than in this miserable treatment the brewers and their hirelings accord their girl slaves.

The foreman also uses his influence, through certain living mediums near at hand, to neutralize any effort having in view the organization of these poor helpless victims of an unholy and brutal profit system, and threats of discharge were made, should these girls attend my meetings.

One of these foremen actually carried a union card, but the writer of this article reported him to the union and had him deprived of it for using such foul language to the girls under him. I learned of him venting his spite by discharging several girls, and I went to the superintendent and told him the character of the foreman. On the strength of my charges, he was called to the office and when he was informed of the nature of the visit, he patted the superintendent familiarly on the back and whined out how loyal he was to the superintendent, the whole performance taking on the character of servile lickspittle. As he fawns on his superior, so he expects to play autocrat with his menials and exact the same cringing from them under him. Such is the petty boss who holds the living of the working-class girls in his hands.

The brewers themselves were always courteous when I called on them, but their underlings were not so tactful, evidently working under instructions. The only brewer who treated me rudely or denied me admittance was Mr. Blatz, who brusquely told me his feelings in the following words: "The Brewers' Association of Milwaukee met when you first came to town and decided not to permit these girls to organize." This Brewers' Association is a strong union of all the brewery plutocrats, composed of Schlitz, Pabst, Miller, and Blatz breweries, who are the principal employers of women. And this union met and decided as above stated, that these women should not be permitted to organize! I then told Mr. Blatz that he could not shut me out of the halls of legislation, that as soon as the legislature assembles I shall appear there and put these conditions on record and demand an investigation and the drafting of suitable laws to protect the womanhood of the state.

Organized labor and humanity demand protection for these helpless victims of insatiable greed, in the interest of motherhood of our future state.

Will the people of this country at large, and the organized wage-workers in particular, tolerate and stand any longer for such conditions as existing in the bottling establishments of these Milwaukee breweries? I hope not! Therefore, I ask all fair-minded people to refrain from purchasing the product of these baron brewers until they will change things for the better for these poor girls working in their bottling establishments.

Exploited by the brewers! Insulted by the petty bosses! Deserted by the press, which completely ignored me and gave no helping hand to these poor girls' cause. Had they had a vote, however, their case would likely have attracted more attention from all sides. Poor peons of the brewers! Neglected by all the Gods! Deserted by all mankind. The present shorn of all that makes life worth living, the future hopeless, without a comforting star or glimmer. What avails our boasted greatness built upon such human wreckage? What is civilization and progress to them? What "message" bears the holy brotherhood in the gorgeous temples of modern worship? What terrors has the over-investigated white-slave traffic for her? What a prolific recruiting station for the red-light district! For after all, the white slave *eats, drinks,* and wears good clothing, and to the hopeless this means living, if it only lasts a minute. What has the beer slave to look forward to—the petty boss will make her job cost her virtue anyhow. This has come to be a price of a job everywhere nowadays. Is it any wonder the white-slave traffic abounds on all sides? No wonder the working class has lost all faith in Gods. Hell itself has no terrors worse than a term in industrial slavery. I will give these brewery lords of Milwaukee notice that my two months' investigation and efforts to organize, in spite of all obstacles placed in my way, will bear fruit, and the sooner they realize their duty the better it will be for themselves. Will they do it?

Think of it, fathers and mothers. Think of it, men and women. When it is asked of thee, "What hast thou done for the economic redemption of the sisters of thy brother Abel?" what will thy answer be?

(1910)

45 • *Emma Goldman*

"THE TRAFFIC IN WOMEN"

Our reformers have suddenly made a great discovery—the white slave traffic. The papers are full of these "unheard-of conditions," and lawmakers are already planning a new set of laws to check the horror.

It is significant that whenever the public mind is to be diverted from a great social wrong, a crusade is inaugurated against indecency, gambling, saloons, etc. And what is the result of such crusades? Gambling is increasing, saloons are doing a lively business through back entrances, prostitution is at its height, and the system of pimps and cadets is but aggravated.

How is it that an institution, known almost to every child, should have been discovered so suddenly? How is it that this evil, known to all sociologists, should now be made such an important issue?

To assume that the recent investigation of the white slave traffic (and, by the way, a very superficial investigation) has discovered anything new, is, to say the least, very foolish. Prostitution has been, and is, a widespread evil, yet mankind goes on its business, perfectly indifferent to the sufferings and distress of the victims of prostitution. As indifferent, indeed, as mankind has remained to our industrial system, or to economic prostitution.

Only when human sorrows are turned into a toy with glaring colors will baby people become interested—for a while at least. The people are a very fickle baby that must have new toys every day. The "righteous" cry against the white slave traffic is such a toy. It serves to amuse the people for a little while, and it will help to create a few more fat political jobs—parasites who stalk about the world as inspectors, investigators, detectives, and so forth.

What is really the cause of the trade in women? Not merely white women, but yellow and black women as well. Exploitation, of course; the merciless Moloch of capitalism that fattens on underpaid labor, thus driving thousands of women and girls into prostitution. With Mrs. Warren these girls feel, "Why waste your life working for a few shillings a week in a scullery, eighteen hours a day?"

Naturally our reformers say nothing about this cause. They know it well enough, but it doesn't pay to say anything about it. It is much more profitable to play the Pharisee, to pretend an outraged morality, than to go to the bottom of things.

However, there is one commendable exception among the young writers: Reginald Wright Kauffman, whose work *The House of Bondage* is the first earnest attempt to treat the social evil—not from a sentimental Philistine viewpoint. A journalist of wide experience, Mr. Kauffman proves that our industrial system leaves most women no alternative except prostitution. The women portrayed in *The House of Bondage* belong to the working class. Had the author portrayed the life of women in other spheres, he would have been confronted with the same state of affairs.

Nowhere is woman treated according to the merit of her work, but rather as a sex. It is therefore almost inevitable that she should pay for her right to exist, to keep a position in whatever line, with sex favors. Thus it is merely a question of degree whether she sells herself to one man, in or out of marriage, or to many men. Whether our reformers admit it or not, the economic and social inferiority of woman is responsible for prostitution.

Just at present our good people are shocked by the disclosures that in New York City alone one out of every ten women works in a factory, that the average wage received by women is six dollars per week for forty-eight to sixty hours of work, and that the majority of female wage workers face many months of

Reprinted from *Anarchism and Other Essays* by Emma Goldman. Third Revised Edition. New York: Mother Earth Publishing Association, 1917.

idleness which leaves the average wage about $280 a year. In view of these economic horrors, is it to be wondered at that prostitution and the white slave trade have become such dominant factors?

Lest the preceding figures be considered an exaggeration, it is well to examine what some authorities on prostitution have to say:

"A prolific cause of female depravity can be found in the several tables, showing the description of the employment pursued, and the wages received, by the women previous to their fall, and it will be a question for the political economist to decide how far mere business consideration should be an apology on the part of employers for a reduction in their rates of remuneration, and whether the savings of a small percentage on wages is not more than counterbalanced by the enormous amount of taxation enforced on the public at large to defray the expenses incurred on account of a system of vice, *which is the direct result, in many cases, of insufficient compensation of honest labor.*"*

Our present-day reformers would do well to look into Dr. Sanger's book. There they will find that out of 2,000 cases under his observation, but few came from the middle classes, from well-ordered conditions, or pleasant homes. By far the largest majority were working girls and working women; some driven into prostitution through sheer want, others because of a cruel, wretched life at home, others again because of thwarted and crippled physical natures (of which I shall speak later on). Also it will do the maintainers of purity and morality good to learn that out of two thousand cases, 490 were married women, women who lived with their husbands. Evidently there was not much of a guaranty for their "safety and purity" in the sanctity of marriage . . .†

. . . It would be one-sided and extremely superficial to maintain that the economic factor is the only cause of prostitution. There are others no less important and vital. That, too, our reformers know, but dare discuss even less than the institution that saps the very life out of both men and women. I refer to the sex question, the very mention of which causes most people moral spasms.

It is a conceded fact that woman is being reared as a sex commodity, and yet she is kept in absolute ignorance of the meaning and importance of sex. Everything dealing with that subject is suppressed, and persons who attempt to bring light into this terrible darkness are persecuted and thrown into prison. Yet it is nevertheless true that so long as a girl is not to know how to take care of herself, not to know the function of the most important part of her life, we need not be surprised if she becomes an easy prey to prostitution, or to any other form of a relationship which degrades her to the position of an object for mere sex gratification.

It is due to this ignorance that the entire life and nature of the girl is thwarted and crippled. We have long ago taken it as a self-evident fact that the boy may follow the call of the wild; that is to say, that the boy may, as soon as his sex nature asserts itself, satisfy that nature; but our moralists are scandalized at the very thought that the nature of a girl should assert itself. To the moralist prostitution does not consist so much in the fact that the woman sells her body, but rather that she sells it out of wedlock. That this is no mere statement is proved by the fact that marriage for monetary considerations is perfectly legitimate, sanctified by law and public opinion, while any other union is condemned and repudiated. Yet a prostitute, if properly defined, means nothing else than "any person for whom sexual relationships are subordinated to gain."*

"Those women are prostitutes who sell their bodies for the exercise of the sexual act and make of this a profession."†

In fact, Banger goes further; he maintains that the act of prostitution is "intrinsically equal to that of a man or woman who contracts a marriage for economic reasons."

Of course, marriage is the goal of every girl, but as thousands of girls cannot marry, our stupid social customs condemn them either to a life of celibacy or prostitution. Human nature asserts itself regardless of all laws, nor is there any plausible reason why

---

*Dr. Sanger, *The History of Prostitution.*
†It is a significant fact that Dr. Sanger's book has been excluded from the U.S. mails. Evidently the authorities are not anxious that the public be informed as to the true cause of prostitution.

---

*Guyot, *La Prostitution.*
†Banger, *Criminalité et Condition Economique.*

nature should adapt itself to a perverted conception of morality.

Society considers the sex experiences of a man as attributes of his general development, while similar experiences in the life of a woman are looked upon as a terrible calamity, a loss of honor and of all that is good and noble in a human being. This double standard of morality has played no little part in the creation and perpetuation of prostitution. It involves the keeping of the young in absolute ignorance on sex matters, which alleged "innocence," together with an overwrought and stifled sex nature, helps to bring about a state of affairs that our Puritans are so anxious to avoid or prevent.

Not that the gratification of sex must needs lead to prostitution; it is the cruel, heartless, criminal persecution of those who dare divert from the beaten track, which is responsible for it.

Girls, mere children, work in crowded, overheated rooms ten to twelve hours daily at a machine, which tends to keep them in a constant over-excited sex state. Many of these girls have no home or comforts of any kind; therefore the street or some place of cheap amusement is the only means of forgetting their daily routine. This naturally brings them into close proximity with the other sex. It is hard to say which of the two factors brings the girl's over-sexed condition to a climax, but it is certainly the most natural thing that a climax should result. That is the first step toward prostitution. Nor is the girl to be held responsible for it. On the contrary, it is altogether the fault of society, the fault of our lack of understanding, of our lack of appreciation of life in the making; especially is it the criminal fault of our moralists, who condemn a girl for all eternity, because she has gone from the "path of virtue"; that is, because her first sex experience has taken place without the sanction of the Church.

The girl feels herself a complete outcast, with the doors of home and society closed in her face. Her entire training and tradition is such that the girl herself feels depraved and fallen, and therefore has no ground to stand upon, or any hold that will lift her up, instead of dragging her down. Thus society creates the victims that it afterwards vainly attempts to get rid of. The meanest, most depraved and decrepit man still considers himself too good to take as his wife the woman whose grace he was quite willing to buy, even though he might thereby save her from a life of horror. Nor can she turn to her own sister for help. In her stupidity the latter deems herself too pure and chaste, not

realizing that her own position is in many respects even more deplorable than her sister's of the street.

"The wife who married for money, compared with the prostitute," says Havelock Ellis, "is the true scab. She is paid less, gives much more in return in labor and care, and is absolutely bound to her master. The prostitute never signs away the right over her own person, she retains her freedom and personal rights, nor is she always compelled to submit to man's embrace."

Nor does the better-than-thou woman realize the apologist claim of Lecky that "though she may be the supreme type of vice, she is also the most efficient guardian of virtue. But for her, happy homes would be polluted, unnatural and harmful practice would abound."

Moralists are ever ready to sacrifice one-half of the human race for the sake of some miserable institution which they can not outgrow. As a matter of fact, prostitution is no more a safeguard for the purity of the home than rigid laws are a safeguard against prostitution. Fully fifty per cent, of married men are patrons of brothels. It is through this virtuous element that the married women—nay, even the children—are infected with venereal diseases. Yet society has not a word of condemnation for the man, while no law is too monstrous to be set in motion against the helpless victim. She is not only preyed upon by those who use her, but she is also absolutely at the mercy of every policeman and miserable detective on the beat, the officials at the station house, the authorities in every prison. . . .

. . . There is not a single modern writer on the subject who does not refer to the utter futility of legislative methods in coping with the issue. Thus Dr. Blaschko finds that governmental suppression and moral crusades accomplish nothing save driving the evil into secret channels, multiplying its dangers to society. Havelock Ellis, the most thorough and humane student of prostitution, proves by a wealth of data that the more stringent the methods of persecution the worse the condition becomes. Among other data we learn that in France, "in 1560, Charles IX. abolished brothels through an edict, but the numbers of prostitutes were only increased, while many new brothels appeared in unsuspected shapes, and were more dangerous. In spite of all such legislation, *or because of it*, there has been no country in which prostitution has played a more conspicuous part."*

Sex and Society.

An educated public opinion, freed from the legal and moral hounding of the prostitute, can alone help to ameliorate present conditions. Wilful shutting of eyes and ignoring of the evil as a social factor of modern life, can but aggravate matters. We must rise above our foolish notions of "better than thou," and learn to recognize in the prostitute a product of social conditions. Such a realization will sweep away the attitude of hypocrisy, and insure a greater understanding and more humane treatment. As to a thorough eradication of prostitution, nothing can accomplish that save a complete transvaluation of all accepted values—especially the moral ones—coupled with the abolition of industrial slavery.

(1910)

46 • *James Oppenheim*

"BREAD AND ROSES"

As we come marching, marching,
Unnumbered women dead
Go crying through our singing
Their ancient song of Bread;
Small art and love and beauty
Their drudging spirits knew—
Yes, it is bread we fight for,
But we fight for roses, too.

As we come marching, marching,
We bring the greater days;
The rising of the women
Means the rising of us all.
No more the drudge and idler,
Ten that toil where one reposes,
But a sharing of life's glories,
Bread and Roses, Bread and Roses.

(1911)

From The American Magazine, December, 1911.

47 • *Rose Schneiderman*

"WE HAVE FOUND YOU WANTING"

One of the greatest industrial tragedies in U.S. history occurred on March 25, 1911, when 146 workers, mostly young immigrant women, died in a fire at the Triangle Shirtwaist company in New York City. Addressing a memorial meeting held in the Metropolitan Opera House on April 2, 1911, Rose Schneiderman (1866–1972), organizer for the International Ladies' Garment Workers' Union (ILGWU) and the Women's Trade Union League read the following lament for the lives lost.

I would be a traitor to those poor burned bodies, if I were to come here to talk good fellowship. We have

First published in *The Survey*, April 8, 1911.

tried you good people of the public—and we have found you wanting.

The old Inquisition had its rack and its thumbscrews and its instruments of torture with iron teeth. We know what these things are today: the iron teeth are our necessities, the thumbscrews are the high-powered and swift machinery close to which we must work, and the rack is here in the firetrap structures that will destroy us the minute they catch fire.

This is not the first time girls have been burned alive in this city. Every week I must learn of the untimely death of one of my sister workers. Every year thousands of us are maimed. The life of men and women is so cheap and property is so sacred! There are so many of us for one job, it matters little if 140-odd are burned to death.

We have tried you, citizens! We are trying you now and you have a couple of dollars for the sorrowing mothers and brothers and sisters by way of a charity gift. But every time the workers come out in the only way they know to protest against conditions which are unbearable, the strong hand of the law is allowed to press down heavily upon us.

Public officials have only words of warning for us—warning that we must be intensely orderly and must be intensely peaceable, and they have the workhouse just back of all their warnings. The strong hand of the law beats us back when we rise—back into the conditions that make life unbearable.

I can't talk fellowship to you who are gathered here. Too much blood has been spilled. I know from experience it is up to the working people to save themselves. And the only way is through a strong working-class movement.

(1911)

48 • *Alexandra Kollotai*

"WORKING WOMAN AND MOTHER"

MASHENKA THE FACTORY DIRECTOR'S WIFE

Mashenka is the factory director's wife. Mashenka is expecting a baby. Although everyone in the factory director's house is a little bit anxious, there is a festive atmosphere. This is not surprising, for Mashenka is going to present her husband with an heir. There will be someone to whom he can leave all his wealth—the wealth created by the hands of working men and women. The doctor has ordered them to look after Mashenka very carefully. Don't let her get tired, don't let her lift anything heavy. Let her eat just what she fancies. Fruit? Give her some fruit. Caviare? Give her caviare.

The important thing is that Mashenka should not feel worried or distressed in any way. Then the baby will be born strong and healthy; the birth will be easy and Mashenka will keep her bloom. That is how they talk in the factory director's family. That is the accepted way of handling an expectant mother, in families where the purses are stuffed with gold and credit notes. They take good care of Mashenka the lady.

Do not tire yourself, Mashenka, do not try and move the armchair. That is what they say to Mashenka the lady.

The humbugs and hypocrites of the bourgeoisie maintain that the expectant mother is sacred to them. But is that really in fact the case?

Originally published as a pamphlet (1914). Reprinted in *Alexandra Kollantai: Selected Writings*, ed. Alix Holt, W. W. Norton (1980).

MASHENKA THE LAUNDRESS

In the same house as the factory director's wife, but in the back part in a corner behind a printed calico curtain, huddles another Mashenka. She does the laundry and the housework. Mashenka is eight months pregnant. But she would open her eyes wide in surprise if they said to her, "Mashenka, you must not carry heavy things, you must look after yourself, for your own sake, for the child's sake, and for the sake of humanity. You are expecting a baby and that means your condition is, in the eyes of society, 'sacred.'" Masha would take this either as uncalled-for interference or as a cruel joke. Where have you seen a woman of the working class given special treatment because she is pregnant? Masha and the hundreds of thousands of other women of the propertyless classes who are forced to sell their working hands know that the owners have no mercy when they see women in need; and they have no other alternative, however exhausted they may be, but to go out to work.

"An expectant mother must have, above all, undisturbed sleep, good food, fresh air, and not too much physical strain." That is what the doctor says. Masha the laundress and the hundreds and thousands of women workers, the slaves of capital, would laugh in his face. A minimum of physical strain? Fresh air? Wholesome food and enough of it? Undisturbed sleep? What working woman knows these blessings? They are only for Mashenka the lady, and for the wives of the factory owners.

Early in the morning before the darkness has given way to dawn and while Mashenka the lady is still having sweet dreams, Mashenka the laundress gets up from her narrow bed and goes into the damp, dark laundry. She is greeted by the fusty smell of dirty linen; she slips around on the wet floor; yesterday's puddles still have not dried. It is not of her own free will that Masha slaves away in the laundry. She is driven by that tireless overseer—need. Masha's husband is a worker, and his pay packet is so small two people could not possibly keep alive on it. And so in silence, gritting her teeth, she stands over the tub until the very last possible day, right up until the birth. Do not be mistaken into thinking that Masha the laundress has "iron health" as the ladies like to say when they are talking about working women. Masha's legs are heavy with swollen veins, through standing at the tub

for such long periods. She can walk only slowly and with difficulty. There are bags under her eyes, her arms are puffed up and she has had no proper sleep for a long time.

The baskets of wet linen are often so heavy that Masha has to lean against the wall to prevent herself from falling. Her head swims and everything becomes dark in front of her eyes. It often feels as if there is a huge rotten tooth lodged at the back of her spine, and that her legs are made of lead. If only she could lie down for an hour . . . have some rest . . . but working women are not allowed to do such things. Such pamperings are not for them. For, after all, they are not ladies. Masha puts up with her hard lot in silence. The only "sacred" women are those expectant mothers who are not driven by that relentless taskmaster, need. . . .

CHILDBIRTH

For the household of Masha the lady the birth is a big event. It is almost a holiday. The house is a flurry of doctors, midwives, and nurses. The mother lies in a clean, soft bed. There are flowers on the tables. Her husband is by her side; letters and telegrams are delivered. A priest gives thanksgiving prayers. The baby is born healthy and strong. That is not surprising. They have taken such care and made such a fuss of Masha.

Masha the laundress is also in labour. Behind the calico curtain, in the corner of a room full of other people, Masha is in pain. She tries to stifle her moaning, burying her head in the pillow. The neighbours are all working people and it would not do to deprive them of their sleep. Towards morning the midwife arrives. She washes and tucks up the baby and then hurries off to another birth. Mashenka is now alone in the room. She looks at the baby. What a thin little mite. Skinny and wrinkled. Its eyes seem to reproach the mother for having given birth at all. Mashenka looks at him and cries silently so as not to disturb the others. . . .

THE CROSS OF MOTHERHOOD

For Masha the lady, motherhood is a joyful occasion. In a bright, tidy nursery the factory owner's heir grows up under the eye of various nannies and the supervision of a doctor. If Masha the lady has too little milk of her own or does not want to spoil her figure, a wet-nurse can be found. Masha the lady amuses herself with the baby and then goes out visiting, goes shopping, or to the theatre, or to a ball. There is someone at hand to look after the baby. Motherhood is amusing, it is entertainment for Masha the lady.

For the other Mashas, the working women—the dyers, weavers, laundresses and the other hundreds and thousands of working-class women—motherhood is a cross. The factory siren calls the woman to work but her child is fretting and crying. How can she leave it? Who will look after it? She pours the milk into a bottle and gives the child to the old woman next door or leaves her young daughter in charge. She goes off to work, but she never stops worrying about the child. The little girl, well-intentioned but ignorant, might try feeding her brother porridge or bits of bread.

Masha the lady's baby looks better every day. Like white sugar or a firm rosy apple; so strong and healthy. The children of the factory worker, the laundress and the craft-worker grow thinner with every day. At nights the baby curls up small and cries. The doctor comes and scolds the mother for not breast-feeding the child or for not feeding it properly. "And you call yourself a mother. Now you have only yourself to blame if the baby dies." The hundreds and thousands of working mothers do not try to explain themselves. They stand with bent heads, furtively wiping away the tears. Could they tell the doctor of the difficulties they face? Would he believe them? Would he understand? . . .

WHAT IS THE ALTERNATIVE?

Imagine a society, a people, a community, where there are no longer Mashenka ladies and Mashenka laundresses. Where there are no parasites and no hired workers. Where all people do the same amount of work and society in return looks after them and helps them in life. Just as now the Mashenka ladies are taken care of by their relatives, those who need more attention—the woman and children—will be taken care of by society, which is like one large, friendly family. When Mashenka, who is now neither a lady nor a servant but simply a citizen, becomes pregnant, she does not have to worry about what will happen to her or her child. Society, that big happy family, will look after everything.

A special home with a garden and flowers will be ready to welcome her. It will be so designed that every pregnant woman and every woman who has just given birth can live there joyfully in health and comfort. The doctors in this society-family are concerned not just about preserving the health of the mother and child but about relieving the woman of the pain of childbirth. Science is making progress in this field, and can help the doctor here. When the child is strong enough, the mother returns to her normal life and takes up again the work that she does for the benefit of the large family-society. She does not have to worry about her child. Society is there to help her. Children will grow up in the kindergarten, the children's colony, the creche and the school under the care of experienced nurses. When the mother wants to be with her children, she only has to say the word; and when she has no time, she knows they are in good hands. Maternity is no longer a cross. Only its joyful aspects remain; only the great happiness of being a mother, which at the moment only the Mashenka ladies enjoy.

But such a society, surely, is only to be found in fairy tales? Could such a society ever exist? The science of economics and the history of society and the state show that such a society must and will come into being. However hard the rich capitalists, factory-owners, landowners and men of property fight, the fairy-tale will come true. The working class all over the world is fighting to make this dream come true. And although society is as yet far from being one happy family, although there are still many struggles and sacrifices ahead, it is at the same time true that the working class in other countries has made great gains. Working men and women are trying to lighten the cross of motherhood by getting laws passed and by taking other measures.

* * *

WHAT MUST EVERY WORKING WOMAN DO?

How are all these demands to be won?[1] What action must be taken? Every working-class woman, every woman who reads this pamphlet must throw off her indifference and begin to support the working-class movement, which is fighting for these demands and is shaping the old world into a better future where mothers will no longer weep bitter tears and where the cross of maternity will become a great joy and a great pride. We must say to ourselves, "There is strength in unity";

the more of us working women join the working-class movement, the greater will be our strength and the quicker we will get what we want. Our happiness and the life and future of our children are at stake.

(1914)

NOTE

1. E.g., maternal protection laws, maternity insurance, maternity homes, child care and kindergartens, plans for which are detailed in omitted passages.

49 • *Crystal Eastman*

"NOW WE CAN BEGIN"

Most women will agree that August 23, the day when the Tennessee legislature finally enacted the Federal suffrage amendment, is a day to begin with, not a day to end with. Men are saying perhaps "Thank God, this everlasting woman's fight is over!" But women, if I know them, are saying. "Now at last we can begin." In fighting for the right to vote, most women have tried to be either noncommittal or thoroughly respectable on every other subject. Now they can say what they are really after and what they are after, in common with all the rest of the struggling world, is *freedom.*

Freedom is a large word.

Many feminists are socialists, many are communists, not a few are active leaders in these movements. But the true feminist, no matter how far to the left she may be in the revolutionary movement, sees the woman's battle as distinct in its objects and different in its methods from the workers' battle for industrial freedom. She knows, of course, that the vast majority of women as well as men are without property, and are of necessity bread and butter slaves under a system of society which allows the very sources of life to be privately owned by a few, and she counts herself a loyal soldier in the working-class army that is marching to overthrow that system. But as a feminist she also knows that the whole of woman's slavery is not summed up in the profit system, nor her complete emancipation assured by the downfall of capitalism.

Woman's freedom, in the feminist sense, can be fought for and conceivably won before the gates open into industrial democracy. On the other hand, woman's freedom, in the feminist sense, is not inherent in the communist ideal. All feminists are familiar with the revolutionary leader who "can't see" the woman's movement. "What's the matter with the women? My wife's all right," he says. And his wife, one usually finds, is raising his children in a Bronx flat or a dreary suburb, to which he returns occasionally for food and sleep when all possible excitement and stimulus have been wrung from the fight. If we should graduate into communism tomorrow this man's attitude to his wife would not be changed. The proletarian dictatorship may or may not free women. We must begin now to enlighten the future dictators.

What, then, is "the matter with women"? What is the problem of women's freedom? It seems to me to be this: how to arrange the world so that women can be human beings, with a chance to exercise their infinitely varied gifts in infinitely varied ways, instead of being destined by the accident of their sex to one field of activity—housework and child-raising. And second, if and when they choose housework and child-raising to have that occupation recognized by the world as work, requiring a definite economic reward and not merely entitling the performer to be dependent on some man.

Speech delivered in 1919. Reprinted in *Crystal Eastman: On Women and Revolution*, ed. Blanche Wiesen Cook. New York: Oxford University Press.

This is not the whole of feminism, of course, but it is enough to begin with. "Oh! don't begin with economics," my friends often protest, "Woman does not live by bread alone. What she needs first of all is a free soul." And I can agree that women will never be great until they achieve a certain emotional freedom, a strong healthy egotism, and some unpersonal sources of joy—that in this inner sense we cannot make woman free by changing her economic status. What we can do, however, is to create conditions of outward freedom in which a free woman's soul can be born and grow. It is these outward conditions with which an organized feminist movement must concern itself.

Freedom of choice in occupation and individual economic independence for women: How shall we approach this next feminist objective? First, by breaking down all remaining barriers, actual as well as legal, which make it difficult for women to enter or succeed in the various professions, to go into and get on in business, to learn trades and practice them, to join trades unions. Chief among these remaining barriers is inequality in pay. Here the ground is already broken. This is the easiest part of our program.

Second, we must institute a revolution in the early training and education of both boys and girls. It must be womanly as well as manly to earn your own living, to stand on your own feet. And it must be manly as well as womanly to know how to cook and sew and clean and take care of yourself in the ordinary exigencies of life. I need not add that the second part of this revolution will be more passionately resisted than the first. Men will not give up their privilege of helplessness without a struggle. The average man has a carefully cultivated ignorance about household matters—from what to do with the crumbs to the grocer's telephone number—a sort of cheerful inefficiency which protects him better than the reputation for having a violent temper. It was his mother's fault in the beginning, but even as a boy he was quick to see how a general reputation for being "no good around the house" would serve him throughout life, and half-consciously he began to cultivate that helplessness until today it is the despair of feminist wives.

A growing number of men admire the woman who has a job, and, especially since the cost of living doubled, rather like the idea of their own wives contributing to the family income by outside work. And of course for generations there have been whole towns full of wives who are forced by the bitterest necessity to spend the same hours at the factory that their husbands spend. But these breadwinning wives have not yet developed home-making husbands. When the two come home from the factory the man sits down while his wife gets supper, and he does so with exactly the same sense of foreordained right as if he were "supporting her." Higher up in the economic scale the same thing is true. The business or professional woman who is married perhaps engages a cook, but the responsibility is not shifted, it is still hers. She "hires and fires," she orders meals, she does the buying, she meets and resolves all domestic crises, she takes charge of moving, furnishing, sending. She may be, like her husband, a busy executive at her office all day, but unlike him, she is also an executive in a small way every night and morning at home. Her noon hour is spent in planning, and too often her Sundays and holidays are spent in "catching up."

Two business women can "make a home" together without either one being over-burdened or over-bored. It is because they both know how and both feel responsible. But it is a rare man who can marry one of them and continue the home-making partnership. Yet if there are no children, there is nothing essentially different in the combination. Two self-supporting adults decide to make a home together: if both are women it is a pleasant partnership, more fun than work; if one is a man, it is almost never a partnership—the woman simply adds running the home to her regular outside job. Unless she is very strong, it is too much for her, she gets tired and bitter over it, and finally perhaps gives up her outside work and condemns herself to the tiresome half-job of housekeeping for two.

Cooperative schemes and electrical devices will simplify the business of home-making, but they will not get rid of it entirely. As far as we can see ahead people will always want homes, and a happy home cannot be had without a certain amount of rather monotonous work and responsibility. How can we change the nature of man so that he will honorably share the work and responsibility and thus make the home-making enterprise a song instead of a burden? Most assuredly not by laws or revolutionary decrees. Perhaps we must cultivate or simulate a little of that highly prized helplessness ourselves. But fundamentally it is a problem of education, of early training—we must bring up feminist sons.

Sons? Daughters? They are born of women—how can women be free to choose their occupation, at all times cherishing their economic independence, unless they stop having children? This is a further question for feminism. If the feminist program goes to pieces on the arrival of the first baby, it is false and useless. For ninety-nine out of every hundred women want children, and seventy-five out of every hundred want to take care of their own children, or at any rate so closely superintend their care as to make any other full-time occupation impossible for at least ten or fifteen years. Is there any such thing then as freedom of choice in occupation for women? And is not the family the inevitable economic unit and woman's individual economic independence, at least during that period, out of the question?

The feminist must have an answer to these questions, and she has. The immediate feminist program must include voluntary motherhood. Freedom of any kind for women is hardly worth considering unless it is assumed that they will know how to control the size of their families. "Birth control" is just as elementary an essential in our propaganda as "equal pay." Women are to have children when they want them, that's the first thing. That ensures some freedom of occupational choice; those who do not wish to be mothers will not have an undesired occupation thrust upon them by accident, and those who do wish to be mothers may choose in a general way how many years of their lives they will devote to the occupation of child-raising.

But is there any way of insuring a woman's economic independence while child-raising is her chosen occupation? Or must she sink into the dependent state from which, as we all know, it is so hard to rise again? That brings us to the fourth feature of our program—motherhood endowment. It seems that the only way we can keep mothers free, at least in a capitalist society, is by the establishment of a principle that the occupation of raising children is peculiarly and directly a service to society, and that the mother upon whom the necessity and privilege of performing this service naturally falls is entitled to an adequate economic reward from the political government. It is idle to talk of real economic independence for women unless this principle is accepted. But with a generous endowment of motherhood provided by legislation, with all laws against voluntary motherhood and education in its methods repealed, with the feminist ideal of education accepted in home and school, and with all special barriers removed in every field of human activity, there is no reason why woman should not become almost a human thing.

It will be time enough then to consider whether she has a soul.

(1919)

50 • *Margaret Sanger*

"MY FIGHT FOR BIRTH CONTROL"

AWAKENING AND REVOLT

Early in the year 1912 I came to a sudden realization that my work as a nurse and my activities in social service were entirely palliative and consequently futile and useless to relieve the misery I saw all about me. . . .

Were it possible for me to depict the revolting conditions existing in the homes of some of the women I attended in that one year, one would find it hard to believe. There was at that time, and doubtless is still today, a sub-stratum of men and women whose lives are absolutely untouched by social agencies.

Reprinted from *The Feminist Papers: From Adams to de Beauvoir*, ed. Alice S. Rossi, 522–528. New York: Bantam, 1974. Reproduced as in the original.

The way they live is almost beyond belief. They hate and fear any prying into their homes or into their lives. They resent being talked to. The women slink in and out of their homes on their way to market like rats from their holes. The men beat their wives sometimes black and blue, but no one interferes. The children are cuffed, kicked and chased about but woe to the child who dares to tell tales out of the home! Crime or drink is often the source of this secret aloofness, usually there is something to hide, a skeleton in the closet somewhere. The men are sullen, unskilled workers, picking up odd jobs now and then, unemployed usually, sauntering in and out of the house at all hours of the day and night.

The women keep apart from other women in the neighborhood. Often they are suspected of picking a pocket or "lifting" an article when occasion arises. Pregnancy is an almost chronic condition amongst them. I knew one woman who had given birth to eight children with no professional care whatever. The last one was born in the kitchen, witnessed by a son of ten years who, under his mother's direction, cleaned the bed, wrapped the placenta and soiled articles in paper, and threw them out of the window into the court below. . . .

In this atmosphere abortions and birth become the main theme of conversation. On Saturday nights I have seen groups of fifty to one hundred women going into questionable offices well known in the community for cheap abortions. I asked several women what took place there, and they all gave the same reply: a quick examination, a probe inserted into the uterus and turned a few times to disturb the fertilized ovum, and then the woman was sent home. Usually the flow began the next day and often continued four or five weeks. Sometimes an ambulance carried the victim to the hospital for a curettage and if she returned home at all she was looked upon as a lucky woman.

This state of things became a nightmare with me. There seemed no sense to it all, no reason for such waste of mother life, no right to exhaust women's vitality and to throw them on the scrap-heap before the age of thirty-five.

Everywhere I looked, misery and fear stalked— men fearful of losing their jobs, women fearful that even worse conditions might come upon them. The menace of another pregnancy hung like a sword over the head of every poor woman I came in contact with that year. The question which met me was always the same: What can I do to keep from it? or, What can I do to get out of this? Sometimes they talked among themselves bitterly.

"It's the rich that know the tricks," they'd say, "while we have all the kids." Then, if the women were Roman Catholics, they talked about "Yankee tricks," and asked me if I knew what the Protestants did to keep their families down. When I said that I didn't believe that the rich knew much more than they did I was laughed at and suspected of holding back information for money. They would nudge each other and say something about paying me before I left the case if I would reveal the "secret." . . .

Finally the thing began to shape itself, to become accumulative during the three weeks I spent in the home of a desperately sick woman living on Grand Street, a lower section of New York's East Side.

Mrs. Sacks was only twenty-eight years old; her husband, an unskilled worker, thirty-two. Three children, aged five, three and one, were none too strong nor sturdy, and it took all the earnings of the father and the ingenuity of the mother to keep them clean, provide them with air and proper food, and give them a chance to grow into decent manhood and womanhood.

Both parents were devoted to these children and to each other. The woman had become pregnant and had taken various drugs and purgatives, as advised by her neighbors. Then, in desperation, she had used some instrument lent to her by a friend. She was found prostrate on the floor amidst the crying children when her husband returned from work. Neighbors advised against the ambulance, and a friendly doctor was called. The husband would not hear of her going to a hospital, and as a little money had been saved in the bank a nurse was called and the battle for that precious life began.

It was in the middle of July. The three-room apartment was turned into a hospital for the dying patient. Never had I worked so fast, never so concentratedly as I did to keep alive that little mother. Neighbor women came and went during the day doing the odds and ends necessary for our comfort. The children were sent to friends and relatives and the doctor and I settled ourselves to outdo the force and power of an outraged nature.

Never had I known such conditions could exist. July's sultry days and nights were melted into a torpid inferno. Day after day, night after night, I slept only in brief snatches ever too anxious about the condition of that feeble heart bravely carrying on, to stay long from the bedside of the patient. . . .

At the end of two weeks recovery was in sight, and at the end of three weeks I was preparing to leave the fragile patient to take up the ordinary duties of her life, including those of wifehood and motherhood. Everyone was congratulating her on her recovery. All the kindness of sympathetic and understanding neighbors poured in upon her in the shape of convalescent dishes, soups, custards, and drinks. Still she appeared to be despondent and worried. She seemed to sit apart in her thoughts as if she had no part in these congratulatory messages and endearing welcomes. I thought at first that she still retained some of her unconscious memories and dwelt upon them in her silences.

But as the hour for my departure came nearer, her anxiety increased, and finally with trembling voice she said: "Another baby will finish me, I suppose."

"It's too early to talk about that," I said, and resolved that I would turn the question over to the doctor for his advice. When he came I said: "Mrs. Sacks is worried about having another baby."

"She well might be," replied the doctor, and then he stood before her and said: "Any more such capers, young woman, and there will be no need to call me."

"Yes, yes—I know, Doctor," said the patient with trembling voice, "but," and she hesitated as if it took all of her courage to say it, "*what* can I do to prevent getting that way again?"

"Oh ho!" laughed the doctor good naturedly, "You want your cake while you eat it too, do you? Well, it can't be done." Then, familiarly slapping her on the back and picking up his hat and bag to depart, he said: "I'll tell you the only sure thing to do. Tell Jake to sleep on the roof!"

With those words he closed the door and went down the stairs, leaving us both petrified and stunned.

Tears sprang to my eyes, and a lump came in my throat as I looked at that face before me. It was stamped with sheer horror. I thought for a moment she might have gone insane, but she conquered her feelings, whatever they may have been, and turning to me in desperation said: "He can't understand, can he?—he's a man after all—but you do, don't you? You're a woman and you'll tell me the secret and I'll never tell it to a soul."

She clasped her hands as if in prayer, she leaned over and looked straight into my eyes and beseechingly implored me to tell her something—something *I really did not know.* It was like being on a rack and

tortured for a crime one had not committed. To plead guilty would stop the agony; otherwise the rack kept turning.

I had to turn away from that imploring face. I could not answer her then. I quieted her as best I could. She saw that I was moved by the tears in my eyes. I promised that I would come back in a few days and tell her what she wanted to know. The few simple means of limiting the family like *coitus interruptus* or the condom were laughed at by the neighboring women when told these were the means used by men in the well-to-do families. That was not believed, and I knew such an answer would be swept aside as useless were I to tell her this at such a time.

A little later when she slept I left the house, and made up my mind that I'd keep away from those cases in the future. I felt helpless to do anything at all. I seemed chained hand and foot, and longed for an earthquake or a volcano to shake the world out of its lethargy into facing these monstrous atrocities.

The intelligent reasoning of the young mother—how to *prevent* getting that way again—how sensible, how just she had been—yes, I promised myself I'd go back and have a long talk with her and tell her more, and perhaps she would not laugh but would believe that those methods were all that were really known.

But time flew past, and weeks rolled into months. That wistful, appealing face haunted me day and night. I could not banish from my mind memories of that trembling voice begging so humbly for knowledge she had a right to have. I was about to retire one night three months later when the telephone rang and an agitated man's voice begged me to come at once to help his wife who was sick again. It was the husband of Mrs. Sacks, and I intuitively knew before I left the telephone that it was almost useless to go.

I dreaded to face that woman. I was tempted to send someone else in my place. I longed for an accident on the subway, or on the street—anything to prevent my going into that home. But on I went just the same. I arrived a few minutes after the doctor, the same one who had given her such noble advice. The woman was dying. She was unconscious. She died within ten minutes after my arrival. It was the same result, the same story told a thousand times before—death from abortion. She had become pregnant, had used drugs, had then consulted a five-dollar professional abortionist, and death followed.

The doctor shook his head as he rose from listening for the heart beat. I knew she had already passed on; without a groan, a sigh or recognition of our belated presence she had gone into the Great Beyond as thousands of mothers go every year. I looked at that drawn face now stilled in death. I placed her thin hands across her breast and recalled how hard they had pleaded with me on that last memorable occasion of parting. The gentle woman, the devoted mother, the loving wife had passed on leaving behind her a frantic husband helpless in his loneliness, bewildered in his helplessness as he paced up and down the room, hands clenching his head, moaning "My God! My God! My God!"

The Revolution came—but not as it has been pictured nor as history relates that revolutions have come. It came in my own life. It began in my very being as I walked home that night after I had closed the eyes and covered with a sheet the body of that little helpless mother whose life had been sacrificed to ignorance.

After I left that desolate house I walked and walked and walked; for hours and hours I kept on, bag in hand, thinking, regretting, dreading to stop; fearful of my conscience, dreading to face my own accusing soul. At three in the morning I arrived home still clutching a heavy load the weight of which I was quite unconscious.

I entered the house quietly, as was my custom, and looked out of the window down upon the dimly lighted, sleeping city. As I stood at the window and looked out, the miseries and problems of that sleeping city arose before me in a clear vision like a panorama: crowded homes, too many children; babies dying in infancy; mothers overworked; baby nurseries; children neglected and hungry—mothers so nervously wrought they could not give the little things the comfort nor care they needed; mothers half sick most of their lives—"always ailing, never failing"; women made into drudges; children working in cellars; children

aged six and seven pushed into the labor market to help earn a living; another baby on the way; still another; yet another; a baby born dead—great relief; an older child dies—sorrow, but nevertheless relief—insurance helps; a mother's death—children scattered into institutions; the father, desperate, drunken; he slinks away to become an outcast in a society which has trapped him. . . .

. . . For hours I stood, motionless and tense, expecting something to happen. I watched the lights go out, I saw the darkness gradually give way to the first shimmer of dawn, and then a colorful sky heralded the rise of the sun. I knew a new day had come for me and a new world as well.

It was like an illumination. I could now see clearly the various social strata of our life; all its mass problems seemed to be centered around uncontrolled breeding. There was only one thing to be done: call out, start the alarm, set the heather on fire! Awaken the womanhood of America to free the motherhood of the world! I released from my almost paralyzed hand the nursing bag which unconsciously I had clutched, threw it across the room, tore the uniform from my body, flung it into a corner, and renounced all palliative work forever.

I would never go back again to nurse women's ailing bodies while their miseries were as vast as the stars. I was now finished with superficial cures, with doctors and nurses and social workers who were brought face to face with this overwhelming truth of women's needs and yet turned to pass on the other side. They must be made to see these facts. I resolved that women should have knowledge of contraception. They have every right to know about their own bodies. I would strike out—I would scream from the housetops. I would tell the world what was going on in the lives of these poor women. I *would* be heard. No matter what it should cost. *I would be heard.*

(1920)

51 • *Tillie Olsen*

"I WANT YOU WOMEN UP NORTH TO KNOW"

I want you women up north to know
how those dainty children's dresses you buy
    at macy's, wannamakers, gimbels, marshall fields,
are dyed in blood, are stitched in wasting flesh,
down in San Antonio, "where sunshine spends the
        winter."
I want you women up north to see
the obsequious smile, the salesladies trill
    "exquisite work, madame, exquisite pleats"
vanish into a bloated face, ordering more dresses,
    gouging the wages down,
dissolve into maria, ambrosa, catalina,
    stitching these dresses from dawn to night,
    In blood, in wasting flesh.

Catalina Rodriguez. 24,
    body shrivelled to a child's at twelve.
catalina rodriguez, last stages of consumption,
    works for three dollars a week from dawn to
        midnight.
A fog of pain thickens over her skull, the parching
        heat
    breaks over her body,
and the bright red blood embroiders the floor
        of her room.
    White rain stitching the night, the bourgeois
        poet would say.
    white gulls of hands, darting, veering.
    white lightning, threading the clouds,
this is the exquisite dance of her hands over
        the cloth,
and her cough, gay, quick, staccato,
    like skeleton's bones clattering,

is appropriate accompaniment for the esthetic dance
    of her fingers,
and the tremolo, tremolo when the hands tremble
        with pain.
Three dollars a week,
two fifty-five,
seventy cents a week,
no wonder two thousand eight hundred ladies of joy
are spending the winter with the sun after he goes
        down—
for five cents (who said this was a rich man's world?)
        you can get all the lovin you want
"clap and syph aint much worse than sore fingers,
        blind eyes, and t.b."

Maria Vasquez, spinster,
    for fifteen cents a dozen stitches garments for
        children she
    has never had,
Catalina Torres, mother of four,
    to keep the starved body starving, embroiders
        from dawn
    to night.
Mother of four, what does she think of,
    as the needle pocked fingers shift over the silk—
    of the stubble-coarse rags that stretch on her
        own brood,
    and jut with the bony ridge that marks hunger's
        landscape
    of fat little prairie-roll bodies that will bulge
        in the
    silk she needles?
(Be not envious, Catalina Torres, look!

on your own children's clothing, embroidery,
more intricate than any a thousand hands could
    fashion,
there where the cloth is ravelled, or darned,
designs, multitudinous, complex and handmade
    by Poverty herself.)
Ambrosa Espinoza trusts in god,
    "Todos es de dios, everything is from god."
    through the dwindling night, the waxing day,
        she bolsters
    herself up with it—
but the pennies to keep god incarnate, from
    ambrosa,
and the pennies to keep the priest in wine, from
    ambrosa,
ambrosa clothes god and priest with hand-made
    children's dresses.

Her brother lies on an iron cot, all day and watches,
    on a mattress of rags he lies.
For twenty-five years he worked for the railroad,
    then they laid him off.
    (racked days, searching for work; rebuffs;
        suspicious eyes of policemen.
    goodbye ambrosa, mebbe in dallas I find work;
        desperate swing for a freight,
    surprised hands, clutching air, and the wheel
        goes over a leg,
    the railroad cuts it off, as it cut off twenty-five
        years of his life.)
She says that he prays and dreams of another world,
    as he lies
    there, a heaven (which he does not know was
        brought to
    earth in 1917 in Russia, by workers like him).
Women up north, I want you to know
when you finger the exquisite hand-made
    dresses
what it means, this working from dawn to
    midnight,

on what strange feet the feverish dawn must come
    to maria, catalina, ambrosa,
how the malignant fingers twitching over the pallid
    faces jerk them to work,
and the sun and the fever mount with the day—
    long plodding hours, the eyes burn like coals,
        heat jellies the flying fingers,
down comes the night like blindness.
    long hours more with the dim eye of the lamp,
        the breaking back,
    weariness crawls in the flesh like worms, gigantic
        like earth's in winter.
And for Catalina Rodriguez comes the night sweat
    and the blood
    embroidering the darkness.
    for Catalina Torres the pinched faces of four
        huddled children,
    the naked bodies of four bony children,
    the chant of their chorale of hunger.
And for twenty eight hundred ladies of joy the
        grotesque act gone
    over—the wink—the grimace—the "feeling
        like it baby?"
And for Maria Vasquez, spinster, emptiness,
    emptiness,
    flaming with dresses for children she can never
        fondle.
And for Ambrosa Espinoza—the skeleton body
    of her brother on his mattress of rags, boring
    twin holes in the dark with his eyes to the
    image of christ, remembering a leg, and
    twenty five years cut off from his life by
    the railroad.

Women up north, I want you to know,
I tell you this can't last forever.

I swear it won't.

                              (1934)

"THE MARRIED WOMAN"

. . . The home has always been the material realization of the ideal of happiness, be it a cottage or a château; it embodies permanence and separation. Inside its walls, the family constitutes an isolated cell and affirms its identity beyond the passage of generations; the past, preserved in the form of furniture and ancestral portraits, prefigures a risk-free future; in the garden, seasons mark their reassuring cycle with edible vegetables; every year the same spring adorned with the same flowers promises the summer's immutable return and autumn's fruits, identical to those of every autumn: neither time nor space escapes into infinity, but instead quietly goes round and round. In every civilization founded on landed property, an abundant literature sings of the poetry and virtues of the home; in Henry Bordeaux's novel precisely titled *La maison* (The Home), the home encapsulates all the bourgeois values: faithfulness to the past, patience, economy, caution, love of family, of native soil, and so forth; the home's champions are often women, since it is their task to ensure the happiness of the familial group; as in the days when the *domina* sat in the atrium, their role is to be "mistress of the house." Today the home has lost its patriarchal splendor; for most men, it is simply a place to live, no longer overrun by memories of deceased generations and no longer imprisoning the centuries to come. But woman still tries to give her "interior" the meaning and value a true home possessed. In *Cannery Row*, Steinbeck describes a woman hobo determined to decorate with rugs and curtains the old abandoned boiler she lives in with her husband; he objects in vain that not having windows makes curtains useless.

This concern is specifically feminine. A normal man considers objects around him as instruments; he arranges them according to the purpose for which they are intended; his "order"—where woman will often only see disorder—is to have his cigarettes, his papers, and his tools within reach. Artists—sculptors and painters, among others—whose work it is to recreate the world through material, are completely insensitive to the surroundings in which they live. Rilke writes about Rodin:

> When I first came to Rodin . . . I knew that his house was nothing to him, a paltry little necessity perhaps, a roof for time of rain and sleep; and that it was no care to him and no weight upon his solitude and composure. Deep in himself he bore the darkness, shelter, and peace of a house, and he himself had become sky above it, and wood around it, and distance and great stream always flowing by.[1]

But to find a home in oneself, one must have realized oneself in works or acts. Man has only a middling interest in his domestic interior because he has access to the entire universe and because he can affirm himself in his projects. Woman, instead, is locked into the conjugal community: she has to change this prison into a kingdom. Her attitude to her home is dictated by this same dialectic that generally defines her conditions: she takes by becoming prey, she liberates herself by abdicating; by renouncing the world, she means to conquer a world.

She regrets closing the doors of her home behind herself; as a young girl, the whole world was her kingdom; the forests belonged to her. Now she is confirmed to a restricted space; Nature is reduced to the size of a geranium pot; walls block out the horizon. . . .

But she is going to make every attempt to refuse this limitation. She encloses faraway countries and past times within her four walls in the form of more or less expensive earthly flora and fauna; she encloses her husband, who personifies human society for her, and the child who gives her the whole future in a portable form. The home becomes the center of the world and even its own one truth; as Bachelard appropriately notes, it is "a sort of counter- or exclusionary universe;"[2] refuge, retreat, grotto, womb, it protects against outside dangers: it is this confused exteriority that becomes unreal. . . .

Thanks to the velvets, silks, and china with which she surrounds herself, woman can in part assuage this grasping sensuality that her erotic life cannot usually satisfy; she will also find in this decor an expression of her personality; it is she who has chosen, made, and "hunted down" furniture and knickknacks, who has aesthetically arranged them in a way where symmetry is important; they reflect her individuality while bearing social witness to her standard of living. Her home is thusly her earthly lot, the expression of her social worth, and her intimate truth. Because she *does* nothing, she avidly seeks herself in what she *has*.

It is through housework that the wife comes to make her "nest" her own; this is why, even if she has "help," she insists on doing things herself; at least by watching over, controlling, and criticizing, she endeavors to make her servants' results her own. By administrating her home, she achieves her social justification; her job is also to oversee the food, clothing, and care of the familial society in general. Thus she too realizes herself as an activity. But, as we will see, it is an activity that brings her no escape from her immanence and allows her no individual affirmation of herself. . . .

Numerous women writers have lovingly spoken of freshly ironed linens, of the whitening agents of soapy water, of white sheets, of shining copper. When the housewife cleans and polishes furniture, "dreams of saturating penetration nourish the gentle patience of the hand striving to bring out the heavy of the wood with wax," says Bachelard. Once the job is finished, the housewife experiences the joy of contemplation. But for the precious qualities to show themselves—the polish of a table, the shine of a chandelier, the icy whiteness and starch of the laundry—a negative action must first be applied; all foul causes must be expelled. . . .

These dialectics can give housework the charm of a game: the little girl readily enjoys shining the silver, polishing doorknobs. But for a woman to find positive satisfaction, she must devote her efforts to an interior she can be proud of; if not, she will never know the pleasure of contemplation, the only pleasure that can repay her efforts. An American reporter, who lived several months among American Southern "poor whites," has described the pathetic destiny of one of these women, overwhelmed with burdens who labored in vain to make a hovel livable.[3] She lived with her husband and seven children in a wooden shack, the walls covered with soot, crawling with cockroaches; she had tried to "make the house pretty," in the main room, the fireplace covered with bluish plaster, a table, and a few pictures hanging on the wall suggested a sort of altar. But the hovel remained a hovel, and Mrs. G. said with tears in her eyes, "Oh, I do *hate* this house *so bad*! Seems like they ain't nothing in the whole world I can do to make it pretty!" Legions of women have in common only endlessly recurrent fatigue in a battle that never leads to victory. Even in the most privileged cases, this victory is never final. Few tasks are more similar to the torment of Sisyphus than those of the housewife; day after day, one must wash dishes, dust furniture, mend clothes that will be dirty, dusty, and torn again. The housewife wears herself out running on the spot; she does nothing; she only perpetuates the present; she never gains the sense that she is conquering a positive Good, but struggles indefinitely against Evil. It is a struggle that begins again every day. We know the story of the valet who despondently refused to polish his master's boots. "What's the point?" he asked. "You have to begin again the next day." Many still unresigned young girls share this discouragement. I recall an essay of a sixteen-year-old student that opened with words like these: "Today is housecleaning day. I hear the noise of the vacuum Mama walks through the living room. I would like to run away. I swear when I grow up, there will never be a housecleaning day in my house." The child thinks of the future as an indefinite ascent toward some unidentified summit. Suddenly in the kitchen, where her mother is washing dishes, the little girl realized that over the years, every afternoon at the same time, these hands have plunged into greasy water and wiped the china with a rough dish towel. And until death they will be subjected to these rites. Eat, sleep, clean . . .

the years no longer reach toward the sky, they spread out identical and gray as a horizontal tablecloth; every day looks like the previous one; the present is eternal, useless, and hopeless. . . .

Washing, ironing, sweeping, routing out tufts of dust in the dark places behind the wardrobe, this is holding away death but also refusing life: for in one movement time is created and destroyed; the housewife only grasps the negative aspect of it. Hers is the attitude of a Manichaean. The essence of Manichaeism is not only to recognize two principles, one good and one evil: it is also to posit that good is attained by the abolition of evil and not by a positive movement; in this sense, Christianity is hardly Manichaean in spite of the existence of the devil, because it is in devoting oneself to God that one best fights the devil and not in trying to conquer him. All doctrines of transcendence and freedom subordinate the defeat of evil to progress toward good. But the wife is not called to build a better world; the house, the bedroom, the dirty laundry, the wooden floors, are fixed things: she can do no more than rout out indefinitely the foul causes that creep in; she attacks the dust, stains, mud, and filth; she fights sin, she fights with Satan. But it is a sad destiny to have to repel an enemy without respite instead of being turned toward positive aims; the housewife often submits to it in rage. Bachelard uses the word "malice" for it; psychoanalysts have written about it. For them, housekeeping mania is a form of sadomasochism; it is characteristic of mania and vice to make freedom want what it does not want; because the maniacal housewife detests having negativity, dirt, and evil as her lot, she furiously pursues dust, accepting a condition that revolts her. She attacks life itself through the rubbish left from any living growth. Whenever a living being enters her sphere, her eye shines with a wicked fire. "Wipe your feet; don't mess up everything, don't touch that." She would like to stop everyone from breathing; the least breath is a threat. Every moment threatens her with more thankless work: a child's somersault is a tear to sew up. Seeing life as a promise of decomposition demanding more endless work, she loses her joie de vivre; her eyes sharpen, her face looks preoccupied and serious, always on guard; she protects herself through prudence and avarice. She closes the windows because sun would bring in insects, germs, and dust; besides, the sun always eats away at the silk wall coverings; the antique

armchairs are hidden under loose covers and embalmed in mothballs: light would fade them. She does not even care to let her visitors see these treasures: admiration sullies. This defiance turns to bitterness and causes hostility to everything that lives. . . .

Preparing meals is more positive work and often more enjoyable than cleaning. First of all, it involves going to the market, which is for many housewives the best time of the day. The loneliness of the household weighs on the woman just as routine tasks leave her head empty. She is happy when, in Midi towns, she can sew, wash, and peel vegetables while chatting on her doorstep; fetching water from the river is a grand adventure for half-cloistered Muslim women: I saw a little village in Kabyle where the women tore down the fountain an official had built on the plaza; going down every morning to the wadi flowing at the foot of the hill was their only distraction. All the time they are doing their marketing, waiting in lines, in shops, on street corners, they talk about things that affirm their "homemaking worth" from which each one draws the sense of her own importance; they feel part of a community that—for an instant—is opposed to the society of men as the essential to the inessential. But above all, making a purchase is a profound pleasure: it is a discovery, almost an invention. Gide observes in his *Journals* that the Muslims, unfamiliar with games of chance, have replaced them with the discovery of hidden treasures; this is poetry and adventure of mercantile civilizations. The housewife is oblivious to the gratuitousness of games: but a good firm cabbage and ripe Camembert are treasures that must be subtly discovered in spite of the cunning shopkeeper; between seller and buyer, relations of dealing and ruse are established: for her, winning means getting the best goods for the lowest price; concern for a restricted budget is not enough to explain the extreme importance given to being economical: winning the game is what counts. When she suspiciously inspects the stalls, the housewife is queen; the world, with its riches and traps, is at her feet, for her taking. She tastes a fleeting triumph when she empties her shopping basket on the table. She puts her canned food and nonperishables in the larder, guarding her against the future, and she contemplates with satisfaction the raw vegetables and meats she is about to submit to her power.

Gas and electricity have killed the magic of fire; but in the countryside, many women still know the joys of kindling live flames from inert wood. With the fire lit, the woman changes into a sorceress. With a simple flip of the hand—beating the eggs or kneading the dough—or by the magic of fire, she effects transmutations of substances; matter becomes food. Colette, again, describes the enchantment of this alchemy:

> All is mystery, magic, spell, all that takes place between the time the casserole, kettle, stewpot, and their contents are put on the fire and the moment of sweet anxiety, of voluptuous expectation, when the dish is brought steaming to the table and its headdress removed. . . .

Here again, it is clear that the little girl passionately enjoys imitating her female elders: with chalk and grass she plays at make-believe; she is happier still when has a real little oven to play with, or when her mother lets her come into the kitchen and roll out the pastry with her palms or cut the hot burning caramel. But this is like housework: repetition soon dispels these pleasures. For Indians who get their nourishment essentially from tortillas, the women spend half their days kneading, cooking, reheating, and kneading again identical tortillas, under every roof, identical throughout the centuries: they are hardly sensitive to the magic of the oven. It is not possible to transform marketing into a treasure hunt every day, nor to delight in a shiny water tap. Women and men writers can lyrically exalt these triumphs because they never or rarely do housework. Done every day, this work becomes monotonous and mechanical; it is laden with waiting: waiting for the water to boil, for the roast to be cooked just right, for the laundry to dry; even if different tasks are well organized, there are long moments of passivity and emptiness; most of the time, they are accomplished in boredom; between present life and the life of tomorrow, they are but an inessential intermediary. If the individual who executes them is himself a producer or creator, they are integrated into his existence as naturally as body functions; this is why everyday chores seem less dismal when performed by men; they represent for them only a negative and contingent moment they hurry to escape. But what makes the lot of the wife-servant ungratifying is the division of labor that dooms her wholly to the general and inessential; home and food are useful for life but do not confer any meaning on it: the housekeeper's immediate goals are only means, not real ends, and they reflect no more anonymous projects. . . .

The saddest thing is that this work does not even result in a lasting creation. Woman is tempted—all the more as she is so attentive to it—to consider her work as an end in itself. Contemplating the cake she takes out of the oven, she sighs: what a pity to eat it! What a pity husband and children drag their muddy feet on the waxed floor. As soon as things are used, they are dirtied or destroyed: she is tempted, as we have already seen, to withdraw them from being used; she keeps the jam until mold invades it; she locks the living room doors. But time cannot be stopped; supplies attract rats; worms start their work. Covers, curtains, and clothes are eaten by moths: the world is not a dream carved in stone, it is made of a suspicious-looking substance threatened by decomposition; edible stuff is as questionable as Dalí's meat monsters: it seemed inert and inorganic but hidden larvae have metamorphosed it into corpses. The housewife who alienates herself in things depends, like things, on the whole world: linens turn gray, the roast burns, china breaks; these are absolute disasters because when things disappear, they disappear irremediably. It is impossible to obtain permanence and security through them. Wars with their looting and bombs threaten wardrobes and the homes.

Thus, the product of housework has to be consumed; constant renunciation is demanded of the wife whose work is finished only with its destruction. For her to consent to it without regret, these small holocausts must spark some joy or pleasure somewhere. But as housework is spent on maintaining the status quo, the husband—when he comes home—notices disorder and negligence but takes order and neatness for granted. He attaches more positive importance to a well-prepared meal. The triumphant moment of the cook is when she places a successful dish on the table: husband and children welcome it warmly, not only with words, but also by consuming it joyously. Culinary alchemy continued with the food becoming chyle and blood. Taking care of a body is of more concrete interest, is more vital than care of a parquet floor; the cook's effort transcends toward the future in an obvious way. However, while it is less futile to depend on an outside freedom than to alienate oneself in things, it is no less dangerous. It is only in the guests' mouths that the cook's work finds its truth; she needs their approval; she demands that they appreciate her dishes, that they take more; she is irritated if they are no longer hungry: to the point that one does not know if the fried potatoes are destined for the husband or the husband for the fried potatoes. . . .

The heavy curse weighing on her is that the very meaning of her existence is not in her hands. This is the reason the successes and failures of her conjugal life have much more importance for her than for the man: he is a citizen, a producer, before being a husband; she is above all, and often exclusively, a wife; her work does not extract her from her condition; it is from her condition, on the contrary, that her work derives its price or not. Loving, generously devoted, she will carry out tasks joyously; these chores will seem insipid to her if she accomplishes them with resentment. They will never play more than an inessential

role in her destiny; in the misadventures of conjugal life they will be of no help. We thus have to see how this condition is concretely lived, one that is essentially defined by bed "service" and housework "service" in which the wife finds her dignity only in accepting her vassalage . . .

(1949)

NOTES

1. Rilke to Lou Andreas-Salomé, August 8, 1903.—TRANS.
2. *La terre et les rêveries du repos* (Earth and Reveries of Repose), trans. Kenneth Haltman.—TRANS.
3. James Agee, Let Us Now Praise Famous Men.

---

53 • *Margaret Benston*

"THE POLITICAL ECONOMY OF WOMEN'S LIBERATION"

The position of women rests, as everything in our complex society, on an economic base.
—*Eleanor Marx and Edward Aveling*

The "woman question" is generally ignored in analyses of the class structure of society. This is so because, on the one hand, classes are generally defined by their relation to the means of production and, on the other hand, women are not supposed to have any unique relation to the means of production. The category seems instead to cut across all classes; one speaks of working-class women, middle-class women, etc. The status of women is clearly inferior to that of men,[1] but analysis of this condition usually falls into discussing socialization, psychology, interpersonal relations, or the role of marriage as a social institution.[2] Are these, however, the primary factors? In arguing that the roots of the secondary status of women are in fact

economic, it can be shown that women as a group do indeed have a definite relation to the means of production and that this is different from that of men. The personal and psychological factors then follow from this special relation to production, and a change in the latter will be a necessary (but not sufficient) condition for changing the former.[3] If this special relation of women to production is accepted, the analysis of the situation of women fits naturally into a class analysis of society . . .

What is needed first is not a complete examination of the symptoms of the secondary status of women, but instead a statement of the material conditions in capitalist (and other) societies which define the group

---

Excerpts from "The Political Economy of Women's Liberation," *Monthly Review*, Vol. 21 (Sept 1969), pp. 13–25. Reprinted by permission of Monthly Review Press. Footnotes have been renumbered.

"women." Upon these conditions are built the specific superstructures which we know. An interesting passage from Mandel points the way to such a definition:

> The commodity . . . is a product created to be exchanged on the market, as opposed to one which has been made for direct consumption. *Every commodity must have both a use-value and an exchange-value.*
>
> It must have a use-value or else nobody would buy it. . . . A commodity without a use-value to anyone would consequently be unsalable, would constitute useless production, would have no exchange-value precisely because it had no use-value.
>
> On the other hand, every product which has use-value does not necessarily have exchange-value. It has an exchange-value only to the extent that the society itself, in which the commodity is produced, is founded on exchange, is a society where exchange is a common practice. . . .
>
> In capitalist society, commodity production, the production of exchange-values, has reached its greatest development. It is the first society in human history where the major part of production consists of commodities. It is not true, however, that all production under capitalism is commodity production. Two classes of products still remain simple use-value.
>
> The first group consists of all things produced by the peasantry for its own consumption, everything directly consumed on the farms where it is produced. . . .
>
> The second group of products in capitalist society which are not commodities but remain simple use-value consists of all things produced in the home. Despite the fact that considerable human labor goes into this type of household production, it still remains a production of use-values and not of commodities. Every time a soup is made or a button sewn on a garment, it constitutes production, but it is not production for the market[4]. . . .

In sheer quantity, household labor, including child care, constitutes a huge amount of socially necessary production. Nevertheless, in a society based on commodity production, it is not usually considered "real work" since it is outside of trade and the market place. It is pre-capitalist in a very real sense. This assignment of household work as the function of a special category "women" means that this group *does* stand in a different relation to production than the group "men." We will tentatively define women, then, as that group of people who are responsible for the production of simple use-values in those activities associated with the home and family . . .

The material basis for the inferior status of women is to be found in just this definition of women. In a society in which money determines value, women are a group who work outside the money economy. Their work is not worth money, is therefore valueless, is therefore not even real work. And women themselves, who do this valueless work, can hardly be expected to be worth as much as men, who work for money. In structural terms, the closest thing to the condition of women is the condition of others who are or were also outside of commodity production, i.e., serfs and peasants. . . .

The argument is often advanced that, under neo-capitalism, the work in the home has been much reduced. Even if this is true, it is not structurally relevant. Except for the very rich, who can hire someone to do it, there is for most women, an irreducible minimum of necessary labor involved in caring for home, husband, and children. For a married woman without children this irreducible minimum of work probably takes fifteen to twenty hours a week; for a woman with small children the minimum is probably seventy or eighty hours a week.[5] (There is some resistance to regarding child-rearing as a job. That labor is involved, i.e., the production of use-value, can be clearly seen when exchange-value is also involved— when the work is done by baby sitters, nurses, child-care centers, or teachers. An economist has already pointed out the paradox that if a man marries his housekeeper, he reduces the national income, since the money he gives her is no longer counted as wages.) The reduction of housework to the minimums given is also expensive; for low-income families more labor is required. In any case, household work remains structurally the same—a matter of private production. . . .

As an economic unit, the nuclear family is a valuable stabilizing force in capitalist society. Since the production which is done in the home is paid for by the husband-father's earnings, his ability to withhold his labor from the market is much reduced. Even his flexibility in changing jobs is limited. The woman, denied an active place in the market, has little control over the conditions that govern her life. Her economic dependence is reflected in emotional dependence, passivity, and other "typical" female personality traits. She is conservative, fearful, supportive of the status quo.

Furthermore, the structure of this family is such that it is an ideal consumption unit. But this fact, which is widely noted in Women's Liberation literature, should not be taken to mean that this is its primary function. If the above analysis is correct, the family should be seen primarily as a production unit for housework and child-rearing. . . .

The history of women in the industrialized sector of the economy has depended simply on the labor needs of that sector. Women function as a massive reserve army of labor. When labor is scarce (early industrialization, the two world wars, etc.) then women form an important part of the labor force. When there is less demand for labor (as now under neocapitalism) women become a surplus labor force—but one for which their husbands and not society are economically responsible. The "cult of the home" makes its reappearance during times of labor surplus and is used to channel women out of the market economy. . . .

At all times household work is the responsibility of women. When they are working outside the home they must somehow manage to get both outside job and housework done (or they supervise a substitute for the housework). Women, particularly married women with children, who work outside the home simply do two jobs; their participation in the labor force is only allowed if they continue to fulfill their first responsibility in the home . . . Equal access to jobs outside the home, while one of the preconditions for women's liberation, will not in itself be sufficient to give equality for women; as long as work in the home remains a matter of private production and is the responsibility of women, they will simply carry a double work-load.

A second prerequisite for women's liberation which follows from the above analysis is the conversion of the work now done in the home as private production into work to be done in the public economy.[6] To be more specific, this means that child-rearing should no longer be the responsibility solely of the parents. Society must begin to take responsibility for children; the economic dependence of women and children on the husband-father must be ended. The other work that goes on in the home must also be changed—communal eating places and laundries for example. When such work is moved into the public sector, then the

material basis for discrimination against women will be gone.

These are only preconditions. The idea of the inferior status of women is deeply rooted in the society and will take a great deal of effort to eradicate. But once the structures which produce and support that idea are changed then, and only then, can we hope to make progress. . . .

The need to keep women in the home arises from two major aspects of the present system. First, the amount of unpaid labor performed by women is very large and very profitable to those who own the means of production. To pay women for their work, even at minimum wage scales, would imply a massive redistribution of wealth. At present, the support of a family is a hidden tax on the wage earner—his wage buys the labor power of two people. And second, there is the problem of whether the economy can expand enough to put all women to work as a part of the normally employed labor force . . . Their incorporation into the labor force on terms of equality—which would create pressure for capitalization of housework—is possible only with an economic expansion so far achieved by neocapitalism only under conditions of full-scale war mobilization. . . .

At best the change to capitalization of housework would only give women the same limited freedom given most men in capitalist society. This does not mean, however, that women should wait to demand freedom from discrimination. There *is* a material basis for women's status; we are not merely discriminated against, we are exploited. At present, our unpaid labor in the home is necessary if the entire system is to function. Pressure created by women who challenge their role will reduce the effectiveness of this exploitation. . . .

(1969)

NOTES AND REFERENCES

1. Marlene Dixon, "Secondary Social Status of Women." (Available from U.S. Voice of Women's Liberation Movement, 1940 Bissell, Chicago, Illinois 60614.)
2. The biological argument is, of course, the first one used, but it is not usually taken seriously by socialist writers. Margaret Mead's *Sex and Temperament* is an early statement of the importance of culture instead of biology.

3. This applies to the group or category as a whole. Women as individuals can and do free themselves from their socialization to a great degree (and they can even come to terms with the economic situation in favorable cases), but the majority of women have no chance to do so.

4. Ernest Mandel, *An Introduction to Marxist Economic Theory* (New York: Merit Publishers, 1967), pp. 10–11.

5. Such figures can easily be estimated. For example, a married woman without children is expected each week to cook and wash up (10 hours), clean house (4 hours), do laundry (1 hour), and shop for food (1 hour). The figures are *minimum* times required each: week for such work. The total, 16 hours, is probably unrealistically low; even so, it is close to half of a regular work week. A mother with young children must spend at least six or seven days a week working close to 12 hours.

6. This is stated clearly by early Marxist writers besides Engels.

---

54 • *Nancy Chodorow*

"GENDER PERSONALITY AND THE REPRODUCTION OF MOTHERING"

In spite of the apparently close tie between women's capacities for childbearing and lactation on the one hand and their responsibilities for child care on the other, and in spite of the probable prehistoric convenience (and perhaps survival necessity) of a sexual division of labor in which women mothered, biology and instinct do not provide adequate explanations for how women come to mother. Women's mothering as a feature of social structure requires an explanation in terms of social structure. Conventional feminist and social psychological explanations for the genesis of gender roles—girls and boys are "taught" appropriate behaviors and "learn" appropriate feelings—are insufficient both empirically and methodologically to account for how women become mothers.

Methodologically, socialization theories rely inappropriately on individual intention. Ongoing social structures include the means for their own reproduction—in the regularized repetition of social processes, in the perpetuation of conditions which require members' participation, in the genesis of legitimating ideologies and institutions, and in the psychological as well as physical reproduction of people to perform necessary roles. Accounts of socialization help to explain the perpetuation of ideologies about gender roles. However, notions of appropriate behavior, like coercion, cannot in themselves produce parenting. Psychological capacities and a particular object-relational stance are central and definitional to parenting in a way that they are not to many other roles and activities.

Women's mothering includes the capacities for its own reproduction. This reproduction consists in the production of women with, and men without, the particular psychological capacities and stance which go into primary parenting. Psychoanalytic theory provides us with a theory of social reproduction that explains major features of personality development and the development of psychic structure, and the differential development of gender personality in particular. Psychoanalysts argue that personality both results from and consists in the ways a child appropriates,

Excerpt from *Reproduction of Mothering: Psychoanalysis and the Sociology of Gender* (Berkeley, Calif.: University of California Press, 1978), pp. 205–209. Reprinted by permission of the Regents of the University of California and the University of California Press.

internalizes, and organizes early experiences in their family—from the fantasies they have, the defenses they use, the ways they channel and redirect drives in this object-relational context. A person subsequently imposes this intrapsychic structure, and the fantasies, defenses, and relational modes and preoccupations which go with it, onto external social situations. This reexternalization (or mutual reexternalization) is a major constituting feature of social and interpersonal situations themselves.

Psychoanalysis, however, has not had an adequate theory of the reproduction of mothering. Because of the teleological assumption that anatomy is destiny, and that women's destiny includes primary parenting, the ontogenesis of women's mothering has been largely ignored, even while the genesis of a wide variety of related disturbances and problems has been accorded widespread clinical attention. Most psychoanalysts agree that the basis for parenting is laid for both genders in the early relationship to a primary caretaker. Beyond that, in order to explain why *women* mother, they tend to rely on vague notions of a girl's subsequent identification with her mother, which makes her and not her brother a primary parent, or on an unspecified and uninvestigated innate femaleness in girls, or on logical leaps from lactation or early vaginal sensations to caretaking abilities and commitments.

The psychoanalytic account of male and female development, when reinterpreted, gives us a developmental theory of the reproduction of women's mothering. Women's mothering reproduces itself through differing object-relational experiences and differing psychic outcomes in women and men. As a result of having been parented by a woman, women are more likely than men to seek to be mothers, that is, to relocate themselves in a primary mother–child relationship, to get gratification from the mothering relationship, and to have psychological and relational capacities for mothering.

The early relation to a primary caretaker provides in children of both genders both the basic capacity to participate in a relationship with the features of the early parent–child one, and the desire to create this intimacy. However, because women mother, the early experience and preoedipal relationship differ for boys and girls. Girls retain more concern with early childhood issues in relation to their mother, and a sense of self involved with these issues. Their attachments

therefore retain more preoedipal aspects. The greater length and different nature of their preoedipal experience, and their continuing preoccupation with the issues of this period, mean that women's sense of self is continuous with others and that they retain capacities for primary identification, both of which enable them to experience the empathy and lack of reality sense needed by a cared-for infant. In men, these qualities have been curtailed, both because they are early treated as an opposite by their mother and because their later attachment to her must be repressed. The relational basis for mothering is thus extended in women, and inhibited in men, who experience themselves as more separate and distinct from others.

The different structure of the feminine and masculine oedipal triangle and process of oedipal experience that results from women's mothering contributes further to gender personality differentiation and the reproduction of women's mothering. As a result of this experience, women's inner object world, and the affects and issues associated with it, are more actively sustained and more complex than men's. This means that women define and experience themselves relationally. Their heterosexual orientation is always in internal dialogue with both oedipal and preoedipal mother–child relational issues. Thus, women's heterosexuality is triangular and requires a third person—a child—for its structural and emotional completion. For men, by contrast, the heterosexual relationship alone recreates the early bond to their mother; a child interrupts it. Men, moreover, do not define themselves in relationship and have come to suppress relational capacities and repress relational needs. This prepares them to participate in the affect-denying world of alienated work, but not to fulfill women's needs for intimacy and primary relationships.

The oedipus complex, as it emerges from the asymmetrical organization of parenting, secures a psychological taboo on parent–child incest and pushes boys and girls in the direction of extrafamilial heterosexual relationships. This is one step toward the reproduction of parenting. The creation and maintenance of the incest taboo and of heterosexuality in girls and boys are different, however. For boys, superego formation and identification with their father, rewarded by the superiority of masculinity, maintain the taboo on incest with their mother, while heterosexual orientation continues from their earliest love relation with her. For girls, creating them as heterosexual in the first place maintains the taboo. However, women's heterosexuality is not so exclusive as men's. This makes it easier for them to accept or seek a male substitute for their fathers. At the same time, in a male-dominant society, women's exclusive emotional heterosexuality is not so necessary, nor is her repression of love for her father. Men are more likely to initiate relationships, and women's economic dependence on men pushes them anyway into heterosexual marriage.

Male dominance in heterosexual couples and marriage solves the problem of women's lack of heterosexual commitment and lack of satisfaction by making women more reactive in the sexual bonding process. At the same time, contradictions in heterosexuality help to perpetuate families and parenting by ensuring that women will seek relations to children and will not find heterosexual relationships alone satisfactory. Thus, men's lack of emotional availability and women's less exclusive heterosexual commitment help ensure women's mothering.

Women's mothering, then, produces psychological self-definition and capacities appropriate to mothering in women, and curtails and inhibits these capacities and this self-definition in men. The early experience of being cared for by a woman produces a fundamental structure of expectations in women and men concerning mothers' lack of separate interests from their infants and total concern for their infants' welfare. Daughters grow up identifying with these mothers, about whom they have such expectations. This set of expectations is generalized to the assumption that women naturally take care of children of all ages and the belief that women's "maternal" qualities can and should be extended to the nonmothering work that they do. All these results of women's mothering have ensured that women will mother infants and will take continuing responsibility for children.

The reproduction of women's mothering is the basis for the reproduction of women's location and responsibilities in the domestic sphere. This mothering, and its generalization to women's structural location in the domestic sphere, links the contemporary social organization of gender and social organization of production and contributes to the reproduction of each. That women mother is a fundamental organizational feature of the sex–gender system: It is basic to the sexual division of labor and generates a psychology and ideology of male dominance as well as an ideology about women's capacities and nature. Women, as wives and mothers, contribute as well to the daily and generational reproduction, both physical and psychological, of male workers and thus to the reproduction of capitalist production.

Women's mothering also reproduces the family as it is constituted in male-dominated society. The sexual and familial division of labor in which women mother creates a sexual division of psychic organization and orientation. It produces socially gendered women and men who enter into asymmetrical heterosexual relationships; it produces men who react to, fear, and act superior to women, and who put most of their energies into the nonfamilial work world and do not parent. Finally, it produces women who turn their energies toward nurturing and caring for children—in turn reproducing the sexual and familial division of labor in which women mother.

Social reproduction is thus asymmetrical. Women in their domestic role reproduce men and children physically, psychologically, and emotionally. Women in their domestic role as houseworkers reconstitute themselves physically on a daily basis and reproduce themselves as mothers, emotionally and psychologically, in the next generation. They thus contribute to the perpetuation of their own social roles and position in the hierarchy of gender.

Institutionalized features of family structure and the social relations of reproduction reproduce themselves. A psychoanalytic investigation shows that women's mothering capacities and commitments, and the general psychological capacities and wants which are the basis of women's emotional work, are built developmentally into feminine personality. Because women are themselves mothered by women, they grow up with the relational capacities and needs, and psychological definition of self-in-relationship, which commits them to mothering. Men, because they are mothered by women, do not. Women mother daughters who, when they become women, mother.

(1978)

55 • *Heidi I. Hartmann*

"THE UNHAPPY MARRIAGE OF MARXISM AND FEMINISM: TOWARDS A MORE PROGRESSIVE UNION"

The "marriage" of marxism and feminism has been like the marriage of husband and wife depicted in English common law: marxism and feminism are one, and that one is marxism.[1] Recent attempts to integrate marxism and feminism are unsatisfactory to us as feminists because they subsume the feminist struggle into the "larger" struggle against capital. To continue our simile further, either we need a healthier marriage or we need a divorce.

The inequalities in this marriage, like most social phenomena, are no accident. Many marxists typically argue that feminism is at best less important than class conflict and at worst divisive of the working class. This political stance produces an analysis that absorbs feminism into the class struggle. Moreover, the analytic power of marxism with respect to capital has obscured its limitations with respect to sexism. We will argue here that while marxist analysis provides essential insight into the laws of historical development, and those of capital in particular, the categories of marxism are sex-blind. Only a specifically feminist analysis reveals the systemic character of relations between men and women. Yet feminist analysis by itself is inadequate because it has been blind to history and insufficiently materialist. Both marxist analysis, particularly its historical and materialist method, and feminist analysis, especially the identification of patriarchy as a social and historical structure, must be drawn upon if we are to understand the development of western capitalist societies and the predicament of women within them. In this essay we suggest a new direction for marxist feminist analysis.

I. MARXISM AND THE WOMAN QUESTION

The woman question has never been the "feminist question." The feminist question is directed at the causes of sexual inequality between women and men, of male dominance over women. Most marxist analyses of women's position take as their question the relationship of women to the economic system, rather than that of women to men, apparently assuming the latter will be explained in their discussion of the former. Marxist analysis of the woman question has taken three main forms. All see women's oppression in our connection (or lack of it) to production. Defining women as part of the working class, these analyses consistently subsume women's relation to men under worker's relation to capital. First, early marxists, including Marx, Engels, Kautsky, and Lenin, saw capitalism drawing all women into the wage labor force, and saw this process destroying the sexual division of labor. Second, contemporary marxists have incorporated women into an analysis of everyday life in capitalism. In this view, all aspects of our lives are seen to reproduce the capitalist system and we are all workers in the system. And third, marxist feminists have focussed on housework and its relation to capital, some arguing that housework produces surplus value and that houseworkers work directly for capitalists. . . .

Marxism enables us to understand many aspects of capitalist societies: the structure of production, the generation of a particular occupational structure, and the nature of the dominant ideology. Marx's theory of

Reprinted from *Capital & Class* 3.2 (1979): 1–33. Used by permission of Sage Publications. Notes have been renumbered.

the development of capitalism is a theory of the development of "empty places." Marx predicted, for example, the growth of the proletariat and the demise of the petit bourgeoisie. More precisely and in more detail, Braverman among others has explained the creation of the "places" clerical worker and service worker in advanced capitalist societies.[2] Just as capital creates these places indifferent to the individuals who fill them, the categories of marxist analysis, class, reserve army of labor, wage-laborer, do not explain why particular people fill particular places. They give no clues about why *women* are subordinate to *men* inside and outside the family and why it is not the other way around. *Marxist categories, like capital itself, are sex-blind.* The categories of marxism cannot tell us who will fill the empty places. Marxist analysis of the woman question has suffered from this basic problem.

* * *

TOWARDS A DEFINITION OF PATRIARCHY

We can usually define patriarchy as a set of social relations between men, which have a material base, and which, though hierarchical, establish or create interdependence and solidarity among men that enable them to dominate women. Though patriarchy is hierarchical and men of different classes, races, or ethnic groups have different places in the patriarchy, they also are united in their shared relationship of dominance over their women; they are dependent on each other to maintain that domination. Hierarchies "work" at least in part because they create vested interests in the status quo. Those at the higher levels can "buy off" those at the lower levels by offering them power over those still lower. In the hierarchy of patriarchy, all men, whatever their rank in the patriarchy, are bought off by being able to control at least some women. There is some evidence to suggest that when patriarchy was first institutionalized in state societies, the ascending rulers literally made men the heads of their families (enforcing their control over their wives and children) in exchange for the men's ceding some of their tribal resources to the new rulers.[3] Men are dependent on one another (despite their hierarchical ordering) to maintain their control over women.

The material base upon which patriarchy rests lies most fundamentally in men's control over women's labor power. Men maintain this control by excluding women from access to some essential productive resources (in capitalist societies, for example, jobs that pay living wages) and by restricting women's sexuality. Monogamous heterosexual marriage is one relatively recent and efficient form that seems to allow men to control both these areas. Controlling women's access to resources and their sexuality, in turn, allows men to control women's labor power, both for the purpose of serving men in many personal and sexual ways and for the purpose of rearing children. The services women render men, and which exonerate men from having to perform many unpleasant tasks (like cleaning toilets) occur outside as well as inside the family setting. Examples outside the family include the harassment of women workers and students by male bosses and professors as well as the common use of secretaries to run personal errands, make coffee, and provide "sexy" surroundings. Rearing children, whether or not the children's labor power is of immediate benefit to their fathers, is nevertheless a crucial task in perpetuating patriarchy as a system. Just as class society must be reproduced by schools, work places, consumption norms, etc., so must patriarchal social relations. In our society children are generally reared by women at home, women socially defined and recognized as inferior to men, while men appear in the domestic picture only rarely. Children raised in this way generally learn their places in the gender hierarchy well. Central to this process, however, are the areas outside the home where patriarchal behaviors are taught and the inferior position of women enforced and reinforced: churches, schools, sports, clubs, unions, armies, factories, offices, health centers, the media, etc.

The material base of patriarchy, then, does not rest solely on childrearing in the family, but on all the social structures that enable men to control women's labor. The aspects of social structures that perpetuate patriarchy are theoretically identifiable, hence separable from their other aspects. Gayle Rubin has increased our ability to identify the patriarchal element of these social structures enormously by identifying "sex/gender systems":

> a "sex/gender system" is the set of arrangements by which a society transforms biological sexuality into products of human activity, and in which these transformed sexual needs are satisfied.[4]

We are born female and male, biological sexes, but we are created woman and man, socially recognized genders. *How* we are so created is that second aspect of the *mode* of production of which Engels spoke, "the production of human beings themselves, the propagation of the species."

How people propagate the species is socially determined. If, biologically, people are sexually polymorphous, and society were organized in such a way that all forms of sexual expression were equally permissible, production would result only from some sexual encounters, the heterosexual ones. The strict division of labor by sex, a social invention common to all known societies, creates two very separate genders and a need for men and women to get together for economic reasons. It thus helps to direct their sexual needs toward heterosexual fulfillment, and helps to ensure biological reproduction. In more imaginative societies, biological reproduction might be ensured by other techniques, but the division of labor by sex appears to be the universal solution to date. Although it is theoretically possible that a sexual division of labor not imply inequality between the sexes, in most known societies, the socially acceptable division of labor by sex is one which accords lower status to women's work. The sexual division of labor is also the underpinning of sexual subcultures in which men and women experience life differently; it is the material base of male power which is exercised (in our society) not just in not doing housework and in securing superior employment, but psychologically as well.

How people meet their sexual needs, how they reproduce, how they inculcate social norms in new generations, how they learn gender, how it feels to be a man or a woman—all occur in the realm Rubin labels the sex/gender system. Rubin emphasizes the influence of kinship (which tells you with whom you can satisfy sexual needs) and the development of gender specific personalities via childrearing and the "oedipal machine." In addition, however, we can use the concept of the sex/gender system to examine all other social institutions for the roles they play in defining and reinforcing gender hierarchies. Rubin notes that theoretically a sex/gender system could be female dominant, male dominant, or egalitarian, but declines to label various known sex/gender systems or to periodize history accordingly. We choose to label our present sex/gender system patriarchy, because it appropriately captures the notion of hierarchy and male dominance which we see as central to the present system.

Economic production (what marxists are used to referring to as *the* mode of production) and the production of people in the sex/gender sphere both determine "the social organization under which the people of a particular historical epoch and a particular country live," according to Engels. The whole of society, then, can be understood by looking at both these types of production and reproduction, people and things.[5] There is no such thing as "pure capitalism," nor does "pure patriarchy" exist, for they must of necessity coexist. What exists is patriarchal capitalism, or patriarchal feudalism, or egalitarian hunting/gathering societies, or matriarchal horticultural societies, or patriarchal horticultural societies, and so on. There appears to be no necessary connection between *changes* in the one aspect of production and changes in the other. A society could undergo transition from capitalism to socialism, for example, and remain patriarchal. Common sense, history, and our experience tell us, however, that these two aspects of production are so closely intertwined that change in one ordinarily creates movement, tension, or contradiction in the other.

Racial hierarchies can also be understood in this context. Further elaboration may be possible along the lines of defining color/race systems, arenas of social life that take biological color and turn it into a social category, race. Racial hierarchies, like gender hierarchies, are aspects of our social organization, of how people are produced and reproduced. They are not fundamentally ideological; they constitute that second aspect of our mode of production, the production and reproduction of people. It might be most accurate then to refer to our societies not as, for example, simply capitalist, but as patriarchal capitalist white supremacist. In Part III below, we illustrate one case of capitalism adapting to and making use of racial orders and several examples of the interrelations between capitalism and patriarchy.

Capitalist development creates the places for a hierarchy of workers, but traditional marxist categories cannot tell us who will fill which places. Gender and racial hierarchies determine who fills the empty places. *Patriarchy is not simply hierarchical organization,* but hierarchy in which *particular* people fill *particular* places. It is in studying patriarchy that we learn why it is women who are dominated and how. While we believe that most known societies have been patriarchal, we do not view patriarchy as a universal, unchanging phenomenon. Rather patriarchy, the set of interrelations among men that allow men to dominate women, has changed in form and intensity over time. It is crucial that the hierarchy among men, and their differential access to patriarchal benefits, be examined. Surely, class, race, nationality, and even marital status and sexual orientation, as well as the obvious age, come into play here. And women of different class, race, national, marital status, or sexual orientation groups are subjected to different degrees of patriarchal power. Women may themselves exercise class, race, or national power, or even patriarchal power (through their family connections) over men lower in the patriarchal hierarchy than their own male kin.

To recapitulate, we define patriarchy as a set of social relations which has a material base and in which there are hierarchical relations between men and solidarity among them which enable them in turn to dominate women. The material base of patriarchy is men's control over women's labor power. That control is maintained by excluding women from access to necessary economically productive resources and by restricting women's sexuality. Men exercise their control in receiving personal service work from women, in not having to do housework or rear children, in having access to women's bodies for sex, and in feeling powerful and being powerful. The crucial elements of patriarchy as we *currently* experience them are: heterosexual marriage (and consequent homophobia), female childrearing and housework, women's economic dependence on men (enforced by arrangements in the labor market), the state, and numerous institutions based on social relations among men—clubs, sports, unions, professions, universities, churches, corporations and armies. All of these elements need to be examined if we are to understand patriarchal capitalism.

Both hierarchy and interdependence among men and the subordination of women are *integral* to the functioning of our society; that is, these relationships are *systemic*. We leave aside the question of the creation of these relations and ask, can we recognize patriarchal relations in capitalist societies? Within capitalist societies we must discover those same bonds between men which both bourgeois and marxist social scientists claim no longer exist or are, at the most, unimportant leftovers. Can we understand how these relations among

men are perpetuated in capitalist societies? Can we identify ways in which patriarchy has shaped the course of capitalist development?

III. THE PARTNERSHIP OF PATRIARCHY AND CAPITAL

How are we to recognize patriarchal social relations in capitalist societies? It appears as if each woman is oppressed by her own man alone; her oppression seems a private affair. Relationships among men and among families seem equally fragmented. It is hard to recognize relationships among men, and between men and women, as *systematically* patriarchal. We argue, however, that patriarchy as a system of relations between men and women exists in capitalism, and that in capitalist societies a healthy and strong partnership exists between patriarchy and capital. Yet if one begins with the concept of patriarchy and an understanding of the capitalist mode of production, one recognizes immediately that the partnership of patriarchy and capital was not inevitable; men and capitalists often have conflicting interests, particularly over the use of women's labor power. Here is one way in which this conflict might manifest itself: the vast majority of men might want their women at home to personally service them. A smaller number of men, who are capitalists, might want most women (not their own) to work in the wage labor market. In examining the tensions of this conflict over women's labor power historically, we will be able to identify the material base of patriarchal relations in capitalist societies, as well as the basis for the partnership between capital and patriarchy.

INDUSTRIALIZATION AND THE DEVELOPMENT OF FAMILY WAGES

Marxists made quite logical inferences from a selection of the social phenomena they witnessed in the nineteenth century. But marxists ultimately underestimated the strength of preexisting patriarchal social forces with which fledgling capital had to contend and the need for capital to adjust to these forces. The industrial revolution was drawing all people into the labor force, including women and children; in fact, the first factories used child and female labor almost exclusively. That women and children could earn wages separately from men both undermined authority relations (as discussed in Part I above) and kept wages low for everyone. . . .

* * *

Male workers resisted the wholesale entrance of women and children into the labor force, and sought to exclude them from union membership and the labor force as well. In 1846 the *Ten-Hours' Advocate* stated:

> It is needless for us to say, that all attempts to improve the morals and physical condition of female factory workers will be abortive, unless their hours are materially reduced. Indeed we may go so far as to say, that married females would be much better occupied in performing the domestic duties of the household, than following the never-tiring motion of machinery. We therefore hope the day is not distant, when the husband will be able to provide for his wife and family, without sending the former to endure the drudgery of a cotton mill.[6]

In the United States in 1854 the National Typographical Union resolved not to "encourage by its act the employment of female compositors." Male unionists did not want to afford union protection to women workers; they tried to exclude them instead. In 1879 Adolph Strasser, president of the Cigar-makers International Union, said: "We cannot drive the females out of the trade, but we can restrict their daily quota of labor through factory laws."[7]

While the problem of cheap competition could have been solved by organizing the wage earning of women and youths, the problem of disrupted family life could not be. Men reserved union protection for men and argued for protective labor laws for women and children. Protective labor laws, while they may have ameliorated some of the worst abuses of female and child labor, also limited the participation of adult women in many "male" jobs. Men sought to keep high wage jobs for themselves and to raise male wages generally. They argued for wages sufficient for their wage labor alone to support their families. This "family wage" system gradually came to be the norm for stable working-class families at the end of the nineteenth century and the beginning of the twentieth. Several observers have declared the non-wage-working wife to be part of the standard of living of male workers. Instead of fighting for equal wages for men and women, male workers sought the family wage, wanting to retain their wives' services at home. In the absence of

patriarchy a unified working class might have confronted capitalism, but patriarchal social relations divided the working class, allowing one part (men) to be bought off at the expense of the other (women). Both the hierarchy between men and the solidarity among them were crucial in this process of resolution. Family wages may be understood as a resolution of the conflict over women's labor power which was occurring between patriarchal and capitalist interests at that time.

* * *

While the family wage shows that capitalism adjusts to patriarchy, the changing status of children shows that patriarchy adjusts to capital. Children, like women, came to be excluded from wage labor. As children's ability to earn money declined, their legal relationship to their parents changed. At the beginning of the industrial era in the United States, fulfilling children's need for their fathers was thought to be crucial, even primary, to their happy development; fathers had legal priority in cases of contested custody. As children's ability to contribute to the economic well-being of the family declined, mothers came increasingly to be viewed as crucial to the happy development of their children, and gained legal priority in cases of contested custody.[8] Here, patriarchy adapted to the changing economic role of children: when children were productive, men claimed them; as children became unproductive, they were given to women.

* * *

THE FAMILY AND THE FAMILY WAGE TODAY

We argued above that with respect to capitalism and patriarchy, the adaptation, or mutual accommodation, took the form of the development of the family wage in the early twentieth century. The family wage cemented the partnership between patriarchy and capital. Despite women's increased labor force participation, particularly rapid since World War II, the family wage is still, we argue, the cornerstone of the present sexual division of labor—in which women are primarily responsible for housework and men primarily for wage work. Women's lower wages in the labor market (combined with the need for children to be reared by someone) assure the continued existence of the family as a necessary income pooling unit. The family, supported by the family wage, thus allows the control of women's labor by men both within and without the family.

Though women's increased wage work may cause stress for the family (similar to the stress Kautsky and Engels noted in the nineteenth century), it would be wrong to think that as a consequence, the concepts and the realities of the family and of the sexual division of labor will soon disappear. The sexual division of labor reappears in the labor market, where women work at women's jobs, often the very jobs they used to do only at home—food preparation and service, cleaning of all kinds, caring for people, and so on. As these jobs are low-status and low-paying, patriarchal relations remain intact, though their material base shifts somewhat from the family to the wage differential, from family-based to industrially-based patriarchy.[9] . . .

It could be that the effects of women's increasing labor force participation are found in a declining sexual division of labor within the family, rather than in more frequent divorce, but evidence for this is also lacking. Statistics on who does housework, even in families with wage-earning wives, show little change in recent years; women still do most of it.[10] The double day is a reality for wage-working women. This is hardly surprising since the sexual division of labor outside the family, in the labor market, keeps women financially dependent on men—even when they earn a wage themselves. The future of patriarchy does not, however, rest solely on the future of familial relations. For patriarchy, like capital, can be surprisingly flexible and adaptable. . . .

* * *

IV. TOWARDS A MORE PROGRESSIVE UNION

Many problems remain for us to explore. Patriarchy as we have used it here remains more a descriptive term than an analytical one. If we think marxism alone inadequate, and radical feminism itself insufficient, then we need to develop new categories.

What makes our task a difficult one is that the same features, such as the division of labor, often reinforce both patriarchy and capitalism, and in a thoroughly patriarchal capitalist society, it is hard to isolate the mechanisms of patriarchy. Nevertheless, this is what we must do. We have pointed to some starting places: looking at who benefits from women's labor power, uncovering the material base of patriarchy, investigating

the mechanisms of hierarchy and solidarity among men. The questions we must ask are endless. . . .

FEMINISM AND THE CLASS STRUGGLE

Historically and in the present, the relation of feminism and class struggle has been either that of fully separate paths ("bourgeois" feminism on one hand, class struggle on the other), or, within the left, the dominance of feminism by marxism. With respect to the latter, this has been a consequence both of the analytic power of marxism, and of the power of men within the left. These have produced both open struggles on the left, and a contradictory position for marxist feminists. . . .

The left has always been ambivalent about the women's movement, often viewing it as dangerous to the cause of socialist revolution. When left women espouse feminism, it may be personally threatening to left men. And of course many left organizations benefit from the labor of women. Therefore, many left analyses (both in progressive and traditional forms) are self-serving, both theoretically and politically. They seek to influence women to abandon attempts to develop an independent understanding of women's situation and to adopt the "left's" analyses of the situation. As for our response to this pressure, it is natural that, as we ourselves have turned to marxist analysis, we would try to join the "fraternity" using this paradigm, and we may end up trying to justify our struggle to the fraternity rather than trying to analyze the situation of women to improve our political practice. Finally, many marxists are satisfied with the traditional marxist analysis of the woman question. They see class as the correct framework with which to understand women's position. Women should be understood as part of the working class; the working class's struggle against capitalism should take precedence over any conflict between men and women. Sex conflict must not be allowed to interfere with class solidarity.

* * *

The struggle against capital and patriarchy cannot be successful if the study and practice of the issues of feminism are abandoned. A struggle aimed only at capitalist relations of oppression will fail, since their underlying supports in patriarchal relations of oppression will be overlooked. And the analysis of patriarchy is essential to a definition of the kind of socialism useful to women. While men and women share a need to overthrow capitalism, they retain interests particular to their gender group. It is not clear—from our sketch, from history, or from male socialists—that the socialism being struggled for is the same for both men and women. For a humane socialism would require not only consensus on what the new society should look like and what a healthy person should look like, but more concretely, it would require that men relinquish their privilege.

As women we must not allow ourselves to be talked out of the urgency and importance of our tasks, as we have so many times in the past. We must fight the attempted coercion, both subtle and not so subtle, to abandon feminist objectives.

This suggests two strategic considerations. First, a struggle to establish socialism must be a struggle in which groups with different interests form an alliance. Women should not trust men to liberate them after the revolution, in part, because there is no reason to think they would know how; in part, because there is no necessity for them to do so. In fact their immediate self-interest lies in our continued oppression. Instead we must have our own organizations and our own power base. Second, we think the sexual division of labor within capitalism has given women a practice in which we have learned to understand what human interdependence and needs are. While men have long struggled *against* capital, women know what to struggle *for*.[11] As a general rule, men's position in patriarchy and capitalism prevents them from recognizing both human needs for nurturance, sharing, and growth, and the potential for meeting those needs in a nonhierarchical, nonpatriarchal society. But even if we raise their consciousness, they might assess the potential gains against the potential losses and choose the status quo. Men have more to lose than their chains.

As feminist socialists, we must organize a practice which addresses both the struggle against patriarchy and the struggle against capitalism. We must insist that the society we want to create is a society in which recognition of interdependence is liberation rather than shame, nurturance is a universal, not an oppressive practice, and in which women do not continue to support the false as well as the concrete freedoms of men.

(1979)

NOTES

1. Often paraphrased as "the husband and wife are one and that one is the husband," English law held that "by marriage, the husband and wife are one person in law; that is, the very being or legal existence of the woman is suspended during the marriage, or at least is incorporated and consolidated into that of the Husband," I. Blackstone, *Commentaries*, 1965, pp. 442–445, cited in Kenneth M. Davidson, Ruth B. Ginsburg, and Herma H. Kay, *Sex Based Discrimination* (St. Paul, Minn.: West Publishing Co., 1974), p. 117.

2. Harry Braverman, *Labor and Monopoly Capital* (New York: Monthly Review Press, 1975).

3. See Viana Muller, "The Formation of the State and the Oppression of Women: Some Theoretical Considerations and a Case Study in England and Wales," *Review of Radical Political Economy*, Vol. 9, no. 3 (Fall 1977), pp. 7–21.

4. Gayle Rubin, "The Traffic in Women," in *Anthropology of Women*, ed. Reiter, p. 159.

5. Himmelweit and Mohun point out that both aspects of production (people and things) are logically necessary to describe a mode of production because by definition a mode of production must be capable of reproducing itself. Either aspect alone is not self-sufficient. To put it simply, the production of things requires people, and the production of people requires things. Marx, though recognizing capitalism's need for people, did not concern himself with how they were produced or what the connections between the two aspects of production were. See Himmelweit and Mohun, "Domestic Labour and Capital." *Cambridge Journal of Economics*, Vol. 1, no. 1 (March 1977), pp. 15–31.

6. Cited in Neil Smelser, *Social Change and the Industrial Revolution* (Chicago: University of Chicago Press, 1959), p. 301.

7. These examples are from Heidi I. Hartmann, "Capitalism, Patriarchy, and Job Segregation by Sex," *Signs: Journal of Women in Culture and Society*, Vol. 1, no. 3, pt. 2 (Spring 1976), pp. 162–163.

8. Carol Brown, "Patriarchal Capitalism and the Female-Headed Family," *Social Scientist* (India); no. 40–41 (November/December 1975), pp. 28–39.

9. Carol Brown, in "Patriarchal Capitalism," argues, for example, that we are moving from a "family-based" to "industrially-based" patriarchy within capitalism.

10. See Kathryn E. Walker and Margaret E. Woods, *Time Use: A Measure of Household Production of Family Goods and Services* (Washington, D.C.: American Home Economics Association, 1976); and Heidi I. Hartmann, "The Family as the Locus of Gender, Class, and Political Struggle: The Example of Housework," *Signs: Journal of Women in Culture and Society*, Vol. 6, no. 3 (Spring 1981).

11. Lise Vogel, "The Earthly Family." *Radical America*, Vol. 7, no. 4–5 (July/October 1973), pp. 9–50.

"THROWING LIKE A GIRL: A PHENOMENOLOGY OF FEMININE BODY COMPORTMENT, MOTILITY, AND SPATIALITY"*

In discussing the fundamental significance of lateral space, which is one of the unique spatial dimensions generated by the human upright posture, Erwin Straus (1966) pauses at "the remarkable difference in the manner of throwing of the two sexes"[1] [p. 157]. Citing a study and photographs of young boys and girls, he (Straus, 1966) describes the difference as follows:

> The girl of five does not make any use of lateral space. She does not stretch her arm sideward; she does not twist her trunk; she does not move her legs, which remain side by side. All she does in preparation for throwing is to lift her right arm forward to the horizontal and to bend the forearm backward in a pronate position. . . . The ball is released without force, speed, or accurate aim. . . . A boy of the same age, when preparing to throw, stretches his right arm sideward and backward; supinates the forearm; twists, turns and bends his trunk; and moves his right foot backward. From this stance, he can support his throwing almost with the full strength of his total motorium. . . . The ball leaves the hand with considerable acceleration; it moves toward its goal in a long flat curve [p. 157–158].[2]

. . . The scope of bodily existence and movement with which I am concerned here is also limited. I concentrate primarily on those sorts of bodily activities which relate to the comportment or orientation of the body as a whole, which entail gross movement, or which require the enlistment of strength and the confrontation of the body's capacities and possibilities with the resistance and malleability of things. Primarily the kind of movement I am concerned with is movement in which the body aims at the accomplishment of a definite purpose or task. There are thus many aspects of feminine bodily existence which I leave out of account here. Most notable of these is the body in its sexual being. Another aspect of bodily existence, among others, which I leave unconsidered is structured body movement which does not have a particular aim—for example, dancing. Besides reasons of space, this limitation of subject is based on the conviction, derived primarily from Merleau-Ponty, that it is the ordinary purposive orientation of the body as a whole toward things and its environment which initially defines the relation of a subject to its world. Thus focus upon ways in which the feminine body frequently or typically conducts itself in such comportment or movement may be particularly revelatory of the structures of feminine existence.[3]

Before entering the analysis, I should clarify what I mean here by "feminine" existence. In accordance with de Beauvoir's understanding, I take "femininity" to designate not a mysterious quality or essence which all women have by virtue of their being biologically female. It is, rather, a set of structures and conditions which delimit the typical *situation* of being a woman in a particular society, as well as the typical way in which this situation is lived by the women themselves. Defined as such, it is not necessary that *any*

Reprinted from *Human Studies* 3, 137–156 (1980). Used by permission of Springer. Notes have been renumbered.

women be "feminine"—that is, it is not necessary that there be distinctive structures and behavior typical of the situation of women.[4] This understanding of "feminine" existence makes it possible to say that some women escape or transcend the typical situation and definition of women in various degrees and respects. I mention this primarily to indicate that the account offered here of the modalities of feminine bodily existence is not to be falsified by referring to some individual women to whom aspects of the account do not apply, or even to some individual men to whom they do.

The account developed here combines the insights of the theory of the lived body as expressed by Merleau-Ponty and the theory of the situation of women as developed by de Beauvoir (1974). I assume that at the most basic descriptive level, Merleau-Ponty's account of the relation of the lived body to its world, as developed in the *Phenomenology of Perception* (1962), applies to any human existence in a general way. At a more specific level, however, there is a particular style of bodily comportment which is typical of feminine existence, and this style consists of particular *modalities* of the structures and conditions of the body's existence in the world.[5]

As a framework for developing these modalities, I rely on de Beauvoir's account of woman's existence in patriarchal society as defined by a basic tension between immanence and transcendence.[6] The culture and society in which the female person dwells defines woman as Other, as the inessential correlate to man, as mere object and immanence. Woman is thereby both culturally and socially denied by the subjectivity, autonomy, and creativity which are definitive of being human and which in patriarchal society are accorded the man. At the same time, however because she is a human existence, the female person necessarily is a subjectivity and transcendence and she knows herself to be. The female person who enacts the existence of women in patriarchal society must therefore live a contradiction: as human she is a free subject who participates in transcendence, but her situation as a woman denies her that subjectivity and transcendence. My suggestion is that the modalities of feminine bodily comportment, motility, and spatiality exhibit this same tension between transcendence and immanence, between subjectivity and being a mere object. . . .

I

The basic difference which Straus observes between the way boys and girls throw is that girls do not bring their whole bodies into the motion as much as the boys. They do not reach back, twist, move backward, step, and lean forward. Rather, the girls tend to remain relatively immobile except for their arms, and even the arm is not extended as far as it could be. Throwing is not the only movement in which there is a typical difference in the way men and women use their bodies. Reflection on feminine comportment and body movement in other physical activities reveals that these also are frequently characterized, much as in the throwing case, by a failure to make full use of the body's spatial and lateral potentialities.

Even in the most simple body orientations of men and women as they sit, stand, and walk, one can observe a typical difference in body style and extension. Women generally are not as open with their bodies as men in their gait and stride. Typically, the masculine stride is longer proportional to a man's body than is the feminine stride to a woman's. The man typically swings his arms in a more open and loose fashion than does a woman and typically has more up and down rhythm in his step. Though we now wear pants more than we used to, and consequently do not have to restrict our sitting postures because of dress, women still tend to sit with their legs relatively close together and their arms across their bodies. When simply standing or leaning, men tend to keep their feet further apart than do woman, and we also tend more to keep our hands and arms touching or shielding our bodies. A final indicative difference is the way each carries books or parcels; girls and women most often carry books embraced to their chests, while boys and men swing them along their sides.

The approach persons of each sex take to the performance of physical tasks that require force, strength, and muscular coordination is frequently different. There are indeed real physical differences between men and woman in the kind and limit of their physical strength. Many of the observed differences between men and women in the performance of tasks requiring coordinated strength, however, are due not so much to brute muscular strength, but to the way each sex *uses* the body in approaching tasks. Women often do not perceive themselves as capable of lifting and carrying heavy things, pushing and shoving with significant force, pulling, squeezing, grasping, or twisting with force. When we attempt such tasks, we frequently fail to summon the full possibilities of our muscular coordination, position, poise, and bearing. Women tend not to put their whole bodies into engagement in a physical task with the same ease and naturalness as men. For example, in attempting to lift something, women more often than men fail to plant themselves firmly and make their thighs bear the greatest proportion of the weight. Instead, we tend to concentrate our effort on those parts of the body most immediately connected to the task—the arms and shoulders—rarely bringing the power of the legs to the task at all. When turning or twisting something, to take another example, we frequently concentrate effort in the hand and wrist, not bringing to the task the power of the shoulder, which is necessary for its efficient performance.[7]

The previously cited throwing example can be extended to a great deal of athletic activity. Now most men are by no means superior athletes, and their sporting efforts more often display bravado than genuine skill and coordination. The relatively untrained man nevertheless engages in sport generally with more free motion and open reach than does his female counterpart. Not only is there a typical style of throwing like a girl, but there is a more or less typical style of running like a girl, climbing like a girl, swinging like a girl, hitting like a girl. They have in common, first, that the whole body is not put into fluid and directed motion, but rather, in swinging and hitting, for example, the motion is concentrated in one body part; and second, that the woman's motion tends not to reach, extend, lean, stretch, and follow through in the direction of her intention.

For many women as they move in sport, a space surrounds them in imagination which we are not free to move beyond; the space available to our movement is a constricted space. Thus, for example, in softball or volley ball women tend to remain in one place more often than men, neither jumping to reach nor running to approach the ball. Men more often move out toward a ball in flight and confront it with their own counter-motion. Women tend to wait for and then *react* to its approach rather than going forth to meet it. We frequently respond to the motion of a ball coming toward us as though it were coming *at* us, and our immediate

bodily impulse is to flee, duck, or otherwise protect ourselves from its flight. Less often than men, moreover, do women give self-conscious direction and placement to their motion in sport. Rather than aiming at a certain place where we wish to hit a ball, for example, we tend to hit it in a "general" direction.

Women often approach a physical engagement with things with timidity, uncertainty, and hesitancy. Typically, we lack an entire trust in our bodies to carry us to our aims. There is, I suggest, a double hesitation here. On the one hand, we often lack confidence that we have the capacity to do what must be done. Many times I have slowed a hiking party in which the men bounded across a harmless stream while I stood on the other side warily testing out my footing on various stones, holding on to overhanging branches. Though the others crossed with ease, I do not believe it is easy for *me*, even though once I take a committed step I am across in a flash. The other side of this tentativeness is, I suggest, a fear of getting hurt, which is greater in women than in men. Our attention is often divided between the aim to be realized in motion and the body that must accomplish it, while at the same time saving itself from harm. We often experience our bodies as a fragile encumbrance, rather than the media for the enactment of our aims. We feel as though we must have our attention directed upon our body to make sure it is doing what we wish it to do, rather than paying attention to what we want to do *through* our bodies.

All the above factors operate to produce in many women a greater or lesser feeling of incapacity, frustration, and self-consciousness. We have more of a tendency than men to greatly underestimate our bodily capacity.[8] We decide beforehand—usually mistakenly—that the task is beyond us, and thus give it less than our full effort. At such a half-hearted level, of course, we cannot perform the tasks, become frustrated, and fulfill our own prophecy. In entering a task we frequently are self-conscious about appearing awkward, and at the same time do not wish to appear too strong. Both worries contribute to our awkwardness and frustration. If we should finally release ourselves from this spiral and really give a physical task our best effort, we are greatly surprised indeed at what our bodies can accomplish. It has been found that women more often than men underestimate the level of achievement they have reached.[9]

None of the observations which have been made thus far about the way women typically move and comport their bodies applies to all women all of the time. Nor do those women who manifest some aspect of this typicality do so in the same degree. There is no inherent, mysterious connection between these sorts of typical comportments and being a female person. Many of them result, as will be developed later, from lack of practice in using the body and performing tasks. Even given these qualifications, one can nevertheless sensibly speak of a general feminine style of body comportment and movement. . . .

IV

. . . The modalities of feminine bodily comportment, motility, and spatiality which I have described here are, I claim, common to the existence of women in contemporary society to one degree or another. They have their source, however, in neither anatomy nor physiology, and certainly not in a mysterious feminine "essence." Rather, they have their source in the particular *situation* of women as conditioned by their sexist oppression in contemporary society.

Women in sexist society are physically handicapped. Insofar as we learn to live out our existence in accordance with the definition that patriarchal culture assigns to us, we are physically inhibited, confined, positioned, and objectified. As lived bodies we are not open and unambiguous transcendences which move out to master a world that belongs to us, a world constituted by our own intentions and projections. To be sure, there are actual women in contemporary society to whom all or part of the above description does not apply. Where these modalities are not manifest in or determinative of the existence of a particular women, however, they are definitive in a negative mode—as that which she has escaped, through accident or good fortune, or more often, as that which she has had to overcome.

One of the sources of the modalities of feminine bodily existence is too obvious to dwell upon at length. For the most part, girls and women are not given the opportunity to use their full bodily capacities in free and open engagement with the world, nor are they encouraged as much as boys to develop specific bodily skills.[10] Girl play is often more sedentary and enclosing than the play of boys. In school and after school activities girls are not encouraged to

engage in sport, in the controlled use of their bodies in achieving well-defined goals. Girls, moreover, get little practice at "tinkering" with things, and thus developing spatial skill. Finally, girls are not asked often to perform tasks demanding physical effort and strength, while as the boys grow older they are asked to do so more and more.[11]

The modalities of feminine bodily existence are not merely privative, however, and thus their source is not merely in lack of practice, though this is certainly an important element. There is a specific positive style of feminine body comportment and movement, which is learned as the girl comes to understand that she is a girl. The young girl acquires many subtle habits of feminine body comportment—walking like a girl, tilting her head like a girl, standing and sitting like a girl, gesturing like a girl, and so on. The girl learns actively to hamper her movements. She is told that she must be careful not to get hurt, not to get dirty, not to tear her clothes, that the things she desires to do are dangerous for her. Thus she develops a bodily timidity which increases with age. In assuming herself as a girl, she takes herself up as fragile. Studies have found that young children of both sexes categorically assert that girls are more likely to get hurt than boys,[12] and that girls ought to remain close to home while boys can roam and explore.[13] The more a girl assumes her status as feminine, the more she takes herself to be fragile and immobile, and the more she actively enacts her own body inhibition. When I was about thirteen, I spent hours practicing a "feminine" walk which was stiff, closed, and rotated from side to side.

Studies which record observations of sex differences in spatial perception, spatial problem solving and motor skills have also found that these differences tend to increase with age. While very young children show virtually no differences in motor skills, movement, spatial perception, etc., differences seem to appear in elementary school and increase with adolescence. If these findings are accurate, they would seem to support the conclusion that it is in the process of growing up as a girl that the modalities of feminine bodily comportment, motility, and spatiality make their appearance.[14]

There is, however, a further source of the modalities of feminine bodily existence which is perhaps even more profound than these. At the root of those modalities, I have stated in the previous section, is the fact that the woman lives her body as *object* as well as subject. The source of this is that patriarchal society defines woman as object, as a mere body, and that in sexist society women are in fact frequently regarded by others as objects and mere bodies. An essential part of the situation of being a woman is that of living the ever present possibility that one will be gazed upon as a mere body, as shape and flesh that presents itself as the potential object of another subject's intentions and manipulations, rather than as a living manifestation of action and intention.[15] The source of this objectified bodily existence is in the attitude of others regarding her, but the woman herself often actively takes up her body as a mere thing. She gazes at it in the mirror, worries about how it looks to others, prunes it, shapes it, molds and decorates it.

This objectified bodily existence accounts for the self-consciousness of the feminine relation to her body and resulting distance she takes from her body. As human, she is a transcendence and subjectivity, and cannot live herself as mere bodily object. Thus, to the degree that she does live herself as mere body, she cannot be in unity with herself, but must take a distance from and exist in discontinuity with her body. The objectifying regard which "keeps her in her place" can also account for the spatial modality of being positioned and for why women frequently tend not to move openly, keeping their limbs enclosed around themselves. To open her body in free active and open extension and bold outward directedness is for a woman to invite objectification.

The threat of being seen is, however, not the only threat of objectification which the woman lives. She also lives the threat of invasion of her body space. The most extreme form of such spatial and bodily invasion is the threat of rape. But we are daily subject to the possibility of bodily invasion in many far more subtle ways as well. It is acceptable, for example, for women to be touched in ways and under circumstances that it is not acceptable for men to be touched, and by persons— i.e. men—whom it is not acceptable for them to touch.[16] I would suggest that the enclosed space which has been described as a modality of feminine spatiality is in part a defense against such invasion. Women tend to project an existential barrier enclosed around them and discontinuous with the "over there" in order to keep the other at a distance. The woman lives her space as confined and enclosed around her at least in part as projecting some small area in which she can exist as a free subject.

The paper is a prolegamenon to the study of aspects of women's experience and situation which have not received the treatment they warrant. I would like to close with some questions which require further thought and research. This paper has concentrated its attention upon the sort of physical tasks and body orientation which involve the whole body in gross movement. Further investigation into woman's bodily existence would require looking at activities which do not involve the whole body and finer movement. If we are going to develop an account of the woman's body experience in situation, moreover, we must reflect on the modalities of a woman's experience of her body in its sexual being, as well as upon less task-oriented body activities, such as dancing. Another question which arises is whether the description given here would apply equally well to any sort of physical tasks. Might the kind of task, and specifically whether it is a task or movement which is sex-typed, have some effect on the modalities of feminine bodily existence? A further question is to what degree we can develop a theoretical account of the connection between the modalities of the bodily existence of women and other aspects of our existence and experience. For example, I have an intuition that the general lack of confidence that we frequently have about our cognitive or leadership abilities, is traceable in part to an original doubt in our body's capacity. None of these questions can be dealt with properly, however, without first performing the kind of guided observation and data collection that my reading has concluded, to a large degree, is yet to be performed.

(1980)

NOTES

1. Erwin W. Straus, The Upright Posture, in *Phenomenological Psychology* (New York: Basic Books, 1966), pp. 137–165. References to particular pages are indicated in the text.
2. Studies continue to be performed which arrive at similar observations. See, for example, Lolas E. Kalverson, Mary Ann Robertson, M. Joanne Safrit, and Thomas W. Roberts, Effect of Guided Practice on Overhand Throw

Ball Velocities of Kindergarten Children, *Research Quarterly*, Vol. 48, No. 2, May 1977, pp. 311–318. The study found that boys had significantly greater velocities than girls.

See also F. J. J. Buytendijk's remarks in *Woman: A Contemporary View* (New York: Newman Press, 1968), pp. 144–115. In raising the example of throwing, Buytendijk is concerned to stress, as am 1 in this paper, that the important thing to investigate is not the strictly physical phenomena, but rather the manner in which each sex projects her or his Being-in-the-world through movement.

3. In his discussion of the "dynamics of feminine existence," Buytendijk focuses precisely on those sorts of motions which are aimless. He claims that it is through these kinds of expressive movements—e.g., walking for the sake of walking—and not through action aimed at the accomplishment of particular purposes, that the pure image of masculine or feminine existence is manifest (pp. 278–9). Such an approach, however, contradicts the basic existentialist assumption that Being-in-the-world consists in projecting purposes and goals which structure one's situatedness. While there is certainly something to be learned from reflecting upon feminine movement in noninstrumental activity, given that accomplishing tasks is basic to the structure of human existence, it serves as a better starting point for investigation of feminine motility. As I point out at the end of this paper, a full phenomenology of feminine existence must take account of this noninstrumental movement.

4. It is not impossible, moreover, for men to be "feminine" in at least some respects, according to the above definition.

5. On this level of specificity there also exist particular modalities of masculine motility, inasmuch as there is a particular style of movement more or less typical of men. I will not, however, be concerned with those in this paper.

6. See de Beauvoir, Chapter XXI, Woman's Situation and Character.

7. It should be noted that this is probably typical only of women in advanced industrial societies, where the model of the Bourgeois woman has been extended to most women. It would not apply to those societies, for example, where most people, including women, do heavy physical work. Nor does this particular observation, of course, hold true of those women in our own society who do heavy physical work.

8. See A. M. Gross, Estimated versus actual physical strength in three ethnic groups, *Child Development*, 39 (1968), pp. 283–90. In a test of children at several different ages, at all but the youngest age-level, girls rated themselves lower than boys and rated themselves on self-estimates of strength, and as the girls grow older, their self-estimates of strength become even lower.

9. See Marguerite A. Cifton and Hope M. Smith, Comparison of Expressed Self-Concept of Highly Skilled Males and Females Concerning Motor Performance, *Perceptual and Motor Skills*, 16 (1963), pp. 199–201. Women consistently underestimated their level of acheivement in skills like running and jumping far more often than men did.

10. Nor are girls provided with examples of girls and women being physically active. See Mary E. Duquin, Differential Sex Role Socialization Toward Amplitude Appropriation, *Research Quarterly* (American Alliance for Health, Physical Education, and Recreation), *48* (1977), pp. 288–292. A survey of textbooks for young children revealed that children are thirteen times more likely to see a vigorously active man than a vigorously active woman, and three times more likely to see a relatively active man than a relatively active woman.

11. Sherman, op. cit., argues that it is the differential socialization of boys and girls in being encouraged to "tinker," explore, etc. that accounts for the difference between the two in spatial ability.

12. See L. Kolberg, A Cognitive-Developmental Analysis of Children's Sex-Role Concepts and Attitudes, in E. E. Maccoby, Ed., *The Development of Sex Differences* (Stanford University Press, 1966), p. 101.

13. Lenore J. Weitzman, Sex Role Socialization, in Freeman, Ed., *Woman: A Feminist Perspective* (Palo Alto, Calif.: Mayfield Publishing Co., 1975), pp. 111–112.

14. Op. cit., Maccoby and Jacklin, pp. 93–94.

15. The manner in which women are objectified by the gaze of the Other is not the same phenomenon as the objectification by the Other which is a condition of self-consciousness in Sartre's account. See *Being and Nothingness*, Hazel E. Barnes, trans. (New York: Philosophical Library, 1956), Pan Three. While the basic ontological category of being-for-others is an objectified for-itself, the objectification which women are subject to is that of being regarded as a mere in-itself. On the particular dynamic of sexual objectification, see Sandra Bartky, Psychological Oppression, in Sharon Bishop and Margorie Weinzweig, Ed., *Philosophy and Women* (Belmont, Calif: Wadsworth Publishing Co., 1979), pp. 33–41.

16. See Nancy Henley and Jo Freeman, The Sexual Politics of Interpersonal Behavior, in Freeman, op. cit., pp. 391–401.

REFERENCES

Bartky, S. Psychological oppression. In S. Bishop & M. Weinzweig (Eds.), *Philosophy and Women.* Belmont, Calif.: Wadsworth Publishing Co., 1979.

Buytendijk, F. J. J. *Woman: A Contemporary View.* New York: Newman Press, 1968.

de Beauvoir, S. *The Second Sex.* New York: Vintage Books, 1974.

Clifton, M. A., & Smith, H. M. Comparison of expressed self-concept of highly skilled males and females concerning motor performance. *Perceptual and Motor Skills*, 1963, 16, 199–201.

Dunquin, M. E. Differential sex role socialization toward amplitude appropriation. *Research Quarterly*, 1977, 48, 288–292.

Erikson, E. H. Inner and outer space: Reflections on Womanhood. *Daedalus*, 1964, 3, 582–606.

Firestone, S. *The Dialectic of Sex.* New York: Bantam Books, 1970.

Fisher, S. Sex differences in body perception. *Psychological Monographs.* 1964, 78, (Whole No. 14).

Fisher, S. *Body Experience in Fantasy and Behavior.* New York: Appleton–Century–Crofts, 1970.

Gross, A. M. Estimated versus actual physical strength in three ethnic groups. *Child Development*, 1968, 39, 283–290.

Henley, N., & Freeman, J. The sexual politics of interpersonal behavior. In J. Freeman (Ed.), *Woman: A Feminist Perspective.* Palo Alto, Calif.: Mayfield Publishing Co., 1975.

Kalverson, L. E., Robertson, M. A., Safrit, M. J., & Roberts, T. W. Effect of guided practice on overhand throw ball velocities of kindergarten children. *Research Quarterly*, (Vol.48). No. 2, *May*, 1977, 311–318.

Kolberg, L. A cognitive-developmental analysis of children's sex-role concepts and attitudes. In E. E. Maccoby (Ed.), *The Development of Sex Differences.* Stanford, Calif: Stanford University Press, 1966.

Maccoby, E. E., & Jacklin, C. N. *The Psychology of Sex Differences.* Stanford, Calif.: Stanford University Press, 1974.

Merleau-Ponty, M. *Phenomenology of Perception.* C. Smith (trans.), New York: Humanities Press, 1962.

Sartre, J. P. *Being and Nothingness.* H. B. Barnes (trans.), New York: Philosophical Library, 1956. (Part Three).

Sherman, J. A. Problems of sex differences in space perception and aspects of intellectual functioning. *Psychological Review*, 1967, 74, 290–299.

Strauss, E. W. The upright posture. *Phenomenological Psychology,* New York: Basic Books, 1966.

Weitzman, L. J. Sex role socialization. In J. Freeman (Ed.), *Woman: A Feminist Perspective.* Palo Alto, Calif.: Mayfield Publishing Co., 1975.

57 • *Ynestra King*

"FEMINISM AND THE REVOLT OF NATURE"

Ecology is a Feminist issue. But why? Is it because women are more a part of nature than men? Is it because women are morally superior to men? Is it because ecological feminists are satisfied with the traditional female stereotypes and wish to be limited to the traditional concerns of women? Is it because the domination of women and the domination of nature are connected?

The feminist debate over ecology has gone back and forth and is assuming major proportions in the movement; but there is a talking-past-each-other, not-getting-to-what's-really-going-on quality to it. The differences derive from unresolved questions in our political and theoretical history, so the connection of ecology to feminism has met with radically different responses from the various feminisms. . . .

From: *Heresies*, no. 13: Earthkeeping/Earthshaking: Feminism & Ecology (1981), 12–16. Notes have been renumbered.

HERE WE GO AGAIN; THIS ARGUMENT IS AT LEAST ONE HUNDRED YEARS OLD!

The radical feminist/socialist feminist debate does sometimes seem to be the romantic feminist/rationalist feminist debate of the late nineteenth century revisited.[1] We can imagine nineteenth-century women watching the development of robber-baron capitalism, "the demise of morality" and the rise of the liberal state which furthered capitalist interests while touting liberty, equality, and fraternity. Small wonder that they saw in the domestic sphere vestiges of a more ethical way of life, and thought its values could be carried into the public sphere. This perspective romanticized women, although it is easy to sympathize with it and share the abhorrence of the pillage and plunder imposed by the masculinist mentality in modern industrial society. But what nineteenth-century women proclaiming the virtues of womanhood did not understand was that they were a repository of organic social values in an increasingly inorganic world. Women placed in male-identified power positions can be as warlike as men. The assimilation or neutralization of enfranchised women into the American political structure has a sad history.

Rationalist feminists in the nineteenth-century, on the other hand, were concerned with acquiring power and representing women's interests. They opposed anything that reinforced the idea that women were "different" and wanted male prerogatives extended to women. They were contemptuous of romantic feminists and were themselves imbued with the modern ethic of progress. They opposed political activity by women over issues not seen as exclusively feminist for the same reasons rationalist radical feminists today oppose the feminism/ecology connection.

THE DIALECTIC OF MODERN FEMINISM

According to the false dichotomy between subjective and objective—one legacy of male Western philosophy to feminist thought—we must root our movement *either* in a rationalist-materialist humanism *or* in a metaphysical-feminist naturalism. This supposed choice is crucial as we approach the ecology issue. *Either* we take the anthropocentric position that nature exists solely to serve the needs of the male bourgeois who has crawled out of the slime to be lord and master of everything, *or* we take the naturalist position that nature has a purpose of its own apart from serving "man." We are *either* concerned with the "environment" because we are dependent on it, *or* we understand ourselves to be *of* it, with human oppression part and parcel of the domination of nature. For some radical feminists, only women are capable of full consciousness.[2] Socialist feminists tend to consider the naturalist position as historically regressive, antirational, and probably fascistic. This is the crux of the anthropocentric/naturalist debate, which is emotionally loaded for both sides, but especially for those who equate progress and rationality.

However, we do not have to make such choices. Feminism is both the product and potentially the negation of the modern rationalist world view and capitalism. There was one benefit for women in the "disenchantment of the world,"[3] the process by which all magical and spiritual beliefs were denigrated as superstitious nonsense and the death of nature was accomplished in the minds of men.[4] This process tore asunder women's traditional sphere of influence, but it also undermined the ideology of "natural" social roles, opening a space for women to question what was "natural" for them to be and to do. In traditional Western societies, social and economic relationships were connected to a land-based way of life. One was assigned a special role based on one's sex, race, class, and place of birth. In the domestic sphere children were socialized, food prepared, and men sheltered from their public cares. But the nineteenth-century "home" also encompassed the production of what people ate, used, and wore. It included much more of human life and filled many more human needs than its modern corollary—the nuclear family—which purchases commodities to meet its needs. The importance of the domestic sphere, and hence women's influence, declined with the advent of market society.

Feminism also negates capitalist social relations by challenging the lopsided male-biased values of our culture. When coupled with an ecological perspective, it insists that we remember our origins in nature, our connections to one another as daughters, sisters, and mothers. It refuses any longer to be the unwitting powerless symbol of all the things men wish to deny in themselves and project onto us—the refusal to be the "other."[5] It can heal the splits in a world divided against itself and built on a fundamental lie: the defining of culture in opposition to nature.

The dialectic moves on. Now it is possible that a conscious visionary feminism could place our technology and productive apparatus in the service of a society based on ecological principles and values, with roots in traditional women's ways of being in the world. This in turn might make possible a total cultural critique. Women can remember what men have denied in themselves (nature), and women can know what men know (culture). Now we must develop a transformative feminism that sparks our utopian imaginations and embodies our deepest knowledge—a feminism that is an affirmation of our vision at the same time it is a negation of patriarchy. The skewed reasoning that opposes matter and spirit and refuses to concern itself with the objects and ends of life, which views internal nature and external nature as one big hunting ground to be quantified and conquered is, in the end, not only irrational but deadly. To fulfill its liberatory potential, feminism needs to pose a *rational reenchantment* that brings together spiritual and material, being and knowing. This is the promise of ecological feminism.

DIALECTICAL FEMINISM: TRANSCENDING THE RADICAL FEMINIST/SOCIALIST FEMINIST DEBATE

The domination of external nature has necessitated the domination of internal nature. Men have denied their own embodied naturalness, repressed memories of infantile pleasure and dependence on the mother and on nature.[6] Much of their denied self has been projected onto women. Objectification is forgetting. The ways in which women have been both included in and excluded from a culture based on gender differences provide a critical ledge from which to view the artificial chasm male culture has placed between itself and nature. Woman has stood with one foot on each side. She has been a bridge for men, back to the parts of themselves they have denied, despite their need of women to attend to the visceral chores they consider beneath them.

An ecological perspective offers the possibility of moving beyond the radical (cultural) feminist/socialist feminist impasse. But it necessitates a feminism that holds out for a separate cultural and political activity so that we can imagine, theorize or envision from the

vantage point of *critical otherness*. The ecology question weights the historic feminist debate in the direction of traditional female values over the overly rationalized, combative male way of being in the world. Rationalist feminism is the Trojan horse of the women's movement. Its piece-of-the-action mentality conceals a capitulation to a culture bent on the betrayal of nature. In that sense it is unwittingly both misogynist and anti-ecological. Denying biology, espousing androgyny and valuing what men have done over what we have done are all forms of self-hatred which threaten to derail the teleology of the feminist challenge to this violent civilization.

The liberation of women is to be found neither in severing all connections that root us in nature nor in believing ourselves to be more natural than men. Both of these positions are unwittingly complicit with nature/culture dualism. Women's oppression is neither strictly historical nor strictly biological. It is both. Gender is a meaningful part of a person's identity. The facts of internal and external genitalia and women's ability to bear children will continue to have social meaning. But we needn't think the choices are external sexual warfare or a denatured (and boring) androgyny. It is possible to take up questions of spirituality and meaning without abandoning the important insights of materialism. We can use the insights of socialist feminism, with its debt to Marxism, to understand how the material conditions of our daily lives interact with our bodies and our psychological heritages. Materialist insights warn us not to assume an *innate* moral or biological superiority and not to depend on alternative culture alone to transform society. Yet a separate radical feminist culture within a patriarchal society is necessary so we can learn to speak our own bodies and our own experiences, so the male culture representing itself as the "universal" does not continue to speak for us.[7]

We have always thought our lives and works, our very beings, were trivial next to male accomplishments. Women's silence is deafening only to those who know it's there. The absence is only beginning to be a presence. Writers like Zora Neale Hurston, Tillie Olsen, Grace Paley, and Toni Morrison depict the beauty and dignity of ordinary women's lives and give us back part of ourselves. Women artists begin to suggest the meanings of female bodies and their relationships to nature.[8] Women musicians give us the sounds of loving ourselves.[9] The enormous and growing lesbian feminist community is an especially fertile ground for women's culture. Lesbians are pioneering in every field and building communities with ecological feminist consciousness. Third-World women are speaking the experience of multiple otherness—of race, sex, and (often) class oppression. We are learning how women's lives are the same and different across these divisions, and we are beginning to engage the complexities of racism in our culture, our movement, and our theory.

There is much that is redemptive for humanity as a whole in women's silent experience, and there are voices that have not yet been heard. Cultural feminism's concern with ecology takes the ideology of womanhood which has been a bludgeon of oppression—the woman/nature connection—and transforms it into a positive factor. If we proceed dialectically and recognize the contributions of both socialist feminism and radical cultural feminism, operating at both the structural and cultural levels, we will be neither materialists nor idealists. We will understand our position historically and attempt to realize the human future emerging in the *feminist present*. Once we have placed ourselves in history, we can move on to the interdependent issues of feminist social transformation and planetary survival.

TOWARD AN ECOLOGICAL CULTURE

Acting on our own consciousness of our own needs, we act in the interests of all. We stand on the biological dividing line. We are the less-rationalized side of humanity in an overly rationalized world, yet we can think as rationally as men and perhaps transform the idea of reason itself. As women, we are naturalized culture in a culture defined against nature. If nature/culture antagonism is the primary contradiction of our time, it is also what weds feminism and ecology and makes woman the historic subject. Without an ecological perspective which asserts the interdependence

of living things, feminism is disembodied. Without a more sophisticated dialectical method which can transcend historic debates and offer a nondualistic theory of history, social transformation and nature/culture interaction, feminism will continue to be mired in the same old impasse. There is more at stake in feminist debates over "the ecology question" than whether feminists should organize against the draft, demonstrate at the Pentagon, or join mixed antinuke organizations. At stake is the range and potential of the feminist social movement . . .

(1981)

NOTES

1. For a social history of the nineteenth-century romanticist/rationalist debate, see Barbara Ehrenreich and Dierdre English, *For Her Own Good* (New York: Doubleday, Anchor, 1979).
2. Mary Daly comes very close to this position. Other naturalist feminists have a less clear stance on *essential* differences between women and men.
3. The "disenchantment of the world" is another way of talking about the process of rationalization discussed above. The term was coined by Max Weber.
4. See Carolyn Merchant, *The Death of Nature: Women, Ecology and the Scientific Revolution* (San Francisco: Harper and Row, 1980).
5. For a full development of the idea of "woman as other," see Simone de Beauvoir, *The Second Sex* (New York: Modern Library, 1968).
6. Dorothy Dinnerstein in *The Mermaid and the Minotaur* (New York: Harper and Row. 1977) makes an important contribution to feminist understanding by showing that although woman is associated with nature because of her mothering role, this does not in itself explain misogyny and the hatred of nature.
7. See de Beauvoir, *Second Sex.*
8. See Lucy Lippard, "Quite Contrary: Body, Nature and Ritual in Women's Art," *Chrysalis* 1, no. 2 (1977): 31–47.
9. Alive, Sweet Honey in the Rock, Meg Christian, Holly Near, Margie Adam—the list is long and growing.

58 • *Dorothy E. Smith*

FROM *THE EVERYDAY WORLD AS PROBLEMATIC*

A Feminist Sociology

THE STANDPOINT OF WOMEN IS OUTSIDE THE EXTRALOCAL RELATIONS OF RULING

When we take up the standpoint of women, we take up a standpoint outside this frame (as an organization of social consciousness). To begin from such a standpoint does not imply a common viewpoint among women. What we have in common is the organization of social relations that has accomplished our exclusion. Taking up this position for the subjects of a sociology, what is the critique? A critique is more than a negative statement. It is an attempt to define an alternative.

We have asked here how it is that sociology as we practice it and recognize its practices does not allow us to begin our work from our experience as women. Women's experience has been a resource, but it has not become the basis for a position from which sociology, as the systematic study of society and social relations, proceeds.

In *The Phenomenology of Mind*, Hegel analyzes the relation of master and servant. This analysis was a model for Marx's analysis of the relation between a ruling class and the working class, including the dynamic process built into the relation that transforms it. Here we have use for a limited aspect of Hegel's "parable," the relation between the master's consciousness and the labor of the servant. Hegel describes how for the master the object of his desire is available to him in a simple and obvious manner such that he can leap directly from the desire to its object, from appetite to consummation, without an intervening labor. The object appears there for him in a simple and direct way. This appearance is, however, the result or product of

the servant's labor. The servant produces the object for the master. In so doing the servant conforms to the will of the master, and his work is in that sense the master's consciousness realized. The servant in relation to the master does not constitute a distinct subject, a consciousness distinctly and authentically present who looks back and reflects the master's will and has no autonomous existence. The servant's labor is present in the relation of the master to the object of his desire, the object of consciousness. The invisibility of that relation from the master's standpoint is a product of the organization of the relation between master and servant. That organization itself is not visible from the standpoint of the master. Within the consciousness of the master there is himself and the object and a servant who is merely a means. For the servant there is the master, the servant's labor producing the object, and there is the simplicity of the relation between the master and the object. The totality of the set of relations is visible.

When Hegel's parable of the master-servant relation is used to interpret Marx's view of the relationship between the consciousness of a ruling class as an ideological consciousness and a science of political economy proceeding from and grounded in the standpoint of the working class, Marx's analysis of the different bases of ideology and knowledge can be applied to the standpoint of women. Our social forms of consciousness have been created by men occupying positions in the extralocal organization of ruling. Discourses, methods of thinking, theories, sociologies take for granted the conditions of that ruling. The actual practices that make that ruling possible are not visible. Women are outside the extralocal relations of ruling, for the most part located in work processes that sustain it and are essential to its existence. There are parallels then between the claims Marx makes for a knowledge based in the class whose labor produces the conditions of existence, indeed the very existence, of a ruling class, and the claims that can be made for a knowledge of society from the standpoint of women.

Established interpretations of Marx understand him to argue that ideological forms of consciousness are determined by their social base, particularly by their base in a class, and that all social forms of consciousness are so determined. It follows, so this interpretation proceeds, that this reasoning applies also to the claims of a science from the standpoint of labor, invalidating its claims to knowledge, hence to Marx's own work. If, however, we apply the Hegelian paradigm to Marx's reasoning, the argument proceeds differently. There is a difference between forms of consciousness arising in the experience of ruling and those arising in the experience of doing the work that creates the conditions of ruling. Ideological forms of consciousness are definite practices of thinking about society that reflect the experience of ruling. From the standpoint of ruling, the actual practices, the labor, and the organization of labor, which makes the existence of a ruling class and their ruling possible, are invisible. It is only possible to see how the whole thing is put together from a standpoint outside the ruling class and in that class whose part in the overall division of labor is to produce the conditions of its own ruling and the existence of a ruling class.

The basis for a political economy from the standpoint of labor, according to Marx, is precisely that it is grounded in the work and activity of actual individuals producing their existence under definite material conditions. The standpoint of labor provides, therefore, a basis for knowledge corresponding to the position of the servant in Hegel's exemplary tale. From the servant's position, the working of the whole process is available in principle since his actual practice brings into being the relation between self and object, appearing as it does from the perspective of the master. From the point of view of the ruling class, the actual practices and the material conditions that form, organize, and provide for the "appearance" of direct action are not visible. Their activities, their work, their consciousness appear simple and complete, their relations

undetermined, because how they are determined is a product of the labor of the working class. The social organization of the forms of consciousness characteristic of a ruling class cannot be examined from the standpoint of the ruling class because that organization is not visible from that perspective or in that mode of action. Thus, when Marx draws attention to how Feuerbach's idealist philosophy ignores its essential dependence on the production of the philosopher's subsistence, and hence his consciousness upon the material processes of labor that produce the world he inhabits and its features including the cherry tree before his window, whose presence is itself a historical product of trading relations, he is not engaging in cheap gibes. He is drawing attention, rather, to an idealism that views the transformation of social forms as taking place in and through conceptual transformations (and therefore as simple) and to how these very idealizations are organized, provided for, and produced by the productive relations and the productive activities, the labor of a working class standing in determinate relation to a ruling class, producing not only the subsistence of a ruling class, but also the basic organization that the social forms of consciousness of the ruling class take for granted. The standpoint of labor thus establishes a site for the knower from which these relations and organization can be made visible as they actually arise in the actual activities of individuals.

Analogous claims can be made for a sociology from the standpoint of women. In the social division of labor the work of articulating the local and particular existence of actors to the abstracted conceptual mode of ruling is done typically by women. The abstracted conceptual mode of ruling exists in and depends upon a world known immediately and directly in the bodily mode. The suppression of that mode of being as a focus, as thematic, depends upon a social organization that produces the conditions of its suppression. To exist as subject and to act in this abstracted mode depend upon an actual work and organization of work by others who make the concrete, the particular, the bodily, thematic of their work and who also produce the invisibility of that work. It is a condition of anyone's being able to enter, become, and remain absorbed in the conceptual mode of action that she does not need to focus her attention on her labors or on her bodily existence. The organization of that work and work expectations in managerial and professional circles both constitute and depend upon the alienation of members of this class from their bodily and local existence. The structure of work in this mode and the structure of career assume the individuals can sustain a mode of consciousness in which interest in the routine aspects of bodily maintenance is never focal and can in general be suppressed. It is taken for granted in the organization of this work that such matters are provided for in a way that will not interfere with action and participation in the conceptual mode.

The sociologist enters the conceptual mode of action when she goes to work. She enters it as a member, and she enters it also as the mode in which she investigates it. She observes, analyzes, explains, and examines as if there were no problem in how that world becomes observable to her. She moves among the doings of organizations, governmental processes, bureaucracies, and so on as a person who is at home in that medium. The nature of that world itself, how it is known to her, and the conditions of its existence or her relation to it are not called into question. Her methods of observation and inquiry extend to it as procedures that are essentially of the same order as those that bring about phenomena with which she is concerned, or that she is concerned to bring under the jurisdiction of that order. Her perspectives and interests may differ, but the substance is the same. She works with facts and information that have been worked up from actualities and appear in the form of documents, which are themselves the product of organizational processes, whether her own or administered by her or of some other agency. She fits that information back into a framework of entities and organizational processes which she takes for granted as known, without asking how she knows them or what are the social processes by which the phenomena corresponding to or providing the empirical events, acts, decisions, and so forth of that world may be recognized. She passes beyond the particular and immediate setting in which she is always located in the body (the office she writes in, the libraries she consults, the streets she travels, the home she returns to) without any sense of having made a transition. She works in the same medium as she studies.

But like everyone else she also exists in the body, in the place in which it is. This, then, is also the place of her sensory organization of immediate experience: the place where her coordinates of here and now, before and after, are organized around herself as center; the place where she confronts people face to face in the physical mode in which she expresses herself to them and they to her as more and other than either can speak. Here there are textures and smells. The irrelevant birds fly away in front of the window. Here she has flu. Here she gives birth. It is a place she dies in. Into this space must come as actual material events, whether as the sounds of speech, the scratchings on the surface of paper that is constituted as document, or directly anything she knows of the world. It has to happen here somehow if she is to experience it at all.

Entering the governing mode of our kind of society lifts the actor out of the immediate local and particular place in which she is in the body. She uses what becomes present to her in this place as a means to pass beyond it to the conceptual order. This mode of action creates a bifurcation of consciousness, a bifurcation, of course, that is present for all those participating in this mode of action. It establishes two modes of knowing, experiencing, and acting—one located in the body and in the space that it occupies and moves into, the other passing beyond it. And although I have made use of the feminine pronoun in general, it is primarily men who are active in this mode.

It is a condition of a person's being able to enter and become absorbed in the conceptual mode that attention to the local and bodily remain, as Schutz says, "horizonal" rather than focal or thematic. Schutz himself, that great ethnographer of the "head" world, provides an account of just this suppression, which locates at least one form of women's work in organizing its own suppression. He writes:

> The corollary to the fact that we live simultaneously in various provinces of reality or meaning is the fact that we put into play various levels of our personality. . . . Only very superficial levels of our personality are involved in such performances as our habitual and even quasi-automatic "household chores", or eating, dressing, and (for normal adults) also in reading and performing simple arithmetical operations. To be sure, when we turn to such routine work, the activities connected with it are constituted as thematic, requiring and receiving our full attention if only momentarily.

Without challenging Schutz's general picture of these various levels of personality and their organization in relation to projects in the world of working, we can also recognize what is presupposed in just that organization, namely, that the routine matters, the household chores, are not problematic, do not become a central focus of man's work, or at least "only momentarily." Once we are alerted to how women's work provides for this organization of consciousness, we can see how this structure depends in actual situations on the working relations of those providing for the logistics of the philosophers bodily existence—those for whom household chores are not horizonal, but are thematic, and whose work makes possible for another the suppression of all but passing attention to the bodily location of consciousness.

If men are to participate fully in the abstract mode of action, they must be liberated from having to attend to their needs in the concrete and particular. Organizing the society in an abstracted conceptual order, mediated symbolically, must be articulated to the concrete and local actualities in which it is necessarily and ineluctably located. That must be a work, must be a product of labor. To a very large extent the direct work of liberating men into abstraction from the Aristotelian categories of time and space of which Bierstedt speaks has been and is the work of women.

The place of women, then, in relation to this mode of action is where the work is done to facilitate men's occupation of the conceptual mode of action. Women keep house, bear and care for children, look after men when they are sick, and in general provide for the logistics of their bodily existence. But this marriage aspect of women's work is only one side of a more general relation. Women work in and around the professional and managerial scene in analogous ways. They do those things that give concrete form to the conceptual activities. They do the clerical work, giving material form to the words or thoughts of the boss. They do the routine computer work, the interviewing for the survey, the nursing, the secretarial work. At almost every point women mediate for men the relation between the conceptual mode of action and the actual concrete forms on which it depends. Women's work is interposed between the abstracted modes and the local and particular actualities in which they are

necessarily anchored. Also, women's work conceals from men acting in the abstract mode just this anchorage.

In the health profession, for example, the routine practices that mediate the actualities of the immediately experienced world and work them up into forms corresponding to the abstracted conceptual forms under which they may be professionally (or "scientifically") known are done largely by women. The psychiatric patient is indeed present to the psychiatrist as a "whole person," but the routines that limit the psychiatrist's relation to the patient, and hence define those aspects that come strictly within his professional focus, are performed in large part by women—nurses, laboratory technicians, social workers, clerks, and so on. To a large extent women have at various points direct and immediate contact with the actual life situation of the patient, before it has been cleaned and tidied up, in all its complexity—just as anyone's life situation is always complex, rooted in others' lives, and multifaceted. Through the work of those who reconstruct the patient's life as a case history, it is obliterated as it was experienced and lived. By the time the patient gets to the psychiatrist, she is already an abstraction. She has been separated from the contexts in which what she was saying and doing were connected. Hence, the psychiatrist encounters the patient as one whose abstraction has already been socially organized. For him there is no war or tension between the direct experience he has in the settings of his work and the ideologies he uses to name, interpret, and order what he observes. He is not exposed to disjunctions between the nature of his psychiatric procedures and the actualities of his patients' lives. He is not exposed in his professional practice to the world before the practices of receptionists, nurses, secretaries, nurses' aides, social workers. Their work brings into being the forms in which what he does, thinks, and says make ordinary sense. His accomplishment of his work in the abstracted conceptual modes depends upon their work in ways that their work itself makes invisible.

Beginning from the standpoint of women locates a subject who begins in a material and local world. It shows the different cognitive domains structuring our realities, not, as Schutz describes, as alternatives—a paramount reality on the one hand and the scientific domain on the other—but rather as a bifurcation of consciousness, with a world directly experienced from oneself as center (in the body) on the one hand and a world organized in the abstracted conceptual mode, external to the local and particular places of one's bodily existence. The abstracted mode of the scientific province is always located in the local and material actualities. Participation in the "head" world is accomplished in actual concrete settings making use of definite material means. Suppression of interest in that setting is organized in a division of labor that accords to others the production and maintenance of the material aspects of a total process. To those who do this work, the local and concrete conditions of the abstracted mode are thematic. The organization that divides the two becomes visible from this base. It is not visible from within the other.

We can see then how the silencing of women of which we spoke earlier suppresses not only women, but the work they represent and the dimension of existence that locates, among other things, that fear of death Schutz holds as the fundamental anxiety. The fear of death is the final announcement to the thinker that his occupancy of the conceptual mode of the bifurcated consciousness is necessarily temporary. He is precipitated into time. Women's lack of authority to speak, their exclusion from the circle of those who make the tradition, who make the discourse, means that the work that suppresses the concrete and material and, with them, the local, particular, and material locus of consciousness, is also silenced. The modes of action in the conceptual mode depend upon this silence.

The theories, concepts, and methods of our discipline claim to be capable of accounting for and analyzing the same world as that which we experience directly. But these theories, concepts, and methods have been built up out of a way of knowing the world that takes for granted the boundaries of experience in the same medium in which it is constituted. It takes for granted and subsumes without examining the conditions of its existence. Its object appears to it, as to Hegel's master, in a direct and simple relation. It is not capable of analyzing its own relation to its conditions nor of locating itself where the social relations organizing and providing for its existence can be seen. The sociologist as actual person in an actual concrete setting, the sociological knower, has been "canceled" from the act of knowing by a procedure that objectifies

and separates him from his knowledge. The essential linkage that is the first clue pointing back to the conditions of his knowledge is lacking.

Locating women's experience as a place to work from in sociology does not, if we follow this line of analysis, land us in a determinante type of position or identify a category of persons from whose various and typical positions in the world we must take our starting point. Women are variously located in society. Their situations are much more various than the topics we recognize somewhat stereotypically as women's topics would suggest. Their position also differs very greatly by class. Even among housewives, who appear to share a universal fate, there are rather wider differences in the conditions, practices, and organization of housework and the social relations in which it is embedded than our studies and the ways in which they have been framed would allow. The identification of the bifurcated consciousness is a potential experience for women members of an intelligentsia or of women otherwise associated with the ruling apparatus that organizes the society. It is clearly not every woman's experience of the world. That is not the issue. At this point the concern is to develop a method of working in sociology that will make it possible to begin from where women in general are, doing the type of work with which we are a sex identified. To develop a sociology from the standpoint of subjects located materially and in a particular place does not involve simply the transfer from one conceptual frame to another, from, say, a Parsonian to a Marxist framework. It does something rather different. A Marxist framework can and has been quite readily assimilated into the modes of the sociological discourse that accord primacy to the conceptual categories and the forms of thought and that subordinate the actualities of the world to them. Nor does the answer lie, as has sometimes been suggested, in the renunciation of the rational, conceptual, scientifically rigorous method or procedure. This is to treat the two sides of the bifurcated consciousness as if they were equal and to locate what is distinctively "female" in the subjective, emotional side, so that the alienative intellectual practices of sociology are eliminated rather than transformed. It has been suggested to me that a phenomenological sociology is a feminist sociology merely because it begins with the consciousness of the knower and is hence "subjective," but the phenomenological perspective remains within the conceptual abstracted world and begins from there, taking for granted the material and social organization of the bifurcated consciousness, and does not render its organization and conditions examinable.

The two sides of the divided consciousness are not equal. As Schutz makes clear and as even minimal attention to the actualities of our own functioning in the world makes clear (you can stop this moment in your reading and attend to the material properties of your reading: chair, paper, ink marks, your own bodily presence, etc.), there is no entry to the abstracted conceptual mode of working without passing through and making use of the concretely and immediately experienced. The symbolic structures that constitute the modes in which we act are necessarily material in transcending that materiality—the sounds we hear that we take up as speech, the scratches on the paper, the material organization that provides for how our consciousness can be thematized in this mode, as well as the social division of labor that sustains us in it. These are not merely essential as prerequisites; they are integral to the organization and existence of the abstracted conceptual mode. It is indeed part of how they are integral that they do not become thematic, that they remain horizonal. The other term of the bifurcated consciousness, which is located not merely in a subjectivity but in a subjectivity located in its body and located not therefore in a definite and particular spatiotemporal existence, is irremediably in what Schutz describes rather ambiguously as the world of working. Beginning, then, from there locates the knower where knowledge must begin.

If we address the problem of the conditions as well as the perceived forms and organization of immediate experience, we should include the events as they actually happen or the ordinary material world that we and others encounter as what is happening to us, to them. When we examine these events, when we examine the actual material organization of our everyday experience, we find that there are many aspects of how these things are and come about of which we have very little, as sociologists, to say. We do not even know how to begin. We have a sense that the events entering our experience originate somewhere in a human intention, but we are unable to track back to find it and to find out how it became and how it got from there to here. Take this room in which I work or that room in which you are reading and treat that as a problem. If we think about the conditions of our activity here, we could track back to how it is that there are chairs, table, walls, our clothing, our presence; how these places (yours and mine) are cleaned and maintained; and so forth. There are human activities, intentions, and relations that are not apparent as such in the actual material conditions of our work. The social organization of the setting is not wholly available to us in its appearance. What is here for us is the product of a social division of labor. If we heard in the things that we make use of—typewriter, paper, chair, table, walls—the voices of those who made them, we would hear the multitudinous voices of a whole society and beyond. Were it not for the time lapse involved, our own voices would be part of them. Locating our work as knowers in the first and fundamental term of the bifurcated consciousness also locates us in the standpoint of the working class, in the location from which Marx's political economy begins. Beginning from the standpoint of women does not follow in any direct way from beginning from the standpoint of labor, but once we have taken this other and momentous step, we can begin to take up the relation established by Marx. It becomes available to us in the mode in which it was originally conceived namely, as having its premises not in the conceptual, abstracted mode but in actual individuals, their work, their actual productive activities, and the material conditions produced by those activities that become their conditions.

(1987)

59 • *Nancy Hartsock*

"FOUCAULT ON POWER: A THEORY FOR WOMEN?"

But to mention the power of women leads immediately to the problem of what is meant by "women." The problem of differences among women has been very prominent in the United States in recent years. We face the task of developing our understanding of difference as part of the theoretical task of developing a theory of power for women. Issues of difference reminds us as well that many of the factors which divide women also unite some women with men—factors such as racial or cultural differences. Perhaps theories of power for women will also be theories of power for others groups as well. We need to develop our understanding of difference by creating a situation in which hitherto marginalized groups can name themselves, speak for themselves, and participate in defining the terms of interaction, a situation in which we can construct an understanding of the world that is sensitive to difference.

What might such a theory look like? Can we develop a general theory, or should we abandon the search for such a theory in favor of making space for a number of heterogeneous voices to be heard? What kinds of common claims can be made about the situations of women and men of color? About those of white women and women and men of color? About the situations of Western peoples and those they have colonized? For example, is it ever legitimate to say "women" without qualification? These kinds of questions make it apparent that the situation we face involves not only substantive claims about the world, but also raises questions about how we come to know the world, about what we can claim for our theories and ultimately about who "we" are. I want to ask what kinds of knowledge claims are required for grounding political action by different groups. Should theories

produced by "minorities" rest on different epistemologies than those of the "majority?" Given the fact that the search for theory has been called into question in majority discourse and has been denounced as totalizing, do we want to ask similar questions of minority proposals or set similar standards?

In our efforts to find ways to include the voices of marginalized groups, one might expect helpful guidance from those who have argued against totalizing and universalistic theories such as those of the Enlightenment. Many radical intellectuals have been attracted to a compilation of diverse writings ranging from literary criticism to the social sciences, generally termed postmodern. The writers, among them figures such as Foucault, Derrida, Rorty, and Lyotard, argue against the faith in a universal reason we have inherited from Enlightenment European philosophy. They reject stories that claim to encompass all of human history: As Lyotard puts it, "let us wage war on totality." In its place they propose a social criticism that is *ad hoc*, contextual, plural, and limited. A number of feminist theorists have joined in the criticism of modernity put forward by these writers. They have endorsed their claims about what can and cannot be known or said or read into/from texts.

Despite their apparent congruence with the project I am proposing, I will argue these theories would hinder rather than help its accomplishment. Despite their own desire to avoid universal claims and despite their stated opposition to these claims, some universalistic assumptions creep back into their work. Thus, postmodernism, despite its stated efforts to avoid the problems of European modernism of the eighteenth and nineteenth centuries, at best manages to criticize these theories

Excerpt from Linda J. Nicholson, ed., *Feminism/Postmodernism* (New York: Routledge, 1990). Reprinted by permission of Taylor and Francis Group LLC.

without putting anything in their place. For those of us who want to understand the world systematically in order to change it, postmodern theories at their best give little guidance. (I should note that I recognize that some postmodernist theorists are committed to ending injustice. But this commitment is not carried through in their theories.) Those of us who are not part of the ruling race, class, or gender, not a part of the minority which controls our world, need to know how it works. Why are we—in all our variousness—systematically excluded and marginalized? What systematic changes would be required to create a more just society? At worst, postmodernist theories can recapitulate the effects of Enlightenment theories which deny the right to participate in defining the terms of interaction. Thus, I contend, in broad terms, that postmodernism represents a dangerous approach for any marginalized group to adopt . . .

THE CONSTRUCTION OF THE COLONIZED OTHER

. . . Foucault calls only for resistance and exposure of the system of power relations. Moreover, he is often vague about what exactly this means. Thus, he argues only that one should "entertain the claims" of subjugated knowledges or bring them "into play." Specifically, he argues that the task for intellectuals is less to become part of movements for fundamental change and more to struggle against the forms of power that can transform these movements into instruments of domination.

Perhaps this stress on resistance rather than transformation is due to Foucault's profound pessimism. Power appears to him as ever expanding and invading. It may even attempt to "annex" the counter-discourses that have developed. The dangers of going beyond resistance to power are nowhere more clearly stated than in Foucault's response to one interviewer who asked what might replace the present system. He responded that to even imagine another system is to extend our participation in the present system. Even more sinister, he added that perhaps this is what happened in the Soviet Union, thus suggesting that Stalinism might be the most likely outcome of efforts at social transformation. Foucault's insistence on simply resisting power is carried even further in his arguments that one must avoid claims to scientific knowledge. In particular, one should not claim Marxism as a science because to do so would invest it with the harmful effects of the power

of science in modern culture. Foucault then, despite his stated aims of producing an account of power which will enable and facilitate resistance and opposition, instead adopts the position of what he has termed official knowledge with regard to the knowledge of the dominated and reinforces the relations of domination in our society by insisting that those of us who have been marginalized remain at the margins. . . .

TOWARD THEORIES FOR WOMEN

Those of us who have been marginalized by the transcendental voice of universalizing theory need to do something other than ignore power relations as Rorty does or resist them as figures such as Foucault and Lyotard suggest. We need to transform them, and to do so, we need a revised and reconstructed theory (indebted to Marx among others) with several important features.

First, rather than getting rid of subjectivity or notions of the subject, as Foucault does and substituting his notion of the individual as an effect of power relations, we need to engage in the historical, political, and theoretical process of constituting ourselves as subjects as well as objects of history. We need to recognize that we can be the makers of history as well as the objects of those who have made history. Our nonbeing was the condition of being of the One, the center, the taken-for-granted ability of one small segment of the population to speak for all; our various efforts to constitute ourselves as subjects (through struggles for colonial independence, racial and sexual liberation struggles, and so on) were fundamental to creating the preconditions for the current questioning of universalist claims. But, I believe, we need to sort out who we really are. Put differently, we need to dissolve the false "we" I have been using into its real multiplicity and variety and out of this concrete multiplicity build an account of the world as seen from the margins, an account which can expose the falseness of the view from the top and can transform the margins as well as the center. The point is to develop an account of the world which treats our perspectives not as subjugated or disruptive knowledges, but as primary and constitutive of a different world. . . .

Second, we must do our work on an epistemological base that indicates that knowledge is possible—not just conversation or a discourse on how it is that power relations work. Conversation as a goal is fine; understanding how power works in oppressive societies is important. But if we are to construct a new society, we need to be assured that some systematic knowledge about our world and ourselves is possible. Those (simply) critical of modernity can call into question whether we ever really knew the world (and a good case can be made that "they" at least did not). They are in fact right that they have not known the world as it is rather than as they wished and needed it to be; they created their world not only in their own image but in the image of their fantasies. To create a world that expresses our own various and diverse images, we need to understand how it works.

Third, we need a theory of power that recognizes that our practical daily activity contains an understanding of the world—subjugated perhaps, but present. Here I am reaffirming Gramsci's argument that everyone is an intellectual and that each of us has an epistemology. The point, then, for "minority" theories is to "read out" the epistemologies in our various practices. I have argued elsewhere for a "standpoint" epistemology—an account of the world with great similarities to Marx's fundamental stance. While I would modify some of what I argued there, I would still insist that we must not give up the claim that material life (class position in Marxist theory) not only structures but sets limits on the understanding of social relations, and that, in systems of domination, the vision available to the rulers will be both partial and will reverse the real order of things.

Fourth, our understanding of power needs to recognize the difficulty of creating alternatives. The ruling class, race, and gender actively structure the material–social relations in which all the parties are forced to participate; their vision, therefore, cannot be dismissed as simply false or misguided. In consequence, the oppressed groups must struggle for their own understandings which will represent achievements requiring both theorizing and the education which grows from political struggle.

Fifth, as an engaged vision, the understanding of the oppressed exposes the relations among people as inhuman and thus contains a call to political action. That is, a theory of power for women, for the oppressed, is not one that leads to a turning away from engagement but rather one that is a call for change and participation in altering power relations.

The critical steps are, first, using what we know about our lives as a basis for critique of the dominant culture and, second, creating alternatives. When the various "minority" experiences have been described and when the significance of these experiences as a ground for critique of the dominant institutions and ideologies of society is better recognized, we will have at least the tools to begin to construct an account of the world sensitive to the realities of race and gender as well as class. To paraphrase Marx, the point is to change the world, not simply to redescribe ourselves or reinterpret the world yet again.

(1990)

60 • *Donna Haraway*

"THE CYBORG MANIFESTO AND FRACTURED IDENTITIES"

This chapter is an effort to build an ironic political myth faithful to feminism, socialism, and materialism. Perhaps more faithful as blasphemy is faithful, than as reverent worship and identification. Blasphemy has always seemed to require taking things very seriously. I know

no better stance to adopt from within the secular-religious, evangelical traditions of United States politics, including the politics of socialist feminism. Blasphemy protects one from the moral majority within, while still insisting on the need for community. Blasphemy is not

Excerpt from *Simians, Cyborgs, and Women: The Reinvention of Nature* (New York: Routledge, 1991).
Reprinted by permission of Taylor and Francis Group LLC.

apostasy. Irony is about contradictions that do not re-solve into larger wholes, even dialectically, about the tension of holding incompatible things together because both or all are necessary and true. Irony is about humour and serious play. It is also a rhetorical strategy and a po-litical method, one I would like to see more honoured within socialist-feminism. At the centre of my ironic faith, my blasphemy, is the image of the cyborg.

A cyborg is a cybernetic organism, a hybrid of ma-chine and organism, a creature of social reality as well as a creature of fiction. Social reality is lived social re-lations, our most important political construction, a world-changing fiction. The international women's movements have constructed "women's experience," as well as uncovered or discovered this crucial collective object. This experience is a fiction and fact of the most crucial, political kind. Liberation rests on the con-struction of the consciousness, the imaginative appre-hension, of oppression, and so of possibility. The cyborg is a matter of fiction and lived experience that changes what counts as women's experience in the late twentieth century. This is a struggle over life and death, but the boundary between science fiction and social reality is an optical illusion.

 . . . The cyborg is a creature in a post-gender world; it has no truck with bisexuality, pre-oedipal symbio-sis, unalienated labour, or other seductions to organic wholeness through a final appropriation of all the powers of the parts into a higher unity. In a sense, the cyborg has no origin story in the Western sense—a "final" irony since the cyborg is also the awful apoca-lyptic *telos* of the "West's" escalating dominations of abstract individuation, an ultimate self untied at last from all dependency, a man in space. An origin story in the "Western," humanist sense depends on the myth of original unity, fullness, bliss and terror, repre-sented by the phallic mother from whom all humans must separate, the task of individual development and of history, the twin potent myths inscribed most pow-erfully for us in psychoanalysis, in Marxism. Hilary Klein has argued that both Marxism and psychoanal-ysis, in their concepts of labour and of individuation and gender formation, depend on the plot of original unity out of which difference must be produced and enlisted in a drama of escalating domination of woman/nature. The cyborg skips the step of original unity, of identification with nature in the Western sense. This is its illegitimate promise that might lead to subversion of its teleology as star wars.

The cyborg is resolutely committed to partiality, irony, intimacy, and perversity. It is oppositional, utopian, and completely without innocence. No longer structured by the polarity of public and private, the cyborg defines a technological polis based partly on a revolution of social relations in the *oikos*, the house-hold. Nature and culture are reworked; the one can no longer be the resource for appropriation or incor-poration by the other. The relationships for forming wholes from parts, including those of polarity and hierarchical domination, are at issue in the cyborg world. Unlike the hopes of Frankenstein's monster, the cyborg does not expect its father to save it through a restoration of the garden; that is, through the fabrication of a heterosexual male, through its completion in a finished whole, a city and cosmos. The cyborg does not dream of community on the model of the organic family, this time without the oe-dipal project. The cyborg would not recognize the Garden of Eden; it is not made of mud and cannot dream of returning to dust. Perhaps that is why I want to see if cyborgs can subvert the apocalypse of returning to nuclear dust in the manic compulsion to name the Enemy. Cyborgs are not reverent; they do not remember the cosmos. They are wary of holism, but needy for connection—they seem to have a natu-ral feel for united front politics, but without the van-guard party. The main trouble with cyborgs, of course, is that they are the illegitimate offspring of militarism and patriarchal capitalism, not to men-tion state socialism. But illegitimate offspring are often exceedingly unfaithful to their origins. Their fathers, after all, are inessential. . . .

So my cyborg myth is about transgressed boundar-ies, potent fusions, and dangerous possibilities which progressive people might explore as one part of needed political work. One of my premises is that most American socialists and feminists see deepened dual-isms of mind and body, animal and machine, idealism and materialism in the social practices, symbolic for-mulations, and physical artefacts associated with "high technology" and scientific culture. From *One-Dimensional Man* (Marcuse, 1964) to *The Death of Nature* (Merchant, 1980), the analytic resources developed by progressives have insisted on the necessary domination of technics and recalled us to an imagined organic body to inte-grate our resistance. Another of my premises is that the need for unity of people trying to resist world-wide intensification of domination has never been more acute. But a slightly perverse shift of perspective might better enable us to contest for meanings, as well as for other forms of power and pleasure in technologically mediated societies.

From one perspective, a cyborg world is about the final imposition of a grid of control on the planet, about the final abstraction embodied in a Star Wars apocalypse waged in the name of defence, about the final appropriation of women's bodies in a masculinist orgy of war. From another perspective, a cyborg world might be about lived social and bodily realities in which people are not afraid of their joint kinship with animals and machines, not afraid of permanently partial identities and contradictory standpoints. The political struggle is to see from both perspectives at once because each reveals both dominations and possibilities unimaginable from the other vantage point. Single vision produces worse illusions than double vision or many-headed monsters. Cyborg unities are monstrous and illegitimate; in our present political circumstances, we could hardly hope for more potent myths for resistance and recoupling. I like to imagine LAG, the Livermore Action Group, as a kind of cyborg society, dedicated to realistically converting the laboratories that most fiercely embody and spew out the tools of technological apocalypse, and committed to building a political form that actually manages to hold together witches, engineers, elders, perverts, Christians, mothers, and Leninists long enough to disarm the state. Fission Impossible is the name of the affinity group in my town. (Affinity: related not by blood but by choice, the appeal of one chemical nuclear group for another, avidity.)

FRACTURED IDENTITIES

It has become difficult to name one's feminism by a single adjective—or even to insist in every circumstance upon the noun. Consciousness of exclusion through naming is acute. Identities seem contradictory, partial, and strategic. With the hard-won recognition of their social and historical constitution, gender, race, and class cannot provide the basis for belief in "essential" unity. There is nothing about being "female" that naturally binds women. There is not even such a state as "being" female, itself a highly complex category constructed in contested sexual scientific discourses and other social practices. Gender,

race, or class consciousness is an achievement forced on us by the terrible historical experience of the contradictory social realities of patriarchy, colonialism, and capitalism. And who counts as "us" in my own rhetoric? Which identities are available to ground such a potent political myth called "us," and what could motivate enlistment in this collectivity? Painful fragmentation among feminists (not to mention among women) along every possible fault line has made the concept of *woman* elusive, an excuse for the matrix of women's dominations of each other. For me—and for many who share a similar historical location in white, professional middle-class, female, radical, North American, mid-adult bodies—the sources of a crisis in political identity are legion. The recent history for much of the US left and US feminism has been a response to this kind of crisis by endless splitting and searches for a new essential unity. But there has also been a growing recognition of another response through coalition—affinity, not identity.

Chela Sandoval, from a consideration of specific historical moments in the formation of the new political voice called women of colour, has theorized a hopeful model of political identity called "oppositional consciousness," born of the skills for reading webs of power by those refused stable membership in the social categories of race, sex, or class. "Women of color," a name contested at its origins by those whom it would incorporate, as well as a historical consciousness marking systematic breakdown of all the signs of Man in "Western" traditions, constructs a kind of postmodernist identity out of otherness, difference, and specificity. This postmodernist identity is fully political, whatever might be said about other possible postmodernisms. Sandoval's oppositional consciousness is about contradictory locations and heterochronic calendars, not about relativisms and pluralisms.

Sandoval emphasizes the lack of any essential criterion for identifying who is a woman of colour. She notes that the definition of the group has been by conscious appropriation of negation. For example, a Chicana or US black woman has not been able to speak as a woman or as a black person or as a Chicano. Thus, she was at the bottom of a cascade of negative identities, left out of even the privileged oppressed authorial categories called "women and blacks," who claimed to make the important revolutions. The category "woman" negated all non-white women; "black" negated all non-black people, as well as all black women. But there was also no "she," no singularity, but a sea of differences among US women who have affirmed their historical identity as US women of colour. This identity marks out a self-consciously constructed space that cannot affirm the capacity to act on the basis of natural identification, but only on the basis of conscious coalition, of affinity, of political kinship. Unlike the "woman" of some streams of the white women's movement in the United States, there is no naturalization of the matrix, or at least this is what Sandoval argues is uniquely available through the power of oppositional consciousness.

Sandoval's argument has to be seen as one potent formulation for feminists out of the world-wide development of anti-colonialist discourse; that is to say, discourse dissolving the "West" and its highest product— the one who is not animal, barbarian, or woman; man, that is, the author of a cosmos called history. As orientalism is deconstructed politically and semiotically, the identities of the occident destabilize, including those of feminists. Sandoval argues that "women of colour" have a chance to build an effective unity that does not replicate the imperializing, totalizing revolutionary subjects of previous Marxisms and feminisms which had not faced the consequences of the disorderly polyphony emerging from decolonization.

Katie King has emphasized the limits of identification and the political/poetic mechanics of identification built into reading "the poem," that generative core of cultural feminism. King criticizes the persistent tendency among contemporary feminists from different "moments" or "conversations" in feminist practice to taxonomize the women's movement to make one's own political tendencies appear to be the *telos* of the whole. These taxonomies tend to remake feminist history so that it appears to be an ideological struggle among coherent types persisting over time, especially those typical units called radical, liberal, and socialist-feminism. Literally, all other feminisms are either incorporated or marginalized, usually by building an explicit ontology and epistemology. Taxonomies of feminism produce epistemologies to police deviation from official women's experience. And of course, "women's culture," like women of colour, is consciously created by mechanisms inducing affinity. The rituals of poetry, music, and certain forms of academic practice have been preeminent. The politics of race and culture in the US women's movements are

intimately interwoven. The common achievement of King and Sandoval is learning how to craft a poetic/political unity without relying on a logic of appropriation, incorporation, and taxonomic identification.

The theoretical and practical struggle against unity-through-domination or unity-through-incorporation ironically not only undermines the justifications for patriarchy, colonialism, humanism, positivism, essentialism, scientism, and other unlamented -isms, but *all* claims for an organic or natural standpoint. I think that radical and socialist/Marxist-feminisms have also undermined their/our own epistemological strategies and that this is a crucially valuable step in imagining possible unities. It remains to be seen whether all "epistemologies" as Western political people have known them fail us in the task to build effective affinities.

It is important to note that the effort to construct revolutionary standpoints, epistemologies as achievements of people committed to changing the world, has been part of the process showing the limits of identification. The acid tools of postmodernist theory and the constructive tools of ontological discourse about revolutionary subjects might be seen as ironic allies in dissolving Western selves in the interests of survival. We are excruciatingly conscious of what it means to have a historically constituted body. But with the loss of innocence in our origin, there is no expulsion from the Garden either. Our politics lose the indulgence of guilt with the *naïveté* of innocence. But what would another political myth for socialist-feminism look like? What kind of politics could embrace partial, contradictory, permanently unclosed constructions of personal and collective selves and still be faithful, effective—and, ironically, socialist-feminist?

I do not know of any other time in history when there was greater need for political unity to confront effectively the dominations of "race," "gender," "sexuality," and "class." I also do not know of any other time when the kind of unity we might help build could have been possible. None of "us" have any longer the symbolic or material capability of dictating the shape of reality to any of "them." Or at least "we" cannot claim innocence from practising such dominations. White women, including socialist feminists, discovered (that is, were forced kicking and screaming to notice) the non-innocence of the category "woman." That consciousness changes the geography of all previous categories; it denatures them as heat denatures a fragile protein. Cyborg feminists have to argue that "we" do not want any more natural matrix of unity and that no construction is whole. Innocence, and the corollary insistence on victimhood as the only ground for insight, has done enough damage. But the constructed revolutionary subject must give late-twentieth-century people pause as well. In the fraying of identities and in the reflexive strategies for constructing them, the possibility opens up for weaving something other than a shroud for the day after the apocalypse that so prophetically ends salvation history.

Both Marxist/socialist-feminisms and radical feminisms have simultaneously naturalized and denatured the category "woman" and consciousness of the social lives of "women." Perhaps a schematic caricature can highlight both kinds of moves. Marxian socialism is rooted in an analysis of wage labour which reveals class structure. The consequence of the wage relationship is systematic alienation, as the worker is dissociated from his (sic) product. Abstraction and illusion rule in knowledge, domination rules in practice. Labour is the pre-eminently privileged category enabling the Marxist to overcome illusion and find that point of view which is necessary for changing the world. Labour is the humanizing activity that makes man; labour is an ontological category permitting the knowledge of a subject, and so the knowledge of subjugation and alienation.

In faithful filiation, socialist-feminism advanced by allying itself with the basic analytic strategies of Marxism. The main achievement of both Marxist feminists and socialist feminists was to expand the category of labour to accommodate what (some) women did, even when the wage relation was subordinated to a more comprehensive view of labour under capitalist patriarchy. In particular, women's labour in the household and women's activity as mothers generally (that is, reproduction in the socialist-feminist sense), entered theory on the authority of analogy to the Marxian concept of labour. The unity of women here rests on an epistemology based on the ontological structure of "labour." Marxist/socialist-feminism does not "naturalize" unity; it is a possible achievement based on a possible standpoint rooted in social relations. The essentializing move is in the ontological structure of labour or of its analogue, women's activity. The inheritance of Marxian humanism, with its preeminently Western self, is the difficulty for me. The contribution from these formulations has been

the emphasis on the daily responsibility of real women to build unities, rather than to naturalize them.

Catharine MacKinnon's version of radical feminism is itself a caricature of the appropriating, incorporating, totalizing tendencies of Western theories of identity grounding action. It is factually and politically wrong to assimilate all of the diverse "moments" or "conversations" in recent women's politics named radical feminism to MacKinnon's version. But the teleological logic of her theory shows how an epistemology and ontology—including their negations—erase or police difference. Only one of the effects of MacKinnon's theory is the rewriting of the history of the polymorphous field called radical feminism. The major effect is the production of a theory of experience, of women's identity, that is a kind of apocalypse for all revolutionary standpoints. That is, the totalization built into this tale of radical feminism achieves its end—the unity of women—by enforcing the experience of and testimony to radical non-being. As for the Marxist/socialist feminist, consciousness is an achievement, not a natural fact. And MacKinnon's theory eliminates some of the difficulties built into humanist revolutionary subjects, but at the cost of radical reductionism.

MacKinnon argues that feminism necessarily adopted a different analytical strategy from Marxism, looking first not at the structure of class, but at the structure of sex/gender and its generative relationship, men's constitution and appropriation of women sexually. Ironically, MacKinnon's "ontology" constructs a non-subject, a non-being. Another's desire, not the self's labour, is the origin of "woman." She therefore develops a theory of consciousness that enforces what can count as "women's" experience—anything that names sexual violation, indeed, sex itself as far as "women" can be concerned. Feminist practice is the construction of this form of consciousness; that is, the self-knowledge of a self-who-is-not.

Perversely, sexual appropriation in this feminism still has the epistemological status of labour; that is to say, the point from which an analysis able to contribute to changing the world must flow. But sexual objectification, not alienation, is the consequence of the structure of sex/gender. In the realm of knowledge, the result of sexual objectification is illusion and abstraction. However, a woman is not simply alienated from her product, but in a deep sense does not exist as a subject, or even potential subject, since she owes her existence as a woman to sexual appropriation. To be constituted by another's desire is not the same thing as to be alienated in the violent separation of the labourer from his product.

MacKinnon's radical theory of experience is totalizing in the extreme; it does not so much marginalize as obliterate the authority of any other women's political speech and action. It is a totalization producing what Western patriarchy itself never succeeded in doing—feminists' consciousness of the non-existence of women, except as products of men's desire. I think MacKinnon correctly argues that no Marxian version of identity can firmly ground women's unity. But in solving the problem of the contradictions of any Western revolutionary subject for feminist purposes, she develops an even more authoritarian doctrine of experience. If my complaint about socialist/Marxian standpoints is their unintended erasure of polyvocal, unassimilable, radical difference made visible in anti-colonial discourse and practice, MacKinnon's intentional erasure of all difference through the device of the "essential" non-existence of women is not reassuring.

In my taxonomy, which like any other taxonomy is a re-inscription of history, radical feminism can accommodate all the activities of women named by socialist feminists as forms of labour only if the activity can somehow be sexualized. Reproduction had different tones of meanings for the two tendencies, one rooted in labour, one in sex, both calling the consequences of domination and ignorance of social and personal reality "false consciousness."

Beyond either the difficulties or the contributions in the argument of any one author, neither Marxist nor radical feminist points of view have tended to embrace the status of a partial explanation; both were regularly constituted as totalities. Western explanation has demanded as much; how else could the "Western" author incorporate its others? Each tried to annex other forms of domination by expanding its basic categories through analogy, simple listing, or addition. Embarrassed silence about race among white radical and socialist feminists was one major, devastating political consequence. History and polyvocality disappear into political taxonomies that try to establish genealogies.

There was no structural room for race (or for much else) in theory claiming to reveal the construction of the category woman and social group women as a unified or totalizable whole. The structure of my caricature looks like this:

socialist feminism—structure of class//wage labour//alienation
labour, by analogy reproduction, by extension sex, by addition race
radical feminism—structure of gender//sexual appropriation//objectification
sex, by analogy labour, by extension reproduction, by addition race

In another context, the French theorist, Julia Kristeva, claimed women appeared as a historical group after the Second World War, along with groups like youth. Her dates are doubtful; but we are now accustomed to remembering that as objects of knowledge and as historical actors, "race" did not always exist, "class" has a historical genesis, and "homosexuals" are quite junior. It is no accident that the symbolic system of the family of man—and so the essence of woman—breaks up at the same moment that networks of connection among people on the planet are unprecedentedly multiple, pregnant, and complex. "Advanced capitalism" is inadequate to convey the structure of this historical moment. In the "Western" sense, the end of man is at stake. It is no accident that woman disintegrates into women in our time. Perhaps socialist feminists were not substantially guilty of producing essentialist theory that suppressed women's particularity and contradictory interests. I think we have been, at least through unreflective participation in the logics, languages, and practices of white humanism and through searching for a single ground of domination to secure our revolutionary voice. Now we have less excuse. But in the consciousness of our failures, we risk lapsing into boundless difference and giving up on the confusing task of making partial, real connection. Some differences are playful; some are poles of world historical systems of domination. "Epistemology" is about knowing the difference.

(1991)

CHAPTER 5

Intersectionality Theories

We are the colored in a white feminist movement.

We are the feminists among the people of our culture.

We are often the lesbians among the straight.

We do this bridging by naming our selves and by telling our stories
 in our own words.

—Cherrie Moraga and Gloria Anzaldúa, 1981

INTRODUCTION

This chapter focuses on a feminist perspective described as "one of the most important contributions that women's studies has made so far" (McCall, 2005: 1771). It was developed by women of color within the United States who felt their concerns were not being adequately addressed by existing feminisms. Born of necessity and neglect, it was based on the profound realization that no one but themselves would adequately address their concerns. In 1989, the term "intersectionality" was coined by legal scholar Kimberle Williams Crenshaw and this term is most frequently used today for this perspective. We must emphasize that it is a *particular* theoretical approach being examined in this chapter, not simply the writings by women of color. Many and diverse feminisms have been embraced by women of color throughout the history of the U.S. women's movement, as we hope this anthology makes clear.

PRECURSORS TO INTERSECTIONAL ANALYSES IN EARLY MODERNITY[1]

The nineteenth-century **cult of domesticity** and the **doctrine of separate spheres** upon which it rested suggested that women required protection from the male-dominated public realm, yet poor and working-class women of all races were not included in the narrow category of white, class-privileged notion of "women" upon which this logic relied. White, class-privileged women also were imbued with chastity, purity, and great maternal importance, whereas women of color and all poor women were regularly subjected to demeaning forms of sexual violence and social control.

A powerful example of this sexual violence can be found in Reading 62 from *Incidents in the Life of a Slave Girl* ([1861] 2001), written by Harriet Jacobs under the pseudonym Linda Brent. Here Jacobs details the incessant sexual threats made by her lecherous white slave master, his removal of her children to force her into sexual submission, the furious jealousy and blame she endured from his wife, and the years she spent in hiding in a small attic to escape his sexual abuse. Jacobs's narrative offers not only a rare and significant historical account of women's experiences of slavery, but also insights into the complex, triangulated relations of power, control, and violence between white men, white mistresses, and black slaves.

Similarly, the harsh demands of slave labor are exposed in Reading 61, ex-slave Sojourner Truth's famous speech "Ain't I a Woman?" This extemporaneous speech took place at a conference on women's rights where white women speakers were heckled by males in the audience who claimed that women had no reasons to complain given how they were put on a pedestal by men. Truth quickly exposed that myth by asserting how she had worked has hard as any man, bore the lash, and seen her children "sold off to slavery" ([1851] 2013: 91). Her insistent refrain "Ain't I a Woman?" exposed the racial and class construction of femininity.

Two famous African American feminist writers of the late nineteenth and early twentieth centuries—Anna Julia Cooper and Ida B. Wells-Barnett—were able to get an advanced education in the small window of opportunity that opened up during the Reconstruction Era. In *A Voice from the South: By a Black Woman of the South* (1892), Cooper discusses the many contributions of black women and highlights a theme that can be found in many of her writings: "no woman can possibly put herself or her sex outside of any interests that affect *humanity*" (Cooper, [1892] 1988: 143, emphasis added). Cooper's awareness of the multiplicity of oppressions that affect people by race, class, gender, and nation, along with her demand that the women's movement address the concerns of *all oppressed peoples*, can be found in Reading 64, titled "Woman versus the Indian" ([1892] 1988) from this book.

Ida B. Wells-Barnett was internationally renowned for her campaigns against lynching and her activism on behalf of women's rights. Reading 65 from her speech "Lynch Law in America" (1900) illustrates the detailed documentation of lynching that characterized her most famous works, *Southern Horrors* ([1892] 1969) and *The Red Record* (1895). Because the rape of white women often was used as an excuse for lynching, white women too often tempered their condemnation of this violence. Wells-Barnett exposed the "myth of the black rapist" and pointed to the irony of the claim that "white women had to be protected from black monsters" given how women of color had been raped by white man with impunity ([1901] 2005: 117).

The violence perpetrated against black men and women became a central issue in the debates over the Fifteenth Amendment to the U.S. Constitution. This amendment—which gave black men the right to vote, but not any women—divided the U.S. women's movement along racial lines with few exceptions. Many white suffragists were enraged that male ex-slaves would get the vote before them and their racism erupted during the heated debates over this amendment. Some black feminists also rejected the Fifteenth Amendment, such as Sojourner Truth, who feared it would make black men masters over black women (Truth, [1867] 2013).

However, most African Americans supported this amendment. One of the most compelling reasons for this consensus was the violence perpetrated by whites against blacks. When confronted with the claim that this violence also affected black women, the abolitionist leader Frederick Douglass replied: "Yes, yes, yes . . . It is true for black women but not because she is a woman, but because she is black!" (Douglass quoted in Giddings, 1984: 67). As Reading 63, "On Woman Suffrage" (Douglass [1888] 2014), demonstrates, Douglass had a long record of supporting women's rights and was one of the few men who attended the Seneca Falls Women's Rights Conference.

PRECURSORS TO INTERSECTIONAL ANALYSES BETWEEN THE WAVES

Some of the most important intersectional writings between the waves came out of the **Harlem Renaissance**—a cultural movement that spanned the period roughly between the 1920s and the 1930s. Its key assumption was that African Americans could challenge racism and transform pervasive racial stereotypes through the production of art, music, and literature. The achievements of black artists, writers, and musicians during the Harlem Renaissance are legendary. Reading 66, "Sweat" ([1926] 1995), is a short story by anthropologist and novelist Zora Neale Hurston. Like her most famous novels *Jonah's Gourd Vine* ([1934] 2008) and *Their Eyes Were Watching God* ([1937] 2006), this short story highlights the intersections of race, class, and gender in the lives of African Americans. Along with Hurston's works, the writings of other novelists, poets, and playwrights of this era became part of the canon of American women's literature, such as those of Nella Larsen, Alice Dunbar-Nelson, and Georgia Douglas Johnson.

Although the Great Depression ended this flourishing period of black culture, the Harlem Renaissance fostered a spirit of self-determination and a foundation of black pride that would be manifest in the civil rights movement and in a simmering black radicalism and militancy that would be ignited in the post–World War II era.

THIS BRIDGE CALLED MY BACK

The 1960s and 1970s witnessed the rise of a number of new social movements that focused on racial/ethnic issues and that embraced **identity politics**. The Native American Movement, the Chicano Movement, the Asian American Movement, and the Puerto Rican Movement followed closely on the heels of the civil rights movement. Second-wave feminists often cut their political teeth in these multiracial struggles against white supremacy for black, brown, red, and yellow power that emerged both practically and symbolically as a new common front of "Third World peoples" *inside* the United States (Gosse, 2005: 168). However, disenchanted with both the sexism that plagued these multiracial struggles and the racism within the white women's movement, a number of second-wave women of color developed their own political organizations and theoretical analyses.

One of these groups was the Combahee River Collective and their signal piece, "A Black Feminist Statement" ([1977] 1983), found in Reading 68, was one of the most influential political statements written during the second wave. This collective of black, socialist, and lesbian feminists used the term "horizontal oppressions" to refer to the differences that divided women on the bases of gender, race, class, and/or sexual orientation. They also pointed to the interlocking nature of multiple oppressions, such as their own experiences as black, lesbian women. This focus on simultaneous and multiple oppressions would come to form the crux of intersectional theory.

In contrast to feminists who had tried to build a unitary, mass movement based on a single identity or oppression—such as the women's movement, the Combahee Collective called for a multiaxis identity politics based on intersectional social locations such as race, class, gender, and sexual orientation where coalitions provide the links that foster mass-based, collective action between the many and diverse identity-based groups (Combahee River Collective, [1977] 1983: 217). The idea here is that identity is taken as a political point of departure, as the motivation for action, and as the basis for delineating political concerns. They write, "This focusing upon our own oppression is embodied in the concept of identity politics. We believe that the most profound and potentially most radical politics come directly out of our own identity, as opposed to working to end someone else's oppression" (212). That their multiaxis perspective arose out of both necessity and neglect is evident in their statement: "We realize that the only people who care enough about us to work consistently for our liberation is us" (212).

The neglect of women on the margins also was highlighted in intersectionality theorists' critique of the "essentialist woman" of the second wave (Spelman, 1988). The term **essentialism** refers to the belief in innate, intrinsic, or indispensable properties that define the core features of a given entity or group. These properties are used not only to distinguish one group from others (such as women from men), but also to bind members of the group together in collective political practice. Second-wave feminists often invoked the notion of "sisterhood" to mobilize women politically and to showcase women's common concerns. Yet, regardless of whether women's shared traits were theorized as biological, psychological, or social, essentialism downplayed differences in their experiences. In *The Inessential Woman* (1988), Elizabeth Spelman named essentialism the "Trojan horse of feminist ethnocentrism"—a painful source of divisions *within* the U.S. women's movement (1988: x).

In *Sister/Outsider* (1984), Audre Lorde argues that generalizations about women qua women are usually false. She points to numerous cases where white feminists ignored differences between women. For example, she says to her white feminist peers: "You fear your children will grow up to join the patriarchy and testify against you, we fear our children will be dragged from a car and shot down in the street, and you turn your backs upon the reasons they are dying" (1984: 119).[2] Lorde also discusses how we all have internalized patterns of oppression that must be altered if we are to build a successful movement based on difference. In Reading 72 from this same book she warns how ". . . the master's tools will never dismantle the master's house" (1984: 110).

Such internalized oppressions are highlighted in Reading 67 from Maya Angelou's novel *I Know Why the Caged Bird Sings* (1969). This story about an African American child, who feels ugly in her dark skin, shows how people in marginalized groups internalize dominant group values and beliefs that undermine their own self-esteem and sense of empowerment. In Reading 69, "Invisibility Is an Unnatural Disaster" (1979), Mitsuye Yamada discusses not only how she felt invisible because of the passive stereotypes associated with Asian Americans, but also how, at times, she was complicit in fostering these stereotypes.

Because of feminism's association with white, class-privileged feminists' concerns, many second-wave women of color preferred not to use the term "feminist." Latinas preferred the terms Chicana feminists, hispanas, and/or xicanistas (Maatita, 2005), whereas African Americans often referred to themselves as "womanists"—a term describe in Reading 71 from Alice Walker's *In Search of Our Mothers' Gardens* (1983). They recognized that different groups of women experience subordination in different ways, depending on their race, class, and sexuality. Thus, what may appear to some women as the most important or urgent issues facing feminism are not seen as the most important issues or concerns to other women.

SIMULTANEOUS AND MULTIPLE OPPRESSIONS

Barbara Smith, a founding member of the Combahee River Collective, describes the simultaneity of multiple oppressions as "one the most significant ideological contributions of black feminist thought" (B. Smith, 1983: xxxii). By simultaneous, multiple oppressions, Smith meant that different forms of oppression, such as race, class, or gender, cannot be torn apart from their interactive impact on people's lives.

Reading 74, "Demarginalizing the Intersection of Race and Sex: A Black Feminist Critique of Antidiscrimination Doctrine, Feminist Theory, and Antiracist Politics" (1989), is the signal piece where legal scholar Kimberlé Crenshaw coined the term "intersectionality." Here Crenshaw focuses on how theoretical frameworks that address only a "single axis" of oppression obscure the multidimensionality of women of color's experiences (Crenshaw, 1989: 151). Her point of departure is the title of one of the most influential anthologies by women of color during this era—*All the Women Are White, All the Men Are Black, but Some of Us Are Brave* (Hull et al., 1981).

Crenshaw presents a number of cases to make her point. For example, in 1976, five black women filed a suit against General Motors alleging that the employer's seniority system perpetuated the effects of past discrimination against black women. General Motors had not hired black women prior to 1964, and all the black women hired after 1970 lost their jobs in a seniority-based layoff. However, because this company had previously hired both "women" (white women) and "blacks" (black men), the court dismissed the case on the grounds that General Motors had not discriminated on the basis of either gender or race. In such ways, Crenshaw illuminates how the intersectionality of multiple oppressions is "greater than the sum of racism and sexism" (1989: 140). Any analysis that does not take intersectionality into account cannot sufficiently address many of the ways in which women of color experience oppression.

Similarly, in her award-winning book *Black Feminist Thought: Knowledge, Consciousness, and the Politics of Empowerment* (1990), Patricia Hill Collins introduces the concept of **matrix of domination** to further explain these multiple oppressions. As shown in Reading 75, Collins describes how people have social structural locations on this matrix in terms of their race, social class, gender, and/or sexual orientation. Some people can even occupy social locations of penalty and privilege simultaneously, thus being both oppressed and oppressors. Wealthy, black males, for example, have privilege by their class and gender positions, but are penalized by their racial location.

Collins uses this matrix to explain the epistemological stance of intersectionality theory. For her, all knowledge is socially situated in the sense that people construct knowledge from different social locations. On the one hand, a specific social location enables people to see realities that are less visible to those in other locations. On the other hand, because no one can view the world from all of the various and diverse social locations, each vantage point is partial or limited. Collins suggests that a more developed understanding of the world can be generated by "pivoting" from the interpretations and knowledge of one group to those of another group (1990: 234). Here, knowledge is constructed in a quilt-like fashion where the social realities of diverse vantage points are interwoven to form a more complete fabric of the whole. She also calls for the retrieval of **subjugated knowledges** or the knowledges of subordinate groups that have been ignored, silenced, or deemed less credible by dominant groups.

FROM MARGIN TO CENTER

Although intersectionality theorists embrace standpoint theory, their standpoint approaches differ from those discussed in the last chapter that focused on the "standpoint of women." As noted earlier, rather than such a single-axis standpoint approach, intersectionality theorists employ a multiaxis standpoint approach that captures the simultaneous, multiple oppressions such as race, class, and gender that affect peoples' vantage points on reality. To capture this multiplicity of oppressions they often speak of margins and centers, rather than gendered standpoints. For example, in bell hooks's *Feminist Theory: From Margin to Center* (1984), hooks argues that marginal social locations generate more critical vantage points for understanding social life precisely because subordinate groups often have to move between two worlds—their world and that of the dominant group to work, to shop and to do their everyday lives, whereas the dominant group has fewer reasons to enter the world of the marginalized. Because the marginalized have knowledge of both the margin and the center, she contends that feminist theory would be enhanced by moving their voices to the center of feminist discourse.

Latina intersectionality theorist Gloria Anzaldúa uses a similar approach in Reading 73 from *Borderlands/La Frontera: The New Mestiza* (1987). Drawing on her own socially lived knowledge, Gloria Anzaldúa highlights the dilemmas faced by people of mixed heritage. She uses "border crossings" as her metaphor for moving from margin to center and interweaves Spanish and Aztec words into her text, so that the very form of the article reflects the experiences of the "mestiza"—a woman of mixed heritage. She asks, to which collectivity does the person of mixed heritage listen? Her answer is to embrace a **new mestiza consciousness** that prizes both the contradictions of multiple identities and the knowledge gained from border crossings as empowering sites of greater freedom and understanding.

Like hooks, Anzaldúa **privileges the knowledge of the oppressed**[3] by viewing the standpoints of the marginalized as having more critical insights than those of dominant groups. However, not all intersectionality theorists privilege the knowledge of subordinate groups. Patricia Hill Collins, for example, is more careful to point out that these critical insights are only *potentials* (1990: 207). For her, the perspectives of the subjugated are neither innocent nor exempt from critical reexamination.[4] Collins recognizes that the costs of oppression can limit access to important opportunities that allow people to expand their awareness of the social world, such as good schools or good health. This view was shared by postcolonial theorist Uma Narayan in Reading 7 from Chapter 1 when she discussed the "dark side of double vision" ([1989] 2013: 376).

DECENTERING AND DIFFERENCE

To provide readers with a better understanding of how intersectionality theorists apply their approach to concrete issues, we included a reading in this anthology that distinguishes intersectional analyses from other feminist approaches on the important topic of reproductive freedom. Freedom of reproductive choice and access to birth control, sex education, and abortion have been extremely contentious issues in the United States over the past half century. These issues were key targets of conservative, antifeminists' efforts to defeat the Equal Rights Amendment and they continue to be volatile issues in the pro-life and pro-natalist politics of the religious right today. Yet *within* the U.S. women's movement, women of color repeatedly pointed out how their key concern was for **reproductive justice**—not only the freedom to control birth, but also the freedom to give birth, to keep their children and not to have contraception forced upon them, something white women in privileged class positions had long enjoyed.

Reading 77 from "Outcast Mothers and Surrogates: Racism and Reproductive Politics in the Nineties" ([1993] 2005) by Angela Davis discusses these issues within the context of new debates that were in the national spotlight in the 1980s and 1990s. By that time, the new reproductive technologies developed for infertile couples, as well as the issue of surrogacy, sparked heated debates in the public at large and between feminists about mothering and childbearing. The second wave split over these issues as Nancy Lublin points out in *Pandora's Box: Feminism Confronts Reproductive Technology* (1998).[5] For example, feminists took very different positions on whose rights should prevail in the event that a surrogate mother changed her mind after she gave birth. Such controversies deconstructed what was meant by mothering—calling into question whether gestation and childbearing or childrearing were the most important issues.

Davis points out how these concerns over the deconstruction of mothering are not something new; rather the meaning of mothering has long been deconstructed on the bases of race and class. She discusses how slavery in the United States effectively denied many aspects of motherhood to African American women as their children were wrenched from their arms to be sold in slave markets. In turn, whereas women of color were (and continue to be) viewed as adequate surrogate nurturers when they serve as "mammies" and nannies to the children of more privileged classes, they are viewed as inadequate nurturers of their own children. Davis also describes how working-class and poor women of all races are "cast like their male counterparts, into the industrial proletariat" ([1993] 2005: 511), where the demands of their jobs often conflict with their ability to mother. She further points to the twentieth-century practices of forced sterilization that disproportionately impacted poor women, women of color, and the disabled.

For Davis, it is telling that the deconstruction of mothering only became salient issues for white feminists when they directly impacted more privileged women. Whereas the debates generated by the new reproductive technologies focus on the reproductive issues of affluent, older, infertile women, the reproductive issues most frequently associated with poor women of color revolve around the so-called excessive fertility of young, single women. Ironically, the latter are denied affordable abortions through restrictions on Medicaid funding of abortions, although the federal government willingly funds their sterilization. For Davis, all of these examples are ways that the bodies of women of color "bear the evidence of colonization" (513).

U.S. THIRD-WORLD FEMINISM

During the 1980s, intersectionality theory was often called "U.S. third world feminism" to link the plight of U.S. women of color to colonized people across the globe and to argue that white feminist thought was a hegemonic feminism that played the same role as a colonialist ideology. Reading 76 from Chela Sandoval's "U.S. Third World Feminism: The Theory and Method of Differential Oppositional Consciousness in a Postmodern World" ([1991] 2003) was one of the most widely read pieces that made this claim. Here Sandoval describes how "U.S. third world feminism provides access to a different way of conceptualizing not only U.S. feminist consciousness" but also a formulation capable of aligning movements for social justice "with what have been identified as world-wide movements of decolonization" ([1991] 2003: 75).

At first glance the term "U.S. third world feminism" sounds like an oxymoron.[6] How can citizens of a major first world country such as the United States be "third world feminists?" The colonization referred to by these theorists is **internal colonialism** (or settler colonialism). In the United States, internal colonialism initially took the form of white settlers either pushing indigenous peoples off their land onto reservations or exterminating them to inhabit the lands themselves (McMichael, 1996: 17). When mercantile traders from the seventeenth through the nineteenth centuries brought thousands of slaves from other parts of the globe to the United States (legally and illegally), African Americans became yet another colonized people. A third internal colony was established when sections of Mexico were annexed after the Mexican–American War (1846–1848). U.S. settler colonialism finally gained hegemony across the North American continent when the western frontier was consolidated after the last of the major Indian Wars in the 1890s—the Battle of Wounded Knee.[7] Reading 70, "I Walk in the History of My People" ([1981] 1983), by the poet Chrystos, harkens back to this battle and the suffering Native Americans have endured as a result of internal colonialism.

Although racism is an integral feature of internal colonialism, other important features of this process include, first, how people of color entered the country involuntarily and/or by force, such as through the slave trade or the military conquest of Mexican and Native American's lands; second, how their native cultures were destroyed and they had to assimilate to the language and culture of the dominant groups; third, how they were relegated to subordinate labor markets meaning low-paying, menial jobs such as harvesting crops, canal and railroad construction, or domestic service; and fourth, how white-dominated state bureaucracies imposed restrictions on these subjugated people that were not imposed on the dominant population, such as segregation laws (Blauner, 1972). In these ways, the twin processes of internal colonialism and racism enriched the white colonizers and maintained the dependency of the colonized. For intersectionality theorists, internal colonialism has been particularly useful in discussing local/global links (see Chapters 8 and 9), as well as struggles for environmental justice.

THE ENVIRONMENTAL JUSTICE MOVEMENT

The major environmental organizations of the nineteenth and twentieth centuries were and continue to be supported and led primarily by white middle- and upper-class men and women (Merchant, 2007). Even the ecofeminist groups of late modernity rarely have been successful in attracting members from different races or social classes (D. E. Taylor, 1997). It was not until the late 1980s that the multiracial, multiclass, grassroots **environmental justice movement** arose. The application of intersectionality theory to environmental issues is most visible in this movement.

Environmental justice activists document how working-class and poor people of color have less access to clean air and water, as well as more exposure to environmental hazards both at home and on the job. They challenge not only the perpetrators of environmental degradation, but also the indifference of mainstream environmental groups to their environmental concerns. Although the overlap of race and social class confounds these issues, numerous studies have found race to be an independent variable, not reducible to social class, in predicting the distribution of air pollution; the location of landfills, incinerators, and toxic waste dumps; and lead poisoning in children (Bryant and Mohai, 1992; Bullard, 1993, 1994). For these reasons, the environmental justice movement highlights the issue of **environmental racism**.

Women of color have been at the forefront of the environmental justice movement and its struggle to bring attention to the environmental problems that harm their communities. They discuss how the successful mobilization of people of color requires a *redefinition of which issues are considered environmental.* Mainstream environmental organizations spend most of their resources on wildlife preservation and conservation. They are less likely to work on issues of greater concern to people of color, such as occupational safety, hazardous wastes, or incinerators and landfills (D. E. Taylor, 1997: 50).

In Reading 78, "Ecofeminism through an Anticolonial Framework" (1997), Andy (Andrea) Smith argues that the failure of mainstream environmental organizations and ecofeminists to embrace an anticolonial framework has led to their failure to understand the origins of environmental problems and patriarchy. She discusses how, prior to U.S. settler colonialism, many indigenous tribes and nations were neither male dominated nor ecologically debilitated. Smith also points to the serious environmental problems facing indigenous people today, such as the nuclear waste left on indigenous lands from uranium mining, as well as from the use of these lands as major test sites for atomic weapons. In this piece, Smith also criticizes spiritual ecofeminists who appropriate native symbols and icons, but who do not give back to these communities.

Her article highlights how the twin practices of internal colonialism and institutional racism left people of color to bear the brunt of environmental risks and hazards. Given past experiences of indifference to their plight, environmental justice activists are less trusting that environmental agencies and white environmental activists or ecofeminists will have concern for their recompense and equity in the future. In these ways, the theory and practice of the environmental justice movement echoes the theory and practice of intersectionality theorists.

INTEGRATING DISABILITY STUDIES WITH INTERSECTIONALITY THEORY

Like other new social movements in the United States during the last half of the twentieth century, the disability rights movement was inspired by the civil rights movement and the women's movement. This movement's first major success was the passage of the Americans with Disabilities Act in May of 1990 (Volion, 2010). A few years later, the interdisciplinary field of disability studies was created to focus on the contributions, experiences, history, and culture of people with disabilities, as well as to formulate their political demands (Society for Disability Studies, n.d.).

One of the major feminist scholars to integrate disability studies with intersectionality theory is Rosemarie Garland-Thomson. In Reading 79, Garland-Thomson points to how disability studies is sorely lacking in feminist analyses, just as feminist studies often is discussed without reference to disabilities (2002: 1–2). She lauds intersectionality theory for being one of the few feminist approaches that has taken into account disability, alongside its focus on gender, race, class, and sexuality.

Garland-Thomson points to various similarities between gendered and disabled social locations. She notes how Western thought historically associated femaleness with disability—with being less rational, less intelligent, and more hysterical than men. She also discusses how the twin ideologies of beauty and normalcy posit female and disabled bodies not only as spectacles to be looked at, but also as pliable bodies to be shaped into conformity with normative cultural standards. She argues that bodies subjugated by race, class, gender, sexuality, and disability all share histories of being depicted as "deficient or profligate" (Garland-Thomson, 2002: 8). They have been targeted for control or elimination through such historical practices as infanticide, forced sterilization, segregation, and normalizing surgical procedures. Garland-Thomson delivers a compelling argument for integrating disability studies with intersectionality theory to enhance our understanding of how these systems of oppression intersect and mutually constitute each other (2002: 28).

CONCLUSION

Overall, intersectionality theorists made significant headway in bridging the racial and ethnic divides that have long characterized the U.S. women's movement by revealing the simultaneous and interlocking nature of the multiple oppressions that affect and mutually constitute us all. Their critical, oppositional gaze contributed to new directions in feminist theory that bridged modern and postmodern thought, highlighted difference, and decentered the white feminisms of the U.S. second wave.

NOTES

1. Parts of this section draw from pp. 162–163 by Jane Ward and Susan Mann (2012b).

2. For example, the "Platform Issues of the Million Woman March" (a political demonstration by African American women first held in Philadelphia in 1997) includes concerns for prisoners, the homeless, and gentrification that are rarely found in the political platforms of white, middle-class feminist organizations. See Million Woman March (1997).

3. The epistemological privileging of the knowledge of oppressed groups has characterized much radical literature and is not unique to intersectional theory (Bar On, 1993).

4. Collins's critique of privileging the knowledge of the oppressed is also shared by Sandra Harding and Dorothy Smith (Harding, 1991: 191; D.E. Smith, 1987: 92).

5. See also Corea (1985) and Purdy (1996).

6. In popular parlance, we tend to use the term "oxymoron" as a contradiction. But the Greek word means something that is surprisingly true despite its appearance—a paradox.

7. The last medals of honor to U.S. soldiers for the American Indian Wars were actually given in 1898 after the Battle of Sugar Point in Minnesota and other smaller skirmishes occurred at later dates.

61 • *Sojourner Truth (Isabella Baumfree)*

"AIN'T I A WOMAN?"

Well, children, where there is so much racket there must be something out of kilter. I think that 'twixt the negroes of the South and the women at the North, all talking about rights, the white men will be in a fix pretty soon. But what's all this here talking about?

That man over there says that women need to be helped into carriages, and lifted over ditches, and to have the best place everywhere. Nobody ever helps me into carriages, or over mud-puddles, or gives me any best place! And ain't I a woman? Look at me! Look at my arm! I have ploughed and planted, and gathered into barns, and no man could head me! And ain't I a woman? I could work as much and eat as much as a man—when I could get it—and bear the lash as well! And ain't I a woman? I have borne thirteen children, and seen them most all sold off to slavery, and when I cried out with my mother's grief, none but Jesus heard me! And ain't I a woman?

Then they talk about this thing in the head; what's this they call it? [Intellect, someone whispers.] That's it, honey. What's that got to do with women's rights or negro's rights? If my cup won't hold but a pint, and yours holds a quart, wouldn't you be mean not to let me have my little half-measure full?

Then that little man in black there, he says women can't have as much rights as men, 'cause Christ wasn't a woman! Where did your Christ come from? From God and a woman! Man had nothing to do with Him.

If the first woman God ever made was strong enough to turn the world upside down all alone, these women together ought to be able to turn it back, and get it right side up again! And now they is asking to do it, the men better let them.

Obliged to you for hearing me, and now old Sojourner ain't got nothing more to say.

(1851)

Speech delivered at the Women's Rights Convention in Akron, Ohio, 1851.

62 • *Harriet Jacobs*

FROM *INCIDENTS IN THE LIFE OF A SLAVE GIRL*

V. THE TRIALS OF GIRLHOOD

During the first years of my service in Dr. Flint's family, I was accustomed to share some indulgences with the children of my mistress. Though this seemed to me no more than right, I was grateful for it, and tried to merit the kindness by the faithful discharge of my duties. But I now entered on my fifteenth year—a sad epoch in the life of a slave girl. My master began

Reprinted from *Incidents in the Life of a Slave Girl* by Linda Brent, ed. L. Maria Child. Boston: Published for the Author, 1861.

to whisper foul words in my ear. Young as I was, I could not remain ignorant of their import. I tried to treat them with indifference or contempt. The master's age, my extreme youth, and the fear that his conduct would be reported to my grandmother, made him bear this treatment for many months. He was a crafty man, and resorted to many means to accomplish his purposes. Sometimes he had stormy, terrific ways, that made his victims tremble; sometimes he assumed a gentleness that he thought must surely subdue. Of the two, I preferred his stormy moods, although they left me trembling. He tried his utmost to corrupt the pure principles my grandmother had instilled. He peopled my young mind with unclean images, such as only a vile monster could think of. I turned from him with disgust and hatred. But he was my master. I was compelled to live under the same roof with him— where I saw a man forty years my senior daily violating the most sacred commandments of nature. He told me I was his property; that I must be subject to his will in all things. My soul revolted against the mean tyranny. But where could I turn for protection? No matter whether the slave girl be as black as ebony or as fair as her mistress. In either case, there is no shadow of law to protect her from insult, from violence, or even from death; all these are inflicted by fiends who bear the shape of men. The mistress, who ought to protect the helpless victim, has no other feelings towards her but those of jealousy and rage. The degradation, the wrongs, the vices, that grow out of slavery, are more than I can describe. They are greater than you would willingly believe. Surely, if you credited one half the truths that are told you concerning the helpless millions suffering in this cruel bondage, you at the north would not help to tighten the yoke. You surely would refuse to do for the master, on your own soil, the mean and cruel work which trained bloodhounds and the lowest class of whites do for him at the south.

Every where the years bring to all enough of sin and sorrow; but in slavery the very dawn of life is darkened by these shadows. Even the little child, who is accustomed to wait on her mistress and her children, will learn, before she is twelve years old, why it is that her mistress hates such and such a one among the slaves. Perhaps the child's own mother is among those hated ones. She listens to violent outbreaks of jealous passion, and cannot help understanding what

is the cause. She will become prematurely knowing in evil things. Soon she will learn to tremble when she hears her master's footfall. She will be compelled to realize that she is no longer a child. If God has bestowed beauty upon her, it will prove her greatest curse. That which commands admiration in the white woman only hastens the degradation of the female slave. I know that some are too much brutalized by slavery to feel the humiliation of their position; but many slaves feel it most acutely, and shrink from the memory of it. I cannot tell how much I suffered in the presence of these wrongs, nor how I am still pained by the retrospect. My master met me at every turn, reminding me that I belonged to him, and swearing by heaven and earth that he would compel me to submit to him. If I went out for a breath of fresh air, after a day of unwearied toil, his footsteps dogged me. If I knelt by my mother's grave, his dark shadow fell on me even there. The light heart which nature had given me became heavy with sad forebodings. The other slaves in my master's house noticed the change. Many of them pitied me; but none dared to ask the cause. They had no need to inquire. They knew too well the guilty practices under that roof; and they were aware that to speak of them was an offence that never went unpunished.

I longed for some one to confide in. I would have given the world to have laid my head on my grandmother's faithful bosom, and told her all my troubles. But Dr. Flint swore he would kill me, if I was not as silent as the grave. Then, although my grandmother was all in all to me, I feared her as well as loved her. I had been accustomed to look up to her with a respect bordering upon awe. I was very young, and felt shamefaced about telling her such impure things, especially as I knew her to be very strict on such subjects. Moreover, she was a woman of a high spirit. She was usually very quiet in her demeanor; but if her indignation was once roused, it was not very easily quelled. I had been told that she once chased a white gentleman with a loaded pistol, because he insulted one of her daughters. I dreaded the consequences of a violent outbreak; and both pride and fear kept me silent. But though I did not confide in my grandmother, and even evaded her vigilant watchfulness and inquiry, her presence in the neighborhood was some protection to me. Though she had been a slave, Dr. Flint was afraid of her. He dreaded her scorching rebukes. Moreover, she was known and patronized by many people; and he did not wish to have his villany made public. It was lucky for me that I did not live on a distant plantation, but in a town not so large that the inhabitants were ignorant of each other's affairs. Bad as are the laws and customs in a slaveholding community, the doctor, as a professional man, deemed it prudent to keep up some outward show of decency.

O, what days and nights of fear and sorrow that man caused me! Reader, it is not to awaken sympathy for myself that I am telling you truthfully what I suffered in slavery. I do it to kindle a flame of compassion in your hearts for my sisters who are still in bondage, suffering as I once suffered.

I once saw two beautiful children playing together. One was a fair white child; the other was her slave, and also her sister. When I saw them embracing each other, and heard their joyous laughter, I turned sadly away from the lovely sight. I foresaw the inevitable blight that would fall on the little slave's heart. I knew how soon her laughter would be changed to sighs. The fair child grew up to be a still fairer woman. From childhood to womanhood her pathway was blooming with flowers, and overarched by a sunny sky. Scarcely one day of her life had been clouded when the sun rose on her happy bridal morning.

How had those years dealt with her slave sister, the little playmate of her childhood? She, also, was very beautiful; but the flowers and sunshine of love were not for her. She drank the cup of sin, and shame, and misery, whereof her persecuted race are compelled to drink.

In view of these things, why are ye silent, ye free men and women of the north? Why do your tongues falter in maintenance of the right? Would that I had more ability! But my heart is so full, and my pen is so weak! There are noble men and women who plead for us, striving to help those who cannot help themselves. God bless them! God give them strength and courage to go on! God bless those, every where, who are laboring to advance the cause of humanity!

(1861)

---

63 • *Frederick Douglass*

"ON WOMAN SUFFRAGE"

Mrs. President, Ladies and Gentlemen: I come to this platform with unusual diffidence. Although I have long been identified with the Woman's Suffrage movement, and have often spoken in its favor, I am somewhat at a loss to know what to say on this really great and uncommon occasion, where so much has been said.

When I look around on this assembly, and see the many able and eloquent women, full of the subject, ready to speak, and who only need the opportunity to impress this audience with their views and thrill them with "thoughts that breathe and words that burn," I do not feel like taking up more than a very small space of your time and attention, and shall not. I would not, even now, presume to speak, but for the circumstance of my early connection with the cause, and of having been called upon to do so by one whose voice in this Council we all gladly obey. Men have very little business here as speakers, anyhow; and if they come here at all they should take back benches and wrap themselves in silence. For this is an International Council, not of men, but of women, and woman should have all the say in it. This is her day in court. I do not mean to exalt the intellect of woman above man's; but I have heard many men speak on this subject, some of them the most eloquent to be found anywhere in the

Published in *Woman's Journal*, April 14, 1888.

country; and I believe no man, however gifted with thought and speech, can voice the wrongs and present the demands of women with the skill and effect, with the power and authority of woman herself. The man struck is the man to cry out. Woman knows and feels her wrongs as man cannot know and feel them, and she also knows as well as he can know, what measures are needed to redress them. I grant all the claims at this point. She is her own best representative. We can neither speak for her, nor vote for her, nor act for her, nor be responsible for her; and the thing for men to do in the premises is just to get out of her way and give her the fullest opportunity to exercise all the powers inherent in her individual personality, and allow her to do it as she herself shall elect to exercise them. Her right to be and to do is as full, complete and perfect as the right of any man on earth. I say of her, as I say of the colored people, "Give her fair play, and hands off." There was a time when, perhaps, we men could help a little. It was when this woman suffrage cause was in its cradle, when it was not big enough to go alone, when it had to be taken in the arms of its mother from Seneca Falls, N.Y., to Rochester, N.Y., for baptism. I then went along with it and offered my services to help it, for then it needed help; but now it can afford to dispense with me and all of my sex. Then its friends were few—now its friends are many. Then it was wrapped in obscurity—now it is lifted in sight of the whole civilized world, and people of all lands and languages give it their hearty support. Truly the change is vast and wonderful.

I thought my eye of faith was tolerably clear when I attended those meetings in Seneca Falls and Rochester, but it was far too dim to see at the end of forty years a result so imposing as this International Council, and to see yourself [Elizabeth Cady Stanton] and Miss Anthony alive and active in its proceedings. Of course, I expected to be alive myself, and am not surprised to find myself so; for such is, perhaps, the presumption and arrogance common to my sex. Nevertheless, I am very glad to see you here to-day, and to see this great assembly of women. I am glad that you are its president. No manufactured "boom," or political contrivance, such as make presidents elsewhere, has made you president of this assembly of women in this Capital of the Nation. You hold your place by reason of eminent fitness, and I give you joy that your life and labors in the cause of woman are

thus crowned with honor and glory. This I say in spite of the warning given us by Miss Anthony's friend against mutual admiration.

There may be some well-meaning people in this audience who have never attended a woman suffrage convention, never heard a woman suffrage speech, never read a woman suffrage newspaper, and they may be surprised that those who speak here do not argue the question. It may be kind to tell them that our cause has passed beyond the period of arguing. The demand of the hour is not argument, but assertion, firm and inflexible assertion, assertion which has more than the force of an argument. If there is any argument to be made, it must be made by opponents, not by the friends of woman suffrage. Let those who want argument examine the ground upon which they base their claim to the right to vote. They will find that there is not one reason, not one consideration, which they can urge in support of man's claim to vote, which does not equally support the right of woman to vote.

There is today, however, a special reason for omitting argument. This is the end of the fought decade of the woman suffrage movement, a kind of jubilee which naturally turns our minds to the past.

Ever since this Council has been in session, my thoughts have been reverting to the past. I have been thinking more or less, of the scene presented forty years ago in the little Methodist church at Seneca Falls, the manger in which this organized suffrage movement was born. It was very small thing then. It was not then big enough to be abused, or loud enough to make itself heard outside, and only a few of those who saw it had any notion that the little thing would live. I have been thinking, too, of the strong conviction, the noble courage, the sublime faith in God and man it required at that time to set this suffrage ball in motion. The history of the world has given to us many sublime undertakings, but none more sublime than this. It was a great thing for the friends of peace to organize in opposition to war; it was a great thing for the friends of temperance to organize against intemperance; it was a great thing for humane people to organize in opposition to slavery; but it was a much greater thing, in view of all the circumstances, for woman to organize herself in opposition to her exclusion from participation in government. The reason is obvious. War, intemperance and slavery are open, undisguised, palpable evils. The best feelings of human nature revolt at them. We could easily make men see the misery, the debasement, the terrible suffering caused by intemperance; we could easily make men see the desolation wrought by war and the hell-black horrors of chattel slavery; but the case was different in the movement for woman suffrage. Men took for granted all that could be said against intemperance, war and slavery. But no such advantage was found in the beginning of the cause of suffrage for women. On the contrary, everything in her condition was supposed to be lovely, just as it should be. She had no rights denied, no wrongs to redress. She herself had no suspicion but that all was going well with her. She floated along on the tide of life as her mother and grandmother had done before her, as in a dream of Paradise. Her wrongs, if she had any, were too occult to be seen, and too light to be felt. It required a daring voice and a determined hand to awake her from this delightful dream and call the nation to account for the rights and opportunities of which it was depriving her. It was well understood at the beginning that woman would not thank us for disturbing her by this call to duty, and it was known that man would denounce and scorn us for such a daring innovation upon the established order of things. But this did not appall or delay the word and work.

At this distance of time from that convention at Rochester, and in view of the present position of the question, it is hard to realize the moral courage it required to launch this unwelcome movement. Any man can be brave when the danger is over, go to the front when there is no resistance, rejoice when the battle is fought and the victory is won; but it is not so easy to venture upon a field untried with one-half the whole world against you, as these women did.

Then who were we, for I count myself in, who did this thing? We were few in numbers, moderate in resources, and very little known in the world. The most that we had to commend us was a firm conviction that we were in the right, and a firm faith that the right must ultimately prevail. But the case was well considered. Let no man imagine that the step was taken recklessly and thoughtlessly. Mrs. Stanton had dwelt upon it at least six years before she declared it in the Rochester convention. Walking with her from the house of Joseph and Thankful Southwick, two of the noblest people I ever knew, Mrs. Stanton, with an earnestness that I shall never forget, unfolded her view on this

woman question precisely as she had in this Council. This was six and forty years ago, and it was not until six years after, that she ventured to make her formal, pronounced and startling demand for the ballot. She had, as I have said, considered well, and knew something of what would be the cost of the reform she was inaugurating. She knew the ridicule, the rivalry, the criticism and the bitter aspersions which she and her co-laborers would have to meet and to endure. But she saw more clearly than most of us that the vital point to be made prominent, and the one that included all others, was the ballot, and she bravely said the word. It was not only necessary to break the silence of woman and make her voice heard, but she must have a clear, palpable and comprehensive measure set before her, one worthy of her highest ambition and her best exertions, and hence the ballot was brought to the front.

There are few facts in my humble history to which I look back with more satisfaction than to the fact, recorded in the history of the woman-suffrage movement, that I was sufficiently enlightened at that early day, and when only a few years from slavery, to support your resolution for woman suffrage. I have done very little in this world in which to glory except this one act—and I certainly glory in that. When I ran away from slavery, it was for myself; when I advocated emancipation, it was for my people; but when I stood up for the rights of woman, self was out of the question, and I found a little nobility in the act.

In estimating the forces with which this suffrage cause has had to contend during these forty years, the fact should be remembered that relations of long standing beget a character in the parties to them in favor of their continuance. Time itself is a conservative power—a very conservative power. One shake of his hoary locks will sometimes paralyze the hand and palsy the tongue of the reformer. The relation of man to woman has the advantage tell us that what is always was and always will be, world without end. But we have heard this old argument before, and if we live very long we shall hear it again. When any aged error shall be assailed, and any old abuse is to be removed, we shall meet this same old argument. Man has been so long the king and woman the subject—man has been so long accustomed to command and woman to obey—that both parties to the relation have been hardened into their respective places, and thus has been piled up a mountain of iron against woman's enfranchisement.

The same thing confronted us in our conflicts with slavery. Long years ago Henry Clay said, on the floor of the American Senate, "I know there is a visionary dogma that man cannot hold property in man," and, with a brow of defiance, he said, "That is property which the law makes property. Two hundred years of legislation has sanctioned and sanctified Negro slaves as property." But neither the power of time nor the might of legislation has been able to keep life in that stupendous barbarism.

The universality of man's rule over woman is another factor in the resistance to the woman-suffrage movement. We are pointed to the fact that men have not only always ruled over women, but that they do so rule everywhere, and they easily think that a thing that is done everywhere must be right. Though the fallacy of this reasoning is too transparent to need refutation, it still exerts a powerful influence. Even our good Brother Jasper yet believes, with the ancient Church, that the sun "do move," notwithstanding all the astronomers of the world are against him. One year ago I stood on the Pincio in Rome and witnessed the unveiling of the statue of Galileo. It was an imposing sight. At no time before had Rome been free enough to permit such a statue to be placed within her walls. It is now there, not with the approval of the Vatican. No priest took part in the ceremonies. It was all the work of laymen. One or two priests passed the statue with averted eyes, but the great truths of the solar system were not angry at the sight, and the same will be true when woman shall be clothed, as she will yet be, with all the rights of American citizenship.

All good causes are mutually helpful. The benefits accruing from this movement for the equal rights of woman are not confined or limited to woman only. They will be shared by every effort to promote the progress and welfare of mankind everywhere and in all ages. It was an example and a prophecy of what can be accomplished against strongly opposing forces, against time-hallowed abuses, against deeply entrenched error, against worldwide usage, and against the settled judgment of mankind, by a few earnest women, clad only in the panoply of truth, and determined to live and die in what they considered a righteous cause.

I do not forget the thoughtful remark of our president in the opening address to this International Council, reminding us of the incompleteness of our work. The remark was wise and timely. Nevertheless, no man can compare the present with the past, the obstacles that then opposed us, and the influences that now favor us, the meeting in the little Methodist chapel forty years ago, and the Council in this vast theater today, without admitting that woman's cause is already a brilliant success. But, however this may be and whatever the future may have in store for us, one thing is certain—this new revolution in human thought will never go backward. When a great truth once gets abroad in the world, no power on earth can imprison it, or prescribe its limits, or suppress it. It is bound to go on till it becomes the thought of the world. Such a truth is woman's right to equal liberty with man. She was born with it. It was hers before she comprehended it. It is inscribed upon all the powers and faculties of her soul, and no custom, law or usage can ever destroy it. Now that it has got fairly fixed in the minds of the few, it is bound to become fixed in the minds of the many, and be supported at last by a great cloud of witnesses, which no man can number and no power can withstand.

The women who have thus far carried on this agitation have already embodied and illustrated Theodore Parker's three grades of human greatness. The first is greatness in executive and administrative ability; second, greatness in the ability to organize; and, thirdly, in the ability to discover truth. Wherever these three elements of power are combined in any movement, there is a reasonable ground to believe in its final success; and these elements of power have been manifest in the women who have had the movement in hand from the beginning. They are seen in the order which has characterized the proceedings of this Council. They are seen in the depth and are seen in the fervid eloquence and downright earnestness with which women advocate their cause. They are seen in the profound attention with which woman is heard in her own behalf. They are seen in the steady growth and onward march of the movement, and they will be seen in the final triumph of woman's cause, not only in this country, but throughout the world.

(1888)

"WOMAN VERSUS THE INDIAN"

When the National Woman's Council convened at Washington in February 1891, among a number of thoughtful and suggestive papers read by eminent women, was one by the Rev. Anna Shaw,[1] bearing the above title . . .

. . . Miss Shaw is one of the most powerful of our leaders, and we feel her voice should give no uncertain note. Woman should not, even by inference, or for the sake of argument, seem to disparage what is weak. For woman's cause is the cause of the weak; and when all the weak shall have received their due consideration, then woman will have her "rights," and the Indian will have his rights, and the Negro will have his rights, and all the strong will have learned at last to deal justly, to love mercy, and to walk humbly; and our fair land will have been taught the secret of universal courtesy which is after all nothing but the art, the science, and the religion of regarding one's neighbor as one's self, and to do for him as we would, were conditions swapped, that he do for us.

It cannot seem less than a blunder, whenever the exponents of a great reform or the harbingers of a noble advance in thought and effort allow themselves to seem distorted by a narrow view of their own aims and principles. All prejudices, whether of race, sect or sex, class pride and caste distinctions are the belittling inheritance and badge of snobs and prigs.

The philosophic mind sees that its own "rights" are the rights of humanity. That in the universe of God nothing trivial is or mean; and the recognition it seeks is not through the robber and wild beast adjustment of the survival of the bullies but through the universal application ultimately of the Golden Rule.

Not unfrequently has it happened that the impetus of a mighty thought wave has done the execution meant by its Creator in spite of the weak and distorted perception of its human embodiment. It is not strange if reformers, who, after all, but think God's thoughts after him, have often "builded more wisely than they knew"; and while fighting consciously for only a narrow gateway for themselves have been driven forward by that irresistible "Power not ourselves which makes for righteousness" to open a high road for humanity. It was so with our sixteenth century reformers. The fathers of the Reformation had no idea that they were inciting an insurrection of the human mind against all domination. None would have been more shocked than they at our nineteenth century deductions from their sixteenth century premises. Emancipation of mind and freedom of thought would have been as appalling to them as it was distasteful to the pope. They were right, they argued, to rebel against Romish absolutism—because Romish preaching and Romish practicing were wrong. They denounced popes for hacking heretics and forthwith began themselves to roast witches. The Spanish Inquisition in the hands of Philip and Alva was an institution of the devil; wielded by the faithful, it would become quite another thing. The only "rights" they were broad enough consciously to fight for was the right to substitute the absolutism of their conceptions, their party, their "*ism*" for an authority whose teaching they conceived to be corrupt and vicious. Persecution for a belief was wrong only when the persecutors were wrong and the persecuted right. The sacred prerogative of the individual to decide on matters of belief they did not dream of maintaining. Universal tolerance and its twin, universal charity, were not conceived yet. The broad foundation stone of all human rights, the great democratic principle "A man's a man, *and his own sovereign* for a' that" they did not dare enunciate. They were incapable of drawing up a Declaration of

Reprinted from *The Voice of Anna Julia Cooper*, ed. Charles Lemert and Esme Bhan. New York: Rowman and Littlefield, Inc., 1998.

Independence for humanity. The Reformation to the Reformers meant one bundle of authoritative opinions vs. another bundle of authoritative opinions. Justification by faith, vs. justification by ritual. Submission to Calvin vs. submission to the Pope. English and Germans vs. the Italians.

To our eye, viewed through a vista of three centuries, it was the death wrestle of the principle of thought enslavement in the throttling grasp for personal freedom; it was the great Emancipation Day of human belief, man's intellectual Independence Day, prefiguring and finally compelling the world-wide enfranchisement of his body and all its activities. Not Protestant vs. Catholic, then; not Luther vs. Leo, not Dominicans vs. Augustinians, nor Geneva vs. Rome;—but humanity rationally free, vs. the clamps of tradition and superstition which had manacled and muzzled it.

The cause of freedom is not the cause of a race or a sect, a party or a class,—it is the cause of human kind, the very birthright of humanity. Now unless we are greatly mistaken the Reform of our day, known as the Woman's Movement, is essentially such an embodiment, if its pioneers could only realize it, of the universal good. And specially important is it that there be no confusion of ideas among its leaders as to its scope and universality. All mists must be cleared from the eyes of woman if she is to be a teacher of morals and manners: the former strikes its roots in the individual and its training and pruning may be accomplished by classes; but the latter is to lubricate the joints and minimize the friction of society, and it is important and fundamental that there be no chromatic or other aberration when the teacher is settling the point, "Who is my neighbor?"

It is not the intelligent woman vs. the ignorant woman; nor the white woman vs. the black, the brown, and the red,—it is not even the cause of woman vs. man. Nay, 'tis woman's strongest vindication for speaking that *the world needs to hear her voice*. It would be subversive of every human interest that the cry of one-half the human family be stifled. Woman in stepping from the pedestal of statue-like inactivity in the domestic shrine, and daring to think and move and speak,—to undertake to help shape, mold, and direct the thought of her age, is merely completing the circle of the world's vision. Hers is every interest that has lacked an interpreter and a defender. Her cause is

linked with that of every agony that has been dumb—every wrong that needs a voice.

It is no fault of man's that he has not been able to see truth from her standpoint. It does credit both to his head and heart that no greater mistakes have been committed or even wrongs perpetrated while she sat making tatting and snipping paper flowers. Man's own innate chivalry and the mutual interdependence of their interests have insured his treating her cause, in the main at least, as his own. And he is pardonably surprised and even a little chagrined, perhaps, to find his legislation not considered "perfectly lovely" in every respect. But in any case his work is only impoverished by her remaining dumb. The world has had to limp along with the wobbling gait and one-sided hesitancy of man with one eye. Suddenly the bandage is removed from the other eye and the whole body is filled with light. It sees a circle where before it saw a segment. The darkened eye restored, every member rejoices with it.

What a travesty of its case for this eye to become plaintiff in a suit, *Eye vs. Foot*. "There is that dull clod, the foot, allowed to roam at will, free and untrammelled; while I, the source and medium of light, brilliant and beautiful, am fettered in darkness and doomed to desuetude." The great burly black man, ignorant and gross and depraved, is allowed to vote; while the franchise is withheld from the intelligent and refined, the pure-minded and lofty souled white woman. Even the untamed and untamable Indian of the prairie, who can answer nothing but "ugh" to great economic and civic questions is thought by some worthy to wield the ballot which is still denied the Puritan maid and the first lady of Virginia.

Is not this hitching our wagon to something much lower than a star? Is not woman's cause broader, and deeper, and grander, than a blue stocking debate or an aristocratic pink tea? Why should woman become plaintiff in a suit versus the Indian, or the Negro or any other race or class who have been crushed under the iron heel of Anglo-Saxon power and selfishness? If the Indian has been wronged and cheated by the puissance of this American government, it is woman's mission to plead with her country to cease to do evil and to pay its honest debts. If the Negro has been deceitfully cajoled or inhumanly cuffed according to selfish expediency or capricious antipathy, let it be woman's mission to plead that he be met as a man and honestly given half the road. If woman's own happiness has been ignored or misunderstood in our country's legislating for bread winners, for rum sellers, for property holders, for the family relations, for any or all the interests that touch her vitally, let her rest her plea, not on Indian inferiority, nor on Negro depravity, but on the obligation of legislators to do for her as they would have others do for them were relations reversed. Let her try to teach her country that every interest in this world is entitled at least to a respectful hearing, that every sentiency is worthy of its own gratification, that a helpless cause should not be trampled down, nor a bruised reed broken; and when the right of the individual is made sacred, when the image of God in human form, whether in marble or in clay, whether in alabaster or in ebony, is consecrated and inviolable, when men have been taught to look beneath the rags and grime, the pomp and pageantry of mere circumstance and have regard unto the celestial kernel uncontaminated at the core,—when race, color, sex, condition, are realized to be the accidents, not the substance of life, and consequently as not obscuring or modifying the inalienable title to life, liberty, and pursuit of happiness,—then is mastered the science of politeness, the art of courteous contact, which is naught but the practical application of the principal of benevolence, the back bone and marrow of all religion; then woman's lesson is taught and woman's cause is won—not the white woman nor the black woman nor the red woman, but the cause of every man or woman who has writhed silently under a mighty wrong. The pleading of the American woman for the right and the opportunity to employ the American method of influencing the disposal to be made of herself, her property, her children in civil, economic, or domestic relations is thus seen to be based on a principle as broad as the human race and as old as human society. Her wrongs are thus indissolubly linked with all undefended woe, all helpless suffering, and the plenitude of her "rights" will mean the final triumph of all right over might, the supremacy of the moral forces of reason and justice and love in the government of the nation.

God hasten the day.

(1892)

---

65 • Ida B. Wells-Barnett

"LYNCH LAW IN AMERICA"

Our country's national crime is *lynching*. It is not the creature of an hour, the sudden outburst of uncontrolled fury, or the unspeakable brutality of an insane mob. It represents the cool, calculating deliberation of intelligent people who openly avow that there is an "unwritten law" that justifies them in putting human beings to death without complaint under oath, without trial by jury, without opportunity to make defense, and without right of appeal . . .

. . . This is the work of the "unwritten law" about which so much is said, and in whose behest butchery is made a pastime and national savagery condoned.

The first statute of this "unwritten law" was written in the blood of thousands of brave men who thought that a government that was good enough to create a citizenship was strong enough to protect it. Under the authority of a national law that gave every citizen the right to vote, the newly-made citizens chose to exercise their suffrage. But the reign of the national law was short-lived and illusionary. Hardly had the sentences dried upon the statute-books before one Southern State after another raised the cry against "negro domination" and proclaimed there was an "unwritten law" that justified any means to resist it.

Published in *The Arena* 23.1 (January 1900): 15–24.

The method then inaugurated was the outrages by the "red-shirt" bands of Louisiana, South Carolina, and other Southern States, which were succeeded by the Ku-Klux Klans. These advocates of the "unwritten law" boldly avowed their purpose to intimidate, suppress, and nullify the negro's right to vote. In support of its plans the Ku-Klux Klans, the "red-shirt" and similar organizations proceeded to beat, exile, and kill negroes until the purpose of their organization was accomplished and the supremacy of the "unwritten law" was effected. Thus lynchings began in the South, rapidly spreading into the various States until the national law was nullified and the reign of the "unwritten law" was supreme. Men were taken from their homes by "red-shirt" bands and stripped, beaten, and exiled; others were assassinated when their political prominence made them obnoxious to their political opponents; while the Ku-Klux barbarism of election days, reveling in the butchery of thousands of colored voters, furnished records in Congressional investigations that are a disgrace to civilization.

The alleged menace of universal suffrage having been avoided by the absolute suppression of the negro vote, the spirit of mob murder should have been satisfied and the butchery of negroes should have ceased. But men, women, and children were the victims of murder by individuals and murder by mobs, just as they had been when killed at the demands of the "unwritten law" to prevent "negro domination." Negroes were killed for disputing over terms of contracts with their employers. If a few barns were burned some colored man was killed to stop it. If a colored man resented the imposition of a white man and the two came to blows, the colored man had to die, either at the hands of the white man then and there or later at the hands of a mob that speedily gathered. If he showed a spirit of courageous manhood he was hanged for his pains, and the killing was justified by the declaration that he was a "saucy nigger." Colored women have been murdered because they refused to tell the mobs where relatives could be found for "lynching bees." Boys of fourteen years have been lynched by white representatives of American civilization. In fact, for all kinds of offenses—and, for no offenses—from murders to misdemeanors, men and women are put to death without judge or jury; so that, although the political excuse was no longer necessary, the wholesale murder of human beings went on just the same. A new name was given to the killings and a new excuse was invented for so doing.

Again the aid of the "unwritten law" is invoked, and again it comes to the rescue. During the last ten years a new statute has been added to the "unwritten law." This statute proclaims that for certain crimes or alleged crimes no negro shall be allowed a trial; that no white woman shall be compelled to charge an assault under oath or to submit any such charge to the investigation of a court of law. The result is that many men have been put to death whose innocence was afterward established; and to-day, under this reign of the "unwritten law," no colored man, no matter what his reputation, is safe from lynching if a white woman, no matter what her standing or motive, cares to charge him with insult or assault.

It is considered a sufficient excuse and reasonable justification to put a prisoner to death under this "unwritten law" for the frequently repeated charge that these lynching horrors are necessary to prevent crimes against women. The sentiment of the country has been appealed to, in describing the isolated condition of white families in thickly populated negro districts; and the charge is made that these homes are in as great danger as if they were surrounded by wild beasts. And the world has accepted this theory without let or hindrance. In many cases there has been open expression that the fate meted out to the victim was only what he deserved. In many other instances there has been a silence that says more forcibly than words can proclaim it that it is right and proper that a human being should be seized by a mob and burned to death upon the unsworn and the uncorroborated charge of his accuser. No matter that our laws presume every man innocent until he is proved guilty; no matter that it leaves a certain class of individuals completely at the mercy of another class; no matter that it encourages those criminally disposed to blacken their faces and commit any crime in the calendar so long as they can throw suspicion on some negro, as is frequently done, and then lead a mob to take his life; no matter that mobs make a farce of the law and a mockery of justice; no matter that hundreds of boys are being hardened in crime and schooled in vice by the repetition of such scenes before their eyes— if a white woman declares herself insulted or assaulted, some life must pay the penalty, with all the horrors of the Spanish Inquisition and all the barbarism of the Middle Ages. The world looks on and says it is well.

Not only are two hundred men and women put to death annually, on the average, in this country by mobs, but these lives are taken with the greatest publicity. In many instances the leading citizens aid and abet by their presence when they do not participate, and the leading journals inflame the public mind to the lynching point with scare-head articles and offers of rewards. Whenever a burning is advertised to take place, the railroads run excursions, photographs are taken, and the same jubilee is indulged in that characterized the public hangings of one hundred years ago. There is, however, this difference: in those old days the multitude that stood by was permitted only to guy or jeer. The nineteenth century lynching mob cuts off ears, toes, and fingers, strips off flesh, and distributes portions of the body as souvenirs among the crowd. If the leaders of the mob are so minded, coal-oil is poured over the body and the victim is then roasted to death. This has been done in Texarkana and Paris, Tex., in Bardswell, Ky., and in Newman, Ga. In Paris the officers of the law delivered the prisoner to the mob. The mayor gave the school children a holiday and the railroads ran excursion trains so that the people might see a human being burned to death. In Texarkana, the year before, men and boys amused themselves by cutting off strips of flesh and thrusting knives into their helpless victim. At Newman, Ga., of the present year, the mob tried every conceivable torture to compel the victim to cry out and confess, before they set fire to the faggots that burned him. But their trouble was all in vain—he never uttered a cry, and they could not make him confess.

This condition of affairs were brutal enough and horrible enough if it were true that lynchings occurred only because of the commission of crimes against women—as is constantly declared by ministers, editors, lawyers, teachers, statesmen, and even by women themselves. It has been to the interest of those who did the lynching to blacken the good name of the helpless and defenseless victims of their hate. For this reason they publish at every possible opportunity this excuse for lynching, hoping thereby not only to palliate their own crime but at the same time to prove the negro a moral monster and unworthy of the respect and sympathy of the civilized world. But this alleged reason adds to the deliberate injustice of the mob's work. Instead of lynchings being caused by assaults upon women, the statistics show that not one-third of the victims of lynchings are even charged with such crimes. The Chicago *Tribune*, which publishes annually lynching statistics, is authority for the following:

In 1892, when lynching reached high-water mark, there were 241 persons lynched. The entire number is divided among the following States:

Alabama	22	Montana	4
Arkansas	25	New York	1
California	3	North Carolina	5
Florida	11	North Dakota	1
Georgia	17	Ohio	3
Idaho	8	South Carolina	5
Illinois	1	Tennessee	28
Kansas	3	Texas	15
Kentucky	9	Virginia	7
Louisiana	29	West Virginia	5
Maryland	1	Wyoming	9
Mississippi	16	Arizona Ter	3
Missouri	6	Oklahoma	2

Of this number, 160 were of negro descent. Four of them were lynched in New York, Ohio, and Kansas; the remainder were murdered in the South. Five of this number were females. The charges for which they were lynched cover a wide range. They are as follows:

Rape	46	Attempted rape	11
Murder	58	Suspected robbery	4
Rioting	3	Larceny	1
Race Prejudice	6	Self-defense	1
No cause given	4	Insulting women	2
Incendiarism	6	Desperadoes	6
Robbery	6	Fraud	1
Assault and battery	1	Attempted murder	2
No offense stated, boy and girl			2

In the case of the boy and girl above referred to, their father, named Hastings, was accused of the murder of a white man. His fourteen-year-old daughter and sixteen-year-old son were hanged and their bodies filled with bullets; then the father was also lynched. This occurred in November, 1892, at Jonesville, La.

Indeed, the record for the last twenty years shows exactly the same or a smaller proportion who have been charged with this horrible crime. Quite a number of the one-third alleged cases of assault that have been personally investigated by the writer have shown that there was no foundation in fact for the charges; yet the claim is not made that there were no real culprits among them. The negro has been too long associated with the white man not to have copied his vices as well as his virtues. But the negro resents and utterly repudiates the efforts to blacken his good name by asserting that assaults upon women are peculiar to his race. The negro has suffered far more from the commission of this crime against the women of his race by white men than the white race has ever suffered through *his* crimes. Very scant notice is taken of the matter when this is the condition of affairs. What becomes a crime deserving capital punishment when the tables are turned is a matter of small moment when the negro woman is the accusing party. . . .

(1900)

66 • *Zora Neale Hurston*

"SWEAT"

It was eleven o'clock of a Spring night in Florida. It was Sunday. Any other night, Delia Jones would have been in bed for two hours by this time. But she was a washwoman, and Monday morning meant a great deal to her. So she collected the soiled clothes on Saturday when she returned the clean things. Sunday night after church, she sorted and put the white things to soak. It saved her almost a half-day's start. A great hamper in the bedroom held the clothes that she brought home. It was so much neater than a number of bundles lying around.

She squatted on the kitchen floor beside the great pile of clothes, sorting them into small heaps according to color, and humming a song in a mournful key, but wondering through it all where Sykes, her husband, had gone with her horse and buckboard.

Just then something long, round, limp and black fell upon her shoulders and slithered to the floor beside her. A great terror took hold of her. It softened her knees and dried her mouth so that it was a full minute before she could cry out or move. Then she saw that it was the big bull whip her husband liked to carry when he drove.

She lifted her eyes to the door and saw him standing there bent over with laughter at her fright. She screamed at him.

"Sykes, what you throw dat whip on me like dat? You know it would skeer me—looks just like a snake, an you knows how skeered Ah is of snakes."

"Course Ah knowed it! That's how come Ah done it." He slapped his leg with his hand and almost rolled on the ground in his mirth. "If you such a big fool dat you got to have a fit over a earth worm or a string, Ah don't keer how bad Ah skeer you."

"You ain't got no business doing it. Gawd knows it's a sin. Some day Ah'm gointuh drop dead from some of yo' foolishness. 'Nother thing, where you been wid mah rig? Ah feeds dat pony. He ain't fuh you to be drivin' wid no bull whip."

"You sho' is one aggravatin' nigger woman!" he declared and stepped into the room. She resumed her work and did not answer him at once. "Ah done tole you time and again to keep them white folks' clothes outa dis house."

He picked up the whip and glared at her. Delia went on with her work. She went out into the yard and returned with a galvanized rub and set it on the washbench. She saw that Sykes had kicked all of the clothes together again, and now stood in her way truculently, his whole manner hoping, *praying*, for an argument. But she walked calmly around him and commenced to re-sort the things.

"Next time, Ah'm gointer kick'em outdoors," he threatened as he struck a match along the leg of his corduroy breeches.

Delia never looked up from her work, and her thin, stooped shoulders sagged further.

"Ah ain't for no fuss t'night Sykes. Ah just come from taking sacrament at the church house."

He snorted scornfully. "Yeah, you just come from de church house on a Sunday night, but heah you is gone to work on them clothes. You ain't nothing but a hypocrite. One of them amen-corner Christians— sing, whoop, and shout, then come home and wash white folks' clothes on the Sabbath."

He stepped roughly upon the whitest pile of things, kicking them helter-skelter as he crossed the room. His wife gave a little scream of dismay, and quickly gathered them together again.

"Sykes, you quit grindin' dirt into these clothes! How can Ah git through by Sat'day if Ah don't start on Sunday?"

"Ah don't keer if you never git through. Anyhow, Ah done promised Gawd and a couple of other men, Ah ain't gointer have it in mah house. Don't gimme no lip neither, else Ah'll throw 'em out and put mah fist up side yo' head to boot."

Delia's habitual meekness seemed to slip from her shoulders like a blown scarf. She was on her feet; her poor little body, her bare knuckly hands bravely defying the strapping hulk before her.

"Looka heah, Sykes, you done gone too fur. Ah been married to you fur fifteen years, and Ah been takin' in washin' fur fifteen years. Sweat, sweat, sweat! Work and sweat, cry and sweat, pray and sweat!"

"What's that got to do with me?" he asked brutally.

"What's it got to do with you, Sykes? Mah tub of suds is filled yo' belly with vittles more times than yo' hands is filled it. Mah sweat is done paid for this house and Ah reckon Ah kin keep on sweatin' in it."

She seized the iron skillet from the stove and struck a defensive pose, which act surprised him greatly, coming from her. It cowed him and he did not strike her as he usually did.

"Naw you won't," she panted, "that ole snaggle-toothed black woman you runnin' with ain't comin' heah to pile up on *mah* sweat and blood. You ain't paid for nothin' on this place, and Ah'm gointer stay right heah till Ah'm toted out foot foremost."

"Well, you better quit gittin' me riled up, else they'll be totin' you out sooner than you expect. Ah'm so tired of you Ah don't know whut to do. Gawd! How Ah hates skinny wimmen!"

A little awed by this new Delia, he sidled out of the door and slammed the back gate after him. He did not say where he had gone, but she knew too well. She knew very well that he would not return until nearly daybreak also. Her work over, she went on to bed but not to sleep at once. Things had come to a pretty pass!

She lay awake, gazing upon the debris that cluttered their matrimonial trail. Not an image left standing along the way. Anything like flowers had long ago been drowned in the salty stream that had been pressed from her heart. Her tears, her sweat, her blood. She had brought love to the union and he had brought a longing after the flesh. Two months after the wedding, he had given her the first brutal beating. She had the memory of his numerous trips to Orlando with all of his wages when he had returned to her penniless, even before the first year had passed. She was young and soft then, but now she thought of her knotty, muscled limbs, her harsh knuckly hands, and drew herself up into an unhappy little ball in the middle of the big feather bed. Too late now to hope for love, even if it were not Bertha it would be someone else. This case differed from the others only in that she was bolder than the others. Too late for everything except her little home. She had built it for her old days, and planted one by one the trees and flowers there. It was lovely to her, lovely.

Somehow, before sleep came, she found herself saying aloud: "Oh well, whatever goes over the Devil's back, is got to come under his belly. Sometime, or ruther, Sykes, like everybody else, is gointer reap his sowing." After that she was able to build a spiritual earthworks against her husband. His shells could no longer reach her. Amen. She went to sleep and slept until he announced his presence in bed by kicking her feet and rudely snatching the covers away.

"Gimme some kivah heah, an' git yo' damn foots over on yo' own side! Ah oughter mash you in yo' mouf fuh drawing dat skillet on me."

Delia went dear to the rail without answering him. A triumphant indifference to all that he was or did.

II

The week was as full of work for Delia as all other weeks, and Saturday found her behind her little pony, collecting and delivering clothes.

It was a hot, hot day near the end of July. The village men on Joe Clarke's porch even chewed cane listlessly. They did not hurl the cane-knots as usual. They let them dribble over the edge of the porch. Even conversation had collapsed under the heat.

"Heah come Delia Jones," Jim Merchant said, as the shaggy pony came 'round the bend of the road toward them. The rusty buckboard was heaped with baskets of crisp, clean laundry.

"Yep," Joe Lindsay agreed. "Hot or col', rain or shine, jes'ez reg'lar ez de weeks roll roun' Delia carries 'em an' fetches 'em on Sat'day."

"She better if she wanter eat," said Moss. "Syke Jones ain't wuth de shot an' powder hit would tek tuh kill 'em. Not to *bub* he ain't."

"He sho' ain't," Walter Thomas chimed in. "It's too bad, too, cause she wuz a right pretty li'l trick when he got huh. Ah'd uh mah'ied huh mahself if he hadnter beat me to it."

Delia nodded briefly at the men as she drove past.

"Too much knockin' will ruin *any* 'oman. He done beat huh 'nough tuh kill three women, let 'lone change they looks," said Elijah Moseley. "How Syke kin stommuck dat big black greasy Mogul he's layin' roun' wid, gits me. Ah swear dat eight-rock couldn't kiss a sardine can Ah done thowed out de back do' 'way las' yeah."

"Aw, she's fat, thass how come. He's allus been crazy 'bout fat women," put in Merchant. "He'd a' been tied up wid one long time ago if he could a' found one tuh have him. Did Ah tell yuh 'bout him come sidlin' roun' *mah* wife—bringin' her a basket uh peecans outa his yard fuh a present? Yessir, mah wife! She tol' him tuh take 'em right straight back home, 'cause Delia works so hard ovah dat washtub she reckon everything on de place taste lak sweat an' soapsuds. Ah jus' wisht Ah'd a' caught 'im 'roun' dere! Ah'd a' made his hips ketch on fiah down dat shell road."

"Ah know he done it, too. Ah sees 'im grinnin' at every 'oman dat passes," Walter Thomas said. "But even so, he useter car some mighty big hunks uh humble pie tuh git dat li'l 'oman he got. She wuz ez pritty ez a speckled pup! Dat wuz fifteen years ago. He

useter be so skeered uh losin' huh, she could make him do some parts of a husband's duty. Dey never wuz de same in de mind."

"There oughter be a law about him," said Lindsay. "He ain't fit tuh carry guts tuh a bear."

Clarke spoke for the first time. "Tain't no law on earth dat kin make a man be decent if it ain't in 'im. There's plenty men dat takes a wife lak dey do a joint uh sugar-cane. It's round, juicy an' sweet when dey gits it. But dey squeeze an' grind, squeeze an' grind an' wring tell dey wring every drop uh pleasure dat's in 'em out. When dey's satisfied dat dey is wrung dry, dey treats 'em jes' lak dey do a cane-chew. Dey thows 'em away. Dey knows whut dey is doin' while dey is at it, an' hates theirselves fuh it but they keeps on hangin' after huh tell she's empty. Den dey hates huh fuh bein' a cane-chew an' in de way."

"We oughter take Syke an' dat stray 'oman uh his'n down in Lake Howell swamp an' lay on de rawhide till they cain't say Lawd a' mussy. He allus wuz uh ovahbearin niggah, but since dat white 'oman from up north done teached 'im how to run a automobile, he done got too beggety to live—an' we oughter kill 'im," Old Man Anderson advised.

A grunt of approval went around the porch. But the heat was melting their civic virtue and Elijah Moseley began to bait Joe Clarke.

"Come on, Joe, git a melon outa dere an' slice it up for yo' customers. We'se all sufferin' wid de heat. De bear's done got *me*!"

"Thass right, Joe, a watermelon is jes' whut Ah needs tuh cure de eppizudicks," Walter Thomas joined forces with Moseley. "Come on dere, Joe. We all is steady customers an' you ain't set us up in a long time. Ah chooses dat long, bowlegged Floridy favorite."

"A god, an' be dough. You all gimme twenty cents and slice away," Clarke retorted. "Ah needs a col' slice m'self. Heah, everybody chip in. Ah'll lend y'all mah meat knife."

The money was all quickly subscribed and the huge melon brought forth. At that moment, Sykes and Bertha arrived. A determined silence fell on the porch and the melon was put away again.

Merchant snapped down the blade of his jackknife and moved toward the store door.

"Come on in, Joe, an' gimme a slab uh sow belly an' uh pound uh coffee—almost fuhgot 'twas Sat'day. Got to git on home." Most of the men left also.

Just then Delia drove past on her way home, as Sykes was ordering magnificently for Bertha. It pleased him for Delia to see.

"Git whutsoever yo' heart desires, Honey. Wait a minute, Joe. Give huh two bottles uh strawberry soda-water, uh quart parched ground-peas, an' a block uh chewin' gum."

With all this they left the store, with Sykes reminding Bertha that this was his town and she could have it if she wanted it.

The men returned soon after they left, and held their watermelon feast.

"Where did Sykes Jones git da 'oman from nohow?" Lindsay asked.

"Ovah Apopka. Guess dey musta been cleanin' out de town when she lef'. She don't look lak a thing but a hunk uh liver wid hair on it."

"Well, she sho' kin squall," Dave Carter contributed. "When she gits ready tuh laff, she jes' opens huh mouf an' latches it back tuh de las' notch. No ole granpa alligator down in Lake Bell ain't got nothin' on huh."

III

Bertha had been in town three months now. Sykes was still paying her room-rent at Della Lewis'—the only house in town that would have taken her in. Sykes took her frequently to Winter Park to 'stomps'. He still assured her that he was the swellest man in the state.

"Sho' you kin have dat li'l ole house soon's Ah git dat 'oman outa dere. Everything b'longs tuh me an' you sho' kin have it. Ah sho' 'bominates uh skinny 'oman. Lawdy, you sho' is got one portly shape on you! You kin git *anything* you wants. Dis is *mah* town an' you sho' kin have it."

Delia's work-worn knees crawled over the earth in Gethsemane and up the rocks of Calvary many, many times during these months. She avoided the villagers and meeting places in her efforts to be blind and deaf. But Bertha nullified this to a degree, by coming to Delia's house to call Sykes out to her at the gate.

Delia and Sykes fought all the time now with no peaceful interludes. They slept and ate in silence. Two or three times Delia had attempted a timid friendliness, but she was repulsed each time. It was plain that the breaches must remain agape.

The sun had burned July to August. The heat streamed down like a million hot arrows, smiting all things living upon the earth. Grass withered, leaves browned, snakes went blind in shedding and men and dogs went mad. Dog days!

Delia came home one day and found Sykes there before her. She wondered, but started to go on into the house without speaking, even though he was standing in the kitchen door and she must either stoop under his arm or ask him to move. He made no room for her. She noticed a soap box beside the steps, but paid no particular attention to it, knowing that he must have brought it there. As she was stooping to pass under his outstretched arm, he suddenly pushed her backward, laughingly.

"Look in de box dere Delia, Ah done brung yuh somethin'!"

She nearly fell upon the box in her stumbling, and when she saw what it held, she all but fainted outright.

"Syke! Syke, mah Gawd! You take dat rattlesnake 'way from heah! You *gottuh*. Oh, Jesus, have mussy!"

"Ah ain't got tuh do nuthin' uh de kin'—fact is Ah ain't got tuh do nothin' but die. Tain't no use uh you puttin' on airs makin' out lak you skeered uh dat snake—he's gointer stay right heah tell he die. He wouldn't bite me cause Ah knows how tuh handle 'im. Nohow he wouldn't risk breakin' out his fangs 'gin *yo* skinny laigs."

"Naw, now Syke, don't keep dat thing 'round tryin' tuh skeer me tuh death. You knows Ah'm even feared uh earth worms. Thass de biggest snake Ah evah did see. Kill 'im Syke, please."

"Doan ast me tuh do nothin' fuh yuh. Goin' 'round tryin' tuh be so damn asterperious. Naw, Ah ain't gonna kill it. Ah think uh damn sight mo' uh him dan you! Dat's a nice snake an' anybody doan lak 'im kin jes' hit de grit."

The village soon heard that Sykes had the snake, and came to see and ask questions.

"How de hen-fire did you ketch dat six-foot rattler, Syke?" Thomas asked.

"He's full uh frogs so he cain't hardly move, thass how Ah eased up on 'm. But Ah'm a snake charmer an' knows how tuh handle 'em. Shux, dat ain't nothin'. Ah could ketch one eve'y day if Ah so wanted tuh."

"Whut he needs is a heavy hick'ry club leaned real heavy on his head. Dat's de bes' way tuh charm a rattlesnake."

"Naw, Walt, y'all jes' don't understand dese diamon' backs lak Ah do," said Sykes in a superior tone of voice.

The village agreed with Walter, but the snake stayed on. His box remained by the kitchen door with its screen wire covering. Two or three days later it had digested its meal of frogs and literally came to life. It rattled at every movement in the kitchen or the yard. One day as Delia came down the kitchen steps she saw his chalky-white fangs curved like scimitars hung in the wire meshes. This time she did not run away with averted eyes as usual. She stood for a long time in the doorway in a red fury that grew bloodier for every second that she regarded the creature that was her torment.

That night she broached the subject as soon as Sykes sat down to the table.

"Sykes, Ah wants you tuh take dat snake 'way fum heah. You done starved me an' Ah put up widcher, you done beat me an Ah took dat, but you done kilt all mah insides bringin' dat varmint heah."

Sykes poured out a saucer full of coffee and drank it deliberately before he answered her.

"A whole lot Ah keer 'bout how you feels inside uh out. Dat snake ain't goin' no damn wheah till Ah gits ready fuh 'im tuh go. So fur as beatin' is concerned, yuh ain't took near all dat you gointer take ef yuh stay 'round *me.*"

Delia pushed back her plate and got up from the table. "Ah hates you, Sykes," she said calmly. "Ah hates you tuh de same degree dat Ah useter love yuh. Ah done took an' took till mah belly is full up tuh mah neck. Dat's de reason Ah got mah letter fum de church an' moved mah membership tuh Woodbridge—so Ah don't haftuh take no sacrament wid yuh. Ah don't wantuh see yuh 'round me atall. Lay 'round wid dat 'oman all yuh wants tuh, but gwan 'way fum me an' mah house. Ah hates yuh lak uh suck-egg dog."

Sykes almost let the huge wad of corn bread and collard greens he was chewing fall out of his mouth in amazement. He had a hard time whipping himself up to the proper fury to try to answer Delia.

"Well, Ah'm glad you does hate me. Ah'm sho' tiahed uh you hangin' ontuh me. Ah don't want yuh. Look at yuh stringey ole neck! Yo' rawbony laigs an' arms is enough tuh cut uh man tuh death. You looks jes' lak de devvul's doll-baby tuh *me.* You cain't hate me no worse dan Ah hates you. Ah been hatin' *you* fuh years."

"Yo' ole black hide don't look lak nothin' tuh me, but uh passle uh wrinkled up rubber, wid yo' big ole

yeahs flappin' on each side lak uh paih uh buzzard wings. Don't think Ah'm gointuh be run 'way fum mah house neither. Ah'm goin' tuh de white folks 'bout *you,* mah young man, de very nex' time you lay yo' han's on me. Mah cup is done run ovah." Delia said this with no signs of fear and Sykes departed from the house, threatening her, but made not the slightest move to carry out any of them.

That night he did not return at all, and the next day being Sunday, Delia was glad she did not have to quarrel before she hitched up her pony and drove the four miles to Woodbridge.

She stayed to the night service—"love feast"—which was very warm and full of spirit. In the emotional winds her domestic trials were borne far and wide so that she sang as she drove homeward,

> Jurden water, black an' col
> Chills de body, not de soul
> An' Ah wantah cross Jurden in uh calm time.

She came from the barn to the kitchen door and stopped.

"What's de mattah, ol' Satan, you ain't kickin' up yo' racket?" She addressed the snake's box. Complete silence. She went on into the house with a new hope in its birth struggles. Perhaps her threat to go to the white folks had frightened Sykes! Perhaps he was sorry! Fifteen years of misery and suppression had brought Delia to the place where she would hope *any-thing* that looked towards a way over or through her wall of inhibitions.

She felt in the match-safe behind the stove at once for a match. There was only one there.

"Dat niggah wouldn't fetch nothin' heah tuh save his rotten neck, but he kin run thew whut Ah brings quick enough. Now he done toted off nigh on tuh haff uh box uh matches. He done had dat 'oman heah in mah house, too."

Nobody but a woman could tell how she knew this even before she struck the match. But she did and it put her into a new fury.

Presently she brought in the tubs to put the white things to soak. This time she decided she need not bring the hamper out of the bedroom; she would go in there and do the sorting. She picked up the pot-bellied lamp and went in. The room was small and the hamper stood hard by the foot of the white iron bed. She could sit and reach through the bedposts—resting as she worked.

"Ah wantah cross Jurden in uh calm time." She was singing again. The mood of the "love feast" had returned. She threw back the lid of the basket almost gaily. Then, moved by both horror and terror, she sprang back toward the door. *There lay the snake in the basket!* He moved sluggishly at first, but even as she turned round and round, jumped up and down in an insanity of fear, he began to stir vigorously. She saw him pouring his awful beauty from the basket upon the bed, then she seized the lamp and ran as fast as she could to the kitchen. The wind from the open door blew out the light and the darkness added to her terror. She sped to the darkness of the yard, slamming the door after her before she thought to set down the lamp. She did not feel safe even on the ground, so she climbed up in the hay barn.

There for an hour or more she lay sprawled upon the hay a gibbering wreck.

Finally she grew quiet, and after that came coherent thought. With this stalked through her a cold, bloody rage. Hours of this. A period of introspection, a space of retrospection, then a mixture of both. Out of this an awful calm.

"Well, Ah done de bes' Ah could. If things ain't right, Gawd knows tain't mah fault."

She went to sleep—a twitch sleep—and woke up to a faint gray sky. There was a loud hollow sound below. She peered out. Sykes was at the wood-pile, demolishing a wire-covered box.

He hurried to the kitchen door, but hung outside there some minutes before he entered, and stood some minutes more inside before he closed it after him.

The gray in the sky was spreading. Delia descended without fear now, and crouched beneath the low bedroom window. The drawn shade shut out the dawn, shut in the night. But the thin walls held back no sound.

"Dat ol' scratch is woke up now!" She mused at the tremendous whirr inside, which every woodsman knows, is one of the sound illusions. The rattler is a ventriloquist. His whirr sounds to the right, to the left, straight ahead, behind, close under foot—everywhere but where it is. Woe to him who guesses wrong unless he is prepared to hold up his end of the argument! Sometimes he strikes without rattling at all.

Inside, Sykes heard nothing until he knocked a pot lid off the stove while trying to reach the match-safe in the dark. He had emptied his pockets at Bertha's.

The snake seemed to wake up under the stove and Sykes made a quick leap into the bedroom. In spite of the gin he had had, his head was clearing now.

"Mah Gawd!" he chattered, "ef Ah could on'y strack uh light!"

The rattling ceased for a moment as he stood paralyzed. He waited. It seemed that the snake waited also.

"Oh, fuh de light! Ah thought he'd be too sick"—Sykes was muttering to himself when the whirr began again, closer, right underfoot this time. Long before this, Sykes' ability to think had been flattened down to primitive instinct and he leaped—onto the bed.

Outside Delia heard a cry that might have come from a maddened chimpanzee, a stricken gorilla. All the terror, all the horror, all the rage that man possibly could express, without a recognizable human sound.

A tremendous stir inside there, another series of animal screams, the intermittent whirr of the reptile. The shade torn violently down from the window, letting in the red dawn, a huge brown hand seizing the window stick, great dull blows upon the wooden floor punctuating the gibberish of sound long after the rattle of the snake had abruptly subsided. All this Delia could see and hear from her place beneath the window, and it made her ill. She crept over to the four-o'clocks and stretched herself on the cool earth to recover.

She lay there. "Delia, Delia!" She could hear Sykes calling in a most despairing tone as one who expected no answer. The sun crept on up, and he called. Delia could not move—her legs had gone flabby. She never moved, he called, and the sun kept rising.

"Mah Gawd!" She heard him moan, "Mah Gawd fum Heben!" She heard him stumbling about and got up from her flower-bed. The sun was growing warm. As she approached the door she heard him call out hopefully, "Delia, is dat you Ah heah?"

She saw him on his hands and knees as soon as she reached the door. He crept an inch or two toward her—all that he was able, and she saw his horribly swollen neck and his one open eye shining with hope. A surge of pity too strong to support bore her away from that eye that must, could not, fail to see the tubs. He would see the lamp. Orlando with its doctors was too far. She could scarcely reach the chinaberry tree, where she waited in the growing heat while inside she knew the cold river was creeping up and up to extinguish that eye which must know by now that she knew.

(1926)

67 • *Maya Angelou*

FROM *I KNOW WHY THE CAGED BIRD SINGS*

"What you looking at me for?
I didn't come to stay . . . "

I hadn't so much forgot as I couldn't bring myself to remember. Other things were more important.

"What you looking at me for?
I didn't come to stay . . . "

Whether I could remember the rest of the poem or not was immaterial. The truth of the statement was like a wadded-up handkerchief, sopping wet in my fists, and the sooner they accepted it the quicker I could let my hands open and the air would cool my palms.

"What you looking at me for . . . ?"

The children's section of the Colored Methodist Episcopal Church was wiggling and giggling over my well-known forgetfulness.

The dress I wore was lavender taffeta, and each time I breathed it rustled, and now that I was sucking in air to breathe out shame it sounded like crepe paper on the back of hearses.

As I'd watched Momma put ruffles on the hem and cute little tucks around the waist, I knew that once I put it on I'd look like a movie star. (It was silk and that made up for the awful color.) I was going to look like one of the sweet little white girls who were everybody's dream of what was right with the world. Hanging softly over the black Singer sewing machine, it looked like magic, and when people saw me wearing it they were going to run up to me and say, "Marguerite [sometimes it was 'dear Marguerite'], forgive us, please, we didn't know who you were," and I would

answer generously, "No, you couldn't have known. Of course I forgive you."

Just thinking about it made me go around with angel's dust sprinkled over my face for days. But Easter's early morning sun had shown the dress to be a plain ugly cut-down from a white woman's once-was-purple throwaway. It was old-lady-long too, but it didn't hide my skinny legs, which had been greased with Blue Seal Vaseline and powdered with the Arkansas red clay. The age-faded color made my skin look dirty like mud, and everyone in church was looking at my skinny legs.

Wouldn't they be surprised when one day I woke out of my black ugly dream, and my real hair, which was long and blond, would take the place of the kinky mass that Momma wouldn't let me straighten? My light-blue eyes were going to hypnotize them, after all the things they said about "my daddy must of been a Chinaman" (I thought they meant made out of china, like a cup) because my eyes were so small and squinty. Then they would understand why I had never picked up a Southern accent, or spoke the common slang, and why I had to be forced to eat pigs' tails and snouts. Because I was really white and because a cruel fairy stepmother, who was understandably jealous of my beauty, had turned me into a too-big Negro girl, with nappy black hair, broad feet and a space between her teeth that would hold a number-two pencil.

"What you looking . . ." The minister's wife leaned toward me, her long yellow face full of sorry. She whispered, "I just come to tell you, it's Easter Day." I repeated, jamming the words together, "Ijustcometo tellyouit'sEasterDay," as low as possible. The giggles hung in the air like melting clouds that were waiting to rain on me. I held up two fingers, close to my chest, which meant that I had to go to the toilet, and tiptoed toward the rear of the church. Dimly, somewhere over my head, I heard ladies saying, "Lord bless the child," and "Praise God." My head was up and my eyes were open, but I didn't see anything. Halfway down the aisle, the church exploded with "Were you there when they crucified my Lord?" and I tripped over a foot stuck out from the children's pew. I stumbled and started to say something, or maybe to scream, but a green persimmon, or it could have been a lemon, caught me between the legs and squeezed. I tasted the sour on my tongue and felt it in the back of my mouth. Then before I reached the door, the sting was burning down my legs and into my Sunday socks. I tried to hold, to squeeze it back, to keep it from speeding, but when I reached the church porch I knew I'd have to let it go, or it would probably run right back up to my head and my poor head would burst like a dropped watermelon, and all the brains and spit and tongue and eyes would roll all over the place. So I ran down into the yard and let it go. I ran, peeing and crying, not toward the toilet out back but to our house. I'd get a whipping for it, to be sure, and the nasty children would have something new to tease me about. I laughed anyway, partially for the sweet release; still, the greater joy came not only from being liberated from the silly church but from the knowledge that I wouldn't die from a busted head.

If growing up is painful for the Southern Black girl, being aware of her displacement is the rust on the razor that threatens the throat.

It is an unnecessary insult.

(1969)

68 • Combahee River Collective*

"A BLACK FEMINIST STATEMENT"

We are a collective of Black feminists who have been meeting together since 1974.[1] During that time we have been involved in the process of defining and clarifying our politics, while at the same time doing political work within our own group and in coalition with other progressive organizations and movements. The most general statement of our politics at the present time would be that we are actively committed to struggling against racial, sexual, heterosexual, and class oppression and see as our particular task the development of integrated analysis and practice based upon the fact that the major systems of oppression are interlocking. The synthesis of these oppressions creates the conditions of our lives. As Black women we see Black feminism as the logical political movement to combat the manifold and simultaneous oppressions that all women of color face.

We will discuss four major topics in the paper that follows: (1) the genesis of contemporary black feminism; (2) what we believe, i.e., the specific province of our politics; (3) the problems in organizing Black

*The Combahee River Collective is a Black feminist group in Boston whose name comes from the guerrilla action conceptualized and led by Harriet Tubman on June 2, 1863, in the Port Royal region of South Carolina. This action freed more than 750 slaves and is the only military campaign in American history planned and led by a woman.

From *Capitalist Patriarchy and the Case for Socialist Feminism*, ed. by Zillah Eisenstein, New York, Monthly Review Press, © 1978. Reprinted by permission of Zillah Eisenstein.

feminists, including a brief herstory of our collective; and (4) Black feminist issues and practice.

1. THE GENESIS OF CONTEMPORARY BLACK FEMINISM

Before looking at the recent development of Black feminism we would like to affirm that we find our origins in the historical reality of Afro-American women's continuous life-and-death struggle for survival and liberation. Black women's extremely negative relationship to the American political system (a system of white male rule) has always been determined by our membership in two oppressed racial and sexual castes. As Angela Davis points out in "Reflections on the Black Woman's Role in the Community of Slaves," Black women have always embodied, if only in their physical manifestation, an adversary stance to white male rule and have actively resisted its inroads upon them and their communities in both dramatic and subtle ways. There have always been Black women activists—some known, like Sojourner Truth, Harriet Tubman, Frances E. W. Harper, Ida B. Wells Barnett, and Mary Church Terrell, and thousands upon thousands unknown—who had a shared awareness of how their sexual identity combined with their racial identity to make their whole life situation and the focus of their political struggles unique. Contemporary Black feminism is the outgrowth of countless generations of personal sacrifice, militancy, and work by our mothers and sisters.

A Black feminist presence has evolved most obviously in connection with the second wave of the American women's movement beginning in the late 1960s. Black, other Third World, and working women have been involved in the feminist movement from its start, but both outside reactionary forces and racism and elitism within the movement itself have served to obscure our participation. In 1973 Black feminists, primarily located in New York, felt the necessity of forming a separate Black feminist group. This became the National Black Feminist Organization (NBFO).

Black feminist politics also have an obvious connection to movements for Black liberation, particularly those of the 1960s and 1970s. Many of us were active in those movements (civil rights, Black nationalism,

the Black Panthers), and all of our lives were greatly affected and changed by their ideology, their goals, and the tactics used to achieve their goals. It was our experience and disillusionment within these liberation movements, as well as experience on the periphery of the white male left, that led to the need to develop a politics that was antiracist, unlike those of white women, and antisexist, unlike those of Black and white men.

There is also undeniably a personal genesis for Black feminism, that is, the political realization that comes from the seemingly personal experiences of individual Black women's lives. Black feminists and many more Black women who do not define themselves as feminists have all experienced sexual oppression as a constant factor in our day-to-day existence. As children we realized that we were different from boys and that we were treated differently. For example, we were told in the same breath to be quiet both for the sake of being "ladylike" and to make us less objectionable in the eyes of white people. As we grew older we became aware of the threat of physical and sexual abuse by men. However, we had no way of conceptualizing what was so apparent to us; what we *knew* was really happening.

Black feminists often talk about their feelings of craziness before becoming conscious of the concepts of sexual politics, patriarchal rule, and most importantly, feminism, the political analysis and practice that we women use to struggle against our oppression. The fact that racial politics and indeed racism are pervasive factors in our lives did not allow us, and still does not allow most Black women, to look more deeply into our own experiences and, from that sharing and growing consciousness, to build a politics that will change our lives and inevitably end our oppression. Our development must also be tied to the contemporary economic and political position of Black people. The post World War II generation of Black youth was the first to be able to minimally partake of certain educational and employment options, previously closed completely to Black people. Although our economic position is still at the very bottom of the American capitalistic economy, a handful of us have been able to gain certain tools as a result of tokenism in education and employment which potentially enable us to more effectively fight our oppression.

A combined antiracist and antisexist position drew us together initially, and as we developed politically we addressed ourselves to hetero-sexism and economic oppression under capitalism.

2. WHAT WE BELIEVE

Above all else, our politics initially sprang from the shared belief that Black women are inherently valuable, that our liberation is a necessity not as an adjunct to somebody else's but because of our need as human persons for autonomy. This may seem so obvious as to sound simplistic, but it is apparent that no other ostensibly progressive movement has ever considered our specific oppression as a priority or worked seriously for the ending of that oppression. Merely naming the pejorative stereotypes attributed to Black women (e.g. mammy, matriarch, Sapphire, whore, bulldagger), let alone cataloguing the cruel, often murderous, treatment we receive, indicates how little value has been placed upon our lives during four centuries of bondage in the Western hemisphere. We realize that the only people who care enough about us to work consistently for our liberation is us. Our politics evolve from a healthy love for ourselves, our sisters and our community which allows us to continue our struggle and work.

This focusing upon our own oppression is embodied in the concept of identity politics. We believe that the most profound and potentially the most radical politics come directly out of our own identity, as opposed to working to end somebody else's oppression. In the case of Black women this is a particularly repugnant, dangerous, threatening, and therefore revolutionary concept because it is obvious from looking at all the political movements that have preceded us that anyone is more worthy of liberation than ourselves. We reject pedestals, queen-hood, and walking ten paces behind. To be recognized as human, levelly human, is enough.

We believe that sexual politics under patriarchy is as pervasive in Black women's lives as are the politics of class and race. We also often find it difficult to separate race from class from sex oppression because in our lives they are most often experienced simultaneously. We know that there is such a thing as racial-sexual oppression which is neither solely racial nor solely sexual, e.g., the history of rape of Black women by white men as a weapon of political repression.

Although we are feminists and lesbians, we feel solidarity with progressive Black men and do not advocate the fractionalization that white women who are separatists demand. Our situation as Black people necessitates that we have solidarity around the fact of race, which white women of course do not need to have with white men, unless it is their negative solidarity as racial oppressors. We struggle together with Black men against racism, while we also struggle with Black men about sexism.

We realize that the liberation of all oppressed peoples necessitates the destruction of the political–economic systems of capitalism and imperialism as well as patriarchy. We are socialists because we believe the work must be organized for the collective benefit of those who do the work and create the products, and not for the profit of the bosses. Material resources must be equally distributed among those who create these resources. We are not convinced, however, that a socialist revolution that is not also a feminist and antiracist revolution will guarantee our liberation. We have arrived at the necessity for developing an understanding of class relationships that takes into account the specific class position of Black women who are generally marginal in the labor force, while at this particular time some of us are temporarily viewed as doubly desirable tokens at white-collar and professional levels. We need to articulate the real class situation of persons who are not merely raceless, sexless workers, but for whom racial and sexual oppression are significant determinants in their working/economic lives. Although we are in essential agreement with Marx's theory as it applied to the very specific economic relationships he analyzed, we know that his analysis must be extended further in order for us to understand our specific economic situation as Black women.

A political contribution which we feel we have already made is the expansion of the feminist principle that the personal is political. In our consciousness-raising sessions, for example, we have in many ways gone beyond white women's revelations because we are dealing with the implications of race and class as well as sex. Even our Black women's style of talking/testifying in Black language about what we have experienced has a resonance that is both cultural and political. We have spent a great deal of energy delving into the cultural and experiential nature of our oppression out of necessity because none of these matters has ever been looked at before. No one before has ever examined the multilayered texture of Black women's lives. An example of this kind of revelation/conceptualization occurred at a meeting as we discussed the ways in which our early intellectual interests had been attacked by our peers, particularly Black males. We discovered that all of us, because we were "smart" had also been considered "ugly", *i.e.*, "smart-ugly." "Smart-ugly" crystallized the way in which most of us had been forced to develop our intellects at great cost to our "social" lives. The sanctions in the Black and white communities against Black women thinkers is comparatively much higher than for white women, particularly ones from the educated middle and upper classes.

As we have already stated, we reject the stance of lesbian separatism because it is not a viable political analysis or strategy for us. It leaves out far too much and far too many people, particularly Black men, women, and children. We have a great deal of criticism and loathing for what men have been socialized to be in this society: what they support, how they act, and how they oppress. But we do not have the misguided notion that it is their maleness, per se—i.e., their biological maleness—that makes them what they are. As Black women we find any type of biological determinism a particularly dangerous and reactionary basis upon which to build a politic. We must also question whether lesbian separatism is an adequate and progressive political analysis and strategy, even for those who practice it, since it so completely denies any but the sexual sources of women's oppression, negating the facts of class and race.

3. PROBLEMS IN ORGANIZING BLACK FEMINISTS

During our years together as a Black feminist collective we have experienced success and defeat, joy and pain, victory and failure. We have found that it is very difficult to organize around Black feminist issues, difficult even to announce in certain contexts that we *are* Black feminists. We have tried to think about the

reasons for our difficulties, particularly since the white women's movement continues to be strong and to grow in many directions. In this section we will discuss some of the general reasons for the organizing problems we face and also talk specifically about the stages in organizing our own collective.

The major source of difficulty in our political work is that we are not just trying to fight oppression on one front or even two, but instead to address a whole range of oppressions. We do not have racial, sexual, heterosexual, or class privilege to rely upon, nor do we have even the minimal access to resources and power that groups who possess any one of these types of privilege have.

The psychological toll of being a Black woman and the difficulties this presents in reaching political consciousness and doing political work can never be underestimated. There is a very low value placed upon Black women's psyches in this society, which is both racist and sexist. As an early group member once said, "We are all damaged people merely by virtue of being Black women." We are dispossessed psychologically and on every other level, and yet we feel the necessity to struggle to change the condition of all Black women. In "A Black Feminist's Search for Sisterhood," Michele Wallace arrives at this conclusion:

"We exist as women who are Black who are feminists, each stranded for the moment, working independently because there is not yet an environment in this society remotely congenial to our struggle—because, being on the bottom, we would have to do what no one else has done: we would have to fight the world."[2]

Wallace is pessimistic but realistic in her assessment of Black feminists' position, particularly in her allusion to the nearly classic isolation most of us face. We might use our position at the bottom, however, to make a clear leap into revolutionary action. If Black women were free, it would mean that everyone else would have to be free since our freedom would necessitate the destruction of all the systems of oppression.

Feminism is, nevertheless, very threatening to the majority of Black people because it calls into question some of the most basic assumptions about our existence, i.e., that sex should be a determinant of power relationships. Here is the way male and female voices were defined in a Black nationalist pamphlet from the early 1970's.

"We understand that it is and has been traditional that the man is the head of the house. He is the leader of the house/nation because his knowledge of the world is broader, his awareness is greater, his understanding is fuller and his application of this information is wiser . . . After all, it is only reasonable that the man be the head of the house because he is able to defend and protect the development of his home . . . Women cannot do the same things as men—they are made by nature to function differently. Equality of men and women is something that cannot happen even in the abstract world. Men are not equal to other men, i.e. ability, experience or even understanding. The value of men and women can be seen as in the value of gold and silver—they are not equal but both have great value. We must realize that men and women are a complement to each other because there is no house/family without a man and his wife. Both are essential to the development of any life."[3]

The material conditions of most Black women would hardly lead them to upset both economic and sexual arrangements that seem to represent some stability in their lives. Many Black women have a good understanding of both sexism and racism, but because of the everyday constrictions of their lives cannot risk struggling against them both.

The reaction of Black men to feminism has been notoriously negative. They are, of course, even more threatened than Black women by the possibility that Black feminists might organize around our own needs. They realize that they might not only lose valuable and hardworking allies in their struggles but that they might also be forced to change their habitually sexist ways of interacting with and oppressing Black women. Accusations that Black feminism divides the Black struggle are powerful deterrents to the growth of an autonomous Black women's movement.

Still, hundreds of women have been active at different times during the three-year existence of our group. And every Black woman who came, came out of a strongly-felt need for some level of possibility that did not previously exist in her life.

When we first started meeting early in 1974 after the NBFO first eastern regional conference, we did not have a strategy for organizing, or even a focus. We just wanted to see what we had. After a period of months of not meeting, we began to meet again late in the year and started doing an intense variety of consciousness-raising. The overwhelming feeling that we had is that after years and years we had finally found each other. Although we were not doing political work as a group, individuals continued their involvement in Lesbian politics, sterilization abuse and abortion rights work, Third World Women's International Women's Day activities, and support activity for the trials of Dr. Kenneth Edelin, Joan Little, and Inez Garcia. During our first summer, when membership had dropped off considerably, those of us remaining devoted serious discussion to the possibility of opening a refuge for battered women in a Black community. (There was no refuge in Boston at that time.) We also decided around that time to become an independent collective since we had serious disagreements with NBFO's bourgeois-feminist stance and their lack of a clear political focus.

We also were contacted at that time by socialist feminists, with whom we had worked on abortion rights activities, who wanted to encourage us to attend the National Socialist Feminist Conference in Yellow Springs. One of our members did attend and despite the narrowness of the ideology that was promoted at that particular conference, we became more aware of the need for us to understand our own economic situation and to make our own economic analysis.

In the fall, when some members returned, we experienced several months of comparative inactivity and internal disagreements which were first conceptualized as a Lesbian–straight split but which were also the result of class and political differences. During the summer those of us who were still meeting had determined the need to do political work and to move beyond consciousness-raising and serving exclusively as an emotional support group. At the beginning of 1976, when some of the women who had not wanted to do political work and who also had voiced disagreements stopped attending of their own accord, we again looked for a focus. We decided at that time, with the addition of new members, to become a study group. We had always shared our reading with each other, and some of us had written papers on Black feminism for group discussion a few months before this decision was made. We began functioning as a study group and also began discussing the possibility of starting a Black feminist publication. We had a retreat in the late spring which provided a time for both political discussion and working out interpersonal issues. Currently we are planning to gather together a collection of Black feminist writing. We feel that it is absolutely essential to demonstrate the reality of our politics to other Black women and believe that we can do this through writing and distributing our work. The fact that individual Black feminists are living in isolation all over the country, that our own numbers are small, and that we have some skills in writing, printing, and publishing makes us want to carry out these kinds of projects as a means of organizing Black feminists as we continue to do political work in coalition with other groups.

4. BLACK FEMINIST ISSUES AND PROJECTS

During our time together we have identified and worked on many issues of particular relevance to Black women. The inclusiveness of our politics makes us concerned with any situation that impinges upon the lives of women, Third World and working people. We are of course particularly committed to working on those struggles in which race, sex and class are simultaneous factors in oppression. We might, for example, become involved in workplace organizing at a factory that employs Third World women or picket a hospital that is cutting back on already inadequate health care to a Third World community, or set up a rape crisis center in a Black neighborhood. Organizing around welfare and daycare concerns might also be a focus. The work to be done and the countless issues that this work represents merely reflect the pervasiveness of our oppression.

Issues and projects that collective members have actually worked on are sterilization abuse, abortion rights, battered women, rape and health care. We have also done many workshops and educationals on Black feminism on college campuses, at women's conferences, and most recently for high school women.

One issue that is of major concern to us and that we have begun to publicly address is racism in the white women's movement. As Black feminists we are made constantly and painfully aware of how little effort white women have made to understand and combat their racism, which requires among other things that they have a more than superficial comprehension of race, color, and black history and culture. Eliminating racism in the white women's movement is by definition work for white women to do, but we will continue to speak to and demand accountability on this issue.

In the practice of our politics we do not believe that the end always justifies the means. Many reactionary and destructive acts have been done in the name of achieving "correct" political goals. As feminists we do not want to mess over people in the name of politics. We believe in collective process and a nonhierarchical distribution of power within our own group and in our vision of a revolutionary society. We are committed to a continual examination of our politics as they develop through criticism and self-criticism as an essential aspect of our practice. In her introduction to *Sisterhood is Powerful* Robin Morgan writes:

"I haven't the faintest notion what possible revolutionary role white heterosexual men could fulfill, since they are the very embodiment of reactionary-vested-interest-power."

As Black feminists and Lesbians we know that we have a very definite revolutionary task to perform and we are ready for the lifetime of work and struggle before us.

(1977)

NOTES

1. This statement is dated April 1977.
2. Michele Wallace, "A Black Feminist's Search for Sisterhood," The Village Voice, 28 July 1975, pp. 6–7.
3. Mumininas of Committee for Unified Newark, Mwanamke Mwananchi (The Nationalist Woman), Newark, N.J., ©1971, pp. 4–5.

69 • *Mitsuye Yamada*

"INVISIBILITY IS AN UNNATURAL DISASTER: REFLECTIONS OF AN ASIAN AMERICAN WOMAN"

Last year for the Asian segment of the Ethnic American Literature course I was teaching, I selected a new anthology entitled *Aiiieeeee!* compiled by a group of outspoken Asian American writers. During the discussion of the long but thought-provoking introduction to this anthology, one of my students blurted out that she was offended by its militant tone and that as a white person she was tired of always being blamed for the oppression of all the minorities. I noticed several of her classmates' eyes nodding in tacit agreement. A discussion of the "militant" voices in some of the other writings we had read in the course ensued. Surely, I pointed out, some of these other writings have been just as, if not more, militant as the words in this introduction? Had they been offended by those also but failed to express their feelings about them? To my surprise, they said they were not offended by any of the Black American, Chicano or American Indian writings, but were hard-pressed to explain why when I asked for an explanation. A little further discussion revealed that they "understood" the anger expressed by the Black and Chicanos and they "empathized" with the frustrations and sorrow expressed by the American Indian. But the Asian Americans??

Then finally, one student said it for all of them: "It made me angry. *Their* anger made *me* angry, because I didn't even know the Asian Americans felt oppressed. I didn't expect their anger."

At this time I was involved in an academic due process procedure begun as a result of a grievance I had filed the previous semester against the administrators at my college. I had filed a grievance for violation of my rights as a teacher who had worked in the district for almost eleven years. My student's remark "Their anger made me angry] . . . I didn't expect their anger," explained for me the reactions of some of my own colleagues as well as the reactions of the administrators during those previous months. The grievance procedure was a time-consuming and emotionally draining process, but the basic principle was too important for me to ignore. That basic principle was that I, an individual teacher, do have certain rights which are given and my superiors cannot, should not, violate them with impunity. When this was pointed out to them, however, they responded with shocked surprise that I, of all people, would take them to task for violation of what was clearly written policy in our college district. They all seemed to exclaim, "We don't understand this; this is so uncharacteristic of her; she seemed such a nice person, so polite, so obedient, so non-trouble-making." What was even more surprising was once they were forced to acknowledge that I was determined to start the due process action, they assumed I was not doing it on my own. One of the administrators suggested someone must have pushed me into this, undoubtedly some of "those feminists" on our campus, he said wryly.

In this age when women are clearly making themselves visible on all fronts, I, an Asian American woman, am still functioning as a "front for those feminists" and therefore invisible. The realization of this sinks in slowly. Asian Americans as a whole are finally coming to claim their own, demanding that they be

Reprinted by permission of Mitsuye Yamada from *This Bridge Called My Back: Writings by Radical Women of Color*, eds. Cherríe Moraga and Gloria Anzaldúa. New York: Kitchen Table Women of Color Press, 1981, 1983.

included in the multicultural history of our country. I like to think, in spite of my administrator's myopia, that the most stereotyped minority of them all, the Asian American woman, is just now emerging to become part of that group. It took forever. Perhaps it is important to ask ourselves why it took so long. We should ask ourselves this question just when we think we are emerging as a viable minority in the fabric of our society. I should add to my student's words, "because I didn't even know they felt oppressed," that it took this long because we Asian American women have not admitted to ourselves that we were oppressed. We, the visible minority that is invisible.

I say this because until a few years ago I have been an Asian American woman working among non-Asians in an educational institution where most of the decision-makers were men[1]; an Asian American woman thriving under the smug illusion that I was *not* the stereotypic image of the Asian woman because I had a career teaching English in a community college. I did not think anything assertive was necessary to make my point. People who know me, I reasoned, the ones who count, know who I am and what I think. Thus, even when what I considered a veiled racist remark was made in a casual social setting, I would "let it go" because it was pointless to argue with people who didn't even know their remark was racist. I had supposed that I was practicing passive resistance while being stereotyped, but it was so passive no one noticed I was resisting; it was so much my expected role that it ultimately rendered me invisible.

My experience leads me to believe that contrary to what I thought, I had actually been contributing to my own stereotyping. Like the hero in Ralph Ellison's novel *The Invisible Man*, I had become invisible to white Americans, and it clung to me like a bad habit. Like most bad habits, this one crept up on me because I took it in minute doses like Mithradates' poison and my mind and body adapted so well to it I hardly noticed it was there.

For the past eleven years I have busied myself with the usual chores of an English teacher, a wife of a research chemist, and a mother of four rapidly growing children. I hadn't even done much to shatter this particular stereotype: the middle class woman happy to be bringing home the extra income and quietly fitting into the man's world of work. When the Asian American woman is lulled into believing that people perceive her as being different from other Asian women (the submissive, subservient, ready-to-please, easy-to-get-along-with Asian woman), she is kept comfortably content with the state of things. She becomes ineffectual in the milieu in which she moves. The seemingly apolitical middle class woman and the apolitical Asian woman constituted a double invisibility.

I had created an underground culture of survival for myself and had become in the eyes of others the person I was trying not to be. Because I was permitted to go to college, permitted to take a stab at a career or two along the way, given "free choice" to marry and have a family, given a "choice" to eventually do both, I had assumed I was more or less free, not realizing that those who are free make and take choices; they do not choose from options proffered by "those out there."

I, personally, had not "emerged" until I was almost fifty years old. Apparently through a long conditioning process, I had learned how *not* to be seen for what I am. A long history of ineffectual activities had been, I realize now, initiation rites toward my eventual invisibility. The training begins in childhood; and for women and minorities, whatever is started in childhood is continued throughout their adult lives. I first recognized just how invisible I was in my first real confrontation with my parents a few years after the outbreak of World War II.

During the early years of the war, my older brother, Mike, and I left the concentration camp in Idaho to work and study at the University of Cincinnati. My parents came to Cincinnati soon after my father's release from Internment Camp (these were POW camps to which many of the Issei[2] men, leaders in their communities, were sent by the FBI), and worked as domestics in the suburbs. I did not see them too often because by this time I had met and was much influenced by a pacifist who was out on a "furlough" from a conscientious objectors' camp in Trenton, North Dakota. When my parents learned about my "boy friend" they were appalled and frightened. After all, this was the period when everyone in the country was expected to

---

[1] It is hoped this will change now that a black woman is Chancellor of our college district.

[2] Issei—Immigrant Japanese, living in the U.S.

be one-hundred percent behind the war effort, and the Nisei[3] boys who had volunteered for the Armed Forces were out there fighting and dying to prove how American we really were. However, during interminable arguments with my father and overheard arguments between my parents, I was devastated to learn they were not so much concerned about my having become a pacifist, but they were more concerned about the possibility of my marrying one. They were understandably frightened (my father's prison years of course were still fresh on his mind) about repercussions on the rest of the family. In an attempt to make my father understand me, I argued that even if I didn't marry him, I'd still be a pacifist; but my father reassured me that it was "all right" for me to be a pacifist because as a Japanese national and a "girl" *it didn't make any difference to anyone.* In frustration I remember shouting, "But can't you see, *I'm* philosophically committed to the pacifist cause," but he dismissed this with "In my college days we used to call philosophy, foolosophy," and that was the end of that. When they were finally convinced I was not going to marry "my pacifist," the subject was dropped and we never discussed it again.

As if to confirm my father's assessment of the harmlessness of my opinions, my brother Mike, an American citizen, was suddenly expelled from the University of Cincinnati while I, "an enemy alien," was permitted to stay. We assumed that his stand as a pacifist, although he was classified a 4-F because of his health, contributed to his expulsion. We were told the Air Force was conducting sensitive wartime research on campus and requested his removal, but they apparently felt my presence on campus was not as threatening.

I left Cincinnati in 1945, hoping to leave behind this and other unpleasant memories gathered there during the war years, and plunged right into the politically active atmosphere at New York University where students, many of them returning veterans, were continuously promoting one cause or other by making speeches in Washington Square, passing out petitions, or staging demonstrations. On one occasion, I tagged along with a group of students who took a train to Albany to demonstrate on the steps of the State Capitol. I think I was the only Asian in this group of predominantly Jewish students from NYU. People who passed us were amused and shouted "Go home and grow up." I suppose Governor Dewey, who refused to see us, assumed we were a group of adolescents without a cause as most college students were considered to be during those days. It appears they weren't expecting any results from our demonstration. There were no newspersons, no security persons, no police. No one tried to stop us from doing what we were doing. We simply did "our thing" and went back to our studies until next time, and my father's words were again confirmed: it made no difference to anyone, being a young student demonstrator in peacetime, 1947.

Not only the young, but those who feel powerless over their own lives know what it is like not to make a difference on anyone or anything. The poor know it only too well, and we women have known it since we were little girls. The most insidious part of this conditioning process, I realize now, was that we have been trained not to expect a response in ways that mattered. We may be listened to and responded to with placating words and gestures, but our psychological mind set has already told us time and again that we were born into a readymade world into which we must fit ourselves, and that many of us do it very well.

This mind set is the result of not believing that the political and social forces affecting our lives are determined by some person, or a group of persons, probably sitting behind a desk or around a conference table.

Just recently I read an article about "the remarkable track record of success" of the Nisei in the United States. One Nisei was quoted as saying he attributed our stamina and endurance to our ancestors whose characters had been shaped, he said, by their living in a country which has been constantly besieged by all manner of natural disasters, such as earthquakes and hurricanes. He said the Nisei has inherited a steely will, a will to endure and hence, to survive.

This evolutionary explanation disturbs me, because it equates the "act of God" (i.e. natural disasters) to the "act of man" (i.e., the war, the evacuation). The former is not within our power to alter, but the latter, I should think, is. By putting the "acts of God" on par with the acts of man, we shrug off personal responsibilities.

I have, for too long a period of time accepted the opinion of others (even though they were directly affecting my life) as if they were objective events totally out of my control. Because I separated such opinions from the persons who were making them, I accepted

---

[3]Nisei—Second generation Japanese, born in the U.S.

them the way I accepted natural disasters; and I endured them as inevitable. I have tried to cope with people whose points of view alarmed me in the same way that I had adjusted to natural phenomena, such as hurricanes, which plowed into my life from time to time. I would readjust my dismantled feelings in the same way that we repaired the broken shutters after the storm. The Japanese have an all-purpose expression in their language for this attitude of resigned acceptance: "Shikataganai." "It can't be helped." "There's nothing I can do about it." It is said with the shrug of the shoulders and tone of finality, perhaps not unlike the "those-were-my-orders" tone that was used at the Nuremberg trials. With all the sociological studies that have been made about the causes of the evacuations of the Japanese Americans during World War II, we should know by now that "they" knew that the West Coast Japanese Americans would go without too much protest, and of course, "they" were right, for most of us (with the exception of those notable few), resigned to our fate, albeit bewildered and not willingly. We were not perceived by our government as responsive Americans; we were objects that happened to be standing in the path of the storm.

Perhaps this kind of acceptance is a way of coping with the "real" world. One stands against the wind for a time, and then succumbs eventually because there is no point to being stubborn against all odds. The wind will not respond to entreaties anyway, one reasons; one should have sense enough to know that. I'm not ready to accept this evolutionary reasoning. It is too rigid for me; I would like to think that my new awareness is going to make me more visible than ever, and to allow me to make some changes in the "man made disaster" I live in at the present time. Part of being visible is refusing to separate the actors from their actions, and demanding that they be responsible for them.

By now, riding along with the minorities' and women's movements, I think we are making a wedge into the main body of American life, but people are still looking right through and around us, assuming we are simply tagging along. Asian American women still remain in the background and we are heard but not really listened to. Like Musak, they think we are piped into the airwaves by someone else. We must remember that one of the most insidious ways of keeping women and minorities powerless is to let them only talk about harmless and inconsequential subjects, or let them speak freely and not listen to them with serious intent.

We need to raise our voices a little more, even as they say to us "This is so uncharacteristic of you." To finally recognize our own invisibility is to finally be on the path toward visibility. Invisibility is not a natural state for anyone.

(1979)

"I WALK IN THE HISTORY OF MY PEOPLE"

There are women locked in my joints
for refusing to speak to the police
My red blood full of those
arrested, in flight, shot
My tendons stretched brittle with anger
do not look like white roots of peace
In my marrow are hungry faces who live on land
    the whites don't want
In my marrow women who walk 5 miles every day
    for water

In my marrow the swollen faces of my people who
    are not allowed
to hunt
to move
to be

In the scars on my knee you can see children torn
    from their families
bludgeoned into government schools
You can see through the pins in my bones that we
    are prisoners of a long war

My knee is so badly wounded no one will look at it
The pus of the past oozes from every pore

The infection has gone on for at least 300 years
My sacred beliefs have been made pencils, names
    of cities, gas stations
My knee is wounded so badly that I limp
    constantly
Anger is my crutch
I hold myself upright with it
My knee is wounded
see
How I Am Still Walking

(1981)

71 • Alice Walker

"WOMANIST"

Womanist 1. From *womanish*. (Opp. of "girlish," i.e., frivolous, irresponsible, not serious.) A black feminist or feminist of color. From the black folk expression of mothers to female children, "You acting womanish," i.e., like a woman. Usually referring to outrageous, audacious, courageous or *willful* behavior. Wanting to know more and in greater depth than is considered "good" for one. Interested in grown-up doings. Acting grown up. Being grown up. Interchangeable with another black folk expression: "You trying to be grown." Responsible. In charge. *Serious*.

* * *

2. *Also:* A woman who loves other women, sexually and/or nonsexually. Appreciates and prefers women's culture, women's emotional flexibility (values tears as natural counterbalance of laughter), and women's strength. Sometimes loves individual men, sexually and/or nonsexually. Committed to survival and

wholeness of entire people, male *and* female. Not a separatist, except periodically, for health. Traditionally universalist, as in: "Mama, why are we brown, pink, and yellow, and our cousins are white, beige, and black?" Ans.: "Well, you know the colored race is just like a flower garden, with every color flower represented." Traditionally capable, as in: "Mama, I'm walking to Canada and I'm taking you and a bunch of other slaves with me." Reply: "It wouldn't be the first time."

* * *

3. Loves music. Loves dance. Loves the moon. *Loves* the Spirit. Loves love and food and roundness. Loves struggle. *Loves* the Folk. Loves herself. *Regardless*.

* * *

4. Womanist is to feminist as purple to lavender.

(1983)

"THE MASTER'S TOOLS WILL NEVER DISMANTLE THE MASTER'S HOUSE"

I agreed to take part in a New York University Institute for the Humanities conference a year ago, with the understanding that I would be commenting upon papers dealing with the role of difference within the lives of American women: difference of race, sexuality, class, and age. The absence of these considerations weakens any feminist discussion of the personal and the political.

It is a particular academic arrogance to assume any discussion of feminist theory without examining our many differences, and without a significant input from poor women, Black and Third World women, and lesbians. And yet, I stand here as a Black lesbian feminist, having been invited to comment within the only panel at this conference where the input of Black feminists and lesbians is represented. What this says about the vision of this conference is sad, in a country where racism, sexism, and homophobia are inseparable. To read this program is to assume that lesbian and Black women have nothing to say about existentialism, the erotic, women's culture and silence, developing feminist theory, or heterosexuality and power. And what does it mean in personal and political terms when even the two Black women who did present here were literally found at the last hour? What does it mean when the tools of a racist patriarchy are used to examine the fruits of that same patriarchy? It means that only the most narrow perimeters of change are possible and allowable.

The absence of any consideration of lesbian consciousness or the consciousness of Third World women leaves a serious gap within this conference and within the papers presented here. For example, in a paper on material relationships between women, I was conscious of an either/or model of nurturing which totally dismissed my knowledge as a Black lesbian. In this paper there was no examination of mutuality between women, no systems of shared support, no interdependence as exists between lesbians and women-identified women. Yet it is only in the patriarchal model of nurturance that women "who attempt to emancipate themselves pay perhaps too high a price for the results," as this paper states.

For women, the need and desire to nurture each other is not pathological but redemptive, and it is within that knowledge that our real power is rediscovered. It is this real connection which is so feared by a patriarchal world. Only within a patriarchal structure is maternity the only social power open to women.

Interdependency between women is the way to a freedom which allows the *I* to *be*, not in order to be used, but in order to be creative. This is a difference between the passive *be* and the active *being*.

Advocating the mere tolerance of difference between women is the grossest reformism. It is a total denial of the creative function of difference in our lives. Difference must be not merely tolerated, but seen as a fund of necessary polarities between which our creativity can spark like a dialectic. Only then does the necessity for interdependency become unthreatening. Only within that interdependency of different strengths, acknowledged and equal, can the power to seek new ways of being in the world generate, as well as the courage and sustenance to act where there are no charters.

Within the interdependence of mutual (nondominant) differences lies that security which enables us to descend into the chaos of knowledge and return with true visions of our future, along with the concomitant power to effect those changes which can bring that future into being. Difference is that raw and powerful connection from which our personal power is forged.

As women, we have been taught either to ignore our differences, or to view them as causes for separation and suspicion rather than as forces for change. Without community there is no liberation, only the most vulnerable and temporary armistice between an individual and her oppression. But community must not mean a shedding of our differences, nor the pathetic pretense that these differences do not exist.

Those of us who stand outside the circle of this society's definition of acceptable women; those of us who have been forged in the crucibles of difference—those of us who are poor, who are lesbians, who are Black, who are older—know that *survival is not an academic skill.* It is learning how to stand alone, unpopular and sometimes reviled, and how to make common cause with those others identified as outside the structures in order to define and seek a world in which we can all flourish. It is learning how to take our differences and make them strengths. *For the master's tools will never dismantle the master's house.* They may allow us temporarily to beat him at his own game, but they will never enable us to bring about genuine change. And this fact is only threatening to those women who still define the master's house as their only source of support.

Poor women and women of Color know there is a difference between the daily manifestations of marital slavery and prostitution because it is our daughters who line 42nd Street. If white American feminist theory need not deal with the differences between us, and the resulting difference in our oppressions, then how do you deal with the fact that the women who clean your houses and tend your children while you attend conferences on feminist theory are, for the most part, poor women and women of Color? What is the theory behind racist feminism?

In a world of possibility for us all, our personal visions help lay the groundwork for political action. The failure of academic feminists to recognize difference as

a crucial strength is a failure to reach beyond the first patriarchal lesson. In our world, divide and conquer must become define and empower.

Why weren't other women of Color found to participate in this conference? Why were two phone calls to me considered a consultation? And I the only possible source of names of Black feminists? And although the Black panelist's paper ends on an important and powerful connection of love between women, what about interracial cooperation between feminists who don't love each other?

In academic feminist circles, the answer to these questions is often, "We did not know who to ask." But that is the same evasion of responsibility, the same cop-out, that keeps Black women's art out of women's exhibitions, Black women's work out of most feminist publications except for the occasional "Special Third World Women's Issue," and Black women's texts off your reading lists. But as Adrienne Rich pointed out in a recent talk, white feminists have educated themselves about such an enormous amount over the past ten years, how come you haven't also educated yourselves about Black women and the differences between us—white and Black—when it is key to our survival as a movement?

Women of today are still being called upon to stretch across the gap of male ignorance and to educate men as to our existence and our needs. This is an old and primary tool of all oppressors to keep the oppressed occupied with the master's concerns. Now we hear that it is the task of women of Color to educate white women—in the face of tremendous resistance—as to our existence, our differences, our relative roles in our joint survival. This is a diversion of energies and a tragic repetition of racist patriarchal thought.

Simone de Beauvoir once said: "It is in the knowledge of the genuine conditions of our lives that we must draw our strength to live and our reasons for acting."

Racism and homophobia are real conditions of all our lives in this place and time. *I urge each one of us here to reach down into that deep place of knowledge inside herself and touch that terror and loathing of any difference that lives there. See whose face it wears.* Then the personal as the political can begin to illuminate all our choices.

(1984)

73 • *Gloria Anzaldúa*

FROM *BORDERLANDS/LA FRONTERA*
The New Mestiza

THE HOMELAND, AZTLÁN
EL OTRO MÉXICO

El otro México que acá hemos construído
el espacio es lo que ha sido
territorio nacional.
Este es el esfuerzo de todos nuestros hermanos
y latinoamericanos que han sabido
progressar.

—Los Tigres del Norte

"The *Aztecas del norte* . . . compose the largest single tribe or nation of Anishinabeg (Indians) found in the United States today. . . . Some call themselves Chicanos and see themselves as people whose true homeland is Aztlán [the U.S. Southwest]."

Wind tugging at my sleeve
feet sinking into the sand
I stand at the edge where earth touches ocean
where the two overlap
a gentle coming together
at other times and places a violent clash.

Across the border in Mexico
  stark silhouette of houses gutted by waves,
    cliffs crumbling into the sea,
      silver waves marbled with spume
        gashing a hole under the border fence.
      Miro el mar atacar
    la cerca en Border Field Park
    con sus buchones de agua,
an Easter Sunday resurrection
of the brown blood in my veins.

Oigo el llorido del mar, el respiro del aire,
  my heart surges to the beat of the sea.
  In the gray haze of the sun
    the gulls' shrill cry of hunger,
      the tangy smell of the sea seeping into me.

    I walk   through the hole in the fence
      to the other side.
  Under my fingers I feel the gritty wire
  rusted by 139 years
    of the salty breath of the sea.

Beneath the iron sky
Mexican children kick their soccer ball across,
run after it, entering the U.S.

    I press my hand to the steel curtain—
  chainlink fence crowned with rolled barbed
    wire—
  rippling from the sea where Tijuana touches
    San Diego
  unrolling over mountains
      and plains
          and deserts,
this "Tortilla Curtain" turning into *el río Grande*
  flowing down to the flatlands
    of the Magic Valley of South Texas
  its mouth emptying into the Gulf.

1,950 mile-long open wound
      dividing a *pueblo,* a culture,
        running down the length of my body,
          staking fence rods in my flesh,
      splits me   splits me
        me raja   me raja

This is my home
this thin edge of
    barbwire.
But the skin of the earth is seamless.
The sea cannot be fenced,
el mar does not stop at borders.
To show the white man what she thought of his
        arrogance,
   Yemayá blew that wire fence down.

   This land was Mexican once,
     was Indian always
      and is.
       And   will be again.

Yo soy un puente tendido
  del mundo gabacho al del mojado,
lo pasado me estira pa' 'trás
  y lo presente pa' 'delante,
Que la Virgen de Guadalupe me cuide
Ay ay ay, soy mexicana de este lado.

The U.S.–Mexican border *es una herida abierta* where the Third World grates against the first and bleeds. And before a scab forms it hemorrhages again, the lifeblood of two worlds merging to form a third country—a border culture. Borders are set up to define the places that are safe and unsafe, to distinguish *us* from *them*. A border is a dividing line, a narrow strip along a steep edge. A borderland is a vague and undetermined place created by the emotional residue of an unnatural boundary. It is in a constant state of transition. The prohibited and forbidden are its inhabitants. *Los atravesados* live here: the squint-eyed, the perverse, the queer, the troublesome, the mongrel, the mulato, the half-breed, the half dead; in short, those who cross over, pass over, or go through the confines of the "normal." Gringos in the U.S. Southwest consider the inhabitants of the borderlands transgressors, aliens—whether they possess documents or not, whether they're Chicanos, Indians or Blacks. Do not enter, trespassers will be raped, maimed, strangled, gassed, shot. The only "legitimate" inhabitants are those in power, the whites and those who align themselves with whites. Tension grips the inhabitants of the borderlands like a virus. Ambivalence and unrest reside there and death is no stranger.

LA CONCIENCIA DE LA MESTIZA
TOWARDS A NEW CONSCIOUSNESS

Por la mujer de mi raza
hablará el espíritu.

José Vasconcelos, Mexican philosopher, envisaged *una raza mestiza, una mezcla de razas afines, una raza de color—la primera raza síntesis del globo.* He called it a cosmic race, *la raza cósmica,* a fifth race embracing the four major races of the world. Opposite to the theory of the pure Aryan, and to the policy of racial purity that white America practices, his theory is one of inclusivity. At the confluence of two or more genetic streams, with chromosomes constantly "crossing over," this mixture of races, rather than resulting in an inferior being, provides hybrid progeny, a mutable, more malleable species with a rich gene pool. From this racial, ideological, cultural and biological cross-pollinization, an "alien" consciousness is presently in the making—a new *mestiza* consciousness, *una conciencia de mujer.* It is a consciousness of the Borderlands.

Una lucha de fronteras/A Struggle of Borders
Because I, a *mestiza,*
continually walk out of one culture
and into another,
because I am in all cultures at the same time,
alma entre dos mundos, tres, cuatro,
me zumba la cabeza con lo contradictorio.
Estoy norteada por todas las voces que me hablan
simultáneamente.

The ambivalence from the clash of voices results in mental and emotional states of perplexity. Internal strife results in insecurity and indecisiveness. The *mestiza's* dual or multiple personality is plagued by psychic restlessness.

In a constant state of mental nepantilism, an Aztec word meaning torn between ways, *la mestiza* is a product of the transfer of the cultural and spiritual values of one group to another. Being tricultural, monolingual, bilingual, or multilingual, speaking a patois, and in a state of perpetual transition, the *mestiza* faces the dilemma of the mixed breed: which collectivity does the daughter of a darkskinned mother listen to?

El choque de un alma atrapado entre el mundo del espíritu y el mundo de la técnica a veces la deja entullada.

Cradled in one culture, sandwiched between two cultures, straddling all three cultures and their value systems, *la mestiza* undergoes a struggle of flesh, a struggle of borders, an inner war. Like all people, we perceive the version of reality that our culture communicates. Like others having or living in more than one culture, we get multiple, often opposing messages. The coming together of two self-consistent but habitually incompatible frames of reference causes *un choque,* a cultural collision.

Within us and within *la cultura chicana,* commonly held beliefs of the white culture attack commonly held beliefs of the Mexican culture, and both attack commonly held beliefs of the indigenous culture. Subconsciously, we see an attack on ourselves and our beliefs as a threat and we attempt to block with a counterstance.

But it is not enough to stand on the opposite river bank, shouting questions, challenging patriarchal, white conventions. A counterstance locks one into a duel of oppressor and oppressed; locked in mortal combat, like the cop and the criminal, both are reduced to a common denominator of violence. The counterstance refutes the dominant culture's views and beliefs, and, for this, it is proudly defiant. All reaction is limited by, and dependent on, what it is reacting against. Because the counter-stance stems from a problem with authority—outer as well as inner—it's a step towards liberation from cultural domination. But it is not a way of life. At some point, on our way to a new consciousness, we will have to leave the opposite bank, the split between the two mortal combatants somehow healed so that we are on both shores at once and, at once, see through serpent and eagle eyes. Or perhaps we will decide to disengage from the dominant culture, write it off altogether as a lost cause, and cross the border into a wholly new and separate territory. Or we might go another route. The possibilities are numerous once we decide to act and not react.

A TOLERANCE FOR AMBIGUITY

These numerous possibilities leave *la mestiza* floundering in uncharted seas. In perceiving conflicting information and points of view, she is subjected to a swamping of her psychological borders. She has discovered that she can't hold concepts or ideas in rigid boundaries. The borders and walls that are supposed to keep the undesirable ideas out are entrenched habits and patterns of behavior; these habits and patterns are the enemy within. Rigidity means death. Only by remaining flexible is she able to stretch the psyche horizontally and vertically. *La mestiza* constantly has to shift out of habitual formations; from convergent thinking, analytical reasoning that tends to use rationality to move toward a single goal (a Western mode), to divergent thinking, characterized by movement away from set patterns and goals and toward a more whole perspective, one that includes rather than excludes.

The new *mestiza* copes by developing a tolerance for contradictions, a tolerance for ambiguity. She learns to be an Indian in Mexican culture, to be Mexican from an Anglo point of view. She learns to juggle cultures. She has a plural personality, she operates in a pluralistic mode—nothing is thrust out, the good the bad and the ugly, nothing rejected, nothing abandoned. Not only does she sustain contradictions, she turns the ambivalence into something else.

She can be jarred out of ambivalence by an intense, and often painful, emotional event which inverts or resolves the ambivalence. I'm not sure exactly how. The work takes place underground—subconsciously. It is work that the soul performs. That focal point or fulcrum, that juncture where the *mestiza* stands, is where phenomena tend to collide. It is where the possibility of uniting all that is separate occurs. This assembly is not one where severed or separated pieces merely come together. Nor is it a balancing of opposing powers. In attempting to work out a synthesis, the self has added a third element which is greater than the sum of its severed parts. That third element is a new consciousness—a *mestiza* consciousness—and though it is a source of intense pain, its energy comes from continual creative motion that keeps breaking down the unitary aspect of each new paradigm.

En unas pocas centurias, the future will belong to the *mestiza.* Because the future depends on the breaking down of paradigms, it depends on the straddling of two or more cultures. By creating a new mythos—that is, a change in the way we perceive reality, the way we see ourselves, and the ways we behave—*la mestiza* creates a new consciousness.

The work of *mestiza* consciousness is to break down the subject–object duality that keeps her a prisoner and to show in the flesh and through the images in her work how duality is transcended. The answer to the problem between the white race and the colored, between males and females, lies in healing the split that originates in the very foundation of our lives, our culture, our languages, our thoughts. A massive uprooting of dualistic thinking in the individual and collective consciousness is the beginning of a long struggle, but one that could, in our best hopes, bring us to the end of rape, of violence, of war.

LA ENCRUCIJADA/THE CROSSROADS

A chicken is being sacrificed
    at a crossroads, a simple mound of earth
a mud shrine for *Esbu*,
    Yoruba god of indeterminacy,
who blesses her choice of path.
    She begins her journey.

Su cuerpo es una bocacalle. La mestiza has gone from being the sacrificial goat to becoming the officiating priestess at the crossroads.

As a *mestiza* I have no country, my homeland cast me out; yet all countries are mine because I am every woman's sister or potential lover. (As a lesbian I have no race, my own people disclaim me; but I am all races because there is the queer of me in all races.) I am cultureless because, as a feminist, I challenge the collective cultural/religious male-derived beliefs of Indo-Hispanics and Anglos; yet I am cultured because I am participating in the creation of yet another culture, a new story to explain the world and our participation in it, a new value system with images and symbols that connect us to each other and to the planet. *Soy un amasamiento*, I am an act of kneading, of uniting and joining that not only has produced both a creature of darkness and a creature of light, but also a creature that questions the definitions of light and dark and gives them new meanings.

We are the people who leap in the dark, we are the people on the knees of the gods. In our very flesh, (r)evolution works out the clash of cultures. It makes us crazy constantly, but if the center holds, we've made some kind of evolutionary step forward. *Nuestra alma el trabajo*, the opus, the great alchemical work; spiritual *mestizaje*, a "morphogenesis," an inevitable unfolding. We have become the quickening serpent movement.

Indigenous like corn, like corn, the *mestiza* is a product of crossbreeding, designed for preservation under a variety of conditions. Like an ear of corn—a female seed-bearing organ—the *mestiza* is tenacious, tightly wrapped in the husks of her culture. Like kernels she clings to the cob; with thick stalks and strong brace roots, she holds tight to the earth—she will survive the crossroads.

(1987)

"DEMARGINALIZING THE INTERSECTION OF RACE AND SEX: A BLACK FEMINIST CRITIQUE OF ANTIDISCRIMINATION DOCTRINE, FEMINIST THEORY, AND ANTIRACIST POLITICS"

One of the very few Black women's studies books is entitled *All the Women Are White, All the Blacks Are Men, but Some of Us Are Brave*.[1] I have chosen this title as a point of departure in my efforts to develop a Black feminist criticism because it sets forth a problematic consequence of the tendency to treat race and gender as mutually exclusive categories of experience and analysis.[2] . . . I want to examine how this tendency is perpetuated by a single-axis framework that is dominant in anti-discrimination law and that is also reflected in feminist theory and antiracist politics.

I will center Black women in this analysis in order to contrast the multidimensionality of Black women's experience with the single-axis analysis that distorts these experiences. Not only will this juxtaposition reveal how Black women are theoretically erased, it will also illustrate how this framework imports its own theoretical limitations that undermine efforts to broaden feminist and antiracist analyses. With Black women as the starting point, it becomes more apparent how dominant conceptions of discrimination condition us to think about subordination as disadvantage occurring along a single categorical axis. I want to suggest further that this single-axis framework erases Black women in the conceptualization, identification and remediation of race and sex discrimination by limiting inquiry to the experiences of otherwise-privileged members of the group. In other words, in race indiscrimination cases, discrimination tends to be viewed in terms of sex- or class-privileged Blacks; in sex discrimination cases, the focus is on race- and class-privileged women.

This focus on the most privileged group members marginalizes those who are multiply-burdened and obscures claims that cannot be understood as resulting from discrete sources of discrimination. I suggest further that this focus on otherwise-privileged group members creates a distorted analysis of racism and sexism because the operative conceptions of race and sex become grounded in experiences that actually represent only a subset of a much more complex phenomenon.

After examining the doctrinal manifestations of this single-axis framework, I will discuss how it contributes to the marginalization of Black women in feminist theory and in antiracist politics. I argue that Black women are sometimes excluded from feminist theory and antiracist policy discourse because both are

Reprinted from "Demarginalizing the Intersection of Race and Sex: A Black Feminist Critique of Antidiscrimination Doctrine, Feminist Theory, and Antiracist Politics" by Kimberlé Crenshaw in *Feminism in the Law: Theory, Practice and Criticism* (vol 1989): 139–167. Copyright 1989 *The University of Chicago Legal Forum.*

predicated on a discrete set of experiences that often does not accurately reflect the interaction of race and gender. These problems of exclusion cannot be solved simply by including Black women within an already established analytical structure. Because the intersectional experience is greater than the sum of racism and sexism, any analysis that does not take intersectionality into account cannot sufficiently address the particular manner in which Black women are subordinated. Thus, for feminist theory and antiracist policy discourse to embrace the experiences and concerns of Black women, the entire framework that has been used as a basis for translating "women's experience" or "the Black experience" into concrete policy demands must be rethought and recast.

As examples of theoretical and political developments that miss the mark with respect to Black women because of their failure to consider intersectionality, I will briefly discuss the feminist critique of rape and separate spheres ideology. . . .

THE ANTIDISCRIMINATION FRAMEWORK

A. THE EXPERIENCE OF INTERSECTIONALITY AND THE DOCTRINAL RESPONSE

One way to approach the problem of intersectionality is to examine how courts frame and interpret the stories of Black women plaintiffs. While I cannot claim to know the circumstances underlying the cases that I will discuss, I nevertheless believe that the way courts interpret claims made by Black women is itself part of Black women's experience and, consequently, a cursory review of cases involving Black female plaintiffs is quite revealing. To illustrate the difficulties inherent in judicial treatment of intersectionality, I will consider three Title VII[3] cases: *DeGraffenreid v General Motors*,[4] *Moore v Hughes Helicopters*[5] and *Payne v Travenol*.[6]

1. DeGraffenreid v General Motors.
In *DeGraffenreid*, five Black women brought suit against General Motors, alleging that the employer's seniority system perpetuated the effects of past discrimination against Black women. Evidence adduced at trial revealed that General Motors simply did not hire Black women prior to 1964 and that all of the Black women hired after 1970 lost their jobs in a seniority-based

layoff during a subsequent recession. The district court granted summary judgment for the defendant, rejecting the plaintiff's attempt to bring a suit not on behalf of Blacks or women, but specifically on behalf of Black women. The court stated:

> [P]laintiffs have failed to cite any decisions which have stated that Black women are a special class to be protected from discrimination. The Court's own research has failed to disclose such a decision. The plaintiffs are clearly entitled to a remedy if they have been discriminated against. However, they should not be allowed to combine statutory remedies to create a new "super-remedy" which would give them relief beyond what the drafters of the relevant statutes intended. Thus, this lawsuit must be examined to see if it states a cause of action for race discrimination, sex discrimination, or alternatively either, but not a combination of both.[7]

Although General Motors did not hire Black women prior to 1964, the court noted that "General Motors has hired . . . female employees for a number of years prior to the enactment of the Civil Rights Act of 1964."[8] Because General Motors did hire women—albeit *white women*—during the period that no Black women were hired, there was, in the court's view, no sex discrimination that the seniority system could conceivably have perpetuated.

After refusing to consider the plaintiffs' sex discrimination claim, the court dismissed the race discrimination complaint and recommended its consolidation with another case alleging race discrimination against the same employer.[9] The plaintiffs responded that such consolidation would defeat the purpose of their suit since theirs was not purely a race claim, but an action brought specifically on behalf of Black women alleging race *and* sex discrimination. . . .

. . .

2. Moore v Hughes Helicopters, Inc.
Moore v Hughes Helicopters, Inc.[10] presents a different way in which courts fail to understand or recognize Black women's claims. *Moore* is typical of a number of cases in which courts refused to certify Black females as class representatives in race *and* sex discrimination actions.[11] In *Moore*, the plaintiff alleged that the employer, Hughes Helicopter, practiced race and sex discrimination in promotions to upper-level craft positions and to supervisory jobs. Moore introduced statistical evidence

establishing a significant disparity between men and women, and somewhat less of a disparity between Black and white men in supervisory jobs.[12]

Affirming the district court's refusal to certify Moore as the class representative in the sex discrimination complaint on behalf of all women at Hughes, the Ninth Circuit noted approvingly:

> . . . Moore had never claimed before the EEOC that she was discriminated against as a female, *but only* as a Black female. . . . [T]his raised serious doubts as to Moore's ability to adequately represent white female employees.[13]

The curious logic in *Moore* reveals not only the narrow scope of antidiscrimination doctrine and its failure to embrace intersectionality, but also the centrality of white female experiences in the conceptualization of gender discrimination. One inference that could be drawn from the court's statement that Moore's complaint did not entail a claim of discrimination "against females" is that discrimination against Black females is something less than discrimination against females. More than likely, however, the court meant to imply that Moore did not claim that *all* females were discriminated against *but only* Black females. But even thus recast, the court's rationale is problematic for Black women. The court rejected Moore's bid to represent all females apparently because her attempt to specify her race was seen as being at odds with the standard allegation that the employer simply discriminated "against females."

The court failed to see that the absence of a racial referent does not necessarily mean that the claim being made is a more inclusive one. A white woman claiming discrimination against females may be in no better position to represent all women than a Black woman who claims discrimination as a Black female and wants to represent all females. The court's preferred articulation of "against females" is not necessarily more inclusive—it just appears to be so because the racial contours of the claim are not specified.

The court's preference for "against females" rather than "against Black females" reveals the implicit grounding of white female experiences in the doctrinal conceptualization of sex discrimination. For white women, claiming sex discrimination is simply a statement that but for gender, they would not have been disadvantaged. For them there is no need to specify

discrimination as *white* females because their race does not contribute to the disadvantage for which they seek redress. The view of discrimination that is derived from this grounding takes race privilege as a given.

Discrimination against a white female is thus the standard sex discrimination claim; claims that diverge from this standard appear to present some sort of hybrid claim. More significantly, because Black females' claims are seen as hybrid, they sometimes cannot represent those who may have "pure" claims of sex discrimination. The effect of this approach is that even though a challenged policy or practice may clearly discriminate against all females, the fact that it has particularly harsh consequences for Black females places Black female plaintiffs at odds with white females.

. . .

3. Payne v Travenol. Black female plaintiffs have also encountered difficulty in their efforts to win certification as class representatives in some race discrimination actions. This problem typically arises in cases where statistics suggest significant disparities between Black and white workers and further disparities between Black men and Black women. Courts in some cases[14] have denied certification based on logic that mirrors the rationale in *Moore:* The sex disparities between Black men and Black women created such conflicting interests that Black women could not possibly represent Black men adequately. In one such case, *Payne v Travenol,*[15] two Black female plaintiffs alleging race discrimination brought a class action suit on behalf of all Black employees at a pharmaceutical plant.[16] The court refused, however, to allow the plaintiffs to represent Black males and granted the defendant's request to narrow the class to Black women only. Ultimately, the district court found that there had been extensive racial discrimination at the plant and awarded back pay and constructive seniority to the class of Black female employees. But, despite its finding of general race discrimination, the court refused to extend the remedy to Black men for fear that their conflicting interests would not be adequately addressed.[17]

. . .

In sum, several courts have proved unable to deal with intersectionality, although for contrasting reasons. In *DeGraffenreid*, the court refused to recognize the possibility of compound discrimination against Black women and analyzed their claim using the employment of white women as the historical base. As a consequence, the employment experiences of white women obscured the distinct discrimination that Black women experienced.

Conversely, in *Moore*, the court held that a Black woman could not use statistics reflecting the overall sex disparity in supervisory and upper-level labor jobs because she had not claimed discrimination as a women, but "only" as a Black woman. The court would not entertain the notion that discrimination experienced by Black women is indeed sex discrimination—provable through disparate impact statistics on women.

Finally, courts, such as the one in *Travenol*, have held that Black women cannot represent an entire class of Blacks due to presumed class conflicts in cases where sex additionally disadvantaged Black women. As a result, in the few cases where Black women are allowed to use overall statistics indicating racially disparate treatment Black men may not be able to share in the remedy.

Perhaps it appears to some that I have offered inconsistent criticisms of how Black women are treated in antidiscrimination law: I seem to be saying that in one case, Black women's claims were rejected and their experiences obscured because the court refused to acknowledge that the employment experience of Black women can be distinct from that of white women, while in other cases, the interests of Black women are harmed because Black women's claims were viewed as so distinct from the claims of either white women or Black men that the court denied to Black females representation of the larger class. It seems that I have to say that Black women are the same and harmed by being treated differently, or that they are different and harmed by being treated the same. But I cannot say both.

This apparent contradiction is but another manifestation of the conceptual limitations of the single-issue analyses that intersectionality challenges. The point is that Black women can experience discrimination in any number of ways and that the contradiction arises from our assumptions that their claims of exclusion must be unidirectional. Consider an analogy to traffic in an intersection, coming and going in all four directions. Discrimination, like traffic through an intersection, may flow in one direction, and it may flow in another. If an accident happens in an intersection, it can be caused by cars traveling from any number of directions and, sometimes, from all of them. Similarly, if a Black women is harmed because she is in the intersection, her injury could result from sex discrimination or race discrimination.

. . .

To bring this back to a non-metaphorical level, I am suggesting that Black women can experience discrimination in ways that are both similar to and different from those experienced by white women and Black men. Black women sometimes experience discrimination in ways similar to white women's experiences; sometimes they share very similar experiences with Black men. Yet often they experience double-discrimination—the combined effects of practices which discriminate on the basis of race, and on the basis of sex. And sometimes, they experience discrimination as Black women—not the sum of race and sex discrimination, but as Black women.

. . .

B. THE SIGNIFICANCE OF DOCTRINAL TREATMENT OF INTERSECTIONALITY

DeGraffenreid, Moore and *Travenol* are doctrinal manifestations of a common political and theoretical approach to discrimination which operates to marginalize Black women. Unable to grasp the importance of Black women's intersectional experiences, not only courts, but feminist and civil rights thinkers as well have treated Black women in ways that deny both the unique compoundedness of their situation and the centrality of their experiences to the larger classes of women and Blacks. Black women are regarded either as too much like women or Blacks and the compounded nature of their experience is absorbed into the collective experiences of either group or as too different, in which case Black women's Blackness or femaleness sometimes has placed their needs and perspectives at the margin of the feminist and Black liberationist agendas.

While it could be argued that this failure represents an absence of political will to include Black women, I believe that it reflects an uncritical and disturbing acceptance of dominant ways of thinking about discrimination. Consider first the definition of discrimination that seems to be operative in antidiscrimination law: Discrimination which is wrongful proceeds from the identification of a specific class or category; either a discriminator intentionally identifies this category, or a process is adopted which somehow disadvantages all members of this category.[18] According to the dominant view, a discriminator treats all people within a race or sex category similarly. Any significant experiential or statistical variation within this group suggests either that the group is not being discriminated against or that conflicting interests exist which defeat any attempts to bring a common claim. Consequently, one generally cannot combine these categories. Race and sex, moreover, become significant only when they operate to explicitly *disadvantage* the victims; because the *privileging* of whiteness or maleness is implicit, it is generally not perceived at all.

Underlying this conception of discrimination is a view that the wrong which antidiscrimination law addresses is the use of race or gender factors to interfere with decisions that would otherwise be fair or neutral. This process-based definition is not grounded in a bottom-up commitment to improve the substantive conditions for those who are victimized by the interplay of numerous factors. Instead, the dominant message of antidiscrimination law is that it will regulate only the limited extent to which race or sex interferes with the process of determining outcomes. This narrow objective is facilitated by the top-down strategy of using a singular "but for" analysis to ascertain the effects of race or sex. Because the scope of antidiscrimination law is so limited, sex and race discrimination have come to be defined in terms of the experiences of those who are privileged *but for* their racial or sexual characteristics. Put differently, the paradigm of sex discrimination tends to be based on the experiences of white women; the model of race discrimination tends to be based on the experiences of the most privileged Blacks. Notions of what constitutes race and sex discrimination are, as a result, narrowly tailored to embrace only a small set of circumstances, none of which include discrimination against Black women.

To the extent that this general description is accurate, the following analogy can be useful in describing how Black women are marginalized in the interface between antidiscrimination law and race and gender hierarchies: Imagine a basement which contains all people who are disadvantaged on the basis of race, sex, class, sexual preference, age and/or physical ability. These people are stacked—feet standing on shoulders—with those on the bottom being disadvantaged by the full array of factors, up to the very top, where the heads of all those disadvantaged by a singular factor brush up against the ceiling. Their ceiling is actually the floor above which only those who are *not* disadvantaged in any way reside. In efforts to correct some aspects of domination, those above the ceiling admit from the basement only those who can say that "but for" the ceiling, they too would be in the upper room. A hatch is developed through which those placed immediately below can crawl. Yet this hatch is generally available only to those who—due to the singularity of their burden and their otherwise privileged position relative to those below—are in the position to crawl through. Those who are multiply-burdened are generally left below unless they can somehow pull themselves into the groups that are permitted to squeeze through the hatch.

As this analogy translates for Black women, the problem is that they can receive protection only to the extent that their experiences are recognizably similar to those whose experiences tend to be reflected in antidiscrimination doctrine. If Black women cannot conclusively say that "but for" their race or "but for" their gender they would be treated differently, they are not invited to climb through the hatch but told to wait in the unprotected margin until they can be absorbed into the broader, protected categories of race and sex. . . .

FEMINISM AND BLACK WOMEN: "AIN'T WE WOMEN?"

. . .

In 1851, Sojourner Truth declared "Ain't I a Woman?" and challenged the sexist imagery used by male critics to justify the disenfranchisement of women. The scene was a Women's Rights Conference in Akron, Ohio; white male hecklers, invoking stereotypical images of "womanhood," argued that women were too frail and delicate to take on the responsibilities of political activity. When Sojourner Truth rose to speak, many white women urged that she be silenced, fearing that she would divert attention from women's suffrage to emancipation. Truth, once permitted to speak, recounted the horrors of slavery, and its particular impact on Black women:

> Look at my arms! I have ploughed and planted and gathered into barns, and no man could head me—and ain't I a woman? I would work as much and eat as much as a man—when I could get it—and bear the lash as well! And ain't I a woman? I have born thirteen children, and seen most of 'em sold into slavery, and when I cried out with my mother's grief, none but Jesus heard me—and ain't I a woman?[19]

By using her own life to reveal the contradiction between the ideological myths of womanhood and the reality of Black women's experience, Truth's oratory provided a powerful rebuttal to the claim that women were categorically weaker than men. Yet Truth's personal challenge to the coherence of the cult of true womanhood was useful only to the extent that white women were willing to reject the racist attempts to rationalize the contradiction—that because Black women were something less than real women, their experiences had no bearing on true womanhood. Thus, this 19th-century Black feminist challenged not only patriarchy, but she also challenged white feminists wishing to embrace Black women's history to relinquish their vestedness in whiteness.

. . .

The value of feminist theory to Black women is diminished because it evolves from a white racial context that is seldom acknowledged. Not only are women of color in fact overlooked, but their exclusion is reinforced when *white* women speak for and as *women*. The authoritative universal voice—usually white male subjectivity masquerading as non-racial, non-gendered objectivity—is merely transferred to those who, but for gender, share many of the same cultural, economic and social characteristics. When feminist theory attempts to describe women's experiences through analyzing patriarchy, sexuality, or separate spheres ideology, it often overlooks the role of race. Feminists thus ignore how their own race functions to mitigate some aspects of sexism and, moreover, how it often privileges them over and contributes to the domination of other women.[20] Consequently, feminist

theory remains *white*, and its potential to broaden and deepen its analysis by addressing non-privileged women remains unrealized.

. . .

Because ideological and descriptive definitions of patriarchy are usually premised upon white female experiences, feminists and others informed by feminist literature may make the mistake of assuming that since the role of Black women in the family and in other Black institutions does not always resemble the familiar manifestations of patriarchy in the white community, Black women are somehow exempt from patriarchal norms. For example, Black women have traditionally worked outside the home in numbers far exceeding the labor participation rate of white women.[21] An analysis of patriarchy that highlights the history of white women's exclusion from the workplace might permit the inference that Black women have not been burdened by this particular gender-based expectation. Yet the very fact that Black women must work conflicts with norms that women should not, often creating personal, emotional and relationship problems in Black women's lives. Thus, Black women are burdened not only because they often have to take on responsibilities that are not traditionally female but, moreover, their assumption of these roles is sometimes interpreted within the Black community as either Black women's failure to live up to such norms or as another manifestation of racism's scourge upon the Black community.[22] This is one of the many aspects of intersectionality that cannot be understood through an analysis of patriarchy rooted in white experience.

Another example of how theory emanating from a white context obscures the multidimensionality of Black women's lives is found in feminist discourse on rape. A central political issue on the feminist agenda has been the pervasive problem of rape. Part of the intellectual and political effort to mobilize around this issue has involved the development of a historical critique of the role that law has played in establishing the bounds of normative sexuality and in regulating female sexual behavior.[23] Early carnal knowledge statutes and rape laws are understood within this discourse to illustrate that the objective of rape statutes traditionally has not been to protect women from coercive intimacy but to protect and maintain a property-like interest in female chastity.[24] Although feminists quite rightly criticize these objectives, to characterize rape law as reflecting male control over female sexuality is for Black women an oversimplified account and an ultimately inadequate account.

Rape statutes generally do not reflect *male* control over *female* sexuality, but *white* male regulation of *white* female sexuality.[25] Historically, there has been absolutely no institutional effort to regulate Black female chastity.[26] Courts in some states had gone so far as to instruct juries that, unlike white women, Black women were not presumed to be chaste.[27] Also, while it was true that the attempt to regulate the sexuality of white women placed unchaste women outside the law's protection, racism restored a fallen white woman's chastity where the alleged assailant was a Black man.[28] No such restoration was available to Black women.

The singular focus on rape as a manifestation of male power over female sexuality tends to eclipse the use of rape as a weapon of racial terror.[29] When Black women were raped by white males, they were being raped not as women generally, but as Black women specifically: Their femaleness made them sexually vulnerable to racist domination, while their Blackness effectively denied them any protection. This white male power was reinforced by a judicial system in which the successful conviction of a white man for raping a Black woman was virtually unthinkable.

In sum, sexist expectations of chastity and racist assumptions of sexual promiscuity combined to create a distinct set of issues confronting Black women.[30] These issues have seldom been explored in feminist literature nor are they prominent in antiracist politics. The lynching of Black males, the institutional practice that was legitimized by the regulation of white women's sexuality, has historically and contemporaneously occupied the Black agenda on sexuality and violence. Consequently, Black women are caught between a Black community that, perhaps understandably, views with suspicion attempts to litigate questions of sexual violence, and a feminist community that reinforces those suspicions by focusing on white female sexuality.[31] The suspicion is compounded by the historical fact that the protection of white female sexuality was often the pretext for terrorizing the Black community. Even today some fear that antirape agendas may undermine antiracist objectives. This is the paradigmatic political and theoretical dilemma created by the intersection of race and gender: Black women are caught between ideological and political currents that combine first to create and then to bury Black women's experiences.

. . .

EXPANDING FEMINIST THEORY AND ANTIRACIST POLITICS BY EMBRACING THE INTERSECTION

If any real efforts are to be made to free Black people of the constraints and conditions that characterize racial subordination, then theories and strategies purporting to reflect the Black community's needs must include an analysis of sexism and patriarchy. Similarly, feminism must include an analysis of race if it hopes to express the aspirations of non-white women. Neither Black liberationist politics nor feminist theory can ignore the intersectional experiences of those whom the movements claim as their respective constituents. In order to include Black women, both movements must distance themselves from earlier approaches in which experiences are relevant only when they are related to certain dearly identifiable causes (for example, the oppression of Blacks is significant when based on race, of women when based on gender). The praxis of both should be centered on the life chances and life situations of people who should be cared about without regard to the source of their difficulties.

I have stated earlier that the failure to embrace the complexities of compoundedness is not simply a matter of political will, but is also due to the influence of a way of thinking about discrimination which structures politics so that struggles are categorized as singular issues. Moreover, this structure imports a descriptive and normative view of society that reinforces the status quo.

It is somewhat ironic that those concerned with alleviating the ills of racism and sexism should adopt such a top-down approach to discrimination. If their efforts instead began with addressing the needs and problems of those who are most disadvantaged and with restructuring and remaking the world where necessary, then others who are singularly disadvantaged would also benefit. In addition, it seems that placing those who currently are marginalized in the center is the most effective way to resist efforts to compartmentalize experiences and undermine potential collective action.

It is not necessary to believe that a political consensus to focus on the lives of the most disadvantaged will happen tomorrow in order to recenter the discrimination discourse at the intersection. It is enough, for now, that such an effort would encourage us to look beneath the prevailing conceptions of discrimination and to challenge the complacency that accompanies belief in the effectiveness of this framework. By so doing, we may develop language which is critical of the dominant view and which provides some basis for unifying activity. The goal of this activity should be to facilitate the inclusion of marginalized groups for whom it can be said: "When they enter, we all enter."

(1989)

NOTES

1. Gloria T. Hull, et al, eds (The Feminist Press, 1982).
2. The most common linguistic manifestation of this analytical dilemma is represented in the conventional usage of the term "Blacks and women." Although it may be true that some people mean to include Black women in either "Blacks" or "women," the context in which the term is used actually suggests that often Black women are not considered. See, for example, Elizabeth Spelman, *The Inessential Woman* 114–15 (Beacon Press, 1988) (discussing an article on Blacks and women in the military where "the racial identity of those identified as 'women' does not become explicit until reference is made to Black women, at which point it also becomes clear that the category of women excludes Black women"). It seems that if Black women were explicitly included, the preferred term would be either "Blacks and white women" or "Black men and all women."
3. Civil Rights Act of 1964, 42 USC & 2000e, et seq as amended (1982).
4. 413 F Supp 142 (E D Mo 1976).
5. 708 F2d 475 (9th Cir 1983).
6. 673 F2d 798 (5th Cir 1982).
7. *De Graffenreid*, 413 F Supp at 143.
8. Id at 144.
9. Id at 145. In *Mosley v General Motors*, 497 F Supp 583 (E D Mo 1980), plaintiffs, alleging broad-based racial discrimination at General Motors' St. Louis facility, prevailed in a portion of their Title VII claim. *The* seniority system challenged in *DeGraffenreid*, however, was not considered in *Mosley*.

10. 708 F2d 475.
11. See also *Moore v National Association of Securities Dealers*, 27 EPD (CCH) ¶32,238 (D DC 1981); but see *Edmondson v Simon*, 86 FRD 375 (N D Ill 1980) (where the court was unwilling to hold as a matter of law that no Black female could represent without conflict the interests of both Blacks and females).
12. 708 F2d at 479. Between January 1976 and June 1979, the three years in which Moore claimed that she was passed over the promotion, the percentage of white males occupying first-level supervisory positions ranged from 70.3 to 76.8%; Black males from 8.9 to 10.9%; white women from 1.8 to 3.3%; and Black females from 0 to 2.2%. The overall male/female ratio in the top five labor grades ranged from 100/0% in 1976 to 98/1.8% in 1979. The white/Black ratio was 85/3.3% in 1976 and 79.6/8% in 1979. The overall ratio of men to women in supervisory positions was 98.2 to 1.8% in 1976 to 93.4 to 6.6% in 1979; the Black to white ratio during the same time period was 78.6 to 8.9% and 73.6 to 13.1%.

For promotions to the top five labor grades, the percentages were worse. Between 1976 and 1979, the percentage of white males in these positions ranged from 85.3 to 77.9%; Black males 3.3 to 8%; white females from 0 to 1.4%, and Black females from 0 to 0%. Overall, in 1979, 98.2% of the highest level employees were male; 1.8% were female.
13. 708 F2d at 480 (emphasis added).
14. See *Strong v Arkansas Blue Cross & Blue Shield, Inc.*, 87 FRD 496 (E D Ark 1980); *Hammons v Folger Coffee Co.*, 87 FRD 600 (W D Mo 1980); *Edmondson v Simon*, 86 FRD 375 (N D Ill 1980); *Vuyanich v Republic National Bank of Dallas*, 82 FRD (N D Tex 1979); *Colston v Maryland Cup Corp.*, 26 Fed Rules Serv 940 (D Md 1978).
15. 416 F Supp 248 (N D Miss 1976).
16. The suit commenced on March 2, 1972, with the filing of a complaint by three employees seeking to represent a class of persons allegedly subjected to racial discrimination at the hands of the defendants. Subsequently, the plaintiffs amended the complaint to add an allegation of sex discrimination. Of the original named plaintiffs, one was a Black male and two were Black females. In the course of the three-year period between the filing of the complaint and the trial, the only named male plaintiff received permission of the court to withdraw for religious reasons. Id at 250.
17. As the dissent in *Travenol* pointed out, there was no reason to exclude Black males from the scope of the remedy *after* counsel had presented sufficient evidence to support a finding of discrimination against Black men. If the rationale for excluding Black males was the potential conflict between Black males and Black females, then

"[i]n this case, to paraphrase an old adage, the proof of plaintiffs' ability to represent the interests of Black males was in the representation thereof." 673 F2d at 837–38.

18. In much of antidiscrimination doctrine, the presence of intent to discriminate distinguishes unlawful from lawful discrimination. See *Washington v Davis*, 426 US 229, 239–45 (1976) (proof of discriminatory purposes required to substantiate Equal Protection violation). Under Title VII, however, the Court has held that statistical data showing a disproportionate impact can suffice to support a finding of discrimination. See *Griggs*, 401 US at 432. Whether the distinction between the two analyses will survive is an open question. See *Wards Cove Packing Co., Inc. v Atonio*, 109 S Ct 2115, 2122–23 (1989) (plaintiffs must show more than mere disparity to support a prima facie case of disparate impact). For a discussion of the competing normative visions that underlie the intent and effects analyses, see Alan David Freeman, *Legitimizing Racial Discrimination Through Antidiscrimination Law: A Critical Review of Supreme Court Doctrine*, 62 Minn L Rev 1049 (1978).

19. Eleanor Flexner, *Century of Struggle: The Women's Rights Movement in the United States* 91 (Belknap Press of Harvard University Press, 1975). See also Bell Hooks, *Ain't I a Woman* 159–60 (South End Press, 1981).

20. For example, many white females were able to gain entry into previously all white male enclaves not through bringing about a fundamental reordering of male versus female work, but in large part by shifting their "female" responsibilities to poor and minority women.

21. See generally Jacqueline Jones, *Labor of Love, Labor of Sorrow: Black Women, Work, and the Family from Slavery to the Present* (Basic Books, 1985); Angela Davis, *Women, Race and Class* (Random House, 1981).

22. As Elizabeth Higginbotham noted, "women, who often fail to conform to 'appropriate' sex roles, have been pictured as, and made to feel, inadequate—even though as women, they possess traits recognized as positive when held by men in the wider society. Such women are stigmatized because their lack of adherence to expected gender roles is seen as a threat to the value system." Elizabeth Higginbotham, *Two Representative Issues in Contemporary Sociological Work on Black Women*, in Hull, et al, eds, *But Some of Us Are Brave* at 95 (cited in note 1).

23. See generally Susan Brownmiller, *Against Our Will* (Simon and Schuster, 1975); Susan Estrich, *Real Rape* (Harvard University Press, 1987).

24. See Brownmiller, *Against Our Will* at 17; see generally Estrich, *Real Rape*.

25. One of the central theoretical dilemmas of feminism that is largely obscured by universalizing the white female experience is that experiences that are described as a manifestation of male control over females can be instead a manifestation of dominant group control over all subordinates. The significance is that other nondominant men may not share in, participate in or connect with the behavior, beliefs or actions at issue, and may be victimized themselves by "male" power. In other contexts, however, "male authority" might include nonwhite men, particularly in private sphere contexts. Efforts to think more clearly about when Black women are dominated as *women* and when they are dominated as *Black women* are directly related to the question of when power is *male* and when it is *white male*.

26. See Note, *Rape, Racism and the Law*, 6 Harv Women's L J 103, 117–23 (1983) (discussing the historical and contemporary evidence suggesting that Black women are generally not thought to be chaste). See also Hooks, *Ain't I a Woman* at 54 (cited in note 19) (stating that stereotypical images of Black womanhood during slavery were based on the myth that "all black women were immoral and sexually loose"); Beverly Smith, *Black Women's Health: Notes for a Course*, in Hull et al, eds, *But Some of Us Are Brave* at 110 (cited in note 1) (noting that " . . . white men for centuries have justified their sexual abuse of Black women by claiming that we are licentious, always 'ready' for any sexual encounter").

27. The following statement is probably unusual only in its candor: "What has been said by some of our courts about an unchaste female being a comparatively rare exception is no doubt true where the population is composed largely of the Caucasian race, but we would blind ourselves to actual conditions if we adopted this rule where another race that is largely immoral constitutes an appreciable part of the population." *Dallas v State*, 76 Fla 358, 79 So 690 (1918), quoted in Note, 6 Harv Women's L J at 121 (cited in note 26).

Espousing precisely this view, one commentator stated in 1902: "I sometimes hear of a virtuous Negro woman but the idea is so absolutely inconceivable to me . . . I cannot imagine such a creature as a virtuous Negro woman." Id at 82. Such images persist in popular culture. See Paul Grein, *Taking Stock of the Latest Pop Record Surprises*, LA Times § 6 at 1 (July 7, 1988) (recalling the controversy in the late 70s over a Rolling Stones recording which included the line "Black girls just wanna get fucked all night") . . .

28. Because the way the legal system viewed chastity, Black women could not be victims of forcible rape. One commentator has noted that "[a]ccording to governing [stereotypes], chastity could not be possessed by Black women. Thus, Black women's rape charges were automatically discounted, and the issue of chastity was contested only in cases where the rape complainant was a

white woman." Note, 6 Harv Women's L J at 126 (cited in note 26). Black women's claims of rape were not taken seriously regardless of the offender's race. A judge in 1912 said: "This court will never take the word of a nigger against the word of a white man [concerning rape]." Id at 120. On the other hand, lynching was considered an effective remedy for a Black man's rape of a white woman. Since rape of a white woman by a Black man was "a crime more horrible than death," the only way to assuage society's rage and to make the woman whole again was to brutally murder the Black man. Id at 125.

29. See *The Rape of Black Women as a Weapon of Terror*, in Gerda Lerner, ed, *Black Women in White America* 172–93 (Pantheon Books, 1972). See also Brownmiller, *Against Our Will* (cited in note 23). Even where Brownmiller acknowledges the use of rape as racial terrorism, she resists making a "special case" for Black women by offering evidence that white women were raped by the Klan as well. Id at 139. Whether or not one considers the racist rape of Black women a "special case," such experiences are probably different. In any case, Brownmiller's treatment of the issue raises serious questions about the ability to sustain an analysis of patriarchy without understanding its multiple intersections with racism.

30. Paula Giddings notes the combined effect of sexual and racial stereotypes: "Black women were seen having all of the inferior qualities of white women without any of their virtues." Giddings, *When and Where I Enter: The Impact of Black Women on Race and Sex in America* 82 (William Morrow and Co, Inc, 1st ed 1984).

31. Susan Brownmiller's treatment of the Emmett Till case illustrates why antirape politicization makes some African Americans uncomfortable. Despite Brownmiller's quite laudable efforts to discuss elsewhere the rape of Black women and the racism involved in much of the hysteria over the Black male threat, her analysis of the Till case places the sexuality of white women, rather than racial terrorism, at center stage. Brownmiller states: "Rarely has one single case exposed so clearly as Till's the underlying group-male antagonisms over access to women, for what began in Bryant's store should not be misconstrued as an innocent flirtation. . . . In concrete terms, the accessibility of all white women was on review." Brownmiller, *Against Our Will* at 272 (cited in note 23). . . .

---

75 • *Patricia Hill Collins*

FROM *BLACK FEMINIST THOUGHT*
Knowledge, Consciousness and the Politics of Empowerment

THE MATRIX OF DOMINATION

Additive models of oppression are firmly rooted in the either/or dichotomous thinking of Eurocentric, masculinist thought. One must be either Black or white in such thought systems—persons of ambiguous racial and ethnic identity constantly battle with questions such as "what are you, anyway?" This emphasis on quantification and categorization occurs in conjunction with the belief that either/or categories must be ranked.

The search for certainty of this sort requires that one side of a dichotomy be privileged while its other is denigrated. Privilege becomes defined in relation to its other.

Replacing additive models of oppression with interlocking ones creates possibilities for new paradigms. The significance of seeing race, class, and gender as interlocking systems of oppression is that such an approach fosters a paradigmatic shift of thinking inclusively about other oppressions, such as age, sexual

Reprinted from *Black Feminist Thought: Knowledge, Consciousness, and the Politics of Empowerment, Perspectives on Gender, Volume 2*, by Patricia Hill Collins, pp. 225–230. Copyright © 1990, 1991, by Routledge. Used by permission of Taylor and Francis Group LLC.

orientation, religion, and ethnicity. Race, class, and gender represent the three systems of oppression that most heavily affect African-American women. But these systems and the economic, political, and ideological conditions that support them may not be the most fundamental oppressions, and they certainly affect many more groups than Black women. Other people of color, Jews, the poor, white women, and gays and lesbians have all had similar ideological justifications offered for their subordination. All categories of humans labeled Others have been equated to one another, to animals, and to nature (Halpin 1989).

Placing African-American women and other excluded groups in the center of analysis opens up possibilities for a both/and conceptual stance, one in which all groups possess varying amounts of penalty and privilege in one historically created system. In this system, for example, white women are penalized by their gender but privileged by their race. Depending on the context, an individual may be an oppressor, a member of an oppressed group, or simultaneously oppressor and oppressed.

Adhering to a both/and conceptual stance does not mean that race, class, and gender oppression are interchangeable. For example, whereas race, class, and gender oppression operate on the social structural level of institutions, gender oppression seems better able to annex the basic power of the erotic and intrude in personal relationships via family dynamics and within individual consciousness. This may be because racial oppression has fostered historically concrete communities among African-Americans and other racial/ethnic groups. These communities have stimulated cultures of resistance (Caulfield 1974; Scott 1985). While these communities segregate Blacks from whites, they simultaneously provide counter-institutional buffers that subordinate groups such as African-Americans use to resist the ideas and institutions of dominant groups. Social class may be similarly structured. Traditionally conceptualized as a relationship of *individual* employees to their employers, social class might be better viewed as a relationship of *communities* to capitalist political economies (Sacks 1989). Moreover, significant overlap exists between racial and social class oppression when viewing them through the collective lens of family and community. Existing community structures provide a primary line of resistance against racial and class oppression. But because gender cross-cuts these structures, it finds fewer comparable institutional bases to foster resistance.

Embracing a both/and conceptual stance moves us from additive, separate systems approaches to oppression and toward what I now see as the more fundamental issue of the social relations of domination. Race, class, and gender constitute axes of oppression that characterize Black women's experiences within a more generalized matrix of domination. Other groups may encounter different dimensions of the matrix, such as sexual orientation, religion, and age, but the overarching relationship is one of domination and the types of activism it generates.

Bell Hooks labels this matrix a "politic of domination" and describes how it operates along interlocking axes of race, class, and gender oppression. This politic of domination

> refers to the ideological ground that they share, which is a belief in domination, and a belief in the notions of superior and inferior, which are components of all of those systems. For me it's like a house, they share the foundation, but the foundation is the ideological beliefs around which notions of domination are constructed. (Hooks 1989, 175)

Johnella Butler claims that new methodologies growing from this new paradigm would be "non-hierarchical" and would "refuse primacy to either race, class, gender, or ethnicity, demanding instead a recognition of their matrix-like interaction" (1989, 16). Race, class, and gender may not be the most fundamental or important systems of oppression, but they have most profoundly affected African-American women. One significant dimension of Black feminist thought is its potential to reveal insights about the social relations of domination organized along other axes such as religion, ethnicity, sexual orientation, and age. Investigating Black women's particular experiences thus promises to reveal much about the more universal process of domination.

MULTIPLE LEVELS OF DOMINATION

In addition to being structured along axes such as race, gender, and social class, the matrix of domination is structured on several levels. People experience and resist oppression on three levels: the level of personal biography; the group or community level of the cultural context created by race, class, and gender; and the systemic level of social institutions. Black feminist thought emphasizes all three levels as sites of domination and as potential sites of resistance.

Each individual has a unique personal biography made up of concrete experiences, values, motivations, and emotions. No two individuals occupy the same social space; thus no two biographies are identical. Human ties can be freeing and empowering, as is the case with Black women's heterosexual love relationships or in the power of motherhood in African-American families and communities. Human ties can also be confining and oppressive. Situations of domestic violence and abuse or cases in which controlling images foster Black women's internalized oppression represent domination on the personal level. The same situation can look quite different depending on the consciousness one brings to interpret it.

This level of individual consciousness is a fundamental area where new knowledge can generate change. Traditional accounts assume that power as domination operates from the top down by forcing and controlling unwilling victims to bend to the will of more powerful superiors. But these accounts fail to account for questions concerning why, for example, women stay with abusive men even with ample opportunity to leave or why slaves did not kill their owners more often. The willingness of the victim to collude in her or his own victimization becomes lost. They also fail to account for sustained resistance by victims, even when chances for victory appear remote. By emphasizing the power of self-definition and the necessity of a free mind, Black feminist thought speaks to the importance African-American women thinkers place on c̲o̲n̲s̲c̲i̲o̲u̲s̲n̲e̲s̲s̲ as a sphere of freedom. Black women intellectuals realize that domination operates not only by structuring power from the top down but by simultaneously annexing the power as energy of those on the bottom for its own ends. In their efforts to rearticulate the standpoint of African-American women as a group, Black feminist thinkers offer individual African-American women the conceptual tools to resist oppression.

The cultural context formed by those experiences and ideas that are shared with other members of a group or community which give meaning to individual biographies constitutes a second level at which domination is experienced and resisted. Each individual biography is rooted in several overlapping cultural contexts—for example, groups defined by race, social class, age, gender, religion, and sexual orientation. The cultural component contributes, among other things,

the concepts used in thinking and acting, group validation of an individual's interpretation of concepts, the "thought models" used in the acquisition of knowledge, and standards used to evaluate individual thought and behavior (Mannheim 1936). The most cohesive cultural contexts are those with identifiable histories, geographic locations, and social institutions. For Black women African-American communities have provided the location for an Afrocentric group perspective to endure.

Subjugated knowledges, such as a Black women's culture of resistance, develop in cultural contexts controlled by oppressed groups. Dominant groups aim to replace subjugated knowledge with their own specialized thought because they realize that gaining control over this dimension of subordinate groups' lives simplifies control (Woodson, 1933; Fanon 1963). While efforts to influence this dimension of an oppressed group's experiences can be partially successful, this level is more difficult to control than dominant groups would have us believe. For example, adhering to externally derived standards of beauty leads many African-American women to dislike their skin color or hair texture. Similarly, internalizing Eurocentric gender ideology leads some Black men to abuse Black women. These are cases of the successful infusion of the dominant group's specialized thought into the everyday cultural context of African-Americans. But the long-standing existence of a Black women's culture of resistance as expressed through Black women's relationships with one another, the Black women's blues tradition, and the voices of contemporary African-American women writers all attest to the difficulty of eliminating the cultural context as a fundamental site of resistance.

Domination is also experienced and resisted on the third level of social institutions controlled by the dominant group: namely, schools, churches, the media, and other formal organizations. These institutions expose individuals to the specialized thought representing the dominant group's standpoint and interests. While such institutions offer the promise of both literacy and other skills that can be used for individual empowerment and social transformation, they simultaneously require docility and passivity. Such institutions would have us believe that the theorizing of elites constitutes the whole of theory. The existence of African-American women thinkers such as Maria Stewart, Sojourner

Truth, Zora Neale Hurston, and Fannie Lou Hamer who, though excluded from and/or marginalized within such institutions, continued to produce theory effectively opposes this hegemonic view. Moreover, the more recent resurgence of Black feminist thought within these institutions, the case of the outpouring of contemporary Black feminist thought in history and literature, directly challenges the Eurocentric masculinist thought pervading these institutions.

RESISTING THE MATRIX OF DOMINATION

Domination operates by seducing, pressuring, or forcing African-American women and members of subordinated groups to replace individual and cultural ways of knowing with the dominant group's specialized thought. As a result, suggests Audre Lorde, "the true focus of revolutionary change is never merely the oppressive situations which we seek to escape, but that piece of the oppressor which is planted deep within each of us" (1984, 123). Or as Toni Cade Bambara succinctly states, "revolution begins with the self, in the self" (1970a, 109).

Lorde and Bambara's suppositions raise an important issue for Black feminist intellectuals and for all scholars and activists working for social change. Although most individuals have little difficulty identifying their own victimization within some major system of oppression—whether it be by race, social class, religion, physical ability, sexual orientation, ethnicity, age or gender—they typically fail to see how their thoughts and actions uphold someone else's subordination. Thus white feminists routinely point with confidence to their oppression as women but resist seeing how much their white skin privileges them. African-Americans who possess eloquent analyses of racism often persist in viewing poor white women as symbols of white power. The radical left fares little better. "If only people of color and women could see their true class interests," they argue, "class solidarity would eliminate racism and sexism." In essence, each group identifies the oppression with which it feels most comfortable as being fundamental and classifies all others as being of lesser importance. Oppression is filled with such contradictions because these approaches fail to recognize that a matrix of domination

contains few pure victims or oppressors. Each individual derives varying amounts of penalty and privilege from the multiple systems of oppression which frame everyone's lives.

A broader focus stresses the interlocking nature of oppressions that are structured on multiple levels, from the individual to the social structural, and which are part of a larger matrix of domination. Adhering to this inclusive model provides the conceptual space needed for each individual to see that she or he is *both* a member of multiple dominant groups *and* a member of multiple subordinate groups. Shifting the analysis to investigating how the matrix of domination is structured along certain axes—race, gender, and class being the axes of investigation for African-American women—reveals that different systems of oppression may rely in varying degrees on systemic versus interpersonal mechanisms of domination.

Empowerment involves rejecting the dimensions of knowledge, whether personal, cultural, or institutional, that perpetuate objectification and dehumanization. African-American women and other individuals in subordinate groups become empowered when we understand and use those dimensions of our individual, group, and disciplinary ways of knowing that foster our humanity as fully human subjects. This is the case when Black women value our self-definitions, participate in a Black women's activist tradition, invoke an Afrocentric feminist epistemology as central to our worldview, and view the skills gained in schools as part of a focused education for Black community development. C. Wright Mills (1959) identifies this holistic epistemology as the "sociological imagination" and identifies its task and its promise as a way of knowing that enables individuals to grasp the relations between history and biography within society. Using one's standpoint to engage the sociological imagination can empower the individual. "My fullest concentration of energy is available to me," Audre Lorde maintains, "only when I integrate all the parts of who I am, openly, allowing power from particular sources of my living to flow back and forth freely through all my different selves, without the restriction of externally imposed definition" (1984, 120–21).

(1990)

"U.S. THIRD WORLD FEMINISM: THE THEORY AND METHOD OF DIFFERENTIAL OPPOSITIONAL CONSCIOUSNESS"[1]

The enigma that is U.S. third world feminism has yet to be fully confronted by theorists of social change. To these late twentieth-century analysts it has remained inconceivable that U.S. third world feminism might represent a form of historical consciousness whose very structure lies outside the conditions of possibility which regulate the oppositional expressions of dominant feminism. In enacting this new form of historical consciousness, U.S. third world feminism provides access to a different way of conceptualizing not only U.S. feminist consciousness but oppositional activity in general; it comprises a formulation capable of aligning such movements for social justice with what have been identified as world-wide movements of decolonization.

Both in spite of and yet because they represent varying internally colonized communities, U.S. third world feminists have generated a common speech, a theoretical structure which, however, remained just outside the purview of the dominant feminist theory emerging in the 1970s, functioning within it—but only as the unimaginable. Even though this unimaginable presence arose to reinvigorate and refocus the politics and priorities of dominant feminist theory during the 1980s, what remains is an uneasy alliance between what appears on the surface to be two different understandings of domination, subordination, and the nature of effective resistance—a shot-gun arrangement at best between what literary critic Gayatri

Spivak characterizes as a "hegemonic feminist theory"[2] on the one side and what I have been naming "U.S. third world feminism" on the other.[3] I do not mean to suggest here, however, that the perplexing situation that exists between U.S. third world and hegemonic feminisms should be understood merely in binary terms. On the contrary, what this investigation reveals is the way in which the new theory of oppositional consciousness considered here and enacted by U.S. third world feminism is at least partially contained, though made deeply invisible by the manner of its appropriation, in the terms of what has become a hegemonic feminist theory.

U.S. third world feminism arose out of the matrix of the very discourses denying, permitting, and producing difference. Out of the imperatives born of necessity arose a mobility of identity that generated the activities of a new citizen-subject, and which reveals yet another model for the self-conscious production of political opposition. In this essay I will lay out U.S. third world feminism as the design for oppositional political activity and consciousness in the United States. In mapping this new design, a model is revealed by which social actors can chart the points through which differing oppositional ideologies can meet, in spite of their varying trajectories. This knowledge becomes important when one begins to wonder, along with late twentieth century cultural critics such as Fredric Jameson, how organized oppositional activity and consciousness can be made possible under the co-opting nature of the so-called "post-modern" cultural condition.[4] . . .

This study identifies five principal categories by which "oppositional consciousness" is organized, and which are politically effective means for changing the dominant order of power. I characterize them as "equal rights," "revolutionary," "supremacist," "separatist," and "differential" ideological forms. All these forms of consciousness are kaleidoscoped into view when the fifth form is utilized as a theoretical model which retroactively clarifies and gives new meaning to the others. Differential consciousness represents the strategy of another form of oppositional ideology that functions on an altogether different register. Its power can be thought of as mobile—not nomadic but rather cinematographic: a kinetic motion that maneuvers, poetically transfigures, and orchestrates while demanding alienation, perversion, and reformation in both spectators and practitioners. Differential consciousness is the expression of the new subject position called for by Althusser—it permits functioning within yet beyond the demands of dominant ideology. This differential form of oppositional consciousness has been enacted in the practice of U.S. third world feminism since the 1960s.

This essay also investigates the forms of oppositional consciousness that were generated within one of the great oppositional movements of the late twentieth century, the second wave of the women's movement. What emerges in this discussion is an outline of the oppositional ideological forms which worked against one another to divide the movement from within. I trace these ideological forms as they are manifested in the critical writings of some of the prominent hegemonic feminist theorists of the 1980s. In their attempts to identify a feminist history of consciousness, many of these thinkers believe they detect four fundamentally distinct phases through which feminists have passed in their quest to end the subordination of women. But viewed in terms of another paradigm, "differential consciousness," here made available for study through the activity of U.S. third world feminism, these four historical phases are revealed as sublimated versions of the very forms of consciousness in opposition which were also conceived within post-1950s U.S. liberation movements.

These earlier movements were involved in seeking effective forms of resistance outside of those determined by the social order itself. My contention is that hegemonic feminist forms of resistance represent only other versions of the forms of oppositional consciousness expressed within all liberation movements active in the United States during the later half of the twentieth century. What I want to do here is systematize in theoretical form a theory of oppositional consciousness as it comes embedded but hidden within U.S. hegemonic feminist theoretical tracts. At the end of this essay, I present the outline of a corresponding theory which engages with these hegemonic feminist theoretical forms while at the same time going beyond them to produce a more general theory and method of oppositional consciousness.

The often discussed race and class conflict between white and third world feminists in the United States allows us a clear view of these forms of consciousness in action. The history of the relationship between first and third world feminists has been tense and rife with antagonisms. My thesis is that at the root of these conflicts is the refusal of U.S. third world feminism to buckle under, to submit to sublimation or assimilation within hegemonic feminist praxis. This refusal is based, in large part, upon loyalty to the differential mode of consciousness and activity outlined in this essay but which has remained largely unaccounted for within the structure of the hegemonic feminist theories of the 1980s. . . .

TOWARD A THEORY OF OPPOSITIONAL CONSCIOUSNESS

. . . Any social order that is hierarchically organized into relations of domination and subordination creates particular subject positions within which the subordinated can legitimately function.[5] These subject positions, once self-consciously recognized by their inhabitants, can become transformed into more effective sites of resistance to the current ordering of power relations. From the perspective of a differential U.S. third world feminism, the histories of consciousness produced by U.S. white feminists are, above all, only other examples of subordinated consciousness in opposition. In order to make U.S. third world feminism visible within U.S. feminist theory, I suggest a topography of consciousness that identifies nothing more and nothing less than the modes the subordinated of the United States (of any gender, race, or class) claim as politicized and oppositional stances in resistance to domination. The topography that follows, unlike its hegemonic feminist version, is not historically organized, no enactment is privileged over any other, and the recognition that each site is as potentially effective in opposition as any other makes possible another mode of consciousness which is particularly effective under late capitalist and postmodern cultural conditions in the United States. I call this mode of consciousness "differential"—it is the ideological mode enacted by U.S. third world feminists over the last thirty years.

The first four enactments of consciousness that I describe next reveal hegemonic feminist political strategies as the forms of oppositional consciousness most often utilized in resistance under earlier (modern, if you will) modes of capitalist production. The following topography, however, does not simply replace previous lists of feminist consciousness with a new set of categories, because the fifth and differential method of oppositional consciousness has a mobile, retroactive, and transformative effect on the previous four forms (the "equal rights," "revolutionary," "supremacist," and "separatist" forms) setting them into new processual relationships. Moreover, this topography compasses the perimeters for a new theory of consciousness in opposition as it gathers up the modes of ideology-praxis represented within previous liberation movements into the fifth, differential, and postmodern paradigm. This paradigm can, among other things, make clear the vital connections that exist between feminist theory in general and other theoretical modes concerned with issues of social hierarchy, race marginality, and resistance. U.S. third world feminism, considered as an enabling theory and method of differential consciousness, brings the following oppositional ideological forms into view:

1. Under an "equal rights" mode of consciousness in opposition, the subordinated group argue that their differences—for which they have been assigned inferior status—are only in appearance, not reality. Behind their exterior physical difference, they argue, is an essence the same as the essence of the human already in power. On the basis that all individuals are created equal, subscribers to this particular ideological tactic will demand that their own humanity be legitimated, recognized as the same under the law, and assimilated

into the most favored form of the human in power. The expression of this mode of political behavior and identity politics can be traced throughout the writings generated from within U.S. liberation movements of the post–World War II era. Hegemonic feminist theorists have claimed this oppositional expression of resistance to social inequality as "liberal feminism."

2. Under the second ideological tactic generated in response to social hierarchy, which I call "revolutionary," the subordinated group claim their *differences* from those in power and call for a social transformation that will accommodate and legitimate those differences, by force if necessary. Unlike the previous tactic, which insists on the similarity between social, racial, and gender classes across their differences, there is no desire for assimilation within the present traditions and values of the social order. Rather, this tactic of revolutionary ideology seeks to affirm subordinated differences through a radical societal reformation. The hope is to produce a new culture beyond the domination/subordination power axis. This second revolutionary mode of consciousness was enacted within the white women's movement under the rubric of either "socialist" or "Marxist" feminisms.

3. In "supremacism," the third ideological tactic, not only do the oppressed claim their differences, but they also assert that those very differences have provided them access to a superior evolutionary level than those currently in power. Whether their differences are of biological or social origin is of little practical concern, of more importance is the result. The belief is that this group has evolved to a higher stage of social and psychological existence than those currently holding power, moreover, their differences now comprise the essence of what is good in human existence. Their mission is to provide the social order with a higher ethical and moral vision and consequently a more effective leadership. Within the hegemonic feminist schema "radical" and "cultural" feminisms are organized under these precepts.

4. "Separatism" is the final of the most commonly utilized tactics of opposition organized under previous modes of capitalist development. As in the previous three forms, practitioners of this form of resistance also recognize that their differences

have been branded as inferior with respect to the category of the most human. Under this mode of thought and activity, however, the subordinated do not desire an "equal rights" type of integration with the dominant order, nor do they seek its leadership or revolutionary transformation. Instead, this form of political resistance is organized to protect and nurture the differences that define it through complete separation from the dominant social order. A utopian landscape beckons these practitioners . . . their hope has inspired the multiple visions of the other forms of consciousness as well.

In the post–WWII period in the United States, we have witnessed how the maturation of a resistance movement means not only that four such ideological positions emerge in response to dominating powers, but that these positions become more and more clearly articulated. Unfortunately, however, as we were able to witness in the late 1970s white women's movement, such ideological positions eventually divide the movement of resistance from within, for each of these sites tends to generate sets of tactics, strategies, and identities which historically have appeared to be mutually exclusive under modernist oppositional practices. What remains all the more profound, however, is that the differential practice of U.S. third world feminism undermines the appearance of the mutual exclusivity of oppositional strategies of consciousness; moreover, it is U.S. third world feminism which allows their reconceptualization on the new terms just proposed. U.S. feminists of color, insofar as they involved themselves with the 1970s white women's liberation movement, were also enacting one or more of the ideological positionings just outlined, but rarely for long, and rarely adopting the kind of fervid belief systems and identity politics that tend to accompany their construction under hegemonic understanding. This unusual affiliation with the movement was variously interpreted as disloyalty, betrayal, absence, or lack: "When they were there, they were rarely there for long" went the usual complaint, or "they seemed to shift from one type of women's group to another." They were the mobile (yet ever present in their "absence") members of this particular liberation movement. It is precisely the significance of this mobility which most inventories of oppositional ideology cannot register.

It is in the activity of weaving "between and among" oppositional ideologies as conceived in this new topological space where another and fifth mode of oppositional consciousness and activity can be found.[6] I have named this activity of consciousness "differential" insofar as it enables movement "between and among" the other equal rights, revolutionary, supremacist, and separatist modes of oppositional consciousness considered as variables, in order to disclose the distinctions among them. In this sense the differential mode of consciousness operates like the clutch of an automobile: the mechanism that permits the driver to select, engage, and disengage gears in a system for the transmission of power.[7] Differential consciousness represents the variant, emerging out of correlations, intensities, junctures, crises. What is differential functions through hierarchy, location, and value—enacting the recovery, revenge, or reparation; its processes produce justice. For analytic purposes I place this mode of differential consciousness in the fifth position, even though it functions as the medium through which the "equal rights," "revolutionary," "supremacist," and "separatist" modes of oppositional consciousness became effectively transformed out of their hegemonic versions. Each is now ideological and *tactical* weaponry for confronting the shifting currents of power.

The differences between this five-location and processual topography of consciousness in opposition, and the previous typology of hegemonic feminism, have been made available for analysis through the praxis of U.S. third world feminism understood as a differential method for understanding oppositional political consciousness and activity. U.S. third world feminism represents a central locus of possibility, an insurgent movement which shatters the construction of any one of the collective ideologies as the single most correct site where truth can be represented. Without making this move beyond each of the four modes of oppositional ideology outlined above, any liberation movement is destined to repeat the oppressive authoritarianism from which it is attempting to free itself and become trapped inside a drive for truth which can only end in producing its own brand of dominations. What U.S. third world feminism demands is a new subjectivity, a political revision that denies any one ideology as the final answer, while instead positing a *tactical subjectivity* with the capacity to recenter depending upon the kinds of oppression to be confronted. This is what the shift from hegemonic oppositional theory and practice to a U.S. third world theory and method of oppositional consciousness requires.

Chicana theorist Aida Hurtado explains the importance of differential consciousness to effective oppositional praxis this way: "by the time women of color reach adulthood, we have developed informal political skills to deal with State intervention. The political skills required by women of color are neither the political skills of the White power structure that White liberal feminists have adopted nor the free spirited experimentation followed by the radical feminists." Rather, "women of color are more like urban guerrillas trained through everyday battle with the state apparatus." As such, "women of color's fighting capabilities are often neither understood by white middle-class feminists" nor leftist activists in general, and up until now, these fighting capabilities have "not been codified anywhere for them to learn."[8] Cherrie Moraga defines U.S. third world feminist "guerrilla warfare" as a way of life: "Our strategy is how we cope" on an everyday basis, she says, "how we measure and weigh what is to be said and when, what is to be done and how, and to whom . . . daily deciding/risking who it is we can call an ally, call a friend (whatever that person's skin, sex, or sexuality)." Feminists of color are "women without a line. We are women who contradict each other."[9]

In 1981, Anzaldua identified the growing coalition between U.S. feminists of color as one of women who do not have the same culture, language, race, or "ideology, nor do we derive similar solutions" to the problems of oppression. For U.S. third world feminism enacted as a differential mode of oppositional consciousness, however, these differences do not become "opposed to each other."[10] Instead, writes Lorde in 1979, ideological differences must be seen as "a fund of necessary polarities between which our creativities spark like a dialectic. Only within that interdependency," each ideological position "acknowledged and equal, can the power to seek new ways of being in the world generate, as well as the courage and sustenance to act where there are no charters."[11] This movement between ideologies along with the concurrent desire for ideological commitment are necessary for enacting differential consciousness. Differential consciousness makes the second topography of consciousness in opposition visible as a new theory and method for comprehending oppositional subjectivities and social movements in the United States.

The differential mode of oppositional consciousness depends upon the ability to read the current situation of power and of self-consciously choosing and adopting the ideological form best suited to push against its configurations, a survival skill well known to oppressed peoples.[12] Differential consciousness requires grace, flexibility, and strength: enough strength to confidently commit to a well-defined structure of identity for one hour, day, week, month, year; enough flexibility to self-consciously transform that identity according to the requisites of another oppositional ideological tactic if readings of power's formation require it; enough grace to recognize alliance with others committed to egalitarian social relations and race, gender, and class justice, when their readings of power call for alternative oppositional stands. Within the realm of differential consciousness, oppositional ideological positions, unlike their incarnations under hegemonic feminist comprehension, are tactics—not strategies. Self-conscious agents of differential consciousness recognize one another as allies, countrywomen and men of the same psychic terrain. As the clutch of a car provides the driver the ability to shift gears, differential consciousness permits the practitioner to choose tactical positions, that is, to self-consciously break and reform ties to ideology, activities which are imperative for the psychological and political practices that permit the achievement of coalition across differences. Differential consciousness occurs within the only possible space where, in the words of third world feminist philosopher Maria Lugones, "cross-cultural and cross-racial loving" can take place, through the ability of the self to shift its identities in an activity she calls "world traveling."[13]

Perhaps we can now better understand the overarching utopian content contained in definitions of U.S. third world feminism, as in this statement made by black literary critic Barbara Christian in 1985 who, writing to other U.S. feminists of color, said: "The struggle is not won. Our vision is still seen, even by many progressives, as secondary, our words trivialized as minority issues," our oppositional stances "characterized by others as divisive. But there is a deep philosophical reordering that is occurring" among us "that is already having its effects on so many of us whose lives and expressions are an increasing revelation of the INTIMATE face of universal struggle."[14] This "philosophical reordering," referred to by Christian, the "different strategy, a different foundation" called for by hooks are, in the words of Audre Lorde, part of "a whole other structure of opposition that touches every aspect of our existence at the same time that we are resisting."[15] I contend that this structure is the recognition of a five-mode theory and method of oppositional consciousness, made visible through one mode in particular, differential consciousness, or U.S. third world feminism, what Gloria Anzaldua has recently named "la conciencia de la mestiza" and what Alice Walker calls "womanism."[16] For Barbara Smith, the recognition of this fundamentally different paradigm can "alter life as we know it" for oppositional actors. In 1981, Merle Woo insisted that U.S. third world feminism represents a "new framework which will not support repression, hatred, exploitation and isolation, but will be a human and beautiful framework, created in a community, bonded not by color, sex or class, but by love and the common goal for the liberation of mind, heart, and spirit."[17] It has been the praxis of a differential form of oppositional consciousness which has stubbornly called up utopian visions such as these. . . .

The praxis of U.S. third world feminism represented by the differential form of oppositional consciousness is threaded throughout the experience of social marginality. As such it is also being woven into the fabric of experiences belonging to more and more citizens who are caught in the crisis of late capitalist conditions and expressed in the cultural angst most often referred to as the postmodern dilemma. The juncture I am proposing, therefore, is extreme. It is a location wherein the praxis of U.S. third world feminism links with the aims of white feminism, studies of race, ethnicity, and marginality, and with postmodern theories of culture as they crosscut and join together in new relationships through a shared comprehension of an emerging theory and method of oppositional consciousness.

(1991)

NOTES

1. This is an early version of a chapter from my book on "Oppositional Consciousness in the Postmodern World." A debt of gratitude is owed the friends, teachers, and politically committed scholars who made the publication of this essay possible, especially Hayden White, Donna Haraway, James Clifford, Ronaldo Balderrama, Ruth Frankenberg, Lata Mani (who coerced me into publishing this now), Rosa Maria Villafane-Sisolak, A. Pearl Sandoval, Mary John, Vivian Sobchak, Helene Moglan, T. de Lauretis, Audre Lorde, Traci Chapman, and the Student of Color Coalition. Haraway's own commitments to social, gender, race, and class justice are embodied in the fact that she discusses and cites an earlier version of this essay in her own work. See especially her 1985 essay where she defines an oppositional postmodern consciousness grounded in multiple identities in her "A Manifesto for Cyborgs: Science, Technology, and Socialist Feminism in the 1980s," *Socialist Review*, no. 80 (March 1985). At a time when theoretical work by women of color is so frequently dismissed, Haraway's recognition and discussion of my work on oppositional consciousness has allowed it to receive wide critical visibility, as reflected in references to the manuscript that appear in the works of authors such as Sandra Harding, Nancy Hartsock, Biddy Martin, and Katherine Hayles. I am happy that my work has also received attention from Caren Kaplan, Katie King, Gloria Anzaldua, Teresa de Lauretis, Chandra Mohanty, and Yvonne Yarboro-Bejarano. Thanks also are due Fredric Jameson, who in 1979 recognized a theory of "oppositional consciousness" in my work. It was he who encouraged its further development.

   This manuscript was first presented publically at the 1981 National Women's Studies Association conference. In the ten years following, five other versions have been circulated. I could not resist the temptation to collapse sections from these earlier manuscripts here in the footnotes; any resulting awkwardness is not due to the vigilance of my editors. This essay is published now to honor the political, intellectual, and personal aspirations of Rosa Maria Villafane-Sisolak, "West Indian Princess," who died April 20, 1990. Ro's compassion, her sharp intellectual prowess and honesty, and her unwavering commitment to social justice continue to inspire, guide, and support many of us. To her, to those named here, and to all new generations of U.S. third world feminists this work is dedicated.

2. Gayatri Spivak, "The Rani of Sirmur," in *Europe and Its Others*, ed. F. Barker, vol. 1 (Essex: University of Essex, 1985), 147.

3. Here, U.S. third world feminism represents the political alliance made during the 1960s and 1970s between a generation of U.S. feminists of color who were separated by culture, race, class, or gender identifications but united through similar responses to the experience of race oppression. The theory and method of oppositional

consciousness outlined in this essay is visible in the activities of the recent political unity variously named "U.S. third world feminist," "feminist women of color," and "womanist." This unity has coalesced across differences in race, class, language, ideology, culture, and color. These differences are painfully manifest: materially marked physiologically or in language, socially value laden, and shot through with power. They confront each feminist of color in any gathering where they serve as constant reminders of their undeniability. These constantly speaking differences stand at the crux of another, mutant unity, for this unity does not occur in the name of all "women," nor in the name of race, class, culture, or "humanity" in general. Instead, as many U.S. third world feminists have pointed out, it is unity mobilized in a location heretofore unrecognized. As Cherrie Moraga argues, this unity mobilizes "between the seemingly irreconcilable lines—class lines, politically correct lines, the daily lines we run to each other to keep difference and desire at a distance," it is *between* these lines "that the truth of our connection lies." This connection is a mobile unity, constantly weaving and reweaving an interaction of differences into coalition. In what follows I demonstrate how it is that inside this coalition, differences are viewed as varying survival tactics constructed in response to recognizable power dynamics. See Cherrie Moraga, "Between the Lines. On Culture, Class and Homophobia," in *This Bridge Called My Back, A Collection of Writings by Radical Women of Color*, ed. Cherrie Moraga and Gloria Anzaldua (Watertown, MA: Persephone Press, 1981), 106. During the national conference of the Women's Studies Association in 1981, three hundred feminists of color met to agree that "it is white men who have access to the greatest amount of freedom from necessity in this culture, with women as their 'helpmates' and chattels, and people of color as their women's servants. People of color form a striated social formation which allow men of color to call upon the circuits of power which charge the category of 'male' with its privileges, leaving women of color as the final chattel, the ultimate servant in a racist and sexist class hierarchy. U.S. third world feminists seek to undo this hierarchy by reconceptualizing the notion of 'freedom' and who may inhabit its realm." See Sandoval, "The Struggle Within: A Report on the 1981 NWSA Conference," published by the Center for Third World Organizing, 1982, reprinted by Gloria Anzaldua in *Making Faces Making Soul, Haciendo Caras* (San Francisco: Spinsters/Aunt Lute, 1990), 55–71. See also "Comment on Krieger's *The Mirror Dance*," a U.S. third world feminist perspective, in *Signs* 9, no. 4 (Summer 1984): 725.

4. See Fredric Jameson's "Postmodernism, or the Cultural Logic of Late Capitalism," *New Left Review* 146 (July–August 1984).

5. In another essay I characterize such legitimated idioms of subordination as "human," "pet," "game," and "wild."

6. Gloria Anzaldua writes that she lives "between and among" cultures in "La Prieta," *This Bridge Called My Back*, 209.

7. Differential consciousness functioning like a "car clutch" is a metaphor suggested by Yves Labissiere in a personal conversation.

8. Aida Hurtado, "Reflections on White Feminism: A Perspective from a Woman of Color" (1985), 25, from an unpublished manuscript. Another version of this quotation appears in Hurtado's essay, "Relating to Privilege: Seduction and Rejection in the Subordination of White Women and Women of Color," in *Signs* 14, no. 4 (Summer 1989): 833–55.

9. Moraga and Anzaldua, *This Bridge Called My Back*, xix. Also see the beautiful passage from Margaret Walker's *Jubilee* which enacts this mobile mode of consciousness from the viewpoint of the female protagonist. See the Bantam Books edition (New York, 1985), 404–407.

10. Gloria Anzaldua, "La Prieta," *This Bridge Called My Back*, 209.

11. Audre Lorde, "Comments at 'The Personal and the Political Panel,'" Second Sex Conference, New York, September 1979. Published in *This Bridge Called My Back*, 98. Also see "The Uses of the Erotic" in *Sister Outsider*, 58–63, which calls for challenging and undoing authority in order to enter a utopian realm only accessible through a processual form of consciousness which she names the "erotic."

12. Anzaldua refers to this survival skill as "la facultad, the capacity to see in surface phenomena the meaning of deeper realities" in *Borderlands, La Frontera*, 38.

The consciousness which typifies la facultad is not naive to the moves of power: it is constantly surveying and negotiating its moves. Often dismissed as "intuition," this kind of "perceptiveness," "sensitivity," consciousness if you will, is not determined by race, sex, or any other genetic status, neither does its activity belong solely to the "proletariat," the "feminist," nor to the oppressed, if the oppressed is considered a unitary category, but it is a learned emotional and intellectual skill which is developed amidst hegemonic powers. It is the recognition of "la facultad" which moves Lorde to say that it is marginality, "whatever its nature . . . which is also the source of our greatest strength," for the cultivation of la facultad creates the opportunity for a particularly effective form of opposition to the dominant culture within which it is formed. The skills required by la facultad are capable of disrupting the dominations and subordinations that scar U.S. culture. But it is not enough to utilize them on an individual and situational basis. Through an ethical and political commitment, U.S. third world feminism requires the development of la facultad to a methodological level capable of generating a political strategy and identity politics from which a new citizenry arises.

Movements of resistance have always relied upon the ability to read below the surfaces—a way of mobilizing—to resee reality and call it by different names. This form of la facultad inspires new visions and strategies for action. But there is always the danger that even the most revolutionary of readings can become bankrupt as a form of resistance when it becomes reified, unchanging. The tendency of la facultad to end in frozen, privileged "readings" is the most divisive dynamic inside of any liberation movement. In order for this survival skill to provide the basis for a differential and unifying methodology, it must be remembered that la facultad is a process. Answers located may be only temporarily effective, so that wedded to the process of la facultad is a flexibility that continually woos change.

13. Maria Lugones, "Playfulness, World-Travelling, and Loving Perception," from *Hypatia: A Journal of Feminist Philosophy* 2, no. 2 (1987).

14. Barbara Christian, "Creating a Universal Literature: Afro-American Women Writers," *KPFA Folio,* Special African History Month Edition, February 1983, front page. Reissued in *Black Feminist Criticism: Perspectives on Black Women Writers* (New York: Pergamon Press, 1985), 163.

15. 15. bell hooks, "Feminist Theory: From Margin to Center," 9; Audre Lorde, "An Interview: Andre Lorde and Adrienne Rich" held in August 1979, *Signs* 6, no. 4 (Summer 1981); and Barbara Smith, *Home Girls: A Black Feminist Anthology,* xxv.

16. Alice Walker coined the neologism "womanist" as one of many attempts by feminists of color to find a name which could signal their commitment to egalitarian social relations, a commitment which the name "feminism" had seemingly betrayed. See Walker, *In Search of Our Mother's Gardens: Womanist Prose* (New York: Harcourt Brace Jovanovich, 1983), xi–xiii. Anzaldua, *Borderlands, La Nueva Frontera.*

17. Merle Woo, "Letter to Ma," *This Bridge Called My Back,* 147.

77 • *Angela Y. Davis*

"OUTCAST MOTHERS AND SURROGATES: RACISM AND REPRODUCTIVE POLITICS IN THE NINETIES"

The historical construction of women's reproductive role, which is largely synonymous with the historical failure to acknowledge the possibility of reproductive self-determination, has been informed by a peculiar constellation of racist and misogynist assumptions. These assumptions have undergone mutations even as they remain tethered to their historical origins. To explore the politics of reproduction in a contemporary context is to recognize the growing intervention of technology into the most intimate spaces of human life: from computerized bombings in the Persian Gulf, that have taken life from thousands of children and adults as if they were nothing more than the abstract statistics of a video game, to the complex technologies awaiting women who wish to transcend biological, or socially induced infertility. I do not mean to suggest that technology is inherently oppressive. Rather, the socioeconomic conditions within which reproductive technologies are being developed, applied, and rendered accessible or inaccessible maneuver them in directions that most often maintain or deepen misogynist, anti-working class, and racist marginalization.

To the extent that fatherhood is denied as a socially significant moment in the process of biological reproduction, the politics of reproduction hinge on the social construction of motherhood. The new developments in reproductive technology have encouraged the contemporary emergence of popular attitudes—at least among the middle classes—that bear a remarkable resemblance to the nineteenth-century cult of motherhood, including the moral, legal, and political taboos it developed against abortion. While the rise of industrial capitalism led to the historical obsolescence of the domestic economy and the ideological imprisonment of (white and middle-class) women within a privatized home sphere, the late twentieth-century breakthroughs in reproductive technology are resuscitating that ideology in bizarre and contradictory ways. Women who can afford to take advantage of the new technology—who are often career women for whom motherhood is no longer a primary or exclusive vocation—now encounter a mystification of maternity emanating from the possibility of transcending biological (and socially defined) reproductive incapacity. It is as if the recognition of infertility is now a catalyst—among some groups of women—for a motherhood quest that has become more compulsive and more openly ideological than during the nineteenth century. Considering the anti-abortion campaign, it is not difficult to envision this contemporary ideological mystification of motherhood as central to the efforts to deny all women the legal rights that would help shift the politics of reproduction toward a recognition of our autonomy with respect to the biological functions of our bodies.

In the United States, the nineteenth-century cult of motherhood was complicated by a number of class- and race-based contradictions. Women who had recently immigrated from Europe were cast, like their male counterparts, into the industrial proletariat, and were therefore compelled to play economic roles that contradicted the increasing representation of women as wives/mothers. Moreover, in conflating slave motherhood and the reproduction of its labor force, the moribund slave economy effectively denied motherhood to vast numbers of African women. . . .

Slave women were *birth mothers* or *genetic mothers*—to employ terms rendered possible by the new reproductive technologies—but they possessed no legal rights as mothers of any kind. Considering the commodification of their children—and indeed, of their own persons— their status was similar to that of the contemporary *surrogate mother.* I am suggesting that the term *surrogate mother* might be invoked as a retroactive description of their status because the economic appropriation of their reproductive capacity reflected the inability of the slave economy to produce and reproduce its own laborers—a limitation with respect to the forces of economic production that is being transformed in this era of advanced capitalism by the increasing computerization and robotization of the economy.

The children of slave mothers could be sold away by their owners for business reasons or as a result of a strategy of repression. They could also be forced to give birth to children fathered by their masters, knowing full well that the white fathers would never recognize their Black children as offspring. As a consequence of the socially constructed invisibility of the white father—a pretended invisibility strangely respected by the white and Black community alike—Black children would grow up in an intimate relation to their white half-brothers and sisters, except that their biological kinship, often revealed by a visible physical resemblance, would remain shrouded in silence. That feature of slave motherhood was something about which no one could speak. Slave women who had been compelled—or had, for their own reasons, agreed—to engage in sexual intercourse with their masters would be committing the equivalent of a crime if they publicly revealed the fathers of their children.[1] These women knew that it was quite likely that their children might also be sold or brutalized or beaten by their own fathers, brothers, uncles, or nephews.

If I have lingered over what I see as some of the salient reproductive issues in African-American women's history, it is because they seem to shed light on the ideological context of contemporary technological intervention in the realm of reproduction. Within the contemporary feminist discourse about the new reproductive technologies—in vitro fertilization, surrogacy, embryo transfer, etc.—concern has been expressed about what is sometimes described as the "deconstruction of motherhood"[2] as a unified biological process. While the new technological developments have rendered the fragmentation of maternity more obvious, the economic system of slavery fundamentally relied upon alienated and fragmented maternities, as women were forced to bear children, whom masters claimed as potentially profitable labor machines. Birth mothers could not therefore expect to be mothers in the legal sense. Legally these children were chattel and therefore motherless. Slave states passed laws to the effect that children of slave women no more belonged to their biological mothers than the young of animals belonged to the females that birthed them.[3]

At the same time, slave women and particularly those who were house slaves were expected to nurture and rear and mother the children of their owners. It was not uncommon for white children of the slave-owning class to have relationships of a far greater emotional intensity with the slave women who were their "mammies" than with their own white biological mothers. We might even question the meaning of this conception of "biological motherhood" in light of the fact that the Black nurturers of these white children were frequently "wet nurses" as well. They nourished the babies in their care with the milk produced by their own hormones. It seems, therefore, that Black women were not only treated as surrogates with respect to the reproduction of slave labor, they also served as surrogate mothers for the white children of the slave-owners.

* * *

The economic history of African-American women—from slavery to the present—like the economic history of immigrant women, both from European and colonized or formerly colonized nations, reveals the persisting theme of work as household servants. Mexican women and Irish women, West Indian women and Chinese women have been compelled, by virtue of their economic standing, to function as servants for the wealthy. They have cleaned their houses and—our present concern—they have nurtured and reared their employers' babies. They have functioned as surrogate mothers. Considering this previous history, is it not possible to imagine the possibility that poor

women—especially poor women of color—might be transformed into a special caste of hired pregnancy carriers? Certainly such fears are not simply the product of an itinerant imagination. In any event, whether or not such a caste of women baby-bearers eventually makes its way into history, these historical experiences constitute a socio-historical backdrop for the present debate around the new reproductive technologies. The very fact that the discussion over surrogacy tends to coincide, by virtue of corporate involvement and intervention in the new technologies, with the debate over surrogacy for profit, makes it necessary to acknowledge historical economic precedents for surrogate motherhood. Those patterns are more or less likely to persist under the impact of the technology in its market context. The commodification of reproductive technologies, and, in particular, the labor services of pregnant surrogate mothers, means that money is being made and that, therefore, someone is being exploited. . . .

If the emerging debate around the new reproductive technologies is presently anchored to the socioeconomic conditions of relatively affluent families, the reproductive issues most frequently associated with poor and working-class women of color revolve around the apparent proliferation of young single parents, especially in the African-American community. For the last decade or so, teenage pregnancy has been ideologically represented as one of the greatest obstacles to social progress in the most impoverished sectors of the Black community. In actuality, the *rate* of teenage pregnancy in the Black community—like that among white teenagers—has been waning for quite a number of years. According to a National Research Council study, fertility rates in 1960 were 156 births per 1,000 Black women aged 15 to 19, and 97 in 1985.[4] What distinguishes teenage pregnancy in the Black community today from its historical counterpart is the deceasing likelihood of teenage marriages. There is a constellation of reasons for the failure of young teenagers to consolidate traditional two-parent families. The most obvious one is that it rarely makes economic sense for an unemployed young woman to marry an unemployed young man. As a consequence of shop closures in industries previously accessible to young Black male workers—and the overarching deindustrialization of the economy—young men capable of contributing to the support of their children are becoming increasingly scarce. For a young woman whose pregnancy results from a relationship with an unemployed youth, it makes little sense to enter into a marriage that will probably bring in an extra adult as well as a child to be supported by her own mother/father/grandmother, etc. . . .

I have chosen to evoke the reproductive issues of single motherhood among teenagers in order to highlight the absurdity of locating motherhood in a transcendent space—as the anti-abortion theorists and activists do—in which involuntary motherhood is as sacred as voluntary motherhood. In this context, there is a glaring exception: motherhood among Black and Latina teens is constructed as a moral and social evil—but even so, they are denied accessible and affordable abortions. Moreover, teen mothers are ideologically assaulted because of their premature and impoverished entrance into the realm of motherhood while older, whiter, and wealthier women are coaxed to buy the technology to assist them in achieving an utterly commodified motherhood.

Further contradictions in the contemporary social compulsion toward motherhood—contradictions rooted in race and class—can be found in the persisting problem of sterilization abuse. While poor women in many states have effectively lost access to abortion, they may be sterilized with the full financial support of the government. While the "right" to opt for surgical sterilization is an important feature of women's control over the reproductive functions of their bodies, the imbalance between the difficulty of access to abortions and the ease of access to sterilization reveals the continued and tenacious insinuation of racism into the politics of reproduction. The astounding high—and continually mounting—statistics regarding the sterilization of Puerto Rican women expose one of the most dramatic ways in which women's bodies bear the evidence of colonization. Likewise, the bodies of vast numbers of sterilized indigenous women within the presumed borders of the U.S. bear the traces of a 500-year-old tradition of genocide. While there is as yet no evidence of large-scale sterilization of African-American and Latina teenage girls, there is documented evidence of the federal government's promotion and funding of sterilization operations for young Black girls during the 1960s and 70s. This historical precedent convinces me that it is not inappropriate to speculate about such a future possibility of preventing teenage pregnancy. Or—to engage in further

speculation—of recruiting healthy young poor women, a disproportionate number of whom would probably be Black, Latina, Native American, Asian, or from the Pacific Islands, to serve as pregnancy carriers for women who can afford to purchase these services.

* * *

In pursuing a few of the ways in which racism—and class bias—inform the contemporary politics of reproduction, I am suggesting that there are numerous unexplored vantage points from which we can reconceptualize reproductive issues. It is no longer acceptable to ground an analysis of the politics of reproduction in a conceptual construction of "woman" as a sex. It is not enough to assume that female beings whose bodies are distinguished by vaginas, ovarian tubes, uteri, and other biological features related to reproduction should be able to claim such "rights" to exercise control over the processes of these organs as the right to abortion. The social/economic/political circumstances that oppress and marginalize women of various racial, ethnic, and class backgrounds, and thus alter the impact of ideological conceptions of motherhood, cannot be ignored without affirming the same structures of domination that have led to such different—but related—politics of reproduction in the first place.

In conclusion, I will point to some of the strategic constellations that should be taken into consideration in reconceiving an agenda of reproductive rights. I do not present the following points as an exhaustive list of such goals, but rather I am trying to allude to a few of the contemporary issues requiring further theoretical examination and practical/political action. While the multiple arenas in which women's legal abortion rights are presently being assaulted and eroded can account for the foregrounding of this struggle, the failure to regard economic accessibility of birth control and abortion has equally important results in the inevitable marginalization of poor women's reproductive rights. With respect to a related issue, the "right" and access to sterilization is important, but again, it is equally important to look at those economic and ideological conditions that track some women toward sterilization, thus denying them the possibility of bearing and rearing children in numbers they themselves choose.

Although the new reproductive technologies cannot be construed as inherently affirmative or violative of women's reproductive rights, the anchoring of the technologies to the profit schemes of their producers and distributors results in a commodification of motherhood that complicates and deepens power relationships based on class and race. Yet, beneath this marriage of technology, profit, and the assertion of a historically obsolete bourgeois individualism lies the critical issue of the right to determine the character of one's family. The assault on this "right"—a term I have used throughout, which is not however, unproblematic—is implicated in the ideological offensive against single motherhood as well as in the homophobic refusal to recognize lesbian and gay family configurations—and especially in the persisting denial of custody (even though some changes have occurred) to lesbians with children from previous heterosexual marriages. This is one of the many ways in which the present-day ideological compulsion toward motherhood that I have attempted to weave into all of my arguments further resonates. Moreover, this ideology of motherhood is wedded to an obdurate denial of the very social services women require in order to make meaningful choices to bear or not to bear children. Such services include health care—from the prenatal period to old age—child care, housing, education, jobs, and all the basic services human beings require to lead decent lives. The privatization of family responsibilities—particularly during an era when so many new family configurations are being invented that the definition of family stretches beyond its own borders—takes on increasingly reactionary implications. This is why I want to close with a point of departure: the reconceptualization of family and of reproductive rights in terms that move from the private to the public, from the individual to the social.

(1993)

NOTES

1. See Harriet A. Jacobs. *Incidents in the Life of a Slave Girl.* Edited and Introduction by Jean Fagan Yellin. Cambridge, Mass.: Harvard University Press, p. 1087.
2. See Michelle Stanworth, ed. *Reproductive Technologies: Gender, Motherhood and Medicine.* Minneapolis: University of Minnesota Press, 1987.
3. See Paula Giddings. *When and Where I Enter: The Impact of Black Women on Race and Sex in America.* New York: William Morrow, 1984.
4. See Marc Mauer, "Young Black Men and the Criminal Justice System: A Growing National Problem." A Report by the Sentencing Project, 918 F Street, N.W. Suite 501, Washington, D.C. 20004, February 1990.

78 • Andy Smith

"ECOFEMINISM THROUGH AN ANTICOLONIAL FRAMEWORK"

Barbara Smith articulates a feminist politics that challenges all forms of social domination: "Feminism is the political theory and practice that struggles to free all women: women of color, working-class women, poor women, disabled women, lesbians, old women—as well as white, economically privileged, heterosexual women. Anything less than this vision of total freedom is not feminism, but merely female self-aggrandizement."[1] Ynestra King extends this analysis to include the domination of nature prevalent in mainstream Western

From *Ecofeminism: Women, Culture, Nature* by Karen J. Warren, ed. Copyright © 1997 by Indiana University Press. Reprinted with permission of Indiana University Press. Notes have been renumbered.

society: "[Ecofeminism's] challenge of social domination extends beyond sex to social domination of all kinds, because the domination of sex, race, and class and the domination of nature are mutually reinforcing."[2]

The term *ecofeminism* may seem to imply that ecofeminists are concerned only about the oppression of women and the oppression of earth. But, as Karen J. Warren argues, "Because all feminists do or must oppose the logic of domination which keeps oppressive conceptual frameworks in place, all feminists must also oppose any isms of domination that are maintained and justified by that logic of domination."[3]

Many ecofeminist theorists argue that there is no primary form of oppression, as all oppressions are related and reinforce each other. However, depending on one's position in society, there is often one form of oppression that seems most pressing in one's everyday life. For instance, King's statement that "domination of woman was the original domination in human society, from which all other hierarchies—of rank, class, and political power—flow"[4] suggests that, for her, sexism is the most pressing form of oppression.

For Native American women, sexism oppression often seems secondary to colonial oppression. As Lorelei Means states,

> We are American Indian women, in that order. We are oppressed, first and foremost, as American Indians, as peoples colonized by the United States of America, not as women. As Indians, we can never forget that. Our survival, the survival of every one of us—man, woman and child—as Indians depends on it. Decolonization is the agenda, the whole agenda, and until it is accomplished, it is the only agenda that counts for American Indians.[5]

Many Native women completely dismiss feminism in light of colonization.[6] I do not necessarily see one oppression as more important than others. However, most Native women probably feel the impact of colonization on our everyday lives more than other forms of oppression.

One reason why colonization seems to be the primary issue for Native women is that most forms of oppression did not exist in most Native societies prior to colonization.[7] As Paula Gunn Allen and Annette Jaimes have shown, prior to colonization, Indian societies were not male dominated. Women served as spiritual, political, and military leaders. Many

societies were matrilineal and matrilocal. Violence against women and children was unheard of. Although there existed at division of labor between women and men, women's labor and men's labor were accorded similar status. Environmental destruction also did not exist in Indian societies. As Winona LaDuke states,

> Traditionally, American Indian women were never subordinate to men. Or vice versa, for that matter. What native societies have always been about is achieving balance in all things, gender relations no less than any other. Nobody needs to tell us how to do it. We've had that all worked out for thousands for years. And, left to our own devices, that's exactly how we'd be living right now.[8]

With colonization begins the domination of women and the domination of nature. As Allen argues, subjugating Indian women was critical in our colonizers' efforts to subjugate Indian societies as a whole: "The assault on the system of woman power requires the replacing of a peaceful, nonpunitive, nonauthoritarian social system wherein women wield power by making social life easy and gentle with one based on child terrorization, male dominance and submission of women to male authority."[9]

Other women, particularly white women, may not experience colonization as a primary form of oppression to the degree that Native women do. However, I do believe it is essential that ecofeminist theory more seriously grapple with the issues of colonization, particularly the colonization of Native lands, in its analysis of oppression.

One reason why this is necessary is because Native lands are the site of the most environmental destruction that takes place in this country. About 60 percent of the energy resources (i.e., coal, oil, uranium) in this country are on Indian land.[10] In addition, 100 percent of uranium production takes place on or near Indian land.[11] In the areas where there is uranium mining, such as Four Corners and the Black Hills, Indian people face skyrocketing incidents of radiation poisoning and birth defects.[12] Many Navajo traditionalists are speculating that the "mystery virus" that is afflicting people in Arizona may be related to the uranium tailings left by mining companies. They think that the uranium has poisoned rats in the area.[13] Children growing up in this area are developing ovarian and testicular cancers at fifteen times the national average.[14] Indian women on Pine Ridge experience a miscarriage rate six times higher than the national average.[15]

Native reservations are often targeted for toxic waste dumps, since companies do not have to meet the same EPA standards that they do on other lands.[16] Over fifty reservations have been targeted for waste dumps.[17] In addition, military and nuclear testing takes place on Native lands. For instance, there have been at least 650 nuclear explosions on Shoshone land at the Nevada test site. Fifty percent of the underground tests have leaked radiation into the atmosphere.[18]

At the historic People of Color Environmental Summit held in October 1991 in Washington, D.C., Native people from across the country reported the environmental destruction taking place on Indian lands through resource development. The Yakima people in Washington State stated that nuclear wastes coming from the Hanford nuclear reactor had been placed in such unstable containers that they were now leaking, and they believed that their underground water was contaminated. They said it would cost $150 billion to clean up these wastes,[19] and plans were being made to relocate the wastes to a repository on Yucca Mountain, where the Shoshone live, at a cost of $3.25 billion. Yucca Mountain is on an active volcanic zone. Kiloton bombs are also exploded nearby, thus increasing the risks of radioactive leakage.[20] . . .

Because Native people suffer the brunt of environmental destruction, it is incumbent upon ecofeminist theorists to analyze colonization as a fundamental aspect of the domination of nature. This is true not just because we should all be concerned about the welfare of Native people but also because what befalls Native people will eventually affect everyone. Radiation will not stay nicely packaged on Indian land; it will eventually affect all of the land. . . .

Another example illustrating colonialist attitudes in the environmental and feminist movements is the increasingly popular concept of "population control." According to the Population Institute, "Burgeoning population is the single greatest threat to the health of the planet."[21] According to the Sierra Club, lack of population control is the cause of infant mortality, famine, poverty, noise pollution, global warming, and most forms of environmental damage: "If we don't act now to stabilize the human population, then the death

factor will act for us. Disease, famine and war will eventually stop the inexorable expansion of our masses."[22] Planned Parenthood echoes that population control contributes "to the process of socio-economic development and to family health, particularly in countries where rapid population growth hinders development efforts."[23]

But as Betsy Hartmann points out, population issues serve to disguise the real causes of environmental destruction:

> dominant economic systems which squander natural and human resources in the drive for short-term profits; and the displacement of peasant farmers and indigenous peoples by agribusiness, timber, mining and energy firms. Ignored also is the role of international lending institutions, war and arms production, and the wasteful consumption patterns of industrialized countries and wealthy elites the world over in creating and exacerbating environmental destruction.[24]

I would argue that colonization and not overpopulation is the cause of poverty in the Third World. Land which formerly supported local subsistence has been appropriated by imperialist countries to produce export crops for the First World. Since much of the land is going to produce export crops rather than crops to meet local needs, people in the Third World find themselves increasingly relying upon imports. The money they spend on imports is more than they make from selling export crops. Consequently, they find themselves in spiraling debt. To maintain these systems of economic inequality, the United States and other colonial powers provide covert and overt support to military regimes to crush popular uprisings. I would argue that is the cause of war, not overpopulation as the Sierra Club would have us believe.

"Overpopulation" is a natural consequence of colonization, since families in colonized lands need as many workers as possible to meet their financial responsibilities. In Bangladesh, boys at age ten are producing more than they consume and by age fifteen have repaid their parents' investment in their upbringing.[25] Consequently, under conditions of colonization, it is in the economic interest of Third World women to have more children in order to raise more export crops. Until the broader social, economic, and political problems are addressed, it will not be in the best interest of the poor to have fewer children.

The average American consumes three hundred times more energy than the average Bangladeshi.[26] The United States constitutes 4 percent of the world's population and consumes 30 percent of its resources. It follows that population control efforts should be directed toward the United States. In fact, some organizations, such as Population-Environment Balance, have argued that the United States is overpopulated. Their solution is to restrict immigration into the United States because it adds "to the United States' rapid population growth (now over three million per year) which already threatens our environment's health" and burdens the taxpayer through "increased funding obligations in AFDC, Medicare, Food Stamps, School Lunch, Unemployment Compensation, [etc.]."[27]

It would seem logical that if U.S. immigrants are poor enough to be on food stamps, then they are probably not the people who are expending most of the energy resources in this country. It would seem we need population control to be directed toward the richest groups in this country. Furthermore, if the United States would stop supporting totalitarian regimes in other countries in order to promote its economic and political interests, we might find that fewer people will need to immigrate.

Again, environmental (and many feminist) organizations blame Third World women and women of color in the United States for all the world's ills, charging that they are having too many babies. It is seen as critical that women of color restrict their births by any means necessary. White middle-class women have been organizing around issues of reproductive freedom, and they have often framed their struggle in terms of "choice" (i.e., they are prochoice). However, when President Bill Clinton reversed the Mexico City policy so that the United States would reinstate funding to organizations that perform abortions as a method of family planning, he stated that his motivation was to "stabilize the world's population," not to increase choices for women. Women of color, in fact, do not get choices regarding our reproductive health. In the efforts to stabilize our population, we are constantly subjected to unsafe drug testing or forced sterilization.

Before Norplant devices were introduced in the United States, nearly one-half million women in Indonesia had been inserted with these devices, often without counseling on their possible side effects (which include menstrual irregularity, nausea, and nervousness). No long-term studies on the effects had been conducted. Many of the women were not told that the devices needed to be removed after five years to avoid an increased risk of ectopic pregnancy.[28] Some 3,500 women in India were implanted with Norplant 2 without being warned about possible side effects or screened to determine if they were suitable candidates. The devices were eventually removed from use owing to concerns about "teratogenicity and carcinogenicity." But in both cases, women who wanted the implant removed had great difficulty finding doctors who would remove them.[29] (Similarly, in the United States many doctors can insert the devices but few know how to remove them.)

Poor women and women of color in the United States are singled out as likely candidates for the devices. State legislatures have been considering bills which would give women on public assistance bonuses if they used them. In California, a black single mother charged with child abuse was given the "choice" of using Norplant or being sentenced to four years in prison. The *Philadelphia Inquirer* ran an editorial suggesting that Norplant could be a useful tool in "reducing the underclass."[30] Every woman I know who is on AFDC has received a call from her caseworker insisting that she go on Norplant and has been advised that there are no side effects to Norplant.[31] I also know that many women who go into Indian health services for contraceptive counseling are often given Depo-Provera or Norplant without being told what they are or even told that other forms of contraception exist. . . .

I have discussed why it is essential for ecofeminist theory to more fully analyze sexism and environmental destruction in terms of colonization. In particular, I have discussed why Native rights have to be on the ecofeminist agenda. I would now like to discuss the process by which ecofeminists can be more inclusive of Native women's struggles.

Environmentalist, ecofeminist thinkers pay tribute to Native people and their ability to live harmoniously with nature. As Judith Plant states, "The shift from the western theological tradition of the hierarchical chain of being to an earth-based spirituality begins the healing of the split between spirit and matter. For ecofeminist spirituality, like the traditions of Native Americans and other tribal peoples, sees the spiritual as alive in us, where spirit and matter, mind and body, are all part of the same living organism."[32]

However, ecofeminist thinkers do not adequately discuss the material conditions in which Indian people live, how these conditions affect non-Indians, and what strategies we can employ to stop the genocide of Indian people and end the destructive forms of resource development on Indian land. Rather, they use Indian people as inspirational symbols for the environmental movement. Ecofeminists quote Native people, but they seldom take the time to develop relationships with Indian communities to struggle along with us. . . .

Carol B. Christ talks at length about Native spirituality.[33] One source she quotes is Lynn Andrews's *Flight of the Seventh Moon*, which has been denounced by most Native people as a thoroughly exploitative and inaccurate rendition of Native spirituality. It appears that Christ has no real ongoing relationship with Indian communities from which to derive her inspiration. Her perceptions of Native reality are not grounded in the present-day lived struggles of Native people but in her (mis)perceptions of Native spirituality based on books.

Ecofeminist thinkers often appropriate Native culture to advance their claims. I have discussed elsewhere the problems of Native cultural appropriation.[34] I think that these white ecofeminist theorists, besides being imperialist when they appropriate Native traditions, also do themselves a disservice.

In my view, mainstream society has very little understanding of spirituality. Our individualist, capitalist society tends to destroy our sense of meaningful connectedness with nature, with all creatures and all people, and to replace these relationships with commodities. Instead of looking for joy in our relationships, we look for joy at the shopping center and what we can buy for ourselves. In mainstream Christianity, we also buy prepackaged spirituality. We go to church once a week and forget about God the rest of the week; we listen to preachers who give us simple solutions to complex problems; we buy books that explain what our spirituality should be. This has little to do with spirituality because spirituality *is* one's life. Spirituality is not something one reads about or something one gets at a certain place at a certain day of the week. It is living one's life with the understanding that one is intimately connected to all of creation, all forces seen and unseen.

Thus for Native people, spirituality is most clearly seen in our everyday struggles for survival. It is not seen in a Lynn Andrews book. It is an integral part of

struggle against genocide. It is what holds us together against the forces of oppression. Many non-Natives, particularly white people, often sense a spiritual void in their religious traditions and look to Native people for spirituality. Ecofeminists look to Native spirituality to help connect them with the earth. Unfortunately, when they appropriate Native spirituality out of its context, when they seek Indian spirituality in a book or a $300 sweat lodge, they are treating Native spirituality as a commodity. What they are receiving has nothing to do with spirituality. Only by becoming unconditional, faithful allies with Native people in their struggles against genocide will non-Native people ever understand anything about Native spirituality. As Chrystos writes in her poem "Shame On" about Indian spiritual exploitation,

America is starving to death for spiritual meaning.
It's the price you pay for taking everything.
It's the price you pay for buying everything.
It's the price you pay for loving your stuff more
    than life.
Everything goes on without you.
You can't hear the grass breathe because you're too
    busy talking about being an Indian holy
    woman 200 years ago.
The wind won't talk to you because you're always
    right, even when you don't know what you're
    talking about.
We've been polite for 500 years and you still don't
    get it.
Take nothing you cannot return.
Give to others; give more.
Walk quietly, do what needs to be done.
Give thanks for your life; respect all beings.
Simple, and it doesn't cost a penny.[35]
. . .

(1997)

NOTES

1. Barbara Smith, "Racism and Women's Studies," *But Some of Us Are Brave* (Old Westbury: Feminist Press, 1982), p. 49.
2. Ynestra King, "The Ecology of Feminism and the Feminism of Ecology," in *Healing the Wounds* (Philadelphia: New Society, 1989), p. 20.
3. Karen J. Warren, "A Feminist Philosophical Perspective on Ecofeminist Spiritualities," in *Ecofeminism and the*

Sacred, ed. Carol J. Adams (New York: Cross-roads, 1993).

4. King, "Ecology of Feminism," p. 25.

5. Lorelei DeCora Means, quoted in M. Annette Jaimes, "American Indian Women: At the Center of Indigenous Resistance in Contemporary North America," in *State of Native America* (Boston: South End Press, 1992), p. 314.

6. See Jaimes, "American Indian Women," pp. 311–37.

7. Some thinkers argue that there was environmental destruction and patriarchal oppression in most Native societies. Riane Eisler in "The Gaia Tradition and the Partnership Future" (in *Healing the Wounds*, p. 32) argues that we must approach tribal societies with caution since they "have all too often been blindly [*sic*] destructive of their environment. . . . there are Western and non-Western peasant and nomadic cultures that have overgrazed and overcultivated land, decimated forests . . . and killed off animals needlessly and indifferently" and "have been as barbarous as the most 'civilized' Roman emperors or the most 'spiritual' Christian inquisitors." What this analysis is based on is not clear. What tribal societies is she referring to that have authored the same kind of mass environmental destruction that is endemic in mainstream Western society? She regurgitates the tired notions that tribal people in general are savages without seeing any need to justify or explain this statement. While no society is perfect, her article does not address the fact that most Native societies in the United States were far more peaceful and socially just than their European counterparts. I think the reason thinkers such as Eisler claim that Native people were in fact savage and disrespectful to the environment is to suggest that Native people are not "innocent" victims of genocide, and consequently white people do not have to feel quite so guilty about the privileges they currently enjoy on the backs of Native people.

8. Quoted in Jaimes, "American Indian Women," p. 318.

9. Paula Gunn Allen, *The Sacred Hoop* (Boston: Beacon Press, 1986), p. 40.

10. Ward Churchill, *Marxism and Native Americans* (Boston: South End Press, 1983).

11. Ward Churchill, "The Political Economy of Radioactive Colonialism," in *State of Native America*, p. 242.

12. See Ward Churchill, "Radioactive Colonization," *Struggle for the Land* (Monroe, ME: Common Courage Press), pp. 261–328.

13. John Flynn, "How Many Legs Do the Rats Have?" *Smoke Signals*, July 1993, p. 1.

14. Valerie Tallman, "The Toxic Waste of Indian Lives," *Covert Action* 17 (Spring 1992), p. 17.

15. Lakota Harden, *Black Hills PAHA SAPA Report*, August–September 1980, p. 15.

16. One reason why Indian lands are targeted for various forms of environmental destruction is that many tribal government leaders are supported by the U.S. government and thus serve the interests of big business rather than the interests of Native people at large. This process began with the Indian Reorganization Act of 1934 in which traditional forms of indigenous government were supplanted in favor of a tribal council structure modeled after corporate boards. The U.S. government or corporations fund those candidates who sell Native lands for energy resource development. See Rebecca Robbins, "Self-Determination and Subordination: The Past, Present, and Future of American Indian Governance," *State of Native America*, pp. 87–122. In effect, tribal governments are similar to colonial governments in the Third World.

17. Conger Beasely, "Dances with Garbage," *E Magazine*, November–December 1991, p. 40.

18. Valerie Tallman, "Tribes Speak Out on Toxic Assault," *Lakota Times*, December 18, 1991.

19. Tallman, "Toxic Waste of Indian Lives," p. 18.

20. Tallman, "Tribes Speak Out on Toxic Assault."

21. 1991 Annual Report, Population Institute.

22. "Population Stabilization: The Real Solution," Sierra Club pamphlet.

23. Mission and Policy Statements, Planned Parenthood, 1984.

24. Betsy Hartmann, "Population Control as Foreign Policy," *Covert Action*, no. 39 (Winter 1991–92), p. 27.

25. *New Internationalist*, October 1987, p. 9.

26. Ibid.

27. *Clearinghouse Bulletin* 1, no. 3 (June 1991), p. 6.

28. Hartmann, "Population Control as Foreign Policy," pp. 29–30.

29. Ammu Joseph, "India's Population Bomb," *Ms.* 3, no. 3 (Nov/Dec. 1992), p. 12.

30. Gretchen Long, "Norplant: A Victory, Not a Panacea for Poverty," *National Lawyers Guild Practitioner* 50, no. 1, p. 11.

31. This includes women I know on a social basis and women I have worked with through my rape crisis center, Women of All Red Nations (WARN), and other women's organizations.

32. Judith Plant, in *Healing the Wounds*, p. 113.

33. Carol B. Christ, "Rethinking Technology and Nature," in *Healing the Wounds*.

34. See n. 44.

35. Chrystos, "Shame On," *Dream On* (Vancouver: Press Gang Publishers, 1991), 100–101.

"INTEGRATING DISABILITY, TRANSFORMING FEMINIST THEORY"

Over the last several years, disability studies has moved out of the applied fields of medicine, social work, and rehabilitation to become a vibrant new field of inquiry within the critical genre of identity studies. Charged with the residual fervor of the Civil Rights Movement, Women's Studies and race studies established a model in the academy for identity-based critical enterprises that followed, such as gender studies, queer studies, disability studies, and a proliferation of ethnic studies, all of which have enriched and complicated our understandings of social justice, subject formation, subjugated knowledges, and collective action.

Even though disability studies is now flourishing in disciplines such as history, literature, religion, theater, and philosophy in precisely the same way feminist studies did twenty-five years ago, many of its practitioners do not recognize that disability studies is part of this larger undertaking that can be called identity studies. Indeed, I must wearily conclude that much of current disability studies does a great deal of wheel reinventing. This is largely because many disability studies scholars simply do not know either feminist theory or the institutional history of Women's Studies. All too often, the pronouncements in disability studies of what we need to start addressing are precisely issues that feminist theory has been grappling with for years. This is not to say that feminist theory can be transferred wholly and intact over to the study of disability studies, but it is to suggest that feminist theory can offer profound insights, methods, and perspectives that would deepen disability studies.

Conversely, feminist theories all too often do not recognize disability in their litanies of identities that inflect the category of woman. Repeatedly, feminist issues that arc intricately entangled with disability—such as reproductive technology, the place of bodily differences, the particularities of oppression, the ethics of care, the construction of the subject—are discussed without any reference to disability. Like disability studies practitioners who are unaware of feminism, feminist scholars are often simply unacquainted with disability studies' perspectives. The most sophisticated and nuanced analyses of disability, in my view, come from scholars conversant with feminist theory. And the most compelling and complex analyses of gender intersectionality take into consideration what I call the ability/disability system—along with race, ethnicity, sexuality, and class. . . .

Disability studies can benefit from feminist theory and feminist theory can benefit from disability studies. Both feminism and disability studies are comparative and concurrent academic enterprises. Just as feminism has expanded the lexicon of what we imagine as womanly, has sought to understand and destigmatize what we call the subject position of woman, so has disability studies examined the identity *disabled* in the service of integrating people with disabilities more fully into our society. As such, both are insurgencies that are becoming institutionalized, underpinning inquiries outside and inside the academy. A feminist disability theory builds on the strengths of both.

FEMINIST DISABILITY THEORY

. . . Academic feminism is a complex and contradictory matrix of theories, strategies, pedagogies, and

Garland-Thomson, Rosemarie. "Integrating Disability, Transforming Feminist Theory." NWSA JOURNAL (now *Feminist Formations*) 14:3 (2002), 1–11, 28. © 2002 NWSA JOURNAL. Reprinted with permission of Johns Hopkins University Press.

practices. One way to think about feminist theory is to say that it investigates how culture saturates the particularities of bodies with meanings and probes the consequences of those meanings. Feminist theory is a collaborative, interdisciplinary inquiry and a self-conscious cultural critique that interrogates how subjects are multiply interpellated: in other words, how the representational systems of gender, race, ethnicity, ability, sexuality, and class mutually construct, inflect, and contradict one another. These systems intersect to produce and sustain ascribed, achieved, and acquired identities—both those that claim us and those that we claim for ourselves. A feminist disability theory introduces the ability/disability system as a category of analysis into this diverse and diffuse enterprise. It aims to extend current notions of cultural diversity and to more fully integrate the academy and the larger world it helps shape. . . .

Integrating disability into feminist theory is generative, broadening our collective inquiries, questioning our assumptions, and contributing to feminism's intersectionality. Introducing a disability analysis does not narrow the inquiry, limit the focus to only women with disabilities, or preclude engaging other manifestations of feminisms. Indeed, the multiplicity of foci we now call feminisms is not a group of fragmented, competing subfields, but rather a vibrant, complex conversation. In talking about feminist disability theory, I am not proposing yet another discrete feminism, but suggesting instead some ways that thinking about disability transforms feminist theory. Integrating disability does not obscure our critical focus on the registers of race, sexuality, ethnicity, or gender, nor is it additive. Rather, considering disability shifts the conceptual framework to strengthen our understanding of how these multiple systems intertwine, redefine, and mutually constitute one another. Integrating disability clarifies how this aggregate of systems operates together, yet distinctly, to support an imaginary norm and structure the relations that grant power, privilege, and status to that norm. Indeed, the cultural function of the disabled figure is to act as a synecdoche for all forms that culture deems non-normative.

We need to study disability in a feminist context to direct our highly honed critical skills toward the dual scholarly tasks of unmasking and re-imagining disability, not only for people with disabilities, but for everyone. As Simi Linton puts it, studying disability is "a prism through which one can gain a broader understanding of society and human experience" (1998, 118). It deepens our understanding of gender and sexuality, individualism and equality, minority group definitions, autonomy, wholeness, independence, dependence, health, physical appearance, aesthetics, the integrity of the body, community, and ideas of progress and perfection in every aspect of cultures. A feminist disability theory introduces what Eve Sedgwick has called a "universalizing view" of disability that will replace an often persisting "minoritizing view." Such a view will cast disability as "an issue of continuing, determinative importance in the lives of people across the spectrum" (1990, 1). In other words, understanding how disability operates as an identity category and cultural concept will enhance how we understand what it is to be human, our relationships with one another, and the experience of embodiment. The constituency for feminist disability studies is all of us, not only women with disabilities: disability is the most human of experiences, touching every family and—if we live long enough—touching us all.

THE ABILITY/DISABILITY SYSTEM

Feminist disability theory's radical critique hinges on a broad understanding of disability as a pervasive cultural system that stigmatizes certain kinds of bodily variations. At the same time, this system has the potential to incite a critical politics. The informing premise of feminist disability theory is that disability, like femaleness, is not a natural state of corporeal inferiority, inadequacy, excess, or a stroke of misfortune. Rather, disability is a culturally fabricated narrative of the body, similar to what we understand as the fictions of race and gender. The disability/ability system produces subjects by differentiating and marking bodies. Although this comparison of bodies is ideological rather than biological, it nevertheless penetrates into the formation of culture, legitimating an unequal distribution of resources, status, and power within a biased social and architectural environment. As such, disability has four aspects: first, it is a system for interpreting and disciplining bodily variations; second, it is a relationship between bodies and their environments; third, it is a set of practices that produce both the able-bodied and the disabled, fourth, it is a way of describing the inherent instability of the embodied self. The disability system excludes the kinds of bodily forms, functions, impairments, changes, or ambiguities that call into question our cultural fantasy of the body as a neutral, compliant instrument of some transcendent will. Moreover, disability is a broad term within which cluster ideological categories as varied as sick, deformed, crazy, ugly, old, maimed, afflicted, mad, abnormal, or debilitated—all of which disadvantage people by devaluing bodies that do not conform to cultural standards. Thus, the disability system functions to preserve and validate such privileged designations as beautiful, healthy, normal, fit, competent, intelligent—all of which provide cultural capital to those who can claim such statuses, who can reside within these subject positions. It is, then, the various interactions between bodies and world that materialize disability from the stuff of human variation and precariousness.

A feminist disability theory denaturalizes disability by unseating the dominant assumption that disability is something that is wrong with someone. By this I mean, of course, that it mobilizes feminism's highly developed and complex critique of gender, class, race, ethnicity, and sexuality as exclusionary and oppressive systems rather than as the natural and appropriate order of things. To do this, feminist disability theory engages several of the fundamental premises of critical theory: (1) that representation structures reality, (2) that the margins define the center, (3) that gender (or disability) is a way of signifying relationships of power, (4) that human identity is multiple and unstable, (5) that all analysis and evaluation have political implications. . . .

REPRESENTATION

The first domain of feminist theory that can be deepened by a disability analysis is representation. Western thought has long conflated femaleness and disability, understanding both as defective departures from a valued standard. Aristotle, for example, defined women as "mutilated males." Women, for Aristotle, have "improper form," we are "monstrosity[ies]" (1944, 27–8, 8–9). As what Nancy Tuana calls "misbegotten men," women thus become the primal freaks in Western history, envisioned as what we might now call congenitally deformed as a result of what we might now term genetic disability (1993, 18). More

recently, feminist theorists have argued that female embodiment is a disabling condition in sexist culture. Iris Marion Young, for instance, examines how enforced feminine comportment delimits women's sense of embodied agency, restricting them to "throwing like a girl" (1990b, 141). Young concludes that, "Women in a sexist society are physically handicapped" (1990b, 153). Even the general American public associates femininity with disability. A recent study on stereotyping showed that housewives, disabled people, blind people, so-called retarded people, and the elderly were all judged as being similarly incompetent. Such a study suggests that intensely normatively feminine positions—such as a housewife—are aligned with negative attitudes about people with disabilities (Fiske, Cuddy, and Glick 2001).[1] . . .

The gender, race, and ability systems intertwine further in representing subjugated people as being pure body, unredeemed by mind or spirit. This sense of embodiment is conceived of as either a lack or an excess. Women, for example, are considered castrated, or to use Marge Piercy's wonderful term, "penis-poor" (1969). They are thought to be hysterical or have overactive hormones. Women have been cast as alternately having insatiable appetites in some eras and as pathologically self-denying in other times. Similarly, disabled people have supposedly extra chromosomes or limb deficiencies. The differences of disability are cast as atrophy, meaning degeneration, or hypertrophy, meaning enlargement. People with disabilities are described as having aplasia, meaning absence or failure of formation, or hypoplasia, meaning underdevelopment. All these terms police variation and reference a hidden norm from which the bodies of people with disabilities and women are imagined to depart.

Female, disabled, and dark bodies are supposed to be dependent, incomplete, vulnerable, and incompetent bodies. Femininity and race are performances of disability. Women and the disabled are portrayed as helpless, dependent, weak, vulnerable, and incapable bodies. Women, the disabled, and people of color are always ready occasions for the aggrandizement of benevolent rescuers, whether strong males, distinguished doctors, abolititionists, or Jerry Lewis hosting his telethons. . . .

Subjugated bodies are pictured as either deficient or as profligate. For instance, what Susan Bordo describes as the too-muchness of women also haunts disability and racial discourses, marking subjugated bodies as ungovernable, intemperate, or threatening (1993). The historical figure of the monster, as well, invokes disability, often to serve racism and sexism. Although the term has expanded to encompass all forms of social and corporeal aberration, *monster* originally described people with congenital impairments. As departures from the normatively human, monsters were seen as category violations or grotesque hybrids. The semantics of monstrosity are recruited to explain gender violations such as Julia Pastrana, for example, the Mexican Indian "bearded woman," whose body was displayed in nineteenth-century freak shows both during her lifetime and after her death. . . .

Such representations ultimately portray subjugated bodies not only as inadequate or unrestrained but at the same time as redundant and expendable. Bodies marked and selected by such systems are targeted for elimination by varying historical and cross-cultural practices. Women, people with disabilities or appearance impairments, ethnic Others, gays and lesbians, and people of color are variously the objects of infanticide, selective abortion, eugenic programs, hate crimes, mercy killing, assisted suicide, lynching, bride burning, honor killings, forced conversion, coercive rehabilitation, domestic violence, genocide, normalizing surgical procedures, racial profiling, and neglect. All these discriminatory practices are legitimated by systems of representation, by collective cultural stories that shape the material world, underwrite exclusionary attitudes, inform human relations, and mold our senses of who we are. Understanding how disability functions along with other systems of representation clarifies how all the systems intersect and mutually constitute one another.

THE BODY

. . . What distinguishes a feminist disability theory from other critical paradigms is that it scrutinizes a wide range of material practices involving the lived body. Perhaps because women and the disabled are cultural signifiers for the body, their actual bodies have been subjected relentlessly to what Michel Foucault calls "discipline" (1979). Together, the gender, race, ethnicity, sexuality, class, and ability systems exert tremendous social pressures to shape, regulate, and normalize subjugated bodies. Such disciplining is

enacted primarily through the two interrelated cultural discourses of medicine and appearance.

Feminist disability theory offers a particularly trenchant analysis of the ways that the female body has been medicalized in modernity. As I have already suggested, both women and the disabled have been imagined as medically abnormal—as the quintessential sick ones. Sickness is gendered feminine. This gendering of illness has entailed distinct consequences in everything from epidemiology and diagnosis to prophylaxis and therapeutics. . . .

Similarly, a feminist disability theory calls into question the separation of reconstructive and cosmetic surgery, recognizing their essentially normalizing function as what Sander L. Gilman calls "aesthetic surgery" (1998). Cosmetic surgery, driven by gender ideology and market demand, now enforces feminine body ideals and standardizes female bodies toward what I have called the "normate"—the corporeal incarnation of culture's collective, unmarked, normative characteristics (1997, 8). Cosmetic surgery's twin, reconstructive surgery, eliminates disability and enforces the ideals of what might be thought of as the normalcy system. Both cosmetic and reconstructive procedures commodify the body and parade mutilations as enhancements that correct flaws to improve the psychological well-being of the patient. The conception of the body as what Susan Bordo terms "cultural plastic" (1993, 246) through surgical and medical interventions increasingly pressures people with disabilities or appearance impairments to become what Michel Foucault calls "docile bodies" (1979, 135). The twin ideologies of normalcy and beauty posit female and disabled bodies, particularly, as not only spectacles to be looked at, but as pliable bodies to be shaped infinitely so as to conform to a set of standards called *normal* and *beautiful*. . . .

. . . Considering disability as a vector of identity that intersects gender is one more internal challenge that threatens the coherence of woman, of course. But feminism can accommodate such complication and the contradictions it cultivates. Indeed the intellectual tolerance I am arguing for espouses the partial, the provisional, the particular. Such an intellectual habit can be informed by disability experience and acceptance. To embrace the supposedly flawed body of disability is to critique the normalizing phallic fantasies of wholeness, unity, coherence, and completeness.

The disabled body is contradiction, ambiguity, and partiality incarnate.

My claim here has been that integrating disability as a category of analysis, an historical community, a set of material practices, a social identity, a political position, and a representational system into the content of feminist—indeed into all—inquiry can strengthen the critique that is feminism. Disability, like gender and race, is everywhere, once we know how to look for it. Integrating disability analyses will enrich and deepen all our teaching and scholarship. Moreover, such critical intellectual work facilitates a fuller integration of the sociopolitical world—for the benefit of everyone. As with gender, race, sexuality, and class: to understand how disability operates is to understand what it is to be fully human.

(2002)

NOTE

1. Interestingly, in Fiske's study, feminists, businesswomen, Asians, Northerners, and black professionals were stereotyped as highly competent, thus envied. In addition to having very low competence, housewives, disabled people, blind people, so-called retarded people, and the elderly were rated as warm, thus pitied.

REFERENCES

Aristotle, 1944. *Generation of Animals.* Trans. A.L. Peck. Cambridge, MA: Harvard University Press.

Bordo, Susan. 1994. "Reading the Male Body." In *The Male Body*, ed. Laurence Goldstein, 265–306. Ann Arbor: University of Michigan Press.

Bordo, Susan. 1993. *Unbearable Weight: Feminism, Western Culture and the Body.* Berkeley: University of California Press.

Fiske, Susan T., Amy J. C. Cuddy, and Peter Glick. 2001. "A Model of (Often Mixed) Stereotype Content: Competence and Warmth Respectively Follow from Perceived Status and Competition." Unpublished study.

Foucault, Michel. 1979. *Discipline and Punish: The Birth of the Prison.* Trans. Alan M. Sheridan-Smith. New York: Vintage Books.

Gilman, Sander L. 1999. *Making the Body Beautiful.* Princeton, NJ: Princeton University Press.

Gilman, Sander L. 1998. *Creating Beauty to Cure the Soul.* Durham, NC: Duke University Press.

Linton, Simi, 1998. *Claiming Disability: Knowledge and Identity.* New York: New York University Press.

Piercy, Marge. 1969. "Unlearning Not to Speak." In her *Circles on Water*, 97. New York: Doubleday.

Sedgwick, Eve Kosofsky. 1990. *Epistemology of the Closet.* Berkeley: University of California Press.

Thomson, Rosemarie Garland. 1999. "Narratives of Deviance and Delight: Staring at Julia Pastrana, 'The Extraordinary Lady.'" In *Beyond the Binary*, ed. Timothy Powell, 81–106. New Brunswick, NJ: Rutgers University Press.

Thomson, Rosemarie Garland. 1997. *Extraordinary Bodies: Figuring Physical Disability in American Culture and Literature.* New York: Columbia University Press

Tuana, Nancy. 1993. *The Less Noble Sex: Scientific, Religious and Philosophical Conceptions of Woman's Nature.* Indianapolis: Indiana University Press.

Young, Iris Marion. 1990a. "Breasted Experience." In her *Throwing Like a Girl and Other Essays in Feminist Philosophy and Social Theory*, 189–209. Bloomington: Indiana University Press.

Young, Iris Marion. 1990b. "Throwing Like a Girl." In her *Throwing Like a Girl and Other Essays in Feminist Philosophy and Social Theory*, 141–59. Bloomington: Indiana University Press.

Feminist Thought After Taking the Postmodern Turn

CHAPTER 6

Postmodernism, Poststructuralism, Queer, and Transgender Theories

Jane Ward and Susan Mann

> There is no gender identity behind the expressions of gender . . . identity is per-
> formatively constituted by the very "expressions" that are said to be its results.
>
> —Judith Butler, 1990

INTRODUCTION[1]

Postmodernism and poststructuralism were developed in France during the1960s
and 1970s. Although references to these writings can be found in feminist works
before 1975, they did not significantly influence U.S. feminism until the late 1970s
and 1980s (Messer-Davidow, 2002: 208). Heavily influenced by Michel Foucault's
poststructuralist perspective, queer theory and transgender studies arose in the last
decade of the twentieth century. The term "queer" came to denote both a new theoretical perspective and a grassroots political movement. The distinct field of transgender studies examines the varied forms of regulation and violence associated
with gender ambiguity and cross-gender identification. For purposes of manage-
ability, at times, we refer to all of these approaches that took the postmodern turn
as the postperspectives below.

CHALLENGING MODERN THOUGHT

Although postmodernism and poststructuralism are umbrella terms that refer to a
vast array of disparate and, at times, competing perspectives, there are common
assumptions underlying these modes of thought that enable them to be discussed
together with some coherence (Featherstone, 1991; Rosenau, 1992; Ritzer, 2011).
As noted in Chapter 1, the lynchpins of postmodern epistemology include a focus
on the social construction of knowledge, the situated and partial nature of knowledges, and their implications for multiple vantage points and realities. These features also characterize standpoint epistemologies, but the similarities stop there. In
postmodern epistemology **judgmental relativism** prevails and no one view is
given epistemic privilege. In contrast, modern epistemologies assume the ability to

adjudicate knowledge claims or to judge the greater or lesser validity of different accounts of the world.

In turn, under the critical lens of postmodernism and poststructuralism, greater knowledge through science did not necessarily result in more freedom. Rather it entailed more regulation and control over social life. By questioning these hallmarks of modern science, postmodern epistemology shook the foundations of modern social thought upon which earlier feminist theories and practices had been based.

MAJOR ASSUMPTIONS OF POSTMODERNISM AND POSTSTRUCTURALISM

A hallmark of postmodernism and poststructuralism is their critique of the **essentialism** that characterizes much modern thought. Modern thinkers frequently used group concepts, such as the working-class or women, without hesitation. In contrast, for postmodernists and poststructuralists, *all group categories* can and should be deconstructed as essentialist; as Judith Grant argues: "groups are not cut out of whole cloth"; they have "no single voice or vision of reality" (1993: 94), but rather are made up of people with heterogeneous experiences. This argument has critical implications for many earlier feminist approaches. For example, whereas intersectionality theorists called into question the essentialist category of "women" for ignoring differences between women by race, social class, and sexual orientation, a similar critique could be leveled against their own group concepts, such as Patricia Hill Collins's "Black feminist thought" (1990) or Gloria Anzaldúa's (1987) "new mestiza consciousness."

Queer theorist Steven Seidman discusses how even "the assertion of a black, middle-class, American, lesbian identity silences differences in this category that relate to religion, regional location . . . to feminism, age or education" (2000: 441). For him, group categories, such as race, class, and gender and the identities based on these categories always entail the silencing or exclusion of differences. It is for these reasons that poststructuralists and queer theorists reject identity politics and share Foucault's vision of freedom as "living in the happy limbo of non-identity" (Foucault quoted in Grant, 1993, 131).

In addition, for postmodernists and poststructuralists, words do not represent or mirror reality; rather, they create and order our sense of reality. For them, group concepts and identities are simply social constructs—social fictions—that serve to regulate behavior and exclude others. They are part of a larger symbolic order—signs and symbols—that construct our notion of social reality. In this sense, social reality is discourse dependent. The goal is to deconstruct these fictions and, thereby, to undermine hegemonic discourses.

TENSIONS BETWEEN FOUCAULT AND FEMINISM

Although the father of poststructuralism, Michel Foucault, supported feminism as a political activist, his actual engagement with feminism in his theoretical writings was marginal. Nevertheless, many features of his work parallel and challenge feminist concerns. His treatments of power and discourse, as well as his views on sex, sexuality, and bodies, have created "tensions between Foucault and feminism," as well as particularly fertile grounds for new directions in feminist thought (Ramazanoglu, 1993: 1).

POWER AND DISCOURSE

Modern theories of power and inequality often conceptualize power as something that an individual or a group either does or does not have—such as material, political, and institutional resources (Gatens, 1992). Despite their variations and nuances, modern feminisms such as liberal feminism, Marxist feminism, socialist feminism, and radical feminism all hold these hierarchical, binary, and top-down views of power. In contrast, poststructuralists call for the demise of binary and dualistic thinking and a view of power that is more dispersed and multidirectional. In Reading 80 from *The History of Sexuality, Volume I* ([1976] 1980), Michel Foucault discusses his views on power and alerts us to the diffuse, microlevel powers that operate in everyday life. Although he recognizes macrolevel forms of power, he argues that power "comes from everywhere" and even "comes from below" (Foucault, [1976] 1980: 93–94). For him, the production of discourses on sex must be understood within "multiple and mobile power relations" ([1976] 1980: 98).

Reading 87 from Riki Wilchins's *Genderqueer: Voices from beyond the Sexual Binary* (2002) interweaves Foucault's insights on power into her own personal narrative of living as a male-to-female trans person and being rebuffed not only by the general public, but also by feminists. The power of discourses on bodies, sex, and gender was ubiquitous in her everyday interactions, even when she was doing such innocuous tasks as purchasing a newspaper or sitting on a bus. She describes this kind of power as "small power exercised in hundreds of everyday transactions" (2002: 51). Wilchins sees modernist thought with its binary thinking and its demand for a single truth—as "a kind of intellectual fascism that squeezes out individual truths" and "stamps out difference" (39 and 41). She offers the notion of "**genderqueer**" to challenge oppressive normative views of sex, gender, and sexuality.

Reading 85 from *Female Masculinity* (1998) by Judith (Jack) Halberstam also focuses on gender policing, referencing a dilemma that Halberstam describes as "littering" queer literature—"the bathroom problem" faced by persons of ambiguous gender (1998: 22). Not only does the persistence of sex-segregated bathrooms "illustrate in remarkably clear ways the flourishing existence of gender binarism" (1998: 22); it also shows how male and female bathrooms do so in entirely different ways. Female bathrooms entail more intense gender scrutiny and surveillance, but they neither operate as highly charged sexual spaces nor entail the same threat of physical violence as do male bathrooms.

Halberstam's book is premised on the claim that masculinity "must not and cannot and should not reduce down to the male body and its effects" (1998: 1). Although female masculinity is often ignored in contemporary studies of masculinity, Halberstam argues that "the shapes and forms of modern masculinity are best showcased by female masculinity" (1998: 3), thus echoing other feminist theorists who see marginalized locations as providing the most critical insights into dominant forms. In addition to decoupling masculinity from men, Halberstam's book also decouples female masculinity from lesbianism by showing how scholars have oversimplified, misunderstood, or elided a wide range of gender and sexual practices (Adams, 2000).

MODERN TECHNIQUES OF POWER

Another hallmark of Foucault's work on power is that he calls into question the Enlightenment version of history as progress toward ever greater human freedom. He shows how the rise of democratic republics was accompanied by the development of more subtle forms of power, control, and discipline than those used in premodern societies where harsh, repressive, absolute forms of power prevailed. Of particular interest to feminists was the way Foucault weaves bodies into his discussion of power. In *Discipline and Punish* ([1975] 1979), he depicts how the harsh punishments that characterized the premodern era reflected a public display of power on the bodies of subjects. Not only were hangings or death by the guillotine public spectacles, but also these forms of punishment literally inscribed power onto bodies. Torture marked the body; "it is intended either by the scar it leaves on the body or by the spectacle that accompanies it, to brand the victim with infamy ([1975] 1979: 179). In modernity, such public executions and torture were largely replaced by more subtle and effective forms of discipline that not only restrained or repressed, but also produced "docile bodies'" ([1975] 1979: 182). He described this new management of life processes as **biopower**—the regulation of subjects through an "explosion of numerous and diverse techniques" for achieving the control of bodies and populations ([1976] 1980: 140).

In Reading 83 from *Unbearable Weight: Feminism, Western Culture and the Body* ([1993] 2003), Susan Bordo argues that Foucault's analysis of how power operates "from below" is especially useful for understanding femininity given how women seem so willing to accept and even to work hard at attaining normative feminine ideals. She examines a number of gender-related and historically specific feminine disorders: hysteria in the late nineteenth century; agoraphobia in the post–World War II era; and anorexia nervosa in recent decades. Bordo exposes the links between these female disorders and "normal" feminine practice, such as how the "emaciated body of the anorectic" presents itself as "a caricature of the contemporary ideal of hyper-slenderness for women" (Bordo [1993] 2003: 170). Her analysis reveals the contradictions that plague the social construction of femininity, as well as how women are complicit in their own domination.

In discussing medical responses to these female disorders, Bordo employs Foucault's analysis of how the more subtle, modern techniques of power were fostered by the rise of new scientific discourses in the nineteenth century, such as the modern medical and social sciences, that specified, for example, which bodies were normal or abnormal, sane or insane. These scientific discourses also delineated and categorized the differences between the sexes, the races, and/or the able-bodied and the disabled. For Foucault, these new discourses "cast a net of surveillance and control over the whole population in the name of science," which is why he referred to modern societies as "disciplinary" or "surveillance" societies (Miller, 2008: 254).

One modern technique of power and surveillance that has received much attention in feminist literature is Foucault's famous discussion of the **panopticon** or gaze. To illustrate this technique, Foucault described the architectural design of the "Panopticon"—a model prison in the nineteenth century. Here a few guards located out of view of the prisoners high in a circular structure at the center of the prison could gaze down on the inmates and their activities. Whether or not guards were present, the effect was to "induce in the prisoners a state of conscious and permanent visibility that assured the automatic functioning of power" such that "each becomes to himself his own jailer" (Foucault, [1975] 1979: 201). For Foucault, the panopticon is a metaphor for how the normative structure of modern societies engenders self-policing and control.

In Reading 81 from "Foucault, Femininity, and the Modernization of Patriarchal Power" ([1988] 1997), Sandra Lee Bartky uses Foucault's notion of the panopticon to explore how women have internalized standards of femininity and beauty. By adhering to disciplinary practices, such as dieting, body sculpting exercises, or cosmetic surgery, women not only police themselves, but also collude in their own subordination. She writes: "A panoptical male connoisseur resides within the consciousness of most women: They stand perpetually before his gaze and under his judgment" (Bartky, [1988] 1997: 101). Like Foucault, she does not treat patriarchal power as a binary form of oppression, but rather as a diffuse and ubiquitous set of decentralized forces. She writes, "the disciplinary power that inscribes femininity on the female body is everywhere and it is nowhere; the disciplinarian is everyone and yet no one in particular" (103). Indeed, the sources of disciplinary power in regard to femininity and beauty ideals are many and diverse. They include magazines, billboards, films, and television—virtually every media outlet. We also learn femininity and beauty ideals from our parents, friends, lovers, and even strangers.

Despite Bartky's poststructuralist analysis of power and its techniques, she sounds more like a modernist when she writes: "We are born male or female, but not masculine or feminine" ([1988] 1997: 95). She treats sex as a biological given and femininity as a cultural artifice—a distinction between sex and gender that was typical of modern feminist thought. By contrast, poststructuralists go farther to argue that *both sex and gender are social constructs*.

Sex, Sexuality, and Deconstructing the "Natural"

Most modern feminist theorists understood biological femaleness and maleness as the fixed, material foundation upon which gender roles (femininity and masculinity) were imposed. Scholars influenced by Foucault's poststructuralism challenged this way of thinking by revealing that even the body and its sexed components (such as genitals, gonads, chromosomes, secondary sex characteristics, hormones, and so forth) are given shape and meaning by preexisting beliefs about gender, including the gendered assumptions of medical authorities. Reading 86 from Anne Fausto-Sterling's "Should There Be Only Two Sexes?" ([2000] 2008) exemplifies this view. For her, the social fiction of "male" and "female" being the only sexes precludes us from recognizing alternatives, such as the multiple sexes she discusses.

Overall, Foucault's insistence on debunking many of our most cherished assumptions about the social world—especially those that expose seemingly natural categories as social constructs—is widely recognized as one of his greatest overall contributions (Jones and Porter, 1994: 5; McWhorter, 1999: 36). In turn, his hostility to the "truths" of the human sciences that attempt to construct our identities and to label what is normal or natural not only alerts us to the damage done by privileged discourses, but also helps foster a healthy skepticism that the social world can be otherwise. Indeed, Foucault has been referred to as the "philosopher of the otherwise" because thinking against the grain of normalizing practices is central to Foucault's view of philosophy (McHoul and Grace, 1993: 125).

QUEER THEORY

Queer theory emerged in the early 1990s as an interdisciplinary synthesis of post-structuralism, feminist theory, and gay and lesbian studies. Although queer theory built on each of these bodies of thought, it also pushed them in new conceptual directions that would place sexuality, and particularly the origins and consequences of *sexual norms*, at the center of analysis.

Like feminist theory, queer theory is a deeply political enterprise, one that evolved from the belief that we must acknowledge, celebrate, and preserve sexual difference. Just as feminist theory feeds into, and is inspired by, feminist activism, queer theory exists in a dynamic relationship with the on-the-ground political work of lesbian, gay, bisexual, and transgendered activists (LGBT).

Perhaps the most important thing to understand about the term "queer" (as queer theorists articulate it) is that it is not a synonym for LGBT identities or a reference to nonheterosexuality. Instead, **queer** is a critique of all things oppressively *normal*. In the influential 1993 anthology *Fear of a Queer Planet*, queer theorist Michael Warner proclaimed that the term queer "rejects . . . simple political interest representation in favor of a more thorough resistance to regimes of the normal" and "define(s) itself against the normal rather than the heterosexual" (Warner, 1993: xxvi). In other words, queerness is not about taking a stand against heterosexual desire, nor is it about being an average, respectable gay or lesbian citizen who lives just like her or his heterosexual counterparts. Instead, resisting the cultural and institutional forces that attempt to make *all people* conform to what is "normal" is a major premise of queer theory.

Reading 88 "Queer Temporality and Postmodern Geographies" from Judith (Jack) Halberstams's *In a Queer Time and Place* (2005) highlights this critique of **normativity** or "conventional forms of association, belonging, and identification" (Halberstam, 2005: 4). Drawing on Foucault's assertion that homosexuality threatens people as a "way of life," rather than a way of having sex, Halberstam argues that "queer" is not a category defined by homosexual sex, but one that describes the experience of living on the margins of domestic safety and sexual respectability. In contrast, the requirements of normativity hinge upon rigid ideas about gender and sexuality, including the dictate to organize our lives around monogamous marriage, the nuclear family, and a gendered division of labor.

Most of us are taught that mature people are those who grow up, enter a monogamous marriage (ideally with a person of the opposite sex), keep their sexuality private, avoid risks, and strive to make as much money as they can so as to buy material objects for their families. Queer theory refuses the notion that these choices are the most fulfilling and politically responsible ways to connect with other people. Queer culture celebrates alternative ways of life often centered on local bars, public performances, art scenes, activist projects, collective sexual exploration, and extended communities. As a result, queer adults remain engaged in activities that heterosexual adults deem immature, self-indulgent, or idealistic (such as performing in drag, playing in a punk band, or organizing street protests)—the very activities that grown-ups are encouraged to leave behind as they become responsible adults. **Queer time**, then, defies the norms associated with heteronormative adulthood, whereas **queer places** are sites that enable queer subculture to survive.

A second major premise of queer theory is that gender and sexual identities—man/woman, heterosexual/homosexual—are artificial and unstable. As queer theorist Judith Butler has famously argued, although most of us take our gender and sexual identities for granted and presume them to be essential aspects of who we are, it is more accurate to view them as sociohistorical inventions that have long been used to classify, rank, and discipline people (Butler, 1990). As Reading 82 titled "Imitation and Gender Insubordination" (1991) reveals, Butler rejects the notion that gender is a role that expresses an interior self or an inner reality of sex. Rather, gender is a **performance**—ritualized acts by an individual that construct the social fiction of a psychological interiority (Butler, 1990: 279). For Butler "there need not be a 'doer' behind the deed, rather the 'doer' is variably constructed in and through the deed" (1990: 181). She uses the concept of performativity to describe how gender acts are derived from gender discourses that are handed down from generation to generation—much as a script survives the particular actors that make use of it. "Like a script," the performance of gender requires individual actors to "actualize and reproduce it as reality once again" (Butler, 1990: 272). The involuntary and repetitive work of displaying that one is a woman or a man, heterosexual or queer, is never complete and it is through this ritualized and disciplined process of performing gender and sexuality that our seemingly coherent and natural "self" is formed. It is for these reasons that Butler describes gender as a "copy for which there is no original" (1990: 95).

A third major premise of queer theory is that, within most cultures, sexual norms constitute a distinct hierarchy that includes, but is not limited to, hierarchies of gender and sexual orientation. This is exemplified in Reading 37 from Gayle Rubin's "Thinking Sex" ([1984] 1993). As noted in Chapter 3, Rubin discusses how, within such hierarchies, there appears to "be a need to draw and maintain an imaginary line between good and bad sex"—a line that stands between "sexual order and chaos" ([1984] 1993: 14). Rubin stood steadfast against any ideologies that attempted to describe sex in term "of sin, disease, neurosis, pathology, decadence, pollution, or the decline and fall of empires" (10). She argues that ideas about normal and ethical sexuality are used to discipline *all* people, including people with considerable gender, racial, and economic privilege. In such ways, her groundbreaking work was a precursor to queer theory.

Heteronormativity—or the assumption that heterosexuality is natural, normal and right—is an especially far-reaching component of the sexual hierarchy, one with consequences well beyond discrimination against lesbians and gay men (Warner, 1993). Queer theorists argue that heteronormativity is core to the very construction of woman, man, masculinity, femininity, romance, intercourse, adulthood, morality, marriage, childbirth, parenting, and aging. For example, sociological research indicates that fear of being called a "fag" in high school looms over nearly *all* boys and results in compulsive displays of masculinity, aggression, and violence (Kimmel and Mahler, 2003; Pascoe, 2007). Such widespread effects explain why queer theory focuses more attention on heteronormativity than on the related but narrow term **homophobia** referring to heterosexuals' fear of, and discrimination against, lesbians and gay men. Placing attention on homophobia can sometimes have the effect of reinforcing the heterosexual–homosexual binary by characterizing heterosexuals as untouched by homophobia and gays as a different type of people in need of tolerance and special protection. Placing heteronormativity at the center of analysis involves shifting one's focus to the cultural beliefs and institutional practices that require *all* of us to account for our sexual practices and gender performances.

By calling attention to the oppressive nature of both normativity and heteronormativity, queer theory serves as a voice for those on the margins. Unlike other marginalized voices, queers do not seek to move to the center. Rather, they posit themselves permanently on the margins as critics of the status quo. In this way, queer theorists and activists make us ever mindful of the power that normative discourses can wield in causing pain to marginalized others.

TRANSGENDER THEORY

A centerpiece of transgender studies is a critique of the **gender binary**, which refers to the idea that humans exist in two essential, biologically determined forms—male and female. The gender binary is sustained by dividing people into gender roles, disciplining people into believing in the naturalness of their gender location, and policing any violations of the male/female gender order. Women's oppression is a pervasive and enduring outcome of the gender binary, but it is not its only troubling effect. Queers, transgendered people, and anyone whose body or gender expression does not adhere to the male/female binary is subject to discipline in a society that believes in only two opposite genders. In fact, since all of us inevitably fail to live up to the rigid gender ideals of our respective cultures, the gender binary has oppressive effects for everyone.

Living up to these rigid gender ideals is especially difficult for some people. For instance, in the United States, close to 2% of children are born **intersex**, possessing some combination of the physical and/or chromosomal features that typically distinguish males and females. Although this is a natural occurrence, the Western belief that people are either exclusively male or female has, for many decades, led doctors in the United States to surgically or otherwise "treat" intersexed children, altering their bodies to ensure their conformity to one sex category or another. In contrast, recognizing that "woman" and "man" are evolving, malleable and contested categories is a key component of transgender theory and its concern with the ways that gendered personhood is mapped onto the physical body. Whereas feminist scholarship generally focused on the *effects* of this mapping, transgender studies centers on how and why this sex assignment happens in the first place and what happens when our sex assignment is contested or disavowed.

Another centerpiece of transgender studies is what we might call the problem of misrecognition. Because sex and gender carry so much meaning, we have all learned to fashion gendered bodies that elicit the most livable circumstances and responses from others. Although all of us work at presenting our bodies in gendered ways, transgender theorists and activists call attention to this process, arguing that every person must be able to fashion the kind of body that will elicit the best available form of recognition, especially in such a gender-obsessed world. This includes being **transgendered**—claiming a gender different from one's assignment at birth—and being able to alter one's body to be recognized according to one's desired gender.

Two readings in this anthology address the problems of misrecognition and discrimination experienced by trans people. Reading 84 from Kate Bornstein's *Gender Outlaw* (1994) uses a personal narrative that juxtaposes humor and gravity to make her points. Reading 89 from Julia Serano's *Whipping Girls* (2009) takes the form of a political manifesto that highlights the particular forms of discrimination faced by trans women and even calls to task many feminists for their complicity in **transphobia** and **trans misogyny**. In particular, Serano is referring to feminists, such as some of the radical feminists discussed in Chapter 3 who limit their notion of women to **cisgender women** (women born women) and who exclude trans-women from their events.[2]

CONCLUSION

The feminist theoretical approaches discussed in this chapter rest on a postmodern epistemology that fundamentally challenged and shook the foundations of modern scientific thought. As a result, the former trend toward seeking universal "truths" and theoretical convergence gave way to the recognition of multiple truths and theoretical pluralism (Cheal, 1991: 153). This recognition, along with a focus on difference, deconstruction, and decentering, has been deemed by some observers a "paradigm shift" in feminist thought that radically breaks with earlier feminisms (Barrett and Phillips, 1992; Hekman, 2004; Mann, 2012). In their aptly titled book, *Destablizing Theory*, Michele Barrett and Ann Phillips write,

> the founding principles of contemporary western feminism have been dramatically challenged with previous shared assumptions and unquestioned orthodoxies relegated almost to history. These changes have been of the order of a 'paradigm shift', in which assumptions rather than conclusions are radically overturned. (1992, 2)

NOTES

1. Sections of this chapter introduction are drawn from Jane Ward and Susan Mann (2012c).
2. For example, an ongoing debate is about the inclusion of trans women at the Michigan Womyn's Music Festival. See http://www.transadvocate.com/national-justice-orgs-say-end-trans-exlcusion-policy-at-michigan-womyns-music-festival_n_14081.htm (retrieved October 26, 2014).

"METHOD"

Hence the objective is to analyze a certain form of knowledge regarding sex, not in terms of repression or law, but in terms of power. But the word *power* is apt to lead to a number of misunderstandings—misunderstandings with respect to its nature, its form, and its unity. By power, I do not mean "Power" as a group of institutions and mechanisms that ensure the subservience of the citizens of a given state. By power, I do not mean, either, a mode of subjugation which, in contrast to violence, has the form of the rule. Finally, I do not have in mind a general system of domination exerted by one group over another, a system whose effects, through successive derivations, pervade the entire social body. The analysis, made in terms of power, must not assume that the sovereignty of the state, the form of the law, or the over-all unity of a domination are given at the outset; rather, these are only the terminal forms power takes. It seems to me that power must be understood in the first instance as the multiplicity of force relations immanent in the sphere in which they operate and which constitute their own organization; as the process which, through ceaseless struggles and confrontations, transforms, strengthens, or reverses them; as the support which these force relations find in one another, thus forming a chain or a system, or on the contrary, the disjunctions and contradictions which isolate them from one another; and lastly, as the strategies in which they take effect, whose general design or institutional crystallization is embodied in the state apparatus, in the formulation of the law, in the various social hegemonies. Power's condition of possibility, or in any case the viewpoint which permits one to understand its exercise, even in its more "peripheral" effects, and which also makes it possible to use its mechanisms as a grid of intelligibility of the social order, must not be sought in the primary existence of a central point, in a unique source of sovereignty from which secondary and descendent forms would emanate; it is the moving substrate of force relations which, by virtue of their inequality, constantly engender states of power, but the latter are always local and unstable. The omnipresence of power: not because it has the privilege of consolidating everything under its invincible unity, but because it is produced from one moment to the next, at every point, or rather in every relation from one point to another. Power is everywhere; not because it embraces everything, but because it comes from everywhere. And "Power," insofar as it is permanent, repetitious, inert, and self-reproducing, is simply the over-all effect that emerges from all these mobilities, the concatenation that rests on each of them and seeks in turn to arrest their movement. One needs to be nominalistic, no doubt: power is not an institution, and not a structure; neither is it a certain strength we are endowed with; it is the name that one attributes to a complex strategical situation in a particular society.

Should we turn the expression around, then, and say that politics is war pursued by other means? If we still wish to maintain a separation between war and politics, perhaps we should postulate rather that this multiplicity of force relations can be coded—in part but never totally—either in the form of "war," or in the form of "politics"; this would imply two different strategies (but the one always liable to switch into the other) for integrating these unbalanced, heterogeneous, unstable, and tense force relations.

Continuing this line of discussion, we can advance a certain number of propositions:

—Power is not something that is acquired, seized, or shared, something that one holds on to or allows to slip away; power is exercised from innumerable points, in the interplay of nonegalitarian and mobile relations.

—Relations of power are not in a position of exteriority with respect to other types of relationships (economic processes, knowledge relationships, sexual relations), but are immanent in the latter; they are the immediate effects of the divisions, inequalities, and disequilibriums which occur in the latter, and conversely they are the internal conditions of these differentiations; relations of power are not in superstructural positions, with merely a role of prohibition or accompaniment; they have a directly productive role, wherever they come into play.

—Power comes from below; that is, there is no binary and all-encompassing opposition between rulers and ruled at the root of power relations, and serving as a general matrix—no such duality extending from the top down and reacting on more and more limited groups to the very depths of the social body. One must suppose rather that the manifold relationships of force that take shape and come into play in the machinery of production, in families, limited groups, and institutions, are the basis for wide-ranging effects of cleavage that run through the social body as a whole. These then form a general line of force that traverses the local oppositions and links them together; to be sure, they also bring about redistributions, realignments, homogenizations, serial arrangements, and convergences of the force relations. Major dominations are the hegemonic effects that are sustained by all these confrontations.

—Power relations are both intentional and nonsubjective. If in fact they are intelligible, this is not because they are the effect of another instance that "explains" them, but rather because they are imbued, through and through, with calculation: there is no power that is exercised without a series of aims and objectives. But this does not mean that it results from the choice or decision of an individual subject; let us not look for the headquarters that presides over its rationality; neither the caste which governs, nor the groups which control the state apparatus, nor those who make the most important economic decisions direct the entire network of power that functions in a society (and makes *it* function); the rationality of power is characterized by tactics that are often quite explicit at the restricted level where they are inscribed (the local cynicism of power), tactics which, becoming connected to one another, attracting and propagating one another, but finding their base of support and their condition elsewhere, end by forming comprehensive systems: the logic is perfectly clear, the aims decipherable, and yet it is often the case that no one is there to have invented them, and few who can be said to have formulated them: an implicit characteristic of the great anonymous, almost unspoken strategies which coordinate the loquacious tactics whose "inventors" or decisionmakers are often without hypocrisy.

—Where there is power, there is resistance, and yet, or rather consequently, this resistance is never in a position of exteriority in relation to power. Should it be said that one is always "inside" power, there is no "escaping" it, there is no absolute outside where it is concerned, because one is subject to the law in any case? Or that, history being the ruse of reason, power is the ruse of history, always emerging the winner? This would be to misunderstand the strictly relational character of power relationships. Their existence depends on a multiplicity of points of resistance: these play the role of adversary, target, support, or handle in power relations. These points of resistance are present everywhere in the power network. Hence there is no single locus of great Refusal, no soul of revolt, source of all rebellions, or pure law of the revolutionary. Instead there is a plurality of resistances, each of them a special case: resistances that are possible, necessary, improbable; others that are spontaneous, savage, solitary, concerted, rampant, or violent; still others that are quick to compromise, interested, or sacrificial; by definition, they can only exist in the strategic field of power relations. But this does not mean that they are only a reaction or rebound, forming with respect to the basic domination an underside that is in the end always passive, doomed to perpetual defeat. Resistances do not derive from a few heterogeneous principles; but neither are they a lure or a promise that is of necessity betrayed. They are the odd term in relations of power; they are inscribed in the latter as an irreducible opposite. Hence they too are distributed in irregular fashion; the points, knots, or focuses of resistance are spread over time and space at varying densities, at times mobilizing groups or individuals in a definitive way, inflaming certain points of the body, certain moments in life, certain types of behavior. Are there no great radical ruptures, massive binary divisions, then? Occasionally, yes. But more often one is dealing with mobile and transitory points of resistance, producing cleavages in a society that shift about, fracturing unities and effecting regroupings, furrowing across individuals themselves, cutting them up and remolding them, marking off irreducible regions in them, in their bodies and minds. Just as the network of power relations ends by forming a dense web that passes through apparatuses and institutions, without being exactly localized in them, so too the swarm of points of resistance traverses social stratifications and individual unities. And it is doubtless the strategic codification of these points of resistance that makes a revolution possible, somewhat similar to the way in which the state relies on the institutional integration of power relationships.

It is in this sphere of force relations that we must try to analyze the mechanisms of power. In this way we will escape from the system of Law-and-Sovereign which has captivated political thought for such a long time. And if it is true that Machiavelli was among the few—and this no doubt was the scandal of his "cynicism"—who conceived the power of the Prince in terms of force relationships, perhaps we need to go one step further, do without the persona of the Prince, and decipher power mechanisms on the basis of a strategy that is immanent in force relationships.

To return to sex and the discourses of truth that have taken charge of it, the question that we must address, then, is not: Given a specific state structure, how and why is it that power needs to establish a knowledge of sex? Neither is the question: What over-all domination was served by the concern, evidenced since the eighteenth century, to produce true discourses on sex? Nor is it: What law presided over both the regularity of sexual behavior and the conformity of what was said about it? It is rather: In a specific type of discourse on sex, in a specific form of extortion of truth, appearing historically and in specific places (around the child's body, apropos of women's sex, in connection with practices restricting births, and so on), what were the most immediate, the most local power relations at work? How did they make possible these kinds of discourses, and conversely, how were these discourses used to support power relations? How was the action of these power relations modified by their very exercise, entailing a strengthening of some terms and a weakening of others, with effects of resistance and counter investments, so that there has never existed one type of stable subjugation, given once and for all? How were these power relations linked to one another according to the logic of a great strategy, which in retrospect takes on the aspect of a unitary and voluntarist politics of sex? In general terms: rather than referring all the infinitesimal violences that are exerted on sex, all the anxious gazes that are directed at it, and all the hiding places whose discovery is made into an impossible task, to the unique form of a great Power, we must immerse the expanding production of discourses on sex in the field of multiple and mobile power relations.

(1976)

81 • *Sandra Lee Bartky*

"FOUCAULT, FEMININITY, AND THE MODERNIZATION OF PATRIARCHAL POWER"

I.

In a striking critique of modern society, Michel Foucault has argued that the rise of parliamentary institutions and of new conceptions of political liberty was accompanied by a darker counter-movement, by the emergence of a new and unprecedented discipline directed against the body. More is required of the body now than mere political allegiance or the appropriation of the products of its labor: the new discipline invades the body and seeks to regulate its very forces and operations, the economy and efficiency of its movements.

The disciplinary practices Foucault describes are tied to peculiarly modern forms of the army, the school, the hospital, the prison, and the manufactory; the aim of these disciplines is to increase the utility of the body, to augment its forces:

> What was then being formed was a policy of coercions that act upon the body, a calculated manipulation of its elements, its gestures, its behaviour. The human body was entering a machinery of power that explores it, breaks it down and rearranges it. A "political anatomy," which was also a "mechanics of power," was being born: it defined how one may have a hold over others' bodies, not only so that they may do what one wishes, but so that they may operate as one wishes, with the techniques, the speed and the efficiency that one determines. Thus, discipline produces subjected and practiced bodies, "docile" bodies.[1]

The production of "docile bodies" requires that an uninterrupted coercion be directed to the very processes of bodily activity, nor just their result; this "microphysics of power" fragments and partitions the body's time, its space, and its movements.[2]

The student, then, is enclosed within a classroom and assigned to a desk he cannot leave; his ranking in the class can be read off the position of his desk in the serially ordered and segmented space of the classroom itself. Foucault tells us that "Jean-Baptiste de la Salle dreamt of a classroom in which the spatial distribution might provide a whole series of distinctions at once, according to the pupil's progress, worth, character, application, cleanliness and parents' fortune."[3] The student must sit upright, feet upon the floor, head erect; he may not slouch or fidget his animate body is brought into a fixed correlation with the inanimate desk.

The minute breakdown of gestures and movements required of soldiers at drill is far more relentless[.] . . . These "body-object articulations" of the soldier and his weapon, the student and his desk effect a "coercive link with the apparatus of production." We are far indeed from older forms of control that "demanded of the body only signs or products, forms of expression or the result of labour."[4]

The body's time, in these regimes of power, is as rigidly controlled as its space: the factory whistle and the school bell mark a division of time into discrete and segmented units that regulate the various

---

activities of the day. . . . Control this rigid and pre-cise cannot be maintained without a minute and relentless surveillance.

Jeremy Bentham's design for the Panopticon, a model prison, captures for Foucault the essence of the disciplinary society. At the periphery of the Panopti-con, a circular structure; at the center, a tower with wide windows that opens onto the inner side of the ring. The structure on the periphery is divided into cells, each with two windows, one facing the windows of the tower, the other facing the outside allowing an effect of backlighting to make any figure visible within the cell. "All that is needed, then, is to place a supervi-sor in a central tower and to shut up in each cell a madman, a patient, a condemned man, a worker or a schoolboy."[5] Each inmate is alone, shut off from effec-tive communication with his fellows, but constantly visible from the tower. The effect of this is "to induce in the inmate a state of conscious and permanent visibility that assures the automatic functioning of power"; each becomes to himself his own jailer.[6] This "state of con-scious and permanent visibility" is a sign that the tight, disciplinary control of the body has gotten a hold on the mind as well. In the perpetual self-surveillance of the inmate lies the genesis of the celebrated "individu-alism" and heightened self-consciousness that are hall-marks of modern times. For Foucault, the structure and effects of the Panopticon resonate throughout society: Is it surprising that "prisons resemble factories, schools, barracks, hospitals, which all resemble prisons"?[7]

Foucault's account in *Discipline and Punish* of the disciplinary practices that produce the "docile bodies" of modernity is a genuine *tour de force*, incorporating a rich theoretical account of the ways in which instru-mental reason takes hold of the body with a mass of historical detail. But Foucault treats the body through-out as if it were one, as if the bodily experiences of men and women did not differ and as if men and women bore the same relationship to the characteristic institutions of modern life. Where is the account of the disciplinary practices that engender the "docile bodies" of women, bodies more docile than the bodies of men? Women, like men, are subject to many of the same disciplinary practices Foucault describes. But he is blind to those disciplines that produce a modality of embodiment that is peculiarly feminine. To overlook the forms of subjection that engender the feminine body is to perpetuate the silence and powerlessness of those upon whom these disciplines have been im-posed. Hence, even though a liberatory note is sounded in Foucault's critique of power, his analysis as a whole reproduces that sexism which is endemic throughout Western political theory.

We are born male or female, but not masculine or feminine. Femininity is artifice, an achievement, "a mode of enacting and reenacting received gender norms which surface as so many styles of the flesh."[8] In what follows, I shall examine those disciplinary prac-tices that produce a body which in gesture and appear-ance is recognizably feminine. I consider three categories of such practices: those that aim to produce a body of a certain size and general configuration; those that bring forth from this body a specific reper-toire of gestures, postures, and movements; and those that are directed toward the display of this body as an ornamented surface. I shall examine the nature of these disciplines, how they are imposed and by whom. I shall probe the effects of the imposition of such dis-cipline on female identity and subjectivity. In the final section I shall argue that these disciplinary practices must be understood in the light of the modernization of patriarchal domination, a modernization that un-folds historically according to the general pattern de-scribed by Foucault.

II.

Styles of the female figure vary over time and across cultures; they reflect cultural obsessions and preoccupa-tions in ways that are still poorly understood. Today, massiveness, power, or abundance in a woman's body is met with distaste. The current body of fashion is taut, small-breasted, narrow-hipped, and of a slimness bordering on emaciation; it is a silhouette that seems more appropriate to an adolescent boy or a newly pu-bescent girl than to an adult woman. Since ordinary women have normally quite different dimensions, they must of course diet.

Mass-circulation women's magazines run articles on dieting in virtually every issue. . . . After the diet-bust-ing Christmas holidays and, later, before summer bikini season, the titles of these features become shriller and more arresting. The reader is now addressed in the imperative mode: Jump into shape for summer! . . . More women than men visit diet doctors, while women greatly outnumber men in such self-help groups as

Weight Watchers and Overeaters Anonymous—in the case of the latter, by well over 90 percent.[9]

Dieting disciplines the body's hungers: appetite must be monitored at all times and governed by an iron will. Since the innocent need of the organism for food will not be denied, the body becomes one's enemy, an alien being bent on thwarting the disciplinary project. Anorexia nervosa, which has now assumed epidemic proportions, is to women of the late twentieth century what hysteria was to women of an earlier day: the crystallization in a pathological mode of a widespread cultural obsession.[10] . . .

Dieting is one discipline imposed upon a body subject to the "tyranny of slenderness"; exercise is another.[11] Since men as well as women exercise, it is not always easy in the case of women to distinguish what is done for the sake of physical fitness from what is done in obedience to the requirements of femininity. Men as well as women lift weights and do yoga, calisthenics, and aerobics, though "jazzercise" is a largely female pursuit. Men and women alike engage themselves with a variety of machines, each designed to call forth from the body a different exertion . . . However, given the widespread female obsession with weight, one suspects that many women are working out . . . with an aim in mind and in a spirit quite different from men's.

. . . [T]here are classes of exercises meant for women alone, these designed not to firm or to reduce the body's size overall, but to resculpture its various pans on the current model. . . . There are exercises to build the breasts and exercises to banish "cellulite," said by "figure consultants" to be a special type of female fat. There is "spot-reducing," an umbrella term that covers dozens of punishing exercises designed to reduce "problem areas" like thick ankles or "saddlebag" thighs. The very idea of "spot-reducing" is both scientifically unsound and cruel, for it raises expectations in women that can never be realized—the pattern in which fat is deposited or removed is known to be genetically determined.

It is not only her natural appetite or unreconstructed contours that pose a danger to woman: the very expressions of her face can subvert the disciplinary project of bodily perfection. An expressive face lines and creases more readily than an inexpressive one. Hence, if women are unable to suppress strong emotions, they can at least learn to inhibit the tendency of the face to register them. Sophia Loren recommends a unique solution to this problem: a piece of tape applied to the forehead or between the brows will tug at the skin when one frowns and act as a reminder to relax the face.[12] The tape is to be worn whenever a woman is home alone. . . .

IV.

We have examined some of the disciplinary practices a woman must master in pursuit of a body of the right size and shape that also displays the proper styles of feminine motility. But woman's body is an ornamented surface too, and there is much discipline involved in this production as well. Here, especially in the application of makeup and the selection of clothes, art and discipline converge, though, as I shall argue, there is less art involved than one might suppose.

A woman's skin must be soft, supple, hairless, and smooth; ideally, it should betray no sign of wear, experience, age, or deep thought. Hair must be removed not only from the face but from large surfaces of the body as well, from legs and thighs . . . With the new high-leg bathing suits and leotards, a substantial amount of pubic hair must be removed too. The removal of facial hair can be more specialized. Eyebrows are plucked out by the roots with a tweezer. Hot wax is sometimes poured onto the mustache and cheeks and then ripped away when it cools. The woman who wants a more permanent result may try electrolysis: this involves the killing of a hair root by the passage of an electric current down a needle that has been inserted into its base. The procedure is painful and expensive.

The development of what one "beauty expert" calls "good skincare habits" requires not only attention to health, the avoidance of strong facial expressions, and the performance of facial exercises, but the regular use of skincare preparations, many to be applied more often than once a day: cleansing lotions (ordinary soap and water "upsets the skin's acid and alkaline balance"), wash-off cleansers (milder than cleansing lotions), astringents, toners, makeup removers, night creams, nourishing creams, eye creams, moisturizers, skin balancers, body lotions, hand creams, lip pomades, suntan lotions, sunscreens, and facial masks. . . . Black women may wish to use "fade creams" to "even skin tone." Skincare preparations are never just sloshed onto the skin, but applied according to precise rules: eye cream is dabbed on gently in movements toward, never away from, the nose; cleansing cream is applied in outward directions only, straight across the forehead, the upper lip, and the chin, never up but straight down the nose and up and out on the cheeks.[13]

The ordinary circumstances of life as well as a wide variety of activities cause a crisis in skincare and require a stepping-up of the regimen as well as an additional laying-on of preparations. Skincare discipline requires a specialized knowledge: a woman must know what to do if she has been skiing, taking medication, doing vigorous exercise, boating, or swimming in chlorinated pools; or if she has been exposed to pollution, heated rooms, cold, sun, harsh weather, the pressurized cabins on airplanes, saunas or steam rooms, fatigue, or stress. Like the schoolchild or prisoner, the woman mastering good skincare habits is put on a timetable: Georgette Klinger requires that a shorter or longer period of attention be paid to the complexion at least four times a day.[14] Hair-care, like skincare, requires a similar investment of time, the use of a wide variety of preparations, the mastery of a set of techniques, and, again, the acquisition of a specialized knowledge.

The crown and pinnacle of good haircare and skincare is, of course, the arrangement of the hair and the application of cosmetics. Here the regimen of haircare, skincare, manicure, and pedicure is recapitulated in another mode. A woman must learn the proper manipulation of a large number of devices—the blow dryer, styling brush, curling iron, hot curlers, wire curlers, eye-liner, lipliner, lipstick brush, eyelash curler, mascara brush—and the correct manner of application of a wide variety of products—foundation, toner, covering stick, mascara, eyeshadow, eyegloss, blusher, lipstick, rouge, lip gloss, hair dye, hair rinse, hair lightener, hair "relaxer," etc.

In the language of fashion magazines and cosmetic ads, making-up is typically portrayed as an aesthetic activity in which a woman can express her individuality. In reality, while cosmetic styles change every decade or so, and while some variation in makeup is permitted depending on the occasion, making-up the face is, in fact, a highly stylized activity that gives little rein to self-expression. Painting the face is not like painting a picture; at best, it might be described as painting the same picture over and over again with minor variations. Little latitude is permitted in what is considered appropriate makeup for the office and for most social occasions; indeed, the woman who uses

cosmetics in a genuinely novel and imaginative way is liable to be seen not as an artist but as an eccentric. Furthermore, since a properly made-up face is, if not a card of entree, at least a badge of acceptability in most social and professional contexts, the woman who chooses not to wear cosmetics at all faces sanctions of a sort that will never be applied to someone who chooses not to paint a watercolor. . . .

VI.

If what we have described is a genuine discipline—a system of "micropower" that is "essentially non-egalitarian and asymmetrical"—who then are the disciplinarians?[15] Who is the top sergeant in the disciplinary regime of femininity? Historically, the law has had some responsibility for enforcement: in times gone by, for example individuals who appeared in public in the clothes of the other sex could be arrested. While cross-dressers are still liable to some harassment, the kind of discipline we are considering is not the business of the police or the courts. Parents and teachers, of course, have extensive influence, admonishing girls to be demure and ladylike, to "smile pretty," to sit with their legs together. The influence of the media is pervasive, too, constructing as it does an image of the female body as spectacle . . .

But none of these individuals—the skincare consultant, the parent, the policeman—does in fact wield the kind of authority that is typically invested in those who manage more straightforward disciplinary institutions. The disciplinary power that inscribes femininity in the female body is everywhere and it is nowhere; the disciplinarian is everyone and yet no one in particular. Women regarded as overweight, for example, report that they are regularly admonished to diet, sometimes by people they scarcely know. These intrusions are often softened by reference to the natural prettiness just waiting to emerge: "People have always said that I had a beautiful face and 'if you'd only lose weight you'd be really beautiful.'"[16] Here, "people"—friends and casual acquaintances alike—act to enforce prevailing standards of body size. . . .

VII.

. . . Whatever its ultimate effect, discipline can provide the individual upon whom it is imposed with a sense of mastery as well as a secure sense of identity. There is a certain contradiction here: while its imposition may promote a larger disempowerment, discipline may bring with it a certain development of a person's powers. Women, then, like other skilled individuals, have a stake in the perpetuation of their skills, whatever it may have cost to acquire them and quite apart from the question whether, as a gender, they would have been better off had they never had to acquire them in the first place. Hence, feminism, especially a genuinely radical feminism that questions the patriarchal construction of the female body, threatens women with a certain de-skilling, something people normally resist: beyond this, it calls into question that aspect of personal identity that is tied to the development of a sense of competence.

Resistance from this source may be joined by a reluctance to part with the rewards of compliance; further, many women will resist the abandonment of an aesthetic that defines what they take to be beautiful. But there is still another source of resistance, one more subtle, perhaps, but tied once again to questions of identity and internalization. To have a body felt to be "feminine"—a body socially constructed through the appropriate practices—is in most cases crucial to a woman's sense of herself as female and, since persons currently can *be* only as male or female, to her sense of herself as an existing individual. To possess such a body may also be essential to her sense of herself as a sexually desiring and desirable subject. Hence, any political project that aims to dismantle the machinery that turns a female body into a feminine one may well be apprehended by a woman as something that threatens her with desexualization, if not outright annihilation.

The categories of masculinity and femininity do more than assist in the construction of personal identities; they are critical elements in our informal social ontology. This may account to some degree for the otherwise puzzling phenomenon of homophobia and for the revulsion felt by many at the sight of female bodybuilders; neither the homosexual nor the muscular woman can be assimilated easily into the categories that structure everyday life. The radical feminist critique of femininity, then, may pose a threat not only to a woman's sense of her own identity and desirability but to the very structure of her social universe.

. . . Foucault has argued that modern bourgeois democracy is deeply flawed in that it seeks political rights for individuals constituted as unfree by a variety of disciplinary micropowers that lie beyond the realm of what is ordinarily defined as the "political." "The man described for us whom we are invited to free," he says, "is already in himself the effect of a subjection much more profound than himself."[17] If, as I have argued, female subjectivity is constituted in any significant measure in and through the disciplinary practices that construct the feminine body, what Foucault says here of "man" is perhaps even truer of "woman.". . . Femininity as a certain "style of the flesh" will have to be surpassed in the direction of something quite different, not masculinity, which is in many ways only its mirror opposite, but a radical and as yet unimagined transformation of the female body. . . .

(1988)

NOTES

1. Michel Foucault, *Discipline and Punish*, trans. Alan Sheridan (New York: Vintage Books, 1979), p. 138.
2. Ibid., p. 28.
3. Ibid., p. 147.
4. Ibid., p. 153.
5. Ibid., p. 200.
6. Ibid., p. 201.
7. Ibid., p. 228.
8. Judith Butler, "Embodied Identity in de Beauvoir's *The Second Sex*" (unpublished manuscript presented to American Philosophical Association, Pacific Division, March 22, 1985), p. 11.
9. Marcia Millman, *Such a Pretty Face: Being Fat in America* (New York: W. W. Norton, 1980), p. 46.
10. Susan Bordo, "Anorexia Nervosa," *Philosophical Forum 17*, no. 2 (Winter 1985–86): 73–104. . . .
11. Phrase taken from the title of Kim Chernin's *The Obsession: Reflections on the Tyranny of Slenderness* (New York: Harper and Row, 1981) . . .
12. Sophia Loren, *Women and Beauty* (New York: William Morrow, 1984), p. 57.
13. Georgette Klinger and Barbara Rowes, *Georgette Klinger's Skincare* (New York: William Morrow, 1978), pp. 102, 105, 151, 188, and passim.
14. Ibid., pp. 137–40.
15. Foucault, *Discipline and Punish*, p. 222.
16. Millman, *Such a Pretty Face*, p. 80. These sorts of remarks are made so commonly to heavy women that sociologist Millman takes the most clichéd as title of her study of the lives of the overweight.
17. Foucault, *Discipline and Punish*, p. 30.

"IMITATION AND GENDER INSUBORDINATION"[1]

> So what is this divided being introduced into language through gender? It is an impossible being, it is a being that does not exist, an ontological joke. (*Monique Wittig*[2])

> Beyond physical repetition and the psychical or metaphysical repetition, is there an *ontological* repetition? . . . This ultimate repetition, this ultimate theater, gathers everything in a certain way; and in another way, it destroys everything; and in yet another way, it selects from everything. (*Gilles Deleuze*[3])

. . . Here is something like a confession which is meant merely to thematize the impossibility of confession: As a young person, I suffered for a long time, and I suspect many people have, from being told, explicitly or implicitly, that what I "am" is a copy, an imitation, a derivative example, a shadow of the real. Compulsory heterosexuality sets itself up as the original, the true, the authentic; the norm that determines the real implies that "being" lesbian is always a kind of miming, a vain effort to participate in the phantasmatic plenitude of naturalized heterosexuality which will always and only fail.[4] And yet, I remember quite distinctly when I first read in Esther Newton's *Mother Camp: Female Impersonators in America*[5] that drag is not an imitation or a copy of some prior and true gender; according to Newton, drag enacts the very structure of impersonation by which *any gender* is assumed. Drag is not the putting on of a gender that belongs properly to some other group, i.e. an act of *ex*propriation or *ap*propriation that assumes that gender is the rightful property of sex, that "masculine" belongs to "male" and "feminine" belongs to "female." There is no "proper" gender, a gender proper to one sex rather than another, which is in some sense that sex's cultural property. Where that notion of the "proper" operates, it is always and only *improperly* installed as the effect of a compulsory system. Drag constitutes the mundane way in which genders are appropriated, theatricalized, worn, and done; it implies that all gendering is a kind of impersonation and approximation. If this is true, it seems, there is no original or primary gender that drag imitates, but *gender is a kind of imitation for which there is no original*; in fact, it is a kind of imitation that produces the very notion of the original as an *effect* and consequence of the imitation itself. In other words, the naturalistic effects of heterosexualized genders are produced through imitative strategies; what they imitate is a phantasmatic ideal of heterosexual identity, one that is produced by the imitation as its effect. In this sense, the "reality" of heterosexual identities is performatively constituted through an imitation that sets itself up as the origin and the ground of all imitations. In other words, heterosexuality is always in the process of imitating and approximating its own phantasmatic idealization of itself—*and failing*. Precisely because it is bound to fail, and yet endeavors to

---

Judith Butler, "Imitation and Gender Subordination," from *Inside/Out: Lesbian Theories, Gay Theories*, edited by Diana Fuss, New York: Routledge, 1991. Reprinted by permission of Taylor and Francis Group LLC. Notes have been renumbered.

succeed, the project of heterosexual identity is propelled into an endless repetition of itself. Indeed, in its efforts to naturalize itself as the original, heterosexuality must be understood as a compulsive and compulsory repetition that can only produce the *effect* of its own originality; in other words, compulsory heterosexual identities, those ontologically consolidated phantasms of "man" and "woman," are theatrically produced effects that posture as grounds, origins, the normative measure of the real.[6]

Reconsider then the homophobic charge that queens and butches and femmes are imitations of the heterosexual real. Here "imitation" carries the meaning of "derivative" or "secondary," a copy of an origin which is itself the ground of all copies, but which is itself a copy of nothing. Logically, this notion of an "origin" is suspect, for how can something operate as an origin if there are no secondary consequences which retrospectively confirm the originality of that origin? The origin requires its derivations in order to affirm itself as an origin, for origins only make sense to the extent that they are differentiated from that which they produce as derivatives. Hence, if it were not for the notion of the homosexual *as* copy, there would be no construct of heterosexuality *as* origin. Heterosexuality here presupposes homosexuality. And if the homosexual *as* copy *precedes* the heterosexual as *origin*, then it seems only fair to concede that the copy comes before the origin, and that homosexuality is thus the origin, and heterosexuality the copy.

But simple inversions are not really possible. For it is only *as* a copy that homosexuality can be argued to *precede* heterosexuality as the origin. In other words, the entire framework of copy and origin proves radically unstable as each position inverts into the other and confounds the possibility of any stable way to locate the temporal or logical priority of either term.

But let us then consider this problematic inversion from a psychic/political perspective. If the structure of gender imitation is such that the imita*ted* is to some degree produced—or, rather, *re*produced—by imitation (see again Derrida's inversion and displacement of mimesis in "The Double Session"), then to claim that gay and lesbian identities are implicated in heterosexual norms or in hegemonic culture generally is not to *derive* gayness from straightness. On the contrary, *imitation* does not copy that which is prior, but produces and *inverts* the very terms of priority and derivativeness. Hence, if gay identities are implicated in heterosexuality, that is not the same as claiming that they are determined or derived from heterosexuality, and it is not the same as claiming that that heterosexuality is the only cultural network in which they are implicated. These are, quite literally, *inverted* imitations, ones which invert the order of imitated and imitation, and which, in the process, expose the fundamental dependency of "the origin" on that which it claims to produce as its secondary effect.

What follows if we concede from the start that gay identities as derivative inversions are in part defined in terms of the very heterosexual identities from which they are differentiated? If heterosexuality is an impossible imitation of itself, an imitation that performatively constitutes itself as the original, then the imitative parody of "heterosexuality"—when and where it exists in gay cultures—is always and only an imitation of an imitation, a copy of a copy, for which there is no original. Put in yet a different way, the parodic or imitative effect of gay identities works neither to copy nor to emulate heterosexuality, but rather, to expose heterosexuality as an incessant and *panicked* imitation of its own naturalized idealization. That heterosexuality is always in the act of elaborating itself is evidence that it is perpetually at risk, that is, that it "knows" its own possibility of becoming undone: hence, its compulsion to repeat which is at once a foreclosure of that which threatens its coherence. That it can never eradicate that risk attests to its profound dependency upon the homosexuality that it seeks fully to eradicate and never can or that it seeks to make second, but which is always already there as a prior possibility.[7] Although this failure of naturalized heterosexuality might constitute a source of pathos for heterosexuality itself—what its theorists often refer to as its constitutive malaise—it can become an occasion for a subversive and proliferating parody of gender norms in which the very claim to originality and to the real is shown to be the effect of a certain kind of naturalized gender mime.

It is important to recognize the ways in which heterosexual norms reappear within gay identities, to affirm that gay and lesbian identities are not only structured in part by dominant heterosexual frames, but that they are *not* for that reason *determined* by them. They are running commentaries on those naturalized positions as well, parodic replays and resignifications of precisely those heterosexual structures that would consign gay life to discursive domains of unreality and unthinkability. But to be constituted or structured in part by the very heterosexual norms by which gay people are oppressed is not, I repeat, to be claimed or determined by those structures. And it is not necessary to think of such heterosexual constructs as the pernicious intrusion of "the straight mind," one that must be rooted out in its entirety. In a way, the presence of heterosexual constructs and positionalities in whatever form in gay and lesbian identities presupposes that there is a gay and lesbian repetition of straightness, a recapitulation of straightness—which is itself a repetition and recapitulation of its own ideality—within its own terms, a site in which all sorts of resignifying and parodic repetitions become possible. The parodic replication and resignification of heterosexual constructs within non-heterosexual frames brings into relief the utterly constructed status of the so-called original, but it shows that heterosexuality only constitutes itself as the original through a convincing act of repetition. The more that "act" is expropriated, the more the heterosexual claim to originality is exposed as illusory.

Although I have concentrated in the above on the reality-effects of gender practices, performances, repetitions, and mimes, I do not mean to suggest that drag is a "role" that can be taken on or taken off at will. There is no volitional subject behind the mime who decides, as it were, which gender it will be today. On the contrary, the very possibility of becoming a viable subject requires that a certain gentler mime be already underway. The "being" of the subject is no more self-identical than the "being" of any gender; in fact, coherent gender, achieved through an apparent repetition of the same, produces as its *effect* the illusion of a prior and volitional subject. In this sense, gender is not a performance that a prior subject elects to do, but gender is *performative* in the sense that it constitutes as an effect the very subject it appears to express. It is a *compulsory* performance in the sense that acting out of line with heterosexual norms brings

with it ostracism, punishment, and violence, not to mention the transgressive pleasures produced by those very prohibitions.

To claim that there is no performer prior to the performed, that the performance is performative, that the performance constitutes the appearance of a "subject" as its effect is difficult to accept. This difficulty is the result of a predisposition to think of sexuality and gender as "expressing" in some indirect or direct way a psychic reality that precedes it. The denial of the *priority* of the subject, however, is not the denial of the subject; in fact, the refusal to conflate the subject with the psyche marks the psychic as that which exceeds the domain of the conscious subject. This psychic excess is precisely what is being systematically denied by the notion of a volitional "subject" who elects at will which gender and/or sexuality to be at any given time and place. It is this excess which erupts within the intervals of those repeated gestures and acts that construct the apparent uniformity of heterosexual positionalities, indeed which compels the repetition itself, and which guarantees its perpetual failure. In this sense, it is this excess which, within the heterosexual economy, implicitly includes homosexuality, that perpetual threat of a disruption which is quelled through a reenforced repetition of the same. And yet, if repetition is the way in which power works to construct the illusion of a seamless heterosexual identity, if heterosexuality is compelled to *repeat itself* in order to establish the illusion of its own uniformity and identity, then this is an identity permanently at risk, for what if it fails to repeat, or if the very exercise of repetition is redeployed for a very different performative purpose? If there is, as it were, always a compulsion to repeat, repetition never fully accomplishes identity. That there is a need for a repetition at all is a sign that identity is not self-identical. It requires to be instituted again and again, which is to say that it runs the risk of becoming *de*-instituted at every interval.

So what is this psychic excess, and what will constitute a subversive or *de*-instituting repetition? First, it is necessary to consider that sexuality always exceeds any given performance, presentation, or narrative which is why it is not possible to derive or read off a sexuality from any given gender presentation. And sexuality may be said to exceed any definitive narrativization. Sexuality is never fully "expressed" in a performance or practice; there will be passive and butchy femmes, femmy and aggressive butches, and both of those, and more, will turn out to describe more or less anatomically stable "males" and "females." There are no direct expressive or causal lines between sex, gender, gender presentation, sexual practice, fantasy and sexuality. None of those terms captures or determines the rest. Part of what constitutes sexuality is precisely that which does not appear and that which, to some degree, can never appear. This is perhaps the most fundamental reason why sexuality is to some degree always closeted, especially to the one who would express it through acts of self-disclosure. That which is excluded for a given gender presentation to "succeed" may be precisely what is played out sexually, that is, an "inverted" relation, as it were, between gender and gender presentation, and gender presentation and sexuality. On the other hand, both gender presentation and sexual practices may corollate such that it appears that the former "expresses" the latter, and yet both are jointly constituted by the very sexual possibilities that they exclude.

This logic of inversion gets played out interestingly in versions of lesbian butch and femme gender stylization. For a butch can present herself as capable, forceful, and all-providing, and a stone butch may well seek to constitute her lover as the exclusive site of erotic attention and pleasure. And yet, this "providing" butch who seems *at first* to replicate a certain husband-like role, can find herself caught in a logic of inversion whereby that "providingness" turns to a self-sacrifice, which implicates her in the most ancient trap of feminine self-abnegation. She may well find herself in a situation of radical need, which is precisely what she sought to locate, find, and fulfill in her femme lover. In effect, the butch inverts into the femme or remains caught up in the specter of that inversion, or takes pleasure in it. On the other hand, the femme who, as Amber Hollibaugh has argued, "orchestrates" sexual exchange,[8] may well eroticize a certain dependency only to learn that the very power to orchestrate that dependency exposes her own incontrovertible power, at which point she inverts into a butch or becomes caught up in the specter of that inversion, or perhaps delights in it . . .

(1991)

NOTES

1. Parts of this essay were given as a presentation at the Conference on Homosexuality at Yale University in October, 1989.

2. "The Mark of Gender," *Feminist Issues* 5, no. 2 (1985): 6.

3. *Différence et répétition* (Paris: PUFm 1968). 374; my translation.

4. Although miming suggests that there is a prior model which is being copied, it can have the effect of exposing that prior model as purely phantasmatic. In Jacques Derrida's "The Double Session" in *Dissemination*, trans. Barbara Johnson (Chicago: University of Chicago Press, 1981), he considers the textual effect of the mime in Mallarmé's "Mimique." There Derrida argues that the mime does not imitate or copy some prior phenomenon, idea, or figure, but constitutes—some might say *performatively*—the phantasm of the original in and through the mime:

   > He represents nothing, imitates nothing, does not have to conform to any prior referent with the aim of achieving adequacy or verisimilitude. One can here foresee an objection: since the mime imitates nothing, reproduces nothing, opens up in its origin the very thing he is tracing out, presenting, or producing, he must be the very movement of truth. Not, of course, truth in the form of adequation between the representation and the present of the thing itself, or between the imitator and the imitated, but truth as the present unveiling of the present. . . . But this is not the case, . . . We are faced then with mimicry imitating nothing: faced, so to speak, with a double that couples no simple, a double that nothing anticipates, nothing at least that is not itself already double. There is no simple reference. . . . This speculum reflects no reality: it produces mere "reality-effects". . . . In this speculum with no reality, in this mirror of a mirror, a difference or dyad does exist, since there are mimes and phantoms. But it is a difference without reference, or rather reference without a referent, without any first or last unit, a ghost that is the phantom of no flesh . . . (206)

5. Esther Newton, *Mother Camp: Female Impersonators in America* (Chicago: University of Chicago Press, 1972).

6. In a sense, one might offer a redescription of the above in Lacanian terms. The sexual "positions" of heterosexually differentiated "man" and "woman" are part of the *Symbolic*, that is, an ideal embodiment of the Law of sexual difference which constitutes the object of imaginary pursuits, but which is always

thwarted by the "real." These symbolic positions for Lacan are by definition impossible to occupy even as they are impossible to resist as the structuring telos of desire. I accept the former point, and reject the latter one. The imputation of universal necessity to such positions simply encodes compulsory heterosexuality at the level of the Symbolic, and the "failure" to achieve it is implicitly lamented as a source of heterosexual pathos.

7. Of course, it is Eve Kosofsky Scdgwick's *Epistemology of the Closet* (Berkeley: University of California Press, 1990) which traces the subtleties of this kind of panic in Western heterosexual epistemes.
8. Amber Hollibaugh and Cherríe Moraga, "What We're Rollin Around in Bed With: Sexual Silences in Feminism," in *Powers of Desire: The Politics of Sexuality*, ed. Ann Snitow, Christine Stansell, and Sharon Thompson (New York: Monthly Review Press, 1983), 394–405.

83 • *Susan Bordo*

"THE BODY AND THE REPRODUCTION OF FEMININITY"

RECONSTRUCTING FEMINIST DISCOURSE ON THE BODY

The body—what we eat, how we dress, the daily rituals through which we attend to the body—is a medium of culture. The body, as anthropologist Mary Douglas has argued, is a powerful symbolic form, a surface on which the central rules, hierarchies, and even metaphysical commitments of a culture are inscribed and thus reinforced through the concrete language of the body.[1] The body may also operate as a metaphor for culture. From quarters as diverse as Plato and Hobbes to French feminist Luce Irigaray, an imagination of body morphology has provided a blueprint for diagnosis and/or vision of social and political life.

The body is not only a *text* of culture. It is also, as anthropologist Pierre Bourdieu and philosopher Michel Foucault (among others) have argued, a *practical*, direct locus of social control. Banally, through table manners and toilet habits, through seemingly trivial routines, rules, and practices, culture is *"made body,"* as Bourdieu puts it—converted into automatic,

habitual activity. As such it is put "beyond the grasp of consciousness . . . [untouchable] by voluntary, deliberate transformations."[2] Our conscious politics, social commitments, strivings for change may be undermined and betrayed by the life of our bodies—not the craving, instinctual body imagined by Plato, Augustine, and Freud, but what Foucault calls the "docile body," regulated by the norms of cultural life.[3]

Throughout his later "genealogical" works (*Discipline and Punish, The History of Sexuality*), Foucault constantly reminds us of the primacy of practice over belief. Not chiefly through ideology, but through the organization and regulation of the time, space, and movements of our daily lives, our bodies are trained, shaped, and impressed with the stamp of prevailing historical forms of selfhood, desire, masculinity, femininity. Such an emphasis casts a dark and disquieting shadow across the contemporary scene. For women, as study after study shows, are spending more time on the management and discipline of our bodies than we have in a long, long time. In a decade marked by a reopening of the public arena to women, the intensification of such regimens appears diversionary and subverting. Through the pursuit of an ever-changing, homogenizing, elusive ideal of femininity—a pursuit without a terminus, requiring that women constantly attend to minute and often whimsical changes in fashion—female bodies become docile bodies—bodies whose forces and energies are habituated to external regulation, subjection, transformation, "improvement." Through the exacting and normalizing disciplines of diet, makeup, and dress—central organizing principles of time and space in the day of many women—we are rendered less socially oriented and more centripetally focused on self-modification. Through these disciplines, we continue to memorize on our bodies the feel and conviction of lack, of insufficiency, of never being good enough. At the farthest extremes, the practices of femininity may lead us to utter demoralization, debilitation, and death.

Viewed historically, the discipline and normalization of the female body—perhaps the only gender oppression that exercises itself, although to different degrees and in different forms, across age, race, class, and sexual orientation—has to be acknowledged as an amazingly durable and flexible strategy of social control. In our own era, it is difficult to avoid the recognition that the contemporary preoccupation with appearance, which still affects women far more powerfully than men, even in our narcissistic and visually oriented culture, may function as a backlash phenomenon, reasserting existing gender configurations against any attempts to shift or transform power relations. . . . In such an era we desperately need an effective political discourse about the female body, a discourse adequate to an analysis of the insidious, and often paradoxical, pathways of modern social control.

Developing such a discourse requires reconstructing the feminist paradigm of the late 1960s and early 1970s, with its political categories of oppressors and oppressed, villains and victims. Here I believe that a feminist appropriation of some of Foucault's later concepts can prove useful. Following Foucault, we must first abandon the idea of power as something possessed by one group and leveled against another; we must instead think of the network of practices, institutions, and technologies that sustain positions of dominance and subordination in a particular domain.

Second, we need an analytics adequate to describe a power whose central mechanisms are not repressive, but *constitutive*: "a power bent on generating forces, making them grow, and ordering them, rather than one dedicated to impeding them, making them submit, or destroying them." Particularly in the realm of femininity, where so much depends on the seemingly willing acceptance of various norms and practices, we need an analysis of power "from below," as Foucault puts it; for example, of the mechanisms that shape and proliferate—rather than repress—desire, generate and focus our energies, construct our conceptions of normalcy and deviance.[4]

And, third, we need a discourse that will enable us to account for the subversion of potential rebellion, a discourse that, while insisting on the necessity of objective analysis of power relations, social hierarchy, political backlash, and so forth, will nonetheless allow us to confront the mechanisms by which the subject at times becomes enmeshed in collusion with forces that sustain her own oppression.

This essay will not attempt to produce a general theory along these lines. Rather, my focus will be the analysis of one particular arena where the interplay of these dynamics is striking and perhaps exemplary. It is a limited and unusual arena, that of a group of gender-related and historically localized disorders: hysteria, agoraphobia, and anorexia nervosa.[5] I recognize that these disorders have also historically been class- and race-biased, largely (although not exclusively) occurring among white middle- and upper-middle-class women. Nonetheless, anorexia, hysteria, and agoraphobia may provide a paradigm of one way in which potential resistance is not merely undercut but *utilized* in the maintenance and reproduction of existing power relations.

The central mechanism I will describe involves a transformation (or, if you wish, duality) of meaning, through which conditions that are objectively (and, on one level, experientially) constraining, enslaving, and even murderous, come to be experienced as liberating, transforming, and life-giving. I offer this analysis, although limited to a specific domain, as an example of how various contemporary critical discourses may be joined to yield an understanding of the subtle and often unwitting role played by our bodies in the symbolization and reproduction of gender.

THE BODY AS A TEXT OF FEMININITY

The continuum between female disorder and "normal" feminine practice is sharply revealed through a close reading of those disorders to which women have been particularly vulnerable. These, of course, have varied historically: neurasthenia and hysteria in the second half of the nineteenth century; agoraphobia and, most dramatically, anorexia nervosa and bulimia in the second half of the twentieth century. This is not to say that anorectics did not exist in the nineteenth century—many cases were described, usually in the context of diagnoses of hysteria[6]—or that women no longer suffer from classical hysterical symptoms in the twentieth century. But the taking up of eating disorders on a mass scale is as unique to the culture of the 1980s as the epidemic of hysteria was to the Victorian era.[7]

The symptomatology of these disorders reveals itself as textuality. Loss of mobility, loss of voice, inability to leave the home, feeding others while starving oneself, taking up space, and whittling down the space one's body takes up—all have symbolic meaning, all have *political* meaning under the varying rules governing the historical construction of gender. Working within this framework, we see that whether we look at hysteria, agoraphobia, or anorexia, we find the body of the sufferer deeply inscribed with an ideological construction of femininity emblematic of the period in question. The construction, of course, is always homogenizing and normalizing, erasing racial, class, and other differences and insisting that all women aspire to a coercive, standardized ideal. Strikingly, in these disorders the construction of femininity is written in disturbingly concrete, hyperbolic terms: exaggerated, extremely literal, at times virtually caricatured presentations of the ruling feminine mystique. The bodies of disordered women in this way offer themselves as an aggressively graphic text for the interpreter—a text that insists, actually demands, that it be read as a cultural statement, a statement about gender.

Both nineteenth-century male physicians and twentieth-century feminist critics have seen, in the symptoms of neurasthenia and hysteria (syndromes that became increasingly less differentiated as the century wore on), an exaggeration of stereotypically feminine traits. The nineteenth-century "lady" was idealized in terms of delicacy and dreaminess, sexual

passivity, and a charmingly labile and capricious emotionality.[8] Such notions were formalized and scientized in the work of male theorists from Acton and Krafft-Ebing to Freud, who described "normal," mature femininity in such terms.[9] In this context, the dissociations, the drifting and fogging of perception, the nervous tremors and faints, the anesthesias, and the extreme mutability of symptomatology associated with nineteenth-century female disorders can be seen to be concretizations of the feminine mystique of the period, produced according to rules that governed the prevailing construction of femininity. . . .

The hysteric's embodiment of the feminine mystique of her era, however, seems subtle and ineffable compared to the ingenious literalism of agoraphobia and anorexia. In the context of our culture this literalism makes sense. With the advent of movies and television, the rules for femininity have come to be culturally transmitted more and more through standardized visual images. As a result, femininity itself has come to be largely a matter of constructing, in the manner described by Erving Goffman, the appropriate surface presentation of the self.[10] We are no longer given verbal descriptions or exemplars of what a lady is or of what femininity consists. Rather, we learn the rules directly through bodily discourse: through images that tell us what clothes, body shape, facial expression, movements, and behavior are required.

In agoraphobia and, even more dramatically, in anorexia, the disorder presents itself as a virtual, though tragic, parody of twentieth-century constructions of femininity. The 1950s and early 1960s, when agoraphobia first began to escalate among women, was a period of reassertion of domesticity and dependency as the feminine ideal. *Career woman* became a dirty word, much more so than it had been during the war, when the economy depended on women's willingness to do "men's work." The reigning ideology of femininity, so well described by Betty Friedan and perfectly captured in the movies and television shows of the era, was childlike, nonassertive, helpless without a man, "content in a world of bedroom and kitchen, sex, babies and home."[11] The housebound agoraphobic lives this construction of femininity literally. "You want me in this home? You'll have me in this home—with a vengeance! . . . "

The emaciated body of the anorectic, of course, immediately presents itself as a caricature of the contemporary ideal of hyper-slenderness for women, an ideal that, despite the game resistance of racial and ethnic difference, has become the norm for women today. . . . On the one hand, our culture still widely advertises domestic conceptions of femininity, the ideological moorings for a rigorously dualistic sexual division of labor that casts woman as chief emotional and physical nurturer. The rules for this construction of femininity (and I speak here in a language both symbolic and literal) require that women learn to feed others, not the self, and to construe any desires for self-nurturance and self-feeding as greedy and excessive. Thus, women must develop a totally other-oriented emotional economy. In this economy, the control of female appetite for food is merely the most concrete expression of the general rule governing the construction of femininity: that female hunger—for public power, for independence, for sexual gratification—be contained, and the public space that women be allowed to take up be circumscribed, limited. . . .

On the other hand, even as young women today continue to be taught traditionally "feminine" virtues, to the degree that the professional arena is open to them they must also learn to embody the "masculine" language and values of that arena—self-control, determination, cool, emotional discipline, mastery, and so on. Female bodies now speak symbolically of this necessity in their slender spare shape and the currently fashionable men's-wear look. . . . Our bodies, too, as we trudge to the gym every day and fiercely resist both our hungers and our desire to soothe ourselves, are becoming more and more practiced at the "male" virtues of control and self-mastery. . . .

PROTEST AND RETREAT IN THE SAME GESTURE

In hysteria, agoraphobia, and anorexia, then, the woman's body may be viewed as a surface on which conventional constructions of femininity are exposed starkly to view, through their inscription in extreme or hyper-literal form. They are written, of course, in languages of horrible suffering. It is as though these bodies are speaking to us of the pathology and violence that lurks just around the corner, waiting at the horizon of "normal" femininity. It is no wonder that a steady motif in the feminist literature on female disorder is that of pathology as embodied *protest*—unconscious,

inchoate, and counterproductive protest without an effective language, voice, or politics, but protest nonetheless. . . .

Although we may talk meaningfully of protest, then, I want to emphasize the counterproductive, tragically self-defeating (indeed, self-deconstructing) nature of that protest. Functionally, the symptoms of these disorders isolate, weaken, and undermine the sufferers; at the same time they turn the life of the body into an all-absorbing fetish, beside which all other objects of attention pale into unreality. On the symbolic level, too, the protest collapses into its opposite and proclaims the utter capitulation of the subject to the contracted female world. The muteness of hysterics and their return to the level of pure, primary bodily expressivity have been interpreted, as we have seen, as rejecting the symbolic order of the patriarchy and recovering a lost world of semiotic, maternal value. But *at the same time*, of course, muteness is the condition of the silent, uncomplaining woman—an ideal of patriarchal culture. Protesting the stifling of the female voice through one's own voicelessness—that is, employing the language of femininity to protest the conditions of the female world—will always involve ambiguities of this sort. . . .

COLLUSION, RESISTANCE, AND THE BODY

The pathologies of female protest function, paradoxically, as if in collusion with the cultural conditions that produce them, reproducing rather than transforming precisely that which is being protested. In this connection, the fact that hysteria and anorexia have peaked during historical periods of cultural backlash against attempts at reorganization and redefinition of male and female roles is significant. Female pathology reveals itself here as an extremely interesting social formation through which one source of potential for resistance and rebellion is pressed into the service of maintaining the established order.

In our attempt to explain this formation, objective accounts of power relations fail us. For whatever the objective social conditions are that create a pathology, the symptoms themselves must still be produced (however unconsciously or inadvertently) by the subject. That is, the individual must invest the body with meanings of various sorts. Only by examining this productive process on the part of the subject can we, as Mark Poster has put it, "illuminate the mechanisms of domination in the processes through which meaning is produced in everyday life"; that is, only then can we see how the desires and dreams of the subject become implicated in the matrix of power relations.[12]

Here, examining the context in which the anorexic syndrome is produced may be illuminating. Anorexia will erupt, typically, in the course of what begins as a fairly moderate diet regime, undertaken because someone, often the father, has made a casual critical remark. Anorexia *begins in*, emerges out of, what is, in our time, conventional feminine practice. In the course of that practice, for any number of individual reasons, the practice is pushed a little beyond the parameters of moderate dieting. The young woman discovers what it feels like to crave and want and need and yet, through the exercise of her own will, to triumph over that need. In the process, a new realm of meanings is discovered, a range of values and possibilities that Western culture has traditionally coded as "male" and rarely made available to women: an ethic and aesthetic of self-mastery and self-transcendence, expertise, and power over others through the example of superior will and control. The experience is intoxicating, habit-forming. . . .

Although the specific cultural practices and meanings are different, similar mechanisms, I suspect, are at work in hysteria and agoraphobia. In these cases too, the language of femininity, when pushed to excess—when shouted and asserted, when disruptive and demanding—deconstructs into its opposite and makes available to the woman an illusory experience of power previously forbidden to her by virtue of her gender. In the case of nineteenth-century femininity, the forbidden experience may have been the bursting of fetters—particularly moral and emotional fetters. John Conolly, the asylum reformer, recommended institutionalization for women who "want that restraint over the passions without which the female character is lost."[13] Hysterics often infuriated male doctors by their lack of precisely this quality. S. Weir Mitchell described these patients as "the despair of physicians," whose "despotic selfishness wrecks the constitution of nurses and devoted relatives, and in unconscious or half-conscious self-indulgence destroys the comfort of everyone around them."[14] It must have given the Victorian patient some illicit pleasure to be viewed as

capable of such disruption of the staid nineteenth-century household. A similar form of power, I believe, is part of the experience of agoraphobia.

This does not mean that the primary reality of these disorders is not one of pain and entrapment. Anorexia, too, clearly contains a dimension of physical addiction to the biochemical effects of starvation. But whatever the physiology involved, the ways in which the subject understands and thematizes her experience cannot be reduced to a mechanical process. The anorectic's ability to live with minimal food intake allows her to feel powerful and worthy of admiration in a "world," as Susie Orbach describes it, "from which at the most profound level [she] feels excluded" and unvalued.[15] The literature on both anorexia and hysteria is strewn with battles of will between the sufferer and those trying to "cure" her; the latter, as Orbach points out, very rarely understand that the psychic values she is fighting for are often more important to the woman than life itself.

TEXTUALITY, PRAXIS, AND THE BODY

The "solutions" offered by anorexia, hysteria, and agoraphobia, I have suggested, develop out of the practice of femininity itself, the pursuit of which is still presented as the chief route to acceptance and success for women in our culture. Too aggressively pursued; that practice leads to its own undoing, in one sense. For if femininity is, as Susan Brownmiller has said, at its core a "tradition of imposed limitations,"[16] then an unwillingness to limit oneself, even in the pursuit of femininity, breaks the rules. But, of course, in another sense the rules remain fully in place. The sufferer becomes wedded to an obsessive practice, unable to make any effective change in her life. She remains, as Toril Moi has put it, "gagged and chained to [the] feminine role," a reproducer of the docile body of femininity.[17]

This tension between the psychological meaning of a disorder, which may enact fantasies of rebellion and embody a language of protest, and the practical life of the disordered body, which may utterly defeat rebellion and subvert protest, may be obscured by too exclusive a focus on the symbolic dimension and insufficient attention to praxis. . . . The shift to the practical dimension is not a turn to biology or nature, but to another "register," as Foucault puts it, of the cultural body, the register of the "useful body" rather than the "intelligible body."[18] The distinction can prove useful, I believe, to feminist discourse.

The intelligible body includes our scientific, philosophic, and aesthetic representations of the body—our cultural *conceptions* of the body, norms of beauty, models of health, and so forth. But the same representations may also be seen as forming a set of *practical* rules and regulations through which the living body is "trained, shaped, obeys, responds," becoming, in short, a socially adapted and "useful body."[19] Consider this particularly clear and appropriate example: the nineteenth-century hourglass figure, emphasizing breasts and hips against a wasp waist, was an intelligible *symbolic* form, representing a domestic, sexualized ideal of femininity. The sharp cultural contrast between the female and the male form, made possible by the use of corsets and bustles, reflected, in symbolic terms, the dualistic division of social and economic life into clearly defined male and female spheres. At the same time, to achieve the specified look, a particular feminine *praxis* was required—straitlacing, minimal eating, reduced mobility—rendering the female body unfit to perform activities outside its designated sphere. This, in Foucauldian terms, would be the "useful body" corresponding to the aesthetic norm.

The intelligible body and the useful body are two arenas of the same discourse; they often mirror and support each other. . . . Another example can be found in the seventeenth-century philosophic conception of the body as a machine, mirroring an increasingly more automated productive machinery of labor. But the two bodies may also contradict and mock each other. A range of contemporary representations and images, as noted earlier, have coded the transcendence of female appetite and its public display in the slenderness ideal in terms of power, will, mastery, the possibilities of success in the professional arena. These associations are carried visually by the slender superwomen of prime-time television and popular movies and promoted explicitly in advertisements and articles appearing routinely in women's fashion magazines, diet books, and weight-training publications. Yet the thousands of slender girls and women who strive to embody these images and who in that service suffer from eating disorders, exercise compulsions, and continual self-scrutiny and self-castigation are anything *but* the "masters" of their lives.

Exposure and productive cultural analysis of such contradictory and mystifying relations between image and practice are possible only if the analysis includes attention to and interpretation of the "useful" or, as I prefer to call it, the practical body. . . .

I view our bodies as a site of struggle, where we must *work* to keep our daily practices in the service of resistance to gender domination, not in the service of docility and gender normalization. This work requires, I believe, a determinedly skeptical attitude toward the routes of seeming liberation and pleasure offered by our culture. It also demands an awareness of the often contradictory relations between image and practice, between rhetoric and reality. Popular representations, as we have seen, may forcefully employ the rhetoric and symbolism of empowerment, personal freedom, "having it all." Yet female bodies, pursuing these ideals, may find themselves as distracted, depressed, and physically ill as female bodies in the nineteenth century were made when pursuing a feminine ideal of dependency, domesticity, and delicacy. The recognition and analysis of such contradictions, and of all the other collusions, subversions, and enticements through which culture enjoins the aid of our bodies in the reproduction of gender, require that we restore a concern for female praxis to its formerly central place in feminist politics.

(1993)

NOTES

1. Mary Douglas, *Natural Symbols* (New York: Pantheon, 1982), and *Purity and Danger* (London: Routledge and Kegan Paul, 1966).
2. Pierre Bourdieu, *Outline of a Theory of Practice* (Cambridge: Cambridge University Press, 1977), p. 94 (emphasis in original).
3. On docility, see Michel Foucault, *Discipline and Punish* (New York: Vintage, 1979), pp. 135–69. For a Foucauldian analysis of feminine practice, see Sandra Bartky, "Foucault, Femininity, and the Modernization of Patriarchal Power," in her *Femininity and Domination* (New York: Routledge, 1990); see also Susan Brownmiller, *Femininity* (New York: Ballantine, 1984).
4. Michel Foucault, *The History of Sexuality*. Vol. 1: *An Introduction* (New York: Vintage, 1980), pp. 136, 94.
5. On the gendered and historical nature of these disorders: the number of female to male hysterics has been estimated at anywhere from 2:1 to 4:1, and as

many as 80 percent of all agoraphobics are female (Annette Brodsky and Rachel Hare-Mustin, *Women and Psychotherapy* [New York: Guilford Press, 1980], pp. 116, 122). Although more cases of male eating disorders have been reported in the late eighties and early nineties, it is estimated that close to 90 percent of all anorectics are female (Paul Garfinkel and David Garner, *Anorexia Nervosa: A Multidimensional Perspective* [New York: Brunner/Mazel, 1982], pp. 112–13).

6. Showalter, *The Female Malady*, pp. 128–29.
7. On the epidemic of hysteria and neurasthenia, see Showalter, *The Female Malady*; Carroll Smith Rosenberg, "The Hysterical Woman: Sex Roles and Role Conflict in Nineteenth-Century America," in her *Disorderly Conduct: Visions of Gender in Victorian America* (Oxford: Oxford University Press, 1985).
8. Martha Vicinus, "Introduction: The Perfect Victorian Lady," in Martha Vicinus, *Suffer and Be Still: Women in the Victorian Age* (Bloomington: Indiana University Press, 1972), pp. x–xi.
9. See Carol Nadelson and Malkah Notman, *The Female Patient* (New York: Plenum, 1982), p. 5; E. M. Sigsworth and T. J. Wyke, "A Study of Victorian Prostitution and Venereal Disease," in Vicinus, *Suffer and Be Still*.
10. Erving Goffman, *The Presentation of the Self in Everyday Life* (Garden City, N.J.: Anchor Doubleday, 1959).
11. Betty Friedan, *The Feminine Mystique* (New York: Dell, 1962), p. 36.
12. Mark Poster, *Foucault, Marxism, and History* (Cambridge: Polity Press, 1984), p. 28.
13. Showalter, *The Female Malady*, p. 48.
14. Smith-Rosenberg, *Disorderly Conduct*, p. 207.
15. Orbach, *Hunger Strike*, p. 103.
16. Brownmiller, *Femininity*, p, 14.
17. Toril Moi, "Representations of Patriarchy: Sex and Epistemology in Freud's *Dora*," in Charles Bernheimer and Claire Kahane, eds., *In Dora's Case: Freud— Hysteria—Feminism* (New York: Columbia University Press, 1985), p. 192.
18. Foucault, *Discipline and Punish*, p. 136.
19. Foucault, *Discipline and Punish*, p. 136.

84 • *Kate Bornstein*

FROM *GENDER OUTLAW*
On Men, Women, and the Rest of Us

10. WHY IS THERE SO MUCH EMPHASIS ON PASSING?

Passing is a form of pretending, which can be fun. In gender, passing is currently defined as the act of appearing in the world as a gender to which one does not belong, or as a gender to which one did not formerly belong. Most passing is undertaken in response to the cultural imperative to be one gender or the other. In this case, passing becomes the outward manifestation of shame and capitulation. Passing becomes silence. Passing becomes invisibility. Passing becomes lies. Passing becomes self-denial.

A more universal and less depressing definition of passing would be the act of appearing in the gender of one's choice. Everyone is passing; some have an easier job of it than others.

There's a reward and punishment mechanism to passing. As much as I go on about this stuff, and as out of the closet as I am on a very broad public level, I still make an effort to walk down the street and pass on a very private level. I do this because I don't want to get beaten up. I do this because all my life it's been something I've wanted—to live as a woman—and by walking through the world looking like one, I have that last

Kate Bornstein, *Gender Outlaw: On Men, Women, and the Rest of Us*, pp. 125–132. New York: Routledge, 1994. Reprinted by permission of Taylor and Francis Group LLC. Notes have been renumbered.

handhold on the illusion, the fantasy, the dream of it all. Passing is seductive—people don't look at you like you're some kind of freak.

On the punishment side of the coin, there's a deep shame involved in any failure to pass. As I was preparing the final draft of this book, someone I know only peripherally came over to my house on an errand—he was with an ex-lover of mine. In casual conversation, he slipped on a pronoun and referred to me as "he."

Let me tell you what happened, the way it looked from inside my head. The world slowed down, like it does in the movies when someone is getting shot and the filmmaker wants you to feel every bullet enter your body. The words echoed in my ears over and over and over. Attached to that simple pronoun was the word *failure*, quickly followed by the word *freak*. All the joy sucked out of my life in that instant, and every moment I'd ever fucked up crashed down on my head. Here was someone who'd never known me as a man, referring to me as a man. Instead of saying or doing anything, I shut down and was polite to him for the rest of the time he was in my house.

Now here's a telling point all three of us (as I later found out) were aware of that slip, and none of us said anything. *He's* a trained sex worker, with a great deal of experience working with sexual and gender minorities. *She* had two transsexual lovers, me having been one of them. I'm a transsexual. We all knew he'd slipped on a pronoun, and none of us said anything— not a giggle, not an "oops," not one comment. Each of us was far too embarrassed to say anything 'til the next day. What does that say about the gender imperative? I think it says everything.

> Who reads us? People whose identity hinges on the need to determine gender: gays and lesbians for sexual reasons, sex workers and street people for economic reasons, children for the reason of trying to establish their own place in the system.

Passing emphatically equals membership, and passing includes all the privileges of gender membership. There is most certainly a privilege to having a gender. Just ask someone who doesn't have a gender, or who can't pass, or who doesn't pass. When you have a gender, or when you are perceived as having a gender, you don't get laughed at in the street. You don't get beat up. You know which public bathroom to use, and

when you use it, people don't stare at you or worse. You know which form to fill out. You know what clothes to wear. You have heroes and role models. You have a past.

Passing by choice can be fantastic fun. Enforced passing is a joyless activity. Any joy that might be generated by the passing cannot be shared. Similarly, the joy of history lies in its telling and in its relevance to current times and relationships. Transgendered people, particularly post-operative transsexuals, are not allowed any history beyond their current gender—we're not supposed to reveal our transgender status or our other-gendered past. Denied the opportunity to speak our stories, transsexuals are denied the joy of our histories. Sometimes it's painful for me to recall having been male: I did some stupid stuff—but that's part of me, and I need my male past as a reference point in my life. Discouraged from examining our past, transgendered people are discouraged from growth.

> The biggest gift for me after having gone through my gender change was getting back in touch with people I'd known when I was a guy. I really thought I'd never hear from them again. I thought they'd all think I was too weird to be in touch with. One by one, as I get back in touch with folks from my past, I can measure the continuity of my life. And I'm so grateful for their open minds and their open hearts.

The concept of passing is built into the culture's definition of transsexuality; and the result is that transsexuals don't question the gender system which their very existence could topple. Instead, through the mandate of passing, the culture uses transsexuals to reinforce the bipolar gender system, as transsexuals strive for recognition within their new gender, and thus the privilege and chains of their new gender.

Ironically, the concept of passing invites and even demands the concept of reading (seeing through someone else's attempt at passing) and being read. The culture desires and will insist upon an unmasking; the culture will have its "truth." The fear of being read as transsexual weighs so heavily on an individual that it focuses even more attention on "passing." It's a conundrum, because more and better passing brings about an increased fear of being read. I know too many transsexuals who deny their lives as transsexual for the sake of appearing "normal."

11. WHAT ABOUT THE CULTURAL EXPLOITATION OF TRANSGENDERED PEOPLE?

I think it's inevitable, I think it's not unique to transgendered people, and I think it will only continue to the degree we allow it to continue. Most minorities have been exoticized by some dominant culture. A dominant culture, to be truly dominant, needs freak populations—be they racial, religious, and gender minorities, or whatever. True exploitation involves the appropriation of the minority's voice.

In the nineteenth century, one venue for the exoticization of minorities was the North American traveling medicine show. It worked like this: the manager of the show wanted to make money by selling some goods. This manager would gather up a group of exotics—usually people of non-white races, or people with physical anomalies (including hermaphrodites)—publicize the attributes of these "freaks," and then charge admission for the general public to come into some tent to look at them. Then the barker would launch into a talk about the exhibited minority person, or freak. The freak would say nothing, or would recite some rehearsed speech approved by the barker, who had a stake in maintaining the dehumanization of the freak so he could charge more money. The barker would proceed to sell his goods, making a double nickel from the attendees.

In this century, there's a similar venue: the television talk show. The barker, or host, still parades the freaks out in front of the audience, but here's the big difference: it's the *sponsor* who sells the goods during the commercial break. The division of labor between barker-as-host and salesperson-as-sponsor has allowed for a whole new window of opportunity for the freak. Because the TV talk show host (barker) is not the person *directly* interested in sales, he or she can afford to be somewhat more interested in the guests (freaks). The talk show host has a stake in a ratings number, not the number of bottles of snake oil sold, so the host/barker can afford to be more sensitive and caring about the guests/freaks. The good television talk show host realizes that he or she has a stake in emphasizing the *humanity* of the guests so that the viewing audience can better identify with them. As a result, the freaks have an opportunity to speak their own words—for the first time, and to a broad audience! In this culture,

I'm a freak—that's why I respect and enjoy doing the talk shows.

I love freaks. I really do. I always have.

When I was a young boy, my father took me to the circus. I don't remember anything about the circus performance. All I remember is the sideshow. And what I remember most is Olaf, the world's tallest man. He was so tall, I had to stretch my neck way back in order to see all of him. He wore a brown suit. I remember that part. His feet were as long as my arm. He was quiet. He had . . . dignity. But, his hands—damn, his hands were enormous. On each of his fingers, he wore rings, which he sold as souvenirs. I remember I was standing up front, close to his stage, as he spoke of his life. I didn't understand a word he said, but I worshipped him. And then he bent down toward me. His already immense head grew larger and larger as his face drew near to mine. And I remember no fear. He knew me, and I knew him. He smiled. I smiled. Then he took one of the rings off his finger, and put it round my wrist. And I knew I was just like him. I knew I was a freak.

Freaks always know that.

I love doing television talk shows—I respect the format. I'm a child of television, so I'm familiar with the venue, and I've learned the language of soundbytes. I know now to prepare ahead of time the point I want to get across, so I don't have to think on my feet. Unlike Olaf, I don't need some barker to approve my material before I present it. I can have fun bantering with the host, and parrying questions and answers with the audience. And I can usually get back to the single point I want to make on that show.

When a politician appears on a talk show, he's called media-savvy. When I appear on a talk show, I'm called self-centered, self-serving, and a freak. Go figure.

There's a comfortable, three-way symbiosis among the talk show hosts, their guests, and their audiences. The relationship between host and guest is a tacit understanding of the need to communicate to the largest possible number of viewers, and to fulfill some "social service" obligation of information dissemination. It's theater, and both host and guest play a role, one in agreement with the other. The relationship between the two of them and the audience is more magical—like the magic between a young child and a circus giant.

But the real cultural exploitation of transgendered people today is evident in comedy skits like "It's Pat," (recently rumored to soon be a major motion picture). When I first heard about the skit, I thought it was a great idea, but I figured the joke would be on all the characters who were desperate to determine Pat's gender. Instead, the joke was consistently on Pat, who is shown as a slobbering, unattractive, simpering nerd. Pat, of course, *cannot* be attractive, because that would return gender ambiguity to its apparently rightful place of being desirable, and that's simply too dangerous. The popularity of this skit is pretty clear evidence that transgendered people are considered fair game for cultural scapegoating. We're still the group that wears no sign proclaiming, "To fuck with me is politically incorrect and social suicide, so hands off." There's no civil rights group to come to Pat's defense or to the defense of those in Pat's position outside the tube. "It's Pat" is the latest installment in a sadly long tradition of comedy that objectifies, vilifies, and dehumanizes an otherwise voiceless minority.

12. IS THERE A ROLE FOR THE TRANSGENDERED IN THIS CULTURE?

I don't believe it's up to the culture to create such a role. I think it's up to the transgendered to claim one for themselves.

Our culture, some say, has no place for the transgendered. There are some who point to other cultures with envy. These other cultures, they say, have established roles for the transgendered. Hijras in India, for example, call themselves "neither men nor women." Their role in Indian culture is a spiritual one, presiding over marriages and births. Yet as India becomes increasingly westernized, the Hijras are being systematically wiped out.

Whereas Westerners feel uncomfortable with the ambiguities and contradictions inherent in such in-between categories as transvestism, homosexuality, hermaphroditism, and transgenderism, and make strenuous attempts to resolve them. Hinduism not only accommodates such ambiguities, but also views them as meaningful and even powerful.

—Serena Nanda, *Neither Men Nor Women: The Hijras of India*, 1990

Our Western culture has no room for any shades of grey, so it wouldn't make much sense to expect this bi-polar culture to create a role for people whose very existence threatens the binary. The transgendered shamans of other cultures earned their roles; their roles as guides and healers were not doled out to them. Similarly, today's transgendered must earn a position in today's culture. That place in the world will certainly not be a gift to us. Left to fate, the roles we have been gifted with in today's culture have been roles of shame and death.

It would be important that any role that the transgendered wind up claiming is not a role that would by its very existence forward the culture that oppresses the transgendered and related border-walkers.

- Any us-versus-them position forwards a culture that oppresses the transgendered. Opt rather for a role that is inclusive, and promotes inclusion.
- Any position which operates non-consensually (violently) forwards a culture that oppresses the transgendered. Choose only positions which trade in mutual agreement.
- Any power-over position forwards a culture that oppresses the transgendered. We should look for positions that allow us to bring out the power we have within us, and to acknowledge the power of others.

13. YOU SAY YOU WANT A REVOLUTION?

Over the past decade, transgendered people have increasingly been speaking in their own voice. It's the beginnings of a revolution.

The problem with revolution, of course, is violence. It would be neat to take part in a non-violent revolution of inclusion, whereby the revolutionaries simply have a good laugh, and welcome anyone else to dinner.

(1994)

85 • *Judith Halberstam*

"AN INTRODUCTION TO FEMALE MASCULINITY: MASCULINITY WITHOUT MEN"

What's the use of being a little boy if you are going to grow up to be a man?
—*Gertrude Stein,* Everybody's Autobiography (1937)

THE REAL THING

What is "masculinity"? This has been probably the most common question that I have faced over the past five years while writing on the topic of female masculinity. If masculinity is not the social and cultural and indeed political expression of maleness, then what is it? I do not claim to have any definitive answer to this question, but I do have a few proposals about why masculinity must not and cannot and should not reduce down to the male body and its effects. I also venture to assert that although we seem to have a difficult time defining masculinity, as a society we have little trouble in recognizing it, and indeed we spend massive amounts of time and money ratifying and supporting the versions of masculinity that we enjoy and trust; many of these "heroic masculinities" depend absolutely on the subordination of alternative masculinities. I claim in this book that far from being an imitation of maleness, female masculinity actually affords us a glimpse of how masculinity is constructed as masculinity. In other words, female masculinities are framed as the rejected scraps of dominant masculinity in order that male masculinity may appear to be the real thing. But what we understand as heroic masculinity has been produced by and across both male and female bodies. . . .

Masculinity in this society inevitably conjures up notions of power and legitimacy and privilege; it often symbolically refers to the power of the state and to uneven distributions of wealth. Masculinity seems to extend outward into patriarchy and inward into the family; masculinity represents the power of inheritance, the consequences of the traffic in women, and the promise of social privilege. But, obviously, many other lines of identification traverse the terrain of masculinity, dividing its power into complicated differentials of class, race, sexuality, and gender. If what we call "dominant masculinity" appears to be a naturalized relation between maleness and power, then it makes little sense to examine men for the contours of that masculinity's social construction. Masculinity, this book will claim, becomes legible as masculinity where and when it leaves the white male middle-class body. Arguments about excessive masculinity tend to focus on black bodies (male and female), latino/a bodies, or working-class bodies, and insufficient masculinity is all too often figured by Asian bodies or upper-class bodies; these stereotypical constructions of variable masculinity mark the process by which masculinity becomes dominant in the sphere of white middle-class maleness. But all too many studies that currently attempt to account for the power of white masculinity recenter this white male body by concentrating all their analytical efforts on detailing the forms and expressions of white male dominance. Numerous studies of Elvis, white male youth, white male feminism, men and marriage, and domestications of maleness amass information about a subject whom we know intimately and ad nauseam. This study professes a degree of indifference to the whiteness of the male and the masculinity of the white male and the project of naming his power: male masculinity figures in my project as a hermeneutic, and as a counterexample to the kinds of masculinity that seem most informative about gender relations and most generative of social change. This book seeks Elvis only in the female Elvis impersonator Elvis Herselvis: it searches for the political contours of masculine privilege not in men but in the lives of aristocratic European cross-dressing women in the 1920s; it describes the details of masculine difference by comparing not men and women but butch lesbians and female-to-male transsexuals; it examines masculinity's iconicity not in the male matinee idol but in a history of butches in cinema; it finds, ultimately, that the shapes and forms of modem masculinity are best showcased within female masculinity. . . .

THE BATHROOM PROBLEM

If three decades of feminist theorizing about gender has thoroughly dislodged the notion that anatomy is destiny, that gender is natural, and that male and female are the only options, why do we still operate in a world that assumes that people who are not male are female, and people who are not female are male (and even that people who are not male are not people!). If gender has been so thoroughly defamiliarized, in other words, why do we not have multiple gender options, multiple gender categories, and real-life nonmale and nonfemale options for embodiment and identification? In a way, gender's very flexibility and seeming fluidity is precisely what allows dimorphic gender to hold sway. Because so few people actually match any given community standards for male or female, in other words, gender can be imprecise and therefore multiply relayed through a solidly binary system. At the same time, because the definitional boundaries of male and female are so elastic, there are very few people in any given public space who are completely unreadable in terms of their gender.

Ambiguous gender, when and where it does appear, is inevitably transformed into deviance, thirdness, or a blurred version of either male or female. As an example, in public bathrooms for women, various bathroom users tend to fail to measure up to expectations of femininity, and those of us who present in some ambiguous way are routinely questioned and challenged about our presence in the "wrong" bathroom. For example, recently, on my way to give a talk in Minneapolis, I was making a connection at Chicago's O'Hare airport. I strode purposefully into the women's bathroom. No sooner had I entered the stall than someone was knocking at the door: "Open up, security here!" I understood immediately what had happened. I had, once again, been mistaken for a man or a boy, and some woman had called security. As soon as I spoke, the two guards at the bathroom stall realized their error, mumbled apologies, and took off. On the way home from the same trip, in the Denver airport, the same sequence of events was repeated. Needless to say, the policing of gender within the bathroom is intensified in the space of the airport, where people are literally moving through space and time in ways that cause them to want to stabilize some boundaries (gender) even as they traverse others (national). However, having one's gender challenged in the women's rest room is a frequent occurrence in the lives of many androgynous or masculine women; indeed, it is so frequent that one wonders whether the category "woman," when used to designate public functions, is completely outmoded."

It is no accident, then, that travel hubs become zones of intense scrutiny and observation. But gender policing within airport bathrooms is merely an intensified version of a larger "bathroom problem." For some gender-ambiguous women, it is relatively easy to "prove" their right to use the women's bathroom—they can reveal some decisive gender trait (a high voice, breasts), and the challenger will generally back off. For others (possibly low-voiced or hairy or breastless people), it is quite difficult to justify their presence in the women's bathroom, and these people may tend to use the men's bathroom, where scrutiny is far less intense. Obviously, in these bathroom confrontations, the gender-ambiguous person first appears as not-woman ("You are in the wrong bathroom!"), but then the person appears as something actually even more scary, not-man ("No. I am not," spoken in a voice recognized as not-male). Not-man and not-woman, the gender-ambiguous bathroom user is also not androgynous or in-between; this person is gender deviant.

For many gender deviants, the notion of passing is singularly unhelpful. Passing as a narrative assumes that there is a self that masquerades as another kind of self and does so successfully; at various moments, the successful pass may cohere into something akin to identity. At such a moment, the passer has *become.* What of a biological female who presents as butch, passes as male in some circumstances and reads as butch in others, and considers herself not to be a woman but maintains distance from the category "man"? For such a subject, identity might best be described as process with multiple sites for becoming and being. To understand such a process, we would need to do more than map psychic and physical journeys between male and female and within queer and straight space; we would need, in fact, to think in fractal terms and about gender geometries. Furthermore, I argue in chapter 4, in my discussion of the stone butch, when and where we discuss the sexualities at stake in certain gender definitions, very different identifications between sexuality, gender, and the body emerge. The stone butch, for example, in her self-definition as a non-feminine, sexually untouchable female, complicates the idea that lesbians share female sexual practices or women share female sexual desires or even that masculine women share a sense of what animates their particular masculinities.

I want to focus on what I am calling "the bathroom problem" because I believe it illustrates in remarkably clear ways the flourishing existence of gender binarism despite rumors of its demise. Furthermore, many normatively gendered women have no idea that a bathroom problem even exists and claim to be completely ignorant about the trials and tribulations that face the butch woman who needs to use a public bathroom. But queer literature is littered with references to the bathroom problem, and it would not be an exaggeration to call it a standard feature of the butch narrative. For example, Leslie Feinberg provides clear illustrations of the dimensions of the bathroom problem in *Stone Butch Blues.* In this narrative of the life of the he-she factory worker, Jess Goldberg, Jess recounts many occasions in which she has to make crucial decisions about whether she can afford to use the women's bathroom. On a shopping outing with same drag

queens, Jess tells Peaches: "I gotta use the bathroom. God, I wish I could wait, but I can't." Jess takes a deep breath and enters the ladies room:

> Two women were freshening their makeup in front of the mirror. One glanced at the other and finished applying her lipstick. "Is that a man or a woman?" She said to her friend as I passed them.
>
> The other woman turned to me. "This is the woman's bathroom," she informed me.
>
> I nodded. "I know."
>
> I locked the stall door behind me. Their laughter cut me to the bone. "You don't really know if that is a man or not," one woman said to the other. "We should call security to make sure."
>
> I flushed the toilet and fumbled with my zipper in fear. Maybe it was just an idle threat. Maybe they really would call security. I hurried out of the bathroom as soon as I heard both women leave.[1]

For Jess, the bathroom represents a limit to her ability to move around in the public sphere. Her body, with its needs and physical functions, imposes a limit on her attempts to function normally despite her variant gender presentation. The women in the rest room, furthermore, are depicted as spiteful, rather than fearful. They toy with Jess by calling into question her right to use the rest room and threatening to call the police. As Jess puts it: "They never would have made fun of a guy like that." In other words, if the women were truly anxious for their safety, they would not have toyed with the intruder, and they would not have hesitated to call the police. Their casualness about calling security indicates that they know Jess is a woman but want to punish her for her inappropriate self-presentation.

Another chronicle of butch life, *Throw It to the River,* by Nice Rodriguez, a Filipina-Canadian writer, also tells of the bathroom encounter. In a story called "Every Full Moon," Rodriguez tells a romantic tale about a butch bus conductor called Remedios who falls in love with a former nun called Julianita. Remedios is "muscular around the arms and shoulders," and her "toughness allows her to bully anyone who will not pay the fare."[2] She aggressively flirts with Julianita until Julianita agrees to go to a movie with Remedios. To prepare for her date, Remedios dresses herself up, carefully flattening out her chest with

Band-Aids over the nipples: "She bought a white shirt in Divisoria just for this date. Now she worries that the cloth may be too thin and transparent, and that Julianita will be turned off when her nipples protrude out like dice" (33). With her "well-ironed jeans," her smooth chest, and even a man's manicure, Remedios heads out for her date. However, once out with Julianita, Remedios, now dressed in her butch best, has to be careful about public spaces. After the movie, Julianita rushes off to the washroom, but Remedios waits outside for her:

> She has a strange fear of ladies rooms. She wishes there was another washroom somewhere between the mens' and the ladies' for queers like her. Most of the time she holds her pee—sometimes as long as half a day—until she finds a washroom where the users are familiar with her. Strangers take to her unkindly, especially elder women who inspect her from head to toe. (40–41)

Another time, Remedios tells of being chased from a ladies' room and beaten by a bouncer. The bathroom problem for Remedios and for Jess severely limits their ability to circulate in public spaces and actually brings them into contact with physical violence as a result of having violated a cardinal rule of gender: one must be readable at a glance. After Remedios is beaten for having entered a ladies' room, her father tells her to be more careful, and Rodriguez notes: "She realized that being cautious means swaying her hips and parading her boobs when she enters any ladies room" (30).

If we use the paradigm of the bathroom as a limit of gender identification, we can measure the distance between binary gender schema and lived multiple gendered experiences. The accusation "you're in the wrong bathroom" really says two different things. First, it announces that your gender seems at odds with your sex (your apparent masculinity or androgyny is at odds with your supposed femaleness); second, it suggests that single-gender bathrooms are only for those who fit clearly into one category (male) or the other (female). Either we need open-access bathrooms or multigendered bathrooms, or we need wider parameters for gender identification. The bathroom, as we know it, actually represents the crumbling edifice of gender in the twentieth century. The frequency with which gender-deviant "women" are mistaken for men in public bathrooms suggests that a large number of feminine women spend a large amount of time and energy policing masculine women. Something very different happens, of course, in the men's public toilet, where the space is more likely to become a sexual cruising zone than a site for gender repression. Lee Edelman, in an essay about the interpenetration of nationalism and sexuality, argues that "the institutional men's room constitutes a site at which the zones of public and private cross with a distinctive psychic charge."[3] The men's room, in other words, constitutes both an architecture of surveillance and an incitement to desire, a space of homosocial interaction and of homoerotic interaction.

So, whereas men's rest rooms tend to operate as a highly charged sexual space in which sexual interactions are both encouraged and punished, women's rest rooms tend to operate as an arena for the enforcement of gender conformity. Sex-segregated bathrooms continue to be necessary to protect women from male predations but also produce and extend a rather outdated notion of a public–private split between male and female society. The bathroom is a domestic space beyond the home that comes to represent domestic order, or a parody of it, out in the world. The women's bathroom accordingly becomes a sanctuary of enhanced femininity, a "little girl's room" to which one retreats to powder one's nose or fix one's hair. The men's bathroom signifies as the extension of the public nature of masculinity—it is precisely not domestic even though the names given to the sexual function of the bathroom—such as cottage or tearoom—suggest it is a parody of the domestic. The codes that dominate within the women's bathroom are primarily gender codes; in the men's room, they are sexual codes. Public sex versus private gender, openly sexual versus discreetly repressive, bathrooms beyond the home take on the proportions of a gender factory.

Marjorie Garber comments on the liminality of the bathroom in *Vested Interests* in a chapter on the perils and privileges of cross-dressing. She discusses the very different modes of passing and cross-dressing for cross-identified genetic males and females, and she observes that the restroom is a "potential waterloo" for both female-to-male (FTM) and male-to-female (MTF) cross-dressers and transsexuals.[4] For the FTM, the men's room represents the most severe test of his ability to pass, and advice frequently circulates within FTM communities about how to go unnoticed in male-only spaces. Garber notes: "The cultural paranoia of being caught in the ultimately wrong place, which may be inseparable from the pleasure of "passing" in that same place, depends in part on the same cultural binarism, the idea that gender categories are sufficiently uncomplicated to permit self-assortment into one of the two 'rooms' without deconstructive reading" (47). It is worth pointing out here (if only because Garber does not) that the perils for passing FTMS in the men's room are very different from the perils of passing MTFS in the women's room. On the one hand, the FTM in the men's room is likely to be less scrutinized because men are not quite as vigilant about intruders as women for obvious reasons. On the other hand, if caught, the FTM may face some version of gender panic from the man who discovers him, and it is quite reasonable to expect and fear violence in the wake of such a discovery. The MTF, by comparison, will be more scrutinized in the women's room but possibly less open to punishment if caught. Because the FTM ventures into male territory with the potential threat of violence hanging over his head, it is crucial to recognize that the bathroom problem is much more than a glitch in the machinery of gender segregation and is better described in terms of the violent enforcement of our current gender system. . . .

In this introduction, I have tried to chart the implications of the suppression of female masculinities in a variety of spheres: in relation to cultural studies discussions, the suppression of female masculinities allows for male masculinity to stand unchallenged as the bearer of gender stability and gender deviance. The tomboy, the masculine woman, and the racialized masculine subject, I argue, all contribute to a mounting cultural indifference to the masculinity of white

males. Gender policing in public bathrooms, furthermore, and gender performances within public spaces produce radically reconfigured notions of proper gender and map new genders onto a utopian vision of radically different bodies and sexualities. By arguing for gender transitivity, for self-conscious forms of female masculinity, for indifference to dominant male masculinities, and for "nonce taxonomies," I do not wish to suggest that we can magically wish into being a new set of properly descriptive genders that would bear down on the outmoded categories "male" and "female." Nor do I mean to suggest that change is simple and that, for example, by simply creating the desegregation of public toilets we will change the function of dominant genders within heteropatriarchal cultures. However, it seems to me that there are some very obvious spaces in which gender difference simply does not work right now, and the breakdown of gender as a signifying system in these arenas can be exploited to hasten the proliferation of alternate gender regimes in other locations. From drag kings to spies with gadgets, from butch bodies to FTM bodies, gender and sexuality and their technologies are already excessively strange. It is simply a matter of keeping them that way.

(1998)

NOTES

1. Leslie Feinberg, *Stone Butch Blues: A Novel* (Ithaca, N.Y.: Firebrand, 1993), 59.
2. Nice Rodriguez, *Throw It to the River* (Toronto, Canada: Women's Press, 1993), 25–26.
3. Lee Edelman, "Tearooms and Sympathy, or The Epistemology of the Water Closet," in *Homographesis: Essays in Gay Literary and Cultural Theory* (New York: Routledge, 1994), 158.
4. Marjorie Garber, *Vested Interests: Cross-Dressing and Cultural Anxiety* (New York: Routledge, 1992), 47.

"SHOULD THERE BE ONLY TWO SEXES?"

HERMAPHRODITIC HERESIES

In 1993 I published a modest proposal suggesting that we replace our two-sex system with a five-sex one.[1] In addition to males and females, I argued, we should also accept the categories herms (named after "true" hermaphrodites), merms (named after male "pseudo-hermaphrodites"), and ferms (named after female "pseudo-hermaphrodites"). I'd intended to be provocative, but I had also been writing tongue in cheek, and so was surprised by the extent of the controversy the article unleashed. Rightwing Christians somehow connected my idea of five sexes to the United Nations–sponsored 4th World Conference on Women, to be held in Beijing two years later, apparently seeing some sort of global conspiracy at work. "It is maddening," says the text of a *New York Times* advertisement paid for by the Catholic League for Religious and Civil Rights,[2] "to listen to discussions of 'five genders' when every sane person knows there are but two sexes, both of which are rooted in nature."[3]

John Money was also horrified by my article, although for different reasons. In a new edition of his guide for those who counsel intersexual children and their families, he wrote: "In the 1970's nurturists . . . become . . . 'social constructionists.' They align themselves against biology and medicine. . . . They consider all sex differences as artifacts of social construction. In cases of birth defects of the sex organs, they attack all medical and surgical interventions as unjustified meddling designed to force babies into fixed social molds of male and female. . . . One writer has gone even to the extreme of proposing that there are five sexes . . . (Fausto-Sterling)."[4] Meanwhile,

those battling against the constraints of our sex/gender system were delighted by the article. The science fiction writer Melissa Scott wrote a novel entitled *Shadow Man*, which includes nine types of sexual preference and several genders, including ferns (people with testes, XY chromosomes, and some aspects of female genitalia), herms (people with ovaries and testes), and mems (people with XX chromosomes and some aspects of male genitalia).[5] Others used the idea of five sexes as a starting point for their own multi-gendered theories.[6]

Clearly I had struck a nerve. The fact that so many people could get riled up by my proposal to revamp our sex/gender system suggested that change (and resistance to it) might be in the offing. Indeed, a lot *has* changed since 1993, and I like to think that my article was one important stimulus. Intersexuals have materialized before our very eyes, like beings beamed up onto the Starship Enterprise. They have become political organizers lobbying physicians and politicians to change treatment practices. More generally, the debate over our cultural conceptions of gender has escalated, and the boundaries separating masculine and feminine seem harder than ever to define.[7] Some find the changes underway deeply disturbing; others find them liberating.

I, of course, am committed to challenging ideas about the male/female divide. In chorus with a growing organization of adult intersexuals, a small group of scholars, and a small but growing cadre of medical practitioners,[8] I argue that medical management of intersexual births needs to change. *First*, let there be no unnecessary infant surgery (by *necessary* I mean to save the infant's life or significantly improve h/her physical well-being). *Second*, let physicians assign a provisional sex (male or female) to the infant (based on existing knowledge of the probability of a particular gender identity formation—penis size be damned!). *Third*, let the medical care team provide full information and long-term counseling to the parents and to the child. However well-intentioned, the methods for managing intersexuality, so entrenched since the 1950s, have done serious harm. . . .

TOWARD THE END OF GENDER TYRANNY: GETTING THERE FROM HERE

Simply recognizing a third category does not assure a flexible gender system. Such flexibility requires political and social struggle. In discussing my "five sexes" proposal Suzanne Kessler drives home this point with great effect:

> The limitation with Fausto-Sterling's proposal is that legitimizing other sets of genitals . . . still gives genitals primary signifying status and ignores the fact that in the everyday world gender attributions are made without access to genital inspection . . . what has primacy in everyday life is the gender that is performed, regardless of the flesh's configuration under the clothes.

Kessler argues that it would be better for intersexuals and their supporters to turn everyone's focus away from genitals and to dispense with claims to a separate intersexual identity. Instead, she suggests, men and women would come in a wider assortment. Some women would have large clitorises or fused labia, while some men would have "small penises or misshapen sorota—phenotypes with no particular clinical or identity meaning."[9] I think Kessler is right, and this is why I am no longer advocating using discrete categories such as herm, merm, and ferm, even tongue in cheek.

The intersexual or transgender person who presents a social gender—what Kessler calls "cultural genitals"—that conflicts with h/her physical genitals often risks h/her life. In a recent court case, a mother charged that her son, a transvestite, died because paramedics stopped treating him after discovering his male genitals. The jury awarded her $2.9 million in damages. While it is heartening that a jury found

such behavior unacceptable, the case underscores the high risk of gender transgression.[10] "Transgender warriors," as Leslie Feinberg calls them, will continue to be in danger until we succeed in moving them onto the "acceptable" side of the imaginary line separating "normal, natural, holy" gender from the "abnormal, unnatural, sick [and] sinful."[11]

A person with ovaries, breasts, and a vagina, but whose "cultural genitals" are male also faces difficulties. In applying for a license or passport, for instance, one must indicate "M" or "F" in the gender box. Suppose such a person checks "F" on his or her license and then later uses the license for identification. The 1998 murder in Wyoming of homosexual Matthew Shepherd makes clear the possible dangers. A masculine-presenting female is in danger of violent attack if she does not "pass" as male. Similarly, she can get into legal trouble if stopped for a traffic violation or passport control, as the legal authority can accuse her of deception—masquerading as a male for possibly illegal purposes. In the 1950s, when police raided lesbian bars, they demanded that women be wearing three items of women's clothing in order to avoid arrest.[12] As Feinberg notes, we have not moved very far beyond that moment.

Given the discrimination and violence faced by those whose cultural and physical genitals don't match, legal protections are needed during the transition to a gender-diverse utopia. It would help to eliminate the "gender" category from licenses, passports, and the like. The transgender activist Leslie Feinberg writes: "Sex categories should be removed from all basic identification papers—from driver's licenses to passports—and since the right of each person to define their own sex is so basic, it should be eliminated from birth certificates as well."[13] Indeed, why are physical genitals necessary for identification? Surely attributes both more visible (such as height, build, and eye color) and less visible (fingerprints and DNA profiles) would be of greater use.

Transgender activists have written "An International Bill of Gender Rights" that includes (among ten gender rights) "the right to define gender identity, the right to control and change one's own body, the right to sexual expression and the right to form committed, loving relationships and enter into marital contracts."[14] The legal bases for such rights are being hammered out in the courts as I write, through the establishment of case law regarding sex discrimination and homo-sexual rights.[15]

Intersexuality, as we have seen, has long been at the center of debates over the connections among sex, gender, and legal and social status. A few years ago the Cornell University historian Mary Beth Norton sent me the transcripts of legal proceedings from the General Court of the Virginia Colony. In 1629, one Thomas Hall appeared in court claiming to be both a man and a woman. Because civil courts expected one's dress to signify one's sex, the examiner declared Thomas was a woman and ordered her to wear women's clothing. Later, a second examiner overruled the first, declaring Hall a man who should, therefore, wear men's clothing. In fact, Thomas Hall had been christened Thomasine and had worn women's clothing until age twenty-two, when he joined the army. Afterward s/he returned to women's clothing so that s/he could make a living sewing lace. The only references to Hall's anatomy say that he had a man's part as big as the top of his little finger, that he did not have the use of this part, and that—as Thomasine herself put it—she had "a peece of an hole." Finally, the Virginia Court, accepting Thomas(ine)'s gender duality, ordered that "it shall be published that the said Hall is a man *and* a woman, that all inhabitants around may take notice thereof and that he shall go clothed in man's apparel, only his head will be attired in a Coiffe with an apron before him."[16]

Today the legal status of operated intersexuals remains uncertain.[17] Over the years the rights of royal succession, differential treatment by social security or insurance laws, gendered labor laws, and voting limitations would all have been at stake in declaring an intersex legally male or female. Despite the lessening of such concerns, the State remains deeply interested in regulating marriage and the family. Consider the Australian case of an XX intersex born with an ovary and fallopian tube on the right side, a small penis, and a left testicle. Reared as a male, he sought surgery in adulthood to masculinize his penis and deal with his developed breasts. The physicians in charge of his case agreed he should remain a male, since this was his psychosexual orientation. He later married, but the Australian courts annulled the union. The ruling held that in a legal system that requires a person to be either one or the other, for the purpose of marriage, he

could be neither male nor female (hence the need for the right to marry in the Bill of Gender Rights).[18]

As usual, the debates over intersexuality are inextricable from those over homosexuality; we cannot consider the challenges one poses to our gender system without considering the parallel challenge posed by the other. In considering the potential marriage of an intersexual, the legal and medical rules often focus on the question of homosexual marriage. In the case of *Corbett v. Corbett 1970*, April Ashley, a British transsexual, married one Mr. Corbett, who later asked the court to annul the marriage because April was really a man. April argued that she was a social female and thus eligible for marriage. The judge, however, ruled that the operation was pure artifact, imposed on a clearly male body. Not only had April Ashley been born a male, but her transforming surgery had not created a vagina large enough to permit penile penetration. Furthermore, sexual intercourse was "the institution on which the family is built, and in which the capacity for natural hetero-sexual intercourse is an essential element." "Marriage," the judge continued, "is a relationship which depends upon sex and not gender."[19]

An earlier British case had annulled a marriage between a man and a woman born without a vagina. The husband testified that he could not penetrate more than two inches into his wife's artificial vagina. Furthermore, he claimed even that channel was artificial, not the biological one due him as a true husband. The divorce commissioner agreed, citing a much earlier case in which the judge ruled, "I am of the opinion that no man ought to be reduced to this state of quasi-natural connexion."[20]

Both British judges declared marriage without the ability for vaginal–penile sex to be illegal, one even adding the criterion that two inches did not a penetration make. In other countries—and even in the several U.S. states that ban anal and oral contact between both same-sex and opposite-sex partners and those that restrict the ban to homosexual encounters[21]—engaging in certain types of sexual encounters can result in felony charges. Similarly, a Dutch physician discussed several cases of XX intersexuals, raised as males, who married females. Defining them as biological females (based on their two X chromosomes and ovaries), the physician called for a discussion of the legality of the marriages. Should they be dissolved "notwithstanding the fact that they are happy ones?" Should they "be recognized legally and ecclesiastically?"[22]

If cultural genitals counted for more than physical genitals, many of the dilemmas just described could be easily resolved. Since the mid-1960s the International Olympic Committee has demanded that all female athletes submit to a chromosome or DNA test, even though some scientists urge the elimination of sex testing.[23] Whether we are deciding who may compete in the women's high jump or whether we should record sex on a newborn's birth certificate, the judgment derives primarily from social conventions. Legally, the interest of the state in maintaining a two-gender system focuses on questions of marriage, family structure, and sexual practices. But the time is drawing near when even these state concerns will seem arcane to us.[24] Laws regulating consensual sexual behavior between adults had religious and moral origins. In the United States, at least, we are supposed to experience complete separation of church and state. As our legal system becomes further secularized (as I believe it will), it seems only a matter of time before the last laws regulating consensual bedroom behavior will become unconstitutional.[25] At that moment the final legal barriers to the emergence of a wide range of gender expression will disappear.

The court of the Virginia Colony required Thomas/Thomasine to signal h/her physical genitals by wearing a dual set of cultural genitals. Now, as then, physical genitals form a poor basis for deciding the rights and privileges of citizenship. Not only are they confusing; they are not even publicly visible. Rather, it is social gender that we see and read. In the future, hearing a birth announced as "boy" or "girl" might enable new parents to envision for their child an expanded range of possibilities, especially if their baby were among the few with unusual genitals. Perhaps we will come to view such children as especially blessed or lucky. It is not so far-fetched to think that some can become the most desirable of all possible mates, able to pleasure their partners in a variety of ways. One study of men with unusually small penises, for example, found them to be "characterized by an experimental attitude to positions and methods."

Many of these men attributed "partner sexual satisfaction and the stability of their relationships to their need to make extra effort including non-penetrating techniques."[26]

My vision is utopian, but I believe in its possibility. All of the elements needed to make it come true already exist, at least in embryonic form. Necessary legal reforms are in reach, spurred forward by what one might call the "gender lobby": political organizations that work for women's rights, gay rights, and the rights of transgendered people. Medical practice has begun to change as a result of pressure from intersexual patients and their supporters. Public discussion about gender and homosexuality continues unabated with a general trend toward greater tolerance for gender multiplicity and ambiguity. The road will be bumpy, but the possibility of a more diverse and equitable future is ours if we choose to make it happen.

(2000)

NOTES

1. Fausto-Sterling 1993a. The piece was reprinted on the Op-Ed page of the *New York Times* under the title "How Many Sexes Are There?" Fausto-Sterling 1994.
2. This is the same organization that tried to close down the Off Broadway play "Corpus Christi" (by Terence McNally) during the fall season of 1998 in New York City.
3. Rights 1995 Section 4, p. 11. The syndicated columnist E. Thomas McClanahan took up the attack as well. "What the heck," he wrote, "why settle for five genders? Why not press for an even dozen?" (McClanahan 1995 p. B6). Pat Buchanan also joined the chorus: "They say there aren't two sexes, there are five genders. . . . I tell you this: God created man and woman—I don't care what Bella Abzug says" (quoted in *The Advocate*, October 31, 1995). Columnist Marilyn vos Savant writes: "There are men and there are women—no matter how they're constructed . . . and that's that" (vos Savant 1996 p. 6).
4. Money 1994.
5. Scott's novel won the Lambda Literary Award in 1995. She specifically acknowledged my work on her web site.
6. See, for example, Rothblatt 1995; Burke 1996; and Diamond 1996.
7. Spence has been writing for some time about the impossibility of these terms. See, e.g., Spence 1984 and 1985.

8. For activists working for change see the Intersex Society of North America (http:/www.isna.org) and Chase 1998a, b; and Harmon-Smith 1998. For academics in addition to myself, see Kessler 1990; Dreger 1993; Diamond and Sigmundson 1997a, b; Dreger 1998b; Kessler 1998; Preves 1998; Kipnis and Diamond 1998; Dreger 1998c. For physicians who are moving toward (or embracing) the new paradigm see Schober 1998; Wilson and Reiner 1998; and Phomphutkul et al. 1999. More cautiously, Meyer-Bahlburg suggests modest changes in medical practice, including giving more thought to gender assignment (an "optimal gender policy"), elimination of nonconsensual surgery for mild degrees of genital abnormalities, and provision of more support services for intersex persons and their parents. He also calls for obtaining more data on long-term outcomes (Meyer-Bahlburg 1998).

9. Kessler 1998, p. 90.

10. Press 1998.

11. Rubin 1984, p. 282.

12. Kennedy and Davis 1993.

13. Feinberg 1996, p. 125.

14. For a complete statement of the International Bill of Gender Rights, see pp. 165–69 of Feinberg 1996.

15. For a thorough and thoughtful treatment of the legal issues (which by extrapolation might apply to intersexuals), see Case 1995. For a discussion of how legal decisions construct the heterosexual and homosexual subject, see Halley 1991, 1993, and 1994.

16. In Norton 1996, pp. 187–88.

17. As sex reassignment surgery became more common in the 1950s, doctors worried about their personal liability. Even though physicians obtained parental approval, could a child—upon reaching the age of majority—sue the surgeon "for changes ranging from malpractice to assault and battery or even mayhem"? Despite "this disagreeable quirk in the law," the worried physician writing this passage felt he ought not shrink from "handling these unfortunate children . . . in whatever way seems . . . to be most suitable and humane" (Gross and Meeker 1955, p. 321).

In 1957, Dr. E. C. Hamblen, reiterating the fear of lawsuit, sought the aid of a law clinic at Duke University. One suggested solution, which never saw the light of day, was to set up state boards or commissions "on sex assignment or reassignment, comparable to boards of eugenics which authorize sterilization." Hamblen hoped such action could protect a physician whose position he feared "might be precarious, indeed, if legal action subsequently resulted in a jury trial" (Hamblen 1957, p. 1,240). After this early flurry of self-concern, the medical literature falls silent on the question of the patient's right to sue. Perhaps doctors have relied both on their near certainty that current medical approaches to intersexuality are both morally and medically correct and on the realization that the vast majority of their patients would never choose to go public about such intimate matters. In the post-Lorena Bobbit era, however, it seems only a matter of time until some medical professional confronts the civil claims of a genitally altered intersexual.

18. O'Donovan 1985. For an up-to-date review of the legal status of the intersexual, see Greenberg 1999.

19. O'Donovan 1985, p. 15; Ormrod 1992.

20. Edwards 1959, p. 118.

21. Halley 1991.

22. Ten Berge 1960, p. 118.

23. See de la Chapelle 1986; Ferguson-Smith et al. 1992; Holden 1992; Kolata 1992; Serrat and Garcia de Herreros 1993; Unsigned 1993.

24. I never would have guessed, when I first drafted this chapter in 1993, that in 1998 homosexual marriages would be on the ballots in two states. Although it lost in both cases, clearly the issue is now open to discussion. I believe it is a matter of time before the debate will be joined again, with different results.

25. Rhode Island repealed its antisodomy law in 1998, the same year that a similar law was found unconstitutional in the state of Georgia.

26. Reilly and Woodhouse 1989, p. 571; see also Woodhouse 1994.

87 • *Riki Wilchins*

"A CERTAIN KIND OF FREEDOM: POWER AND THE TRUTH OF BODIES"

. . . Queer bodies are always defined by gender norms that are constructed in their absence. In fact, such norms are constructed only *by* their absence, because if they were there at the inception, the norm couldn't exist. It would be queered from the start.

It's particularly intriguing to hear charges of Realness coming from lesbians and feminists. Barely 100 years ago suffragettes were not considered to be "real women" because they shunned passivity to invade men's social prerogatives. Only 40 years ago, lesbians were accused of not being "real women" because they didn't want to marry men and become mothers. Twenty years ago femmes were ridiculed for not being "real lesbians" because they looked like straight women—yet another kind of displacement that ceded femininity to heterosexuality.

And, of course, through it all, any man who slept with or desired the same sex gave up forever the hope of ever being a "real man." In fact, the United States may be the only country in the world where we are so insecure about gender that the words *man* and *woman* have no meaning unless they are preceded by *real*.

Realness circulates in so many different contexts because it is very politically effective. As a form of knowledge, it empowers some bodies, discourages others, and teaches all to stay within the lines.

DOUBLE VISION

"Can I ask you something—are you a man or a woman?"
—*attendee at women's conference*

"Not always, but sometimes I think I am."
—*smart-ass author*

What is it about binaries that so captivates our thinking: men/women, gay/straight, M-to-F/F-to-M, white/black, real/artificial, male/female, lesbian/feminist. Whoops . . . sorry. Scratch that. If there are more than two genders, it's a cinch that, with our bifocal glasses, we'll never see them. Actually, that's backward. Two-ness is not something "out there" but a product of the way we see. We look for that two-ness. Our categories assure that we see it. That's why no matter what gender I do, the only question is "Are you a man or a woman?" because that exhausts all the available possibilities.

When we pick up complex things—like desire or gender—with primitive mental tools like binaries, we lose nuance and multiplicity. Binaries don't give us much information. But then, they're not supposed to.

Quick: What is the meaning of masculinity? Mannish, not feminine, right? What about being straight? That means not being gay.

To say that I'm still really a man is only meaningful in terms of my not being a woman. I am feminine only to the exact degree that I am . . . not masculine. I am gay only as much as I'm not straight or to the exact number of songs I've memorized from *The Sound of Music*.

There's really not very much meaning or information circulating here, because with only two possibilities, meaning is confined to what something is not. As a form of thinking, binaries prevent other kinds of information from emerging. That is why no other genders ever appear. Binaries are the black holes of knowledge. Nothing is allowed to escape, so we get the same answers every time.

From *Genderqueer: Voices from beyond the Sexual Binary.* Edited by Joan Nestle, Clare Howell, and Riki Wilchins, 2002. Reprinted by permission of Magnus Books, an imprint of Riverdale Avenue Books.

TWO'S A CROWD

So in binaries all knowledge is broken down into two equal halves, right? Actually, no. Despite the name, binary thinking is not like two, like two halves of an aspirin you break down the middle.

At this point in my life, I have spoken to hundreds of people about my body. Some of them even standing up. In 20 years, not one has asked me anything about "gaining a vagina." If they mentioned my surgery at all, every one said something, often in the form of a crude joke that was related to my losing the big Magic Wand. Now, I'm as impressed with my genitals as the next person. Maybe more so. This is the same sort of question posed to F-to-Ms. It seems no matter what sex it is, it's about male.

At this point, it should surprise no one that binaries are about power, a form of doing politics through language. Binaries create the smallest possible hierarchy of one thing over another. They are not really about two things, but only one.

Consider Man. We understand Man as a given, universal, and inclusive. That's why we say "all of Mankind" or "the study of Man." Woman is defined as what is left over: sex, procreation, and mystery. In this sense Woman is always "Other." Confined to what is not-man—sex, procreation, and mystery—Woman is always genderqueer. In terms of color, this would be equivalent to Asian being racially queered. Asians are seen through the lens of Orientalism. What is Western and white is universal, while the Orient as Other is confined to the mysterious, exotic, and primitive.

The second term of a binary exists only to support the first term. Thus Woman functions not as an equal half but as a support and prop, derivative from and dependent on Man. So both terms of the binary are really in the first. This gives the first term of any binary a lot of power. It defines the terms in which we talk. By doing so, it is itself insulated from discussion. We debate what Woman is, what women want, etc., etc. ad nauseam. But Man is immune from such debate. We endlessly debate the "meaning" of blackness, but whiteness—until very recently—is a given.

Only by overturning binaries and binary thinking will we really be able to open up more room for the second terms to come into their own, for things now obscured at the margins to emerge. But toppling binaries is not easy. They are very compelling forms of thinking. For instance, I can promote genderqueerness all I want. But questioning "real" sexes and genders, whether male and female, man and woman really exist, just leaves me looking like a fool.

And as long as I can't question the existence of normative sexes and genders, it will be *my* body and my gender that are on the firing line, that I will be forced to define, defend, and write books about, over and over again.

Genderqueerness maybe a failed project from the outset. Our challenge is not promoting genderqueerness—as if it weren't already another way of promoting normative genders—but rather challenging the whole narrow, outdated notion of applying binary norms to bodies and genders.

SEEING THROUGH TRANSPARENCY

In the beginning was the Word, and the Word was with God, and the Word was God . . . and the Word was made flesh. . . .

—The Gospel According to John

In the beginning was Sex, and Binary Sex was with God, and Binary Sex was from God . . . and Binary Sex was made flesh, and it became The One, True Thing about everyone's body.

—The Gospel According to Us

As a panel member at a gay journalists' conference, I wanted to talk about issues, politics, gender-based hate crimes and job discrimination. But first audience members wanted to know what I "was." As reporters, they needed a label to identify me to their readers, not to mention their editors. The predictable questions flew. Did I consider myself transgendered? Was I presenting myself as male or female? Did I use male or female pronouns? Was I pre-op or post-op? Did I want to sleep with men or women (short menu in this restaurant)?

As I insisted on ignoring my personal life to focus on issues, their questioning grew more insistent. The more I deflected them, the more demanding they became. Finally several audience members became openly hostile, standing to verbally attack me with epithets and slurs, and finally physically assaulting me onstage with fists, chairs, and broken bottles.

No, wait a minute. I'm sorry. That was an *S/M* panel I was on. But at the gay journalism conference, my audience *did* repeatedly question what I was and express their frustration with my refusal to answer.

The question is whether language is transparent. Does it faithfully reveal the world, as though beneath a clear sheet of glass, or does it first create the world we say it reveals?

What kind of information did these journalists want?

Was I gay or straight?

Is it true I was transgendered?

Had I had surgery?

I wonder what in the world these things had to do with creating gender equality for all Americans. Is there anything I could say about my body or identity to those journalists that wouldn't obscure everything I really wanted to tell them? Are there any names for myself I could have given them with which I did not completely disagree, which wouldn't have made me complicit in my own silencing?

Our belief in language is based on our naive faith that the world is right here: finite, knowable, immediately and totally available to us. Thus what isn't named doesn't exist. What is named must therefore exist.

I'LL SEE IT WHEN I BELIEVE IT WHEN YOU'VE NAMED IT

But is the world really "right here?" Do words really describe the world accurately, exhausting what's "there"? Or are they limited only to what is repeatable and shared, and thus communicable? What about all those messy spaces between words and around their borders? Many of them are populated by our life's more profound experiences. Can language capture why you prefer wearing a nice dress to a new suit, why you want to penetrate instead of being penetrated, why you enjoy having a chest but don't want breasts, how you feel when you're stoned (not that the author has any experience here), or why you like Big Macs but hate sashimi (Japanese for "tastes like shit")?

Indeed, what about all those messy spaces between words like *feminine* and *masculine* and around the borders of words like *male* and *female* that are populated by bodies that don't fit the language? Or any of us

whose gender experience confounds words when we transcend the narrow, outdated language of norms?

Words work well for things we can repeat, that we hold in common. What is unique or private is lost to language. But gender is a system of meanings that shapes our experience of bodies. Genderqueerness is by definition unique, private, and profoundly different. That's what makes it "queer." When we force all people to answer to a single language that excludes their experience of themselves in the world, we not only increase their pain and marginalization, we make them accomplices in their own erasure.

It is bad enough to render them silent, even worse to make them speak a lie, worse yet if speaking the lie erases them.

A recurrent theme of this anthology is writers struggling with language used about them and against them, even as it struggles back, twists in their hands, erases their sounds. All of us have those small, private experiences that we can never truly put into words. Our belief in language tells us that they aren't as real, as important, as the things we can say and share.

But I think it's just the opposite. For nowhere are we more ourselves than in those small, private moments when we transcend the common reality, when we experience ourselves in ways that cannot be said or understood or repeated. It is to those moments that we are called, and it is to those moments that we must listen.

HOW TO BE HIP

Nor are the effects of such forms of knowledge confined to the political sphere. For instance, when I first decided to change my body, I was told I was transsexual. I just wanted to change my body, but I was told the reason for this was that I was a "woman trapped in a man's body." I had a gender identity disorder. But I learned to think of myself as having a "birth defect," characterized by my new mental disorder.

When I entered the lesbian-feminist community of Cleveland Heights, Ohio, I was told I was still "really a man" or a "surgically altered she-male": in short, some kind of gender freak. I was kicked out of my apartment, shunned in bars, and barred from local events. Painful as this was, even worse was my buying into what was being said about me. I learned to think of myself as some sort of man-woman, neither male nor female: not even appropriate for my (lesbian) lover.

With the advent of transgenderism, I finally had a way of thinking of myself that gave me a sense of pride. I began to understand myself as transgendered. And, of course, at some point, that didn't work either, because like everything that preceded it, it didn't really fit.

It's not that I'm especially impressionable. To understand our bodies at all, we must make a stand somewhere. There is no neutral place, no position outside of language. We seek ways of understanding our bodies that solve what we perceive to be their problems.

In my case, the problem that was created about my body was its genderqueerness. And I sought ways of understanding it that would resolve that problem: some painful, some empowering. The problem could have been many other things. For instance, there's the gentlewoman who sat next to me on the bus, saying, "Please excuse my fat hips." When I asked her about this, she said, "I know, my feminist friends said I should think of them as nurturing and maternal." We had a long talk about her hips and my body and how miserable they'd made each of us.

Was she especially susceptible? I doubt it. But someone had explained to her that her hips were "width-queer," that they transcended some norm somewhere. She had internalized this as a problem of her body and sought ways of understanding it, just as I had, that would explain its "meaning."

Indeed, two things stand out most about our stories. First is how feminism's counterdiscourse on women's bodies has in its own way become as narrow and inflexible as the one from which it was supposed to free us. Second is how much the understanding of our bodies has colored how we feel about them. I doubt my wanting to change my body or that woman's hips had much implicit meaning. But the attachment of meaning is a powerful tool for making us experience ourselves in the world in very specific ways.

YOU CUT ME UP

Which brings me to my second concern: How are such effects achieved? As good progressives, when we think of Power, we imagine something above us,

overwhelming, and harsh that we need laws to rein in. This works well with big, institutional power, like the police powers of arrest, the power of courts, and the government's power to spy on us or restrict our speech. But that kind of power doesn't go very far in explaining that woman's hips or my body. After all, there was no central registry tracking us, no government agency compelling our experiences.

For that kind of power, we need another model: discourse. I seldom use the word, because when I do, Clare thrusts two fingers down her throat and makes rude gagging sounds. Academics may overuse it, but I think it's useful here. Discourse simply refers to power "from the bottom up." This is the kind of small power exercised in hundreds of little everyday transactions.

Think of the body's surface as a sheet of cookie dough. Because the dough has no inherent meaning, you can cut it all into circles, stars, or squares, or a mixture of different shapes all at once. When you're done, no doubt the cookies are "real." But there is no "truth" behind them, nothing to be learned from why one is a star and not a triangle, and no shape was any more *there* beforehand than any other. What truths there are lie with the cutter, not its product. Discourse is the cookie cutter.

But wait. All this is too abstract. Why don't you take a break for a minute, go down to the corner newsstand, and buy a *Times*?

NEWS TO ME

Fine. Does the man ahead of you hold the door for you as you leave your building? Do people step aside when you walk down the crowded street, or do they unconsciously expect you to step aside?

When you get to the newsstand, does the newspaper vendor address you as "Sir," "Ma'am," or "Miss"? Perhaps he finds you sexually confusing and stumbles awkwardly over pronouns. When he hands you your change, does he look down in respect, meet your eyes, or perhaps refuse to acknowledge you at all? Does he smile in friendliness or frown in disgust? If he's the guy you always see, before you leave, does he swap a dirty joke or ask about "the wife and kids"? Or maybe he flirts just a little, asking if you've lost weight and telling you that you need a young man in your life.

Even in this tiny exchange, a small fraction of your day, are piled up one interaction after another that stamp us with our sex, gender, or class. This is not power from the "top down," but from the "bottom up." It is not the big, familiar power of concrete buildings and visible institutions, power that is both massed and massive. Rather, it's the power of what is said and thought about us: the small, diffuse, invisible power created and instantly destroyed in thousands of little, insignificant exchanges.

It is through just such interactions that fat hips and queer bodies are made, interactions that tell us what we are, what we mean, and to what names we must answer.

(2002)

88 • *Judith Halberstam*

"QUEER TEMPORALITY AND POSTMODERN GEOGRAPHIES"

How can a relational system be reached through sexual practices? Is it possible to create a homosexual mode of life? . . . To be "gay," I think, is not to identify with the psychological traits and the visible masks of the homosexual, but to try to define and develop a way of life.

—Michel Foucault, "Friendship as a Way of Life"

There is never one geography of authority and there is never one geography of resistance. Further, the map of resistance is not simply the underside of the map of domination—if only because each is a lie to the other, and each gives the lie to the other.

—Steve Pile, "Opposition, Political Identities, and Spaces of Resistance"

This book makes the perhaps overly ambitious claim that there is such a thing as "queer time" and "queer space." Queer uses of time and space develop, at least in part, in opposition to the institutions of family, heterosexuality, and reproduction. They also develop according to other logics of location, movement, and identification. If we try to think about queerness as an outcome of strange temporalities, imaginative life schedules, and eccentric economic practices, we detach queerness from sexual identity and come closer to understanding Foucault's comment in "Friendship as a Way of Life" that "homosexuality threatens people as a 'way of life' rather than as a way of having sex" (310). In Foucault's radical formulation, queer friendships, queer networks, and the existence of these relations in space and in relation to the use of time mark out the particularity and indeed the perceived menace of homosexual life. In this book, the queer "way of life" will encompass subcultural practices, alternative methods of alliance, forms of transgender embodiment, and those forms of representation dedicated to capturing these willfully eccentric modes of being.

Obviously not all gay, lesbian, and transgender people live their lives in radically different ways from their heterosexual counterparts, but part of what has made queerness compelling as a form of self-description in the past decade or so has to do with the way it has the potential to open up new life narratives and alternative relations to time and space.

Queer time perhaps emerges most spectacularly, at the end of the twentieth century, from within those gay communities whose horizons of possibility have been severely diminished by the AIDS epidemic. In his memoir of his lover's death from AIDS, poet Mark Doty writes: "All my life I've lived with a future which constantly diminishes but never vanishes" (Dory 1996, 4). The constantly diminishing future creates a new emphasis on the here, the present, the now, and while the threat of no future hovers overhead like a storm cloud, the urgency of being also expands the potential of the moment and, as Dory explores, squeezes new possibilities out of the time at hand. In his poem "In Time of Plague," Thom Gunn explores the erotics of compressed time and impending mortality: "My thoughts are crowded with death / and it draws so oddly on the sexual / that I am confused/confused to be attracted / by, in effect, my own annihilation" (Gunn 1993, 59). Queer time, as it flashes into view in the heart of a crisis, exploits the potential of what Charles-Pierre Baudelaire called in relation to modernism "The transient, the fleeting, the contingent." Some gay men have responded to the threat of AIDS, for example, by rethinking the conventional emphasis on longevity and futurity, and by making community in relation to risk, disease, infection, and death (Bersani 1996; Edelman 1998). And yet queer time, even as it emerges from the AIDS crisis, is not only about compression and annihilation; it is also about the potentiality of a life unscripted by the conventions of family, inheritance, and child rearing. In the sections on subcultures in this book, I will examine the queer temporalities that are proper to subcultural activities, and will propose that we rethink the adult/youth binary in relation to an "epistemology of youth" that disrupts conventional accounts of youth culture, adulthood, and maturity.[1] Queer subcultures produce alternative temporalities by allowing their participants to believe that their futures can be imagined according to logics that lie outside of those paradigmatic markers of life experience—namely, birth, marriage, reproduction, and death. . . .

Queer time and space are useful frameworks for assessing political and cultural change in the late twentieth and early twenty-first centuries (both what has changed and what must change). The critical languages that we have developed to try to assess the obstacles to social change have a way of both stymieing our political agendas and alienating nonacademic constituencies. I try here to make queer time and queer space into useful terms for academic and nonacademic considerations of life, location, and transformation. To give an example of the way in which critical languages can sometimes weigh us down, consider the fact that we have become adept within postmodernism at talking about "normativity," but far less adept at describing in rich detail the practices and structures that both oppose and sustain conventional forms of association, belonging, and identification. I try to use the concept of queer time to make clear how respectability, and notions of the normal on which it depends, may be upheld by a middle-class logic of reproductive temporality. And so, in Western cultures, we chart the emergence of the adult from the dangerous and unruly period of adolescence as a desired process of maturation; and we create longevity as the most desirable future, applaud the pursuit of long life (under any circumstances), and pathologize modes of living that show little or no concern for longevity. Within the life cycle of the Western human subject, long periods of stability are considered to be desirable, and people who live in rapid bursts (drug addicts, for example) are characterized as immature and even dangerous. But the ludic temporality created by drugs (captured by Salvador Dali as a melting clock and by William Burroughs as "junk time") reveals the artificiality of our privileged constructions of time and activity. In the works of queer postmodern writers like Lynn Breedlove (*Godspeed*), Eileen Myles (*Chelsea Girls*), and others, speed itself (the drug as well as the motion) becomes the motor of an alternative history as their queer heroes rewrite completely narratives of female rebellion (Myles 1994; Breedlove 2002).

The time of reproduction is ruled by a biological clock for women and by strict bourgeois rules of respectability and scheduling for married couples. Obviously, not all people who have children keep or even are able to keep reproductive time, but many and possibly most people believe that the scheduling of repro-time is natural and desirable. Family time refers to the normative scheduling of daily life (early to bed, early to rise) that accompanies the practice of child rearing. This timetable is governed by an imagined set of children's needs, and it relates to beliefs about children's health and healthful environments for child rearing. The time of inheritance refers to an overview of generational time within which values, wealth, goods, and morals are passed through family ties from one generation to the next. It also connects the family to the historical past of the nation, and glances ahead to connect the family to the future of both familial and national stability. In this category we can include the kinds of hypothetical temporality—the time of "what if"—that demands protection in the way of insurance policies, health care, and wills.

In queer renderings of postmodern geography, the notion of a body-centered identity gives way to a model that locates sexual subjectivities within and between embodiment, place, and practice. But queer work on sexuality and space, like queer work on sexuality and time, has had to respond to canonical work on "postmodern geography" by Edward Soja, Fredric Jameson, David Harvey, and others that has actively excluded sexuality as a category for analysis precisely because desire has been cast by neo-Marxists as part of a ludic body politics that obstructs the "real" work of activism (Soja 1989; Harvey 1990; Jameson 1997). This foundational exclusion, which assigned sexuality to body/local/personal and took class/global/political as its proper frame of reference, has made it difficult to introduce questions of sexuality and space into the more general conversations about globalization and transnational capitalism. Both Anna Tsing and Steve Pile refer this problem as the issue of "scale." Pile, for example, rejects the notion that certain political arenas of struggle (say, class) are more important than others (say, sexuality), and instead he offers that we rethink these seemingly competing struggles in terms of scale by recognizing that while we tend to view local struggles as less significant than global ones, ultimately "the local and the global are not natural scales, but formed precisely out of the struggles that seemingly they only contain" (Pile 1997, 13).

A "queer" adjustment in the way in which we think about time, in fact, requires and produces new conceptions of space. And in fact, much of the contemporary theory seeking to disconnect queerness from an essential definition of homosexual embodiment has focused on queer space and queer practices. By articulating and elaborating a concept of queer time, I suggest new ways of understanding the nonnormative behaviors that have clear but not essential relations to gay and lesbian subjects. For the purpose of this book, "queer" refers to nonnormative logics and organizations of community, sexual identity, embodiment, and activity in space and time. "Queer time" is a term for those specific models of temporality that emerge within postmodernism once one leaves the temporal frames of bourgeois reproduction and family, longevity, risk/safety, and inheritance. "Queer space" refers to the place-making practices within postmodernism in which queer people engage and it also describes the new understandings of space enabled by the production of queer counterpublics. Meanwhile, "postmodernism" in this project takes on meaning in relation to new forms of cultural production that emerge both in sync with and running counter to what Jameson has called the "logic" of late capitalism in his book *Postmodernism* (1997). I see postmodernism as simultaneously a crisis and an opportunity—a crisis in the stability of form and meaning, and an opportunity to rethink the practice of cultural production, its hierarchies and power dynamics, its tendency to resist or capitulate. In his work on postmodern geography, Pile also locates postmodernism in terms of the changing relationship between opposition and authority; he reminds us, crucially, that "the map of resistance is not simply the underside of the map of domination" (6).

In *The Condition of Postmodernity*, Harvey demonstrates that our conceptions of space and time are social constructions forged out of vibrant and volatile social relations (Harvey 1990). Harvey's analysis of postmodern time and space is worth examining in detail both because he energetically deconstructs the naturalization of modes of temporality and because he does so with no awareness of having instituted and presumed a normative framework for his alternative understanding of time. Furthermore, Harvey's concept of "time/space compression" and his accounts of the role of culture in late capitalism have become hegemonic in academic contexts. Harvey asserts that because we experience time as some form of natural progression, we fail to realize or notice its construction. Accordingly, we have concepts like "industrial" time and "family" time, time of "progress," "austerity" versus "instant" gratification, "postponement" versus "immediacy." And to all of these different kinds of temporality, we assign value and meaning. Time, Harvey explains, is organized according to the logic of capital accumulation, but those who benefit from capitalism in particular experience this logic as inevitable, and they are therefore able to ignore, repress, or erase the demands made on them and others by an unjust system. We like to imagine, Harvey implies, both that our time is our own and, as the cliché goes, "there is a time and a place for everything." These formulaic responses to time and temporal logics produce emotional and even physical responses to different kinds of time; thus people feel guilty about leisure, frustrated by waiting, satisfied by punctuality, and so on. These emotional responses add to our sense of time as "natural." . . .

The different forms of time management that Harvey mentions and highlights are all adjusted to the schedule of normativity without ever being discussed as such. In fact, we could say that normativity, as it has been defined and theorized within queer studies, is the big word missing from almost all the discussions of postmodern geography within a Marxist tradition. Since most of these discussions are dependent on the work of Foucault and since normativity was Foucault's primary understanding of the function of modern power, this is a huge oversight, and one with consequences for the discussion of sexuality in relation to time and space. Harvey's concept of time/space compressions, for instance, explains that all of the time cycles that we have naturalized and Internalized (leisure, inertia, recreation, work/industrial, family/domesticity) are also spatial practices, but again, Harvey misses the opportunity to deconstruct the meaning of naturalization with regard to specific normalized ways of being. The meaning of space, Harvey asserts, undergoes a double process of naturalization: first, it is naturalized in relation to use values (we presume that our use of space is the only and inevitable use of space—private property, for example); but second, we naturalize space by subordinating it to time. The construction of spatial practices, in other words, is obscured by the

naturalization of both time and space, Harvey argues for multiple conceptions of time and space, but he does not adequately describe how time/space becomes naturalized, on the one hand, and how hegemonic constructions of time and space are uniquely gendered and sexualized, on the other. His is an avowedly materialist analysis of time/space dedicated understandably to uncovering the processes of capitalism, but it lacks a simultaneous desire to uncover the processes of heteronormativity, racism, and sexism. . . .

In relation to gender, race, and alternative or subcultural production, therefore, Harvey's grand theory of "the experience of space and time" in postmodernity leaves the power structures of biased differentiation intact, and presumes that, in Pile's formulation, opposition can only be an "echo of domination" (Pile 1997, 13). But while Harvey, like Soja and Jameson, can be counted on at least to nod to the racialization and gendering of postmodern space, also like Soja and Jameson, he has nothing to say about sexuality and space. Both Soja and Harvey claim that it was Foucault's interviews on space and published lecture notes on "heterotopia" that, as Soja puts it, created the conditions for a postmodern geography. The Foucault who inspires the postmodern Marxist geographers is clearly the Foucault of *Discipline and Punish*, but not that of *The History of Sexuality*. Indeed, Harvey misses several obvious opportunities to discuss the naturalization of time and space in relation to sexuality. Reproductive time and family time are, above all, heteronormative time/space constructs. But while Harvey hints at the gender politics of these forms of time/space, he does not mention the possibility that all kinds of people, especially in postmodernity, will and do opt to live outside of reproductive and familial time as well as on the edges of logics of labor and production. By doing so, they also often live outside the logic of capital accumulation: here we could consider ravers, club kids, HIV-positive barebackers, rent boys, sex workers, homeless people, drug dealers, and the unemployed. Perhaps such people could productively be called "queer subjects" in terms of the ways they live (deliberately, accidentally, or of necessity) during the hours when others sleep and in the spaces (physical, metaphysical, and economic) that others have abandoned, and in terms of the ways they might work in the domains that other people assign to privacy and family. Finally, as

I will trace in this book, for some queer subjects, time and space are limned by risks they are willing to take: the transgender person who risks his life by passing in a small town, the subcultural musicians who risk their livelihoods by immersing themselves in nonlucrative practices, the queer performers who destabilize the normative values that make everyone else feel safe and secure; but also those people who live without financial safety nets, without homes, without steady jobs, outside the organizations of time and space that have been established for the purposes of protecting the rich few from everyone else. . . .

(2005)

89 • *Julia Serano*

"TRANS WOMAN MANIFESTO"

This manifesto calls for the end of the scapegoating, deriding, and dehumanizing of trans women everywhere. For the purposes of this manifesto, *trans woman is defined as* any person who was assigned a male sex at birth, but who identifies as and/or lives as a woman. No qualifications should be placed on the term "trans woman" based on a person's ability to "pass" as female, her hormone levels, or the state of her genitals—after all, it is downright sexist to reduce any woman (trans or otherwise) down to her mere body parts or to require her to live up to a certain societally-dictated ideal regarding appearance.

Perhaps no sexual minority is more maligned or misunderstood than trans women. As a group, we have been systematically pathologized by the medical and psychological establishment, sensationalized and ridiculed by the media, marginalized by mainstream lesbian and gay organizations, dismissed by certain segments of the feminist community, and, in too many instances, been made the victims of violence at the hands of men who feel that we somehow threaten their masculinity and heterosexuality. Rather than being given the opportunity to speak for ourselves on the very issues that affect our own lives, trans women are instead treated more like research subjects: Others place us under their microscopes, dissect our lives, and assign motivations and desires to us that validate their own theories and agendas regarding gender and sexuality.

Trans women are so ridiculed and despised because we are uniquely positioned at the intersection of multiple binary gender-based forms of prejudice: transphobia, cissexism, and misogyny.

Transphobia is an irrational fear of, aversion to, or discrimination against people whose gendered identities, appearances, or behaviors deviate from societal norms. In much the same way that homophobic people are often driven by their own repressed homosexual tendencies, we believe that transphobia is first and foremost an expression of one's own insecurity about having to live up to cultural gender ideals. The fact that transphobia is so rampant in our society reflects the reality that we place an extraordinary amount of pressure on individuals to conform to all of the expectations, restrictions, assumptions, and privileges associated with the sex they were assigned at birth.

While all transgender people experience transphobia, transsexuals additionally experience a related (albeit distinct) form of prejudice: cissexism, which is the belief that transsexuals' identified genders are inferior to, or less authentic than, those of cissexuals (i.e., people who are not transsexual and who have only ever experienced their subconscious and physical sexes as being aligned). The most common expression of cissexism occurs when people attempt to deny trans people the basic privileges that are associated with the gender the trans person self-identifies as. Common examples include purposeful misuse of pronouns, insisting that the trans person use a different public restroom, etc. The justification for these denials is generally founded on the assumption that the trans person's gender is not authentic because it does not correlate with their birth sex. In making this assumption, the transphobe attempts to create an artificial hierarchy—by insisting that the trans person's gender is "fake," they attempt to validate their own gender as "real" or "natural." This sort of thinking is extraordinarily naive, as it denies the basic truth that everyday we make assumptions about other people's genders without ever seeing their birth certificates, their chromosomes, their genitals, their reproductive systems, their childhood socialization, or their legal sex. There is no such thing as a "real" gender—there is only the gender we identify as and the gender we perceive others to be.

While often different in practice, cissexism, transphobia, and homophobia are all rooted in *oppositional sexism*, which is the belief that female and male are rigid, mutually exclusive categories, each possessing a unique and non-overlapping set of attributes, aptitudes, abilities, and desires. Oppositional sexists attempt to punish or dismiss those of us who fall outside of gender or sexual norms because our existence threatens the idea that women and men are opposite sexes. This explains why bisexuals, lesbians, gays, transsexuals, and other transgender people—who may experience their genders and sexualities in very different ways—are so often confused or lumped into the same category (i.e., queer) by society at large. Our natural inclinations to be the other sex, or to be attracted to the same sex, challenge the assumption that women and men are mutually exclusive categories, each possessing a unique set of attributes, aptitudes, abilities, and desires. By breaking these gender and sexual norms, we essentially blur the boundaries that are required to maintain the male-centered gender hierarchy that exists in our culture today.

In addition to the rigid, mutually exclusive gender categories established by oppositional sexism, the other requirement for maintaining a male-centered gender hierarchy is to enforce *traditional sexism*—the

belief that maleness and masculinity are superior to femaleness and femininity. Traditional and oppositional sexism work hand in hand to ensure that those who are masculine have power over those who are feminine, and that only those born male will be seen as authentically masculine. For the purposes of this manifesto, the word misogyny will be used to describe this tendency to dismiss and deride femaleness and femininity in our culture.

Just as all trans people experience transphobia and cissexism to different extents (depending on how often, obvious, or out we are as transgender), we experience misogyny to different extents too. This is most evident from the fact that, while there are many different types of transgender people, our society tends to single-out trans women and others on the male-to-female [MTF] spectrum for attention and ridicule. This is not merely because we transgress gender norms per se, but because we, by necessity, embrace our own femaleness and femininity. Indeed, more often than not, it is our expressions of femininity and our desire to be female that become sensationalized, sexualized, and trivialized by others. While trans people on the female-to-male (FTM) spectrum face discrimination for breaking gender norms (aka, transphobia), their expressions of maleness or masculinity themselves are not targeted for ridicule—to do so would require one to question masculinity itself.

When a trans person is ridiculed or dismissed not merely for transgressing gender norms, but for their expressions of femaleness or femininity, they become the victims of a specific form of discrimination: *transmisogyny*. When the majority of jokes made at the expense of trans people center on "men wearing dresses" or "men who want their penises cut off," that is not transphobia—it is trans misogyny. When the majority of violence and sexual assault committed against trans people is directed at trans women, that is not transphobia—it is trans misogyny[1]. When it's OK for women to wear "men's" clothing, but men who wear "women's" clothing can be diagnosed with the "psychological disorder" Transvestic Fetishism, that is not transphobia—it is trans misogyny[2]. When women's or lesbian organizations and events open their doors to trans men but not trans women, that is not transphobia—it is trans misogyny.

In a male-centered gender hierarchy, where it is assumed that men are better than women and that masculinity is superior to femininity, there is no greater perceived threat than the existence of trans women, who despite being born male and inheriting male privilege, "choose" to be female instead. By embracing our own femaleness and femininity, we in a sense cast a shadow of doubt over the supposed supremacy of maleness and masculinity. In order to lessen the threat we pose to the male-centered gender hierarchy, our culture (primarily via the media) uses every tactic in its arsenal of traditional sexism to dismiss us.

1. The media hyper-feminizes us: by accompanying stories about trans women with pictures of us putting on make-up, dresses, and heels, in an attempt to highlight the "frivolous" nature of our femaleness, or by portraying trans woman as having derogatory feminine-associated character traits such as being weak, confused, passive, or mousy.

2. The media hyper-sexualizes us: by creating the impression that most trans women are sex workers or sexual deceivers, and by asserting that we transition for primarily sexual reasons (e.g., to prey on innocent straight men or to fulfill some kind of bizarre sex fantasy). Such depictions not only belittle trans women's motives for transitioning, but implicitly suggest that women as a whole have no worth beyond their ability to be sexualized.

3. The media objectifies our bodies: by sensationalizing sex reassignment surgery and openly discussing our "man-made" vaginas without any of the discretion that normally accompanies discussions about genitals. Further, those of us who have not had surgery are constantly being reduced to our body parts, whether it be by the creators of tranny porn who overemphasize and exaggerate our penises, thus distorting trans women into "she-males" and "chicks with dicks," or by other people who have been so brainwashed by phallocentrism that they believe that the mere presence of a penis can trump the femaleness of our identities, our personalities, and the rest of our bodies.

Because anti-trans discrimination is steeped in traditional sexism, it is not simply enough for trans activists to challenge binary gender norms (i.e., oppositional sexism)—we must also challenge the idea that femininity is inferior to masculinity and that femaleness is inferior to maleness. In other words, by necessity, trans activism must be at its core a feminist movement.

Some might consider this contention to be controversial. Over the years, many self-described feminists have gone out of their way to dismiss trans people, and in particular trans women, often resorting to many of the same tactics (hyper-feminization, hyper-sexualization, and objectification of our bodies) that the mainstream media regularly uses against us. These pseudo-feminists proclaim that "Women can do anything that men can" then ridicule trans women for any perceived masculine tendency we may have. They argue that women should be strong and unafraid to speak our minds then tell trans women that we act like men when we voice our opinions. They claim that it is misogynistic when men create standards and expectations for women to meet then they dismiss us for not meeting their standard of "woman." These pseudo-feminists consistently preach feminism with one hand, while practicing traditional sexism with the other.

It is time for us to take back the word "feminism" from these pseudo-feminists. After all, feminism is much like the ideas of "democracy" or "Christianity." Each has a major tenet at its core, but there are an infinite number of ways in which one can practice that belief. And just as some forms of democracy and Christianity are corrupt and hypocritical while others are more just and righteous, we trans women must join trans-positive women and allies of all genders to forge a new type of feminism, one that understands that the only way for us to achieve true gender equity is to abolish both oppositional sexism and traditional sexism.

It is no longer enough for feminism to fight solely for the rights of those born female. That strategy has furthered the prospects of many women over the years, but now it bumps up against a glass ceiling that is partly of its own making. Though the movement worked hard to encourage women to enter into previously male-dominated areas of life, many feminists have been ambivalent at best, and resistant at worst, to the idea of men expressing or exhibiting feminine traits and moving into certain traditionally female realms. And while we credit previous feminist movements for helping to create a society where most sensible people would agree with the statement "women are men's equals," we lament the fact that we remain light years away from being able to say that most people believe that femininity is masculinity's equal.

Instead of attempting to empower those born female by encouraging them to move further away from femininity, we should instead learn to empower femininity itself. We must stop dismissing it as "artificial" or as a "performance," and instead recognize that certain aspects of femininity (as well masculinity) transcend both socialization and biological sex—otherwise there would not be feminine boy and masculine girl children. We must challenge all those who assume that feminine vulnerability is a sign of weakness. For when we do open ourselves up, whether it be honestly communicating our thoughts and feelings or expressing our emotions, it is a daring act, one that takes more courage and inner strength than the alpha-male facade of silence and stoicism.

We must challenge all those who insist that women who act or dress in a feminine manner necessarily take on a submissive or passive posture. For many of us, dressing or acting feminine is something we do for ourselves, not for others. It is our way of reclaiming our own bodies and fearlessly expressing our own personalities and sexualities. It is not us, but rather those who foolishly assume that our feminine style is a signal that we sexually subjugate ourselves to men, who are the ones guilty of trying to reduce our bodies to the mere status of playthings.

In a world where masculinity is assumed to represent strength and power, those who are butch and boyish are able to contemplate their identities within the relative safety of those connotations. In contrast, those of us who are feminine are forced to define ourselves on our own terms and develop our own sense of self-worth. It takes guts, determination, and fearlessness for those of us who are feminine to lift ourselves up out of the inferior meanings that are constantly being projected onto us. If you require any evidence that femininity can be more fierce and dangerous than masculinity, then all you need to do is simply ask the average man to hold your handbag or a bouquet of flowers for a minute, and watch how far away he holds it from his body. Or tell him you would like to put your lipstick on him and watch how fast he runs off in the other direction. In a world where masculinity is respected and femininity is regularly dismissed, it takes loads of strength and confidence for any person to embrace their femme self.

But it is not enough for us to empower femaleness and femininity. We must also stop pretending that there are essential differences between women and men. This begins with the acknowledgement that there are exceptions to every gender rule and stereotype, and this simply stated fact disproves all gender theories that purport that female and male are mutually exclusive categories. We must move away from pretending that women and men are "opposite" sexes, because when we buy into that myth it establishes a dangerous precedent. For if men are big, then women must be small; and if men are strong then women must be weak. And if being butch is to make yourself rock solid, then being femme becomes allowing yourself to be malleable; and if being a man means taking control of your own situation, then being a woman becomes living up to other people's expectations. When we buy into the idea that female and male are "opposites," it becomes impossible for us to empower women without either ridiculing men or else pulling the rug out from under ourselves.

It is only when we move away from the idea that there are "opposite" sexes, and let go of the culturally-derived values that are assigned to expressions of femininity and masculinity, that we may finally approach gender equity. By challenging both oppositional and traditional sexism simultaneously, we can make the world safe for those of us who are queer, those of us who are feminine, and for those of us who are female, while simultaneously empowering people of all sexualities and genders.

(2009)

NOTES

1. Viviane K. Namaste, *Invisible Lives: The Erasure of Transsexual and Transgendered People* (Chicago: University of Chicago Press, 2000), 145, 215–216; Viviane Namaste, *Sex Change, Social Change: Reflections on Identity, Institutions, and Imperialism* (Toronto: Women's Press, 2005), 92–93.

2. American Psychiatric Association, *Diagnostic and Statistical Manual of Mental Disorders, Fourth Edition, Text Revision (DSM-IV-TR)* (Washington D.C.: American Psychiatric Association, 2000), 574–575.

CHAPTER 7

Third-Wave Feminisms

Gently swelling, rising and then crashing, waves evoke images of both beauty and power. As feminists, we could do much worse than be associated with this phenomenon.

—Cathryn Bailey, 1997

INTRODUCTION[1]

In the 1990s, the women's movement in the United States witnessed a resurgence of feminist activism and scholarship among a new generation of young feminists that was so large and unexpected that some referred to it as a "genderquake" (Wolf, [1993] 1994: 25). In 1992, these feminist activists founded Third Wave Direct Action—an organization designed to mobilize young people politically and to foster young women's leadership skills. By 1996, they had established the Third Wave Foundation—a national organization committed to supporting women from ages 15 to 30 in activities devoted toward gender, racial, social, and economic justice.

The surge of third-wave activism, in part, was a response to media claims that feminism was dead or no longer relevant—claims that had begun as early as 1982 when journalists labeled women in their teens and twenties as the "postfeminist" generation (Bolotin, 1982).[2] When Rebecca Walker asserted on the pages of *Ms.* magazine: "I am not a postfeminist feminist. I *am* the third wave" (1992: 41, her emphasis), it was an act of defiance to these obituaries for feminism (Henry, 2004).[3] Although the THIRD WAVE became the banner under which these young women identified their new brand of feminism, clearly delineating who constitutes this new wave is not without difficulty. They have been referred to in myriad ways that focus more on age than on their contributions to feminist theory and activism. For example, some writers use specific dates of birth, such as birth dates between 1963 and 1974, whereas others use more collective imagery, such as "Generation X," the "twenty-somethings," or the "Jane Generation" (Heywood and Drake, 1997; Kamen, 1991; Johnson, 2002). "Mother–daughter tropes" also have been used to describe these younger feminists' relationship to their second-wave predecessors, often resulting in themes of generational conflict or rebellion (Quinn, 1997; Henry, 2004).

The focus of this chapter is on U.S. third-wave feminism as a *theoretical perspective*, one that any feminist—young, old, or middle-aged—could embrace. Although clearly not all U.S. third wavers share a uniform perspective, their major publications share a number of important theoretical assumptions that enable us to discuss their unique contributions to feminist thought. In particular, we will examine how U.S. third-wave feminism is based on a synthesis of poststructuralism and intersectionality theory (Siegel, 1997; Mann, 2013). Calling this theoretical approach a synthetic derivation is not meant to suggest that the third-wave agenda lacks originality. Rather, the complex ways that the third wave interweaves features of these earlier feminisms make their third-wave agenda novel.

HISTORICALLY GROUNDING THE THIRD WAVE

The world encountered by third wavers when they reached adulthood in the 1980s and 1990s was immensely different from the world encountered by their second-wave predecessors in the 1960s and 1970s. Politically, they were confronted with a highly mobilized, conservative backlash to feminism by the "New Right" who had a significant voice in national politics through the Reagan/Bush Sr. years. The rise of the New Right was in large part the result of how Reagan's 1980 presidential campaign and the STOP-ERA movement had coalesced evangelical Christians with more secular conservatives. In contrast, the second wave arose amid vibrant, liberal, and left-wing social movements, such as the civil rights movement and the anti-Vietnam War movement.

Economically, third-wave feminists faced the worst job market since World War II and were the first postwar generation expected to fare worse than their parents (Heywood and Drake, 1997). Given the decline of U.S. manufacture in the face of increased globalization and the rise of low-paying service jobs, third-wave feminist Michelle Sidler referred to this bleak economic era as "living in McJobdom" (Sidler, 1997: 25). She discussed how the high price of college tuition left many of her peers with huge debts and how, even after obtaining college degrees, high-paying jobs were few and far between. This period of economic uncertainty and downward mobility for many Americans contrasted sharply with the post–World War II era of economic prosperity when the second wave came to adulthood.

The third wave also grew up in the midst of the "New Information Society" and a global "technoculture" made possible by the rise of the new electronic and digital technologies (Heywood and Drake, 2004: 20). The lives of third wavers have been saturated with a mass culture devoted to consumerism and advertising, where sound bites parade as news. Thus it is not surprising that this new wave identified mass culture as one of their major sites of struggle. On the positive side, these new technologies created new ways for the third wave to spread their ideas and to engage in online organizing, options not available to their second-wave predecessors (Alfonso and Trigilio, 1997; Duncan, 2005).

In terms of gender issues, the third wave's path had been paved, in part, by the earlier accomplishments of the first and second waves. Although third wavers have been accused of spending too much energy criticizing their feminist predecessors rather than feminism's external foes (Henry, 2004: 82), many third wavers have paid tribute to these earlier feminist movements. Reading 93 from Jennifer Baumgardner and Amy Richards' *Third Wave Manifesta* (2000) is a tribute to the second wave's achievements that reminds us what the United States was like for women in 1970 before the successes of the second wave.

TRACING THE THIRD WAVE'S LINEAGE TO INTERSECTIONALITY THEORY

Many third-wave authors, regardless of their own racial or ethnic backgrounds, trace their lineage to the U.S. second-wave women of color who pioneered intersectionality theory. For example, in *Third Wave Agenda* (1997), editors Leslie Heywood and Jennifer Drake state, "It was U.S. Third World Feminism that modeled a language and a politics of hybridity that can account for our lives at the century's turn" (1997, 13). Astrid Henry, author of *Not My Mother's Sister* (2004), describes "the insight into the simultaneous, interlocking nature of multiple oppressions" as "the second wave's most influential and vital lesson" for the third wave (2004, 32). Reading 95 from the introduction to Daisy Hernandez and Bushra Rehman's *Colonize This! Young Women of Color in Today's Feminism* (2002) describes this anthology as "continuing the conversations" first initiated by second-wave intersectionality theorists (2002, xxi).

An intersectional commitment to polyvocality and the retrieval of subjugated knowledges can be found in many major third-wave publications. The editors of third-wave anthologies are careful to include authors of diverse races, ethnicities, genders, and sexualities. Along with *Colonize This!* (2002), anthologies such as *To Be Real* (R. Walker, 1995), *Listen Up* (Findlen, 1995), and *Different Wavelengths* (Reger, 2005) exemplify this approach to voicing difference. Most third-wave authors are critical of essentialism and have a keen awareness of differences between women.

Notably, women of color and biracial women are in key leadership positions of the third wave, making it the first wave of U.S. feminism to be led by women of color (Henry, 2004: 163). Third-wave activism, as well as theory, draws its inspiration from the writings of second-wave women of color. The focus on multiple, interlocking oppressions led activists in the third wave to embrace broader notions of inequality and justice. Vivian Labaton and Dawn Lundy Martin, the editors of *The Fire This Time: Young Activists and the New Feminism* (2004) write:

> Woman as a primary identity category has ceased to be the entry point for much young activist work. Instead, it has become one of the many investigatory means used to affect an indefinite number of issues . . . the real work takes place at the ground level, where young women and men are getting down and dirty on the front lines of the struggle for equality and justice. (2004: xxxi)

The idea here is that, rather than bringing activists into the women's movement, they bring their feminism to other sites of activism (Mack-Canty, 2005; Dicker, 2008).

Reading 97 from "It's all about the Benjamins': Economic Determinants of Third Wave Feminism in the U.S." (2004) by Leslie Heywood and Jennifer Drake offers additional reasons for the dispersed forms of activism that characterize the third wave. Heywood and Drake agree that, because their generation was "raised on a multicultural diet" (2004: 16), third wavers are more likely to branch out into other movements for social justice that reflect their commitment to intersectional differences. However, they also argue that third wavers' preference for creating their own media sites and networks as forms of "localized," "radical dispersal" better resists "co-optation by global technoculture" than does identity politics (Heywood and Drake, 2004: 20). In turn, they consider a focus on women's issues or "patriarchal oppression" as "useful only in some contexts" for their generation (Heywood and Drake, 2004: 18). They discuss how globalization and deindustrialization resulted not only in downward mobility for most Americans, but also in greater income parity for men and women of their generation. Because "it's all about the Benjamins," third wavers "have more in common with men of their own age group than they do with women of previous generations" (Heywood and Drake, 2004: 16). For all of these reasons, third-wave feminism as a political movement becomes "less visible," but "more widely dispersed" (Heywood and Drake, 2004: 20).

Like intersectionality theorists, third-wave authors also call for a broader description of the activity that customarily qualifies as theoretical—pointing to multiple sites of theory production both inside and outside of the academy. In particular, they share with intersectionality theorists a deep appreciation for **socially lived knowledge** that is visible in their frequent use of personal narratives to express their views. Analysts of third-wave texts have argued that: "the majority of third wave feminists have been quick to define themselves as primarily non-academic" (Gillis and Munford, 2004: 168). For example, third-wave authors Veronica Chambers and Joan Morgan highlight distinctions between the socially lived knowledge they drew from their everyday lives and the academic knowledge they acquired in women's studies classes (Chambers, 1995; J. Morgan, 1999). Both are critical of how "academic feminism" is too often viewed as the only form of knowledge authorized to wear the title of feminism with a capital "F" (Henry, 2004: 172). In her hip hop classic, *When Chickenheads Come Home to Roost* (1999), Joan Morgan calls for a feminism that speaks to young Black women, the way that hip hop does. She states, "If feminism is to have any relevance in the lives of the majority of black women . . . it has to rescue itself from the ivory towers of academia" (J. Morgan, 1999: 76). Morgan also analyzes the race, class, and gender contradictions that pervade hip hop music and explains how she deals with her love for this music, despite its misogynist language.

Such political engagement with popular culture is prevalent within the third wave. For example, many third wavers were inspired by **Riot Grrrls**, who made a space for women within punk rock by creating their own music and zines, developing their own record labels, and ensuring mosh pits were safe for women (Klein, 1997). The do-it-yourself approach employed by the Riot Grrrls is embraced by many third wavers who often describe the empowerment they experience by producing their own zines and creating home places online to disseminate their political messages (Bates and McHugh, 2005; Duncan, 2005). Reading 90 is a Bikini Kill zine cover produced circa 1991 that can be found today in *The Riot Grrrl Collection* (Darms, 2013: 122). Bikini Kill was a punk band that consisted of Kathleen Hanna, Billy Karren, Kathi Wilcox, and Tobi Vail and is considered a pioneer of the Riot Grrrl movement. Such zines illustrate the creativity that can be unleashed by such multiple forms of theorizing.

TRACING THE THIRD WAVE'S LINEAGE TO POST-STRUCTURALISM AND QUEER THEORY

Along with mass culture, sexuality is another major site of third-wave activism and their treatment of sexual practices illustrates well the influence of poststructuralism and queer theory. In *"Bad Girls"/"Good Girls"* (1996), editors Nan Bauer Maglin and Donna Perry describe "sexuality in all its guises" as the "lightning rod of their generation's hopes and discontents," likening it to how civil rights and the Vietnam war galvanized the generation of the 1960s (1996, xvi). Like poststructuralists and queer theorists, third wavers focus on transgressive acts that challenge and subvert the status quo and revel in a "feminist badass" image (Siegel, 2007: 124 and 155–157). Queer theoretical assumptions are prevalent in third-wave works that embrace a profusion of gendered subjects, as well as a lusty, "no sex toy unturned" approach to sexual practices (Stoller, 1999: 84). As one author put it: "the term 'queer' has been used to mark a new formulation of politics for this new generation of feminists" (Henry, 2004: 115).

The third wave also follows in the footsteps of poststructuralists and queer theorists by rejecting identity politics. Rebecca Walker writes, "We fear that identity will dictate and regulate our lives, instantaneously pitting us against someone, forcing us to choose inflexible and unchanging sides, female against male, black against white, oppressed against oppressor, good against bad (1995: xxxiii). Similarly, Danzy Senna argues that "breaking free of identity politics" gave her "an awareness of the complexity and ambiguity of the world we have inherited" (Senna, 1995: 20). Third wavers' desire for more fluid notions of identity has fondly been described as "the lived messiness" of the third wave (Heywood and Drake, 1997: 8).

Third-wave authors also have taken to heart Foucault's warning that theories—*even emancipatory theories*—are often blind to their dominating tendencies (Ramazanoglu, 1993). For some third-wave authors, these ideas have provided particularly fertile grounds for critiquing feminism itself. Claims that feminism (especially second-wave feminism) is a disciplinary discourse that restricts individual freedom and sits authoritatively in judgment over women's ideas and practices can be found in a number of third-wave publications (Henry, 2004: 39).

Barbara Findlen, editor of *Listen Up*, describes how her peers think that "if something is appealing, fun or popular, it can't be feminist" (1995: xiv). The refrain that second-wave feminists are their dowdy, austere, and too "serious sisters" is echoed by other third-wave writers (Baumgardner and Richards, 2000: 161). To counter this, the playful use of humor and contradictions is interwoven in many third-wave writings and political practices, as Reading 92 from *Adios, Barbie* (1998) by Susan Jane Gilman illustrates.

A far more serious and damning description of the disciplinary nature of second-wave feminism is voiced by Rebecca Walker in Reading 91 from *To Be Real* (1995: xxix).

> A year before I started this book, my life was like a feminist ghetto. Every decision I made, person I spent time with, word I uttered had to measure up to an image I had in my mind of what was morally and politically right according to my vision of female empowerment. Everything had a gendered explanation, and what didn't fit into my concept of feminist was "bad, patriarchal, and problematic."

In the "Afterword" of *To Be Real*, second-wave intersectionality theorist Angela Davis expresses her dismay at how many contributors to Walker's anthology felt feminism had "incarcerated their individuality—their desires, aims, and sexual practices" (Davis in R. Walker, 1995: 281).[4]

This imagery of incarceration evokes Foucault's notion of the panopticon prison and how the panoptical gaze leads people to police their own behaviors to measure up to normative prescriptions (Foucault, [1975] 1979: 155). Gina Dent's article "Missionary Position" (1995) (also in Rebecca Walker's anthology) warns us against a feminism that "polices its borders" and prescribes proper feminist behaviors— much as missionaries prescribed the proper way to have sex (Dent, 1995: 71). In short, second-wave feminism appears as an austere and disciplinary force to many third wavers.

A thoughtful discussion of the tensions between second- and third-wave feminists can be found in Reading 94 from "Unpacking the Mother/Daughter Baggage: Reassessing Second- and Third-Wave Tensions" (2002), by Cathryn Bailey. Using Foucaultian imagery, she writes,

> Many younger women see themselves as struggling against becoming the kind of feminist subjects they thought that they were supposed to become. As such, they may be offering a kind of resistance that is not immediately directed at actual feminists, but rather to an internalized version of a feminist governor—a "panoptical feminist connoisseur." (Bailey, 2002: 150)

Bailey provides examples of how both second- and third-wave feminists fail to communicate adequately and she offers suggestions for reducing the tensions between these waves.

Bailey also confronts the postmodern epistemological relativism embraced by many third-wave writers. She uses the example of Donna Minkowitz's contribution to Rebecca Walker's anthology *To Be Real* (1995) where Minkowitz describes how she found the violent rape of a child with a baseball bat erotic and how she wanted to be free to reveal such feelings. Rebecca Walker praised all of her contributing authors for "being real" and for their "courageous reckoning" with "anti-revolutionary acts"—meaning acts that would have been criticized by most second wavers (R. Walker, 1995: xxxviii).[5] And, indeed, second-wave feminist Gloria Steinem, who wrote the foreword to R. Walker's anthology, is critical of Minkowitz's narrative. Bailey too is uncomfortable with Minkowitz's relativist notions of being free or authentic to one self. She argues that it is not sufficient for a person to simply think her or his actions are subversive or in the interests of freedom and resistance, there "must be a balance between the subject's own interpretation and that of others" (Bailey, 2002: 149). Here Bailey seriously grapples with the problem of postmodern relativism that plagues many third-wave writings.

The authors of *Catching a Wave* (2003), Rory Dicker and Alison Piepmeier also address the relativism that plagues third-wave writings. In their view, the absence of any boundaries on what feminism means "empties feminism of any core set of values and politics" and results in a "feminist free-for-all" where anyone can be a feminist regardless of their views or behaviors (Dicker and Piepmeier, 2003: 17). For them, this is the "worst interpretation" of intersectionality theorist bell hooks's edict that "feminism is for everybody" (17). Although other critics have pointed to the problems that arise from the third wave's "unhappy marriage" of poststructuralism and intersectionality theory (Mann, 2013: 1), below we discuss one of the third wave's most successful mergers of these diverse theoretical perspectives.

THIRD-WAVE THEORY APPLICATIONS

Reading 96 provides excerpts from Julie Bettie's *Women without Class: Girls, Race and Identity* (2003), which interweaves intersectionality theory and poststructuralism to provide one of the most impressive contemporary works on gender, race, and class.[6] Her book is based on an ethnographic study of the lives of Mexican American and Anglo girls in a senior high school. She uses an intersectional analysis to examine how race, gender, and class are interlocking, mutually constitutive, and inseparable features of these young girls' lives. She also draws heavily from Judith Butler's poststructuralist approach to examine social class as performance. As Bettie points out, this type of class analysis had made only "cameo" appearances in feminist literature before her book was published (Bettie, 2003: 51).

Different class performances were evident in the various student cliques at the high school she studied. Here Bettie highlights the importance of understanding the cultural dimensions of social class—how class differences are reflected in consumer practices and subcultural styles—such as the hairstyles, clothing, and even the color of the lipstick the girls wore. Such differences often were perceived as markers of sexual morals, whereby the working-class Chicanas were viewed by teachers and other students as the most sexually active girls, regardless of whether this was actually the case. Class differences were further evident in the students' study habits, their classroom behavior, and their extracurricular activities. In short, Bettie exposed how class warfare was played out in the everyday life of high school cliques.

When Mexican American girls acted like "preps," they were accused of "acting white" by their Mexican American peers (Bettie, 2003: 83–86). Some theorists have called this a **strategy of dismissal**—a strategy used to control and to ostracize the actions of group members that are found threatening (see Chapter 10). Although Bettie recognizes this, she also highlights how such accusations confuse racial and class categories. For example, Bettie asked why acting white was associated with class-privileged preps rather than with working-class "smokers" (since both cliques were largely white). In response, the Mexican American students dismissed the smokers as irrelevant. For Bettie, the relative invisibility or unimportance of working-class whites to these students was precisely because the preps inflicted the most class injuries in the school (2003: 84). Here she is not referring to physical injuries, but rather to what some theorists have called **the hidden injuries of social class**—the damage done to people's self-esteem when people feel inadequate or lesser because of their lower class positions (Sennett and Cobb, 1972).

Like other third-wave writers, Bettie is comfortable drawing from both modern and postmodern theoretical approaches. Rather than seeing these perspectives as contradictory, Bettie feels free to employ what she sees as the strengths of both. Overall, her work demonstrates the richness that can be garnered from such a theoretical synthesis.

SOLITARY SISTERHOOD?

In Reading 98, "Solitary Sisterhood: Individualism Meets Collectivity in Feminism's Third Wave" (2005), Astrid Henry focuses on the strong strain of individualism that undergirds many third-wave writings. She describes third-wave texts as "replete with individual definitions of feminism" (2005: 82–83)—a point other third wavers have acknowledged. For example, in *Third Wave Agenda* (1997), Heywood and Drake write, "Despite our knowing better, despite our knowing its emptiness, the ideology of individualism is still a major motivating force in many third wave lives" (11). More than a decade later, Shelley Budgeon describes third-wave authors as still "privileging individual experience" and names one her chapters "A Politics of Self" in *Third Wave Feminism and the Politics of Gender in Late Modernity* (2011: 103 and 191).

Henry points out how individualism is reflected in the third wave's penchant for personal narratives. Much like diaries or journals, these personal narratives highlight the contradictions, uncertainties, and dilemmas that they face in their individual everyday lives. Rarely did second-wave feminists write in such a personal manner. Rather they argued that analysis should move from an individual, personal response to a collective, political response. Some second-wave authors have been especially critical of this third-wave writing style. One critic referred to the contributors to *Listen Up: Voices from the Next Feminist Generation* (1995) as "amateur memoirists" who confuse "feeling bad" with oppression and who "believe their lives are intrinsically interesting to strangers" (Kaminer quoted in Siegel, 1997: 67).

Henry is not so harsh. She recognizes that the third wave's individualistic approach to writing reflects their resistance to using the essentialist, second wave's collective "we" and speaking for other women (Henry, 2005: 43)—a welcome critical stance they learned from poststructuralism and intersectionality theory. However, she thinks it is time for third-wave feminists to move beyond personal accounts, to engage in larger political and theoretical explorations, and to move from the individual to the collective.

Henry is particularly critical of individualistic definitions of feminism, such as the one voiced by Marcelle Karp, the co-editor of *The Bust Guide to the New Girl Order* (1999): "We've entered an era of DIY feminism—sistah, do-it-yourself—we have all kinds of names for ourselves lipstick lesbians, do-me feminists . . . No matter what the flava is, we're still feminists. Your feminism is what you want it to be and what you make of it" (Karp quoted in Karp and Stoller, 1999: 310–311). Although Henry applauds the intent of third wavers, such as Karp, to make feminism appealing to more women and men, she argues that when feminism is represented as whatever an individual wants it to be, it "loses it critical political perspective" and becomes nothing more than a "meaningless bumper sticker announcing 'girl power'" (Henry, 2005: 84).

Henry fears that such individualistic notions of feminism fit too well with the conservative realities of U.S. politics in the twenty-first century that highlight individual solutions to collective social problems (2005: 84). She laments the loss of shared struggles, definable political goals and targeted enemies (2005: 91). She concludes that by building shared political goals, the third wave can move from merely "a generational stance taken by individuals to a critical political perspective that acknowledges diversity and differences within feminism while simultaneously stressing the need for collective action to affect social change" (2005: 93–94).

CONCLUSION

There are signs that third-wave feminists are moving in the direction of addressing larger political and economic issues in their writings. Certainly the reading in this chapter by Heywood and Drake addresses important economic and technological developments that have impacted the third wave. Similarly, the reading by Alison Symington in Chapter 10 examines how powerful financial institutions affect global developments today. Such concern with the economic and political realities of the New World Order also can be found in the works of European third-wave feminists (Van der Tuin, 2011) or in the transnational approaches employed by various contributors to international third-wave anthologies such as *Defending Our Dreams: Global Feminist Voices for a New Generation* (Wilson et al., 2005) and *Third Wave Feminism: A Critical Exploration* (Gillis et al., ([2004] 2007). Given time, it is likely that we will speak of different third-wave feminisms, just as we speak of different feminisms *within* both the first and second waves.

NOTES

1. Sections of this chapter first appeared in S. A. Mann, "Third Wave Feminism's Unhappy Marriage of Poststructuralism and Intersectionality Theory, *Journal of Feminist Scholarship*, (May, 2013). The author wishes to thank the *Journal of Feminist Scholarship* and the College of Liberal Arts at the University of Massachusetts, Dartmouth, for permission to print them.

2. Even the *New York Times*—usually considered the bastion of liberal journalism—struck up a dirge with a cover story in its weekly magazine that began "The women's movement is over. . . ." (quoted in Faludi, 1991: 76).

3. Third wavers also cite the confirmation hearings for Clarence Thomas's nomination to the U.S. Supreme Court in 1991 after he was accused of sexual harassment by Anita Hill as sparking their feminist activism. As Astrid Henry writes, "The Thomas hearing helped put feminist issues back into the media spotlight after the bleak anti-feminist 1980s" (2004: 161).

4. Davis views the third wave's portrayal of feminism as austere and disciplinary as an "imaginary feminist status quo" (Davis in R. Walker, 1995: 281).

5. The relativist stance that pervades Walker's book is most explicit in her statement: "If feminism is to continue to be radical and alive, it must avoid reordering the world in terms of any polarity, be it female/male, good/evil" (R. Walker, 1995: xxxv).

6. Bettie's book has won numerous awards, including the American Sociological Association Sex and Gender Section's most prestigious book award for 2004.

90

BIKINI KILL ZINE COVER

(circa 1991)

Bikini Kill no. 2. Copyright held by the Kathleen Hanna Papers. Reprinted by permission of Kathi Wilcox. Image courtesy of the New York University Fales Library & Special Collections.

"BEING REAL: AN INTRODUCTION"

A year before I started this book, my life was like a feminist ghetto. Every decision I made, person I spent time with, word I uttered, had to measure up to an image I had in my mind of what was morally and politically right according to my vision of female empowerment. Everything had a gendered explanation, and what didn't fit into my concept of feminist was "bad, patriarchal, and problematic." I couldn't stay intimate with a male friend who called someone a "pussy" derogatorily and revealed an un-decolonized mind, I couldn't live with a partner because I would never be able to maintain my independence and artistic strength as a woman, I couldn't utter thoughts of dislike or jealousy for another woman because that would mean I was horribly unfeminist, and so, horribly bad.

My existence was an ongoing state of saying no to many elements of the universe, and picking and choosing to allow only what I thought should belong. The parts of myself that didn't fit into my ideal were hidden down deep, and when I faced them for fleeting moments they made me feel insecure and confused about my values and identity. Curiosity about pornography, attraction to a stable domestic partnership, a desire to start a business and pursue traditional individual power, interest in the world of S/M, a love for people who challenged and sometimes flatly opposed my feminist beliefs—these feelings in themselves were not terribly terrible, and I think that for most who consider them they seem terribly trivial, but for me and my sense of how to make feminist revolution, they represented contradictions that I had no idea how to reconcile.

Linked with my desire to be a good feminist was, of course, not just a desire to change my behavior to change the world, but a deep desire to be accepted, claimed, and loved by a feminist community that included my mother, godmother, aunts, and close friends. For all intents and purposes their beliefs were my own, and we mirrored each other in the most affirming of ways. As is common in familial relationships, I feared that our love was dependent upon that mirroring. Once I offered a face different from the one they expected, I thought the loyalty, the bond of our shared outlook and understanding, would be damaged forever.

The thought of exploring myself and the world and coming up with new questions and different answers was not half as terrifying as the thought of sharing these revelations with people I admired and loved. That moment of articulating my difference, when I imagined it in my mind, was not one of power, of me coming to voice about my own truths, it was one filled with the guilt of betrayal. If the Goddess didn't work for me, if I didn't think violence on TV translated into real-life violence, if I didn't believe in the essential goodness of women's culture, I thought I might be perceived as betraying "The Movement" rather than celebrating it. I feared that this betrayal, which was grounded in staying true to myself, could mean banishment from the community for questioning the status quo. Because feminism has always been so close to home, I worried that I might also be banished from there.

The ever-shifting but ever-present ideals of feminism can't help but leave young women and men struggling with the reality of who we are. Constantly measuring up to some cohesive fully down-for-the-feminist-cause identity without contradictions and messiness and lusts for power and luxury items is not a fun or easy task. As one woman said to me at a small Midwestern college where I was giving a lecture, "I feel I can't be a feminist because I am not strong enough, not good enough, not disciplined enough." At an all women's college in Virginia, another young woman expressed relief when I told the group that there was no one correct way to be a feminist, no seamless narrative to assume and fit into. This soft-spoken young woman told the group hesitantly, "I have always believed in equal rights and been involved in speaking up, but I didn't think I could call myself a feminist because I am also Christian." The concept of a strictly defined and all-encompassing feminist identity is so prevalent that when I read the section in my talk about all the different things you can do and still be a feminist, like shave your legs every day, get married, be a man, be in the army, whatever, audience members clap spontaneously. This simple reassurance paves the way for more openness and communication from young women and men than anything else I say.

Buried in these vibrant young women's words are a host of mystifications, imagistic idealizations, and ingrained social definitions of what it means to be a feminist. For each young woman there is a different set of qualifiers, a different image which embodies an ideal to measure up to, a far-reaching ideological position to uphold at any cost. Depending on which mythology she was exposed to, she believes that in order to be a feminist one must live in poverty, always critique, never marry, want to censor pornography and/or worship the Goddess. A feminist must never compromise herself, must never make concessions for money or for love, must always be devoted to the uplift of her gender, must only make an admirable and selfless livelihood, preferably working for a women's organization. She fears that if she wants to be spanked before sex, wants to own a BMW, is a Zen priest, wants to be treated "like a lady," prioritizes racial oppression over gender oppression, loves misogynist hip-hop music, still speaks to the father that abused her, gets married, wants to raise three kids on a farm in Montana, etc., that she can't be a feminist. That is, she can't join a community of women and men working for equality, and can't consider herself a part of a history of societal transformation on behalf of women.

From my experience talking with young women and being one myself, it has become clear to me that young women are struggling with the feminist label not only, as some prominent Second Wavers have asserted, because we lack a knowledge of women's history and have been alienated by the media's generally horrific characterization of feminists, and not only because it is tedious to always criticize world politics, popular culture, and the nuances of social interaction. Young women coming of age today wrestle with the term because we have a very different vantage point on the world than that of our foremothers. We shy from or modify the label in an attempt to begin to articulate our differences while simultaneously avoiding meaningful confrontation. For many of us it seems that to be a feminist in the way that we have seen or understood feminism is to conform to an identity and way of living that doesn't allow for individuality, complexity, or less than perfect personal histories. We fear that the identity will dictate and regulate our lives, instantaneously pitting us against someone, forcing us to choose inflexible and unchanging sides, female against male, black against white, oppressed against oppressor, good against bad.

This way of ordering the world is especially difficult for a generation that has grown up transgender, bisexual, interracial, and knowing and loving people who are racist, sexist, and otherwise afflicted. We have trouble formulating and perpetuating theories that compartmentalize and divide according to race and gender and all of the other signifiers. For us the lines between Us and Them are often blurred, and as a result we find ourselves seeking to create identities that accommodate ambiguity and our multiple positionalities: including more than excluding, exploring more than defining, searching more than arriving.

Whether the young women who refuse the label realize it or not, on some level they recognize that an ideal woman born of prevalent notions of how empowered women look, act, and think is simply another impossible contrivance of perfect womanhood, another scripted role to perform in the name of biology and virtue. But tragically, rather than struggling to locate themselves within some continuum of feminism, rather than upset the boat a little by reconciling the feminism they see and learn about with their own ideas and desires, many young women and men simply bow out altogether, avoiding the dreaded confrontation with some of the people who presently define and represent feminism, and with their own beliefs.

Neither myself nor the young women and men in this book have bowed out. Instead, the writers here have done the difficult work of being real (refusing to be bound by a feminist ideal not of their own making) and telling the truth (honoring the complexity and contradiction in their lives by adding their experiences to the feminist dialogue). They change the face of feminism as each new generation will, bringing a different set of experiences to draw from, an entirely different set of reference points, and a whole new set of questions. . . .

These voices are important because if feminism is to continue to be radical and alive, it must avoid reordering the world in terms of any polarity, be it female/male, good/evil, or, that easy allegation of false consciousness which can so quickly and silently negate another's agency: evolved/unconscious. It must continue to be responsive to new situations, needs, and especially desires, ever expanding to incorporate and entertain all those who wrestle with and swear by it, including those who may not explicitly call its name. . . .

As they shared their stories, I gradually revealed more about the book I wanted to read. I wanted to explore the ways that choices or actions seemingly at odds with mainstream ideas of feminism push us to new definitions and understandings of female empowerment and social change. I wanted to know more about how people reconciled aspects of their lives that they felt ashamed of with politics they believed in. I especially wanted to hear experiences of people attempting to live their lives envisioning or experiencing identities beyond those inscribed on them by the surrounding culture. . . .

It was extraordinarily difficult for writers to produce works for this book. I spent innumerable hours alternating between therapist and editor. Many pieces didn't make it because writers were afraid to expose themselves. The pieces that did make it are strong pieces which open doors of understanding and prioritize political commitment *and* self-acceptance. Whether it is Jocelyn Taylor writing on her quest for public eroticism as activism rather than as objectification, Jason Schultz on the conundrum of straight white male sexuality within feminist practice, Veena Cabreros-Sud on reclaiming violence within a movement that prizes nonviolence, or mocha jean herrup using the Internet as a facilitator of a politics of ambiguity, these essays

provoke us and enlarge our view, challenging us to accept other patterns of thought. Other essays, like bell hooks's on the role beauty and material objects play in her sense of progressive struggle, and Jeannine DeLombard's on her insistence on being a *femme*nist, make a space for us to forge new meanings from our attraction to things that may be considered "anti-revolution." Some of the more shocking pieces, like Donna Minkowitz's courageous reckoning with her own eroticization of violence, are disturbing journeys that may leave some readers in agony from having their norms so questioned . . .

This book is a testament to the realities that there is no betrayal in being yourself, home must be made within, and the best communities are those built on mutual respect. The complex, multi-issue nature of our lives, the instinct not to categorize and shut oneself off from others, and the enormous contradictions we embody are all fodder for making new theories of living and relating. This continuing legacy of feminism, which demands that we know and accept ourselves, jettisoning societal norms that don't allow for our experiences, is a politically powerful decision. For, in these days of conservative and exclusionary politics predicated upon notions of black and white, of who is entitled to resources and who is not, of who is good and who should be incarcerated, it is more important than ever to fight to be all of who we are. Rather than allowing ourselves and others to be put into boxes meant to categorize and dismiss, we can use the complexity of our lives to challenge the belief that any person or group is more righteous, more correct, more deserving of life than any other. . . .

And so what you have in your hands now is the book that I struggled for two years to even allow myself to bring into being. The one that came out of the late-night wonderings and intense conversations about difference, desire, and the things we fear most within our emerging selves. I hope the journeys in this collection encourage you to reach into the spaces of yourself where you are most afraid to go, to create feminist space in which you can be real. I hope these writers encourage you to pull your truths, your questions, and your so-called demons out, out into the open, where you can get a better look and lead us all into the future.

(1995)

"KLAUS BARBIE, AND OTHER DOLLS I'D LIKE TO SEE"

Dinner Roll Barbie. A Barbie with multiple love handles, double chin, a real, curvy belly, generous tits and ass and voluminous thighs to show girls that voluptuousness is also beautiful. Comes with miniature basket of dinner rolls, bucket o'fried chicken, tiny Entenmann's walnut ring, a brick of Sealtest ice cream, three packs of potato chips, a T-shirt reading "Only the Weak Don't Eat" and, of course, an appetite.

Birkenstack Barbie. Finally, a doll made with horizontal feet and comfortable sandals. Made from recycled materials.

Bisexual Barbie. Comes in a package with Skipper and Ken.

Butch Barbie. Comes with short hair, leather jacket, "Silence = Death" T-shirt, pink triangle buttons, Doc Martens, pool cue and dental dams. Packaged in cardboard closet with doors flung wide open. Barbie Carpentry Business sold separately.

Our Barbies, Ourselves. Anatomically correct Barbie, both inside and out, comes with spreadable legs, her own speculum, magnifying glass and detailed diagrams of female anatomy so that little girls can learn about their bodies in a friendly, nonthreatening way. Also included: tiny Kotex, booklets on sexual responsibility. Accessories such as contraceptives, sex toys, expanding uterus with fetus at various stages of development and breast pump are all optional, underscoring that each young women has the right to choose what she does with her own Barbie.

Harley Barbie. Equipped with motorcycle, helmet, shades. Tattoos are non-toxic and can be removed with baby oil.

Body Piercings Barbie. Why should Earring Ken have all the fun? Body Piercings Barbie comes with changeable multiple earrings, nose ring, nipple rings, lip ring, navel ring and tiny piercing gun. Enables girls to rebel, express alienation and gross out elders without actually having to puncture themselves.

Blue Collar Barbie. Comes with overalls, protective goggles, lunch pail, UAW membership, pamphlet on union organizing and pay scales for women as compared to men. Waitressing outfits and cashier's register may be purchased separately for Barbies who are holding down second jobs to make ends meet.

Rebbe Barbie. So why not? Women rabbis are on the cutting edge in Judaism. Rebbe Barbie comes with tiny satin *yarmulke*, prayer shawl, *tefillin*, silver *kaddish* cup, Torah scrolls. Optional: tiny *mezuzah* for doorway of Barbie Dreamhouse.

B-Girl Barbie. Truly fly Barbie in midriff-baring shirt and baggy jeans. Comes with skateboard, hip hop accessories and plenty of attitude. Pull her cord, and she says things like, "I don't *think* so," "Dang, get outta my face" and "You go, girl." Teaches girls not to take shit from men and condescending white people.

The Barbie Dream Team. Featuring Quadratic Equation Barbie (a Nobel Prize–winning mathematician with her own tiny books and calculator), Microbiologist Barbie (comes with petri dishes, computer and Barbie Laboratory) and Bite-the-Bullet Barbie, an anthropologist with pith helmet, camera, detachable limbs, fake blood and kit for performing surgery on herself in the outback.

Transgender Barbie. Formerly known as G.I. Joe.

(1998)

"A DAY WITHOUT FEMINISM"

We were both born in 1970, the baptismal moment of a decade that would change dramatically the lives of American women. The two of us grew up thousands of miles apart, in entirely different kinds of families, yet we both came of age with the awareness that certain rights had been won by the women's movement. We've never doubted how important feminism is to people's lives—men's and women's. Both of our mothers went to consciousness-raising-type groups. Amy's mother raised Amy on her own, and Jennifer's mother, questioning the politics of housework, staged laundry strikes.

With the dawn of not just a new century but a new millennium, people are looking back and taking stock of feminism. Do we need new strategies? Is feminism dead? Has society changed so much that the idea of a feminist movement is obsolete? For us, the only way to answer these questions is to imagine what our lives would have been if the women's movement had never happened and the conditions for women had remained as they were in the year of our births.

Imagine that for a day it's still 1970, and women have only the rights they had then. Sly and the Family Stone and Dionne Warwick are on the radio, the kitchen appliances are Harvest Gold, and the name of your Whirlpool gas stove is Mrs. America. What is it like to be female?

Babies born on this day are automatically given their father's name. If no father is listed, "illegitimate" is likely to be typed on the birth certificate. There are virtually no child-care centers, so all preschool children are in the hands of their mothers, a baby-sitter, or an expensive nursery school. In elementary school, girls can't play in Little League and almost all of the teachers are female. (The latter is still true.) In a few states, it may be against the law for a male to teach grades lower than the sixth, on the basis that it's unnatural, or that men can't be trusted with young children.

In junior high, girls probably take home ec; boys take shop or small-engine repair. Boys who want to learn how to cook or sew on a button are out of luck, as are girls who want to learn how to fix a car. *Seventeen* magazine doesn't run feminist-influenced current columns like "Sex + Body" and "Traumarama." Instead the magazine encourages girls not to have sex; pleasure isn't part of its vocabulary. Judy Blume's books are just beginning to be published, and *Free to Be . . . You and Me* does not exist. No one reads much about masturbation as a natural activity; nor do they learn that sex is for anything other than procreation. Girls do read mystery stories about Nancy Drew, for whom there is no sex, only her blue roadster and having "luncheon." (The real mystery is how Nancy gets along without a purse and manages to meet only white people.) Boys read about the Hardy Boys, for whom there are no girls.

In high school, the principal is a man. Girls have physical-education class and play half-court basketball, but not soccer, track, or cross country; nor do they have any varsity sports teams. The only prestigious physical activity for girls is cheer-leading, or being a drum majorette. Most girls don't take calculus or physics; they plan the dances and decorate the gym. Even when girls get better grades than their male counterparts, they are half as likely to qualify for a National Merit Scholarship because many of the test questions favor boys. Standardized tests refer to males and male experiences much more than to females and their experiences. If a girl "gets herself pregnant," she loses her membership in the National Honor Society (which is still true today) and is expelled.

Girls and young women might have sex while they're unmarried, but they may be ruining their chances of landing a guy full-time, and they're probably getting a bad reputation. If a pregnancy happens, an enterprising gal can get a legal abortion only if she lives in New York or is rich enough to fly there, or to Cuba, London, or Scandinavia. There's also the Chicago-based Jane Collective, an underground abortion-referral service, which can hook you up with an illegal or legal termination. (Any of these options are going to cost you. Illegal abortions average $300 to $500, sometimes as much as $2,000.) To prevent pregnancy, a sexually active woman might go to a doctor to be fitted for a diaphragm, or take the high-dose birth-control pill, but her doctor isn't likely to inform her of the possibility of deadly blood clots. Those who do take the Pill also may have to endure this contraceptive's crappy side effects: migraine headaches, severe weight gain, irregular bleeding, and hair loss (or gain), plus the possibility of an increased risk of breast cancer in the long run. It is unlikely that women or their male partners know much about the clitoris and its role in orgasm unless someone happens to fumble upon it. Instead, the myth that vaginal orgasms from penile penetration are the only "mature" (according to Freud) climaxes prevails.

Lesbians are rarely "out," except in certain bars owned by organized crime (the only businessmen who recognize this untapped market), and if lesbians don't know about the bars, they're less likely to know whether there are any other women like them. Radclyffe Hall's depressing early-twentieth-century novel *The Well of Loneliness* pretty much indicates their fate.

The Miss America Pageant is the biggest source of scholarship money for women. Women can't be students at Dartmouth, Columbia, Harvard, West Point, Boston College, or the Citadel, among other all-male institutions. Women's colleges are referred to as "girls' schools." There are no Take Back the Night marches to protest women's lack of safety after dark, but that's okay because college girls aren't allowed out much after dark anyway. Curfew is likely to be midnight on Saturday and 9 or 10 p.m. the rest of the week. Guys get to stay our as late as they want. Women tend to major in teaching, home economics, English, or maybe a language—a good skill for translating someone else's words. The women's studies major does

not exist, although you can take a women's studies course at six universities, including Cornell and San Diego State College. The absence of women's history, black history, Chicano studies, Asian-American history, queer studies, and Native American history from college curricula implies that they are not worth studying. A student is lucky if he or she learns that women were "given" the vote in 1920, just as Columbus "discovered" America in 1492. They might also learn that Sojourner Truth, Mary Church Terrell, and Fannie Lou Hamer were black abolitionists or civil-rights leaders, but not that they were feminists. There are practically no tenured female professors at any school, and campuses are not racially diverse. Women of color are either not there or they're lonely as hell. There is no nationally recognized Women's History Month or Black History Month. Only 14 percent of doctorates are awarded to women. Only 3.5 percent of MBAs are female.

Only 2 percent of everybody in the military is female, and these women are mostly nurses. There are no female generals in the U.S. Air Force, no female naval pilots, and no Marine brigadier generals. On the religious front, there are no female cantors or rabbis, Episcopal canons, or Catholic priests. (This is still true of Catholic priests.)

Only 44 percent of women are employed outside the home. And those women make, on average, fifty-two cents to the dollar earned by males. Want ads are segregated into "Help Wanted Male" and "Help Wanted Female." The female side is preponderantly for secretaries, domestic workers, and other low-wage service jobs, so if you're a female lawyer you must look under "Help Wanted Male." There are female doctors, but twenty states have only five female gynecologists or fewer. Women workers can be fired or demoted for being pregnant, especially if they are teachers, since the kids they teach aren't supposed to think that women have sex. If a boss demands sex, refers to his female employee exclusively as "Baby," or says he won't pay her unless she gives him a blow job, she either has to quit or succumb—no pun intended. Women can't be airline pilots. Flight attendants are "stewardesses"— waitresses in the sky—and necessarily female. Sex appeal is a job requirement, wearing makeup is a rule, and women are fired if they exceed the age or weight deemed sexy. Stewardesses can get married without getting canned, but this is a new development. (In 1968 the Equal Employment Opportunity Commission—EEOC—made it illegal to forcibly retire stewardesses for getting hitched.) Less than 2 percent of dentists are women; 100 percent of dental assistants are women. The "glass ceiling" that keeps women from moving naturally up the ranks, as well as the sticky floor that keeps them unnaturally down in low-wage work, has not been named, much less challenged.

When a woman gets married, she vows to love, honor, and obey her husband, though he gets off doing just the first two to uphold his end of the bargain. A married woman can't obtain credit without her husband's signature. She doesn't have her own credit rating, legal domicile, or even her own name unless she goes to court to get it back. If she gets a loan with her husband—and she has a job—she may have to sign a "baby letter" swearing that she won't have one and have to leave her job.

Women have been voting for up to fifty years, but their turnout rate is lower than that for men; and they tend to vote right along with their husbands, not with their own interests in mind. The divorce rate is about the same as it is in 2000, contrary to popular fiction's blaming the women's movement for divorce. However, divorce required that one person be at fault, therefore if you just want out of your marriage, you have to lie or blame your spouse. Property division and settlements, too, are based on fault. (And at a time when domestic violence isn't a term, much less a crime, women are legally encouraged to remain in abusive marriages.) If fathers ask for custody of the children, they get it in 60 to 80 percent of the cases. (This is still true.) If a husband or a lover hits his partner, she has no shelter to go to unless she happens to live near the one in northern California or the other in upper Michigan. If a woman is downsized from her role as a housewife (a.k.a. left by her husband), there is no word for being a displaced homemaker. As a divorcée, she may be regarded as a family disgrace or as easy sexual prey. After all, she had sex with one guy, so why not *all* guys?

If a woman is not a Mrs., she's a Miss. A woman without makeup and a hairdo is as suspect as a man with them. Without a male escort she may be refused

service in a restaurant or a bar, and a woman alone is hard-pressed to find a landlord who will rent her an apartment. After all, she'll probably be leaving to get married soon, and, if she isn't, the landlord doesn't want to deal with a potential brothel.

Except among the very poor or in very rural areas, babies are born in hospitals. There are no certified midwives, and women are knocked out during birth. Most likely, they are also strapped down and lying down, made to have the baby against gravity for the doctor's convenience. If he has a schedule to keep, the likelihood of a cesarean is also very high. *Our Bodies, Ourselves* doesn't exist, nor does the women's health movement. Women aren't taught how to look at their cervixes, and their bodies are nothing to worry their pretty little heads about; however, they are supposed to worry about keeping their little heads pretty. If a woman goes under the knife to see if she has breast cancer, the surgeon won't wake her up to consult about her options before performing a Halsted mastectomy (a disfiguring radical procedure, in which the breast, the muscle wall, and the nodes under the arm, right down to the bone, are removed). She'll just wake up and find that the choice has been made for her.

Husbands are likely to die eight years earlier than their same-age wives due to the stress of having to support a family and repress an emotional life, and a lot earlier than that if women have followed the custom of marrying older, authoritative; paternal men. The stress of raising kids, managing a household, and being undervalued by society doesn't seem to kill off women at the same rate. Upon a man's death, his beloved gets a portion of his Social Security. Even if she has worked outside the home for her entire adult life, she is probably better off with that portion than with hers in its entirety, because she has earned less and is likely to have taken time out for such unproductive acts as having kids.

Has feminism changed our lives? Was it necessary? After thirty years of feminism, the world we inhabit barely resembles the world we were born into. And there's still a lot left to do.

(2000)

"UNPACKING THE MOTHER/DAUGHTER BAGGAGE: REASSESSING SECOND- AND THIRD-WAVE TENSIONS"

. . . In this essay, I look at how feminism, especially the academic feminism born of the second wave, can be understood as significantly affecting younger feminists in their very constitution as emerging feminist subjects. Through an appropriation of some Foucauldian ideas, I show how a movement such as feminism must contain the very kinds of pressures that serve to produce feminist subjects who can then be expected to resist that same feminism. . . . As I see it, the generation gap between these groups of feminists is not based so much on disagreement about particular issues as on a failure to communicate honestly in the first place. There is a disingenuousness about the nature of power and resistance on both sides, one that not only results in gross misunderstandings as reflected in the popular media, but that also will affect the nature and quality of cross-generational collaboration in the academy.

REGIMES OF FEMINISM

One of Michel Foucault's most useful insights is that power need not be located in one site or wielded by one readily identifiable authority to be effective (*Discipline and Punish* 1979). Thus, for example, Foucault could write about the effectiveness of modern educational practices to mold students even though he understood that such power did not merely trickle unidirectionally from a dictator to the masses through a clearly visible hierarchy (*Discipline and Punish* 1979).

Similarly, the fact that we cannot speak of a singularly identifiable feminist power does not mean that it does not exist with the capacity to affect subjects. In the wake of the current backlash against feminism, many of us are accustomed to thinking of it as an increasingly disempowered movement, but we need to see how it continues to be enmeshed in power relations. If not, we can never comprehend why someone who has some appreciation for feminism might, nevertheless, feel a need to resist aspects of it, as many younger women clearly do.[1] . . .

Additionally, whether we are discussing patriarchal sites of power or feminist ones, we should sometimes expect to find a conflation between aspects that are empowering and those that are not. What can serve liberatory interests can also function repressively. For example, initiatives to document paternity for the collection of child support can be exploited to threaten mothers' custody. Modern science serves as a more dramatic example. Initially a movement that served to empower individuals against state and religious authority, modern science has also aided in the oppression of whole populations in the contemporary world (Harding 96). Social movements must, by their very natures, repress some possibilities while they foster others. "All order is, after all, double edged, at once prohibitive and productive" (Cocks 70). . . .

The crucial point here is that feminism does not cease to exert normalizing power over subjects simply because it is an ideology associated with a genuinely liberatory movement. The particular ways of being a feminist may never be fully enumerated, but it is necessary, in order for the concept of feminism to be meaningful, that certain options be experienced by subjects as foreclosed. In addition, "it is only through the process of subjectification that we become subjects capable of resisting the institutions, discourses, and practices that constitute us as subjects" (McLaren 119). Part of what feminist teaching encourages is the recognition and respect of one's own ideas, desires, and so forth. Thus, to some extent it is a testament to the success of feminism that such teaching produces younger feminist subjects who resist, on feminist terms, the very feminism that has helped to shape them. . . .

* * *

CONTEXTUALIZING SOME YOUNGER WOMEN'S CHALLENGES

Defining third-wave feminism has itself been a focus of many third-wave writings largely because there have been no watershed political events to mark either the death of the second wave or the birth of the third.[2] Here, I limit my discussion to works in which the editors explicitly identify as third-wave feminists, although individual contributors may not. Some may be more comfortable with the punk feminist identity of "Riot Grrl," while others simply call themselves and their peers "younger feminists" or, simply, "younger women." In general, third-wave feminists tend to position themselves by age and attitude; they see themselves as being able to take for granted some of the things for which older feminists had to fight, although there is often appreciation expressed to second wavers. Although it is really no easier to define the agenda of third-wave feminism than that of second-wave feminism, I have mostly restricted my focus to issues of sexuality and bodily aesthetics as these figure most prominently in the third-wave material I have encountered.

In her introductory essay, Rebecca Walker, editor of the seminal third-wave anthology *To Be Real: Telling the Truth and Changing the Face of Feminism*, claims that "to be a feminist in the way that we have seen or understood feminism is to conform to an identity and way of living that doesn't allow for individuality, complexity, or less than perfect personal histories"

(xxxii–iii). Like Walker, many of the other contributors to the anthology focus on sexuality and bodily aesthetics. Another contributor remembers her experience with an activist, feminist mother:

> My sister, brother, and I were mortified as we ran alongside the march, giggling and pointing at the marching women chanting "Women Unite—Take Back the Night!" The throngs were letting it all hang out: Their breasts hung low, their leg hair grew wild, their thighs were wide in their faded blue jeans. Some of them donned Earth shoes and t-shirts with slogans like "A Woman Needs a Man Like a Fish Needs a Bicycle." They weren't the least bit ashamed. But I was. I remember thinking, "I will never let myself look like that." (Senna 7–8)

Another contributor also defines her young adult identity reactively, against what she perceived to be the prevailing second-wave aesthetic (or lack of it): "I felt part of a new generation of feminists. We wanted to make room for play in our lives—dying our hair, shaving our legs, dressing in ways that made us happy" (Allyn 144). More recently, aesthetic and sexual issues remain central to younger women's complaints with the insistence that one can "wear makeup, shave your legs, wear dresses, have a traditional wedding, or celebrate your femininity and still be considered a 'feminist'" (Jacob). Amy Richards, one of the authors of *Manifesta: Young Women, Feminism, and the Future*, explains in an interview, "I don't think these women are saying 'I'm going to be female, going to be objectified, going to wear sexy clothes and so on and be part of the backlash against feminism.' I think they're saying, 'I'm going to do all these things because I want to embrace my femininity'" (Straus).

Despite the fact that this woman's conception of second-wave feminism is, I think, conditioned by backlash stereotypes (the "hairy, humorless, man-hater"?), clearly, for some younger women, one important perceived site of dissent is the personal experience of the body. This is not the only locus of concern. *Manifesta*, in particular, has some focus on traditional political issues, at least, liberal political issues, but here, too, issues of bodily aesthetics and sexuality are quite prominent, and not in a way that is likely to comfort older feminists. Referring to the "Third Wave revalorization of beauty, sexual power and femininity," one critic of *Manifesta* worries: "What happens to feminism when it reclaims the very sources of power the patriarchy has always been happy to grant us?" (Jensen 4). Certainly, there is a rich understanding among many second wavers about the risks of embracing traditionally feminine qualities that younger feminists ought to consider.

Nonetheless, I think that the intense focus on these kinds of issues, however misguided some of them are in the details, is a wake-up call for older feminists that what appears, from one perspective, to be conformist, may, from another perspective, have subversive potential. Since the 1970s, things may not have changed as much as any of us would have liked, but they have changed. We cannot assess the meaning of younger women's actions and attitudes without recognizing that the backdrop against which their actions are performed is, in many cases, significantly different. As one younger feminist explains: "The legacy of second wave feminism had taught me that, as a girl, I could do anything I wanted to do, but the backlash let me know that this was possible only as long as I wasn't a girl—as long as I wasn't soft and feminine and weak" (Shoemaker 115). Another younger feminist puts it this way: "We want not to get rid of the trappings of traditional femininity or sexuality so much as to pair them with demonstrations of strength or power. We are much less likely to burn our bras communally than to run down the street clad in nothing but our bras yelling 'Fuck you!' " (Klein 223). Whether such an action is usefully subversive would be a worthwhile question for discussion, but that cannot occur if older feminists simply assume that it is patriarchally conformist now simply because it would have been thirty years ago.

FEMINIST CHOICE AND THE COMMUNICATION GAP

While I think Walker is simply incorrect in her claim that feminism typically involves "policing morality" (xxxv) or rabid "identity politics" (xxxiv), we can take seriously her kind of resistance to older feminism without invalidating or oversimplifying the message of the second wave. Here, we are at an impasse based on problematic understandings and uses of the concept of feminist choice. My analysis highlights not so much a disagreement between younger and older feminists as an inability to communicate effectively enough to even get to the point of fruitful disagreement.

The difficulty begins, I think, with feminists who attempt to hide behind the tired liberal rhetoric of individual freedom to avoid the charge that feminism advocates some values while eschewing others. It is a maneuver designed precisely to avoid been seen as "policing morality." On this view, the shift in consciousness that leads a woman to identify herself as a feminist is understood as one that helps her gain access to a more authentic self. It is not, then, the content of the choices themselves that are significant, but the fact that they emerged from an authentically feminist subjectivity.

The concept of an "authentic self," however, is too slippery to be useful in any kind of political context. Even if it were true that each of us had such a self (and I'm not at all sure that it is) we could still have no way of knowing which desires emerged from that true self and which from one's "patriarchal self." There simply is no readily available, external standard of authenticity relative to which individuals' desires can be assessed. This is one of the theoretical difficulties that underlies many historically important feminist debates. For example, is the woman who "chooses" sadomasochistic sex merely acting from her patriarchal conditioning or is it possible that her motives emanate from her true self?

Consider, for example, another of the third-wave contributors who asks, "Is it horrible to say that reading about real-world rape and torture sometimes turns me on?" (Minkowitz 79). She goes on to offer an explanation and defense of her behavior including a plausible account of its psychological genesis in her childhood abuse. In her foreword to the anthology in which Minkowitz's essay appears, Gloria Steinem writes that reading it "makes [her] as sorrowful as reading about a gay person, someone who is Jewish, or a person of color who finds homophobic, anti-Semitic, or racist violence to be a sexual turn-on." Steinem further claims that Minkowitzs' essay "is a powerful reminder of the power of socialization" (xxi).

Minkowitz implies that her desires are traceable to her own socialization, but also attempts to validate them, suggesting that her desires are at least partly a function of her nature, that is, who she is without the veneer of society (85). Steinem suggests that the content of Minkowitz's desires is itself enough to show that they are inauthentically patriarchal in their origin. According to Steinem, the fact that Minkowitz would claim to freely choose to masturbate while reading actual accounts of rape is itself enough to mark her behavior as coerced by socialization. Adopting a model that relies this way upon the concept of authentic choice, Steinem cannot help but feel sorry for Minkowitz and Minkowitz cannot help but feel patronized by the suggestion that Steinem seems to think she has better access to Minkowitzs' true self (and others like her) than has Minkowitz herself. While Walker claims to offer a new brand of feminism that emphasizes "self possession" and "self determination," Steinem responds that feminism has always encouraged such ideals. In her foreword to *To Be Real*, Steinem expresses a general resentment to charges such as Walker's: "Imagine how frustrating it is to be held responsible for some of the very divisions you've been fighting against, and you'll know how feminists of the 1980s and earlier may feel as they read some of these pages" (xxiii). However, when confronted by what women such as Minkowitz claim to be their choices, Steinem denies that they are real choices. This is a denial that, to Walker's eyes, must look a bit like denial of individual freedom itself. . . .

. . . But skepticism about the very possibility of pure choice based on the recognition that sexism shapes the nature and range of the choices is what has always motivated feminist ambivalence about such things as women's involvement in sadomasochistic sex, pornography, prostitution, and surrogate motherhood. The knee-jerk response is to deny that any such choices, under patriarchy, truly qualify as free. This type of response, though, risks suggesting that one has, as a feminist judge, access to an objective standard against which to assess others' choices. No wonder younger feminists might feel the need to rebel. One younger woman refers specifically to Steinem, who has placed herself in public conversation with third wavers and whose name appears regularly in their essays: "A woman—sorry, an *icon*—more than twice my age, as old (older than) my mother—was going to tell *me* what I think about . . . myself?" (Leibovich 2).

Younger feminists who complain about the restrictive nature of second-wave feminism may be picking up on the sheer falsity of the claim that feminism is simply interested in increasing the number of choices available to women without regard to the content of those choices. Surely, it's more honest to describe feminism as aiming to increase the number of *feminist* choices available to women, even if we do not claim to know in advance (or, perhaps, ever) precisely what would count as such a choice. We may even need to commit to the circular claim that part of what conditions a choice as feminist is that it was chosen by a feminist, taking some of the emphasis away from the content of the choice and placing it on the nature and context of the agent's intention. Being up front about the fact that not all choices can possibly count as feminist ones is the sort of step towards honesty that might improve generational communication. . . .

FORMS OF YOUNGER WOMEN'S RESISTANCE

{A}n Iraqi woman wearing a mini-skirt may be making a political statement in the expression of gender quite different from a U.S. woman wearing the same skirt. The illusion of sameness, the parallax, arises from ignoring different points of departure.

—Nancy J. Finley (4)

What counts as resistance is, to some extent, a relative matter. For example, in a traditionally heterosexually oriented club, a woman's appearance in a very short skirt, heels, and dramatic makeup might be easy to dismiss as patriarchally complicit. In the context of a lesbian bar where the prevailing aesthetic is quite different, such a woman's presence might have a different meaning. It is reasonable in the second context to consider this woman's costume to be a sign of resistance. I am not so much interested in convincing readers that this actually is the case; rather, I want to push the point that part of what makes an act count as subversive is the context in which it occurs.

For example, contextualizing third-wave feminist Eisa Davis' continued devotion to hip-hop music, which she acknowledges as sexist, may allow us to appreciate her position as resistance to racism. As she claims: "Hip hop, after all, is the chosen whipping boy for a misogyny that is fundamental to Western culture. Why should I deny myself hip hop but get a good grounding in Aristotle?" (132). Listening to hip-hop, even hip-hop that is blatantly sexist, may reasonably be understood as an act performed to counter the racist currents that may too selectively focus on the sexism of Black men. It is clear that differences in context can give one and the same act different meanings.

One of the factors that contributes to whether or not an act should be considered one of resistance is the agent's intention. On the other hand, there must be some external criteria to help define an act; otherwise, the fact that I believe myself to be waving in greeting would determine that that is what I would be doing even if my arm were actually anesthetized and hanging by my side. Similarly, acts of resistance should be defined by considerations both of intention and relevant external factors.

However, the difficulties in engaging in an enumeration of the "proper" criteria for determining what counts as genuine resistance are prohibitive. Should Minkowitz be solely responsible for accurately naming her intention or might Steinem legitimately be thought to have a voice in the matter? There must be a balance between the subject's own interpretation and that of others. But there is no practical way, beyond some vague recommendation for dialogue, to arrive at that balance of interpretations. The important point, though, is that some acknowledgment be made that in naming what counts as resistance, factors that are both internal and external to the agent must be considered. Thus, actions that may not have been subversive in the 1970s may be so today, but the simple fact that the agent thinks that this is the case is not enough to guarantee that it actually is.

It is especially important that subtler forms of resistance be recognized, especially given that some "forms of third wave activism don't always look 'activist' enough to second wave feminists" (Heywood and Drake 4). This is especially true when what an agent is resisting is the process of subjectification itself, that is, the processes through which one becomes tied to a particular identity. Many younger women see themselves as struggling against becoming the kind of feminist subjects they thought they

were supposed to become. As such, they may be offering a kind of resistance that is not immediately directed at actual feminists, but rather to an internalized version of a feminist governor—a "panoptical feminist connoisseur"—to adapt Bartky's term (71). I am not arguing that there actually exist such policing figures in the world, but rather suggesting that we acknowledge how young feminists might come to internalize a judgmental feminist eye. Utilizing the "social parallax lens" in this way might permit us to understand more of what younger women say and do as gestures towards progressive resistance rather than as merely whiney and/or ignorantly complicit with the backlash.

CONCLUSION: BEYOND THE MOTHER/DAUGHTER IMPASSE

I have been emphasizing similarities in how feminism operates as a disciplinary power and how other social forces, especially sexist ones, exert their pressures. I've done this not so much because I think that feminism is like the patriarchy, but because, as feminists, it is patriarchal forces that we've done the most thinking about. In particular, we need to uncover the "costs of our self-constitution," the price we pay for the benefits of becoming who we are (Sawicki 165). The urgency for self-criticism is made greater by the realization that many younger women are critical of feminism. We do not need to agree that feminism is fundamentally repressive in order to be concerned about those elements that may be experienced as repressive, especially by younger women.

Feminism principally exerts the kind of disciplinary power that produces subjects, agents capable of acting in various ways, rather than exerting it on women as objects. To borrow from the language of Foucault's later work, feminism exerts power, but it is not dominating. "Whereas 'domination' refers to a situation in which the subject is unable to overturn or reverse the domination relation—a situation where resistance is impossible—'power' refers to relations that are flexible, mutable, fluid, and even reversible" (Sawicki 170). Some younger feminists have incorrectly suggested that feminism is dominating, but there have always been voices within second-wave feminism crying out for diversity and individual variance. There is a level of ignorance about second-wave feminism in some third-wave critiques that is disappointing. Even worse, it is an ignorance that is rarely honestly acknowledged. It is, in part, the second wave's capacity for being so openly self-critical that has made concerns about diversity such a focal point for everyone else, including third wavers. . . .

Only if we take seriously that feminist power exists, power that works to shape subjects, rather than innocently facilitating the emergence of young women's "authentic selves," can we appreciate that there might be something in these young women's experiences of their own feminist identities to be resisted. In addition, the resistance that feminism has inspired in younger women may tell us something worth reflecting upon, but not necessarily that older feminists are simply wrong. As Foucault's analysis suggests, power need not be simplistically authoritarian or totalizing in order to have great impact. Even though feminists have not, by and large, been dictatorial, we still have the responsibility to appreciate how younger women may have felt themselves to be structured and limited by second-wave values. . . .

The biggest problem is not so much that second- and third-wave feminists disagree as that they have not yet even gotten to the point of honest disagreement. What is needed from older feminists is a more realistic acknowledgement of feminist power that does not lead to a brushing aside of younger women's complaints. From younger women there must be a commitment to engage with the women and work of the second wave in ways that are politically and academically serious, rather than token acknowledgements of its merely "historical" importance. As the authors of *Manifesta* have put it so well, second wavers are not third wavers' mothers. As such, older feminists should not expect automatic and uncritical deference. But it is equally worth emphasizing that third wavers should not be indulged as rebellious daughters whose limitations are to be explained away as mere symptoms of their inexperience or growing pains. If we approach the table, not as mothers and daughters, but as peers with different strengths and weakness, we might get somewhere. Maybe then, at least, honest communication will take us to the point of productive disagreement.

(2002)

NOTES

1. An ambivalence toward feminism both as a general ideology and as it is practiced in women's studies classrooms figures prominently in much third-wave work. See, for example, Findlen, and Heywood and Drake.

2. This point is developed more fully in Bailey.

REFERENCES

Allyn, Jennifer, and David Allyn. "Identity Politics." *To Be Real: Telling the Truth and Changing the Face of Feminism.* Ed. Rebecca Walker. New York: Anchor, 1995. 143–55.

Bailey, Cathryn. "Making Waves and Drawing Lines: The Politics of Defining the Vicissitudes of Feminism." *Hypatia* 12.3 (1997): 17–28.

Bartky. Sandra. "Foucault, Feminism, and the Modernization of Patriarchal Power." *Feminism and Foucault: Reflections on Resistance.* Ed. Irene Diamond and Lee Quinby. Boston; Northeastern University Press, 1988, 61–68.

Baumgardner, Jennifer, and Amy Richards. *Manifesta: Young Women, Feminism, and the Future of Feminism.* New York: Farrar, 2000.

Cocks, Joan. *The Oppositional Imagination: Feminism, Critique, and Political Theory.* New York: Routledge, 1989.

Davis, Eisa. "Sexism and the Art of Feminist Hip-Hop Maintenance." Walker, *To Be Real.* 127–41.

Finley, Nancy J. "The Concept of Social Parallax." *Women and Language* 20.1 (1997): 5–8 (4).

Foucault, Michel. "Afterword: The Subject and Power." Dreyfus and Rabinow, *Beyond Structuralism.* 208–26.

Foucault, Michel. *Discipline and Punish: The Birth of the Prison.* Trans., Alan Sheridan. New York: Vintage, 1979.

Foucault, Michel. *The History of Sexuality, Volume I: An Introduction.* Trans., Robert Hurley. New York: Vintage, 1990.

Foucault, Michel. "On the Genealogy of Ethics: An Overview of Work in Progress." Dreyfus and Rabinow, *Beyond Structuralism.* 229–52.

Harding, Sandra. *Whose Science? Whose Knowledge? Thinking From Women's Lives.* Ithaca, NY: Cornell UP, 1991.

Heywood, Leslie, and Jennifer Drake, eds. *Third Wave Agenda: Being Feminist, Doing Feminism.* Minneapolis: U of Minnesota P, 1997.

Jacob, Krista. "Engendering Change: What's Up with Third Wave?" *Sexing the Political: A Journal of Third Wave Feminists On Sexuality.* Online, available: http://www.sexingthepolitical.com/.2001.

Jensen, Michelle. "Riding the Third Wave." Rev. of *Manifesta: Young Women, Feminism, and the Future*, by Jennifer Baumgardner and Amy Richards. *The Nation Online.* Available: http://www.thenation.com/. December 2000: 11.

Klein, Melissa. "Duality and Redefinition: Young Feminism and the Alternative Music Community." Heywood and Drake, *Third Wave Agenda*. 207–25.

Leibovich, Lori. "Hey Hey, Ho, Ho, The Matriarchy's Got to Go!" *Salon*. Online, available: http://www.salon.com/. 1998.

McLaren, Margaret A. "Foucault and the Subject of Feminism." *Social Theory and Practice*. 23.1 (1997). 109–29.

Minkowitz, Donna. "Giving it Up: Orgasm, Fear, and Femaleness." Walker, *To Be Real*. 77–85.

Sawicki, Jana. "'Subjects' of Power and Freedom." Hekman, *Feminist Interpretations*.

Senna, Danzy. "To Be Real." Walker, *To Be Real*. 5–20.

Shoemaker, Leigh. "Part Animal, Part Machine: Self-Definition, Rollins Style." Heywood and Drake, *Third Wave Agenda*. 103–21.

Steinem, Gloria. "Foreword." Walker, *To Be Real*. xiii–xviii.

Straus, Tamara. "A Manifesto for Third Wave Feminism." *Alternet*. Online, available: http://www.alternet.org/. October 24, 2000.

Walker, Rebecca, ed. *To Be Real: Telling the Truth and Changing the Face of Feminism*. New York: Anchor, 1995.

95 • *Bushra Rehman and Daisy Hernández*

"INTRODUCTION"

From *Colonize This! Young Women of Color on Today's Feminism*

December 7, 2001

This morning I woke up to the news radio. Women were throwing off their veils in Afghanistan and I thought about how for years the women I have known have wanted this to happen. But now what a hollow victory it all is. I am disgusted by the us-and-them mentality. "We" the liberated Americans must save "them" the oppressed women. What kind of feminist victory is it when we liberate women by killing their men and any woman or child who happens to be where a bomb hits? I feel myself as a Muslim-American woman, as a woman of color fearing walking down the street, feeling the pain that my friends felt as they were beaten down in the weeks after September 11th. Solemnly, we counted as the numbers rose: two, five, seven . . . My friend telling me: They told me I smelled—they touched me everywhere—and when I talked back, they made fun of me, grabbed me, held my arms back, told me to go back to my country, took my money and ran. My other friend telling me: they punched me, kicked me, called me queer—they had found the pamphlets in my bag, and I'm here on asylum, for being a queer activist— my papers were just going through—I'm not safe in this country as a gay man. My other friends telling me: We didn't want to report it to the police, why just start another case of racial profiling? They're not going to find the guys who did it. They're just going to use our pain as an excuse for more violence. Use our pain as an excuse for more violence. It's what I hear again and again in a city that is grieving, that is beginning to see what other countries live every day.

But where does women of color feminism fit into all of this? Everywhere. As women of color feminists, this is what we have to think about.

—Bushra Rehman

February 12, 2002

At first I think the teacups have fallen. Broken, they sit on a shelf in the attic apartment Bushra and her sister Sa'dia share. The teacups look antique, etched with thin lines that loop like the penmanship from old textbooks. I imagine they have been in the family for years, but then I find out they were created by Sa'dia for her art exhibit. She made the cups and inscribed each one with the name of a woman from her family. Each cup represents that woman and is broken to the degree of her rebellions. Some are cracked a little, others shattered. They are piled on top of each other, as if someone needs to do the dishes.

The teacups broken and the women broken. That's how it feels sitting on this thin carpet, editing these essays on feminism while Washington wages war against terrorism. Life feels like something broken on purpose. During the Spanish evening news, a man in Afghanistan says, "It was an enemy plane and a woman cried." His words stay with me as if they were a poem. It was an enemy plane and a woman cried. I think of that woman and TV cameras in Colombia, my mother's country. The footage shows bloodied streets and women crying. My mother refuses to look. I can't look away. Her eyes are sad and grateful: my American daughter who can just watch this on TV. My aunt gives us cups of tea and tells me to watch what I say on the phone. Rumors are spreading that the FBI is making people disappear. My aunt with the wide smile. She tapes an American flag to my window, determined to keep us safe.

—Daisy Hernández

When we began editing this book, we knew only a little about each other. We were two dark-haired women who moved in overlapping circles of writers, queers, artists and feminists. We had met in New York City through the collective Women in Literature and Letters (WILL), which organized affordable writing programs that were women of color-centered. It was while editing this book, however, that we realized how much a Pakistani-Muslim girl from Queens could have in common with a Catholic, Cuban-Colombian girl from New Jersey.

We both grew up bilingual in working-class immigrant neighborhoods. Our childhoods had been steeped in the religions and traditions of our parents' homelands, and at an early age, we were well acquainted with going through customs, both at home and at the airports. We followed our parents' faith like good daughters until we became women: At fifteen, Daisy left obligatory Sunday mass and Catholicism when a nun said the Bible didn't have to be interpreted literally and no, Noah's ark had never existed. At sixteen, Bushra discovered her body—and stopped praying five times a day.

Of course, there were also differences. Bushra had been raised knowing that violence was as common as

friendship between people of color. Her family had moved from Pakistan to New York City to Saudi Arabia to Pakistan and then back to New York City. Daisy, on the other hand, had grown up with white European immigrants who were becoming white Americans, and her familia had only moved from one side of town to the other. We also broke with our families in different ways: Bushra left home without getting married; Daisy stayed home and began dating women.

Our personal rebellions led to a loss of family that took us on another path, where we met other not-so-perfect South-Asian and Latina women also working for social change. It felt like it had taken us a lifetime to find these spaces with women who gave us a feeling of familiarity and of belonging, something that had never been a given in our lives. With these women we could talk about our families and find the understanding that would help us go back home. We began to realize, however, that working with our own was only the groundwork. To make change happen we needed to partner up with other women of color. To work on this book we had to venture out of our safe zones.

And then 9/11 happened. People from our communities turned on each other in new ways. Girls wearing the hijab to elementary school were being slapped by other colored girls. Any mujer dating an Arab man was now suspect in her own community. People we considered friends were now suspicious of Middle Eastern men, Muslims and Arab immigrants, even if they were immigrants themselves. Living near Ground Zero, we watched people respond to their grief and fear with violence that escalated in both action and conversation, and we felt our own fear close to home: Daisy was afraid that, with the surge of pro-American sentiments, her mother would be mistreated for not speaking English, and Bushra feared for her mother and sisters who veil, and for her father and brothers with beards who fit the look of "terrorists."

In response to the war, we wanted to do "traditional" activist work, to organize rallies and protest on the street, but abandoning this book project didn't feel right. Darice Jones, one of our contributors, reminded us of Angela Davis's words: "We are living in a world for which old forms of activism are not enough and today's activism is about creating coalitions between communities." This is exactly our hope for this book. Despite differences of language, skin color and class, we have a long, shared history of oppression and resistance. For us, this book is activism, a way to continue the conversations among young women of color found in earlier books like *This Bridge Called My Back* and *Making Face, Making Soul.*

After many late night talks, we chose the title of Cristina Tzintzún's essay for this book in order to acknowledge how the stories of women and colonization are intimately tied. But when we first sat down to write this introduction and looked in the dictionary, we found that colonize means "to create a settlement." It sounds so simple and peaceful. We rewrote the definition. To colonize is "to strip a people of their culture, language, land, family structure, who they are as a person and as a people." Ironically, the dictionary helped us better articulate the meaning of this book. It reminded us that it's important for women of color to write. We can't have someone else defining our lives or our feminism.

Like many other women of color, the two of us first learned the language of feminism in college through a white, middle-class perspective, one form of colonization. Feminism should have brought us closer to our mothers and sisters and to our aunties in the Third World. Instead it took us further away. The academic feminism didn't teach us how to talk with the women in our families about why they stayed with alcoholic husbands or chose to veil. In rejecting their life choices as women, we lost a part of ourselves and our own history.

This is difficult to write because, initially, white feminism felt so liberating. It gave us a framework for understanding the silences and tempers of our fathers and the religious piety of our mothers. It gave us Ani Di Franco's music to sing to and professors telling us that no, patriarchy isn't only in our colored homes, it is everywhere. There is actually a system in place that we can analyze and even change.

But our experience with white feminism was bittersweet at best. Daisy felt uncomfortable talking about her parents' factory work in the middle-class living rooms where feminists met to talk about sweatshops. Bushra realized how different she was from her feminist sisters whenever there was a flare-up in the Middle East and she was asked to choose between her identity as a Muslim and an American. There was always a dualism at play between our "enlightened" feminist friends at college and the "unenlightened"

nonfeminist women in our families. We wondered how it could be that, according to feminist thought, our mothers were considered passive when they raised six children; worked night and day at stores, in factories and at home; and when they were feared and respected even by the bully on the block.

It was only after college, through word of mouth from other women of color, that we learned about another kind of feminism. These groups practiced women of color feminism, sometimes naming it as such and sometimes not saying it at all. Daisy joined WILL, a collective founded by three Latinas to use writing as a political weapon, and that's how she first read Cherríe Moraga's writings on homosexuality and began publishing her own work. Bushra joined SAWCC (South Asian Women's Creative Collective), where she found a desi audience and began performing her poetry first in New York City and eventually around the country. It was among these women that we both began developing a feminist way of looking at la vida that linked the shit we got as women to the color of our skin, the languages we spoke and the zip codes we knew as home.

Our feminism lies where other people don't expect it to. As we write this introduction, the cop who (allegedly) took part in sodomizing Abner Louima has just been released from jail. We see pictures of the cop kissing his wife splattered across the newspapers. This sanctioning of sexual violence and police brutality against a black Haitian immigrant feels like a slap in the face. As women of color, this is where our feminism lies. When the media vilifies a whole race, when a woman breaks the image of a model minority, when she leaves her entire community behind only to recreate it continually in her art and her writing, or when our neighborhoods are being gentrified, this is also where our feminism lies.

As young women of color, we have both a different and similar relationship to feminism as the women in our mothers' generation. We've grown up with legalized abortion, the legacy of the Civil Rights movement and gay liberation, but we still deal with sexual harassment, racist remarks from feminists and the homophobia within our communities. The difference is that now we talk about these issues in women's studies classes, in classrooms that are multicultural but xenophobic and in a society that pretends to be racially integrated but remains racially profiled.

We have also grown up with a body of literature created by women of color in the last thirty years—Alice Walker's words about womanism, Gloria Anzaldúa's theories about living in the borderlands and Audre Lorde's writings about silences and survival. In reading the submissions for this anthology, we found that it was the books that kept young women of color sane through college, abortions and first romances with women. Many of us just needed the books: We needed another woman of color writing about her fear of loving a dark woman's body or about being black and pregnant and feeling the scarcity of her choices.

In working with the writers in this book, we often thought of Audre Lorde's words from her poem, "A Litany for Survival": *We were never meant to survive.* Who would think that we would survive—we, young girls prey to the hands of men, the insults of teachers, the restrictive laws of holy texts and a world that tells us "this is not your world." For the young women in this book, creating lives on their own terms is an act of survival and resistance. It's also a part of a larger liberation struggle for women and people of color.

With these ideas and essays in hand, we locked ourselves up for weeks at a time until the book took form. We chose to focus on the four major themes of family and community, mothers, cultural customs and talking back. Our first section, "Family and Community: A Litany for Survival," describes how we band closer to our birth or chosen families because of the hostility in the world, of someone calling us "spic," "nigger," "fag," "terrorist" or because political and economic wars are only a phone call away to aunties living in Nicaragua or the Philippines. But family is only a safe zone until you kiss another woman, question the faith or go to the movies with a white boy. With our communities we're expected to suppress our individual selves and our dissent in order to look strong in the face of racism. In this section, mixed-race women write to those of us who question their belonging to a women of color community. Women search for chosen families, act like the "man of the house" because there isn't any man and choose different lives after being diagnosed with HIV. Their feminism and community activism are based on the model of family.

"Our Mothers, Refugees from a World on Fire" is about our inclination as young women of color to see our mothers as the "real" feminists, the ones who practice rather than preach. While college may have given us the theories, many of us return home for a working definition of what it means to be a feminist—whether that means learning lesbian femme tactics from a mom who did sex work or taking after a fearless auntie who owned a brothel in Colombia. The mothers in this section are strong women who told us to get married, go to school, pray and avoid sex. They depended on each other, on sisters, neighbors and best friends to watch over us while they themselves were coping with mental illness, poverty or raising too many kids. They are the women Cherríe Moraga wrote about twenty years ago when she said our parents were "refugees from a world on fire." We were just kids then, playing on the streets and translating for our mothers in supermarkets and at the doctor's office.

"Going through Customs," our third section, is about when every part of us is vulnerable at the checkpoint, when we're asked to check our language, our clothing, our food at the door. Many of us have been negotiating identities from the time we first step out of our parents' homes. When our parents came here with stars in their eyes and fear in their guts, they didn't realize all they would have to give up. When they hoped for a better future for us, they didn't realize they were giving up a chance to have good Hindu, good Nigerian, good Mexican daughters. "Going through customs" is our own way of picking and choosing what we will keep from our traditions and what we will bring into our lives now. It is a young black woman with guitar in hand, playing with the cultures of black and white America.

Our last section, "Talking Back, Taking Back," borrows from the title of bell hooks's book and shows women talking back to white feminists, white Americans, men on the streets, their mothers and liberals. For young women of color, so much of feminism has meant talking back and taking back the world that we live in. It is a taking back of our image, and a breaking down of roles imposed on us, whether it's that of the model minority or the affirmative action kid. These women talk back when someone tells us that racism is over because there are a handful of African Americans in the honors class, when we can't walk down the street wearing what we want because we'll be sexually harassed, when they tell us that Black women have no problem with body image just because all the women in the magazines are white. Here are women talking back to stereotypes and taking back a history that has been denied to us.

We hope that this book will introduce some of the ideas of woman of color feminism to women who have thought that feminism is just a philosophy about white men and women and has nothing to do with our communities. We also want this book to deepen conversations between young women of color. We believe that hearing each other out about our differences and similarities is an important step toward figuring out how to work with whatever divides us.

We have learned so much from the process and from each contributor. Our own work as writers has taken on more urgency because of this book and we hope other young women will also be moved to action. We know, of course, that one book can't do it all, and ironically, our lack of money and time made it difficult to reach women who also lacked those resources. But we hope that this anthology will inspire other women to fill in our gaps and move the work forward and deeper. As shani jamila writes at the end of her essay in this book: "The most important thing we can do as a generation is to see our new positions of power as weapons to be used strategically in the struggle rather than as spoils of war. Because this shit is far from finished."

(2002)

96 • *Julie Bettie*

FROM *WOMEN WITHOUT CLASS*

CLASS AS PERFORMANCE AND PERFORMATIVE

I entered the field with a good deal of cynicism about subcultural styles in the United States, in particular among white youth, assuming they would not be linked in any way to class politics. I was prepared to find that youth of color would be more able to articulate race awareness, and a related nascent class awareness, through a politics of style. For the most part, I expected to find that subcultural genres were politically vacuous styles performed by middle-class youth who were victims of the mass culture industry. In short, I did not go looking to romanticize subculture style as resistance, and especially not among girls.

But a primary way students understand class and racial/ethnic differences among themselves is through their informal peer hierarchy, with cliques and their corresponding styles largely organized by racial/ethnic and class identities. The social roles linked to group membership include curriculum choices (whether a student is on the college-prep or vocational track) and extracurricular activities (whether a student was involved in what are considered either college-prep or non-prep activities). These courses and activities combine to shape class futures, leading some girls to four-year colleges, others to vocational programs at community colleges, and still others directly to low-wage jobs directly out of high school.

While there is a strong correlation between a girl's class of "origin" (by which I mean her parents socioeconomic status), and her class performance at school (which includes academic achievement, prep or non-prep activities, and membership in friendship groups and their corresponding style), it is an imperfect one, and there are exceptions where middle-class girls perform working-class identity and vice versa. In other words, in a kind of class "passing," some students choose to perform class identities which are sometimes not their "own."

Although clique membership is not entirely determined by class, there was certainly "a polarization of attitudes toward class characteristics," and group categories (such as preps, smokers, and chola/os) were "embodiment[s] of the middle and working class[es]" (Eckert 1989, 4–5) and led to differential class futures. On the one hand, embracing and publicly performing a particular class culture mattered significantly more than origins in terms of a student's aspirations, her treatment by teachers and other students, and potentially her class future. On the other hand, class origins did matter, of course, as girls drew upon different resources from home, both economic and cultural, which shaped their life chances. Families are a crucial site where cultural capital is acquired and where class identity is formed, which individuals then bring to mixed-class settings. Class-differentiated experiences within the family provide us with different sets of symbolic and material resources (Roman 1988) and shape our experience of mixed-class public settings like schools, peer culture, and sites of leisure and consumption, where we then routinely experience and inflict class injuries upon each other. It is important to explore the way in which the construction of self is shaped by family and community life, and the way in which the family contributes to the "ideological construction of 'other'" (Weis 1990).

Because of the imperfect correlation, I came to define students not only as working- or middle-class in origin (problematic in itself), but also as working- or middle-class *performers* (and synonymously as non-prep or prep students). Girls who were passing, or metaphorically cross-dressing, had to negotiate their "inherited" identity from home with their "chosen" public identity at school. There was a disparity for them between what people looked like and talked like at home, and their own class performance at school and what their friends' parents were like. As I came to understand these negotiations of class as cultural (not political) identities, it became useful to conceptualize class not only as a material location, but also as a performance. Although my reference to middle-class and working-class performers is cumbersome, I choose it nonetheless as a constant reminder to the reader of my point that class can be conceptualized, in part, as a

performance and that there are exceptions to the class-origin-equals-class-performance rule. Many educational ethnographies make claims and generalizations about working-class students and middle-class students. If I employ the same terminology, my work may be indistinguishable from those, and my key point about class as performance and about exceptions may be lost by the end of the reading.

Exceptions to the rule aside, social actors largely display the cultural capital that is a consequence of the material and cultural resources to which they have had access. Cultural performances most often reflect one's *habitus*—that is; our unconsciously enacted, socially learned dispositions, which are not natural or inherent or prior to the social organization of class inequality, but are in fact produced by it. Here it is useful to think of class as *performative*, in the sense that class as cultural identity is an *effect* of social structure.

Little attention has been paid to thinking about *class* as a performance or as performative. To conceptualize class in this way is not to ignore its materiality. There is always the materiality of the body in thinking about race and gender (the continua of phenotype and of sex), whose meaning is negotiated and made more or less salient by culture (or, more strongly, whose materiality is created by culture). And with class there is the materiality of economic and cultural resources about which we make meaning. Cultural and political discourses that naturalize and sanction kinds of class relations and normalize institutionalized class inequality produce kinds of class subjects (poor, working, middle, rich, etc.) and material inequalities. In turn, those class subjects and material inequalities produce discourses that naturalize and normalize class inequality. . . .

In short, what is necessary to understand about my use of and distinction between the terms *performance* and *performative* is that the former refers to agency and a conscious attempt at passing. Applied to class this might mean consciously imitating middle-class expressions of cultural capital in an attempt at mobility. *Performativity*, on the other hand, refers to the fact that class subjects are the effects of the social structure of class inequality, caught in unconscious displays of cultural capital that are a consequence of class origin or habitus. Here there is no "doer behind the deed" (Hood-Williams and Harrison 1998). The dual concepts of performance and performativity thus allow me analytical room to explain the extent to which class identity is both fluid and fixed . . .

The work on performativity that comes out of cultural studies and poststructuralist feminism (Butler 1990, 1993, in particular), both of which offer a radical constructionist analysis of gender, race, and sexuality, holds something in common with the constructionism of symbolic interactionist sociology and ethnomethodology (Goffman 1959, 1967, 1974; and West and Fenstermaker 1995, in particular). There are important differences between the two, however, which are reflected in the long-standing structure/agency debate. Symbolic interactionist sociology and ethnomethodology have been long critiqued for tending toward a subject too readily construed as an active agent outside of the autonomy of social structures that preexist and produce various performances. A widespread misreading of Judith Butler's notion of performance also conceptualizes actors as agents who are free to choose identity performances. In actuality, in her poststructuralist framework there is no actor/agent who preexists the performance; rather the subject is constructed by the performance. Within the latter understanding, post-structuralism has been criticized for tending toward an overdetermined subject, one who is always already interpellated by discourse. I attempt to address both this fixity and fluidity, structure and agency, as I query how girls are constructed by and construct themselves in and with cultural discourses. . . .

I proceed by asking: What are the cultural gestures involved in the performance of class? How is class "authenticity" accomplished? And how is it imbued with racial/ethnic, sexual, and gender meaning? I hope to provide a "thick description" (Geertz 1973) of these performative intersections. Little attention has been paid to the ways in which class subjectivity, as a cultural identity, is experienced in relationship to the cultural meanings of race/ethnicity, gender, and sexuality. These various gestures of class performance never exist outside of and are always imbued with race and gender meanings. For example, as we will see among Mexican-American students, class performance was made complex by the ongoing negotiation between themselves, peers, and parents around the meanings of and links between class mobility, assimilation, and a race-based politic and identity. Because middle- or working-class performances were experienced differently across race/ethnicity, and further, because those performances

were read differently by others, dependent on the race/ethnicity of the performer, and because it is impossible to uncouple these meanings, I use the hyphenated "race-class performances of femininity" as a way to indicate that class performances have race and gender specific meanings. But I could just as well speak of "gender-class performances of race" or "race-gender performances of class." That race, class, gender, and sexual meanings and identities intersect is not simply an abstract theoretical insight. This is a multiplicity "born of history and geography" (Mohanty 1991, 37). Race/ethnicity and class and gender and sexuality are always produced and read in relationship to one another in the social world. . . .

THE SYMBOLIC ECONOMY OF STYLE

There was, at the school, a symbolic economy of style that was the ground on which class and racial/ethnic relations were played out. A whole array of gender-specific commodities were used as markers of distinction among different groups of girls, who performed race-class-specific versions of femininity. Hairstyles, clothes, shoes, and the colors of lipstick, lip liner, and nail polish, in particular, were key markers in the symbolic economy that were employed to express group membership as the body became a resource and a site on which difference was inscribed. For example, las chicas preferred darker colors for lips and nails in comparison to preps, who either went without or wore clear lip gloss, pastel lip and nail color or French manicures (the natural look). Each group was fully aware of the other's stylistic preference and knew that their own style was in opposition. In short, girls created and maintained symbolic oppositions, where "elements of behavior that come to represent one category [are] rejected by the other, and . . . may be exploited by the other category through the development of a clearly opposed element" (Eckert 1989, 50). . . .

Further, las chicas explained to me that the darker colors they chose and the lighter colors preps wore were not simply related to skin color. As Lorena explained, "It's not that, 'cause some Mexican girls who look kinda white, they wear real dark lip color" so no one will mistake them as white. And when I mentioned that I rarely saw white girls in dark lipstick, Lisa, a white prep, explained, scoffing and rolling her eyes,

Oh, there are some, but they're girls who are trying to be hard-core [meaning these were white girls who were performing chola identity]. And those hick girls [white working-class], some of them wear that bright pink crap on their lips and like *ba-loo* eye shadow!

The dissident femininity performed by both white and Mexican-American working-class girls were ethnic-specific styles, but nonetheless both sets of girls rejected the school-sanctioned femininity performed by college prep students. Working-class performers across race were perceived similarly by preps as wearing too much makeup. . . .

In spite of the meanings that working-class girls themselves gave to their gender-specific cultural markers—a desire to remain differentiated from preps—their performances were overdetermined by broader cultural meanings that code women in heavy makeup and tight clothes as low class and oversexed, in short, cheap. In other words, class differences are often understood as sexual differences, as Sherry Ortner usefully explains, where "the working class is cast as the bearer of an exaggerated sexuality, against which middle-class respectability is defined" (1991, 177). Among women, "clothing and cosmetic differences are taken to be indexes of the differences in sexual morals" between classes (178). And indeed, this was the case, as middle-class performing prep girls (both white and Mexican-American) perceived las chicas, as well as working-class performing white girls, as overly sexually active. But non-prep Mexican-American girls were seen as especially so because, although there was no evidence that they were more sexually active, they were more likely to keep their babies if they became pregnant, so there was more often a visible indicator of their sexual activity . . .

ON ACTING WHITE

Mexican-American students did have a way in which they simultaneously recognized and displaced class, at times explaining differences among themselves in racial/ethnic terms as "acting white" versus acting "the Mexican role." The class coding of these descriptions is revealed when the categories are pushed only slightly. When I asked Lorena what she meant by "acting white," she gave an animated imitation of a girl she'd met at a Future Business Leaders of America

(FBLA) meeting, affecting a stereotypical "valley girl" demeanor and speech pattern:

Ohmigod, like I can't believe I left my cell phone in my car. It was so nice to meet you girls, do keep in touch.

Lorena perceived this sentiment as quite disingenuous since they had just met. Indeed, part of working-class girls' interpretation of preps was that they were "fake"; their friendships were considered phony and insincere, always working in the interests of social ambition. Lorena went on,

I'm going to play volleyball for Harvard next year.

Clearly "Harvard" was an exaggeration on Lorena's part, but for her any university may as well have been Harvard, as it was just as distant a possibility. When I pointed out to her that she was using a "valley girl" accent, she explained:

But it's not just how they talk, it's what they talk about. Like "Let's go shopping at Nordstrom's." They brag about their clothes and cars.

I pushed for whether she thought preps really were purposefully bragging or were just unaware of how their talk affected those around them. She was convinced it was intentional: "They know. They brag."

Erica, a Filipina-American girl who had been befriended by and accepted as one of las chicas confided to me, "There's a lot of trashing of white girls really, and Mexican girls who act white." When I asked her what she meant by "acting white," her answer was straightforward:

ERICA: The preps.

JULIE: Not the smokers or the hicks or—

ERICA: Oh, no, never smokers, basically preps.

At some level, the girls knew that "acting white" didn't refer to whites generally, but to preps specifically (that is, a middle-class version of white), but class as a way of making distinctions among whites was not easily articulated. The whites most visible to them were those who inflicted the most class injuries, the preps. In fact, working-class whites were invisible in their talk, unless I asked specifically about them. The most marginalized, hard-living, working-class whites, known as the smokers, were either unknown or perplexing to most Mexican-American students. As Mariana, a Mexican-American middle-class performer, said to me, almost exasperated:

> I mean, they're white. They've had the opportunity. What's wrong with them?

The utility or necessity of describing class performances in racial terms as "acting white" is found in the difficulty all students had coming up with a more apt way of describing class differences in a society in which class discourse as such is absent. It is also found in the reality of the lives of Mexican-American students for whom the fact that race and class correlate (that people of color are overrepresented among the poor) was highly visible. This is not to say that there is nothing racial/ethnic-specific that might be named "acting white" outside of middle-classness, but it was not made clear in girls' talk what that might be.

In popular discourse, class is often not a present category of thought at all or is considered temporary (a condition of immigration) and not institutionalized. As a result, categories like race and gender, which appear to be essentially there, fixed, and natural, readily take the place of class in causal reasoning rather than being understood as intertwined with one another (for example, when class difference is read as sexual morality). In other words, class appears in popular discourse, "just not in terms we recognize as 'about class'" (Ortner 1991, 170). Read through gender and through race, class meaning is articulated in other terms. . . .

The notion of racial/ethnic authenticity is a discursive resource mobilized to perform the work of constructing racial/ethnic boundaries, boundaries that are inevitably class coded. In short, race and class are always already mutually implicated and read in relationship to one another. But when class is couched in race and ethnicity, and vice versa, it impairs our understanding of *both* social forces. Not only do we fail to learn something about class as a shaper of identity, but further, because of the conflation, we fail to learn much about the existence of racial/ethnic cultural forms and experience *across* class categories.

(2003)

---

97 • *Leslie Heywood and Jennifer Drake*

" 'IT'S ALL ABOUT THE BENJAMINS': ECONOMIC DETERMINANTS OF THIRD WAVE FEMINISM IN THE UNITED STATES"

Although conversation and debates about third wave feminism have been ongoing since the nineties, there has been a lack of theory that delineates and contextualises third wave feminist perspectives, especially in the US. This chapter provides a partial redress of this through illustrating how third wave perspectives are shaped by the material conditions created by economic globalisation and technoculture, and by bodies of thought such as postmodernism and postcolonialism. Since writers usually identified as the "third wave" are

From *Third Wave Feminism: A Critical Exploration* (Palgrave Macmillan), eds. Stacy Gillis, Becky Munford and Gill Howie (2004), pp. 13–17, 19–21. Reprinted by permission of the author. Notes have been renumbered.

most likely to be part of a generation that has come of age in these contexts, the chapter outlines some of the economic variables that have heavily impacted the current generation in the US, and demonstrates how they have resulted in a feminist movement that is not focused on narrowly defined "women's issues," but rather an interrelated set of topics including environmentalism, human rights, and anti-corporate activism. While discussions of third wave feminism have tended to limit themselves to the context of North American consumer culture—and have thus largely been identified with writers living in the US—these discussions can only have theoretical and practical value if they are set within the larger frames of globalisation and technoculture, and do not prioritise the US.

THE ECONOMICS AND DEMOGRAPHICS OF POST-BOOMER GENERATIONS IN THE US

The following are definitional criteria that delineate the economic and demographic determinants of a generational perspective, a perspective that influences critical strategies employed by women and men who identify as third wave feminists in the US. This perspective is not monolithic and it does not exclude persons of other generations, but most third wave feminists (although not all who identify as such) were born after the baby boom.[1] Transnational capital, downsizing, privatisation, and a shift to a service economy have had a drastic impact on the world these generations have inherited.

The shift away from the public works philosophy of the Roosevelt years to the free market fundamentalism of the Reagan/Thatcher years clearly contextualises the third wave tendency to focus on individual narratives and to think of feminism as a form of individual empowerment. In collections such as Barbara Findlen's *Listen Up*, Rebecca Walker's *To Be Real*, Marcelle Karp and Debbie Stoller's *The BUST Guide to the New Girl Order*, and Ophira Edut's *Adios, Barbie*, third wave writers took the second wave feminist mantra of "the personal is political" seriously, using their own experiences to help name and situate their own feminist views. This valuation of the personal as a theoretical mode has led to charges that the third wave is "a youthful continuation of individualist, middle-class liberal feminism," and that its preoccupation with

popular culture and media images is "not serious enough" (Messner 204). These charges misunderstand third wave work, which can be understood through an examination of how the lives of post-boomer women and men in the US have been impacted by economic globalisation and technoculture.

Gender-based wage and education gaps are closing, especially in younger age groups, and this relative gender equality has shaped third wave perspectives. The 1994 US census provides evidence that the wage gap has closed to within five per cent for women and men aged 20–24, and that more women now earn BA and MA degrees than do men. While women only make 78 cents overall for every dollar that men make, this varies widely depending on the group of women. The United States Department of Labor's report *Highlights of Women's Earnings in 2001* states that

> [t]he women's-to-men's earnings ration varies significantly by demographic group. Among blacks and Hispanics, for example, the ratios were about 87 and 88 percent, respectively, in 2001; for whites, the ratio was about 75 percent. Young women and men had fairly similar earnings; however, in the older age groups, women's earnings were much lower than men's. (1)

However, gender inequality persists on the highest levels of the economic ladder. The article "Women Relatively Scarce in Realms of Top Earners" makes the case that

> far more men are earning high salaries than women, with the gap narrowing only in the lowest income categories, according to a report in the New York Times on a study by the Internal Revenue Service. The IRS examined wages reported by employers in 1998 and found that 43,662 men had annual salaries of $1 million or more, while 3253 women had top earnings; a 13 to 1 ratio. Men outnumbered women 10 to 1 in the $500,000 to $1 million category, and 9 to 1 in the $250,000 to $500,000 range. The gap closed as salary range decreased, with women and men roughly equally represented in the $25,000 to $30,000 category. (1–2)

This data reveals the feminisation of poverty. It also reveals a blind spot in standard feminist analysis of women's wages. According to the United States Congress Joint Committee on Taxation, 90 per cent of American families make less than $100,000 a year, and, according to Bernie Sander, the annual income per person in the US is $28,553. This makes the $25,000–30,000 category—in which women's and men's wages are largely equal—very close to the national average. However, feminist analyses of these numbers often emphasise the fact that men comprise the vast majority of top wage earners, despite the fact that the majority of women are not "topped" in this particular manner. For example, Rory Dicker and Alison Piepmeier refer to the data that "97.3 percent of top earners are men" to help make their valid point that there is still very much a need for feminism today (6). Yet, as is characteristic of much feminist work on the gender wage gap, they fail to mention the situation of men who are not "top earners," and the relatively equal wages of men and women at lower income levels. If feminist analysis is truly differentiated for class, it becomes clear that for the majority of American women, especially in post-boomer generations, there is more gender parity in terms of wages except for the richest ten per cent of the population. . . .

Third wave feminist thinking, then, is informed by the fact that the majority of young Americans have experienced relative gender equality in the context of economic downward mobility. It has also been shaped by the racial and ethnic diversity of post-boomer generations. According to the 2000 US census, non-Hispanic whites account for 73 per cent of baby boomers and an even larger proportion of older Americans, but they account for only 64 per cent of Generation Xers and 62 per cent of the Millennial Generation (United States Census Bureau 1). These post-civil-rights generations were raised on a multicultural diet, and their attitudes about racial, cultural and sexual diversity have continued to be shaped by the increasing globalisation of entertainment and image-based industries, including the import of Asian cultural products such as anime and kung-fu films; the national dissemination of grassroots cultural practices like grunge, hip hop, and car culture; the increasing visibility of gays and lesbians in the media; and the normalisation of porn imagery.

The economic and demographic determinants of third wave feminist thinking can be catalogued as follows. First, women are *as* likely or *more* likely to identify with their generation as with their gender. Because post-boomer men and women have substantially narrowed the wage gap, because they are likely to occupy

similar entry-level to mid-level positions in workplace power structures, and because these realities mean economic struggle, women now often have more in common with men of their own age group than they do with women of previous generations.[2] Secondly, codes for "good" and "bad" as well as gender ideals are no longer polarised. This shapes the third wave's simultaneous endorsement and critique of media representations, particularly sexual imagery.[3] It also shapes third wave cultural production. For example, various aspects of girlie culture use the humorous reappropriation of traditions and symbols to craft identities in the context of structural disempowerment, such as reclaiming words like girl, bitch, and cunt. This playful reappropriation of stereotypes is often interpreted as marking a lack of seriousness, but such play is a serious part of the third wave's critical negotiations with the culture industries. Thirdly, women and men of the third wave tend not to locate meaning and identity in one place, particularly not in a job or profession. Owing to corporate downsizing and the shift to the service sector that occurred just as the oldest post-boomers reached their full-time employment years, these generations cannot expect to spend their entire lives in one workplace accruing benefits and advancing over time. While women in this demographic expect to work, the satisfaction that work offers is most often diminished. As is necessary in a global economy and workforce, workers' identities tend to be flexible and multifaceted, even contradictory. Finally, worldwide globalisation has contributed to a further concentration of wealth at the very top of the pyramid, shifting venues of political struggle from patriarchy to the World Trade Organization. The "enemy" has been decentralised. While feminist perspectives are still valuable in what Peggy Orenstein calls "this era of half-change," an economic and demographic analysis has shown that these perspectives cannot fully describe the lived conditions experienced by post-boomer generations (11).

Thus, it is clear that third wave feminists are not simply daughters rebelling for rebellion's sake.[4] Third wave lives have been and will continue to be profoundly shaped by globalisation and the new economy it fosters. What is common to the diversity of third-wave thinking is a complicated legacy; the third wave is torn between the hope bequeathed by the successes of the civil rights movement and second wave feminism, and the hopelessness born of generational downward mobility and seemingly insurmountable social and political problems worldwide. Of necessity, the third wave locates activism in a broad field that includes the kinds of issues often called "women's issues," but that also encompasses environmentalism, anticorporate activism, human rights issues, cultural production and the connections between these. In this era of half-change, when it is clear how global events intersect local lives, here is what the third wave knows: women's issues—and women activists—cannot and do not stand in isolation.

TECHNOCULTURE AND THIRD WAVE FEMINISM

Although third wave thinking can be understood in the context of post-boomer economics and demographics, it must be acknowledged that many women and men choose to identify with third wave feminist perspectives whether or not they are part of a post-boomer generation. The third wave, then, refers *both* to a feminist generation *and* to emerging forms of feminist activism. These uses of the term overlap but are not the same. They both, however, emphasise that feminism takes shape in relation to its time and place. As feminists of all generations craft responses to our current context of technoculture, new forms of activism are emerging. A discussion of feminism and technoculture demonstrates how feminist activism has shifted and why that shift cannot be wholly attributed to generational difference.

Jodi Dean describes technoculture as an economic–political–cultural formation characterised

> by the rise of networked communication [such as] the Internet, satellite broadcasting, and the global production and dissemination of motion pictures; by the consolidation of wealth in the hands of transnational corporations and the migration and immigration of people, technologies, and capital; [and] by the rise of a consumerist entertainment culture and the corresponding production of sites of impoverishment, violence, starvation, and death. (1)

. . . Through its celebratory and critical engagement with consumer culture, the third wave attempts

to navigate the fact that there are few alternatives for the construction of subjectivity outside the production/consumption cycle of global commodification. . . . The attraction of large segments of the contemporary youth market to rap music and hip hop culture cannot be merely understood as a pathological interest in violence or a "White Negro" appropriation of black male cultural expression. It also indicates a strong post-boomer identification with rap's harsh representation of economic struggle and its obsessive fantasies of economic success. These identifications occur because young women and men of all races have come of age in a contracting economy. It is interesting, then, that the primary third wave feminist texts have tended to avoid the kinds of harsh economic truths found in rap, instead favouring stories of successful sex-gender rebellion and emphasising the pleasures of girl-culture consumption enroute to cultural critique.

However, as third wave feminists grow up and out of youth culture, having come of age through claiming power, the problems created and perpetuated by technoculture must be addressed. As Dean puts it, "if this is post-patriarchy, something is definitely missing" (3). A paradox for the third wave is that this "something" is missing when it seems like alternative images are part of dominant culture like never before. Multicultural fashion models, images of female athletes like Mia Hamm and Marion Jones, the commodified male body, lesbian chic—as corporate America searched for new markets in the 1990s, difference was glorified and on display. But in this brave new world of niche marketing, everyone is valued as a potential consumer, and no one is valued intrinsically. What looked like progress was a fundamental incorporation into the global machine. As Naomi Klein points out in *No Logo*, a documentation of the rise of anticorporate activism, "for the media activists who had, at one point not so long ago, believed that better media representation would make for a more just world, one thing had become abundantly clear: identity politics weren't fighting the system, or even subverting it. When it came to the vast new industry of corporate branding, they were feeding it" (113). Third wave approaches to activism, and the third wave suspicion of traditional forms of activism, have been forged in this crucible of empowerment and exploitation. Australian third wave feminist Anita Harris argues that young women's alternative ways of conducting political organisation, protest, debate, and agitation have been shaped in response to

> the co-optation of left politics as merely a marketable style . . . The trend towards an increased surveillance of youth, the re-discovery of young women in particular as the new consumers, and the cultural fascination with girlhood, have all resulted in a deep suspicion of overt activism as the best method for protest and the creation of social change. (13)

As such, the third wave is a movement committed to local action and characterised by dispersal and diversity, as opposed to a single-leader and single-issue movement, a strategy that resists co-optation and supports survival in global technoculture.[5] Committed to cultural production as activism, and cognizant that it is impossible for most Americans to wholly exit consumer culture, third wave feminists both use and resist the mainstream media and create their own media sites and networks, both of which are key components of successful activism in technoculture. As Harris argues, "these new practices of resistance respond to corporate concentration with a maze of fragmentation, to globalization with its own kind of localization, to power consolidation with radical power dispersal" (14).

As socialist feminists have long argued, feminism is an integral part of larger social justice struggles that are framed by global capitalism. The hip hop phrase "It's all about the Benjamins" titles this chapter because it signals that the global markets that have made difference visible only value difference for its carriers' ability to consume. This has necessitated the reconceptualisation of "feminism as a movement to end all forms of oppression" (Warren 328).[6] Therefore, anti-corporate activism like the 1999 Seattle protests has, of necessity, become part of feminism's focus, which makes feminism as a movement less visible than it once was—less visible and more widely dispersed simultaneously, part of multiple social struggles. To think about third wave feminism globally is to understand that "young feminist membership is much larger than may be initially imagined, and . . . is concerned with a feminism beyond merely claiming girls' power" (Harris 9). Feminism has become part of a global struggle for human rights that incorporates women's and gender issues. Third wave theory is a theory broad enough to account for various axes of difference, and to recognise multiple forms of feminist work, including environmentalism, anti-corporate activism, and struggles for human rights. While gender play and cultural production are important parts of a third wave approach to feminist action, they are only one part of the third wave and they take place in only one site. Third wave perspectives recognise these forms of activism, and place them alongside many other kinds of work.

(2004)

NOTES

1. Generational designations—usually developed for marketers and workplace executives—are always somewhat arbitrary. The "baby-boomer" generation is commonly designated as those born between 1943–1960, "Generation X" as 1961–1981, and the "Millennial Generation" as those born between 1982 and 1998 ("Guide to Recent U.S. 'Generations'").
2. This situation parallels that of African Americans and Hispanics, who have also seen a drastic decline in real wages during the past thirty years, who have continued to identify primarily with their communities, and who have had an enormous impact on post-boomer generations in terms of both demographic numbers and cultural influence.
3. For examples of third wave perspectives on sexual imagery, see the magazines *Bitch*, *BUST*, and *Fierce*.
4. For more on this view of the third wave see Phyllis Chesler's *Letters to a Young Feminist* or Anna Bondoc and Meg Daly's collection *Letters of Intent*.
5. On the question of leaders in the third wave, see Jennifer Baumgardner and Amy Richards' "Who's the Next Gloria?"
6. While Karen Warren, who is known for her work on ecofeminism, is not identified as a third wave feminist, her insistence that "at a conceptual level the eradication of sexist oppression requires the eradication of the other forms of oppression" (327) is a concept that has been thoroughly internalised in the third wave.

"SOLITARY SISTERHOOD: INDIVIDUALISM MEETS COLLECTIVITY IN FEMINISM'S THIRD WAVE"

A third wave of feminism has emerged in the United States since the mid-1990s, grounded in the distinct generational experiences of women who have come of age after feminism's second wave. As Jennifer Baumgardner and Amy Richards describe in *Manifesta*, "For anyone born after the early 1960s, the presence of feminism in our lives is taken for granted. For our generation, feminism is like fluoride. We scarcely notice that we have it—it's simply in the water."[1] . . . Taking feminism for granted, however, has seemingly led to a more ambivalent relationship to it; while third wavers see feminism as "our birthright," to quote one commentator, when compared to the second wave feminists who came before us we seem much less secure in our ability to affect real political change, particularly if such change is premised on collective action.[2]

Self-described third wave feminists have used the term as a way to distinguish themselves, both generationally and ideologically, from second wave feminists, the generation of feminists who came of age in the late 1960s and 1970s. The publication of a number of anthologies since the mid-1990s has helped to further define what is meant by third wave feminism.[3] The feminism that has emerged from these texts makes clear that positing a shared "sisterhood," in the second wave sense of the term, has not been a major priority for third wavers. Rather than arguing for a feminism based on the shared identity "woman" or on shared political goals, as the rhetorical gesture of sisterhood once suggested, younger feminists today seem to find their collectivity mainly through a *shared generational stance* against second wave feminism and second wave feminists. . . .

Taking a generational stance against the second wave has given many third wave feminists a way to enter into feminism. Articulating this new wave primarily in generational terms, however, has hindered the development of third wave feminism as a political movement or as a critical perspective, particularly because such a movement or perspective requires solidarity premised on more than just generational location. Although the third wave has coalesced by taking a unified stance as the first post-second-wave generation, it appears to lack the other forms of collectivity that were so central to much second wave feminism. Third wave feminists rarely articulate unified political goals, nor do they often represent the third wave as sharing a critical perspective on the world. Rather, third wave texts are replete with individual definitions of feminism and individualistic narratives of coming to feminist consciousness.

The third wave's "ideology of individualism," to quote Leslie Heywood and Jennifer Drake, has found its ideal form in the autobiographical essay, the preferred writing genre of third wavers and one that shares little with the group manifestos of a previous generation.[4] The majority of third wave anthologies published since the mid-1990s have been structured around such personal essays and, correspondingly, personal definitions of feminism. As Baumgardner notes, "the personal frontier is where my generation is doing most of its work."[5] Such essays can be seen as the first step in the consciousness-raising process developed

From *Different Wavelengths: Studies of the Contemporary Women's Movement*, edited by Jo Reger. New York: Routledge, 2005. Reprinted by permission of Taylor and Francis Group LLC. Notes have been renumbered.

from the earlier women's liberation movement.[6] That is, they provide a means by which to express individual experiences and to analyze those experiences in larger social and political terms. Where the third wave has often appeared stuck, however, is in moving beyond self-expression to developing a larger analysis of the relationship between individual and collective experience, culminating in theory and political action.[7] As Gina Dent has warned, "where there is no process through which legitimate self-exploration is translated into collective benefit, the feminism drops out of Feminism and the personal fails to become political."[8]

Third wave feminists' preference for defining feminism in their own terms—that is, for each individual feminist to define feminism for herself as an individual—can be seen in the original declaration of the third wave, Rebecca Walker's "Becoming the Third Wave," written in response to the Clarence Thomas hearings and published in *Ms. Magazine* in January 1992. Her essay, devoted to explaining why feminism is still needed and why a new generation of feminists must begin to mobilize, ends with the following words: "I am not a postfeminism feminist. *I am* the Third Wave."[9] In calling for a new wave, Walker does not speak in a collective voice. There is no "we" in this statement, just an "I." An early expression of what was to become a common theme within third wave discourse, Walker's essay does not attempt to speak in the name of other women. Rather, she writes about her own individual desire to devote her life to feminism.

This approach to feminism has been echoed in many subsequent third wave texts since the mid-1990s, including *The Bust Guide to the New Girl Order* in which *Bust* editor Marcelle Karp proclaims: "We've entered an era of DIY feminism—sistah, do-it-yourself. . . . Your feminism is what you want it to be and what you make of it. Define your agenda. Claim and reclaim your F-word."[10] Comments such as these are meant to offer an alternative to the perceived dogmatism of second wave feminism in which there is only one right way to be a feminist and to do feminism. Like many third wavers, Karp steers clear of prescribing a particular feminist agenda and instead celebrates the ways in which feminism can be defined by each woman in her own terms. She tries to make feminism an open space, one which is available to all. Naomi Wolf's *Fire with Fire: The New Female Power and How It Will Change the 21st Century* has a similar goal;

ultimately, however, Wolf argues for a feminism so devoid of politics that anyone—no matter how homophobic, antichoice, or racist—can claim it for herself, as long as she's for what Wolf terms "power feminism." In the preface to the paperback edition, Wolf responds to criticisms of her project with the following:

> The question arose as to whether I redefine "feminism" so loosely that it's meaningless. One critic attacked my definition because it was one "no one could argue with." To me that is its virtue. . . . This redefinition is important because all the negative associations attached to the term are now paralyzing women.[11]

On the one hand, this call for redefinition is meant to invite more women and men into feminism, to make the term *feminist* appealing so that more people will want to claim it for themselves. Given the ways in which feminism and feminists are routinely caricaturized within the mainstream media and culture, this rehabilitation of feminism is important work, to be sure. However, when this rehab project represents feminism as nothing more than whatever one wants it to be, feminism loses its critical political perspective. Without its critiques of white supremacy and privilege, heterosexism, and capitalism—not to mention its continued insistence on examining the ways in which sexism and misogyny continue to operate in the world—feminism becomes nothing but a meaningless bumper sticker announcing "girl power." . . .

Some third wave writers have rightly cautioned against these recent trends toward redefining feminism to make it as appealing as possible or narrowly envisioning feminism around the needs of the individual. In their introduction to *Catching a Wave: Reclaiming Feminism for the 21st Century*, Rory Dicker and Alison Piepmeier write:

> [S]ometimes it seems as if everything and anyone can fit within the third wave—it doesn't matter what they actually think, do, or believe. We call this the "feminist free-for-all": under this rubric, feminism doesn't involve a set of core beliefs that one shares or goals that one works for. . . . This is the worst interpretation of bell hooks's edict that "feminism is for everybody": it implies that anybody can be a feminist, regardless of her or his actions.[12]

In insisting that feminism "must be politically rigorous" if it is to "transform our lives and our world,"

Dicker and Piepmeier offer an important alternative to many of the individualistic definitions of feminism currently being offered.[13] Yet, as they themselves acknowledge, insisting that third wave feminism be grounded in shared political goals and beliefs is a challenge to those who value the "new" feminism precisely because of its amorphous quality. As the next generation of U.S. feminists continues to define itself over the next decade, it is an open question as to which direction the third wave will take. Will third wave feminism begin to take a more overtly political and collective stance, or will it continue to develop as an individual and generational perspective?

The third wave's penchant for individual definitions of feminism is particularly striking when put against the universal claims and group manifestos characteristic of the early second wave. Slogans such as "Sisterhood is Powerful," the ubiquitous catchphrase of the late 1960s and early 1970s, stressed a common sisterhood based on the shared oppression of all women. Much early feminist theory was founded on this vision, such as the "Redstockings Manifesto," from 1969, in which the radical feminist group relies on a shared sisterhood to call women to action: "We identify with all women"; "We repudiate all economic, racial, education, or status privileges that divide us from other women"; "We call on all our sisters to unite with us in struggle."[14] In its best intentions, the feminist argument that women are sisters in a common struggle was an attempt to look beyond divisions among women toward a definition of sisterhood—and feminism—that included all women. As has been widely discussed by feminist scholars however, the rhetoric of universal sisterhood was often not accompanied by a careful analysis of differences between women, whether of race, class, sexuality, or nationality, in both the first and second waves. As the second wave of feminism developed throughout the 1970s, the idealism expressed in the frequent claim of sisterhood would rightly be challenged, and feminists would be forced to address the very real differences, that divide women and which complicate any monolithic definition of "woman"—or of feminism itself.

The feminism "in the water" that third wave feminists take for granted is decidedly postsisterhood in its assumption that feminism cannot be founded on a universal definition of women or women's experience. Critiques of second wave feminism's racism, its homophobia,

its class bias, and its inattention to other forms of oppression among women have been at the center of what many third wave feminists have learned as feminist theory and the history of the women's movement. As Ednie Kaeh Garrison notes in 2000, "It is clear now that feminist critiques of feminism are part of the very origins of Third Wave feminism rather than trailing behind an already unitary model of the movement."[15] The foundational role of "feminist critiques of feminism" to the third wave can be attributed, in part, to the central role feminists of color have played in shaping this wave's understanding of feminist theory and feminist practice, a point routinely stressed by third wave feminists of all races. . . .

In their insistence that neither "women" nor "sisterhood" can provide the natural alliance these terms once were presumed to convey, third wave feminists critique the concept of identity politics that an earlier generation saw as instrumental to political mobilization. As it was conceived by second wave feminists, as well as other civil rights groups, identity politics posits a relationship between one's gender, racial, or class experience and one's political interests, as in the Redstockings' "[w]e identify with all women." In contrast, third wave writers rarely use identity categories to make claims for an entire group, whether women or otherwise; there is little sense in these contemporary texts that identity categories can provide a coalescing structure to bring people together toward a collective political agenda. . . .

The eschewing of universal claims in the name of sisterhood can also be attributed to the political realities faced by feminists at the beginning of the twenty-first century. As Dicker and Piepmeier note:

> [T]hird wave feminism's political activism on behalf of women's rights is shaped by—and responds to—a world of global capitalism and information technology, postmodernism and postcolonialism, and environmental degradation. We no longer live in the world that feminists of the second wave faced. Third wavers . . . are therefore concerned not simply with "women's issues" but with a broad range of interlocking topics.[16]

Dicker and Piepmeier highlight the ways in which new world realities shape new forms of feminist activism, suggesting that third wave feminists will have to tackle multiple and interlocking issues rather than any one singular and clearly definable "women's issue," as could second wave feminists. Ednie Garrison echoes this point when she writes, "In the Third Wave, feminist collective consciousness may not necessarily manifest itself in a nationalized and highly mobilized social movement unified around a single goal or identity. At the moment, this hardly seems imaginable."[17] In fact, in its current manifestation, third wave feminism is more about textual and cultural production, local forms of activism, and a particular form of feminist consciousness than it is a large-scale social justice movement with unified goals.

In much of this contemporary writing, the third wave is celebrated for its more complicated, nuanced, and multifaceted understanding of women's experiences and political action—often in terms which contrast this new wave with the perceived simplistic nature of the monolithic second wave. Yet, at moments in this new writing, the inability to speak in a collective voice and for a unified goal is lamented. As Elizabeth Mitchell writes:

> The women of my mother's generation seemed given to this . . . communal effort, winning victories for the feminist movement, for their sisters, for their daughters. They had the comfort of knowing that what they fought for was needed by all members of their gender; sexual freedom, equal opportunity in the workplace, access to all the institutions of power. They also had more clear-cut antagonists to act against.[18]

Haunting Mitchell's passage is a sense of loss for what the third wave has missed out on: shared struggle, definable political goals, and targeted enemies. She seems to suggest that her generation lacks the clarity of purpose which was indicative of an earlier era . . .

In some of the third wave anthologies, one can see signs that younger feminists are beginning to move beyond their individual self-explorations of feminism toward some form of collectivity—albeit one skeptical of any easy or natural sisterhood between women. Take, for example, Joan Morgan's *When Chickenheads Come Home to Roost: My Life as Hip-Hop Feminist* (1999). As with other third wave writers, Morgan takes issue with what she perceives as dogmatic and overly prescriptive second wave feminism. Yet, like many third wave feminists of color, Morgan doesn't resort to defining feminism in solely individualistic terms, as Lehrman, Katie Roiphe, and other more conservative, and usually white, feminists have tended to do, but rather she tries to forge connections with her fellow

African-American feminists, even when to do so is difficult and painful.[19] She closes her book with the following words to her readers:

> I know that ours has never been an easy relationship. Sistahood ain't sainthood. That nonsense about if women had power there would no wars is feminist delusion at best. . . . That being said, know that when it comes to sistahood, I am deadly serious about my commitment to you. . . . sistahood is critical to our mutual survival.[20]

Making sisterhood her own by infusing it with black slang, Morgan calls for a "sistahood" for a new generation, one committed to the "mutual survival" of African-American women. Rather than distancing herself from her generational peers, she concludes her book by arguing that some form of sisterhood—no matter how difficult—is essential to the future of feminism.

Morgan's point that sisterhood, or collective action, isn't easy has been repeated by other third wave writers in their call to mobilize a new generation. JeeYeun Lee, for example, writes: "This thing called 'feminism' takes a great deal of hard work, and I think this is one of the primary hallmarks of young feminists' activism today: We realize that coming together and working together are by no means natural or easy."[21] Second wave feminists have taught us the difficulties in working with other women on shared political goals; these are the lessons inherited by the third wave, the feminism that we grow up with "in the water." While a nostalgic longing may continue to exist for that clear and unifying agenda of the past—even if that vision of the past is itself a fiction—some third wave feminists have begun to insist that we need to work toward a communal vision of feminism in the present, one that acknowledges differences among women while simultaneously arguing for a shared political commitment. As Sarah Boonin argues in "Please—Stop Thinking about Tomorrow: Building a Feminist Movement on College Campuses for *Today*":

> While feminism does not need to—and should not— mean sameness, it does imply a certain philosophical and ideological connection. We share a commitment to the pursuit of equality. That common pursuit forms the basis of our community. . . . Unless we think of ourselves as a "we"—a community of students, activists,

scholars, and national leaders—we can never be true partners in change.[22]

. . . But if Boonin's call is any indication, perhaps a "we" can still be found in that shared commitment to equality, to ending sexist oppression—and all the interlocking forms of oppression that shape women's and men's experience—in the twenty-first century. Ideally, this "we" can encompass more than just-the members of one generation. Built on the shared political goals across generations of feminists, this "we" has the possibility to transform third wave feminism from "merely" a generational stance taken by individuals to a critical political perspective that acknowledges diversity and differences within feminism while simultaneously stressing the need for collective action to affect social change.

(2005)

NOTES

1. Jennifer Baumgardner and Amy Richards, *Manifesta: Young Women, Feminism, and the Future* (New York: Farrar, Straus and Giroux, 2000), 17.

2. Rene Denfeld, *The New Victorians: A Young Woman's Challenge to the Old Feminist Order* (New York: Warner Books, 1995), 2.

3. Including Barbara Findlen, ed., *Listen Up: Voices from the Next Feminist Generation* (Seattle, WA: Seal Press, 1995); Rebecca Walker, ed., *To Be Real: Telling the Truth and Changing the Face of Feminism* (New York: Anchor, 1995); Leslie Heywood and Jennifer Drake, eds., *Third Wave Agenda: Being Feminist, Doing Feminism* (Minneapolis: University of Minnesota Press, 1997); Ophira Edut, ed., *Adiós Barbie: Young Women Write About Body Image and Identity* (New York: Seal Press, 1998); Anna Bondoc and Meg Daly, eds., *Letters of Intent: Women Cross the Generations to Talk About Family, Work, Sex, Love and the Future of Feminism* (New York: Simon and Schuster, 1999); Daisy Hernández and Bushra Rehman, eds., *Colonize This! Young Women of Color and Today's Feminism* (New York: Seal Press, 2002); Rory Dicker and Alison Piepmeier, eds., *Catching a Wave: Reclaiming Feminism for the 21st Century* (Boston: Northeastern University Press, 2003).

4. Leslie Heywood and Jennifer Drake, "Introduction," in *Third Wave Agenda,* 11.

5. Jennifer Baumgardner in Katha Pollitt and Jennifer Baumgardner, "Afterword: A Correspondence Between Katha Pollitt and Jennifer Baumgardner," in *Catching a Wave,* 316.

6. Jennifer Baumgardner and Amy Richards seem hopeful in this regard when they write that such autobiographical anthologies provide "the foundation of the personal ethics upon which a political women's movement will be built." Baumgardner and Richards, *Manifesta,* 20.

7. An exception can be found in *Catching a Wave,* where editors Rory Dicker and Alison Piepmeier explicitly describe their anthology's format as following the second wave principle of consciousness raising in order to move the reader from personal experience to theory and action. See Dicker and Piepmeier, "Introduction," in *Catching a Wave,* 3–28.

8. Gina Dent, "Missionary Position," in *To Be Real,* 64.

9. Rebecca Walker, "Becoming the Third Wave," *Ms. Magazine,* (January/February 1992): 41; emphasis added.

10. Marcelle Karp, "Herstory: Girl on Girls," in *The Bust Guide to the New Girl Order,* ed. Marcelle Karp and Debbie Stoller (New York: Penguin Books, 1999), 310.

11. Naomi Wolf, *Fire with Fire: The New Female Power and How It Will Change the 21st Century* (New York: Random House, 1993), xix.

12. Dicker and Piepmeier, "Introduction," 17.

13. Ibid., 18.

14. Redstockings, "Redstockings Manifesto," in *Sisterhood is Powerful: An Anthology of Writings from the Women's Liberation Movement,* ed. Robin Morgan (New York: Vintage Books, 1970), 535.

15. Ednie Kaéh Garrison, "U.S. Feminism-Grrrl Style! Young (Sub)Cultures and the Technologies of the Third Wave," *Feminist Studies* 26, no. 1 (Spring 2000): 145.

16. Dicker and Peipmeier, "Introduction," 10. As Daisy Hernandez and Bushra Rehman write in their introduction to Colonize This!: "We are living in a world for which old forms of activism are not enough and today's activism is about creating coalitions between communities." Rehman and Hernandez, "Introduction," xxi.

17. Garrison, "U.S. Feminism-Grrrl Style!" 164.

18. Mitchell, "An Odd Break with the Human Heart," 52.

19. See Lehrman, *The Lipstick Proviso*; Katie Roiphe, *The Morning After: Sex, Fear, and Feminism on Campus* (Boston, MA: Little, Brown, 1993).

20. Joan Morgan, *When Chickenheads Come Home to Roost: My Life as Hip-Hop Feminist* (New York: Simon and Schuster, 1999), 231–32. For more on black feminist texts, see Springer, chapter 1.

21. Lee, "Beyond Bean Counting," 211.

22. Sarah Boonin, "Please—Stop Thinking about Tomorrow: Building a Feminist Movement on College Campuses for *Today*," in *Catching a Wave,* 149.

SECTION THREE

Bridging the Local and the Global: Feminist Discourses on Colonialism, Imperialism, and Globalization

INTRODUCTION

Global issues appeared to be placed solidly on the feminist agenda when the United Nations' "Decade of the Women" (1975–1985) was followed a decade later by the United Nations' Fourth World Conference on Women in Beijing, China, and the Forum for Non-Governmental Organizations in Huairou, China. These historic conferences provided feminists with hope for the future and valuable insights into the ways their own lives locally were intertwined with the lives of women across the globe. However, they also revealed how the increasing feminization of global labor fragmented women's solidarity by pitting women of diverse classes, races, ethnicities, and nations against each other. Global divisions between women were sorely exacerbated by the traumatic events surrounding September 11, 2001, and the military conflicts the United States and its allies waged in Iraq and Afghanistan. These conflicts were accompanied by the resurgence of nationalism and religious fundamentalism at home and abroad—both of which have a long history of dividing women's solidarity and circumscribing their rights.

To enhance our understanding of global issues, this section of the anthology focuses on how feminists applied their theoretical perspectives to the topics of colonialism, imperialism and globalization from the mid-nineteenth century to the present. By holding the topic constant, paradigm shifts in global feminist thought from early modernity to postmodernity should become more visible.

CONCEPTUALIZING IMPERIALISM AND COLONIALISM

The last three chapters of this anthology will show how new conceptual schemes arose to address global processes in early modernity, late modernity, and post-modernity. We begin by introducing some major concepts that were used to distinguish forms of imperialism and colonialism in early modernity following the analytical distinctions made by one of the earliest feminist theorists of imperialism, Rosa Luxemburg. Her book, *The Accumulation of Capital*, first published in 1913, stands today as one of the major theoretical works on imperialism written in early modernity.

Imperialism refers to a foreign power's forceful extension of economic, political, and cultural domination over other nations or geopolitical formations. However, Luxemburg distinguished between premodern and modern forms of imperialism. Premodern forms, such as the imperial conquests of Ancient Rome, subjugated indigenous populations and exploited them largely through heavy taxation, but generally left their forms of production in place. By contrast, **modern imperialism** destroys indigenous forms of production by usurping and privatizing land and forcing premodern economies into market economies (Luxemburg, [1913] 1951: 416; and [1908] 2004: 110).

Colonialism refers to a foreign power holding direct political control over another country or geopolitical region. In **colonies of rule** foreign governments use an oligarchy of colonial administrators to organize the social, cultural, economic, and political life of indigenous people in the colonies and to facilitate their home country's economic and political aims (McMichael, 1996: 17). British rule in India exemplifies this type of colonialism. By contrast, in **settler colonialism** or **internal colonialism** the rule by colonial administrators is accompanied by immigrants who settle on the lands of indigenous peoples and who wield social, cultural, economic, and political domination over them (McMichael, 1996: 17). As discussed in Chapter 5, internal colonies are groups subjugated in the following ways: their entry to the host country is often by brute force; they are forced to assimilate the dominant group's language and culture; they are denied the same "citizenship" rights enjoyed by the dominant group; and they often are relegated to subordinate labor markets or lowly paid, menial forms of work (Blauner, 1972). Institutional racism is an integral part of this process (Memmi, [1957] 1991: 73–74).

Despite the long history of various forms of imperialism and colonialism that have impacted the area we now call the United States, theories of modern imperialism were late-nineteenth and early-twentieth-century inventions. These theories were Western or Eurocentric in the sense that whether the theorist was a supporter or critic of imperialism, all of these theories were written from the vantage point of Western or European global social locations.[1] This Western approach to analyses of imperialism and colonialism would influence U.S. feminist thought for much of the next century.

CHAPTER 8

Feminism and Imperialism in Early Modernity

Militarism is the oldest and has been the most unyielding enemy of woman.

—Carrie Chapman Catt, 1901

INTRODUCTION[2]

In earlier chapters, we discussed how U.S. feminists responded to the forms of internal colonialism experienced by African Americans as a result of slavery, as well as the postemancipation segregation laws that operated in much of the United States until the victories of the civil rights movement. The readings in this chapter examine how first-wave feminists responded to the U.S. government's annexation of new lands both at home and abroad in the nineteenth and early twentieth centuries. As Allison Sneider points out in *Suffragists in an Imperial Age: U.S. Expansion and the Woman Question* (2008), for most first-wave suffragists colonialism and imperialism were associated with expansion onto new lands (115–116). When new lands were annexed, whether in the American West or overseas, legal and constitutional issues over citizenship and suffrage were reopened. In this way, debates over "the Woman Question" remained integrally interwoven with debates over U.S. colonialism and imperialism.

U.S. WESTERN EXPANSION AND THE WOMAN QUESTION

Given that the first women's rights convention in the United States—the Seneca Falls Convention—took place in 1848, U.S. feminists were not sufficiently mobilized to adequately address as a women's movement the annexation of Mexican lands and the Mexican–American War which took place in that same year. Nevertheless, one of the most influential political tracts ever written on nonviolent forms of resistance was a protest against the Mexican–American War—"Civil Disobedience" ([1849] 2013). Excerpts from this iconic work by abolitionist and women's rights activist Henry David Thoreau can be found in Reading 99, which focuses on the individual's relationship to the state and how to deal with laws believed to be unjust. Because tax revenues provide the funds for wars, Thoreau refused to pay taxes and was jailed for his nonviolent resistance.

The first published Chicana narrative written in English from the perspective of the conquered Mexican population after the Mexican–American War was by María Amparo Ruiz de Burton. Selections from her novel *The Squatter and the Don* ([1885] 1997) in Reading 102 reveal how Mexican ranchers living in California viewed the Treaty of Guadalupe Hidalgo signed at the end of that war. Although her novel is a historical romance, Ruiz de Burton interweaves the voices of the conquered Mexicans to challenge dominant discourses of that era that touted the "American way" as a just and democratic system (Sanchez and Pita, 1997: 7).

The bloodiest American battle of the nineteenth century was the Civil War. Indeed, the death and injury toll from this war far exceeds that of any war the United States has been involved in from the American Revolution to the present. Few people today realize that the first Mother's Day Proclamation, written by Julia Ward Howe in 1870,[3] spoke directly to this carnage and was designed to unify women against any future wars. This anti-war proclamation can be found in Reading 100.

As federal troops withdrew from the South, the federal government increasingly turned its attention westward. As early as 1871, Congress passed legislation declaring that "hereafter no Indian nation or tribe within the territory of the United States shall be acknowledged or recognized as an independent nation, tribe, or power with whom the United States may contract by treaty" (Sneider, 2008: 62). Between 1860 and 1880, the population of the western states and territories nearly doubled. The conflicts that flared between indigenous peoples and the settler colonialists represented a clash between distinct modes of production and social formations. As hunters and gatherers, many Native Americans lived within more communal, subsistence-oriented social formations that depended on open access to the land and natural resources. By contrast, the way of life of the settler colonialists was predicated on privatized land ownership and commercial production, which meant dividing and fencing in these lands. Family farmers, as well as the capitalist farmers, ranchers, and railroad companies, had vested interests in making commodity forms transcontinental so as to expand the markets for their commodities. The settlers saw the West as an "open frontier" for social and economic development. That this "frontier" was inhabited by indigenous peoples whose way of life was predicated on its continued openness created the social contradictions that erupted in the Indian Wars that raged across the West in the late nineteenth century.

The extent of what Rosa Luxemburg called the devastation of premodern societies was visible in western colonization. In 1850 Native peoples still had control over approximately one half of the land mass of the area now called the United States. By 1880 they controlled about one eighth of this area, whereas today the 314 reservations scattered across the United States account for just 2 percent of the country's land area. When the first Europeans arrived in the late fifteenth century it is estimated that the indigenous population numbered in the millions. By the beginning of the twentieth century, they numbered a mere 250,000 (Macionis, [2002] 2011; Dobyns, 1966; Tyler, 1973). The decimation of the indigenous population was the result of a number of factors, including their inability to cope with the new diseases brought by white settlers, the scarcity of wild game that accompanied western settlement, and outright **genocide** by the U.S. military.

Although Native Americans would not obtain U.S. citizenship and suffrage until 1924, as early as the 1870s a number of national legislators increasingly favored giving Native Americans citizenship to "resolve the hostilities"; this was the major impetus of a proposed bill in 1877 that sought to turn indigenous peoples across the continent into U.S. citizens (Sneider, 2008: 57 and 61). This bill generated intense debates. Many Native Americans rejected citizenship because it would mean that their tribal lands would be broken up and privatized and their communal strength weakened.

A few white, middle-class suffragists took up the Native Americans' cause. These suffragists were often women who had grown up in close proximity to indigenous tribes and who, from their early childhood, had closer associations with native peoples. Reading 101 is by one of the presidents of the National Women's Suffrage Association, Matilda Joslyn Gage, who was raised in New York near the Iroquois nation. Her article "Indian Citizenship" ([1878] 1998) described how this proposed "gift of citizenship" would enable the U.S. government to end tribal sovereignty and "would open wide the door to the grasping avarice of the white man for Indian lands" (Gage [1878] 1998: 36).

Although Gage decried the brutal treatment of indigenous people in her writings and was even admitted to the Iroquois Council of Matrons, she was angered when the federal government seemed poised to give citizenship and suffrage to Native American males. Like many other white, middle-class suffragists, Gage feared that extending voting rights to Native American men would make it even harder for women to gain the vote. This latter view was the position taken at the National Women's Suffrage Association convention of 1877, where the question of Native American citizenship and suffrage became a topic of movement concern. Signed by the Association's new president, Clemence Lozier, as well as by Susan B. Anthony, this convention's announcement declared that "Indian men" as voters would create "an additional peril" to the women citizens of the United States and that they were likely to "vote solid against woman suffrage" like "Mexicans, half-breeds, [and other] ignorant, vicious men" (quoted in Sneider, 2008: 63). In this same announcement, they claimed that "Indian men turned their women into beasts of burden" (Sneider, 2008: 64). In this way, they targeted the vileness of indigenous men, but could still show sympathy for indigenous women.

These suffragists failed to make the connection between Native American women's productive labor as gatherers and horticulturalists and their political rights within their tribes, unlike Friedrich Engels's analysis in Reading 41 of Chapter 4. Indeed, one of the real tragedies for indigenous women was that when settler colonialists imposed their "civilized views" on indigenous peoples, they eroded the equality that Native American women shared with men in some tribes. For example, in tribes where Native American women were the major cultivators, U.S. government officials encouraged and even legislated that Native American men take over farming. As contemporary Native American feminist activist Wilma Mankiller writes,

> Our tribe and others which were matriarchal[4] have become assimilated and have adopted the cultural value of the larger society, and, in doing, we've adopted sexism. We're going forward and backward at the same time. As we see a dilution of the original values, we see more sexism. (Mankiller quoted in Mihesuah, 2003: 42)

Although many indigenous voices from this era have been lost to history, a few survived.[5] Reading 110 by Waheenee from the Hidatsa tribe bemoans the loss of "our Indian ways" and laments how her son, who grew up in a "white man's school," helps teach her people how to "follow the white man's road" (Waheenee, [1921] 1987).[6] Reading 109 by Zitkala-Sa (Gertrude Bonnin) from the Dakota Sioux tribe discusses her harsh experiences in the Indian school she attended. She also describes how her mother cursed the white settlers who lived in camps on a hillside near their wigwam, waiting like vultures to make claims on their land (Zitkala-Sa, ([1921] 2008: 40–43). Reading 103 is a poem by Tekahionwake (Emily Pauline Johnson) describing an Indian wife's farewell to her warrior husband who is fighting to protect their land from the "greed of the white men's hands" (Tekahionwake, 1885).[7]

Aside from these indigenous voices, one of the most empathetic and politically progressive positions taken toward Native Americans by first-wave feminists can be found in Anna Julia Cooper's *A Voice from the South* (1892). In Reading 64 titled "Women versus the Indian" ([1892] 1998), Cooper directly responds to papers presented at the National Woman's Council of 1891 by Susan B. Anthony and Anna Shaw who had highlighted the "inferiority" of Native American men to underscore why these men should not be given the vote. Cooper writes,

> The cause of freedom is not the cause of race or a sect, a party or a class—it is the cause of human kind. . . . If the Indian has been wronged and cheated by the puissance of this American Government, it is woman's mission to plead with her country to cease to do evil and to pay its honest debts . . . Let her rest her plea, not on Indian inferiority, nor on Negro depravity, but on the obligation of legislators to do for her as they would have others do for them were relations reversed. ([1892] 1998: 107–108)

Notably, Cooper also criticized overseas imperialism in her 1925 doctoral dissertation, "L'Attitude de la France à l'égard de l'esclavage pendant la Révolution" ("France's Attitudes toward Slavery during the Revolution").[8] This study focused on how the French dealt with the contradiction of maintaining slavery in their colonies, while heralding liberty, equality, and fraternity at home. Cooper concluded that the fate of the colonies was not a result of their alleged backwardness, but because of the ways colonizing powers exerted their influence and appropriated natural and human resources (Lemert and Bhan, 1998: 268–269).

U.S. OVERSEAS EXPANSION AND THE WOMAN QUESTION

The Spanish–American War is considered the turning point in American history, when the United States translated its growing industrial might into military and political power on a global scale. From the last decade of the nineteenth century to World War I, the United States took possession of Hawaii, the Philippines, Puerto Rico, Guam, and Samoa. It established protectorates over Cuba, Panama, and the Dominican Republic and mounted armed interventions in Mexico, Haiti, and Nicaragua (Fain, 2005).

In the 1890s the two major suffrage organizations combined to form the National American Women's Suffrage Association (NAWSA) in an effort to provide a more powerful, united front to win suffrage for American women. Yet, NAWSA did not side with anti-imperialists. Rather, it split over this issue. Many white, middle-class suffragists claimed that ignorant and illiterate people were incapable of self-government (Giddings, 1984; Terborg-Penn, 1998). They also did not hesitate to reveal their fears of people of color as violent and savage. Susan B. Anthony writes, "It is nonsense to talk about giving those guerrillas in the Philippines their liberty for that's all they are that are waging this war. If we did, the first thing they would do would be to murder and pillage every white person on the island" (Anthony quoted in Hoganson, 2001: 13–14).

Even in later years when many of these same feminists argued for women's suffrage in Hawaii, Puerto Rico, and the Philippines, they only supported suffrage for literate people (Sneider, 2008: 109). Such limits would mean, for example, that of the 110,000 inhabitants of Hawaii in 1893, the number of eligible voters would have been around 2,700 (98). Reading 104 is one of Elizabeth Cady Stanton's writings "On Educated Suffrage" ([1897] 2013). Reading 105 includes a "Petition for the Women of Hawaii" written by Susan B. Anthony and Elizabeth Cady Stanton ([1899] 2013), as well as a response to this petition by Samuel Gompers on behalf of the American Federation of Labor (Gompers, [1899] 2013). Anthony and Stanton urge the U.S. government to allow women's suffrage in Hawaii, whereas Samuel Gompers criticizes these suffragists for their colonialist stance. Although his organization supported suffrage for U.S. women, he states that neither these U.S. feminists nor the U.S. government have the right to decide the laws of Hawaii. Rather, if these suffragists really believed in self-government, then Hawaiians should decide how their laws and government are framed.

An issue that generated some anti-imperialist sentiment among suffragists during the Philippine–American War was the revival of assertions that women should not vote because they did not render military service. In her address as president of NAWSA in 1901, Carrie Chapman Catt highlighted this point, arguing that "militarism is the oldest and has been the most unyielding enemy of woman" (quoted in Hoganson, 1998: 195). As claims of male privilege based on military service grew in strength, Catt formally endorsed Philippine independence while visiting Manila for a suffrage meeting of Filipina and U.S. activists (Hoganson, 2001: 26).

The major organization that protested U.S. imperial policies was the **Anti-Imperialist League** founded in 1898 during the Spanish–American War (Beisner, 1968).[9] Although the Anti-Imperialist League did not support suffrage, a number of suffragists were members of the league. Jane Addams, who was active in Chicago's Anti-Imperialist League, spoke adamantly against the brutality of the armed interventions undertaken by the United States (Winant, 2007). Charlotte Perkins Gilman was also a member, although she did not write extensively on the issue of imperialism. The prominent feminist and pacifist from Montana, Jeannette Rankin, was active in the league and was the first woman elected to the U.S. House of Representatives in 1916. She was one of only fifty Representatives to cast votes against the United States entering World War I.

The anarchist feminist Emma Goldman was among the most vocal first-wave feminists in condemning U.S. imperialism. In Reading 106, from *Patriotism: a Menace to Liberty* (1911), she specifically attacked U.S. policies in the Mexican–American War, in Cuba, and in the Spanish–American War:

Indeed, conceit, arrogance, and egotism are the essentials of patriotism . . . Patriotism assumes that our globe is divided into little spots . . . Those who have had the fortune of being born on some particular spot, consider themselves better, nobler, grander, more intelligent than the living beings inhabiting any other spot. It is, therefore, the duty of everyone living on that chosen spot to fight, kill, and die in the attempt to impose his superiority upon all the others. (Goldman, ([1911] 1917: 134–135)[10]

Although jailed many times for her activism, Goldman's longest jail term was for her activism against the involuntary conscription of men during World War I.

Some U.S. feminists kept up the struggle against imperialism throughout World War I and even after the American Anti-Imperialist League disbanded in 1921. Carrie Chapman Catt and Jane Addams formed the first Women's Peace Party (WPP) in 1915 that called for global women's suffrage and for U.S. women to attend an international conference to seek ways of ending war. That same year, the WPP sent representatives to an International Women's Congress for Peace and Freedom[11] where more than 1,000 participants from both neutral and warring nations adopted the resolutions that can be found in Reading 108 (Addams et al., 1915). Even attending this meeting was an act of heroism because participants faced severe censure at home for undercutting their nation's war efforts (Sklar et al., 1998: 43 and 205). Addams writes,

> The great achievement of this congress to my mind is the getting together of these women from all parts of Europe, when their men-folks are shooting each other from opposite trenches . . . it is a supreme effort of heroism to rise to the feeling of internationalism, without losing patriotism. (Addams quoted in Sklar et al., 1998: 204)

In later years the WPP became the U.S. section of the Women's International League for Peace and Freedom, which is the oldest international women's peace organization in the world (Alonso, 1993; Schott, 1997; Rupp, 1997).

ROSA LUXEMBURG ON IMPERIALISM AND THE WOMAN QUESTION

Marxist feminist Rosa Luxemburg's writings on women are sparse compared with her writings on social class and imperialism. Not surprisingly, her views on women's suffrage reveal her ever close attention to class issues. For example, in "Women's Suffrage and Class Struggle" (1912), Luxemburg argued that governments who refused to allow women's suffrage were primarily concerned about working-class women winning the vote and voting against laws that favor big business. Also evident in this reading is her disdain for bourgeois women, whom she views as parasites who live off the labor of others.

In her major treatise on imperialism, *The Accumulation of Capital* ([1913] 1951), she focused on the economic factors that compelled capitalist enterprises to expand beyond their national borders. For Luxemburg, the imperialist destruction of natural economies exemplified the process of **primitive accumulation** or the use of brute force and violence to subjugate premodern peoples, to usurp and privatize their land, and to turn premodern subsistence economies into market economies. Because of this, she saw militarism an integral part of the logic of modern imperialism. Reading 107 titled "Militarism as a Province of Accumulation" (1913) is from the last chapter of her book and discusses how militarism drained tax dollars that could be used for more humane purposes, as well as how imperial governments' constant demands for new, more technologically sophisticated weaponry filled the coffers of the capitalist armaments industries. Thus, Luxemburg's theory of imperialism recognized the rise of both a permanent arms economy and the military–industrial complex—insights that would be more fully developed decades later by other neo-Marxists (Magdoff, 1969).

Few Marxists of her era ever matched Luxemburg's depth of concern over the Western imperialist destruction of premodern social relations (Hudis and Anderson, 2004: 17). Instead of highlighting the backwardness of such formations, she focused on their extraordinary tenacity, elasticity, and adaptability. In particular, she emphasized how European imperialism destroyed the world's remaining indigenous communal formations—formations that had "afforded the most productive labor process and the best assurance of its continuity and development for many epochs" (Luxemburg quoted in Hudis and Anderson, 2004: 16). In her *Introduction to Political Economy* ([1908] 2004) Luxemburg writes,

> The intrusion of European civilization was a disaster in every sense for primitive social relations. . . . ripping the land from underneath the feet of the native population . . . What emerges is something that is worse than all oppression and exploitation, total anarchy and a specifically European phenomenon, the uncertainty of existence. (Luxemburg, [1908] 2004: 110)

This theme of the ruination of natural economies pervades Luxemburg's critiques of the impact of French imperialism in Algeria, of British imperialism in India and China, of U.S. imperialism in the Pacific and Latin America, and of various European colonial ventures in Southern Africa. Her focus on how imperialism devastated premodern societies would inspire a number of contemporary global feminist theorists, as we shall see in the next chapter.

ANTI-WAR WRITINGS BETWEEN THE WAVES

We end this chapter with one of the most celebrated feminist anti-war writings written between the first and second waves. Reading 111 provides excerpts from Virginia Woolf's famous anti-war essay *Three Guineas* (1938). It is structured as her response to an upper-class man's request to join his efforts to prevent war. Although Woolf was a pacifist, she uses this format to level a scathing critique of patriarchal privilege and to explain why the standpoint of women is (or should be) entirely different from the standpoint of men on militarism and war. Here readers can find her celebrated statement: ". . . in fact, as a woman, I have no country. As a woman I want no country. As a woman my country is the whole world." (2008: 313).

CONCLUSION

The readings in this chapter exemplify the importance of reclaiming our historical past for enhancing our understanding of the theories and practices of the U.S. women's movement. Nevertheless, compared to feminist scholarly work on other topics, far less attention has focused on how the first wave of the women's movement responded to U.S. overseas imperialism.[12] It is rare to find references to this topic in any feminist texts. Consequently, we hope this chapter will spur more research on the relationship between feminism, imperialism, and militarism in early modernity.

NOTES

1. Other major nineteenth- and early-twentieth-century works on modern imperialism include John Hobson's *Imperialism: A Study* ([1902] 1971), Rudolf Hilferding's *Finance Capital* ([1910] 2007), V. I. Lenin's *Imperialism: The Highest Stage of Capitalism* ([1917] 1996), and Joseph Schumpeter's *Imperialism and Social Classes* ([1919] 1955).

2. Parts of this introduction are drawn from Susan. A. Mann, "Feminism & Imperialism, 1890–1920: Our Anti-Imperialist Sisters—Missing in Action from American Feminist Sociology," *Sociological Inquiry*, 2008, 59 (4): 461–489). The author thanks John Wiley and Sons for permission to reprint them.

3. See http://www.peace.ca/mothersdayproclamation.htm (retrieved March 3, 2014).

4. There are debates over whether the term "matrilineal" is a more accurate description of these tribes. Whereas "matrilineal" refers to tracing lines of descent through the mother, "matriarchal" implies domination of men and children by women. Some anthropologists argue that there never have been any matriarchal societies.

5. The Native American writings in this chapter survived because Zitkala-Sa learned English in an Indian school, Tekahionwake was of mixed ancestry having a Mohawk father and a British mother, and Waheenee told her stories to an interested anthropologist.

6. See http://www.californiaindianeducation.org/inspire/traditional/ (retrieved October 8, 2013).

7. See http://www.poemhunter.com/i/ebooks/pdf/emily_pauline_johnson_ tekahionwake__2012_5.pdf (retrieved October 28, 2014) for Tekahionwake's poem.

8. Anna Julia Cooper's 1925 dissertation was later published in 1988 as *Slavery and the French Revolutionists: 1788–1805*, Trans. Frances Richardson Keller. Lewiston, N.Y.: Mellon Press.

9. The politics of Anti-Imperialist League members crossed the political spectrum. The League included leftists such as W. E. B. Dubois, who was committed to self-government abroad, as well racists such as Varina Howell Davis (Jefferson Davis's wife) whose "most serious objection to making the Philippines American territory" was because "three-fourths of the population is made up of Negroes" (Davis quoted in Foner and Winchester, 1984: 235). However, the vast majority of members objected to the antidemocratic nature of U.S. imperialism and to the irony that a former colony would become a colonial master.

10. See http://ucblibrary3.berkeley.edu/Goldman/Writings/Anarchism/patriotism.html (retrieved October 28, 2014).

11. Although these first-wave organizations are called "international" organizations, they only included representatives from First World countries in Europe and North America (Ferree and Tripp, 2006).

12. Allison Sneider's *Suffragists in an Imperial Age: U.S. Expansion and the Woman Question* (2008) and Kristin Hoganson's *Fighting for American Manhood: How Gender Politics Provoked the Spanish–American and Philippine–American Wars, 1870–1929* (1998) provide some of the best feminist scholarship to date on the response of first-wave suffragists to imperialism.

"CIVIL DISOBEDIENCE"

I HEARTILY ACCEPT the motto,—"That government is best which governs least"; and I should like to see it acted up to more rapidly and systematically. Carried out, it finally amounts to this, which also I believe,—"That government is best which governs not at all"; and when men are prepared for it, that will be the kind of government which they will have. Government is at best but an expedient; but most governments are usually, and all governments are sometimes, inexpedient. The objections which have been brought against a standing army, and they are many and weighty, and deserve to prevail, may also at last be brought against a standing government. The standing army is only an arm of the standing government. The government itself, which is only the mode which the people have chosen to execute their will, is equally liable to be abused and perverted before the people can act through it. Witness the present Mexican war, the work of comparatively a few individuals using the standing government as their tool; for, in the outset, the people would not have consented to this measure. . . .

But, to speak practically and as a citizen, unlike those who call themselves no-government men, I ask for, not at once no government, but *at once* a better government. Let every man make known what kind of government would command his respect, and that will be one step toward obtaining it . . .

Can there not be a government in which majorities do not virtually decide right and wrong, but conscience?—in which majorities decide only those questions to which the rule of expediency is applicable? Must the citizen ever for a moment, or in the least degree, resign his conscience to the legislator? Why has every man a conscience, then? I think that we should be men first, and subjects afterward. It is not desirable to cultivate a respect for the law, so much as for the right.

The only obligation which I have a right to assume is to do at any time what I think right. It is truly enough said that a corporation has no conscience; but a corporation of conscientious men is a corporation *with* a conscience. Law never made men a whit more just; and, by means of their respect for it, even the well-disposed are daily made the agents of injustice. A common and natural result of an undue respect for law is, that you may see a file of soldiers, colonel, captain, corporal, privates, powder-monkeys, and all, marching in admirable order over hill and dale to the wars, against their wills, ay, against their common sense and consciences, which makes it very steep marching indeed, and produces a palpitation of the heart. They have no doubt that it is a damnable business in which they are concerned; they are all peaceably inclined. Now, what are they? Men at all? or small movable forts and magazines, at the service of some unscrupulous man in power? . . .

How does it become a man to behave toward this American government to-day? I answer, that he cannot without disgrace be associated with it. I cannot for an instant recognize that political organization as *my* government which is the *slave's* government also . . .

In other words, when a sixth of the population of a nation which has undertaken to be the refuge of liberty are slaves, and a whole country is unjustly overrun and conquered by a foreign army, and subjected to military law, I think that it is not too soon for honest men to rebel and revolutionize. What makes this duty the more urgent is the fact that the country so overrun is not our own, but ours is the invading army. . . .

There are thousands who are *in opinion* opposed to slavery and to the war, who yet in effect do nothing to put an end to them; who, esteeming themselves

Originally published as "Resistance to Civil Government" in the periodical *Aesthetic Papers* (1849).

children of Washington and Franklin, sit down with their hands in their pockets, and say that they know not what to do, and do nothing; who even postpone the question of freedom to the question of free-trade, and quietly read the prices-current along with the latest advices from Mexico, after dinner, and, it may be, fall asleep over them both. What is the price-current of an honest man and patriot to-day? They hesitate, and they regret, and sometimes they petition; but they do nothing in earnest and with effect. They will wait, well disposed, for others to remedy the evil, that they may no longer have it to regret. At most, they give only a cheap vote, and a feeble countenance and Godspeed, to the right, as it goes by them. There are nine hundred and ninety-nine patrons of virtue to one virtuous man; but it is easier to deal with the real possessor of a thing than with the temporary guardian of it. . . .

It is not a man's duty, as a matter of course, to devote himself to the eradication of any, even the most enormous wrong; he may still properly have other concerns to engage him; but it is his duty, at least, to wash his hands of it, and, if he gives it no thought longer, not to give it practically his support. If I devote myself to other pursuits and contemplations, I must first see, at least, that I do not pursue them sitting upon another man's shoulders. I must get off him first, that he may pursue his contemplations too. See what gross inconsistency is tolerated. I have heard some of my townsmen say, "I should like to have them order me out to help put down an insurrection of the slaves, or to march to Mexico;—see if I would go"; and yet these very men have each, directly by their allegiance, and so indirectly, at least, by their money, furnished a substitute . . .

I do not hesitate to say, that those who call themselves Abolitionists should at once effectually withdraw their support, both in person and property, from the government of Massachusetts, and not wait till they constitute a majority of one, before they suffer the right to prevail through them. I think that it is enough if they have God on their side, without waiting for that other one. Moreover, any man more right than his neighbors constitutes a majority of one already.

I meet this American government, or its representative, the State government, directly, and face to face, once a year—no more—in the person of its tax-gatherer; this is the only mode in which a man situated as I am necessarily meets it; and it then says distinctly,

Recognize me; and the simplest, the most effectual, and, in the present posture of affairs, the indispensablest mode of treating with it on this head, of expressing your little satisfaction with and love for it, is to deny it then. My civil neighbor, the tax-gatherer, is the very man I have to deal with—for it is, after all, with men and not with parchment that I quarrel—and he has voluntarily chosen to be an agent of the government. How shall he ever know well what he is and does as an officer of the government, or as a man, until he is obliged to consider whether he shall treat me, his neighbor, for whom he has respect, as a neighbor and well-disposed man, or as a maniac and disturber of the peace, and see if he can get over this obstruction to his neighborliness without a ruder and more impetuous thought or speech corresponding with his action? I know this well, that if one thousand, if one hundred, if ten men whom I could name—if ten *honest* men only—ay, if *one* HONEST man, in this State of Massachusetts, *ceasing to hold slaves*, were actually to withdraw from this copartnership, and be locked up in the county jail therefor, it would be the abolition of slavery in America. For it matters not how small the beginning may seem to be: what is once well done is done forever. . . .

Under a government which imprisons any unjustly, the true place for a just man is also a prison. The proper place to-day, the only place which Massachusetts has provided for her freer and less desponding spirits, is in her prisons, to be put out and locked out of the State by her own act, as they have already put themselves out by their principles. It is there that the fugitive slave, and the Mexican prisoner on parole, and the Indian come to plead the wrongs of his race, should find them; on that separate, but more free and honorable ground, where the State places those who are not *with* her, but *against* her—the only house in a slave State in which a free man can abide with honor. If any think that their influence would be lost there, and their voices no longer afflict the ear of the State, that they would not be as an enemy within its walls, they do not know by how much truth is stronger than error, nor how much more eloquently and effectively he can combat injustice who has experienced a little in his own person. Cast your whole vote, not a strip of paper merely, but your whole influence. A minority is powerless while it conforms to the majority; it is not even a minority then; but it is irresistible when it clogs by its whole weight. If the alternative is to keep all just men in prison, or give up war and slavery, the State will not hesitate which to choose. If a thousand men were not to pay their tax-bills this year, that would not be a violent and bloody measure, as it would be to pay them, and enable the State to commit violence and shed innocent blood. This is, in fact, the definition of a peaceable revolution, if any such is possible. If the tax-gatherer, or any other public officer, asks me, as one has done, "But what shall I do?" my answer is, "If you really wish to do anything, resign your office." When the subject has refused allegiance, and the officer has resigned his office, then the revolution is accomplished. But even suppose blood should flow. Is there not a sort of blood shed when the conscience is wounded? Through this wound a man's real manhood and immortality flow out, and he bleeds to an everlasting death. I see this blood flowing now. . . .

I have paid no poll-tax for six years. I was put into a jail once on this account, for one night; and, as I stood considering the walls of solid stone, two or three feet thick, the door of wood and iron, a foot thick, and the iron grating which strained the light, I could not help being struck with the foolishness of that institution which treated me as if I were mere flesh and blood and bones, to be locked up. I wondered that it should have concluded at length that this was the best use it could put me to, and had never thought to avail itself of my services in some way. I saw that, if there was a wall of stone between me and my townsmen, there was a still more difficult one to climb or break through, before they could get to be as free as I was. I did not for a moment feel confined, and the walls seemed a great waste of stone and mortar. I felt as if I alone of all my townsmen had paid my tax. They plainly did not know how to treat me, but behaved like persons who are underbred. In every threat and in every compliment there was a blunder; for they thought that my chief desire was to stand the other side of that stone wall. I could not but smile to see how industriously they locked the door on my meditations, which followed them out again without let or hindrance, and they were really all that was dangerous. As they could not reach me, they had resolved to punish my body; just as boys, if they cannot come at some person against whom they have a spite, will abuse his dog. I saw that the State was half-witted, that it was timid as a lone woman with her silver spoons, and that it did not know its friends from its foes, and I lost all my remaining respect for it, and pitied it.

Thus the State never intentionally confronts a man's sense, intellectual or moral, but only his body, his senses. It is not armed with superior wit or honesty, but with superior physical strength. I was not born to be forced. I will breathe after my own fashion. Let us see who is the strongest. What force has a multitude? They only can force me who obey a higher law than I. They force me to become like themselves. I do not hear of *men* being *forced* to have this way or that by masses of men. What sort of life were that to live? . . . If a plant cannot live according to its nature, it dies; and so a man. . . .

The authority of government, even such as I am willing to submit to—for I will cheerfully obey those who know and can do better than I, and in many things even those who neither know nor can do so well—is still an impure one: to be strictly just, it must have the sanction and consent of the governed. It can have no pure right over my person and property but what I concede to it. The progress from an absolute to a limited monarchy, from a limited monarchy to a democracy, is a progress toward a true respect for the individual. Even the Chinese philosopher was wise enough to regard the individual as the basis of the empire. Is a democracy, such as we know it, the last improvement possible in government? Is it not possible to take a step further towards recognizing and organizing the rights of man? There will never be a really free and enlightened State until the State comes to recognize the individual as a higher and independent power, from which all its own power and authority are derived, and treats him accordingly. I please myself with imagining a State at least which can afford to be just to all men, and to treat the individual with respect as a neighbor; which even would not think it inconsistent with its own repose if a few were to live aloof from it, not meddling with it, nor embraced by it, who fulfilled all the duties of neighbors and fellow-men. A State which bore this kind of fruit, and suffered it to drop off as fast as it ripened, would prepare the way for a still more perfect and glorious State, which also I have imagined, but not yet anywhere seen.

(1849)

100 • *Julia Ward Howe*

"MOTHERS' DAY PROCLAMATION"

Arise, then, women of this day! Arise all women who have hearts, whether our baptism be that of water or of fears!

Say firmly: "We will not have great questions decided by irrelevant agencies. Our husbands shall not come to us, reeking with carnage, for caresses and applause. Our sons shall not be taken from us to unlearn all that we have been able to teach them of charity, mercy and patience.

We women of one country will be too tender of those of another country to allow our sons to be trained to injure theirs. From the bosom of the devastated earth a voice goes up with our own. It says "Disarm, Disarm! The sword of murder is not the balance of justice."

Blood does not wipe our dishonor nor violence indicate possession. As men have often forsaken the plow and the anvil at the summons of war, let women now leave all that may be left of home for a great and earnest day of counsel. Let them meet first, as women, to bewail and commemorate the dead.

Let them then solemnly take counsel with each other as to the means whereby the great human family can live in peace, each bearing after their own time the sacred impress, not of Caesar, but of God.

In the name of womanhood and of humanity, I earnestly ask that a general congress of women without limit of nationality may be appointed and held at some place deemed most convenient and at the earliest period consistent with its objects, to promote the alliance of the different nationalities, the amicable settlement of international questions, the great and general interests of peace.

(1870)

Julia Ward Howe, Boston, 1870.

101 • *Matilda Joslyn Gage*

"INDIAN CITIZENSHIP"

While the United States is trying to force citizenship upon the Indians, the latter are everywhere protesting against it. The famous Iroquois, or Six Nations, held a council at Onondaga the last of March, upon the old, original council grounds where, before the advent of Columbus, they were wont to meet in settlement of grave questions.

No such important questions ever came up during their old barbaric life as were discussed at the council in March. First among them was the bill recently introduced in the United States Senate by Mr. Kernan of N. Y., to give those tribes the rights of citizenship and allow them to sell their lands in this State.

Published in *National Citizen and Ballot Box*, edited by Matilda Gage, May 1878 p. 2.

The Indians decline the gift of citizenship and although Judge Wallace of the Northern District of New York recently decided in favor of the right of an Oneida Indian who voted at the presidential election of 1876, Chief Skenandoah of the Oneidas was one of the principal speakers against this innovation.

The Mohammeds {Muslims} have a saying that one hour of justice is worth seventy years of prayer; the Indians seem to think one hour of justice worth a thousand years of citizenship, as the drift of their talk was against any law that should either allow or compel them to become citizens, as such a course would open wide the door to the grasping avarice of the white man. They discussed plans to compel the payment due them for lands once deeded them by the United States in treaty but which were afterwards seized and sold for the benefit of our government.

Over one hundred chiefs and warriors of the different nations took part in this discussion. This council of Indians at Onondaga Castle, in the center of the great Empire State, and the convention of the women of the country at Washington in January, the one protesting against citizenship about to be forced upon them, because with it would come further deprivation of their rights,—the other demanding citizenship denied them, in order to protect their rights, are two forcible commentaries upon our so-called republican form of government.

. . . That the Indians have been oppressed—are now—is true, but the United States has treaties with them, recognizing them as distinct political communities, and duty towards them demands not an enforced citizenship but a faithful living up to its obligations on the part of the Government.

Our Indians are in reality foreign powers, though living among us. With them our country not only has treaty obligations, but pays them, or professes to, annual sums in consideration of such treaties; the U.S. Government paying the Iroquois their annuities in June, the State of New York in September. One great aversion the Iroquois have to citizenship is that they would then be compelled to pay taxes, which they look upon as a species of tribute. From an early day they were accustomed to receiving tribute, sending among the conquered tribes of Long Island for their annual dues of wampum. As poor, as oppressed as they are, surrounded as they now are by the conquering white man, they still preserve their olden spirit of independence, still look upon themselves as distinct nations and in the payment of their annuities, fancy they are receiving, as of old, tribute from their enemies. Compelling them to become citizens would be like the forcible annexation of Cuba, Mexico, or Canada to our government, and as unjust.

A delegation of Indians called at the White House on New Year's day. As a sarcasm of justice, on their "Happy New Year" cards were inscribed extracts from various treaties made with them, and disregarded rights guaranteed them in treaty by the Government.

The women of the nation might take hint from the Indians and on July 4th, send to the legislative, judicial and executive bodies, cards inscribed with such sentiments as "Governments derive their just powers from the consent of the governed." "Taxation without representation is tyranny," and others of like character.

The black man had the right of suffrage conferred upon him without his asking for it, and now an attempt is made to force it upon the red man in direct opposition to his wishes, while women citizens, already members of the nation, to whom it rightfully belongs, are denied its exercise. Truly, consistency is a jewel so rare its only abode is the toad's head.

(1878)

FROM *THE SQUATTER AND THE DON*

"I thought that the rights of the Spanish people were protected by our treaty with Mexico,"[1] George said.

"Mexico did not pay much attention to the future welfare of the children she left to their fate in the hands of a nation which had no sympathies for us," said Doña Josefa, feelingly.

"I remember," calmly said Don Mariano, "that when I first read the text of the treaty of Guadalupe Hidalgo, I felt a bitter resentment against my people; against Mexico, the mother country, who abandoned us—her children—with so slight a provision of obligatory stipulations for protection. But afterwards, upon mature reflection, I saw that Mexico did as much as could have been reasonably expected at the time. In the very preamble of the treaty the spirit of peace and friendship, which animated both nations, was carefully made manifest. That spirit was to be the *foundation* of the relations between the conqueror and conquered. How could Mexico have foreseen then that when scarcely half a dozen years should have elapsed the trusted conquerors would, *In Congress Assembled,* pass laws which were to be retroactive upon the defenseless, helpless, conquered people, in order to despoil them? The treaty said that our rights would be the same as those enjoyed by all other American citizens. But, you see, Congress takes very good care not to enact retroactive laws for Americans, laws to take away from American citizens the property which they hold now, already, with a recognized legal title. No, indeed. But they do so quickly enough with us—with us, the Spano-Americans, who were to enjoy equal rights, mind you, according to the treaty of peace. This is what seems to me a breach of faith, which Mexico could neither presuppose nor prevent."

"It is nothing else, I am sorry and ashamed to say," George said. "I never knew much about the treaty with Mexico, but I never imagined we had acted so badly."

"I think but few Americans know or believe to what extent we have been wronged by Congressional action. And truly, I believe that Congress itself did not anticipate the effect of its laws upon us and how we would be despoiled, we, the conquered people," said Don Mariano, sadly.

"It is the duty of law-givers to foresee the effect of the laws they impose upon people," said Doña Josefa.

"That I don't deny, but I fear that the conquered have always but a weak voice, which nobody hears," said Don Mariano.

"We have had no one to speak for us. By the treaty of Guadalupe Hidalgo the American nation pledged its honor to respect our land titles just the same as Mexico would have done. Unfortunately, however, the discovery of gold brought to California the riff-raff of the world, and with it a horde of land-sharks, all possessing the privilege of voting, and most of them coveting our lands, for which they very quickly began to clamor. There was, and still is, plenty of good government land, which anyone can take. But no. The forbidden fruit is the sweetest. They do not want government land. They want the land of the Spanish people, because we 'have too much,' they say. So, to win their votes, the votes of the squatters, our representatives in Congress helped to pass laws declaring all lands in California open to preemption, as in Louisiana, for instance. Then, as a coating of whitewash to the stain on the nation's honor, a 'land commission' was established to examine land titles. Because, having pledged the national word to respect our rights, it would be an act of despoliation, besides an open violation of pledged honor, to take the lands without some pretext of a legal process. So then, we became obliged to

Pages 65–66 & 162–163 are reprinted with permission from the publisher of "The Squatter and the Don" by Maria Amparo Ruiz de Burton (© 1997 Arte Público Press–University of Houston).

present our titles before the said land commission to be examined and approved or rejected. While these legal proceedings are going on, the squatters locate their claims and raise crops on our lands, which they convert into money to fight our titles. . . .

. . .

"Why did they favor such legislation?"

"Because California was expected to be filled with a population of farmers, of industrious settlers who would have votes and would want their one hundred and sixty acres each of the best land to be had. As our legislators thought "that we, the Spano-American natives, had the best lands, and but few votes, there was nothing else to be done but to despoil us, to take our lands and give them to the coming population.""

"But that was outrageous. Their motive was a political object."

"Certainly. The motive was that our politicians wanted *votes*. The squatters were in increasing majority; the Spanish natives, in diminishing minority. Then the cry was raised that our land grants were too large; that a few lazy, thriftless, ignorant natives, holding such large tracts of land would be a hindrance to the prosperity of the State, because such lazy people would never cultivate their lands, and were even too sluggish to sell them. The cry was taken up and became popular. It was so easy to upbraid, to deride, to despise the conquered race! Then to despoil them, to make them beggars, seemed to be, if not absolutely righteous, certainly highly justifiable. Anyone not acquainted with the real facts might have supposed that there was no more land to be had in California but that which belonged to the natives. Everybody seemed to have forgotten that for each acre that was owned by them, there were thousands vacant, belonging to the Government and which anyone can have at one dollar and twenty-five cents per acre. No, they didn't want Government land. The settlers want the lands of the lazy, the thriftless Spaniards. Such good-for-nothing, helpless wretches are not fit to own such lordly tracts of land. It was wicked to tolerate the waste, the extravagance of the Mexican Government, in giving such large tracts of land to a few individuals. The American government never could have been, or ever could be, guilty of such a thing. No, never! But, behold! Hardly a dozen years had passed, when this same economical, far-seeing Congress, which was so ready to snatch away from the Spanish people their lands (which rightfully belonged to them) on the plea that such large tracts of land ought not to belong to a *few* individuals, this same Congress mind you, goes to work and gives to railroad companies millions upon millions of acres of land. . . .

(1885)

NOTE

1. Treaty of Guadalupe-Hidalgo (1848) after the United States–Mexican War. See Introduction 18.

---

103 • *Tekahionwake (Emily Pauline Johnson)*

"A CRY FROM AN INDIAN WIFE"

My forest brave, my Red-skin love, farewell;
We may not meet to-morrow; who can tell
What mighty ills befall our little band,
Or what you'll suffer from the white man's hand?

Here is your knife! I thought 'twas sheathed for aye.
No roaming bison calls for it to-day;
No hide of prairie cattle will it maim;
The plains are bare, it seeks a nobler game:

In 1885, Charles G. D. Roberts published Johnson's "A Cry from an Indian Wife" in *The Week*, Goldwin Smith's Toronto magazine.

'Twill drink the life-blood of a soldier host.
Go; rise and strike, no matter what the cost.
Yet stay. Revolt not at the Union Jack,
Nor raise Thy hand against this stripling pack
Of white-faced warriors, marching West to quell
Our fallen tribe that rises to rebel.
They all are young and beautiful and good;
Curse to the war that drinks their harmless blood.
Curse to the fate that brought them from the East
To be our chiefs—to make our nation least
That breathes the air of this vast continent.
Still their new rule and council is well meant.
They but forget we Indians owned the land
From ocean unto ocean; that they stand
Upon a soil that centuries agone
Was our sole kingdom and our right alone.
They never think how they would feel to-day,
If some great nation came from far away,
Wresting their country from their hapless braves,
Giving what they gave us—but wars and graves.
Then go and strike for liberty and life,
And bring back honour to your Indian wife.
Your wife? Ah, what of that, who cares for me?
Who pities my poor love and agony?
What white-robed priest prays for your safety here,
As prayer is said for every volunteer
That swells the ranks that Canada sends out?
Who prays for vict'ry for the Indian scout?

Who prays for our poor nation lying low?
None—therefore take your tomahawk and go.
My heart may break and burn into its core,
But I am strong to bid you go to war.
Yet stay, my heart is not the only one
That grieves the loss of husband and of son;
Think of the mothers o'er the inland seas;
Think of the pale-faced maiden on her knees;
One pleads her God to guard some sweet-faced
   child
That marches on toward the North-West wild.
The other prays to shield her love from harm,
To strengthen his young, proud uplifted arm.
Ah, how her white face quivers thus to think,
Your tomahawk his life's best blood will drink.
She never thinks of my wild aching breast,
Nor prays for your dark face and eagle crest
Endangered by a thousand rifle balls,
My heart the target if my warrior falls.
O! coward self I hesitate no more;
Go forth, and win the glories of the war.
Go forth, nor bend to greed of white men's hands,
By right, by birth we Indians own these lands,
Though starved, crushed, plundered, lies our
   nation low . . .
Perhaps the white man's God has willed it so

(1885)

---

104 • *Elizabeth Cady Stanton*

"ON EDUCATED SUFFRAGE"

26 West 61st   N.Y. Sept 21st [1897]
Dear Mrs Colby,
I send you a copy of the resolutions I shall try to have passed at every state convention & at our fiftieth anniversary if possible.

The greatest block in the way of woman suffrage today, is the fear of the ignorant vote. They say to extend suffrage to woman is to double the ignorant vote, already so large that it threatens to swamp our free institutions.

New York & London: Mother Earth Publishing Association, 1911. pp. 133–150. Notes have been deleted.

The most speedy way to limit the ignorant vote is to require an educational qualification. To this end we should demand that after the dawn of the next century, no one shall be permitted to exercise the right of suffrage unless they can read & write the English language intelligently. This would lengthen the way from the steerage to the polls, as it would take the ordinary foreigner at least five years, to acquire this knowledge, & stimulate our native population to prepare themselves early for citizenship. The boys in the streets would say to each other, you better go to school or you cannot vote when you are twenty one. Those who prize this right would be willing to work, in order to secure it.

An educational qualification being an attainable one in in no way conflicts with our cherished idea of universal suffrage. We say now the voter must be twenty one before he can exercise this right, it is equally just & logical to say that he must read & write, intelligence is quite as important as years.

The women of this nation should take the lead in this important reform. As they have no party ties nor official positions to lose they are in a position free ↑free↓ to advocate vital principles in government. When our fathers made haste to establish free schools, they saw the importance of educated citizens in a republic Moreover as women have no choice in their laws or lawmakers, they have at least the right to demand that their rulers shall be able to read & write

What an anomaly it is in a Republic that a large class of citizens, representing the virtue & intelligence, the wealth & position of the nation should be under the heels of the ignorant masses, foreign & native. In all national conflicts ↑it was considered↓ the most grievous accident of war, was for the native population should be left under a foreign yoke, yet that is the position of our educated women today.

The teachers in schools Professors in colleges, Lawyers, Doctors, Editors, ordained ministers, all wear a foreign yoke. Our Judges, Jurors, legislators, are foreigners so are our policemen who patrol the streets at night. A girl of sixteen running for a physician for a dying father, & a woman accoucher hastening to her patient at midnight were both arrested & kept in the station house all night. Although they protested & told the importance of their errands, the ↑policemen↓

laughed in their faces & said "they had heard such excuses before, women had no business to be in the streets at night." It seems these women had very important business. Laws denying women the freedom of the city at night are an insult to the whole sex, & the excuse for such laws are is as ridiculous as oppressive. Suppose a disreputable woman assaults a good man, has he not the strength in ordinary cases to push her aside & run home? Why deny freedom to all good women on errands of mercy, at night to protect men, when they are abundantly able to protect themselves.

This is one of the penalties of disfranchisement, under a foreign yoke. It is truly lamentable to see the apathy with which women submit to to such indignities. Must each one of us, feel the iron teeth of the law in our own flesh before we can be roused to rebellion. It is absolutely necessary for the safety of the republic as well as ourselves that the educated women of the nation should have a voice in making & administering the laws. Our demand for educated rulers would give rise to a new & more heated agitation of our question, yours sincerely

Elizabeth Cady Stanton

SECOND ENCLOSURE

Resolved, That a Republic based on universal suffrage, in which a large class of educated women, representing the virtue and wealth of the nation are disfranchised, is an anomaly in government, especially when all men, foreign and native, black and white, ignorant and vicious, vote on the laws and rules for this superior class.

Resolved, That in convention assembled we demand, that as women have no voice in their rulers, those who administer the laws hereafter shall be required to read and write the English language intelligently, before they are allowed to exercise the right of suffrage. This qualification should be adopted at once in every State in the union.

Resolved, That an educational qualification of voters, in no way conflicts with our cherished idea of universal suffrage, as it is an attainable qualification. All are born citizens in a republic, but the boy must be twenty-one before he can exercise the right of suffrage. It is equally just and logical to require that he shall read and write the English language intelligently.

Resolved, That laws should be passed at once demanding that at the dawn of the next century, all who exercise the right of suffrage, must be required to read and write the English language. As women have no party ties, they constitute the only independent class to lead in the agitation of this question.

Resolved, That as politicians are afraid to advocate suffrage lest they risk their official positions and as some reformers do not see the wisdom of such a measure, it remains for those who do, to create a widespread public sentiment in favor of this important measure.

Woman's Tribune, 9 October 1897.

(1897)

---

105 • *Susan B. Anthony and Elizabeth Cady Stanton*

"PETITION FOR THE WOMEN OF HAWAII"

TO THE SENATE AND HOUSE OF REPRESENTATIVES IN CONGRESS ASSEMBLED

The undersigned earnestly pray your honorable body that in the proposed government for our newly acquired territories you recognize for women the highest position of citizenship yet attained in this republic.

As in four States of the Union women now enjoy civil and political equality, to create a male oligarchy, by restricting the right to vote and hold office to men, would be to ignore all the steps of progress made during the last fifty years and reestablish at the very dawn of the new century a government based upon the invidious distinctions of sex, which have ever blocked the way to a higher civilization.

When the emancipation of black men was under discussion the Women's Loyal League sent 400,000 petitions to Congress in favor of that measure. Shall we do less for the political freedom of the women of Hawaii? On the contrary, let us of the several States vie with each other

in our efforts to roll up the largest petition ever presented in Congress against any form of class legislation.

Elizabeth Cady Stanton.
Susan B. Anthony.

(15 January 1899)

LETTER FROM SAMUEL GOMPERS TO SUSAN B. ANTHONY

Dear Madam:

Your favor of the 27th inst., together with enclosed petition, came duly to hand; and I beg to assure you that I fully appreciate your courtesy in asking the co-operation of our organization for the purpose of further agitation and securing equal suffrage for women and men. You say that you propose starting out on new lines of agitation. One is to insist upon the incorporation of a clause in the constitutions which may be adopted for the government of "Hawaiian

---

Islands, for Cuba, Porto Rico, and the Philippines" so as to leave the adjective "male" out of the suffrage clause, and to petition the Federal Government to adopt an amendment to the constitution that shall prohibit the states from "disfranchising citizens on account of sex."

In regard to the latter proposition I would say that the American Federation of Labor some years ago circulated a petition of this character, and that within a few months more than 300,000 signatures were obtained and presented to Congress. Thus, you will see we are with you on this proposition, and have been for a very long time, and I am sure we shall have no hesitation at all in rendering whatever assistance we could to follow in the same lines.

But, in regard to your petition to the 56th Congress not to insert the word "male" in the suffrage clause of the constitution for the governments of Hawaii, Cuba, Porto Rico, and the Philippines, and in which the petitions are asked in the name of justice and equality for all citizens of our republic, I think very peculiar, more particularly when it is asked upon the fundamental principle of the "consent of the governed." I do not believe that the American Federation of Labor is likely to concede the right of our Congress to form constitutions for the islands you name. To petition Congress to incorporate such a qualification, or rather, to omit such a qualification for suffrage, is to recognize that the government of the United States has the right to foist itself upon the people of those islands, not only against the "consent of the governed," but in spite of their protests, the protests that they are manifesting by sacrificing their very lives, if necessary, to make effective. You will not make friends for the cause of woman's suffrage by following the course to which I refer, I imagine.

It should require no assurance of my earnest desire for equal suffrage. So far as it lies within my power, I have been a consistent advocate and defender of that proposition, and am still willing to do all that lies in my power to further that cause; but I can not consent, and I do not think that the organized working people of our country will consent, to a movement which recognizes and practically sanctions a violation of the fundamental principles upon which the institutions of our country are based, and as involved in the wars of conquest. Very respectfully yours,

Sam Gompers
President, American Federation of Labor

(31 October 1899)

---

106 • *Emma Goldman*

FROM *PATRIOTISM*

A Menace to Liberty

. . . What, then, is patriotism? "Patriotism, sir, is the last resort of scoundrels," said Dr. Johnson. Leo Tolstoy, the greatest anti-patriot of our times, defines patriotism as the principle that will justify the training of wholesale murderers; a trade that requires better equipment for the exercise of man-killing than the making of such necessities of life as shoes, clothing, and houses; a trade that guarantees better returns and greater glory than that of the average workingman.

Excerpt from Emma Goldman's *Anarchism and Other Essays*. Second Revised Edition. New York & London: Mother Earth Publishing Association, 1911. pp. 133–150.

Gustave Hervé, another great anti-patriot, justly calls patriotism a superstition—one far more injurious, brutal, and inhumane than religion. The superstition of religion originated in man's inability to explain natural phenomena. That is, when primitive man heard thunder or saw the lightning, he could not account for either, and therefore concluded that back of them must be a force greater than himself. Similarly he saw a supernatural force in the rain, and in the various other changes in nature. Patriotism, on the other hand, is a superstition artificially created and maintained through a network of lies and falsehoods; a superstition that robs man of his self-respect and dignity, and increases his arrogance and conceit.

Indeed, conceit, arrogance, and egotism are the essentials of patriotism. Let me illustrate. Patriotism assumes that our globe is divided into little spots, each one surrounded by an iron gate. Those who have had the fortune of being born on some particular spot, consider themselves better, nobler, grander, more intelligent than the living beings inhabiting any other spot. It is, therefore, the duty of everyone living on that chosen spot to fight, kill, and die in the attempt to impose his superiority upon all the others.

The inhabitants of the other spots reason in like manner, of course, with the result that, from early infancy, the mind of the child is poisoned with blood-curdling stories about the Germans, the French, the Italians, Russians, etc. When the child has reached manhood, he is thoroughly saturated with the belief that he is chosen by the Lord himself to defend *his* country against the attack or invasion of any foreigner. It is for that purpose that we are clamoring for a greater army and navy, more battleships and ammunition. It is for that purpose that America has within a short time spent four hundred million dollars. Just think of it—four hundred million dollars taken from the produce of *the people*. For surely it is not the rich who contribute to patriotism. They are cosmopolitans, perfectly at home in every land. We in America know well the truth of this. Are not our rich Americans Frenchmen in France, Germans in Germany, or Englishmen in England? And do they not squandor with cosmopolitan grace fortunes coined by American factory children and cotton slaves? Yes, theirs is the patriotism that will make it possible to send messages of condolence to a despot like the Russian Tsar, when any mishap befalls him, as President Roosevelt did in the name of *his* people, when Sergius was punished by the Russian revolutionists.

It is a patriotism that will assist the arch-murderer, Diaz, in destroying thousands of lives in Mexico, or that will even aid in arresting Mexican revolutionists on American soil and keep them incarcerated in American prisons, without the slightest cause or reason.

But, then, patriotism is not for those who represent wealth and power. It is good enough for the people. It reminds one of the historic wisdom of Frederick the Great, the bosom friend of Voltaire, who said: "Religion is a fraud, but it must be maintained for the masses."

That patriotism is rather a costly institution, no one will doubt after considering the following statistics. The progressive increase of the expenditures for the leading armies and navies of the world during the last quarter of a century is a fact of such gravity as to startle every thoughtful student of economic problems. It may be briefly indicated by dividing the time from 1881 to 1905 into five-year periods, and noting the disbursements of several great nations for army and navy purposes during the first and last of those periods. From the first to the last of the periods noted the expenditures of Great Britain increased from $2,101,848,936 to $4,143,226,885, those of France from $3,324,500,000 to $3,455,109,900, those of Germany from $725,000,200 to $2,700,375,600, those of the United States from $1,275,500,750 to $2,650,900,450, those of Russia from $1,900,975,500 to $5,250,445,100, those of Italy from $1,600,975,750 to $1,755,500,100, and those of Japan from $182,900,500 to $700,925,475.

The military expenditures of each of the nations mentioned increased in each of the five-year periods under review. During the entire interval from 1881 to 1905 Great Britain's outlay for her army increased fourfold, that of the United States was tripled, Russia's was doubled, that of Germany increased 35 per cent., that of France about 15 per cent., and that of Japan nearly 500 per cent. . . . .

The awful waste that patriotism necessitates ought to be sufficient to cure the man of even average intelligence from this disease. Yet patriotism demands still more. The people are urged to be patriotic and for that luxury they pay, not only by supporting their "defenders," but even by sacrificing their own children. Patriotism requires allegiance to the flag, which means obedience and readiness to kill father, mother, brother, sister.

The usual contention is that we need a standing army to protect the country from foreign invasion. Every intelligent man and woman knows, however, that this is a myth maintained to frighten and coerce the foolish. The governments of the world, knowing each other's interests, do not invade each other. They have learned that they can gain much more by international arbitration of disputes than by war and conquest. Indeed, as Carlyle said, "War is a quarrel between two thieves too cowardly to fight their own battle; therefore they take boys from one village and another village, stick them into uniforms, equip them with guns, and let them loose like wild beasts against each other."

It does not require much wisdom to trace every war back to a similar cause. Let us take our own Spanish–American war, supposedly a great and patriotic event in the history of the United States. How our hearts burned with indignation against the atrocious Spaniards! True, our indignation did not flare up spontaneously. It was nurtured by months of newspaper agitation, and long after Butcher Weyler had killed off many noble Cubans and outraged many Cuban women. Still, in justice to the American Nation be it said, it did grow indignant and was willing to fight, and that it fought bravely. But when the smoke was over, the dead buried, and the cost of the war came back to the people in an increase in the price of commodities and rent—that is, when we sobered up from our patriotic spree it suddenly dawned on us that the cause of the Spanish–American war was the consideration of the price of sugar; or, to be more explicit, that the lives, blood, and money of the American people were used to protect the interests of American capitalists, which were threatened by the Spanish government. That this is not an exaggeration, but is based on absolute facts and figures, is best proven by the attitude of the American government to Cuban labor. When Cuba was firmly in the clutches of the United States, the very soldiers sent to liberate Cuba were ordered to shoot Cuban workingmen during the great cigarmakers' strike, which took place shortly after the war. . . .

However, the clamor for an increased army and navy is not due to any foreign danger. It is owing to the dread of the growing discontent of the masses and of the international spirit among the workers. It is to meet the internal enemy that the Powers of various countries are preparing themselves; an enemy, who, once awakened to consciousness, will prove more dangerous than any foreign invader.

The powers that have for centuries been engaged in enslaving the masses have made a thorough study of their psychology. They know that the people at large are like children whose despair, sorrow, and tears can be turned into joy with a little toy. And the more gorgeously the toy is dressed, the louder the colors, the more it will appeal to the million-headed child.

An army and navy represent the people's toys. To make them more attractive and acceptable, hundreds and thousands of dollars are being spent for the display of these toys. That was the purpose of the American government in equipping a fleet and sending it along the Pacific coast, that every American citizen should be made to feel the pride and glory of the United States. The city of San Francisco spent one hundred thousand dollars for the entertainment of the fleet; Los Angeles, sixty thousand; Seattle and Tacoma, about one hundred thousand. To entertain the fleet, did I say? To dine and wine a few superior officers, while the "brave boys" had to mutiny to get sufficient food. Yes, two hundred and sixty thousand dollars were spent on fireworks, theatre parties, and revelries, at a time when men, women, and children through the breadth and length of the country were starving in the streets; when thousands of unemployed were ready to sell their labor at any price.

Two hundred and sixty thousand dollars! What could not have been accomplished with such an enormous sum? But instead of bread and shelter, the children of those cities were taken to see the fleet, that it may remain, as one of the newspapers said, "a lasting memory for the child."

A wonderful thing to remember, is it not? The implements of civilized slaughter. If the mind of the child is to be poisoned with such memories, what hope is there for a true realization of human brotherhood?

We Americans claim to be a peace-loving people. We hate bloodshed; we are opposed to violence. Yet we go into spasms of joy over the possibility of projecting dynamite bombs from flying machines upon helpless citizens. We are ready to hang, electrocute, or lynch anyone, who, from economic necessity, will risk his own life in the attempt upon that of some industrial magnate. Yet our hearts swell with pride at the thought that America is becoming the most powerful nation on earth, and that it will eventually plant her iron foot on the necks of all other nations.

Such is the logic of patriotism.

Considering the evil results that patriotism is fraught with for the average man, it is as nothing compared with the insult and injury that patriotism heaps upon the soldier himself,—that poor, deluded victim of superstition and ignorance. He, the savior of his country, the protector of his nation,—what has patriotism in store for him? A life of slavish submission, vice, and perversion, during peace; a life of danger, exposure, and death, during war. . . .

Thinking men and women the world over are beginning to realize that patriotism is too narrow and limited a conception to meet the necessities of our time. The centralization of power has brought into being an international feeling of solidarity among the oppressed nations of the world; a solidarity which represents a greater harmony of interests between the workingman of America and his brothers abroad than between the American miner and his exploiting compatriot; a solidarity which fears not foreign invasion, because it is bringing all the workers to the point when they will say to their masters, "Go and do your own killing. We have done it long enough for you." . . .

The American workingman has suffered so much at the hands of the soldier, State and Federal, that he is quite justified in his disgust with, and his opposition to, the uniformed parasite. However, mere denunciation will not solve this great problem. What we need is a propaganda of education for the soldier: antipatriotic literature that will enlighten him as to the real horrors of his trade, and that will awaken his consciousness to his true relation to the man to whose labor he owes his very existence. It is precisely this that the authorities fear most. It is already high treason for a soldier to attend a radical meeting. No doubt they will also stamp it high treason for a soldier to read a radical pamphlet. But, then, has not authority from time immemorial stamped every step of progress as treasonable? Those, however, who earnestly strive for social reconstruction can well afford to face all that; for it is probably even more important to carry the truth into the barracks than into the factory. When we have undermined the patriotic lie, we shall have cleared the path for that great structure wherein all nationalities shall be united into a universal brotherhood,—a truly FREE SOCIETY.

(1911)

107 • *Rosa Luxemburg*

"MILITARISM AS A PROVINCE OF ACCUMULATION"

Militarism fulfills a quite definite function in the history of capital, accompanying as it does every historical phase of accumulation. It plays a decisive part in the first stages of European capitalism, in the period of the so-called "primitive accumulation," as a means of conquering the New World and the spice-producing countries of India. Later, it is employed to subject the modern colonies, to destroy the social organisations of primitive societies so that their means of production may be appropriated, forcibly to introduce commodity trade in countries where the social structure had been unfavourable to it, and to turn the natives into a proletariat by compelling them to work for wages in the colonies. It is responsible for the creation and expansion of spheres of interest for European capital in non-European regions, for extorting railway concessions in backward countries, and for enforcing the claims of European capital as international lender. Finally, militarism is a weapon in the competitive struggle between capitalist countries for areas of non-capitalist civilisation.

In addition, militarism has yet another important function. From the purely economic point of view, it is a pre-eminent means for the realisation of surplus value; it is in itself a province of accumulation. In examining the question who should count as a buyer for the mass of products containing the capitalised surplus value, we have again and again refused to consider the state and its organs as consumers. . . . But when the monies concentrated in the exchequer by taxation are used for the production of armaments, the picture is changed.

With indirect taxation and high protective tariffs the bill of militarism is footed mainly by the working class and the peasants . . . The transfer of some of the purchasing power from the working class to the state entails a proportionate decrease in the consumption of means of subsistence by the working class . . . For capital as a whole, it means producing a smaller quantity of consumer goods for the working class . . .

Capital has won with the left hand only what it has lost with the right. Or we might say that the large number of capitalists producing means of subsistence have lost the effective demand in favour of a small group of big armament manufacturers.

But this picture is only valid for individual capital. Here {in capitalism as a whole} it makes no difference indeed whether production engages in one sphere of activity or another . . . There are only commodities and buyers, and it is completely immaterial to him whether he produces instruments of life or instruments of death, corned beef or armour plating . . .

On the basis of indirect taxation, militarism in practice works both ways. By lowering the normal standard of living for the working class, it ensures both that capital should be able to maintain a regular army, the organ of capitalist rule, and that it may tap an impressive field for further accumulation. . . .

And the satisfaction of this demand presupposes a big industry of the highest order. It requires the most favourable conditions for the production of surplus value and for accumulation. In the form of government contracts for army supplies the scattered purchasing power of the consumers is concentrated in large quantities and, free of the vagaries and subjective fluctuations of personal consumption, it achieves an almost automatic regularity and rhythmic growth . . . All other attempts to expand markets and set up operational bases for capital largely depend on historical, social and political factors beyond the control of capital, whereas production for militarism represents a province whose regular and progressive expansion seems primarily determined by capital itself.

In this way capital turns historical necessity into a virtue: the ever fiercer "competition" in the capitalist world itself provides a field for accumulation of the first magnitude. Capital increasingly employs militarism for implementing a foreign and colonial policy to get hold of the means of production and labour power of non-capitalist countries and societies. . . .

(1913)

108 • *The International Congress of Women*

"RESOLUTIONS ADOPTED"

I. WOMEN AND WAR

1. PROTEST

We women, in International Congress assembled, protest against the madness and the horror of war, involving as it does a reckless sacrifice of human life and the destruction of so much that humanity has laboured through centuries to build up.

2. WOMEN'S SUFFERINGS IN WAR

This International Congress of Women opposes the assumption that women can be protected under the conditions of modern warfare. It protests vehemently against the odious wrongs of which women are the victims in time of war, and especially against the horrible violation of women which attends all war.

II. ACTION TOWARDS PEACE

3. THE PEACE SETTLEMENT

This International Congress of Women of different nations, classes, creeds and parties is united in expressing sympathy with the suffering of all, whatever their nationality, who are fighting for their country or labouring under the burden of war.

Since the mass of the people in each of the countries now at war believe themselves to be fighting, not as aggressors but in self-defence and for their national existence, there can be no irreconcilable differences between them, and their common ideals afford a basis upon which a magnanimous and honourable peace might be established. The Congress therefore urges the Governments of the world to put an end to this bloodshed, and to begin peace negociations. It demands that the peace which follows shall be permanent and therefore based on principles of justice, including those laid down in the resolutions) adopted by this Congress, namely:

That no territory should be transferred without the consent of the men and women in it, and that the right of conquest should not be recognized.

That autonomy and a democratic parliament should not be refused to any people.

That the Governments of all nations should come to an agreement to refer future international disputes to arbitration or conciliation and to bring social, moral and economic pressure to bear upon any country which resorts to arms.

That foreign politics should be subject to democratic control.

That women should be granted equal political rights with men.

4. CONTINUOUS MEDIATION

This International Congress of Women resolves to ask the neutral countries to take immediate steps to create a conference of neutral nations which shall without delay offer continuous mediation. The Conference shall invite suggestions for settlement from each of the belligerent nations and in any case shall submit to all of them simultaneously, reasonable proposals as a basis of peace.

(1915)

International Congress of Women, the Hague, April 28–May 1, 1915. Notes have been deleted.

FROM *AMERICAN INDIAN STORIES*

III. MY MOTHER'S CURSE UPON WHITE SETTLERS

One black night mother and I sat alone in the dim starlight, in front of our wigwam. We were facing the river, as we talked about the shrinking limits of the village. She told me about the poverty-stricken white settlers, who lived in caves dug in the long ravines of the high hills across the river.

A whole tribe of broad-footed white beggars had rushed hither to make claims on those wild lands. Even as she was telling this I spied a small glimmering light in the bluffs.

"That is a white man's lodge where you see the burning fire," she said. Then, a short distance from it, only a little lower than the first, was another light. As I became accustomed to the night, I saw more and more twinkling lights, here and there, scattered all along the wide black margin of the river.

Still looking toward the distant firelight, my mother continued: "My daughter, beware of the paleface. It was the cruel paleface who caused the death of your sister and your uncle, my brave brother. It is this same paleface who offers in one palm the holy papers, and with the other gives a holy baptism of firewater. He is the hypocrite who reads with one eye, 'Thou shalt not kill,' and with the other gloats upon the sufferings of the Indian race." Then suddenly discovering a new fire in the bluffs, she exclaimed, "Well, well, my daughter, there is the light of another white rascal!"

She sprang to her feet, and, standing firm beside her wigwam, she sent a curse upon those who sat around the hated white man's light. Raising her right arm forcibly into line with her eye, she threw her whole might into her doubled fist as she shot it vehemently at the strangers. Long she held her outstretched fingers toward the settler's lodge, as if an invisible power passed from them to the evil at which she aimed.

IV. RETROSPECTION

Leaving my mother, I returned to the school in the East. As months passed over me, I slowly comprehended that the large army of white teachers in Indian schools had a larger missionary creed than I had suspected.

It was one which included self-preservation quite as much as Indian education. When I saw an opium-eater holding a position as teacher of Indians, I did not understand what good was expected, until a Christian in power replied that this pumpkin-colored creature had a feeble mother to support. An inebriate paleface sat stupid in a doctor's chair, while Indian patients carried their ailments to untimely graves, because his fair wife was dependent upon him for her daily food.

I find it hard to count that white man a teacher who tortured an ambitious Indian youth by frequently reminding the brave changeling that he was nothing but a "government pauper."

Though I burned with indignation upon discovering on every side instances no less shameful than those I have mentioned, there was no present help. Even the few rare ones who have worked nobly for my race were powerless to choose workmen like themselves. To be sure, a man was sent from the Great Father to inspect Indian schools, but what he saw was usually the students' sample work *made* for exhibition. I was nettled by this sly cunning of the workmen who hoodwinked the Indian's pale Father at Washington.

My illness, which prevented the conclusion of my college course, together with my mother's stories of the encroaching frontier settlers, left me in no mood to

---

strain my eyes in searching for latent good in my white co-workers.

At this stage of my own evolution, I was ready to curse men of small capacity for being the dwarfs their God had made them. In the process of my education I had lost all consciousness of the nature world about me. Thus, when a hidden rage took me to the small white-walled prison which I then called my room, I unknowingly turned away from my one salvation.

Alone in my room, I sat like the petrified Indian woman of whom my mother used to tell me. I wished my heart's burdens would turn me to unfeeling stone. But alive, in my tomb, I was destitute!

For the white man's papers I had given up my faith in the Great Spirit. For these same papers I had forgotten the healing in trees and brooks. On account of my mother's simple view of life, and my lack of any, I gave her up, also. I made no friends among the race of people I loathed. Like a slender tree, I had been uprooted from my mother, nature, and God. I was shorn of my branches, which had waved in sympathy and love for home and friends. The natural coat of bark which had protected my oversensitive nature was scraped off to the very quick.

Now a cold bare pole I seemed to be, planted in a strange earth. Still, I seemed to hope a day would come when my mute aching head, reared upward to the sky, would flash a zigzag lightning across the heavens. With this dream of vent for a long-pent consciousness, I walked again amid the crowds.

At last, one weary day in the schoolroom, a new idea presented itself to me. It was a new way of solving the problem of my inner self. I liked it. Thus I resigned my position as teacher; and now I am in an Eastern city, following the long course of study I have set for myself. Now, as I look back upon the recent past, I see it from a distance, as a whole. I remember how, from morning till evening, many specimens of civilized peoples visited the Indian school. The city folks with canes and eyeglasses, the countrymen with sunburnt cheeks and clumsy feet, forgot their relative social ranks in an ignorant curiosity. Both sorts of these Christian palefaces were alike astounded at seeing the children of savage warriors so docile and industrious.

As answers to their shallow inquiries they received the students' sample work to look upon. Examining the neatly figured pages, and gazing upon the Indian girls and boys bending over their books, the white visitors walked out of the schoolhouse well satisfied: they were educating the children of the red man! They were paying a liberal fee to the government employees in whose able hands lay the small forest of Indian timber.

In this fashion many have passed idly through the Indian schools during the last decade, afterward to boast of their charity to the North American Indian. But few there are who have paused to question whether real life or long-lasting death lies beneath this semblance of civilization.

(1921)

---

110 • *Waheenee (Buffalo Bird Woman)*

FROM *AN INDIAN GIRL'S STORY TOLD BY HERSELF TO GILBERT L. WILSON*

I am an old woman now.

The buffaloes and black-tail deer are gone, and our Indian ways are almost gone. Sometimes I find it hard to believe that I ever lived them.

My little son grew up in the white man's school. He can read books, and he owns cattle and has a farm. He is a leader among our Hidatsa people, helping teach them to follow the white man's road.

Waheenee: An Indian Girl's Story Told by Herself to Gilbert L. Wilson. 1921. Reprint, St. Paul: Minnesota Historical Society Press, 1987.

He is kind to me. We no longer live in an earth lodge, but in a house with chimneys, and my son's wife cooks by a stove.

But for me, I cannot forget our old ways.

Often in summer I rise at daybreak and steal out to the corn fields, and as I hoe the corn I sing to it, as we did when I was young. No one cares for our corn songs now.

Sometimes in the evening I sit, looking out on the big Missouri. The sun sets, and dusk steals over the water.

In the shadows I see again to see our Indian village, with smoke curling upward from the earth lodges, and in the river's roar I hear the yells of the warriors, and the laughter of little children of old.

It is but an old woman's dream.

Then I see but shadows and hear only the roar of the river, and tears come into my eyes. Our Indian life, I know, is gone forever.

(1921)

III • *Virginia Woolf*

FROM *THREE GUINEAS*

ONE

Three years is a long time to leave a letter unanswered, and your letter has been lying without an answer even longer than that. I had hoped that it would answer itself, or that other people would answer it for me. But there it is with its question—How in your opinion are we to prevent war?—still unanswered. . . .

In the first place let us draw what all letter-writers instinctively draw, a sketch of the person to whom the letter is addressed. Without someone warm and breathing on the other side of the page, letters are worthless. You, then, who ask the question, are a little grey on the temples; the hair is no longer thick on the top of your head. You have reached the middle years of life not without effort, at the Bar; but on the whole your journey has been prosperous. There is nothing parched, mean or dissatisfied in your expression. And without wishing to flatter you, your prosperity—wife, children, house—has been deserved. You have never sunk into the contented apathy of middle life, for, as your letter from an office in the heart of London shows, instead of turning on your pillow and prodding your pigs, pruning your pear trees—you have a few acres in Norfolk—you are writing letters, attending meetings,

presiding over this and that, asking questions, with the sound of the guns in your ears. For the rest, you began your education at one of the great public schools and finished it at the university.

It is now that the first difficulty of communication between us appears. Let us rapidly indicate the reason. We both come of what, in this hybrid age when, though birth is mixed, classes still remain fixed, it is convenient to call the educated class. When we meet in the flesh we speak with the same accent; use knives and forks in the same way; expect maids to cook dinner and wash up after dinner; and can talk during dinner without much difficulty about politics and people; war and peace; barbarism and civilization—all the questions indeed suggested by your letter. Moreover, we both earn our livings. But . . . those three dots mark a precipice, a gulf so deeply cut between us that for three years and more I have been sitting on my side of it wondering whether it is any use to try to speak across it. Let us then ask someone else—it is Mary Kingsley—to speak for us. "I don't know if I ever revealed to you the fact that being allowed to learn German was *all* the paid-for education I ever had. Two thousand pounds was spent on my brother's, I still

---

hope not in vain." Mary Kingsley is not speaking for herself alone; she is speaking, still, for many of the daughters of educated men. And she is not merely speaking for them; she is also pointing to a very important fact about them, a fact that must profoundly influence all that follows: the fact of Arthur's Education Fund. You, who have read *Pendennis*, will remember how the mysterious letters A.E.F. figured in the household ledgers. Ever since the thirteenth century English families have been paying money into that account. From the Pastons to the Pendennises, all educated families from the thirteenth century to the present moment have paid money into that account. It is a voracious receptacle. Where there were many sons to educate it required a great effort on the part of the family to keep it full. For your education was not merely in book-learning; games educated your body; friends taught you more than books or games. Talk with them broadened your outlook and enriched your mind. In the holidays you travelled; acquired a taste for art; a knowledge of foreign politics; and then, before you could earn your own living, your father made you an allowance upon which it was possible for you to live while you learnt the profession which now entitles you to add the letters K.C. to your name. All this came out of Arthur's Education Fund. And to this your sisters, as Mary Kingsley indicates, made their contribution. Not only did their own education, save for such small sums as paid the German teacher, go into it; but many of those luxuries and trimmings which are, after all, an essential part of education—travel, society, solitude, a lodging apart from the family house—they were paid into it too. It was a voracious receptacle, a solid fact—Arthur's Education Fund—a fact so solid indeed that it cast a shadow over the entire landscape. And the result is that though we look at the same things, we see them differently. . . .

Here, immediately, are three reasons which lead your sex to fight; war is a profession; a source of happiness and excitement; and it is also an outlet for manly qualities, without which men would deteriorate. But that these feelings and opinions are by no means universally held by your sex is proved by the following extract from another biography, the life of a poet who was killed in the European war: Wilfred Owen.

Already I have comprehended a light which never will filter into the dogma of any national church: namely, that one of Christ's essential commands was: Passivity

at any price! Suffer dishonour and disgrace, but never resort to arms. Be bullied, be outraged, be killed; but do not kill . . . Thus you see how pure Christianity will not fit in with pure patriotism.

And among some notes for poems that he did not live to write are these:

The unnaturalness of weapons . . . Inhumanity of war . . . The insupportability of war . . . Horrible beastliness of war . . . Foolishness of war.

From these quotations it is obvious that the same sex holds very different opinions about the same thing. But also it is obvious, from today's newspaper, that however many dissentients there are, the great majority of your sex are today in favour of war. The Scarborough Conference of educated men, the Bournemouth Conference of working men are both agreed that to spend £300,000,000 annually upon arms is a necessity. They are of opinion that Wilfred Owen was wrong; that it is better to kill than to be killed. Yet since biography shows that differences of opinion are many, it is plain that there must be some one reason which prevails in order to bring about this overpowering unanimity. Shall we call it, for the sake of brevity, "patriotism"? What then, we must ask next, is this "patriotism" which leads you to go to war? Let the Lord Chief Justice of England interpret it for us:

Englishmen are proud of England. For those who have been trained in English schools and universities, and who have done the work of their lives in England, there are few loves stronger than the love we have for our country. When we consider other nations, when we judge the merits of the policy of this country or of that, it is the standard of our own country that we apply. . . . Liberty has made her abode in England. England is the home of democratic institutions . . . It is true that in our midst there are many enemies of liberty—some of them, perhaps, in rather unexpected quarters. But we are standing firm. It has been said that an Englishman's Home is his Castle. The home of Liberty is in England. And it is a castle indeed—a castle that will be defended to the last . . . Yes, we are greatly blessed, we Englishmen.

That is a fair general statement of what patriotism means to an educated man and what duties it imposes upon him. But the educated man's sister—what does "patriotism" mean to her? Has she the same reasons for being proud of England, for loving England, for defending England? Has she been "greatly blessed" in

England? History and biography when questioned would seem to show that her position in the home of freedom has been different from her brother's; and psychology would seem to hint that history is not without its effect upon mind and body. Therefore her interpretation of the word "patriotism" may well differ from his. And that difference may make it extremely difficult for her to understand his definition of patriotism and the duties it imposes. If then our answer to your question. "How in your opinion are we to prevent war?" depends upon understanding the reasons, the emotions, the loyalties which lead men to go to war, this letter had better be torn across and thrown into the waste-paper basket. For it seems plain that we cannot understand each other because of these differences. . . . When he says, as history proves that he has said, and may say again, "I am fighting to protect our country" and thus seeks to rouse her patriotic emotion, she will ask herself, "What does 'our country' mean to me an outsider?" To decide this she will analyse the meaning of patriotism in her own case. She will inform herself of the position of her sex and her class in the past. She will inform herself of the amount of land, wealth and property in the possession of her own sex and class in the present—how much of "England" in fact belongs to her. From the same sources she will inform herself of the legal protection which the law has given her in the past and now gives her. And if he adds that he is fighting to protect her body, she will reflect upon the degree of physical protection that she now enjoys when the words "Air Raid Precaution" are written on blank walls. And if he says that he is fighting to protect England from foreign rule, she will reflect that for her there are no "foreigners," since by law she becomes a foreigner if she marries a foreigner. And she will do her best to make this a fact, not by forced fraternity, but by human sympathy. All these facts will convince her reason (to put it in a nutshell) that her sex and class has very little to thank England for in the past; nor much to thank England for in the present; while the security of her person in the future is highly dubious. But probably she will have imbibed, even from the governess, some romantic notion that Englishmen, those fathers and grandfathers whom she sees marching in the picture of history, are "superior" to the men of other countries. This she will consider it her duty to check by comparing French historians with English; German with French; the testimony of the ruled—the Indians or the Irish, say—with the claims made by their rulers. Still some "patriotic" emotion, some ingrained belief in the intellectual superiority of her own country over other countries may remain. Then she will compare English painting with French painting; English music with German music; English literature with Greek literature, for translations abound. When all these comparisons have been faithfully made by the use of reason, the outsider will find herself in possession of very good reasons for her indifference. She will find that she has no good reason to ask her brother to fight on her behalf to protect "our" country. "'Our country,'" she will say, "throughout the greater part of its history has treated me as a slave; it has denied me education or any share in its possessions. 'Our' country still ceases to be mine if I marry a foreigner. 'Our' country denies me the means of protecting myself, forces me to pay others a very large sum annually to protect me, and is so little able, even so, to protect me that Air Raid precautions are written on the wall. Therefore if you insist upon fighting to protect me, or 'our' country, let it be understood, soberly and rationally between us, that you are fighting to gratify a sex instinct which I cannot share; to procure benefits which I have not shared and probably will not share; but not to gratify my instincts, or to protect either myself or my country. For, the outsider will say, "in fact, as a woman, I have no country. As a woman I want no country. As a woman my country is the whole world." And if, when reason has said its say, still some obstinate emotion remains, some love of England dropped into a child's ears by the cawing of rooks in an elm tree, by the splash of waves on a beach, or by English voices murmuring nursery rhymes, this drop of pure, if irrational, emotion she will make serve her to give to England first what she desires of peace and freedom for the whole world.

Such then will be the nature of her "indifference" and from this indifference certain actions must follow. She will bind herself to take no share in patriotic demonstrations; to assent to no form of national self-praise; to make no part of any claque or audience that encourages war; to absent herself from military displays, tournaments, tattoos, prize-givings and all such ceremonies as encourage the desire to impose "our" civilization or "our" dominion upon other people. The psychology of private life, moreover, warrants the belief that this use of indifference by the daughters of educated men would help materially to prevent war. For psychology would seem to show that it is far harder for human beings to take action when other people are indifferent and allow them complete freedom of action, than when their actions are made the centre of excited emotion. The small boy struts and trumpets outside the window: implore him to stop; he goes on: say nothing; he stops. That the daughters of educated men then should give their brothers neither the white feather of cowardice nor the red feather of courage, but no feather at all; that they should shut the bright eyes that rain influence, or let those eyes look elsewhere when war is discussed—that is the duty to which outsiders will train themselves in peace before the threat of death inevitably makes reason powerless.

Such then are some of the methods by which the society, the anonymous and secret Society of Outsiders would help you, Sir, to prevent war and to ensure freedom. . . .

(1938)

CHAPTER 9

Feminism and Imperialism in Late Modernity

Central Intelligence Agency interventions overseas, support for "friendly" dictators, the overthrow of the Allende government in Chile, Watergate, the efforts to overthrow the Sandinista regime [in Nicaragua], the nuclear arms buildup—all have served to strengthen the image of the United Sates as an aggressive, ruthless and unethical nation. For Americans to understand anti-Americanism they must take off their cultural blinders and see their country as others see it.

—Margarita Chant Papandreou, 1988

INTRODUCTION

This chapter focuses on modernist approaches to globalization written by second-wave feminists. The readings in this chapter span the time period from the 1970s through to the new millennium given that many second-wave feminists are still writing today. In short, it is not the date of their publication that that makes these readings late modern, but rather the approach taken to the issues of colonialism, imperialism, and militarism.

By the end of World War II, the sun had set on the European empires. Many former colonies had gained their independence through successful national liberation movements and/or because the European powers could not sustain their colonial rule during and after the devastation wrought by this war.[1] Yet colonial independence did not transform the uneven nature of global stratification. Although national liberation movements had promised greater freedom and democracy in their anticolonialist zeal, they often ended up with small, indigenous elites enjoying great wealth and power amid the poverty of the masses or what Franz Fanon called "the wretched of the earth" (Fanon, [1961] 1967). The reasons for this extremely unequal global development became the central questions debated by theorists of globalization after World War II.

Because the post–World War II era was also the Cold War era, many theorists' conceptual schemes reflected the politics of the Cold War. The Iron Curtain divide between capitalist and socialist/communist countries was used to distinguish between the First, Second, and Third Worlds. The **first world** referred to industrially developed, capitalist countries; the **second world** to industrially developed, socialist/communist countries; and the **third world** to countries that were still largely agrarian, whether capitalist or socialist.[2] Because many former colonies had achieved their political independence, the new term **neocolonialism** was used to describe the *indirect* political, economic, and cultural control by a foreign power(s)—a form of control over Third-World countries that many Western powers continued to maintain.

The post–World War II era also witnessed a significant increase in the role of global **finance capital**. Finance capital makes profits off of lending, investing, and/or manipulating money and currencies. Two major international financial agencies that were established after World War II became major players in global development policies. The **World Bank**,[3] which was established in 1944 to oversee the rebuilding of Europe after World War II, shifted its role dramatically in later decades to become the world's largest supplier of development capital and advice. The **International Monetary Fund (IMF)**, also established in 1944, significantly enlarged its scope of activities over time to include overseeing global exchange rate policies, providing financial assistance to members with balance-of-payments problems, and giving technical assistance for policies, institutions, and statistics (Symington, 2005).

The visibility of these financial institutions on the global economic landscape became clearer as their impact became harsher. In the 1980s, the World Bank and the IMF began to impose requirements on countries that had accepted loans through policies known as **structural adjustment programs (SAPs)**. To repay their debts, SAP prescriptions required cutting government expenditures on local health, education, and welfare programs, slashing wages, fostering export commodities and cash crops, and devaluing local currency—all of which had a negative effect on the lives of many Third-World peoples—especially women and children.

Of all the new developments in the post–World War II era, the Vietnam War was the major event that fostered U.S. second-wave feminists' engagement with the issues of imperialism and militarism. The carnage from this war was severe. In 1967 about 200 U.S. soldiers were killed *every week* and considerably more at the war's peak in 1968 (Gosse, 2005: 94). By the end of the war, 58,000 U.S. soldiers had died and more than 153,000 were wounded; at least 2 million Indochinese had perished (86 and 109).

THE ANTI–VIETNAM WAR MOVEMENT

The Vietnam War directly impacted second-wave feminists as their husbands, lovers, brothers, and friends were conscripted into the U.S. armed forces. Such a direct impact made them pay more attention to global issues and to the role of the U.S. military and the Central Intelligence Agency in overt and covert ventures abroad. The anti–Vietnam War movement was the largest peace movement in U.S. history. In the spring of 1970, after the campus shootings of demonstrators at Kent State and Jackson State,[4] student strikes shut down more than 500 colleges and universities across the country and it was estimated that approximately 100,000 antiwar protestors marched in the nation's capital (Anderson, 2007: 247). In the following year, antiwar demonstrations in Washington, D.C. swelled, reaching numbers ranging from 500,000 to 750,000 (Gosse, 2005: 106).

Using both Old and New Left theories, antiwar activists criticized the U.S. government for bolstering an antidemocratic government in South Vietnam and for intervening in the Vietnamese people's right to self-determination. They viewed the U.S. military as an occupying force and strongly contested their use of torture and chemical weapons like napalm and Agent Orange.[5] Reading 117, Minerva Salado's "Report from Vietnam on International Women's Day" ([1985] 1988), is a poem that first appears to describe a woman burning with passion, but she is actually burning from napalm. This poem evokes an iconic photograph from the Vietnam War era of a naked Vietnamese child screaming while she is running down a road after a napalm attack on her village.

Many women who were (or who would become) second-wave feminists were engaged in the anti–Vietnam war movement. There they learned important political and organizing skills and were immersed in the theory and political practice of the Old and New Left. However, just as first-wave activists came to realize their second-class status as women within the abolitionist movement, many second-wave activists came to feminism because of the sexism within the New Left and the Anti–Vietnam War movement. Radical feminist Robin Morgan describes this sexism below:

> Thinking we were involved in the struggle to build a new society, it was a slowly dawning and depressing realization that we were doing the same work and playing the same roles in the Movement as out of it: typing speeches that men delivered, making coffee but not policy. (R. Morgan, 1970: xxiii)

Feminists' antiwar activism would be used against them during their efforts to pass the Equal Rights Amendment. In particular, the claims that feminists were unpatriotic and that the Equal Rights Amendment would place women in combat added converts to the conservative STOP-ERA movement (Marshall, [1989] 1995; Schlafly, 1977).

MODERNIZATION THEORY AND DEPENDENCY THEORY

After World War II, the major theories used to explain uneven global development also reflected the capitalist versus socialist battle grounds of the Cold War. Modernization theorists tended to be either conservatives or moderate liberals, who were procapitalist and who located the problems of third-world countries in *internal factors* that hindered their development such as overpopulation, illiteracy, traditional values/cultures, and/or these countries' lack of resources and technology. Dependency theorists tended to be left-wing liberals, anticolonialists, and/or prosocialists who argued that the uneven and unequal development of third world countries was caused by *external factors*—namely neocolonialism by first-world governments and the exploitation of cheap labor by multinational corporations that funneled wealth from the third to the first world. Dependency theorists referred to this first-world enrichment through third-world exploitation as the "**development of underdevelopment**" (Frank, 1976; Amin, 1977).

LIBERAL FEMINISMS INSPIRED BY MODERNIZATION THEORY

A critical role played by liberal feminist global scholars in the early 1970s was to illuminate the gender issues entailed in modernization and development. One of the first and most influential works to do this was Ester Boserup's *Woman's Role in Economic Development* (1970). Using an impressive array of quantitative and qualitative cross-cultural data, she documented how women were more negatively affected by modernization than were their male counterparts. She argued that if third-world women had greater access to birth control and gained more education and opportunities to participate in the modernized sectors of the economy, their lives would be enhanced (Boserup, 1970: 224–225). Thus, Boserup did not fundamentally critique modernization itself, but rather wanted women included equally in this process.

Reading 112, "The Adverse Impact of Development on Women" (1976) by Irene Tinker,[6] summarizes the findings of some of these early global feminist studies. Tinker discusses how a gender-blind approach to modernization meant that by the time she was writing "in virtually all countries and among all classes, women have lost ground relative to men" (22). The major reason for this "deplorable phenomenon" (ibid) was that development planners too often ignored women's dual responsibilities for work inside and outside the home. Tinker describes, for example, how European colonial administrators assumed men were better farmers than women even in locales where women had been the primary cultivators. Hence, these women were not provided instruction when new agricultural techniques were introduced. Even in the post–World War II era after many former colonies became independent, development experts continued to ignore the negative impacts on women's traditional roles, their workloads, and/or their wages when they introduced advanced technologies (27). It took the work of feminist scholars, such as Tinker and Boserup, to show how "gender matters" in development.

FEMINISMS INSPIRED BY DEPENDENCY THEORY

The more revolutionary U.S. feminisms of the 1970s and early 1980s—such as Marxist feminism, socialist feminism, and intersectionality theory—were inspired by dependency theory and its focus on neocolonialism. Many of these feminists focused on two important global developments witnessed in the post–World War II era—the rise of labor-intensive, global factories and the feminization of migration. The former employed third-world women's labor in the production of commodities for the world market, whereas the latter employed third-world women's labor in the social reproduction of the everyday lives of wealthier families in more developed countries.

The 1960s witnessed the rapid expansion of multinational, labor-intensive industries in the Third World. These global factories found lucrative homes in third-world countries with first-world-friendly elites and political regimes, low levels of unionization and regulation, and cheap labor and high unemployment. This era also was characterized by the proliferation of export processing zones (EPZs) and tax-free zones (TFZs) where governments offered concessions such as infrastructural subsidies and/or tax breaks to attract foreign investment. Especially significant to feminists was how young, third-world women overwhelmingly constituted the labor force of these global factories (McMichael, 2008: 92). Reading 114, "Life on the Global Assembly Line" ([1981] 1993), by Barbara Ehrenreich and Annette

Fuentes, reveals the high levels of exploitation in these factories. When these women organized to improve their working conditions, they were met with police brutality and/or companies simply moved to other countries where the labor force was more docile.

Feminist dependency theorists also highlighted how off-shoring and outsourcing not only impacts the lives of third-world workers, but also impacts the lives of first-world working-class people who lose their jobs as a result of these processes. Between 1965 and 1985, employment in U.S. industrial manufacturing dropped from 60 percent to 26 percent, whereas employment in service jobs rose from 40 percent to 74 percent (Stacey, 1991: 18). The new jobs in the service sector did not compensate for the loss of blue-collar manufacturing jobs since many of them were lowly paid and lacked the medical and pension benefits associated with blue-collar, unionized labor. As a consequence of this wage erosion, many U.S. families, of necessity, became dual-income families. Whereas in the 1950s only 15 percent of mothers with children under the age of six were employed in the U.S. labor force, by 2002 that percentage had increased to 65 percent (Ehrenreich and Hochschild, [2002] 2004: 8).

Many people from the third world migrated to fill the growing, low-paid, service sector jobs of first-world countries, as well as the roles that first-world stay-at-home moms had once played. The **feminization of global migration** refers to the increasing number of women migrant workers crossing the globe in search of jobs. Whereas in earlier decades men had constituted the vast majority of global migrant laborers, by 1980 women began to outnumber men as global migrant laborers (Castles and Miller [1993] 1998).

Reading 121 from "The Global Trade in Filipina Workers" (1997) by Grace Chang describes the global migration of women from poor countries to rich countries where they serve as sex-workers; as nannies and maids in private homes; and as caregivers in institutional settings like hospitals, hospices, child-care centers, and nursing homes. She notes how the implementation of SAPs in the 1980s helped foster the feminization of migration (Chang, 1997: 132). Third-world governments often recruited women and men to migrate abroad because of the foreign dollars migrant workers sent back to their families. These remittances from overseas workers provided much-needed currency for their national debt payments.

Chang also discusses the third-world "brain drain" that results from these migrations. When she was writing, for example, of the approximately 100,000 registered nurses in the Philippines almost none resided in their home country (Chang, 1997: 133). In *Global Woman* ([2002] 2004), Barbara Ehrenreich and Arlie Hochschild describe how this brain drain is accompanied by a "care drain":

> As rich nations become richer and poor nations become poorer, this one-way flow of talent and training continuously widens the gap between the two. But in addition to this brain drain, there is now a parallel but more hidden and wrenching trend, as women who normally care for the young, the old, and the sick in poor countries move to care for the young, the old, and the sick in rich countries . . . It's a care drain. ([2002] 2004: 17)

The "**care drain**" refers to the children, the elderly, and the sick left behind in the third world when their mothers or fathers migrate to seek work. Today an estimated 30 percent of Filipino children live in households where at least one parent has gone overseas.

Chang's work was published in the anthology *Dragon Ladies: Asian American Feminists Breathe Fire* (1997). Many other contributors to this anthology discuss the role U.S. imperialism played their lives. Not only has U.S. imperialism in the Philippines, in the Pacific Islands, and in many countries of the Far East had a long history, but also the Korean War and the Vietnam War were conflicts that directly impacted the lives of these women and their families. By linking racism at home with imperialism abroad, these feminists provided important insights into how the global is local.

A more personal narrative that wrestles with the issue of neocolonialism can be found in Reading 118 from intersectionality theorist June Jordan's "Report from the Bahamas" ([1985] 2013). Jordan's ever-conscious awareness of race, class, gender, and neocolonialism shadow her visit to the sunny Bahamas for a brief vacation in disturbing and discomfiting ways. Her relative privilege compared to the woman who cleans her room and the women who sell hand-made goods at a local market cannot be escaped and force her to critically interrogate the bases for political connection.

Overall, feminist dependency theorists call for more first-world accountability for third-world problems, as well as policies that protect the interests of poor and working-class women globally. They also call for collective political action, such as the unionization of workers hired by multinational corporations or demonstrations against decisions harmful to working-class and poor people by international bodies such as the World Bank.

RADICAL FEMINIST GLOBAL ANALYSES

Beginning in the 1970s, radical feminists took a leading role in highlighting how patriarchal practices placed obstacles in the path of women's liberation globally. Mary Daly's *Gyn/Ecology: The MetaEthics of Radical Feminism* ([1978] 1990) was one of the most widely read radical feminist books on global, patriarchal practices. Her book had chapters on Indian suttee (sati), Chinese foot-binding, and African genital mutilation as architypes of violence against third-world women. She stated that her book would "analyze a number of barbaric rituals" to seek out the "basic patterns they have in common" that comprise a patriarchal "sado-ritual syndrome" ([1978] 1990: 111). In Reading 113 Daly describes this "sado-ritual syndrome" and discusses Indian sati as an example. This reading also shows how Daly emphasizes the "universal sameness of phallocratic morality" (112).

Radical feminists' goal was to get women across the globe to recognize their common oppression. Their notion of women globally as victims of oppression is visible in the imagery on the cover of the one of the more famous second-wave feminist journals *Off Our Backs* displayed in Reading 115. This journal, published by a nonprofit feminist collective, had a rather long lifespan covering the period from 1970 to 2008. In turn, radical feminists' focus on similarities between women across the globe is reflected in the title of Robin Morgan's book *Sisterhood Is Global* (1984) and an excerpt from this book can be found in Reading 116. Compiling the information for this book required an extraordinary degree of international networking and research. It included moving essays as well as detailed statistical information on the status of women in more than eighty countries. When it was published in 1984 it was described by Western reviewers as an "international feminist encyclopedia" and as "the definitive text on the international women's movement" (Morgan, [1984]

1996: vii). Radical feminists' global politics differed from the liberal feminist approach in that it enjoined women to create alternative social institutions separate from men where women could organize in their own interests.

Together the work of feminists locally and globally and representing various political persuasions was instrumental in the U.N.'s adoption of the **Convention on the Elimination of All Forms of Discrimination against Women (CEDAW)** in 1979, which called on member states to transform customs, attitudes, and practices that discriminated against women. As of July 2014, the United States still had not ratified CEDAW. Although the Obama administration supports its ratification, two thirds of the Senate must also agree. Over the past thirty years, more than 180 countries have become signatories of CEDAW and the U.S stands alone as the only Western industrialized country that has not done so.[7]

GLOBAL FEMINIST ANALYSES INSPIRED BY ROSA LUXEMBURG'S WORK

Given Rosa Luxemburg's focus on the devastation of premodern societies wrought by colonialism and imperialism, second-wave feminists inspired by her work went the farthest in critically interrogating Western models of development and in recognizing the negative ecological implications entailed in these models. Reading 119 from Maria Mies's *Patriarchy and Accumulation on a World Scale: Women in the International Division of Labor* (1986) discusses this devastation and highlights how women fare far worse than men as a consequence.

Similarly, in her earlier, coauthored book, *Women: The Last Colony*, she describes the impact of capitalism on women in India as follows:

> available data permits the formulation of a thesis: namely, *that capitalist penetration leads to the pauperization and marginalization of large masses of subsistence producers; and secondly, that women are more affected by these processes than men*, who may still be partly absorbed into the actual wage labour force . . . There is a growing inequality and polarization between the sexes. The capitalist penetration [of noncapitalist forms abroad], far from bringing about more equality between men and women . . . has, in fact introduced new elements of patriarchalism and sexism. (Mies et al., 1988: 40 and 41, her emphasis)

Mies explains how this process has led to the feminization of poverty and an increase in violence against women as their position deteriorates relative to men. She also discusses the dissolution of families as pauperized men migrate to the cities for wage labor while wives and daughters stay in the local villages doing subsistence farming or turning to prostitution to make ends meet (42–43).

Vandana Shiva, another feminist inspired by Luxemburg's work, uses the concept of "**maldevelopment**" to describe this devastation (Shiva, 1989: 1). An excerpt from her book *Staying Alive: Women, Ecology and Development* (1989) can be found in Reading 120. Shiva's critical interrogation of what is meant by development marks a paradigm shift in global feminist analysis.

> The old assumption that with the development process the availability of goods and services will automatically be increased and poverty will be removed is now under serious challenge from women's ecology movements in the Third World, even while it continues to guide development thinking in the centers of patriarchal power. (13)

Previous analyses of development, whether politically left, right, or center, primarily used economic growth as their major indicator of development. They argued that to increase production and alleviate third-world poverty, industrialization has to replace less efficient, premodern forms of production. This view was held by both modernization and dependency theorists and the benefits of industrialization were the common thread in these otherwise opposing capitalist and socialist paths to development.

Shiva rejects these paths to development. Her vision for the future is most clearly articulated in *Ecofeminism* (1993), coauthored with Maria Mies. They use the terms subsistence perspective and survival perspective interchangeably to refer to their alternative vision. A major feature of this subsistence perspective is changing the aim of economic activity from producing an ever-expanding "mountain of commodities" to satisfying fundamental human needs (Mies and Shiva, 1993: 319–321). Reliance on barter and social bonds of community replace the market and financial institutions, whereas natural resources such as water, soil, and oil are neither privatized nor commercialized but treated as community responsibilities. Their preference is for simple, sustainable living. This type of populist solution[8] is popular in global feminist and ecofeminist circles today and is embraced by feminists of various political persuasions including anarcha-feminists, cultural and spiritual ecofeminists, and many younger feminists of the third wave (Merchant, 1995: 3–26; Reger, 2005: 207–208).

FEMINISM AND THE MILITARY

The last half century has witnessed an increasing number of women in the U.S. military, as well as significant changes in the roles that they play. Today, women serve in many and diverse capacities, even at the highest ranks of the military. After a decade of fighting in Iraq and Afghanistan, the U.S. military had sent more than 280,000 female troops into war zones (Lerman, 2013). In July 2013, officials from all branches of the military told Congress that they will open combat positions to women by 2016. The legal battles fought for women's rights helped foster these changes, but the shortage of soldiers with the end of conscription and the new landscape of modern warfare where combat zones are everywhere and anywhere clearly hastened them (Horton, 2014).

Although the increased role of women in a hypermasculine institution like the U.S. military has been viewed by many feminists as a significant advance, it has not occurred without serious problems. Not only have women in war zones long been victims of soldier rapes (Copelon, 1994), but also even *within* the U.S. military an alarming number of women soldiers have reported rapes and sexual harassment by their male counterparts. For example, close on the heels of the Navy's "Tailhook" scandal in 2003 came the army's Aberdeen training base scandal, followed by other revelations of gay bashing, sexual harassment, and rapes by U.S. military personnel (Enloe, 1989 and 2000).

Reading 122 from Cynthia Enloe's "Wielding Masculinity inside Abu Ghraib and Guantánamo" (2007) addresses these important issues. Enloe is a second-wave feminist who has devoted her life's work to studying the impact of U.S. militarism on women abroad, as well as on women serving in the U.S. military. In this reading from *Globalization & Militarism: Feminists Make the Link* (2007), Enloe discusses an event that took place in Abu Ghraib prison in Iraq, when American soldiers, including women soldiers, used torture and sexual violence to intimidate the prisoners. Whereas the military explained this horror by pointing to a "few bad apples" (Enloe, 2007: 102) within its troops, Enloe uses the insights of second-wave feminists on sexual harassment and sexual violence to discuss how the "organizational climate" (2007: 105) of the military, itself, is the problem. She also discusses how this organizational climate is a key factor in explaining the sexual harassment and sexual violence experienced by women soldiers themselves (2007: 106–107).

CONCLUSION

Despite their many differences, late modern feminist theories heightened our awareness of how *gender matters* in global development. Prior to the work of these second-wave feminists, rarely did theorists of modernization and development—whether politically left, right, or center—have any discussion of the differential impact of modernization on men versus women. Rather, the subjects of their global studies were without gender.

NOTES

1. Between 1945 and 1981 more than 100 new countries joined the United Nations, tripling its ranks from 51 to 156 nations (McMichael, 1996: 25).
2. "Third world" is the English translation of *le tiers monde*, a term that emerged in France in the 1950s alongside the heightened anticolonial consciousness that accompanied the newly independent nations in Africa and Asia (Parpart et al., 2000: 28).
3. The proper name is the International Bank for Reconstruction and Development.
4. In May of 1970, four unarmed students were killed at Kent State University in Ohio and two more were killed later that same month at Jackson State College in Mississippi (Anderson, 2007: 249).
5. Agent Orange was the nickname given to an herbicide/defoliant used by the U.S. armed forces. This chemical not only ruined crops, but also caused a number of health problems for those exposed to it.
6. Irene Tinker cites Ester Boserup as one of her major mentors. See http://www.irenetinker.com (retrieved April 23, 2014).
7. For reasons why the U.S. has not ratified CEDAW, see Women Engaging Globally, "CEDAW in the United States: Why a Treaty for the Rights of Women?" http://www.wedo.org/files/CEDAW. Retrieved June 2, 2014 and http://www.unfinishedbusiness.org/20140717-34-years-after-signing-united-states-still-hasnt-ratified-cedaw/ Retrieved October 31, 2014.
8. A subsistence-based, populist alternative existed during Luxemburg's era. However, Luxemburg rejected the populist path and favored the socialist road to development (Nettl, 1969: 28 and 42; Mann, 1990: 22).

"THE ADVERSE IMPACT OF DEVELOPMENT ON WOMEN"

During much of the last quarter century, "development" has been viewed as the panacea for the economic ills of all less developed countries: create a modern infrastructure and the economy will take off, providing a better life for everyone. Yet in virtually all countries and among all classes, women have lost ground relative to men; development, by widening the gap between incomes of men and women, has not helped improve women's lives, but rather has had an adverse effect upon them.

The major reason for this deplorable phenomenon is that planners, generally men—whether in donor-country agencies or in recipient countries—have been unable to deal with the fact that women must perform two roles in society, whereas men perform only one. In subsistence societies, it is understood that women bear children and at the same time carry out economic activities that are essential to the family unit. Western industrial societies have chosen to celebrate the child-bearing role, glorifying motherhood while downgrading the economic functions attached to child bearing and household care, and erecting barriers to paid work for women. Accepting this stereotype of women's roles, economic theorists in the West imbued their students, indigenous and foreign, with the cliché that "women's place is in the home," classifying them forever as economically dependent. In doing so, they followed the unequivocal depiction of women in the law as legally dependent minors. Small wonder that the spread of Western "civilization," with its view of woman as "child-mother," has had an adverse impact on the more sexually equal subsistence societies. Communist doctrine errs in the opposite direction: women are economic units

first, mothers second. Since children interfere with work, the government provides day care; but little has been done in the Soviet Union or Eastern Europe to encourage men to share the responsibilities of children and home. This leaves women two time-consuming jobs: full-time work plus daily shopping, cooking, cleaning, and care of the children in the evening. Not surprisingly, the result is a drastic fall in birthrates throughout Eastern Europe—accompanied (at least in the Soviet Union) by evidence of increased marital instability and a high incidence of alcoholism among men. Yet even in these societies, where doctrine asserts that women and men are supposed to be economic equals, employment data show that women hold the least prestigious jobs.[1] It may be that in these countries also, men "subtract" a woman's home and child-care responsibilities from her ability to hold down important positions. Whatever the explanation, it would seem women lose twice.

Development planners must begin to recognize women's dual roles and stop using mythical stereotypes as a base for their development plans. A first step is to recognize the actual economic contributions of women. Even this is difficult. Statistics, the "holy building blocks" of developers, are made of the same mythical assumptions: (a) "work" is performed for *money*, and (b) "work" is located only in the *modern* sector. Thus the U.S. Department of Labor can issue a statement saying that in Africa only 5 per cent of the women work![2] This clearly is an absurd assertion about a continent where women are reported to be doing 60–80 per cent of the work in the fields and working up to 16 hours a day during the planting

From *Women and World Development*, edited by Irene Tinker and Michèle Bo Bramsen. Copyright © 1975 Irene Tinker. Used with permission.

season.[3] The "explanation" for the 5 per cent figure is that agricultural work done by family members is not recorded as "work." Nor are exchange labor, household work, child care, or many activities in the tertiary of informal sector counted as work. And since statistics do not show women working, planners do not plan for women to work. Too often new projects actually intrude on activities in which women already are engaged; but instead of providing services or training to women, assumptions about proper sex roles dictate that *men* receive the new training, new seeds, or new loans. The gap widens.

Unfortunately, this phenomenon of increased dependency of women on men is not new. The pattern has been repeated time and time again, whenever a given society developed beyond sheer subsistence and created a civilization which required functional specialization. Documenting the erosion of women's position in ancient Greece and Rome, for example, Evelyne Sullerot has observed that "as a rule it is in the early periods of each civilization that the least difference exists between the position of men and that of women. As a civilization asserts and refines itself, the gap between the relative status of men and women widens."[4] May Ebihara has noted similar "reductions" of women's status in Southeast Asia's past. She points out that a Chinese visitor to the Khmer empire in Angkor in the thirteenth century recorded that women held many positions in the court; yet within a century, due to the spread of Chinese influence after the fall of the Khmer empire, women were reduced to being legal minors of their husbands.[5]

Historically, these bureaucratic states produced a stratified society with the higher classes living in towns. It seemed to follow inevitably that women, separated from their essential food production functions, became more dependent upon men, especially as upper-class men commanded large incomes and generally adopted a more ostentatious style of living. Women lost their economic base and came to be valued mainly for their female attributes of child bearing and providing sexual gratification. Thus they increasingly came to be "protected" or "confined"—perceived as "jewels" for men to play with or as vehicles for perpetuating the family line. However, they were then also perceived—accurately—as *economic liabilities*. In subsistence societies, where women are a valuable economic commodity, a man pays a bride price to the bride's father to buy her services; in societies where women have lost their economic function, the exchange of money is reversed, and the bride's family pays the groom to accept her.

Recent studies recording women's roles in subsistence economies show a panoply of traditional roles, both economic and familial, whose patterns more often add up to near serfdom than to any significant degree of independence and personal dignity for women. Yet those studies show that, however onerous women's lives, development plans have seldom helped them. Rather, development has tended to put obstacles in women's way that frequently prevent them even from maintaining what little economic independence they do have. Laws and customs designed to protect women also can cause hardship. Even education can widen the gap between men and women. This is not to say that development never helps women; the case being made is that, *compared to men*, women almost universally have lost as development has proceeded. If economic planners would only look at recent (and long-standing) anthropological evidence, they hopefully would recognize that women's productive contributions to the economy have been and can continue to be important, and perhaps would begin to plan projects which not only support women's work but also open up opportunities for women to become part of the modern economic system. With this objective in mind, this paper will now review the existing evidence which shows how development has negatively affected the productivity of women in different areas of life.

CHANGE IN SUBSISTENCE ECONOMIES

In subsistence economies every family member traditionally is assigned roles which are essential to the survival of the unit, whether that unit is a small "nuclear" family or an extended one. Men as well as women have dual functions: family roles are integrated with economic roles. While in any given society these roles generally are sex-specific, they vary from culture to culture. Almost everywhere change has meant a diminution of men's roles in caring for and training children or assisting in household tasks. Since development is primarily concerned with economic activity, and since it is women's traditional economic role that has been ignored, we shall focus on this function and how it has changed for both men and women.

Ester Boserup—in her landmark book, *Woman's Role in Economic Development*—has linked the variation of sex roles in farming to different types of agriculture. In subsistence farming where land is plentiful, a slash-and-burn technique is the typical agricultural style; generally men clear the land and women do the bulk of the farming. This agricultural technique is still predominant in Africa but is also found in many parts of Asia and Central and South America When population increase limits land availability, draft animals are brought in to increase productivity through the use of the plough.

> And the advent of the plough usually entails a radical shift in sex roles in agriculture; men take over the ploughing even in regions where the hoeing had formerly been women's work. At the same time, the amount of weeding to be done by the women may decline on land ploughed before sowing and planting, and either men or women may get a new job of collecting feed for the animals and feeding them.[6]

As population pressure on land increases further, more labor-intensive crops are introduced and grown year-round in irrigated fields. Women are drawn back into the fields—to plant, weed, and harvest alongside the men.

In addition to their important role in farming, women in subsistence economies traditionally have engaged in a variety of other economic activities— spinning fibers, weaving cloth, drawing water, tending market gardens, and processing and preserving foods gathered from communal property. Women in Southeast Asia boil palm sugar. West African women brew beer. Women in parts of Mexico and elsewhere make pottery. Women in most countries weave cloth and make clothes. Women in most cultures sell their surplus food in local markets. Profits from these activities generally belong to the women themselves. Thus women in many parts of the world have become known for their astuteness in the marketplace. Javanese women have a reputation for being thrifty, while Javanese men consider themselves incapable of handling money wisely. In Nicaragua, women continue to dominate the traditional marketplace, which caters to the lower classes, despite the availability of modern supermarkets nearby.[7] Market women of West Africa have parlayed their

economic strength into political power as well. In contrast, Hindu and Arab women seldom are seen in the markets as buyers and never as sellers. But these women come from societies that have long been bureaucratized and in which women have lost some of their earlier economic independence.

Erosion of the role that women played in subsistence economies began under colonial rule. Policies aimed at improving or modernizing the farming systems, particularly the introduction of the concept of private property and the encouragement of cash crops, favored men. Under tribal custom, women who were farmers had users' rights to land. Colonial regimes, past and recent, seldom have felt comfortable with customary communal land-tenure rights and have tended to convert land to private ownership—in some cultures thereby dispossessing the women, in disregard of local tradition, by recognizing men as the new owners. This was as true of the Chinese in Southeast Asia and the Spanish in Latin America as it was of the Europeans in Asia and Africa. Thus woman still farmed the land but no longer owned it and therefore became dependent on their fathers or their brothers. Wherever colonial governments introduced cash crops, these were considered to be men's work. Much of the agricultural development was focused on improving these crops. To encourage the men to take jobs on plantations or to grow cash crops on their own land, governments frequently introduced taxes—thereby forcing men (who were more mobile) into the modern money economy, while women (with child-rearing responsibilities) remained in rural areas and hence in the subsistence economy. Their lack of access to money and loss of control of land left women with little incentive to improve either crops or the land in areas where they continued to dominate the farming system. Furthermore, access to the modern sector, whether in agriculture or industry, has drawn men away from their households and often even from their land, and thus has given women additional tasks that formerly were men's work. Not surprisingly, productivity has declined as "development" has proceeded.

Efforts to reverse this trend have been undertaken by development agencies, but their stereotypes concerning the sex of the farmer often have led to ridiculous results. In 1974 Liberia decided to try to encourage wet-rice cultivation and brought to the country a team of Taiwanese farmers. To assure attendance at the demonstration planting, the government offered wages to the observers. Many unemployed men participated in the experiment while the women continued their work in the fields. Throughout Africa, rural extension services, modeled on those in the United States, have been staffed and attended by men only; custom prevented rural women from attending courses taught by men, and the courses taught by women—mainly home economics courses on canning and sewing—were irrelevant to their needs. Cooperatives, too, tended to assume that farmers were males. Thus the men had access to credit or to improved seeds which they used to produce cash crops; women in the subsistence sector were barred from membership as well as from growing cash crops.

Perhaps because the economic position of women in Africa was deteriorating so quickly, active opposition to this trend started there. Nigerian women formed all-female cooperatives and demanded credit to buy more efficient oil pressers to use in processing palm-oil nuts. Under pressure from women's groups, the government of Kenya reinterpreted the cooperative regulations to allow membership to women, and then formed a special task force to show women how to utilize this new opportunity. Zambian women were taught how to grow onions as a cash crop, in between rows of the usual subsistence crops. They were so successful that men demanded similar assistance: this venture turned sour when the women refused to tend the men's onions, claiming it was not a traditional obligation! In Tanzania the government is encouraging the establishment of Ujamaa villages, where land is held communally and workers are paid according to their efforts; in these villages, women for the first time are being paid for growing subsistence crops. Marjorie Mbilinyi writes that "it is therefore not surprising that women are the most ardent supporters of socialist rural policies in many areas of Tanzania."[8]

The ways in which development agencies have introduced new technologies likewise have tended to contribute to the undermining of women's traditional roles. Small implements such as presses, grinders, or cutters generally have been introduced to men, even when the work for which they are a substitute traditionally has been done by women. The availability of corn grinders in Kenya, for example, clearly saves women many hours of manual effort—though they also spend hours going to the grinding center. But why are women

themselves not taught to operate these grinders? Oil presses in Nigeria, tortilla-making machines in Mexico, and sago-processing machines in Sarawak also are purchased and operated by men—because only men have access to credit or to money.[9] Stereotypes that women cannot manage technology are reinforced by the fact that illiteracy is more widespread among women, who therefore cannot read instructions.

Agricultural technology has produced the "green revolution" and has altered traditional agricultural practices. The high capitalization involved in buying improved seed varieties and fertilizers has pressured farmers into more efficient harvesting arrangements which often utilize fewer laborers and increase unemployment. Planners know this and often have tried to create alternative employment for the displaced *men*. But, in most economies that rely on wet-rice cultivation, it is the women who do the harvesting. A detailed study on Central Java, for example, noted that the women formerly accepted low wages for planting in order to receive payment in rice itself for harvesting work. Today the harvesting is done by mobile teams of men using the more efficient scythe; women, who harvested with a hand knife, have lost their rights to harvest and have not yet been able to obtain higher wages for planting.[10]

Improved transportation systems have affected traditional markets in both positive and negative ways. In Mexico, for example, improved transport has increased demand for locally made ceramic animal figures, thereby increasing rural earnings. It has made manufactured fabrics available in even the smallest towns, enabling women to make clothing without having to weave the cloth. Moreover, travel to markets in town has eased the drudgery of women's lives in rural areas.[11] On the other hand, improved transport has made many traditional occupations redundant. It has opened new markets for manufactured goods that compete with local, hand-made artifacts. Traders from more distant towns are taking over local markets, undercutting the traditional suppliers: women traders from outlying villages. In Java, the importation of Coca-Cola and Australian ice cream ruined local soft drink manufacture and ice cream production; both enterprises had been dominated by women. Sago processing by women in Sarawak was replaced by machine processing run by Chinese men. Men's enterprises also have suffered from competition with national or international firms.

A study of governmental policies in Zaria, Nigeria, showed that small businesses run by men suffered from the lack of basic services—particularly water, light, and credit—and that this prevented their expansion; in contrast, two large local factories, producing tobacco and textiles, were fostered by governmental policy.[12] Planners usually are aware of and try to ease the demise of small businesses in the wake of modern industrialization. What they have forgotten, however, is the sex of the entrepreneurs—and hence have attempted to provide alternative employment for *men only*. . . .

CONCLUSION

In subsistence economies, the process of development has tended to restrict the economic independence of women as their traditional jobs have been challenged by new methods and technologies. Because Western stereotypes of appropriate roles and occupations for women tend to be exported with aid, modernization continually increases the gap between women's and men's ability to cope with the modern world. Elites in these countries are imbued with middle-class Western values relegating women to a subordinate place—values often transmitted by the industrial world's bureaucratic systems, which frequently reinforce such stereotypes in their own societies.

In the developed, "modern" world, women continue to experience restricted economic opportunities while at the same time finding increased family obligations thrust upon them. The strange contrast of this reality with the Western ideal of "equality for all" increasingly has made women aware of this injustice. Instead of docilely accepting their fate, women are becoming increasingly hostile, leaving marriage behind, and taking on the dual functions of work and family without the added burden of husband. A redress is overdue. Planners must not only consider and support women's economic activities but must also find ways of mitigating the drudgery of housework and the responsibility of child rearing. The roles assigned each sex must again be made more equal—with men as well as women accepting their dual functions of work and family.

For a time after World War II, there was great optimism about the ability of the world to proceed apace with economic development. Today there is a growing realization that development is a more elusive concept than had been previously thought. Even where countries are able to boast of a rising gross national product in the face of population growth, it is recognized that Western-style development approaches of the past have tended to make the rich richer and the poor poorer, both within countries and among countries. Not only women but the poor generally have been left out.

Not surprisingly, many economists are looking for alternative paths to development, and are showing an increasing interest in the experiences of such non-Western countries as the Soviet Union and China. In their impact on women, however, these non-Western models also are inadequate; in a sense they err twice, for while women's nurturing roles are deemphasized in favor of their economic roles, women continue to have access only to the less important economic and political roles. Clearly these models—whatever the impact of their policies on the women in their own countries—also cannot and should not be exported without major adaptation, or they too will undermine women's traditional roles. What is needed, therefore, is not an imported model, but rather an adaptation of development goals to each society—an adaptation that will ensure benefits for women as well as men.

(1976)

NOTES

1. Barbara W. Jancar, "Women Under Communism," in Jane S. Jaquette, ed., *Women in Politics* (New York: John Wiley & Sons. 1974), pp. 217–42.
2. U.S. Congress, House of Representatives, Committee on Foreign Affairs, Subcommittee on International Organizations and Movements, "International Protection of Human Rights" (hearings August–December 1973), 93rd Congress, p. 444.
3. U.N. Economic Commission for Africa, Women's Programme Unit. "The Integration of Women in African Development," paper prepared for the 14th Conference of the Society for International Development, Abidjan, Ivory Coast, 1974.
4. Evelyne Sullerot, *Women, Society, and Change* (New York: McGraw–Hill, World University Library, 1971), p. 19.
5. May Ebihara, "Khmer Village Women in Cambodia," in Carolyn S. Matthiasson, ed., *Many Sisters: Women in*

Cross-Cultural Perspective (New York: The Free Press, 1974), pp. 305–48.

6. Ester Boserup, *Woman's Role in Economic Development* (London: George Allen and Unwin, Ltd., 1970), p. 33.

7. Hildred Geertz, *The Javanese Family* (New York. The Free Press, 1961); and Margaret Hagen, "Notes on the Public Markets and Marketing System of Managua, Nicaragua" (Managua: Institute Centroamericano de Administración de Empresas, 1974).

8. Marjorie J. Mbilinyi, "Barriers to the Full Participation of Women in the Socialist Transformation of Tanzania," paper presented at the Conference on the Role of Rural Women in Development, sponsored by the Agricultural Development Council, Princeton, New Jersey, 1974.

9. Charlotte Stolmaker, "Examples of Stability and Change from Santa Maria Atzompa," paper presented at the Southwestern Anthropological Association Meeting,

Tucson, Arizona, 1971; and Barbara E. Ward, "Women and Technology in Developing Countries," *Impact of Science on Society*, Vol. 20, No. 1 (1970). Describing the adverse effects of technology, Beverly Chiñas observes: "Modern technology imported by foreigners brings with it a preference for male employees." (Beverly Chiñas, "La participación femenina en el sistema educacional Venezolano," Documento técnico 2 (Caracas: Centro de Estudios Sociales con la Cooperación de AITEC, 1975).

10. Ann Stoler, "Land, Labor and Female Autonomy in a Javanese Village," unpublished manuscript, 1975.

11. Stolmaker, "Examples of Stability," op. cit., p. 23; and Ward, "Women and Technology," op. cit., p. 96.

12. Dorothy Remy and John Weeks, "Employment, Occupation and Inequality in a Non-Industrialized City," in K. Wohlmuth, ed., *Employment in Emerging Societies* (New York: Praeger, 1973).

113 • *Mary Daly*

FROM *GYN/ECOLOGY*
The Metaethics of Radical Feminism

INDIAN *SUTTEE*:
THE ULTIMATE CONSUMMATION OF MARRIAGE

> Slow advancing, halting, creeping,
> Comes the Woman to the hour!
> She walketh veiled and sleeping,
> For she knoweth not her power.
>
> Charlotte Perkins Gilman,
> from "She Walketh Veiled and Sleeping,"
> *In This Our World*

> "I have not deserved it. . . . Why must I die like this, alone with my mortal enemy?"
>
> Willa Cather,
> *My Mortal Enemy*

"Widow" is a harsh and hurtful word. It comes from the Sanskrit and it means "empty." . . . I resent what the term has come to mean. I am alive. I am part of the world.

Lynn Caine,
Widow

They speak together of the threat they have constituted towards authority, they tell how they were burned on pyres to prevent them from assembling in future.

Monique Wittig,
Les Guérillères

The Indian rite of *suttee*, or widow-burning, might at first appear totally alien to contemporary Western society, where widows are not ceremoniously burned alive on the funeral pyres of their husbands.* Closer examination unveils its connectedness with "our" rituals. Moreover, the very attempt to examine the ritual and its social context through the re-sources of Western scholarship demonstrates this connectedness. For the

scholars who produced these re-sources exhibit by their very language their complicity in the same social order which was/is the radical source of such rites of female sacrifice.

The hindu rite of *suttee* spared widows from the temptations of impurity by forcing them to "immolate themselves," that is to be burned alive, on the funeral pyres of their husbands. This ritual sacrifice must be

---

*Although *suttee* was legally banned in 1829, and despite the existence of other legal reforms, it should not be imagined that the lot of most Indian women has changed dramatically since then, or since the publication of Katherine Mayo's *Mother India* in 1927. The situation of most widows is pitiable. An article in an Indian paper, the *Sunday Standard*, May 11, 1975, described the wretched existence of the 7,000 widows of the town of Brindaban, "the living spectres whose life has been eroded by another's death." These poverty-stricken women with shaved heads and with a single white cloth draped over their bare bodies are forced every morning to chant praise ("*Hare Rama, Hare Rama, Rama Rama, Hare Hare, Hare Krishna*" . . . ad nauseam) for four hours in order to get a small bowl of rice. In mid-afternoon they must chant for four more hours in order to receive the price of a glass of tea. A not unusual case is that of a sixty-nine-year-old widow who was married at the age of nine and widowed at eleven, and has been waiting ever since for the "day of deliverance." Surveys carried out by an Indian Committee on the Status of Women revealed that a large percentage of the Indian population still approves of such oppression of widows.

An Indian woman need not be widowed to be victimized. Many are literally starved to death. An article in an Indian magazine, *Youth Times*, March 7, 1975, states: "Our marriage ceremony puts her two steps behind the sacrificial fire—like a puppy that must follow its master. It is a place that spells disaster for millions. For it is a medical fact that the malnutrition and anaemia that plague such a vast number of our women have a basis in the habit of the women eating after they have served their husbands, a practice which in poor homes means virtual starvation" (p. 23). A look at tables of

age-specific death rates is revealing. In 1969, in rural India, it was estimated that 70.2 females per thousand under the age of four died, while the death rate for males was 58.3. Since infant mortality generally is higher among males, it is reasonable to believe that these girl children got less to eat or were purposefully starved. The death rate for females is significantly higher in each age group up to the age of thirty-four (Devaki Jain, ed., *Indian Women* [Publications Division, Ministry of Information and Broadcasting, Government of India, 1975], p. 148). A number of sources, including Jain, refer obliquely to the high rate of "suicide" among women. Jain suggests that suicide "must seem an attractive way out of an intolerable situation" (p. 77). Jain is here referring to victims of the dowry system. The bride is often tormented and pressured to extract more money from her parents. In some cases she is murdered by her in-laws when her parents fail to come through. On January 13, 1977, the *New York Times* reported the details of one such murder of a twenty-year-old wife, who was strangled and burned in kerosene by her husband and in-laws. The article suggested that there are many such "dowry murders" in India each year, most of them disguised as kitchen accidents. These are occasionally reported in the Indian press in brief notices (as are cases of women murdered for not bearing sons). Although there was a Dowry Prohibition Act in 1961, according to the *Sunday Standard* (New Delhi, November 10, 1974), it is doubtful whether there has been even one instance of its enforcement. In addition to these horrors there is high maternal mortality resulting from extremely early marriage, too many pregnancies, maternal malnutrition, and unspeakably filthy and destructive methods of "delivery."

understood within its social context. Since their religion forbade remarriage and at the same time taught that the husband's death was the fault of the widow (because of her sins in a previous incarnation if not in this one), everyone was free to despise and mistreat her for the rest of her life. Since it was a common practice for men of fifty, sixty, or seventy years of age to marry child-brides, the quantitative surplus of such unmarriageable widows boggles the imagination. Lest we allow our minds to be carried away with astronomic numerical calculations, we should realize that this ritual was largely confined to the upper caste, although there was a tendency to spread downward. We should also realize that in some cases—particularly if the widow was an extremely young child before her husband's unfortunate (for her) death—there was the option of turning to a life of prostitution, which would entail premature death from venereal disease. This, however, would be her only possible escape from persecution by in-laws, sons, and other relatives. As a prostitute, of course, she would be held responsible for the spread of more moral and physical impurity.

If the general situation of widowhood in India was not a sufficient inducement for the woman of higher caste to throw herself gratefully and ceremoniously into the fire, she was often pushed and poked in with long stakes after having been bathed, ritually attired, and drugged out of her mind. In case these facts should interfere with our clear misunderstanding of the situation, Webster's invites us to re-*cover* women's history with the following definition of suttee: "the act or custom of a Hindu woman *willingly* cremating herself or being cremated on the funeral pyre of her husband as an indication of her *devotion* to him [emphases mine]." It is thought-provoking to consider the reality behind the term *devotion*, for indeed a wife must have shown signs of extraordinarily slavish devotion during her husband's lifetime, since her very life depended upon her husband's state of health. A thirteen-year-old wife might well be concerned over the health of her sixty-year-old husband.

Joseph Campbell discusses *suttee* as the Hindu form of the widely practiced "custom" of sending the family or part of it "into the other world along with the chief member." The time-honored practice of "human sacrifice," sometimes taking the form of live burial, was common also in other cultures, for example in ancient Egypt. Campbell notes that Professor George Reisner

excavated an immense necropolis in Nubia, an Egyptian province, and found, without exception, "a pattern of burial with human sacrifice—specifically, female sacrifice: of the wife and, in the more opulent tombs, the entire harem, together with the attendants." After citing Reisner's descriptions of female skeletons, which indicated that the victims had died hideous deaths from suffocation, Campbell writes:

> In spite of these signs of suffering and even panic in the actual moment of the pain of suffocation, we should certainly not think of the mental-state and experience of these individuals after any model of our own more or less imaginable reactions to such a fate. For these sacrifices were not properly, in fact, individuals at all; that is to say, they were not particular beings, distinguished from a class or group by virtue of any sense or realization of a personal, individual destiny or responsibility.

I have not italicized any of the words in this citation because it seemed necessary to stress *every* word. It is impossible to make any adequate comment.

At first, *suttee* was restricted to the wives of princes and warriors, but as one scholar (Benjamin Walker) deceptively puts it, "in course of time *the widows* of weavers, masons, barbers and others of lower caste *adopted the practice* [emphases mine]." The use of the active voice here suggests that the widows actively sought out, enforced, and accepted this "practice." Apparently without any sense of inconsistency the same author supplies evidence that relatives forced widows to the pyre. He describes a case reported in 1796, in which a widow escaped from the pyre during the night in the rain. A search was made and she was dragged from her hiding place. Walker concludes the story of this woman who "adopted the practice" as follows:

> She pleaded to be spared but her own son insisted that she throw herself on the pile as he would lose caste and suffer everlasting humiliation. When she still refused, the son with the help of some others present bound her hands and feet and hurled her into the blaze.

The same author gives information about the numerical escalation of *suttee*:

> Among the Rājputs and other warrior nations of northern India, the observance of suttee took on staggering proportions, since wives and concubines *immolated themselves* by the hundred. It became customary not

only for wives but for mistresses, sisters, mothers, sisters-in-law and other near female relatives and retainers *to burn themselves* along with their deceased master. With Rājputs it evolved into the terrible rite of *jauhar* which took place in times of war or great peril *in order to save the honour of the womenfolk of the clan* [emphases mine].

Again the victims, through grammatical sleight of hand, are made to appear as the agents of their own destruction. The rite of *jauhar* consisted in heaping all the females of the clan into the fire when there was danger of defeat by the enemy. Thousands of hindu women were murdered this way during the muslim invasion of India. Their masters could not bear that they should be raped, tortured, and killed by foreign males adhering to "different" religious beliefs, rather than by themselves.

The term *custom*—a casual and neutral term—is often used by scholars to describe these barbarous rituals of female slaughter. Clearly, however, they were religious rites. Some scholars assert that an unscrupulous priesthood provided the religious legitimation for the practice by rigging the text of the Rig Veda. Priests justified the ritual atrocity by their interpretations of the law of Karma. Furthermore, the typical mind-diverting orderliness of murderous religious ritual was manifested not only in the ceremonial bathing and dressing of the widows, but included other details of timing and placement. If the widow was menstruating, she was considered impure, and thus a week had to pass after the cessation of her period before she could commit *suttee*. Since impurity also resulted from pregnancy, *suttee* had to be delayed two months after the birth of the child. For the event itself, the widow was often required to sit with the corpse's head in her lap or on her breast. The orderliness is that of ritual: repetitive, compulsive, delusional.

This horror show was made possible by the legitimating role of religious rite, which allows the individual to distinguish between the real self, who may be fearful or scrupulous, and the self as role-performer. This schizoid perception on the part of those participating in the ritual carries over to the scholars who, though temporally or spatially distanced from the rite, identify with *it* rather than with the victims. Joseph Campbell placidly writes of the tortured and sacrificed woman:

Sati, the feminine participle of *sat*, then, is the female who really is something in as much as she is truly and properly a player of the female part: she is not only good and true in the ethical sense but true and real ontologically. In her faithful death, she is at one with her own true being.

Thus the ontological and moral problems surrounding female massacre are blandly dismissed. Campbell is simply discussing a social context in which, for a woman, to be killed is "good and true," and to cease to exist is to be. His androcratically attached de-tachment from women's agony is manifested in paragraph after paragraph. After describing the live burial of a young widow which took place in 1813, this devotee of the rites of de-tached scholarship describes the event as "an *illuminating*, though *somewhat* appalling, glimpse into the deep, silent pool of the Oriental, archaic soul . . . [emphases mine]." What eludes this scholar is the fact that the "archaic soul" was a woman destroyed by Patriarchal Religion (in which he is a true believer), which demands female sacrifice.

The bland rituals of patriarchal scholarship perpetuate the legitimation of female sacrifice. The social reality, unacknowledged by such myth-masters, is that of minds and bodies mutilated by degradation. The real social context included the common practice of marrying off small girls to old men, since brahmans have what has been called a "strange preference for children of very tender years." Katherine Mayo, in an excellent work entitled with appropriate irony, *Mother India*, shows an understanding of the situation which more famous scholars entirely lack. Her work is, in the precise sense of the word, exceptional. She writes:

That so hideous a fate as widowhood should befall a woman can be but for one cause—the enormity of her sins in a former incarnation. From the moment of her husband's decease till the last hour of her own life, she must expiate those sins in shame and suffering and self-immolation, chained in every thought to the service of his soul. Be she a child of three, who knows nothing of the marriage that bound her, or be she a wife in fact, having lived with her husband, her case is the same. By his death she is revealed as a creature of innate guilt and evil portent, herself convinced when she is old enough to think at all, of the justice of her fate.

. . .

THE PATTERN OF THE SADO-RITUAL SYNDROME

In order to re-member female divinity, it is important for Hags/Spinsters to look carefully at the pattern of the maze of gynocidal ritual illustrated in *suttee* and its aftereffects. I have shown that there are a number of layers/levels of erasure. These are all designed to stop the Journey of women finding our Selves—a Journey which is quest-ing, be-ing. They are also designed to stop women from finding each other, for this is essential to finding our Selves. Thus feminist Searchers are blocked/divided from knowing their sisters who have been erased by ritual atrocities, and the rituals of re-search function to ensure this blockage, sending feminist would-be Searchers repeatedly down blind alleys. The few who find their way at last through the maze are often too far ahead of their sister Searchers for the latter to catch up. Meanwhile the researchers have time to spread propaganda discrediting these dis-coverers, and their findings are effectively re-covered. All of these elements are parts of the Sado-Ritual Syndrome. We are now in a position to perceive the operative pattern of this Syndrome, which is illustrated in the ritual of *suttee* and its aftereffects, and which we can find—if we look wildly, listen keenly—over and over again in the other ritual atrocities of androcracy.

I

In the Sado-Ritual we find, first, an obsession with purity. This obsession legitimates the fact that the women who are the primary victims of the original rites are erased physically as well as spiritually. These primary victims are often killed, as in the case of the rite of *suttee.* In other cases, such as Chinese footbinding, as we shall see later, they are physically and psychically maimed. This original erasure obviously keeps the primary victims from being witnesses. In the name of "purity," they are effectively silenced. Thus the widows' sexual purity is "safeguarded" by ritual murder. In preparation for this ultimate purification they are ceremoniously bathed, and care is taken to kill them at a "pure" time, that is, when they are not menstruating or pregnant. Thus "society" is purified of these "wicked" widows and also of all traces of female rebelliousness, for the women and girl-children who witness these

events or hear of them must be perfectly brainwashed with terror of the same fate.

II

Second, there is total erasure of responsibility for the atrocities performed through such rituals. Those doing the destruction commonly have recourse to the idea that they are acting "under orders," or following tradition (serving a Higher Order). This allows the self as role-carrier to commit acts which the personal/private self would find frightening or evil.

III

Third, gynocidal ritual practices have an inherent tendency to "catch on" and spread, since they appeal to imaginations conditioned by the omnipresent ideology of male domination. Moreover, since the patriarchal imagination is hierarchical, there is a proliferation of atrocities from an elite to the upwardly aspiring lower echelons of society.

IV

Fourth, women are used as scapegoats and token torturers (for example, by the "setting up" of mothers-in-law as to blame for the widows' doom). This masks the male-centeredness of the ritualized atrocity and turns women against each other.

V

Fifth, we find compulsive orderliness, obsessive repetitiveness, and fixation upon minute details, which divert attention from the horror. In short, attention is focused upon what is proper and ceremonial, rather than upon the woman's horrible suffering and death.

VI

Sixth, behavior which at other times and places is unacceptable becomes acceptable and even normative as a consequence of conditioning through the ritual atrocity. Such value judgments are easily interchangeable in the swinging-pendulum society characterized by consciousness split into false opposites. Thus it is not surprising that the practice is desired and sometimes continued even after it has officially/legally been terminated, as in the recurring instances of "practical *suttee*."

VII

Seventh, there is legitimation of the ritual by the rituals of "objective" scholarship—despite appearances of disapproval. The basic cultural assumptions which make the atrocious ritual possible and plausible remain unquestioned, and the practice itself is misnamed and isolated from other parallel symptoms of the planetary patriarchal practice of female maiming and massacre.

Jan Raymond has suggested that such scholarship could be called *meta-ritual*. The name is accurate, for this kind of writing not only "records" (erases) the original rituals but also provides "explanations" and legitimations for them, purporting to see beyond their materiality into their "soul" or meaning. This legitimation by the Rites of Re-search is an extension of the primordial gynocidal acts. The practitioners of these Last Rites re-enact the original rites by erasing their meaning and by effacing those Searchers who did weave their way through the mazes of re-search with integrity, dis-covering the forbidden fruit of their labors, that is, the *facts*.

(1978)

114 • *Barbara Ehrenreich and Annette Fuentes*

"LIFE ON THE GLOBAL ASSEMBLY LINE"

In Ciudad Juarez, Mexico, Anna M. rises at 5 A.M. to feed her son before starting on the two-hour bus trip to the maquiladora (factory). He will spend the day along with four other children in a neighbor's one-room home. Anna's husband, frustrated by being unable to find work for himself, left for the United States six months ago. She wonders, as she carefully applies her new lip gloss, whether she ought to consider herself still married. It might be good to take a night course, become a secretary. But she seldom gets home before eight at night, and the factory, where she stitches brassieres that will be sold in the United States through J.C. Penney, pays only $48 a week.

In Penang, Malaysia, Julie K. is up before the three other young women with whom she shares a room, and starts heating the leftover rice from last night's supper. She looks good in the company's green-trimmed uniform, and she's proud to work in a modern, American-owned factory. Only not quite so proud as when she started working three years ago—she thinks as *she squints out the door at a passing group of women. Her job involves peering all day through a microscope, bonding hair-thin gold wires to a silicon chip destined to end up inside a pocket calculator, and at 21, she is afraid she can no longer see very clearly.*

Every morning between four and seven, thousands of women like Anna and Julie head out for the day shift. In Ciudad Juárez, they crowd into ruteras (run-down vans) for the trip from the slum neighborhoods to the industrial parks on the outskirts of the city. In Penang they squeeze, 60 or more at a time, into buses for the trip from the village to the low, modem factory buildings of the Bayan Lepas free trade zone. In Taiwan, they walk from the dormitories—where the night shift is already asleep in the still-warm beds—through the checkpoints in the high fence surrounding the factory zone.

This is the world's new industrial proletariat: young, female. Third World, Viewed from the "first world," they are still faceless, genderless "cheap labor," signaling their existence only through a label or tiny imprint— "made in Hong Kong," or Taiwan, Korea, the Dominican Republic, Mexico, the Philippines. But they may be one of the most strategic blocks of womenpower in the world of the 1980s. Conservatively, there are 2 million Third World female industrial workers employed now, millions more looking for work, and their numbers are rising every year. Anyone whose image of Third World women features picturesque peasants with babies slung on their backs should be prepared to update it. Just in the last decade, Third World women have become a critical element in the global economy and a key "resource" for expanding multinational corporations.

It doesn't take more than second-grade arithmetic to understand what's happening. In the United States, an assembly-line worker is likely to earn, depending on her length of employment, between $3.10 and $5 an hour. In many Third World countries, a woman doing the same work will earn $3 to $5 a *day*. According to the magazine "Business Asia," in 1976 the average hourly wage for unskilled work (male or female) was 55 cents in Hong Kong, 52 cents in South Korea, 32 cents in the Philippines, and 17 cents in Indonesia. The logic of the situation is compelling: why pay someone in Massachusetts $5 an hour to do what someone in Manila will do for $2.50 a day? Or as a corollary, why pay a male worker anywhere to do what a female worker will do for 40 to 60 percent less?

And so, almost everything that can be packed up is being moved out to the Third World; not heavy industry, but just about anything light enough to travel—garment manufacture, textiles, toys, footwear, pharmaceuticals, wigs, appliance parts, tape decks, computer components, plastic goods. In some industries, like garment and textile, American jobs are lost in the process, and the biggest losers are women, often black and Hispanic. But what's going on is much more than a matter of runaway shops. Economists are talking about a "new international division of labor," in which the process of production is broken down and the fragments are dispersed to different parts of the world. In general, the low-skilled jobs are farmed out to the Third World, where labor costs are minuscule, while control over the overall process and technology remains safely at

company headquarters in "first world" countries like the United States and Japan.

The American electronics industry provides a classic example: circuits are printed on silicon wafers and tested in California; then the wafers are shipped to Asia for the labor-intensive process by which they are cut into tiny chips and bonded to circuit boards; final assembly into products such as calculators or military equipment usually takes place in the United States. Garment manufacture too is often broken into geographically separated steps, with the most repetitive, labor-intensive jobs going to the poor countries of the southern hemisphere. Most Third World countries welcome whatever jobs come their way in the new division of labor, and the major international development agencies—like the World Bank and the United States Agency for International Development (AID)— encourage them to take what they can get.

So much any economist could tell you. What is less often noted is the *gender* breakdown of the emerging international division of labor. Eighty to 90 percent of the low-skilled assembly jobs that go to the Third World are performed by women—in a remarkable switch from earlier patterns of foreign-dominated industrialization. Until now, "development" under the aegis of foreign corporations has usually meant more jobs for men and—compared to traditional agricultural society—a diminished economic status for women. But multinational corporations and Third World governments alike consider assembly-line work—whether the product is Barbie dolls or missile parts—to be "women's work."

One reason is that women can, in many countries, still be legally paid less than men. But the sheer tedium of the jobs adds to the multinationals' preference for women workers—a preference made clear, for example, by this ad from a Mexican newspaper: *We need female workers; older than 17, younger than 30; single and without children; minimum education primary school, maximum education one year of preparatory school* {high school}; *available for all shifts.*

It's an article of faith with management that only women can do, or will do, the monotonous, painstaking work that American business is exporting to the Third World. Bill Mitchell, whose job is to attract United States businesses to the Bermudez Industrial Park in Ciudad Juárez told us with a certain macho pride: "A man just won't stay in this tedious kind of work. He'd walk out in a couple of hours." The personnel manager of a light assembly plant in Taiwan told anthropologist Linda Gail Arrigo: "Young male workers are too restless and impatient to do monotonous work with no career value. If displeased, they sabotage the machines and even threaten the foreman. But girls? At most, they cry a little."

In fact, the American businessmen we talked to claimed that Third World women genuinely enjoy doing the very things that would drive a man to assault and sabotage. "You should watch these kids going into work," Bill Mitchell told us. "You don't have any sullenness here. They smile." A top-level management consultant who specializes in advising American companies on where to relocate their factories gave us this global generalization: "The [factory] girls genuinely enjoy themselves. They're away from their families. They have spending money. They can buy motorbikes, whatever. Of course it's a regulated experience too—with dormitories to live in—so it's a healthful experience."

What is the real experience of the women in the emerging Third World industrial work force? The conventional Western stereotypes leap to mind: You can't really compare, the standards are so different. . . . Everything's easier in warm countries. . . . They really don't have any alternatives, . . . Commenting on the low wages his company pays its women workers in Singapore, a Hewlett-Packard vice-president said, "They live much differently here than we do. . . ." But the differences are ultimately very simple. To start with, they have less money.

The great majority of the women in the new Third World work force live at or near the subsistence level for one person, whether they work for a multinational corporation or a locally owned factory. In the Philippines, for example, starting wages in U.S. owned electronics plants are between $34 to $46 a month, compared to a cost of living of $37 a month; in Indonesia the starting wages are actually about $7 a month less than the cost of living. "Living," in these cases, should be interpreted minimally: a diet of rice, dried fish, and water—a Coke might cost a half-day's wages—lodging in a room occupied by four or more other people. Rachael Grossman, a researcher with the Southeast Asia Resource Center, found women employees of U.S. multinational firms in Malaysia and the Philippines living four to eight in a room in boardinghouses, or squeezing into tiny extensions built onto squatter huts near the factory.

Where companies do provide dormitories for their employees, they are not of the "healthful," collegiate variety implied by our corporate informant. Staff from the American Friends Service Committee report that dormitory space is "likely to be crowded with bed rotation paralleling shift rotation—while one shift works, another sleeps, as many as twenty to a room." In one case in Thailand, they found the dormitory "filthy," with workers forced to find their own place to sleep among "splintered floorboards, rusting sheets of metal, and scraps of dirty cloth."

Wages do increase with seniority, but the money does not go to pay for studio apartments or, very likely, motorbikes. A 1970 study of young women factory workers in Hong Kong found that 88 percent of them were turning more than half their earnings over to their parents. In areas that are still largely agricultural (such as parts of the Philippines and Malaysia), or places where male unemployment runs high (such as northern Mexico), a woman factory worker may be the sole source of cash income for an entire extended family.

But wages on a par with what an 11-year-old American could earn on a paper route and living conditions resembling what Engels found in 19th-century Manchester are only part of the story. The rest begins at the factory gate. The work that multinational corporations export to the Third World is not only the most tedious, but often the most hazardous part of the production process. The countries they go to are, for the most part, those that will guarantee no interference from health and safety inspectors, trade unions, or even free-lance reformers. As a result, most Third World factory women work under conditions that already have broken or will break their health—or their nerves—within a few years, and often before they've worked long enough to earn any more than a subsistence wage.

Consider first the electronics industry, which is generally thought to be the safest and cleanest of the exported industries. . . .

One study in South Korea found that most electronics assembly workers developed severe eye problems after only one year of employment: 88 percent had chronic conjunctivitis; 44 percent became nearsighted; and 19 percent developed astigmatism. A manager for Hewlett-Packard's Malaysia plant, in an interview with Rachael Grossman, denied that there were any eye problems. "These girls are used to working with 'scopes.' We've found no eye problems. But it sure makes me dizzy to look through those things."

Electronics, recall, is the "cleanest" of the exported industries. Conditions in the garment and textile industry rival those of any 19th-century (or 20th—see below) sweatshop. The firms, generally local subcontractors to large American chains such as J.C. Penney and Sears, as well as smaller manufacturers, are usually even more indifferent to the health of their employees than the multinationals. Some of the worst conditions have been documented in South Korea, where the garment and textile industries have helped spark that country's "economic miracle." Workers are packed into poorly lit rooms, where summer temperatures rise above 100 degrees. Textile dust, which can cause permanent lung damage, fills the air. When there are rush orders, management may require forced overtime of as much as 48 hours at a stretch, and if that seems to go beyond the limits of human endurance, pep pills and amphetamine injections are thoughtfully provided. In her diary (originally published in a magazine now banned by the South Korean government) Min Chong Suk, 30, a sewing-machine operator, wrote of working from 7 a.m. to 11:30 p.m. in a garment factory: "When [the apprentices] shake the waste threads from the clothes, the whole room fills with dust, and it is hard to breathe. Since we've been working in such dusty air, there have been increasing numbers of people getting tuberculosis, bronchitis, and eye diseases. Since we are women, it makes us so sad when we have pale, unhealthy, wrinkled faces like dried-up spinach. . . . It seems to me that no one knows our blood dissolves into the threads and seams, with sighs and sorrow." . . .

There has been no international protest about the exploitation of Third World women by multinational corporations—no thundering denunciations from the floor of the United Nations' general assembly, no angry resolutions from the Conference of the Non-Aligned Countries. Sociologist Robert Snow, who has been tracing the multinationals on their way south and eastward for years, explained why: "The Third World governments *want* the multinationals to move in. There's cutthroat competition to attract the corporations." . . .

Then there is the World Bank, which over the past decade has lent several billion dollars to finance the roads, airports, power plants, and even the first-class hotels that multinational corporations need in order to set up business in Third World countries. The Sri Lankan garment industry, which like other Third World garment industries survives by subcontracting to major Western firms, was set up on the advice of the World Bank and with a $20 million World Bank loan. This particular experiment in "development" offers young women jobs at a global low of $5 for a six-day week. Gloria Scott, the head of the World Bank's Women and Development Program, sounded distinctly uncomfortable when we asked her about the bank's role in promoting the exploitation of Third World women. "Our job is to help eliminate poverty. It is not our responsibility if the multinationals come in and offer such low wages. It's the responsibility of the governments." However, the Bank's 1979 World Development Report speaks strongly of the need for "wage restraint" in poor countries. . . .

But the most obvious form of United States involvement, according to Lenny Siegel, the director of the Pacific Studies Center, is through "our consistent record of military aid to Third World governments that are capitalist, politically repressive, and are not striving for economic independence." Ironically, says Siegel, there are "cases where the United States made a big investment—through groups like AAFLI or other kinds of political pressure—to make sure that any unions that formed would be pretty tame. Then we put in even more money to support some dictator who doesn't allow unions at all." And if that doesn't seem like a sufficient case of duplicate spending, the U.S. government also insures (through the Overseas Private Investment Corporation) outward-bound multinationals against any lingering possibility of insurrection or expropriation.

What does our government have to say for itself? It's hard to get a straight answer—the few parts of the bureaucracy that deal with women and development seem to have little connection with those that are concerned with larger foreign policy issues. A spokesman for the Department of State told us that if multinationals offer poor working conditions (which he questioned), this was not their fault: "There are just different standards in different countries." Offering further evidence of a sheltered life, he told us that "corporations today are generally more socially responsible than even ten years ago. . . . We can expect them to treat their employees in the best way they can." But he conceded in response to a barrage of unpleasant examples, "Of course, you're going to have problems wherever you have human beings doing things." Our next stop was the Women's Division within AID. Staffer Emmy Simmons was aware of the criticisms of the quality of employment multinationals offer, but cautioned that "we can get hung up in the idea that it's exploitation without really looking at the alternatives for women." AID's concern, she said, was with the fact that population is outgrowing the agricultural capacity of many Third World countries, dislocating millions of people. From her point of view, multinationals at least provide some sort of alternative: "These people have to go somewhere." . . .

Yet thousands of women in the Third World's industrial work force have chosen to fight for better wages and working conditions. Few of these struggles reach the North American media. We know of them from reports, often fragmentary, from church and support groups.

- Nuevo Laredo, Mexico, 1973: 2,000 workers at Transitron Electronics walked out in solidarity with a small number of workers who had been unjustly fired. Two days later, 8,000 striking workers met and elected a more militant union leadership.
- Mexicali, Mexico, 1974: 3,000 workers, locked out by Mextel (a Mattel subsidiary), set up a 24-hour guard to prevent the company from moving in search of cheaper labor. After two months of confrontations, the company moved away.
- South Korea, 1978: 1,000 workers at the Mattel toy company in Seoul, which makes Barbie dolls and Marie Osmond dolls, staged a work slowdown to protest their 25 cents-an-hour wages and 12-hour shifts.
- South Korea, 1979: 200 young women employees of the YH textile-and-wig factory staged a peaceful vigil and fast to protest the company's threatened closing of the plant. On August 11, the fifth day of the vigil, more than 1,000 riot police, armed with clubs and steel shields, broke into the building where the women were staying and forcibly dragged the women out. Twenty-one-year-old Kim Kyong-suk was killed during the melee. It was her death that touched off widespread rioting throughout Korea that many thought led to the overthrow of President Park Chung Hee.

Saralee Hamilton, an AFSC staff organizer of a 1978 conference on "Women and Global Corporations" (held in Des Moines, Iowa) says: "The multinational corporations have deliberately targeted women for exploitation. If feminism is going to mean anything to women all over the world, it's going to have to find new ways to resist corporate power internationally." She envisions a global network of grass-roots women capable of sharing experiences, transmitting information, and—eventually—providing direct support for each other's struggles. It's a long way off; few women anywhere have the money for intercontinental plane flights or even long-distance calls, but at least we are beginning to see the way. "We all have the same hard life," wrote Korean garment worker Min Chong Suk. "We are bound together with one string."

(1981)

OFF OUR BACKS COVER

(1983)

Off Our Backs, Vol. 13, No. 10. Washington, D.C., November, 1983. Reprinted by permission of Off Our Backs Collective.

"INTRODUCTION: PLANETARY FEMINISM: THE POLITICS OF THE 21ST CENTURY"

Sisterhood Is Global is being published in the year 1984, the year George Orwell chose, almost four decades earlier, for the title and the time period of his now classic dystopian novel. Orwell's *1984* predicted a nightmarish future: a world in chronic war, its peoples cynically manipulated by three megapowers, its societies mirror images of each other in terms of sophisticated technology, mind control, rigid job, class, racial, and ethnic classification, sentimental quasi-religiosity, literary and political censorship, total suppression of human rights including sexual and reproductive freedom, and communication through patriotic propagandistic double-talk. "War is Peace," proclaims Big Brother, the Dictator, "Freedom is Slavery," "Ignorance is Strength." To rebel is to invite torture, "attitude reprogramming," or death. Indeed, there is no rebellion that has not been anticipated and prepared against in advance through the co-optation or the crushing of those who revolt.

The year 1984 has arrived in reality. The planet is manipulated by a few superpower nations promulgating adversarial ideologies but acting in mirror-image fashion. Corporate capitalism and State capitalism between them control sophisticated technology and world markets. Propaganda—whether from government ministries, advertising agencies, or the two in league with each other—manipulates human attitudes. Religious fundamentalism breathes its hoarse condemnation across entire regions. Literary and political censorship ranges from the brutal (torture of the outspoken) to the subtle (simple erasure of the utterance). "Human rights" in any full sense has become as much an empty

cliché as the double-talk phrases "pacification battle," "pre-emptive defense attack," and "armaments buildup for maintaining the peace." Wars are chronic; natural resources are being depleted or polluted rapidly and beyond revitalization; hunger and homelessness increase along with the population; revolutions become counterrevolutionary since there is no rebellion not anticipated and prepared against in advance. Big Brother smiles patriarchally from television sets in the United States and Western and Eastern Europe, from posters in Moscow and Beijing, from podiums in Africa and the Middle East, from military-review grandstands in Latin America.

But there is one factor neither Orwell nor Big Brother anticipated or prepared against: women as a world political force.

Because virtually all existing countries are structured by patriarchal mentality, the standard for being human is being male—and female human beings *per se* become "other," and invisible. This permits governments and international bodies to discuss "the world's problems"—war, poverty, refugees, hunger, disease, illiteracy, overpopulation, ecological imbalance, the abuse or exploitation of children and the elderly, etc.—without noticing that those who suffer most from "the world's problems" are *women*, who, in addition, are not consulted about possible solutions.

"While women represent half the global population and one-third of the labor force, they receive only one-tenth of the world income and own less than one percent of world property. They also are responsible for two-thirds of all working hours," said former UN Secretary General Kurt Waldheim in his "Report to the UN Commission on the Status of Women."[1] This was a diplomatic understatement of the situation.

Two out of three of the world's illiterates are now women, and while the general illiteracy rate is falling, the female illiteracy rate is rising. One third of all families in the world are headed by women. In the developing countries, almost half of all single women over age fifteen are mothers. Only one third of the world's women have any access to contraceptive information or devices, and more than one half have no access to trained help during pregnancy and childbirth. Women in the developing world are responsible for more than 50 percent of all food production (on the African continent women do 60 to 80 percent of all agricultural work, 50 percent of all animal husbandry, and 100 percent of all food processing). In industrialized countries, women still are paid only one half to three quarters of what men earn at the same jobs, still are ghettoized into lower-paying "female-intensive" job categories, and still are the last hired and the first fired; in Europe and North America, women constitute over 40 percent of the paid labor force, *in addition* to contributing more than 40 percent of the Gross Domestic Product in *un*paid labor in the home. As of 1982, 30 million people were unemployed in the industrialized countries and 800 million people in the Third World were living in absolute poverty; most of those affected are migrant workers and their families, youth, the disabled, and the aged—and the majority of all those categories are women. Approximately 500 million people suffer from hunger and malnutrition; the most seriously affected are children under age five and women. Twenty million persons die annually of hunger-related causes and one billion endure chronic undernourishment and other poverty deprivations; the majority are women and children.[2] And this is only part of the picture.

Not only are females most of the poor, the starving, and the illiterate, but women and children constitute more than 90 percent of all refugee populations. Women outlive men in most cultures and therefore *are* the elderly of the world, as well as being the primary caretakers of the elderly. The abuse of children is a women's problem because women must bear responsibility for children in virtually all cultures, and also because it is mostly female children who are abused—nutritionally,

educationally, sexually, psychologically, etc. Since women face such physical changes as menarche, menstruation, pregnancy, childbearing, lactation, and menopause—in addition to the general health problems we share with men—the crisis in world health is a crisis of women. Toxic pesticides and herbicides, chemical warfare, leakage from nuclear wastes, acid rain, and other such deadly pollutants usually take their first toll as a rise in cancers of the female reproductive system, and in miscarriages, stillbirths, and congenital deformities. Furthermore, it is women's work which must compensate for the destruction of ecological balance, the cash benefits of which accrue to various Big Brothers: deforestation (for lumber sales as export or for construction materials) results in a lowering of the water table, which in turn causes parched grasslands and erosion of topsoil; women, as the world's principal water haulers and fuel gatherers, must walk farther to find water, to find fodder for animals, to find cooking-fire fuel.[3] This land loss, combined with the careless application of advanced technology (whether appropriate to a region or not), has created a major worldwide trend: rural migration to the cities. That, in turn, has a doubly devastating effect on women. Either they remain behind trying to support their children on unworkable land while men go to urban centers in search of jobs, or they also migrate—only to find that they are considered less educable and less employable than men, their survival options being mainly domestic servitude (the job category of two out of five women in Latin America), factory work (mostly for multinational corporations at less than $2 US per day), or prostitution (which is growing rapidly in the urban centers of developing countries). Since women everywhere bear the "double job" burden of housework in addition to outside work, we are most gravely affected by the acknowledged world crisis in housing—and not only in less developed countries. In Britain, the Netherlands, and the United States, women were the founders of spontaneous squatters' movements; in Hungary, the problem is so severe that women have been pressuring to have lack of housing declared as a ground for abortion; in Portugal, Mexico, and the USSR, women have been articulating the connections between the housing crisis, overcrowding, and a rise in the incidence of wife battery and child sexual abuse.

But the overlooked—and most important—factor in the power of women as a world political force is the magnitude of suffering combined with the magnitude of women: *women constitute not an oppressed minority, but a majority—of almost all national populations, and of the entire human species.* As that species approaches critical mass and the capacity to eradicate all life on the planet, more than ever before in recorded history, that majority of humanity now is mobilizing. The goal not only is to change drastically our own powerless status worldwide, but to redefine all existing societal structures and modes of existence.

The book you hold in your hands reflects the intense network of contacts and interlocking activities the world's women have built over the past two decades. It reflects the fact that this foundation now is solid enough to support a genuine global movement of women which will have enormous political impact through the end of this century, and will create a transnational transformation in the next century. This movement will affect every aspect of life and society: reproduction and production, natural resources, political systems, nationalism, human sexuality and psychology, science and technology, youth and age and "the family," economics, religion, communication, health, and philosophy—and many other aspects we cannot yet imagine.

It is a multiplicitous movement, as befits the majority of humankind, and its styles, strategies, and theoretical approaches are as varied as its composition is and its effects will be. Just as *Sisterhood Is Global* is a cross-cultural, cross-age-group, cross-occupation/class, cross-racial, cross-sexual-preference, and cross-ideological assemblage of women's voices, so is the movement itself. It has come into being through diverse means—informal one-to-one contacts, feminist meetings, demonstrations, solidarity actions, issue-focused networks, academic research and popular media, electoral processes and underground organizing, unofficial forums and official conferences.

A growing awareness of the vast resources of womanpower is becoming evident in a proliferation of plans of action, resolutions, legislative reforms, and other blueprints for change being put forward by national governments, international congresses and agencies, and multinational corporations. Women have served or are serving as heads of states and governments in more nations than ever before, including Belize, Bolivia,

Dominica, Iceland, India, Israel, Norway, Portugal, Sri Lanka, the United Kingdom, and Yugoslavia. Yet these women still must function within systems devised and controlled by men and imbued with androcentric values. What resonates with even greater potential is what "ordinary" women all over the globe are beginning to whisper, say, and shout, to ourselves and one another, *autonomously*—and what we are proceeding to *do*, in our own countries and across their borders.

The quality of feminist political philosophy (in all its myriad forms) makes possible a totally new way of viewing international affairs, one less concerned with diplomatic postures and abstractions, but focused instead on concrete, *unifying* realities of priority importance to the survival and betterment of living beings. For example, the historical, cross-cultural opposition women express to war and our healthy skepticism of certain technological advances (by which most men seem overly impressed at first and disillusioned at last) are only two instances of shared attitudes among women which seem basic to a common world view. Nor is there anything mystical or biologically deterministic about this commonality. It is the result of a *common condition* which, despite variations in degree, is experienced by all human beings who are born female.

(1984)

NOTES

1. Statistics from Development Issue Paper No. 12, UNDP.
2. Statistics from the World Conference of the United Nations Decade for Women (Copenhagen, 1980), from the Oxford Committee for Famine Relief, and from the 1982 UN *Report on the World Situation*. The 1982 UN *Report* also noted that military research and development expenditures, estimated at $35 billion for 1980, surpassed all public funds spent on research and development in the fields of energy, health, pollution control, and agriculture *combined*, and amounted to at least six times the total research-and-development expenditures of all developing countries.
3. In 1872, 14 percent of all potentially arable land was desert; in 1952, 33 percent; by 1982, almost 66 percent was dry and barren. The United Nations estimates that there will be half as much farm land per person by the year 2000 as there is now, given the rates of population growth and agricultural land loss.

117 • *Minerva Salado*

"REPORT FROM VIETNAM FOR INTERNATIONAL WOMEN'S DAY"

A woman is aflame.
She is twenty-one years old
and her flesh is on fire.
Her womb trembles;
her erect breasts are consumed by fire.
Her hips contort.

The muscles of her thighs boil.
Anh Dai's flesh is ignited by flames,
but she does not burn with passion.
It is napalm.
(*Translated by Daniela Gioseffi with Enildo Garcia*)

(1985)

Translated by Daniela Gioseffi and appearing in her book *Women on War: International Writings from Antiquity to the Present* (Feminist Press: CUNY: NY 2003.) Reprinted by permission.

118 • *June Jordan*

"REPORT FROM THE BAHAMAS"

I am staying in a hotel that calls itself the Sheraton British Colonial. One of the photographs advertising the place displays a middle-aged Black man in a waiter's tuxedo, smiling. What intrigues me most about the picture is just this: while the Black man bears a tray full of "colorful" drinks above his left shoulder, both of his feet, shoes and trouserlegs, up to ten inches above his ankles, stand in the also "colorful" Caribbean salt water. He is so delighted to serve you he will wade into the water to bring you Banana Daquiris while you float! More precisely, he will wade into the water, fully clothed, oblivious to the ruin of his shoes, his trousers, his health, and he will do it with a smile.

I am in the Bahamas. On the phone in my room, a spinning complement of plastic pages offers handy index clues such as CAR RENTAL and CASINOS. A message from the Ministry of Tourism appears among these travelers tips. Opening with a paragraph

"Report from the Bahamas" by June Jordan, from *On Call: Political Essays*, South End Press, Boston, MA, 1985. Copyright 2014 June Jordan Literary Estate Trust; reprinted by permission. www.junejordan.com

of "WELCOME," the message then proceeds to "A PAGE OF HISTORY," which reads as follows:

New World History begins on the same day that modern Bahamian history begins—October 12, 1492. That's when Columbus stepped ashore—British influence came first with the Eleutherian Adventurers of 1647—After the Revolutions. American Loyalists fled from the newly independent states and settled in the Bahamas. Confederate blockade-runners used the island as a haven during the War between the States, and after the War, a number of Southerners moved to the Bahamas.

There it is again. Something proclaims itself a legitimate history and all it does is track white Mr. Columbus to the British Eleutherians through the Confederate Southerners as they barge into New World surf, land on New World turf, and nobody saving one word about the Bahamian people, the Black peoples, to whom the only thing new in their island world was this weird succession of crude intruders and its colonial consequences.

This is my consciousness of race as I unpack my bathing suit in the Sheraton British Colonial. Neither this hotel nor the British nor the long ago Italians nor the white Delta airline pilots belong here, of course. And every time I look at the photograph of that fool standing in the water with his shoes on I'm about to have a West Indian fit, even though I know he's no fool; he's a middle-aged Black man who needs a job and this is his job—pretending himself a servile ancillary to the pleasures of the rich. (Compared to his options in life, I am a rich woman. Compared to most of the Black Americans arriving for this Easter weekend on a three nights four days' deal of bargain rates, the middle-aged waiter is a poor Black man.)

We will jostle along with the other (white) visitors and join them in the tee shirt shops or, laughing together, learn ruthless rules of negotiation as we, Black Americans as well as white, argue down the price of handwoven goods at the nearby straw market while the merchants, frequently toothless Black women seated on the concrete in their only presentable dress, humble themselves to our careless games:

"Yes? You like it? Eight dollar."

"Five."

"I give it to you. Seven."

And so it continues, this weird succession of crude intruders that, now, includes me and my brothers and my sisters from the North.

This is my consciousness of class as I try to decide how much money I can spend on Bahamian gifts for my family back in Brooklyn. No matter that these other Black women incessantly weave words and flowers into the straw hats and bags piled beside them on the burning dusty street. No matter that these other Black women must work their sense of beauty into these things that we will take away as cheaply as we dare, or they will do without food.

We are not white, after all. The budget is limited. And we are harmlessly killing time between the poolside rum punch and "The Native Show on the Patio" that will play tonight outside the hotel restaurant.

This is my consciousness of race and class and gender identity as I notice the fixed relations between these other Black women and myself. They sell and I buy or I don't. They risk not eating. I risk going broke on my first vacation afternoon.

We are not particularly women anymore; we are parties to a transaction designed to set us against each other.

"Olive" is the name of the Black woman who cleans my hotel room. On my way to the beach I am wondering what "Olive" would say if I told her why I chose the Sheraton British Colonial; if I told her I wanted to swim. I wanted to sleep. I did not want to be harassed by the middle-aged waiter, or his nephew. I did not want to be raped by anybody (white or Black) at all and I calculated that my safety as a Black woman alone would best be assured by a multinational hotel corporation. In my experience, the big guys take customer complaints more seriously than the little ones. I would suppose that's one reason why they're big; they don't like to lose money anymore than I like to be bothered when I'm trying to read a goddamned book underneath a palm tree I paid $264 to get next to. A Black woman seeking refuge in a multinational corporation may seem like a contradiction to some, but there you are. In this case it's a coincidence of entirely different self-interests; Sheraton/cash = June Jordan's short run safety.

Anyway, I'm pretty sure "Olive" would look at me as though I came from someplace as far away as Brooklyn. Then she'd probably allow herself one indignant query before righteously removing her vacuum cleaner from my room; "and why in the first place you come down you without your husband?"

I cannot imagine how I would begin to answer her.

•

My "rights" and my "freedom" and my "desire" and a slew of other New World values; what would they sound like to this Black woman described on the card atop my hotel bureau as "Olive the Maid"? "Olive" is older than I am and I may smoke a cigarette while she changes the sheets on my bed. Whose rights? Whose freedom? Whose desire?

And why should she give a shit about mine unless I do something, for real, about hers? . . .

It's time to pack it up. Catch my plane. I scan the hotel room for things not to forget. There's that white report card on the bureau.

"Dear Guests:" it says, under the name "Olive." "I am your maid for the day. Please rate me: Excellent. Good. Average. Poor. Thank you."

I tuck this momento from the Sheraton British Colonial into my notebook. How would "Olive" rate *me*? What would it mean for us to seem "good" to each other? What would that rating require?

But I am hastening to leave. Neither turtle soup nor kidney pie nor any conch shell delight shall delay my departure. I have rested, here, in the Bahamas, and I'm ready to return to my usual job, my usual work. But the skin on my body has changed and so has my mind. On the Delta flight home I realize I am burning up, indeed.

So far as I can see, the usual race and class concepts of connection, or gender assumptions of unity, do not apply very well. I doubt that they ever did. Otherwise why would Black folks forever bemoan our lack of solidarity when the deal turns real. And if unity on the basis of sexual oppression is something natural, then why do we women, the majority people on the planet, still have a problem?

The plane's ready for takeoff. I fasten my seatbelt and let the tumult inside my head run free. Yes: race and class and gender remain as real as the weather. But what they must mean about the contact between two individuals is less obvious and, like the weather, not predictable.

And when these factors of race and class and gender absolutely collapse is whenever you try to use them as automatic concepts of connection. They may serve well as indicators of commonly felt conflict, but as elements of connection they seem about as reliable as precipitation probability for the day after the night before the day.

It occurs to me that much organizational grief could be avoided if people understood that partnership in misery does not necessarily provide for partnership for change: *When we get the monsters off our backs all of us may want to run in very different directions.*

And not only that: even though both "Olive" and "I" live inside a conflict neither one of us created, and even though both of us therefore hurt inside that conflict, I may be one of the monsters she needs to eliminate from her universe and, in a sense, she may be one of the monsters in mine.

I am reaching for the words to describe the difference between a common identity that has been imposed and the individual identity any one of us will choose, once she gains that chance.

That difference is the one that keeps us stupid in the face of new, specific information about somebody else with whom we are supposed to have a connection because a third party, hostile to both of us, has worked it so that the two of us, like it or not, share a common enemy. *What happens beyond the idea of that enemy and beyond the consequences of that enemy?*

I am saying that the ultimate connection cannot be the enemy. The ultimate connection must be the need that we find between us. It is not only who you are, in other words, but what we can do for each other that will determine the connection.

I am flying back to my job. I have been teaching contemporary women's poetry this semester. One quandary I have set myself to explore with my students is the one of taking responsibility without power. We had been wrestling ideas to the floor for several sessions when a young Black woman, a South African, asked me for help, after class.

Sokutu told me she was "in a trance" and that she'd been unable to eat for two weeks.

"What's going on?" I asked her, even as my eyes startled at her trembling and emaciated appearance.

"My husband. He drinks all the time. He beats me up. I go to the hospital. I can't eat. I don't know what/ anything."

In my office, she described her situation. I did not dare to let her sense my fear and horror. She was dragging about, hour by hour, in dread. Her husband, a young Black South African, was drinking himself into more and more deadly violence against her.

Sokutu told me how she could keep nothing down. She weighed 90 lbs. at the outside, as she spoke to me. She'd already been hospitalized as a result of her husband's battering rage.

I knew both of them because I had organized a campus group to aid the liberation struggles of Southern Africa.

Nausea rose in my throat. What about this presumable connection: this husband and this wife fled from that homeland of hatred against them, and now what? He was destroying himself. If not stopped, he would certainly murder his wife.

She needed a doctor, right away. It was a medical emergency. She needed protection. It was a security crisis. She needed refuge for battered wives and personal therapy and legal counsel. She needed a friend.

I got on the phone and called every number in the campus directory that I could imagine might prove helpful. Nothing worked. There were no institutional resources designed to meet her enormous, multifaceted, and ordinary woman's need.

I called various students. I asked the Chairperson of the English Department for advice. I asked everyone for help.

Finally, another one of my students, Cathy, a young Irish woman active in campus IRA activities, responded. She asked for further details. I gave them to her.

"Her husband," Cathy told me, "is an alcoholic. You have to understand about alcoholics. It's not the same as anything else. And it's a disease you can't treat any old way."

I listened, fearfully. Did this mean there was nothing we could do?

"That's not what I'm saying," she said. "But you have to keep the alcoholic part of the thing central in everybody's mind, otherwise her husband will kill her. Or he'll kill himself."

She spoke calmly. I felt there was nothing to do but to assume she knew what she was talking about.

"Will you come with me?" I asked her, after a silence. "Will you come with me and help us figure out what to do next?"

Cathy said she would but that she felt shy: Sokutu comes from South Africa. What would she think about Cathy?

"I don't know," I said. "But let's go."

We left to find a dormitory room for the young battered wife.

It was late, now, and dark outside.

On Cathy's VW that I followed behind with my own car, was the sticker that reads BOBBY SANDS FREE AT LAST. My eyes blurred as I read and reread the words. This was another connection: Bobby Sands and Martin Luther King Jr. and who would believe it? I would not have believed it; I grew up terrorized by Irish kids who introduced me to the word "nigga."

And here I was following an Irish woman to the room of a Black South African. We were going to that room to try to save a life together.

When we reached the little room, we found ourselves awkward and large. Sokutu attempted to treat us with utmost courtesy, as though we were honored guests. She seemed surprised by Cathy, but mostly Sokutu was flushed with relief and joy because we were there, with her.

I did not know how we should ever terminate her heartfelt courtesies and address, directly, the reason for our visit: her starvation and her extreme physical danger.

Finally, Cathy sat on the floor and reached out her hands to Sokutu.

"I'm here," she said quietly, "Because June has told me what has happened to you. And I know what it is. Your husband is an alcoholic. He has a disease. I know what it is. My father was an alcoholic. He killed himself. He almost killed my mother. I want to be your friend."

"Oh," was the only small sound that escaped from Sokutu's mouth. And then she embraced the other student. And then everything changed and I watched all of this happen so I know that this happened: this connection.

And after we called the police and exchanged phone numbers and plans were made for the night and for the next morning, the young South African woman walked down the dormitory hallway, saying goodbye and saying thank you to us.

I walked behind them, the young Irish woman and the young South African, and I saw them walking as sisters walk, hugging each other, and whispering and sure of each other and I felt how it was not who they were but what they both know and what they were both preparing to do about what they know that was going to make them both free at last.

And I look out the windows of the plane and I see clouds that will not kill me and I know that someday soon other clouds may erupt to kill us all.

And I tell the stewardess No thanks to the cocktails she offers me. But I look about the cabin at the hundred strangers drinking as they fly and I think even here and even now I must make the connection real between me and these strangers everywhere before those other clouds unify this ragged bunch of us, too late.

(1985)

FROM *PATRIARCHY AND ACCUMULATION ON A WORLD SCALE*

Women in the International Division of Labour

The idea of writing this book arose out of my desire to clarify some of the recurring confusions regarding the issue of feminism. I realized that, while the feminist movement was spreading to ever more regions of the world, while women's issues were becoming more and more "acceptable" to the rulers of the world, the questions of what this movement was fighting against and what it was fighting for were becoming increasingly blurred.

While many of us would agree that our enemy is capitalist patriarchy as a system, and not just men, we cannot deny that many feminists do not even talk of capitalism, or if they do, have a rather limited notion of this system and simply try to add the feminist analysis to the traditional Marxist analysis. Others only want more equality with men, like the Equal Rights Amendment (ERA) supporters in the USA, and do not even aspire to transcend capitalist patriarchy as a system.

Similarly, most of us feel that the feminist rebellion has crossed all barriers of class, race and imperialism, because women everywhere are victims of sexism and male dominance. We, therefore, feel that there is a realistic base for international solidarity among women, or for global sisterhood. On the other hand, we cannot close our eyes to the stark fact that women of all classes in the West, and middle-class women in the Third World, are also among those whose standard of living is based on the ongoing exploitation of poor women and men in the underdeveloped regions and classes.

Obviously, it is not enough to say that all women are exploited and oppressed by men. There is not only the hierarchical division between the sexes; there are also other social and international divisions intrinsically interwoven with the dominance relation of men over women. That means the feminist movement cannot ignore the issues of class, or the exploitative international division of labour, and imperialism. On the other hand, the old argument, put forward by scientific socialists, that the "woman question" is a secondary contradiction and belongs to the sphere of ideology, the superstructure or culture, can no longer be upheld to explain reality for women, particularly since everywhere the feminist rebellion was sparked off around the issue of violence.

The unresolved questions concern the relationship between patriarchy and capitalism, in other words, the relationship between women's oppression and exploitation and the paradigm of never-ending accumulation and "growth," between capitalist patriarchy and the exploitation and subordination of colonies. These are not academic questions. They concern every woman in her everyday life, and the feminist movement in its political goals and existence. If we are unable to find plausible answers to these questions, the danger arises that the feminist rebellion may be co-opted by the forces that only want to continue the destructive model of capital accumulation and which need the vitality of this movement to feed the slackening "growth" process . . . .

From *Patriarchy and Accumulation on a World Scale* by Maria Mies. New York: Zed Books, 1998. Reprinted by permission of the publisher. Notes have been deleted.

DISCONTINUITIES: WOMEN'S WORK

Another area where the feminist movement broke with the traditions of the old women's movement as well as with those of the orthodox left was the area of women's work. Whereas the old movement and the orthodox left had accepted the capitalist division between private housework or—in Marxist terminology—reproductive work, and public and productive work—or wage-work, the only sphere from which they expected revolution as well as women's emancipation—the feminists not only challenged this division of labour but also the very definitions of "work" and "non-work." This approach also put into question the accepted division, following from the other dualistic divisions, between politics and economics. It was only logical that, once women had begun to consider the personal and the "private" as political, that they also began to re-evaluate and re-define the work that most women did in this "private" sphere, namely housework.

One of the most fruitful debates which feminism had started was the debate on domestic labour. This debate, more than others, was a challenge not only to the concept of politics of the traditional left but also to some of its fundamental theoretical positions. Significantly, the debate on housework was the first instance that men participated in the feminist discourse.

But before this debate on domestic labour started and before it degenerated into a more or less academic discourse, the issue of housework was raised as a *political issue* in the context of the labour struggles in Italy in the early seventies. The first challenge to the orthodox Marxist theory on women's work came from Italy, from Maria-Rosa Dalla Costa's essay, "The Power of Women and the Subversion of the Community," which was published together with Selma James's "A Woman's Place" in 1972 in Padua and in the same year in Bristol.

In this essay the classical Marxist position that housework is "non-productive" is challenged for the first time. Dalla Costa points out that what the housewife produces in the family are not simply use-values but the commodity "labour power" which the husband then can sell as a "free" wage labourer in the labour market. She clearly states that the productivity of the housewife is the precondition for the productivity of the (male) wage labourer. The nuclear family, organized and protected by the state, is the social factory where this commodity "labour power" is produced. Hence, the housewife and her labour are not outside the process of surplus value production, but constitute the very foundation upon which this process can get started. The housewife and her labour are, in other words, the basis of the process of capital accumulation. With the help of the state and its legal machinery women have been shut up in the isolated nuclear family, whereby their work there was made socially invisible, and was hence defined—by Marxist and non-Marxist theoreticians—as "non-productive." It appeared under the form of love, care, emotionality, motherhood and wifehood. Dalla Costa challenged the orthodox left notion, first spelt out by Engels, but then dogmatized and codified by all communist parties, and still upheld today, that women had to leave the "private" household and enter "social production" as wage-workers along with the men if they wanted to create the preconditions for their emancipation. Contrary to this position, Dalla Costa identified the strategic link created by capital and state between the unpaid housework of women and the paid wage-work of men. Capital is able to hide behind the figure of the husband, called "breadwinner," with whom the woman, called "housewife," has to deal directly and for whom she is supposed to work out of "love," not for a wage. "The wage commands more work than what collective bargaining in the factories shows us. *Women's work appears as personal service outside of capital."* (Dalla Costa, 1973: 34; transl. M.M.)

Dalla Costa rejects the artificial division and hierarchy capital has created between wage-workers on the one side and non-wage-workers on the other:

> In the measure that capital has subordinated the man to itself by making him a wage-labourer it has created a cleavage between him—the wage labourer—and all other proletarians who do not receive a wage. Those who are not considered capable of becoming a subject of social revolt because they do not participate directly in social production. (Dalla Costa, 1973: 33)

On the basis of this analysis, Dalla Costa also criticizes the notion held by many men and women of the left, that women are only "oppressed," that their problem is "male chauvinism." As capital is able to command the unpaid labour of the housewife as well as the paid labour of the wage labourer, the domestic slavery of women is called *exploitation*. According to Dalla Costa, one cannot understand the exploitation of wage-labour unless one understands the exploitation of non-wage-labour.

The recognition of housework as productive labour and as an area of exploitation and a source for capital accumulation also meant a challenge to the traditional policies and strategies of left parties and trade unions which had never included housework in their concept of work and their struggles. They have always colluded with capital in its strategy to remove all non-wage work from public perception.

It is not accidental that the issue of domestic labour was first raised in Italy, one of the more "underdeveloped" countries of Europe which nevertheless had a strong communist party. As Selma James points out in her introduction, Italy had only a small number of female factory workers, the majority of women being "housewives" or peasant women. On the other hand, Italy had seen a number of labour struggles, influenced by the non-parliamentary opposition which had included "reproductive struggles," that is, non-payment of rent, struggles in neighbourhoods and schools. In all these struggles women had played a prominent role.

Moreover, Dalla Costa already saw a structural similarity between women's struggles and the struggles of Third World countries against imperialism as well as that of the blacks in the United States and the youth rebellion as the revolt of all those who had been defined as being *outside* of capitalism (or as belonging to "pre-capitalist," "feudal," etc., formations). With Frans Fanon she interprets the divisions among women (as housewives and wage-workers) as a result of a colonizing process because the family and the household to her is a colony, dominated by the "metropolis," capital and state (Dalla Costa, 1973: 53). Dalla Costa and James wanted to reintroduce women into history as revolutionary subjects.

As a strategy to overthrow capitalism they launched the "Wages for Housework" campaign. Many women in Europe and Canada were mobilized by this campaign and a lively discussion took place about the prospects of this strategy. Eventually the campaign petered out because several questions inherent in it could not be solved, for instance, the problem that "wages for housework" would not end the isolation and atomization of housewives, or that the total generalization of wage

labour would not necessarily lead to an overthrow of capitalism but rather to a totalization of alienation and commodity production, or the question, who would pay the wages for housework, the capitalists, the state or the husband?

In spite of these unresolved questions, the "Wages for Housework" campaign had put the issue of women's domestic labour on the agenda of feminist theorizing. The "domestic labour debate" which followed the book of Dalla Costa and James, particularly in Britain, but also in West Germany, has been an important contribution to a feminist theory of work. However, as many of the women and men who participated in this debate came from the traditional left, their concern eventually seemed to be rather to "save their Marx" than to promote women's liberation.

Hence much of the debate ended in typically academic arguments at the centre of which was the question whether Marx's theory of value could be applied to domestic labour or not. Following from this, the dividing line between orthodox Marxists and feminists continued to be the question whether housework was considered "socially productive" labour or not.

I do not intend to go back to the domestic labour debate here. As far as the politics of the feminist movement are concerned, its contribution was limited. But it did confront the left organizations for the first time with the unresolved question of women's housework under capitalism. Today many women and men of the left admit that Marx left out housework in his analysis of capitalism, but they then proceed to say that this does not invalidate the central role Marx assigned to wage labour, as the wage-labour relation to capital still constitutes *the* capitalist production relation.

The domestic labour debate, which took place between 1973 and 1979, did not include other areas of non-wage work which are tapped by capital in its process of accumulation. This is particularly all the work performed by subsistence peasants, petty commodity producers, marginalized people, most of whom are women, in the underdeveloped countries. Thus, most people involved in the discussion on housework did not transcend the Eurocentric view of capitalism. According to this view, these other areas of human labour are considered to be lying outside of capitalism and society proper. They are called "pre-capitalist," "peripheral-capitalist," "feudal" or "semi-feudal," or simply underdeveloped or backward. Sometimes they are referred to as areas of "uneven development."

The discovery, however, that housework under capitalism had also been excluded per definition from the analysis of capitalism proper, and that this was the mechanism by which it became a "colony" and a source for unregulated exploitation, opened our eyes to the analysis of other such colonies of non-wage-labour exploitation, particularly the work of small peasants and women in Third World countries. This discussion was mainly led by feminists in West Germany who extended the critique of Marx's blindness regarding women's work to the blindness regarding the other types of non-wage-work in the colonies.

In an article called "Women's work, the blind spot in the critique of political economy," Claudia v. Werlhof challenged the classical notion of capital versus wage labour as *the only* capitalist production relation. She identified two more production relations based on non-wage labour, namely housework and subsistence work in the colonies, as prerequisites for the "privileged" (male) wage-labour relation. In the discussions that took place between Claudia v. Werlhof, Veronika Bennholdt-Thomsen and myself in these years on the various forms of non-wage labour relations and their place in a worldwide system of capital accumulation, Rosa Luxemburg's work on imperialism played a decisive role (Luxemburg, 1923).

Rosa Luxemburg had tried to use Marx's analysis of the process of extended reproduction of capital or capital accumulation (Marx, *Capital*, Vol. II) for the analysis of imperialism or colonialism. She had come to the conclusion that Marx's model of accumulation was based on the assumption that capitalism was a closed system where there were only wage labourers and capitalists. Rosa Luxemburg showed that historically such a system never existed, that capitalism had always needed what she called "non-capitalist milieux and strata" for the extension of labour force, resources and above all the extension of markets. These non-capitalist milieux and strata were initially the peasants and artisans with their "natural economy," later the colonies. Colonialism for Rosa Luxemburg is therefore not only the last stage of capitalism (Lenin, 1917), but its constant necessary condition. In other words, without colonies capital accumulation or extended reproduction of capital would come to a stop (Luxemburg, 1923: 254–367).

This is not the place to go further into the debate which followed Rosa Luxemburg's work. With the tendencies governing the Comintern in the twenties it is not surprising that her views were criticized and rejected. I am also not concerned with Rosa Luxemburg's final expectation that if all "non-capitalist milieux and strata" have been integrated into the accumulation process, capitalism would come to its logical breakdown. But what her work opened up for our feminist analysis of women's labour worldwide was a perspective which went beyond the limited horizon of industrialized societies and the housewives in these countries. It further helped to transcend theoretically the various artificial divisions of labour created by capital, particularly the sexual division of labour and the international division of labour by which precisely those areas are made invisible which are to be exploited in non-wage labour relations and where the rules and regulations governing wage-labour are suspended. We consider it the most important task of feminism *to include all these relations* in an analysis of women's work under capitalism, because today there can be no doubt that capital has already reached the stage of which Rosa Luxemburg spoke. All milieux and strata are already tapped by capital in its global greed for ever-expanding accumulation. It would be self-defeating to confine our struggles and analysis to the compartmentalizations capitalist patriarchy has created: if Western feminists would only try to understand women's problems in overdeveloped societies, and if Third World women would only restrict their analysis to problems in underdeveloped societies. Because capitalist patriarchy, by dividing and simultaneously linking these different parts of the world, has already created a worldwide context of accumulation within which the manipulation of women's labour and the sexual division of labour plays a crucial role.

A look at the brief history of the feminist movement can teach us that the rejection of all dualistic and hierarchical divisions, created by capitalist patriarchy, viz., between public and private, political and economic, body and mind, head and heart, etc., was a correct and successful strategy. This was not a pre-planned programme of action, but the issues raised were of such a nature that feminists could expect success only by radically transcending these colonizing divisions, for it became increasingly clear that the capitalist mode of production was not identical with the famous capital-wage-labour relation, but that it needed different categories of colonies, particularly women, other peoples and nature, to uphold the model of ever-expanding growth.

At present, I think it is necessary that feminists worldwide began to identify and demystify all colonizing divisions created by capitalist patriarchy, particularly by the interplay between the sexual and the international division of labour.

An emphasis on these colonial divisions is also necessary from another point of view. Many feminists in the United States and Europe have, together with critical scientists and ecologists, begun to criticize the dualistic and destructive paradigm of Western science and technology. Drawing their inspiration from C.G. Jung's psychology, humanistic psychology, nondualistic "Eastern" spirituality, particularly Taoism and other oriental philosophies, they propose a new holistic paradigm, the New Age paradigm (Fergusson, 1980; Capra, 1982; Bateson, 1972). This emphasis on the fact that in our world everything is connected with everything and influences everything is definitely an approach which goes along with much of the feminist rebellion and vision of a future society. However, if this desire to "become whole" again, and to build bridges across all the cleavages and segmentations White Man has created is not to be frustrated again, it is necessary that the New Age feminists, the eco-feminists and others open their eyes and minds to the real colonies whose exploitation also guarantees them the luxury of indulging in "Eastern spirituality" and "therapy." In other words, if the holistic paradigm is nothing but an affair of a new spiritualism or consciousness, if it does not identify and fight against the global system of capitalist accumulation and exploitation, it will end up by becoming a pioneering movement for the legitimization of the next round of the destructive production of capitalism. This round will not focus on the production and marketing of such crude material commodities as cars and refrigerators, but on non-material commodities like religion, therapies, friendship, spirituality, and also on violence and warfare, of course with the full use of the "New Age" technologies. . . .

(1986)

"DEVELOPMENT, ECOLOGY AND WOMEN"

DEVELOPMENT AS A NEW PROJECT OF WESTERN PATRIARCHY

"Development" was to have been a post-colonial project, a choice for accepting a model of progress in which the entire world remade itself on the model of the colonising modern west, without having to undergo the subjugation and exploitation that colonialism entailed. The assumption was that western style progress was possible for all. Development, as the improved well-being of all, was thus equated with the westernisation of economic categories—of needs, of productivity, of growth. Concepts and categories about economic development and natural resource utilisation that had emerged in the specific context of industrialisation and capitalist growth in a centre of colonial power, were raised to the level of universal assumptions and applicability in the entirely different context of basic needs satisfaction for the people of the newly independent Third World countries. Yet, as Rosa Luxemberg has pointed out, early industrial development in western Europe necessitated the permanent occupation of the colonies by the colonial powers and the destruction of the local "natural economy."[1] According to her, colonialism is a constant necessary condition for capitalist growth: without colonies, capital accumulation would grind to a halt. "Development" as capital accumulation and the commercialisation of the economy for the generation of "surplus" and profits thus involved the reproduction not merely of a particular form of creation of wealth, but also of the associated creation of poverty and dispossession. A replication of economic development based on commercialisation of resource use for commodity production in the newly independent countries created the internal colonies.[2] Development was thus reduced to a continuation of the process of colonisation; it became an extension of the project of wealth creation in modern western patriarchy's economic vision, which was based on the exploitation or exclusion of women (of the west and non-west), on the exploitation and degradation of nature, and on the exploitation and erosion of other cultures. "Development" could not but entail destruction for women, nature and subjugated cultures, which is why, throughout the Third World, women, peasants and tribals are struggling for liberation from "development" just as they earlier struggled for liberation from colonialism.

The UN Decade for Women was based on the assumption that the improvement of women's economic position would automatically flow from an expansion and diffusion of the development process. Yet, by the end of the Decade, it was becoming clear that development itself was the problem. Insufficient and inadequate "participation" in "development" was not the cause for women's increasing under-development; it was rather, their enforced but asymmetric participation in it, by which they bore the costs but were excluded from the benefits, that was responsible. Development exclusivity and dispossession aggravated and deepened the colonial processes of ecological degradation and the loss of political control over nature's sustenance base. Economic growth was a new colonialism, draining resources away from those who needed them most. The discontinuity lay in the fact that it was now new national elites, not colonial powers, that masterminded the exploitation on

grounds of "national interest" and growing GNPs, and it was accomplished with more powerful technologies of appropriation and destruction.

Ester Boserup[3] has documented how women's impoverishment increased during colonial rule; those rulers who had spent a few centuries in subjugating and crippling their own women into de-skilled, de-intellectualised appendages, disfavoured the women of the colonies on matters of access to land, technology and employment. The economic and political processes of colonial under-development bore the clear mark of modern western patriarchy, and while large numbers of women and men were impoverished by these processes, women tended to lose more. The privatisation of land for revenue generation displaced women more critically, eroding their traditional land use rights. The expansion of cash crops undermined food production, and women were often left with meagre resources to feed and care for children, the aged and the infirm, when men migrated or were conscripted into forced labour by the colonisers. As a collective document by women activists, organisers and researchers stated at the end of the UN Decade for Women, "The almost uniform conclusion of the Decade's research is that with a few exceptions, women's relative access to economic resources, incomes and employment has worsened, their burden of work has increased, and their relative and even absolute health, nutritional and educational status has declined."[4]

The displacement of women from productive activity by the expansion of development was rooted largely in the manner in which development projects appropriated or destroyed the natural resource base for the production of sustenance and survival. It destroyed women's productivity both by removing land, water and forests from their management and control, as well as through the ecological destruction of soil, water and vegetation systems so that nature's productivity and renewability were impaired. While gender subordination and patriarchy are the oldest of oppressions, they have taken on new and more violent forms through the project of development. Patriarchal categories which understand destruction as "production" and regeneration of life as "passivity" have generated a crisis of survival. Passivity, as an assumed category of the "nature" of nature and of women, denies the activity of nature and life. Fragmentation and uniformity as assumed categories of progress and development destroy the living forces which arise from relationships within the "web of life" and the diversity in the elements and patterns of these relationships.

The economic biases and values against nature, women and indigenous peoples are captured in this typical analysis of the "unproductiveness" of traditional natural societies:

> Production is achieved through human and animal, rather than mechanical, power. Most agriculture is unproductive; human or animal manure may be used but chemical fertilisers and pesticides are unknown. . . . For the masses, these conditions mean poverty.[5]

The assumptions are evident: nature is unproductive; organic agriculture based on nature's cycles of renewability spells poverty; women and tribal and peasant societies embedded in nature are similarly unproductive, not because it has been demonstrated that in cooperation they produce *less* goods and services for needs, but because it is assumed that "production" takes place only when mediated by technologies for commodity production, even when such technologies destroy life. A stable and clean river is not a productive resource in this view: it needs to be "developed" with dams in order to become so. Women, sharing the river as a commons to satisfy the water needs of their families and society are not involved in productive labour: when substituted by the engineering man, water management and water use become productive activities. Natural forests remain unproductive till they are developed into monoculture plantations of commercial species. Development thus, is equivalent to maldevelopment, a development bereft of the feminine, the conservation, the ecological principle. The neglect of nature's work in renewing herself, and women's work in producing sustenance in the form of basic, vital needs is an essential part of the paradigm of maldevelopment, which sees all work that does not produce profits and capital as non or unproductive work. As Maria Mies[6] has pointed out, this concept of surplus has a patriarchal bias because, from the point of view of nature and women, it is not based on material surplus produced *over and above* the requirements of the community: it is stolen and appropriated through violent modes from nature (who needs a share of her produce to reproduce herself) and from women (who need a share of nature's produce to produce sustenance and ensure survival).

From the perspective of Third World women, productivity is a measure of producing life and sustenance; that this kind of productivity has been rendered invisible does not reduce its centrality to survival—it merely reflects the domination of modern patriarchal economic categories which see only profits, not life.

MALDEVELOPMENT AS THE DEATH OF THE FEMININE PRINCIPLE

In this analysis, maldevelopment becomes a new source of male-female inequality. "Modernisation" has been associated with the introduction of new forms of dominance. Alice Schlegel[7] has shown that under conditions of subsistence, the interdependence and complementarity of the separate male and female domains of work is the characteristic mode, based on diversity, not inequality. Maldevelopment militates against this equality in diversity, and superimposes the ideologically constructed category of western technological man as a uniform measure of the worth of classes, cultures and genders. Dominant modes of perception based on reductionism, duality and linearity are unable to cope with equality in diversity, with forms and activities that are significant and valid, even though different. The reductionist mind superimposes the roles and forms of power of western male-oriented concepts on women, all non-western peoples and even on nature, rendering all three "deficient," and in need of "development." Diversity, and unity and harmony in diversity, become epistemologically unattainable in the context of maldevelopment, which then becomes synonymous with women's underdevelopment (increasing sexist domination), and nature's depletion (deepening ecological crises). Commodities have grown, but nature has shrunk. The poverty crisis of the South arises from the growing scarcity of water, food, fodder and fuel, associated with increasing maldevelopment and ecological destruction. This poverty crisis touches women most severely, first because they are the poorest among the poor, and then because, with nature, they are the primary sustainers of society.

Maldevelopment is the violation of the integrity of organic, interconnected and interdependent systems, that sets in motion a process of exploitation, inequality, injustice and violence. It is blind to the fact that a recognition of nature's harmony and action to maintain it are preconditions for distributive justice. This is why

Mahatma Gandhi said, "There is enough in the world for everyone's need, but not for some people's greed."

Maldevelopment is maldevelopment in thought and action. In practice, this fragmented, reductionist, dualist perspective violates the integrity and harmony of man in nature, and the harmony between men and women. It ruptures the co-operative unity of masculine and feminine, and places man, shorn of the feminine principle, above nature and women, and separated from both. The violence to nature as symptomatised by the ecological crisis, and the violence to women, as symptomatised by their subjugation and exploitation arise from this subjugation of the feminine principle. I want to argue that what is currently called development is essentially maldevelopment, based on the introduction or accentuation of the domination of man over nature and women. In it, both are viewed as the "other," the passive non-self. Activity, productivity, creativity which were associated with the feminine principle are expropriated as qualities of nature and women, and transformed into the exclusive qualities of man. Nature and women are turned into passive objects, to be used and exploited for the uncontrolled and uncontrollable desires of alienated man. From being the creators and sustainers of life, nature and women are reduced to being "resources" in the fragmented, anti-life model of maldevelopment. . . .

. . . The paradox and crisis of development arises from the mistaken identification of culturally perceived poverty with real material poverty, and the mistaken identification of the growth of commodity production as better satisfaction of basic needs. In actual fact, there is less water, less fertile soil, less genetic wealth as a result of the development process. Since these natural resources are the basis of nature's economy and women's survival economy, their scarcity is impoverishing women and marginalised peoples in an unprecedented manner. Their new impoverishment lies in the fact that resources which supported their survival were absorbed into the market economy while they themselves were excluded and displaced by it.

The old assumption that with the development process the availability of goods and services will automatically be increased and poverty will be removed, is now under serious challenge from women's ecology movements in the Third World, even while it continues to guide development thinking in centres of patriarchal power. Survival is based on the assumption of the sanctity of life; maldevelopment is based on the assumption of the sacredness of "development." Gustavo Esteva asserts that the sacredness of development has to be refuted because it threatens survival itself. "My people are tired of development," he says, "they just want to live."[8]

The recovery of the feminine principle allows a transcendance and transformation of these patriarchal foundations of maldevelopment. It allows a redefinition of growth and productivity as categories linked to the production, not the destruction, of life. It is thus simultaneously an ecological and a feminist political project which legitimises the way of knowing and being that create wealth by enhancing life and diversity, and which deligitimises the knowledge and practise of a culture of death as the basis for capital accumulation.

(1989)

NOTES

1. Rosa Luxemberg, *The Accumulation of Capital*, London: Routledge and Kegan Paul, 1951.
2. An elaboration of how "development" transfers resources from the poor to the well-endowed is contained in J. Bandyopadhyay and V. Shiva, "Political Economy of Technological Polarisations" in *Economic and Political Weekly*, Vol. XVIII, 1982, pp. 1827–32; and J. Bandyopadhyay and V. Shiva, "Political Economy of Ecology Movements," in *Economic and Political Weekly*, forthcoming.
3. Ester Boserup, *Women's Role in Economic Development*, London: Allen and Unwin, 1970.
4. DAWN, Development Crisis and Alternative Visions: Third World Women's Perspectives, Bergen: Christian Michelsen Institute, 1985, p. 21.
5. M. George Foster, *Traditional Societies and Technological Change*, Delhi: Allied Publishers, 1973.
6. Maria Mies, Patriarchy and Accumulation on a World Scale, London: Zed Books. 1986.
7. Alice Schlegel (ed.), *Sexual Stratification: A Cross-Cultural Study*, New York: Columbia University Press, 1977.
8. G. Esteva, Remarks made at a Conference of the Society for International Development, Rome, 1985.

"THE GLOBAL TRADE IN FILIPINA WORKERS"

Since the 1980s, the World Bank, the International Monetary Fund, and other international lending institutions based in the North have routinely prescribed structural adjustment policies (SAPs) to the governments of indebted countries of the South as pre-conditions for loans. These prescriptions have included cutting government expenditures on social programs, slashing wages, liberalizing imports, opening markets to foreign investment, expanding exports, devaluing local currency, and privatizing state enterprises. While SAPs are ostensibly intended to promote efficiency and sustained economic growth in the "adjusting" country, in reality they function to open up developing nations' economies and peoples to imperialist exploitation.

SAPs strike women in these nations the hardest and render them most vulnerable to exploitation both at home and in the global labor market. When wages and food subsidies are cut, wives and mothers must adjust household budgets, often at the expense of their own and their children's nutrition. As public healthcare and education vanishes, women suffer from a lack of prenatal care and become nurses to ill family members at home, while girls are the first to be kept from school to help at home or go to work. When export-oriented agriculture is encouraged, indeed coerced, peasant families are evicted from their lands to make room for corporate farms, and women become seasonal workers in the fields or in processing areas. Many women are forced to find work in the service industry, in manufacturing, or in home work, producing garments for export.[1]

When women take on these extra burdens and are still unable to sustain their families, many have no other viable option but to leave their families and migrate in search of work. Asian women migrate by the millions each year to work as servants, service workers, and sex workers in the United States, Canada, Europe, the Middle East, and Japan. Not coincidentally, the demand for service workers, and especially for private household caregivers and domestic workers, is exploding in wealthy nations of the First World undergoing their own versions of adjustment.

For example, in the United States, domestic forms of structural adjustment, including cutbacks in healthcare and the continued lack of subsidized childcare, contribute to an expanded demand among dual-career, middle-class households for workers in child-care, eldercare, and housekeeping. The slashing of benefits and social services under "welfare reform" helps to guarantee that this demand is met by eager migrant women workers. The dismantling of public supports in the United States in general, and the denial of benefits and services to immigrants in particular, act in tandem with structural adjustment abroad to force migrant women into low-wage labor in the United States. Migrant women workers from indebted nations are kept pliable not only by the dependence of their home countries and families on remittances, but also by stringent restrictions on immigrant access to almost all forms of assistance in the United States. Their vulnerability is further reinforced by U.S. immigration policies, designed to recruit migrant women as contract laborers or temporary workers who are ineligible for the protections and rights afforded to citizens.[2]

Both in their indebted home countries and abroad, women suffer the most from the dismantling of social programs under structural adjustment. In the Third World, women absorb the costs of cuts in food subsidies and healthcare by going hungry and foregoing proper medical care. Ironically, these same women continue to take up the slack for vanishing social supports in the First World, by nursing the elderly parents and young children of their employers for extremely low wages. Thus, there is a transfer of costs from the governments of both sending and receiving countries to migrant women workers from indebted nations. In both their home and "host" countries, and for both their own and their employers' families, these women pay most dearly for "adjustment." . . .

TESTIMONIES OF WOMEN LIVING UNDER SAPS

. . . Consistently, women from around the Third World testified that, as women have been displaced from their lands and homes under structural adjustment, women who were once small farmers have been forced to do home work, to migrate to the cities to work in manufacturing and the electronic industry, or to migrate overseas to do nursing, domestic work, sex work, and "entertainment."[3] The women's testimony demonstrates their clear recognition that they bear the brunt of hardships under structural adjustment, while their nations' governments and elites reap fat rewards in the form of women's cheap or unpaid labor and remittances from migrant women workers abroad. Commentary of women organizing in countries affected by SAPs reflects an acute awareness of the ways in which the governments and economic elites of their countries and First World countries profit at the expense of women's labor conditions, education, nutrition, health, and safety. As one labor organizer from India remarked:

> Our governments are surrendering to these multinational corporations and Western agencies. These magnate[s] and mafias, in the name of globalization, want to exploit our workers and resources. Our real concerns are food, water, clean sanitary conditions, health, shelter, and no exploitation. These are the human rights we want. All these

governments are telling us to talk about human rights. What are they doing?[4]

EXPORTING WOMEN: THE "NEW HEROES"

Each day, thousands of Filipinas leave their homes and families in search of work abroad. The Philippine government estimates that more than 4 percent of the country's total population are contract workers overseas. About 700,000 Filipinas/os were deployed through a government agency, the Philippine Overseas Employment Administration (POEA), in each of the past two years.[5] In 1991, women constituted a larger proportion of the country's overseas workforce (41 percent) than its domestic workforce (36 percent). Of those overseas, approximately 70 percent are women working as domestic servants in middle- and upper-class homes in the United States, Britain, Europe, Japan, and the Middle East. Many of the others work as nurses, sex workers, and entertainers.[6] Such massive migrations of women have led to public charges that the Philippines government is selling or trafficking in women.

Indeed, this massive migration is no mere coincidence of individual women's choices to leave the Philippines. The Philippine government receives huge sums of remittances from its overseas workers each year. "Host" country governments and private employers welcome the migrant women workers for the cheap labor they provide. These governments and employers save money not only by paying abominably low wages, but by failing to provide public benefits or social services to these temporary workers. Finally, recruiting agencies and other entrepreneurs on each end of the trade route reap tremendous profits for providing employers in "host" countries with ready and willing service workers and caregivers of all kinds. . . .

. . . As many countries of the North undergo downsizing and the dismantling of public supports, migrant women workers offer the perfect solution. The steady flow of migrant women provides an ideal source of cheap, highly exploitable labor. These women are channeled directly into the service sector, where they do every form of care work for a pittance and no benefits. Ironically, immigrant domestic workers, nannies, in-home caregivers, and nurses pick up the slack for cuts in government services and supports that pervade the North as well as the South. Overseas, they provide care for the ill, elderly, and children, while their own families forego this care because of the economic restructuring that drives them overseas.

FILIPINA NURSES AND HOMECARE WORKERS

Currently, there are 100,000 registered nurses in the Philippines, but almost none actually reside in the country. Similarly, 90 percent of all Filipino/a medical school graduates do not live in the Philippines. Since the 1970s, the United States has imported women from the Philippines to work as nurses, ostensibly in response to domestic shortages in trained nurses. This importation system became institutionalized with the H-1 nursing visa, which enables a hospital or nursing home to sponsor or bring a nurse with a professional license from abroad to work in the United States for two years. . . .

Ninotchka Rosca of Gabriela Network USA observes the ironic history of Filipina nurses in the United States. In the 1980s, the nursing profession was extremely low-paying, with salaries at about $20,000 a year in the United States, so the country experienced a drastic shortage of nurses. With few U.S. citizens going into the field or willing to do nursing at such low wages, many Jamaican and Filipina women migrated here to do this work. With the downsizing in healthcare, many of the migrant nurses who have been here for over a decade are now finding themselves just as vulnerable as new migrants. Hospitals are attempting to reduce costs by firing their most experienced, and thus highest-paid, nurses. Rosca suggests that U.S. hospitals and the healthcare industry would collapse without Filipina nurses. "We take care of everybody else's weaker members of society, while we let our own society go to hell."[7]

HOMECARE WORKERS

Home healthcare is another industry in which immigrant women are highly concentrated and fall prey to both profit-seeking agencies and the cost-cutting U.S. government. Many homecare workers are employees of the state, under a state-funded program called "in-home support services" (IHSS). Some of these women are registered nurses, while others are not trained as nurses at all. The program provides no training, no regulations, and no monitoring of the work, which includes everything from performing medical procedures, preparing meals, and cleaning to helping elderly, frail, or ill clients go to the toilet, bathe, and move about. To keep costs down, the state pays workers a minimum wage of $4.50 an hour and provides no benefits, including no sick leave, family leave, overtime pay, compensation for injuries on the job, or reimbursement for bus fares or gasoline used to run errands for patients or to take them to the doctor.[8] In California, there are 170,000 of these workers statewide, of which approximately 80 percent are women, 60 to 70 percent are people of color, and 40 percent are immigrants. . . .

Employing an IHSS worker saves taxpayers approximately $30,000 a year, the difference between the cost of keeping a patient in a nursing home and the typical salary of $7,000 a year earned by an IHSS worker who works 30 hours a week. This savings is reaped by the state, county, and (through Medicaid) federal governments, which all share the program's annual cost. Robert Barton, manager of the adult services branch of the California Department of Social Services overseeing the program, commented: "It's a good deal for the government." The union's director of organizing in Washington, D.C., David Snapp, retorts: "It's a scam."[9] The IHSS program provides perhaps the best illustration available of the tremendous savings to local, state, and federal governments through the low-wage labor of migrant care workers. Other savings to the state and employers have not been measured, such as those reaped from not providing public benefits, services, and protections to these workers. . . .

DOMESTIC WORKERS AND NANNIES

The majority of migrant Filipina workers are domestic workers and nannies. Many of them work in Canada, which has had a "live-in caregiver program" since 1992 to facilitate the importation of these migrants. . . .

The film *Brown Women, Blonde Babies*, produced by Marie Boti, documents the conditions for Filipina migrant women working as domestics and nannies in

Canada. Typically, women work around the clock, from 7 a.m. to 10 p.m. and beyond, and are always considered on call. They earn an average of $130 a month after taxes. Women who wish to leave their employers must persuade an immigration officer to let them. In response to one woman's pleas for release from an employer, one immigration officer coldly responded, "You didn't come here to be happy." . . .

According to the Kanlungan Foundation Centre, an advocacy group for Filipina migrant workers,

> We do not migrate as totally free and independent individuals. At times, we have no choice but to migrate, to brave the odds. . . . Even from the very start, we are already victims of illegal recruitment, victims of our government's active marketing of our cheap labor, . . . and suffering the backlash of states that fail to provide adequate support for childcare services, we enter first world countries that seek to preserve patriarchal ideology.[10]

This statement reflects migrant women workers' clear understanding that they are being used to maintain patriarchy in the First World, as governments in these wealthy nations cut social supports. . . .

WOMEN'S RESISTANCE

. . . Teresita Tristan is a widow who left two children behind in the Philippines for a job in Britain as a domestic worker. Before leaving, she had been promised a salary of $400 a month, but when she arrived, her employers took her passport and informed her she would be paid $108 a month. On her first day in the country, she was taken for a medical exam, given medicine to clean her stomach, and was instructed to take a bath and not to touch the dishes with her bare hands until five days had passed. Her daily work consisted of cleaning the entire house, taking the children to school, and preparing the family's meals, while she ate leftovers. She was not allowed to eat from plates or glasses or to use the toilet inside the house. When her employer kept making sexual advances and asking her to go to the guest house with him, she asked to be released so she could return home. Instead, she was transferred to her employers' daughter's home, where she was likewise treated badly.[11] . . .

Tristan's story is typical of that of migrant workers, according to Kalayaan, an organization working for justice for overseas domestic workers in Britain. Between January 1992 and December 1994, Kalayaan interviewed 755 migrant domestic workers who had left their employers. The results of these interviews revealed widespread abuses of migrant domestic workers from the Philippines, Sri Lanka, India, Ghana, Nigeria, Colombia, and Brazil. Eighty-eight percent had experienced psychological abuse, including name-calling, threats, and insults, and 38 percent had endured physical abuse of some form. Eleven percent had experienced attempted, threatened, or actual sexual assault or rape. A full 60 percent had received no regular meals, 42 percent had no bed, and 51 percent had no bedroom and were forced to sleep in a hallway, kitchen, bathroom, or storeroom. Thirty-one percent reported being imprisoned or not being allowed to leave the house. Ninety-one percent reported working for an average of 17 hours a day with no time off. Fifty-five percent were not paid regularly, and 81 percent were paid less than was agreed upon in their contracts, with an average monthly wage of USD $105. . . .

Migrant workers have mobilized worldwide to expose these abuses and to fight for protection of their rights. Women in many "host" countries, including Canada, Japan, Britain, and the United States, have organized grassroots organizations to offer support and legal advocacy, and to lobby for the protection of Filipina and other migrant workers abroad. . . .

Groups such as Kalayaan, INTERCEDE, and SEIU focus on organizing migrant workers and providing direct services to them in "host" countries while lobbying these "host" governments to change oppressive immigration and labor policies. Other organizations have a different emphasis, putting pressure on the Philippine government to recognize the impact of SAPs on poor women of the Third World at home and abroad. They aim to expose how the Philippine government facilitates the exportation of women migrant workers, sacrificing women in the futile effort to keep up with debt payments. Finally, they pressure the Philippine government to redirect expenditures away from debt servicing, to institute protections for migrant workers abroad, and to stop the export of women from the Philippines and other impoverished countries. . . .

Mainstream U.S. feminist responses to the trade in women have been lukewarm at best. When Gabriela called on women's organizations around the world to put the issue of global trafficking of women on their agendas, the National Organization for Women (NOW) declined to do so, stating that it does not deal with international issues.[12] The real issue may be that privileged women of the First World, even self-avowed feminists, are some of the primary consumers and beneficiaries in this trade. Middle-and upper-class professional women generally have not joined efforts to improve wages or conditions for care workers in the United States, since they have historically relied on the "affordability" of women of color and migrant women working in their homes, daycare centers, and nursing homes. . . .

Asian/Pacific Islander and other women of color feminists in the First World would do well to take the lead from groups like INTERCEDE and many of our Third World sisters who have been mobilizing around the issues of SAPs and the traffic in women for years now. At the NGO Forum, many First World women remarked that they were the least well-informed or organized on global economic issues. Many First World feminists of color came home from the Forum resolved to undertake or redouble efforts to understand and expose the links between economic restructuring in the First World, SAPs in the Third World, and the global trade in women. . . .

(1997)

NOTES

This article is extracted from a chapter in my forthcoming book, *Disposable Domestics*. I would like to thank Luisa Blue, Josie Camacho, Mayee Crispin, Ninotchka Rosca, Carole Salmon, and Felicita Villasin for sharing their great insights, expertise, and time in interviews. I am also indebted to Miriam Ching Louie and Linda Burnham for bravely leading the Women of Color Resource Center delegation to Huairou, and for their pioneering work on Women's Education in the Global Economy. I am grateful to Nathaniel Silva for his insights and comments in developing this piece.

1. Sparr, Pamela. *Mortgaging Women's Lives: Feminist Critiques of Structural Adjustment*. London: Zed Books, 1994.

2. Chang, Grace. "Disposable Nannies: Women's Work and the Politics of Latina Immigration." *Radical America* 26, 2 (October 1996): 5–20.

3. Testimony of representative from International Organization of Prostitutes. Gabriela Workshop, NGO Forum, September 3, 1995.

4. Plenary on Globalization, NGO Forum, September 3, 1995.

5. This number does not include women who are trafficked or illegally recruited, those who migrate for marriage, students, or tourists who eventually become undocumented workers. Compiled by Kanlungan Center Foundation from Philippine Overseas Employment Administration (POEA) and Department of Labor and Employment (DOLE) statistics.

6. Vincent, Isabel. "Canada Beckons Cream of Nannies: Much-sought Filipinas Prefer Work Conditions." *The Globe and Mail*. 20 January 1996: A1, A6. Other authors address more extensively trafficking in women for the sex work, entertainment, and mail-order bride industries. See Rosca, Ninotchka. "The Philippines' Shameful Export." *The Nation*. 17 April 1995: 523–525; Kim, Elaine. "Sex Tourism in Asia: A Reflection of Political and Economic Equality." *Critical Perspectives of Third World America* 2.1 (Fall 1984): 215–231; *Sisters and Daughters Betrayed: The Trafficking of Women and Girls and the Fight to End It*. Video. Prod. Chela Blitt. Global Fund for Women.

7. Rosca, Ninotchka. Personal interview. 29 April 1996.

8. Kilborn, Peter T. "Union Gets the Lowly to Sign Up: Home Care Aides Are Fresh Target." *New York Times*. 21 November 1995.

9. Kilborn, op cit.

10. *A Framework on Women and Migration*. Kanlungan Center Foundation; prepared for the NGO Forum of 1995.

11. Testimony, Workshop on Violence and Migration, NGO Forum, 1995.

12. Rosca, Ninotchka. Personal Interview. 29 April 1996.

"WIELDING MASCULINITY INSIDE ABU GHRAIB AND GUANTÁNAMO: THE GLOBALIZED DYNAMICS"

In June 2006, two years after the Abu Ghraib scandal broke and set off worldwide consternation, a short article appeared in the *New York Times* reporting that an American army dog handler had been found guilty by a military court-martial. He had been charged with having used his dog to intimidate Iraqi male prisoners being held by the U.S. military at Abu Ghraib (Associated Press 2006). Sergeant Santos A. Cardona was the eleventh American soldier serving in Iraq's infamous Abu Ghraib, a U.S. military jail and interrogation center, to have been convicted of violations of the U.S. military code of conduct. His defense lawyers had argued, unsuccessfully, that Sergeant Cardona was doing only what he had been trained to do and what his military superiors had commanded him to do.

Three of the eleven American soldiers convicted of committing abuses at Abu Ghraib were women, eight were men. All eleven soldiers who were court-martialed and convicted were enlisted personnel or noncommissioned officers. None were higher-ranking officers. None were Washington-based civilian policymakers (Hillman 2005).

The only senior officer to receive an official reprimand and demotion was a woman, General Janis Karpinski. She was the army reserve officer then in charge of the U.S. occupation authority's cobbled-together military prison system in Iraq. Her own telling of the Abu Ghraib story is full of descriptions of wartime unpreparedness, lack of senior command support, autonomous actions by military and CIA interrogators, and

routine behaviors in what has become the military's institutional culture of sexism (Karpinski 2005).

On the same June day in 2006 that the *New York Times* reported Sergeant Cardona's conviction, the paper's editors included two other reports that one could read as possibly connected to the short article about Abu Ghraib. First, there was another brief report of the last of the U.S. Army's trials concerning abuses at a U.S. detention center at the Bagram military base in Afghanistan. The last soldier to be prosecuted for abuse and the deaths of prisoners held at Bagram was Private First Class Damien M. Corsetti. He was one of more than a dozen U.S. soldiers—all men—charged with abusing and causing the deaths of Afghan prisoners at Bagram. The military jury acquitted Private Corsetti (Golden 2006).

The Geneva Conventions are international agreements negotiated by governments in the mid-twentieth century. The agreements are not designed so much to reverse militarization as they are intended to globalize the ethics that should guide governments' war-waging behavior. War waging can continue but should be conducted according to these agreed-upon rules. The U.S. government is a signatory to the Geneva Conventions. Prescriptions for the treatment of prisoners captured in wartime is one of the major elements of the Geneva Conventions. That is, a soldier may be in the enemy's forces, but he or she is still a human being and, as a human being, deserves to be treated humanely.

Avoiding these internationally agreed upon requirements to treat prisoners of war humanely was a strategy adopted by U.S. government officials in the name of

- "urgency," coupled with
- "national security," in order to wage
- "the global war on terror."

Those who devised the political rationales, legal interpretations, and bureaucratic strategies for this avoidance were overwhelmingly civilians. They were civilians posted inside the Defense Department, the Justice Department, the White House legal counsel's office, and the office of the vice president (Danner 2004; Mayer 2005a; Mayer 2005b; Mayer 2005c; Mayer 2006).

Witnesses for both the defense and the prosecution at the June 2006 Corsetti court-martial described how the pressures imposed on guards and interrogators at Bagram to get more information from their prisoners increased in late 2002. It was then two months into the U.S.-led military invasion of Afghanistan. President Bush had declared that prisoners captured in Afghanistan were not to be deemed eligible for the international protections guaranteed to enemy combatants under the Geneva Conventions. Many of those male prisoners first detained and questioned at Bagram would soon be flown in large cargo planes—after they had been dressed in orange jump suits, shackled, and had burlap bags placed over their heads—to the detention center the U.S. had recently constructed at its naval base in Guantánamo, Cuba (Lipman forthcoming). The links between Bagram and Guantánamo were being forged.

A year later, those forged links would be extended to Abu Ghraib. Trying to make sense of what happened inside Abu Ghraib in the fall and winter of 2003 turns out to be nearly impossible if one treats Abu Ghraib as an island. It was not an island. It was a link in a globalized chain (Greenberg and Dratel 2005). Among the materials used to weld those chain links—Bagram to Guantánamo, Guantánamo to Abu Ghraib—were American ideas about *feminization*.

Feminization is a process of imposing allegedly feminine characteristics on a person—man or woman—or a group or a kind of activity. Often the goal of feminizing someone (or something) is to lower his (or its) status. Feminization provokes anxiety when particular forms of masculinity are culturally, academically, politically, or economically privileged (Carver 2003; Elias forthcoming). Stitching sneakers

for the global market has been feminized in the corporate hope of lowering labor costs. Military nursing has become feminized in an effort to use women in the military without diluting the military's prized image as a masculinized institution. A male candidate running for election against another male candidate may try to gain an advantage with voters by feminizing his opponent—for instance, by portraying his rival as "weak on national security." A male prisoner is feminized when his captors force him to look or act in ways those captors think will make him feel feminine. The presumption motivating his taunters is that a man who is being feminized will become more cooperative out of his sense of shame and helplessness.

In a patriarchal culture—in rich countries and poor countries, in countries with diverse cultural traditions—any person, group, or activity that can be feminized risks losing his or her (or its) influence, authority, and even self-respect. So long as any culture remains patriarchal, then, feminization can be wielded as an instrument of intimidation.

Using a feminist curiosity to make sense of what happened in Abu Ghraib means both investigating any efforts to wield feminization in imprisonment and interrogation and looking for the women in all their various roles. Those roles can be both obvious and obscure. Ann Wright served as an army officer for twenty-nine years and then as a U.S. diplomat before resigning in opposition to the administration's preemptive war. After resigning, Ann Wright decided to use her new independence to find out where all the women were on the broad canvas that became "Abu Ghraib." She found Major General Barbara Fast, chief of military intelligence, serving in the U.S. military command's headquarters in Baghdad. She found Captain Carolyn Wood, a military intelligence officer who had been the leader of the interrogation team in Bagram and then, with her unit, transferred to Abu Ghraib. Wright found two lower-ranking women interrogators deployed to Abu Ghraib, as well as two women employed as interpreters by a civilian contractor, the Titan Company, working with a military intelligence unit inside the prison. Ann Wright also found three Army linguists working in interrogation teams at Guantánamo during 2003 and 2004. She discovered that during these same crucial months at least three other Army women were conducting interrogations at Guantánamo. An unknown number of additional women were serving at Guantánamo at the same time as private contract interrogators. None of these women came forward to stop the abuses they witnessed. Several of them, according to firsthand accounts, helped devise some of the practices meant to humiliate the male prisoners (Wright 2006; Saar 2005).

Is it surprising that there were so many American women inside Bagram, Guantánamo, and Abu Ghraib who, in 2003 and 2004, were playing roles up and down the chain of command as guards, interpreters, and interrogators? Probably not. After all, over the past two decades, in devising gender strategies for recruiting women while still maintaining the military's masculinized core—combat—officials of the U.S. Defense Department had channeled women soldiers into not just nursing and administration but such seemingly noncontroversial jobs as military police, military interpreters, and intelligence. By 2004, women, who made up only 15 percent of total U.S. Army personnel, represented 22 percent of military police and 25 percent of military interrogators (Wright 2006).

Still, using a feminist curiosity to make sense of Abu Ghraib, Bagram, and Guantánamo allows one to do more than look for where the women are—as revealing as that exploration is. Using a feminist curiosity prompts one to also pursue the answer to a question that most commentators fail to ask: what are the causes and consequences of wielding ideas about masculinity and femininity?

Feminization has been used during the Afghanistan and Iraq wars mainly by American militarized men (civilian and military), but with the complicity and sometimes the direct involvement of a handful of American militarized women. Evidence gathered thus far suggests that feminization was intended by its wartime wielders to humiliate and thereby gain information from foreign men, mostly men identified by their American captors as "Muslim," "dangerous," and "the enemy." As they were transported by U.S. officials from Washington to Bagram to Guantánamo to Abu Ghraib, these practices of coercive feminization might be thought of as being *globally militarized.*

Back at Private Corsetti's June 2006 barely reported court-martial, defense witnesses sought to undercut the prosecution's case against Corsetti by noting that there were almost-daily phone calls to interrogators at Bagram from their civilian Defense Department superiors in Washington. Their superiors were infused with a sense of urgency. They demanded quick results from the interrogations being conducted at the Bagram base. The witnesses recalled how this pressure from Washington officials served to increase the aggressiveness of the physical tactics that Bagram soldiers and interrogators used on prisoners deemed uncooperative (Golden 2006). The jury seemed convinced.

American military interrogators' and guards' adoption of both painful "stress positions" and feminization to intimidate captive men can be traded globally, just as rifles can be traded globally, just as ideas about national security and creating "cheap labor" can be traded globally.

American male and female soldiers serving during late 2003 and early 2004 as prison guards in Abu Ghraib became the best known actors in this fast-globalizing drama. As individuals, they seemed far from being global players. They appeared quite parochial and isolated. The photographs that showed them deliberately humiliating and torturing scores of Iraqi men held in detention and under interrogation were taken apparently for their own private amusement, not for prime-time television or headline stories. But their audience expanded beyond their wildest dreams—or nightmares. Between April and June 2004, millions of viewers were looking at these private photos: American soldiers smiling broadly as they appeared to be taking enormous pleasure in frightening and humiliating their wartime Iraqi charges.

Most people who saw these photographs can still describe the scenes. An American male soldier standing in a self-satisfied pose, facing his army colleague holding the camera with his arms crossed and wearing surgical blue rubber gloves, a sign that this abuse was occurring in the age of AIDS. In front of him, we, the globalized viewers of these photographs, could see an American woman soldier smiling at the camera as she leaned on top of a pile of naked Iraqi men who were being forced to contort themselves into a human pyramid.

Other pictures whizzed around the planet. An American woman soldier, again smiling, holding an Iraqi male prisoner on a leash. An American woman soldier pointing to a naked Iraqi man's genitals, apparently treating them as a joke. American male soldiers intimidating naked Iraqi male prisoners with snarling guard dogs. An Iraqi male prisoner standing alone on a box, his head covered with a hood and electrical wires attached to different parts of his body. An Iraqi male prisoner forced to wear women's underwear. Not pictured, but substantiated, were Iraqi men forced to masturbate and to simulate oral sex with each other, as well as an Iraqi woman prisoner coerced by several American male soldiers into kissing them (Hersh 2004)....

Several things proved shocking to the millions of viewers of the clandestine prison photos. First, the Abu Ghraib scenes suggested there existed a gaping chasm between, on the one hand, the Bush administration's claim that its military invasion and overthrow of the brutal Saddam Hussein regime would bring a civilizing sort of "freedom" to the Iraqi people and, on the other hand, the seemingly barbaric treatment that American soldiers were willfully meting out to Iraqis held in captivity without trial. Second, it was shocking to witness such blatant abuse of imprisoned detainees by soldiers representing a government that had passed its own antitorture laws and had signed both the international Geneva Conventions against mistreatment of wartime combatants and the UN Convention against Torture and Other Cruel, Inhuman or Degrading Treatment or Punishment (sometimes referred to simply as the "Convention Against Torture").

Yet there was a third source of shock that prompted scores of early media commentaries and intense conversations among ordinary viewers: seeing women engage in torture. Of the seven American soldiers initially court-martialed (and eleven soldiers eventually court-martialed), all low-ranking army reserve military police guards, three were women. Somehow, the American male soldier in the blue surgical gloves (Charles Graner) was not shocking to most viewers and so did not inspire much private consternation or a stream of op-ed columns. Women, by contrast, were conventionally expected by most editors and news watchers to appear in wartime as mothers and wives of soldiers, occasionally as military nurses and truck mechanics, and most often as victims of wartime violence. Women were not—according to the conventional presumption—supposed to be the wielders of violence and certainly not the perpetrators of torture. When those deeply gendered presumptions were turned upside down, many people felt a sense of shock. "This is awful; how could this have happened?"

Private First Class Lynndie England, the young female military clerk (not a guard) photographed

holding the man on a leash, thus became the source of intense public curiosity. The news photographers could not restrain themselves two months later, in early August 2004, from showing England in her camouflaged army maternity uniform when she appeared at Fort Bragg for her pretrial hearing. She had become pregnant as a result of her sexual liaison with another enlisted reservist while on duty in Abu Ghraib. Her sexual partner was Charles Graner. Yet Charles Graner's name was scarcely mentioned. He apparently was doing what men are expected to do in wartime: have sex and wield violence. The public's curiosity and its lack of curiosity thus matched its pattern of shock. All three—curiosity, lack of curiosity, and shock—were conventionally gendered. Using a feminist investigatory approach, one should find this lack of public and media curiosity about Charles Graner just as revealing as the public's and media's fascination with Lynndie England.

Yet more than Charles Graner was pushed aside. The government policymaking that implicitly approved the use of torture was never put on trial. In fact, one reporter who, with a handful of her colleagues followed the Abu Ghraib trials for months, all the way through to the trial of Lynndie England (the last of the low-ranking Abu Ghraib soldiers to be tried) and heard Lynndie England's sentence pronounced in the court room at Fort Hood, Texas, in September 2005, noted how narrow the focus remained throughout all the trials. Bigger issues were deemed irrelevant (Wypijewski 2006). In fact, it was considered quite exceptional when General Geoffrey Miller, the Guantánamo commander who had brought the message to Iraq in the fall of 2003 that pressure on captured suspected insurgents needed to be increased, appeared briefly at just one of the many court sessions. No senior civilian officials from the Defense or Justice Department made any appearances. This legalistic narrowing of the focus served to normalize in the minds of many ordinary people those government interrogation policies and the resultant practice of inflicting physical pain and feminized humiliation that flowed from them.

Responding to the torrent of Abu Ghraib stories coming out of Iraq during the spring and summer of 2004, President George W. Bush and Secretary of Defense Donald Rumsfeld, the president's appointee, tried to reassure the public that the abusive behavior inside the prison was not representative of America, nor did it reflect the Bush administration's own foreign policies. Rather, the Abu Ghraib abuses were the work of "rogue" soldiers, a "few bad apples."

The "bad apple" explanation always goes like this: the institution is working fine, its values are appropriate, its internal dynamics are of a sort that sustain positive values, along with respectful, productive behavior. Thus, according to the "bad apple" explanation, nothing needs to be reassessed or reformed in the way the organization works; all that needs to happen to stop the abuse is to prosecute and remove those few individuals who refused to play by the established rules. Sometimes this may be true. Some listeners to the administration's "bad apple" explanation, however, weren't reassured. They wondered if the Abu Ghraib abuses were not produced by just a few bad apples found in a solid, reliable barrel but instead were produced by an essentially "bad barrel." They also wondered whether this "barrel" embraced not only the Abu Ghraib prison, but the larger U.S. military, intelligence, and civilian command structures (Hersh 2004; Human Rights Watch 2004).

What makes a "barrel" go bad? That is, what turns an organization, an institution, or a whole system into one that ignores, perhaps even fosters, abusive behavior by the individuals operating inside it? This question is relevant for every workplace, every political system, every international alliance. Here, too, feminists have been working hard over the past three decades to develop a curiosity and a set of analytical tools with which we can all answer this important question. So many of us today live much of our lives within complex organizations, large and small—workplaces, local and national governments, health care systems, criminal justice systems, international organizations. Feminist researchers have revealed that virtually all organizations are gendered; that is, all organizations are shaped by the ideas about, and daily practices of wielding, norms of masculinity and femininity (Bunster-Burotto 1985; Ehrenreich 2004; Enloe 2000; Whitworth 2004; Burke 2004). Ignoring the workings of gender, feminist investigators have found, makes it impossible for us to explain accurately what makes any organization "tick." That failure makes it impossible for us to hold an organization accountable. . . .

Since the mid-1970s, feminists have been introducing new questions to pose and crafting skills to explain when and why organizations become arenas for sexist

abuse. One of the great contributions of the work done by what is often referred to as the "Second Wave" of the international women's movement (that is, feminist activism of the 1960s to 1990s) has been to shed light on what breeds sex discrimination and sexual harassment inside organizations otherwise as dissimilar as a factory, a stockbrokerage, a legislature, a university, a student movement, and a military (Bowers 2004; Kwon 2000; Ogasawara 1998; Stockford 2004; Whitworth 2004; Murphy 2005). All of the authors of the reports on Abu Ghraib talked about a "climate," an "environment," or a "culture," having been created inside Abu Ghraib that fostered abusive acts. The conditions inside Abu Ghraib were portrayed as having been part of a climate of "confusion," of "chaos." It is important to note that it was feminists who gave us this innovative concept of organizational climate.

When trying to figure out why women employees in some organizations were subjected to sexist jokes, unwanted advances, and retribution for not going along with the jokes or not accepting those advances, feminist lawyers, advocates, and scholars began to look beyond the formal policies and the written rules. They explored something more amorphous but just as potent, and maybe even more so: the set of unofficial presumptions that shapes workplace interactions between men and men and between men and women. They followed the bread crumbs to the casual, informal interactions between people up and down the organization's ladder. They investigated who drinks with whom after work, who sends sexist jokes to whom over office e-mail, who pins up which sorts of pictures of women in their lockers or next to the coffee machine. And they looked into what those people in authority did *not* do. They discovered that inaction is a form of action: "turning a blind eye" is itself a form of action. Inaction sends out signals to everyone in the organization about what is condoned. Feminists labeled these webs of presumptions, informal interactions, and deliberate inaction as an organization's "climate." As feminists argued successfully in court, it is not sufficient for a stockbrokerage or a college to include anti-sexual-harassment guidelines in its official handbook; employers have to take explicit steps to create a workplace climate in which women are treated with fairness and respect.

By 2004, this feminist explanatory concept—organizational "climate"—had become so accepted by so many analysts that their debt to feminists had been forgotten. Generals Taguba, Jones, and Fay, as well as former defense secretary Schlesinger, may never have taken a women's studies course, but when they were assigned the job of investigating Abu Ghraib they were drawing on the ideas and investigatory skills crafted for them by feminists.

However, more worrisome than the failure by such investigators to acknowledge their intellectual and political debts was their ignoring the feminist lessons that went hand in hand with the concept of "climate." The first lesson: to make sense of any organization, we always must dig deep into the group's dominant presumptions about femininity and masculinity. The second lesson: we need to take seriously the experiences of women as they try to adapt to, or sometimes resist, those dominant gendered presumptions—not because all women are angels, but because paying close attention to women's ideas and actions will shed light on why men with power act the way they do.

It is not as if the potency of ideas about masculinity and femininity had been totally absent from the U.S. military's thinking. Between 1991 and 2004, there had been a string of military scandals that had compelled even those American senior officials who preferred to look the other way to face sexism straight on. The first stemmed from the September 1991 gathering of American navy pilots at a Hilton hotel in Las Vegas. Male pilots (all officers), fresh from their victory in the first Gulf War, lined a hotel corridor and physically assaulted every woman who stepped off the elevator. They made the "mistake" of assaulting a woman navy helicopter pilot who was serving as an aide to an admiral. Within months, members of Congress and the media were telling the public about "Tailhook"— why it happened and who tried to cover it up (Office of the Inspector General 2003). Close on the heels of the navy's "Tailhook" scandal came the army's Aberdeen training base sexual harassment scandal, followed by other revelations of gay bashing, sexual harassment, and rapes by American male military personnel (Enloe 1993, 2000).

Then in September 1995, the rape of a local school girl by two American male marines and a sailor in Okinawa sparked public demonstrations, the formation of new Okinawan women's advocacy groups, and more congressional investigations in the United States. At the start of the twenty-first century, American media

began to notice the patterns of international trafficking in Eastern European and Filipino women around American bases in South Korea, prompting official embarrassment in Washington (embarrassment that had not been demonstrated earlier when American base commanders turned a classic "blind eye" to a prostitution industry organized locally to service those commanders' own male soldiers, because it employed "just" local South Korean women). And in 2003, three new American military sexism scandals caught Washington policymakers' attention: four American male soldiers returning from combat missions in Afghanistan murdered their female partners at Fort Bragg, North Carolina; a pattern of sexual harassment and rape by male cadets of female cadets—and superiors' refusal to treat these acts seriously—was revealed at the U.S. Air Force Academy; and at least sixty American women soldiers returning from tours of duty in Kuwait and Iraq testified that they had been sexually assaulted by their male colleagues there— once again, with senior officers choosing inaction and advising the American women soldiers to "get over it" (Jargon 2003; Lutz and Elliston 2004; Miles Foundation 2004; Moffeit and Herder 2004).

Carol Burke, a professor of folklore, taught at the U.S. Naval Academy at Annapolis. When the evidence of abuses perpetrated in Abu Ghraib started to become news, she immediately drew the parallels between what had gone on inside the prison and what she herself had witnessed routinely among American male cadets at the naval academy: men using feminized rituals of hazing to try to humiliate other male cadets, which simultaneously reinforced the collective contempt with which anything "tainted" with femininity was held. Even the use of women's underwear and the coerced sexual acts were identical (Burke 2004, 2006).

So it should have come as no surprise to senior uniformed and civilian policymakers seeking to make sense of the abuses perpetrated in Abu Ghraib that a culture of sexism had come to permeate many sectors of U.S. military life. If they had thought about what they had all learned in the last thirteen years—from Tailhook, Aberdeen, Fort Bragg, Okinawa, South Korea, and the U.S. Air Force Academy—they should have put the workings of masculinity and femininity at the top of their investigatory agendas. They should have made feminist curiosity one of their own principal tools. Perhaps Tillie Fowler did suggest to her colleagues that they think about these military scandals when they began to delve into Abu Ghraib. A former Republican congresswoman from Florida, Tillie Fowler had been a principal investigator on the team that looked into the rapes (and their cover-ups) at the U.S. Air Force Academy. Because of her leadership in that role, Fowler was appointed to the commission headed by James Schlesinger investigating Abu Ghraib. Did she raise this comparison between the Air Force Academy case and Abu Ghraib? If she did, did her male colleagues take her suggestion seriously?

Perhaps ultimately the investigators did not make use of the feminist lessons and tools because they imagined that the lessons of Tailhook, Aberdeen, Fort Bragg, Okinawa, South Korea, and the Air Force Academy were relevant only when all the perpetrators of sexual abuse are men and all the victims are women. Perhaps they ignored their knowledge of the sexualized hazing practices common in American military organizations (and in fraternities and sports teams at American colleges) because, after all, those could be dismissed as "boys being boys" and could be imagined as having no serious consequences on either the men being hazed or the women implicitly being denigrated.

The presence of Lynndie England and the other women in Abu Ghraib's military police unit, they might have assumed, made the feminist tools sharpened in those earlier gendered military scandals inappropriate for their current investigation. But the lesson of Tailhook and the other military scandals was *not* that the politics of masculinity and femininity matter only when men are the perpetrators and women are the victims. Instead, the deeper lesson of all those other military scandals is that we must always ask "has this organization (or this system of interlocking organizations) become masculinized in ways that privilege certain forms of masculinity, feminize its opposition, and trivialize most forms of femininity?"

With this core gender question in mind, we might uncover significant dynamics operating in Abu Ghraib and in the American military and civilian organizations that were supposed to be supervising the prison's personnel. American military police and their military and CIA intelligence colleagues might have been guided by their *own* masculinized fears of humiliation when they forced Iraqi men to go naked for days, to wear women's underwear, and to masturbate in front of each other and American women guards. That is, the Americans' belief in an allegedly "exotic," frail Iraqi masculinity, fraught with fears of nakedness and homosexuality, might not have been the chief motivator for the American police and intelligence personnel; it may have been their own homegrown American sense of masculinity's fragility—how easily manliness can be feminized—that prompted them to craft these prison humiliations, Either belief could encourage the guards to wield feminization as a technique of prisoner humiliation. In this distorted masculinized scenario, the presence of women serving as military police might have proved especially useful. Choreographing the women guards feminized roles so that they could act as ridiculing feminized spectators of male prisoners might have been imagined to intensify the demasculinizing demoralization. As histories of international conflicts in Vietnam, Rwanda, and Western Europe have revealed, dominant men trying to use women in ways that undermine the masculinized self-esteem of rival men is not new.

What about the American women soldiers themselves? In the U.S. military of 2004, women constituted 15 percent of active duty personnel, 17 percent of all reserves and the National Guard, and a surprising 24 percent of the army reserves alone. From the very time these particular young women joined this military police unit, they, like their fellow male recruits, probably sought to fit into the group. If the unit's evolving culture—perhaps fostered by their superiors for the sake of "morale" and "unit cohesion"—was one that privileged a certain form of masculinized humor, racism, and bravado, each woman would have had to decide how to deal with that. At least some of the women reservists might have decided to join in, to play the roles assigned to them in order to gain the hoped-for reward of male acceptance. The fact that the Abu Ghraib prison was grossly understaffed during the fall of 2003 (too few guards for the spiraling numbers of Iraqi detainees), that it was isolated from other military operations, and that its residents endured daily and nightly mortar attacks would only serve to intensify the pressures on each soldier to gain acceptance from those unit members who seemed to represent the group's dominant masculinized culture. And what about the fact that Lynndie England entered into a sexual liaison with Charles Graner? We need to treat this as more than merely a "lack of discipline." Looking back on the masculinized and sexualized climate inside the both internally troubled and externally besieged prison, Janis Karpinski, the army reserve general in charge of the prison, recalled how, over the years of her career, she had seen so many young women soldiers "seek protection" from older, more senior male soldiers, usually with those men more than willing to serve as their female subordinates' "protectors" (Karpinski forthcoming). It would be more useful to ask about the cause and effect dynamics between these soldiers' sexual behaviors and their abuses of Iraqi prisoners (including the staged photographs). Feminists have taught us never to brush off sexual relations as if they have nothing to do with organizational and political practices.

Then there is the masculinization of the military interrogators' organizational culture, the masculinization of the CIA's field operatives, and the ideas about "manliness" shaping the entire U.S. political system. Many men and women—lawyers, generals, cabinet members, elected officials—knew full well that aggressive interrogation techniques violated both the spirit and the language of the Geneva Conventions, the UN Convention against Torture, and U.S. federal law against torture. Yet during the months of waging wars in Afghanistan and Iraq, most of these men and women kept silent. Feminists have taught us always to be curious about silence. Thus, we need to ask: did any of the American men involved in interrogations keep silent because they were afraid of being labeled "soft" or "weak," thereby jeopardizing their status as "manly" men? We need also to discover if any of the women who knew better kept silent because they were afraid that they would be labeled "feminine," thus risking being deemed by their colleagues to be untrustworthy outsiders.

We are not going to get to the bottom of the tortures perpetrated by Americans at Abu Ghraib unless we make use of a feminist curiosity and unless we revisit the feminist lessons derived from the scandals that have been revealed at the Tailhook convention, Fort Bragg, the U.S. Naval Academy, Okinawa, and the Air Force Academy. A feminist curiosity, combined with those lessons, might shed a harsh light on an entire American military institutional culture and maybe even the climate of contemporary American political life. That military culture and that political climate together have profound implications for both

Americans and for all those citizens in countries where the U.S. military is being held up as a model to emulate as they modernize their own armed forces. . . .

Furthermore, it is by tracking the gendered assumptions about how to wield feminization to humiliate male prisoners inside Abu Ghraib, *not* in isolation, but with the understanding that those assumptions were linked to the ideas, assumptions, and policies shaping detention and interrogation practices at Bagram and Guantánamo—and the unknown number of secret prisons used by the U.S. government around the world—that we are likely to get a clearer picture of why "Abu Ghraib" happened—and whether it will happen again.

(2007)

NOTE

1. An earlier, quite different, version of this chapter was published as: "Wielding Masculinity inside Abu Ghraib," *Asian Journal of Women's Studies* 10, no. 3 (September 2004): 235–243.

REFERENCES

Associated Press. 2006. "Dog Handler Convicted in Abu Ghraib Abuse." *New York Times*, June 2.

Bowers, Simon. 2004. "Merrill Lynch Accused of 'Institutional Sexism'." *Guardian* (London), June 12.

Bunster-Burotto, Ximena. 1985. "Surviving Beyond Fear: Women and Torture in Latin America." In *Women and Change in Latin America*, ed. June Nash and Helen Safa, 297–325. South Hadley, MA: Bergin & Garvey.

Burke, Carol. 2004. *Camp All-American, Hanoi Jane, and the High-and-Tight*. Boston: Beacon Press.

Carver, Terrell. 2003. "Gender/Feminism/IR." *International Studies Review* 5 (2): 288–290.

Danner, Mark, ed. 2004. *Torture and Truth: America, Abu Ghraib, and the War on Terror*. New York: New York Review of Books.

Ehrenreich, Barbara. 2004. "All Together Now." Op-Ed, *New York Times*, July 15.

Elias, Juanita, ed. Forthcoming. "Hegemonic masculinities in International Politics." Special Issue, *Men and Masculinities*.

Enloe, Cynthia. 1993. *The Morning After: Sexual Politics at the End of the Cold War*. Berkeley: University of California Press.

_____. 2000. *Maneuvers: The International Politics of Militarizing Women's Lives*. Berkeley: University of California Press.

Golden, Tim. 2006. "The Battle for Guantanamo." *New York Times Magazine*, September 17, 60–71, 140–145.

Greenberg, Karen and Joshua Dratel, eds. 2005. *The Torture Papers: The Road to Abu Ghraib.* New York: Cambridge University Press.

Hersh, Seymour, M. 2004. *Chain of Command: The Road to Abu Ghraib.* New York: HarperCollins.

Hillman, Elizabeth Lutes. 2005. *Defending America: Military Culture and the Cold War Court-Martial.* Princeton: Princeton University Press.

Human Rights Watch. 2004. *The Road to Abu Ghraib.* New York: Human Rights Watch.

Jargon, Julie. 2003. "The War Within." Westowrd, Jnaurary 30. http//www.westword.com/issues/2003-01-30/feature.html.

Karpinksi, Janis. 2005. *One Woman's Army: The Commanding General of Abu Ghraib Tells Her Story.* New York: Hyperion.

_____. Forthcoming. "Lynndie England in Love." In Women as Aggressors and Torturers, ed. Tara McKelvey. Seattle: Seal Press.

Kwon, Insook. 2000. "Miltarism in My Heart: Militarization of Women's Consciousness and Culture in South Korea." Phd dissertation, MA, Clark University.

Lipman, Jana K. Forthcoming. "Guantanamo: A Working Class History of Revolution and Empire, 1939–1979." Ph.D. diss., Yale University.

Lutz, Catherine and Jon Elliston. 2004. "Domestic Terror." In Interventions: Activists' and Academics' *Perspectives on Violence*, ed. Elizaberh Castelli and Janet Jackson. New York: Palgrave Macmillan.

Mayer, Jane. 2005a. "Outsourcing Terror." *New Yorker*, February 14–21, 106–123.

_____. 2005b. "The Memo." *New Yorker*, February 27, 32–41.

_____. 2005c. "The Experiment." *New Yorker*, July 11–18, 60–71.

_____. 2006. "The Hidden Power." *New Yorker*, July 3, 44–55.

Miles Foundation. 2004. "Brownback/Fitz Amendment to S. 2400" e-mail message to Miles Foundation mailing list, June 14.

Moffeit, Miles and Amy Herder. 2004. "Returning Female GIs Report Rapes, Poor Care." http://www.sirnosir.com/the_film/resistor_84.html.

Murphy, Evelyn, with E. J. Graff. 2005. *Getting Even: Why Women Don't Get Paid Like Men – and What to Do about It.* New York: Simon & Schuster.

Office of the Inspector General, U.S. Department of Defense. 2003. *The Tailhook Report.* New York: St. Martin's.

Ogasawara, Yuko. 1998. *Office Ladies and Salaried Men: Power, Gender, and Work in Japanese Companies.* Berkeley: University of California Press.

Saar, Eric. 2005. *Inside the Wire: A Military Intelligence Soldier's Eyewitness Account of Life at Guantanamo.* New York: Penquin.

Stockford, Marjorie A. 2004. *The Bellwomen: The Story of the Landmark AT&T Sex & Discrimination Case.* New Brunswick, NJ: Rutgers University Press.

Whitworth, Sandra. 2004. *Men, Militarism and UN Peacekeeping.* Boulder, CO: Lynne Rienner.

Wright, Ann. 2006. "Women Involved in Prisoner Abuse: Perpetrators, Enablers, and Victims." In *Proceedings of the Conference Women in the Military Today*, 19–20 May 2005, ed. Lory Manning, 64–111. Washington, DC: Women's Research and Education Institute.

Wypijewski, JoAnn. 2006. "Judgment Days: Lessons from the Abu Ghraib Courts-Martial," *Harper's*, February, 39–50.

CHAPTER 10

Feminism and Imperialism in Postmodernity

The West is painfully made to realize the existence of the Third World in the First World, and vice versa. The Master is bound to recognize that His Culture is not as homogeneous, as monolithic as He believes it to be. He discovers with much reluctance, He is just an other among others.

—Trinh T. Minh-ha, 1989

INTRODUCTION

In postmodernity the operation of global forces blurred and unsettled economic and geopolitical boundaries such that theorists now speak more fluidly of scapes, circuits, and networks as opposed to more rigid, stable, hierarchical, national, and international social relationships. This blurring of boundaries is evident in the new conceptual schemes that replaced the nation-focused and Cold War–inspired concepts of first-world, second-world, and third-world countries. By the 1990s, the concepts of the **Global North** and **Global South** came to be used more frequently to distinguish high-income/high-consumption areas of the globe from those characterized by low income/low consumption. Here the "North" and "South" do not designate specific geographic locations, but rather locations of inequality. The concept of **transnational** also replaced international and refers to social forms that fail to correspond to or transcend the boundaries of the nation state. Transnational forms have confounded earlier conceptual schemes and have "challenged theory to catch up with lived realities" (Ong, 1991: 279). Indeed, there is a growing sense among theorists that an adequate understanding of social life can no longer be derived from an analysis that is conceptually limited to a geopolitical order based on nation-states (Smart, 1993: 135).

Economic power also appears more fluid and difficult to locate in national terms today. As transnational feminist theorists Inderpal Grewal and Caren Kaplan point out, it is difficult to maintain national distinctions in the conventional sense if the

Japanese-headquartered corporation SONY owns a Hollywood studio or if a Saudi Arabian investor owns the U.S. news organization UPI (Grewal and Kaplan, [1994] 2006: 10–11). The rise of transnational economic units such as the **European Union (EU)** and the **North American Free Trade Agreement (NAFTA)** further blur national boundaries. The North American Free Trade Agreement includes the countries of the United States, Mexico, and Canada, whereas the European Union includes more than two dozen countries and even has its own currency. These transnational forms were developed to enhance the movement of commodities and capital across international borders so as to compete more successfully in world markets.

Flexible capitalism is another name given to these economic developments because of the new ways corporations move and adapt to existing circumstances. Unlike earlier multinational corporations where research, design, and corporate control were located in the most developed countries, today transnational corporations tap into different labor pools (skilled or unskilled, blue collar or white collar, foreign or domestic) regardless of where they are located. Here concerns focus on optimal production, marketing, infrastructural, and political conditions (Harvey, 1989; Ong, 1991: 281–282).

The rise of flexible capitalism, the enhanced role of finance capital, and the implementation of harsh structural adjustment programs (SAPs) were fostered by **neoliberalism**—an economic ideology that arose in response to the international debt crises of the late 1970s and 1980s. Neoliberalism is based on promoting free markets, competitive capitalism, private ownership, free trade, export-led growth, strict controls on balances of payments and deficits, and drastic reductions in government social spending. This laissez-faire economic philosophy fostered the deregulation of economic practices both at home and abroad. Although corporate capital was decentered in the sense of being relocated globally, it was not weakened, but became more powerful and anarchic as regulations over economic behavior were removed (Touraine, 1998).

The increased volume of economic exchanges and the enhanced mobility of capital and firms required new forms of authority that bridged the local, national, and global. The establishment of the **World Trade Organization (WTO)** in 1995 as a new addition to the dynamic duo of the World Bank and the International Monetary Fund (IMF) exemplifies these developments. The WTO was established to oversee trade agreements and negotiate disputes that emerged from the General Agreement on Tariffs and Trade (GATT). It has been described as the "institutional face of globalization" and is one of the most wide reaching of all international players today (Symington, 2005: 36). Together this powerful trio—the World Bank, the International Monetary Fund, and the World Trade Organization—have been referred to as the driving forces of globalization policies in the contemporary era.

Reading 133 by Alison Symington (2005) discusses these organizations and how important it is for feminists to understand these financial developments. Her article was included in the "first international collection by young feminists"— *Defending Our Dreams: Global Feminist Voices for a New Generation* (Wilson et al., 2005). This book was written by young feminists from more than eleven countries and was fostered by the Development Alternatives with Women for a New Era (DAWN) Training Institute in Feminist Advocacy for young women (ages twenty-five to thirty-five). Many of the contributing authors combine personal introspection with their analyses of global issues, but they focus more on structural and material analyses than do most U.S. third-wave authors.

Along with the increase in transnational finance, military clashes are increasingly transnational today. Although communism was a transnational ideology, U.S. military clashes with communist insurgents usually took the form of nations fighting nations, such as in the Vietnam War or the Korean War. Funding or military aid may have come from other countries in these previous wars. However the actual participants represented particular countries or areas within countries. In contrast, international clashes today often involve **transnational combatants** who represent transnational cultural/ethnic/religious communities and garner volunteer armies from multiple countries, such as Al-Qaeda. These developments resulted in important changes in warfare as, for example, when the U.S. government declared that transnational combatants do not fall under the protections of the Geneva Convention. Moreover, agencies that deal with the social problems generated by militarism and war also have taken transnational forms, such as Amnesty International or Doctors without Borders.

POSTCOLONIAL AND TRANSNATIONAL FEMINISMS

The rise of postcolonial and transnational feminist perspectives witnessed a significant paradigm shift in global feminist analyses. Many feminists today prefer to use transnational analysis rather than following the conceptual paths of earlier, modern global feminist analyses with their first-world/third-world frameworks. As Inderpal Grewal and Caren Kaplan explain, these earlier theoretical frameworks contain remnants of a "Euro-North-American-centric" worldview where global power brokers at the core are portrayed as the movers and shakers of world history, while the complex class divisions at the local level are ignored ([1994] 2006: 12). These feminists also challenge and break with the "inadequate and inaccurate binary divisions" (13) embedded in these earlier frameworks, highlighting how social forces operate in multiple directions that reflect a process of hybridization rather than of simple, unidirectional homogenization.

In Reading 131 from *Talking Visions: Multicultural Feminism in a Transnational Age* ([1999] 2001), Ella Shohat discusses some of the differences between her transnational, multicultural approach and intersectionality theory. Although Shohat applauds the contributions of intersectional analyses, she criticizes U.S. intersectionality theorists for only rarely discussing their own privileged positions as citizens of a first-world nation and global superpower. Shohat states that opposition to racism, classism, sexism, and homophobia within the United States has never guaranteed opposition to U.S. global hegemony. For example, she discusses how people of color often have used the U.S. military as a path to upward mobility and have served in numerous U.S. military imperialist endeavors abroad. Shohat argues that "First Worldness," even when experienced from the bottom, entails certain privileges that must be acknowledged in discussions of local/global links ([1999] 2001: 37–38).

The term **postcolonial** is a critical concept that refers to engaging with and contesting the legacy of colonialism's discourses, power structures, and social hierarchies. Postcolonial theorists also place a heavier focus on cultural and discursive manifestations of globalization. They do not ignore political economy, but view political and economic concerns as so interwoven with cultural and discursive analyses that the old modern dividing line between materialist and idealist theories becomes more fluid and ambiguous. They also reject linear views of history that depict the social world as moving from traditional to modern societies where time is accumulated vertically (such that some social formations are viewed as more advanced than others). For postcolonial theorists, time is "scrambled and **palimpsestic**" (Alexander, 2005: 190). A palimpsest is a parchment that has been inscribed and reinscribed such that the previous text is imperfectly erased and remains partly visible. Using this metaphor, sociohistorical time is an imperfect erasure, with the past always visible in the present (190).

Reading 123 is from Edward Said's *Orientalism* ([1978] 1979), one of the founding works of postcolonial theory. Said was concerned with the persistent Western prejudice again Arabo-Islamic and Asian peoples/cultures from the Near East, Middle East, and Far East, which he referred to as "**Orientalism**." Using a blend of poststructuralism and Marxist theory, he described how "the Orient" is a material-discursive construct of "the West" that was then projected onto the lands and peoples of the colonized East. This process entailed an "othering" of "the Orient" that, in turn, helped to define and solidify "the West" (Said [1978] 1979: 12). As such, Orientalism says as much about the West as it does about the East as filtered through Western eyes. The object of postcolonial theory is to critically analyze the *social implications of such mutually constitutive processes between the colonizer and the colonized.*[1]

DECOLONIZING FEMINIST THOUGHT

Reading 124 from Chandra Talpade Mohanty's "Under Western Eyes: Feminist Scholarship and Colonial Discourses" (1984) is a signal piece that introduced U.S. feminists to feminist postcolonial theory. Mohanty's goal is to deconstruct and dismantle the privilege and ethnocentrism found in many first-world global feminist discourses (Mohanty, [1984] 2005: 372). She especially criticizes the essentialism that pervades these discourses where Western feminists construct a singular, composite notion of "third world women" as a group with identical interests and desires, regardless of their actual class, ethnic, or racial locations. She argues that this homogenous construction of "third world women" frequently implies that they are poor, ignorant, tradition bound, and victimized. Unspoken, but assumed here, is that first-world women by contrast are educated and modern, have control over their own bodies and sexualities, and are free to make their own decisions (Mohanty, [1984] 2005: 374). This type of binary discourse not only entails a "paternalistic attitude towards women in the third world," but also reduces third-world women to victimized objects, "robbing them of their historical and political agency" (Mohanty, [1984] 2005: 377–378). An example of this can be found on the cover of the U.S. second-wave feminist journal *Off Our Backs* (1983) shown in Reading 115 from Chapter 9. This particular edition of *Off Our Backs* was titled "Latin American Feminists Meet" and the woman on the cover evokes the poor, victimized third-world woman that Mohanty argued was so representative of Western feminist thought.

Like Mohanty's work, Uma Narayan's writings also unveiled Western feminists' eyes to their implicit colonialist assumptions. In Reading 129 from *Dislocating Cultures: Identities, Traditions, and Third-World Feminism* (1997), Narayan explores representations of "third world traditions" that replicate a **"colonialist stance"** toward third-world women using the work of U.S. radical feminist Mary Daly (see Reading 113 in Chapter 9) as her example (Narayan, 1997: 43). Narayan makes clear that not all Western feminist criticisms of third-world cultural practices are inherently colonialist or ethnocentric (1997: 58–59). Rather, taking a colonialist stance entails representations that employ a **missionary framework** where third-world women are viewed as victims that must be rescued from their own cultural traditions. As such, they are viewed as without agency, as unable to represent themselves. Colonialist stances also erase the historical and contextual framework in which cultural traditions arose and developed. These cultural traditions are treated as if they are unchanging and "perennially in place," making third-world countries appear as "places with no history" (Narayan, 1997: 48–49) and with no indigenous forms of resistance.

Narayan also deconstructs the meaning given to terms such as "Westernization." She discusses how the term "Westernized" is often used as a **strategy of dismissal"** where third-world feminists who advocate for women's rights are categorized as Westernized "traitors to their communities" (Narayan, 1997: 31) to undermine their feminist demands and actions. She points to how her opponents selectively choose what is deemed Westernized; they drive cars or use computers but do not consider these actions traitorous. In sum, she calls for more critical debate about what terms such as Westernization mean, so as to deconstruct the uses and abuses of this term.

CAN THE SUBALTERN SPEAK?

By merging features of Marxism and poststructuralism, postcolonial theorists focus not only on the economic and political impacts of colonialism and imperialism, but also on their discursive implications. The latter is highlighted in Reading 125 from Gayatri Chakravorty Spivak's essay "Can the Subaltern Speak?" ([1985] 1988). Spivak was a member of the Indian-based Subaltern Studies Collective who used the term **"subaltern"** to refer to "the general attribute of subordination whether this is expressed in terms of class, caste, age, gender, or any other way" (Morton, 2003: 48).[2]

For Spivak, the imposition of imperial codes and practices on the colonized fractures all indigenous sign-systems of the colonized—a process Spivak terms **epistemic violence**. The cultural effects of this violent rupture are complex, but they include the silencing of authentic native cultures. For Spivak, those who are truly subaltern—the most marginalized—cannot speak. If the subaltern could speak, she or he would no longer occupy the place of the subaltern. Some writers have interpreted this position as a dismissal or silencing of the native as a historical subject and combatant (Parry, 1987: 34). However, Spivak means something very different from this. For her, anti-imperialist writers and activists are clearly not outside the field of imperialism as a discursive field since they address it directly. Those positioned to engage in a theoretical critique of colonial discourse can hardly occupy the place of the subaltern (Morton, 2003: 66–67). Their own privilege and hybridity must be recognized and acknowledged (Landry and Maclean, 1993: 200).

Spivak's position differs from that of feminist standpoint theorists who privilege the knowledge of the oppressed (or subaltern) by arguing that marginalized people have the most critical vantage points. In contrast, Spivak views such a project as "in the long run deeply insulting" (1989: 86). She argues that it can only be under the guise of "representing" the subaltern that these writers make such claims. That is, when feminists privilege the knowledge of the oppressed, it is actually the feminist intellectual who *interprets* and *speaks for* the standpoint of the marginalized. In this way feminist intellectuals foreground the standpoint of the marginalized, but actually hide in the background by not acknowledging their interpretative role or the displacement involved when they speak for and interpret the standpoint of subjugated peoples (Pels, 2004). For Spivak, if one pretends to actually represent the other without acknowledging this displacement, then one would be complicit in a new form of domination even if it is constructed on the bases of radical or liberatory practice.

Spivak's work is valuable in the way it makes such careful analytical distinctions while at the same time insisting on forging connections between women—often of a difficult global kind. She urges feminists to acknowledge that all feminist thought—whether written by Western whites, Western women of color, or postcolonial theorists—must be interrogated and deconstructed for its possible imperial logic. She teaches us to critically "read the world" (Sanders, 2006: 93) and to "unlearn one's privilege" (Spivak, 1990: 30 and 42) as an ethical and political responsibility.

DIASPORAS AND THE GENDER POLITICS OF POSTCOLONIAL SPACE

Whereas modern global feminist writers focused on labor migrations that flowed from one country to another, postcolonial feminists highlight a more fluid sense of global migrations captured in the term **diaspora** derived from the Greek *dia*, "through," and *speirein*, "to scatter." Modern thought is more fixed and nation oriented, such as the concept of Mexican American, which denotes the country of origin and the country of arrival. The concept of diaspora signals the processes of multilocationality across geographical, cultural, and psychic boundaries (Brah, 2003: 625).

Rather than simply portraying global migrants as victims of dominant cultures, postcolonial theorists such as Avtar Brah (1996) and Trinh T. Minh-Ha (1989) point out how migrants constantly challenge the peripheralizing impulses of the cultures of dominance. Hence, dominant cultures also change in the process. For example, Brah's *Cartographies of Diaspora* (1996) discusses how Britishness has been disassembled and reconstituted since World War II as a result of the vast migration to Great Britain by people from its former colonies. Through this process, Englishness becomes just another ethnicity among many (Brah, 2003: 632–633). This idea is captured well in Reading 126 from Trinh T. Minh-ha's *Woman, Native, Other: Writing Postcoloniality and Feminism* (1989):

> The West is painfully made to realize the existence of the Third World in the First World, and vice versa. The Master is bound to recognize that His Culture is not as homogeneous, as monolithic as He believes it to be. He discovers with much reluctance, He is just an other among others. (Minh-ha, 1989: 99–100)

Minh-ha's work undermines the notion of "authentic insiders" to any culture and reveals how every cultural formation is a hybrid. By contrast, "the dominant Western attitude toward hybridity is that it is always elsewhere or it is infiltrating an identity or location that is assumed to be, to always have been, pure and unchanging" (Grewal and Kaplan, [1994] 2006: 8). Correcting this assumption is a goal of "decolonizing" Western thought.

Just as Minh-ha argues that the "first world/third world" binary must be challenged and rejected in understanding the hybridity of existing multicultural societies, so too does the "West versus the rest" binary need to be deconstructed and dismantled in social thought. Indeed, many postcolonial theorists view the very idea of "modernity" as one of the "central tropes" through which the industrially, developed West constructed itself as the center and the rest of the world as its more backward periphery, rather than recognizing their intertwined histories (Mary Louise Pratt in Spurlin, 2006: 23).

The short story "Fireweed" (2009) by Skye Brannon in Reading 135 is about a migrant refugee who was part of a diaspora from a brutal war in Liberia where his young sister was raped and killed by soldiers. Hired to do carpentry work in the home of an American woman, his traumatic experiences are revealed through this woman's petty concerns over the color of paint used for her bedroom walls. The story highlights not only the ignorance of many Americans in regard to global issues, but also the trivial concerns of the American woman compared to those of the refugee who had faced the horrors of warfare and displacement. Nevertheless, the woman's world was the center and the refugee was merely a peripheral being in her life. Such stories help us to understand why Mohandas Gandhi, the leader of India's anti-colonialist struggle against the British, could reply when he was asked what he thought of Western civilization: "I think it would be a very good idea."[3]

FEMINISM AND RELIGIOUS FUNDAMENTALISMS

In Reading 127 from *Scattered Hegemonies: Postmodernity and Transnational Feminist Practices* ([1994] 2006), Inderpal Grewal and Caren Kaplan discuss the importance of theorizing the seismic changes that have taken place in postmodernity. In particular, they focus on the challenges created by the growth of transnational forms of militarism and religious fundamentalism in the post-9/11 era. Rather than viewing these transnational global clashes simply as "culture wars," Grewal and Kaplan ([1994] 2006: 19) call for a materialist-deconstructive approach that examines the political and economic roots of the intensification of religious fundamentalisms today.

The portrayal of global clashes today as *culture wars* is frequently found in the U.S. mass media where the West becomes associated with either its Judeo-Christian traditions or its modern, secular culture—both of which are portrayed as enemies of fundamentalist Islam. Even a number of contemporary theorists view global clashes as backlashes by traditional communities to the discursive frameworks fostered by modernity, such as the Western ideals of the separation of church and state, freedom of speech, and individualism (Ritzer, 2011). Here again, the focus is on cultural differences.

Grewal and Kaplan argue that if we view anti-Western sentiments abroad as fomented, not simply by culture wars, but also by the earlier impacts of colonialist and neocolonialist policies, we can better see how the hegemonic Western powers created their own global hotspots. For example, the U.S. Central Intelligence Agency helped foster the coup that brought Mohammad Reza Pahlavi, Shah of Iran, to power in 1953. It was his autocratic rule that was eventually overthrown in 1979 by the Islamic fundamentalists that rule Iran today (Gasiorowski and Byrne, 2004). In the 1980s, the U.S. government gave military and financial support to the Taliban in Afghanistan when it was fighting the Soviets. Two decades later, the United States was at war with the Taliban as part of its war on terror.

Grewal and Kaplan warn feminists not to allow historical amnesia to blind us to how the West's previous support of repressive regimes played a role in creating contemporary global clashes. They also urge U.S. feminists not to focus only on the patriarchal nature of fundamentalist Islam, but to examine Christian fundamentalism and how its influence on the Republican Party has affected the lives of millions of women worldwide through funding and development practices that restrict reproductive choice.

Portrayals of Muslim women as victims of repressive religious/cultural practices often have been used to garner support for the U.S. government's war on terror. President George W. Bush, for example, used the war against the Taliban in Afghanistan as evidence of his commitment to women's rights and as an attempt to woo women voters to support the Republican Party (Walter, 2004).[4] In Reading 132, Lila Abu-Lughod asks the question: "Do Muslim Women Really Need Saving?" ([2002] 2012). She cautions feminists to be wary of how "neat cultural icons are plastered over messier historical and political narratives" (Abu-Lughod, [2002] 2012: 488) that claim to be liberating Muslim women—particularly when military troops are standing behind these messages.

In discussing the politics of veiling and the burqa, Abu-Lughod also discusses how feminists "need to work against the reductive interpretation of veiling as the quintessential sign of women's unfreedom" ([2002] 2012: 490). Feminists must accept difference—the possibility that other women may have different views of freedom and justice. At the same time Abu-Lughod warns feminists against falling into the trap of cultural relativism—with its refusal to judge or to try to end oppressive practices. For Abu-Lughod, the very construction of Muslim women as people in need of saving evokes the paternalistic colonialist image of white Westerners saving brown women from brown men. It reinforces a sense of superiority by Westerners—a form of arrogance that deserves to be challenged (492).

QUEERING GLOBAL ANALYSES

William Spurlin points out in *Imperialism without Margins* (2006) how postcolonial queer theorists undertake the two-prong task of decolonizing the Western biases of queer theory and queering the heterosexist biases of postcolonial theory (2006: 7). In Reading 130 titled "Erotophobia and the Colonization of Queer(s)/Nature" (1997), Greta Gaard uses a palimpsestic approach that draws from historical works to show how the early history of European colonialism in North America, Latin America, and Asia entailed the imposition of European regimes of gender and sexuality on a variety of heterosexual and nonheterosexual erotic practices of indigenous peoples.

Colonialists used what they saw as the "aberrant" sexual behaviors of indigenous peoples as proof of their heathen and uncivilized nature and, thereby, as justification for their colonization. One explorer wrote of the Choctaw nation, "They are morally quite perverted and most of them are addicted to sodomy" (quoted in Gaard, 1997: 126–127). The conquerors sought to eliminate indigenous forms of Indian homosexuality as part of their attempt to destroy Native cultures and as an excuse for exterminating natives. Heterosexual practices devoid of the restrictions imposed by Christianity also were objectionable to European colonizers. Missionaries viewed the "muher supra virum" (woman above the man) as "absolutely contrary to the order of nature" (quoted in Gaard, 1997: 129). Although people today joke about how the "missionary position" has governed Western ideas of sexual practices, few are aware of the horrors that befell indigenous peoples when European conquistadors and colonialists enforced their sexual regimes. For example, postcolonial theorist M. Jacqui Alexander relays the grisly story of how the conquistador Vasco Nunez d'Balboa killed forty Panamanian male Indians he "found dressed in women's apparel" and fed them to his dogs (Alexander, 2005: 196).

By excavating this history, postcolonial queer theorists show how the discourses and practices of colonialism contained specific conceptions not only of race and gender, but also of sex and sexuality that authorized their colonial and imperialist ventures. To these theorists, colonization is an act of nationalist self-assertion of identity and definition over and against the other, "whereby the queer erotic of non-westernized peoples, as well as their culture and their land is subdued into the missionary position—with the conqueror 'on top'" (Gaard, 1997: 131).

TRANSNATIONAL FEMINIST ORGANIZING

By the 1990s, global feminist organizing had adopted new forms and operated through different sites that reflect the rise of transnational global politics. The challenges posed by women from the "global South" to the ideological dominance of the "global North" in framing the international women's agenda had become sufficiently concerted to be effective (Tripp in Ferree and Tripp, 2006: 60–61). The blending together of two strands of transnational women's organizing—human rights issues and sustainable development concerns—portended an even greater role to the concerns of women from the global South. The merger of these concerns was consolidated during the 1995 world conferences in Beijing and Huairou, as can be seen in Reading 128 from the Beijing Declaration. Internet linkages, cheaper airfares, and global phone service also enabled organizations to be more fluid. People across the globe could interact routinely and could even participate in world conferences without being sponsored as a representative of a particular nation, as occurred in Huairo (Ferree in Ferree and Tripp, 2006: 12).

In Reading 134, "Towards Transnational Feminisms" (2006), Jyotsna Agnihotri Gupta discusses what is meant by "transnational feminisms" and how this concept differs from the earlier notion of "global sisterhood." The latter starts out from a focus on the commonalities between women, whereas the concept of transnational feminisms begins with the recognition of differences between women (Gupta, 2006: 25). A transnational feminist approach also acknowledges how one's privilege in the world-system is linked to another's oppression. It requires a comparative analysis of multiple, overlapping, and discrete oppressions rather than the construction of a universal theory of gender that assumes a unified feminist agenda as did the earlier global sisterhood approach (34).

Although committed to intersectional analysis, **transversal politics**, and praxis rooted in postcolonial critiques, a transnational feminist approach also seeks to overcome the undertheorization of political economic issues in feminist postcolonial approaches that remain ensnared in cultural/discursive debates (Gupta, 2006: 25). To explain this, Gupta draws insights from the progression over time of Chandra Talpade Mohanty's postcolonial approach. Mohanty's earlier works, such as "Under Western Eyes" (1984), found in Reading 124 focused on decolonizing Western feminist thought. In her later works, such as *Feminism without Borders: Decolonizing Theory, Practicing Solidarity* ([2003] 2006), Mohanty views "the politics and economics of capitalism as a far more urgent locus of struggle" (230). Mohanty makes clear that she does not sever the link between political economy and culture/discourse, but simply shifts the focus. For Gupta, such a materialist-deconstructive approach that is attentive to the micropolitics of local context, subjectivity, and struggle as well as to the macropolitics of global economic and political systems and processes is the core of transnational feminisms.

CONCLUSION

Both supporters and critics agree that postcolonial and transnational thought are expressive not only of a real crisis in the ideology of linear progress and development, but also of a crisis in the modes of comprehending and conceptualizing the world today. Thus, a major contribution of these paradigm shifts in global feminist thought from late modernity to postmodernity is that they "answered the conceptual needs of the social, political and cultural problems thrown up by this New World Order" (Dirlik, 1997: 502).

NOTES

1. Some genealogists of postcolonial theory trace its origins back to other classic works on colonialism, such as Albert Memmi's *The Colonizer and the Colonized* ([1957] 1991) or Frantz Fanon's *The Wretched of the Earth* ([1961] 1967) and *Black Skins, White Masks* (1967).
2. The term subaltern was first used in critical theory by the Italian Marxist Antonio Gramsci to refer to subordinate groups who were undertheorized in Marx's writings.
3. This quote can be found at http://www.brainyquote.com/quotes/quotes/m/mahatmagan141784.html (Retrieved October 30, 2014).
4. Even in some of her speeches, Laura Bush highlighted how "the fight against terrorism is a fight for the rights and dignity of women" (Laura Bush quoted in Abu-Lughod [2002] 2012: 487).

FROM *ORIENTALISM*

. . . I have begun with the assumption that the Orient is not an inert fact of nature. It is not merely *there*, just as the Occident itself is not just *there* either. We must take seriously Vico's great observation that men make their own history, that what they can know is what they have made, and extend it to geography: as both geographical and cultural entities—to say nothing of historical entities—such locales, regions, geographical sectors as "Orient" and "Occident" are man-made. Therefore as much as the West itself, the Orient is an idea that has a history and a tradition of thought, imagery, and vocabulary that have given it reality and presence in and for the West. The two geographical entities thus support and to an extent reflect each other.

Having said that, one must go on to state a number of reasonable qualifications. In the first place, it would be wrong to conclude that the Orient was *essentially* an idea, or a creation with no corresponding reality. When Disraeli said in his novel *Tancred* that the East was a career, he meant that to be interested in the East was something bright young Westerners would find to be an all-consuming passion; he should not be interpreted as saying that the East was *only* a career for Westerners. There were—and are—cultures and nations whose location is in the East, and their lives, histories, and customs have a brute reality obviously greater than anything that could be said about them in the West. About that fact this study of Orientalism has very little to contribute, except to acknowledge it tacitly. But the phenomenon of Orientalism as I study it here deals principally, not with a correspondence between Orientalism and Orient, but with the internal consistency of Orientalism and its ideas about the Orient (the East as career) despite or beyond any correspondence, or lack thereof, with a "real" Orient. My point is that Disraeli's statement about the East refers mainly to that created consistency, that regular constellation of ideas as the pre-eminent thing about the Orient, and not to its mere being, as Wallace Stevens's phrase has it.

A second qualification is that ideas, cultures, and histories cannot seriously be understood or studied without their force, or more precisely their configurations of power, also being studied. To believe that the Orient was created—or, as I call it, "Orientalized"—and to believe that such things happen simply as a necessity of the imagination, is to be disingenuous. The relationship between Occident and Orient is a relationship of power, of domination, of varying degrees of a complex hegemony, and is quite accurately indicated in the title of K. M. Panikkar's classic *Asia and Western Dominance*. The Orient was Orientalized not only because it was discovered to be "Oriental" in all those ways considered commonplace by an average nineteenth-century European, but also because it *could be*—that is, submitted to being—*made* Oriental. There is very little consent to be found, for example, in the fact that Flaubert's encounter with an Egyptian courtesan produced a widely influential model of the Oriental woman; she never spoke of herself, she never represented her emotions, presence, or history. *He* spoke for and represented her. He was foreign, comparatively wealthy, male, and these were historical facts of domination that allowed him not only to possess Kuchuk Hanem physically but to speak for her and tell his readers in what way she was "typically Oriental." My argument is that Flaubert's situation of strength in relation to Kuchuk Hanem was not an isolated instance. It fairly stands for the pattern of relative strength between East and West, and the discourse about the Orient that it enabled.

This brings us to a third qualification. One ought never to assume that the structure of Orientalism is nothing more than a structure of lies or of myths which, were the truth about them to be told, would simply blow away. I myself believe that Orientalism is more particularly valuable as a sign of European-Atlantic power over the Orient than it is as a veridic discourse about the Orient (which is what, in its academic or scholarly form, it claims to be). Nevertheless, what we must respect and try to grasp is the sheer knitted-together strength of Orientalist discourse, its very close ties to the enabling socio-economic and political institutions, and its redoubtable durability. After all, any system of ideas that can remain unchanged as teachable wisdom (in academies, books, congresses, universities, foreign-service institutes) from the period of Ernest Renan in the late 1840s until the present in the United States must be something more formidable than a mere collection of lies. Orientalism, therefore, is not an airy European fantasy about the Orient, but a created body of theory and practice in which, for many generations, there has been a considerable material investment. Continued investment made Orientalism, as a system of knowledge about the Orient, an accepted grid for filtering through the Orient into Western consciousness, just as that same investment multiplied—indeed, made truly productive—the statements proliferating out from Orientalism into the general culture.

Gramsci has made the useful analytic distinction between civil and political society in which the former is made up of voluntary (or at least rational and noncoercive) affiliations like schools, families, and unions, the latter of state institutions (the army, the police, the central bureaucracy) whose role in the polity is direct domination. Culture, of course, is to be found operating within civil society, where the influence of ideas, of institutions, and of other persons works not through domination but by what Gramsci calls consent. In any society not totalitarian, then, certain cultural forms predominate over others, just as certain ideas are more influential than others; the form of this cultural leadership is what Gramsci has identified as *hegemony*, an indispensable concept for any understanding of cultural life in the industrial West. It is hegemony, or rather the result of cultural hegemony at work, that gives Orientalism the durability and the strength I have been speaking about so far. Orientalism is never far from what Denys Hay has called the idea of Europe, a collective notion identifying "us" Europeans as against all "those" non-Europeans, and indeed it can be argued that the major component in European culture is precisely what made that culture hegemonic both in and outside Europe: the idea of European identity as a superior one in comparison with all the non-European peoples and cultures. There is in addition the hegemony of European ideas about the Orient, themselves reiterating European superiority over Oriental backwardness, usually over-riding the possibility that a more independent, or more skeptical, thinker might have had different views on the matter.

In a quite constant way, Orientalism depends for its strategy on this flexible *positional* superiority, which puts the Westerner in a whole series of possible relationships with the Orient without ever losing him the relative upper hand. And why should it have been otherwise, especially during the period of extraordinary European ascendancy from the late Renaissance to the present? The scientist, the scholar, the missionary, the trader, or the soldier was in, or thought about, the Orient because he *could be there*, or could think about it, with very little resistance on the Orient's part. Under the general heading of knowledge of the Orient, and within the umbrella of Western hegemony over the Orient during the period from the end of the eighteenth century, there emerged a complex Orient suitable for study in the academy, for display in the museum, for reconstruction in the colonial office, for theoretical illustration in anthropological, biological, linguistic, racial, and historical theses about mankind and the universe, for instances of economic and sociological theories of development, revolution, cultural personality, national or religious character. Additionally, the imaginative examination of things Oriental was based more or less exclusively upon a sovereign Western consciousness out of whose unchallenged centrality an Oriental world emerged, first according to general ideas about who or what was an Oriental, then according to a detailed logic governed not simply by empirical reality but by a battery of desires, repressions, investments, and projections. . . .

. . . My idea is that European and then American interest in the Orient was political according to some of the obvious historical accounts of it that I have given here, but that it was the culture that created that interest, that acted dynamically along with brute political, economic, and military rationales to make the Orient the varied and complicated place that it obviously was in the field I call Orientalism.

Therefore, Orientalism is not a mere political subject matter or field that is reflected passively by culture, scholarship, or institutions; nor is it a large and diffuse collection of texts about the Orient; nor is it representative and expressive of some nefarious "Western" imperialist plot to hold down the "Oriental" world. It is rather a *distribution* of geopolitical awareness into aesthetic, scholarly, economic, sociological, historical, and philological texts; it is an *elaboration* not only of a basic geographical distinction (the world is made up of two unequal halves, Orient and Occident) but also of a whole series of "interests" which, by such means as scholarly discovery, philological reconstruction, psychological analysis, landscape and sociological description, it not only creates but also maintains; it *is*, rather than expresses, a certain *will* or *intention* to understand, in some cases to control, manipulate, even to incorporate,

what is a manifestly different (or alternative and novel) world; it is, above all, a discourse that is by no means in direct, corresponding relationship with political power in the raw, but rather is produced and exists in an uneven exchange with various kinds of power, shaped to a degree by the exchange with power political (as with a colonial or imperial establishment), power intellectual (as with reigning sciences like comparative linguistics or anatomy, or any of the modern policy sciences), power cultural (as with orthodoxies and canons of taste, texts, values), power moral (as with ideas about what "we" do and what "they" cannot do or understand as "we" do). Indeed, my real argument is, that Orientalism is—and does not simply represent—a considerable dimension of modern political–intellectual culture, and as such has less to do with the Orient than it does with "our" world . . .

(1978)

---

124 • *Chandra Talpade Mohanty*

"UNDER WESTERN EYES: FEMINIST SCHOLARSHIP AND COLONIAL DISCOURSES"

Any discussion of the intellectual and political construction of "third world feminisms" must address itself to two simultaneous projects: the internal critique of hegemonic "Western" feminisms, and the formulation of autonomous, geographically, historically, and culturally grounded feminist concerns and strategies. The first project is one of deconstructing and dismantling; the second, one of building and constructing. While these projects appear to be contradictory, the one working negatively and the other positively, unless these

two tasks are addressed simultaneously, "third world" feminisms run the risk of marginalization or ghettoization from both mainstream (right and left) and Western feminist discourses.

It is to the first project that I address myself. What I wish to analyze is specifically the production of the "third world woman" as a singular monolithic subject in some recent (Western) feminist texts. The definition of colonization I wish to invoke here is a predominantly *discursive* one, focusing on a certain mode of

From *Third World Women* by Chandra Talpade Mohanty. Copyright © 1991 by Indiana University Press. Reprinted with permission of Indiana University Press.

appropriation and codification of "scholarship" and "knowledge" about women in the third world by particular analytic categories employed in specific writings on the subject which take as their referent feminist interests as they have been articulated in the U.S. and Western Europe. If one of the tasks of formulating and understanding the locus of "third world feminisms" is delineating the way in which it resists and *works against* what I am referring to as "Western feminist discourse," an analysis of the discursive construction of "third world women" in Western feminism is an important first step.

Clearly Western feminist discourse and political practice is neither singular nor homogeneous in its goals, interests, or analyses. However, it is possible to trace a coherence of *effects* resulting from the implicit assumption of "the West" (in all its complexities and contradictions) as the primary referent in theory and praxis. My reference to "Western feminism" is by no means intended to imply that it is a monolith. Rather, I am attempting to draw attention to the similar effects of various textual strategies used by writers which codify Others as non-Western and hence themselves as (implicitly) Western. It is in this sense that I use the term *Western feminist*. Similar arguments can be made in terms of middle-class urban African or Asian scholars producing scholarship on or about their rural or working-class sisters which assumes their own middle-class cultures as the norm, and codifies working-class histories and cultures as Other. Thus, while this essay focuses specifically on what I refer to as "Western feminist" discourse on women in the third world, the critiques I offer also pertain to third world scholars writing about their own cultures, who employ identical analytic strategies.

It ought to be of some political significance, at least, that the term *colonization* has come to denote a variety of phenomena in recent feminist and left writings in general. From its analytic value as a category of exploitative economic exchange in both traditional and contemporary Marxisms (cf. particularly contemporary theorists such as Baran 1962, Amin 1977, and Gunder-Frank 1967) to its use by feminist women of color in the U.S. to describe the appropriation of their experiences and struggles by hegemonic white women's movements (cf. especially Moraga and Anzaldúa 1983, Smith 1983, Joseph and Lewis 1981, and Moraga 1984), colonization has been used to characterize everything from the most evident economic and political hierarchies to the production of a particular cultural discourse abut what is called the "third world."[1] However sophisticated or problematical its use as an explanatory construct, colonization almost invariably implies a relation of structural domination and a suppression—often violent—of the heterogeneity of the subject(s) in question.

My concern about such writings derives from my own implication and investment in contemporary debates in feminist theory, and the urgent political necessity (especially in the age of Reagan/Bush) of forming strategic coalitions across class, race, and national boundaries. The analytic principles discussed below serve to distort Western feminist political practices, and limit the possibility of coalitions among (usually white) Western feminists and working-class feminists and feminists of color around the world. These limitations are evident in the construction of the (implicitly consensual) priority of issues around which apparently all women are expected to organize. The necessary and integral connection between feminist scholarship and feminist political practice and organizing determines the significance and status of Western feminist writings on women in the third world, for feminist scholarship, like most other kinds of scholarship, is not the mere production of knowledge about a certain subject. It is a directly political and discursive *practice* in that it is purposeful and ideological. It is best seen as a mode of intervention into particular hegemonic discourses (for example, traditional anthropology, sociology, literary criticism, etc.); it is a political praxis which counters and resists the totalizing imperative of age-old "legitimate" and "scientific" bodies of knowledge. Thus, feminist scholarly practices (whether reading, writing, critical, or textual) are inscribed in relations of power—relations which they counter, resist, or even perhaps implicitly support. There can, of course, be no apolitical scholarship.

The relationship between "Woman"—a cultural and ideological composite Other constructed through diverse representational discourses (scientific literary juridical, linguistic, cinematic, etc.)—and "women"— real, material subjects of their collective histories—is one of the central questions the practice of feminist scholarship seeks to address. This connection between women as historical subjects and the representation of Woman produced by hegemonic discourses is not a relation of direct identity, or a relation of correspondence or simple implication.[2] It is an arbitrary relation set up by particular cultures. I would like to suggest that the feminist writings I analyze here discursively colonize the material and historical heterogeneities of the lives of women in the third world, thereby producing/re-presenting a composite, singular "third world woman"—an image which appears arbitrarily constructed, but nevertheless carries with it the authorizing signature of Western humanist discourse.[3]

I argue that assumption of privilege and ethnocentric universality, on the one hand, and inadequate self-consciousness about the effect of Western scholarship on the "third world" in the context of a world system dominated by the West, on the other, characterize a sizeable extent of Western feminist work on women in the third world. An analysis of "sexual difference" in the form of a cross-culturally singular, monolithic, notion of patriarchy or male dominance leads to the construction of a similarly reductive and homogeneous notion of what I call the "third world difference"—that stable, ahistorical something that apparently oppresses most if not all the women in these countries. And it is in the production of this "third world difference" that Western feminisms appropriate and "colonize" the constitutive complexities which characterize the lives of women in these countries. It is in this process of discursive homogenization and systematization of the oppression of women in the third world that power is exercised in much of recent Western feminist discourse, and this power needs to be defined and named.

. . .

The first analytic presupposition I focus on is involved in the strategic location of the category "women" vis-à-vis the context of analysis. The assumption of women as an already constituted, coherent group with identical interests and desires, regardless of class, ethnic or racial location, or contradictions, implies a notion of gender or sexual difference or even patriarchy which can be applied universally and cross-culturally. (The context of analysis can be anything from kinship structures and the organization of labor to media representations.) The second analytical presupposition is evident on the methodological level, in the uncritical way "proof" of universality and cross-cultural validity are provided. The third is a more specifically political presupposition underlying the methodologies and the analytic strategies, i.e., the model of power and struggle they imply and suggest. I argue that as a result of the two modes—or, rather, frames—of analysis described

above, a homogeneous notion of the oppression of women as a group is assumed, which, in turn, produces the image of an "average third world woman." This average third world woman leads an essentially truncated life based on her feminine gender (read: sexually constrained) and her being "third world" (read: ignorant, poor, uneducated, tradition-bound, domestic, family-oriented, victimized, etc.). This, I suggest, is in contrast to the (implicit) self-representation of Western women as educated, as modern, as having control over their own bodies and sexualities and the freedom to make their own decisions.

The distinction between Western feminist representation of women in the third world and Western feminist self-presentation is a distinction of the same order as that made by some Marxists between the "maintenance" function of the housewife and real "productive" role of wage labor, or the characterization by developmentalists of the third world as being engaged in the lesser production of "raw materials" in contrast to the "real" productive activity of the first world. These distinctions are made on the basis of the privileging of a particular group as the norm or referent. Men involved in wage labor, first world producers, and, I suggest, Western feminists who sometimes cast third world women in terms of "ourselves undressed" (Michelle Rosaldo's [1980] term), all construct themselves as the normative referent in such a binary analytic.

"WOMEN" AS CATEGORY OF ANALYSIS, OR: WE ARE ALL SISTERS IN STRUGGLE

By women as a category of analysis, I am referring to the crucial assumption that all of us of the same gender, across classes and cultures, are somehow socially constituted as a homogeneous group identified prior to the process of analysis. This is an assumption which characterizes much feminist discourse. The homogeneity of women as a group is produced not on the basis of biological essentials but rather on the basis of secondary sociological and anthropological universals. Thus, for instance, in any given piece of feminist analysis, women are characterized as a singular group on the basis of a shared oppression. What binds women together is a sociological notion of the "sameness" of their oppression. It is at this point that an elision takes place between "women" as a discursively constructed group and "women" as material subjects of their own history. Thus, the discursively consensual homogeneity of "women" as a group is mistaken for the historically specific material reality of groups of women. This results in an assumption of women as an always already constituted group, one which has been labeled "powerless," "exploited," "sexually harassed," etc., by feminist scientific, economic, legal, and sociological discourses. (Notice that this is quite similar to sexual discourse labeling women weak, emotional, having math anxiety, etc.) This focus is not on uncovering the material and ideological specificities that constitute a particular group of women as "powerless" in a particular context. It is, rather, on finding a variety of cases of "powerless" groups of women to prove the general point that women as a group are powerless.

. . .

METHODOLOGICAL UNIVERSALISMS, OR: WOMEN'S OPPRESSION IS A GLOBAL PHENOMENON

Western feminist writings on women in the third world subscribe to a variety of methodologies to demonstrate the universal cross-cultural operation of male dominance and female exploitation. I summarize and critique three such methods below, moving from the simplest to the most complex.

First, proof of universalism is provided through the use of an arithmetic method. The argument goes like this: the greater the number of women who wear the veil, the more universal is the sexual segregation and control of women (Deardon 1975, 4–5). Similarly, a large number of different, fragmented examples from a variety of countries also apparently add up to a universal fact. For instance, Muslim women in Saudi Arabia, Iran, Pakistan, India, and Egypt all wear some sort of a veil. Hence, this indicates that the sexual control of women is a universal fact in those countries in which the women are veiled (Deardon 1975, 7, 10). Fran Hosken writes, "Rape, forced prostitution, polygamy, genital mutilation, pornography, the beating of girls and women, purdah (segregation of women) are all violations of basic human rights" (1981, 15). By equating purdah with rape, domestic violence, and forced prostitution, Hosken asserts its "sexual control" function as the

primary explanation for purdah, whatever the context. Institutions of purdah are thus denied any cultural and historical specificity, and contradictions and potentially subversive aspects are totally ruled out.

In both these examples, the problem is not in asserting that the practice of wearing a veil is widespread. This assertion can be made on the basis of numbers. It is a descriptive generalization. However, it is the analytic leap from the practice of veiling to an assertion of its general significance in controlling women that must be questioned. While there may be a physical similarity in the veils worn by women in Saudi Arabia and Iran, the specific meaning attached to this practice varies according to the cultural and ideological context. In addition, the symbolic space occupied by the practice of purdah may be similar in certain contexts, but this does not automatically indicate that the practices themselves have identical significance in the social realm. For example, as is well known, Iranian middle-class women veiled themselves during the 1979 revolution to indicate solidarity with their veiled working-class sisters, while in contemporary Iran, mandatory Islamic laws dictate that all Iranian women wear veils. While in both these instances, similar reasons might be offered for the veil (opposition to the Shah and Western cultural colonization the first case, and the true Islamicization of Iran in the second), the concrete *meanings* attached to Iranian women wearing the veil are clearly different in both historical contexts. In the first case, wearing the veil is both an oppositional and a revolutionary gesture on the part of Iranian middle-class women; in the second case, it is a coercive, institutional mandate (see Tabari 1980 for detailed discussion). It is on the basis of such context-specific differentiated analysis that effective political strategies can be generated. To assume that the mere practice of veiling women in a number of Muslim countries indicates the universal oppression of women through sexual segregation not only is analytically reductive, but also proves quite useless when it comes to the elaboration of oppositional political strategy.

Second, concepts such as reproduction, the sexual division of labor, the family, marriage, household, patriarchy, etc., are often used without their specification in local cultural and historical contexts. Feminists use these concepts in providing explanations for women's subordination, apparently assuming their universal applicability. For instance, how is it possible to refer to "the" sexual division of labor when the *content* of this division changes radically from one environment to the next, and from one historical juncture to another? At its most abstract level, it is the fact of the differential assignation of tasks according to sex that is significant; however, this is quite different from the *meaning* or *value* that the content of this sexual division of labor assumes in different contexts. . . .

Finally, some writers confuse the use of gender as a superordinate category of analysis with the universalistic proof and instantiation of this category. In other words, empirical studies of gender differences are confused with the analytical organization of cross-cultural work. . . .

To summarize: I have discussed three methodological moves identifiable in feminist (and other academic) cross-cultural work which seeks to uncover a universality in women's subordinate position in society. The next and final section pulls together the previous sections, attempting to outline the political effects on the analytical strategies in the context of Western feminist writing on women in the third world. These arguments are not against generalization as much as they are for careful, historically specific generalizations responsive to complex realities. Nor do these arguments deny the necessity of forming strategic political identities and affinities. Thus, while Indian women of different religions, castes, and classes might forge a political unity on the basis of organizing against police brutality toward women (see Kishwar and Vanita 1984), an *analysis* of police brutality must be contextual. Strategic coalitions which construct oppositional political identities for themselves are based on generalization and provisional unities, but the analysis of these group identities can be based on universalistic, ahistorical categories.

. . .

THE SUBJECT(S) OF POWER

. . .

What happens when this assumption of "women as an oppressed group" is situated in the context of Western feminist writing about third world women? It is here that I locate the colonialist move. By contrasting the representation of women in the third world with what I referred to earlier as Western feminisms' self-presentation in the same context, we see how Western feminists alone become the true "subjects" of this counterhistory. Third world women, on the other hand, never rise above the debilitating generality of their "object" status.

While radical and liberal feminist assumptions of women as a sex class might elucidate (however inadequately) the autonomy of particular women's struggles in the West, the application of the notion of women as a homogeneous category to women in the third world colonizes and appropriates the pluralities of the simultaneous location of different groups of women in social class and ethnic frameworks; in doing so it ultimately robs them of their historical and political *agency*. Similarly, many Zed Press authors who ground themselves in the basic analytical strategies of traditional Marxism also implicitly create a "unity" of women by substituting "women's activity" for "labor" as the primary theoretical determinant of women's situation. Here again, women are constituted as a coherent group not on the basis of "natural" qualities or needs but on the basis of the sociological "unity" of their role in domestic production and wage labor (see Haraway 1985, esp., p. 76). In other words, Western feminist discourse, by assuming women as a coherent, already constituted group which is placed in kinship, legal, and other structures, defines third world women as subjects *outside* social relations, instead of looking at the way women are constituted *through* these very structures.

Legal, economic, religious, and familial structures are treated as phenomena to be judged by Western standards. It is here that ethnocentric universality comes into play. When these structures are defined as "underdeveloped" or "developing" and women are placed within them, an implicit image of the "average third world woman" is produced. This is the transformation of the (implicitly Western) "oppressed woman" into the "oppressed third world woman." While the category of "oppressed woman" is generated through an exclusive focus on gender difference, "the oppressed third world woman" category has an additional attribute—the "third world difference!" The "third world difference" includes a paternalistic attitude toward women in the third world. Since discussions of the various themes I identified earlier (kinship, education, religion, etc.) are conducted in the context of the relative "underdevelopment" of the third world (which is nothing less than unjustifiably confusing development with the separate path taken by the West in its development, as well as ignoring the directionality of the first-third world power relationship), third world women as a group or category are automatically and necessarily defined as religious (read "not progressive"), family-oriented (read "traditional"), legal minors (read "they-are-still-not-conscious-of-their-rights"), illiterate (read "ignorant"), domestic (read "backward"), and sometimes revolutionary (read "their-country-is-in-a-state-of-war; they-must-fight!"). This is how the "third world difference" is produced.

When the category of "sexually oppressed women" is located within particular systems in the third world which are defined on a scale which is normed through Eurocentric assumptions, not only are third world women defined in a particular way prior to their entry into social relations, but since no connections are made between first and third world power shifts, the assumption is reinforced that the third world has just not evolved to the extent that the West has. This mode of feminist analysis, by homogenizing and systematizing the experiences of different groups of women in these countries, erases all marginal and resistant modes and experiences. It is significant that none of the texts I reviewed in the Zed Press series focuses on lesbian politics or the politics of ethnic and religious marginal organizations in third world women's groups. Resistance can thus be defined only as cumulative reactive, not as something inherent in the operation of power. If power, as Michel Foucault has argued recently, can really be understood only in the context of resistance,[4] this misconceptualization is both analytically and strategically problematical. It limits theoretical analysis as well as reinforces Western cultural imperialism. For in the context of a first/third world balance of power, feminist analyses which perpetrate and sustain the hegemony of the idea of the superiority of the West produce a corresponding set of universal images of the "third world woman," images such as the veiled woman, the powerful mother, the chaste virgin, the obedient wife, etc. These images exist in universal, ahistorical splendor, setting in motion a colonialist discourse which exercises a very specific power in defining, coding, and maintaining existing first/third world connections.

To conclude, then, let me suggest some disconcerting similarities between the typically authorizing signature of such Western feminist writings on women in the third world, and the authorizing signature of the project of humanism in general—humanism as a Western ideological and political project which involves the necessary recuperation of the "East" and "Woman" as Others.

. . .

As discussed earlier, a comparison between Western feminist self-presentation and Western feminist representation of women in the third world yields significant results. Universal images of "the third world woman" (the veiled woman, chaste virgin, etc.), images constructed from adding the "third world difference" to "sexual difference," are predicated upon (and hence obviously bring into sharper focus) assumptions about Western women as secular, liberated, and having control over their own lives. This is not to suggest that Western women *are* secular, liberated, and in control over their own lives. I am referring to a *discursive* self-presentation, not necessarily to material reality. If this were a material reality, there would be no need for political movements in the West. Similarly, only from the vantage point of the West is it possible to define the "third world" as underdeveloped and economically dependent. Without the overdetermined discourse that creates the *third* world, there would be no (singular and privileged) first world. Without the "third world woman," the particular self-presentation of Western women mentioned above would be problematical. I am suggesting, then, that the one enables and sustains the other. This is not to say that the signature of Western feminist writings on the third world has the same authority as the project of Western humanism. However, in the context of the hegemony of the Western scholarly establishment in the production and dissemination of texts, and in the context of the legitimating imperative of humanistic and scientific discourse, the definition of "the third world woman" as a monolith might well tie into the larger economic and ideological praxis of "disinterested" scientific inquiry and pluralism which are the surface manifestations of a latent economic and cultural colonization of the "non-Western" world. It is time to move beyond the Marx who found it possible to say: They cannot represent themselves; they must be represented.

(1984)

NOTES

1. Terms such as *third* and *first world* are very problematical, both in suggesting oversimplified similarities between and among countries labeled thus, and in implicitly

reinforcing existing economic, cultural, and ideological hierarchies which are conjured up in using such terminology. I use the term *"third world"* with full awareness of its problems, only because this is the terminology available to us at the moment. The use of quotation marks is meant to suggest a continuous questioning of the designation. Even when I do not use quotation marks, I mean to use the term critically:

2. I am indebted to Teresa de Lauretis for this particular formulation of the project of feminist theorizing. See especially her introduction in de Lauretis, *Alice Doesn't: Feminism, Semiotics, Cinema* (Bloomington: Indiana University Press, 1984); see also Sylvia Wynter, "The Politics of Domination," unpublished manuscript.

3. This argument is similar to Homi Bhabha's definition of colonial discourse as strategically creating a space for a subject people through the production of knowledges and the exercise of power. The full quote reads: "[colonial discourse is] an apparatus of power. . . . an apparatus that turns on the recognition and disavowal of racial/cultural/historical differences. Its predominant strategic function is the creation of a space for a subject people through the production of knowledges in terms of which surveillance is exercised and a complex form of pleasure/unpleasure is incited. It (i.e., colonial discourse) seeks authorization for its strategies by the production of knowledges by coloniser and colonised which are stereotypical but antithetically evaluated" (1983, 23).

4. This is one of M. Foucault's (1978, 1980) central points in his reconceptualization of the strategies and workings of power networks.

REFERENCES

Amin, Samir. 1977. *Imperialism and Unequal Development*, New York: Monthly Review Press.

Baran, Paul A. 1962. *The Political Economy of Growth*, New York: Monthly Review Press.

Brown, Beverly. 1983. *"Displacing the Difference: Review of Nature, Culture Gender."* m/f: 8:79–89.

Deardon, Ann, ed. 1975. *Arab Women*. London: Minority Rights Group Report No. 27.

Foucault, Michel. 1978. *History of Sexuality: Volume One*, New York: Random House.

Foucault, Michel. 1980. *Power/Knowledge*. New York: Pantheon.

Gunder-Frank, Audre, 1967. *Capitalism and Underdevelopment in Latin America*. New York: Monthly Review Press.

Haraway, Donna. 1985. "A Manifesto for Cyborgs: Science Technology and Socialist Feminism in the 1980s." *Socialist Review* 80 (March/April): 65–108.

Hosken, Fran. 1981. "Female Genital Mutilation and Human Rights." *Feminist Issues* 1, no. 3.

Joseph, Gloria, and Jill Lewis. 1981. *Common Differences: Conflicts in Black and White Feminist Perspectives*. Boston: Beacon Press.

Kishwar, Madhu, and Ruth Vanita. 1984. *In Search of Answers: Indian Women's Voices from Manushi*. London: Zed Press.

Mies, Maria. 1982. *The Lace Makers of Naraspur: Indian Housewives Produce for the World Market*. London: Zed Press.

Moraga, Cherrie. 1984. *Loving in the War Years*. Boston: South End Press.

Moraga, Cherrie, and Gloria Anzaldúa, eds. 1983. *This Bridge Called My Back: Writings by Radical Women of Color*. New York: Kitchen Table Press.

Rosaldo, M.A. 1980. "The Use and Abuse of Anthropology: Reflections on Feminism and Cross-Cultural Understanding." *Signs* 53:389–417.

Smith, Barbara, ed. 1983. *Home Girls: A Black Feminist Anthology*. New York: Kitchen Table Press.

Tabari, Azar. 1980. "The Enigma of the Veiled Iranian Women." *Feminist Review* 5:19–32.

125 • *Gayatri Chakravorty Spivak*

"CAN THE SUBALTERN SPEAK?"

... The first part of my proposition—that the phased development of the subaltern is complicated by the imperialist project—is confronted by the "Subaltern Studies" group. They *must* ask, Can the subaltern speak? Here we are within Foucault's own discipline of history and with people who acknowledge his influence. Their project is to rethink Indian colonial historiography from the perspective of the discontinuous chain of peasant insurgencies during the colonial occupation. This is indeed the problem of "the permission to narrate" discussed by Said.[1] As Ranajit Guha, the founding editor of the collective, argues,

> The historiography of Indian nationalism has for a long time been dominated by elitism—colonialist elitism and bourgeois-nationalist elitism . . . shar[ing] the prejudice that the making of the Indian nation and the development of the consciousness—nationalism—which confirmed this process were exclusively or predominantly elite achievements. In the colonialist and neo-colonialist historiographies these achievements are credited to British colonial rulers, administrators, policies, institutions, and culture; in the nationalist and neonationalist writings—to Indian elite personalities, institutions, activities and ideas.[2]

Certain members of the Indian elite are of course native informants for first-world intellectuals interested in the voice of the Other. But one must nevertheless insist that the colonized subaltern subject is irretrievably heterogeneous . . . .

Can the subaltern speak? What might the elite do to watch out for the continuing construction of the subaltern? The question of "woman" seems most problematic in this context. Confronted by the ferocious standardizing benevolence of most U.S. and Western European human-scientific radicalism (recognition by assimilation) today, and the exclusion of the margins of even the center–periphery articulation (the "true and differential subaltern"), the analogue of class-consciousness rather than race-consciousness in this area seems historically, disciplinarily, and practically forbidden by Right and Left alike.

In so fraught a field, it is not easy to ask the question of the subaltern woman as subject; it is thus all the more necessary to remind pragmatic radicals that such a question is not an idealist red herring. Though all feminist or antisexist projects cannot be reduced to this one, to ignore it is an unacknowledged political gesture that has a long history and collaborates with a masculist radicalism that operates by strategic exclusions, equating "nationalist" and "people" (as counterproductive as the equation of "feminist" and "woman").

If I ask myself, How is it possible to want to die by fire to mourn a husband ritually? I am asking the question of the (gendered) subaltern woman as subject, not, as my friend Jonathan Culler somewhat tendentiously suggests, trying to "produce difference by differing" or to "appeal . . . to a sexual identity defined as essential and privileg[ing] experiences associated with that identity."[3] Culler is here a part of that mainstream project of Western feminism that both continues and displaces the battle over the right to individualism between women and men in situations of upward class mobility. One suspects that the debate between U.S. feminism and European "theory" (as theory is generally represented by women from the United States or Britain) occupies a significant corner of that very terrain. I am generally sympathetic with the call to make U.S.

Reprinted by permission of the publisher from *A Critique of Postcolonial Reason* by Gayatri Chakravorty Spivak, pp. 270, 281–289. Cambridge, Mass.: Harvard University Press, Copyright © 1999 by the President and Fellows of Harvard College. Notes have been renumbered.

feminism more "theoretical." It seems, however, that the problem of the muted subject of the subaltern woman, though not solved by an "essentialist" search for lost origins, cannot be served by the call for more theory in Anglo-America either.

That call is often given in the name of a critique of "positivism," which is seen here as identical with "essentialism." Yet Hegel, the modern inaugurator of "the work of the negative," was not a stranger to the notion of essences. For Marx, the curious persistence of essentialism within the dialectic was a profound and productive problem. Thus, the stringent binary opposition between positivism/essentialism (read, U.S.) and "theory" (read, French or Franco-German via Anglo-American) may be spurious. Apart from repressing the ambiguous complicity between essentialism and critiques of positivism (acknowledged by Derrida in "Of Grammatology as a Positive Science"), it also errs by implying that positivism is not a theory. This move allows the emergence of a proper name, a positive essence, Theory. And once again, the position of the investigator remains unquestioned. If and when this territorial debate turns toward the Third World, no change in the question of method is to be discerned. This debate cannot take into account that, in the case of the woman as subaltern, rather few ingredients for the constitution of the itinerary of the trace of a sexed subject (rather than an anthropological object) can be gathered to locate the possibility of dissemination.

Yet I remain generally sympathetic to aligning feminism with the critique of positivism and the defetishization of the concrete. I am also far from averse to learning from the work of Western theorists, though I have learned to insist on marking their positionality as investigating subjects. Given these conditions, and as a literary critic, I tactically confronted the immense problem of the consciousness of the woman as subaltern. I reinvented the problem in a sentence and transformed it into the object of a simple semiosis. What can such a transformation mean?

This gesture of transformation marks the fact that knowledge of the other subject is theoretically impossible. Empirical work in the discipline constantly performs this transformation tacitly. It is a transformation from a first–second person performance to the constatation in the third person. It is, in other words, at once a gesture of control and an acknowledgment of limits. Freud provides a homology for such positional hazards.

Sarah Kofman has suggested that the deep ambiguity of Freud's use of women as a scapegoat may be read as a reaction-formation to an initial and continuing desire to give the hysteric a voice, to transform her into the *subject* of hysteria.[4] The masculine-imperialist ideological formation that shaped that desire into "the daughter's seduction" is part of the same formation that constructs the monolithic "third-world woman." No contemporary metropolitan investigator is not influenced by that formation. Part of our "unlearning" project is to articulate our participation in that formation—by *measuring* silences, if necessary—into the *object* of investigation. Thus, when confronted with the questions, Can the subaltern speak? and Can the subaltern (as woman) speak? our efforts to give the subaltern a voice in history will be doubly open to the dangers run by Freud's discourse. It is in acknowledgment of these dangers rather than as solution to a problem that I put together the sentence "White men are saving brown women from brown men," a sentence that runs like a red thread through today's "gender and development." My impulse is not unlike the one to be encountered in Freud's investigation of the sentence "A child is being beaten."[5]

The use of Freud here does not imply an isomorphic analogy between subject-formation and the behavior of social collectives, a frequent practice, often accompanied by a reference to Reich, in the conversation between Deleuze and Foucault. I am, in other words, not suggesting that "White men are saving brown women from brown men" is a sentence indicating a *collective* fantasy symptomatic of a *collective* itinerary of sadomasochistic repression in a *collective* imperialist enterprise. There is a satisfying symmetry in such an allegory, but I would rather invite the reader to consider it a problem in "wild psychoanalysis" than a clinching solution.[6] Just as Freud's insistence on making the woman the scapegoat in "A child is being beaten" and elsewhere discloses his political interests, however imperfectly, so my insistence on imperialist subject-production as the occasion for this sentence discloses a politics that I cannot step around.

Further, I am attempting to borrow the general methodological aura of Freud's strategy toward the sentence he constructed *as a sentence* out of the many similar substantive accounts his patients gave him. This does not mean I will offer a case of transference-in-analysis as an isomorphic model for the transaction between reader and text (here the constructed sentence). As I repeat in this chapter, the analogy between transference and literary criticism or historiography is no more than a productive catachresis. To say that the subject is a text does not authorize the converse pronouncement: that the verbal text is a subject.

I am fascinated, rather, by how Freud predicates a *history* of repression that produces the final sentence. It is a history with a double origin, one hidden in the amnesia of the infant, the other lodged in our archaic past, assuming by implication a preoriginary space where human and animal were not yet differentiated.[7] We are driven to impose a homology of this Freudian strategy on the Marxist narrative to explain the ideological dissimulation of imperialist political economy and outline a history of repression that produces a sentence like the one I have sketched: "White men are saving brown women from brown men"—giving honorary whiteness to the colonial subject on precisely this issue. This history also has a double origin, one hidden in the maneuverings behind the British abolition of widow sacrifice in 1829,[8] the other lodged in the classical and Vedic past of "Hindu" India, the *Rg-Veda* and the *Dharmasastra*. An undifferentiated transcendental preoriginary space can only too easily be predicated for this other history.

The sentence I have constructed is one among many displacements describing the relationship between brown and white men (sometimes brown and white women worked in).[9] It takes its place among some sentences of "hyperbolic admiration" or of pious guilt that Derrida speaks of in connection with the "hieroglyphist prejudice." The relationship between the imperialist subject and the subject of imperialism is at least ambiguous.

The Hindu widow ascends the pyre of the dead husband and immolates herself upon it. This is widow sacrifice. (The conventional transcription of the Sanskrit word for the widow would be *sati*. The early colonial British transcribed it *suttee*.) The rite was not practiced universally and was not caste- or class-fixed. The abolition of this rite by the British has been generally understood as a case of "White men saving brown women from brown men." White women—from the nineteenth-century British Missionary Registers to Mary Daly—have not produced an alternative understanding. Against this is the Indian nativist statement,

a parody of the nostalgia for lost origins: "The women wanted to die," still being advanced . . .[10]

The two sentences go a long way to legitimize each other. One never encounters the testimony of the women's voice consciousness. Such a testimony would not be ideology-transcendent or "fully" subjective, of course, but it would constitute the ingredients for producing a countersentence. As one goes down the grotesquely mistranscibed names of these women, the sacrificed widows, in the police reports included in the records of the East India Company, one cannot put together a "voice." The most one can sense is the immense heterogeneity breaking through even such a skeletal and ignorant account (castes, for example, are regularly described as tribes). Faced with the dialectically interlocking sentences that are constructible as "White men are saving brown women from brown men" and "The women wanted to die," the metropolitan feminist migrant (removed from the actual theater of decolonization) asks the question of simple semiosis—What does this signify?—and begins to plot a history.

As I have suggested in the previous chapter, to mark the moment when not only a civil but a good society is born out of domestic confusion, singular events that break the letter of the law to institute its spirit are often invoked. The protection of women by men often provides such an event. If we remember that the British boasted of their absolute equity toward and noninterference with native custom/law, an invocation of this sanctioned transgression of the letter for the sake of the spirit may be read in J. D. M. Derrett's remark: "The very first legislation upon Hindu Law was carried through without the assent of a single Hindu." The legislation is not named here. The next sentence, where the measure is named, is equally interesting if one considers the implications of the survival of a colonially established "good" society after decolonization: "The recurrence of *sati* in independent India is probably an obscurantist revival which cannot long survive even in a very backward part of the country."[11]

Whether this observation is correct or not, what interests me is that the protection of woman (today the "third-world woman") becomes a signifier for the establishment of a *good* society (now a good planet) which must, at such inaugurative moments, transgress mere legality, or equity of legal policy. In this particular case, the process also allowed the redefinition as a crime of what had been tolerated, known, or adulated as ritual. In other words, this one item in Hindu law jumped the frontier between the private and the public domain.

Although Foucault's *historical narrative*, focusing solely on Western Europe, sees merely a tolerance for the criminal antedating the development of criminology in the late eighteenth century (*PK* 41), his *theoretical description* of the "episteme" is pertinent here: "The *episteme* is the 'apparatus' which makes possible the separation not of the true from the false, but of what may not be characterized as scientific" (*PK* 197)—ritual as opposed to crime, the one fixed by superstition, the other by legal science.[12]

The leap of *suttee* from private to public has a clear but complex relationship with the changeover from a mercantile and commercial to a territorial and administrative British presence; it can be followed in correspondence among the police stations, the lower and higher courts, the courts of directors, the prince regent's court, and the like.[13] (It is interesting to note that, from the point of view of the native "colonial subject," also emergent from the "feudalism-capitalism" transition—necessarily askew because "colonial"—*sati* is a signifier with the reverse social charge: "Groups rendered psychologically marginal by their exposure to Western impact . . . had come under pressure to demonstrate, to others as well as to themselves, their ritual purity and allegiance to traditional high culture. To many of them *sati* became an important proof of their conformity to older norms at a time when these norms had become shaky within.")[14] . . .

(1985)

NOTES

1. Edward W. Said, "Permission to Narrate," *London Review of Books* (16 Feb. 1984).
2. Guha, *Subaltern Studies*, (Delhi: Oxford Univ. Press, 1982), 1:1.
3. Jonathan Culler, *On Deconstruction: Theory and Criticism after Structuralism* (Ithaca: Cornell Univ. Press, 1982), p. 48.
4. Sarah Kofman, *The Enigma of Woman: Woman in Freud's Writings, tr. Catherine Porter* (Ithaca: Cornell Univ. Press, 1985).
5. Freud, "'A Child Is Being Beaten': A Contribution to the Study of the Origin of Sexual Perversion," *SE* 17. For a list of ways in which Western criticism constructs "third world woman," see Chandra Talpade Mohanty, "Under Western Eyes: Feminist Scholarship and Colonial Discourses," in Mohanty et al., eds., *Third World Women and the Politics of Feminism* (Bloomington: Indiana Univ. Press, 1991), pp. 51–80.
6. Freud, "'Wild' Psycho-Analysis," *SE* vol. 11, pp. 221–227. A good deal of psychoanalytic social critique would fit this description.
7. Freud, "A Child Is Being Beaten,'" p. 188.
8. For a brilliant account of how the "reality" of widow-sacrificing was constituted or "textualized" during the colonial period, see Lata Mani, "Contentious Traditions: The Debate on *Sati* in Colonial India," in *Recasting Women: Essays in Colonial History* (Delhi: Kali for Women, 1989), pp. 88–126. I profited from discussion with Dr. Mani at the inception of this project. Here I present some of my differences from her position. The "printing mistake in the Bengali translation" (p. 109) that she cites is not the same as the mistake I discuss, which is in the ancient Sanskrit. It is of course altogether interesting that there should be all these errancies in the justification of the practice. A regulative psychobiography is not identical with "textual hegemony" (p. 96). I agree with Mani that the latter mode of explanation cannot take "regional variations" into account. A regulative psychobiography is another mode of "textualist oppression" when it produces not only "women's consciousness" but a "gendered episteme" (mechanics of the construction of objects of knowledge together with validity-criteria for statements of knowledge). You do not have to "read verbal texts" here. It is something comparable to Gramsci's "inventory without traces" (Antonio Gramsci, *Selections from the Prison Notebooks*, tr. Quintin Hoare and Geoffrey Nowell Smith [New York: International Publishers, 1971], p. 324). Like Mani (p. 125, n. 90), I too wish to "add" to Kosambi's "strategies." To the "supplement[ation of the linguistic study of problems of ancient Indian culture] by intelligent use of archaeology, anthropology, sociology and a suitable historical perspective" (Kosambi, "Combined Methods in Indology," *Indo-Iranian Journal* 6 [1963]: 177), I would add the insights of psychoanalysis, though not the regulative psychobiography of its choice. Alas, in spite of our factualist fetish, "facts" alone may account for women's oppression, but they will never allow us to approach gendering, a net where we ourselves are enmeshed, as we decide what (the) facts are. Because of epistemic prejudice, Kosambi's bold and plain speech can and has been misunderstood; but his word "live"

can take on board a more complex notion of the mental theater as Mani cannot: "Indian peasants in villages far from any city *live* in a manner closer to the days when the Puranas were written than do the descendants of the brahmins who wrote the Puranas" (emphasis mine). Precisely. The self-representation in gendering is regulated by the Puranic psychobiography, with the Brahmin as the model. In the last chapter I will consider what Kosambi mentions in the next sentence: "A stage further back are the pitiful fragments of tribal groups, usually sunk to the level of marginal castes; they rely heavily upon food-gathering and have the corresponding mentality." Kosambi's somewhat doctrinaire Marxism would not allow him to think of the tribal episteme as anything but only backward, of course. After the *sati* of Rup Kanwar in September 1987, a body of literature on the contemporary situation has emerged. That requires quite a different engagement (see Radha Kumar, "Agitation against Sati, 1987–88," in *The History of Doing* [Delhi: Kali for Women, 1993], pp. 172–181.)

9. See Kumari Jayawardena, *The White Woman's Other Burden: Western Women and South Asia during British Colonial Rule* (New York: Routledge, 1995). Envy, backlash, reaction-formation; these are the routes by which such efforts may, in the absence of ethical responsibility, lead to opposite results. I have repeatedly invoked Melanie Klein and Assia Djebar in this context. See also Spivak, "Psychoanalysis in Left Field," pp. 66–69.

10. The examples of female ventriloquist complicity, quoted by Lata Mani in her brilliant article "Production of an Official Discourse on *Sati* in early Nineteenth Century Bengal," *Economic and Political Weekly* 21.17 (26 Apr. 1986), women's studies supp., p. 36, proves my point. The point is not that a refusal would not be ventriloquism for Women's Rights. One is not suggesting that only the latter is correct free will. One is suggesting that the freedom of the will is negotiable, and it is not on the grounds of a disinterested free will that we will be able to justify an action, in this case against the burning of widows, to the adequate satisfaction of all. The ethical aporia is not negotiable. We must act in view of this.

11. J. D. M. Derrett, *Hindu Law Past and Present: Being an Account of the Controversy Which Preceded the Enactment of the Hindu Code, and Text of the Code as Enacted, and Some Comments Thereon* (Calcutta: A. Mukherjee and Co., 1957), p. 46.

12. Kosambi comments on such shifts as a matter of course. Of the much admired widow remarriage reform, e.g., he writes: "[t]hat he [R. G. Bhandarkar] spoke for a very narrow class in the attempt to speak for the whole of India never struck him, nor for that matter other contemporary 'reformers'. Still, *the silent change of emphasis from caste to class was a necessary advance*" (D. D. Kosambi, *Myth and Reality: Studies in the Formation of Indian Culture* [Bombay: Popular Prakashan, 1962], p. 38, n. 2; emphasis mine). We would say "shift" rather than "advance"; for it is this silent century-old epistemic shift that allows today's Hindu nationalism to proclaim itself anti-casteist, nationalist—even "secular." Incidentally, to confine the construction of *Sati* to colonial negotiations, and finally to the Ram Mohun Roy–Lord William Bentinck exchange, is also to avoid the question of "subaltern consciousness." For further commentary on the differences between Mani and Spivak, see Sumit Sarkar, "Orientalism Revisited: Saidian Frameworks in the Writing of Modern Indian History," *Oxford Literary Review* 16 (1994): 223. I remain grateful to Professor Sarkar for noticing that "Mani's article stands in marked contrast to the much more substantive discussion of pre-colonial and colonial discourses on sati in Spivak, 'Can the Subaltern Speak?'" To claim that caste or clitoridectomy is no more than a colonial construction advances nothing today. Romila Thapar tells me that the seventh-century historian Banabhatta objected to *Sati*. There may be something Eurocentric about assuming that imperialism began with Europe.

13. Today, interference in women's cultural privacy remains a project of making rural women available for micro-enterprise in the economic sphere, and a project of bettering women's lives in the political. Demands for a more responsible tempo—woman's time—so that the violence of the change does not scar the episteme, are often impatiently rejected as cultural conservatism.

14. Ashis Nandy, "Sati: A Nineteenth Century Tale of Women, Violence and Protest," *Rammohun Roy and the Process of Modernization in India*, ed. V. C. Joshi (Delhi: Vikas Publishing House, 1975), p. 68.

"INFINITE LAYERS/THIRD WORLD?"

To survive, "Third World" must necessarily have negative *and* positive connotations: negative when viewed in a vertical ranking system—"underdeveloped" compared to over-industrialized, "underprivileged" within the already Second sex—and positive when understood sociopolitically as a subversive, "non-aligned" force. Whether "Third World" sounds negative or positive also depends on *who* uses it. Coming from you Westerners, the word can hardly mean the same as when it comes from Us members of the Third World. Quite predictably, you/we who condemn it most are both we who buy in and they who deny any participation in the bourgeois mentality of the West. For it was in the context of such mentality that "Third World" stood out as a new semantic finding to designate what was known as "the savages" before the Independences. Today, hegemony is much more subtle, much more pernicious than the form of blatant racism once exercised by the colonial West. I/i always find myself asking, in this one-dimension society, where I/i should draw the line between tracking down the oppressive mechanisms of the system and aiding their spread. "Third World" commonly refers to those states in Africa, Asia and Latin America which called themselves "non-aligned," that is to say, affiliated with neither the Western (capitalist) nor the Eastern (communist) power blocs. Thus, if "Third World" is often rejected for its judged-to-be-derogatory connotations, it is not so much because of the hierarchical, first-second-third order implied, as some invariably repeat, but because of the growing threat "Third World" consistently presents to the Western bloc the last few decades. The emergence of repressed voices into the worldwide political arena has already prompted her (Julia Kristeva) to ask: "How will the West greet the awakening of the 'third world'

as the Chinese call it? Can we [Westerners] participate, actively and lucidly, in this awakening when the center of the planet is in the process of moving toward the East?" Exploited, looked down upon, and lumped together in a convenient term that denies their individualities, a group of "poor" (nations), having once sided with neither of the dominating forces, has slowly learned to turn this denial to the best account. "The Third World to Third World peoples" thus becomes an empowering tool, and one which politically includes all non-whites in their solidarist struggle against all forms of Western dominance. And since "Third World" now refers to more than the geographically and economically determined nations of the "South" (versus "North"), since the term comprises such "developed" countries as Japan and those which have opted for socialist reconstruction of their system (China, Cuba, Ethiopia, Angola, Mozambique) as well as those which have favored a capitalist mode of development (Nigeria, India, Brazil), there no longer exists such a thing as a unified unaligned Third World bloc. Moreover, Third World has moved West (or North, depending on where the dividing line falls) and has expanded so as to include even the remote parts of the First World. What is at stake is not only the hegemony of Western cultures, but also their identities as unified cultures. Third World dwells on diversity; so does First World. This is our strength and our misery. The West is painfully made to realize the existence of a Third World in the First World, and vice versa. The Master is bound to recognize that His Culture is not as homogeneous, as monolithic as He believed it to be. He discovers, with much reluctance, He is just an other among others.

Thus, whenever it is a question of "Third World women" or, more disquietingly, of "Third World Women in the U.S.," the reaction provoked among many whites almost never fails to be that of annoyance, irritation, or vexation. "Why Third World in the U.S.?" they say angrily; "You mean those who still have relatives in South East Asia?" "Third World! I don't understand how one can use such a term, it doesn't mean anything." Or even better, "Why use such a term to defeat yourself?" Alternatives like "Western" and "non-Western" or "Euro-American" and "non-Euro-American" may sound a bit less charged, but they are certainly neither neutral nor satisfactory, for they still take the dominant group as point of reference, and they reflect well the West's ideology of dominance (it is as if we were to use the term "non-Afro-Asian," for example, to designate all white peoples). More recently, we have been hearing of the Fourth World which, we are told, "is a world populated by indigenous people who still continue to bear a spiritual relationship to their traditional lands." The colonialist creed "Divide and Conquer" is here again, alive and well. Often ill at ease with the outspoken educated natives who represent the Third World in debates and paternalistically scornful of those who remain reserved, the dominant thus decides to weaken this term of solidarity, both by invalidating it as empowering tool and by inciting divisiveness within the Third World—a

Third World within the Third World. Aggressive Third World (educated "savages") with its awareness and resistance to domination must therefore be classified apart from gentle Fourth World (uneducated "savages"). Every unaligned voice should necessarily/consequently be either a personal or a minority voice. The (impersonal) majority, as logic dictates, has to be the (aligned) dominant.

> It is, apparently, inconvenient, if not downright mind stretching [notes Alice Walker], for white women scholars to think of black women as women, perhaps because "woman" (like "man" among white males) is a name they are claiming for themselves, and themselves alone. Racism decrees that if they are now women (years ago they were ladies, but fashions change) then black women must, perforce, be something else. (While they were "ladies" black women could be "women" and so on.)

Another revealing example of this separatist majority mentality is the story Walker relates of an exhibit of women painters at the Brooklyn Museum: when asked "Are there no black women painters represented here?" (none of them is, apparently), a white woman feminist simply replies "It's a *women's* exhibit!" Different historical contexts, different semantic contents . . .

(1989)

127 • *Inderpal Grewal and Caren Kaplan*

"POSTMODERNISM AND TRANSNATIONAL FEMINIST PRACTICES"

If feminist political practices do not acknowledge transnational cultural flows, feminist movements will fail to understand the material conditions that structure women's lives in diverse locations. If feminist movements cannot understand the dynamics of these material conditions, they will be unable to construct an effective

opposition to current economic and cultural hegemonies that are taking new global forms. Without an analysis of transnational scattered hegemonies that reveal themselves in gender relations, feminist movements will remain isolated and prone to reproducing the universalizing gestures of dominant Western cultures.

Notions such as "global feminism" have failed to respond to such needs and have increasingly been subject to critique.[1] Conventionally, "global feminism" has stood for a kind of Western cultural imperialism. The term "global feminism" has elided the diversity of women's agency in favor of a universalized Western model of women's liberation that celebrates individuality and modernity. Anti-imperialist movements have legitimately decried this form of "feminist" globalizing (albeit often for a continuation of their own agendas). Many women who participate in decolonizing efforts both within and outside the United States have rejected the term "feminism" in favor of "womanist" or have defined their feminism through class or race or other ethnic, religious, or regional struggles.

Yet we know that there is an imperative need to address the concerns of women around the world in the historicized particularity of their relationship to multiple patriarchies as well as to international economic hegemonies. We seek creative ways to move beyond constructed oppositions without ignoring the histories that have informed these conflicts or the valid concerns about power relations that have represented or structured the conflicts up to this point. We need to articulate the relationship of gender to scattered hegemonies such as global economic structures, patriarchal nationalisms, "authentic" forms of tradition, local structures of domination, and legal–juridical oppression on multiple levels.

Transnational feminist practices require this kind of comparative work rather than the relativistic linking of "differences" undertaken by proponents of "global feminism"; that is, to compare multiple, overlapping, and discrete oppressions rather than to construct a theory of hegemonic oppression under a unified category of gender. . . .

Feminists must continually question the narratives in which they are embedded, including but not limiting ourselves to the master narratives of mainstream feminism. As Kumkum Sangari and Sudesh Vaid assert:

> If feminism is to be different, it must acknowledge the ideological and problematic significance of its own past. Instead of creating yet another grand tradition or a cumulative history of emancipation, neither of which can

deal with our present problems, we need to be attentive to how the past enters differently into the consciousness of other historical periods and is further subdivided by a host of other factors including gender, caste, and class.[2]

. . . Feminist movements must be open to rethinking and self-reflexivity as an ongoing process if we are to avoid creating new orthodoxies that are exclusionary and reifying. The issue of who counts as a feminist is much less important than creating coalitions based on the practices that different women use in various locations to counter the scattered hegemonies that affect their lives. . . .

Part of any feminist self-examination necessitates a rigorous critique of emerging orthodoxies. In debates within the United States, for example, it is important to examine the ways in which race, class, and gender are fast becoming the holy trinity that every feminist feels compelled to address even as this trinity delimits the range of discussion around women's lives. What is often left out of these U.S.-focused debates are other complex categories of identity and affiliation that apply to non-U.S. cultures and situations. U.S. feminists often have to be reminded that all peoples of the world are not solely constructed by the trinity of race–sex–class; for that matter, other categories also enter into the issues of subject formation both within and outside the borders of the United States, requiring more nuanced and complex theories of social relations. For example, emerging theories of homosexual formations in various locations demonstrate that the category of sexuality can be multiply constituted in the context of transnational cultures, pointing the way for detailed feminist studies of cultural production and reception.[3]

The question becomes how to link diverse feminisms without requiring either equivalence or a master theory. How to make these links without replicating cultural and economic hegemony? For white, Western feminists or elite women in other world locations, such questions demand an examination of the links between daily life and academic work and an acknowledgment that one's privileges in the world-system are always linked to another woman's oppression or exploitation. As Cynthia Enloe's recent work demonstrates, the old

From *Scattered Hegemonies: Postmodernity and Transnational Feminist Practices*, eds. Inderpal Grewal and Caren Kaplan. University of Minnesota Press, 1994, pp. 17–20, 23–28. Copyright 1995 by the Regents of the University of Minnesota. Notes have been renumbered.

sisterhood model of missionary work, of intervention and salvation, is clearly tied to the older models of center–periphery relations.[4] As these models have become obsolete in the face of proliferating, multiple centers and peripheries, we need new analyses of how gender works in the dynamic of globalization and the countermeasures of new nationalisms, and ethnic and racial fundamentalisms. Feminists can begin to map these scattered hegemonies and link diverse local practices to formulate a transnational sec of solidarities. For instance, we need to examine fundamentalisms around the world and seek to understand why Muslim fundamentalism appears in the media today as the primary progenitor of oppressive conditions for women when Christian, Jewish, Hindu, Confucian, and other forms of extreme fundamentalisms exert profound controls over women's lives.

What is the relationship between transnational economies and the intensification of religious fundamentalism? For example, when the United States gave billions to General Zia of Pakistan to fight the Soviets in Afghanistan, the United States propped up a regime that was inimical to women. U.S. feminists need to fight against this kind of aid on their home ground instead of abstractly condemning Islam as the center of patriarchal oppression. Simultaneously, we need to examine how the importance of Christian fundamentalism within the Republican party in the United States affects the lives of millions of women worldwide through funding and development practices that structure reproductive and other politics. Transnational feminist approaches link the impact of such policies on women on public assistance in the United States and women who have little agency in their dealing with U.S.-sponsored clinics and health centers that have been established in the so-called peripheries. The concept of multiple peripheries, therefore, can link directly the domestic policies of a world power such as the United States to its foreign policies. Transnational feminist alliances can work to change these policies only when such congruencies are accounted for and transformed into the basis for multiple, allied, solidarity projects. . . .

In an important article in *Feminist Review*, "Washing Our Linen: One Year of Women Against Fundamentalism," Clara Connolly argues that fundamentalism is the "mobilization of religious affiliation for political ends" with detrimental results on women's lives.[5]

Connolly chronicles the formation of the Women Against Fundamentalism group as a coalition of Asian, Black, and other ethnic minority feminists that struggles against every form of fundamentalism but, most importantly, critiques the Christian dominance of the English nation-state and the place of multiculturalism within it. Women Against Fundamentalism target "the *state* rather than the fundamentalists of any religion" and seek not only the complete separation of church and state but a "measure of legal and social protection against the efforts of fundamentalists to restrict our life-choices and sexualities."[6]

Many fundamentalist interests in states that have been through nationalist, supposedly decolonizing struggles present themselves as anti-Western and antimodernization even though such a West/non-West opposition is too simplistic a duality. Islamic fundamentalism, as Deniz Kandiyoti argues, has been a "constant vehicle for popular classes to express their alienation from 'Westernized' elites."[7] Yet certain "fundamentalist" dictums and beliefs are hardly "authentic" expressions of indigenous Islamic culture. For example, the well-publicized Islamic laws that prevent the prosecution of husbands who murder adulterous wives do not date from time immemorial but are borrowed from the nineteenth-century French Penal Code.[8] What needs to be examined in light of such transnational hegemonic "borrowings" are the ways in which various patriarchies collaborate and borrow from each other in order to reinforce specific practices that are oppressive to women.

Feminists have great stakes in understanding and theorizing these distinct fundamentalist formations. In the United States, for example, feminists need to examine how fundamentalist agendas pervade supposedly secular states, enabling Christian doctrines to masquerade as law. A transnational feminist practice, therefore, examines the ways in which Christian fundamentalism in different countries has an impact on women's lives in different ways, just as does Islamic, Jewish, or Hindu fundamentalism in different groups and locations. Each fundamentalism uses and disciplines women in different ways. As a result, we must examine the similarities and differences between anti-abortion politics sponsored by fundamentalists in the United States and the crackdown on reproductive rights in formerly socialist countries in Europe. In addition, the relationship between an entity like the Vatican and the practices of social control in Latin America may vary from the Baptist-oriented, U.S. TV evangelism that permeates the same geographical region.

We need to learn more about the varied ways in which a state becomes fundamentalist and how women fare in those locations. Although there are now twenty-three countries that can be considered to be Muslim fundamentalist, such states as Pakistan, Saudi Arabia, and Iran differ greatly in their political and global affiliations.[9] For instance, against the opposition of many women, Saudi Arabia gives aid to groups in Bangladesh that are fundamentalist, hoping to assist in the creation of an Islamic state.

Such transnational links between religious and state formations are the least clearly formulated. As Sara Diamond points out in her book on Christian fundamentalism, "many social science studies of right-wing movements ignore the national and international political context in which movement organizations operate."[10] U.S. Christian fundamentalism has an increasingly global reach through the development of televangelist broadcasting in Latin America and the Middle East. In addition, Diamond describes the comprehensive attempts by large evangelical denominations to win the allegiance of recent Latino immigrants to the United States who are particularly vulnerable to offers of assistance with immigration, language acquisition, and other valuable services. Spanish-language broadcasts "offering material success and a ready-made Christian 'family' to born-again believers," Diamond warns, are designed to increase dramatically the number of "Hispanic" churches throughout the decade.[11] In addition to studies on this domestic phenomenon, we need to examine the impact of the religious right on U.S. foreign policy. Diamond's work on the links between Christian fundamentalism and contra aid during the 1980s, for example, points the way for complex, multi-leveled, and interdisciplinary work on the transnational politics of cultures of fundamentalism.

Another coalition organized to address such transnational feminist issues is the international group constructing the Women Living Under Muslim Laws dossiers. By collecting dossiers on the condition of women in various Islamic countries, the women in this group gather information on the diverse political and social implications of Islamic laws as they are carried

out in various countries. For instance, in some countries it is mainly poor women who feel the force of these laws while upper-class women have various means to escape them. Thus, these dossiers reveal that there is not one homogeneous Muslim world. Rather, as the introduction to Dossier 3 states:

> while similarities exist, the notion of a uniform Muslim world is a misconception imposed on us. We have erroneously been led to believe that the only way of "being" is the one we currently live in each of our contexts. Depriving us of even dreaming of a different reality is one of the most debilitating forms of oppression we suffer.[12]

What concerns this group of women is the widespread promulgation of the view that there is one interpretation of Islam and one way of living that reality as Muslim women. Yet, in only one instance of resistance to fundamentalism, Bangladesh women have organized by remembering what happened in Iran, where women participated in the revolution against the Shah only to find themselves outside the power structures once an Islamic state became established. One has only to look at the various essays in Deniz Kandiyoti's collection *Women, Islam, and the State* in order to see how differently Islamization becomes state law in various countries as it interacts with specific historical conditions, how varied the political interests are that are fostering Islamization, and the specific purposes that each of these groups of interests has in order to create Islamic states. As Kandiyoti writes:

> The legitimacy crises engendered by these processes have favored the rise of organized oppositional movements with Islamist platforms, as well as attempts at social control by governments emphasizing their own commitment to orthodoxy. The arena in which these political projects can most easily be played out and achieve a measure of consensus is . . . the control of women.[13]

As Kandiyoti argues, the political interest Islamic fundamentalist groups have in common is that of basing their movements on the control of women; how and why they push this goal is specific and varied. The purpose of the dossiers is to record this variety of experiences. The documents that comprise the dossiers are not only collected by women in the countries themselves, they are used in any number of ways, including the documentation of oppressive conditions that can aid in some women's efforts to argue for refugee status. Reinterpreting the Koran, providing new translations and interpretations is, therefore, an important part of this movement. Such practices, of course, run counter to the various fundamentalist groups that wish to create a Muslim homogeneity. Therefore it can be argued that these practices refuse to play into the hands of both the U.S. "democratic, free-world" agenda as well as the Islamic fundamentalist states and groups. It is the collusion of interests and not their "authentic" homogeneity that needs to be examined, both in the patriarchies and in the groups that oppose them.

These examples suggest roles for women everywhere to play in the politics of solidarity in transnational feminist practices. Women in the United States can work on opposing various state policies that promote and collude with fundamentalisms (Christian, Muslim, Jewish, Hindu, or any other). Women from so-called minority communities can work to form alliances that oppose all these fundamentalisms (including Christian formations in the West) and to resist the agendas of a racist state. These activities do not collaborate with Eurocentric feminism, nor do they work for the patriarchal power groups within their own communities. Instead, they create affiliations between women from different communities who are interested in examining and working against the links that support and connect very diverse patriarchal practices.

An example of such a transnational affiliative group in the United States is the coalition of women from very diverse Asian communities in the San Francisco area who have organized the Asian Women's Shelter.[14] This group examines how the so-called cultural defense is used against women in the U.S. courts today. In focusing on what counts as "cultural defense," the group examines the implementation of this argument during sentencing for crimes committed by men from minority groups against women from minority communities, or committed by minority women who internalize and act upon the patriarchal ideologies of their particular cultures. It is part of this group's agenda to explore the links between who can define "culture," who can be legitimated as "expert" testifiers, and what kind of problematic, misogynist notions underlie this kind of authoritative legal testimony. The variety of "cultural defense" arguments highlights the diversity of the communities; from the Hmong woman who

reports rape while the man involved claims marriage-by-capture, to the Japanese-American woman who attempts "*oyaku-shinju*" (parent–child suicide) in response to her husband's infidelity and is then accused of the murder of her children. In their analysis of the "cultural defense" argument, the Asian Women's Shelter group demonstrates how a patriarchal, Judeo-Christian legal system reinforces and institutionalizes racist stereotypes about Asian women rather than differentiating between the ethnic, regional, caste, and class practices of women of different cultures.

The Asian Women's Shelter group in San Francisco works from the assumption that women from diverse Asian cultures are constructed differently as women even though there are links between the ways that their communities and the dominant culture collaborate (although not always consciously) to oppress them. For example, in arguing that the "battered woman" syndrome is culture-specific rather than cross-cultural, the group is theorizing how U.S. immigration laws, historical circumstances, and cultural responses all figure in interpretations of domestic violence. In identifying these collaborations between powerful interests and by working collaboratively themselves, the members of the group can help to make changes in their communities. Although support for this project has not come from those feminists who view Asian culture as a monolithic category nor from women who participate in ethnic nationalist agendas, the example of such groups as Women Against Fundamentalism has been helpful in understanding how collaborative coalitions can be formed and maintained.

All three of the groups we have discussed acknowledge differences in women's lives as well as links between transnational power structures. Emphasizing a variety of cultural hegemonies, they are neither homogenizing nor relativistic in their use of the category "woman." Above all, how these groups use the term "woman" recalls Tani Barlow's argument that this category enables both oppression and opposition. Barlow's essay examines how the term "woman" comes into use in China in a variety of ways: through the state, through religious fundamentalism, or as an oppositional term. Barlow argues that "woman" as a universal term only came into use with colonialism and became a disciplinary category during state-deployed decolonization. As Barlow suggests, if the Chinese state's movements toward modernity can be seen in the creation of a category called "woman" that brought together all female persons, it did so also as a disciplinary, modernizing practice. Studies such as Barlow's clearly demonstrate that universalizing, anti-poststructuralist, anti-postmodernist movements toward an albeit nonessentialist but universal category called woman allows state power and the power of fundamentalist groups to mobilize forces against all female persons.

Given contemporary global conditions, transnational feminist practices will emerge only through questioning the conditions of postmodernity. Rather than attempt to account for or definitively circumscribe either "theory" or "practice," the essays in this collection engage political and narrative strategies as they proliferate in transnational cultures. The first section of the book, "Gender, Nation, and Critiques of Modernity," problematizes the relationship between feminism and nationalism, asking how feminist practices can exist outside certain master narratives. The second section, "Global-Colonial Limits," points toward feminist practices that acknowledge the scattered hegemonies that intersect discourses of gender. The essays in each section provide varied political engagements while deconstructing monolithic categories and mythic binaries. We hope this collection provokes further discussion and debate to rework the terms of theory and practice of gender across cultural divides.

(1994)

NOTES

1. See in particular Chandra Talpade Mohanty's critique of Robin Morgan's *Sisterhood is Global*, "The Politics of Experience," 33.

2. Kumkum Sangari and Sudesh Vaid, "*Recasting Women*: An Introduction," in *Recasting Women*, 18.

3. See Karie King. "Lesbianism in Multi-National Reception: Global Gay Formations and Local Homosexualities." *Camera Obscura* 28 (1992): 79–99; Lourdes Arguelles and B. Ruby Rich, "Homosexuality, Homophobia, and Revolution: Notes toward an Understanding of the Cuban Lesbian and Gay Male Experience," Part I. *Signs* 9 (1984): 683–99, and Part II, *Signs* 11 (Autumn 1985): 120–36; Ana Maria Alonso and Maria Teresa Koreck, "Silences: 'Hispanics,' AIDS, and Sexual Practices," *differences* 1, no. 1 (Winter 1989): 101–24; and Lourdes Arguelles, *Homosexualities and Transnational Migration* (forthcoming).

4. Enloe, *Bananas, Beaches, and Bases*.

5. Clara Connolly, "Washing Our Linen: One Year of Women Against Fundmentalism," *Feminist Review* 37 (Spring 1991): 69.

6. Ibid., 76.

7. Deniz Kandiyoti, "Introduction," *Women, Islam and the State* (Philadelphia: Temple University Press, 1991), 8.

8. Melissa Spatz, "A 'Lesser' Crime A: Comparative Study of Legal Defenses for Men Who Kill Their Wives," *Columbia Journal of Law and Social Problems* 24 (1991): 600.

9. Spatz, "A 'Lesser' Crime," 597.

10. Sara Diamond, *Spiritual Warfare* (Boston: South End Press, 1989), 48.

11. Ibid., 42.

12. Cited in Pragna Patel, "Review Essay: Alert for Action," *Feminist Review* 37 (Spring 1991): 95–105.

13. Deniz Kandiyoti, "Introduction," 17.

14. We are indebted to the Cultural Defense Study group for their analysis of how cultural defense works in the U.S. courts. Thanks to Jacqueline Agtuca, Deanna Jang, Mimi Kim, Debbie Lee, Jayne Lee, Lata Mani, Leni Marin, Beckie Masaki, Alexandra Saur, and Leti Volpp. In particular, we would like to thank Jayne Lee for sharing her research and her work.

"BEIJING DECLARATION"

1. We, the Governments participating in the Fourth World Conference on Women,

2. Gathered here in Beijing in September 1995, the year of the fiftieth anniversary of the founding of the United Nations,

3. Determined to advance the goals of equality, development and peace for all women everywhere in the interest of all humanity,

4. Acknowledging the voices of all women everywhere and taking note of the diversity of women and their roles and circumstances, honoring the women who paved the way and inspired by the hope present in the world's youth,

5. Recognize that the status of women has advanced in some important respects in the past decade but that progress has been uneven, inequalities between women and men have persisted and major obstacles remain, with serious consequences for the well-being of all people,

6. Also recognize that this situation is exacerbated by the increasing poverty that is affecting the lives of the majority of the world's people, in particular women and children, with origins in both the national and international domains,

7. Dedicate ourselves unreservedly to addressing these constraints and obstacles and thus enhancing further the advancement and empowerment of women all over the world, and agree that this requires urgent action in the spirit of determination, hope, cooperation and solidarity, now and to carry us forward into the next century.

We reaffirm our commitment to:

8. The equal rights and inherent human dignity of women and men and other purposes and principles enshrined in the Charter of the United Nations, to the Universal Declaration of Human Rights and other international human rights instruments, in particular the Convention on the Elimination of All Forms of Discrimination against Women and the Convention on the Rights of the Child, as well as the Declaration on the Elimination of Violence against Women and the Declaration on the Right to Development;

9. Ensure the full implementation of the human rights of women and of the girl child as an inalienable, integral and indivisible part of all human rights and fundamental freedoms;

10. Build on consensus and progress made at previous United Nations conferences and summits—on women in Nairobi in 1985, on children in New York in 1990, on environment and development in Rio de Janeiro in1992, on human rights in Vienna in 1993, on population and development in Cairo in 1994 and on social development in Copenhagen in 1995 with the objective of achieving equality, development and peace;

11. Achieve the full and effective implementation of the Nairobi Forward-looking Strategies for the Advancement of Women;

12. The empowerment and advancement of women, including the right to freedom of thought, conscience, religion and belief, thus contributing to the moral, ethical, spiritual and intellectual needs of women and men, individually or in community with others and thereby guaranteeing them the possibility of realizing their full potential in society and shaping their lives in accordance with their own aspirations.

We are convinced that:

13. Women's empowerment and their full participation on the basis of equality in all spheres of society, including participation in the decision-making

United Nations Fourth World Conference on Women. http://www.un.org/womenwatch/daw/beijing/platform/declar.htm

process and access to power, are fundamental for the achievement of equality, development and peace;

14. Women's rights are human rights;

15. Equal rights, opportunities and access to resources, equal sharing of responsibilities for the family by men and women, and a harmonious partnership between them are critical to their well-being and that of their families as well as to the consolidation of democracy;

16. Eradication of poverty based on sustained economic growth, social development, environmental protection and social justice requires the involvement of women in economic and social development, equal opportunities and the full and equal participation of women and men as agents and beneficiaries of people-centered sustainable development;

17. The explicit recognition and reaffirmation of the right of all women to control all aspects of their health, in particular their own fertility, is basic to their empowerment;

18. Local, national, regional and global peace is attainable and is inextricably linked with the advancement of women, who are a fundamental force for leadership, conflict resolution and the promotion of lasting peace at all levels;

19. It is essential to design, implement and monitor, with the full participation of women, effective, efficient and mutually reinforcing gender-sensitive policies and programmes, including development policies and programmes, at all levels that will foster the empowerment and advancement of women;

20. The participation and contribution of all actors of civil society, particularly women's groups and networks and other non-governmental organizations and community-based organizations, with full respect for their autonomy, in cooperation with Governments, are important to the effective implementation and follow-up of the Platform for Action;

21. The implementation of the Platform for Action requires commitment from Governments and the international community. By making national and international commitments for action, including those made at the Conference, Governments and the international community recognize the need to take priority action for the empowerment and advancement of women.

We are determined to:

22. Intensify efforts and actions to achieve the goals of the Nairobi Forward-looking Strategies for the Advancement of Women by the end of this century;

23. Ensure the full enjoyment by women and the girl child of all human rights and fundamental freedoms and take effective action against violations of these rights and freedoms;

24. Take all necessary measures to eliminate all forms of discrimination against women and the girl child and remove all obstacles to gender equality and the advancement and empowerment of women;

25. Encourage men to participate fully in all actions towards equality;

26. Promote women's economic independence, including employment, and eradicate the persistent and increasing burden of poverty on women by addressing the structural causes of poverty through changes uneconomic, ensuring equal access for all women, including those in rural areas, as vital development agents, to productive resources, opportunities and public services;

27. Promote people-centred sustainable development, including sustained economic growth, through the provision of basic education, life-long education, literacy and training, and primary health care for girls and women;

28. Take positive steps to ensure peace for the advancement of women and, recognizing the leading role that women have played in the peace movement, work actively towards general and complete disarmament under strict and effective international control, and support negotiations on the conclusion, without delay, of a universal and multilaterally and effectively verifiable comprehensive nuclear-test-ban treaty which contributes to nuclear disarmament and the prevention of the proliferation of nuclear weapons in all its aspects;

29. Prevent and eliminate all forms of violence against women and girls;

30. Ensure equal access to and equal treatment of women and men in education and health care and enhance women's sexual and reproductive health as well as education;

31. Promote and protect all human rights of women and girls;

32. Intensify efforts to ensure equal enjoyment of all human rights and fundamental freedoms for all women and girls who face multiple barriers to their empowerment and advancement because of such factors as their race, age, language, ethnicity, culture, religion, or disability, or because they are indigenous people;

33. Ensure respect for international law, including humanitarian law, in order to protect women and girls in particular;

34. Develop the fullest potential of girls and women of all ages, ensure their full and equal participation in building a better world for all and enhance their role in the development process.

We are determined to:

35. Ensure women's equal access to economic resources, including land, credit, science and technology, vocational training, information, communication and markets, as a means to further the advancement and empowerment of women and girls, including through the enhancement of their capacities to enjoy the benefits of equal access to these resources, interalia, by means of international cooperation;

36. Ensure the success of the Platform for Action, which will require a strong commitment on the part of Governments, international organizations and institutions at all levels. We are deeply convinced that economic development, social development and environmental protection are interdependent and mutually reinforcing components of sustainable development, which is the framework for our efforts to achieve a higher quality of life for all people. Equitable social development that recognizes empowering the poor, particularly women living in poverty, to utilize environmental resources sustainably is a necessary foundation for sustainable development. We also recognize that broad-based and sustained economic growth in the context of sustainable development is necessary to sustain social development and social justice. The success of the Platform for Action will also require adequate mobilization of resources at the national and international levels as well as new and additional resources to the developing countries from all available funding mechanisms, including multilateral, bilateral and private sources for the advancement of women; financial resources to strengthen the capacity of national, sub regional, regional and international institutions; a commitment to equal rights, equal responsibilities and equal opportunities and to the equal participation of women and men in all national, regional and international bodies and policy-making processes; and the establishment or strengthening of mechanisms at all levels for accountability to the world's women;

37. Ensure also the success of the Platform for Action in countries with economies in transition, which will require continued international cooperation and assistance;

38. We hereby adopt and commit ourselves as Governments to implement the following Platform for Action, ensuring that a gender perspective is reflected in all our policies and programmes. We urge the United Nations system, regional and international financial institutions, other relevant regional and international institutions and all women and men, as well as non-governmental organizations, with full respect for their autonomy, and all sectors of civil society, in cooperation with Governments, to fully commit themselves and contribute to the implementation of this Platform for Action.

(1995)

FROM *DISLOCATING CULTURES*
Identities, Traditions, and Third-World Feminism

INTRODUCTION

My aim in this essay is to explore representations of "Third-World traditions" that seem to replicate what I shall call a "colonialist stance" toward Third-World cultures, to explain why these representations are both problematic and "colonialist," and to describe other representations of "Third-World traditions" that present a very different picture of what these "traditions" are. To make my task of exploring "colonialist representation" manageable, I shall confine myself to a close examination of the discussion of the "Indian tradition" of *sati* or widow-immolation in Mary Daly's chapter on "Indian Sutee" in her book *Gyn/Ecology: The Metaethics of Radical Feminism*. The first section attempts to show both what is wrong with Daly's representation of *sati* and how these problems replicate a "colonialist stance." In the second section, I attempt to contrast the notion of "tradition" that is operative in Daly's chapter to a more *historical* and *political* understanding of "tradition" that is at work in recent historical work on *sati* in the colonial period. I wish to argue that these historically and politically grounded understandings of Third-World "traditions" avoid "colonialist" representations of these "traditions," and provide an analysis that is more useful for a feminist understanding of the issues raised by such "traditions." The third section explores contemporary Indian feminist contestations around *sati*, with the aim of showing that the political issues raised by *sati* are far different from, and more complex than, the picture suggested by a reading of Daly's text. In the concluding section of the essay,

I look at some of the broader implications of these contemporary Indian feminist contestations of *sati* for feminist politics, both in Western and Third-World national contexts.

While I focus on the problematic representations of one particular "Third-World practice" in one specific Western feminist text, my analysis of the representation of *sati* in Daly's chapter is motivated by the belief that similar problems occur in other Western feminist representations of issues affecting women in Third-World contexts. Ahistorical and apolitical Western feminist understandings of "Third-World traditions" continue to appear, for instance, in more contemporary work on issues such as *sati* and dowry-murder, and in discussions relating to human rights-based interventions into "cultural practices" affecting Third-World women. I have no desire, however, to suggest that these problems are characteristic of *all* work on Third-World women done by Western feminists, or are somehow "representative" of Western feminist work on Third-World women. Understanding the nature of the "colonialist stance," with respect to representations of "Third-World traditions," is additionally important because these problems are, I believe, not exclusive to academic feminist writing but perhaps even more common in general Western public understandings of "Third-World cultures," "Third-World traditions," and "Third-World women's problems." I approach my project in this paper both as someone who has learnt a great deal from many Western feminist works, during my time in

India as well as my years in the United States, and as someone who has had problems with some Western feminist analyses and perspectives. I also approach this task as someone who is particularly indebted to the critiques of mainstream Western feminism generated by feminists of color.

Colonialism as an historical phenomenon does not only connect and divide Westerners from subjects in various Third-World nations in a series of complicated and unequal relationships. It also connects and divides mainstream Western subjects from Others in their *own* societies whose unequal relationships to the mainstream are themselves products of Western colonial history. Colonial history is not only the history of Western domination of "non-Western" populations, but is also a history of the creation of racially distinct and oppressed populations within Western countries such as the United States. Thus several aspects of "colonialist" representation that I analyze are, I believe, potentially applicable to mainstream Western feminist representations of the "cultures" and "traditions" of Third-World nation-states as well as to representations of the "cultures" and "traditions" of Third-World communities in Western contexts. However, this paper is an attempt to illuminate aspects of "colonialist representation" by focusing on the colonialist representations of the *specific* practice of *sati*. I leave to my readers the task of assessing whether my analysis of colonialist representation helps illuminate similar problems in other Western and Western feminist representations of different "cultural" practices pertaining to Third-World women.

Many mainstream Western feminist perspectives have been criticized by Third-World feminists for excluding or marginalizing from their analyses and agendas the interests and concerns of women who are additionally marginalized in terms of class, race, ethnicity, and sexual orientation. It has been argued that such exclusions not only generate inadequate feminist theories but also result in political agendas and public policies that fail to be adequately responsive to the interests of women from these marginalized groups. However, exclusion, marginalization, and lack of attention have not been the only source of unhappiness with the projects and perspectives of such mainstream Western feminist analyses. In this essay I wish to focus on a different set of problems, ones that have less to do with *exclusion* than with the manner and the mode of *inclusion*.

The terms "exclusion" and "inclusion" are not, in one sense, pure opposites. Since feminist analyses that did not explicitly concern themselves with the applicability and relevance of their analyses to "women on the margins" often perceived themselves as applicable to *all* women, that form of "exclusion" was simultaneously a problematic form of "inclusion." Attending specifically to problems affecting women in Third-World contexts, as Daly does, is a *form* of "inclusion" and is, in one respect, preferable to simply *assuming* that one's feminist perspective applies to *all* women. However, the terms in which such analyses are carried out might still be embedded in theoretical frameworks and conceptual assumptions that have problematic implications. Thus, while Daly's work addresses "Third-World women's issues," I shall argue that it does so in a manner that misrepresents what is at stake, and that these misrepresentations replicate some common and problematic Western understandings of Third-World contexts and communities.

While I focus on "colonialist representation" in one Western feminist text, I would like to insist that the characteristic of "being a colonialist representation" does *not* require that the representation be "produced" by a Western subject. A representation that is "colonialist" would be so when produced by anyone, including Third-World men or women. A "colonialist representation," as I wish to use the term, is one that replicates problematic aspects of Western representations of Third-World nations and communities, aspects that have their roots in the history of colonization. Precisely because of this history and its complex effects on Third-World subjects, it is hardly surprising that one can find "colonialist representations" produced by members of Third-World communities, a point I shall return to. Why then do I focus on colonialist representations in a Western feminist text? The answer is simple. I believe that "colonialist representation" by Western feminists poses an obstacle to the urgent need for feminists to form "communities of resistance" across boundaries of class, race, ethnicity, and national background.

I turn to a critical examination of Mary Daly's chapter on "Indian Suttee" to show how Daly's misrepresentations of the practice of *sati* replicate aspects of a "colonialist stance" toward Third-World contexts. I have chosen to use this particular text for two reasons. It is a text that both provides good examples of various facets of a "colonialist stance" and that sharply contrasts with representations of *sati* in recent work by feminists of Indian background. My choice of text is *not* driven by a desire to "attack" Mary Daly in particular; that these problems are *not unique* to Daly's work is precisely why they are worth discussing.

Like a good deal of Western feminist writing on Third-World women, Daly's chapter on *sati* is both directed at, and likely to be predominantly read by, Western readers unfamiliar with the historical, social, political, and cultural contexts of the practice being discussed. Such contextual unfamiliarity is likely to enable problematic representations to be accepted uncritically and without awareness that the text contains an interrelated cluster of misrepresentations that collaboratively constitute a "colonialist stance." Understanding various facets of what a "colonialist stance" involves might help readers approach such texts more cautiously and critically. I invite readers who are ignorant about the Indian context to read Daly's chapter on *sati* before proceeding to read the rest of my analysis, so that they may judge for themselves the difference that such awareness might make. . . .

THE LIMITATIONS OF THE MISSIONARY POSITION: THE 'COLONIALIST STANCE' IN MARY DALY'S DISCUSSION OF "INDIAN SUTTEE"

I. THE "COLONIALIST STANCE" AND THE ERASING OF HISTORY

Daly's chapter on "Indian Suttee" begins by excluding the issue of history and historical change. After four lines of text that seem intended to introduce the practice of *sati* to Western readers, the rest of the first page of this chapter consists of an extended footnote that also takes up a third of the next page. In this footnote, Daly begins by saying, "Although suttee was legally banned in 1829 . . . it should not be imagined that the lot of most Indian women has changed dramatically since then." Daly's footnote goes on to refer to contemporary incidents of the ill-treatment of Indian widows, dowry-harassment and dowry-murders, high rates of female malnutrition and female maternal mortality, and higher mortality rates for Indian women in general, and cites recent Indian publications and newspaper reports as sources for her information.

What do I find problematic about this introduction? Daly's introduction leads readers to believe that all of the several problems mentioned in the footnote exist in the same "temporal frame" as the problem of *sati*, which is the central topic of Daly's chapter. The footnote conveys the impression that *sati* as well as the various problems mentioned in the footnote, have all afflicted "Indian women" in the past and that each continues to afflict them today. What tend to vanish in Daly's introductory framing are the specific historical contexts and time frames of the various problems strung together on this list as "problems affecting Indian women." Neither in the introduction nor in the rest of the chapter is the reader informed that the practice of *sati* was never a widespread practice in all "Hindu" communities, let alone "Indian" communities. Neither is it made clear that incidents of *sati* were more common in the *past* than they are at present, or that incidents of *sati* were *extremely rare* by 1978, when Daly's book was published. Although there have been a few incidents of *sati* recently, incidents whose political import I will discuss later in the essay, Daly's chapter is highly misleading in creating the impression that widow immolation is a widespread and ongoing practice that threatens the lives of many Indian women today. . . .

Daly's failure to historically contextualize the practice of *sati* is compounded by her linkage of *sati*, in her footnote, to contemporary phenomena such as dowry-murder, producing a problematic effect that I call an "erasing of history." This linkage of *sati* and dowry-murder has the effect of simultaneously suggesting that the *historical* phenomenon of *sati* is an ongoing "Indian tradition" and that the *contemporary* phenomenon of dowry-murder is a longstanding "traditional" practice. As a result, two historically distinct phenomena are *each* misleadingly portrayed in a manner that suggests that they are both instances of "traditional practices that afflict contemporary Indian women." (Even though dowry itself is a "traditional" institution of longstanding, dowry-murders seem to be a fairly recent phenomenon, one where the number of incidents seem to be *increasing*. Dowry-murder is thus not a "traditional" practice, neither being endorsed by "tradition" nor seeming to have taken place in noticeable numbers until recent times.) Daly's juxtaposition of *sati* and dowry-murder suggests a common temporal framework that these phenomena do not in fact share, since one is a virtually extinct practice and the other a fairly recent problem. . . .

Daly's introduction operates to convey an impression of the "Duration" of the practices of *sati* and of dowry-murder without any attention to "Change"—to the historical contexts of their emergence or decline. Daly's "erasing of history" hence contributes to reinforcing problematic colonial (and still persistent) Western pictures of Third-World countries as "places without history." The only function of the Present in such representations of Third-World contexts is to testify to the stubborn persistence of the Past in the guise of "unchanging traditions." Daly's discussion suggests an India whose present is possessed by the past, a place whose contemporary reality is neither one where past practices yield to the effects of political contestation and social change, nor one that generates new and complex problems of its own. All patriarchal practices in the Indian context seem *perennially in place*— Unchanging Legacies of the Past. One does not get the sense that some historical practices have virtually disappeared (as with *sati*) nor the sense that new problems, such as dowry-murders, have arisen in the course of modernization and social change. Given Daly's framing, Indian women seem to go up in flames—on the funeral pyres of their husbands and in the "kitchen accidents" that are the characteristic mode of dowry-murder—without historical pause.

Daly's representation of *sati* replicates a "colonialist stance" because it reproduces a Western tendency to portray Third-World contexts as dominated by the grip of "traditional practices" that insulate these contexts from the effects of historical change. I am *not* arguing that Daly *deliberately intends* to collude with this colonialist picture of Third-World contexts. Daly's mode of representation in her chapter on *sati* is in keeping with the overall project of her book, which seems motivated by a desire to testify to the transhistorical and global persistence of patriarchal institutions and practices. However, while her overall discussion of patriarchy in Western contexts tends to convey the picture that "practices change but Patriarchy goes on," the discussion in her chapter on *sati* suggests that Third-World patriarchy goes on differently, without any substantial historical changes in the practices that guarantee its regime. In short, Daly's overall picture suggests that Western patriarchy persists within and despite historical change, while Third-World patriarchy

seems to persist without significant historical change. Especially when framed by Daly's astonishing suggestion that "the lot of Indian women" has not changed substantially since 1829, *sati* and all the other problems affecting Indian women that Daly mentions seem to be problems rooted in "Ancient Indian Patriarchal Traditions," which have somehow managed to remain entirely insulated from the tremendous changes of the last hundred fifty years.

2. DANGEROUS LACKS OF DETAIL AND THE POLITICS OF SPECIFICITY

Daly's account of *sati* not only erases its *temporal* context but also blurs other important *contextual* features of the practice with respect to its variations across class, caste, religion, and geographical location. Alternately characterizing *sati* as a "Hindu rite" and as an "Indian rite," Daly notes that "at first, suttee was restricted to the wives of princes and warriors" and goes on to cite a Western scholar on its spread to "others of lower caste." This facet of her discussion has the effect of suggesting that although *sati* had its origin in a particular social group, it eventually spread widely so as to become a practice prevalent virtually across *all* Indian castes. What Daly fails to mention is that *sati* was a practice limited to particular castes and specific regions of India, and a practice unknown in many Indian communities. Daly completely fails to make clear that *sati* was not practiced by *all* Hindu communities, and was never practiced by various non-Hindu communities in the Indian population. (Nor does Daly seem to register that if in fact the practice began among communities of "princes and warriors," it must have also "spread to those of higher caste" given that a large number of *satis* in British colonial times took place among the *Brahmin* community of Bengal!)

My motivation in stressing the fact of "limited practice" is not to vindicate "Indian Culture" by pointing out that not all Indian communities immolated widows. I believe that these contextual features of incidence are important for quite different reasons. Attending to these specificities of incidence serves to counter a colonialist Western tendency to represent Third-World contexts as uniform and monolithic spaces, with no important internal cultural differentiations, complexities, and variations. While Western contexts are represented both as spaces of historical change and internal complexity,

Third-World contexts tend to be portrayed as places where "time stands still" and where "one culture rules all." The effacement of *cultural change* within historical time, which I previously discussed, collaborates with the effacement of *cultural variations* across communities and regions to suggest a "Third-World culture" that is "frozen" with respect to both Space and Time.

Failure to attend to features of contextual variation and heterogeneity within Third-World communities produces two sharp contrasts between how Western women and Third-World women are often represented by Western feminists. First, largely as a result of critiques of mainstream Western feminism by feminists of color, there is a great deal more caution about generalizing about categories such as "American women" or "European women" without attending to specificities such as class, race, ethnicity, sexual orientation, and religion. However, this lesson of caution about generalization is often quickly forgotten when it comes to "Third-World Women," a point forcefully made by Chandra Mohanty with respect to a recent publication entitled *Women of Africa: Roots of Oppression*, when she asks, "In the 1980's, is it possible to imagine writing a book entitled *Women of Europe: Roots of Oppression?*"

The second difference is that problems that affect particular groups of Third-World women are more often assumed to be primarily, if not entirely, results of an imagined and unitary complex called "their Traditions/ Religions/Cultures"—where these terms are represented as virtually synonymous with each other. As a result, problems that have very little to do with traditions, religions, or culture are represented as if they are the effects of this imagined complex, reinforcing "ethnic" stereotypes and completely misrepresenting the real nature of these problems. An interesting example of this phenomenon is provided by Radhika Parameswaran's discussion of the *Dallas Observer* coverage of the murder of an Indian Christian woman, a member of the diasporic Indian community in Texas, who was set ablaze by her husband after a bitter family dispute. According to Parameswaran, the coverage was studded with references to both *sati* and dowry-murder, with a headline that indicated Aleyamma Mathew to be a "victim of her culture." What is astounding about the *Dallas Observer* coverage is that the references to sati and to dowry-murder were entirely gratuitous, given that Aleyamma's death had nothing to do with either

sati or dowry, and everything to do with her husband's alcoholism, history of abusiveness, and family conflicts over whether to return to India! . . .

Daly's unnuanced and totalizing picture of "Indian culture and traditions" contributes to an ongoing practice of "blaming culture" for problems in Third-World contexts and communities, a practice that sharply contrasts with "noncultural" accounts of problems where mainstream Western subjects bear culpability. . . .

Discussions such as those found in Daly's chapter on *sati* represent Third-World contexts not only as "places without History" but as "places suffused by Unchanging Religious Worldviews." These two axes of (mis)representation are connected to each other in important ways. The portrayal of Third-World contexts as "places without History" proceeds by depicting them as places governed instead by Unchanging Religious Traditions, whose very lack of susceptibility to change appears as a key symptom of the absence of "History." The unnuanced resort to "Religion" as a category of explanation for practices oppressive to Third-World women constitutes part of a "colonialist stance" toward Third-World contexts because of an intimate linkage between such explanatory uses of "Religion" and colonialist depictions of Third-World contexts as "places without History." . . .

It is important for Western feminists engaged in scholarship on Third-World women to remember that *colonial* discourses that positioned Third-World cultures "outside history" have dangerous echoes in the discourses of *contemporary* religious-fundamentalist political movements, which have their own reasons for misportraying certain practices and traditions as "timeless" elements of "National Culture." They also need to attend to the fact that "an insistence on History" is often crucial to feminists and others in these Third-World contexts who are engaged in politically contesting such fundamentalist views. For example, historical data about *sati*—about its historical origins, the increases and decreases in the practice at various historical moments, the specificities of its incidence in particular classes, castes, and geographical areas–is critical to Indian feminist contestations of Hindu fundamentalist attempts to portray *sati* as an unchanging and widely endorsed "Indian Tradition." Daly-type misrepresentations of *sati* are not simple mistakes but constitute *dangerous lacks of detail*. Western feminist analyses that replicate such problems often only add to "the brown woman's burden"—functioning as obstacles rather than as assets to ongoing Third-World feminist political agendas. . . .

DIFFERENCES OF "CULTURE" AND DIFFERENCES IN "CULTURE AS EXPLANATION"

I would like to end by considering an interesting asymmetry that exists between explanations of violence against women in "mainstream Western culture" and such "death by culture" explanations of violence against women specific to "Third-World cultural contexts." The best way I can think of to point to this asymmetry is the following kind of "thought experiment," which is also a kind of wicked fantasy whose "fantastical" elements are actually more interesting than its wickedness. Imagine yourself meeting a young Indian woman journalist who, after reading Bumiller's book, has decided to retaliate by working on a book entitled, *May You Be the Loser of A Hundred Pounds: A Journey Among the Women of the United States.* The young journalist plans to travel throughout the United States talking to an assortment of American women, trying to learn about "American women and American culture." The chapters she hopes to include in her book include vignettes on American women suffering from eating disorders; American women in weight-loss programs; American women who have undergone liposuctions, breast implants, and other types of cosmetic surgery; American women victims of domestic violence; American women in politics, and American women media stars. . . .

Permit me to imagine the interesting difficulties that would confront our imaginary journalist as she attempted to write this chapter on "domestic violence and American culture." . . .

Among the things she will learn in her readings and conversations are that American men batter their partners for "reasons" that range from sexual jealousy, alcoholism, stress, and pure unmitigated rage, to the desire to control the woman or to "prevent her leaving." She will learn that economic dependency, worries about the custody and welfare of children, low self-esteem due to abuse, and the threats and violence that have followed upon previous attempts at leaving are often given as reasons for American women staying in abusive relationships. With the possible exception of "low

self-esteem," these sorts of reasons will seem similar to those that work to keep Indian women in abusive marriages, though they are often eclipsed in explanations that rely on elements such as Hindu mythology or the status of women in the Laws of Manu. She will notice that in U.S. accounts of domestic violence the sorts of reasons mentioned above appear to provide explanation enough, and that there is no felt need to explain why domestic violence in America is "American." None of this, she realizes, is helping her write a chapter that easily links U.S. domestic violence to "American culture."

Suddenly, she has a flash of inspiration! "Guns," she exclaims to herself, "gun-related domestic violence against women is what my chapter should be about. That will provide the tie into 'American culture' I have been looking for, since guns are so quintessentially 'American.' I need to find out how many women are injured annually by guns and how seriously, and how many of these injuries are inflicted by domestic partners. I need to find out how many domestic shooting incidents are claimed to be 'accidents' and how often there is good reason to doubt that they are. I need to find out how many American women are murdered annually by guns, and how many of them by their partners. Finding this information might help me depict guns as an 'icon' of violence against U.S. women, just as 'fire' seems to have become an icon of violence against Indian women."

What our imaginary Indian journalist might run up against as she tries to write this improbable chapter is revealing. Guns and lack of gun control, she will find in her conversations with Americans, are often acknowledged to be fairly distinctively "American" problems. However, in her attempts to relate gun-related violence to women and domestic violence, she will find that gun control and gun-related violence have not widely emerged specifically as "women's issues" or "domestic-violence issues." . . .

In short, she will predominantly find that figures pertaining to U.S. domestic violence do not specifically focus on guns, and that data on gun-related violence in the U.S. lacks specific attention to domestic violence. The intersection between "domestic violence suffered by U.S. women" and "American gun-related violence"—which would be the space of "domestic violence against American women mediated by the use of guns"—seems not to be well marked either as an

"American" or as a "women's" issue. If she eventually finds the data, she will be struck by the fact that although the majority of women murdered by partners are in fact murdered with firearms, gun control has not emerged strongly as a U.S. feminist issue or even as a "visible" issue in much of the literature on domestic violence. The journalist will discover that her idea about linking "domestic violence" to "American culture" by focusing on gun-related violence against women is not a project easy to carry out, since the two issues seem not to be frequently connected by those engaged with gun-control issues or domestic-violence agendas. She might, however, acquire some interesting "cross-cultural insights" as a result of her frustrations. She might come to see that while Indian women repeatedly suffer "death by culture" in a range of scholarly and popular works,

even as the elements of "culture" proffered do little to explain their deaths, American women seem relatively immune to such analyses of "death or injury by culture" even as they are victimized by the fairly distinctively American phenomenon of wide-spread gun-related violence.

Given these difficulties, it is perhaps for the best that this is an imaginary chapter in an improbable book. I would like to end with the suggestion that books that cannot be written and chapters that are oddly difficult to write might have more to teach us about particular cultures and their relationships to "Other cultures" than many books and chapters that face few difficulties in being either imagined or written.

(1997)

"EROTOPHOBIA AND THE COLONIZATION OF QUEER(S)/NATURE"

The rhetoric and institution of Christianity, coupled with the imperialist drives of militarist nation-states, have been used for nearly two thousand years to portray heterosexuality, sexism, racism, classism, and the oppression of the natural world as divinely ordained. Today, although twentieth-century Western industrialized nations purport to be largely secular, those countries with Christian and colonial origins retain the ideology of divinely inspired domination nonetheless. . . .

It is interesting that both the monarchs and the explorers felt the need to justify their colonialist desires for more land, more wealth, and more slaves. From medieval theologians, Christianity had inherited the message that the "fruits of any conquest could only be legitimate if the war that won them had been just";

conveniently, through the Crusades, Christianity developed the principle that "war conducted in the interests of the Holy Church was automatically just" (Jennings 1975, 4). Because the church had been engaged in persecuting the erotic since its inception, choosing the sexual behaviors of indigenous peoples as proof of their heathenism and lack of civilization seemed adequate justification for their colonization.

Katz's valuable research in Gay American History offers numerous observations of native sexual practices, dating from the sixteenth-century explorers on. These records clearly express the explorers' erotophobic, imperialist attitudes. "The people of this nation [the Choctaw] are generally of a brutal and coarse nature," wrote Jean Bernard Bossu. "They are morally quite

Reprinted from *Hypatia* 12:1, 1997. Used by permission of John Wiley & Sons. Notes have been renumbered.

perverted, and most of them are addicted to sodomy. These corrupt men . . . have long hair and wear short skirts like women" (Katz 1976, 291). "The sin of sodomy prevails more among them than in any other nation, although there are four women to one man," wrote Pierre Liette about the Miamis in 1702 (Katz 1976, 288). The role of the nadleeh, or transgendered person, particularly offended Western European sensibilities.[1] Of the Iroquois, the Illinois, and other tribes in the Louisiana area, Jesuit explorer and historian Pierre Franæois Xavier de Charlevoix wrote in 1721, "these effeminate persons never marry, and abandon themselves to the most infamous passions" (Katz 1976, 290). When Jesuit Father Pedro Font found "some men dressed like women" among the California Yumas, he inquired about their clothing and learned that "they were sodomites, dedicated to nefarious practices." Font concluded, "there will be much to do when the Holy Faith and the Christian religion are established among them" (Katz 1976, 291). The Franciscan missionary Francisco Palou reported with shock that "almost every village" in what is now Southern California "has two or three" transgendered persons, but prayed "that these accursed people will disappear with the growth of the missions. The abominable vice will be eliminated to the extent that the Catholic faith and all the other virtues are firmly implanted there, for the glory of God and the benefit of those poor ignorants" (Katz 1976, 292). In the rhetoric of Christian colonialism, the Europeans filled the role of benevolent culture "civilizing" savage nature—and this "civilizing" involved taking the natives' homelands, eliminating their cultural and spiritual practices, and raping and enslaving their people.

A specific example of the role erotophobia played in authorizing colonization may be of use. In his book, The Elder Brothers, Alan Ereira reports on the Kogi, who live deep in Colombia's Sierra Nevada mountains, and who may be "the last surviving high civilisation of pre-conquest America" (1992, 1). In 1498, the land around what is now the Colombian city of Santa Marta was discovered by the Spanish in their search for gold, and on June 12, 1514, a Spanish galleon arrived and began the process of colonization. That process involved reading a decree declaring the natives' new servitude to King Ferdinand and the Christian God, in both Spanish and Carib languages, although the native people did not

speak either one. The Spanish conquistador Pedrarias Davila concluded his proclamation with the warning that if the native people did not submit to this rule:

> I assure you that with the help of God I will enter powerfuly against you, and I will make war on you in every place and in every way that I can, and I will subject you to the yoke and obedience of the church and their highnesses, and I will take your persons and your women and your children, and I will make them slaves, and as such I will sell them, and dispose of them as their highnesses command: I will take your goods, and I will do you all the evils and harms which I can, just as to vassals who do not obey and do not want to receive their lord, resist him and contradict him. And I declare that the deaths and harms which arise from this will be your fault, and not that of their highnesses, nor mine, nor of the gentlemen who have come with me here. (Ereira 1992, 74)

The Spanish invasion proceeded accordingly. As Ereira observes, gender and sexuality played a prominent role in the rhetoric and the justification of colonial conquest. "The Spanish could not endure the Indians' relationship between the sexes," he writes. "It was so fundamentally different from their own as to be an outrage. The men did not dominate the women" (Ereira 1992, 136). The Spanish were horrified, moreover, by the acceptance of homosexual behaviors and transgendered identities: "it was an inner fear, a fear of their own nature. And so they set out to eliminate sodomy among the Indians" (137; emphasis added). After nearly a century of colonial enslavement and missionary zeal, the Spanish concluded their most vicious assault on the native population in 1599. The governor of Santa Marta called together all the native chiefs at the base of the Sierras and told them he would put an end to their "'wicked sinfulness'" (138). The native population planned a revolt, but news of their plans was leaked to the Spanish through two missionaries, and the Spanish were prepared. For three months, the Spanish carried out their own plan of torture and genocide against the indigenous people. When it was over, the governor declared:

> And if any other Indian is found to have committed or to practice the wicked and unnatural sin of sodomy he is condemned so that in the part and place that I shall

specify he shall be garrotted in the customary manner and next he shall be burned alive and utterly consumed to dust so that he shall have no memorial and it is to be understood by the Indians that this punishment shall be extended to all who commit this offense. (Ereira 1992, 140)

Those persons "who wish to live" were required to pay a fine of "pacification" amounting to fifteen hundred pounds of gold (Ereira 1992, 140). Gender-role deviance and the accepted presence of nonheterosexual erotic practices had become the rhetorical justification for genocide and colonialism.

Not only did transgender practices and sodomy disturb the colonizers; even heterosexual practices devoid of the restrictions imposed by Christianity were objectionable. Among the Hopi of the Southwest, for example, those who had been successfully converted to Christianity were forbidden to attend the traditional snake dance because there, "male cross-dressing, adultery, and bestiality could be observed publicly" (D'Emilio and Freedman 1988, 93). Missionaries objected to the heterosexual practices of the Pueblo Indians, calling them "bestial" because "'like animals, the female plac[ed] herself publicly on all fours'" (Gutiérrez 1991, 72–73). What became known as the "missionary position" was advocated by the seventeenth-century Spanish theologian Tomás Sánchez, in his De sancto matrimond sacramento, as the "natural manner of intercourse. . . . The man must lie on top and the woman on her back beneath. Because this manner is more appropriate for the effusion of male seed, for its reception into the female vessel" (Gutiérrez 1991, 212). Sánchez likened the phallus to a plow and the woman to the earth; the missionary position would be the one most conducive to procreation and hence the most "natural." In contrast, the mulier supra virum (woman above man) position was "absolutely contrary to the order of nature" (Gutiérrez 1991, 212).

Appeals to nature have often been used to justify social norms, to the detriment of women, nature, queers, and persons of color. The range of colonial assaults on sexuality—from gender roles to same-sex behaviors to heterosexual practices—is the reason I name the colonizers' perspective erotophobic rather than simply homophobic. This colonial erotophobia remained intact through the arrival of the Pilgrims, the establishment of the United States, and the waves of westward expansion that followed. . . .

As I have argued elsewhere, when nature is feminized and thereby eroticized, and culture is masculinized, the culture–nature relationship becomes one of compulsory heterosexuality (Gaard 1993). Colonization can therefore be seen as a relationship of compulsory heterosexuality whereby the queer erotic of non-westernized peoples, their culture, and their land, is subdued into the missionary position—with the conqueror "on top."[2]

TOWARD A QUEER ECOFEMINISM

Today, all those associated with nature and the erotic continue to experience the impact of centuries of Western culture's colonization, in our very bodies and in our daily lives. Rejecting that colonization requires embracing the erotic in all its diversity and building coalitions for creating a democratic, ecological culture based on our shared liberation.

To create that culture, we must combine the insights of queer and ecofeminist theories. As feminists have long argued, the way out of this system of endemic violence requires liberating the erotic—not in some facile liberal scheme, which would authorize increased access to pornography or child sexual encounters, but through a genuine transformation of Western conceptions of the erotic as fundamentally opposed to reason, culture, humanity, and masculinity. A queer ecofeminist perspective would argue that liberating the erotic requires reconceptualizing humans as equal participants in culture and in nature, able to explore the eroticism of reason and the unique rationality of the erotic. Ecofeminists must be concerned with queer liberation, just as queers must be concerned with the liberation of women and of nature; our parallel oppressions have stemmed from our perceived associations. It is time to build our common liberation on more concrete coalitions.

(1997)

NOTES

1. The more common term, berdache, I reject here on the basis of its original meaning as "a boy kept for unnatural purposes." The word originated with the European colonizers, and reflects their erotophobic perspective, just

as it virtually erases the various cultural, spiritual, and economic aspects of this particular gender role. Male and female transgenders have been found in more than 130 North American tribes (Roscoe 1991, 5), and have been named accordingly in each culture. I prefer the Navajo term nadleeh both for its indigenous rather than colonial origins and because the Navajo used the same term for both men and women transgenders (Gay American Indians 1988).

2. Suzanne Zantop has arrived at a similar conclusion in her study of a German debate regarding the colonization of the Americas. The debate took place in the years following 1768 between the Dutch canon Cornelius de Pauw and the Prussian royal librarian Antoine Pernety. Zantop finds that "by imposing a gender framework on the encounter between colonizer and colonized, and by grounding this gender structure in a particular biology, de Pauw render[ed] the violent appropriation of the New World natural and inevitable, even desirable" and that "the power relationship of colonizer to colonized [became] the model for a successful matrimony" (1993, 312–13).

REFERENCES

D'John Emilio, and Estelle B. Freedman. 1988. Intimate matters: A history of sexuality in America. New York: Harper and Row.

Ereira, Alan. 1992. The elder brothers: A lost South American people and their wisdom. New York: Random House.

Gaard, Greta, ed. 1993. Ecofeminism: Women, animals, nature. Philadelphia: Temple University Press.

Gutiérrez, Ramón A. 1989. "Must we deracinate Indians to find gay roots?" Out/Look 1(4):61–67.

Gutiérrez, Ramón A. 1991 . When Jesus came, the corn mothers went away: Marriage, sexuality, and power in New Mexico, 1500–1846. Stanford: Stanford University Press.

Jennings, Francis. 1975. The invasion of America: Indians, colonialism, and the cant of conquest. New York: W. W. Norton.

Katz, Jonathan Ned. 1976. Gay American history: Lesbians and gay men in the U.S.A. New York: Penguin.

131 • *Ella Shohat*

"AFTER THE METANARRATIVES OF LIBERATION"

Produced also in a moment of postmodern dissolution of metanarratives, *Talking Visions* offers neither grand salvations nor total revolutions. Indeed, the fact that the era of national liberation in the Third World has now ebbed is more or less obvious. In many regions, the powerful framework of nationalism, which once held such enormous liberationist promise, has begun to fall apart. Third Worldist euphoria has given way to the collapse of communism, the indefinite postponement of "tricontinental revolution," the realization that the "wretched of the earth" are not unanimously revolutionary, and the recognition that international geopolitics and the global economic system have forced even the "Second World" to be incorporated into transnational capitalism. The slogans of nationalism, its mythos of hearth and home, are now trumpeted by

Shohat, Ella Habiba, ed., *Talking Visions: Multicultural Feminism in a Transnational Age*, pp. 10–11, 13, 15, 35–38, © 1999 Massachusetts Institute of Technology, by permission of The MIT Press. Notes have been deleted.

national elites often repressive toward those who wanted to go beyond a purely nationalist revolution to restructure class, caste, gender, sexuality, religion, racial, and ethnic relations. The choice of the term "multicultural feminism" as opposed to "Third World feminism" in my title is not simply a matter of fashion; it signals a different historical moment and different set of discourses. The anticolonial struggle is echoed in contemporary efforts to decolonize Eurocentric culture; but the critique is now articulated within what I would call a "post-Third Worldist" perspective. Moving beyond the ideology of Third Worldism, this perspective assumes the validity of antiracist and anticolonialist movements, but also interrogates the multiple fissures in the "Third World" nation and U.S. sixties national power movements. Contemporary postcolonial and diasporic writings testify to the difficulties of redefining and reestablishing a relationship to the icons, symbolic complexes, and discourses of anti-colonial and anti-racist nationalism after the decline of its liberationist thrust. . . .

We have traveled a long road since the publication of such groundbreaking multi-racial feminist anthologies as Cherríe Moraga and Gloria Anzaldúa's *This Bridge Called My Back: Writings by Radical Women of Color*. Using personal experience as a trampoline for an analysis of the social and historical forces shaping the consciousness of women of color, their anthologies filled important "gaps" both in the (white) feminist movement and in Third Worldist revolutions. By "giving name to the nameless" (Audre Lorde), they transformed silence into speech. In fact, for feminists of color, language, voice, and writing have been key tropes articulated as "being silenced," "to be heard," "talking back," "speaking out," "gaining voice." It is not simply a case, as Aimé Césaire suggested in his rewriting of Shakespeare's *Tempest*, of using Prospero's language to curse him, but also, I would suggest, of hearing the voice of the absent dark woman, the missing "Calibana" of Césaire's anti-colonial text. Correcting a serious lacuna in the field of knowledge production, radical writings by feminists of color offered "theory in the flesh," (Moraga/Anzaldúa), and a search for an authentic expression beneath the alienating scars of colonialism and hetero/sexism, which inspired many women of color. (See here images by Amalia Mesa-Bains, Marta Maria Perez Bravo, Dolores Zorreguieta, Maria Magdalena Campos-Pons, and Jossette Urso for more recent visual reworkings of the "biomythography" (Lorde) of bodily memory and counter spirituality.) Such works have reflected the fact that Third World feminists, and "minority" feminists in the First World, have found no cozy home in the communities of white First World feminism. Their longing for a "home," or a bonding site free from oppression, was accompanied by concerns about how to create such a space of emotional knowledge and feminist language while doing away with the "master's tools" (Audre Lorde).

Anthologies by and about diverse women of color emerged out of a period when one could still speak of *the* movement, whether that movement was black power, *la raza*, the antiwar movement, or the women's movement; a period when one could still speak of "revolution" in the Leftist-Marxist, Third World, anti-colonial sense. From the seventies the writing of women of color has been characterized by a complex and conflicted relation to the (Euro-American) women's liberation movement and to the diverse heteromasculinist race-based movements (Black Power, la raza). In the past decade meanwhile, one finds, even on the left, a self-reflexive and ironic distance from revolutionary rhetoric, eclipsed by an idiom of "resistance"; Substantive nouns like "revolution" and "liberation" transmute into a largely adjectival opposition: "counter-hegemonic," and "resistant practices," indicative of a crisis of totalizing narratives and a shifting vision of what constitutes an emancipatory project. Recent multicultural feminist writings are very much indebted to the earlier texts, but they differ in their tone, in their modes of analysis, and in their ways of formulating transformative politics. The gradual shift from the revolutionary spirit characteristic of the early activism of feminists of color forms part of a more general eclipse of revolutionary projects. *A luta continua*, even in the late 1990s, then, but it *continuas* in a different way.

The shift from the unitary subject of "revolution" to a fragmented and dispersed scene of multiple resistances has also been evident in more recent volumes, such as *Scattered Hegemonies: Postmodernity and Transnational Feminist Practices*, edited by Inderpal Grewal and Caren Kaplan, and *Feminist Genealogies, Colonial Legacies and Democratic Futures*, edited by M. Jacqui Alexander and Chandra Talpade Mohanty, both of which articulate a complex theory and practice of feminism, unfolded within the realities of neocolonialism and transnationalism. *Talking Visions* straddles this same postmodern fault line. It does not erase earlier writings by radical women of color; on the contrary, it draws nourishment from them, while at the same time recognizes that it has to formulate its vision within an altered theoretical and political framework that allows only for contingent forms of resistance. The volume, then, offers no single "safe house" but rather a makeshift network of dwellings, a mobile cohabitation of alliances. We may create a "safe house for difference" (here Audre Lorde's collective spatial metaphor has to be seen in contrast to Virginia Woolf's more individualist trope of "a room of one's own"); but even collective "houses" assembled from alliances will be constantly on the move in a world simultaneously undergoing globalization and fragmentation, a world where transnational corporations claim that "we're all connected" (to cite the New York Telephone ad) but where, at the same time, borders and passports are kept under thorough surveillance, a constant reminder that some have more "connections" than others. The goal of this book is to stage a shifting, multifronted constellation of struggles that can synergistically meet and mutually reinforce one another. . . .

. . . Tensions within and between communities oblige us to go beyond a discourse of "common oppression" sisterhood. In the case of immigration, the divisive issues are many, making coalition work a challenge. Some immigrants to the U.S. bring with them racist attitudes, especially in relation to African-Americans. When immigrants got off the boat, Toni Morrison suggests, the "second word they learned was 'nigger.'" Immigrants, including even black Africans, arrive to the U.S. already having been exposed to stereotypes transmitted by global media, for example the phobic hypersexualization of African-Americans, even if at the same time they have been induced to admire African-American musicians and athletes. (The same asymmetrical flow that disseminates African-American popular culture globally, also disseminates the hierarchical raced/gendered codes of the U.S. dominant society.) Immigrants of color, pressured by the reigning black/white binarism, may adopt ambivalent attitudes, identifying with fellow "minorities" but may also be tempted to affirm their precarious sense of American

belonging by themselves rejecting blacks. We are all accountable not only to fight the discriminations of which we are victims but also the discriminations perpetrated by members of our own communities.

That some lower-middle-class immigrants manage to achieve a simulacrum of the American dream reinforces a public discourse that indirectly blames African-Americans for their social plight. Media images of (black) welfare queens and gangs, on the one hand, and of "model minority" Asians on the other, obscures the traumatic violence done to the black family by slavery and segregation. Another related issue revolves around the ways in which immigrants from South Asia, West Asia (Middle East) or Africa fight against their own discrimination in the U.S., while simultaneously harassing community-based women's organizations on such issues as domestic violence; and while also remaining affiliated with the home country reactionary institutions that discriminate against their own religious or ethnic "minorities" (e.g., see here Meena Alexander's account of this contradictory positionality of U.S. Hindu fundamentalist immigrants' mobilization against Muslims). The feminist coalitionary work of postcolonial diasporas, addressed in this volume, for example, by Chandra Talpade Mohanty, rearticulates the experience of racism and heteropatriarchalism, not simply in the context of one immigrant community, but also in conjunction with other anti-racist feminist struggles, such as those of Latina and African-American women.

A multicultural feminist alliance confronts the limitations of a black/white framing of identities. The multiracial conflicts involving Koreans, African-Americans, and Latino/as in Los Angeles in 1992 speak volumes about these limitations. Although the black/white binarism is strongly inscribed in the material and ideological structures of the U.S., it is crucial for multicultural feminist alliances to examine the interplay of diverse communities—especially since the 1965 Immigration Act, by democratizing access to the U.S., has added even more "dark" layers to an already multi-layered amalgam. Yet recent waves of immigration by people of color are a result, not only of the inclusiveness of the 1965 Immigration Act, but also of U.S. imperial interventions, and of a globalized economic structure in which the U.S. has played a central role. In the context of rampant downsizing, recent Third World immigrants to the U.S. compete with people of color and white working class people over shrinking resources. Not only "Anglos" make up the marching troops of the "English-only" movement: they are sometimes joined ironically, by people of color who had themselves been brutally shorn of their own languages, just as Proposition 187 in California has been applauded by some people of color who feel disadvantaged vis-à-vis recent immigrants. At the same time, the military remains one relatively secure avenue to a scaled-down version of the American Dream, promising a measure of racial and gender (but not yet sexual) equality within a neo-imperial nationalist framework. . . .

"First Worldness," even when experienced from the bottom, brings certain privileges that must be considered as we reconceptualize a multicultural, transnational, cross-regional feminism. Living in the U.S. given the unequal global flow of economic, technological, and cultural production can generate certain advantages, such as a powerful currency and an open-sesame passport. Struggles on behalf of African-American women and Latinas, for example, are not necessarily liberatory for women in Africa or Latin America, and vice versa. Being a U.S. feminist of color does not automatically guarantee a critical attitude toward the consequences of U.S. national interests for Third World women, whose cheap labor indirectly allows First World working-class women of color to consume products at lower prices. Multicultural feminism has to address these economic structures and the "structure of feeling" of Third World feminists toward U.S. power in the world. Applying globally the idea of "women of color" cannot paper over the asymmetries implicit in the gendered flow of capital and labor across nation-state borders.

Opposition to racism, sexism, and homophobia in the U.S., furthermore, has never guaranteed opposition to U.S. global hegemony. Mervat Hatem's and Wahneema Lubiano's essays offer gendered analyses of the global/local contradictions in relation to the Gulf War. For U.S. people of color the path to upward mobility has often passed through the obligatory display of patriotic devotion to the "American nation." Many people of color and gays/lesbians have fought as soldiers on the U.S.'s behalf in the last decade—in the Middle East, in Panama, in Somalia, in Haiti—occasionally alongside soldiers whose origins are in these countries. In times of national war efforts, hegemonic discourse transforms the usually black and Latino men from crack dealers and absent fathers into heroes in uniform, privileged, as Lubiano shows, in the hetero/masculinist narrative of the returning father soldier. The interwovenness of geopolitics and global economy suggests that our "hands are not clean." "Such an understanding," writes Lubiano, "disrupt[s] the tendency on the part of some black women to think that 'we' have a lock on the oppression sweepstakes and remind[s] us that the contempt that many of us direct toward something understood (or caricatured) as 'mainstream feminism' or 'a middle-class white feminist movement'—a contempt directed at white feminists for talking and behaving as though their particular oppression is absolutely primary—could in some measure be directed as ourselves." The essays in *Talking Visions*, then, try to account for precisely this relational web of contradictory positionalities.

(1999)

"DO MUSLIM WOMEN REALLY NEED SAVING? ANTHROPOLOGICAL REFLECTIONS ON CULTURAL RELATIVISM AND ITS OTHERS"

What are the ethics of the current "War on Terrorism," a war that justifies itself by purporting to liberate, or save, Afghan women? Does anthropology have anything to offer in our search for a viable position to take regarding this rationale for war?

I was led to pose the question of my title in part because of the way I personally experienced the response to the U.S. war in Afghanistan. Like many colleagues whose work has focused on women and gender in the Middle East, I was deluged with invitations to speak—not just on news programs but also to various departments at colleges and universities, especially women's studies programs. Why did this not please me, a scholar who has devoted more than 20 years of her life to this subject and who has some complicated personal connection to this identity? Here was an opportunity to spread the word, disseminate my knowledge, and correct misunderstandings. The urgent search for knowledge about our sister "women of cover" (as President George Bush so marvelously called them) is laudable and when it comes from women's studies programs where "transnational feminism" is now being taken seriously, it has a certain integrity (see Safire 2001).

My discomfort led me to reflect on why, as feminists in or from the West, or simply as people who have concerns about women's lives, we need to be wary of this response to the events and aftermath of September 11, 2001. I want to point out the minefields—a metaphor that is sadly too apt for a country like Afghanistan, with the world's highest number of mines per capita—of this obsession with the plight of Muslim women. I hope to show some way through them using insights from anthropology, the discipline whose charge has been to understand and manage cultural difference. At the same time, I want to remain critical of anthropology's complicity in the reification of cultural difference.

CULTURAL EXPLANATIONS AND THE MOBILIZATION OF WOMEN

It is easier to see why one should be skeptical about the focus on the "Muslim woman" if one begins with the U.S. public response. I will analyze two manifestations of this response: some conversations I had with a reporter from the PBS *NewsHour with Jim Lehrer* and First Lady Laura Bush's radio address to the nation on November 17, 2001. The presenter from the *NewsHour* show first contacted me in October to see if I was willing to give some background for a segment on Women and Islam. I mischievously asked whether she had done segments on the women of Guatemala, Ireland, Palestine, or Bosnia when the show covered wars in those regions; but I finally agreed to look at the questions she was going to pose to panelists. The questions were hopelessly general. Do Muslim women believe "x"? Are Muslim women "y"? Does Islam allow "z" for women? I asked her: If you were to substitute Christian or Jewish wherever you have Muslim, would

From *American Anthropologist* 104, no. 3 (2002). Copyright © 2002 by the American Anthropological Association. Reprinted with permission.

these questions make sense? I did not imagine she would call me back. But she did, twice, once with an idea for a segment on the meaning of Ramadan and another time on Muslim women in politics. One was in response to the bombing and the other to the speeches by Laura Bush and Cherie Blair, wife of the British Prime Minister.

What is striking about these three ideas for news programs is that there was a consistent resort to the cultural, as if knowing something about women and Islam or the meaning of a religious ritual would help one understand the tragic attack on New York's World Trade Center and the U.S. Pentagon, or how Afghanistan had come to be ruled by the Taliban, or what interests might have fueled U.S. and other interventions in the region over the past 25 years, or what the history of American support for conservative groups funded to undermine the Soviets might have been, or why the caves and bunkers out of which Bin Laden was to be smoked "dead or alive," as President Bush announced on television, were paid for and built by the CIA.

In other words, the question is why knowing about the "culture" of the region, and particularly its religious beliefs and treatment of women, was more urgent than exploring the history of the development of repressive regimes in the region and the U.S. role in this history. Such cultural framing, it seemed to me, prevented the serious exploration of the roots and nature of human suffering in this part of the world. Instead of political and historical explanations, experts were being asked to give religio-cultural ones. Instead of questions that might lead to the exploration of global interconnections, we were offered ones that worked to artificially divide the world into separate spheres—recreating an imaginative geography of West versus East, us versus Muslims, cultures in which First Ladies give speeches versus others where women shuffle around silently in burqas.

Most pressing for me was why the Muslim woman in general, and the Afghan woman in particular, were so crucial to this cultural mode of explanation, which ignored the complex entanglements in which we are all implicated, in sometimes surprising alignments. Why were these female symbols being mobilized in this "War against Terrorism" in a way they were not in other conflicts? Laura Bush's radio address on November 17 reveals the political work such mobilization accomplishes. On the one hand, her address collapsed important

distinctions that should have been maintained. There was a constant slippage between the Taliban and the terrorists, so that they became almost one word—a kind of hyphenated monster identity: the Taliban-and-the-terrorists. Then there was the blurring of the very separate causes in Afghanistan of women's continuing malnutrition, poverty, and ill health, and their more recent exclusion under the Taliban from employment, schooling, and the joys of wearing nail polish. On the other hand, her speech reinforced chasmic divides, primarily between the "civilized people throughout the world" whose hearts break for the women and children of Afghanistan and the Taliban-and-the-terrorists, the cultural monsters who want to, as she put it, "impose their world on the rest of us."

Most revealingly, the speech enlisted women to justify American bombing and intervention in Afghanistan and to make a case for the "War on Terrorism" of which it was allegedly a part. As Laura Bush said, "Because of our recent military gains in much of Afghanistan, women are no longer imprisoned in their homes. They can listen to music and teach their daughters without fear of punishment. . . . The fight against terrorism is also a fight for the rights and dignity of women" (U.S. Government 2002).

These words have haunting resonances for anyone who has studied colonial history. Many who have worked on British colonialism in South Asia have noted the use of the woman question in colonial policies where intervention into sati (the practice of widows immolating themselves on their husbands' funeral pyres), child marriage, and other practices was used to justify rule. As Gayatri Chakravorty Spivak (1988) has cynically put it: white men saving brown women from brown men. The historical record is full of similar cases, including in the Middle East. In Turn of the Century Egypt, what Leila Ahmed (1992) has called "colonial feminism" was hard at work. This was a selective concern about the plight of Egyptian women that focused on the veil as a sign of oppression but gave no support to women's education and was professed loudly by the same Englishman, Lord Cromer, who opposed women's suffrage back home. . . .

Lazreg (1994) also gives memorable examples of the way in which the French had earlier sought to transform Arab women and girls. She describes skits at awards ceremonies at the Muslim Girls' School in Algiers in 1851 and 1852. In the first skit, written by "a French lady from Algiers," two Algerian Arab girls reminisced about their trip to France with words including the following:

> Oh! Protective France: Oh! Hospitable France! . . .
> Noble land, where I felt free
> Under Christian skies to pray to our God. . . .
> God bless you for the happiness you bring us!
> And you, adoptive mother, who taught us
> That we have a share of this world,
> We will cherish you forever! (Lazreg 1994:68–69) . . .

Just as I argued above that we need to be suspicious when neat cultural icons are plastered over messier historical and political narratives, so we need to be wary when Lord Cromer in British-ruled Egypt, French ladies in Algeria, and Laura Bush, all with military troops behind them, claim to be saving or liberating Muslim women.

POLITICS OF THE VEIL

. . . It is common popular knowledge that the ultimate sign of the oppression of Afghan women under the Taliban-and-the-terrorists is that they were forced to wear the burqa. Liberals sometimes confess their surprise that even though Afghanistan has been liberated from the Taliban, women do not seem to be throwing off their burqas. Someone who has worked in Muslim regions must ask why this is so surprising. Did we expect that once "free" from the Taliban they would go "back" to belly shirts and blue jeans, or dust off their Chanel suits? We need to be more sensible about the clothing of "women of cover," and so there is perhaps a need to make some basic points about veiling.

First, it should be recalled that the Taliban did not invent the burqa. It was the local form of covering that Pashtun women in one region wore when they went out. The Pashtun are one of several ethnic groups in Afghanistan and the burqa was one of many forms of covering in the subcontinent and Southwest Asia that has developed as a convention for symbolizing women's modesty or respectability. The burqa, like some other forms of "cover" has, in many settings, marked the symbolic separation of men's and women's spheres, as part of the general association of women with family and home, not with public space where strangers mingled.

Twenty years ago the anthropologist Hanna Papanek (1982), who worked in Pakistan, described the burqa as "portable seclusion." She noted that many saw it as a liberating invention because it enabled women to move out of segregated living spaces while still observing the basic moral requirements of separating and protecting women from unrelated men. Ever since I came across her phrase "portable seclusion," I have thought of these enveloping robes as "mobile homes." Everywhere, such veiling signifies belonging to a particular community and participating in a moral way of life in which families are paramount in the organization of communities and the home is associated with the sanctity of women.

The obvious question that follows is this: If this were the case, why would women suddenly become immodest? Why would they suddenly throw off the markers of their respectability, markers, whether burqas or other forms of cover, which were supposed to assure their protection in the public sphere from the harassment of strange men by symbolically signaling to all that they were still in the inviolable space of their homes, even though moving in the public realm? Especially when these are forms of dress that had become so conventional that most women gave little thought to their meaning. . . .

Two points emerge from this fairly basic discussion of the meanings of veiling in the contemporary Muslim world. First, we need to work against the reductive interpretation of veiling as the quintessential sign of women's unfreedom, even if we object to state imposition of this form, as in Iran or with the Taliban. (It must be recalled that the modernizing states of Turkey and Iran had earlier in the century banned veiling and required men, except religious clerics, to adopt Western dress.) What does freedom mean if we accept the fundamental premise that humans are social beings, always raised in certain social and historical contexts and belonging to particular communities that shape their desires and understandings of the world? Is it not a gross violation of women's own understandings of what they are doing to simply denounce the burqa as a medieval imposition? Second, we must take care not to reduce the diverse situations and attitudes of millions of Muslim women to a single item of clothing. Perhaps it is time to give up the Western obsession with the veil and focus on some serious issues with which feminists and others should indeed be concerned.

Ultimately, the significant political–ethical problem the burqa raises is how to deal with cultural "others." How are we to deal with difference without accepting the passivity implied by the cultural relativism for which anthropologists are justly famous—a relativism that says it's their culture and it's not my business to judge or interfere, only to try to understand. Cultural relativism is certainly an improvement on ethnocentrism and the racism, cultural imperialism, and imperiousness that underlie it; the problem is that it is too late not to interfere. The forms of lives we find around the world are already products of long histories of interactions. . . .

To be critical of this celebration of women's rights in Afghanistan is not to pass judgment on any local women's organizations, such as RAWA, whose members have courageously worked since 1977 for a democratic secular Afghanistan in which women's human rights are respected, against Soviet-backed regimes or U.S.-, Saudi-, and Pakistani-supported conservatives. Their documentation of abuse and their work through clinics and schools have been enormously important. . . .

It is, however, to suggest that we need to look closely at what we are supporting (and what we are not) and to think carefully about why. How should we manage the complicated politics and ethics of finding ourselves in agreement with those with whom we normally disagree? I do not know how many feminists who felt good about saving Afghan women from the Taliban are also asking for a global redistribution of wealth or contemplating sacrificing their own consumption radically so that African or Afghan women could have some chance of having what I do believe should be a universal human right—the right to freedom from the structural violence of global inequality and from the ravages of war, the everyday rights of having enough to eat, having homes for their families in which to live and thrive, having ways to make decent livings so their children can grow, and having the strength and security to work out, within their communities and with whatever alliances they want, how to live a good life, which might very well include changing the ways those communities are organized.

Suspicion about bedfellows is only a first step; it will not give us a way to think more positively about what to do or where to stand. For that, we need to confront two more big issues. First is the acceptance of the possibility of difference. Can we only free Afghan women to be like us or might we have to recognize that even after "liberation" from the Taliban, they might want different things than we would want for them?

What do we do about that? Second, we need to be vigilant about the rhetoric of saving people because of what it implies about our attitudes.

Again, when I talk about accepting difference, I am not implying that we should resign ourselves to being cultural relativists who respect whatever goes on elsewhere as "just their culture." I have already discussed the dangers of "cultural" explanations; "their" cultures are just as much part of history and an interconnected world as ours are. What I am advocating is the hard work involved in recognizing and respecting differences—precisely as products of different histories, as expressions of different circumstances, and as manifestations of differently structured desires. We may want justice for women, but can we accept that there might be different ideas about justice and that different women might want, or choose, different futures from what we envision as best (see Ong 1988)? We must consider that they might be called to personhood, so to speak, in a different language. . . .

One of the things we have to be most careful about in thinking about Third World feminisms, and feminism in different parts of the Muslim world, is how not to fall into polarizations that place feminism on the side of the West. I have written about the dilemmas faced by Arab feminists when Western feminists initiate campaigns that make them vulnerable to local denunciations by conservatives of various sorts, whether Islamist or nationalist, of being traitors (Abu-Lughod 2001). . . .

My point is to remind us to be aware of differences, respectful of other paths toward social change that might give women better lives. Can there be a liberation that is Islamic? And, beyond this, is liberation even a goal for which all women or people strive? Are emancipation, equality, and rights part of a universal language we must use? To quote Saba Mahmood, writing about the women in Egypt who are seeking to become pious Muslims, "The desire for freedom and liberation is a historically situated desire whose motivational force cannot be assumed a priori, but needs to be reconsidered in light of other desires aspirations, and capacities that inhere in a culturally and historically located subject" (2001:223). In other words, might other desires be more meaningful for different groups of people? Living in close families? Living in a godly way? Living without war? . . .

BEYOND THE RHETORIC OF SALVATION

Let us return, finally, to my title, "Do Muslim Women Really Need Saving?" The discussion of culture, veiling, and how one can navigate the shoals of cultural difference should put Laura Bush's self-congratulation about the rejoicing of Afghan women liberated by American troops in a different light. It is deeply problematic to construct the Afghan woman as someone in need of saving. When you save someone, you imply that you are saving her from something. You are also saving her to something. What violences are entailed in this transformation, and what presumptions are being made about the superiority of that to which you are saving her? Projects of saving other women depend on and reinforce a sense of superiority by Westerners, a form of arrogance that deserves to be challenged. . . .

Could we not leave veils and vocations of saving others behind and instead train our sights on ways to make the world a more just place? The reason respect for difference should not be confused with cultural relativism is that it does not preclude asking how we, living in this privileged and powerful part of the world, might examine our own responsibilities for the situations in which others in distant places have found themselves. We do not stand outside the world, looking out over this sea of poor benighted people, living under the shadow—or veil—of oppressive cultures; we are part of that world. Islamic movements themselves have arisen in a world shaped by the intense engagements of Western powers in Middle Eastern lives.

A more productive approach, it seems to me, is to ask how we might contribute to making the world a more just place. A world not organized around strategic military and economic demands; a place where certain kinds of forces and values that we may still consider important could have an appeal and where there is the peace necessary for discussions, debates, and transformations to occur within communities. We need to ask ourselves what kinds of world conditions we could contribute to making such that popular desires will not be overdetermined by an overwhelming sense of helplessness in the face of forms of global injustice. Where we seek to be active in the affairs of distant places, can we do so in the spirit of support for those within those communities whose goals are to make women's (and men's) lives better (as Walley has argued in relation to practices of genital cutting in Africa [1997])? Can we use a more egalitarian language of alliances, coalitions, and solidarity, instead of salvation? . . .

(2002)

REFERENCES

Abu-Lughod, Lila. 2001. Orientalism and Middle East Feminist Studies. *Feminist Studies* 27(1):101–113.

Ahmed, Leila. 1992. *Women and Gender in Islam.* New Haven, CT: Yale University Press.

Lazreg, Marnia. 1994. *The Eloquence of Silence: Algerian Women in Question.* New York: Routledge.

Mahmood, Saba. 2001. Feminist Theory, Embodiment, and the Docile Agent: Some Reflections on the Egyptian Islamic Revival. *Cultural Anthropology* 16(2):202–235.

Ong, Aihwa. 1988. Colonialism and Modernity: Feminist RePresentations of Women in Non-Western Societies. *Inscriptions* 3–4:79–93.

Papanek, Hanna. 1982. Purdah in Pakistan: Seclusion and Modern Occupations for Women. In *Separate Worlds.* Hanna Papanek and Gail Minault, eds. Pp. 190–216. Columbia, MO: South Asia Books.

Safire, William. 2001. "On Language." *New York Times Magazine,* October 28:22.

Spivak, Gayatri Chakravorty. 1988. Can the Subaltern Speak? In *Marxism and the Interpretation of Culture.* Cary Nelson and Lawrence Grossberg, eds. Pp. 271–313. Urbana: University of Illinois Press.

U.S. Government. 2002. Electronic document, http://www.whitehouse.gov/news/releases/2001/11/20011117. Accessed January 10.

Walley, Christine. 1997. Searching for "Voices": Feminism, Anthropology, and the Global Debate over Female Genital Operations. *Cultural Anthropology* 12(3):405–438.

"FROM TRAGEDY AND INJUSTICE TO RIGHTS AND EMPOWERMENT: ACCOUNTABILITY IN THE ECONOMIC REALM"

There is no common perspective or view of young women today. Our ideas, interests and goals are as diverse as our appearances and our homes.[1] Yet it is fair to say that we have some common experiences, which shape both who we are and who we will become. For example, as young people we have universally experienced a lack of power, whether because of our age and our dependence on others to meet our needs and fulfil our rights, or because of poverty, discrimination, lack of opportunity or limits placed upon our freedoms. Moreover, we all live in consumerist cultures; no matter where we live in the world, McDonald's, Levi's and Coca-Cola and the values of profit, consumption and accumulation have crept into our societies (although their manifestations and impacts can be quite distinct). And for the vast majority of young women in the world, a sense of unfairness and/or injustice at the institutions and ideologies that structure our lives and our world is also a common experience. How we, as diverse young women, respond to this unfairness is the focus of this chapter.

In focusing on questions of how young women today are responding to and shaping our world, a key area to consider is necessarily that of economic rights, macro-economic institutions and the predominant international economic ideologies. If we look at the structures and actors that have the power to influence policies and behaviours around the world, rich country governments and finance ministers the world over, chief executive officers of transnational corporations, international and regional financial institutions and wealthy individuals figure at the top of the list. Comparing these contemporary powerhouses to those that dominated 20, 50, and even 100 years ago, we see both new actors and new ways of exerting power. We also see more global uniformity in the exertion of this power and the global reach of the powerful, which have become greatly amplified with the advent of new communication and transportation technologies that enable constant communication and exchange without geographic or time limitations. This is a whole new world.

Some of the most powerful economic forces in the world today are relatively new to their positions of power and have been structuring the rules by which they will play the game as they go along. Their influence and what it means to engage with them will only really be known by those who are in the younger generations today, and in particular by those who continue to be excluded from their bounty, including women, indigenous peoples, the disabled, racialized peoples, the poor, migrants, and others who are marginalized by patriarchal and colonial structures and ideologies. The intention of this chapter is modest: to sketch out a preliminary picture of this economics-dominated world and its implications for young women today, and to consider some of the diverse responses and modes of

This chapter originally appeared in *Defending Our Dreams: Global Feminist Voices For A New Generation*, 2005, produced through the Young Women and Leadership theme of the Association for Women's Rights in Development (AWID). Reprinted by permission of Alison Symington. Notes have been renumbered.

engagement that are beginning to take hold and will continue to unfold and develop in the coming years. It is hoped that this contribution will add to an understanding of why and how young women act, react and engage distinctly from older generations and in diverse ways from each other, not only with respect to economic justice issues but also in terms of the broader and more complete picture of their lives.

MONEY MAKES THE WORLD GO ROUND

. . . So if we want to understand this new world of challenges faced by young women today, we need first to understand the cast of characters.

First and foremost, there is the World Trade Organization (WTO). While it has been described as the "institutional face of globalization" and is perhaps the most powerful and wide-reaching of all international players today, the institution is in fact only ten years old. Based in Geneva, it was formed to oversee the series of trade agreements that had emerged from the "Uruguay Round" of negotiations on an international trade agreement called the General Agreement on Tariffs and Trade (GATT) and to implement a dispute settlement process with respect to members' rights and obligations under these agreements.[2] As of February 2005, 148 states are members of the WTO.[3] Officially, the WTO is a member-driven "one-country, one-vote" organization. In practice, however, there is a long-standing custom of decision-making "by consensus," and the richer countries exert disproportionate influence within the organization. While some of the world's least-developed countries have minimal capacity to participate in negotiating sessions, the richer countries have large staffs of trade specialists, lawyers and expert negotiating teams. In addition to this global trading body, numerous regional trading bodies (such as MERCOSUR, CAFRA and NAFTA) serve similar roles at the regional level.[4]

The World Bank (the International Bank for Reconstruction and Development, in full) plays a close supporting role to the WTO.[5] Originally established in 1944, the Bank is the world's largest supplier of development capital and advice. It is headquartered in Washington, DC, and has 100 country offices. The Bank is primarily engaged in three activities: lending, development research and economic analysis, and technical assistance. It provides funding from public sources for development programmes in areas such as health, education and environmental protection, focusing on national legal, political and economic structures. It promotes reforms that it believes will create long-term growth and stability, while lending to governments and using the profits generated from the loans to finance its operations.

Over the years, the activities and policies of the World Bank have shifted significantly, from its original role in rebuilding Europe after the war, to its central role in development finance today. Over the past ten years, significant shifts can be seen in the terminology used by the Bank to describe its work, including, in more recent times, venturing into the realms of gender equality and rights. What remains steadfast through these shifts, however, is the underlying policy framework, which is based on an unwavering belief in neo-liberalism (see description below) as the only way. In terms of the evolution of these players, it is critical to understand that many of the policies that are being cemented today in international law through the WTO were initially put into place through World Bank structural adjustment policies and development programmes. Working with the World Bank, which has a global scope, are the regional development banks (such as the Asian Development Bank), which have similar operations and missions.[6]

The third in this trio of international financial institutions is the International Monetary Fund (IMF).[7] The IMF was also established in 1944. Its focus is short-term balance-of-payments crises. Its three main areas of activity are surveillance of exchange rate policies, financial assistance to members with balance-of-payments problems, and technical assistance with respect to policies, institutions and statistics. In a nutshell, the IMF formulates economic policy based on the mantra "tighten your belt" and it has created a body of international monetary law.

Together, these three institutions have set in place the set of economic policies and prescriptions that pervade our world today and are the driving force behind globalization. Commonly referred to as neo-liberalism, this policy framework primarily arose as a response to the economic downturn and international debt crises of the 1970s. It is based on an unwavering belief in "free markets," promoting competitive market capitalism, private ownership, "free trade," export-led growth, strict controls on balance of payments and deficits, and drastic reductions in government social spending. More than a theoretical model or set of economic tools, neo-liberalism has become *the only way*. In the 1980s, the international financial institutions began to impose these economic prescriptions on countries that accepted loans or aid through them as "conditionality," a central feature of structural adjustment policies, which were intended to pull poor countries into conformity with this model and hence propel them into "development." In most areas of the world, marginalized peoples have not benefited from neo-liberal policies and it is common for women to suffer disproportionately from disruptions to their local economies, from the continual under-valuing of their work, and from the increased insecurity brought about by the increasing prevalence of casual and flexible jobs alongside the privatization of essential services.[8]

The other key actors that have gained awesome power in recent years are corporations. The statistics on the magnitude of corporate power are now well known: of the world's 100 largest economies, 51 are corporations, not countries; the world's top 200 corporations account for over a quarter of the economic activity on the global level, while employing less than 1 per cent of the global workforce; and the average CEO in the United States made 531 times what the average worker was paid in 2000.[9] Most transnational corporations are headquartered in developed countries but may have operations, supply chains and distribution networks that stretch across many borders. Corporations have been granted extensive rights as investors and have wielded increasing power to influence policy at the international level and within countries.

Where do people fit within this system? Well, primarily they are consumers. People buy things, they consume products and services. If the good is valued, then people will pay for it. The limited purchasing power of poor people means that they are quite invisible in the system. To the extent that they are explicitly considered, they are most seen as anomalies, as recipients of charity and as drains on an otherwise efficient system.

The point of this sketch is in terms of understanding the structures, influences and realities of young women today. These economic institutions and the ideologies that they promote and enforce are essential components of the fabric of our lives. If we pour ourselves a glass of water to drink, take our mother to see a doctor, go to a dance club with our friends or participate in an employment training programme, these institutions and ideologies have influenced the availability and accessibility of the services and products available to us, and they impose restrictions on the types of regulations governments can impose on products and service-providers. Whether we live in peace or conflict, in health or illness, if we are restricted by religious and cultural tradition or free to explore and experiment, these institutions and ideologies put parameters around the choices our governments can make, and the options and opportunities available to us. . . .

I believe it is important to start with the recognition of the place of money and economic institutions in the lives of young women today. I do not want to oversimplify the complexity of the rich experiences of young women or to under-emphasize the importance of the pursuit of wealth in the colonial project and throughout history, but this everyday lived reality is the necessary starting point for most young women as they engage with issues of social justice, with gender roles and discrimination, and with technology and with cross-cultural interactions, among other issues. Of course it does not determine who a young woman is and what her dreams are, but it does structure her existence in a multitude of ways. Moreover, young women necessarily come to issues of social justice, development and equality differently from older generations simply because of this different starting point. This is a reality that I believe is often overlooked in discussions of "intergenerational dialogue" and "movement-building" within feminist circles, yet is essential in moving forward meaningfully.

ALTERNATIVES IN THE WORKS

While the neo-liberal economic system has a firm grasp today and dominates almost everywhere, that of course does not mean that it is universally accepted, welcomed or left to function without contestation. Young women are active among those struggling against the tragedies and injustices brought about by this system and all it entails. For example, in Seattle in 1999 and Cancun in 2003, many young women took to the streets to protest about the World Trade Organization and have been involved in the numerous "anti-globalization" rallies ever since. Many young women are active members of local anarchist groups and radical anti-poverty organizations such as the Ontario Coalition Against Poverty in Canada, and anti-corporate protests such as those against Chevron in Nigeria.[10] And many young women are embarking on careers in the public service, in NGOs, as lawyers, economists and policy analysts and as educators and organizers to challenge the system.

By now, it is well established in extensive academic and popular literature that the international trade, aid and investment regimes do not work for women, young or old. They do not contribute to the eradication of poverty, nor do they advance women's rights and gender equality. It is probably safe to say that few young women today could imagine a world without international trade, foreign investors or overseas development assistance, but can they imagine a system in which these forces contribute to equality, peace and justice? Many young women just try to get the best deal they can for themselves within the existing system, paying little attention to notions of social and economic justice. But on the other hand, many are extremely active and committed to the causes, taking part in diverse forms of action, activism and studies towards a more fair and just world.

One of the interesting phenomena with respect to globalization and neo-liberalism is that they are often discussed as if they are inevitable and as if they exist in a complete vacuum. Somehow, policy-makers and "experts" have become adept at debating development as if it does not involve people, trade as if it is an end in itself, and international investment and production supply chains as if they are the only option. Most financial institutions and international economic actors talk of human rights as if they are unnecessary, purely political, confrontational, and really just a distraction from the important matters at hand. In fact, discussions often go on as if human rights do not exist, alternative models and values are absent and irrelevant, and by and large, humans and the environment are similarly irrelevant. But surely for most of humanity, the values of human rights, of equality, justice, dignity and happiness, are much more in line with what we truly value. Surely the stark disjunctures between these competing value systems and discourses are the intersection points at

which people really live, struggle and survive. To my mind, it is at these points of disjuncture and collision that alternatives are concocted, gestated and experienced.

YOUNG WOMEN USING HUMAN RIGHTS

International human rights law is one of the tools that we have at our disposal in the quest for a fairer global economic system, and a tool that seems to appeal to many young women. I can only speculate as to why, but I believe it is at least in part because human rights present a principled, alternative and comprehensive vision of how our world can be organized. Using human rights tools makes one *for* something concrete, opposing the complex, multi-faceted and seemingly seamless world of global capitalism with an equally complex, multi-faceted and rigorous set of principles and prescriptions. . . .

As young human rights advocates know, non-discrimination is one of the most fundamental principles of human rights, and poverty is increasingly understood as a total lack of economic, social and cultural rights. By using the analytical frameworks, the legal principles, the moral imperatives and the mobilizing power of human rights, we could effectively work towards an international economic system that is supportive of poverty eradication, sustainable development and the full attainment of human rights for everyone. This is a truly exciting and inspirational prospect! The challenge for young women who are stepping into this area is to figure out how to apply and fully implement human rights in our globalized world. A central part of this challenge is to determine how to apply human rights principles practically, to ensure that the rules of international trade contribute to the type of world, characterized by justice and equality, which many young women want.

INCOHERENCE IN INTERNATIONAL LAW

. . . Many young women are discovering how the language of human rights can be an effective tool for mobilizing and motivating people to demand accountability and justice. In designing effective campaign messages, for example, it is extremely useful to reveal the hands of power at work in a particular situation. It is easy for the average person to understand as tragic the fact that approximately 40 million people are living with HIV/AIDS today, a growing percentage of whom are women,[11] or to feel distressed that there were 700,000 new HIV infections in children in 2003, most of which resulted from mother-to-child transmission because most women do not have access to treatments aimed at preventing transmission to their children.[12] Similarly, hunger, drought and food insecurity in poor countries and the extreme malnutrition suffered by so many throughout the world can readily be understood as a terrible thing by most. But until the powerful actors and institutions that created and/or are maintaining this situation are revealed, people may only recognize this deprivation as a misfortune.

But the HIV/AIDS pandemic, hunger and food insecurity are *injustices*, with national and international institutions and actors significantly responsible. In other words, they are largely preventable and solvable problems, if human will is there to resolve them. Injustices require corrective action and redress. The human rights framework is a valuable tool for revealing some of the injustices behind ill health, malnutrition, homelessness, the lack of access to essential services, unsafe working conditions and gender inequality. By naming a specific human rights violation, identifying the persons or institutions responsible for that violation, and claiming redress, the injustice is laid bare and can be used to mobilize a constituency to advocate for change. While misfortune elicits sympathy, injustice evokes outrage, passion and motivation to make a concerted effort to bring about change. Young women are using human rights frameworks to mobilize action against injustice in this way.

Human rights can also be used to lobby governments, demanding that they fulfil their international obligations (this is a more "traditional" form of feminist activism). But what is more novel, and also promising, is using international mechanisms such as investor-state dispute resolution panels, domestic tort claims provisions, the World Bank Inspection Panel and other economic mechanisms within economic institutions and other areas to challenge injustices by asserting principles of equality, accountability, transparency and human rights.[13] Truly innovative work is being done to stop environmentally damaging mining practices, to protect indigenous rights, to guarantee access to essential services such as safe drinking water, and to empower workers to claim their rights in factories all over the world. And finally, tools and principles are being developed that use human rights as the basis for policy development, so that governments implement policies that are based on their rights obligations rather than their perceptions of "need" or "charity," or, as is so often the case, purely in response to political expedience and interest group demands.[14] These developments are taking human rights into their next stage of development, moving into empowerment and accountability for women and excluded peoples. . . .

From a gender equality perspective, the provisions of the WTO agreements, as well as most regional trade agreements, are quite interesting in that they aim to create a rule-based, predictable, transparent system where each member is equal (often referred to as creating "a level playing field"). But years of feminist theory and gender equality activism have made it clear that treating unequal parties equally does *not* produce equality. Treating all poor countries and all rich countries alike does not result in equality any more than does treating all men and all women equally, or applying the same rules to persons of different ethnicities, different sexual orientations, different levels of ability, or any number of other attributes. "Level playing fields" puts the stronger in a position to do better. Substantive equality, the standard used in human rights, produces equal outcomes.

What would the international trade regime look like if it operated under the principles of substantive equality and attempted to put all countries, large or small, rich or poor, into a position where they could obtain the same substantive results in consideration of their actual means? What would trade policy look like if it considered the differing capabilities of individuals and groups all over the world, and attempted to put in place policies and programmes that would allow them to achieve substantively equal outcomes? There is a tremendous amount of diversity in terms of levels of wealth, industrialization and trade capacity in trading blocs, and in terms of genders, classes, races and levels of capabilities within our societies. Only approaches grounded in ideas of substantive equality can bring about equality and justice. Herein lies the challenge. Young women can start fresh from their experiences and perspectives to help develop these doctrines. As we go forward, we do not have to be tied to given meanings and past experiences that privilege elite interests and profit-maximization values. . . .

AN ECONOMICALLY JUST FUTURE?

Trade is only one component of the macro-economic system. Investment, currency exchange and aid are also important elements, and all of these are tied to the provision of basic services, employment and educational opportunities, and to equality and empowerment within our communities. We do not need complex statistics or deep theoretical analysis to understand how dire the situation is in the world right now—extreme poverty thrives, millions lack access to basic shelter, water and food necessary for survival, and the natural environment is being decimated at the same time as wealth accumulates and luxury overflows for a select few. Within the so-called "global feminist movement," basic issues of poverty are not always front and centre, with "sexier" issues such as erotic justice, spatial theory and reproductive technologies garnering more attention. But to my mind, poverty and economic rights are the most fundamental issues there are. Our humanity rests on our ability to solve this disaster, which is not natural or inevitable but is located in institutions and structures created by humans (mostly men, of course).

We must work from foundational principles such as justice, equality and accountability. Discussions of aid, development and concessions will not get us anywhere without people and humanity being centred and the values we are working towards being clearly articulated. Civil society must generate the will for change to happen and average people must choose to live their lives differently. There is no magical formula or perfect disciplinary approach to social justice and gender equality.

Many young women are facing up to this challenge, mastering a critical analysis of economics and developing skills in advocacy, policy-formulation, public protest and mobilization. It is up to us to decide how to address the neo-liberal global economic system—whether to challenge it, work within it, attempt to reform it or disengage from it. But if we want to really change it, to divert the present course towards one of justice and equality, we must resist the current tendency to shy away from "smarts." Intellectual leadership is as important as charismatic leadership in implementing rights

and articulating alternatives. These systems and ideologies are complex: life is not simple, and the problems of poverty and injustice are monstrous. We need a dose of humility alongside our confidence, some silence in addition to the noise we can generate, and a critical analysis with solid evidence and proposals to back up our dreams and visions.

Much of this work is done by young women outside the "global feminist movement," including research done in universities and research institutions, activism through non-feminist organizations and initiatives, service provision by various institutions, and policy work by women who do not define themselves as activists or their work as internationally oriented. A mosaic of approaches, experiences and perspectives, from all over the world, come together to create alternatives based on rights, empowerment and accountability. There is a new world of challenges from and for young women, but also a new world of possibilities.

(2005)

NOTES

1. It should be stated off-the-top that I am a young, middle-class white woman who lives in Toronto, Canada. I am a researcher for an international organization, educated in the fields of international development and international law. My comments necessarily emanate from my position, location and experiences, representing only my own personal and ever-evolving perspectives and realities.
2. See the WTO website for an explanation on the WTO: <http://www.wto.org/english/thewto_e/thewto_e.htm>. See also M. Trebilcock and R. Howse (1999), *The Regulation of International Trade*, 2nd edn (London and New York: Routledge); L. Wallach and P. Woodall (2003), *Whose Trade Organization? A Field Guide to the World Trade Organization* (New York: New Press); or M. Matsushita, P. C. Mavroidis, P. Mavroidis, T. Schoenbaum and T. J. Schoenbaum (2003), *World Trade Organization: Law, Practice and Policy* (Oxford: Oxford University Press).
3. WTO (2005), "Members and observers," see <http://www.wto.org/english/thewto_e/whatis_e/tif_e/org6_e.htm>.
4. For more information see: NAFTA Secretariat at: http://www.nafta-sec-alena.org/DefaultSite/index_e.aspx; the Regional Trade Agreements section of the WTO website is: <http://www.wto.org/english/tratop_e/region_e/region_e.htm>.

5. See World Bank website: <http://www.worldbank.org>, <www.imf.org> or A. Symington (2002), "AWID Facts and Issues No. 5: The World Bank and Women's Rights in Development."

6. See Asian Development Bank website: <http://www.adb.org>.

7. See IMF website: <http://www.imf.org>.

8. See for example D. Elson and N. Cagatay (2000), "The social content of macroeconomic policy," *World Development*, 28(7); D. Elson and H. Keklik (2002), *Progress of the World's Women 2002: Gender Equality and the Millennium Development Goals*; UNIFEM (2003), *Progress of the World's Women 2000* (New York: UNIFEM).

9. The Corporate Accountability Project (2004), "How the system works (or doesn't work) and what to do about it," see <http://www.corporations.org/system>.

10. CorpWatch (2002), "Youth protesters take over Chevron oil rig, leave peacefully," see <http://www.corpwatch.org/article.php?id=2428>, or CorpWatch (2002), "Women protesters say deal with Chevron off," see <http://www.corpwatch.org/article.php?id=3088>.

11. Centers for Disease Control and Prevention (2004), "Division of HIV/AIDS prevention: basic statistics," see <http://www.cdc.gov/hiv/stats. htm#international>.

12. WHO (2004), "International women's day: women and HIV/AIDS 8 March 2004," see <http://www.who.int/fch/depts/gwh/en/IWDtwo-pagers0403. pdf>.

13. For example, claims under the North American Agreement on Labor Cooperation (NAALC), a side agreement of the North American Free Trade Agreement (NAFTA), with respect to labour rights violations in *maquilladoras* in Mexico; use of the Alien Tort Claims Act in the United States to sue corporations for their actions overseas; and use of the World Bank Inspection Panel to challenge government decisions with respect to access to health services.

14. See the reports of the UN Special Rapporteur on the Right to Health, Paul Hunt, for a discussion of rights-based approaches to policy-making, including Report to the General Assembly, 10 October 2003, A/58/427, *Report to the Commission on Human Rights: Addendum on Mission to the World Trade Organization*, 1 March 2004, E/CN.4/2004/49/Add.1, and others.

134 • *Jyotsna Agnihotri Gupta*

"TOWARDS TRANSNATIONAL FEMINISMS"

TRANSNATIONAL FEMINISMS: A NEW CONCEPT

In the early 1980s, I was a student pursuing the "women and development" (sub) specialization within the masters programme in development studies, at the Institute of Social Studies in The Hague. This programme was one of the pioneers in the field of women's studies in the Netherlands, under the stewardship of Maria Mies and Kumari Jayawardena. We were a group of international students drawn from all continents. For our first International Women's Day celebration on 8 March 1982, we made a poster with the slogan "Divided in Culture, United in Struggle" and launched a newsletter called *Insisterhood*. During the course, we had become aware of the differences in our social positioning due to our diversity not only in terms of culture, but also race, class, religion, sexual orientation, etc. And yet we felt the bond of sisterhood in terms of the shared discrimination, subordination and oppression that either we had experienced personally as women or had learnt of

From *European Journal of Women's Studies* Copyright © 2006 SAGE Publications. Vol. 13(1): 23–38. Reprinted by permission from SAGE Publications.

through our work, as well as the need for feminist scholarship and political organizing to fight against it. Were we being too naive then in discounting our differences? And were we too optimistic regarding forging solidarity, speaking from our own privileged positions within our own societies, or could we actually see the commonalities beyond the differences?

Now, we are more than 20 years further. Over the years, in our postmodern, "posthuman," and perhaps for some, even "postfeminism" (Braithwaite, 2002) times, the idea of "universal truths" has been replaced by "diversity." The category "woman" has been deconstructed to take cognizance of the differences among women. Also, the idea of our individual "situatedness" within intersections has gained ground, and there is a multiplicity of world's feminisms. At the same time, the concept "transnational feminisms" has been introduced to mark the shift from "global sisterhood" (Morgan, 1984), which according to some bears the bias of ethnocentrism. "Transnational feminisms" is a fairly new concept to emerge in western academia. So, what does this term encompass? What does it have to offer feminists at the beginning of the 21st century? Is it just a new buzzword, or does it have an added value over the old concept of "global sisterhood" used during the second wave of the women's movement mainly by first world, white, middle-class feminists, a term that allegedly glossed over the differences between women? Is the concept "transnational feminisms" adequate to describe women's organizing across the globe from their different social positioning and interests? Is transnational solidarity possible and on what grounds will it be built under the conditions of transnational capitalism in this era of globalization? In particular, women's use of technologies for assisted conception and the local and global transactions in reproductive body parts form a testing ground for transnational feminisms.

As a point of departure for reflecting on these questions, I make use of the insights of Breny Mendoza (2002) and Chandra Talpade Mohanty (2003a). According to Mendoza, the concept "transnational feminisms" builds on feminist postcolonial criticism within western academia, and seems to imply a shared context of exploitation and domination across North and South. Used in the plural, it "points to the multiplicity of the world's feminisms and to the increasing tendency of national feminisms to politicize women's issues beyond the borders of the nation state, for instance, in United

Nations (UN) women's world conferences, or on the Internet. The term points simultaneously to the position feminists worldwide have taken against the processes of globalization of the economy, the demise of the nation state and the development of a global mass culture, as well as to the nascent global women's studies research into the ways in which globalization affects women around the globe" (Mendoza, 2002: 296). "But foremost," Mendoza continues, "it takes its meaning from Third and First World feminist theorizations on race, class and sexuality, and feminist postcolonial studies that make us aware of the artificiality of the idea of nation and its patriarchal nature" (Mendoza, 2002:296). It envisages the desirability and possibility of a political solidarity of feminists across the globe transcending race, class, sexuality and national boundaries, based on the concrete experiences of transnational organizing of women.

While "global sisterhood" starts out from the commonalities between women, "transnational feminisms" departs from the differences between women. Mendoza (2002: 310), however, puts the finger on the problem in saying that although committed to intersectional analysis and transversal politics as well as dedicated to praxis rooted in postcolonial critiques of racism, ethnocentrism, sexism and heteronormativity and committed to the subversion of multiple oppressions, transnational feminist debates still reveal important gaps between the intentions—in terms of its theory and tactics— and outcomes of transnational feminist mobilizations. Many of these gaps derive from an undertheorization or an inadequate treatment of political economic issues within feminist postcolonial criticism and their entrapment in cultural debates. I share this concern of Mendoza and find the insights developed by Mohanty (1986, 2003a, 2003b) useful to approach these concerns.

Mohanty (1986) argued that "cross-cultural feminist work must be attentive to the micropolitics of context, subjectivity, and struggle, as well as to the macropolitics of global economic and political systems and processes." Inspired by Maria Mies's and Vandana Shiva's writings, she places feminist solidarity firmly within a broad framework of anti-capitalist struggles. UN conferences—such as the International Conference on Population and Development in Cairo (including its NGO counterpart) and the World Conferences on Women—as well as the campaigns around WTO negotiations, such as the popularly known "Battle of

Seattle," have acted as important catalysts for global solidarity, and not only among feminists. For instance, events such as the regional Social Forums, and the World Social Forum last held in Mumbai in January 2004, were manifestations of global solidarity of men and women, on myriad issues, and in particular against the neoliberal development model now also embraced by many developing countries. These transnational forms of politicization and social movements, invoking the idea of a global citizenship, have also been referred to as "globalization from below" . . . .

ETHICAL UNIVERSALS AND TRANSNATIONAL FEMINISMS

Transnational feminist analyses and practices require an acknowledgement of the fact that one's privileges in the world-system are always linked to another woman's oppression or exploitation. This implies that the perpetual inequalities between women produced by their location in the world-system in themselves foreclose the possibility of solidarity (Grewal and Kaplan, 1994). Transnational feminist practices require comparative work rather than the relativistic thinking of "differences" undertaken by proponents of "global feminism"; that is, to compare multiple, overlapping and discrete oppressions rather than to construct a theory of hegemonic oppression under a unified category of gender. Amrita Basu (1995), too, has shown the importance of attending to "local feminisms" instead, even if the cost of doing so means abandoning hopes for a "master theory" of gender or a unified feminist agenda. Mohanty (2003b: 250) is more optimistic, and believes that "global capitalism" both destroys the possibilities [for a transnational feminist practice] and also offers up new ones. She suggests the thorough embeddedness of the local and the particular within the global and the universal, and envisions a feminism without borders to address the injustices of global capitalism.

The challenges posed by new socioeconomic and political developments in a globalized world constantly require new responses and new strategies at a practical level; at an analytical level, they require re-examining old concepts and theoretical paradigms and developing new ones. Mohanty (2003a: 518) suggests that a "comparative feminist studies" or "feminist solidarity" model is the most useful and productive pedagogical

strategy for feminist cross-cultural work. "It is through this model that we can put into practice the idea of 'common difference' as the basis for deeper solidarity across differences and unequal power relations." . . .

(2006)

NOTES

The research on the transaction in body parts for this article was conducted within a research project, "Body Parts, Property and Gender," funded by a grant from the Netherlands Foundation for the Advancement of Tropical Research (NWOWOTRO), project number WB 52-871 during my affiliation as postdoctoral researcher at Leiden University Medical Centre. I am extremely grateful to Professor Dr Annemiek Richters, Leiden University Medical Centre, Department of Culture, Health and Illness, for comments and suggestions on earlier drafts of this article and to Professor Dr Indu Agnihotri, Centre for Women's Development Studies, New Delhi, for her input. I also thank the anonymous reviewers for their sharp comments and suggestions.

This article is a revised version of my presentation at the conference "Passing on Feminism" held to commemorate the 10th anniversary of the *European Journal of Women's Studies*, Belle van Zuylen Institute, Amsterdam, 23 January 2004.

REFERENCES

Basu, Amrita, ed. (1995) *Women's Movements in Global Perspective*. Boulder, CO and Oxford: Westview Press.

Braithwaite, Ann (2002) "The Personal, the Political, Third-Wave and Postfeminisms," *Feminist Theory* 3(3): 335–44.

Grewal, Inderpal and Caren Kaplan, eds (1994) *Scattered Hegemonies: Postmodernity and Transnational Feminist Practices*. Minneapolis and London: University of Minnesota Press.

Mendoza, Breny (2002) "Transnational Feminisms in Question," *Feminist Theory* 3(3): 295–314.

Mohanty, Chandra Talpade (1986) "Under Western Eyes: Feminist Scholarship and Colonial Discourses," *Boundary* 2 12(3): 333–58.

Mohanty, Chandra Talpade (2003a) "'Under Western Eyes' Revisited: Feminist Solidarity through Anticapitalist Struggles," *Signs: Journal of Women in Culture and Society* 28(2): 499–535.

Mohanty, Chandra Talpade (2003b) *Feminism Without Borders: Decolonizing Theory, Practicing Solidarity*. Durham, NC: Duke University Press.

Morgan, Robin (1984) *Sisterhood is Global: The International Women's Movement Anthology*. New York: Anchor Press/Doubleday.

135 • *Skye Brannon*

"FIREWEED"

It was a remembering day for Baluta. It began with laughter, or a dream of laughter. It was Alanso's laugh, flowing like doves out of her bright smiling mouth. It was Alanso's laugh, out from between those cheeks that caught the sun and held it in a warm glow the rest of the day. It was Alanso's laugh, stirred from the dead to wake Baluta. Sometimes remembering began later in the day, but not today. Baluta had to lift from beneath a stone of grief, so heavy with his sister's memory, to get out of his cot. He had work today, after all.

Baluta washed in the shower, cold after his brother and sister-in-law had had theirs. Cold like Kpatawee Falls back home, Baluta thought. Yes. Today would be a remembering day. He pulled a work shirt over his head. The name "Joel" was simply embroidered over the heart. The name had been his brother's idea.

"Dese Americans," Jato said, "if you tell dem your Mandika name, dey look like you've given dem a riddle. You tell dem your name is Bob, and dey are all smiles." Jato grinned at his younger brother. "But you can't have Bob, dat is mine."

Jato and his wife, Sama, had already gone. Since Baluta had to have the car to go where the bus route didn't, it was Jato and Sama who had to wake at five a.m. to catch buses to work. Baluta felt awful for this, but he had to work to get a car, and needed a car to get to work. So, here he was, walking toward the family vehicle. Jato called it the Swiss Chevy. The old Camero had so many holes in its body, the attempts at duct-tape patchwork had been abandoned, and Baluta heard the wind whistle through them as he drove through the ghettos of his neighborhood, through the factory district, out to the country, past golf resorts, and finally in through a large gate toward his work site.

Just the week before, he'd taken a left at the cross-roads in the neighborhood, to work on a banister for Mrs Giles. She'd nodded, pleased at Baluta's work, and as a reward referred him for more work. "This couple has some cabinet problems that are really bothersome, Jim." Even remembering Baluta's fake name was too difficult for Mrs Giles. "I'll give you a call if they want you to come over."

She had and Baluta was on his way. This time, he would take a right after entering the gate, and drive past the large man-made pond. It was only a lip, a small man-made lip on one side of the water's body, but it was just the same curve as the pond where he and Alanso played, splashing and laughing. She could pull fish from that pond, like plucking flowers from a field, and would howl good-naturedly at Baluta's empty handed attempts. When they would get back to their hut, a square in the shanty-town quilt shadowed by a mountain, Alanso would always tell Grandma Awa that Baluta had caught some fish. She'd smile at Baluta, and he'd kick the dirt embarrassed.

Baluta pulled his attention from the pond, from his remembering. He noted the wrought-iron numbers on the mansions he passed. When he was several numbers away, he took his foot off the gas. He hoped he could glide to a stop in front of the correct house, otherwise, the Swiss Chevy would let out a loud squeal when he hit the brake. He had timed it just right to slow to a dead stop just at the start of brownstone path that led to the palatial home.

He saw a lady, pretty, laid back inside the house, behind the glass of a large bay window. In his side vision, he saw her sit up straight at Swiss Chevy's approach. When he got out of the car, he noticed a frightened look on her face and that she clutched a phone in her hand.

From *One World: A Global Anthology of Short Stories.* Oxford: New Internationalist Publications Ltd., 2009.
Reprinted by permission of New Internationalist.

That posture, that clutching, that frightened look, it made Baluta remember his father's monkey traps. They were just small boxes with a drilled hole and a nut inside. The monkeys could put their hands in the box to grab the nut, but they could not pull their fists out, and refused to let go of the treasures. This lady in the square of the window, she had the same posture, still and frightened, as those monkeys when Baluta's father would collect them.

By the time Baluta had gotten out of the car, she was gone from the window and standing behind the door, opened only slightly.

"Did you need something?" she called out.

Baluta smiled a wide smile, standing still next to his car. "Hello der, Miss! I am Joel, the carpenter."

"Okay." The woman stayed still behind the door, closing it a little more.

"Mrs Giles said you needed some cabinets fixed?"

"Oh!" Suddenly, the woman became comfortable. The scared monkey in her had run away. "That's right. I forgot Cindy had said you were coming today."

Joel nodded, starting up the path.

"Oh, wait." The lady seemed to shout as an afterthought. She pointed out toward where Joel was walking. "Could you please smash down that pile of dirt?"

"Sorry, Miss?" Joel looked around and saw a small mound of earth, piled up around a hole.

"Yes, that. The real-estate agent just left that hole there when she pulled out her sign. I'll have to use someone else next time. Could you go ahead and fill up that hole?"

"Sure, Miss." He didn't know this lady's name, Baluta thought, and was already at work for her. He approached the mound and the remembering began. It was the mound of dirt full of ants that he and Alanso used to torment. He had been stung once, and then twice, and then a third time. Every time he had cried, and watched the welts rise on the bites. These ant stings were more painful than any other, little fire irons on the skin. Alanso told him that it must have been because he was a sweet boy, and she a sour little girl.

It was only a moment, and the dirt was back in its place, a dot of black in the lush green. The lady watched from the steps, pleased. She introduced herself as Tiffany, and moved through the large entry way, into the extravagant kitchen. She teetered on tall, skinny high heels as she walked, stopped at a cabinet above the sink, and opened it accusingly.

"This has *got* to be fixed." She looked at Baluta for confirmation.

Baluta nodded, but saw nothing wrong. The cabinet was of beautiful hardwood. "What is it, Miss?"

"This," Tiffany tried to push the cabinet door back, and it remained straight out. "This, this door needs to go *all* the way back, not just straight out. *All* the way back. *All* of them. All of them should go *all* the way back."

"Okay, Miss. Dis is not a problem. I can fix dis today. Mrs Giles told you of my terms, yes?"

"Yes. Fine." Tiffany waved absently. "She said you were from Africa?'

"Liberia." Baluta clarified.

"Oh, sorry." Tiffany looked at the cabinet again. "Cindy said you were from Africa. How long will this take?"

"Only a few hours, Miss."

"Fine. I'll just be right there." Tiffany pointed her slender finger toward the granite counter tops. The sunlight bounced from her diamond ring and danced dazzles across Baluta's face. Diamonds.

"They think they've found diamonds in our mountain." Baluta's father, Idirissa, had once told him gravely. "The war will be coming our way soon." Baluta remembered; it was the first time he had seen fear behind his father's strong eyes.

Tiffany scooted up to the granite counter while Baluta began his work. Slick magazines splayed in front of her. Pouting models wearing high skinny heels. Grand dining room and kitchen displays. A collage of movie stars caught in the act of living, with the byline "who got fat, who got skinny, who got married, who got surgery." She flipped through the magazines absently while Baluta lost himself in the work, the sawdust, and the remembering.

Tiffany's cellphone rang. It was a custom ring of a song called "I still haven't found what I'm looking for" by U2. She flipped the phone. "Yes?" She turned a page absently, and then slammed her fist on the counter. "What do you mean they don't have it? It said right there on the website that it was in stock! Have you gone to the paint store on 78th Street?" Baluta tried to shut his ears to this woman's trill. "Are you sure you are asking for the right color? F-I-R-E-W-E-E-D? Fireweed?" The word hit Baluta right in the heart. It knocked his breath from his lungs, and stilled his hands. Fireweed.

"Go! Go you! Go get de fireweed now! You are a very bad boy!" Grandma Awa had caught Baluta with his hand in the cassava pile. He had been so hungry and wanted only a small slice, but Grandma Awa, her eyes usually full of kindness, was irate at this. She never spanked him, no, but ordered something far worse—fireweed. Even in mouths long used to hot peppers, sucking on the bitter red leaves would make your eyes water in pain.

"Fireweed!" Tiffany screeched. "That's the only one that will work. Chet, what are we going to do? We already have two walls painted fireweed in the second guest bedroom? Are we going to have two fucking mismatched walls? Not in my house we aren't. Go to the store on 78th. I don't care. The painters will be here tomorrow and then are booked up for a month with the Tremmel's renovation. Chet, get that paint or I swear to God. Just go."

"Just go! Go now!" Grandma Awa had said, looking down at her mortar, smashing the rice.

"Can I go with him?" Alanso had chimed in, her eyes sparkling.

"Do you want de fireweed too?" Grandma raised her eyebrows to Alanso, who looked down silent.

Baluta's hands stopped working on the cabinets. The remembering had captured him. That day, the day he went to get fireweed. He never wanted to remember that day. With this woman's screaming about paint, it was accosting him now. His trip, past the ant pile, past the pond where Alanso caught her fish, past his father's monkey traps to the small fireweed bush stretched out in his mind. He'd picked the largest leaf he could find. The larger the leaf, the less the sting, he and Alanso had decided.

He held the stem of the fireweed gingerly, ready to hold it up to Grandma Awa for inspection when he returned, before putting it in his mouth. Past the monkey traps, past the pond, he stopped still at the ant pile. Fear had frozen him. From the ant pile, he saw the dust surrounding their shanty. He saw the jeeps and men with guns and machetes. He saw his father, swinging from a tree, on a rope. He saw a hill on the ground the same colored pattern as Grandma Awa's dress, still, in a growing circle of red.

"Are you there, Chet? On 78th? Do you see the fireweed?"

Baluta held tightly to the fireweed stem, he could not move even though troupes of ants attacked his feet. Sting, sting, sting, he stood still, holding tightly onto his fireweed. He saw little Alanso's ten-year old body, limp, naked in the sun, being passed from one soldier to another, his pants mingling with the dust. Sting, sting, sting.

"Chet, if I don't get that fireweed, I'm just going to die!"

(2009)

Glossary

A

Androgyny: Where people display such a melding of masculine and feminine characteristics that the performance of distinct gender roles is no longer visible or necessary.

Anti-Imperialist League: Founded in 1898 to oppose the United States' acquisition of colonies and territories abroad. It included more than 100 affiliated organizations, approximately 30,000 members, and more than 500,000 contributors by the turn of the twentieth century.

B

Biopower: Michel Foucault's term for how modern states regulate their subjects through a number of subtle techniques to achieve control over bodies and populations. He especially focused on the role played by medical and social scientific discourses in creating a discourse of normality where people's bodies and social practices were categorized as normal or abnormal.

Bourgeoisie: A Marxist term for the capitalist class who own businesses or capital assets and hire wage labor. He further divided this class into finance, industrial, and mercantile capitalists.

Bread and Roses: "Bread and Roses" was first published as a poem by James Oppenheim in 1911 and later became an anthem for working women's rights. It is often associated with a strike of women textile workers in Lawrence, Massachusetts, in 1912 called the Bread and Roses Strike.

C

Capitalist-patriarchy: A concept used by socialist feminist Heidi Hartmann to argue that feminist theory must examine two realms of society—social production and social reproduction—for class oppression and gender oppression to be given equal importance.

Care drain: Refers to the children, the elderly, and the sick left behind in the third world when their mothers or fathers migrate to seek work abroad.

Cisgender person: A cisgender person is someone who identifies as the gender/sex they were assigned at birth.

Colonialism: Refers to direct social, economic, political, and cultural control of a region or country by a foreign power. In *colonies of rule*, an oligarchy of colonial administrators organizes the life of indigenous people in the colonies to facilitate the home country's economic and political aims. In *settler colonialism* the colonial administrators are accompanied by immigrants who settle on the lands of indigenous peoples (see also "internal colonialism").

Colonialist stance (or missionary stance): Used in postcolonial theory to criticize Western feminists when they portray third-world women as victims of stagnant, backward cultural traditions, such that they are unable to politically act on their own behalf and need to be rescued by modern, enlightened feminists from the West.

Colonies of rule: (See colonialism.)

Comparable worth: The demand that jobs which require comparable skills, ability, and educational requirements should receive similar wages or salaries. This is especially relevant to sex-segregated areas of the work where jobs traditionally held by women often are paid less than traditionally male jobs that require less skill or education.

Compulsory heterosexuality: Adrienne Rich's concept that challenges the "naturalness" of heterosexuality. It refers to how heterosexuality has been rigidly enforced by patriarchal institutions to maintain women's subservience through emotional and erotic loyalty to men. Rich asks, If heterosexuality is natural, why do societies need such violent strictures to enforce it?

Convention on the Elimination of All Forms of Discrimination against Women (CEDAW): Adopted by the United Nations in 1979, this legislation called on all UN member-states to eliminate attitudes and practices that discriminate against women. Although at least 180 countries have signed this legislation, the United States had not done so as of July 2014.

Cult of domesticity (or cult of true womanhood): A set of ideals stemming from the doctrine of separate spheres that romanticized women's place in the home as loving wife, nurturing mother, and moral servant.

D

Development of underdevelopment: A term used by dependency theorists to highlight the interrelated processes that foster first-world enrichment through the exploitation of third-world countries, whereby the rich countries get richer and the poor countries get poorer.

Diaspora: A term used to capture the notion of a dispersal or scattering of peoples from their homelands to multiple locations as a consequence of global labor migrations.

Doctrine of coverture: Common law doctrine that held that, once a man and woman were married, they were one in front of the law. This "one" was the man who controlled the property and income of the household and had the right to chastise or punish his wife and children.

Doctrine of separate spheres: A nineteenth-century ideology that relegated women's roles to the private sphere of the home and men's roles to the public sphere outside of the home.

E

Empirical: Evidence is said to be empirical when it is observable through one's sense of sight, sound, smell, taste, or touch and is verifiable by others.

Environmental justice movement: A multiracial, multiclass grassroots movement that emerged in the 1980s and organized around environmental issues that disproportionately affect communities of color, such as pollution, toxic hazards, and the location of waste facilities.

Environmental racism: Refers to how race is an independent variable, not reducible to social class, in predicting the distribution of environmental hazards and pollution in societies.

Epistemology: Refers to the study of who can be a knowledge producer, how knowledge is produced, and what constitutes privileged knowledge.

Epistemic violence: A term coined by postcolonial feminist Gayatri Spivak to refer to the destruction of indigenous languages, culture, and thought that accompanies colonial conquest.

Equal pay: Equal pay for work of equal value has long been a feminist demand. The Equal Pay Act was passed in 1963 and although women's earnings vis-à-vis men's have risen, they still stand at less than men's earnings for similar work.

Essentialism: An approach that attributes certain qualities, traits, or behaviors to all members of a group.

Ethic of care: Emphasizes interconnectedness and emerges to a greater degree in girls because of their early connection in identity formation with their mothers, according to some feminist psychoanalytical theorists.

Ethic of justice: Emphasizes adherence to formal rules based on masculine identity formation that requires separation and individualism from the mother, according to some feminist psychoanalytical theorists.

European Union (EU): An agreement among European nations to remove restrictions on the movement of commodities, services, capital, and labor with the goal of competing more successfully on the world market. Established in 1993, it now includes more than two dozen nations.

Expressive roles: In sex role theory, these are emotional, people-oriented, caretaking roles assigned to women that contrast with the impersonal, instrumental roles assigned to men.

F

Feminine mystique: Betty Friedan introduced this concept in 1963 to refer to how learned femininity undermined gender equality. She lamented how young women were taught to pity unfeminine career women and how they eschewed the opportunities for higher education, political rights, and financial independence that the first wave had struggled to achieve in favor of marriage and childrearing.

Feminist separatism: Women's conscious and willful separation from various aspects of patriarchal control. In its purest form it would mean not living with or having anything to do with adult males.

Feminization of global migration: A phenomenon witnessed in the 1980s when women made up an increasing proportion of people who migrated from poor to rich countries to take jobs.

Finance capital: Enterprises that generate profits from lending money, investments, and/or manipulating currencies (such as banks or insurance companies) in contrast to industrial capitalist enterprises, where profits are generated from the actual production of commodities.

First wave: The surge of U.S. women's rights activism beginning in the 1830s and culminating around the campaign for women's suffrage that ended or at least went into abeyance in 1920 with the passage of the Nineteenth Amendment to the U.S. Constitution.

First world: Developed during the Cold War, this concept referred to highly developed, industrial, capitalist countries.

Flexible capitalism: A term used to reflect how transnational corporations adapt to changing political and economic conditions and tap into different labor pools (skilled or unskilled, blue collar or white collar, foreign or domestic) regardless of where they are located so long as optimal production, infrastructural, marketing, and political conditions exist.

Free love: (See sex love.)

G

Gender binary: Refers to the idea that humans exist in two essential, biologically determined forms (male and female). This binary is sustained by dividing people into gender roles based on their presumed location as male or female, disciplining people into believing in the naturalness of their gender location, and policing any violations to the male/female gender order.

Genderqueer: This movement celebrates and works in the political interests of those who break free of the constraints of the gender binary by subversively playing with gender norms, living between genders, and embodying both, neither, or multiple genders.

Genocide: The deliberate, systematic killing of a racial, cultural, or religious group.

Global North: A term used by contemporary theorists to refer to high-income, high-consumption societies.

Global South: A term used by contemporary theorists to refer to low-income, low-consumption societies.

God trick: A critical term used to refer to scientists' claims that they can view the world in a detached, impartial, objective, and value-free manner.

H

Harlem Renaissance: A cultural movement that spanned the period roughly between the 1920s and the 1930s that enabled African Americans to challenge racism and transform negative racial stereotypes through their intellect and the production of art, music, and literature.

Heteronormativity: The assumption that heterosexuality is natural, normal, and socially appropriate. It becomes the standard by which other sexual practices are deemed deviant.

Hidden injuries of social class: A term used to describe the damage done to people's self-esteem when they are made to feel inadequate because of their lower class position.

Historical specificity: A term used by feminists who call for concrete analyses of a specific time and place to avoid the dangers of making broad, sweeping generalizations that often ignore differences between women and differences in how various social phenomena affect women.

Homophobia: Heterosexuals' fear of and discrimination against lesbians and gay men.

I

Identity politics: Where people's politics are rooted in group identities, such as race, class, gender, or sexual orientation. Identity is the motivation for political action and the basis for delineating political concerns. **Single-axis identity politics** address one form of oppression, such as the women's movement. **Multiaxis identity politics** address more than one form of oppression, such as those often found in intersectional analysis.

Imperialism: A foreign power's forceful economic, political, and cultural domination over another nation or geopolitical formation. As contrasted with premodern forms of imperialism, modern imperialism destroys indigenous forms of production by usurping and privatizing land and forcing premodern economies into market economies.

Institutional ethnography: A term Dorothy Smith uses to describe her research, which examines how the social practices of everyday life affect, are affected by, and are linked to the social practices undertaken in social institutions and organizations. It shows how social practices are the anatomy of social life and how they can reproduce or resist the status quo.

Instrumental roles: In sex role theory, these are the impersonal and task-oriented roles assigned to men that contrast with the expressive, emotional roles played by women.

Internal colonialism (or settler colonialism): Refers to colonies existing *within* a country where subordinate groups (often of a different race) are relegated to menial and low-paying jobs, denied the citizenship rights held by the dominant group, and are forced to assimilate the language and culture of the dominant group. The peoples and lands that comprise these internal colonies were historically established by force, such as through slavery and/or military conquest.

International Monetary Fund (IMF): An agency established at the end of World War II to oversee the international monetary system to ensure the stability of currency and to stimulate trade. Its efforts later expanded to regulate repayments of loans made to indebted countries.

International Women's Day: Celebrated each year on March 8 to honor the social, political, and cultural achievements of women. It was established by the Second International in 1910 to commemorate major strikes by women workers.

Intersex: A term used for people who are born with a reproductive or sexual anatomy and/or chromosome pattern that does not seem to fit typical definitions of male or female.

J

Judgmental relativism: The postmodern epistemological stance that, because all knowledge is socially situated and socially constructed, no one knowledge claim or vantage point can be judged as superior or more valid than any other.

L

Lavender menace: A term used to describe the fears of some feminists that lesbians were undermining and discrediting the women's movement. It arose in the 1960s after Betty Friedan called lesbian issues the "lavender herring" of the women's movement.

Lesbian continuum: A concept used by Adrienne Rich to highlight the importance of a wide range of women-centered experiences, such as mother–daughter relationships, sister-to-sister relations, women's friendships, and sexual intimacy between women. This continuum was used not only to describe lesbianism as more than simply a sexual issue, but also to foster common ground for unifying lesbian and straight women.

M

Maldevelopment: A term introduced by Vandana Shiva to critically interrogate what is meant by "development" by highlighting the negative impacts of the economic development on indigenous societies.

Matrix of domination: A concept developed by Patricia Hill Collins to describe multiple axes of privilege and oppression. Within this matrix, people have a social location in terms of structural forms of oppression such as race, ethnicity, social class, gender, and/or sexual orientation. Thus people can simultaneously be both oppressed and oppressors because they could occupy social locations of penalty and privilege. Wealthy black males, for example, have privilege by their class and gender positions, but are penalized by their racial location.

Missionary framework: (See colonialist stance.)

Modern imperialism: (See imperialism.)

Municipal housekeeping: A term used for women's environmental activism in the nineteenth and early twentieth centuries. In an era when political activism by women was viewed as improper, framing their concerns over municipal sanitation and clean air, water, and food as extensions of domestic roles within the home gave their environmental activism more legitimacy.

N

National American Woman Suffrage Association (NAWSA): Formed in the 1890's through a merger of the National Women's Suffrage Association and the American Women's Suffrage Association, it was the largest suffrage organization during the first wave.

National Organization for Women (NOW): Founded in 1966 by liberal feminists, it has been the largest feminist organization in the United States over the past half century.

Neocolonialism: A term developed to describe the indirect economic, political, and cultural control of a formally independent country by a foreign power.

Neoliberalism: An economic ideology that arose in the late 1970s based on open, unrestricted markets and free trade. It promotes competitive capitalism, deregulation, and reductions in government size and government spending in favor of privatization.

New Left: Refers to the new social movements of late modernity such as the civil rights movement, the women's movement, the gay and lesbian rights movement, and the anti–Vietnam war movement. Along with a focus social class, the New Left addressed the conflicts and cleavages generated by inequalities of race, gender, sexuality, and global location.

New mestiza consciousness: A term developed by Gloria Anzaldúa to express how people of mixed heritage can empower themselves by recognizing the richness of the contradictions and ambiguities entailed in their hybridity. This new consciousness is a powerful critique of binary thought because it treasures diversity and the fluidity of identities.

Normativity: A term used by queer theorists to refer to conventional forms of association, belonging, and identification that are prescribed as socially appropriate in a given time and place. Critiquing normativity is a major premise of queer theory.

North American Free Trade Agreement (NAFTA): Signed into law in 1993, this agreement among Canada, the United States, and Mexico reduced barriers to trade and investment between these countries.

O

Old Left: The term "Old Left" refers to political perspectives that arose in the nineteenth century, such as Marxism and anarchism, whose aim was to make societies free from oppression. Although they struggled against many forms of oppression, they focused on class oppression and championed the working class as the primary agent of revolutionary social change.

Orientalism: A term developed by Edward Said to point out the socially constructed and mythic notion of the "Orient" imposed on the land and peoples of the colonized East that served to "other" this region and to define and solidify the concept of the "West."

P

Palimpsestic: A palimpsest is a parchment that has been inscribed and reinscribed with the previous text being imperfectly erased and partly visible. Postcolonial theorists use this concept as a metaphor for their view of social change and sociohistorical time as imperfect erasures whereby the past is always visible in the present.

Panopticon (or panoptical gaze): Michel Foucault's term to describe the powerful effects on individuals when institutional and normative surveillance is internalized. This modern technique of power leads people to police their own behaviors and practices to avoid stigma or punishment, thereby reducing the need for direct force in dealing with deviance.

Paradigm shift: A fundamental change in the theoretical assumptions underlying an entire school of thought or worldview. It results not only in different scientific conclusions, but also in a transformation of the entire conceptual framework of social thought that prevails in a given discipline or area of study.

Patriarchy: Institutionalized male dominion over women and children.

Performance: Ritualized acts or practices by an individual that construct the social fiction of a psychological interiority to identities, such as race, gender, or social class.

Personal is political: This slogan of the second wave refers to how gender-related problems that were often treated as personal problems should be addressed politically as problems rooted in social institutions. It also enjoined feminists to live their politics in their everyday lives, thus motivating transformations of both the individual and society.

Polyvocality: A term that highlights the value of including many diverse voices or multiple vantage points in the creation of knowledge.

Postcolonial: A critical concept that refers to engaging with and challenging colonial discourses as well as the social, economic, political, and cultural legacies of colonialism.

Primitive accumulation: Marx's term for how the origins of capitalism entailed brute force and violence to transform premodern economies into modern industrial capitalist societies. Rosa Luxemburg argued that primitive accumulation is a recurring process in the imperial drive of capitalism into foreign lands.

Privileging the knowledge of the oppressed: An epistemological stance taken by many standpoint theorists that argues that the social locations of marginalized or subordinated people provide superior vantage points for critically understanding power relations.

Problem that has no name: Betty Friedan's term for the persistent depression found among housewives, which she attributed to traditional gender roles that provided few avenues for individual self-fulfillment for these women.

Production for exchange: A Marxist phrase used by Marxist and socialist feminists to describe labor that produces commodities (goods for sale) or garners an income. It served to analytically distinguish different types of work done by women.

Production for use: A Marxist phrase used by Marxist and socialist feminists to describe unpaid labor performed for immediate use or consumption. It was used to highlight how the unpaid work done by homemakers (such as cooking, cleaning, and child care) places women in a dependent position financially in market economies.

Proletariat: A Marxist term for the wage laborers or the working class in a capitalist system. In Marx's era, these wage laborers were primarily blue-collar workers.

Q

Queer: A critique of all things oppressively normal, especially conventional ideas about sex. As such, it embraces sexual and gender difference.

Queer places: Queer culture celebrates alternative ways of life often centered on local bars, public performances, art scenes, activist projects, collective sexual exploration, and extended communities. As a result, queer adults remain engaged in activities that heterosexual adults often deem immature, deviant, or irresponsible. Queer places refer to the sites that enable queer subculture to survive (see also queer time).

Queer time: Queer time defies the norms associated with heteronormative adulthood, such as having a stable job, entering a monogamous marriage (ideally with a person of the opposite sex), keeping one's sexuality private, avoiding risks, and striving to make as much money as possible to buy material objects for one's family. As a result, queer adults remain engaged in activities that heterosexual adults deem immature, self-indulgent, or idealistic (such as performing in drag, playing in a punk band, or organizing street protests)—the very activities that grown-ups are encouraged to leave behind as they become responsible adults.

R

Redstockings: A radical feminist organization that reclaimed the pejorative label "bluestockings" used for educated women in the nineteenth century using the color red to signify their radical politics. Their 1968 "Redstockings Manifesto" was one of the earliest statements of the assumptions and goals of radical feminism.

Reflexivity: The recognition that one's ideas and behaviors are influenced by one's own social location and how one's ideas and behaviors affect other people. A reflexive approach to research methods requires that researchers acknowledge their roles in knowledge production and how their own social locations may influence their studies. It also requires that they consider how their studies may impact their own views, as well as other people.

Reform-oriented politics: Politics that involve working within the existing institutional system through legitimate electoral, legislative, and judicial processes. Reform-oriented politics are often contrasted with revolutionary politics that call for a qualitative change of the system itself.

Reproductive justice: A term used by women of color to emphasize their concerns with having the freedom to give birth, to keep their children, and not to have contraception or sterilization forced upon them.

Riot Grrrls: These feminists made space for women within punk rock by creating their own music and zines, developing their own record labels, and ensuring mosh pits were safe for women. They inspired many third-wave feminists to engage in political activism.

Roe v. Wade: The 1973 U.S. Supreme Court's decision that established a constitutional right to privacy, a woman's right to control her body, and the legalization of abortion.

S

Second wave: The resurgence of U.S. feminist activism in the 1960s that ended or at least suffered major setbacks with the defeat of the Equal Rights Amendment (ERA) in 1982.

Second world: Developed during the Cold War era, this concept referred to industrially developed socialist and/or communist countries.

Settler colonialism: (See internal colonialism.)

Sex love (or free love): Used by first-wave feminists to refer to the right to marry for love, to have sex with someone you loved, and for women to have the same sexual rights as men.

Sex-segregated occupations: This refers to how some occupations traditionally have been gender specific, whereby women dominate in certain areas of work such as teachers and nurses, whereas men dominate in other areas of work such as plumbers or electricians. (See comparable worth.)

Sexual reformism: A thread of feminist theorizing beginning in the late eighteenth century that emphasized a woman's right to make sexual choices based on rationality, dignity, and autonomy.

Sex wars: The term "sex wars" has been used to describe heated debates that took place *within* the second wave of U.S. feminism from the late 1970s through the mid-1980s. These debates focused on the implications of various sexual practices for women's liberation. Feminists argued over pornography, sex work, censorship, sadomasochism, and other erotic practices in terms of what constituted nonpatriarchal forms of sex or whether there should even be such a notion.

Shakespeare's sister: A fictional character developed by Virginia Woolf to lament how women voices were missing from literature because they were denied opportunities for education and writing. She calls on women to take up the pen and write their way into history.

Socially lived knowledge: Refers to knowledge gained from everyday life experiences in contrast to knowledge garnered from formal education or training.

Social reproduction of labor power: A term used by second-wave Marxist and socialist feminists to refer to the labor involved in domestic labor, such as cooking, cleaning, and caretaking, which enables the people cared for to go back to work each day refueled and rejuvenated. It also includes the intergenerational reproduction of labor power through childbirth and childrearing.

STOP-ERA movement: An antifeminist movement led by Phyllis Schlafly in the 1970s and early 1980s to stop the passage of the Equal Rights Amendment to the U.S. Constitution.

Strategy of dismissal: Ostracizing the ideas or actions of group members that are found to be threatening to group cohesion or control.

Structural adjustment programs (SAPs): Methods of repayment imposed on heavily indebted countries by the International Monetary Fund and the World Bank to ensure loans would not go into default. These measures include reducing government funds spent on social programs (such as health care, education, and welfare) and focusing economic activity on export production.

Subaltern: A concept used by Antonio Gramsci for subordinate groups in general and especially for groups (such as peasants) that did not fit easily into Marxist class categories. Feminist postcolonial theorist Gayatri Spivak extended the utility of this term to include women and other postcolonial subjects.

Subjugated knowledges: Refers to knowledges (often of subordinate groups and marginalized people) that have been ignored, silenced, or deemed less credible by dominant groups.

T

Third wave: The resurgence of U.S. feminist activism in the 1990s, especially by younger feminists who came of adult age after the second wave.

Third world: A concept that referred to all countries (whether capitalist or socialist) that were not industrialized, but where large proportions of the population were still engaged in direct agricultural production in the post–World War II era.

Transgender: Transgender is a term for people whose gender identity, expression, or behavior is different from that typically associated with their assigned sex at birth.

Trans misogyny: Trans misogyny is steeped in the assumption that femaleness and femininity are inferior to, and exist primarily for the benefit of, maleness and masculinity. It is visible in the greater stigma and marginalization associated with trans female/feminine spectrum people.

Transnational: A term that highlights how new social forms transcend or fail to correspond to the boundaries of the national state. This term is used to highlight the multidirectionality of global influences, the multi-locationality of many people's lives, and the social relations that cut across global locations.

Transnational combatants: Transnational combatants often represent transnational cultural, ethnic, and/or religious communities and garner volunteer armies from multiple countries, such as Al-Qaeda. The rise of transnational combatants in recent decades has resulted in important changes in warfare as, for example, when the U.S. government declared that transnational combatants do not fall under the protections of the Geneva Convention.

Transphobia: Transphobia is an irrational fear of, and/or hostility toward, people who are transgender or who otherwise transgress traditional gender norms.

Transversal politics: An approach to transnational feminist politics aimed at enhancing polyvocality and reducing conflicts between women by dialog that crosses borders both horizontally (such as shared experiences by race, class, and sexuality) and vertically (such as different positions of power and privilege). A person cannot speak for others unless democratically elected and advocates do not have to be members of the constituency for whom they advocate as in the case of identity politics. It is the message not the messenger that is important and all views are recognized as partial.

V

Voluntary motherhood: A nineteenth-century feminist demand that women have the right to abstain from having sexual relations with their husbands. It was a position taken by first-wave feminists who did not support birth control or abortion but who wanted some control over reproduction.

W

Woman-identified-woman: A term used by radical feminists to describe women who are committed to meeting each other's political, economic, and emotional needs rather than giving their primary commitments to men.

Woman's Party: Formed by Alice Paul in 1916 to work exclusively for a federal women's suffrage amendment using a wider array of tactics that Paul had learned from her contact with militant British suffragists. The Woman's Party formed the nucleus for the National Woman's Party that was established a year later.

World Bank: Established as the International Bank for Reconstruction and Development in 1944 to oversee the rebuilding of Europe after World War II. In later decades it became the largest dispenser of development capital to third-world countries.

World Trade Organization (WTO): Established in 1995 to oversee and regulate international trade agreements.

Special thanks to Kristin Schwartz, Laura Dean Shapiro, Dimitra Cupo, and Kristin Lewis for their help in constructing this glossary.

References

Abu-Lughod, Lila. 2002. "Do Muslim Women Really Need Saving? Anthropological Reflections on Cultural Relativism and Its Others." *American Anthropologist* 104, no. 3.

Abu-Lughod, Lila. [2002] 2012. "Do Muslim Women Really Need Saving? Anthropological Reflections on Cultural Relativism and Its Others." Pp. 486–495 in *Feminist Frontiers*, 9th ed. Eds. Verta Taylor, Nancy Whittier, and Leila J. Rupp. Boston: McGraw–Hill.

Adams, Abigail and John Adams. [1776] 1974. "Selected Letters from the Adams Family Correspondence." Pp. 10 and 11 in *The Feminist Papers: From Adams to de Beauvoir*, ed. Alice S. Rossi, 10–11. New York: Bantam.

Adams, Rachel. 2000. "Masculinity without Men." *GLQ: A Journal of Lesbian and Gay Studies* 6(3): 467–478.

Addams, Jane. 1907. "On Municipal Housekeeping." In *Newer Ideals of Peace*. Chatauqua, New York: The Chatauqua Press.

Addams, Jane. [1907] 1973. "On Municipal Housekeeping." Pp. 605–608 in *The Feminist Papers: From Adams to de Beauvoir*. Ed. Alice S. Rossi. New York: Bantam Books.

Addams, Jane, Emily Green Balch, and Alice Hamilton. 1915. "International Congress of Women: The Hague, April 28–May 1, 1915, Resolutions Adopted." http://www.ub .gu.se/kvinn/portaler/fred/samarbete/pdf/resolutions_1915 .pdf/. Retrieved May 30, 2014.

Alexander, M. Jacqui. 2005. *Pedagogies of Crossing: Meditations on Feminism, Sexual Politics, Memory, and the Sacred*. Durham, N.C.: Duke University Press.

Alfonso, Rita, and Jo Trigilio. 1997. "Surfing the Third Wave: A Dialogue between Two Third Wave Feminists." *Hypatia: A Journal of Feminist Philosophy* 12(3): 8–16.

Alonso, Harriet Hyman. 1993. *Peace as a Woman's Issue: A History of the U.S. Movement for World Peace and Women's Rights*. Syracuse, N.Y.: Syracuse University Press.

"American Suffragettes." 1896. Photo by MPI/Getty Images.

Amin, Samir. 1977. *Unequal Development: An Essay on the Social Formations of Peripheral Capitalism*. New York: Monthly Review.

Anderson, Terry H. 2007. "Vietnam Is Here: The Anti-War Movement." Pp. 245–264 in *The War That Never Ends: New Perspectives on the Vietnam War*. Eds. David Anderson and John Ernst. Lexington, K.Y.: University of Kentucky Press.

Angelou, Maya. 1969. *I Know Why the Caged Bird Sings*. New York: Random House.

Anthony, Susan B. [1872] 1992. "Constitutional Argument: Speech after Arrest for Illegal Voting." Pp. 152–164 in *The Elizabeth Cady Stanton–Susan B. Anthony Reader: Correspondence, Writings, Speeches*. Ed. Ellen Carol DuBois. Boston: Northeastern University Press.

Anthony, Susan B., and Elizabeth Cady Stanton. [1899] 1997. "Petition for the Women of Hawaii." Pp. 270–271 in *The Selected Papers of Elizabeth Cady Stanton & Susan B. Anthony, Volume VI: An Awful Hush 1895–1906*. Ed. Ann D. Gordon. New Brunswick, N.J.: Rutgers University Press.

Anthony, Susan B., and Elizabeth Cady Stanton. [1899] 2013. "Petition for the Women of Hawaii." Pp. 270–271 in *The Selected Papers of Elizabeth Cady Stanton & Susan B. Anthony, Volume VI: An Awful Hush 1895–1906*. Ed. Ann D. Gordon. New Brunswick, N.J.: Rutgers University Press.

Anzaldúa, Gloria. 1987. *Borderlands/LaFrontera: The New Mestiza*. San Francisco, Calif.: Aunt Lute Books.

Bailey, Cathryn. 1997. "Making Waves and Drawing Lines: The Politics of Defining the Vicissitudes of Feminism." *Hypatia: A Journal of Feminist Philosophy* 12(3): 17–28.

Bailey, Cathryn. 2002. "Unpacking the Mother/Daughter Baggage: Reassessing Second- and Third-Wave Tensions." *Women's Studies Quarterly* 30(3–4): 138–154.

Bamrah, Amrita. 2014. "34 Years After Signing, United States Still Hasn't Ratified CEDAW." http://www .unfinishedbusiness.org/20140717-34-years-after-signing

-united-states-still-hasnt-ratified-cedaw/. Retrieved October, 31 2014.

Bar On, Bat-Ami. 1993. "Marginality and Epistemic Privilege." Pp. 83–100 in *Feminist Epistemologies*. Eds. Linda Alcoff and Elizabeth Potter. New York: Routledge.

Barrett, Michele, and Anne Phillips, eds. 1992. *Destabilizing Theory: Contemporary Feminist Debates*. Stanford, Calif.: Stanford University Press.

Barrett, Michele. 1980. *Women's Oppression Today: Problems in Marxist Feminist Analyses*. London: Verso.

Bartky, Sandra. 1988. "Foucault, Femininity, and the Modernization of Patriarchal Power." Pp. 61–80 in *Feminism and Foucault: Paths of Resistance* Ed. Lee Quinby and Irene Diamond. Boston: Northeastern University Press.

Bartky, Sandra. [1988] 1997. "Foucault, Femininity, and the Modernization of Patriarchal Power." Pp. 92–111 in *Feminist Social Thought: A Reader* Ed. Diana Tietjens Meyers. New York: Routledge.

Bates, Dawn, and Maureen C. McHugh. 2005. "Zines: Voices of Third Wave Feminists." Pp. 179–194 in *Different Wavelengths: Studies of the Contemporary Women's Movement* Ed. Jo Reger. New York: Routledge.

Bauer-Maglin, Nan, and Donna Perry, eds. 1996. *"Bad Girls"/"Good Girls": Women, Sex, and Power in the Nineties*. New Brunswick, N.J.: Rutgers University Press.

Baumgardner, Jennifer, and Amy Richards. 2000. *Manifesta: Young Women, Feminism, and the Future*. New York: Farrar, Straus and Giroux.

Bebel, August. 1904. *Women under Socialism*. New York: Labor News.

Beisner, Robert L. 1968. *Twelve against Empire: The Anti-Imperialists, 1898–1900*. New York: McGraw–Hill.

Benston, Margaret. 1969. "The Political Economy of Women's Liberation." *Monthly Review* 21(September): 13–25.

Berger, Ronald J., Patricia Searles, and Charles E. Cottle. 1991. *Feminism and Pornography*. Westport, Conn.: Praeger.

Best, Steven, and Douglas Kellner. 2001. *The Postmodern Adventure: Science, Technology, and Cultural Studies at the Third Millenium*. New York: Guilford.

Bettie, Julie. 2003. *Women without Class: Girls, Race, and Identity*. Berkeley: University of California Press.

Bikini Kill [1991] 2013. Bikini Kill Zine Cover. P. 122 in *The Riot Grrrl Collection*, edited by Lisa Darms. 2013. New York: The Feminist Press.

Blauner, Robert. 1972. *Racial Oppression in America*. New York: Harper & Row.

Bolotin, Susan. 1982. "Views from the Postfeminist Generation." *New York Times Magazine*, October 17.

Bordo, Susan. [1993] 1995. *Unbearable Weight: Feminism, Western Culture, and the Body*. Berkeley: University of California Press.

Bordo, Susan. [1993] 2003. *Unbearable Weight: Feminism, Western Culture, and the Body*. Berkeley: University of California Press.

Bornstein, Kate. 1994. *Gender Outlaw: On Men, Women, and the Rest of Us*. New York: Vintage.

Boserup, Esther. 1970. *Women's Role in Economic Development*. London: Allen & Unwin.

Brah, Avtar. 1996. *Cartographies of Diaspora: Contesting Identities*. New York: Routledge.

Brah, Avtar. 2003. "Diaspora, Border, and Transnational Identities." Pp. 613–634 in *Feminist Postcolonial Theory: A Reader*. Eds. Reina Lewis and Sara Mills. New York: Routledge.

Brannon, Skye. 2009. "Fireweed." Pp. 155–159 in *One World: A Global Anthology of Short Stories*. Oxford, U.K.: New Internationalist.

Bryant, Bunyan, and Paul Mohai, eds. 1992. *Race and the Incidence of Environmental Hazards: A Time for Discourse*. Boulder, Colo.: Westview Press.

Budgeon, Shelly. 2011. *Third Wave Feminism and the Politics of Gender in Late Modernity*. New York: Palgrave/Macmillan.

Bullard, Robert, ed. 1993. *Confronting Environmental Racism: Voices from the Grassroots*. Boston: South End Press.

Bullard, Robert, ed. 1994. *Unequal Protection: Environmental Justice and Communities of Color*. San Francisco, Calif.: Sierra Club.

Bunch, Charlotte. [1972] 1987. "Lesbians in Revolt." Pp. 161–167 in *Passionate Politics: Feminist Theory in Action* by Charlotte Bunch. New York: St. Martin's Press.

Bunch, Charlotte. [1979] 1987. "Not by Degrees: Feminist Theory and Education." Pp. 240–253 in *Passionate Politics: Feminist Theory in Action* by Charlotte Bunch. New York: St. Martin's Press.

Butler, Judith. 1990. *Gender Trouble: Feminism and the Subversion of Identity*. New York: Routledge.

Butler, Judith. 1991. "Imitation and Gender Insubordination." Pp. 13–31 in *Inside/Out: Lesbian Theories, Gay Theories*. Ed. Diana Fuss. New York: Routledge.

Butterfield, L. H., Marc Friedlaender, and Mary-Jo Kline. 1975. *The Book of Abigail and John: Selected Letters of the Adams Family, 1762–1784*. Cambridge, Mass.: Harvard University Press.

Castles, Stephen, and Mark J. Miller. [1993] 1998. *The Age of Migration: International Population Movements in the Modern World*, 2nd ed. Basingstoke, U.K.: Macmillan.

Cavallaro, Dani. 2003. *Beyond the Big Three: French Feminist Theory Today*. New York: Continuum.

Chambers, Veronica. 1995. "Betrayal Feminism." Pp. 21–28 in *Listen Up: Voices of the Next Feminist Generation*. Ed. Barbara Findlen. Seattle, Wa.: Seal.

Chang, Grace. 1997. "The Global Trade in Filipina Workers." Pp. 132–152 in *Dragon Ladies: Asian American Feminists Breath Fire*. Ed. Sonia Shah. Cambridge, Mass.: South End.

Cheal, David. 1991: *Family and the State of Theory*. Toronto: University of Toronto Press.

Chodorow, Nancy. [1978] 1999. *The Reproduction of Mothering: Psychoanalysis and the Sociology of Gender*. Berkeley: University of California Press.

Chopin, Kate. 1894/1975. "The Story of an Hour." Pp. 15–18 in *Women & Fiction: Short Stories by and about Women*. Ed. Susan Cahill. New York: New American Library/Penguin.

Christ, Carol P. 1978. "Why Women Need the Goddess: Phenomenological, Psychological, and Political Reflections." In "The Great Goddess Re-Emerging," from keynote address at the University of California at Santa Cruz Extension conference. Spring, 1978.

Christ, Carol P. 1979. "Why Women Need the Goddess." Pp. 275–287 in *Womanspirit Rising: A Feminist Reader in Religion*. Eds. Carol P. Christ and Judith Plaskow. San Francisco, Ca.: Harper Collins.

Chrystos. [1981] 1983. "I Walk in the History of My People." P. 57 in *This Bridge Called My Back: Writings by Radical Women of Color*. EdS. Cherríe Moraga and Gloria Anzaldúa. New York: Kitchen Table–Women of Color Press.

Collins, Patricia Hill. 1990. *Black Feminist Thought: Knowledge, Consciousness, and Empowerment*. Boston: Unwin Hyman.

Combahee River Collective. [1977] 1978. "A Black Feminist Statement." Pp. 362–372 in *Capitalist Patriarchy and the Case for Socialist Feminism* edited by Zillah Eisenstein. New York: Monthly Review Press.

Combahee River Collective. [1977] 1983. "A Black Feminist Statement." Pp. 210–218 in *This Bridge Called My Back: Writings by Radical Women of Color*. Eds. Cherrie Moraga and Gloria Anzaldua. New York: Kitchen Table–Women of Color Press.

Cooper, Anna Julia. [1892] 1988. *A Voice from the South*. New York: Oxford University Press.

Cooper, Anna Julia. [1892] 1998. "Excerpt from 'Woman versus the Indian.'" Pp. 184–189 in *The Women Founders: Sociology and Social Theory, 1830–1930*. Eds. Patricia Madoo Lengermann and Jill Niebrugge-Brantley. Boston: McGraw–Hill.

Cooper, Anna Julia. [1925] 1988. *Slavery and the French Revolutionists: 1788–1805*. Trans. Frances Richardson Keller. Lewiston, N.Y.: Mellow Press.

Cooper, Anna Julia. 1998. "The Social Conditions of the French-American Colonies: The Class Structure." Pp. 272–279 in *The Voice of Anna Julia Cooper*. Eds. Charles Lemert and Esme Bhan. Lanham, Md.: Rowman & Littlefield.

Copelon, Rhonda. 1994. "Surfacing Gender: Reconceptualizing Crimes against Women in Time of War." Pp. 197–218 in *Mass Rape: The War against Women in Bosnia-Herzegovina*, Ed. Alexandra Stilmayer. Lincoln, Neb.: University of Nebraska Press.

Corea, Gena. 1985. *The Mother Machine*. London: Women's Press.

Cott, Nancy. 1987. *The Grounding of Modern Feminism*. New Haven, Conn.: Yale University Press.

Crenshaw, Kimberlé. 1989. "Demarginalizing the Intersection of Race and Sex: A Black Feminist Critique of Antidiscrimination Doctrine, Feminist Theory and Antiracist Politics." *University of Chicago Legal Forum* 1989: 139–167.

Dalla Costa, Mariarosa, and Selma James. 1975. *The Power of Women and the Subversion of the Community*. Bristol, U.K.: Falling Wall.

Daly, Mary. [1978] 1990. *Gyn/Ecology: Metaethics of Radical Feminism*. Boston: Beacon.

Darms, Lisa, ed. 2013. *The Riot Grrrl Collection*. New York: The Feminist Press.

Davis, Angela. 1993. "Outcast Mothers and Surrogates: Racism and Reproductive Politics in the Nineties." Pp. 355–366 in *American Feminist Thought at Century's End* edited by Linda S. Kauffman. Cambridge, MA: Blackwell.

Davis, Angela. [1993] 2005. "Outcast Mothers and Surrogates: Racism and Reproductive Politics in the Nineties." Pp. 509–514 in *Feminist Theory: A Reader*, 2nd ed. Eds. Wendy K. Kolmar and Frances Bartkowski. Boston: McGraw–Hill.

de Beauvoir, Simone. [1949] 2011. *The Second Sex*. Trans. Constance Borde and Sheila Malovany-Chevallier. New York: Vintage Books/Random House.

Deckard, Barbara Sinclair. [1979] 1983. *The Women's Movement: Political, Socioeconomic, and Psychological Issues*. New York: Harper & Row.

Denfeld, Rene. 1995. *The New Victorians: A Young Woman's Challenge to the Old Feminist Order*. New York: Warner.

Dent, Gina. 1995. "Missionary Position." Pp. 61–76 in *To Be Real: Telling the Truth and Changing the Face of Feminism*. Ed. Rebecca Walker. New York: Anchor.

Dicker, Rory. 2008. *A History of U.S. Feminisms*. Berkeley, CA: Seal Press.

Dicker, Rory, and Alison Piepmeier, eds. 2003. *Catching a Wave: Reclaiming Feminism for the 21st Century*. Boston: Northeastern University Press.

Dirlik, Arif. 1997. "The Postcolonial Aura: Third World Criticism in the Age of Global Capitalism." Pp. 501–528 in *Dangerous Liaisons: Gender, Nation, and Postcolonial Perspectives*. Eds. Anne McClintock, Aamir Mufti, and Ella Shohat. Minneapolis: University of Minnesota Press.

Dobyns, Henry. 1966. "An Appraisal of Techniques with a New Hemispheric Estimate." *Current Anthropology* 7(4): 395–446.

Douglass, Frederick. 1888. "On Woman Suffrage." *Woman's Journal*, April 14.

Douglass, Frederick. [1888] 2014. "On Woman Suffrage." http://www.blackpast.org/1888-frederick-douglass-woman-suffrage/. Retrieved January 2, 2014.

Duncan, Barbara. 2005. "Searching for a Home Place: Online in the Third Wave." Pp. 161–178 in *Different Wavelengths: Studies of the Contemporary Women's Movement*. Ed. Jo Reger. New York: Routledge.

Dworkin, Andrea, and Catharine A. MacKinnon. 1988. *Pornography and Civil Rights: A New Day for Women's Equality*. Minneapolis, Minn.: Organizing against Pornography.

Dworkin, Andrea, and Catharine A. MacKinnon. 1988. "An Excerpt from Model Antipornography Civil Rights Ordinance." http://www.nostatusquo.com/ACLU/dworkin/OrdinanceModelExcerpt.html/. Retrieved September 6, 2013 (also published in *Ms.* magazine [January/February] 1994).

Eastman, Crystal. [1919] 1978. *On Women and Revolution*. Edited by Blanche Wiesen Cook. New York: Oxford University Press.

Ehrenreich, Barbara, and Annette Fuentes. 1981. "Life on the Global Assembly Line." *Ms.* magazine January 1981.

Ehrenreich, Barbara, and Annette Fuentes. [1981] 1993. "Life on the Global Assembly Line." Pp. 259–266 in *Feminist Frameworks: Alternative Theoretical Accounts of the Relations between Women and Men*, 3rd ed. Eds. Alison M. Jaggar and Paula S. Rothenberg. New York: McGraw–Hill.

Ehrenreich, Barbara, and Arlie Russell Hochschild. [2002] 2004. *Global Woman: Nannies, Maids, and Sex Workers in the New Economy*. New York: Metropolitan.

Eisenstein, Zillah, ed. 1979. *Capitalist Patriarchy and the Case for Socialist Feminism*. New York: Monthly Review.

Engels, Friedrich. [1884] 1972. *The Origin of the Family, Private Property, and the State*. New York: International.

England, Paula. 1992. *Comparable Worth: Theories and Evidence*. New York: Aldine de Gruyter.

Enloe, Cynthia. 1989. *Bananas, Beaches, and Bases: Making Feminist Sense of International Politics*. Berkeley: University of California Press.

Enloe, Cynthia. 2000. *Maneuvers: The International Politics of Militarizing Women's Lives*. Berkeley: University of California Press.

Enloe, Cynthia. 2007. "Wielding Masculinity inside Abu Ghraib and Guantanamo: The Globalized Dynamics." Pp. 93–115 in *Globalization and Militarism: Feminists Make the Link*. New York: Rowman & Littlefield.

Fain, W. Taylor. 2005. "Neighborhoods and Markets: The United States in Latin America and Asia, 1890–1917."

Virginia Center for Digital History; http://www.vcdh.virginia.edu/solguide/VUS09/essay09a.html/. Retrieved September 5, 2008.

Faludi, Susan. 1991. *Backlash: The Undeclared War against American Women*. New York: Crown.

Fanon, Frantz. [1961] 1967. *The Wretched of the Earth*. New York: Penguin.

Fanon, Frantz. 1967. *Black Skins, White Masks*. New York: Grove.

Fausto-Sterling, Anne. 2000. "Should There Be Only Two Sexes?" Pp. 78–114 in *Sexing the Body: Gender Politics and the Construction of Sexuality*. New York: Perseus Books Group.

Fausto-Sterling, Anne. [2000] 2008. "Should There Be Only Two Sexes?" Pp. 124–143 in *The Feminist Philosophy Reader*. Eds. Alison Bailey and Chris Cuomo. Boston: McGraw–Hill.

Featherstone, Mike. 1991. *Consumer Culture and Postmodernism*. London: Sage.

Ferree, Myra Marx, and Aili Mari Tripp, eds. 2006. *Global Feminism: Transnational Women's Activism, Organizing, and Human Rights*. New York: New York University Press.

Findlen, Barbara, ed. 1995. *Listen Up: Voices from the Next Feminist Generation*. Seattle, Wa.: Seal.

Firestone, Shulamith. [1970] 2003. *The Dialectic of Sex: The Case for Feminist Revolution*. New York: Farrar, Straus and Giroux.

Flax, Jane. 1992. "The End of Innocence." Pp. 445–463 in *Feminists Theorize the Political*. Eds. Judith Butler and Joan W. Scott. New York: Routledge.

Foner, Philip, and Richard Winchester, eds. 1984. *The Anti-Imperialist Reader: A Documentary History of Anti-Imperialism in the United States*, vol. 1, *From the Mexican War to the Election of 1900*. New York: Holmes & Meier.

Foucault, Michel. [1975] 1979. *Discipline and Punish: The Birth of the Prison*. New York: Vintage.

Foucault, Michel. 1976. *History of Sexuality, Volume 1: An Introduction*. Paris, France: Gallimard.

Foucault, Michel. [1976] 1980. *History of Sexuality, Volume 1: An Introduction*. London: Penguin.

Fourth World Conference on Women. 1995. "Beijing Declaration." http://www.un.org/womenwatch/daw/beijing/platform/declar.htm/. Retrieved January 2, 2014.

Fox, Bonnie, ed. 1980. *Hidden in the Household: Women's Domestic Labour under Capitalism*. Toronto: Women's Press.

Frank, Andre Gunder. 1976. *On Capitalist Underdevelopment*. New York: Oxford University Press.

Friedan, Betty. [1963] 1997. *The Feminine Mystique*. New York: W. W. Norton.

Gaard, Greta. 1997. "Toward a Queer Ecofeminism." *Hypatia: A Journal of Feminist Philosophy* 12(1): 114–137.

Gage, Matilda Joselyn. 1878. "Indian Citizenship." *National Citizen and Ballot Box* 5: 2

Gage, Matilda Joselyn. [1878] 1998. "Indian Citizenship." Pp. 35–37 in *Matilda Joselyn Gage: She Who Holds the Sky*, by Sally Roesch Wagner. Aberdeen, S.D.: Sky Carrier Press.

Gandhi, Mohandas. 2014. http://www.brainyquote.com/quotes/quotes/m/mahatmagan141784.html. Retrieved October 28, 2014.

Garland-Thomson, Rosemarie. 2002. "Integrating Disability, Transforming Feminist Theory." *NWSA Journal* 14:3 (fall): 1–32.

Gasiorowski, Mark, and Malcolm Byrne, eds. 2004. *Mohammed Mosaddeq and the 1953 Coup in Iran*. Boulder, Colo.: Westview.

Gatens, Moira. 1992. "Power, Bodies, and Difference." Pp. 120–137 in *Destabilizing Theory: Contemporary Feminist Debates*. Eds. Michele Barrett and Anne Phillips. Stanford, Calif.: Stanford University Press.

Giddings, Paula. 1984. *When and Where I Enter: The Impact of Black Women on Race and Sex in America*. New York: Bantam.

Gilligan, Carol. 1982. *In a Different Voice: Psychological Theory and Women's Development*. Cambridge, Mass.: Harvard University Press.

Gillis, Stacy, and Rebecca Munford. 2004. "Genealogies and Generations: The Politics and Praxis of Third Wave Feminism." *Women's History Review* 13(2): 165–182.

Gillis, Stacy, Gillian Howe, and Rebecca Munford, eds. [2004] 2007. *Third Wave Feminism: A Critical Exploration*. New York: Palgrave Macmillian.

Gilman, Charlotte Perkins. [1892] 1995. "The Yellow Wallpaper." Pp. 41–55 in *The Oxford Book of Women's Writing in the United States*. Eds. Linda Wagner-Martin and Cathy N. Davidson. New York: Oxford University Press.

Gilman, Charlotte Perkins. [1898] 1966. *Women and Economics*. New York: Harper & Row.

Gilman, Charlotte Perkins. [1898] 1974. "From *Women and Economics*", Pp. 591–598 in *The Feminist Papers: From Adams to de Beauvoir*, edited by Alice S. Rossi. New York: Bantam.

Gilman, Charlotte Perkins. 1900. *Concerning Children*. Boston: Small, Maynard.

Gilman, Charlotte Perkins. 1903. *The Home: Its Work and Influence*. New York: Macmillan.

Gilman, Charlotte Perkins. 1904. *Human Work*. New York: McClure, Phillips.

Gillman, Charlotte Perkins. [1915] 1979. *Herland*. New York: Pantheon.

Gilman, Susan Jane. 1998. "Klaus Barbie, and Other Dolls I'd Like to See." Pp. 20–21 in *Adiós Barbie: Young Women Write about Body Image and Identity*. Ed. Ophira Edut. Seattle, Wa.: Seal.

Goldman, Emma. 1911. *Anarchism and Other Essays, Second Revised Edition*. New York. Mother Earth Publishing Association.

Goldman, Emma. [1911] 1917. *Anarchism and Other Essays, Third Edition*. New York: Mother Earth.

Goldman, Emma. [1910] 2005. "'The Traffic in Women' from *Anarchism and Other Essays*." Pp. 120–123 in *Feminist Theory: A Reader*, 2nd ed. Eds. Wendy K. Kolmar and Frances Bartkowski. Boston: McGraw–Hill.

Goldman, Emma. 1911. "Patriotism: A Menace to Liberty." http://ucblibrary3.berkeley.edu/Goldman/Writings/Anarchism/patriotism.html Retrieved October, 28, 2014.

Goldman, Emma. 1912. BrainyQuote.com. http://www.brainyquote.com/quotes/authors/e/emma_goldman.html/. Retrieved August 20, 2011.

Goldsmith, Barbara. 1998. "The Woman Who Set American on Its Ear." *Parade Magazine*, March 8.

Gompers, Samuel. [1899] 2013. "Reply on Behalf of the American Federation of Labor." Pp. 310–312 in *The Selected Papers of Elizabeth Cady Stanton & Susan B. Anthony, Volume VI: An Awful Hush 1895–1906*. Ed. Ann D. Gordon. New Brunswick, N.J.: Rutgers University Press.

Gosse, Van. 2005. *Rethinking the New Left: An Interpretative History*. New York: Palgrave Macmillan.

Grahame, Peter R. 1998. "Ethnography, Institutions, and the Problematic of the Everyday World." *Human Studies* 21(4): 1–10.

Grant, Judith. 1993. *Fundamental Feminism: Contesting the Core Concepts of Feminist Theory*. New York: Routledge.

Grewal, Inderpal, and Caren Kaplan, eds. [1994] 2006. *Scattered Hegemonies: Postmodernity and Transnational Feminist Practices*. Minneapolis: University of Minnesota Press.

Griffin, Susan. [1978] 1980. "Use." Pp. 52–54 in *Woman and Nature: The Roaring inside Her*. New York: Harper Colophon.

Grimké, Sarah M. [1837] 1974. "Letter VIII." *Letters on the Equality of the Sexes and the Condition of Women*. Pp. 311–316 in *The Feminist Papers: From Adams to de Beauvoir*. Ed. Alice S. Rossi. New York: Bantam Books.

Grimshaw, Jean. 1993. "Practices of Freedom." Pp. 51–72 in *Up against Foucault: Explorations of Some Tensions between Foucault and Feminism*, ed. Caroline Ramazanoglu, New York: Routledge.

Gupta, Jyostna Angihorti. 2006. "Towards Transnational Feminisms: Some Reflections and Concerns in Relation to the Globalization of Reproductive Technologies." *European Journal of Women's Studies* 13(23): 23–38.

Halberstam, Judith. 1998. *Female Masculinity*. Durham, N.C.: Duke University Press.

Halberstam, Judith. 2005. *In a Queer Time and Place: Transgender Bodies, Subcultural Lives*. New York: NYU Press.

Hall, Radclyffe. 1928. *The Well of Loneliness*. London: Wordsworth.

Hanisch, Carol. 1969. "The Personal Is Political." carolhanish .org. http://www.carolhanisch.org/CHwritings/PIP.html/. Retrieved August 15, 2011.

Haraway, Donna. 1985. "A Manifesto for Cyborgs: Science, Technology, and Socialist Feminism in the 1980s." *Socialist Review* 80(1985): 65–108.

Haraway, Donna. 1991. *Simians, Cyborgs, and Women: The Reinvention of Nature*. New York: Routledge.

Harding, Sandra. 1986. "From the Woman Question in Science to the Science Question in Feminism." Pp. 15–29 in *The Science Question in Feminism* by Sandra Harding. Ithaca, N.Y.: Cornell University Press.

Harding, Sandra. 1991. *Whose Science? Whose Knowledge? Thinking from Women's Lives*. Ithaca, N.Y.: Cornell University Press.

Harding, Sandra. 1993. "Rethinking Standpoint Epistemology: 'What Is Strong Objectivity'?" Pp. 49–82 in *Feminist Epistemologies*, ed. Linda Alcoff and Elizabeth Potter. New York: Routledge.

Harding, Sandra. 2004. *The Feminist Standpoint Reader: Intellectual and Political Controversies*. New York: Routledge.

Hartmann, Heidi I. 1979. "The Unhappy Marriage of Marxism and Feminism: Towards a More Progressive Union." *Capital & Class* 3(2): 1–33.

Hartsock, Nancy. 1990. "Foucault on Power: A Theory for Women?" Pp. 157–175 in *Feminism/Postmodernism* edited by Linda J. Nicholson. New York: Routledge.

Hartsock, Nancy. [1990] 1993. "Foucault on Power: A Theory for Women?" Pp. 545–554 in *Social Theory: The Multicultural and Classic Readings*. Ed. Charles Lemert. Boulder, Colo.: Westview Press.

Harvey, David. 1989. *The Condition of Postmodernity: An Enquiry into the Origins of Cultural Change*. Oxford: Blackwell.

Hayden, Dolores. 1982. *The Grand Domestic Revolution: A History of Feminist Designs for American Homes, Neighborhoods, and Cities*. Cambridge, Mass.: MIT Press.

Hekman, Susan. 2004. "Truth and Method: Feminist Standpoint Theory Revisited." Pp. 225–241 in *The Feminist Standpoint Reader: Intellectual and Political Controversies*. Ed. Sandra G. Harding. New York: Routledge.

Henry, Astrid. 2004. *Not My Mother's Sister: Generational Conflict and Third Wave Feminism* Bloomington: University of Indiana Press.

Henry, Astrid. 2005. "Solitary Sisterhood: Individualism Meets Collectivity in Feminism's Third Wave." Pp. 81–96 in *Different Wavelengths: Studies of the Contemporary Women's Movement*, by Jo Reger. New York: Routledge.

Hernandez, Daisy, and Bushra Rehman. 2002. *Colonize This! Young Women of Color on Today's Feminism*. New York: Seal.

Hesse-Biber, Sharlene Nagy, Patricia Leavy, and Michelle Yaiser. 2004. "Feminist Approaches to Research as a *Process*: Reconceptualizing Epistemology, Methodology, and Method." Pp. 3–26 in *Feminist Perspectives on Social Research*. Eds. Sharlene Nage Hesse-Biber and Michelle Yaiser. New York: Oxford University Press.

Heywood, Leslie, and Jennifer Drake, eds. 1997. *Third Wave Agenda: Being Feminist, Doing Feminism*. Minneapolis: University of Minnesota Press.

Heywood, Leslie, and Jennifer Drake, eds. 2004. "'It's all about the Benjamins': Economic Determinants of Third Wave Feminism in the United States." Pp. 13–23 in *Third Wave Feminism: A Critical Exploration* Eds. Stacy Gillis, Gillian Howe, and Rebecca Munford. New York: Palgrave Macmillan.

Hilferding, Rudolph. [1910] 2007. *Finance Capital: A Study in the Latest Phase of Capitalist Development*. London: Routledge.

Hobson, John Atkinson. [1902] 1971. *Imperialism: A Study*. Ann Arbor: University of Michigan Press.

Hoganson, Kristin L. 1998. *Fighting for American Manhood: How Gender Politics Provoked the Spanish–American and Philippine–American Wars*. New Haven, Conn.: Yale University Press.

Hoganson, Kristin L. 2001. "'As Badly Off as the Filipinos': U.S. Women's Suffragists and the Imperial Issue at the Turn of the Twentieth Century." *Journal of Women's History* 13(2): 9–33.

Hole, Judith, and Ellen Levine. 1979. "The First Feminists." Pp. 543–556 in *Women: A Feminist Perspective*, 2nd ed. Ed. Jo Freeman. Palo Alto, Calif.: Mayfield.

Holley, Joe. 2007. "Obituary for Tillie Olsen." *Washington Post*, January 5.

hooks, bell. 1984. *Feminist Theory: From Margin to Center*. Boston: South End.

hooks, bell. 1994. *Teaching to Transgress: Education as the Practice of Freedom*. New York: Routledge.

Horton, Heather. 2014. "Gendered Bodies and the U.S. Military: Exploring the Institutionalized Regulation of Bodies." M.A. Thesis. University of New Orleans.

Howe, Julia Ward. 1870. "Mother's Day Proclamation." Boston.

Howe, Julia Ward. [1870] 2012. "Mother's Day Proclamation." http://www.peace.ca/mothersdayproclamation.html/. Retrieved June 25, 2012.

Hudis, Peter, and Kevin B. Anderson, eds. 2004. *The Rosa Luxemburg Reader*. New York: Monthly Review.

Hull, Gloria, Patricia Bell Scott, and Barbara Smith, 1981. *All the Women Are White, All the Men Are Black, but Some of Us Are Brave*. Old Westbury, N.Y.: Feminist Press.

Hurston, Zora Neale. [1926] 1995. "Sweat." Pp. 101–110 in *The Oxford Book of Women's Writing in the United States*. Eds. Linda Wagner-Martin and Cathy N. Davidson. New York: Oxford University Press.

Hurston, Zora Neale. [1934] 2008. *Jonah's Gourd Vine*. New York: Harper Perennial.

Hurston, Zora Neale. [1937] 2006. *Their Eyes Were Watching God*. New York: Harper Perennial.

Jacobs, Harriet. 1861. *Incidents in the Live of a Slave Girl*. Edited by L. Maria Child. Boston: Published for the Author.

Jacobs, Harriet. [1861] 2001. *Incidents in the Live of a Slave Girl*. Mineola, N.Y.: Dover.

Jaggar, Alison M., and Paula S. Rothenberg, eds. 1984. *Feminist Frameworks: Alternative Theoretical Accounts of the Relations between Women and Men*, 2nd ed. New York: McGraw–Hill.

Jaggar, Alison M., and Paula S. Rothenberg. 1993. *Feminist Frameworks: Alternative Theoretical Accounts of the Relations between Women and Men*, 3rd ed. New York: McGraw–Hill.

Johnson, Merri Lisa, ed. 2002. *Jane Sexes It Up: True Confessions of Feminist Desire*. New York: Four Walls Eight Windows.

Jones, Colin and Roy Porter, eds. 1994. *Reassessing Foucault: Power, Medicine and the Body*. New York: Routledge.

Jones, Mother (Mary). 1910. "Girl Slaves of the Milwaukee Breweries". *United Mine Workers Journal*. 1910. April 7, 20 (47):2.

Jones, Mother (Mary). [1910] 1990. "Girl Slaves of the Milwaukee Breweries." Pp. 105–108 in *Calling Home: Working-Class Women's Writings, An Anthology*. Ed. Janet Zandy. New Brunswick, N.J.: Rutgers University Press.

Jordan, June. [1985] 2013. "Report from the Bahamas." Pp. 268–276 in *Feminist Theory Reader: Local and Global Perspective*, 3rd ed. Eds. Carole R. McCann and Sung-Kyung Kim. New York: Routledge.

Jordan, June. [1985] 2014. "Report from the Bahamas." Pp. 39–51 in *On Call: Political Essays*. Boston: South End Press.

Joreen. [Jo Freeman]. 1969. "The BITCH Manifesto." http://www.jofreeman.com/joreen/bitch.htm/. Retrieved January 5, 2014.

Kamen, Paula. 1991. *Feminist Fatale: Voices from the "Twentysomething" Generation Explore the Future of the "Women's Movement."* New York: Donald I. Fine.

Karp, Marcell, and Debbie Stoller, eds. 1999. *The Bust Guide to the New Girl Order*. New York: Penguin.

Kemp, Alice Abel. 1993. *Women's Work: Devalued and Degraded*. Englewood Cliffs, N.J.: Prentice Hall.

Kimmel, Michael, and Matthew Mahler. 2003. "Adolescent Masculinity, Homophobia, and Violence." *American Behavioral Scientist* 46(10): 1439–1458.

King, Katie. 1990. "Producing Sex, Theory, and Culture: Gay/Straight Remappings in Contemporary Feminism."

Pp. 82–101 in *Conflicts in Feminism*. Eds. Marianne Hirsch and Evelyn Fox Keller. New York: Routledge.

King, Ynestra. 1981. "Feminism and the Revolt of Nature." *Heresies* 13: 12–16.

Klein, Melissa. 1997. "Duality and Redefinition: Young Feminism and the Alternative Music Community." Pp. 207–225 in *Third Wave Agenda: Being Feminist, Doing Feminism*. Eds. Leslie Heywood and Jennifer Drake. Minneapolis: University of Minnesota Press

Knott, Sarah, and Barbara Taylor. 2005. *Women, Gender, and the Enlightenment*. New York: Palgrave Macmillan.

Kollontai, Alexandra. [1914] 1980. "Working Woman and Mother." Pp. 127–139 in *Alexandra Kollontai: Selected Writings*, edited by Alix Holt. New York: W.W. Norton.

Kollontai, Alexandra. [1914] 2005. "Working Woman and Mother." Pp. 126–130 in *Feminist Theory: A Reader*, 2nd ed. Eds. Wendy K. Kolmar and Frances Bartkowski. Boston: McGraw–Hill.

Kramarae, Cheris, and Paula A. Treichler, eds. 1985. *A Feminist Dictionary*. Boston: Pandora.

Labaton, Vivien, and Dawn Lundy Martin, eds. 2004. *The Fire This Time: Young Activists and the New Feminism*. New York: Anchor.

Landry, Donna, and Gerald MacLean. 1993. *Materialist Feminisms*. Cambridge, Mass.: Blackwell.

Landsman, Gail. H. 1992. "The 'Other' as Political Symbol: Images of the Indians in the Woman Suffrage Movement." *Ethnohistory* 39(1): 247–284.

Lazarus, Emma. 1883. "The New Colossus." http://xroads.virginia.edu/~cap/liberty/lazaruspoem.html. Retrieved October 22, 2014.

Lemert, Charles C., and Esme Bhan. 1998. *The Voice of Anna Julia Cooper: Including "A Voice from the South" and Other Important Essays, Papers, and Letters*. Lanham, Md.: Rowman & Littlefield.

Lenin, V. I. [1917] 1996. *Imperialism: The Highest Stage of Capitalism*. London: Pluto.

Lenin, V. I. [1934] 1995. *The Emancipation of Women: From the Writings of V. I. Lenin*. New York: International.

Lerman, David. 2013. "U.S. Military Vows to Put Women in Combat Roles by 2016." http://www.bloomberg.com/news/2013-07-24/u-s-military-vows-to-put-women-in-combat-roles-by-2016.html. Retrieved November 2, 2014.

Lerner, Gerda. 1979. *The Majority Finds Its Past: Placing Women in History*. New York: Oxford University Press.

Lorde, Audre. 1984. *Sister/Outsider*. Trumansburg, N.Y.: Crossing Press.

Lublin, Nancy. 1998. *Pandora's Box: Feminism Confronts Reproductive Technology*. Lanham, Md.: Rowman & Littlefield.

Lugones, Maria C., and Elizabeth V. Spelman. [1983] 2005. "Have We Got a Theory for You! Feminist Theory, Cultural Imperialism, and the Demand for 'The Woman's

Voice." Pp. 17–26 in *Feminist Theory: A Reader*, 2nd ed. Eds. Wendy K. Kolmar and Frances Bartkowski. Boston: McGraw–Hill.

Lugones, Maria C., and Elizabeth V. Spelman. 1983. "Have We Got a Theory for You! Feminist Theory, Cultural Imperialism, and the Demand for 'The Woman's Voice." *Women's Studies International Forum*, 6(6): 573–581.

Luxemburg, Rosa. [1908] 2004. "The Dissolution of Primitive Communism: Introduction to Political Economy." Pp. 71–110 in *The Rosa Luxemburg Reader*. Eds. Peter Hudis and Kevin Anderson. New York: Monthly Review.

Luxemburg, Rosa. 1912. "Women's Suffrage and Class Struggle." http://www.marxists.org/archive/luxemburg/ 1912/05/12.htm/. Retrieved May 30, 2014.

Luxemburg, Rosa. [1913] 1951. "Militarism as a Province of Accumulation". http://www.marxists.org/archive/ luxemburg/1913/accumulation-capital/ch32.htm/. Retrieved October 18, 2013.

Luxemburg, Rosa. [1913] 1951. *The Accumulation of Capital*. New Haven, Conn.: Yale University Press.

Luxemburg, Rosa. [1913] 2003. *The Accumulation of Capital*. New York: Routledge.

Maatita, Florence. 2005. "Que Viva La Mujer: Negotiating Chicana Feminist Identities." Pp. 23–38 in *Different Wavelengths: Studies of the Contemporary Women's Movement*. Ed. Jo Reger. New York: Routledge.

Macionis, John. [2002] 2011. *Society: The Basics*. Upper Saddle River, N.J.: Prentice Hall.

Mack-Canty, Colleen. 2005. "Third Wave Feminism and Ecofeminism: Reweaving the Nature/Culture Duality." Pp. 195–211 in *Different Wavelengths: Studies of the Contemporary Women's Movement*. Ed. Jo Reger. New York: Routledge.

Magdoff, Harry. 1969. *The Age of Imperialism*. New York: Monthly Review.

Mann, Susan A. 1990. *Agrarian Capitalism in Theory and Practice*. Chapel Hill: University of North Carolina Press.

Mann, Susan A. 2008. "Feminism and Imperialism, 1890– 1920: Our Anti-Imperialist Sisters—Missing in Action from American Feminist Sociology." *Sociological Inquiry* 78(4): 461–489.

Mann, Susan A. 2011. "Pioneers of Ecofeminism and Environmental Justice." *Feminist Formations* 23(2): 1–25.

Mann, Susan A. 2012. *Doing Feminist Theory: Paradigm Shifts from Modernity to Postmodernity*. New York: Oxford University Press.

Mann, Susan A. 2013. "Third Wave Feminism's Unhappy Marriage of Poststructuralism and Intersectionality Theory." *Journal of Feminist Scholarship* (Spring).

Mann, Susan A., and Lori R. Kelley. 1997. "Standing at the Crossroads of Modernist Thought: Collins, Smith and the New Feminist Epistemologies." *Gender & Society* 11(4): 391–408.

Marshall, Susan. [1989] 1995. "Keep Us on the Pedestal: Women against Feminism in Twentieth-Century America." Pp. 567–580 in *Women: A Feminist Perspective*. Ed. Jo Freeman. Palo Alto, Calif.: Mayfield.

Marx, Karl. [1882] 1986. *Ethnological Notebooks of Karl Marx*. Ed. Lawrence Krader. New York: Irvington.

McCall, Leslie. (2005). "The Complexity of Intersectionality." *Signs* 30(3): 1771–1800.

McHoul, Alec, and Wendy Grace. 1993. *A Foucault Primer: Discourse, Power, and the Subject*. New York: NYU Press.

McMichael, Philip. 1996 . *Development and Social Change: A Global Perspective*. Thousand Oaks, Calif.: Pine Forge/Sage.

McMichael, Philip. 2008. *Development and Social Change: A Global Perspective*. 3rd ed. Thousand Oaks, Calif.: Pine Forge/Sage.

McWhorter, Ladelle. 1999. *Bodies and Pleasures: Foucault and the Politics of Sexual Normalization*. Bloomington: Indiana University Press.

Mead, Margaret. 1928. *Coming of Age in Samoa: A Psychological Study of Primitive Youth for Western Civilization*. New York: Blue Ribbon.

Mead, Margaret. [1935] 1963. *Sex and Temperament in Three Primitive Societies*. San Francisco, CA: HarperCollins Publishers.

Memmi, Albert. [1957] 1991. *The Colonizer and the Colonized*. Boston: Beacon.

Merchant, Carolyn. 1995. *Earthcare: Women and the Environment*. New York: Routledge.

Merchant, Carolyn. 2007. *American Environmental History: An Introduction*. New York: Columbia University Press.

Merchant, Carolyn, ed. 1999. *Ecology: Key Concepts in Critical Theory*. Amherst, N.Y.: Humanity.

Messer-Davidow, Ellen. 2002. *Disciplining Feminism: From Social Activism to Academic Discourse*. Durham, N.C.: Duke University Press.

Mies, Maria. 1986. *Patriarchy and Accumulation on a World Scale: Women in the International Division of Labor*. London: Zed.

Mies, Maria. [1986] 1998. *Patriarchy and Accumulation on a World Scale: Women in the International Division of Labor*. New York: Zed Books.

Mies, Maria, Veronika Bennholdt-Thomsen, and Claudia Von Werlhof. 1988. *Women: The Last Colony*. London: Zed.

Mies, Maria, and Vandana Shiva. 1993. *Ecofeminism*. London: Zed.

Mihesuah, Devon Abbott. 2003. *Indigenous American Women: Decolonization, Empowerment, Activism*. Lincoln: University of Nebraska Press.

Mill, Harriet Taylor. [1851] 1970. "Enfranchisement of Women." Pp. 89–122 in *Essays on Sex Equality: John Stuart*

Mill and Harriet Taylor Mill. Ed. Alice Rossi. Chicago: University of Chicago Press.

Mill, John Stuart. [1869] 1972. *The Subjection of Women*. Pp. 125–242 in *Essays on Sex Equality: John Stuart Mill and Harriet Taylor Mill*. Ed. Alice Rossi. Chicago: University of Chicago Press.

Mill, John Stuart, and Harriet Taylor. [1832] 1970. "Early Essays on Marriage and Divorce." Pp. 67–87 in *Essays on Sex Equality: John Stuart Mill and Harriet Taylor Mill*. Ed. Alice Rossi. Chicago: University of Chicago Press.

Miller, Leslie. 2008. "Foucauldian Constructionism." Pp. 251–274 in *Handbook of Constructionist Research*. Eds. James Holstein and Jaber Gubrium. New York: Guilford.

Million Woman March. 1997. "Our Platform Issues," October 25. http:webspace.webring.com/people/wk/khandi_pages/mwm/platform-issues.htm/. Retrieved August 22, 2001.

Minh-ha, Trinh. 1989. *Woman, Native, Other: Writing Postcoloniality and Feminism*. Bloomington: Indiana University Press.

Mohanty, Chandra Talpade. 1984. "Under Western Eyes: Feminist Scholarship and Colonial Discourses." *Boundary 2* 12(3)–13(1): 333–358.

Mohanty, Chandra Talpade. [1984] 1991. "Under Western Eyes: Feminist Scholarship and Colonial Discourses." Pp. 51–80 in *Third World Women and the Politics of Feminism*. Bloomington: Indiana University Press.

Mohanty, Chandra Talpade. [1984] 2005. "'Under Western Eyes: Feminist Scholarship and Colonial Discourses' from *Third World Women and the Politics of Feminism*." Pp. 372–379 in *Feminist Theory: A Reader*, 2nd ed. Eds. Wendy K. Kolmar and Frances Bartkowski. Boston: McGraw–Hill.

Mohanty, Chandra Talpade. [2003] 2006. *Feminism without Borders: Decolonizing Theory, Practicing Solidarity*. Durham, N.C.: Duke University Press.

Moraga, Cherríe, and Gloria Anzaldúa, eds. [1981] 1983. *This Bridge Called My Back: Writings by Radical Women of Color*. New York: Kitchen Table–Women of Color Press.

Morgan, Joan. 1999. *When Chickenheads Come Home to Roost: A Hip-Hop Feminist Breaks It Down*. New York: Simon & Schuster.

Morgan, Lewis Henry. [1877] 1964. *Ancient Society; or, Researches in the Lines of Human Progress from Savagery through Barbarism to Civilization*. New York: Henry Holt.

Morgan, Robin, ed. 1970. *Sisterhood Is Powerful: An Anthology of Writings from the Women's Liberation Movement*. New York: Random House.

Morgan, Robin. [1977] 1992. "Theory and Practice: Pornography and Rape." Pp. 78–89 in *The Word of a Woman: Feminist Dispatches*, 2nd ed. New York: W. W. Norton.

Morgan, Robin. [1984] 1996. *Sisterhood Is Global: The International Women's Movement Anthology*. Garden City, N.Y.: Anchor/Doubleday.

Morgan, Robin. [1984] 1996. "Preface to the Feminist Press Edition." Pp. vii–xii in *Sisterhood Is Global: The International Women's Movement Anthology*. Ed. Robin Morgan. New York: Feminist Press.

Morton, Stephen. 2003. *Gayatri Chakravorty Spivak*. New York: Routledge.

Narayan, Uma. [1989] 2013. "The Project of Feminist Epistemology: Perspectives from a Nonwestern Feminist." Pp. 370–378 in *Feminist Theory: A Reader, Local and Global Perspectives*, 3rd ed. Eds. Carole R. McCann and Seung-Kyung Kim. New York: Routledge.

Narayan, Uma. 1989. "The Project of Feminist Epistemology: Perspectives from a Nonwestern Feminist." Pp. 256–269 in *Gender/Body/Knowledge*, eds. A. M. Jaggar and S. R. Bordo, 256–269. New Brunswick: Rutgers University Press..

Narayan, Uma. 1997. *Dislocating Cultures/Identities, Traditions, and Third World Feminism*. New York: Routledge.

National Organization for Women. 1966. "Statement of Purpose." http://coursesa.matrix.msu.edu/~hst306/documents/nowstate.html. Retrieved October, 26, 2014.

Nestle, Joan, Clare Howell, and Riki Wilchins, eds. 2002. *GenderQueer: Voices from Beyond the Sexual Binary*. New York: Alyson.

Nettl, Peter. 1969. *Rosa Luxemburg*. New York: Oxford University Press.

Nin, Anais. [1979] 1995. "Mandra, II" from *Little Birds: Erotica*. Pp. 578–560 in *The Oxford Book of Women's Writing in the United States*. Eds. Linda Wagner-Martin and Cathy N. Davidson. New York: Oxford University Press.

O'Brien, Karen. 2009. *Women and Enlightenment in 18th-Century Britain*. Cambridge, U.K.: Cambridge University Press.

O'Connor, James.1997. "Socialism and Ecology." *Capitalism, Nature, Socialism* 2(3): 1–12.

Oakley, Ann. 1974a. *Housewife*. New York: Pantheon.

Oakley, Ann. 1974b. *The Sociology of Housework*. New York: Pantheon.

Off Our Backs: A Women's News Journal. 1983. Cover of "Latin American Feminist Meet." xiii(10).

Olsen, Tillie. [1934] 1990. "I Want You Women Up North to Know." Pp. 91–994 in *Calling Home: Working-Class Women's Writings, an Anthology*. Ed. Janet Zandy. New Brunswick, N.J.: Rutgers University Press.

Olsen, Tillie. 2013. *Tell Me a Riddle, Requa I, and Other Works*. Lincoln, Nebraska: University of Nebraska Press.

Ong, Aihwa. 1991. "The Gender and Labor Politics of Postmodernity." *Annual Review of Anthropology* 20(1): 279–309.

Oppenheim, James. 1911. "Bread and Roses". *American Magazine* (December).

Papandreou, Margarita Chant. 1988. "Causes and Cures of Anti-Americanism." Pp. 152–154 in *Women on War: Essential Voices for the Nuclear Age*. Ed. Daniela Gioseffi. New York: Simon & Schuster.

Parpart, Jane, Patricia Connelly, and Eudine Barriteau. 2000. *Theoretical Perspectives on Gender and Development*. Ottawa, Ontario: International Development Research Centre.

Parry, Benita. 1987. "Problems in Current Theories of Colonial Discourse." *Oxford Literary Review* 9(1–2): 27–58.

Pascoe, C. J. 2007. *Dude You're a Fag: Masculinity and Sexuality in High School*. Berkeley: University of California Press.

Pels, Dick. 2004. "Strange Standpoints, or How to Define the Situation for Situated Knowledge." Pp. 273–289 in *The Feminist Standpoint Theory Reader: Intellectual and Political Controversies*. Ed. Sandra G. Harding. New York: Routledge.

Purdy, Laura. 1996. *Reproducing Persons: Issues in Feminist Bioethics*. Ithaca, N.Y.: Cornell University Press.

Quinn, Rebecca. 1997. "An Open Letter to Institutional Mothers." Pp. 174–182 in *Generations: Academic Feminists in Dialogue*. Eds. Devoney Looser and Ann Kaplan. Minneapolis: University of Minnesota Press.

Radicalesbians. [1970] 1997. "The Woman-Identified Woman." Pp. 153–157 in *The Second Wave: A Reader in Feminist Theory*. Ed. Linda Nicholson. New York: Routledge.

Ramazanoglu, Caroline, ed. 1993. *Up against Foucault: Explorations of Some Tensions between Foucault and Feminism*. New York: Routledge.

Redstockings. 1969. "Redstockings Manifesto." http://www .historyisaweapon.com/defcon1/redstockingsmanifesto .html/. Retrieved September 27, 2013.

Redstockings. 1969. "Redstockings Manifesto." In Redstockings Women's Liberation Archives for Action at www .redstockings.org. Retrieved September 30, 2013.

Reger, Jo, ed. 2005. *Different Wavelengths: Studies of the Contemporary Women's Movement*. New York: Routledge.

Rich, Adrienne. [1976] 1977. *Of Woman Born: Motherhood as Experience and Institution*. New York: Bantam.

Rich, Adrienne. [1980] 1994. "Compulsory Heterosexuality and Lesbian Existence." Pp. 26–68 in *Blood, Bread, and Poetry: Selected Prose 1979–1985* by Adrienne Rich. New York: W. W. Norton.

Ritzer, George. 2011. *Sociological Theory*, 8th ed. Boston: McGraw-Hill.

Roiphe, Katie. 1993. *The Morning After: Sex, Fear, and Feminism on Campus*. Boston: Little, Brown.

Rosenau, Pauline Marie. 1992. *Post-modernism and the Social Sciences: Insights, Inroads, and Intrusions*. Princeton, N.J.: Princeton University Press.

Rossi, Alice. 1970. *Essays on Sex Equality: John Stuart Mill and Harriet Taylor Mill*. Chicago: University of Chicago Press.

Rossi, Alice. 1974. *The Feminist Papers from Adams to de Beauvoir*. Toronto: Bantam.

Rowbotham, Sheila. 1975. *Hidden from History: 300 Years of Women's Oppression and the Fight against It*. London: Pluto.

Rowbotham, Sheila. 1978. *Women's Consciousness, Man's World*. Baltimore: Penguin.

Rubin, Gayle. 1984. "Thinking Sex: Notes for a Radical Theory of the Politics of Sexuality." Pp. 267–391 in *Pleasure and Danger: Exploring Female Sexuality*. Ed. Carole S. Vance. Boston: Routledge and Kegan Paul. [Reprinted as pp. 3–44 in *The Lesbian and Gay Studies Reader*. Eds. Henry Abelove, Michèle Aina Barale, and David M. Halperin. New York: Routledge, 1993.]

Ruiz de Burton, María Amparo. [1885] 1997. *The Squatter and the Don*. Eds. Rosaura Sanchez and Beatrice Pita. Houston, Tex.: Arte Publica Press.

Rupp, Leila J. 1997. *Worlds of Women: The Making of an International Women's Movement*. Princeton, N.J.: Princeton University Press.

Said, Edward W. [1978] 1979. *Orientalism*. New York: Random House.

Salado, Minerva. [1985] 1988. "Report from Vietnam for International Women's Day." Pp. 247 in *Women on War: Essential Voices for the Nuclear Age*. Ed. Daniela Gioseffi. New York: Simon & Schuster.

Sanders, Mark. 2006. *Gayatri Chakravorty Spivak: Live Theory*. New York: Continuum.

Sandoval, Chela. 1991. "U.S. Third-World Feminism: The Theory and Method of Oppositional Consciousness in the Postmodern World." *Genders*, #10: 1–24.

Sandoval, Chela. [1991] 2003. "U.S. Third-World Feminism: The Theory and Method of Oppositional Consciousness in the Postmodern World." Pp. 75–99 in *Feminist Postcolonial Theory: A Reader*. Eds. Reina Lewis and Sara Mills. New York: Routledge.

Sanger, Margaret. 1920. *Woman and the New Race*. New York: Truth.

Sanger, Margaret. [1920] 1974. "My Fight for Birth Control." Pp. 522–532 in *The Feminist Papers: From Adams to de Beauvoir*. Ed. Alice S. Rossi. New York: Bantam Books.

Sanchez, Rosaura, and Beatrice Pita. 1997. "Introduction" to *The Squatter and the Don* by Maria Amparo Ruiz de Burton. Houston, Tex.: Arte Publica Press.

Schlafly, Phyllis. 1977. *The Power of the Positive Woman*. New Rochelle, N.Y.: Arlington House.

Schneiderman, Rose. 1911. "We Have Found You Wanting." *The Survey*, April 8.

Schneiderman, Rose. [1911] 1962. "We Have Found You Wanting." Pp. 144–145 in *The Triangle Fire*. Ed. Leon Stein. New York: Carroll and Graf.

Schott, Linda. 1997. *Reconstructing Women's Thoughts: The Women's International League for Peace and Freedom before World War II*. Stanford, Calif.: Stanford University Press.

Schumpeter, Joseph. [1919] 1955. *Imperialism and Social Classes*. New York: Meridian.

Seccombe, Wally. 1973. "The Housewife and Her Labour under Capitalism." *New Left Review* 83(January–February): 3–24.

Seidman, Steven. 2000. "Queer-ing Sociology, Sociologizing Queer Theory." Pp. 434–455 in *Social Theory: Roots and Branches*. Ed. Peter Kivisto. Los Angeles: Roxbury.

Senna, Danzy. 1995. "To Be Real." Pp. 5–20 in *To Be Real: Telling the Truth and Changing the Face of Feminism*. Ed. Rebecca Walker. New York: Anchor.

Sennett, Richard, and Jonathan Cobb. 1972. *The Hidden Injuries of Social Class*. New York: Vintage.

Serano, Julia. 2009. *Whipping Girl: A Transexual Woman on Sexism and the Scapegoating of Femininity*. Seattle, Wa.: Seal Press.

Shaw, Stephanie. 1995. "Black Club Women and the Creation of the National Association of Colored Women." Pp. 443–447 in *We Specialize in the Wholly Impossible: A Reader in Black Women's History*. Eds. Darlene Clark Hine, Wilma King, and Linda Reed. Brooklyn, N.Y.: Carlson.

Shiva, Vandana. 1989. *Staying Alive: Women, Ecology, and Development*. London: Zed.

Shohat, Ella, ed. [1999] 2001. *Talking Visions: Multicultural Feminism in a Transnational Age*. Cambridge, Mass.: MIT Press.

Sidler, Michelle. 1997. "Living in McJobdom: Third Wave Feminism and Class Inequity." Pp. 25–39 in *Third Wave Agenda: Being Feminist, Doing Feminism*. Eds. Leslie Heywood and Jennifer Drake. Minneapolis: University of Minnesota Press.

Siegel, Deborah L. 1997. "The Legacy of the Personal: Generating Theory in Feminism's Third Wave." *Hypatia: A Journal of Feminist Philosophy* 12(3): 46–75.

Siegel, Deborah L. 2007. *Sisterhood Interrupted: From Radical Women to Grrls Gone Wild*. New York: Palgrave Macmillan.

Sklar, Kathryn Kish, Anja Schuler, and Susan Strasser, eds. 1998. *Social Justice: Feminists in the United States and Germany: A Dialogue in Documents, 1855–1933*. Ithaca, N.Y.: Cornell University Press.

Smart, Barry. 1993. *Postmodernity: Key Ideas*. New York: Routledge.

Smith, Andy. 1997. "Ecofeminism through an Anticolonial Framework." Pp. 21–37 in *Ecofeminism: Women, Culture,*

Nature. Ed. Karen J. Warren. Bloomington: Indiana University Press.

Smith, Barbara, ed. 1983. *Home Girls: A Black Feminist Anthology*. Lantham, N.Y.: Kitchen Table–Women of Color Press.

Smith, Dorothy E. 1987. *The Everyday World as Problematic: A Feminist Sociology*. Boston: Northeastern University Press.

Smith, Dorothy E. 1990. *The Conceptual Practices of Power: A Feminist Sociology of Knowledge*. Boston: Northeastern University Press.

Smith, Dorothy E. 1993. "High Noon in Textland: A Critique of Clough." *Sociological Quarterly* 34(1): 183–192.

Smith, Dorothy E. 1996. "Telling the Truth after Postmodernism." *Symbolic Interaction* 19(3): 171–202.

Smith, Dorothy E. 2004. "Comment on Hekman's "Truth and Method: Feminist Standpoint Theory Revisited." Pp. 263–268 in *The Feminist Standpoint Theory Reader: Intellectual and Political Controversies*. Ed. Sandra G. Harding. New York: Routledge.

Smith, Dorothy E. 2005. *Institutional Ethnography: A Sociology for People*. New York: Rowman & Littlefield.

Sneider, Allison L. 2008. *Suffragists in an Imperial Age: U. S. Expansion and the Woman Question, 1870–1929*. New York: Oxford University Press.

Society for Disability Studies. n.d. "Mission Statement." https://www.disstudies.org/about/mission-and-history. Retrieved November 2, 2014.

Sokoloff, Natalie J. 1980. *Between Money and Love: The Dialectics of Women's Home and Market Work*. New York: Praeger.

Solway, Jacqueline S. 2006. *The Politics of Egalitarianism: Theory and Practice*. New York: Berghahn.

Spelman, Elizabeth. 1988. *Inessential Woman: Problems of Exclusion in Feminist Thought*. Boston: Beacon.

Spivak, Gayatri Chakravorty. [1985] 1988. "Can the Subaltern Speak?" Pp. 271–316 in *Marxism and the Interpretation of Culture*. Ed. Cary Nelson and Lawrence Grossberg. Urbana: University of Illinois Press.

Spivak, Gayatri Chakravorty. 1999. "Can the Subaltern Speak?" Pp. 270–289 in *A Critique of Postcolonial Reason*. Cambridge, Mass.: Harvard University Press.

Spivak, Gayatri Chakravorty. 1989. "Naming Gayatri Spivak" (Interview). *Stanford Humanities Review* 1(1): 84–97.

Spivak, Gayatri Chakravorty. 1990. *The Post-colonial Critique: Interviews, Strategies, Dialogues*. London: Routledge.

Spivak, Gayatri Chakravorty. [1999] 2006. *A Critique of Post-colonial Reason: Toward a History of the Vanishing Present*. Cambridge, Mass.: Harvard University Press.

Spurlin, William J. 2006. *Imperialism within the Margins: Queer Representation and the Politics of Culture in South Africa*. New York: Palgrave Macmillan.

Stacey, Judith. 1991. *Brave New Families*. New York: Basic.

Stanton, Elizabeth Cady. [1848] 2005. "'Declaration of Sentiments' from *The History of Women's Suffrage*." Pp. 71–73 in *Feminist Theory: A Reader*, 2nd ed. Eds. Wendy K. Kolmar and Frances Bartkowski. Boston: McGraw–Hill.

Stanton, Elizabeth Cady. [1848] 1881. "Declaration of Sentiments." In *The History of Women's Suffrage*. New York: Fowler and Wells.

Stanton, Elizabeth Cady. [1897] 1997. "On Educated Suffrage." Pp. 165–168 in *The Selected Papers of Elizabeth Cady Stanton & Susan B. Anthony, Volume VI: An Awful Hush 1895–1906*. Ed. Ann D. Gordon. New Brunswick, N.J.: Rutgers University Press.

Stanton, Elizabeth Cady. [1897] 2013. "On Educated Suffrage." Pp. 165–168 in *The Selected Papers of Elizabeth Cady Stanton & Susan B. Anthony, Volume VI: An Awful Hush 1895–1906*. Ed. Ann D. Gordon. New Brunswick, N.J.: Rutgers University Press.

Stanton, Elizabeth, and Susan B. Anthony. [1897] 2013. *The Selected Papers of Elizabeth Cady Stanton & Susan B. Anthony, Volume VI: An Awful Hush 1895–1906*. Ed. Ann D. Gordon. New Brunswick, N.J.: Rutgers University Press.

Stein, Gertrude. [1922] 1984. "Miss Furr and Miss Skeene." Pp. 30–36 in *Women and Fiction: Volume 1*. Ed. Susan Cahill. New York: New American Library. See also http://www.gutenberg.org/cache/epub/33403/pg33403.txt/. Retrieved January 6, 2014.

Steinem, Gloria. 1980. *Outrageous Acts and Everyday Rebellions*. New York: Macmillan.

Steinem, Gloria. [1983]1995. "If Men Could Menstruate." Pp. 372–375 in *The Oxford Book of Women's Writing in the United States*. Eds. Linda Wagner-Martin and Cathy N. Davidson. New York: Oxford University Press.

Stoller, Debbie. 1999. "Sex and the Thinking Girl." Pp. 74–84 in *The Bust Guide to the New Girl Order*. Eds. Marcelle Karp and Debbie Stoller. New York: Penguin.

Symington, Alison. 2005. "From Tragedy and Injustice to Rights and Empowerment: Accountability in the Economic Realm." Pp. 34–48 in *Defending Our Dreams: Global Feminist Voices for a New Generation*. Eds. Shamillah Wilson, Anasuya Sengupta, and Kristy Evans. London: Zed.

Taylor, Dorceta E. 1997. "Women of Color, Environmental Justice, and Ecofeminism." Pp. 38–81 in *Ecofeminism: Women, Culture, Nature*. Ed. Karen Warren. Bloomington: Indiana University Press.

Taylor, Verta. 1989. "Social Movement Continuity: The Women's Movement in Abeyance." *American Sociological Review* 54(5): 761–775.

Tekahionwake. 1885. "A Cry from an Indian Wife." *The Week* June 18th, Goldwin Smith's Toronto Magazine.

Tekahionwake (Emily Pauline Johnson). [1885] 2012. "A Cry from an Indian Wife." http://www.poemhunter.com/i/ ebooks/pdf/emily_pauline_johnson_tekahionwake__ 2012_5.pdf. Retrieved 10/28/14.

Terborg-Penn, Rosalyn. 1998. "Enfranchising Women of Color: Woman Suffragists as Agents of Imperialism." Pp. 41–56 in *Nation, Empire, Colony: Historicizing Gender and Race*. Eds. Ruth Roach Pierson and Nupur Chaudhuri. Bloomington: Indiana University Press.

Thoreau, Henry David. 1849. "Resistance to Civil Government." *Aesthetic Papers*.

Thoreau, Henry David. [1849] 2013. "Civil Disobedience." http://thoreau.eserver.org/civil.html/. Retrieved October 17, 2013.

Tinker, Irene. 1976. "The Adverse Impact of Development on Women." Pp. 22–34 in *Women and World Development*. Eds. Irene Tinker and Michele Bo Bramsen. Washington, D.C.: Overseas Development Council.

Tong, Rosemarie Putnam. 1998. *Feminist Thought: A More Comprehensive Introduction*. 2nd ed. Boulder, Colo.: Westview.

Touraine, Allen. 1998. "Sociology without Society." *Current Sociology* 46(2): 119–143.

Trotsky, Leon. 1973. *Women and the Family*. New York: Pathfinder.

Truth, Sojourner. [1851] 2013. "Ain't I a Woman." Pp. 91 in *Feminist Theory: A Reader*, 4th ed. Eds. Wendy K. Kolmar and Frances Bartkowski. Boston: McGraw–Hill.

Truth, Sojourner. [1867] 2013. "Keeping the Thing Going while Things Are Stirring." Pp. 91–92 in *Feminist Theory A Reader*, 4th ed. Eds. Wendy K. Kolmar and Frances Bartkowski. Boston: McGraw–Hill.

Tyler, S. Lyman. 1973. *A History of Indian Policy*. Washington, D.C.: U.S. Department of the Interior, Bureau of Indian Affairs.

Van der Tuin, Iris. 2011. "New Feminist Materialisms." *Women's Studies International Forum*, 34(4): 271–277.

Vogel, Lise. [1973] 1983. *Marxism and the Oppression of Women: Towards a Unitary Theory*. New Brunswick, N.J.: Rutgers University Press.

Vogel, Lise. 1981. "Marxism and Socialist-Feminist Theory: A Decade of Debate." *Current Perspectives in Social Theory* 2: 209–231.

Volion, Ashley Maria. 2010. "Everyday Lived-Experiences and the Domain of the Sexual as Explored by Four Physically Disabled Women." Master's thesis, University of New Orleans.

Walker, Alice. 1983. *In Search of our Mothers' Gardens: Womanist Prose*. Orlando, Fla.: Harcourt.

Walker, Rebecca. 1992. "Becoming the Third Wave." *Ms.* January–February.

Walker, Rebecca, ed. 1995. *To Be Real: Telling the Truth and Changing the Face of Feminism*. New York: Doubleday.

Walter, Natasha, 2004. "The Winners are Warlords, Not Women." *Guardian.* http://www.theguardian.com/ world/2004/oct/12/gender.afghanistan. Retrieved November 2, 2014.

Walters, Suzanna. [1996] 2013. "From Here to Queer: Feminism, Postmodernism, and the Lesbian Menace (Or, Why Can't a Woman be More Like a Fag?)." Pp. 553–570 in *Feminist Theory Reader: Local and Global Perspective*, 3rd ed. Eds. Carole R. McCann and Sung-Kyung Kim. New York: Routledge.

Walters, Suzanna. 1996. "From Here to Queer: Feminism, Postmodernism, and the Lesbian Menace (Or, Why Can't a Woman be More Like a Fag?)." *Signs: Journal of Women in Culture and Society* Summer (21)4: 830–869.

Waheenee, Buffalo Bird Woman. [1921] 1987. *Waheenee: An Indian Girl's Story Told by Herself to Gilbert L. Wilson.* St. Paul: Minnesota Historical Society Press.

Ward, Jane, and Susan Mann. 2012a. "Liberal Feminists on Love, Marriage, and Sex in Early Modernity." Pp. 40–45 in *Doing Feminist Theory: From Modernity to Postmodernity* by Susan Archer Mann. New York: Oxford.

Ward, Jane, and Susan Mann. 2012b. "Precursors to Intersectional Analyses in Early Modernity." Pp. 162–168 in *Doing Feminist Theory: From Modernity to Postmodernity* by Susan Archer Mann. New York: Oxford.

Ward, Jane, and Susan Mann. 2012c. "Chapter 6: Postmodernism, Poststructuralism, Queer, and Transgender Theories." Pp. 211–255 in *Doing Feminist Theory: From Modernity to Postmodernity* by Susan Archer Mann. New York: Oxford.

Warner, Michael. 1993. *Fear of a Queer Planet: Queer Politics and Social Theory.* Minneapolis: University of Minnesota Press

Wells-Barnett, Ida B. [1892] 1969. "Southern Horrors." In *On Lynchings.* New York: Arno.

Wells-Barnett, Ida B. 1895. *The Red Record.* Chicago: Donohue & Henneberry.

Wells-Barnett, Ida B. 1900. "Lynch Law in America." *The Arena* 23(January): 15–24. (See also http://courses .washington.edu/spcmu/speeches/idabwells.htm/. Retrieved May 28, 2014).

Wells-Barnett, Ida B. [1901] 2005. "Lynching and the Excuse for It." Pp. 117–119 in *Feminist Theory: A Reader*, 2nd ed. Eds. Wendy K. Kolmar and Frances Bartkowski. Boston: McGraw–Hill.

Welter, Barbara. 1973. "The Cult of True Womanhood: 1820–1860." Pp. 224–250 in *The American Family in Social-Historical Perspective.* Ed. Michael Gordon. New York: St. Martin's.

Wilchins, Riki. 2002. "A Certain Kind of Freedom: Power and the Truth of Bodies—Four Essays on Bodies." Pp. 23–63 in *GenderQueer: Voices from Beyond the Sexual Binary.* Ed. Joan Nestle, Clare Howell, and Riki Wilchins. New York: Alyson.

Wilson, Shamillah, Anasuya Sengupta, and Kristy Evans, eds. 2005. *Defending our Dreams: Global Feminist Voices for a New Generation.* London: Zed.

Winant, Howard. 2007. "The Dark Side of the Force: One Hundred Years of the Sociology of Race." Pp. 535–571 in *Sociology in America: A History.* Ed. Craig Calhoun. Chicago: University of Chicago Press.

Wolf, Naomi. [1993] 1994. *Fire with Fire: The New Female Power and How It Will Change the 21st Century.* New York: Random House.

Wollstonecraft, Mary. [1792] 1975. *A Vindication of the Rights of Woman.* New York: W. W. Norton.

Women Engaging Globally. 2014. "CEDAW in the United States: Why A Treaty for the Rights of Women?" http:// www.wedo.org/files/CEDAW/. Retrieved June 2, 2014.

Woodhull, Victoria. [1871] 2010. "And the Truth Shall Make You Free." Pp. 51–65 in *Selected Writings of Victoria Woodhull: Suffrage, Free Love, and Eugenics.* Ed. Cari M. Carpenter. Lincoln: University of Nebraska Press.

Woolf, Virginia. 1929. *A Room of One's Own.* New York: Harcourt, Brace and Company.

Woolf, Virginia. 1938. *Three Guineas.* New York: Harcourt, Brace and Company.

Woolf, Virginia. 2008. *A Room of One's Own and Three Guineas.* Ed. Morag Shiach. New York: Oxford University Press.

Yamada, Mitsuye. 1979. "Invisibility Is an Unnatural Disaster: Reflections of an Asian American Woman." *Bridge, an Asian Perspective* 7(1): 11–13. Reprinted [1981] (1983). Pp. 35–40 in *This Bridge Called My Back: Writings by Radical Women of Color.* Eds. Cherríe Moraga and Gloria Anzaldúa, New York: Kitchen Table–Women of Color Press.

Young, Iris Marion. 1980. "Throwing Like a Girl: A Phenomenology of Feminine Body Comportment, Motility, and Spatiality." *Human Studies.* 3: 137–156.

Young, Iris Marion. 2005. *On Female Body Experience: "Throwing Like a Girl" and Other Essays.* New York: Oxford University Press.

Zeitlin. Irving M. 1981. *Ideology and the Development of Sociological Theory.* Englewood Cliffs, N.J.: Prentice Hall.

Zitkala-Sa (Gertrude Bonnin). 1921 [2008]. *American Indian Stories.* Gloucester, U.K.: Dodo Press.